1765 Parliament passes the Stamp Act, the seemingly onerous terms of which help to unify the colonies in their conflict with the Mother Country

1775 Minutemen meet Redcoats at Lexington and Concord and fire "the shot heard round the world"

1776 The Declaration of Independence announces the birth of a new nation

1783 The Treaty of Paris marks the successful termination of the Revolution

1787 The Constitutional Convention in Philadelphia draws up the basic instrument of government for the new nation

1789 George Washington is inaugurated as first President of the United States

1800 Thomas Jefferson's election gives a strong impulse to the spread of political democracy

1803 The Louisiana Purchase, in one spectacular stroke, doubles the territory of the United States

1804-6 Lewis and Clark explore the country from St. Louis to the Pacific and heighten Americans' belief in their "continental destiny"

1812 A second war with England arouses the spirit of nationalism in the young Republic

1820 The Missouri Compromise settles the first ominous conflict over extending slavery to new territory

1823 The Monroe Doctrine warns Europe to abandon its territorial ambitions in North and South America

1825 The opening of the Erie Canal strengthens the commercial ties between the East and the West, and heightens the isolation of the South

1828 Andrew Jackson's election as president strengthens the democratic tendencies of the older Jeffersonian regime

THE UNITED STATES

THE UNITED

RICHARD HOFSTADTER
Columbia University

WILLIAM MILLER
Co-author, The Age of Enterprise

DANIEL AARON
Smith College

STATES

THE

HISTORY

OF A

REPUBLIC

PRENTICE-HALL, INC.
Englewood Cliffs, N.J.

First printing .... *March, 1957*
Second printing ...... *July, 1957*
Third printing ...... *August, 1957*
Fourth printing ...... *June, 1958*
Fifth printing ..... *February, 1959*
Sixth printing .... *February, 1960*
Seventh printing .. *September, 1960*
Eighth printing .... *January, 1961*
Ninth printing ...... *March, 1961*

Printed in the United States of America

93835—C

PREFACE

The vigor and the resiliency, the desire for change, and the belief in progress that characterize American life in today's troubled world give the impression that we are still a young and growing country. And so we are—compared with most other countries of the earth. For us, as for our children, the future of the United States is far more important than its past. Yet it is a full three hundred and fifty years since the first permanent settlement was made, at Jamestown, Virginia, on the territory that was to become the United States. And we can be sure that any future we may have will emerge out of the deep and varied experiences of that long period.

What we are has been shaped by what our forefathers were and by what they did—not only on the American continent, but in the far older societies of Europe, Africa, and Asia from which most of us are descended. To know our heritage takes us far toward improving our knowledge of ourselves. And to know ourselves is indispensable if we are to act with understanding and realism in the making of our future.

Three and a half centuries of historical development—short though they may seem on the scale of human history—offer a formidable challenge to authors who try to compress them into a one-volume book. Much, obviously, cannot be told. On the other hand, a short history has the advantage of being able to focus on the main themes of our development as a nation. Many fascinating paths we must leave, reluctantly, unvisited. Yet it is possible, while keeping to the main highway, to point out the byways of the American experience and to invite their exploration.

The main highway itself seems always to alter its course as time passes; that is why each generation, as it approaches maturity, rewrites the history of the past. Its vantage point has become different from that of earlier generations; its perspective is altered by its own experience; its hopes have changed shape because of frustrations in some areas, fulfillment in others. Once, the making of the American Constitution and the development of its history seemed to be the main road of American historical study. Later, constitutional history appeared for a time to be arid and purposeless, while the development of communication and industry seemed to be the most rewarding path for students and scholars to take. Still later, it seemed impossible fully to understand either constitutional history or industrial progress without first getting to know more about the different segments of our entire population and the consequences of their competitive aspirations, goals, and ideals.

Once again, perhaps, as a new wave of nationalism sweeps the world and we are thrown increasingly on ourselves, we are ready to return to an examination of our political institutions and practices as the most promising ground on which to seek self-understanding. Yet historians today study politics with their perceptions heightened and their awareness deepened by knowledge of our economy and our

v

social structure—and by familiarity with the philosophy, religion, literature, and art through which we arrive at self-realization as a nation and a people.

This book was written to provide a synthesis of American history for this generation. Within the necessary chronological framework we have treated each facet of our subject—politics, diplomacy, war, industry, religion, literature, and art—as a sequence having internal coherence of its own, so that each portion of the book would offer not a mere compilation of events but rather a meaningful narrative. At the same time, we have tried to see American civilization whole and to do justice to the interrelationships among various aspects of American life.

Although the political development of the nation occupies the foreground of our story, many of the problems of our politics have been connected with our economic growth, and we have treated them accordingly. We have assumed, too, that economic life has an intrinsic interest of its own and lends itself to narrative history as readily as explorations, battles, or elections. As for our approach to American culture, we have tried to treat it in its relation to politics and social developments without falling victim to the assumption that all important cultural matters can be reduced to matters of politics. Art, like economics and politics, has a life of its own, and we have tried to make the reader aware of this as well as of the unity of art and economics and politics in our national existence.

ACKNOWLEDGMENTS

Those who prepare a general work are singularly dependent upon the counsel of friends and the advice of experts. This volume has been read in whole or in large part by Professors Henry F. Graff, Fletcher M. Green, James P. Shenton, and Kenneth M. Stampp. Chapters in the areas of their respective specialties have been read by Professors John M. Blum, Alfred D. Chandler, Jr., Thomas C. Cochran, David Donald, John Hope Franklin, Peter Gay, Nellie Schargo Hoyt, William E. Leuchtenburg, Arthur S. Link, Edmund S. Morgan, Henry L. Roberts, Donald Sheehan, Fritz Stern, and C. Vann Woodward. Mr. Clyde Griffen checked the accuracy of the manuscript with zeal. All these critics have saved us errors of fact and interpretation; for any errors that remain, the authors alone are responsible.

To Everett Sims and his co-workers on the editorial staff of Prentice-Hall, Inc., for their devoted attention to this volume and for the seemingly infinite patience which they extended to the vagaries of its authors, we owe many thanks. To our publishers we are grateful for a generosity in the planning and production of this book which goes far beyond customary practice in the relations between publishers and authors. We are obliged to Vaughn Gray for his fine maps.

R. H.
W. M.
D. A.

CONTENTS

vii

T NINE
Toward a Sectional Economy 191

T TEN
The Jacksonian Era 211

A ELEVEN
America in Ferment 236

M TWELVE
Manifest Destiny 264

MAPS

by Vaughn Gray

xv

THE UNITED STATES

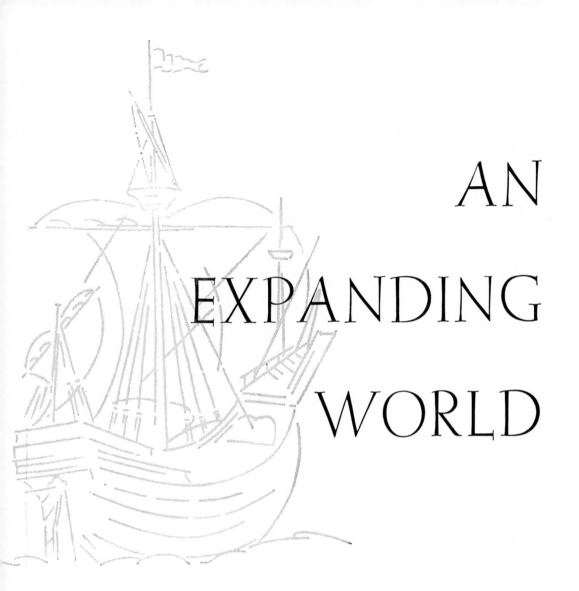

AN
EXPANDING
WORLD

C H A P T E R   O N E

America has been discovered many times. Centuries before voyagers verified its existence, legend had predicted it. Some have held that an Irish monk, St. Brendan, approached the North American continent in the sixth century, but this seems unlikely. And so does the shadowy theory that Buddhist missionaries from China reached the fiords of British Columbia at approximately the same time. Yet a Chinese chronicle, riddled with internal contradictions and distorted by fable, about the land of Fusan, still suggests a country not unlike the California coast. Perhaps so great a land mass as North and South America was simply too large to miss. Mariners approaching from the eastern or western oceans, driven by currents and storms, may have touched on its fringes even

1

before the Greek philosopher, Plato, invented his mythical continent, Atlantis, or before ancient geographers charted the imaginary islands beyond the Pillars of Hercules.

well-timbered, and with small knolls upon it." Where Leif Ericsson landed and spent the winter is disputed. Some scholars hold for Cape Cod, others for eastern Maine. But he apparently beheld Baffins Island, Labrador, and Newfoundland, and possibly land farther

The perils of the deep: a sixteenth-century impression of ocean travel.

Even authenticated voyages of the intrepid Norsemen in the tenth and eleventh centuries have an air of legend. For generations, the reports of their expeditions were handed down by word of mouth, and the accounts that were written later lack precise details. During this period of Scandinavian expansion (850-1050), land-hungry Norsemen, sailing from their base in Ireland, settled Iceland in 874 and then Greenland in 986. From a small settlement in Greenland, three-fourths of the way across the Atlantic, Leif Ericsson sailed about the year 1000 to investigate reports of a land sighted earlier by Bjarni Herjulfson, a country "not mountainous,

south. The fate of Leif's colony will probably remain a mystery.

Little came of Leif's adventures. Europeans may have heard about his voyages, but at this time they felt no impulse to venture into the western sea. For many more years, it was the eastern Mediterranean that absorbed their attention. By the time of the Columbian voyages almost 500 years later, there were no known records of that "region in the recesses of the Northern Ocean," as the medieval cartographers called it. But rumors persisted of an island "called Vinland because grapes from which the most delicious wine could be made grew there."

I.   THE IMPULSE TO DISCOVERY

Europe's discovery of America was but one act in a world drama in which rival nations contended for the wealth of the Indies. Before the age of discovery, the advantage had rested with such enterprising independent Italian city-states as Genoa and Venice, whose merchants competed for the trade of Asia, Africa, and the Middle East. Italian traders in the late Middle Ages were busy in Constantinople, the Crimea, and the upper

reaches of the Nile, exchanging textiles, minerals, tar, and gold and silver coins for spices, chinaware, carpets, perfumes, drugs, and precious gems. These exotic products reached Antioch, Constantinople, Alexandria, and other Levantine terminals from the East by overland and sea routes. And traders from Italy (as well as a lesser number from northern Europe), set up their warehouses in these depots. From here the precious goods were re-shipped to the home ports to be distributed throughout western Europe.

As oriental products came into wider use after the Crusades, the newly emerging nation-states of Portugal, Spain, France, and England began to resent their dependence upon the Italian distributors. The enormous cost of articles that Europeans by the late fourteenth century were beginning to regard almost as necessities drained away specie from the towns of western Europe. A direct route to the Indies would wipe out the whole succession of charges levied on goods as they moved slowly from East to West. English, French, and Spanish consumers, living far away from the trade centers, felt that they were in effect paying tribute to Arab and Italian middlemen. A short cut to the Orient would divert these profits to the country that was fortunate enough to discover it.

The voyagers who finally succeeded in discovering this short cut benefited from a gradual accumulation of knowledge—the reports of travelers, scientific discoveries, and technological improvements. A few travelers managed to penetrate the eastern recesses as early as the thirteenth century, and they described China as bordering on an eastern sea. Asia was not simply a vast extension of land, then; conceivably it could be reached by water. The best-known traveler by land, Marco Polo, visited the court of Kubla Khan, the Emperor of China, with his father and uncle in 1275. Awarded official posts by the great Khan, Marco Polo traveled throughout the Chinese empire. When he finally returned to Venice in 1295, he set down his knowledge "concerning the Kingdoms and Marvels of the East." Marco Polo's chronicle, dictated in a Genoese prison (after the defeat of the Venetian fleet in 1296), described the China of Kubla Khan and the island of Cipangu (Japan) stretching some 1,500 leagues out to sea.

Interest in a water-route to the East was also shown by Renaissance scholars stimulated by Greek thought and Arab learning. These scholars made remarkable strides in astronomy, geography, and mathematics during the fifteenth and sixteenth centuries, and

their theories were put to practical tests. The roundness of the earth, for example, had been known to the Greeks and accepted by European savants since the twelfth century (despite all folklore to the contrary), but now voyagers actually set out to prove it. First, though, improvements had to be made in methods of navigation, shipbuilding, and the related arts. Navigating by instinct, with the polestar as guide, sufficed for the Mediterranean, but unknown oceans called for a more exact science. Voyagers needed stouter vessels, more accurate maps, and more reliable navigational instruments.

Until the thirteenth century, navigational methods had been crude, but from the fourteenth century on a series of technological aids reduced the uncertainties of ocean travel. The compass came into use, and with it the astrolabe and the cross-staff, instruments that provided a rough way of measuring latitude. By 1450, cartographers had correctly charted the coast lines of familiar territory. The simultaneous appearance of an improved printing press and of movable metal type meant that the reports of travelers and scientists could be more widely distributed. Finally, a sturdy ocean-going vessel, the Portuguese caravel, had been evolved by the fifteenth century to supplant the less seaworthy Genoese carrack. The caravel was highly maneuverable and designed for shallow coastal waters and windward sailing.

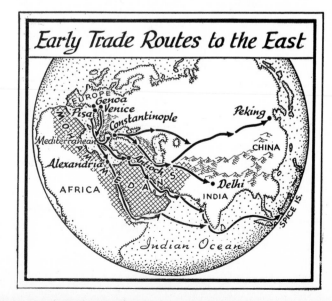

Early Trade Routes to the East

II. THE EUROPEAN BACKGROUND

Mercantilism
and the National States.   European society under feudalism had been conservative in thought if not in action. The breakdown of the old relationships between noble and peasant, the development of towns under the impetus of commercial expansion, and the emergence of national states between the thirteenth and seventeenth centuries created new conditions that led to the settling of the New World. In Portugal, Spain, France, and England, enough capital accumulated to finance exploratory voyages. In England, the dispossession of the peasants and the growth of towns created a landless population from which colonists could ultimately be drawn. During the period of state unification, a fierce national pride, almost unknown in the Middle Ages, quickened the economic rivalry between European states.

Throughout the late Middle Ages and in fact until the middle of the fifteenth century, European nations were dominated by a turbulent feudal nobility who made national unity impossible and narrowly confined the authority of the sovereign. But with the help of the urban bourgeoisie, ambitious "New Monarchs" crushed the feudal lords and exalted their own power. Mercenary armies financed by the merchants and recruited from the lower classes enabled the kings of Portugal, Spain, England, and France to unify their countries and engage in foreign wars. As Portugal achieved unity between the twelfth and fourteenth centuries, she was at the same time developing into the leading commercial power of Europe. Spanish consolidation came somewhat later, and here again the merchants had a hand in welding the five principalities into one nation-state. Centuries of civil and dynastic wars in France and England postponed national integration until the fifteenth century. France, after bringing the Hundred Years' War with England to a successful conclusion (1453), finally became unified by the end of the century; England's strife ended after 1485, when the first of the Tudors, Henry VII, brought order to his country.

The economic impetus provided by national centralization and the autocratic authority of the monarch was immense. The king dispensed with traditional legal restraints against his power and claimed, by sanction of the newly revived Roman law, to represent the will of the people through his own wishes and deeds. The medieval church had distrusted trade and had denounced the taking of interest as sinful. But these religious restraints lost their force in the period of nationalism and nascent capitalism. With the growth of a merchant class in the early towns, and the vigorous state support of commerce that followed national unification, large-scale commercial activity became possible for the first time. Economic practices that were formerly prohibited or frowned upon—the granting of monopolies, high interest rates, profiteering—were encouraged by ambitious rulers who regarded commerce as a kind of war against rival nation-states.

The objectives of "Mercantilism," as the prevailing economic philosophy of the sixteenth and seventeenth centuries has come to be called, were, at bottom, the enrichment of the nation and the impoverishment of its competitors. Every country tried to sell more than it bought in order to preserve its supply of precious metal. The less reliance it placed on other nations for essential goods, the less vulnerable it would be during times of war. Colonies and trading stations, many believed, increased the self-sufficiency of the nation by supplying it with vital raw materials that must otherwise be bought somewhere else. And colonies might also serve as outlets for surplus population.

The Reformation. If the political and economic transformations in western Europe were important in bringing about the trans-Atlantic colonization, so was the far-reaching religious upheaval known as the Reformation.

Until the Reformation, the medieval church maintained religious uniformity. But during the Renaissance, men's attention began to turn from the next world to this, and an audacious mental outlook grew up that often did violence to Catholic doctrine. Corruption in the Church, moreover, provoked a bitter opposition among religious reformers that the new monarchs (in substituting their own sovereignty for Rome's) unwittingly or deliberately encouraged.

Until Martin Luther, a German monk and professor, challenged the authority of the Pope early in the sixteenth century, most reformers had been content to work inside the Church. But Luther was forced either to break from Rome or abandon his beliefs. Modifying the Catholic creed, he preached that men were not saved by performing good works or by observing outward forms of holiness, but only by the faith that comes directly from God. He believed that Christians should learn about religion not through priestly intermediaries but directly from the Bible, the word of God, and he translated the Bible into magnificent vernacular German. Luther attacked monastic seclusion and the celibacy of priests, and he called for the marriage of the clergy. His conservative political views, his appeal for German independence from Rome, and his conviction that the state should control religion brought to his support a number of German princes and later the support of other northern rulers who saw in Luther's program an excuse for confiscating church property and a chance to strengthen their own authority.

Jean Calvin, a French theologian and lawyer and a younger contemporary of Luther, lifted the arguments of the Protestant Reformation from their German and Scandinavian setting and made them more fully international. In 1536, he published his celebrated *Institutes of the Christian Religion,* a work that appealed to religious dissenters throughout Europe. Calvin shared many of Luther's convictions, including belief in justification by faith rather than works. Most important among their theological differences was the idea of predestination, which Calvin made central to his doctrine. Men are so depraved, he held, that no one has merit enough to save his own soul. God arbitrarily chooses—predestines—some (Calvin called them "the elect") to be saved, and leaves the majority to the eternal damnation that their sinfulness justifies.

It may seem odd that a faith so paralyzing in its implications, a faith that saved the few and damned the many, that made eternal bliss dependent upon the arbitrary act of God, should prove so satisfying. Yet this stern Protestant creed unleashed a special kind of energy. Calvinists tried hard to lead the kind of disciplined and saintly lives that would give them reason to believe that they were recipients of God's grace. Convinced that they had the true faith and a divine mission, that the Almighty was on their side, and that many of them were among the "elect," they acquired a militant confidence that distinguished them throughout Europe. The later Calvinists pursued the business of this world with the same passionate intensity that the medieval saints had shown in contemplating the next. Since God, according to Calvin, blessed every "calling," no matter how mean, the virtues of thrift, abstinence, and frugality eventually took on a religious significance.

Calvin, unlike Luther, rejected the idea that the state could be supreme over religion and make laws for it. He proposed that the church should be self-governing and that it should be strong enough to influence, indeed to Christianize, the state. Geneva, in Switzerland, became the Calvinist model community. Here religion permeated all civic activities, and non-Calvinists—Papists as well as those who questioned Christ's divinity—were harshly persecuted. But Calvinism also spread in Germany, France, the Netherlands,

England, Scotland, and Bohemia. The rising class of merchants and traders found it especially congenial. Although Calvinism was in theory undemocratic, it strengthened the cause of individual freedom in the end by insisting on the privacy of religious experience, by making all "callings" honorable, by giving laymen a vital role in church government, and by teaching that the authority of the state was limited by divine law.

The religious revolution begun by Luther and Calvin spawned a number of sects throughout Europe that carried reformation to the extreme. Men who believed themselves in direct communication with God—mystics and perfectionists—excited the anger of Catholic and Protestant alike. The Catholic Church rigorously reformed itself in the middle of the sixteenth century. The Council of Trent, which met irregularly from 1545 to 1563, developed a program for reform and redefined Catholic doctrine. Henceforth the Church sought to reconvert the "heretics" and to enforce conformity through the machinery of church courts (the Inquisition). The lines were now drawn for the great religious persecutions and wars that erupted in the sixteenth and seventeenth centuries. Before these ended, thousands of Lutheran, Calvinist, Catholic, and sectarian refugees were driven to seek religious as well as economic security in the New World.

III.   VOYAGERS AND CONQUISTADORES

Portugal Takes the Lead.   The young and vigorous Portugal was the first of the newly arisen nation-states to challenge the Italians' control of the seas. Early in the

Portuguese Sea Routes to the East

fourteenth century, a Portuguese navy and merchant-marine (with many Italian officers) began to operate in the Mediterranean, the northern European waters, and off the coast of Africa. Under the leadership of Prince Henry the Navigator (1394-1460), the Portuguese cut through the murk of ancient tradition—the legends of ship-devouring monsters and boiling oceans—and proved old fears groundless. Henry's sea captains exploded the classical theory that an uninhabitable torrid zone lay to the south by sending his ships down the African coast. Prince Henry himself combined the most advanced scientific knowledge of his day with practical seafaring, and he systematized geographical information. By the fifteenth century, Portugal had become the center of nautical science. As Portuguese expeditions pushed farther and farther along the African coast, the lure of Indian riches was certainly a strong motive, but not the only one. Prince Henry had dreamed of converting the natives of Guinea to Christianity and using them as allies against the Moslems who had been assailing Portugal from their base in North Africa. Legend also told of a mysterious Christian king, Prester John, beleaguered by Moslems somewhere in the region of the Upper Nile, and Henry envisaged a Christian confederacy capable of striking at the Arab strongholds from the south. Then, too, there was the appeal of knowledge for its own sake—the excitement of the quest.

A series of successful voyages finally produced the long-anticipated result: Vasco da Gama arrived in Calicut in 1498. This was 38 years after Prince Henry's death and 11 years after Bartholomew Diaz first sailed around the *Cabo Tormentoso* (the Cape of Storms), later renamed the Cape of Good

revolutionized commerce and had created an empire.

Columbus.   Some years before Da Gama's epoch-making voyage, a Genoese mariner, Christopher Columbus, hit on the idea of reaching the Indies by sailing west. Where

A 1493 Florentine woodcut depicting the landing of Columbus.

Hope. When Da Gama returned to Lisbon in 1499 with a cargo of spices and jewels, the commercial supremacy of the Italian states was in effect at an end. The Portuguese drove the Moslem merchants out of the Indian Ocean, reduced their strongholds, and destroyed their navy. Lisbon now became the principal depot for oriental trade, the center from which eastern wares were distributed by traders to every part of Europe. A country of less than 2 million people had

Columbus got this idea is not certain. It may have been from his reading of Marco Polo's marvelous narrative about the China of Kubla Khan and the island of Cipangu. Authorities from Aristotle and Ptolemy to Cardinal Pierre d'Ailly, a fifteenth-century geographer whose *Imago Mundi* served as Columbus' bedside reading, may have persuaded him that Asia lay only a short distance beyond the last Atlantic landfall, the Azores.

According to one theory, Columbus learned from a famous Florentine astronomer, Paolo Toscanelli, that the Chinese city of Kinsay (Hang Chow) lay 3,900 miles due west of Lisbon. "The passage, in my opinion," Toscanelli is alleged to have written to Columbus, "will be found easy and safe, in the quarters which I have pointed out. . . . You may be certain of meeting with extensive kingdoms, populous cities, and rich provinces, abounding in all sorts of precious stones." Some scholars believe that Toscanelli never wrote this letter. Others believe that Columbus learned of fabled isles from a Portuguese sailor. One thing is clear: by 1484 Columbus was seeking help to finance an expedition.

Columbus applied first to the King of Portugal, who turned him down. There seemed little more likelihood that he would find support in the Spanish court, though the Spaniards, who had been excluded from African waters by a treaty with Portugal (1479), were particularly interested in finding another route to the Indies. But the Spanish monarchs, Ferdinand and Isabella, were warned by their advisers that the theories of Columbus conflicted with reason and with Biblical teaching. After eight years of fruitless intrigue, Columbus was ready to give up. Suddenly help came from two mariners in Palos, the Pinzón brothers, and through their influence he finally caught the attention of the Queen. In 1492, the same year in which the Spaniards expelled the Moors from Granada, Columbus obtained a commission from Isabella. Now an admiral, he sailed on August 3 from Palos with a fleet of three ships. His route took him first to the Canary Islands and then to one of the Bahamas, which he reached on October 12. Columbus named this island "San Salvador." Exploring further, he sailed on to the island of Cuba (which he at first mistook for Japan or the mainland of Asia) and from there to Haiti (which he again hopefully identified as Japan). Even after three more voyages, in 1493, 1498, and 1502-1504, Columbus never suspected that a continent lay athwart the passage to China and Japan. No great distance, he believed, separated his lush islands in the West Indies from the palaces of the great Khan. Columbus died in 1506, still convinced that he had reached the Orient.

The New World took its name from a controversial Florentine businessman and

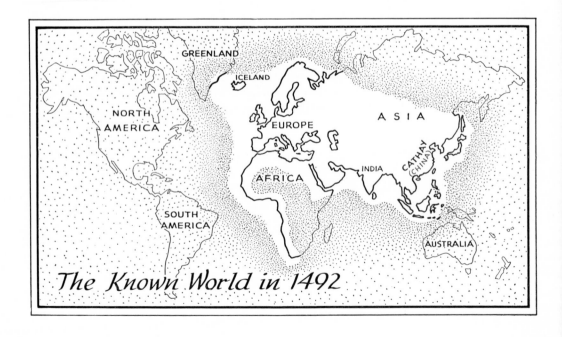

The Known World in 1492

voyager, Americus Vespucius, who claimed to have seen the South American mainland a year before Columbus reached the mouth of the Orinoco in 1498. He probably pre-dated by four years his first contact with American shores, and there is no reason to believe that he saw the American mainland before Columbus did. But he publicized his alleged achievement in a famous and widely circulated letter. In 1507, a German geographer proposed to call the new land "America," after its discoverer, Americus, and the mapmakers complied. This was not to be the last time that shrewd publicity circumvented the truth about the New World.

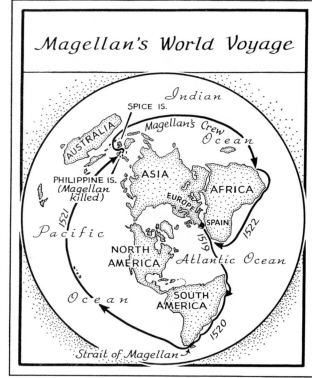

Magellan's World Voyage

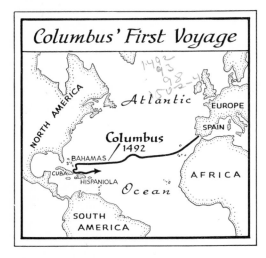

Columbus' First Voyage

In the late Middle Ages, scholars had exaggerated the portion of the earth's surface that was covered by the Eurasian continental land mass. Hence they thought China much nearer and easier to reach than in fact it was. At first, when mariners struck upon America, they hoped that the portions they saw were no more than small island obstructions, through which they could find passages that would lead them to the East. For more than a century after Ferdinand Magellan set forth on his incredible voyage of discovery, the search for a new passage to the East continued. The new continent remained a mystery even after the Spanish and the French had explored the trans-Allegheny country in the sixteenth and seventeenth centuries. It was a long time before

Europeans were convinced that there were no hidden waterways linking the Atlantic to the Pacific, that more land lay west of the Mississippi than east of it, that no lions roared in Massachusetts, that no fountains of youth gushed forth in Florida. The search for an elusive short cut to the Orient served to stimulate the zeal for exploration, but so long as Europeans preferred East Indian spices to the humbler products of North America they felt little urge to colonize the New World. For over a century after England and France knew about North America, they did not think it worth while to colonize in that part of the world.

The Rise of Spain. On the eve of American colonization, the strongest powers were Catholic—and the most Catholic and the most powerful was Spain. She had supplanted Portugal about 1550, when Portugal —too small and impoverished to maintain its restive and far-flung empire—began to decline. A more populous Spain, recently unified, strongly armed, and spiritually aroused,

9

seized the leadership in colonial enterprise many years before she finally absorbed her tottering neighbor in 1580. The Spanish wars for national unity, culminating in the expulsion of the Moors in 1492, whipped up the crusading spirit of the country. Columbus' discovery in the same year inflamed the minds of the pious and the mercenary, and brought to Spain immense territories outside the Portuguese sphere of influence in Africa and the southern Atlantic.

In 1493, Spanish-born Pope Alexander VI granted to Spain the lands that Columbus had discovered. This ruling ran counter to Portugal's claim, which had been upheld until now by the Pope. In 1494, Spain and Portugal agreed on a demarcation line running north and south some 370 leagues west of the Cape Verde Islands. East of this line, Portugal received all rights of discovery. Lands lying to the west fell to Spain. Since the tip of the Brazilian coastline extended into the Portuguese sphere, the Spanish were excluded from that section of South America. But most of the land in the Western Hemisphere lay open to her men of arms, the conquistadores. This agreement, later much disputed, was given papal sanction in 1506 and imposed on Spain the responsibility of converting the heathen peoples.

Out of their base of Santo Domingo—or Hispaniola, as it was called—Spain's explorer-captains, like Balboa and Ponce de Léon, led small bands to Cuba, the Central American isthmus, and Florida, searching for the mythical El Dorado where gold and jewels were as common as stones. Only twice did the gold-seekers discover bonanzas. The first occurred when the young soldier-adventurer, Hernando Cortés, led an expedition of 550 men from Cuba into Mexico and overthrew the rich and mighty Aztec nation. With the help of Indian allies and aided by Aztec legends that prophesied the return of the white god, Quetzalcoatl, the outnumbered but well-armed Spaniards reached the magnificent capital, Tenochtitlán, and finally subdued it in 1521. Spanish coffers were

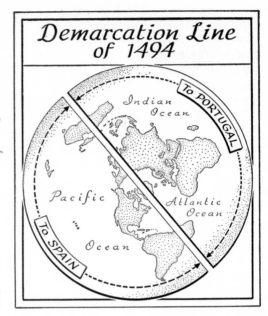

soon being replenished by Mexican silver. A decade later, in Peru, the rapacious Francisco Pizarro crushed the well-organized Inca rulers by treachery and uncovered more precious metals than the conquerors of Mexico.

Elsewhere the conquistadores found little treasure. The tough Spanish soldiers, more resistant to tropical heat than the northern Europeans and famed for their endurance on the march, pressed forward in their desperate undertakings. Pertinacious greed carried the Spanish into the Mississippi country in 1541 under the leadership of Hernando de Soto, and Francisco Vásquez de Coronado searched in vain for the Seven Cities of Cíbola in southwestern America. By 1600, Spanish ships had ranged as far south as Chile and the Argentine, and as far north as the upper coast of California.

Long before the other Atlantic nations were ready to challenge Spain's dominion in America, she had already established a vast empire bearing the unmistakable stamp of her institutions. The Spanish regime was in many respects cruel and inflexible. The *encomienda,* a system of enforced native labor, sometimes resulted in frightful abuses; the highly centralized Spanish administration was authoritarian to an extreme; both *creoles* (native-born whites) and *mestizos* (natives of mixed Indian and white ancestry) suffered social discrimination.

Yet despite the continued harshness of her imperial policy, Spain's colonial venture was remarkably successful. Under the Spaniards, bloody Indian tribal warfare ceased. Intermarriage of white and Indian peoples facilitated the Europeanizing of Spain's possessions and saved the natives from extermination, a fate they sometimes suffered in other New World regions. Spanish officials built churches, founded universities in Peru and Mexico more than three-quarters of a century before the founding of Harvard in 1636, and instructed the Indians in husbandry and handicrafts. Spanish annals in the New World are full of blood and violence, but they also contain accounts of humanitarians, like the noble priest, Bartholomew de Las Casas, who devoted their lives to combating Indian enslavement. Ironically, it was Las Casas' passionate exposure of colonial exploitation (*La Brevissima Relación*) that furnished Spain's enemies (who behaved no less cruelly) with a powerful propaganda weapon and made "Spanish cruelty" a byword for generations.

Spain and Her Rivals. Although Spain throughout most of the sixteenth century was the strongest European state, enriched by the treasures of the Aztecs and the Incas and the bullion from the Peruvian silver mines of Potosí, her decline had already begun with the accession of Philip II in 1556. Philip squandered his treasures in an anti-Protestant crusade against the Netherlands and England. Spain's gold supply was drained off to German and Flemish bankers to pay for her expeditionary armies in Europe and the Americas and for the manufactured goods required by her overseas possessions. The expulsion of the Jews and Moors deprived her of merchants and artisans who might have competed with the aggressive trading classes of her rivals. Spain swarmed with proud aristocrats, who had already become anachronistic by the seven-

teenth century; her manufacturers could not compete with foreign sellers, even with the help of protective tariffs. Weakened by declining production, a grafting and ponderous

Indian versions of the Spanish conquest.

bureaucracy, and the burdens of war, Spain gradually lost out to her Dutch, English, and French competitors. Supreme as late as 1560, and still a formidable power for another century, she never completely recovered from the disasters that fell upon her during and after the reign of Philip II (1556-1598). The catastrophic defeat of Spain's "Invincible Armada," destroyed in 1588 by a swifter and more maneuverable English fleet, was only a prologue to future humiliations.

During the seventeenth century, when the first important settlements in North America were established, the center of power in Europe shifted dramatically. In 1500, the Italians had dominated the Mediterranean; Portugal had jealously guarded her African and Asiatic trade monopoly; Spain had claimed the vast stretches of the New World. By 1630, the picture was quite different.

Spain's contentions that the Atlantic Ocean was her private lake, and that Spanish discoveries gave her a perpetual monopoly in the New World, were disputed by the new powers of western Europe. Even while

Europe remained officially at peace, Dutch, French, and English privateers were snapping up the Spanish gold fleet, raiding Spanish towns, and planting stations in areas claimed by the Spanish Crown. Spain retaliated during the sixteenth century by fortifying her Caribbean towns and by establishing convoy systems, but as the century waned she combated the foreign freebooters with diminishing success.

Her rivals had become formidable. The Dutch revolted against Spanish domination in 1566 and declared themselves independent in 1581. By 1609, the northern provinces of the Netherlands had virtually freed themselves from Spain. During the same period, the Dutch supplanted the Portuguese as the dominant power in the East Indies. The French, wracked by religious civil war in the late sixteenth century, were finally pacified by the accession of Henry IV in 1594. Accepting Catholicism in the interests of national harmony, this popular king removed political restraints on the French Protestants (Huguenots), encouraged commerce and manufacturing, and made extensive plans for establishing a French empire in America.

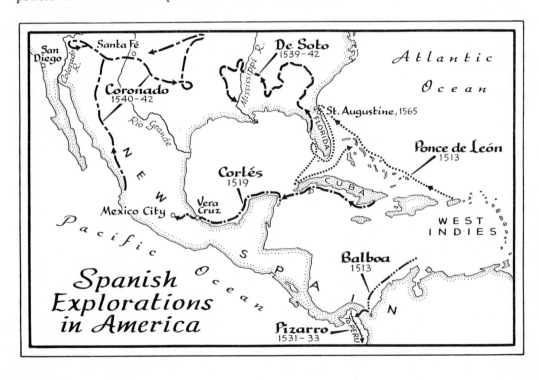

Spanish Explorations in America

IV. EARLY ENGLISH COLONIZATION

The Rise of England.   French and Dutch sea-raiders exposed the weakness of Spain's hold on America, but it was England that most effectively contested Spanish claims to exclusive rights in the New World, most successfully colonized North America, and finally ousted her Spanish, French, and Dutch rivals. And it is with the foundation of the English colonies that American history really begins.

England had achieved political unity under the Tudor kings, the first of whom, Henry VII (1485-1509), ended the baronial Wars of the Roses and established the supremacy of kingship. His successor, Henry VIII (1509-1547), centralized national power and strengthened his own authority when he detached the Church of England from Rome and distributed church lands among his supporters. Since the national English church sprang from a political rather than a religious difference, English Protestantism developed in a different fashion from that of the Continent. The brief reign of Mary Tudor, a Catholic, and her marriage to Philip II of Spain, only sharpened anti-Catholic feeling in England. Under Elizabeth I (1558-1603), English Protestantism came to be centered in a state church that retained a few Catholic vestiges but that resolutely opposed papal interference in England as well as Rome's claim that the Pope was the Vicar of Christ. English Protestants read the Bible in the vernacular, and English clergymen married. During Elizabeth's reign, a split could already be detected between the "Anglicans" or High Church adherents, who were closer to Rome in doctrine and church organization, and the Puritans, who were pressing for a radical "purifying" reformation. Elizabeth, however, subordinated sectarian differences to patriotic aspiration, and religious dissensions did not break out again until the Stuarts came to the throne after her death.

Anti-Catholicism injected a strong religious element into the commercial wars that England carried on against Spain and France in the seventeenth and eighteenth centuries, and inspired an aggressive imperialism. But the English impulse to colonize sprang not only from the patriotic desire to block Spanish ambitions. The dream of extending the dominions of Christ by bringing the light to heathen peoples was also an important motive, and one that happened to coincide with the commercial interests of the English merchants.

By Elizabeth's time, the merchants were self-confident enough to risk more capital on distant ventures. Two hundred and fifty years of growth had transformed a small nation into the most dynamic of the European states. England's prosperity rested on two unexotic commodities: wool and coal. High profits gained from exporting wool and woolen products had induced landowners to substitute sheep-raising for agriculture and to enclose fields and grazing lands that had formerly been apportioned among tenants. From about 1350 on, the extension of the enclosure movement and the rise of the woolen industry transformed the society and economy of England. Dispossessed farm-laborers and yeomen moved into the towns, the medieval guild system gradually disintegrated, and an alert class of merchant-capitalists supported by commercial-minded noblemen assumed control over the English economy.

The depletion of the forests brought coal into use as an industrial and domestic fuel. Its increased consumption after 1550 stimulated an expansion of British industry and quickened an economic revolution between 1570 and 1620. The substitution of coal for wood increased the production of salt, glass, pottery, and metals, and it also fathered a number of derived industries. Coal traffic necessitated the dredging of harbors, and, most important, a heavy ship-building program.

On the eve of the first migrations to America, England had constructed a solid base for her commercial and industrial supremacy, and had also developed appropriate machinery for launching colonial enterprises. By pooling resources, or by permitting the public to participate in cooperatively owned or joint-stock corporations, merchants were able to extend their operations into the Mediterranean, Russia, India, and the Levant. "Regulated" companies, like the Merchant Adventurers, chartered in 1564, imposed business codes on their members but allowed them to trade directly in areas where the company enjoyed market privileges. The joint-stock company was designed for remote lands where the risks were too great for the individual trader. It also provided a means whereby investors might buy shares in privateering expeditions and finance voyages of exploration.

Although England had made extraordinary economic advances since the Middle Ages, by 1600 she had still not reached the status of a first-class power. From the mercantilist point of view, she lacked sufficient markets and an adequate supply of precious metals, and her prosperity was too closely geared to the easily disrupted continental trade. Overseas colonies, the expansionists felt, would provide outlets for her excess population and would satisfy the prodigious hunger for land. Plantations in North America might in addition furnish England with raw materials she now had to purchase elsewhere: fish, lumber, furs, potash, naval stores. Finally, bases in the New World would thwart the expansion of the Catholic powers. Commerce, patriotism, and religion conspired to propel a crowded and restless people into the establishment of overseas colonies. To carry out these colonial enterprises, English energies were not wanting.

The Colony as an Idea. England's wars with Spain had postponed the planting of settlements in the sixteenth century, but the English disinclination to colonize cannot be explained by this fact alone. Prejudice, inertia, and fear also had been deterrents.

The English had no word for "colony" in the overseas sense until the sixteenth century, and the verb "to colonize" was first used by Francis Bacon in 1622. The English undoubtedly knew about the trading posts that the Italians and the Portuguese had set up in the Levant and southern Asia, but the idea of a "plantation" or settlement attracted popular attention only with the attempt to colonize Ireland during Elizabeth's reign. The miseries suffered in subjugating the Irish, and the ferocity of Irish resistance against the would-be settlers, evoked a strong popular repugnance against the plantation idea in the 1580's and 1590's. The reluctance of the English to pull up stakes and move prompted the same kind of propaganda or "promotion" literature that was written later to attract reluctant settlers to America.

This natural hesitation to embark for unknown shores was partially overcome by appeals to national pride, missionary zeal, the lure of adventure, and the promise of gain. For a long time the colony was conceived of as a military base garrisoned by a kind of warrior-settler. Richard Hakluyt the younger, clergyman and cosmographer, did a great deal to change this attitude. He collected every scrap of information he could find about foreign lands, and in his *Principall Navigations, Voiages, and Discoveries of the English Nation* (1589) he revealed the outside world to his insular countrymen. In other writings, Hakluyt argued persuasively for a North American settlement as a source of raw materials and as a market for English trade. Just as Ireland had drawn the wicked, the needy, and the land-hungry, so the American plantations might attract the "able men" who now "pestered" English prisons, "which for small robberies are daily hanged up in great numbers, even twenty at a clap, out of one gaol."

When Hakluyt wrote, the British statute books listed some 400 capital crimes. Many felons in the sixteenth century—given the

The American bison as it appeared to a Spanish artist in the sixteenth century.

choice of deportation or death—preferred the perils of the newly discovered world to the mysteries of that "undiscovered country" from which (as Shakespeare reminded them) no one ever returned. But not all Englishmen who left for the New World acted from such desperate motives. Some dutifully followed the religious injunction to "advance the gospel of Jesus Christ," as John Donne urged them to in a sermon before one of the Trading Companies. "You shall have made this island," he said, "which is but as the suburbs of the Old World a bridge, a gallery to the New, to join all to that world that shall never grow old, the Kingdom of Heaven."

For those who were not overly concerned with the converting of the heathen, "the goodliest and most pleasing Territorie of the world" offered a variety of inducements and challenges. Even the hazards graphically recorded by Hakluyt tempted the adventurous:

How dangerous [he wrote] it is to attempt new Discoveries, either for length of the voyage, or the ignorance of the language, the want of Interpreters, new and unaccustomed Elements and ayres, strange and unsavoury meates, hugenesse of woods, dangerousnesse of Seas, dread of tempests, feare of hidden rockes, steepnesse of mountaines, darknesse of sudden falling fogges, continuall paines taking without any rest, and infinite others.

These sobering realities, however, could not dispel the appeal of discovery, the fascination of strangeness so congenial to the Elizabethan mind. Reports of exotic animals and plants, variations in climate, unusual customs, and rare "objects for contemplation" proved endlessly entertaining and satisfied the appetite for the marvelous. The voyager dreamed of finding cities like Sir Walter Raleigh's fabulous Manoa, where the humblest articles were made of gold. Nothing seemed incredible to an age in which actuality out-dazzled myth.

The prospects of new Inca hoards and richer Potosí mines sharpened the greed of the soldier-adventurers. But philosophers like Sir Thomas More looked beyond these narrow horizons. In his famous *Utopia* (1516), which was colored by the discovery of the New World, the inhabitants have abandoned the corruptions of Europe, regard precious jewels as baubles for children, and contemptuously use gold only to make chamber pots.

English Seafaring and Discovery.

English claims to the Atlantic coast of North America rested on the 1497 voyage of John Cabot, a naturalized Venetian who had been sent out by Henry VII to discover new territories. Like Columbus, Cabot thought he had reached Asia. Nothing important came of this pioneer voyage, though it was proclaimed that Cabot had "won a part of Asia without a stroke of the sword." An English expedition to reach Asia by a northeast route failed in 1553, but the English established trade relations with Russia in 1555 with the formation of the Muscovy Company. At about the same time, English fishermen began to contest the Newfoundland banks with the fishermen of Portugal, Spain, and France. Interest in America was stimulated in 1576 when Sir Humphrey Gilbert, in a celebrated essay (*Discourse of a Discovery of a New Passage to Cataia*), "proved" by ingenious logic that America was in fact an island cut off from Asia. North America, he argued, harbored no Asiatic animals, no

Scythians or Tartars. A study of the currents along the Atlantic coast proved to his satisfaction the existence of a northwest passage running somewhere along the 62nd to the 72nd parallel. The voyages of Martin Frobisher tested Gilbert's theory, but neither these nor the subsequent voyages of John Davis and Gilbert himself led to the discovery of this elusive passage.

During the next two decades, when the undeclared war between Britain and Spain flared into the open, English adventurers found it more profitable to plunder Spanish treasure ships and to raid Spanish colonies, with Elizabeth's blessing, than to try to plant colonies of their own. Spanish intrigues against the English queen, together with stern prohibitions against trade between outsiders and the Spanish colonies, provoked widespread English attacks in which freebooters like Sir John Hawkins and Sir Francis Drake enriched both themselves and their country. Drake's daring voyage around the world (1577-1580) exposed the vulner-

ability of Spain's overextended dominions, and the defeat of the Armada in 1588 forcibly demonstrated that Spain could not defend her claims in the New World. The chartering of the East India Company in 1600 meant that England, having tapped the oriental trade, no longer needed to look for a shorter passage to Asia—though the search went on. Elizabeth's sailors, now boldly following the lanes once dominated by Spain and Portugal, established English trading stations in Surat and Madras (India). America, however, was to be the site of England's true settlements.

England During the Atlantic Migration.

After the death of Elizabeth I in 1603, the quarrel between Puritan and Anglican (see p. 13) grew more bitter and finally broke out into civil war. The first of the Stuarts, James I, who succeeded Elizabeth, believed strongly in the divine right of kings. He hated non-conformists, not only because they opposed the national church, but also because they supported the powerful middle-class party in Parliament that wanted to limit his royal authority. By upholding the Anglican establishment, James bolstered his own prerogatives. During his reign (1603-1625), the Puritans (that is, those who wished to "purify" the Anglican Church) and the separatists (who wished to separate themselves from it completely) were persecuted more severely than they had been in Elizabeth's time, but their situation really became acute when James' son, Charles I, succeeded his father.

Charles' ecclesiastical watchdog, Archbishop William Laud, a well-intentioned but inflexible autocrat, immediately launched a campaign against the Puritans and separatists. He outlawed their forms of worship and punished their communicants. Non-conformists had the choice of practicing their religion secretly and at the risk of punishment, of conforming to the established church, or of seeking religious refuge elsewhere. Had England been politically and economically stable

English Voyages to America

at this time, the dissenters might have accepted their religious disabilities. Between 1620 and 1635, however, crop failures, rising food prices, and widespread unemployment added to the miseries of religious persecution. The 70,000 people who migrated to the West Indies and the North American mainland in the two decades after 1620 were persuaded to take this drastic step by both economic and religious considerations.

The Puritan exodus to America continued until the overthrow and execution of Charles I. From 1629 to 1640, the king had managed to rule without parliamentary assistance, but an unsuccessful war against the Scots Presbyterians forced him to summon Parliament, which promptly reduced his royal privileges. When Charles attempted to arrest the parliamentary leaders in the House of Commons and refused the demands that would have placed parliamentary over royal authority, he started a civil war and paved the way for the dictatorship of Oliver Cromwell. This powerful and earnest Puritan leader had welded his army of "Roundheads" into an irresistible force and had routed the royalist troops of King Charles. He became Lord Protector of the country soon after the beheading of Charles in 1649, and his regime, known as the Commonwealth, lasted until 1660 when Charles II, son of the "martyred" king, was restored to the throne.

During the Puritan Commonwealth, the flow of dissenters to America slackened, and only a few royalists were now ready to leave even a joyless and austere land for the uncertainties of the New World.

The English Birthright.   The English colonists brought with them certain characteristic traits and attitudes, certain traditional ways of thinking and doing, that worked to their advantage in America.

Consider the matter of class. Though class distinctions were taken for granted in Tudor and Stuart England, they were much less inflexible than in Spain or France, and men could more easily rise and fall from one class to another. At the time of active colonization, a new aristocracy was in the process of being created. Scions of noblemen, unlike their Spanish or French counterparts, did not feel it beneath their dignity to engage in trade, and any man—student, soldier, or doctor—could claim the title of gentleman so long as he did not perform menial labor. This liberal conception of social class gave the English a distinct advantage over their competitors in the New World, for it meant that men of all classes and aptitudes could work together in the great adventure.

Then, too, the English were accustomed to cooperate in private associations and to rely less upon governmental initiative than the French, the Spanish, or the Dutch. The English government made the conditions possible for the planting of settlements abroad, but private enterprise provided the means for this community effort as well as the intelligence to direct it. Once settled in America, the English colonists were likely to flout directives from home, nor did they customarily look to the mother country for guidance.

Again, their social traditions had prepared them for civic responsibility. Since medieval times, people of several classes in English towns and villages had been called on to fill various civic offices. Men of no rank or substance performed the duties of churchwardens, constables, and a variety of lesser jobs. In themselves, these petty offices were of little significance, but they reveal a good deal about English society. The elective assemblies soon to emerge in the English colonies did not grow by accident nor did they derive from the experiments of an isolated people. They had their origins in the British shires where common classes of men, the yeoman freeholders, shared in community management.

The settlers brought with them their arts and their institutions—the jury system, the common law, their insistence on certain rights and privileges. They also brought a less enlightened legacy from the past: harsh punishments, outlandish medical opinions, and a vast store of misinformation about the world. With all their intellectual handicaps, however, the English settlers looked neither to their king nor to Rome for their sanctions.

For them, ultimate truth lay in the Bible, their talisman and the source of both their orthodoxy and their heresies. It was these immigrants—earthy and contentious, tough and serious-minded—who laid the foundation for a new civilization in North America.

Readings

A well-written and sophisticated survey of European history, useful as background reading for Chapter I, is R. R. Palmer and Joel Colton, *A History of the Modern World* (2nd ed., 1956). For more detail on the European scene in relation to America, see E. P. Cheyney, *The European Background of American History, 1300-1600* (1904), and his *The Dawn of a New Era, 1250-1453* (1936); W. C. Abbott, *The Expansion of Europe* (1938); J. E. Gillespie, *A History of Geographical Discovery, 1400-1800* (1933); and L. B. Packard, *The Commercial Revolution, 1400-1776* (1927). More detailed accounts of early voyages and explorations can be found in Halldór Hermansson, *The Problem of Wineland* (1936); S. E. Morison's biography of Columbus, *Admiral of the Ocean Sea* (2 vols., 1942); J. B. Brebner, *The Explorers of North America, 1492-1806* (1933); H. V. Livermore, *A History of Portugal* (1933); E. G. Bourne, *Spain in America, 1450-1580* (1905); and H. I. Priestley, *The Coming of the White Man, 1492-1848* (1929). On the economic backgrounds of English development and colonization, J. U. Nef, *Industry and Government in France and England, 1540-1640* (1940), is distinctive and important. Wallace Notestein's *The English People on the Eve of Colonization, 1603-1630* (1954), is a charmingly written and deeply informed book on the background of the English migrations. On the colonial idea, see K. E. Knorr, *British Colonial Theories, 1570-1850* (1944).

A substantial and detailed history of the colonies is C. M. Andrews' *The Colonial Period of American History* (4 vols., 1934-1938). An excellent one-volume colonial history, particularly full on economic development, is Curtis P. Nettels, *The Roots of American Civilization* (1938). The reader will also profit by consulting Max Savelle, *The Foundations of American Civilization* (1942); O. P. Chitwood, *A History of Colonial America* (1948); and Frank J. Klingberg, *The Morning of America* (1941).

Among special works, the following are of interest: J. N. L. Baker, *History of Geographical Discovery and Exploration* (1932); L. B. Wright, *The Atlantic Frontier* (1947); H. E. Bolton, *Rim of Christendom* (1936); F. A. Kirkpatrick, *The Spanish Conquistadores* (1936); Francis Parkman, *Pioneers of France in the New World* (1865)—still a fresh and interesting work; and W. E. Lingelbach, *The Merchant Adventurers of England* (1902).

SETTLING

AMERICA

CHAPTER TWO

When Pope Alexander VI divided the New World between Spain and Portugal in 1493, he failed to take into account the response of the French king, Francis I—a response that was typical of most of Europe: "The sun shines on me as well as on others," he said. "I should be very happy to see the clause in Adam's will which excluded me from my share when the world should come to be divided." A century later, Holland, France, and England had gone far beyond harassing Spanish shipping in the Caribbean. They had seized islands in the West Indies, had planted bases along the South American coast, and had founded colonies on the North American mainland that served both as military posts and as sources of raw materials.

I. THE REALITIES OF THE NEW WORLD

The Economics

of the Wilderness. The European powers engaged in dismembering the Spanish colonial empire soon discovered that the colony in theory did not correspond to the colony in fact. The French, English, and Dutch promoters who financed the North American experiments in colony-making had hoped for immediate profits from their investments. But they minimized the difficulties involved in trying to survive in a forest wilderness. Europeans were not accustomed to the savage extremes in temperature that they found in the New World. They suffered from strange diseases, and sometimes starved in the midst of a fertile land teeming with animal life. Finding no precious metals or jewels on the North American mainland, they turned to fur-trading and lumbering; instead of spices, they sent back soap, ashes, pitch, and deer hides. Although they sometimes penetrated the hinterlands in order to trade with the Indians, they usually clung to the coasts and built their houses by the bays and rivers—the St. Lawrence, the Hudson, the Delaware, the Chesapeake. Their financial backers soon realized that such primitive settlements were much riskier ventures than were the well-established tobacco and sugar plantations of the West Indies. Throughout the seventeenth century, the economic importance of the Caribbean area exceeded that of the mainland colonies.

The old expectations of quick profits from gold and silver mines, and of unobstructed routes to the Orient, still attracted European adventurers as late as the eighteenth century. But by the 1640's the Western Hemisphere had taken on an importance of its own; fish, fur, tobacco, lumber, and sugar were adding to European wealth and were sustaining a colonial society. In fact, competition for New World products began to involve large investments of capital and important concessions to the colonists. The colony was gradually assuming an importance in the eyes of Europe that its early projectors had hardly dreamed of.

The Indian.

The Old World man in America immediately found himself in touch with an Indian population comprising hundreds of tribes and speaking languages that seemed as different from one another as English from Chinese. Europeans tended to lump all the Indians together in one category, but in reality the tribes or nations varied significantly in culture and in social organization. Some, like those of the lower South, were primarily agricultural peoples who made up great confederacies. Others lived in isolated groups, and depended more on hunting. Tribes like the Iroquois in Upper New York were highly organized politically; others had no government at all in the European sense. Among the eastern Indians, government was based on the clan council, which was composed of all tribal members who belonged to the same "totem" or animal-ancestor. The clan elected both sachems (chiefs), who represented the clan at the councils, and military chieftains.

The early whites often misunderstood Indian tribal organization and treated Indian leaders as if they were European potentates. And they failed to grasp the Indian conception of landownership, a misunderstanding that provoked much bloodshed. The Indian, though an individualist, could not conceive of private ownership of land. To him, land belonged to the clan. Hunting districts were reserved to the clan or to the nation, and village agriculture was a communal affair. When the whites attributed undesirable qualities to the Indians, they were usually displaying the ignorance of civilized men con-

A late sixteenth-century impression of an Indian village in what is now North Carolina. An engraving by Theodore De Bry of a water color by John White.

fronted by a primitive people whose values were different from their own but not necessarily debased.

From the Indians the white settlers learned how to accommodate themselves to the forest world. They borrowed the "milpa" or slash-and-burn system of clearing the land. First the trees were "girdled" in order to kill them and make them fall; then the trunks were burned and the wood-ash was spread over the cleared ground to prepare it for the first planting of "maize," or corn. Maize grew everywhere and quickly became the staple for a number of colonial recipes. Other Indian culinary inventions were the baked clam, planked shad, and baked beans. The settlers also learned to use white and sweet potatoes, tomatoes, tobacco, squash, and cotton. From the whites, in turn, the Indians acquired a knowledge of tools and firearms—as well as a taste for whisky. Both as friend and as enemy, the Indian was an important element in the white man's "discovery" of America, and in the struggle between the European powers in North America his friendship or hostility was of decisive importance.

II.   PATTERNS OF COLONIZATION

The Way of the French.   When Jacques Cartier, looking for a short cut to the Orient, reached the Gulf of the St. Lawrence in 1534, he found sailors from his native Brittany already there fishing for cod. They had been exploiting these fisheries at least a generation before Cartier's voyage, and even before that of the Italian seaman, Verrazano, employed by the French in 1524 to find a northwest passage to India. Cartier sailed up the St. Lawrence River in 1535 and wintered on the site of present-day Quebec, but his attempt to plant a colony there in 1541 ended disastrously. Internal disturbances at home postponed further French efforts to colonize the St. Lawrence region until 1608, when Samuel de Champlain, an experienced geographer and administrator, and a passionate explorer, founded Quebec. He established a base at Port Royal in Acadia (now Annapolis Royal, Nova Scotia), and accurately charted the Atlantic coast as far south as Cape Cod. During his last years, Champlain discovered the lake that bears his name and reached the upper Great Lakes by an inland route that circumvented the hostile Iroquois, whom Champlain had unwisely antagonized. When he died in 1635, the French controlled the St. Lawrence and were in a position to dominate the Great Lakes area.

From Champlain's arrival until 1627, the white population in New France never reached a hundred. The middle-class entrepreneurs who managed the trading companies found it almost impossible to attract qualified colonists. Religious bickering, royal indifference, and jealousies among the merchants themselves prevented the working out of a consistent colonial policy. When Cardinal Richelieu took over colonial affairs in the 1620's, he tried to give New France vitality and direction by withdrawing the charters of the old trading companies and substituting in their place one government-sponsored company known as the "Company of the One Hundred Associates," or the Company of New France.

But the Company of New France did not bring prosperity. Supply ships fell to English privateers; Quebec was seized by the English in 1629 and held for three years. A catastrophic series of Indian wars during the next decades so weakened New France that the Crown assumed control in 1663 and moved belatedly to strengthen the ailing colony. French troops pacified the Iroquois. Land grants and subsidies were offered to prospective settlers, and shiploads of unmarried women sailed from France to become their wives. Although attempts to improve agricultural techniques and to build up a variety of industries met with some success, the new policy failed to attract the peasants, who still had no strong motive for emigrating. New France remained a country of priests, traders, soldiers, and officials whose needs were too great to be met by the small corps of farmers and artisans.

A semi-feudal society slowly took form in New France. The *seigneurs,* or large landowners, served as the colonial nobility; the *habitants,* or small farmers, tilled the land. Actually, the landowners did not constitute a true aristocracy, nor did they live very differently from the *habitants* who performed only the lightest and most casual services for them—a few days of work each year. The settlers lived in villages rather than in isolated homesteads and looked to the Church and to the military for direction.

Many reasons have been offered to explain the weakness of New France. An inhospitable climate and soil cannot be discounted, nor can the reluctance of the French to emigrate to the New World. France, like other European nations, had her religious dissidents, but the French Protestants were excluded from Canada and chose to contribute their energies and talents to France's enemies. The French government paralyzed colonial

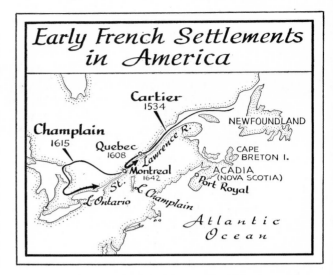

initiative by scrutinizing and interfering with every aspect of religious, political, and economic activity.

As explorers and traders, however, the French performed brilliantly. From the outset, individual fur-traders, or *coureurs de bois,* defied the law requiring Indians to bring their furs to the settlements and disappeared into the forests where they could deal with the Indians without governmental restraints.

Champlain helps his Indian allies defeat the Iroquois.

Ranging deep into the interior, they acquired an expert knowledge of the forests and a profound understanding of Indian psychology. Their tact and the willingness with which they acquired Indian ways and wives had enormous economic and military consequences. Their Indian allies procured furs for them, fought their battles, and guided the expeditions that took French explorers as far west as the Rockies and as far south as the Gulf of Mexico. As a result, France was able to stake her claim to interior America and to formulate her grandiose plans for a colonial empire long before her European rivals.

But the Canadian population was still less than 7,000 in 1700. Scarcity of settlers meant that New France had to depend upon the mother country for food and protection, and this dependency invited a debilitating governmental intervention. "It was the nature of French colonization," wrote the American historian, Francis Parkman, "to seize upon detached strategic points, and hold them by the bayonet, forming no agricultural base, but attracting the Indians by trade and holding them by conversion. A musket, a rosary, and a pack of beaver skins may serve to represent it, and in fact it consisted in little else." In these symbols we can find both the power and the weakness of New France.

The Way of the Dutch.

During the seventeenth century, Holland became the leading commercial nation in Europe and, though her population was small, the financial and cultural center of the world. Dutch enterprise reached into the East Indies, Africa, and the Americas. Concerned only with economic exploitation, the Dutch set up trading stations and forts. They showed even less interest in planting true colonies than the French, and preferred to serve as the middlemen and carriers of Europe.

Dutch activity in America began in 1609, when the Englishman, Henry Hudson, explored the Hudson River for the Dutch East India Company. In the next two decades,

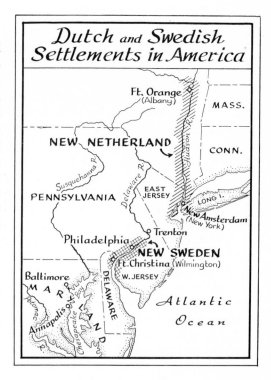

Dutch merchants erected fur-trading posts in the neighborhood of present-day Albany and made their celebrated purchase of the island of Manhattan for $24 worth of goods (1626). The minute regulations laid down by the Dutch West India Company (which controlled New Netherland after 1621), left little room for private initiative, and few Hollanders cared to settle in America. In order to attract settlers, the company offered "patroonships," large tracts of land, to anyone who would transport 50 people across the Atlantic. The "patroons" were virtually independent feudal lords.

The Dutch consolidated their power in 1655, when they expelled a colony of Swedes (established since 1638) from a base on the Delaware River and pushed small settlements into the Hudson River Valley, Long Island, and New Jersey. Having struck up a trading agreement with the formidable Iroquois, they brutally exterminated the Indian foes of their ally, but subsequent Indian wars weakened the colony. The autocratic policies of the company, and its overriding pursuit of trade, moreover, prevented the growth of a substantial farming class that might have resisted hostile pressures from the outside. On the eve of its conquest by the English (1664), New Netherland had a mixed population of Walloons, Huguenots, Swedes, Dutchmen, and Negroes numbering around 8,000. In New Amsterdam alone, 18 languages were spoken. Before the idea of the "melting pot" was thought of, New Amsterdam had become the most cosmopolitan community in North America. But a long period of unwise direction had destroyed any possibility of the colony's survival as a Dutch possession.

The Way of the English.

At the end of the sixteenth century, England, like France and Holland, conceived of a colony as primarily a trading venture or as a base for piratical adventures against Spain; her first experiments in colony-planting were as inept as those of her rivals. The ultimate success of the English in America cannot be attributed to an enlightened and far-seeing colonial policy. Rather, it derived from other factors: from social and political unrest, from the English character, and from English institutions.

Throughout the early years of English colonial expansion, the home country was torn by religious and political dissensions and racked by depression and revolution. Puritan and Royalist, Irishman and Scotsman, Catholic, Anglican, and Dissenter sought refuge in turn as his cause suffered in the mother country. In contrast to New France, British America and the West Indies were peopled by malcontents and rebels, who were promising prospects for colonization but not the safest architects for the building of loyal British dependencies. Had life in England been more serene and more stable economically during the seventeenth century, overseas expansion would have been much slower. As it was, economic and political unrest spurred the advance.

Chaotic conditions at home and a lack of funds prevented the Crown from taking a direct part in planting the original colonies.

That responsibility was left to a small number of capitalists and merchants in southern England and to several wealthy promoters. Privately associated, or operating through joint-stock companies, these were the men who financed the pioneer expeditions. They agreed to pay the costs of transporting settlers and of supplying them with food and implements for a stated period. In return, they expected to enjoy exclusive trading rights with the colonies and to retain a voice in colonial affairs. Some of the companies sank large sums in American plantations, often with no returns. Most colonial enterprises were launched without enough capital, and there were simply no quick profits for the promoters.

The first settlers worried more about their own survival than about company dividends. Insufficient knowledge of colonial conditions and the absence of any clear-cut administrative authority made realistic planning impossible. And, since each company limited its financial obligations, the colonists were left in an awkward situation; additional sums to meet emergencies could be raised only by the company's issuing more stock.

Despite these obstacles, three types of colonies had emerged by the middle of the seventeenth century: the corporate or joint-stock company, the proprietary colony, and the royal colony. In the *joint-stock company,* colonial affairs were in the hands of a number of shareholders operating under the authority of a charter granted by the king. Under the *proprietary system,* the proprietor obtained a charter from the king, established the colony at his own risk, and appointed its officials. In the *royal colony,* affairs were directed by crown officials. Organizers of the first two types performed the job of getting the colonists across the ocean and settling them in the New World. What the Crown regarded as dangerous weaknesses soon began to show themselves in both the corporate and proprietary colonies and eventually some of these colonies were taken over by the king.

The West Indies.   Shortly before and during the English colonization of the American mainland, English merchants had been attracted by the possibility of raising tobacco on the islands of the Caribbean. By 1627, the English colonists were exporting dyewood and tobacco from St. Christopher and Barbados; four years later, the colonial population of Barbados had risen to 1,600.

For the next century and a half, the West Indies played a decisive role in the history of America. Spain's loosening hold on her New World possessions and the vulnerability of the Spanish Main to ferocious assaults by French, Dutch, and English buccaneers ultimately forced Spain to limit her claims of sovereignty in the Caribbean. Populations in the Dutch and French West Indian Islands remained small, but English colonists continued to pour into Barbados; there were approximately 40,000 of them in the West Indies by 1640. This was the high point of colonization, for during the next decade declining tobacco prices brought on by competition from Virginia produced an acute depression in the overcrowded islands. The introduction of sugar cane from Brazil in 1642 quickly restored prosperity, but it also created a remarkable social transformation. The profits from sugar encouraged successful planters to buy out their smaller neighbors and to purchase Negro slaves from the Dutch. White indentured servants (p. 30) and displaced planters, who thus lost their small holdings, went buccaneering, drifted to the mainland colonies, or simply perished. The white population in Barbados decreased from 36,500 in 1645 to 23,000 in 1655.

West Indian sugar turned out to be a vital product in the commerce between England and the American colonies, and the West Indies became the most valuable of England's overseas possessions. The sugar planters not only produced an indispensable crop for the mother country, but they also bought English manufactured goods, and fish, lumber, and horses from the American mainland. The early histories of the American colonies were closely bound up with events in the West Indies.

III. THE CHESAPEAKE COUNTRY

Virginia.   England's first attempts to colonize the New World took place while she was carrying on a costly war with Spain. Sir Humphrey Gilbert's failure at Newfoundland (1583) and Sir Walter Raleigh's abortive effort to settle 150 colonists on Roanoke Island off the coast of North Carolina (1587) demonstrated two things: that successful colonization could not be carried out under wartime conditions and that only a well-financed enterprise, drawing upon the resources of many people, could plant and sustain a colony.

England got its first permanent foothold in America in 1607, when an expedition, after sighting "the Bay of Chesupiac" (Chesapeake), landed amidst "faire meddows and goodly tall Trees," and fell into a skirmish with Indians. A few days later, the three ships, carrying more than 140 passengers (most of them disbanded soldiers and fortune-hunters), sailed some 50 miles up the James River and selected a spot strategically situated for trading and defense, but malaria-ridden.

This pioneer venture had been launched by a group of London promoters who had applied for and received a charter from King James I in 1606. The most important figures in this London (later Virginia) Company were Sir Thomas Smith, a founder of the East India Company, and the Puritan nobleman, Sir Edwin Sandys. The London shareholders had expected immediate profits, but they were soon disillusioned. Company "servants" in Virginia preferred gold-hunting to work, and they were physically and morally unequipped to meet the challenge of the American frontier. As company employees, they had no real stake in the land, and they found no incentive in communal agriculture. During the bleak days of 1609-1610, only the efforts of Captain John Smith held the starving colony together.

Virginia's economic future remained uncertain until, between 1612 and 1614, the settlers discovered a cash crop—tobacco. Englishmen had acquired a taste for what the Elizabethans called "drinking tobacco" in the 1550's. As a result of experiments by the colonist John Rolfe (the future husband of Pocahontas) in the growing and curing of tobacco, Virginia was able to ship 30,000 pounds to England in 1618 and 500,000 by 1627.

Until 1619, political and social conditions

John Smith landing in Virginia—an early eighteenth-century conception.

within the colony remained unsettled. The new charters that Virginia had received in 1609 and again in 1612 had not affected the lives of the colonists very much. A more liberal policy was instituted on July 30, 1619, when the first representative assembly (later known as the House of Burgesses) met at Jamestown. Although the governor and his councilors were company appointees, the people selected the "burgesses." From these simple beginnings arose the form of colonial government that endured until the Revolution.

Increased political stability, the abrogation of harsh laws, the promise of voting privileges and religious toleration, all helped to attract a better type of settler. Under the "head-right" system, introduced in 1618, any person who transported himself to the colony and stayed for three years was given 50 acres. Later, the head of a family could claim an additional 50 acres for any dependent or servant he brought with him. Some men made a business of importing colonists, and acquired large tracts of land in this way.

Yet despite these political and social improvements, the colony did not flourish, and in 1624, when the Virginia Company lost its charter, Virginia became a crown possession. Disputes among company leaders had destroyed its chance to win a tobacco monopoly in England, and a frightful Indian massacre in 1622 lowered company prestige even further. A royal investigation of the company in 1623 revealed some melancholy statistics: of the 6,000 colonists who had taken part in the colonial adventure since 1606, some 4,000 had died. The Virginia enterprise was also a financial failure. Two hundred thousand pounds had been invested, without a single pound of return.

Yet it would be a mistake to minimize the accomplishments of this colonial experiment: (1) The blunders committed in Virginia served as warnings to later colonial promoters. (2) Virginia demonstrated that tobacco was an admirable crop for the pioneer farmer in the lower latitudes. (3) Virginia

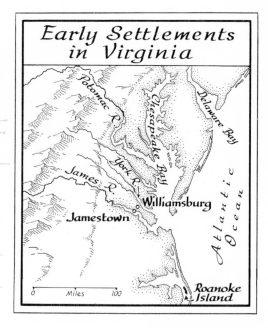

Early Settlements in Virginia

had worked out a pattern of colonial government that was repeated, with important modifications, in the later settlements.

Maryland. Unlike Virginia, the settling of Maryland involved no joint-stock companies and shareholders. Maryland was under the control of a single family during its formative years. Its founder, Sir George Calvert, first Lord Baltimore, had been a favorite of James I, but he resigned his offices after embracing Catholicism in 1625. Religious zeal as well as a wish to improve his family estate prompted him to establish a refuge for English Catholics in America. After experimenting unsuccessfully with a colony in Newfoundland (1622-1627), Calvert obtained a grant of land from Charles I in northern Virginia. He died while negotiations were still in process, but in 1632 his son Cecilius received the charter for a tract that lay between the Potomac River and the fortieth degree of latitude. This "sprout from Virginia" was named Maryland in honor of the English Queen Henrietta Maria.

The younger Baltimore, Cecilius Calvert, an able and humane administrator, successfully planned and directed the initial colonization. St. Mary's, situated near the mouth of the Potomac, turned out to be an ideal location for the first settlers who landed in the spring of 1634, and by dealing fairly with the local tribes Baltimore spared his colony the horrors of an Indian war during its critical period. Most of the colonists began to raise tobacco after a short term of subsistence farming, and the colony almost immediately enjoyed a modest prosperity.

Cecilius Calvert, who remained in England, and Leonard, his younger brother who acted for him in Maryland, proceeded to lay out the new colony in manors of from 1,000 to 3,000 acres. The manor lords (largely Catholic) held their property directly from Cecilius Calvert, but they rented land to smaller planters who paid them in produce. Both small and large planters paid a kind of land tax, called a quit-rent, to the proprietor. The settler was freed or "quit" from any further feudal obligations and became, in effect, an owner of the land. But his tax was still a relic of institutions that had long passed away in England, and it was a symbol of social hierarchy. Such a practice was not likely to take root in a wilderness where land was plentiful and where the people were hostile to feudal ideas.

Until 1660, domestic affairs were turbulent in Maryland in spite of Calvert's toleration. The gentry were mostly Catholic, but the farmers and artisans were usually Protestants who had backed Parliament during the English Civil War. Because they wanted more voice in local government, they made trouble for the political oligarchy who managed the colony's affairs. During this same period, many Puritans left Virginia, where Anglicanism was the established religion, for the tolerant atmosphere of Maryland. This influx swelled the Protestant majority there and complicated the problems of the Catholic proprietors.

In order to safeguard the Catholic minority from Puritan intolerance, the Maryland assembly passed the famous Toleration Act in 1649. This act provided that any person who believed in the divinity of Jesus Christ should be permitted to worship without being molested. The use of reproachful epithets like "heretic," "popish priest," or "Puritan" was made punishable. Although a provision which made the denial of the Trinity a capital offense invalidated the spirit of toleration, Maryland achieved at least a partial success in furthering the cause of liberty of conscience.

By 1650, proprietary authority had somewhat diminished in Maryland as the result of concessions made by the Calverts to popular rule. For many years, the freemen had enjoyed only the privilege of advising the governor, but in 1650 they won the right to propose and approve legislation. In this year, the legislature (hitherto a single-chambered body chosen by the governor) met for the first time as two separate bodies. Calvert still reserved the right to veto legislation even if it had been approved by his governor, and by appointing his own men to key places he maintained his control over the colony. The Calverts ruled unchecked until 1691, when Maryland became a royal colony, and so it remained until it was returned to them in 1715.

The Chesapeake Economy. The first American frontier in Virginia and Maryland was a fertile area of coastal plains which

First Settlements in Maryland.

BALTIMORE'S CHARTER BOUNDARY OF 1632
Susquehanna R.
PRESENT BOUNDARY
40°
Patapsco R.
Potomac R.
Patuxent R.
Severn R.
Delaware R.
St. George's R.
Preston
VIRGINIA
Mattapony
St. Marys
Chesapeake Bay
Watkins Pt.

0   Miles   100

became known as the tidewater region. Through this territory ran numerous navigable estuaries and streams. Since ocean-going vessels could sail right up to the plantation wharves, there was no need to transport produce to export centers. This geographical advantage helps to explain the development of an independent and self-sufficient plantation society.

The marshy tidewater country was decidedly unhealthful—malaria was endemic there —but very fertile. The tidewater soil, though thin and quickly exhausted, produced fine crops of tobacco. By 1619 in Virginia, and by 1650 in Maryland, tobacco had supplanted the pioneer crops of maize, pork, and vegetables, and the basic unit of production had become the independent tobacco farm. In early Virginia, small farms had predominated, but by 1700, when the colony numbered some 40,000, the large one-crop plantation had already appeared. This was particularly true in the coastal areas, where marked social stratification first became evident. By 1700, yeoman farmers had been pushed out of the older sections into the interior and were practicing a subsistence agriculture with tobacco as a side crop.

The monopolizing of the best land by large speculators was made possible by the very laws designed to prevent it. Theoretically, the head-right system (see above, p. 28) should have peopled the wilderness with small holdings; actually it conferred special benefits on speculators and colony officials. Many obtained head-rights by the baldest frauds. By law, land had to be put under cultivation within a three-year period, but since this proviso was largely ignored and since land taxes were hard to extract on the frontier, it was almost impossible to prevent speculators from buying up land and then withholding it from resale for indefinite periods.

Most of the residents of the Chesapeake country were lower-class and middle-class Englishmen, at least half of whom had come to America as servants. In the usual contract, which was drawn up before departure, a person agreed to serve a fixed period of indenture (usually from five to seven years) in payment for his passage. During this time, he was not supposed to marry; violation of this and other restrictions might lengthen his servitude. Sometimes, whole families of servants might cross without signing any contracts. These "redemptioners" would then seek buyers after their arrival. Convicts supplied another source of white indentured or slave labor, and many poor men and unfortunate vagrants were kidnapped in English slums to satisfy the ever-increasing demand for workers. The servants and convicts who survived the hideous ordeal of the Atlantic voyage, the heart-breaking conditions following their arrival, and the actual terms of service, often became rich and respected citizens. In 1663, for example, over one-third of the members of the Virginia House of Burgesses had begun their colonial life as servants.

The need for contract labor, however, was always greater than the supply. There were just not enough white bonded servants to meet the demand, and their terms of indenture ended just as they were becoming well trained. Once free, the former servants would compete with their masters. The best of them became independent farmers, for the proximity of cheap land on the frontier stimulated independent enterprise.

To complicate the problem even further, the widely held theory that England was overpopulated was abandoned after 1660, and the flow of settlers almost stopped except for "the very rubbish and off-scouring of his majesty's dominions." Hence Negro workers, who had been present in Virginia as early as 1619 as servants, were introduced in increasingly larger numbers. Their uncertain status was clarified in 1661 when Virginia legally recognized slavery, and after 1687 strict laws were passed controlling their activities. By 1708, Virginia's Negro population had risen to 12,000, and Negro slavery was well established in the tobacco belt.

Tobacco brought wealth to Virginia and Maryland, especially after the West Indies gave up tobacco for sugar raising. But excessive and unplanned production had reduced the price of tobacco on the London market by the 1620's, and during the next three decades the industry suffered from a variety of causes. Tobacco producers were required to send their crop to England in English or colonial vessels, even though roughly three-quarters of it was then reexported to the Continent. Colonial producers resented paying the English tax on every pound of tobacco shipped, and they complained of burdensome freight rates. Actually, the producers gained far more than they lost by these British regulations. The Crown remitted most of the import duties on re-exported tobacco and protected colonial commerce with its sea power. British credit supported the industry. The high carrying charges, as British officials frequently pointed out, were caused by the growers' refusal to ship their tobacco from a centralized port. The periodic tobacco slumps in the seventeenth century were simply an early indication of the uncertainties of an unregulated one-crop agricultural economy.

In both Virginia and Maryland, economic hardships fell most heavily on the small, often unrepresented class of farmers who were excluded from county and parish offices. A privileged clique controlled the legislature and reaped the economic fruits of patronage. This was particularly true in Virginia during the 1660's and 1670's, when the reactionary governor, William Berkeley, was working closely with the nascent aristocracy. Berkeley and his favorites monopolized the fur trade. What is more, they refused to send the militia against the Susquehanna Indians, who had been terrorizing Maryland and Virginia settlements, lest the fur trade suffer as a result of the Indians' resentment. Berkeley's decision provoked a rebellion among the small farmers in the region of the upper James River.

In 1676, Nathaniel Bacon, a young member of the Governor's Council and a comparative newcomer to Virginia, became impatient with Berkeley's policies, and upon being refused a military commission by the Governor, took the leadership of the discontented farmers, organized a volunteer force, and led them in successful attacks against the Indians. Bacon, now extremely popular, forced Berkeley to hold new elections, and in these Bacon was chosen to go to the Burgesses. But when he arrived at Jamestown to take his seat, he was arrested, and his demand for a military commission was again refused. Bacon then collected a body of infuriated supporters who terrorized Berkeley into granting him a commission. When Bacon departed to put down renewed Indian raids on the frontier, the Governor raised an army against him. Bacon turned east, captured Jamestown, and, as the Governor fled, set up a reform government. Once again, conflict on two fronts was too much for him: when Bacon left for still further campaigns against the Indians, the Governor stubbornly returned. This time the rebels came back to capture and burn Jamestown; but Bacon himself died of a fever in October, 1676. His following became a disorderly mob, and Berkeley, returning for a final assault with a force of eastern planters, suppressed them. The vindictive Berkeley hanged 23 of the rebels before King Charles' commissioners arrived to relieve him of his office.

IV.   THE NEW ENGLAND SETTLEMENTS

Plymouth.   Thirteen years after the settling of Jamestown, a small band of English Pilgrims who had "separated" from the Anglican church, landed from the *Mayflower* at Plymouth, Massachusetts, on December 21, 1620. An earlier New England post, set up at the mouth of the Kennebec River in 1607, had been abandoned after one Maine winter. In 1614, Captain John Smith, sailing from Virginia, mapped the northern New England coast but did not attempt to settle it. The first permanent English post in New England, the second on the American mainland, was that of the Pilgrims.

The passengers aboard the *Mayflower* consisted of a minority of the separatists who had fled to Holland between 1607 and 1609, together with other miscellaneous Englishmen —102 in all. Through a historic concession, James I had given them permission to settle in the Virginia territory "in order to enjoy their own way of thinking, called gospel-privileges, in peace and purity." A group of 70 London merchants had invested some £700 in the venture, and in return for this backing the Pilgrims were expected to work seven years for the promoters. At the end of this period, all property would be divided between the settlers and the merchants. When the Pilgrims discovered that they had come ashore at a point outside the boundaries of the Virginia Company, they obtained permission from the Council for New England to remain. This land company had obtained a patent in 1620-1621 granting it title to an area roughly equivalent to what is today New England.

The story of the Pilgrims is eloquently recorded in Governor William Bradford's *Of Plimouth Plantation*. Neither the menacing landscape nor the hostility of men shook Bradford's faith in God. It was God, he relates, who filled the voyagers' restless hearts with courage to undertake the ocean passage. God reserved the New World as His bounty to the Pilgrims and destroyed a majority of the benighted aborigines of Cape Cod before the Pilgrims landed. It was God who sustained the Pilgrims through illness and starvation, who "heard their voice and looked on their adversity."

The Pilgrims never reached such desperate straits as the first settlers of Jamestown, but they too came close to starvation and were plagued by disease and mutinies. Before landing in 1620, the Pilgrim leaders signed an agreement, known as the Mayflower Compact, to "covenant & combine ourselves to-

geather into a civill body politick for our better ordering & preservation," and to frame "just & equall lawes ... for ye generall good of ye Colonie." The government of the early Pilgrims was thus hardly more than an agreement, a social compact, to create the rules for a cooperative society and to abide by them. The community was in reality a church body, and every member had a voice in determining policy by electing the governor and his assistants. As the colony grew, however, and as society became decentralized in small towns, a representative system supplanted what had formerly been a kind of direct democracy. Plymouth's importance, which was never great, lessened as the century waned. It became a satellite of Massachusetts Bay even before it was absorbed by that colony in 1691.

Massachusetts Bay.

The Puritan commonwealth of Massachusetts Bay differed in important respects from the earlier settlements at Jamestown and Plymouth. Better organized, more richly endowed, and more efficiently led, it wore from the very outset an air of success. This was the first migration of a large community from the Old World to the New.

In 1628, a vanguard of 40 Puritans landed at Naumkeag (Salem) under the leadership of an unattractive zealot, John Endecott. Two years later, in 1630, a far more gracious and humane man, John Winthrop, reached New England with the main body of 1,000 colonists and founded the Puritan capital of Boston. Smaller villages immediately sprang up around it—among them Charlestown, Roxbury, Dorchester, Newtown (Cambridge), Watertown, Agawam (Ipswich), and Saugus (Lynn).

The Massachusetts Bay Company, incorporated by a group of wealthy Puritans in 1629, had been started as a commercial venture. Its character changed when some of the members, led by John Winthrop, decided to remove themselves from the persecutions under Charles I. Having obtained a charter from the King, they got the company's permission to take it with them to America, which meant that the powers of government were vested in a small oligarchy far removed from Old World interference. With the charter safely in Massachusetts, no godless investors in the mother country could wrest company control away from the Puritan "insiders."

The Puritan leaders were not humanitarian democrats who were out to create a haven for dissenters in America. In fact, they made certain that power stayed in the hands of a godly minority. According to their charter, author-

first step. Since ministers were given the privilege of screening the candidates and excluding the unsanctified, the pulpit was in effect transformed into a barrier of conservatism.

The anti-democratic bias of the Puritan authorities, however, can easily be overemphasized. We must remember that the General Court in the 1640's had a hard time getting freemen to exercise their political prerogatives or to perform their civic duties.

The Fairbanks House, Dedham, Massachusetts, built about 1637—the oldest wooden house now standing in America.

ity rested with a legislature or "General Court," composed of share-holders or "freemen," and a governor, deputy governor, and council of "assistants" elected by the freemen. Upon arrival, the freemen in the colony made up less than 1 per cent of the population, but in a few months Winthrop enlarged the number of voters. Soon after, the freemen (or voting citizens) claimed their right to elect colony officials annually, and by 1644 the General Court was composed of an upper chamber of assistants and a lower chamber of deputies, two from each town. Despite this representative machinery, the magistrates and ministers maintained their power by requiring church membership (distinguished from compulsory church attendance) as a prerequisite for the franchise. Admission to church membership did not automatically confer the right to vote, but it was the indispensable

Non-freemen often voted on local matters and occupied town offices. The alliance between clergyman and magistrate was in no sense a conspiracy against the lower orders but a testament to the Puritan recognition that civil and religious matters were closely intertwined. Any deviation from orthodox belief—whether in matters of politics, religion, or personal behavior—was sternly corrected. The Puritan leaders assumed that the good society operated according to the laws of God as interpreted by a learned ministry. And the Bible was the infallible clue to God's intentions. The alternative to godly government was chaos. What might seem to us mere theological quibbling had explosive implications for Massachusetts magistrates, who knew that the visions of religious enthusiasts often led to political as well as to religious heresy.

The Radicals

of Rhode Island. During the decade between 1630 and 1640, the Massachusetts leaders were in fact challenged on political, social, and religious grounds. One of the consequences of the struggle that followed was the founding of Rhode Island by a heretical refugee from Massachusetts orthodoxy.

Roger Williams, "a man," to quote Bradford, "having very many precious parts, but very unsettled in judgment," had proved troublesome to Archbishop Laud back in England because of his uncompromising views, and the leaders of the Bay Colony found him no less obnoxious. Not only did he raise embarrassing issues, such as his assertion that Massachusetts Bay had no just claim to Indian lands, but he also charged the Bay authorities to admit that the colony had in fact separated itself from the Church of England. Williams' tactlessness reached its height when he accused Massachusetts of setting up its own national church and when he denied the right of the Puritan rulers to compel religious observances. He was attacking the citadel of Massachusetts theocracy: the inseparability of church and state.

The magistrates insisted that "the powers that be are ordained by God. Whosoever therefore resisteth the power, resisteth the ordinance of God; and they that resist shall receive to themselves damnation." Williams' repudiation of this doctrine was not an expression of secular liberalism but the response of a deeply religious man who doubted that "Judges are Gode upon earthe." The Puritan leaders understood the dangerous undercurrent of his thinking, and, being logical and consistent men, they threw him out. Expelled from Massachusetts, Williams established his own community in the region of Narragansett Bay in 1636. Providence, as he named his settlement, later became the center of the colony of Rhode Island and the Providence Plantations.

Anne Hutchinson, another rebel who sought asylum in Rhode Island, fared no better in her dealings with the Puritan orthodoxy. Had she held her tongue, she might have remained in Boston and continued to conduct her discussions on midwifery. But Anne Hutchinson began to hold forth on doctrinal matters as well, and her incautious speculations split the town in two. Behind the jargon of Puritan theology lay an all-important question: Was it possible for a person to communicate directly with God without confirmation by scripture, ministerial authority, or logic? When she insisted that it was, her enemies in Boston were convinced that Satan, not God, was the source of her inspirations, and the more this "modern Jezebel" prophesied, the more certain they became "that Mrs. Hutchinson" was "deluded by the Devil." Her theologizing, like Williams', threatened the foundations of the state, and in 1638 the magistrates expelled her. After a sojourn in Rhode Island, Anne Hutchinson moved to present-day New York, where she and her family were massacred by Indians.

From this point on, Rhode Island became a magnet for dissenting settlers and a symbol of anarchy and heresy to its neighbors. Four loosely federated settlements existed there by 1643, and one year later Rhode Island got official sanction and a charter from Parliament. In 1647, a union of towns similar to that of Massachusetts was inaugurated. For a long time, Rhode Island was the only

Massachusetts, Rhode Island and Connecticut Settlements

Miles 0 — 100
PRESENT BOUNDARIES

MASS. BAY COLONY, 1629
Salem
Watertown, Boston
Roxbury
Dorchester
Springfield
Plymouth
PLYMOUTH COLONY, 1630
Windsor
Newtown
Hartford
Providence
Wethersfield
Warwick
Portsmouth
CONN. COLONY, 1662
New Haven
Guilford
Milford
Newport
PROVIDENCE PLANTATIONS, 1636
Stamford
Ft. Saybrook
RHODE I. COLONY, 1638

Atlantic Ocean

colony in which all religious sects enjoyed freedom of worship according to the doctrine of toleration stated in Williams' famous tract, *The Bloudy Tenent of Persecution for Cause of Conscience.* Other New England colonies continued to regard Rhode Island as "Rogues' Island" and excluded it from their confederation (see p. 36).

The Expansion of New England.

By 1643, the Puritan settlements extended westward to the Connecticut River, southward to Long Island Sound, and northward to New Hampshire and Maine. The expansion into the fertile Connecticut Valley took place under the direction of a formidable minister, Thomas Hooker. His congregation had grown dissatisfied with the poor land around the village of Newtown (Cambridge), and Hooker himself was too powerful and ambitious a man to be content with a subordinate role in Massachusetts affairs. Moreover, he was disturbed by the absence in Massachusetts of a codified body of law. Hooker was no radical, but the new colony of Connecticut that took shape between 1636 and 1639 under his direction seemed to be more liberal in politics than Massachusetts.

The Fundamental Orders of Connecticut, drawn up in 1639 by delegates from the newly established towns of Hartford, Wethersfield, and Windsor, has been hailed as "the first written constitution of modern democracy." Actually, it was not democratic in our sense of the word, and it followed pretty closely the Puritan conceptions of civil government. It dispensed with religious qualifications for citizenship so long as the candidate was "acceptable," but in effect only good Puritans were regarded as acceptable. Under its provisions, a General Assembly or Court was established to which each town might send four deputies. The General Assembly chose a governor each year, and no governor could serve two years consecutively. It also elected a body of assistants who functioned as an upper house with the right (after 1645) to veto the legislation of the deputies. Similar

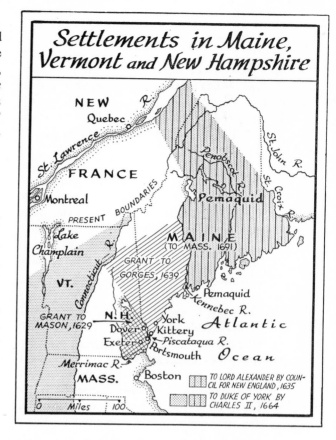

Settlements in Maine, Vermont and New Hampshire

patterns of government took form in the New Haven settlement, founded by the Reverend John Davenport and Theophilus Eaton in 1638, and in the nucleus of other towns that affiliated themselves with New Haven (1643-1656). Here Puritan orthodoxy was not relaxed, and church membership continued to be a prerequisite for the franchise. Connecticut emerged as a separate colony in 1662, when the Crown joined New Haven with the river towns.

The colonies of New Hampshire and Maine were another result of the settlers' going where they had no legal right to be: into the possessions of Captain John Mason and Sir Ferdinando Gorges, who between them owned all the land between the Merrimac and Kennebec rivers. Small settlements sprang up in this country, though the two proprietors neglected to do anything themselves to develop their holdings. The gradual occupation of the New Hampshire area by Massachusetts emigrants foreshadowed its absorption into the Bay Colony in 1644.

35

Charles II detached it again in 1679, and New Hampshire became a royal province. The Massachusetts penetration of Maine proceeded along the same lines. After the death of Gorges, it was officially joined to Massachusetts in 1668.

The expansion of the English colonists into areas claimed or occupied by the Indians and by other European powers inevitably led to friction. To the north lay the settlements of the French, and to the southwest the Dutch were entrenched. In every direction, powerful Indian tribes impeded the New England advance. To meet these combined dangers, Massachusetts, Plymouth, Connecticut, and New Haven joined together in 1643 to form "The Confederation of the United Colonies of New England," the first of a series of colonial efforts to work together. The union indicated that New England considered itself perfectly capable of negotiating with the French and Dutch without consulting the mother country. The Confederation refused to admit Rhode Island (whose lands were coveted by the other settlements as much as its principles were detested), and it also turned down Maine's petition for entrance. According to the agreement, each of the four colonies elected two representatives who determined policy on Indian affairs, negotiated with foreign powers, and arbitrated differences among themselves. The Confederation, which was an active force only until 1665, broke up in 1684. Massachusetts' sometimes overbearing behavior and her refusal on occasion to submit to majority rule may have been one reason for its disintegration.

The New England Economy.

New England, with the exception of the Connecticut and Merrimac valleys, was less fertile than the Chesapeake region, and was destined to be settled with small farms and compact villages. When a group wanted to establish a new town (for, unlike the practice in Virginia, expansion was planned beforehand), they obtained permission from the General Court to settle a new territory of approximately six square miles adjoining an older one. The settlers or "Proprietors" laid out the main street, the village green, the centrally located church, the school, the town lots, and fields or strips adjacent to the village. All freemen were eligible to draw for the town lots and to make use of the undistributed woods and meadows. The richer settlers sometimes got additional lots, but even the most favored never received more than two or three times as much land as the poorest. Only freemen could vote in the town meeting, where local business was transacted, but anyone might attend.

This system of establishing new towns carried with it certain disadvantages. The original proprietors tended to become a local upper class. And because they retained control over the further distribution of undivided land, they clashed with the late-comers: freemen, who owned small amounts of land and who voted but who were denied the land-distributing privilege of the original proprietors; and the landless renters or laborers, who were not even voting citizens. Together these late-comers formed a disgruntled majority. Disputes between the old settlers and the new often ended with the latter moving west to newer settlements, and gradually the old New England system of planned expansion broke down. By 1725, townships were being sold to speculators in Massachusetts, Connecticut, and New Hampshire instead of to communities of settlers. But during the middle decades of the seventeenth century, the New England plan of settlement worked effectively, preserving culture and religion.

The success of New England's controlled expansion was due partly to careful planning and centralized administration and partly to inhospitable nature. Had the soils to the westward been temptingly fertile, the westward movement of New England towns might not have been so orderly. But New England's physiography as well as her institutions prevented the emergence of large plantations worked by servants or slaves; its rock-studded soil and harsh climate produced no cash crops. The industrious pioneers (some 85 per cent of them) turned to subsistence farming and the remaining 15 per cent to fishing, lumbering, shipbuilding, and small-scale manufacturing. They smelted iron as early as 1644, manufactured rum from

molasses, and developed a lively trade with the West Indies. The foundations of New England's commercial prosperity were well established by the 1670's.

V. PROPRIETORS AND PHILANTHROPISTS

The Carolinas. The founding of Carolina was merely one of the many important colonial enterprises that were launched during the first decade of Charles II's reign. From Hudson's Bay to the West Indies, new

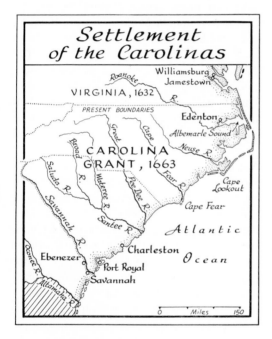

territories were being annexed and old territories reorganized. Although the eight friends of the King who directed the establishment of Carolina obtained their grant in 1663, no permanent settlement was effected until seven years had passed. Two earlier attempts to plant a settlement at the mouth of the Cape Fear River had failed, but in 1670 an expedition founded the city of Charles Towne (Charleston) at Albemarle Point. Charles Towne was relocated in 1680 at the confluence of the Ashley and Cooper rivers.

First called "New Charles Towne," it did not become Charleston until 1783. Even before 1670, squatters from Virginia had begun to filter into the northern section of the Carolina grant along what is now the Albemarle Sound. This area, later to become North Carolina, was administered from Virginia.

The eight proprietors wished to create a colony somewhat along the lines of Maryland. John Locke, the most famous philosopher of his age, drew up for them a remarkable document known as the "Fundamental Constitutions of Carolina." Here was a blueprint that made Maryland's manorial plan seem like a model of practical wisdom. Locke's constitution provided for an elaborate hierarchy ranging from a hereditary nobility ("seignors") down through "landgraves," "caciques," and "commoners." The titles Locke conferred upon the eight proprietors have a grandeur ironically inappropriate to the American scene: "Lord Palatine," the "Lord High Chamberlain." Needless to say, the Fundamental Constitutions was not welcomed by the colonists. Only a few of its provisions were accepted, but the proprietors, even without their grandiose paper government, gave an aristocratic tone to Carolina society and helped to create the basis of a plantation gentry.

Charles Towne soon became a cosmopolitan community. French Protestant refugees came to the town after 1685 (when Louis XIV resumed the persecution of the Huguenots) as well as settlers from New England and the West Indies. The economy of the colony first centered around foodstuffs and naval stores, but in the early 1700's rice became South Carolina's staple crop. A representative system roughly similar to Maryland's gradually evolved, but the proprietors remained unpopular.

North Carolina, which became a separate colony in 1691, offered a striking contrast to its aristocratic sister to the south. Settled by malcontents from Virginia, it soon became notorious as a center for smugglers and pirates. Well-born Virginians of a later generation, men like William Byrd II, sneered at North Carolina as a "lubberland," a haunt for runaway slaves, debtors, and fugitives. Like Rhode Island in the north, it stood as an oasis between two aristocratic societies, and later on it became a center of paper-money agitation and other economic heresies (see pp. 61-62).

New York and New Jersey.

The proprietorship of Charles II's brother James, Duke of York, over what had been New Netherland, gave him almost absolute powers. Happily, the Duke and his first deputy, Richard Nichols, preferred to conciliate the mixed Dutch and English population, and his regime in some respects was more liberal than that of the Dutch had been. The so-called "Duke's Laws" (1665) granted religious toleration, confirmed existing land titles, and permitted the Long Island towns to run their local affairs. New York's government was still the least democratic in the colonies, but agitation to liberalize it met with no success until the colony became a royal province in 1685 at the accession of James II.

In the same year in which New Netherland passed to the English (1664), the Duke of York detached the part of his grant that lay between the Delaware and the Hudson and gave it to his loyal followers, Sir George Carteret and John, Lord Berkeley. The name New Jersey was given to this area to commemorate the Island of Jersey, where Carteret had served as governor. After New York had been reconquered by the Dutch (1673) and returned (1674), the charter had to be reissued to the two proprietors. but in the meantime Berkeley had sold his share of New Jersey to some Quakers (1680). The Duke therefore reissued the grant to Carteret, who retained control of East Jersey (see map on p. 24), and West Jersey became a Quaker colony. After the death of Carteret, another group of Quaker proprietors bought the East Jersey province. During the Quaker proprietorship, the Jerseys enjoyed a liberal government and became a haven for the persecuted. The two sections remained separate until 1692, and in 1702 the Crown made New Jersey a royal province.

Pennsylvania.

In 1681, William Penn, who had been largely responsible for the liberal government of West Jersey, acquired a charter from Charles II which enabled him to found a colony of his own. Penn (1644-1718), the son of an aristocratic and wealthy British admiral, had been infected with Quaker ideas as a young boy, and kept them despite the attempts of an angry father to make him renounce the principles of this despised sect.

Like other dissenters, the Quakers rejected both the ritual and hierarchical organization of the Anglican church and the Calvinism of the Puritans. George Fox (1624-1691), the founder of the Religious Society of Friends, as the Quakers called themselves, was a mystic who felt himself divinely commissioned to preach the new creed: that man's love for God could be best shown by man's love for man, and that salvation was possible for all. Fox and his followers ardently propagandized for the new faith and outraged the world by their demands and condemnations. Every Quaker was a member of the priesthood, since all men possessed the "inner light" that enabled them to hear God's voice. The radical equalitarianism of the Quakers —their refusal to swear oaths, to fight, to accept class distinctions—seemed to subvert the standing order, and they were savagely persecuted both in Europe and America. At the same time, their diligence and frugality made them prosperous. Fifty years after George Fox's preachings, the Quakers had grown from the lowliest to one of the most influential of the dissenting sects.

After the death of his father, Penn was able to carry out his dream of providing a refuge for his persecuted brethren. In exchange for a debt the King had owed his father, Penn obtained a grant to a large area in the Delaware region north of Maryland that had once been part of New Netherland but that lay outside the Duke of York's original proprietorship. The terms of Penn's charter did not give him the sweeping powers enjoyed by the earlier proprietors; British officials, by this time, had begun to check colonial pretensions to self-rule. Nevertheless, Penn laid down a plan of government that was certainly the most liberal in the colonies and perhaps in the world. It called for a two-chambered parliament, both houses to be elected by the freemen. The upper house would propose legislation; the lower house would ratify or reject it. Since the ownership of a small amount of land or the payment of taxes entitled a man to vote, suffrage was widely held. Only Rhode Islanders could claim so liberal a franchise.

Even though Penn's government and humane legal code proved attractive to settlers, the non-Quaker element fought his administration from the start. Boundary disputes with New York and Maryland, together with charges in 1692 that he favored the cause of the exiled James II, made his position insecure. Between 1692 and 1696, he in fact lost his charter, and his colony was governed during the interim by the governor of New York. Penn's disgust with his enemies did not prevent him from returning in 1699 and liberalizing his government even further. The "Charter of Privileges" granted in 1701 met some of the demands of his critics and gave partial self-government to the counties west of the Delaware that once had belonged to the Swedes. Delaware itself, granted to Penn in 1682, had its own legislature by 1704, but had the same governor as Pennsylvania until the Revolution.

The immediate success of Pennsylvania and its extraordinary progress from its founding in 1682 indicate how much prac-

tical wisdom the colonists had accumulated since the days of Jamestown and Plymouth. Penn carefully selected the site for Philadelphia before the first settlers had even arrived, and he planned its dimensions with foresight. He had made friends with the Indians and thus insured an interval of peace that lasted for 75 years. That his province turned out to be fertile and that its beginnings happened to coincide with religious persecutions on the Continent, were, of course, accidental. But Penn skillfully took advantage of his opportunities. He advertised his colony and persuaded large numbers of German sectarians from the Rhineland to migrate to the Pennsylvania back-country. Complete religious toleration for anyone who worshiped God attracted colonists of all faiths. In 1682, Pennsylvania's population amounted to about 1,000. By 1689 there were 12,000 inhabitants. A flourishing trade quickly developed with the West Indies, where Pennsylvania's pork, beef, wheat, and flour were in great demand. Pennsylvania soon became the richest colony in North America.

Georgia.   The settling of Pennsylvania marked the end of British colonization in the seventeenth century. Only one strip of coast

lay open between Spanish Florida and South Carolina. This gap was closed in 1733 when James Oglethorpe, acting for a group of British philanthropists, landed a hundred settlers above the mouth of the Savannah River and founded the town of Savannah. Legally, Spain had better claims to this area based on her explorations here in the sixteenth century, but she could do nothing to prevent the English occupation.

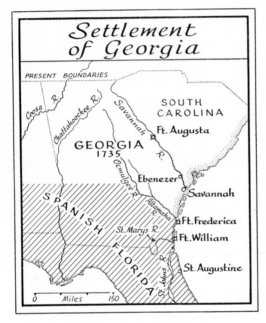

Settlement of Georgia

PRESENT BOUNDARIES

SOUTH CAROLINA

Ft. Augusta

GEORGIA 1735

Ebenezer

Savannah

SPANISH FLORIDA

St. Marys R.

Ft. Frederica

Ft. William

St. Augustine

0   Miles   150

Coosa R.   Chattahoochee R.   Savannah R.   Ocmulgee R.   Altamaha R.   St. Johns R.

Georgia was neither a corporate colony nor, strictly speaking, a proprietary colony. The Crown regarded it as a military outpost, and the directors or trustees hoped to make it an asylum for Englishmen imprisoned for debt. Oglethorpe himself envisioned a community of small farmers who might also comprise a yeoman militia. No person, the trustees ruled, could own more than 50 acres, and the land could be passed on only to male heirs. Slavery was prohibited, for humanitarian and commercial reasons. The trustees had unrealistically planned an economy based on the production of wine and silk, neither of which required slave labor. They felt that Negroes would be a military hazard if the Spaniards succeeded in making them revolt against their masters. Finally, the trustees banned the importation of rum and brandy.

These regulations did not sit well with the mixed group of Welsh, Scots, English, and Germans who had come to Georgia to improve their fortunes. The Georgians needed slave labor and larger holdings of land. They resented the interdict against importing rum, for it prevented them from selling lumber to the West Indies. But here as elsewhere in the American colonies, impractical expectations gave way before local conditions. In time the trustees had to yield to the unidealistic colonial demands, and Georgia became a plantation and slave-owning society.

VI.   ENGLAND AND THE COLONIES, 1650-1733

The First Navigation Acts.   As the colonies grew in size and wealth, and as they consumed more and more English manufactured goods, Englishmen began to point out the "irregular and disorderly state" of trade between the kingdom and its plantations; and, as imperial conflicts increased, statesmen began to give thought to the question of how the colonies could be made to contribute most to English self-sufficiency and English profits. Gradually, over a period of many decades, a series of acts regulating colonial trade was passed by Parliament and a num-

ber of administrative agencies were set up to enforce the regulations.

The first measures originated during the struggles with the Dutch that followed hard upon the Civil War in England. Seizing the English disorders as an opportunity to cut into the trade of the English merchants, the Dutch soon began to undersell their British rivals and to take away much of their shipping trade. Under Cromwell, the Puritan Parliament retaliated by passing two Navigation Acts, in 1650 and 1651, which were intended to shut the Dutch out of the commerce of the English colonies and from the entire carrying trade between England and other countries.

Many of the deeds of Cromwell and the Puritans were undone after the Stuart restoration (in the person of Charles II) in 1660. But the Navigation Acts, far from being abandoned, were re-enacted and systematized, and served as the basis of the imperial trade for more than a century. The Navigation Act of 1660 (re-enacted by the first regular Restoration Parliament in 1661) provided that no goods or commodities, wherever they came from, could be brought to or sent out of any English colony, except in ships that were owned by Englishmen and operated by an English master and a three-fourths English crew. This requirement worked no hardship on the colonials, because the term "English" was always understood to include English subjects in the colonies. The Act also required that certain "enumerated articles"—chiefly sugar, tobacco, indigo, and cotton-wool—that were grown or manufactured in the colonies be sold only to England or to another colony. Among the first list of enumerated articles only tobacco was of major importance, but other items were added from time to time. This measure aimed to keep important supplies out of other countries, and the mother country had no intention of harming the trade of the colonies. To assure the colonials the full benefit of the English market, the growing of tobacco in England was forbidden, as well as its importation from foreign countries. These prohibitions, however, did not prevent occasional gluts in the tobacco market, such as the one in the 1660's which led to a drastic fall in prices.

The Navigation Act of 1663, passed to give to English merchants a monopoly of colonial trade, affected the colonists more seriously. It required, with a few exceptions (salt, wine from Madeira and the Azores, and provisions, horses, and servants from Scotland and Ireland), that European goods destined for the colonies must be shipped through England and on English ships. Import and export duties were charged on this trans-shipment, but a system of rebates to the

colonists enabled them to buy foreign goods coming by way of England about as cheaply as Englishmen could buy them at home. The colonial merchants, none the less, regarded the measure as a serious limitation and inconvenience, since in some cases it called for an extra leg on their voyages to secure goods from the Continent. They began to violate the enumerated-articles law by shipping directly to European ports and to violate the Act of 1663 by smuggling European goods directly back to the colonies without stopping at England.

A third Navigation Act, which became effective in 1673, was intended to stop up some of the loopholes. Colonial shippers, for example, would pretend that they were taking enumerated articles to another colonial port, but would then clear that port for Europe. To stop this easy practice, the Act of 1673 assessed duties in the colonies *at the port of clearance,* unless the captain would bind himself to take the cargo to England. Since a staff of officials had to be set up in the colonies to collect the export duties, the Act of 1673 provoked a good deal of friction between colonials and royal officials. One of the most officious of these officers sent to New England in 1676 was Edward Randolph, who harassed the New Englanders for many years, drew the attention of royal officials to various facets of law-evasion in Massachusetts, and helped to bring about the train of events that cost Massachusetts her charter in 1684.

After the Restoration, a great deal of authority to make recommendations on colonial policy and colonial trade had been given to the Committee for Trade and Plantations of the Privy Council, usually called more simply the Lords of Trade. As early as 1664, a royal commission had been sent to investigate the infringements of crown authority in Massachusetts. Finally, after Randolph's charges convinced the Privy Council of the outrageousness of Massachusetts' actions, the Council annulled her charter and made plans to overhaul colonial administration.

Between 1684 and 1688, all the northern colonies were consolidated into one, called the "Territory and Dominion of New England." This "Dominion" included all the New England colonies together with New York and East and West New Jersey—an unwieldy realm administered by the stubborn and dictatorial Sir Edmund Andros. The Council hoped to modify the economy of the New England and Middle colonies and to encourage the production of metals, hemp, and naval stores in place of commerce and manufacturing. Under Andros' regime the colonial assemblies were abolished, and an attempt was made to enforce Anglican worship. No one could have reconciled the Massachusetts Puritans to the religious features of the Dominion of New England, but Andros made matters worse by the insolence with which he offended their sentiments. Everyone felt threatened by his policies, and when the joyous news arrived from England that King James II had been deposed in the Glorious Revolution of 1689, Andros was immediately overthrown and imprisoned.

The English System

After 1689.   William and Mary, called to the throne by the deposers of James II, found their authority somewhat curtailed, for the celebrated Bill of Rights, passed in 1689 and accepted by William, forbade the king to suspend a parliamentary act, gave Parliament the sole right to raise taxes and maintain an army, and guaranteed legal rights to every English subject.

Massachusetts hailed the Glorious Revolution with joy, but its elation was premature. No effort was made to restore the Dominion of New England, but the new government of William III faced serious problems of colonial administration. In one of its first decisions, it converted several colonies from proprietary or partial self-government to royal government, which meant that sovereign authority was represented in the province by a governor appointed by the Crown. The new charter granted to Massachusetts in 1691 replaced the old elected governor of the period before 1684 with a royal governor with veto power over legislation. New Hampshire, now again separated from Massachusetts, received a royal governor, as did New York and (for an interim until 1715) Maryland. The proprietors of Pennsylvania lost their control for several years. After 1752, the only remaining proprietary colonies were Pennsylvania, Delaware, and Maryland. Except for Connecticut and Rhode Island, which still lived under independent corporate charters, the rest were crown colonies presided over by royal governors.

What did it mean to be a royal governor? As the Crown's chief representative in the colonies, the royal governor possessed broad powers. He could summon and dissolve the assembly, veto its legislation, and appoint minor officials. The council or upper house, which served as his advisory board, with executive, legislative, and judicial functions, was chosen (except in Massachusetts) by the Board of Trade in England from among leading colonials. But since the governor's recommendations affected the choice of council members, his influence and patronage were great among the rich and able in the colonies. With all his dignity and authority, the governor found himself caught between colonial and royal crossfire. As the symbol and spokesman of royal supremacy, he was expected to follow instructions from England that reflected the rigid policies of British officialdom, the interests of British merchants that clashed with those of the colonists, and the conclusions of the Board of Trade whose members were not familiar at first-hand with American conditions. Yet he had to respect the needs of the colony and not offend its leaders, among whom he had to live. The job called for remarkable tact, a genius for knowing when to compromise and when to stand firm. Much has been made of the governor's dependence on the assembly for his salary, but in only four provinces (New York, New Jersey, New Hampshire, and Massachusetts) was salary control of vital importance in the struggle between governor and assembly.

The Crown under William III continued the series of commercial regulations with a reorganized Board of Trade. The Navigation Act of 1696, for example, was intended to tighten administrative enforcement. Colonial laws contrary to the earlier Navigation Acts were declared void. Colonial naval officers were given new responsibilities, and provincial customs officers were given the same rights as those in England, including the right to enter forcibly where examination of premises was deemed necessary. Governors not appointed directly by the Crown had to win the King's approval. Bonds had to be posted to assure the proper delivery of enumerated articles.

And the list of enumerated articles was lengthened. In 1705, rice (now an important Carolina crop) was added, along with molasses, the key item in the West Indies economy. Naval stores were also enumerated, but because they were now much needed in England, the Crown offered welcome bounties for their production. In 1721, beaver skins, furs, and copper were also enumerated. The Molasses Act of 1733, the most threatening of the measures adopted between 1696 and the American Revolution, aimed to force the colonists to buy West Indies products from the English islands only, and to forsake trade with the foreign West Indies. Since the English islands, both as markets and sources of supply, were inadequate to the needs of the American merchants, this act, which placed prohibitive duties on all sugar, molasses, spirits, and rum imported from foreign plantations, would have been disastrous if enforced. Fortunately, it became law during the period when Sir Robert Walpole, with his policy of "salutary neglect" of the colonies, dominated the English government. Under his regime, the colonists violated the Molasses Act freely, and on the whole continued to prosper.

Less laden with potential trouble for the empire were the measures taken by the mother country to prevent the development of any manufacturing industry in the colonies formidable enough to spoil them as a market for her own goods. The Wool Act of 1699 forbade the export of wool products from any American colony either overseas or to another colony. The Hat Act of 1732, passed under pressure from London felt-makers, banned the exportation of hats from one colony to another and placed limits on the apprenticeship system in the colonies in order to check the growth of a large reservoir of skilled labor in this trade. The Iron Act of 1750, forbade the erection in America of rolling and slitting mills, forges, and steel furnaces. The ban was meant to prevent the colonists from making finished products that would compete with England's. But the act also allowed colonial pig and bar iron to enter England duty-free, because these supplies were in great demand in the mother country.

The modern reader may easily imagine that English regulation of American affairs was more burdensome to the colonies than it actually was. American as well as English merchants benefited from the exclusion of the Dutch and others from the imperial trade. Generous bounties were given to producers of colonial goods such as naval stores, which were in great demand in England. Merchant-smugglers violated freely and frequently the more onerous regulations, and British administration was either too inefficient or too easy-going to do much about it. The trade of the colonies—threatened by competition from their French neighbors and hampered by Indian forays—was protected by British arms on land and sea. To draw up a balance sheet of the gains and losses of American membership in the empire would be difficult. What seems certain, however, is that the apparatus of colonial regulation and control schooled the Americans first in the arts of evasion and then in the defiance of authority. Although on principle they accepted most of the regulations of the old colonial system, in practice they were extremely uneasy about conforming with the demands of any external authority. The friction engendered under colonial regulations went far to encourage the spirit of restless independence that erupted in 1776.

In 1614, Captain John Smith had written of North America:

> As for the goodness and fine substance of the land, we are for the most part yet altogether ignorant of them, but only here and there where we have touched or seen a little, the edges of those large dominions which do stretch themselves into the main, God doth know how many thousand miles.

By the time Georgia was settled, the English and the world had a better notion of America's dimensions and a better understanding of how to live within them. The early settlers had approached the shores of the New World pitifully unequipped for its rigors. The agonies of Jamestown, the deaths from "cruel diseases as swellings, fluxes, burning fevers" but mostly from famine—have been mentioned. In Plymouth, to quote from the ironical Captain Smith again, the Pilgrims' "humorous ignorances caused them for more than a year to endure a wonderful deal of misery with infinite patience . . . thinking to find things better than I advised them."

Such were the unpromising beginnings. During the next century, the English came across in greater numbers to clinch their hold on the Atlantic seaboard. Transplanted to America, they gradually learned to adapt themselves to new conditions, to slough off old ways, and to follow what became a well-worn American injunction: "Root, hog, or die." By the end of the seventeenth century, a hybrid culture had emerged reflecting European ideas as applied to the American scene. Regional differences had already begun to appear, differences in "constitutions and complexions, air and government," as one observer put it. A new civilization was in the making.

Readings

An excellent and informative account of the North American aborigines that corrects a good deal of traditional misinformation is C. T. Foreman's *Indians Abroad, 1493-1938* (1943). For a comprehensive one-volume study of colonizing in the Western Hemisphere, with interesting comparisons between the culture and institutions of the respective Portuguese, Spanish, French, and English settlements, the reader may consult Vera Brown Holmes, *A History of the Americas* (1950). A classic account of French settlement in North America is Francis Parkman, *Pioneers of France in the New World* (rev. ed., 1885), a work that should be supplemented by more recent studies like G. M. Wrong, *The Rise and Fall of New France* (2 vols., 1928), and G. L. Nute, *Caesars of the Wilderness: Médard Chouart, Sieur des Groseilliers, and Pierre Esprit Radisson, 1618-1710* (1943). A convenient summary of the Dutch in America may be found in T. J. Wertenbaker, *The Founding of American Civilization: The Middle Colonies* (1938).

Material on the founding and early history of the English colonies in North America is so extensive that only some of the more standard works will be mentioned here. Besides the works of Nettels, Savelle, and Andrews, previously cited for Chapter 1, readable accounts can be found in the first volume of Edward Channing's *History of the United States* (6 vols., 1905-1925), and T. J. Wertenbaker's, *The First Americans* (1927). The most up-to-date volume on the southern colonies is W. F. Craven, *The Southern Colonies in the Seventeenth Century* (1949). G. F. Willison, *Behold Virginia: The Fifth Crown* (1951), is an informal but scholarly account of the early Virginia settlers. Early New England history is covered in J. T. Adams' strongly anti-Puritan *The Founding of New England* (1921), and S. E. Morison's sympathetically written *Builders of the Bay Colony* (1930). G. F. Willison, *Saints and Strangers* (1945), is a readable and balanced account of the Plymouth experiment. If possible, the reader should consult some biographies of important New England personalities, such as L. S. Mayo, *John Endecott, a Biography* (1936); S. H. Brockunier, *The Irrepressible Democrat: Roger Williams* (1940); and Edith Curtis, *Anne Hutchinson* (1930). Particularly recommended is an anthology of Puritan writing, P. Miller and T. H. Johnson, *The Puritans* (1938).

A good introduction to the Middle colonies is T. J. Wertenbaker, *The Founding of American Civilization: The Middle Colonies* (1938). An adequate account of early New York history can be found in *The History of the State of New York* (1933, Vols. I, II), edited by A. C. Flick. S. G. Fisher, *The Making of Pennsylvania* (1896, reprinted 1932), is a good introduction to Pennsylvania history, which ought to be supplemented by a biography of William Penn. Two satisfactory ones are Bonamy Dobrée, *William Penn, Quaker and Pioneer* (1932), and W. W. Comfort, *William Penn* (1944).

On the complicated matter of Britain's administration of her colonies, Nettels is again recommended, but more specialized studies should be noted. L. A. Harper, *The English Navigation Laws: A Seventeenth Century Experiment in Social Engineering* (1939), is detailed and scholarly. Valuable also is Bernard Bailyn, *The New England Merchants in the Seventeenth Century* (1955). G. L. Beer has written most extensively on this topic. His books—*The Commercial Policy of England toward the American Colonies* (1893); *The Origins of the British Colonial System, 1578-1660* (1908); *The Old Colonial System, 1660-1754* (2 vols., 1912); and *British Colonial Policy, 1754-1765* (1907)—constitute the fullest treatment of English-colonial relations, along with another great history, L. H. Gipson, *The British Empire before the American Revolution* (9 vols., 1936-1956).

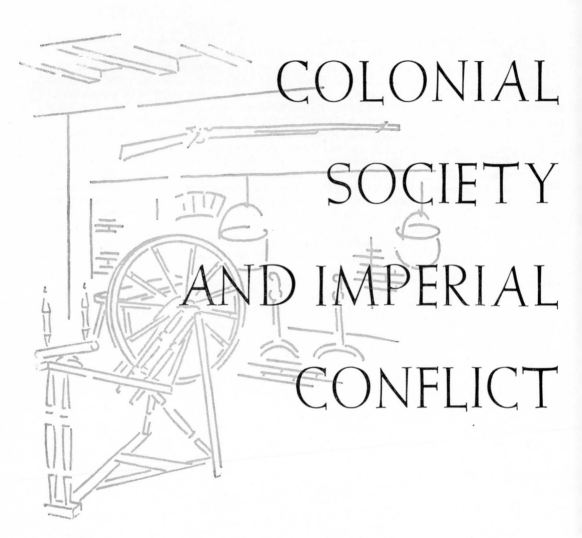

COLONIAL SOCIETY AND IMPERIAL CONFLICT

C H A P T E R   T H R E E

By the year of England's "Glorious Revolution" (1688-1689), when William III peacefully acceded to the English throne, and the troubled days of James II's reign finally ended, the English had consolidated their power on the American mainland. A chain of English settlements fronted the 1,200 miles of the Atlantic seaboard and stretched inland to where the Appalachians rise from the coastal plain. Having outmaneuvered the Dutch in both hemispheres, the English now prepared for a worldwide struggle with the French that was to last for over a century. The English, of course, could not foresee that their eventual victory over the French in America would greatly lessen the colonists' need for the protection provided by the mother country.

I. THE COLONIAL POPULATION

England's ultimate success in North America sprang largely from the astonishing growth of her American colonies, whose population after 1700 almost doubled every 25 years. There were about 200,000 people in the mainland colonies in 1688; by 1750, the number had increased to about 1,-500,000. At that time, there were only 65,000 Europeans in New France. The most densely populated area of the English colonies was the South, which contained some 700,000 inhabitants, 300,000 of them Negro slaves. Most of the slaves were West Africans who were transported in the slave ships of Britishers and New Englanders to the West Indian and southern plantations.

Approximately a half-million people lived in New England during the 1750's, some 400,000 in the Middle colonies (which were expanding at the fastest rate), and about 400,000 in the West Indies. The high birth rate among the English colonists accounts in large part for this remarkable population growth—it has been estimated that the average colonial family increased at the rate of one child every two years. Another reason was immigration from the British Isles, from the Continent, and (to a lesser degree) from the West Indies to the mainland colonies.

From the early decades of the seventeenth century, America had been a catch-all for Europe. Swedes, Finns, Netherlanders, Huguenots (who had arrived before the revocation of the Edict of Nantes in 1685, see p. 6), and Spanish and Portuguese Jews, together with a sprinkling of more exotic nationalities, had all reached North America before the 1680's. After that decade, however, the largest numbers of immigrants came from Germany and Northern Ireland. Most of the new arrivals settled in Pennsylvania or filtered southward into that vast stretch of territory lying between the Allegheny foothills and the southern lowlands and spreading out some 600 miles southwest from the Maryland-Pennsylvania boundary.

The history of German immigration begins in 1683, when small groups of Mennonites and Quakers established Germantown, a settlement in southeastern Pennsylvania. During the next three decades, numbers of other radical German Protestants (most of whom had migrated from their homeland for religious reasons) founded such towns as Bethlehem, Lititz, and Nazareth. Most of these early Germans were substantial people, many of them well educated, who came with some property, paid for their own passages, and bought land on their arrival. They must be distinguished from the so-called "church people" (Lutherans and German-Reformed) who poured into Pennsylvania in the eighteenth century to escape the exorbitant taxes and the pillaging armies in their native land, the Rhine Valley. For a hundred years after 1618 the Rhine Valley had been the battleground for a half-dozen European armies. The peasants, periodically despoiled by military foragers and feudal overlords, responded enthusiastically to reports of a country where there were no feudal obligations and where land was plentiful. These "church people" came as redemptioners (see p. 30), drawn by the advertisements of promoters or the reports of friends, and many received 50 acres after serving their indenture. They gradually filled up the rich farm land in the Lehigh, Susquehanna, and Cumberland valleys. When they reached less fertile lands to the north, they swung south into the Shenandoah Valley. German immigration reached its high point in the colonial period between 1749 and 1754 when (much to the dismay of the English colonists, who feared they might be engulfed) the Germans were arriving in American ports at the rate of over 5,000 a year.

The Germans did their best to duplicate

the kind of life they had known at home. They hoped to settle down in the quiet valleys, to develop their farms, and to cultivate their traditional arts, religion, and ways of life. But the village pattern they had known in Germany could not be maintained in Pennsylvania, where individual holdings were so large that farmhouses were far apart. So they led instead the more isolated lives of independent farmers. They retained many of their old agricultural practices but sometimes discarded the intensive, careful farming methods they had used in Europe. Only as land grew scarcer did the Germans return to the old techniques.

Even so, their influence on both the agricultural and industrial development of Pennsylvania was profound. They became celebrated for their gardens and orchards, for their stout barns and well-tended livestock, and for their sturdy self-sufficiency. Many skilled craftsmen, both German and Swiss, had settled in the Pennsylvania interior, where they introduced their techniques for knitting, weaving, shoemaking, and carving. German artisans developed the famous long rifle, which was first manufactured in Lancaster and was later adopted by the frontiersmen. Perhaps more important innovations were the iron stove and the Conestoga wagon. The stove was a vast improvement over the heat-wasting open hearth of the English-style dwelling, and the new wagon was a durable, efficient vehicle for transporting inland produce to the seaboard.

Ulstermen from the North of Ireland, preceded by small numbers of Irish Quakers, began to emigrate at about the same time as the Germans. Of lowland Scot origin, the Ulstermen had settled in Northern Ireland during the reign of James I. Here they had prospered as farmers and as household manufacturers until discriminatory laws shut off the English markets for their linen and woolen products. As Presbyterians, moreover, they resented paying taxes to support the official Anglican church. The migration from Northern Ireland to America had begun

during the Puritan revolution, but parliamentary legislation between 1660 and 1718 provoked a mass exodus. For example, to protect English farmers and the woolen interests, Parliament excluded Ulster meat, dairy products, and woolens from England and the colonies. The final blow came when British absentee landlords raised the rents of their Irish tenants. Around 1718, the Scotch-Irish began to leave for America in large numbers. During the next decades, shiploads of new settlers continued to arrive from Ulster. Most of them headed for Pennsylvania or the Carolinas, though the other colonies attracted some of them. Successive waves of tough Scotch-Irish pushed farther and farther into the interior, and southward along the well-traveled route to the upland South. By 1750, they were most heavily concentrated in the Cumberland Valley, and after 1763 there were many in southwestern Pennsylvania.

Unlike the Germans, the men from Ulster were flinty, aggressive, and political-minded. More restless than the placid and stable men from the Palatinate, they served as the cutting edge of the southward migration. They took easily to the frontier life and made up for their indifference to the arts by their zeal in warfare and their passion for politics. Later they distinguished themselves as minis-

ters, teachers, and statesmen, as well as soldiers, and formed a strong anti-British nucleus on the eve of the Revolution.

II. THE SOUTHERN COLONIES

The Tidewater.   The South has always been a section of contrasts. In colonial times, most of the population of tidewater Virginia and Maryland and northeastern North Carolina was of English extraction. Here the economy was based on tobacco. The Carolina low country, extending southward along the coast to the mouth of the Savannah River and inland about 60 miles, with its center at Charleston, was settled later than the Chesapeake region. Its staple crops were rice and indigo. Last to be settled was the southern hinterland, the "back country" or "back parts," a fertile country covered with hardwood and pine forests and teeming with wildlife—deer, bear, buffalo, and many other kinds of animals—which made the area a paradise for hunter and trapper. This upland region, virtually empty until the 1730's, filled up rapidly during the next 40 years. By 1776, some 250,000 inhabitants, white and Negro, occupied the country from western Maryland to western Georgia. A mixed population of Germans, Ulster and Highland Scots, Pennsylvania Quakers, Englishmen, and migrants from the tidewater region made up a society that differed radically from the Chesapeake settlements.

The Chesapeake planters kept close ties with the mother country and aped the manners of the English aristocracy. An élite group of large landed proprietors evolved that furnished the social and political leadership of the region. The Carters, Lees, Byrds, Randolphs, and Fitzhughs of Virginia, and the Carrolls, Dulanys, and Galloways of Maryland are good examples of this tidewater aristocracy. They lived in Georgian mansions far grander than the smaller and plainer seventeenth-century farmhouses of their grandfathers, and they filled their well-

proportioned rooms with the finest imported furniture. Able artisans were employed to carry out the plans of English architects or local amateurs and the designs of foreign cabinet-makers. The evidence of their extraordinary talents can be seen today in the Byrd mansion, "Westover," and in the stylish town houses of Annapolis.

Contemporary observers noted that these planters were an outdoor people, fonder of fox-hunting and horse-racing and long weekend house parties than of polite learning. Some of them boasted large libraries—William Byrd II, for example, who began his long day by reading passages in Hebrew and Greek, and Robert Carter of a later generation with his collection of some 1,500 books. But these men were the exceptions. What

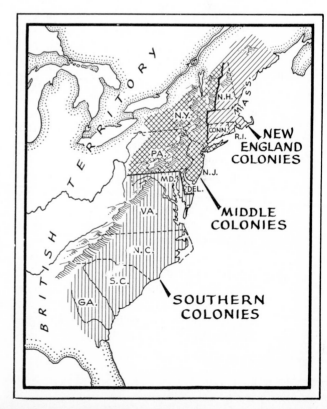

Westover, Charles City County, Virginia, home of William Byrd II (1674-1744), planter, author, wit.

reading the planters did usually dealt with practical subjects like law, medicine, commerce, and surveying. They were at their most typical pursuits on election days when the county centers were crowded with yokels and gentlemen, or during their interminable visiting when the men got together and discussed horses and tobacco prices. Education they respected, and many sent their sons abroad for sound classical instruction. But the planters feared rusticity and inelegance more than ignorance. The dancing master was as much in demand as the well-qualified northern tutor.

Although highly conscious of their rank and thoroughly undemocratic, the planters took their duties seriously and performed them efficiently. The management of plantations and related commercial enterprises produced no exciting culture, but it trained the tidewater gentry in the arts of government and administration.

Carolina differed from the Chesapeake colonies in its ethnic composition, its economy, and its culture. Here Englishmen (many of them from Barbados) mixed with Huguenots, Scots, Welsh, Germans, and Scotch-Irish. Unlike the Chesapeake planters,

who relied entirely on tobacco for their cash crop, the Carolina planters and merchants prospered on rice production, indigo, and hides. Indigo, introduced from the West Indies in 1740, was supported by a crown bounty after 1748. Production increased rapidly under this official encouragement and, together with rice, indigo gave the Carolinians an income that was less subject to price fluctuations and competition than was Chesapeake tobacco.

Rich Carolina planters like the Draytons, the Izards, the Manigaults, and the Pinckneys lived on a very handsome scale. If they did not go north to Newport, Rhode Island, during the dangerous summer months, they stayed in their Charleston houses and enjoyed the genteel entertainment this cosmopolitan city afforded: music, the theater, dancing parties, and horse-racing. What gave a distinctive and exotic charm to eighteenth-century Charleston was the architectural styles borrowed from the West Indies—the pastel-shaded brick and stucco Georgian houses embellished with wrought-iron balconies and gates, and the lush private gardens. Handsome churches and public buildings lent an added dignity. Clustered around the wharves were wholesale and retail establishments, warehouses, and business offices—evidences of Charleston's commercial vigor.

Charleston's economic burgeoning (a result of the expanding market for her staples and a favorable trade balance) permitted ambitious businessmen to make fortunes, buy land, marry into older families, and set themselves up as grandees. South Carolina in the 1760's probably had more really rich men than any other colony. Plantations of more than 20,000 acres were not unknown, and men who started out as humble craftsmen often ended up as prosperous landholders. All this new money gave a parvenu tone to the society and helped create its materialistic values. The Carolina aristocracy was remarkable neither for its intellectual attainments nor for its capacity to govern. Charleston was a pleasure capital, flourishing at the expense of a badly administered province. No developing middle class contested the authority of the plantation lords, and everyone seemed to be scrambling for higher status:

Their whole lives are one continued Race [declared the *South Carolina Gazette* in 1773] in which everyone is endeavoring to distance all behind him; and to overtake or pass by, all before him; everyone is flying from his inferiors in Pursuit of his Superiors. . . . Every Tradesman is a Merchant, every Merchant is a Gentleman, and every Gentleman one of the Noblesse. We are a Country of Gentry. . . . We have no such Thing as a common People among us: Between Vanity and Fashion, the Species is utterly destroyd.

The Back Country.

Although tidewater society was largely English in origin and interest, and was economically and culturally dependent on the mother country, the southern back country was a conglomeration of immigrant communities. Differing in religion, in origin, and in social degree, and cooperating only during emergencies, it remained culturally disunited. Only gradually did the tidewater institutions, both legal and political, impose a kind of uniformity on western Maryland and Virginia and ultimately on South Carolina and Georgia.

During the first year, the poorer settlers in the back country usually lived in crude log shanties enclosed on only three sides; they constructed more substantial log houses later. Throughout the area a mixed subsistence agriculture (cereals, flax, hemp, potatoes, peaches, apples, livestock) sprang up, and soon small market centers emerged along the chief roads or at the ferries where the surplus could be disposed of. A half-century before the Revolution, thriving communities had arisen around such economic crossroads as Frederick, Hagerstown, Martinsburg, Winchester, Charlotte, Camden, and Augusta. The back country, by European standards still sparsely populated, slowly became a network of agricultural villages, orchards and wheat fields, grist mills, and country stores. It was a self-sufficient area, with its own craftsmen—bakers, masons, carpenters, millers, coopers, brickmakers, and stocking-weavers.

Rough conditions bred rough manners in the early days of the migration into the unpopulated upland South. Travelers often remarked on the primitiveness of the early pioneer life in this region and on the shiftlessness and intemperance of the "poor whites" who formed an illiterate yeomanry. These people were heroic consumers of peach brandy and renowned for their rough-and-tumble fighting as well as for their generous hospitality. Below them stood the servant and the convict class, whose position was superior only to that of the Negro slaves. Most travelers agreed that both the well-to-do and poorer yeomanry lacked the initiative of their counterparts in the Middle colonies and New England. Itinerant clergymen reported with dismay the roistering life in frontier South Carolina, where people lived together in "Concubinage, swapping their wives as Cattel, and living in a State of Nature, more irregularly and unchastely than the Indians." Spending lonely years in a country still ringing with the cries of wolves and panthers, suffering from malaria and other endemic diseases, and facing the prospects of unending labor must have been particularly hard on a people fresh from Ulster or German villages. But in time, conditions for the poorer and middle classes improved in the "back parts," and life took on more of the characteristics of the tidewater. The use of slave labor increased and a kind of loose aristocracy grew up; cabins gave way to farmhouses and the frontier rawness disappeared. Not until well after the Revolution, however, did the back country cease to be a region of diversity and conflict.

III. THE MIDDLE COLONIES

Pennsylvania. Throughout the eighteenth century, the Middle colonies drew the largest number of immigrants and formed the most heterogeneous part of England's North American dominions. Philadelphia had forged ahead of Boston after 1755 and, with a population of about 28,000 in the 1760's, was the largest and richest of the colonial cities.

The Quaker aristocrats of Pennsylvania had prospered by practicing their religious precepts of industry, thrift, and reliability in their everyday affairs. In the mid-eighteenth century, the Quakers were no longer in the majority in Philadelphia, but they comprised the wealthiest group in the city. They grew rich on the extensive trade with the West Indies and Europe, and upon a foundation of grain, flour, bread, pork, hoops, and barrel staves they erected princely fortunes which they re-invested in mining, manufacturing, and real estate.

Class lines were not so tightly drawn in Pennsylvania society as they were in the South, but it was by no means an equalitarian society. William Penn held the same notions of low and high degree as any wellborn seventeenth-century man, and he hoped to see his colony managed by a country gentry. But he disapproved strongly of vast landed estates and laws of primogeniture, a prejudice that made any sort of planter or patroon aristocracy impossible in Pennsylvania. The city merchant assumed the first rank; in the trading atmosphere of Philadelphia, the way to wealth was open to the talented of all classes. Less than 50 years after the founding of Pennsylvania, its affairs were being run by a Quaker clique, a union sealed by family alliances, religion, and common interest among the Norrises, the Lloyds, the Pembertons, the Logans, and other English Quaker families.

Prosperity and the intricacies of business led to a loosening of the restrictions against worldly pleasures. A great Quaker merchant in 1719 might declare: "I always suspect the furniture of the Inside Where too much application is Shewn for a Gay or fantasticall outside." But the next generation was not so suspicious. They cultivated an expensive simplicity. Their clothes, though unadorned, were cut from the most expensive materials. Their Georgian houses might lack the external decoration and the more elaborate doorways of non-Quaker mansions, but the interiors were just as sumptuous. Quaker gentry patronized the silversmiths and cabinetmakers. Objections to the fine arts still lingered on in the mid-eighteenth century, but some rich Quakers had their portraits done in England and even orthodox Friends tolerated profile silhouettes. Like the Chesapeake and Carolina aristocracy, the Philadelphia merchants kept elaborate carriages to carry them back and forth to their country estates. They entertained lavishly, cultivated magnificent gardens, and enjoyed "free sociable Conversation." But gambling, dancing, theater-going, and tippling, the "world's" pleasures, were not condoned by the orthodox.

By the early years of the eighteenth century, the liberal government provided by William Penn was already being criticized by the Pennsylvania Quakers, who wanted to strengthen the local assembly at the expense of the proprietors. After 1740, the struggle between the proprietary party (which stood for centralized authority in the hands of the Governor and Council) and the popular party (composed of city merchants and property-holding farmers) became more intense. Liberal suffrage laws and the support of the German element enabled the anti-proprietary Quaker party to outmaneuver the deputies of the Penns.

The Assembly enjoyed the confidence of all sections until its failure to protect the frontier from marauding Indians led to charges that it was being dominated by mercantile politicians. Actually, the Assembly was not averse to voting funds for frontier defense, but it insisted that the proprietors share the burden of expense by permitting their lands to be taxed. A deadlock resulted. Meanwhile, thousands of Scotch-Irish beyond the Susquehanna, facing annihilation by the Indians, were on the point of abandoning their homes. Relief finally came when the proprietors gave £5,000 to colonial defense and the Assembly voted the necessary funds.

Despite the differences between the proprietors and the Quaker party—led by the resourceful Benjamin Franklin—the colony continued to prosper. Pennsylvania enjoyed a favorable balance of trade, a stable currency, and a relaxed social atmosphere. Less avid for education than New England, the heterogeneous population, with its different religious and cultural traditions, relied upon denominational schools to train the young.

New Jersey.   About 70,000 people were living in New Jersey in the 1750's. The colony had already become a "keg tapped at

Portrait of Isaac Royall and family, by Robert Feke, an artist who revealed the aspirations of the New England and Pennsylvania aristocracy by delineating their silks and satins.

both ends," with its surplus transported either to New York or Philadelphia for shipment to Europe. Hemp, grain, flax, hay, and Indian corn made up its principal exports.

East Jersey had cultural ties with New England, and the New England influence was dominant in such towns as Newark, Elizabeth, and Woodbridge. The movement of settlers from New England to East Jersey, which had begun while the Dutch still held New Netherland, was perhaps the first significant intercolonial migration. It belongs properly to the story of New England expansion, since the settlers moved from Massachusetts Bay to Rhode Island and Connecticut, or down the Connecticut Valley, before they founded the Jersey towns. Some of them were Quakers fleeing from their Puritan persecutors; others, shocked by the growing religious laxity in New England, sought to establish a stricter Puritan community. The old New England ways were modified in the new environment, and by the eighteenth century the transplanted village community, with its town meetings, its close social and religious supervision, had broken down.

New York.   Although travelers passing through New Jersey in the eighteenth century might stop to comment on its natural beauty, its prosperity, or the succulence of its oysters, there was nothing more to detain the curious, who usually hastened on to New York. Crossing over on the Staten Island ferry, the visitor discovered the city emerging out of a delightful vista "of rivers, islands, fields, hills, woods," of "vessels sailing to and fro, and

View across the East River of the lower end of New York City, 1717.

innumerable porpoises playing upon the surface of the water." In the 1750's, New York City, lying between the North and East rivers, had about 13,000 inhabitants. Shade trees grew along the paved streets, which were clean by colonial standards, and the public and private buildings usually drew favorable comments.

At mid-century, New York City was beginning to lose many of its Dutch features. The absence of a Dutch press or a Dutch colonial literature meant that a dying culture was left with no supports. Its weakening can be traced in the architectural changes from the period of 1650, when New York, with its steep-gabled houses, resembled a transplanted Dutch city, to a century later when the English Georgian influence prevailed. One English traveler, describing this city of "industrious" and "parsimonious" traders in 1759, confessed that differences in language and national origin among the inhabitants made it "almost impossible to give them any precise or determined character." As cosmopolitan as Philadelphia, New York's wealthy inhabitants enjoyed the same pleasures as their Pennsylvania neighbors, but with easier consciences.

New York (outranked only by Boston and Philadelphia as a commercial center) relied upon the produce of the back country for its extensive trade with the West Indies, England, and the Continent, and with New England and the Southern colonies. Dairy products, livestock, bread, cereals, lumber, and furs were shipped to New York from New Jersey, Connecticut, Long Island, and the Hudson Valley, and were then exchanged for West Indian staples (rum, molasses, sugar), wines from Madeira and the Azores, and manufactured goods from England.

The Hudson Valley.

The Hudson Valley was already well settled by the 1740's, although huge empty tracts were held by a few great landowners who leased them to tenant farmers. From the beginning of the eighteenth century, British governors of the province had emulated the old patroon system by rewarding favorites with land grants ranging from 50,000 to 1 million acres. This monopoly of the richest areas by owners who sometimes paid nothing but a token tax on their property discouraged bona-fide settlers and encouraged squatting. Nevertheless, the province filled up. Between 1720 and 1756, the population grew from about 30,000 to 85,000.

As the traveler proceeded north to Albany by sloop, he was struck by the predominance of Dutch civilization and the increased use of the Dutch language. The voyage up the picturesque river was punctuated by stops at small settlements like Poughkeepsie. At the end of this scenic route was Albany, still very Dutch in 1744, and suggesting some idea of how the Dutch had lived, behaved, and thought before the English conquest.

Albany's exposure to Indian raiders from Canada explains its frontier-like aspect prior to the defeat of the French in 1763 (see p. 67). Wooden palisades enclosed this city of 4,000 in the 1750's. In the center of the town stood a square stone fortress manned by 300 of the king's troops. Observers noticed that the gable ends of the provincial wooden and brick houses faced the street, and that the snug, simple interiors had a "superstitiously clean" look.

Eighteenth-century travel accounts make frequent references to what one Swedish observer spoke of as "the avarice, selfishness, and immeasurable love of money" of the Albany Dutch. They were even charged with trading with the enemy when Indian war-parties led by the French were burning New England settlements (1702-1706). Their materialism, however, could not be described as an untypical colonial trait. An English nobleman writing in 1765 said that they showed "an unwearied attention to their own personal and particular interests, and an abhorrence to all superior powers." Another traveler found them slovenly and over-frugal, but criticized their "hard favored" women and the custom of indiscriminate kissing more than he did their business ethics.

IV. THE NEW ENGLAND WAY

Rhode Island. From Albany, the traveler could choose between sailing down the Hudson and beginning his New England tour from New York, and striking overland by way of Great Barrington. From here he could ride southward to Canaan, Connecticut, and thence southeast by way of Norfolk and Simsbury to Hartford. To travel from Hartford to Boston he might proceed up the Connecticut Valley by post road to Springfield, and thence to Boston via Palmer, Leicester, and Worcester. From Worcester to Boston, the roads were good, with houses and villages lining the way. Boston was regarded by many as the most impressive as well as the most English city in all the colonies.

More common ways of reaching Boston from the Middle colonies were to embark on a ship from New York or to journey the length of Long Island and then to cross by ferry from Oyster Pond to New London, Connecticut.

Most travelers making the New England tour stopped at Newport, Rhode Island, already renowned among vacationists for its pleasing and healthful climate. Newport was a center of wealth and refinement in the mid-eighteenth century. Its businessmen, having no colonial staple to export, grew rich on "a kind of circular commerce" that involved a complicated interchange of imports and exports. Approximately 7,000 people lived in Newport in the 1750's. Though it was only

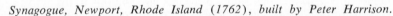

Synagogue, Newport, Rhode Island (1762), built by Peter Harrison.

the fifth largest city in the colonies, the magnificence of its private and public buildings rivaled those of Boston, Philadelphia, and Charleston. In Peter Harrison, Newport could claim "the most distinguished architect of colonial America," whose genius was recognized throughout New England.

Despite the wealth of its aristocracy, Rhode Island remained a byword for radicalism and unreliability, a place too "entirely democratical" to please conservatives. "The private people," declared one English visitor, "are cunning, deceitful, and selfish; they live almost entirely by unfair and illicit trading." To Rhode Island's critics, the colony was a paradise for unscrupulous debtors and a nursery for heretical doctrines—political, economic, and religious.

Massachusetts.   From Newport, the traveler reached Boston by way of Bristol and Providence, through prosperous country that called forth the admiration of all who made the trip. The Massachusetts capital in the 1750's was a flourishing town with more than 15,000 inhabitants. It was blessed with a fine, stoutly defended harbor, extensive wharves, and handsome buildings. With no single cash crop, Massachusetts relied principally on fish, rum, and shipbuilding to pay for her imports. The merchants of Boston, Salem, and Marblehead, like those of Newport, grew rich on their multiple transactions. English visitors regarded Boston as having "much the air of our best country towns in England." Even prejudiced observers from other sections, who came with preconceived notions about the "enthusiastical" or "canting" Yankees, were amazed by the richness and graciousness of upper-class life in Boston.

To appreciate the change that had come over the old Puritan stronghold since the days of Winthrop and John Cotton a hundred years before, we must glance back again to seventeenth-century New England. What had given distinction to New England society had been less economic and political than moral and religious. Since Puritanism has exercised such an enormous influence on American civilization—both early and late —it is important to understand something about Puritan beliefs, which were most clearly revealed during Puritanism's "golden age" (1630-1670).

New England's Calvinism was not essentially different from continental Calvinism (see Chapter 1), but it was less dogmatic and legalistic. God was unknowable and all-powerful. He determined beforehand the destiny of every mortal, and saved or damned whom He willed (*predestination*). Man, inheriting Adam's sin, was by nature depraved and incapable of discovering the truth through his natural reason. But God might freely offer regeneration (*grace*) to a person, who could then either receive or reject it. Outward acts of merit would not in themselves bring about "election," but good behavior might be a sign of inward sanctity. So would an unshakable belief in Christ. When God flooded the sinner with His irresistible grace, the soul's insulation from God was dissolved, and the regenerate man was expected to proclaim his mystical experience publicly in church.

Puritan ministers supervised every aspect of social life, decided on the authenticity of conversions or the significance of thunderstorms, and counseled the magistrates. No event was too large or too small for their concern. Although New England was technically committed to the independence of the separate congregations, associations of ministers saw to it that unsound doctrines got no hearing in New England pulpits. Quakers and Baptists in particular came under the ban of the magistrates, and for a few years after 1658 a death penalty was prescribed for any Quaker who returned to Massachusetts after he had been banished. Four Quakers were actually executed and others were publicly whipped, but the laws against them were never popular or systematically enforced. The persecution of heretics ended in the 1660's.

It is easy to exaggerate Puritan intolerance and to label later "blue laws" Puritanical.

Actually, the Puritans valued faith more highly than outward shows of piety and did not object to what Calvin called "the right use of terrestial blessings." They consumed rum, beer, cider, and applejack in huge quantities, relished the beauties of nature, and were not excessively harsh in punishing the sins of the flesh. Their ideal, in Calvin's words, was simply "to enjoy abundance with moderation," and they ordinarily expected the "saints" to dramatize their election by maintaining decent behavior.

Seventeenth-century New England communities (except for Rhode Island) regarded education as an indispensable condition for right conduct. The "ignorant sinner," according to Thomas Hooker, was like a sick man searching for medicine in an apothecary's shop during the black of night. Though "the choycest of all receipts" are available, "yet because he cannot see what he takes, he may kill himself or encrease his distempers, but never cure any disease." The Bible was a beacon for the sinner, and the purpose of the schools was to teach unregenerate man how to read it. So the authorities passed compulsory education laws in order to foil "that old deluder Satan" who would "keep man from the knowledge of the Scriptures." In 1647, Massachusetts required towns of 50 or more houses to set up elementary schools; towns of 100 or more houses had to establish secondary schools as well. In 1636, Harvard College was founded as a "nursery" for ministers. Of the roughly 24,000 New Englanders in the 1650's, more than 130 had graduated from English universities. The ordinary people, inured to two- or three-hour sermons, and experts in theological niceties, respected the culture of their leaders. Education was not so much an ornament as a necessity.

As the religious fires subsided, Bostonians became more self-indulgent and less alarmed by the warnings of ministers lamenting the colony's spiritual decline. Soon the families of wealth and eminence—the Winthrops, Dudleys, Mathers, Faneuils, and Belchers—began to intermarry and build up the foundation for the celebrated "Brahmin caste" of the next century.

In their elegant town houses, filled with imported furniture and fine silver, rich Bostonians indulged in the same refinements as the English gentry. A prejudice against the theater and secular novels still held on

John Greenwood, "Sea Captains Carousing in Surinam." In this early-morning scene, Greenwood painted himself carrying a candle attempting to leave his boisterous friends, one of whom, Captain Nicholas Cooke (seated in profile at the table smoking a pipe), later became governor of Rhode Island.

Mr. and Mrs. Isaac Winslow—an example of John Singleton Copley's realistic portraiture.

in some quarters, in contrast to the South and New York, but the genteel Bostonians dressed richly, attended concerts, and sat for their portraits. The distance between the pious colony and the secularized eighteenth-century province is reflected in the contrast between the size and luxury of the new Georgian houses and the severe medieval lines of the seventeenth-century dwellings. John Singleton Copley's realistic portraits of the brocaded merchants and their wives not only reveal their frills and finery but also their down-to-earth materialistic outlook. The new preference for easy manners and politeness could be detected, too, in the abandonment of thorny seventeenth-century prose for a smooth and easy diction that would be less jarring to refined ears.

The growing secularization so characteristic of colonial society everywhere in the eighteenth century showed itself clearly in the turbulence and irreverence of urban life. Samuel Sewall, judge, spirited diarist, and the epitome of the new bourgeoisie, was reporting the tumults and riots in the Boston streets as early as the 1680's. Fifty years later, Boston mobs attacked bawdy houses and public market houses indiscriminately, according to one contemporary, and the warning of Boston's leading minister and savant, Cotton Mather, to a Boston reprobate—that every time he drank rum, he was selling the blood of Christ—was met by the rejoinder "Truly, Sir, when we are going to make ourselves drunk, we never think of that." To the orthodox, the revival of Christmas revels and pagan customs like the celebrations of Shrove Tuesday (the "most horrid and Shocking profanity"), the increase of drunkenness, and even dueling in the Common, suggested that God had withdrawn His favor.

Rural New England. To the west, north, and south of Boston, the rural traditions persisted. Here the people were sometimes said to be "Indianizing" themselves by the first third of the eighteenth century. New settlements, freed from the controls of the old authorities, had sprung up. To Cotton Mather, these were the "ungospelized" plantations, "the very Brothel houses of Satan." But to the outsider, New England villages

59

were remarkable for their tidiness, decency, and good order. The yeomanry of Massachusetts, Connecticut, and New Hampshire were known for their curiosity and readiness to debate nice theological distinctions. One observer from the South seemed surprised that these people, who looked "rather more like clowns, than the riff-raff of our Maryland planters," should discuss matters "that in our parts would be like Greek, Hebrew, or Arabick."

By mid-century, the Yankee had already emerged, dry, hard-working, independent, and better educated than his rural counterpart in the other provinces. Living frugally in simple frame houses, tilling an indifferent soil, the New England farmers developed into the tough, uncommunicative (though sometimes garrulous) American stereotype. Travelers thought them too democratic and oblivious of social distinctions. "They seem to be a good substantial Kind of Farmers," remarked one visitor, "but there is no break in their Society; their Government, Religion, and Manners all tend to support an equality. Whoever brings in your Victuals sits down and chats to you." Another attributed this independence to "that ancient and rugged Spirit of Levelling, early imported from home." Actually, however, the plain people in New England, and especially in Massachusetts, did not condone unlimited democracy, and observed their own social distinctions. The large landowners in southern and western New England were accepted as acknowledged leaders, along with the ministers, physicians, and innkeepers. The church meeting enforced a practical social discipline, and what often seemed like loose behavior (for example, the custom of courtship known as "bundling" or "tarrying") simply testified to rural innocence.

The Yankee, tight with his money yet philanthropic for the public good, loyal to his neighbors but regarding the world beyond his village as fair game, became a kind of colonial paradox. He was admired for his industry and his institutions, but disdained for his shrewdness. Though deeply conservative and wary of sudden innovation, he was susceptible to emotional appeals in religion and to political and economic heresies.

V. PROVINCIAL POLITICS

Intercolonial Ties. Insularity and provincialism undoubtedly existed throughout colonial America, as American and foreign travelers frequently observed. But long before the Revolution, these intellectual barriers were being broken down. Roads and waterways brought the businessmen of New York, Philadelphia, Boston, and Charleston into a vital economic network. Itinerant peddlers, printers, and artists passed from colony to colony; invalids took long journeys to improve their health; families paid visits to distant kin; Quakers and Jews sought out their co-religionists. The colleges at Princeton, New Haven, and Cambridge attracted students from the South and the West Indies as well as from neighboring colonies. John Bartram of Philadelphia, like other naturalists, botanized in many parts of America and entertained fellow enthusiasts who came from distant places to see his celebrated gardens. Fraternal societies, which were organized in the principal cities as early as the 1730's, welcomed members from other colonies; Washington, Franklin, and other colonial leaders were Masons before civil and military emergencies brought them together. Finally, colonists read one another's newspapers, circular letters, sermons, pamphlets, and almanacs. The literate colonial had at his disposal a variety of information on matters outside his immediate sphere of interest—political, cultural, and economic—that linked him with the destiny of his continent. When the time came, colonial spokesmen were able to appeal to a set of shared beliefs and experiences.

Colonial self-consciousness became evident to English observers early in the eighteenth century. They noted a new sense of independence and restlessness. According to one visitor in 1749, the visionary idea was being spread "that empire is travelling westward." It seemed that "everyone is looking forward with eager and impatient expectation to that destined moment when America is to give law to the rest of the world." Such notions seemed farfetched at the time, and most English authorities agreed that "America is formed for happiness, but not for empire." There were good reasons for this assumption.

Internal Differences. A country so diverse, geographically and culturally, was not likely to unify itself. Idiom, custom, and economic interest divided the colonies; distance and unreliable communications hampered their cooperation. And even should the colonies surmount the physical and social obstacles that prevented their amalgamation, where could they expand? To the west, beyond the fringe of settlements, lay the formidable Indian nations. The extended coastline could not be defended without a navy. Neither the fisheries nor the West Indian trade, on which colonial prosperity depended, could survive without the help of British seapower. In fact, to English eyes, only the stabilizing control of the mother country prevented colonial anarchy.

Certainly the points of friction in British North America were numerous and unconcealed, but they have probably been exaggerated by historians. It is now suspected, for example, that property requirements for voting were not so high as they were once thought to be, and that society was less class-riven. In eighteenth-century Pennsylvania, the vote was granted to any Christian male who resided two years in the colony and owned 50 acres of land (12 of them cleared) or property valued at £50. Although this provision discriminated against the landless urban population, most of the rural male population probably could qualify. Nearly all adult males could vote in Massa-

chusetts, and the situation was about the same in New Jersey. In the South, the franchise was less liberal, and property qualifications for office were much higher. A member of the South Carolina assembly had to own at least 500 acres of land, 10 slaves, or property worth £1,000.

But if there was not much agitation to widen the franchise, sharp class differences did exist. An aristocracy of large merchants, landowners, and lawyers—an alliance of the favored and the energetic—was able to accumulate wealth and power. By supporting legislation prejudicial to popular interests, they sometimes antagonized the less successful in the cities and villages.

The quarrels between the aristocratic and popular forces in the colonies were primarily over questions of land and money, though religion and politics complicated the picture. The colonies also engaged in acrimonious boundary disputes—Maryland with Virginia, Massachusetts with New York. Sectional hostility expressed itself in provincial prejudices against outsiders. But these differences were hardly profound. Far more serious were the divisions within the colonies themselves between the East and the West, the tidewater and the frontier. Here the blindness and selfishness of the conservative East, together with the sometimes impulsive brutality and ignorance of the West, produced dangerous repercussions.

Throughout the eighteenth century, the small farmer, who was often a debtor removed from the centers of influence, opposed the claims of the land-speculators and proprietors. Bedeviled by demands for quit-rents, insecure in his title, and enraged by the failure of the eastern-dominated governments to protect his life and liberty, he waged political and sometimes physical war against his eastern enemies. In North Carolina between 1734 and 1752, for example, the small farmers in the back country stopped paying quit-rents. In 1771, their fury against land monopolies and unfair taxes was aggravated by sluggish trade, low prices, and high court fees. Their protests ended in outright rebellion. The Regulators, an association of small farmers in North Carolina's western counties formed in 1768, captured the lower house of the assembly in 1769. Governor Tryon countered by dissolving it. He had tried to do something about mismanagement and dishonesty and to remedy the grievances of the back country, but his officers were venal and inefficient. In any event, the Regulators disliked not only bad government but any government at all. They did not hesitate to dragoon reluctant colonists into their ranks, and they offended moderate elements even in their own counties by beating up their opponents and destroying their property. After Tryon and his troop of tidewater gentry surprised and defeated the Regulators' badly equipped army at Alamance in 1771, the insurgents collapsed. Some of the remnants moved into Tennessee, and in 1776 many of the small farmers in both North and South Carolina chose to join the English rather than cooperate with the tidewater gentry.

The North Carolina pattern was repeated, though with significant differences, in South Carolina, Pennsylvania, New Jersey, and Massachusetts. In Pennsylvania, the antagonism between the western and eastern counties had become evident by 1720. The western settlements, made up for the most part of Scotch-Irish and Germans, showed the same aversion to paying taxes that the other back-country regions showed. They particularly resented the reluctance of both the proprietors and the Quaker-dominated assembly to protect them from Indian attacks. Until 1763, both eastern speculators and western small farmers opposed the Penns, who refused to allow their lands to be taxed. In that year, the Indians, under their chief, Pontiac, struck hard at the unprotected Pennsylvania frontier. Unable to repulse the attack, a group of frontiersmen calling themselves the "Paxton Boys" retaliated by massacring 20 peaceful Indians at Lancaster. Then they marched toward Phil-

adelphia, where the government had stationed troops to protect the lives of 140 other Indians. Benjamin Franklin pacified these "Christian White Savages," as he called them in one of his sardonic pamphlets, but the westerners continued to protest against the minority in the eastern counties who elected a majority of the representatives in the assembly.

No serious violence occurred in New Jersey and New England, though the farmers did riot against absentee proprietors and land-speculators. And conflicts over currency sharpened class and sectional cleavages in these areas as well as in most of the other colonies.

From the farmer's point of view, a money shortage was sure to bring distress. He noted that while prices for his produce might fluctuate, his debts remained fixed no matter how much or how little he made. Easy money meant high prices and reduced debts. Therefore, the farmer favored the establishment of "land banks" by the colonial governments, banks that would lend money at low rates of interest and with land as security.

The creditors, on the other hand, feared— and with good reason—paper money, which worked to their disadvantage. It often depreciated rapidly and raised the farmer's bargaining power. The farmer borrowed from the land banks at a lower rate of interest than he could from private lenders, and the colony-backed bank treated him more leniently when he could not meet his obligations. Thus the creditors opposed any attempt to make paper currency legal tender, and they won the support of the crown authorities in their efforts to foil the schemes of the "needy, idle and extravagant."

Controversies over paper money raged in South Carolina and the other colonies. But the classic battle took place in Massachusetts in 1741, when the debtor farmers tried to establish a land bank against the will of Governor Belcher and his conservative supporters. A thousand farmers, "grown so brassy and hardy," said the angry Governor, "as to be now combining in a body to raise a rebellion," prepared to march on Boston on election day and join their allies among the town laborers. Belcher jailed the leaders and election day passed quietly. But when the election results showed a heavy majority in favor of the land bank, Parliament came to the rescue of the defeated creditors by declaring land banks illegal. This decision, though popular among the moneyed gentry, increased the hostility between rich and poor. Ten years later, largely owing to the scandalous depreciation of paper currency in Rhode Island, Parliament passed the Currency Act of 1751. New land banks were prohibited in New England, old issues of currency were to be called in at the date of their retirement, and new issues had to be guaranteed by taxes and retired after a limited period. These regulations widened the split between Parliament and rural New Englanders, whose violent response a few years later bore out Franklin's warning to London in 1764: "I wish some good Angel would forever whisper in the Ears of your great Men that Dominion is founded in Opinion."

Considering how disunited the colonies were in 1763, the British observers who rejected the possibility of American separation from the mother country had good reason for their conviction. Each province seemed hopelessly divided over matters of taxation and representation. Everywhere the rich and well-born seemed bent upon maintaining their economic and political control with or without the aid of the Crown. Disgruntled elements on the frontier and the urban democracy remained restive. And yet in the space of a few years internal disharmony

had abated. Old enmities, of course, were not forgotten. The merchant-creditors who were soon to enlist the support of the farmer "mobocracy" against the aggressions of Parliament still found the lower orders more avid for liberty than they were themselves. But common grievances had created a temporary alliance between creditor and debtor, East and West, speculator and squatter. By the 1770's, English mismanagement had produced a unity that the colonies had been unable and unwilling to achieve by themselves.

British Territory in 1713

VI. ANGLO-FRENCH RIVALRY

The French Domain. England's mercantile policy from the very beginning had been devised as a way of combating her commercial rivals, Spain, Holland, and France. The subordination of the Atlantic colonies to national grand strategy, the imposition of trade restrictions on the colonies, and the exclusion of foreign competition from co-

lonial trade were all war-like maneuvers in the battle to dominate world trade. Spain and Holland gave ground to the British before 1700. Only France remained to contest England's expanding power.

In the cycle of Anglo-French wars that began in 1689 and ended in 1763, France pitted herself against England in an effort to retain supremacy in Europe as well as to win the North American fur trade, the riches of the Caribbean, and markets and empire in India. In the first three of these contests, known in America as "King William's War" (1689-1697), "Queen Anne's War" (1701-1713), and "King George's War," (1744-1748), America was simply one of the lesser theaters of action in a remote corner of the world. In the first two conflicts, the British had tried to take Quebec and had failed. In the second, with the help of Massachusetts men, they won the province of Acadia (now Nova Scotia). In the third, the colonials helped the British to capture the fortress of Louisbourg, which the French had built on Cape Breton Island. To the colonials' disgust, England returned

the fortress to France in the peace treaty in exchange for Madras in India.

None of these actions settled the struggle for North America, but the last of the imperial conflicts, known in Europe as the Seven Years' War and in America as the French and Indian War (1756-1763), determined the future of North America.

For 150 years France had been consolidating her hold on North America. After the settlement of Quebec and Montreal (see p. 22), her explorers had pushed west and south along the great water routes as far as the Gulf of Mexico. Reports of the upper lake country had been followed by rumors of a great river flowing westward. France's ambitious empire-builder in the New World, Jean Talon, sent Louis Joliet and Father Jacques Marquette to find out if these rumors were true. In the spring of 1673, they reached the Mississippi via the Wisconsin River after a month's journey that had taken them up the Green Bay and the Fox River and across Lake Winnebago. The expedition then proceeded down the Father of Waters until it became clear that the Mississippi emptied into the Gulf and not into the Atlantic or the Pacific ocean. Joliet and Marquette had traveled as far south as Arkansas before they turned back.

They were followed by the most intrepid of French explorers, Robert Cavelier, Sieur de La Salle, who not only made the journey down the Mississippi all the way to the Gulf, but also claimed the entire Mississippi Valley for the King of France. This solemn event, which took place after he had reached the mouth of the river on April 9, 1682, has been described in Francis Parkman's epic history:

On that day, the realm of France received on parchment a stupendous accession. The fertile plains of Texas; the vast basin of the Mississippi, from its frozen northern springs to the sultry borders of the Gulf; from the woody ridges of the Alleghenies to the bare peaks of the Rocky Mountains,—a region of savannas and forests, sun-cracked deserts, and grassy prairies, watered by a thousand rivers, ranged by a thousand warlike tribes, passed beneath the sceptre of the Sultan of Versailles; and all

French Explorations and Settlements in the Mississippi Valley

NEW FRANCE

Montreal
Saulte Ste.Marie
L. Superior   L. Huron
St. Lawrence R.
L. Ontario
Green Bay   L.
Fox R.   Michigan   L. Erie
Mississippi R.   Detroit
Illinois R.   ENGLISH COLONIES
Ohio R.

Marquette
and Joliet

Arkansas R.   Mississippi R.
La Salle
Mobile   SPANISH
Biloxi
New Orleans
Gulf of Mexico

0   Miles   500

by virtue of a feeble human voice, inaudible at half a mile.

French claims were bolstered by a chain of forts extending from the lake country into Illinois and eventually into the Louisiana country. Biloxi (1699), Mobile (1711), and finally New Orleans (1718) completed a line of settlements that had been begun a century before at Quebec.

The French and Indian War.

By the middle of the eighteenth century, the English colonies on the coast of North America were hemmed in by a vast expanse of French territory stretching from Quebec down to the southern borders of Georgia and extending inland far beyond the Mississippi. But this domain was loosely held. French Canada's population of only 50,000 or 60,000 farmers and fur traders faced English colonies that outnumbered them by approximately 20 to 1. Since the British had superior sea power as well, it may have seemed that British victory was simply a matter of time. In fact, the British won control of North America only after more than seven years of bitter fighting.

Although the war could have been touched off at any point along the Anglo-French border, the immediate provocation came in western Pennsylvania. The French had been building a chain of fortifications in the region, where a group of important Virginia land speculators, the Ohio Company, held claims from which they expected great profit. Governor Dinwiddie of Virginia, who supported the Ohio Company, had learned through a preliminary expedition (1753-1754) under young George Washington that the French were fortifying the whole Ohio River Valley and could be driven out only by force. In 1754, he again sent Washington into the region, but Washington arrived only to find that the French had already built Fort Duquesne on the site of what is now Pittsburgh. After a brief skirmish at Great Meadows, Washington found it advisable to return home. Informally, the conflict was on, though

The War in the West 1753-1754

the declaration of war did not come until two years afterward.

Less than a month after Washington's defeat in western Pennsylvana, colonial delegates assembled at Albany, under the sponsorship of the Crown, to try to make a common peace with the Indians and to win the support of the Iroquois in the coming war with the French. The most important result was the acceptance by the conference of a plan drawn up by Benjamin Franklin for intercolonial union. The Albany Plan called for a "General Government . . . under which Government each Colony may retain its present constitution" except for certain particulars. The super-government would consist of a grand council made up of representatives from each colony according to population and wealth. A president-general

65

(to be appointed by the king) and a treasurer would comprise the executive branch, advised by the grand council but with final authority in matters of peace and war. The grand council would handle Indian affairs, administer the disposal of western lands, govern the frontier territories beyond the precincts of the colonies until the Crown took over, and levy taxes to maintain a colonial army.

Neither the English nor the individual colonial governments would even consider this enlightened proposal. Land-speculators (particularly strong in the Virginia government, which had not bothered to send delegates to Albany) did not wish to entrust the distribution of the Ohio lands to an intercolonial congress, and every colonial assembly wanted to retain its control of taxation. The colonies were not ready for union in 1754, and the war against the French was conducted inefficiently and with constant bickering among the colonies themselves and between the colonies and England.

Both Virginia, with its western land interests, and New England, with its perennial desire to reduce the strength of the French in Canada, were prepared for war in 1755. But neither the French nor the British wanted to fight at this point, and the Duke

of Newcastle, the First Secretary of State, hoped at first that the war might be localized. Events dashed his hope. An expedition dispatched under the command of General Edward Braddock to capture Fort Duquesne was ambushed and savagely mauled by a force of French and Indians on the Monongahela River about eight miles below the fort. Braddock was mortally wounded. This defeat exposed the western settlements of Pennsylvania, Maryland, and Virginia to a series of French raids and weakened the waning prestige of the English among the Indians. The rest of the English operations that year were largely unsuccessful, for they failed to take Fort Niagara, the key to French control of the West, or Crown Point on Lake Champlain.

In the meantime, the European powers had undergone a shift in alliances. France, Austria, Russia, Sweden, many of the German states, and later Spain, were allied against England, Portugal, and Prussia. The struggle for America had become one phase of a world war raging on the Continent, in the Atlantic, the Mediterranean, the Indian Ocean, the West Indies, and finally even the Philippines. Until 1758, the contest went badly for England and her allies almost everywhere. But in that year, when the brilliant organizer and strategist, William Pitt, became Secretary of State, English fortunes began to pick up. Perceiving the central importance of the North American theater of action, Pitt subsidized Frederick the Great of Prussia to carry the burden of war in Europe, used the English fleet to bottle up French ships in French ports, and brought greater energy to bear in the New World.

In 1758 the English recaptured Louisbourg, and George Washington, now on the staff of General John Forbes, had the satisfaction at last of taking part in the capture of Fort Duquesne. Frederick turned the tide on the Continent, and Clive began to tame the French in India. But the climax among the victories of the following year came when a brilliant young brigadier general, James Wolfe, stormed the Heights of Abraham outside Quebec, and took the city from a

Campaigns in the North 1755 – 1760

■ CAPTURED BY BRITISH

C A N A D A

Quebec 1759
Montreal 1760
Ft. Frontenac 1758
L. Ontario
L. Erie
Ft. Niagara 1759
St. Lawrence R.
L. Champlain
Crown Point 1759
Ft. Ticonderoga 1759
NOVA SCOTIA
Louisbourg 1758
Ft. Duquesne 1758
BRADDOCK DEFEATED 1755
ACADIANS EXPELLED 1755
Atlantic Ocean

smaller force under General Montcalm, thus gaining strategic control of the St. Lawrence. Both generals were killed in the battle, but Wolfe lived long enough to know that he had won Canada for the Empire. Since the English were also winning on the sea, in the West Indies, in India, and in the American West, the crisis in the war had passed. But the war dragged on until 1763, when the opposing coalition, which now included Spain, agreed to make peace.

By the Treaty of Paris, concluded in February, 1763, Britain won from France all of Canada and all the great interior east of the Mississippi except for the port of New Orleans. France retained fishing rights on the Newfoundland banks and two small islands as fishing bases there, and England returned to her the captured West Indies islands of Martinique and Guadeloupe. Spain gave up East and West Florida to the British in return for the restoration of Cuba, which had been overrun the preceding year. By a treaty contracted in 1762, France, which had induced Spain to enter the war, compensated her ally by yielding to her all the French territories west of the Mississippi and the Isle of Orleans.

Long before the conquest of Canada, Britons had regarded the American colonies as an increasingly important part of the British Empire, and indeed they were steadily becoming more significant as markets, not merely as sources of raw material. Consequently, the mainland colonies, which were doubling in population with every generation, took on a new and special value, and British attention was somewhat diverted

"The Death of Wolfe," a painting by Benjamin West (1738-1820). West was not the first to give up dressing heroes in classic togas, but he made his version of Wolfe's death more lifelike than earlier representations of this event.

from the West Indies, which had hitherto been more highly prized. Within the North American colonies, the "bread colonies" of the middle region and the New England colonies offered a particularly attractive market for English exports. In 1698, seven-eighths of Britain's colonial trade had been with the West Indies, Virginia, Maryland, and the Carolinas, and only one-eighth with the Middle and New England colonies. By 1767, however, two-thirds of English exports to the colonies were going to the areas north of Maryland.

Even before the negotiations leading to the Treaty of Paris, English statesman realized that they could not have both Guadeloupe and Canada—that if they demanded both, the French would continue the fight. Debate went on in England over this choice, but Pitt felt that the possession of Canada would make the empire more secure militarily and also provide a valuable source of trade. England, proudly victorious, now became committed to the development of a great continental domain in North America. During the argument over Canada and Guadeloupe, it was asked whether this immense domain would not some day revolt, announce its independence, and even become an enemy of England's. Benjamin Franklin, then in London as a colonial agent, wrote a pamphlet on the subject in which he argued for keeping Canada as an addition to a great and fabulously rich American agricultural empire that would serve as an immense and rapidly expanding market for English manufactures. The idea of independence Franklin brushed lightly aside. If the North American colonists had been incapable of uniting against their murderous enemies, the French and Indians, he asked, was there any likelihood that they would unite against "their own nation" which protected and encouraged

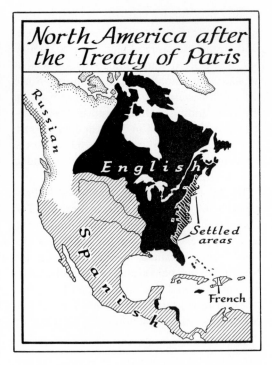

North America after the Treaty of Paris

them and which "they love much more than they love one another?" A union among the colonies, he went on, "is not merely improbable, it is impossible."

But here Franklin added an explanation which, though he did not mean it as a warning, might well have been taken as such: "When I say such a union is impossible, I mean without the most grievous tyranny and oppression." There was no assurance, of course, that Englishmen and Americans would agree on what constituted grievous tyranny, and the British victory over the French brought with it many problems that cried for solution and that laid the ground for serious differences between the colonies and the mother country. When Franklin published his essay in 1760, he could hardly have imagined that 16 years later he would put his signature to a Declaration of Independence and negotiate for loans with the enemies of England.

Readings

The fascinating story of emigration from the Old World to the New is told in M. L. Hansen, *The Atlantic Migration, 1607-1860* (1940), and Carl Wittke, *We Who Built America: The Saga of the Immigrant* (1939). A. B. Faust, *The German Element in the United States* (2 vols., 1909), is still the standard work. For the Scotch-Irish, H. J. Ford, *The Scotch-Irish in America* (1915), is recommended.

An outstanding book on colonial southern life is Carl Bridenbaugh's *Myths and Realities: Societies of the Colonial South* (1952). T. J. Wertenbaker's *The Old South: The Founding of American Civilization* (1942), provides additional information on the Chesapeake society, and A. H. Hirsch, *The Huguenots of Colonial South Carolina* (1928), is suggestive in its treatment of Charleston society.

Particularly valuable on the cultural, social, and political life of colonial Pennsylvania are: Carl and Jessica Bridenbaugh, *Rebels and Gentlemen: Philadelphia in the Age of Franklin* (1942); F. B. Tolles, *Meeting House and Counting House, the Quaker Merchants of Colonial Philadelphia* (1948); and T. J. Wertenbaker, *The Founding of American Civilization: The Middle Colonies* (1938).

New England society is adequately if not impartially covered in J. T. Adams, *Revolutionary New England, 1691-1776* (1923). To correct Adams' anti-Puritan bias, the reader should consult S. E. Morison, *Intellectual Life of Colonial New England* (1956), and the pro-Puritan biography of an important Massachusetts leader, K. B. Murdock's *Increase Mather, the Foremost American Puritan* (1925), and Barrett Wendell's *Cotton Mather* (1891). Indispensable for an understanding of New England thought and society are Perry Miller's *The New England Mind: The Seventeenth Century* (1939), and *The New England Mind: From Colony to Province* (1953). Information on the New England back country can be found in L. K. Mathews, *The Expansion of New England* (1909), and the early chapters of L. N. Newcomer, *The Embattled Farmers: A Massachusetts Countryside in the American Revolution* (1953).

Family life in colonial America is touched upon in E. A. Dexter, *Colonial Women* (1924); A. W. Calhoun, *A Social History of the American Family* (3 vols., 1917-1919); and E. S. Morgan, *The Puritan Family* (1944).

New investigations have modified earlier views on the degree of internal conflict within the colonies and the limitation of the franchise. The following titles present the revisionist position. Robert E. Brown, *Middle-Class Democracy and the Revolution in Massachusetts, 1691-1780* (1955); Theodore Thayer, *Pennsylvania Politics and the Growth of Democracy, 1740-1776* (1953); and R. P. McCormick, *The History of Voting in New Jersey* (1953). For a solid treatment of the traditional attitude toward internal controversy, C. P. Nettels' *The Roots of American Civilization* (1938) is excellent.

Parkman's chronicle of Anglo-French rivalry is conveniently abridged in S. E. Morison's *The Parkman Reader* (1955). In addition to G. M. Wrong, *The Rise and Fall of New France* (2 vols., 1928), the reader might consult D. G. Creighton, *Dominion of the North, A History of Canada* (1944), and an excellent account of Pontiac's conspiracy, H. H. Peckham, *Pontiac and the Indian Uprising* (1947). Braddock's defeat is covered in D. S. Freeman's *Young Washington* (1948), the first two volumes of a six-volume study. Another important book dealing with English problems is C. W. Alvord, *The Mississippi Valley in British Politics* (2 vols., 1916).

Some important general studies on the life and culture of colonial America are Carl Bridenbaugh's richly detailed *Cities in the Wilderness: The First Century of Urban Life in America, 1625-1742* (1938), and *Cities in Revolt: Urban Life in America, 1743-1776* (1955); and Michael Kraus' *The Atlantic Civilization: Eighteenth Century Origins* (1949), valuable for its discussion of cultural ties between the colonies and England. For a discussion of colonial architecture, see Oliver Larkin, *Art and Life in America* (1949). Dr. Alexander Hamilton's amusing and instructive account of his trip from Maryland to New England in 1744 has been edited by Carl Bridenbaugh as *Gentlemen's Progress* (1948).

THE MATURE
COLONIAL
MIND

C H A P T E R F O U R

In 1608, Captain John Smith had testily referred to those "gentlemen" who

because they found not English cities, nor such fair houses, nor at their own wishes any of their accustomed dainties, with feather beds and down pillows, taverns and alehouses in every breathing place, neither such plenty of gold and silver and dissolute liberty as they expected,

had little or no care of anything but to pamper their bellies, to fly away with our pinnaces, or procure their means to return for England; for the country was to them a misery, a ruin, a death, a hell.

A century later, even the most severe critic of America could not have described it as a "misery" or a "hell." The colonies not only provided "dainties" and "alehouses" but also a culture—imitative and provincial, to be sure, but bearing the stamp of a distinctive experience. The idler, the trifler, the unproductive gentleman, was no more suited to eighteenth-century America than he had been to John Smith's wilderness, but economic prosperity permitted a cultivated

minority, at least, to engage in non-utilitarian pursuits and to keep in touch with the latest intellectual developments on the Continent. And it was this minority that shared in the intellectual "Enlightenment" of the eighteenth-century world.

I. THE SECULAR MIND

The Enlightenment. In the last part of the seventeenth century, a relatively small number of savants, philosophers, and scientists began to look at man and his environment in a new way—to make objective scientific inquiries, to emphasize the power of reason instead of appeals to religion and authority, and to affirm the innate goodness of man. These architects of the Enlightenment, or the "Age of Reason," were in turn carrying on empirical traditions of thought that went back before the Renaissance. When Nicholas Copernicus, a Polish-born mathematician and astronomer, published his *Concerning the Revolutions of Heavenly Bodies* in 1543, he changed the conception of the cosmos from an earth-centered universe around which the planets revolved to a sun-centered universe. In so doing, he cast suspicion on man's kinship with the angels and subordinated the universe to unchanging natural laws. Further scientific discoveries after Copernicus in astronomy, physics, anatomy, geology, and chemistry, weakened the old religious dogmas even more, and by the eighteenth century the learned world accepted the idea of the universe as it appeared in the treatises of the great English mathematician, Sir Isaac Newton (1642-1727).

Newton's universe was not ruled by chance and governed by miracle; it operated mechanically according to fixed mathematical laws. Theology and priests were of less help than right reason in winning the good life and in understanding God's ways. Virtue needed no theological sanction; its advantages could be scientifically demonstrated. By means of reason, an ideal environment

could be created in which the potentially virtuous man might develop harmoniously. Bad environment, rather than original sin, was responsible for social evils. As one rational child of the Enlightenment, Thomas Jefferson, wrote to John Adams, Calvin's God

. . . is not the God whom you and I acknowledge and adore, the creator and benevolent Governor of the world; but a daemon of malignant spirit. It would be more pardonable to believe in no God at all, than to blaspheme him by the atrocious attributes of Calvin.

Most men of the Enlightenment did not deny the value of religion, but they tended to present God as a skilled engineer rather than as a hurler of thunderbolts and a watcher of sparrows; He was far more removed from the world and far more impersonal than the Biblical God of the pre-Newtonian era. The eighteenth-century philosophers held no brief for miracles, "the refuge of the ignorant." They extended their rationalistic probings not only into the natural and physical sciences but also into the arts and social sciences. They derived new rules of writing and revised systems of aesthetics from the canons of reason; and they made the mental qualities most valued in the study of physics or political economy—reasonableness, clarity, exactness—the criteria of eighteenth-century literary expression as well.

The Enlightenment
in America. The shift in interest from spiritual to earthly affairs in the colonies had already begun before the advent of the En-

lightenment. Anticipations of the "eighteenth-century outlook" can be discovered among the Puritan exponents of Calvin, who, notwithstanding their conviction that man's nature was sinful, held forth on the rational order of the universe before they had even heard of Newton's laws. "The structure and organization of the world," Calvin himself had written, "bear witness to God which the dullest ear cannot fail to hear."

Portrait of Cotton Mather (1663-1728), attributed to Peter Pelham.

Cotton Mather (1663-1728), the last great figure of the Mather dynasty, had no difficulty in reconciling the faith of his fathers with the new science. He was the grandson of Richard Mather, one of the original Massachusetts "Saints," a "very hard student" and eminent minister who lived and died an inflexible Puritan. Richard Mather's famous son, Increase, the father of Cotton, "swam quietly in a stream of impiety and carnal security for many years together," as he phrased it, and was converted in 1654. Educated at Harvard and at Trinity College, Dublin, he served as colonial agent for Massachusetts and preached in a leading Boston church. From 1685 to 1701, he was President of Harvard College, and his learning was almost as prodigious as his son's. Cotton Mather, who wrote of himself— "I began to pray, even when I began to speak"—was the leading figure in New England during the transition between the age of faith and the age of reason. An understanding of Nature, he believed, was the best antidote to atheism, and his religious zeal in no way interfered with his lively interest in medicine and agriculture. In fact, his curiosity about every aspect of the natural world, his loving attention to the humblest practical problem, and his unflagging dedication to human betterment sprang directly from his Christian piety.

Mather's concern for man, his preoccupation with the useful that drew from him the characteristic observation—"The very wheelbarrow is to be with respect looked upon"—illustrate the change in colonial thinking that had occurred between 1620 and 1720. Eighteenth-century America tended to become humanitarian, secular, liberal, to turn its attention away from God to man. Time and prosperity dulled the early religious fervor. Society slowly became secularized, earth-bound, man-controlled, less subject to heavenly direction.

The seventeenth-century Puritan, to be sure, had never renounced this world. In fact, he displayed his piety by working with a holy zeal to transform the Devil's playground into God's vineyard. But his chief end was "to glorify God and enjoy him forever." He could not, as one orthodox minister put it, "be his own felicity. He is a dependent creature. . . . He doth not enjoy in himself a self-sufficiency."

And yet this is precisely what the American colonists began to enjoy. As their attentions turned increasingly to the solid things of the earth, they came to resemble (as one successful Virginia planter regretfully admitted in 1720) "muckworms . . . that is, in other words, too great lovers of this world." And as the colonists changed, so did their God. The fierce and magnificent Autocrat, who worked mysteriously for His own glory, grew more tractable and kindly, less capricious, more concerned about the happiness of His children.

Thus by the mid-eighteenth century, a social and mental climate favorable to scientific and secular thinking had evolved that prepared the way for the reception of Deism, as the religion of reason was called. Deism posited a mechanical universe run by a Heavenly Engineer who had no need to resort to miracles to demonstrate His glory. It dismissed the Trinity, the divinity of Christ, and the Biblical account of human origins as superstitions and maintained that the moral truths of Christianity were better defended by science than by revelation. In marked contrast to Calvinism, Deism emphasized the morality of Jesus, attacked sectarian dogma, and encouraged humanitarianism. The Deists were not atheists (although they were so labeled by their enemies); they believed in a benevolent God who rewarded virtue and punished vice. As rational men, the truest was for them the clearest; the most logical was the most easily explained; and scientific laws were the architecture of religion. Deism, a philosophy of life rather than a religion, held sway chiefly among a small number of educated men in the seaboard cities.

Benjamin Franklin.

The exemplar of the American Enlightenment and one of the greatest men of his age was the renegade Bostonian and adopted Philadelphian, Benjamin Franklin. He was himself a living proof of the Enlightenment, an illustration of what might be accomplished by reason, measure, and clarity:

Printer, postmaster, almanac maker, essayist, chemist, orator, tinker, professor of housewifery, ambassador, projector, maxim-monger, herb-doctor, wit;—Jack of all trades, master of each and mastered by none—the type and genius of the land.

So Herman Melville, the great nineteenth-century American novelist, later described

This unusual portrait of Benjamin Franklin has been attributed to both Robert Feke and John Greenwood. It shows Franklin in the guise of a sophisticated man of the world rather than a homely philosopher.

him, observing at the same time that Franklin was "everything but a poet." Melville was right. Franklin abhorred mysteries and found metaphysical reasonings disgusting. Incapable of feeling deep religious emotions, he developed a bland and complacent practical faith of his own while remaining completely tolerant of the beliefs of others. In his own eyes, he never "sinned"; rather, he "erred." And in that distinction we can measure the gulf between the piety of Franklin's seventeenth-century antecedents and the easier morality of the eighteenth century.

Franklin's admirable utilitarianism was neither greedy nor materialistic. He respected

73

tools and the people who used them, and his close attention to problems arising from the humblest occupations as well as from the loftier ones grew out of his desire to produce "something for the common benefit of mankind." When he had acquired enough money to support himself, he gave up business and devoted his energies to science, public affairs, and writing. He wanted people, he once confessed, to say after his death that "He lived usefully" rather than that "He died rich." And so Franklin improved the printing press, tinkered successfully with smoky chimneys, suggested changes in the shape and rigging of ships, plotted cyclonic storms, introduced new plants into America, drained lands skillfully, coined the terms "positive" and "negative" electricity, improved carriage wheels, founded the first American club for mutual improvement, invented the bifocal lens, designed an effective iron stove, recommended a more practical watering trough for horses, showed navigators how to shorten the eastern crossing by following the Gulf Stream, showed how public buildings could be heated, and constructed a fan for his chair to keep off the flies. This is only a partial list of his accomplishments, which included pioneer work in the science of electricity, studies in American population growth, and a fantastically successful public career. He asked for no rewards, took out no patents on his inventions, because "as we enjoy great advantages from the inventions of others, we should be glad of an opportunity to serve others by any invention of ours." His entire life was a fulfillment of one of his most deeply felt beliefs: "Serving God is doing good to men."

It is this very many-sidedness of Franklin and his zeal for the practical that make it hard to think of him as a philosopher and man of letters. Yet he took to writing as he took to politics, religion, ethics, science, agriculture, and mechanics—easily and engagingly. Through his writings he expressed the values of thousands of his fellow Americans, the common citizens whose virtues he so uncommonly represented. Their materialistic aspirations he caught in his capitalistic homily, "The Way to Wealth." But his shrewd, cynical, and humorous maxims went beyond vulgar pragmatism and embodied the folk-wisdom of the American people: *Fish and visitors stink in three days. Write with the learned, pronounce with the vulgar. Eat to please thyself but dress to please others. Neither a fortress nor a maid will hold out long after they begin to parley. Let thy maidservant be faithful, strong, and homely. Keep your eyes wide open before marriage, half shut afterwards. Where there's marriage without love there will be love without marriage. The most exquisite folly is made of wisdom spun too fine.*

In his hostility to authoritarian restraint, in his humanitarianism, his faith in progress or "the power of man over matter," Franklin epitomized the Enlightenment, but he retained (perhaps as a Puritan legacy) a certain distrust for uninstructed human nature and a canny insight into human frailty.

II.   THE RELIGIOUS MIND

Jonathan Edwards and Puritanism.   At the very time when Deism was enjoying a vogue among the colonial intelligentsia and religious liberals, old-fashioned orthodoxy held its ground among the farmers and artisans who made up the bulk of the colonial population. But many of them no longer felt that religion was a vital force in their lives. In New England, piety had been sapped by prosperity, especially in the towns, and by the declining prestige of the ministerial class.

The Puritan orthodoxy suffered its first serious blow when the children of regenerate church members, having no religious experiences to confess in public, were permitted by the terms of the "Half-Way Covenant" of 1662 to remain in the church and have their children baptized. A series of dramatic setbacks then followed. Under the short administration of Governor Andros (1686-1689), the legal foundations of Puritanism were undermined in the Bay Colony and Anglicanism was introduced. Massachusetts' revised charter of 1691 substituted property for religious tests as a qualification for voting, and made the governorship an appointed office, thereby removing it from popular control. The excesses of the Salem witchcraft hysteria that followed immediately in 1692 further weakened the authority of the ministerial class.

This episode began when two Salem girls accused some townspeople of bewitching them, and soon a perfect epidemic of witch-hunting infected the community. Before the scare had died down, 20 victims had been executed and more than a hundred others were awaiting trial. The clerical interrogators and the magistrates who conducted the witch trials soon came to their senses when the most eminent and respected citizens were branded as the Devil's emissaries. Both Increase and Cotton Mather had inadvertently encouraged the outbreak by publishing books proving the existence of witches—and this at a time when William Penn dismissed a case against a woman charged with riding on a broomstick by saying "that there was no law in Pennsylvania against riding on broomsticks." During the trials, the Mathers had cautioned the court not to accept as evidence the reports of persons allegedly afflicted by witchcraft; but since neither the Mathers nor other ministers actively opposed the trials, they were subsequently blamed and lost considerable prestige.

Elsewhere throughout the colonies, religion had fallen to a low condition. Many settlers in the back country, particularly in the South, rarely saw a minister. In some areas, no provisions had been made for religious instruction even as late as the eighteenth century. It was during this time of religious apathy in the 1730's that a great religious revival began. Known as the Great Awakening, it was one of the most

significant intercolonial experiences to take place before 1776. This widespread phenomenon indicated a deep-seated emotional need that a formalized and intellectualized religion had failed to meet. The Great Awakening was actually part of a world-wide evangelical movement that had its roots in Germany and England. Its leading spirits in the colonies were men of various denominations: Theodore Frelinghuysen, a Dutch-Reformed minister, living in New Jersey; William Tennent and his sons, Pennsylvania Presbyterians; and Jonathan Edwards, a Massachusetts Congregationalist and the greatest theologian of them all.

Edwards was a speculative theologian who investigated less practical problems than Franklin's lightning conductors and smoking chimneys. In his concern for truths that lay beyond concrete experience, in his rapturous and at the same time astute analysis of religious feeling, evil, and grace, Edwards demonstrated another kind of concern that was as characteristically American as Franklin's. Both these great men showed that the American mind, soon to be recognized as having a characteristic outlook, would be as diverse and contradictory as the country itself: visionary and down-to-earth, deeply radical and solidly conservative, coldly prudent and unexpectedly wild.

Edwards had succeeded his grandfather, the eminent Solomon Stoddard, in the Northampton pastorate where he served for 21 years before his congregation dismissed him. The significance—and the tragedy—of Edwards' career was his unsuccessful attempt to restore the sense of God's omnipotence to a people for whom religion had become a meaningless routine. Because his own religious experience was so intense, he sought to awaken in his congregation a similar emotion. Ever since his days at Yale, Edwards had been a reader of Newton and John Locke; the science and philosophy of the Enlightenment interested him enormously. But his mystical and poetic disposition prevented him from becoming a rationalist like the cool and anti-emotional Charles Chauncy of Boston, Edwards' chief theological opponent. Locke taught Edwards that men's hearts could be touched only by making the abstract come alive. A later generation was to abuse him for his apparent pleasure in threatening his listeners with hell-fire. Actually, most of his sermons dealt with God's mercy, but by occasionally playing on the nerves of his auditors, by reducing hell to something vividly physical, he awakened slumbering hearts.

Between 1733 and 1735, Northampton underwent an intense religious revival. Edwards attacked the widely held doctrine that salvation depended upon reputability and good works, that man possessed the power to save himself. In place of the humanized Deity, genial and benevolent, who made salvation easy (the God of Franklin), he presented the omnipotent and splendid God of Calvin. His own revival efforts prepared the way seven years later for the American tour of the electrifying English evangelist, George Whitefield.

The Great Awakening.   Arriving from England in 1739, Whitefield spoke to enormous crowds in New England, New York, Philadelphia, Charleston, and Savannah. Many of his listeners traveled for miles to hear him. He preached theatrically, using human-interest stories and appealing to the emotions of his audience rather than emphasizing doctrinal distinctions. Although Whitefield did not mix politics with religion, some of his enthusiastic co-workers offended the conservatives by their extravagance and upset the social order by rejecting forms and creeds. Too often they mistook weeping and screaming and bodily gyrations for the spirit of God. Enemies of the revival questioned these grotesque manifestations and were shocked by the actions of ministers who enacted the sufferings of Christ from the pulpit. They deplored especially the itinerant ministers who passed from place to place censuring the local clergy for their lack of piety.

It is easy to play up the excesses of the Great Awakening in the spirit of its severest critics but it cannot be dismissed as a mere emotional orgy. Its consequences can be summarized as follows:

1. *The religious consequences.* The Great Awakening split the old denominations into two main groups, one espousing the traditional conservative doctrines or forms, the other adopting the "New Divinity." The latter was a religion of personal experience as against a religion of custom or habit. The "New Light" or "New Side" wing, as the revivalists were called, demanded a universal priesthood of believers, a kind of spiritual democracy. The great revival increased the membership of the small dissenting sects at the expense of the established denominations.

2. *Political and economic consequences.* The weakening of the established Anglican church helped to loosen British authority in the colonies, particularly in Virginia where the Baptists and Methodists led the fight against the Anglicans. Elsewhere, too, the Great Awakening served as a leveling movement to prepare the way for the separation of church and state. Men trained to stand up for their religion made good revolutionaries in 1776, and radical preachers often anticipated the better-known ideas of the anti-British pamphleteers. It required no great stretch of the imagination to extend the liberties of conscience to economic and political liberties. The Great Awakening was opposed by the old orthodoxy and the fashionable rationalists, for both groups were disturbed by its political and social implications. It had its greatest effect among the economically as well as the spiritually impoverished.

3. *Social and cultural consequences.* Provincial jealousies and localism were weakened by the itinerant ministers who traveled through the colonies. The huge crowds who flocked to hear Whitefield and the other preachers were starved for social contact. In the vast outdoor meetings that were to

become a common feature of subsequent revivals, they found release for emotions long repressed—social and spiritual. Despite the excesses accompanying the Great Awakening and the backsliding that followed, morals and manners improved as a result of it. Especially among the Baptists, the followers of Wesley, and the Presbyterians, righteous conduct was the test of grace.

Although some of the revivalists were suspicious of an educated clergy and encouraged lay-preaching, the Great Awakening produced a small educational renaissance. William Tennent's famous "Log College" at Neshaminy, Pennsylvania, founded in 1736, fathered similar schools for the preparation of Presbyterian ministers. The Baptists lagged behind the Presbyterians, but they established their own schools—Hopewell Academy, and later the College of Rhode Island (Brown) in 1764. Princeton (Presbyterian), Rutgers (Dutch-Reformed), and Dartmouth (Congregational) were all founded under the impetus of the revival movement.

The Great Awakening, furthermore, quick-

ened the humanitarian spirit of the eighteenth century by forcing men to pay attention to their social as well as their spiritual condition. When Jonathan Edwards defined virtue as "love of Being in general," he was suggesting that there was a divine element in everyone that ought to be recognized out of love for God. Orphans, Negroes, Indians, and paupers shared in this Being and became the objects of Christian concern. Notable Quakers like Anthony Benezet and John Woolman intensified Quaker humanitarianism by protesting against slavery and injustice.

Religion and the Churches. At the end of the colonial period, there was approximately one church for every 900 people. Despite the Great Awakening, the majority of the colonial population had no church affiliation. Established churches (those that were officially supported by the state)

Nassau Hall, College of New Jersey (now Princeton University), 1763, with the President's house on the right.

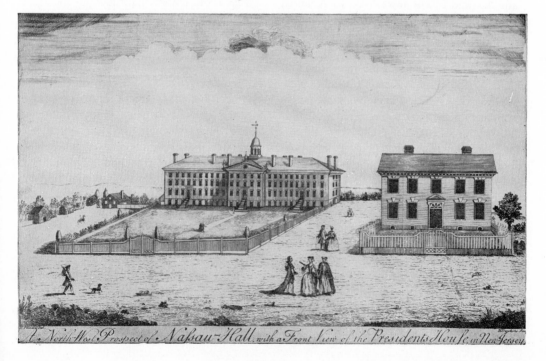

existed in some colonies—Anglican in the South and Congregational in New England. But almost from the beginning many colonies had been battlegrounds for competing sects. When Quakers, Anglicans, Presbyterians, Dutch-Reformed, Catholics, and Jews lived in the same province, as they did in Pennsylvania, an established church became inadvisable if not impossible. The dissenting spirit of Protestantism did not fade away in America. Rather, it took on a new energy as denominations splintered and new sects sprang up. The very multiplicity of religions insured a practical tolerance and the acceptance of what finally came to be the American principle of the separation of church and state.

Despite the variety of sects and the ethnic and geographical divisions among the denominations, the following generalizations about colonial religion in the 1750's seem valid:

First, colonial religion was overwhelmingly Protestant. Although the colonies provided a refuge for the persecuted of all the Old World religions, only about 25,000 Catholics and 2,000 Jews lived in America on the eve of the Revolution. The colonists were in a real sense the children of the Reformation, differing radically among themselves in creed and doctrine yet joined in common opposition to Rome. Catholics were not physically molested in eighteenth-century America, but they were the victims of anti-Catholic propaganda spread by Protestant ministers, educators, editors, and publishers of the popular almanacs. England's wars with Catholic France partly explain this anti-Catholic feeling, but the hostility went far deeper. Particularly in New England, but elsewhere as well, the inhabitants passed on their inherited prejudices against Catholic practices.

Second, the doctrine and organization of American churches reflected the social background of the members. The most powerful and influential denominations in the New World were the New England Congregationalists, the Presbyterians, and the Anglicans. These churches numbered among their adherents many plain folk in addition to most of the established mercantile and landed middle-class families. A higher proportion of persons of modest means was found in the Baptist churches, among the Methodists who emerged in the late 1760's, and in various small sects.

In the early days of colonial settlement, the religious establishments, both Puritan and Church of England, had been intolerant of the dissenting sects and only grudgingly accepted their right to exist. By the 1760's, however, the Quakers, Baptists, and a host of other imported sects no longer suffered active persecution. Some groups, like the Quakers, had become rich and respectable, and the Baptists made many converts among the poor and illiterate. Depending less on an educated clergy, and making frankly evangelical appeals, the dissenting churches aroused the fear and disgust of the established denominations. But they reached elements in the colonial population that had hitherto been neglected by the older churches, and they often joined the fight for religious and political liberty.

Third, the tendency throughout the eighteenth century was toward greater religious freedom and the separation of church and state. America had been settled by men eager to "shake off the dust of Babylon." To the sectarian-minded worshiper of the seventeenth century, tolerance or "polypiety" was the greatest impiety. But no state-enforced religion could survive where dissenters continued to dissent and where men of diverse backgrounds and religions lived side by side. Even in orthodox New England the persecution of Quakers and Baptists had ceased by 1700, and a robust minister like John Wise of Ipswich could almost single-handedly foil the attempt of an organized clique of ministers to centralize church government and destroy the autonomy of the independent congregation. In defending the congregational principle and church democracy (*The Churches' Quarrel Espoused,* 1710, and *The Vindication of the Govern-*

Wise introduced arguments that were later adopted by the Revolutionary patriots in defense of political democracy. All men are born free, he said, and "Democracy is Christ's government in Church and State." The cause of religious liberalism was also supported from abroad. Since 1689, when Parliament passed the Act of Toleration granting religious freedom to Protestant Dissenters, although still excluding them from public office, English poets, philosophers, and statesmen had attacked religious discrimination.

Most influential in the war against an official church were the dissenting sects (Quakers, Baptists, and Presbyterians, in particular) whose protests against discrimination grew more persistent during the eighteenth century. With the breakdown of Puritan control in New England after 1691, all the Protestant sects could ally themselves against the Anglican church, which was regarded by many colonists as the tool of British absolutism. In 1763, the possibility that an Anglican bishop might be appointed for New England aroused as much heat as the Stamp Act was to raise a few years later.

By 1776, the atmosphere in the colonies made wide religious toleration inevitable. Colonial proprietors found that toleration was good for business since it attracted foreign settlers. The experience of colonies like Rhode Island and Pennsylvania, which had prospered without an established church, and the opposition of the unchurched and dissenters also contributed to religious liberty.

III. CULTURAL PROGRESS

Education. The educational system of the colonies was largely English in origin. The idea of the public grammar school was already a century old before its introduction to North America in 1642, and English universities served as the models for the first colleges in the New World. The Dutch system of public schools, municipally supported, may have had some influence in the colonies, but English pedagogy and textbooks held sway in colonial schools, and English schoolmasters and scholars enjoyed great prestige.

In the seventeenth century, education had been closely tied up with religion and the church. But in the eighteenth century, the introduction of secular subjects modified the religious emphasis, though religious teaching was not forsaken. Social usefulness became as important an educational goal as morality, and both were essential to the eighteenth-century ideal—the public-spirited man.

Education reflected the social cleavages that existed not only in the South, where class lines were very sharply drawn, but also in the Middle and New England colonies. Rich children received a different kind of education from that received by poor children, who, if they were educated at all, were prepared only for their limited stations in life. Even liberal-minded men in the mid-eighteenth century—revolutionists in the making—accepted these social distinctions as natural and proper.

The kind and quality of education in eighteenth-century America depended also upon the national origin of the settlers, their religion, their section, their closeness to settled areas, and the availability of trained teachers.

Education in the South, for example, lagged behind education in the colonies to the north. Here there was no strong religious motive to create an interest in learning, and it was difficult to establish any kind of organized educational system in the scattered southern settlements. Pauper schools gave rudimentary instruction to orphans and the children of the poor, but in general only the children of the rich were educated. Standards were higher in the Middle colonies, where the dissenting Protestant denominations emphasized Bible-reading. But, since no sect enjoyed a privileged position, the state kept hands off and left schooling to private schools and church schools. Orphans and pauper children received only a minimum of religious and vocational training; the amount and quality of education that most children received was limited to what their parents could afford.

Only in Massachusetts and Connecticut did education become a public concern. The Massachusetts school laws of 1642 and 1647 meant, in effect, that all children must be taught to read. These stringent standards—unique in the English-speaking world at the time—deteriorated as New England society became more decentralized and as educational control passed to the local authorities. By 1700, education was at a low ebb in New England, and illiteracy was prevalent on the frontier. But conditions rapidly improved.

During the 40-year period from 1720 to 1760, a number of excellent semi-private academies were established, and New Englanders once again could proudly assert that they were the best-educated people in all North America.

In the cities, several interesting educational experiments were carried on in the eighteenth century. Philadelphia, Boston, and New York, besides having the best private academies, also had a number of private evening schools that featured practical courses ignored by the classical academies. Such subjects as geography, navigation, bookkeeping, mathematics, and surveying had a high practical value in a commercial society. All classes attended evening schools but the majority of students, of both sexes, came from middle-class homes. Although experiments in practical education were mostly confined to the seaport towns, a group of German sectarians in Bethlehem, Pennsylvania, did make innovations in the teaching of music. Elsewhere, too, men

Pages from the 1767 edition of The New England Primer.

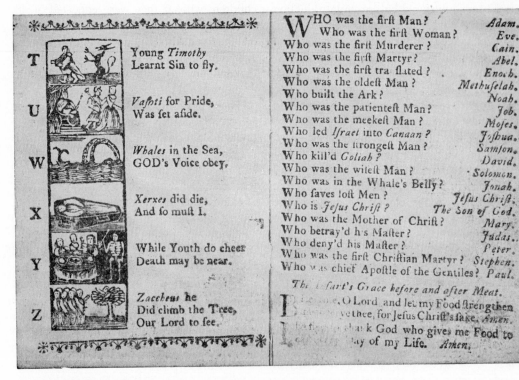

began to think of an education that was freed from traditional European forms and that would deal more directly with American needs. By the 1750's, many private secondary schools had introduced drawing, geography, commerce, and related studies that would offer a useful preparation for the commercial-minded.

A relatively small number of students, drawn almost entirely from the middle and upper classes, attended the seven colonial colleges that had been established by 1764. These and the private academies retained the European curriculum (Latin, Greek, Hebrew, and Science) and fostered aristocratic, conservative ideals. In the higher as well as the lower schools, however, the liberal and rational influences of the age began to be felt as the century waned. The students of the second-oldest college chartered in America, William and Mary, began to debate the philosophy of politics and natural rights. Such eminently practical leaders as Thomas Jefferson and James Monroe were trained here. Harvard became a center of science; the College of Philadelphia an advocate of *"every thing* that is useful, and *every thing* that is ornamental."* King's College (later Columbia) advertised that while the teaching of religion was its principal objective, "it is further the Design of this College, to instruct and perfect the Youth in . . . the Arts of *Numbering* and *Measuring,* of *Surveying* and *Navigation,* of *Geography* and *History,* of *Husbandry, Commerce* and Government."

Naturally enough, the colleges had become the centers of the new science by the first quarter of the eighteenth century. True, no college professor ever matched the self-taught Benjamin Franklin in originality, nor did the most eminent colonial botanist, John Bartram (whose European reputation antedated Franklin's), have university connections. But America's ablest astronomer, John Winthrop, taught at Harvard College, and David Rittenhouse, astronomer and mathematician, lectured at the College of Philadelphia, as did Dr. Benjamin Rush, the first professor of chemistry in America. These

colonial scientists—many of whom were contributing members of the British Royal Society—sent news of their studies in astronomy, mathematics, botany, medicine, and cartography to their learned brethren abroad.

Journalism and Letters.

By 1765, twenty-five weekly newspapers were being published in eleven colonies. Most of the columns were filled with excerpts from English papers, but after the famous trial of John Peter Zenger in 1735 greater opportunities opened up for independent reporting. Zenger, a German printer, was charged with libel for printing an unfavorable report about a crown official. His supporters hired an eminent Philadelphia lawyer, Andrew Hamilton, to defend him, and Hamilton appealed to the jury to define libel in a way contrary to the current British theory. For the judges, the question was merely whether Zenger published the offending articles; for Hamilton, the question was whether the contents of the articles were true. The jury accepted his version of libel and held that since the articles were true, Zenger was not guilty as charged. This decision proved to be a landmark in the history of American journalism, for it established the principle that the jury —not judges—should decide on questions of libel, and that the publication of truthful statements could not be considered libelous. The Zenger case therefore encouraged the press to comment more boldly on political matters than it would have dared to do had Zenger been found guilty.

During Franklin's term as Deputy Postmaster for the colonies (1753-1755), he succeeded in reducing postal rates for newspapers and in speeding up their distribution. But they remained throughout the pre-Revolutionary period too expensive for the poor, and only a small percentage of the people read them.

A more popular medium for disseminating social, scientific, and political information to the uneducated reading public, particularly rural Americans, was the almanac. Almanacs were an old English institution. The first colonial almanac appeared in New England in 1639; by 1731, almanacs were being read in all the colonies. Almanacs were pocket-sized and paper-bound. They served as calendars, astrological guides, recipe books, and children's primers. Sandwiched in between bits of practical information were jokes, poems, and maxims. The better ones (published by Nathaniel Ames and Benjamin Franklin) punctured superstition, provided simplified and palatable summaries of the new science, and presented tasteful selections from the best British authors. Franklin's *Poor Richard's Almanac,* first published in Philadelphia in 1732, soon became a colonial institution, and sold 10,000 copies annually.

Literature received more attention in the eighteenth century than in the seventeenth, though the Puritan suspicion of the secular imagination had not entirely relaxed. A commercially and politically minded population, however, had little interest in *belles lettres,* and the absence of cultural centers, great universities, a national system of education, and a substantial reading public doomed the cause of polite letters. In the South, literary activity was confined mostly to histories, tracts, pamphlets, and newspaper squibs, although some derivative verse was published from time to time. By the 1740's, Philadelphia had become the literary center of the colonies and the first city in which a literary self-consciousness was manifested. There a coterie of young men gathered around the educator and magazine editor, William Smith. But these young writers were even more fettered by English literary conventions than their predecessors had been. Not one measured up to the gifted Puritan poet, Edward Taylor, whose verse blended homely details of New England life with magnificent visions of God. None wrote with the urbanity, robustness, and wit of William Byrd II, with the charm and lucidity

of Franklin, or with the passionate exactness of Jonathan Edwards.

Until the appearance of Philip Freneau's earliest poems in the 1770's American writing remained derivative and provincial, and yet the American experience was preparing the ground for a fresher and more original kind of expression. Literally as well as metaphorically, Americans had begun to speak a different language from the English. In the seventeenth and eighteenth centuries, English lexicographers and scholars like Dr. Samuel Johnson had pruned and refined Elizabethan English, but many of the barbarisms they eliminated continued to be good usage in the colonies. Surviving archaisms like *I guess, chump, flap-jack, homespun, to hustle, cord-wood, Bub* (an expression for a boy), and hundreds of others came to be regarded as Americanisms. American speech also absorbed words from the Dutch, French, German, and Spanish; it adopted words from the Indians, and invented new words like *cow-hide, no-account,* and *hoe-cake.* New plants, animals, and birds tested the imagination and wit of the colonists, as did the peculiar American geography. *Poke-weed, bottom-land, rolling-country, back-woods, roasting-ear, snow-plow, land office,* and *crazy-quilt* were all colonial words that described new scenery, new objects, and new situations.

Political Ideas.　　The most important and solid colonial writing during the eighteenth century was not the work of literary men but of theologians, scientists, and political theorists. The political writers were preoccupied with the political and economic issues that convulsed the American colonies from 1763 to 1776, and among them were some of the ablest minds in the New World. During this period, it was more natural for an ambitious young man to write a pamphlet than to compose a poem, to read political philosophers than to study literary critics. But these political writers were men of education and culture who clashed with their British or loyalist opponents on terms of intellectual equality. Moreover, they found a readier audience than did the more imaginative writers, because they were dealing with ideas that touched most deeply the traditions and aspirations of colonial society.

The political philosophy of most thinking Americans before the Revolution derived partly from colonial experience and partly from English and continental sources. Even during the seventeenth century, when faith, revelation, and authority carried more weight than the cult of reason, the foreshadowings of democracy were dimly visible. Puritanism, as well as the Enlightenment, taught men to appeal to higher truths; both encouraged education, worldly success, and individual self-fulfillment. As rationalism gradually undermined old dogmas and as democratic tendencies grew more noticeable, Americans became receptive to ideas from abroad that seemed to corroborate their own experiences.

Chief among these ideas was the doctrine of natural rights, which received its classic formulation in John Locke's *Two Treatises of Government*. Published in 1690, and taken as an ideological prop for the Revolution of 1688 and for the supremacy of Parliament, Locke's essays were used in the colonies after the 1760's to support resistance to Parliament. Locke had postulated a state of nature that existed before the organization of official government. Here each man possessed the "natural rights" of life, liberty, and property. To escape from the anarchy of the natural state and yet to protect their natural rights, men formed a civil government. By terms of the "social contract," they agreed to yield certain liberties in return for greater security, but they retained the right to overthrow the government if it failed to fulfill the trust they put in it, by violating their inalienable natural rights. In effect, then, government rested upon the continuing consent of the people.

This natural-rights philosophy was strengthened by other beliefs that were widely entertained in the colonies. The common-law rights of freeborn Englishmen, for example, were closely identified with the natural rights of men. And these legal rights were sustained by two English authorities who were immensely influential in America: Sir William Blackstone, known through his *Commentaries on the Laws of England* (1765-1769), and Sir Edward Coke, an eminent seventeenth-century English lawyer. From Blackstone the colonists quoted that man's first allegiance was to God, whose will was the universal law of nature, and that human laws were clearly invalid when they conflicted with natural law.

Ideas about natural rights were in the air, then, before the Declaration of Independence was written. They had been popularized by American lawyers in petty local issues touching on matters of religion, taxation, and the rights of proprietors. When larger issues overshadowed these local concerns, colonial pamphleteers were quick to adopt the natural-rights doctrines for the higher levels of British-American debate. The philosophy of John Locke, thus domesticated for American consumption, seemed especially appropriate to a people who had in fact created government while still living in a state of nature, and colonial experience also provided a basis for argument. The arguments of John Wise in defense of the Congregational principle (see p. 78) or the theories of the Boston minister, Jonathan Mayhew, turned out to have a close bearing on the quarrel between the colonies and England. Mayhew admitted that civil authority required obedience, that disobedience was morally as well as politically sinful. But, he added, when rulers pillage the public instead of protecting it, they stop being emissaries of God and become "common pirates and highwaymen." To support a tyrant was to abet him in promoting misery. For Mayhew, the doctrine of the divine right of kings (with its corollary of non-resistance) was "altogether as fabulous and chimerical as transubstantiation; or any reveries of ancient or modern visionaries." The form that a government took was less important than the need for it to have popular support. If government derived from God, as the absolutists said, it was because God moved the people to organize it.

Here was a reasonable and religious basis for popular assemblies that made sense to the learned and the unlearned alike. A century and a half of colonial history, as a conservative Swedish observer noted in 1775, had created a new kind of political animal peculiar to the North American continent:

The chief trait in the character of an American is an immoderate love of liberty, or rather license.... And this enthusiasm rules in the breasts of all from the highest to the lowest. Education, manner of life, religion, and government—all contribute to it. Parents exercise no authority over children, beyond letting them for the most part do what pleases them. Everyone can maintain himself without trouble, for here there is room enough, and wages are high. No one, therefore, knows oppression or depend-

ence. All are equally good; birth, office, and merits do not make much distinction. Freedom of conscience is unlimited, without the least control by secular law, and church discipline means nothing. The English method of government is in itself quite mild, and is all the less able, in this remote part of the empire, to exercise a reasonable strictness. The reins of government lie so slack that they seldom are noticed, and the hand that guides is never seen. The result of all this is that the people neither know nor will know of any control, and everyone regards himself as an independent Prince.

The French writer, Hector St. John de Crèvecoeur, wrote that a "surprising metamorphosis" had taken place in America. A "new man" had appeared in a miraculous country that demanded little and gave much. "The American," he wrote, "is a new man, who acts upon new principles; he must therefore entertain new ideas, and form new opinions." By 1776, the colonists were ready to go even further. They were ready to test their new opinions in deeds.

Readings

Merle Curti, *The Growth of American Thought* (1943), is a standard work of great importance, not only for colonial ideas but for American intellectual history as a whole. Michael Kraus' *The Atlantic Civilization* (1949), already cited, contains much information relevant to the material covered in this chapter, as do Max Savelle's *Seeds of Liberty* (1948), Clinton Rossiter's *Seedtime of the Republic* (1953), Brooke Hindle's *The Pursuit of Science in Revolutionary America, 1735-1789* (1956), and Daniel Boorstin's perceptive essay on the social philosophy of the Jeffersonian circle, *The Lost World of Thomas Jefferson* (1948).

James Parton, *Life and Times of Benjamin Franklin* (2 vols., 1864), has long been out of print, but in some ways it is still the best biography. The standard modern biography is Carl Van Doren, *Benjamin Franklin* (1938); two other volumes, V. W. Crane, *Benjamin Franklin, Englishman and American* (1936), and I. Bernard Cohen, *Benjamin Franklin* (1953), a well-edited selection, are most readable. There are many cheap editions of Franklin's classic *Autobiography*. A convenient selection from his other writings has been edited by F. L. Mott and C. E. Jorgenson, *Benjamin Franklin* (1936); and *The Letters of Benjamin Franklin and Jane Mecom* (1950), edited by Carl Van Doren, are also worth reading. For a very critical estimate of Franklin, see D. H. Lawrence's malicious essay included in his *Studies in Classic American Literature* (new edition, 1953), and the sardonic portrait of Franklin in Herman Melville's novel, *Israel Potter* (1855, reprinted 1924).

No completely satisfactory book on colonial religion exists, but W. W. Sweet, *Religion in Colonial America* (1942), is helpful. The Great Awakening figures prominently in three interesting books: O. E. Winslow, *Jonathan Edwards, 1703-1758* (1940); Perry Miller, *Jonathan Edwards* (1949); and A. D. Belden, *George Whitefield, the Awakener* (1930). Perry Miller has an excellent discussion of the Salem witchcraft hysteria in *The New England Mind: From Colony to Province* (1953). For a fuller account, M. L. Starkey, *The Devil in Massachusetts, A Modern Inquiry into the Salem Witch Trials* (1949), should be consulted.

Colonial education is dealt with in Paul Monroe, *The Founding of the American Public School System: A History of Education in the United States, from the Early Settlements to the Close of the Civil War Period* (Vol. I, 1940). The most recent and complete summary of higher education in colonial times is Chapter III of R. Hofstadter and W. P. Metzger, *The Development of Academic Freedom in the United States* (1955).

The volumes listed in the first paragraph all contain information on aspects of popular culture, but Sidney Kobre, *The Development of the Colonial Newspaper* (1944), and F. L. Mott, *A History of American Magazines* (Vol. I, 1930-1938), should be added. Oliver Larkin's *Art and Life in America* (1949) is a good introduction to American painting. There is a vast amount of material on colonial literature, both of a specialized and general nature, but the following are all worth looking at: V. L. Parrington's *The Colonial Mind, 1620-1800,* the first volume of his *Main Currents in American Thought* (1927), has been much criticized for its over-simplifications, but it is still vigorous and entertaining reading. Moses Coit Tyler's classic studies of colonial literature have recently been assembled in one volume, *A History of American Literature, 1607-1765* (1949). Worth glancing at for a quick survey are the first chapter of Marcus Cunliffe's *The Literature of the United States* (1954), and an excellent essay on colonial writing is H. M. Jones, *Ideas in America* (1944). Chapters I and II of Robert Spiller *et al., Literary History of the United States* (3 vols., 1948), contain up-to-date and scholarly treatments by specialists in colonial literature.

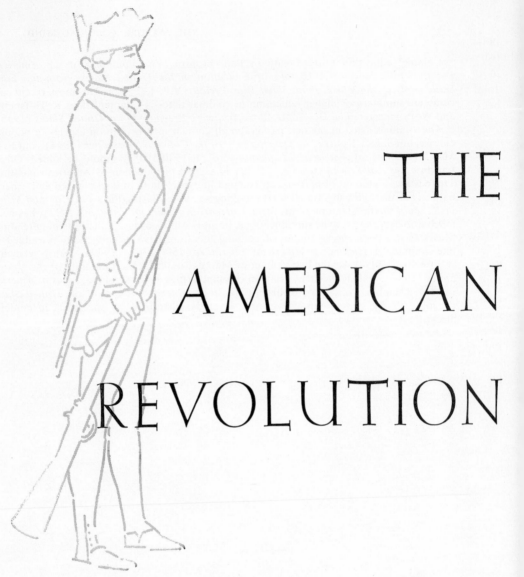

THE
AMERICAN
REVOLUTION

CHAPTER FIVE

In 1818, John Adams declared that "The Revolution was effected before the war commenced. The Revolution was in the minds and hearts of the people." Adams had the advantage of hindsight, but it is easy to see that American loyalty had been undermined before shots were fired at Lexington. Many of the settlers who came to America felt no deep attachment for old England. Religious

dissenters who had been harried out of their homes, convicts who had escaped the hangman's noose, and refugees from the Continent did not make the most dutiful subjects. But neither the original settlers nor their descendants nourished rebellion. After all, British colonials had prospered as members of a benevolent empire, and their institutions and culture were English. They read English books, retained their connections with English church bodies, followed English styles in dress, architecture, and social behavior. John Adams also said that Americans "had been educated in an habitual affection for

England." How was it, then, that the most enlightened and powerful European state lost its most cherished colonial possessions?

I. AN IMPERIAL CRISIS

Problems of Empire.   To the superficial observer, the prospects of the British Empire in 1763 at the close of the French and Indian War (see p. 67) looked bright indeed. Everywhere the British armies and fleets had been successful—in Europe, Africa, the West Indies, North America, and India. France was ruined, though not (as William Pitt warned) incapable of recovery. To the world and to herself, Britain was the model of successful imperial conquest.

Underneath the bright surface, however, lurked a number of difficulties and dangers with which, as time was to show, English officialdom was not imaginative enough to deal. In many ways the American Revolution was the outcome of imperial problems arising out of the French and Indian War. The seeds of rebellion, though planted long ago in early colonial America, flowered in the postwar climate.

Strangely enough, England's acquisition of Canada was one of the main reasons for her eventual loss of the American colonies. So long as the French occupied Canada, the colonists were drawn close to the mother country by the threat of an alien neighbor. But the departure of the French dissolved this bond, and with English control of Canada there arose a new source of controversy. Britain, inheriting both the trade and the administrative problems of Canada, attempted to protect that trade and settle those problems in ways that proved offensive to the colonials.

The events of the French and Indian War also changed the administration of trade regulations in ways that were disadvantageous to colonial merchants. One of the most irksome of these regulations limited trade with the French West Indies. But this trade had been so profitable to the northern merchants and so important a part of their operations that they continued their illegal commerce with the French. Before the war these violations had usually been overlooked, but during the war, they took on the treasonous guise of trading with the enemy. In fact, it was widely believed in England that the French West Indies would have fallen easily if they had not been illegally supplied by colonial merchants. Resentment over these illegal activities induced the English to impose stricter laws regulating colonial trade, a step that inevitably led to ill-will between the colonies and the mother country.

But the most acute problem arising from the war was taxation. The war, which was the climax of a long series of costly eighteenth-century struggles for empire, left the British taxpayers staggering under a crushing tax burden. The expenses came to £82 million, the exchequer now carried a debt of about £130 million, and British landowners were already paying about one-third of their incomes to meet it. The old and newly acquired parts of the empire needed to be garrisoned (it was calculated that 10,000 troops would be needed in America alone), and the English felt that the Americans should be willing to share in the costs of the imperial burden.

The colonists, however, for all their English customs and manners and their sincerely professed loyalty to the Crown, did not accept the idea that Parliament could make laws that governed their internal affairs or that drew upon them as a source of revenue. In general, they were in the habit of managing their home affairs and leaving commercial and diplomatic matters to the Crown. Technically, every act passed by a colonial assembly could be disallowed—that is, thrown out—by the English Privy Council; but imperfect communications and long delays meant that English control was elastic at best. The colonial assemblies learned from experience to ignore rather than to fight over royal instructions defining the extent of their authority. Of 8,563 laws passed by the home assemblies between 1691 and 1775, 469 were vetoed by the British government. But most of these did not reach deep into domestic affairs; they were vetoed because they affected British commercial interests.

In short, the ideas of Englishmen and colonials on the power of the mother country over the colonies were not, and had not been, in agreement, but the long-standing differences had never been argued out. Instead, there had been a system of accommodation by neglect: the English authorities had frequently overlooked colonial violations of parliamentary regulations, and the colonists had preferred to go on quietly breaking these laws when they could rather than openly challenge Parliament's right to pass them. After 1763, these neglected differences suddenly moved into the center of the political arena and led to a fatal conflict before a satisfactory formula for resolving them could be worked out.

English authorities failed to grasp one essential truth: that the Americans had a passion to manage their own affairs without interference. Even as early as the time of the English Civil War in the 1640's, the Massachusetts General Court had rejected the authority of Parliament over its internal affairs because "our allegiance binds us not to the laws of England any longer than we live in England." Under George III, just at the time when the colonists were ready to press for more freedom in self-government and for full equality with the people of England, the English officials decided to try to enforce a system of mercantile regulation, to impose new and unfamiliar taxes. The makers of English policy, men who did not know the colonies at first-hand, thus showed their ignorance of the colonial state of mind

But there was more than a failure of understanding; there was a clash of material ambitions, for the colonial assemblies and Parliament had become representatives of two sets of opposing interests. Parliament was under the influence of English taxpayers, merchants, land speculators, and creditors; the colonial assemblies were under the influence of colonial merchants, colonial land-speculators, and debtors. Parliament, thinking largely of solving English rather than colonial problems, passed a series of measures after 1763 that damaged colonial commercial interests and offended colonial sentiments— and then, after offering this provocation, showed weakness rather than strength. The relative mildness of British authority in America—as reflected in the unfettered agitations of merchants' groups and patriotic organizations, the terrorizing of the Tories in the colonies—suggests that the Revolution came not because of English tyranny but because of English weakness and inconsistency. The one thing most lacking after 1763 to make a revolution possible was enough sense of unity among the colonies to carry it through—and the fumbling policies of Parliament provided just the necessary unifying provocation.

For all this, it would be a mistake to imagine that most colonists plotted and planned for independence. They wanted only the right to manage their affairs within—not outside —the empire. Even a month after fighting broke out at Lexington and Concord, the Continental Congress voted to make a careful list of the supplies captured from the English at Fort Ticonderoga so that they could be properly returned when "restoration of the former harmony" made it possible. But the colonists were driven to demand independence when they finally concluded that without it they would not have the measure of self-government they wanted.

The Grenville Ministry. The task of solving colonial problems after the French and Indian War fell first upon the ministry of George Grenville, which lasted from 1763 to 1765. The situation in Parliament was most confusing, for a clear-cut two-party system did not exist, and politics was carried on by a number of factions organized around varying interests and ambitions. George III, who came to the throne in 1760, while still in his twenties, has been much maligned by both English and American historians. He was conscientious and earnest, and sought to function not as a tyrant but as a constitutional monarch; but he lacked the imagination to conceive a strategy for the solution of imperial problems too complex even for

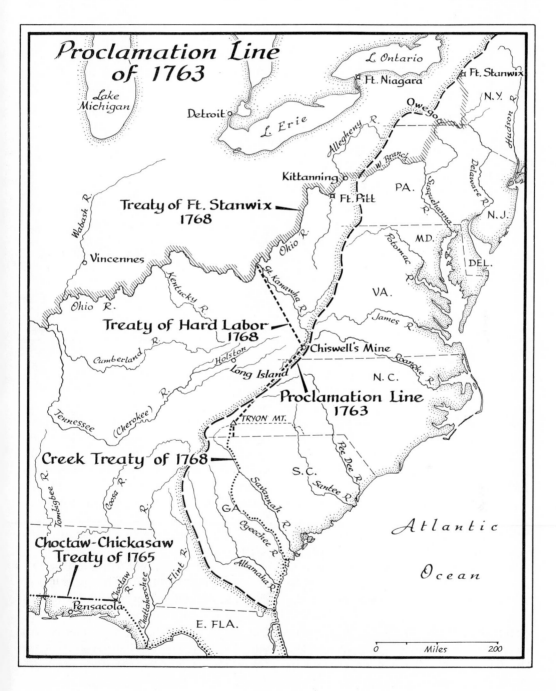

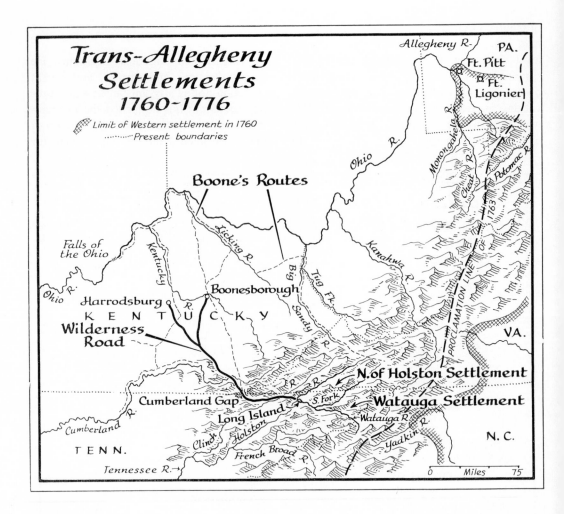

Trans-Allegheny Settlements 1760-1776

Limit of Western settlement in 1760

Present boundaries

Boone's Routes

Allegheny R.

PA.

Ft. Pitt

Ft. Ligonier

Ohio R.

Monongahela R.

Cheat R.

Potomac R.

1763

PROCLAMATION LINE OF

VA.

Falls of the Ohio

Kentucky R.

Licking R.

Big Sandy R.

Tug Fk.

Kanawha R.

Ohio R.

Harrodsburg

Boonesborough

K E N T U C K Y

Wilderness Road

Cumberland R.

Clinch R.

Holston R.

S. Fork

N. of Holston Settlement

Watauga Settlement

Cumberland Gap

Long Island

Watauga R.

Yadkin R.

TENN.

French Broad R.

Tennessee R.

N. C.

0   Miles   75

wiser heads, and after 1765 he was troubled by intermittent attacks of the insanity that eventually clouded his last years. It was not George himself, but the politicians, organized in shifting alliances and susceptible to the pressure of parliamentary factions that were at times grasping or corrupt, who chiefly determined colonial policy.

The program of the Grenville ministry ignored the unruly realities of colonial society that clashed with its orderly plans. Its first measure was the Proclamation of 1763, intended to solve the pressing problem of administering the great interior along the frontier and the new provinces of Canada. Pioneers were settling in the Ohio country; speculators and land companies were asking for grants through their agents in London. The Indians along the frontier, aroused by

the advance of settlement and irritated by traders who defrauded them of their furs, were on the warpath. Encouraged by French fur-traders (with whom they had close relations) to believe that the French were ready to return, the tribes of the Northwest region, led by Pontiac, an Ottawa chief, organized a series of successful attacks on the British posts. By May, 1763, they had destroyed all the posts west of Niagara except Detroit, and it took many months of counter-attack to pacify them.

The Proclamation of 1763, issued in October, at the instance of Lord Shelburne of the Board of Trade, set boundaries for the three new crown colonies of the mainland: Quebec, East Florida, and West Florida. All other lands lying west of the sources of the rivers flowing into the sea from the north or northwest, and not yet acquired from the Indians by purchase or cession, were for the moment reserved for the Indians, and thus, provocatively, were closed to settlement. As a result, settlers and speculators were now prevented from advancing further into the huge territory from the Alleghenies to the Mississippi between Florida and 50° north latitude. To insure peace on the frontier, the Crown arranged a preliminary treaty with the Choctaw and Chickasaw in 1765, and treaties with the Iroquois at Fort Stanwix and with the Cherokee at Hard Labor in 1768. But settlers ignored the Proclamation Line and pushed into the Watauga Valley in western North Carolina (see p. 121). Even before 1776, Daniel Boone and his axmen had followed the "Wilderness Road" from the Holston River, through the Cumberland Gap, and into the fertile and bloody ground of Kentucky.

Grenville also wanted the colonists to contribute at least half of the £300,000 estimated as the cost of defending American possessions. Partly to raise some of this money and partly to stop smuggling, the Revenue Act—or "Sugar" Act—of 1764 was passed. This measure, which replaced the poorly enforced Molasses Act of 1733 (see p. 43), lowered the duty on foreign molasses brought to the colonies from six to three cents a gallon; it also raised the tariff on refined sugar, and put a tax on certain textiles, wines, coffee, and pimientos, unless these were shipped to the colonies via England.

Plans for the serious enforcement of this measure were made in order to end the connivance of customs officials with American smugglers. The law struck a blow at the triangular trade, which involved the foreign West Indies (see p. 43), and at the profitable business in rum, fish, and slaves. Until the 1760's, New England merchants and distillers had smuggled in much of their molasses and sugar from the French West Indies, since the supply from the British sugar islands was insufficient for the manufacture of rum, a staple of Yankee foreign trade. Enforcement now threatened to put an end to these activities. The Sugar Act

also struck at the colonists' extensive lumber trade with the Continent by requiring that all consignments be sent directly to England for reshipment elsewhere. The new duties on Madeira wine from the Azores blocked another profitable source of income. The Sugar Act, moreover, in cutting off the French West Indies trade, deprived the northern colonies of the leading source of the hard cash they needed both to pay for imports from England and to meet the new taxes.

Against the Sugar Act, the northern merchants protested firmly but peacefully. After many years of solid prosperity and cheerful smuggling, the hand of empire had been laid heavily upon them. All the commercial colonies joined in the protest, and Rhode Island went so far as to say to the Board of Trade that the colony could not continue to exist without the foreign West Indies trade.

The southern colonies, with Virginia in the vanguard, had their own set of grievances, different in character but hardly less acute than those of the trading colonies. Their internal lands were now settled, and tobacco had so depleted the soil that the planters were looking eagerly to western lands as a solution to their problems. Now the Proclamation of 1763 dashed their plans for expansion beyond the Alleghenies.

Moreover, the planters suffered from a wasteful system of marketing, which became increasingly burdensome as the years went by. Instead of doing their own selling, they bought and sold through English merchants. Freight charges, commissions to the dealers, and insurance on tobacco cargoes, together with the costs of the goods they imported, threw the planters into debt. As their returns from the depleted lands dwindled, their debts mounted significantly. Jefferson once estimated that Virginia planters owed at least £2 million to British merchants, and complained that these charges "had become hereditary from father to son, for many generations, so that the planters were a species of property annexed to certain mercantile houses in London." When the planters tried to ease the problem of payments by making debts payable in a depreciated currency, their English creditors strongly objected. During the French and Indian War, Virginia had issued £250,000 in bills of credit which the assembly made legal tender in payment of both past and future debts. But in response to complaints from the British merchants, Parliament forbade this practice and laid a heavy penalty on any colonial governor who would sign such a measure. The Currency Act of 1764 extended to all the colonies the provisions of a paper-money prohibition of 1751 that had originally been directed against New England.

The Virginians, shut off from westward expansion and prevented from resorting to easy expedients to lighten their debt burden, were doubly restive under English authority. It would be far too much to say that the Virginians supported resistance because they expected to repudiate their debts; but it is reasonable to believe that their economic difficulties heightened their irritation with English measures and prepared them to co-operate with their brethren to the north.

A still more troublesome measure than the Proclamation of 1763 was the Stamp Act of March, 1765, from which Grenville hoped to raise £60,000 a year. Tax stamps, ranging from a half-penny to ten pounds, were required for commercial and legal documents and licenses, newspapers, pamphlets, almanacs, playing cards, dice, and liquor licenses. Violations were punishable by heavy fines. No measure could have been better calculated to arouse a wide public opposition or to unify the colonies around a single issue. Although the Sugar Act had struck at merchants and those associated with them, the Stamp Act affected not only the mercantile interests, but all other classes —printers, editors, tavern-owners, and lawyers—that influenced the public.

Less than a month after the passage of the Stamp Act came the Quartering Act, which arranged for the housing of British troops in the colonies. Where barracks were insufficient, public inns and even private houses or barns might be used; soldiers were to be supplied with certain materials. Persons furnishing quarters or supplies were, of course, to be paid, but the very prospect of quartering soldiers angered the colonists.

II. THE ROAD TO REVOLUTION

Taxation and Representation.

Taxation and

Representation. Against the Stamp Act an effective protest arose, led by lawyers and publishers. Massachusetts, always quick to cry out when its privileges were abridged, had indicated the line that colonial opposition was to take as early as 1764, when passage of the act was still being discussed. In that year, Boston declared, in instructing its representatives in the Assembly:

For if our Trade may be taxed, why not our Lands? Why not the produce of our Lands and every Thing we possess or make use of? This we apprehend annihilates our Charter Rights to Govern and Tax ourselves. It strikes at our British Privileges which as we have never forfeited them we hold in common with our Fellow Subjects who are Natives of Britain: If

Taxes are laid upon us in any shape without ever having a Legal Representation where they are laid, are we not reduced from the Character of Free Subjects to the miserable state of Tributary Slaves?

Action followed these strong words. In Boston, Philadelphia, Newport, and New York, mobs organized by the merchants rioted in the streets, attacked and pillaged the houses of supporters of the Stamp Act, and intimidated the king's officials. When the mobs began to indulge in indiscriminate wrecking, even their respectable leaders became alarmed. But leading agitators throughout the colonies set up an intercolonial organization, the Sons of Liberty, to keep the fires of opposition burning bright.

In October, 1765, delegates from nine of the thirteen provinces met at New York in the Stamp Act Congress. Of the four absent states, three (Virginia, Georgia, and North Carolina) failed to send representatives only because their royal governors would not permit any to be selected. The Stamp Act Congress issued a moderately phrased "Declaration of Rights and Grievances," in which it acknowledged that the colonies owed allegiance to the Crown, claimed all the rights of Englishmen, and asserted that among these rights was freedom from taxation except "with their own consent, given personally or by their representatives." Since it was impossible for the colonists to be represented in the House of Commons, the resolutions declared, only their own legislatures could tax them. Any money coming from the colonists to the Crown must come as "free gifts of the people" and could not rightly be taken for the Crown by the people of Great Britain. Recent trade regulations and changes in the admiralty courts were denounced along with the Stamp Act, and their repeal was politely petitioned. But there was no mention of the idea of independence.

Real force was put behind the Congress' protests during the same month when merchants in the major ports, beginning with New York, signed agreements not to buy English goods until the Stamp Act and the objectionable trade regulations were repealed. On November 1, when the Stamp Act went into effect, business in general was suspended throughout the colonies.

From the resolutions of the Stamp Act Congress, as well as from pamphlets written during the period by colonial lawyers like James Otis of Massachusetts, Daniel Dulany of Maryland, and John Dickinson of Pennsylvania, we can see what position thoughtful colonial leaders were taking on Parliament's right to tax. It was indeed a strong position, fateful for Grenville's ambition to raise revenue in America to help run the empire. The colonists, in brief, accepted the right of Parliament to regulate their commerce just as it had in the past. They accepted this right even though they knew

that trade regulation required import and export duties that would yield what Daniel Dulany in 1766 called "incidental revenue." (He was able to show that the small sums that were normally collected when trade was regulated could not be considered taxation for revenue—for it cost more to collect them than they were worth.) But as for the right to levy taxes for the purpose of *raising money*—this the colonists could not and would not accept. Since they were not represented in Parliament, Parliament had no right under the British constitution to tax them. Only their own legislatures could do that.

English writers replied that even at home not all Englishmen were actually represented in Parliament by their own representatives. As an example, they cited the people of Manchester and Birmingham, who sent no members to the House of Commons. Yet even these Englishmen, they said, and the colonists as well, were "virtually" represented by the members chosen by their fellow-Englishmen. But this argument left the colonists unimpressed, for they did not see how their interests were or could be represented by men sitting in a Parliament 3,000 miles away, who never saw them. To them, "virtual representation" was no representation.

The issue was further complicated by the failure of the English lawmakers to understand the scope of the colonists' objection to taxes. The English thought that the colonists would accept Parliament's right to impose external taxes (such as duties and imposts) but not internal taxes (such as land taxes or poll taxes). In fact, the colonists soon gave up this distinction when they found it unworkable. Their true object was to reject *all* taxation whose *purpose* was to raise a revenue.

The Sugar Act presented a knotty problem to the colonial pamphleteers who were writing on the issues of the day. Everyone knew that the purpose of the act was to raise money, and its official title said so. But it was passed in the form of an act to regulate trade. To many men it became clear that if the colonists were to uphold their determination not to be taxed by Parliament, they must not let their argument rest upon the intentions of Parliament or the purposes of laws; rather, they would have to stand on the highest possible ground. "No middle ground can be well maintained," Benjamin Franklin concluded in 1768. "Something might be made of either of the extremes: that Parliament has a power to make *all* laws for us . . . or *no laws* for us; and I think the arguments for the latter more numerous and weighty, than those for the former." What the argument pointed to, then, was that the colonists should be completely independent of Parliament and united to Britain only by their loyalty to the Crown. Such a solution—to grant dominion status—was unthinkable in England at the time of the Revolution; and not until after the American Civil War would Parliament adopt such a policy for the newly united Canadas.

The Developing Crisis.   In 1766, just after the fall of the Grenville government, the Stamp Act was repealed. British merchants, hostile to Grenville's methods of tax collection and frightened by growing losses from an organized American boycott of British goods, had brought pressure on Parliament to give way. Yet even the most pro-American among them were alarmed by the violence of the colonial protest and began to wonder if the Americans were not thinking of cutting themselves off from the empire. It was impossible for English authorities to admit that Parliament had no right to tax the colonies. So that there would be no mistake about where it stood on this principle, Parliament passed, along with the repeal of the Stamp Act, the Declaratory Act, asserting that Parliament had full power to make laws "to bind the colonies and people of America . . . in all cases whatsoever." Only

a few colonists chose to make a stand against this last ominous proviso, and amid the general rejoicing over the repeal of the Stamp Act it was largely ignored. In the colonies, the radicals chose to see repeal as a victory for their tactics. In England, the ultra-conservatives concluded only that the Crown had been too lenient.

The Grenville ministry was followed by the Rockingham ministry, which lasted from 1765 to 1766. The new ministry reduced the duty on all molasses (whether British or foreign-supplied) from threepence to one penny a gallon in 1766; but the central issue of taxation and revenue remained unsolved. When Rockingham's ministry gave way to that of the Duke of Grafton in 1766, America's friend, William Pitt, became a key figure. His illness, however, permitted Charles Townshend, Chancellor of the Exchequer, to dominate the cabinet.

Townshend proposed new taxes in 1767 to meet a government deficit and to support the British troops quartered in America. These Townshend Acts added a new list of import duties on a few products—glass, white lead, paper, and tea—that had hitherto entered duty-free. Their most annoying feature, however, was the creation of a Board of Customs Commissioners, centered in Boston, with powers to punish infringements of the Navigation Acts (see p. 43). The revenue derived from fines and judgments against delinquent colonists was to be used to pay the salaries of the king's appointees and to make them independent of both Parliament and the colonial assemblies. Boston, which had suffered heavily under the Sugar Act, again bore the brunt of the financial burden, but feeling ran high against the Townshend Acts throughout the colonies. According to one of the provisions, the New York Assembly's legislative power was suspended for failure to comply satisfactorily with the Quartering Act. This action was everywhere regarded as an attack on American liberties. Even moderates like John Dickinson of Pennsylvania began to resent the harassing of legitimate trade by the customs commissioners.

Systematic agreements among the colonial merchants to cut off all imports from abroad went into effect in 1768 and 1769—an action that carried more weight than mere indignation. A circular letter drafted by Samuel Adams for the Massachusetts Assembly in 1768 and sent to the other colonies fused American sentiment against British taxation and stimulated resistance to it. The heavy shrinkage in American imports of British goods, moreover, provided the best kind of weapon for the anti-Townshendites in England, and the government once more backed down, in March, 1770, and repealed the Townshend Acts. All duties except the one on tea were withdrawn. Meanwhile the boycott had spread everywhere, especially after the publication of a particularly arrogant circular letter written by the Earl of Hillsborough, Secretary of State for the Colonies, in reply to the Massachusetts circular letter. Hillsborough's lofty dismissal of the Massachusetts letter as treasonable nonsense, and his warning that all assemblies that approved it would be dissolved, only strengthened the American resolve. The patriot showed his defiance by wearing homespun clothes, by sacrificing "the most darling Appurtances (sic) of the Toilet on the Altar of public Emolument," and by drinking rye whiskey instead of imported liquor. Actually, the colonies were not nearly so self-sufficient as they would have liked to be, but their threat to construct workshops and factories alarmed and antagonized the British merchants. Although the merchants were prepared to back the colonists against the trade-wrecking consequences of parliamentary legislation, they could not encourage the colonists to become economically independent.

Tension relaxed after the repeal of the Townshend Acts in 1770 and the accession of a new ministry headed by Lord North. But just at this time a disturbing incident took place in Boston. This was the so-called "Boston Massacre" of March 5, 1770, which was exploited to the hilt by American propagandists. Some British soldiers, goaded by a mob, lost their heads and killed five Americans and wounded others. John Adams, though an ardent patriot, defended the soldiers. All were acquitted of murder, and two men found guilty of manslaughter were released after minor punishment. But the "massacre" produced much persuasive oratory. Here is how one Bostonian responded:

Has the grim savage rushed again from the wilderness? Or does some fiend, fierce from the depths of hell, with all the rancorous malice which the apostate damned can feel, twang her deadly arrows at our breast? No: none of these . . . it is the hand of Britain that inflicts the wound.

Better feeling between the mother country and the colonies developed after 1770, but the issue of Parliament's right to tax still went unresolved. Between 1770 and 1772, the colonists seemed to have forgotten their truculence, and conservative businessmen dissociated themselves from the radical extremists. But the lull was only temporary. In 1772, friction between Rhode Island merchants and customs officials culminated in the burning of the beached *Gaspee,* a British revenue cutter engaged in catching colonial smugglers. Nor did the Rhode Islanders cooperate with the royal commission in its effort to apprehend the culprits.

The flames of rebellion among the rural yeomanry and the town laborers were fanned by Samuel Adams, who was hostile to the colonial aristocracy and inveterately anti-British. Adams' father had been ruined when Parliament outlawed the Massachusetts land bank in which he was a large stockholder. His son remained a persistent foe of Britain, an egalitarian political philosopher, and an irrepressible fomenter of American independence. A Harvard graduate, trained for the law, Adams was by temperament a political intriguer of the first class and a true apostle of revolution. In 1772, the Boston Town Meeting adopted his plan to form a committee of correspondence to keep in touch with similar committees in the other towns and to forge a union of dissent. Influential Virginia and the other provinces followed suit, and soon a veritable network of seditious organizations spread out over the country.

The Eve of Revolution.

With characteristic ineptness, the British government now provided the radicals with an ideal grievance. In May of 1773, the government, seeking to assist the almost bankrupt East India Company, granted to it the right to reship its heavy stocks of tea to America without paying the regular import duties in England. Even when the three-pence duty per pound had been paid to customs in America, the colonists were able to buy tea from the East India Company at a lower cost than ever before—cheaper than

The Boston Tea Party (from an illustration in a German Almanac, 1784).

English buyers in fact. But the colonists rejected this lure of cheap tea, for the following reasons: (1) Since the tea was to be distributed in America by a picked group of merchants, the merchants who had bought their tea through middlemen at higher prices were being discriminated against. (2) The large stocks of tea already smuggled in by American merchants could be undersold by the East India Company. (3) Most important, the colonists pointed out that if Parliament could bestow a tea monopoly on the East India Company, what was to stop it from granting similar monopolies on other commodities? So John Hancock, a rich Boston merchant, argued, and all his fellow smugglers agreed.

The merchants of Rhode Island, Philadelphia, and New York made the loudest outcries and roused the city mobs to "persuade" the pro-British merchants not to sell company tea. Everywhere the tea shipments were refused. But in Boston, where Governor Hutchinson protected the pro-English merchants with British troops, the tea cargoes were neither returned to England nor locked up in government warehouses as the colonists demanded. The baffled patriots then hit upon the by no means novel device of disguising themselves as Indians, boarding the tea ships, and throwing the tea into the harbor. This feat, performed on December 16, 1773, was an act so defiant that neither the ministry of Lord North nor the colonies' friends in Parliament dared to condone it. English retaliation against Massachusetts was immediate and drastic.

The punitive acts passed by Parliament early in 1774 (the so-called Coercive or "Intolerable Acts") were the prelude to revolution: (1) The port of Boston was to be closed to shipping until the East India Company had been reimbursed for its losses. (2) English officials indicted by Massachusetts courts for acts they committed while enforcing English laws were to be tried either in another colony or in England. (3) Town meetings were forbidden unless the governor gave his permission; the upper house of the Assembly was henceforth to be appointed by the governor, not elected. (4) A new quartering act for all the colonies required that adequate housing be provided for resident British troops within 24 hours after they had been ordered.

These coercive measures struck at most of the principles that the colonies had been fighting for since 1763. Then, on top of everything, Parliament passed the Quebec Act. This long-planned measure had much to recommend it, so far as Canadians were concerned. It recognized certain features of French law for the government of Canada (including trial without jury) and granted complete toleration to Catholics. Most important for the Americans, the Province of Quebec was enlarged to include the territory north of the Ohio and east of the Mississippi. The western land claims of Massachusetts, Connecticut, and Virginia were completely ignored. Moreover, the recognition extended to Catholicism aroused the intolerance of American Protestants. The American radicals now had all the combustible material they needed. They no longer had to exaggerate the dangers that were threatening their traditional liberties, and they had good grounds for believing, as Edmund Burke advised the New York Assembly from London, that the Quebec Act had been passed to hem in the colonies and to cut off their growth. When the Massachusetts House of Representatives suggested that all the colonies send delegates to convene in Philadel-

"The Bostonians in Distress," a cartoon showing the consequences of the closing of the port of Boston in 1774.

phia in September, 1774, in opposition to the Coercive Acts, the proposal met with almost universal agreement. Twelve of the thirteen colonies—all but Georgia—were represented.

When the delegates to the First Continental Congress gathered, both moderates and radicals decided that some kind of remonstrance was in order, but they differed on just what course of action to take. Joseph Galloway of Pennsylvania suggested a new plan of union between the colonies and the mother country. He proposed the creation of a Grand Council composed of delegates elected by the colonial assemblies, a body that would divide authority with Parliament. It could initiate laws relating to the colonies as a whole and could ratify measures originating in Parliament; the consent of both bodies would be necessary for the enactment of a law. A president general, appointed by

97

the Crown, would have veto power over the council's decisions. Had this plan, which was defeated by a 6-5 vote, succeeded, reconciliation with England might have been possible.

But the Congress, spurred on perhaps by false rumors that General Gage (recently appointed governor of Massachusetts) had ordered his regulars to level Boston, supported resolutions made by Massachusetts to flout the Coercive Acts. Furthermore, it organized a "Continental Association" to prevent any kind of economic intercourse with England. Nothing English was to be imported or consumed. Nothing would be sent to England. Local committees in all the colonies supported the Association and used every means from persuasion to tar and feathering to enforce the boycott of English goods. Militia companies began to drill, and some Americans displayed their patriotic fervor by refusing to pay their debts to English creditors. When it became clear that the southern and Middle colonies were prepared to stand with New England, the hopes of the conservatives for reconciliation faded. The fence-straddlers now had to decide to stand either with England or with America.

The Tory Mind.   The men who cast their lot with the patriot cause made up a cross section of colonial America, with political opinions ranging from the radical to the conservative extremes. Many finally made their choice after an agonizing period of indecision; they were alarmed by the extravagance of the radicals and reluctant to link their lives and fortunes with their social inferiors. A tiny minority of Americans had worked for independence and had done what they could to destroy ties of loyalty between the colonies and England. For the majority, however, the movement toward overt rebellion progressed slowly and often imperceptibly.

The leading patriot pamphleteers who propagandized for colonial rights in the 1760's and 1770's usually coupled their arguments with expressions of loyalty to the Crown and of abhorrence toward independence. But the colonists, sometimes upheld by radicals like James Otis and Samuel Adams, and sometimes by moderates like John Dickinson and Daniel Dulany, failed to persuade Parliament that their cause was just. Reluctantly, the American patriots had to accept the logical consequences of their position. Men like James Wilson of Pennsylvania, though judicious and flexible in their attitudes, finally admitted that the benefits derived from membership in the British empire were less than the advantages of home rule. Back-country farmers in the North sided with the patriots as a way of getting back at the pro-British local aristocracy. In some other areas, notably Virginia, sectional animosities were dropped for the time being, as tidewater and hinterland joined against the common oppressor. In a few instances, however, farmers held back from the patriot cause simply because the eastern aristocrats led it. The most noteworthy case of this sort occurred in North Carolina, where a faction of back-country farmers, the Regulators, fought openly with the aristocracy over taxes for several years before the Revolution. To many of the Regulators, the eastern aristocracy was the enemy, and they preferred to support the British cause (see p. 62).

The middle and lower classes were thus not unanimous in their support of the revolutionists. Many farmers and laborers remained loyal, or else shared the sentiments of one vehement Tory farmer from western Massachusetts who shouted defiantly to his enemies: "Damn the Rebels. . . . I would cut them in hunks, boil them on the coals and eat them. . . . I wish I had the Keys of Hell I would turn on all the damned Rebels and kick them along. . . . I wish they all were Scalped: damn the Congress to hell."

It is hard to say just who the Tories (or Loyalists) were, because they differed so widely in class, education, and religion, and because they allied themselves with King and Parliament from such a wide variety of motives. Anglican clergymen and English officials tended to remain loyal, as did many of the rich merchants and large land-owners and conservative lawyers. And so did recent arrivals from the British Isles who had not lived in the colonies long enough to lose their affection for England. Certainly it would be wrong to conclude that the Tories were invariably richer and socially more prominent than the Whigs, or to exaggerate their numbers. In all probability, a substantial number of the colonial population in all classes were Tory before and after the outbreak of war.

In the war of words that preceded the resort to arms in 1776, outstanding Tory spokesmen ably answered the patriotic argument. The Tory position, stemming from the divine-right theory of government, was anti-democratic and authoritarian. Daniel Leonard, a talented and forceful Boston lawyer, grimly described the fate of society when brute force prevailed and rebels defied their God-appointed rulers. He observed with

Tory bluntness that the common people, "confined to the humbler walks of business or retirement," had little knowledge of state affairs, and he warned of the swift retribution that would come if the colonists tried to fight the king's armies. The thoughts of Leonard and his fellow loyalists were clearly and elegantly expressed. But such men were not representative of popular attitudes.

A hundred years earlier, the colonists might have accepted the definition of freedom given by Tory Jonathan Boucher, an Anglican divine from Maryland: the liberty to obey the laws created by one's betters. By 1776 the Tories were out of step with the main trend of American sentiments, and from 1774 on, they suffered more than harsh words for their continued loyalty to the Crown. Zealous patriots had begun to resort to tar and feathers and beatings.

III. THE WAR FOR INDEPENDENCE

From Lexington

to Independence. Symbolic of colonial resolution during 1774 was the formation of extra-legal provincial congresses which acted as state governments. By the end of the year, these congresses were operating in ten of the colonies, gathering arms and preparing for future emergencies. Joseph Warren and John Hancock headed the Massachusetts provincial congress. When General Gage tried to arrest Hancock and Samuel Adams and destroy the military stores collected at Concord, he inadvertently started a war.

Gage was unable to carry out his order to seize the two rebel leaders, and he was not altogether successful in his plan to destroy the military supplies that the patriots had stored at Concord. A troop of 700 regulars did manage to reach Concord on April 19, 1775, after scattering some slight resistance at Lexington. And they succeeded in destroying a part of the matériel the forewarned colonists had been unable to hide. But when the British retreated to Boston, they were

harassed by angry swarms of Minute Men who peppered them from behind fence and tree. Gage's raid cost the British 273 dead, wounded, and missing; the Americans lost 93. But far more important than the skirmish itself was the propaganda victory it made possible for the patriots. Their reports of British atrocities and rapine had no basis in fact, but they convinced the other colonists that Britain thirsted for American blood.

Amid spirited preparations for resistance, the Second Continental Congress met in Philadelphia on May 10, 1775. Men already distinguished, and others soon to become so, attended the opening sessions—among them were the first three presidents-to-be of the United States. In selecting the Virginia aristocrat, George Washington, to lead the new army, the Congress may have intended to conciliate the conservatives and to flatter the South, but whatever the motives it proved to be a fortunate choice. Washington did not turn out to be a brilliant tactician. Yet he inspired confidence, and he persisted stubbornly despite the many setbacks that he suffered—often as a result of his own mistakes. His courage, tenacity, honesty, and dignity were in the long run more vital to the success of his difficult assignment than military genius.

On July 6, the Congress issued a "Declaration of Causes of Taking up Arms," in which the reasons for resisting General Gage were set forth. "We are reduced [read the "Declaration"] to the alternative of choosing an unconditional submission to the tyranny of irritated ministers or resistance by force." Moderate voices still carried some influence, however, for the respected John Dickinson and John Jay did succeed in getting the Congress to adopt a petition to the king known as the "Olive Branch." This petition put the blame for colonial disorders on the policies of the king's ministers, and begged the king to effect a reconciliation by curtailing the tyranny of Parliament. After some delay, the petition found its way to the only sympathetic member of the British cabinet, the Earl of Dartmouth. But it arrived too late, and the British government refused to negotiate with an "illegal" congressional body.

Less than a month after adopting the Olive Branch petition, the Congress itself had rejected an English plan of compromise. Parliament had passed this conciliatory plan, devised by Lord North, which provided that any American colony that taxed itself for the common defense and the costs of civil government through its own assembly would be immune from taxation by Parliament. But by the time this plan had come before the Congress, Parliament had nullified its effect by passing a "Restraining Act" on March 30, 1775, which cut off New England (later all colonial) commerce outside the empire and closed the northern fisheries to the people of New England. This measure made Lord North's plan of conciliation unpalatable, and the drift toward complete separation went on.

Before Washington arrived from Philadelphia to take command of the colonial army surrounding Boston, General Gage, strengthened by fresh contingents, tried to drive the patriot besiegers from their entrenched positions on Breed's Hill. In the engagement of June 17, 1775, now known as the Battle of Bunker Hill, British troops dislodged the Americans, but at a frightful

The Battle of Lexington, engraved from a drawing by Ralph Earl (1775).

Boston and Concord 1775

North Bridge — British Route April 19, 1775
Concord — Lexington — Medford
Menotomy — Bunker Hill
Cambridge
Watertown — Boston
MASS. — Brookline — Dorchester
Roxbury
American Lines 1775-76
0 Mi. 5

pathy for the colonial cause. Even after the war had started, many Whigs openly expressed their feeling that the fight for freedom was being fought in America. But petitions from Whig merchants did not persuade the king and his cabinet to alter their course. George feared that if the colonies were not subdued, other British possessions would hurry to detach themselves from the empire. Ireland might revolt. Merchants might leave England for America, and England might sink into unimportance.

Because Englishmen felt disinclined to fight the colonials, the government looked around for foreign mercenaries to send to America. The Empress of Russia refused to oblige, but six petty princes in south and west Germany were happy to sell the services of their subjects for cash. Almost 30,000 (subsequently known as "Hessians," because many of them came from the German prin-

cost. The Americans lost 400, and the English losses came to more than 1,000—over 40 per cent of the English troops involved. In March, 1776, Washington mounted heavy cannon, which had been drawn all the way from captured Fort Ticonderoga, on Dorchester Heights overlooking Boston. General Howe, successor of General Gage, found his position untenable and evacuated his army to Halifax, Nova Scotia.

Elsewhere, the patriots fared less well. After Ethan Allen had taken Crown Point and Ticonderoga from the British early in 1775, two separate American columns, one led by Richard Montgomery and the other by Benedict Arnold, invaded Canada in the fall and winter of 1775. Montgomery took Montreal, but a joint assault against Quebec failed. Montgomery was killed, Arnold wounded. Finally the colonial army, ravaged by smallpox and unprepared to face a strengthened British army, retired slowly southward. But the British invasion of New York from Canada had been delayed—a very fateful delay, as General John Burgoyne's disastrous expedition two years later was to prove.

As full-scale war got under way, the military problems facing the royal government loomed ominously large. The debt-burdened English people did not relish the prospect of another expensive war, especially against America. An influential minority both in and out of Parliament openly expressed sym-

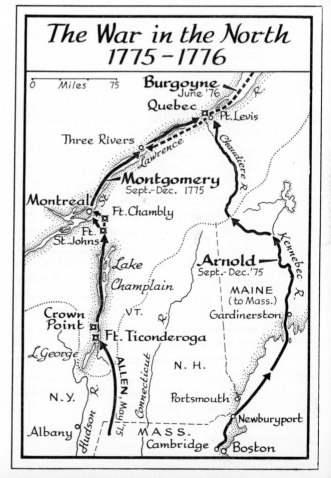

The War in the North 1775-1776

0 Miles 75
Burgoyne June '76
Quebec
Pt. Levis
Three Rivers
St. Lawrence
Chaudière R.
Montgomery Sept.-Dec. 1775
Montreal
Ft. Chambly
Ft. St. Johns
Lake Champlain
Arnold Sept.-Dec. '75
Kennebec R.
MAINE (to Mass.)
Gardinerston
Crown Point
VT.
Ft. Ticonderoga
L. George
N. H.
ALLEN, May '75
Connecticut R.
Portsmouth
N.Y.
Hudson R.
Newburyport
Albany
MASS.
Cambridge — Boston

cipality of Hesse) served with the British army in America. Colonial propagandists, notably Benjamin Franklin, were quick to exploit the employment of these mercenaries.

The British resolution to press the war, and the announcement that German mercenaries had been hired to help fight it, stiffened the will of those Americans who already wanted independence. Still, as late as a year after Lexington and Concord most Americans seem not yet to have decided that it was independence they were fighting for. Yet their repudiation of Parliament's authority, the argument over the British Constitution, their failure to come to an agreement over taxation, the outbreak of fighting, the rejection of the Olive Branch petition, the Restraining Act, the necessity of making plans for continued resistance while the English were making plans to subdue them—all pointed toward independence rather than reconciliation.

Early in 1776 there appeared in Philadelphia a pamphlet from the hand of Thomas Paine which did much to push public opinion over the dividing line. In clear and persuasive prose, Paine argued the advantages of a separate national existence: free trade with the nations of the world, freedom from Europe's wars when the obligation to fight by the side of Britons was removed, freedom from having petitions and grievances carried to a court of resort 3,000 miles away. "There is something very absurd," he insisted, "in supposing a Continent to be perpetually governed by an island." "To know whether it be the interest of this continent to be Independent, we need only ask this easy simple question: Is it the interest of a man to be a boy all his life?" Since Americans, rejecting Parliament entirely, still held sentiments of loyalty toward the Crown, Paine did not hesitate to ridicule monarchy: "Of more worth is one honest man to society, and in the sight of God, than all the crowned ruffians that ever lived." Where argument ceased, rhetoric continued:

O ye that love mankind! Ye that dare oppose not only the tyranny but the tyrant, stand forth! Every spot of the old world is overrun with oppression. Freedom hath been hunted round the globe. Asia and Africa have long expelled her. Europe regards her like a stranger, and England hath given her warning to depart. O receive the fugitive, and prepare in time an asylum for mankind.

Americans bought 150,000 copies of this exciting tract—an astonishing number for that day.

Many of the colonists had already begun to accept the logic and consequences of separation. They were undeterred by talk of former English tenderness and future English punishment, and they felt that the gains of independence would outweigh the economic and political advantages of British protection. On July 2, 1776, the Congress at Philadelphia voted for independence. On July 4th, it adopted the Declaration of Independence.

The Declaration was in effect a moral defense of the Revolution that placed the blame on George III, an undeserving but tangible symbol of tyranny. It cannot be taken as an accurate historical examination of the causes. Thomas Jefferson (who wrote most of it, with some judicious revisions by Franklin) set about to make clear to the world why rebellion was in some circumstances legitimate, and to enumerate the grievances suffered by the colonies before they took their drastic step. The Declaration implied that it was not the abuses themselves that made rebellion necessary, but rather what they stood for: an intention to place the colonies under the autocratic will of a royal despot. Jefferson rested his arguments on natural law. Men were created equal and shared the natural rights of life, liberty, and happiness. Governments were established to achieve these ends. When the King violated his sacred obligations and broke the civil compact, then the people had the right "to alter or abolish" his government.

Commenting later on this document, Jefferson remarked: "I did not consider it as any part of my charge to invent new ideas

"The Signing of the Declaration of Independence," begun by Robert E. Pine and, upon his death in 1788, completed by Edward Savage.

altogether and to offer no sentiment which had ever been expressed before." The ideas of the Declaration had been common property for a generation. They had been set forth in pamphlets, speeches, and sermons. John Locke supplied the main outlines of the theory, but the Declaration derived also from classical and European political philosophy and from the political notions previously worked out by Whig pamphleteers like John Dickinson and John Adams.

The Opposing Powers. The Loyalist warning that Britain possessed enormous military advantages over the disorganized and inexperienced colonial troops was well founded. By the summer of 1776, some 10,000 redcoats and Hessians were poised in Canada for an invasion of New York.

General William Howe, with 32,000 soldiers, was planning to take New York City, and, after destroying the rebel opposition there, to strike at New England—the center of colonial resistance. The British troops were well equipped and thoroughly experienced. True, their experience was in the open warfare practiced on the Continent; but in Lord George Germain, the Colonial Secretary, they had an intelligent and meticulous organizer who fully appreciated the difficulties "of opposing an enemy that avoids facing you in the open field." Germain gave his American commanders wide latitude in planning their maneuvers under the new conditions. As time proved, however, he was too optimistic about loyalist assistance and trusted too much in generals who lacked energy and imagination.

The British military superiority was offset by other factors as well. A nation of 10 million people had difficulty mustering an army large enough to fight a long war. The day of the conscript army had not yet arrived and only professionals enlisted in the king's forces. Members of the Lord North ministry, moreover, felt that France was still the principal adversary and were reluctant to detach needed regiments and ships for the American campaign. One group even wanted to limit British efforts in North America to a naval blockade and to keep the regular troops in Europe. But Lord Sandwich, the shrewd and hard-working (though personally notorious) First Lord of the Admiralty, recognized that the English navy was not strong enough to operate in European and American waters at the same time. Lord North, not Sandwich, must bear the onus for reducing England's naval strength in 1772, an economy measure that had fatal consequences. To wage a campaign in a huge and unsettled country thousands of miles away from the base of supply would have been hazardous under the happiest of circumstances, but in 1776 England was unprepared for war. The mediocre Lord North had national backing, but he faced an unrelenting opposition in Parliament, and he had none of the abilities of a great war leader, no grand strategy, and no inspired military commander.

General Wolfe, the hero of Quebec, had described colonial soldiers as

... in general the dirtiest, most contemptible cowardly dogs that you can conceive. There is no depending on them in action. They fall down dead in their own dirt and desert by battalions, officers and all. Such rascals as those are rather an encumbrance than any real strength to an army.

Some of the British officers who shared Wolfe's views lived to change their minds, but before Lexington they had no reason to. The Continental army was poorly equipped, badly disciplined, and pitifully small. Numbering between 14,000 to 16,000 at full strength, it dropped to as low as 2,000 in the darkest days of the war and was hardly more than that at Yorktown. The state militias swelled patriot ranks and performed well when defending their homes, but Washington soon learned to his sorrow that these "summer soldiers," as Paine called them, would drift back to their farms after serving for a few months. And Washington knew that he had little to offer them.

From Long Island to Yorktown.

In June, 1776, before their main forces attacked New York, the British tried to establish contact with Loyalist elements in the Carolinas through a combined sea and land operation. A premature uprising of Loyalists had been crushed at Moore's Creek Bridge, North Carolina, three months earlier. Though deprived of

Northern and Central Campaigns, 1776-78

0   Miles   100

CANADA

Montreal
Ft. St. Johns
St. Lawrence R.
L. Champlain

St. Leger
1777

Burgoyne
1777

Ft. Ticonderoga

L. Ontario
Ft. Oswego

Ft. Niagara

Saratoga
Herkimer
Oriskany
Mohawk R.
Arnold
Cherry Valley
Gates
Bennington
MASS.

N. Y.

Hudson R.
CONN.

Butler, 1778

PROCLAMATION LINE OF 1763

Susquehanna R.
PA.

WYOMING VALLEY

Washington's Retreat
1776

Morristown

Princeton

Philadelphia

Delaware R.

N. J.

Trenton

New York

Howe
from
Halifax
1776

MD.

Tory support, General Henry Clinton, supported by Sir Peter Parker's fleet, attacked the city of Charleston by sea; but they withdrew with heavy losses on June 28, 1776, after failing to destroy the garrison on Sullivan's Island, and rejoined Howe. For two years afterward, the British suspended active operations in the South.

The long-delayed British assault on New York finally took place in August, 1776, initiating a series of defeats for the Americans. Badly beaten at Brooklyn Heights on August 27, 1776, Washington ferried his mauled army across the East River, aided by wind, tide, and Marblehead boatmen. He retreated again from Harlem Heights to White Plains and thence across the Hudson to New Jersey. Washington had extricated his troops, but was forced to abandon Fort Washington on the northern end of Manhattan and Fort Lee on the other side of the Hudson. Had General Howe pursued the retreating patriot army or if he had invaded New England in November, 1776, he might have crushed colonial resistance. But instead, he ordered Clinton to take Newport, and moved his army into winter quarters. Washington retreated into Pennsylvania as winter and gloom descended over his ragged Continentals. The first number of Thomas Paine's *The Crisis,* a series of essays published at irregular intervals, with its ringing declaration, "These are the times that try men's souls," raised morale in Washington's camp. And the brilliantly conceived attack against a Hessian garrison at Trenton on Christmas night, 1776, did a great deal to buoy up patriot hopes. Following the Trenton raid, Washington retired to Morristown, after defeating a British force sent to trap him at Princeton.

The tactical blunders of the British now paved the way for portentous American victories in the campaigns of 1777. Lord George Germain devised a plan of campaign that looked good on the map: New York would be subdued and occupied; New England and the Middle and southern colonies would thus be cut off from each other, and could be conquered separately. The conquest of New York would be a three-pronged operation: A main army under General Burgoyne would come down from Canada along Lake Champlain and the upper Hudson; an auxiliary force under Colonel St. Leger would come eastward from Lake Ontario along the Mohawk Valley; and General Howe, after taking Philadelphia, would bring a strong force up the Hudson; the three would converge at Albany, and New England would be shut off.

Howe, arriving by sea from New York, defeated the Americans, who had moved down from Morristown, at Brandywine Creek, and on September 26, 1777, occupied Philadelphia. Howe repulsed another attack by Washington at Germantown in October. But he did not learn, until too late, that he was supposed to meet Burgoyne. While he was defending Philadelphia, and enjoying its social life, the English cause suffered disaster. St. Leger, who had been

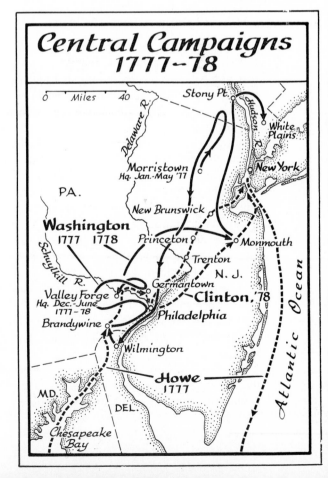

Central Campaigns 1777-78

temporarily checked at Oriskany by a small and valiant force under General Nicholas Herkimer, soon lost his Indian auxiliaries through a clever ruse of Benedict Arnold's, and retired to Fort Oswego on Lake Ontario. Burgoyne, unwittingly left to carry on alone, fought a losing battle all summer with his own supply problem as he came down through difficult wilderness terrain, suffered much from harassment by Vermont and Massachusetts militiamen, and arrived at Saratoga greatly weakened. Opposed there by overwhelming numbers under Generals Gates and Arnold, he surrendered his battered forces on October 17, 1777 (see map, p. 104).

As one British officer captured at Saratoga wrote:

The courage and obstinacy with which the Americans fought were the astonishment of every one, and we now become fully convinced, they are not that contemptible enemy we had hitherto imagined them, incapable of standing a regular engagement, and that they would only fight behind strong and powerful works.

The victory at Saratoga frustrated the British plan to cut off New England, and it had international reverberations in England and on the Continent. Two months later, France recognized the independence of the United States. Burgoyne's defeat elated the opposition in Parliament and nearly brought about the collapse of the North ministry. North, now thoroughly alarmed by rumors of a military treaty between France and the colonies, tried to deal unofficially with the American commissioners in Paris and sent a peace commission to America with an offer to revoke all laws passed after 1763. When the Continental Congress demanded that British troops withdraw and that the Crown recognize the independence of the colonies, the peace commission broke off negotiations. Lord North had waited too long.

After many dark hours, Saratoga gave the Americans reason to believe that they could win. But the most important consequence of the victory was the American-French alliance, February 6, 1778. Negotiated chiefly by the captivating Franklin, who was immensely popular in France, the treaty brought the French, eager to humble England and redress the balance of European power, into the war on America's side. The two powers agreed not to make peace without the consent of the other, and opened their ports to each other's commerce. France agreed not to ask for additional territory on the North American mainland, and the United States promised to guarantee the West Indies to the French.

The signing of the French alliance made the war of American independence a European war. France induced her ally, Spain, to join the war in 1779, with the promise of retaking Gibraltar and Florida. In 1781, Holland came in. England became more isolated when Russia, antagonized by the English practice of searching non-belligerent vessels for contraband, organized a coalition of European states in 1780, the League of Armed Neutrality, to protect their commerce and keep armed vessels out of the Baltic.

To the American cause, the French brought troops and loans, but, above all, naval power. Ships were the key to supremacy in the New World. Having failed to quiet the Americans with Lord North's plan of conciliation, the English were forced to conduct a largely defensive war on the North American continent, while planning to strike at the French and Spanish navies and regain supremacy on the high seas. After the action at Saratoga, important land operations on the American mainland took place only in the South. At sea, American privateers began to operate out of French ports, playing havoc with British shipping in the Channel and raiding the English and Irish coasts.

The stimulus given to American hopes by the Saratoga victory, however, was only temporary. Washington's army, which had retired to Valley Forge, shivered through the grueling winter of 1777-1778, and fared no better in subsequent winter encampments. In the spring of 1778, Howe was recalled, and his successor, General Clinton, was ordered to evacuate Philadelphia and retire to New York to prepare for a new campaign.

After the first spurt of hope, the French alliance actually brought a lapse into lethargy. Civilians and soldiers alike lacked the patience and will to carry on the war. The states responded poorly to requisitions; supplies and troops were short. Members of the underfed, underclothed, and unpaid army began to desert and finally to mutiny. In May, 1780, and again in January, 1781, disturbances among Washington's troops had to be suppressed.

In the meantime, the British tried to capitalize on low colonial morale by offering bribes to influential leaders. Benedict Arnold, who had fought so bravely for the patriot cause, succumbed to British gold in the summer of 1779, but his plot to turn over West Point to General Henry Clinton collapsed after a British agent, Major John André, was trapped behind the American lines with evidence of the conspiracy and hanged as a spy. All in all, British cloak-and-dagger schemes had little success.

Combined British and Loyalist units, however, severely impaired colonial property and morale in destructive raids against the Connecticut and Virginia coastal areas. And royal privateers were almost as effective in punishing American commerce as the patriot privateers were in damaging British shipping. The Wyoming Valley of Pennsylvania and

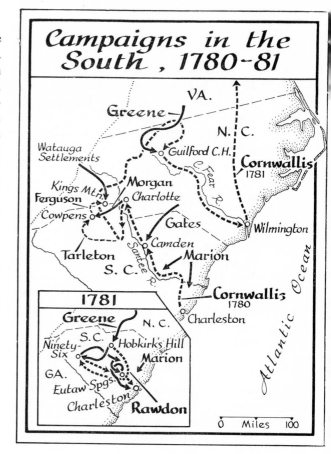

the Cherry Valley region of New York bled from repeated attacks by Indians and Tories (see map, p. 104).

The Indian threat abated after an American army of 5,000 marched into central New York in 1779 and burned the Iroquois villages there, and after George Rogers Clark retaliated against the British-Indian forces in the Ohio Valley. Early in 1778, with a small company of riflemen, Clark had floated down the Ohio River, joined another party at the falls of the Ohio, and proceeded to capture the undefended old French towns of Kaskaskia, Cahokia, and Vincennes. Colonel William Hamilton, the hated English commandant at Detroit who paid his Indian auxiliaries for American scalps, counterattacked and recaptured Vincennes. Clark then performed one of the most remarkable feats of the war. With an "army" of 127 men, half of them French, he marched 180 miles from Kaskaskia to Vincennes—triumphing over cold, floods, and hunger—and forced

Hamilton to surrender on February 24, 1779. Clark never reached Detroit, as he hoped, nor did his victories clinch the lower Ohio and Illinois country for the Americans. But he lifted the Indian pressure from the settlements in Kentucky and West Virginia.

The final battles of the Revolutionary War were fought in the South. A series of decisive British victories beginning in 1778 led General Clinton to believe that the southern colonies had been permanently rewon. Savannah fell on December 29, 1778, and Georgia was overrun. General Benjamin Lincoln's surrender at Charleston on May 6, 1780, cost the patriots over 5,000 soldiers and 300 cannon. Lord Cornwallis followed up with a smashing victory over General Gates at Camden, South Carolina, on August 16, 1780. With Georgia and South Carolina firmly held (despite the partisan warfare of South Carolina guerrillas like the daring "Swamp Fox," Francis Marion), the British commanders now turned to North Carolina. British confidence, however, was

suddenly checked by a number of stunning reversals. At King's Mountain, near the border between North and South Carolina, an army of 1,100 Tories under Patrick Ferguson was shot up by back-country marksmen on October 7, 1780. General Daniel Morgan's victory over Lt. Col. Tarleton at Cowpens on January 16, 1781, and a severe engagement with the Continentals at Guilford Courthouse in March, persuaded Cornwallis to evacuate North Carolina. He marched a 2,000-man army to Wilmington and thence to Yorktown, Virginia. General Nathanael Greene, who had taken over the command of the Continental army in the South from Gates after the latter's defeat at Camden, then forced the British out of Charleston, December 14, 1782 (see map, p. 107).

When Cornwallis took up his position at Yorktown, he believed that British naval superiority would assure the evacuation of his troops, if such a move became necessary. But he was not aware that a French fleet had left France for the West Indies in the spring of 1781 under the command of Admiral de Grasse. Facing him in Virginia was a small Continental army led by the Marquis de Lafayette, a French officer who had volunteered his services to the American cause in 1777. Meanwhile, Washington's troops, who had tried to cut off Clinton's withdrawal from Philadelphia, at Monmouth, New Jersey, in 1778, and a French army of 6,000 men that had arrived the preceding summer, were encamped near the city of New York. At the suggestion of the French commander, Comte de Rochambeau, Washington gave up his idea of attacking New York and arranged to remove his forces to Virginia in time to meet De Grasse moving up from the West Indies with 3,000 more French troops.

The joint land and sea operation was carried out smoothly. French naval units bottled up Chesapeake Bay and foiled Clinton's efforts to reinforce Cornwallis by sea. Washington's main army met up at Yorktown with advance detachments led by Lafayette and General Anthony Wayne. Pinned down between the French fleet and the com-

Virginia Campaign 1781

Washington & Rochambeau
Philadelphia
N. J.
Baltimore
MD.
DEL.
Lafayette
Wayne
VA.
Richmond
Petersburg
Yorktown
Bedford
Graves from N.Y.
De Barras from R.I.
C. Charles
Tarleton's Raid
C. Henry
Cornwallis
De Grasse from West Indies
N. C.

bined French-American army of 16,000 men, Cornwallis had to yield, and his defeated troops, numbering about 7,000 stacked their arms while the bands played a march called "The World's Turned Upside Down." The British surrender at Yorktown on October 19, 1781, virtually ended hostilities between England and America. Lord North, who had long wanted to retire, now resigned in March, 1782, and a new government got ready to grant independence.

The American peace commissioners, Benjamin Franklin, John Jay, and John Adams, who were sent by Congress to Paris in 1782, had to proceed very delicately in their negotiations. Congress had instructed them to consult with France on matters of diplomacy, but the commissioners knew that Spain had never approved of American independence and that she opposed the Mississippi River boundary the envoys were seeking. It seemed likely that France would support her. Hence the three Americans happily ignored their instructions and reached a preliminary agreement with the British delegation that gave America the Mississippi boundary. In return, America renounced all claims to Canada. Vergennes, the French minister, was chagrined by these behind-the-scenes deals, but the adroit Franklin managed to soothe him and even to extract another fat loan for the United States.

The treaty between the United States of America and England was signed on September 3, 1783, and was ratified in Philadelphia on January 14, 1784. Known as the Treaty of Paris, it included the following provisions: (1) Britain recognized Amer-

"The American Peace Commissioners," 1782, an unfinished painting by Benjamin West of John Jay, John Adams, Benjamin Franklin, William Temple Franklin, and Henry Laurens. Only John Jay, John Adams, and Benjamin Franklin (from left to right) took an active part in the negotiations.

ican independence. (2) America obtained all the territory bounded by the Mississippi River on the West, the 31st parallel on the south (the line agreed upon if England ceded Florida to Spain, which she did), and the Great Lakes on the north. (3) England acknowledged America's right to the Newfoundland fisheries, but (4) retained the privilege with America of navigating the Mississippi. The United States agreed (5) to impose "no lawful impediment" to the recovery by British creditors of private debts due them but (6) consented only to "recommend" that the states restore Loyalist property.

The American negotiators had done well. Although the treaty left many important issues unresolved, many commercial agreements uncertain, and some boundaries dangerously inexact, American independence was a recognized fact, and a vast area from the Alleghenies to the Mississippi lay open to settlement. An epoch had begun, a New Jersey congressman observed. "It opens a new scene to Mankind, and is big with inconceivable Effects in the political and I hope in the moral world."

IV.   THE HERITAGE OF THE REVOLUTION

The Economics

of Revolution.

When the war began, American economic machinery was simple, if not primitive. Colonial businessmen had amassed considerable capital, but most business enterprises were personally managed rather than group investments. No commercial banks existed. Merchants and planters relied on British credit, and new avenues for capital investment were blocked by imperial restrictions. More significant, most of the colonists tended to distrust merchants, speculation, and all the paraphernalia of finance. They were agrarians and distrusted manufacturing. Although colonial businessmen were certainly acquisitive, they were reluctant to surrender traditional forms of enterprise (commerce and land speculation) so long as they brought adequate returns.

After 1776, a new climate of economic freedom encouraged the development of new techniques. The removal of British restraints unfettered economic enterprise and offered opportunities hitherto unknown to an aggressive group of young entrepreneurs. In this atmosphere of revolution and change, former prejudices and the old fear of innovation gave way. Businessmen, whether ardent Tories, Whigs, or middle-of-the-roaders, found ways to profit from the war. Some conducted an illegal trade with England via Amsterdam, importing prized English manufactured goods for a luxury-loving clientele. Internal trade between mutually dependent regions increased. Since the patriot armies had to be provisioned, often with supplies sent over considerable distances, the services of businessmen were in great demand. American independence automatically opened new outlets in northern Europe that had previously been denied to colonial shippers by the English Navigation Acts, and a lively Franco-American trade developed. Colonial ports now received the vessels of foreign nations as well as the American

privateers (about 2,000 in all, mostly from New England) that ravaged the English merchant-marine and brought home handsome profits for their lucky crews and shareholders.

There were also profits to be made in marine insurance, and in speculating in the highly erratic paper currency and other forms of negotiable notes. This speculation was bitterly criticized by Washington and others, but there is every reason to believe that the freedom that made it possible accomplished more for the American cause than a strictly controlled economy could have done. It is helpful to remember, too, that Adam Smith's great treatise, *The Wealth of Nations*, was published in the same year that the Declaration of Independence was written. American businessmen shared Smith's opinion that self-interest resulted in the public good. In short, the Revolution provided much useful experience for the business community that emerged after 1783.

The war left the American economy unstable. Agriculture had suffered little, since only a small percentage (from one-eighth to one-sixteenth of the roughly 700,000 men capable of bearing arms) had been drawn from the farms into the army. French and English troops paid for their provisions in gold, and the farmers were glad to sell to either. In the South, tobacco production soared during the war years, even though the tobacco ships had to run the English blockade. But many of the planters in the areas where the fighting had taken place were ruined.

American manufacturing made moderate but important progress during the war years. The closing of British markets and the release from English mercantile restrictions stimulated textile production, and the demand for war materials increased the number of small gun factories, foundries, and mines. During this period of nascent manufacturing (1774-1784), labor costs doubled as a result of the manpower shortage and inflation, but British prisoners and deserters with experience in factories contributed valuable services. So long as commerce provided

steps taken to control inflation. The establishment of the Bank of North America (chartered in Pennsylvania and opened in 1782), a less wasteful system of supplying the Continental army, and timely loans from France and the Netherlands brought some improvement, but financial and economic conditions remained chaotic throughout the war. Washington had to wheedle supplies

Pennsylvania troops rough up General Anthony Wayne on their march on Congress to demand overdue pay, January 1, 1781.

safer channels for investment, however, American capitalists were not eager to turn to industry.

Under the Second Continental Congress and the Articles of Confederation (see p. 115), the Congress could not tax effectively, and the promissory notes and certificates issued by the Congress and the state governments (some $450 million in all) were hardly worth the paper they were printed on. Financing the war by inflationary paper money turned out to be a kind of piecemeal confiscation. It was inferior to a fairly designed tax system, but since the Congress had no power to tax, it was the only possible substitute. Foreign loans and subsidies were neither big enough nor steady enough to stabilize colonial finances. Some $9 million came from France and Spain, but by 1780 eighty paper dollars were equal to one dollar in gold or silver. Not until the appointment of Robert Morris as Superintendent of Finance in 1781 were practical

from suspicious delegates. Profiteering and stock-jobbing made him question the colonies' ability to sustain a war. To James Warren he wrote in 1779:

Nothing I am convinced, but the depreciation of our currency ... aided by stockjobbing and party dissensions, has fed the hopes of the Enemy and kept the B. arms in America to this day. . . . Is the paltry consideration of a little dirty pelf to individuals to be placed in competition with the essential rights and liberties of the present generation, and of millions yet unborn? Shall a few designing men, for their own aggrandizement, & to gratify their own avarice, overset the goodly fabric we have been rearing at the expense of so much time, blood, & treasure? And shall we at last become the victims of our own abominable lust of gain? Forbid it Heaven!

But so long as the currency fluctuated it was impossible to establish price and wage controls, despite a series of abortive efforts by state and regional groups.

State Governments and Social Changes.

Even before the Declaration of Independence, four states, at the suggestion of the Congress, had begun to draw up constitutions. With the adoption of the Declaration of Independence, the legal basis upon which the American states had been governed—their royal charters— was swept away. It now became necessary for most of the remaining states to create their own instruments of government. Rhode Island and Connecticut, the corporate colonies, were able to go along under their former charters, which they found satisfactory; but between 1776 and 1780 the other states drew up new constitutions.

In most of the states, the legislatures drew up the new constitutions without consulting the voters. Massachusetts, however, set an example that was later adopted by the other states when they came to rewrite their basic law. In Massachusetts, a written constitution was drafted by a special convention and adopted in 1780 after its provisions had been referred to the towns for approval. The Massachusetts constitution declared, in the spirit of John Locke:

The body politic is formed by a voluntary association of individuals; it is a social compact, by which the whole people covenants with each citizen, and each with the whole people that all be governed by certain laws for the common good.

The conception that so fundamental a thing as a constitution is different from ordinary laws and should hence be acted upon by a special convention elected only for that purpose was quite consistent with the political theory accepted by most educated men in the colonies. But Massachusetts, by acting on the theory for the first time, set an important precedent for the conventions by which the states later ratified the Federal Constitution.

For the most part, the new state constitutions followed colonial forms of organization. Usually the legislature had two houses (both elective), though Pennsylvania experimented by having only one. The most important single change was the drastic reduction in the power of the governors, for many of the states, having had experience with powerful royal governors, wanted to limit the executive. In nine of the states he did not enjoy the veto power, and in the same number he had to be re-elected every year. Most of the states had bills of rights, guaranteeing the fundamental liberties of the citizens. The most famous of these documents, that of Virginia, which was written in 1776 by George Mason, set an example for other states and still later for the Federal Constitution.

The state constitutions varied widely in their assignment of political rights to the people. Four states (Pennsylvania, North Carolina, Delaware, and Georgia) adopted a democratic form of government with broad suffrage. In Pennsylvania, North Carolina, and Georgia, for example, all adult male taxpayers, which included most citizens, were allowed to vote; in New Hampshire, all who paid a small poll tax could vote. Virginia gave the vote to all who owned 25 acres of settled land. Most of the state constitutions also specified that legislators be elected annually, which was considered by the democratic theorists of the time to be an important safeguard for popular control. In more conservative states, property requirements for suffrage were kept; and in some, like South Carolina, New Jersey, and Maryland, rather high property-holding requirements were established for members of the legislature.

On the whole, the new state constitutions tended to favor greater democracy and humane reforms. The spirit of the Revolution fostered change, and the conservative classes were weakened by the death or departure of nearly 100,000 Loyalists, who came from or supported the propertied classes, and by the fact that exciting political events stirred up many people who might otherwise have taken little interest in politics. The popular spirit of the new America was caught in the following manifesto of a Massachusetts town meeting in 1778:

> The oftener power Returns into the hands of the people the Better, and when for the good of the whole the power is Delligated it ought to be done by the whole. . . . Where can the power be lodged so Safe as in the Hands of the people and who can Delligate it So Well as they, or who has the boldness without Blushing to Say that the people are not Suitable to putt in their own officers—if so why do we wast our blood and Treasure to obtaine that which when obtained we are not fitt to Enjoy, or if but a Selected few only are fitt to appoint our Rulers, why were we uneasie under George?

In spite of this assertive spirit, perhaps the most noteworthy thing about the temper of the American Revolution was the moderation with which social and legal changes were instituted. It is true that some Loyalists were tarred and feathered, some driven out, and that those with the largest property holdings usually saw them confiscated. But many Tories, especially the inconspicuous ones, were permitted to live quietly through the Revolution. There were no jacqueries, there was no revolutionary terror, no system of mass executions. The holdings of rich men who supported the Revolution were left intact, and very often even their direction of political affairs was only mildly qualified. Free manhood suffrage was not established. Slavery, though widely condemned even in the South, and given up in a few northern states, was not abolished in any place where it had economic importance. Even indentured servitude was not much affected by the Revolution: as an institution it was modified in most places but not abolished until many years later.

In some respects, however, the humanitarians and reformers, as well as the democrats, made real gains. The Revolution resulted in a gradual redistribution of land, partly because of the confiscation of Loyalist estates, partly because of the opening of the West. Some of the Tory estates passed through the hands of speculators and large

holders, but other portions went to dirt farmers. In Virginia, the old institutions of primogeniture and entail, which had in fact become a nuisance to most planters, were easily abolished—an act perhaps more symbolic of the liberalism of the times than important for the Virginia land system. Religious changes were of considerable significance. Only two of the states removed all religious disabilities: Rhode Island, with its long tradition of religious liberalism; and Virginia, where Jefferson, Madison, and Mason overcame the advocates of a state-supported church after a bitter fight. Elsewhere the established Anglican churches—never the churches of a majority, and now identified with Toryism and aristocracy—went down before the combined attack of other Protestant denominations. In New England, Congregationalism remained the established church (until 1818 in Connecticut and 1833 in Massachusetts), and 11 states kept religious qualifications for office-holding.

Toward Political Union:
The Confederation.

Between 1776 and 1781, the Second Continental Congress had the well-nigh impossible task of coordinating the war effort. Historians have tended to slight the accomplishments of this unglamorous body, which was hounded from Philadelphia to Baltimore and from Baltimore to York by the British redcoats. They have contrasted its impotency with the domineering states, who considered themselves sovereign and independent and who jealously guarded their prerogatives. Its weaknesses were notorious, but its members did more than bicker and make feeble recommendations. They declared American independence and organized the military and civil arms of the new government. They borrowed and issued money and sometimes acted without permission of the states.

The war had done much to break down narrow provincialism. Virginians had served at Saratoga, New Englanders had died in Pennsylvania, Marylanders had campaigned in South Carolina. After 1776 it became clear that disunited states could not wage an efficient war for independence, and that one government would have a better chance of winning than thirteen.

Although preliminary steps had been taken in this direction in 1775 when Franklin prepared the first "Articles of Confederation and Perpetual Union," the Congress did not debate the issue until the next year. In June, 1776, a 13-man committee was appointed to draw up a constitution, which was presented to the states in November, 1776. John Dickinson, the Pennsylvania representative, was the principal architect of the plan of union that provided for a national government without weakening the sovereignty of the states. Under the Articles, each state elected and paid the salaries of its own delegates and reserved the right to recall them. Voting in the single-chambered legislature was by state, and each state had only one vote, no matter how many delegates it sent. Important legislation required a two-thirds majority of the states. The provision nullifying a state's vote if its delegation were evenly split made law-making even more difficult.

The Articles gave the new government considerable powers and yet kept it weak in salient particulars: Congress might (1) make war or peace and fix state quotas of men and money for the national army; (2) make treaties and alliances; (3) decide interstate disputes, limit state boundaries, and admit new states; (4) borrow money and regulate standards of coinage and weights and measures; and (5) establish post offices. The assurance, however, that "Each state retains its sovereignty, freedom, and independence, and every Power, Jurisdiction, and right, which is not by this confederation expressly delegated to the United States, in Congress assembled," indicated where the real power lay. Many of the important powers could be exercised only with the consent of nine states. Congress could not levy taxes, nor could it regulate commerce. These powers were reserved to the states, and the Articles could be amended only after the Congress and every state legislature had agreed.

The drafters of the Articles had expected quick approval by the state governments, but Maryland refused to sign the Articles unless the seven "landed" states (New York, Virginia, the two Carolinas, Georgia, Massachusetts, and Connecticut), whose original charters defined their western boundaries as the Mississippi River or the Pacific, renounced their claims. Maryland, representing the views of the "landless" states, argued that since the war was a common effort, new territories should be "considered as common property, subject to be parcelled by Congress into free, convenient, and independent governments." Influential land-speculators in Pennsylvania and Maryland, motivated by less patriotic reasons, also urged congressional control. They had bought large tracts in territory claimed by Virginia, and they knew their claims would not be valid if the "landed" states retained title to the land. Finally, the magnanimity of the patriots from Virginia and New York, and the pressure of military necessity, broke the deadlock. Virginia, "preferring the good of the country to every object of smaller importance," agreed to renounce her trans-Allegheny claims, and Connecticut gave up a part of its share in the western lands. Recalcitrant Maryland dropped its objections in February, 1781, and in March the Articles went into effect.

The ratification drew the applause of the world and sustained the union at home. Some American leaders, refusing to minimize the defects of the Articles, saw them as only a step to something better. But it was an achievement not to be discounted. The much-abused Articles had many weaknesses, as future events showed, but their acceptance by a people who had unhesitatingly repudiated the plan of the Albany Congress (see p. 65) 27 years before was enormously significant. When, shortly after their adoption, Congress succeeded in settling a long-standing dispute between Pennsylvania and

Connecticut over the question of their western land claims, Robert R. Livingston of New York predicted:

There are few instances of independent States submitting their cause to a court of justice. The day will come when all disputes in the great republic of Europe will be tried in the same way, and America will be quoted to exemplify the wisdom of the measure.

In sum, the accomplishments of the American states since Lexington and Concord were in many ways remarkable. True, the Revolution had been financed with difficulty and miserably supplied, morale had been spotty, and strategy had been poor. Sacrifices had been unevenly and unfairly distributed, and innumerable problems had been postponed rather than overcome. But a population of 2,781,000 had defied the world's most powerful empire, had fought a difficult and exhausting war for seven years, had gained the respect and aid of foreign powers, had written a series of workable state constitutions and had supported political revolution with social reforms, had won independence and the cession of a great unsettled internal domain, and had taken the first steps, however faltering, toward a more satisfactory union among themselves. As George Washington declared in 1783, a great opportunity awaited the young Republic:

The citizens of America, placed in the most enviable condition, as the sole lords and proprietors of a vast tract of continent, comprehending all the various soils and climates of the world, and abounding with all the necessaries and conveniences of life, are now, by the late satisfactory pacification, acknowledged to be possessed of absolute freedom and independency. They are, from this period, to be considered as the actors on a most conspicuous theatre, which seems to be peculiarly designated by Providence for the display of human greatness and felicity.

Readings

For the events leading up to the American Revolution, L. H. Gipson, *The Coming of the Revolution, 1763-1775* (1954), is an informative recent summary; but C. L. Becker, *The Eve of the Revolution* (1921), and J. C. Miller, *Origins of the American Revolution* (1943), are also excellent. J. C. Wahlke has conveniently assembled a number of differing points of view in *The Causes of the American Revolution* (1950). Eric Robson, *The American Revolution, 1763-1783* (1955), is a recent contribution of an English scholar that succinctly discusses the Revolution as a problem of English policy. In this connection, L. B. Namier's *England in the Age of the American Revolution* (1930), should be consulted, as should the documents in Max Beloff, ed., *The Debate on the American Revolution, 1761-1783* (1949). Edmund S. Morgan, *The Birth of the Republic: 1763-89* (1956), is an authoritative brief summary.

The impact of British policies in the colonies is treated in A. M. Schlesinger, *The Colonial Merchants and the American Revolution, 1763-1776* (1918); E. S. and H. M. Morgan, *The Stamp Act Crisis: Prologue to Revolution* (1953); and Clinton Rossiter, *Seedtime of the Republic* (1953). Biographies of leading Revolutionary and anti-Revolutionary figures also shed much light on the period. Some of the more revealing are: D. S. Freeman, *George Washington: A Biography* (6 vols., 1948-1954); R. V. Harlow, *Samuel Adams, Promoter of the American Revolution* (1923); J. C. Miller, *Sam Adams: Pioneer in Propaganda* (1936); Jacob Axelrad, *Patrick Henry, The Voice of Freedom* (1947); C. J. Stillé, *The Life and Times of John Dickinson, 1732-1808* (1891); J. K. Hosmer, *The Life of Thomas Hutchinson* (1896); Nathan Schachner, *Thomas Jefferson* (2 vols., 1951); Esther Forbes, *Paul Revere and the World He Lived In* (1942); Catherine Bowen, *John Adams and the American Revolution* (1950); Curtis P. Nettels, *George Washington and American Independence* (1951); and Bernhard Knollenberg, *Washington and the Revolution* (1940).

The military aspect of the Revolution is briefly but clearly presented in J. R. Alden's *The American Revolution, 1775-1783* (1954). Other pertinent treatments are S. G. Fisher, *The Struggle for American Independence* (2 vols., 1908); J. C. Miller, *Triumph of Freedom* (1948); and C. H. Van Tyne, *The War of Independence* (1929). On the Continental Congress, see Lynn Montross, *The Reluctant Rebels* (1950), and E. C. Burnett, *The Continental Congress* (1941).

For the war of ideas, Carl L. Becker, *The Declaration of Independence: A Study in the History of Political Ideas* (1922), is excellent; but it should be supplemented with Dumas Malone, *Jefferson, the Virginian* (1948), and Adrienne Koch, *The Philosophy of Thomas Jefferson* (1943). Thomas Paine's important role is thoroughly treated in M. D. Conway, *The Life of Thomas Paine* (2 vols., 1892), and Hesketh Pearson, *Tom Paine, Friend of Mankind* (1937). Revolutionary propaganda is interestingly discussed in Philip Davidson, *Propaganda and the American Revolution, 1763-1783* (1941); and the influence of the patriot newspapers is dealt with in an essay by S. I. Pomerantz included in *The Era of the American Revolution* (1939), edited by R. B. Morris, a book with several other essays of general interest.

S. F. Bemis, *The Diplomacy of the American Revolution* (1935), is a scholarly and reliable account of Revolutionary diplomacy. A well-written survey can also be found in T. A. Bailey, *A Diplomatic History of the American People* (1950). American relations with France are fully presented in E. S. Corwin, *French Policy and the American Alliance* (1916); and cultural ties between the two countries are dealt with in Bernard Fäy, *The Revolutionary Spirit in France and America* (1927).

For a picture of the social changes occurring within the colonies during the Revolutionary period, J. F. Jameson's *The American Revolution Considered as a Social Movement* (1926), is still important, although historians now seriously question whether the social upheaval Jameson assumed was really as thorough-going as he thought. For a fair-minded critique see the article by F. B. Tolles in *American Historical Review*, October 1954. A more generalized account of social and economic changes during the Revolutionary period is E. B. Greene, *The Revolutionary Generation, 1763-1790* (1943).

Interesting material on the part played by the colonial clergy during the Revolutionary era is contained in A. M. Baldwin, *The New England Clergy and the American Revolution* (1928), and E. F. Humphrey, *Nationalism and Religion in America, 1774-1789* (1924). G. A. Koch, *Republican Religion: The American Revolution and the Cult of Reason* (1933), is also relevant here.

A SOVEREIGN NATION

CHAPTER SIX

The Revolution freed the American states from England, but it did not forge a new nation. Although the people of the several states had just fought successfully in a common cause, they still thought of themselves not primarily as Americans, but as South Carolinians, New Yorkers, and Rhode Islanders. Even a man of such broad views as Thomas Jefferson meant Virginia when he spoke of "my country." In the past the provinces had often been quarrelsome, and their populations had been almost as suspicious of one another as Europeans were. They never cooperated spontaneously in a common cause; they were usually motivated by fear of a common enemy. The Albany Congress (see p. 65), a British-inspired meeting, had been called to increase mutual strength against the French and to achieve unity in dealings with the Indians. Subsequent movements toward organization, such as the Committees of Correspondence, the Continental Congresses, and the Articles of Confederation, had all been created out of the need to defend common rights against British rule or to wage the Revolutionary War. The American states had proved that they could submerge their differences and unite temporarily during an emergency, but it remained to be seen whether they could bind themselves together permanently to form a nation.

I. THE NATION UNDER THE ARTICLES

The Problems of Union. Many leading Americans even wondered whether a permanent, general union was desirable. The Americans still lived on the edge of a great continent, and presumably their descendants, whether or not they united under a single sovereignty, would in some sense share a common fate, would constitute some kind of community. Europe, too, could be regarded as a community, but Americans knew all too well that Europe was a fragmented continent composed of many quarreling nationalities. Most Europeans and Americans believed that it was utterly impossible to organize so large a territory as either continent under one republican government. Only the firm hand of a monarch or a tyrant could impose such a unity, and of monarchs and tyrants the Americans felt they had had their fill. Any effort to organize them as a single people would have to overcome this healthy prejudice and quiet this natural suspicion.

The American people, of course, had lived under the centralizing government of the mother country. But this experience made them all the more suspicious of any new centralizing agency that might interfere in what they considered to be their own local affairs. The men who drew up the weak Articles of Confederation understood this attitude very well. Even at the risk of leaving the new Confederation without the means of keeping itself alive, they had refrained from giving it the power to tax individuals. The Congress of the Confederation could make requisitions on the several states for funds, but could do nothing to collect them when the states failed to comply. So far as most Americans were concerned, government meant snooping tax-collectors, mortgage-foreclosing courts, unpalatable regulations, and little else—and the less of it the better.

Nevertheless, the American states had shared many common experiences in their history and were now facing a set of common problems. Farseeing men realized that although these experiences and problems might be a source of further friction, they might also draw the states together for effective common action. At the very least, the states had a common debt to pay off, inherited from the Revolutionary struggle. Then there was the great western domain, which was rapidly becoming an area of settlement and speculation. Conflicting claims to the western lands themselves, and differing conceptions of the relation of the newly settled areas to the existing states, had to be ironed out. We have already seen (p. 115) that some of these claims had to be settled even before the weak Articles of Confederation themselves could be ratified. In carrying on external relations—with the nations of Europe and with the Indian tribes on their own frontiers—the states would obviously be far stronger if they could act together. Common problems arising out of commercial relations with the rest of the world and among the states themselves made interstate action particularly urgent.

These were the problems, then, that made the defects of the Articles clearer with each passing year and led eventually to the Philadelphia Convention of 1787.

The Confederation
and the West.

The ratification of the Articles of Confederation (under which the states, led by Virginia, agreed to cede their western claims to the central government) imposed upon Congress the administration of a large domain. Virginia's cession, delayed by technicalities, was completed by 1784. Meanwhile New York had relinquished her claims in 1780 (a step made final in 1782), and Massachusetts, Connecticut, and the southern states soon fell in line.

By this time, settlers had begun to break into the rich territory between the Alleghenies and the Mississippi. In these newer areas, and also in many partly settled regions of the existing states, the rich promise of the land attracted farmers and speculators alike.

The spirit of enterprise and settlement, at work on all frontiers, was best exemplified in two areas—in the rapidly growing Vermont country, claimed by both New York and New Hampshire, and in the Southwest. In Vermont, the three Allen brothers, Ethan, Ira, and Levi, staked out large holdings for themselves and succeeded in having

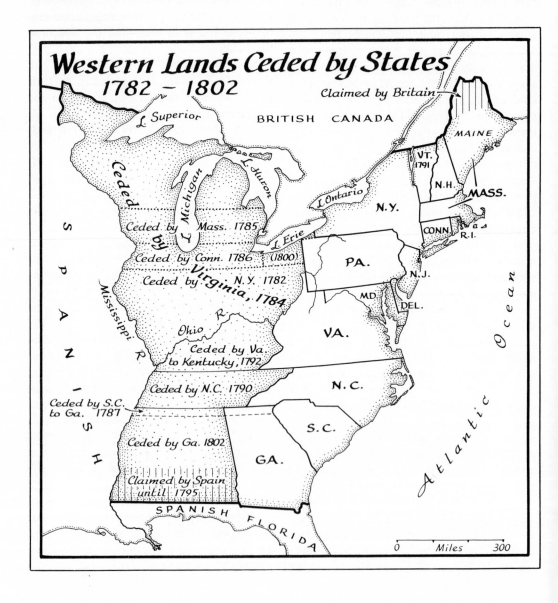

A newly cleared farm on the frontier.

Vermont admitted in 1791 as the Union's fourteenth state. In the Southwest, where Virginians were particularly active, James Robertson and John Sevier, two speculators from that state, took settlers into the region of the Watauga and Holston rivers during the 1770's. In 1784, when North Carolina finally ceded her old claims to this region, the Wataugans set up the independent state of Franklin, with Sevier as governor. However, by 1788, North Carolina reversed its decision, and the Wataugans, tired of "self-government" under the imperious Sevier, returned to North Carolina jurisdiction. Ultimately the Watauga country became part of Tennessee (see map, p. 90).

Another private state was staked out in the vicinity of Nashville in the Cumberland Valley by Judge Richard Henderson of North Carolina. In 1780, Henderson's settlers formed a government; but two years later, when North Carolina recognized the region by creating Davidson County, the settlers returned to that state's jurisdiction.

In Kentucky, the most heavily settled of the western areas, many conventions were held to work out plans for separate statehood. Virginia, after years of delay, acceded to this demand, but Congress acted even more slowly, and Kentucky did not become a state until 1792. Still another group organized a territory in western Virginia called Westsylvania, but this region remained a part of Virginia.

The Northwest Territory. The organization of the southwestern frontier was thus haphazard and disorderly. In the Northwest Territory, however, as the area above the Ohio River between the Appalachians and the Mississippi was to be called, the Yankee traditions of orderly survey and purchase came to dominate. Here, though settlement was left to individuals, as elsewhere, Congress made the rules even in the days of the Confederation.

After New York ceded her lands in the

Northwest Territory to Congress in 1780, Congress resolved that they be formed into states having the same rights as the existing states. In 1784, when Congress named a committee to decide what kind of government should be set up for the Northwest Territory, Jefferson, its chairman, followed this resolve. The result of the committee's work was the Northwest Ordinance of 1784, the first document to outline procedures for the establishment of territorial government and an orderly transition to statehood.

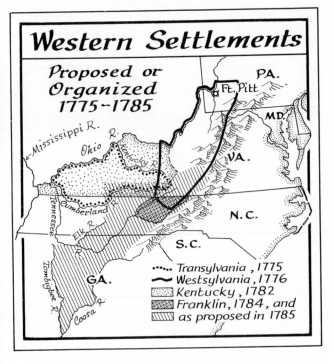

Western Settlements

Proposed or Organized 1775~1785

PA.
Ft. Pitt
Mississippi R.
Ohio R.
MD.
Kentucky
VA.
Tennessee
Cumberland R.
Elk R.
N.C.
S.C.
Tombigbee R.
GA.
Coosa R.

····· *Transylvania , 1775*
~ *Westsylvania , 1776*
▒ *Kentucky , 1782*
▓ *Franklin , 1784, and*
▨ *as proposed in 1785*

Congress never put the details of this ordinance into effect, but it became the basis of the more famous Northwest Ordinance of 1787, under which the Northwest Territory was actually organized. Before the Ordinance of 1787 itself was put into effect, Congress had also adopted the Land Ordinance of 1785, under which the land of the Northwest Territory was apportioned and sold. Also the work of a committee headed by Jefferson, the Land Ordinance required that the Northwest Territory (except for a small part retained by Connecticut as its Western Reserve) be surveyed into townships of 36 sections. Each section was made up of 640 acres, or one square mile. Four sections in each township were to be kept for the United States government, and one section was to be used for the support of local education. The rest was to be auctioned off through land offices set up at convenient locations. The minimum purchase was to be one 640-acre section, and the minimum price was to be $1 per acre. Congress hoped that good land would command a better price.

Desperate for funds to carry on the government, Congress hoped to raise revenue from the sale of its newly organized public domain. But the results were disappointing. The minimum requirement of $640 in cash effectively shut out most of the small settlers. In later years reductions were made in the minimum acreage and the minimum price, and extended credit eased the problem of payment.

Although sales to small settlers lagged at first, organized speculators were quick to come forth with offers for large tracts. In 1786 two army officers from Massachusetts organized the Ohio Company to purchase a million dollars' worth of new land. They planned to pay for it by distributing company stock to fellow ex-officers in exchange for the warrants these veterans had received from Congress for back pay. The company sent the Reverend Manasseh Cutler as a lobbyist to promote the scheme. He succeeded only after he agreed that a group of congressmen and their friends be allowed to take part in the deal through another agency, the Scioto Company. The Ohio Company got 1,500,000 acres at about 9 cents an acre. The Scioto Company, however, became entangled in various frauds and lawsuits and never earned anything for the schemers.

Having made the deal, the Ohio Company prodded Congress to get the government of the new territory in order so that sale and settlement could proceed legally and peacefully. The result was the Northwest Ordinance of 1787, probably the most important act passed by Congress under the Confederation. Under its terms, the Northwest Territory was to be set up as a single unit with a governor at its head and three judges for its new courts, all to be appointed by Congress. When 5,000 free male inhabitants had settled in the territory, those who owned at least 50 acres were to elect a territorial legislature whose acts would be subject only to the appointed governor's veto. The voters would also elect a non-voting delegate to Congress. No less than three and no more than five states were to be carved out of the territory, and the boundaries of three future states were tentatively laid out. When a potential state had 60,000 free inhabitants, it was to be admitted to the Union on an equal footing with the original states. Entail and primogeniture were banned; slavery was prohibited in the territory and in all the states to be carved from it.

Organized settlement followed hard upon this enactment. The Ohio Company sent out a small group of settlers in December, 1787, and in the spring of the next year they established the settlement of Marietta at the junction of the Ohio and Muskingum rivers. The Scioto Company brought a company of 600 Frenchmen to the area in 1790, but they had to be settled on Ohio Company lands because the Scioto Company had none to give them. A third group, sent out by the New Jersey speculator John Cleves Symmes to settle a tract he had purchased from Congress, laid the foundations of Cincinnati in 1788. Eight years later, Moses Cleaveland led a band of pioneers to begin developing the Connecticut Land Company's holdings in the Western Reserve. Here, on the Ohio lake front, the town of Cleveland was founded.

Foreign Affairs
Under the Confederation.
The Treaty of Paris, which was ratified by Congress in January, 1784, left many problems unsolved. Loyalist debts, British posts in the West, and western commerce were particularly vexing. According to the treaty, the British were to abandon their military and fur-trading posts

in the Northwest as soon as possible. But instead they continued to hold the posts and set about organizing the Indians in order to maintain the power with which to protect the rich Scottish-Canadian fur trade in the region. Hoping that the new nation would collapse and leave the whole Northwest open to reoccupation, the British repeatedly ignored requests from Congress to evacuate their posts. Moreover, they denied the use of the Great Lakes to Americans.

The British were not alone in failing to carry out the terms of the treaty. The treaty had declared that no legal impediments would hinder creditors on either side from collecting their debts; but Congress did not in fact have the power to prevent the states from passing measures obstructing English creditors. The attitude of a number of states was expressed by those Virginians who began asking in 1783: "If we are now to pay the debts due the British merchants, what have we been fighting for all this while?" Not until 1802 did the United States settle American pre-Revolutionary private debts by agreeing to pay £600,000 to British creditors.

Under the terms of the treaty, Congress had also made "earnest recommendation" to the states to restore confiscated Loyalist property. But most states ignored the recommendation, and even after the war patriots continued to confiscate Loyalist lands without being punished by the courts. The treaty also permitted Loyalists to return for twelve months to try to recoup their losses; but many who came got only tar and feathers for their pains. Years later, Britain herself awarded £3,300,000 to about 5,000 Loyalists for property they had lost in America.

The British seized upon such failures as an excuse for retaining the forts and for pursuing the fur trade that depended upon them.

The Indians supplied them with still another excuse for holding fast to the posts indefinitely. In 1783, the British still remembered Pontiac's conspiracy of 20 years earlier (see p. 90). Although the Treaty of Paris gave the United States control of the northwest country, it made no provision for the local tribes. Fearing that American settlement of the West would lead to new native uprisings, the British wanted to keep the posts for protection against the Indians. During the years 1784-1786 and in 1789, Congress negotiated four separate treaties with the Indians in this territory and forbade Americans to settle on any land that was not ceded by these treaties. But Congress had neither the money nor the military power to remove the Indians from the purchased land or to keep the Americans off forbidden ground. The British were aware of this weakness. As they foresaw, the Indians renounced the treaties, the Americans ignored them, and warfare was quickly resumed.

Indian problems also arose in the Southwest, where Spain was determined to keep American settlers out. During the Revolution, Spain had offered to mediate between the colonists and Britain if they would cede to her the territory between the Ohio River and the Gulf of Mexico and between the Appalachians and the Mississippi. Congress had refused this offer, but Spain had entered the war anyway in support of France. In a separate treaty in 1783, she received East and West Florida from Britain. Here she established forts of her own, from which she proceeded in 1784 to make treaties with the Indians of the region. These agreements required the Indians to join in the harassment of American frontiersmen.

According to the terms of the Treaty of Paris, Britain had agreed that Americans had the right to navigate the Mississippi, which presumably meant that they could deposit their goods for export at New Orleans. But now Spain insisted that these rights had not been Britain's to grant. Spain had acquired control of New Orleans on the west bank of the Mississippi from France in 1763, and she had captured the port of Natchez, on the east bank, from the British in 1779. At the end of the war Spain refused to yield Natchez to the United States, in whose territory it lay, and Congress had no means of forcing her to give it up. This failure cost Congress support on the southwest frontier, just as its weakness with the British and the Indians had cost it support in the Northwest.

More costly still were the efforts of John Jay, appointed by Congress as Secretary for Foreign Affairs, to negotiate a commercial treaty with Spain in 1785. Spain had played on the westerners' discontent with Congress by suggesting that they secede from the United States and become part of the Spanish empire. As bait, she offered them the use of the Mississippi and free deposit at New Orleans. Jay, an extremely conservative New Yorker, would have been pleased to see the westerners go. Pioneers, he thought, would "fill the wilderness with white savages . . . more formidable to us than the tawny ones which now inhabit it." With this prejudice in mind, he concluded long negotiations with Don Diego de Gardoqui, the first Spanish Minister to the United States. According to the agreement reached between the two, the United States would surrender claims to use of the Mississippi for 25 years, in exchange for favorable commercial treatment of American ships in Spanish ports elsewhere.

Although Congress failed to ratify this agreement, seven of the 13 states, most of them in the commercial North, supported it against the opposition of the southern states, which had ambitions of their own in the Southwest. The fact that Jay had negotiated this treaty, however, made him—and the commercial interests generally—suspect in the West and in the South for decades.

Congress was now in an embarrassing position: it had lost credit in the West by failing to control the Indians, and in the West and the South by appearing to be willing to sacrifice their interests to those of the commercial seaboard; and yet it had not succeeded in winning any gains of importance for the commercial interests of the East.

II. THE POSTWAR ECONOMIC CRISIS

Commerce and Enterprise.   Historians still disagree about how dark or how bright economic conditions actually were during the years from 1783 to 1787—years in which the American people lived under the Articles of Confederation. Conditions undoubtedly varied from place to place and from time to time, and the testimony of contemporaries is mixed. But it is certain that in many areas of economic life a postwar depression prevailed.

The American states suffered a great deal from the disruption of commercial relations with Britain brought about by independence. Before the war, legitimate trade had been carried on chiefly with the mother country and her West Indian possessions. After the war, however, American ships entering Britain's home ports were subject to the same heavy charges that other non-British vessels paid in British ports, and an attempt was made to exclude them altogether from trading with the British West Indies. American commerce suffered severe losses from these discriminations, which were only in part offset by increased trade with the Baltic area, the new trade opened up with China in 1784, and the conclusion of commercial treaties with France, Holland, Sweden, Prussia, and Morocco. The envoys of Congress, moreover, were laughed out of court when they tried to get Britain to reopen the West Indian trade to American goods and American ships. John Adams' experience in these negotiations (he was once asked whether he represented one government or thirteen) served to strengthen his support of a stronger central government.

Congress tried to retaliate against the British commercial affronts but succeeded only in displaying its own impotence and the weakness of the new nation. Congress was unable to control state ports, and the states themselves sought only their own advantage. Lord Sheffield, who promoted the British anti-American policy, wrote in his *Observations on the Commerce of the American States* (1783): "America cannot retaliate. It will not be an easy matter to bring the American States to act as a nation. They are not to be feared as such by us."

Immediately after the war, British policy and American weakness had combined to give the American importer a taste of prosperity. But once the splurge on English finery and other goods was over, the importer added his voice to the chorus of protest raised against Congress. Blaming his plight on the shortage of domestic currency and the insecurity of domestic credit, he demanded financial reforms. American manufacturers, in turn, who had had the American market so largely to themselves during the conflict, also demanded protection against the influx of British goods and sought subsidies to support their own programs of industrial expansion—neither of which Congress was in a position to provide.

Fortunately, most Americans, especially the inarticulate farmers who made up 90 per cent of the population, did not depend on Congress for their well-being. Even those who looked to it to better their condition often got along well enough by themselves while Congress itself languished. Philadelphia, New York, and Baltimore merchants profited from the illicit trade with the British West Indies and from the world trade that was opened up during and after the war. Creditors, though unpaid and angry, apparently still had enough capital to sponsor many new business ventures; for the years immediately following the war saw unprecedented activity in canal construction, bridge-building, river improvement, road construction, house-building, insurance, stagecoach transportation, land transactions, and banking.

The United States after the war was still a wild, poor country, and its people were far from being industrial-minded. Even so, a new business spirit showed itself in America after the Revolution. In Pennsylvania in 1784, Washington found a "spirit of commerce [that] may achieve almost anything." In New York, he noted a "temper, genius, and policy" directed single-mindedly toward capturing trade. He advised his fellow Virginians to adopt this commercial spirit and show "to our countrymen the superior advantages we possess beyond others." Otherwise Virginia must "submit to the evils arising [from commercial competition] without receiving its benefits." Perhaps the most encouraging signs during the postwar "critical period" were the resumption of immigration to America, the rapid growth in the number and size of families, and the settlement of new lands on the frontiers, especially in the West. These gains, made despite Congress, attest to the vigor of the people, most of whom were content to develop the country with neither the help nor the interference of political bodies.

Debts—Public and Private. Congress, meanwhile, lacking the power to tax, became desperate for funds and was threatened with the disgrace of disbanding the army unpaid. Many other money claims arising from the war came pouring in every day. The national government had foreign debts to pay and a huge war debt to meet that rose steadily because back interest had to go unpaid. Its requests to the states for funds were not cordially received, for the states had their own unpaid Revolutionary debts—some of them very substantial—and they had a tendency to hang back, each hoping that the others would share the common obligation more generously. When Congress requested $10 million from the states in 1782-1783, it received less than $1½ million.

Plainly, some independent source of funds was needed. In 1781, at the urging of Robert Morris, the new Secretary of Finance, Congress had asked for authority to levy a 5 per cent duty on imports. But this authority would have required an amendment to the Articles that every state would have had to pass on. Since Rhode Island refused to consent to the proposed duty, no amendment could pass. Morris had also proposed a land tax, a poll tax, and an excise on distilled liquors. But Congress would vote none of these. Morris tried again in 1782, with no greater success. In 1783, with the army growing restive and with some sectors of it in mutiny, with the federal debt at over $36 million and with overdue interest at more than $2 million, Morris modified his proposals—but again with no more luck than before. In January, 1783, Morris tried to resign. No one could be found to take over the thankless job, however, and Morris was prevailed upon to remain at least until the army was satisfied. The men finally agreed to go home in June, and their eventual compensation took the form of warrants to western land—land in which the Indians were violently opposed to settlement. The warrants served to encourage people to go west, but Congress had neither the money nor the armed power to protect them. When Morris finally left his post in September, 1784, having won no financial concessions from the states, he was a stauncher proponent of a strong central government than ever before, and many of the settlers who were exposed to Indian depredations on the far frontier had become his allies.

While Congress sat troubled by its inability to raise funds, the states were struggling with their own internal problems—particularly an agricultural depression and the absence of a satisfactory system of currency and credit. By 1785, with the withdrawal of the last of the foreign troops and the disbanding of the American army, the farmers' market had begun to contract. At the same time, impatient war-time creditors of the states were pressing for back interest, and the farmers' taxes began to go up. This sudden reversal of fortune led the farmers and the harassed small retailers who depended upon them to demand relief. They agitated for the states to issue paper money that would be legal tender for all debts, public and private; and they pressed for the enactment of "stay laws" that would delay the foreclosure of farms on which mortgage payments were in arrears.

In most of the states, the farmers did win concessions. Seven states issued some form of paper money, often with good effects. But in states like Massachusetts, the creditors and conservatives resisted the farmers' demands. There the seaboard commercial towns succeeded in passing a disproportionate part of the tax burden on to the inland farmers. It has been estimated that after 1780 the average Massachusetts farmer had to surrender a third of his income for taxes.

Even in Rhode Island, where the debtors were strong, the farmers suffered setbacks. After a good bit of pressure, they prevailed upon the legislature to issue paper money in 1786, but the money that was issued rapidly depreciated in value. Merchants refused to accept it, and even began avoiding their debtors. The legislature responded by passing a law that made refusal to accept the paper money a crime punishable by fines without even the ceremony of a jury trial. One Rhode Island butcher, John Weeden by name, appealed his conviction under this law to the state supreme court. In the famous case of *Trevett* v. *Weeden* (1786), the court dismissed the complaint on the ground that it had no jurisdiction, but established one of the chief precedents for judicial review (see p. 133) by announcing its opinion that the law was repugnant to the provisions of the Rhode Island charter and was therefore unconstitutional.

In New Hampshire, the militia had to be called out in 1786 to disperse a mob that had surrounded the legislative meeting house in an effort to coerce the members to issue paper money. It was in Massachusetts, however, that conservatives felt the greatest fright. Here the legislature, its upper house dominated by merchants, not only failed to heed the back-country farmers' demands for relief, but actually pressed them further by levying still higher taxes that had to be paid in specie. This action set the stage for Shays' famous rebellion, one of the most dramatic of the violent outbreaks that developed during this period.

In the summer of 1786, after several courthouses in western Massachusetts had been attacked, Captain Daniel Shays, a veteran of Bunker Hill and other battles, led some 2,000 of the newly embattled farmers in a raid on Springfield, Massachusetts. The raid succeeded in forcing the state court to adjourn, which meant that foreclosure proceedings and actions against delinquent taxpayers were suspended. Governor Bowdoin immediately sent General Benjamin Lincoln with the militia to put down Shays' "rebellion." Shays and a number of his straggling followers were finally captured in December, but the legislature freed them in June. The strong feeling behind this uprising emerged clearly in the subsequent elections, when the aging John Hancock defeated Governor Bowdoin.

Shays' rebellion shocked conservatives throughout the states. They now felt more acutely than before the necessity of preventing attacks on courts of law and physical intimidation of legislatures. They also sought to prevent legislatures from impairing the obligations of private contracts and from establishing depreciated currencies as legal tender for the payment of debts. By the winter of 1786, with Shays' rebels suppressed, the movement for a new constitution was already well under way.

III. DRAFTING A CONSTITUTION

Preliminaries. The weakness of the Confederation government, along with the economic distress and social conflict of the time, convinced many patriotic Americans that a new form of government had to be set up. Some talked vaguely of monarchy or a military dictatorship; others predicted that the states would split up into two or three confederations, each more tightly knit than the existing government. A number of political leaders, however, continued to hope that all 13 states could be kept together in one nation, and that this nation could be kept republican in form. As early as 1780, Alexander Hamilton had asked for a new and more energetic government to press the war forward. In the next six years, several proposals were made to call interstate conventions to revise or supplant the Articles, but none of them led to action. In 1782 the New York legislature and in 1785 the Massachusetts legislature passed resolutions calling for conventions, but nothing came of them.

Finally, a strong movement for a new form of government emerged from the efforts of practical men to achieve what the Articles themselves could not—that is, a more satisfactory regulation of interstate commerce. Early in 1785, delegates from Maryland and Virginia met at Alexandria in an attempt to settle differences between the two states over navigation of the Potomac River and Chesapeake Bay. The delegates moved on to Washington's home in Mount Vernon, where they extended their sessions so that delegates from neighboring Delaware and Pennsylvania could attend. Finally, these discussions resulted in a recommendation to the Virginia legislature that it call a general meeting of all the states, to take place at Annapolis, in September, 1786. Only five states actually sent delegates to Annapolis. But one of them was New York—and among New York's delegates was the far-seeing and indefatigable Hamilton. The Annapolis Convention was supposed to deal only with matters of commerce, but the occasion to do more than that was too good to miss.

The Convention adjourned promptly. Its report, written by Hamilton, spoke of the numerous and important defects of the Articles of Confederation, not merely those relating to commerce. It ended with a call for a great new convention to amend the Articles to meet at Philadelphia the following May. The states listened to Hamilton's proposal much more seriously than they had to the Virginia legislature's call to the Annapolis Convention. All the state legislatures save Rhode Island sent delegates to the Philadelphia Convention of 1787.

The Great Convention. In arguing for the Constitution in the Federalist papers, John Jay wrote: "When once an efficient national government is established, the best men in the country will not only consent to serve but also will be generally appointed to manage it." Questionable as this prediction became in later years, the new government, from the first, not only elicited the services of the country's best men but was set up by them.

Not all the eminent leaders were on hand in Philadelphia, however. Jay himself, Jefferson, and John Adams were absent on other duties; Sam Adams was not named as a delegate; Patrick Henry, appointed by Virginia, refused to attend. But from Pennsylvania came Benjamin Franklin, Gouverneur Morris, Robert Morris, and James Wilson; from Massachusetts, Rufus King and Elbridge Gerry; from Connecticut, Roger Sherman; from Delaware, John Dickinson; from New York, Alexander Hamilton; from New Jersey, William Paterson; from Maryland, Luther Martin; and from Virginia came the most brilliant delegation of all, reluctantly headed by the silent Washington, and including James Madison, George Wythe, Edmund Randolph, and George Mason.

No limitation was placed on the number of delegates a state might send. Rhode Island refused to appoint any; most of the states, for reasons of economy, sent only a few. Of the 74 men named, only 55 appeared. Their average age was but 42 years. Many of them had been young officers in the Revolution, and 27 belonged to the Society of Cincinnati, an organization of such officers. Only eight had signed the Declaration. A majority of the delegates were college graduates. Lawyers predominated, although many were young merchants, and almost all were men of affairs.

The Convention had been called for May 14, 1787, but not until May 25 did delegates from a majority of the states reach Philadelphia. Foreshadowing their ready agreement later, the 29 delegates in attendance that day unanimously elected Washington as presiding officer. Next they decided to protect themselves from the pressures of the populace and the press by keeping the sessions secret. There was then debate about their purpose in coming together, with some maintaining that they must adhere to the instructions from their states, which empowered them only to amend the Articles. But those who were determined to supplant the Articles had their way.

Agreement

in the Convention. Although the Constitutional Convention spent a good bit of time settling differences among the delegates, it is important to realize that in their general philosophy of "balanced government" and on a great number of specific objectives the majority were in substantial agreement. As enlightened and worldly-wise men, the delegates felt that no soundly based theory of government could rely on the generosity or goodness of men for its operation. On the contrary, government should be built on the assumption that men would pursue their own interests so far as they could go without damaging themselves or without being checked by equal or superior force. If any single interest in society or any particular arm of government could go on indefinitely adding to its power, it would certainly become tyrannical. Therefore, architects of government had to find ways of harnessing the evil and selfish impulses in men, and of seeing to it that they limited and counterbalanced one another. In short, the various interests in society—the slave-owning interest, the manufacturing interest, the commercial interest, and the like—must be made to balance, and the government must

contain the mechanisms for this self-balancing operation.

Thus, although the Founding Fathers believed that the people must have a voice in government—for sovereignty properly rested in them—they placed no great trust in popular wisdom. They knew from the record of ancient republics and Italian city-states, as well as from recent experience, that the people could be stampeded into following demagogues and tyrants, that unchecked they would plunder the rich. Hence, the people must be limited and controlled—but they did not apply this thinking only to the poor. Although they were themselves men of property and distrusted democracy, the framers of the Constitution had no illusions about the benevolence of the rich, who they felt would plunder the poor if they could. They sought to create a legislative system that would give both "the people" and the well-to-do a distinct voice in the government, and to limit both by a strong, but not unchecked, executive.

Assuming that each special and local interest would seek its own advantage, the framers aimed to create a political society in which no one interest could completely dominate, because it would be restrained by the others. To do this, they hoped to establish a government with a division of powers among executive, legislative, and judicial branches. Even within the legislative branch, two divisions were to exert a mutual check, just as the state governments and the national government were to distribute power between them and hamper the excessive use of power in any one place.

Naturally, the delegates did not agree unanimously, even on the application of these general principles. Some delegates from New York and Maryland were so concerned lest state power be eclipsed that they could not enter sympathetically into the proceedings; others, like George Mason of Virginia, were more concerned with preventing the establishment of a national sovereignty that would swallow up traditional personal liberties than they were with creating a balanced government.

On the extreme conservative side of the Convention stood Alexander Hamilton, who admired British monarchical government and looked with candid disdain upon popular judgment and democratic procedures. "The people," he said, "seldom judge or determine right," and he would have reduced their role in government almost to nothing. He favored a centralization of power so drastic that the delegates, for all his valuable services to the movement for the Constitution, hardly gave him a serious hearing. "The gentleman from New York," it was said, "has been praised by everybody, he has been supported by none." By and large, the delegates preferred a compromising, moderately conservative approach to the problem of federal union. It is one of the ironies of history that Hamilton, who worked so hard for the Constitution, and indeed for its ratification, felt that it fell far short of his ideals, and referred to

Alexander Hamilton (1757?-1804).

it in later years as "a frail and worthless fabric."

Although the Convention delegates occasionally differed on the general problems of government and politics, they were almost unanimous on certain specific powers that the new government should have. The propositions dealing with the economic powers of the new government won general approval: (1) that the new Congress should have what Congress under the Articles so sadly lacked —the power to levy and collect taxes, tariffs, and excises; (2) that Congress should be able to coin and borrow money; (3) that it should be able to pay all debts contracted by the United States before the adoption of the Constitution; (4) that it should be able to raise and maintain an army and a navy; and (5) that it should be able to regulate interstate and foreign commerce.

These propertied and conservative men, distrustful and fearful of the debtor element in society, also agreed that the state governments, though still left in possession of a wide range of powers and responsibilities, should be forbidden to coin money, to issue bills of credit, to make anything but gold and silver legal tender for the payment of debts, and that they should be barred from making any laws impairing the obligation of contracts, or from levying any duties on imports or exports. Thus the framers acted decisively and without major disagreement to check what Madison called "the mutability of the laws of the states."

Compromise
in the Convention.
Although the delegates agreed on many of the problems before them, fundamental differences on the question of the distribution of power could be settled only by compromise. In fact, the so-called "Great Compromise" became the chief business of the convention for several days.

No sooner had the delegates agreed to give up the idea of amending the Articles than Randolph came forward with the Virginia Plan for a new government embodying proposals that were attractive chiefly to the large states. He proposed a two-house "National Legislature" with membership in both houses allotted among the states in proportion to their free population. Members of the "second house" (or upper house) were to be elected by the members of the first, who were themselves to be elected by the people. The whole "National Legislature" was then to elect the "National Executive" and the "National Judiciary." This plan violated the prevailing theory of the separation of the executive, legislative, and judicial powers—a theory that was cherished even among strong nationalists and was widely practiced in the state governments. Advocates of this theory believed that if separation and mutual checks and balances were not carefully planned, a determined grasp for power by the unchecked and unbalanced branch would lead to tyranny.

Still more important was the vigorous objection put forward by delegates from the small states. They feared that they would be overwhelmed in the popularly elected house by the heavily populated states, and that some states might get no representatives at all in the second house. To protect themselves the small states offered a plan of their own, presented first by William Paterson of New Jersey and known since as the New Jersey Plan. According to this plan Congress was to remain, as under the Articles, in a single house, and all the states, large and small alike, would continue to have only one vote apiece. In spite of the nominal "supremacy" of the proposed national government, its fund-raising power, besides the familiar and unsuccessful requisitions on the states, now included only tariffs and a few other taxes. The delegates quickly rejected the New Jersey Plan.

Dissatisfied though the delegates were with the Virginia Plan, they adopted it as a preliminary model from which to construct their final document. But the issue of representation, which involved a conflict of interests between the large and small states, presented the most difficult problem of all. As the debate grew keener, tempers flared in the hot Philadelphia summer. At one point the small states were on the verge of leaving and disrupting the entire Convention.

Finally, cooler heads averted catastrophe. A special committee, headed by Gerry, was named to restudy the whole issue of representation. After deliberating the question, the committee presented to the Convention a compromise scheme devised largely by Franklin. There would be a two-house legislature, and membership in the lower house would be apportioned according to population, thus satisfying the large states. Membership in the upper house would be equal for all states, thus satisfying the small ones. This arrangement, eventually adopted after much argument, provided the basis for the "Great Compromise" of the Constitution. It determined the general character of the two bodies that soon came to be called the House of Representatives and the Senate, and removed the main obstacle that was preventing the Convention from getting on with its business.

In the end, the two-house plan also enabled the delegates to incorporate another feature of balanced government into the Constitution, the establishment of the lower house as the people's branch. Its members were to be elected by all voters in the states who were eligible to vote for "the most numerous branch of the State Legislature." This opened the choice of representatives to a broad electorate, and was considered adequate to protect "the people." The upper house, whose senators were to be chosen, more restrictively, by the state legislatures, was expected to have members who would be more congenial to propertied interests and more conservative. Thus the two parts of the legislature would counterbalance one another, and would give adequate representation to both the general public and the special propertied interests.

By the time Gerry's special committee offered the "Great Compromise," the Convention as a whole had already decided that the "direct taxes" the new government had the new power to levy were to be apportioned among the states according to their population, just as representation was to be apportioned in the lower house. The scheme, however, opened up a new rift—this time between the slave states and the free states. The South wanted Negro slaves, if they were counted at all in apportioning taxes, to be given less weight than free men. The North wanted Negroes to be given less weight only in apportioning congressional representation. The upshot was a second compromise, the "three-fifths compromise," which specified that for both direct taxes and representation, five Negroes were to be counted as equivalent to three whites.

Representatives of the commercial North in the Convention had urged that the new government be granted full power to regulate interstate and foreign commerce and to make treaties which the states must honor and obey. The Convention readily agreed on this point, but the South, fearful of being outvoted in the new Congress, demanded that commercial regulations and all treaties require the consent of a two-thirds majority of the Senate rather than a simple majority. The southerners were particularly fearful of taxes on exports, for they were heavily dependent upon selling their tobacco and other staples in competitive world markets. They were also worried lest the slave trade be tampered with.

To settle these matters, the Convention negotiated a third compromise. To satisfy the South, the Constitution prohibited any taxes on exports and guaranteed that for at least 20 years there would be no ban on the importation of slaves. It also required the free states to return any fugitive slaves who sought refuge there. Finally, the South won the provision requiring a two-thirds vote in the Senate for the ratification of all treaties. In exchange for these concessions, the northerners were permitted to retain the requirement that a simple congressional majority would be sufficient to pass acts regulating commerce.

Toward Sovereign Power. The delegates to the Great Convention succeeded in designing a system of government that was specific enough to remedy all the major defects of the Articles of Confederation and yet flexible enough to anticipate the distant future.

Two fateful weaknesses had impaired the effectiveness of the Confederation: it had neither the power of the purse nor the power of the sword. The Constitution remedied these weaknesses by unequivocally granting the new Congress power to tax the people, to raise and maintain armies and a navy, to declare war, suppress insurrections, regulate commerce, coin money, and—very broadly—to provide for the "general welfare of the United States." As if to guarantee that these powers would be exercised, the framers added the famous "elastic clause," enabling Congress "to make all laws which shall be necessary and proper for carrying into execution the foregoing powers." And its members were to be paid by the United States, rather than by their respective states.

A third weakness of the Confederation had been that its executive was not a responsible individual but an executive committee with too many heads. The Constitution created a president—a single responsible executive—elected independently of Congress. After many arguments—especially between the centralists, who wanted the president elected by the people, and the state sovereignty men, who wanted him chosen by the state legislatures—the Convention devised the electoral-college plan. This left the method of choosing the electors up to the legislature of each state, and mollified the state sovereignty men. The centralists were consoled by the virtual apportionment of the electors by population. Each state was to have as many electors as it had representatives and senators.

The president was empowered (with the consent of the Senate) to appoint his own administrators. (The power of removing these appointees, though not specifically mentioned, was later held to be included.) The president was to be commander-in-chief of the army and navy, and to have power (with the consent of two-thirds of the Senate) to make treaties, call Congress into extraordinary session, and to enforce the laws. He was to have the veto power over acts of Congress—though his veto could be overridden by a two-thirds vote in both houses. In the future, of course, the effectiveness of presidential leadership grew even beyond the expectations of the framers, partly because of the dynamic qualities of certain individual leaders, but also because of the development of the American party system and presidential patronage.

A fourth weakness of the Confederation was its lack of a judiciary independent of state courts. This fault the Constitution remedied by setting up a complete judicial system. At the head of the system was the Supreme Court of the United States. It could decide cases on appeal from all the lower federal courts (which Congress was empowered to establish), and from the state courts in cases involving the Constitution, the laws of the United States, or treaties with other nations.

The Constitution made no specific provision for what has become known as "judicial review"—that is, the power of the Court to declare legislative acts unconstitutional and void. But the framers knew about the practice of judicial review, and Article VI, section 2, made it clear that any state acts or laws that encroached on the supreme powers of Congress must be found unconstitutional. The Constitution was less clear on whether or not and to what extent acts of Congress were to be subject to judicial review. Some scholars deny that the framers even intended to give the Court such power. The safest assumption seems to be that most of them expected the Supreme Court to exercise this power. In any case, John Marshall, who became Chief Justice in 1801, firmly established this power in the Supreme Court (see p. 156).

Thus, in place of a weak Confederation, a pawn of the states, and a frequent victim of their disagreements, the Convention erected a government that could act with speed and sovereign dignity. By the Tenth Amendment (in force after 1791) the states were permitted to retain all powers not specifically delegated by the Constitution to the new federal government. But in the exercise of the powers it received, the new government was supreme.

Building for the Ages.   If the framers sought primarily to substitute a strong central government for the weak Articles, they also hoped to create a government, as Madison put it, "for the ages." What, then, were some of the features that the framers of the Constitution believed would help the document to endure down through the years?

One, surely, was the system of checks and balances. For example, all bills, to become laws, must be passed by the House and the Senate, and then must have the president's signature. Even then, they could be contested in the courts and overthrown. Again, treaties, though made by the executive, must have the approval of the Senate; and measures making appropriations required by treaties must, like all financial measures, originate in the House. Although the Constitution named the president commander-in-chief of the armed forces, it stated that only Congress could declare war.

A second source of the Constitution's lasting strength is the amending process, which allows an amendment passed by Congress to become part of the Constitution after ratification by three-fourths of the states. The futility of trying to amend the Articles of Confederation, under which the consent of every state was needed, was one of the factors that hastened their demise. But it was the right to propose amendments to the new Constitution, and indeed the promise that the first ten amendments would be added after ratification, that won some of the opponents of the Constitution to its support (see p. 136). Only the prospect of early amendment prompted Patrick Henry to accept the new government once the ratification battle had been won: "I will be a peaceable citizen," he said. "My head, my hand, and my heart shall be at liberty to retrieve the loss of liberty, and remove the defects of that system in a constitutional way."

The endurance of the Constitution rests in part on a paradox. On the one hand, statesmanship prompted the framers to leave many important powers to the jealous states. On the other hand, they wrote the Constitution in such general terms—no accident, but a result of their classical training and universal way of thinking—that these powers could be retrieved by the federal government when the advance of industry and changes in international relations made it important that the powers be used on a national level.

The Constitutional Convention, for all its conservatism, set up what was surely by world-wide standards a radical government, a democratic nation among aristocratic ones, a republic among oppressive monarchies. For all its inhibitions on direct democratic action, moreover, the Constitution had its "democratical branch," which John Adams prescribed as essential to all free governments. Under the Constitution, said John Marshall, who rose as a new leader during the ratification controversy in Virginia, "It is the people that give power, and can take it back. What shall restrain them? They are the masters who give it, and of whom their servants hold it."

IV.   ADOPTING A NEW GOVERNMENT

Ratification. The Constitutional Convention was in session from May 25 to September 17, 1787. Of the 55 delegates who took some part in the deliberations, 42 stayed to the end. Some, like Luther Martin and John Mercer of Maryland, and Robert Yates and John Lansing of New York, had deserted the Convention, disturbed by its disregard of the Articles. Although 39 delegates signed the document at the end, the other three, Gerry of Massachusetts, and Randolph and Mason of Virginia, refused to go along, their reasons accumulating as the sessions drew out. These defections and refusals were warnings of the storm that would blow up when the Constitution was presented to the states for ratification.

It had been possible to amend the Articles only by the consent of all thirteen states; the framers of the Constitution made things easier for themselves by providing that their document would go into effect after nine state conventions had ratified it. The process of ratifying by special conventions of delegates in each state, chosen only for the purpose of accepting or rejecting the Constitution, was more democratic than any previous major interstate act. The Declaration of Independence, for instance, had not been submitted for ratification, and the Articles themselves had been ratified only by the state legislatures. The procedure of ratification through special conventions gave the Convention members who were not members of state legislatures a chance to carry on the fight for ratification. But it was also deemed appropriate to refer the document to the people for approval because the Convention, in drawing up a new Constitution instead of proposing amendments to the Articles, had completely exceeded its instructions. The Convention members did refer the document to Congress, but Congress, without voting on it, merely advised the states to elect ratifying conventions.

While these elections were in progress, the Constitution began to be discussed and debated throughout the country. Interest was especially high because the Convention had met in secret and the results of its deliberations had not become generally known until it was over. In press and pulpit, at public meetings and in personal correspondence, the new proposal was attacked, defended, dissected, and sometimes disavowed. Its opponents aroused the old suspicion of central-

Signing the Constitution in Independence Hall. Benjamin Franklin is standing second from the left and George Washington is seated behind the desk in the center.

ized government, and with it the old fear of governmental power as a threat to personal freedom. Rufus King, a member of the Massachusetts ratifying convention, summed up the feelings of the opposition, though he did not share them, when he wrote to James Madison in January, 1788: "An apprehension that the liberties of the people are in danger, and a distrust of men of property and education have a more powerful effect upon the minds of our opponents than any specific objections against the Constitution."

But the Constitution's critics offered plenty of specific objections: there was no bill of rights guaranteeing traditional liberties; state sovereignty would be destroyed; the president might become king; the standing army would be everywhere; only the rich and well-born could afford to hold office; tax collectors would swarm over the countryside; the people could not bear to be taxed by both state and national governments; commercial treaties would sell out the West and the South; debtors would no longer be able to defend themselves through recourse to state paper money and state stay

laws. In March, 1787, George Washington had remarked that "A thirst for power [has] taken fast hold of the states individually; . . . the many whose personal consequence in the control of state politics will be annihilated [by a national government] will form a strong phalanx against it." But it was not merely the local lions who felt themselves threatened by the proposal. Many honest citizens shrank back from an innovation so drastic, whose consequences they found it so hard to calculate.

At the beginning, however, ratification went along smoothly. Between December 7, 1787, and January 9, 1788, five states ratified, and the conventions of three (Delaware, New Jersey, Georgia) did so without a single opposing vote; while a fourth, Connecticut, ratified with the overwhelming majority of 128 to 40. In Pennsylvania alone, the second among the first five, heated controversy sprang up in the legislature. By staying away, the opponents of the Constitution (now generally called Antifederalists) tried to prevent the Pennsylvania legislature from forming the quorum it needed before

135

it could vote to call a ratifying convention. The Federalists then resorted to strong-arm tactics, seizing some of their opponents and forcibly dragging them into the chamber to make up a quorum. But in the convention itself the Federalists won handily, by a vote of 46 to 23.

In Massachusetts, the sixth state to ratify, the contest was close. Its convention debated from early January to early February, but Federalist leaders maneuvered ingeniously to win over such popular opponents as John Hancock and Sam Adams, and placated many opponents by promising to support amendments guaranteeing popular liberties. Finally, by the close vote of 187 to 168, Massachusetts voted for the Constitution.

In Maryland and South Carolina ratification went smoothly and won easily. In New Hampshire, the opposition was powerful, and after a first convention failed to reach a vote, a second convention ratified on June 21, 1788, by the narrow margin of 57 to 46. Technically speaking, the new government could now go into effect, for nine states had accepted it. But no one believed that it could be successful without Virginia and New York, and in these two states the outcome was very doubtful.

In Virginia, an extraordinarily thorough and brilliant review of the issue took place, with the opposition led by the scholarly George Mason and the inflammatory Patrick Henry. Washington's influence and the knowledge that he would consent to serve as first president was responsible for the unexpected conversion of Edmund Randolph, who had refused to sign the Constitution; and the promised addition of a bill of rights softened the opposition and helped to swing the convention. Four days after New Hampshire had ratified, Virginia fell in line, 89 to 79. By arrangement between Madison and Hamilton, couriers were immediately dispatched to carry the good news to New York, where a desperately close struggle was in process.

In New York, Hamilton led the Federalist fight in support of ratification. Lansing and Yates joined Governor Clinton in opposition. Well aware of Clinton's strength, Hamilton, assisted on a few occasions by John Jay and more elaborately by Madison, began to write articles in the press supporting the Constitution. The various essays written by these three under the pseudonym "Publius" put forward almost every conceivable argument in support of the Constitution. Later published as *The Federalist,* these articles provide the leading commentary on the Constitution by its contemporary advocates and are the most important American contribution to the literature of political theory. The *Federalist* papers did not create a landslide for the Constitution in New York, however, for there the Federalist victory was the narrowest of all. News of the Federalist successes in New Hampshire and Virginia did influence New York, since it changed the issue from creating a new union to joining one that seemed almost certain to be established. And—once again—the promise of amendments overcame some of the opposition. Having agreed to support amendments for a bill of rights, the Federalists finally won on July 26 by the narrow margin of 30 to 27.

Rhode Island and North Carolina were so hostile to the Constitution that they did not join the Union until after the new government was already in operation. North Carolina, by a wide margin, decided to join in November, 1789; but Rhode Island, always reluctant to take part in interstate efforts, held out until May, 1790, and even then made her decision to enter only by the narrowest of margins.

It was now assured that the federal experiment would be tried, and that the Antifederalists had lost. But again and again they had succeeded in raising one persistent doubt about the Constitution. Why did it not contain a guarantee of the rights of the people, as almost all of the state constitutions did? Why was there no bill of rights to assure freedom of religion, speech, and the press, security against unreasonable searches and seizures and excessive bail, jury trials in criminal prosecutions, and to guarantee life, liberty, or property through due process of law? This was a hard question to answer. In the Convention a bill of rights had been suggested only in the closing days, by George Mason. And most of the delegates seem to have agreed with Roger Sherman, who stated that a bill of rights was unnecessary because these guarantees already existed in the state constitutions—after all, there had been no bill of rights in the Articles of Confederation. But the Articles had left the basic powers of government in the hands of the states, whereas the Constitution transferred most of them to the federal government. Many men wanted explicit guarantees against such a powerful government, and the Antifederalists worked to have them included in the Constitution.

Many of the more flexible Federalist leaders in Massachusetts, Virginia, New York, and elsewhere also realized that the framers had made a serious omission in failing to include a bill of rights. In fact they reassured the opposition in the ratifying conventions by promising to support measures to correct this oversight. It was to redeem this promise that James Madison arose in the first Congress to introduce the proposals for the first ten amendments, which finally became the Constitution's Bill of Rights.

The Meaning of Ratification.

Over 40 years ago, the distinguished historian, Charles A. Beard, tried to show that the vote for and against the ratification of the Constitution took place along class and sectional lines. Speculators, men with large holdings in public securities, and other investors favored the proposal, Beard wrote, while the frontiersmen, small farmers, and debtors opposed it. The bitter struggle that raged over the Constitution, he argued, was won by the Federalists against the wishes of the majority largely because so many of the opponents were disfranchised and because the Federalists were better organized and better educated, more aware of their interests, and better able to act together.

More than a generation of further re-search has made it clear that the simple lines of division set forth in Beard's pioneer work cannot be sustained. A great many historical forces were at work, and no historian has been able to formulate a simple theory that fully explains the action of a single important state, to say nothing of the action of all the states taken together. In the Virginia ratifying convention, to give but one instance, the Antifederalists were, as a social group, pretty much the same sort of people as the Federalists—so far as landholdings, slaveholdings, military offices held, and other measurable qualities go. So no simple economic or historical explanations of the division between them will hold. Again, in Massachusetts, we might expect the former Shaysites to have been vigorous opponents of ratification, and it is true that the delegates from a number of counties in the center of the state did oppose it. But the delegates from almost all the Shaysite territory north and west of Springfield voted in favor of ratification. Finally, although the great financial center of New York City supported the Constitution, as we would expect if Beard's thesis was sound, the predominantly agricultural state of New Jersey was just as strong in the support it gave to the new system of government.

Nor was the struggle waged over democratic principles. In the public debates over the merits of the Constitution, many Antifederalists attacked the Constitution as an effort to restrict democracy, to thwart the popular will, and to subvert popular liberties. But recent research has shown that leading Antifederalists—among them George Mason and Elbridge Gerry—were as skeptical about the merits of democracy as the Federalists were. The Constitution was not framed in a democratic age, but the participation of the common man in political decisions was as advanced in the American states as it was anywhere; and there is every evidence that none of the leading elements in American society were willing to accept unrestrained popular decision. In assigning the people a voice through their own branch of the legislature, the framers of the Constitution had gone about as far as most men of property and learning were willing to go toward democracy.

It is possible, though not certain, that the Constitution was accepted by the majority of those who cared about political matters. The election of members of the ratifying conventions was thrown open to a very extensive electorate—everyone was allowed to vote who satisfied the minimum qualifications for the election of state officers.* Although we do not know what the popular vote on the Constitution was, we do know the votes of the delegates the people chose. In the 11 states that ratified the Constitution before it went into effect, the elected delegates voted 844 to 467 to adopt it. Many of them were uninstructed, and it is impossible to know whether they voted the wishes of their constituents. Some of them were simply endorsed as trusted representatives and went to the conventions to make up their own minds. And some of them, following the distinguished example of Edmund Randolph, changed their minds in the course of the debates.

Had all adult males been able to vote, would the opposition to the Constitution have been more powerful? It is impossible to know for sure, for a wider electorate may have meant simply that the proportion of non-voters would have been greater. Despite all the emphasis that historians have put upon the bitterness and the closeness of the contest, the fact remains that, as Robert E. Brown has pointed out, "the Constitution was adopted with a great show of indifference." Although some men felt the issue keenly and discussed it hotly with their neighbors, many people who had the right

to go to the polls and vote did not care to do so. They had not yet developed a lively interest in political matters outside their own states. In Philadelphia, for example, the voting turnout was only a fraction of what it had been years before in a hotly contested local election. In Massachusetts, the vote was smaller than it had been in the relatively exciting Bowdoin-Hancock election that followed Shays' Rebellion. Perhaps part of the explanation is that the ordinary citizen in the American states was not yet a very active political man, and he had a tendency to trust, to an extraordinary degree, the judgment of the established political leaders.

Moreover, alongside those who felt strongly on one side of the issue or the other, there were a great many men of lukewarm sentiments, perhaps a bit skeptical of the experiment in federal union but willing to give it a try. Many may have agreed with young John Quincy Adams, who wrote in his diary when he heard that his state had ratified the Constitution:

In this town [Newburyport, Mass.] the satisfaction is almost universal; for my own part, I have not been pleased with this system.... But I am now converted, though not convinced. My feelings upon the occasion have not been passionate nor violent; and, as upon the decision of this question I find myself on the weaker side, I think it my duty to submit without murmuring against what is not to be helped.

Perhaps all that we can say with full confidence is that the Constitution had been conceived, drawn up, and promoted by an extraordinary generation of political leaders; that, for all the controversy their work stirred up, these leaders had persuaded the politically active public to make a drastic change in the structure of their government without violence, without bloodshed, without coercion; and finally that these leaders were given an ample opportunity to show that the Constitution which had been won on paper could now be made to work in actuality.

* Except in New York, where manhood suffrage was allowed, and in Connecticut, where all voters in town meetings were permitted to vote.

Readings

The classic commentary on the Constitution is *The Federalist,* written in 1787 and 1788 by Alexander Hamilton, James Madison, and John Jay, and since reprinted in innumerable editions. The view that conditions under the Confederation were bad to the point of being extremely critical for the country is developed by John Fiske in *The Critical Period of American History* (1888), an old but interesting and well-written book. A more recent scholarly work, *The New Nation,* by Merrill Jensen (1950), develops the idea that conditions were not as bad as the proponents of the Constitution claimed. Jensen's work derives from Charles A. Beard's outstanding scholarly monograph, *An Economic Interpretation of the Constitution of the United States* (1913). For an extremely close and hostile critique of Beard, see Robert E. Brown, *Charles Beard and the Constitution* (1956). For another view that differs from Beard's see Charles Warren, *The Making of the Constitution* (1928). The most substantial general account of the Confederation period is Allan Nevins, *The American States During and After the Revolution, 1775-1789* (1924). The state of American business under the Articles is described in Robert A. East, *Business Enterprise in the American Revolutionary Era* (1938). On the problems of the West, see Beverly W. Bond, Jr., *The Civilization of the Old Northwest* (1934), and Arthur P. Whitaker, *The Spanish American Frontier, 1783-1795* (1927).

Two good introductions to the making of the Constitution are Robert L. Schuyler, *The Constitution of the United States* (1923), and Carl Van Doren, *The Great Rehearsal* (1948). Leading biographies of proponents of the Constitution include Irving Brant, *James Madison: The Nationalist, 1780-1787* (1948), and *James Madison: Father of the Constitution, 1787-1800* (1950), two parts of a many-volume life of Madison; Nathan Schachner, *Alexander Hamilton* (1946); and Frank Monaghan, *John Jay* (1935). Interesting accounts of opponents of the Constitution include E. W. Spaulding, *His Excellency George Clinton, Critic of the Constitution* (1938), and Helen Hill, *George Mason, Constitutionalist* (1938).

The spirit of the Constitution and its makers is best revealed in *Records of the Federal Convention,* edited by Max Farrand (4 vols., 1911-1937); and the spirit of its reception among the people is shown in *The Debates of the Several State Conventions on the Adoption of the Federal Constitution,* edited by Jonathan Elliot (5 vols., 1836-1845). Among the state studies which shed light on the ratification process, see F. G. Bates, *Rhode Island and the Formation of the Union* (1898); R. L. Brunhouse, *The Counter-Revolution in Pennsylvania, 1776-1790* (1942); S. B. Harding, *The Contest over Ratification of the Federal Constitution in the State of Massachusetts* (1896); C. H. Ambler, *Sectionalism in Virginia from 1776 to 1851* (1910); J. B. McMaster and F. D. Stone, *Pennsylvania and the Federal Constitution, 1787-1788;* L. I. Trenholme, *The Ratification of the Federal Constitution in North Carolina* (1932). See also O. G. Libby, *The Geographical Distribution of the Vote of the Thirteen States on the Federal Constitution, 1787-1788* (1894), for sectional aspects. On the bill of rights and its adoption, consult R. A. Rutland, *The Birth of the Bill of Rights, 1776-1791* (1955).

FEDERALISTS AND JEFFERSONIANS

CHAPTER SEVEN

March 4, 1789, was the date set for the assembling of the new Congress in New York City. At dawn, the guns at the Battery on the southern tip of Manhattan saluted the great day, and the city's church bells rang out. But it was an empty gesture. As late as March 30, a quorum of neither representatives nor senators had completed the rough journey to the capital. New York's old City Hall, at Broad and Wall streets, had been carefully remodeled under the supervision of the French architect, L'Enfant, and now, as Federal Hall, it stood ready for the lawmakers. Its elegance, one historian has said, "was enough to disturb the republican souls of members from the rural districts and the small towns." It was the emptiness of Federal Hall, however, that disturbed the Federalist leaders already in New York awaiting their tardy colleagues. "The people will forget the new government before it is born," moaned Fisher Ames of Boston, the conservative who had defeated Sam Adams for Congress.

I. THE NEW NATIONAL GOVERNMENT

The First Congress Meets. By April 1 the House of Representatives was ready to convene, and by April 6 the Senate had its quorum and could join the House in examining the ballots of the presidential electors. Washington, with 69 votes, was chosen president, and John Adams, second in the balloting with 34 votes, was named vice-president. After a triumphal journey from Mount Vernon, Washington arrived in New York on April 23, 1789. On April 30, with the sun shining on the gaily decorated streets, he was inaugurated.

The choice of New York as the first national capital gave a fillip to the already dashing social life of the country's second largest city. Madison's unhappiness over the "scanty proportion" of representatives "who will share in the drudgery of the business" was scarcely dispelled by the round of dinners, dances, and great balls that quickly caught up his colleagues. The sun shone on the American economy as brightly as it had on the inauguration. Overseas markets for Virginia tobacco, Carolina rice, Pennsylvania wheat, and New England fish had revived. A growing home market stimulated northern manufactures. New England shipbuilders were busy. The number of American merchantmen on the West Indian run—in either legitimate trade or smuggling—was nearing the prewar high. The port of New York, especially, hummed with European commerce and the beginnings of the China trade. New fortunes were reflected in the boisterousness and ostentation of the capital's entertainments.

Congress, nevertheless, got on with its business. The leaders of the first Congress were determined to make good—and to make a good impression. John Adams, for example, as President of the Senate, an office which Gouverneur Morris hoped would "show us the might of aristocracy," was so insistent upon dignified titles and procedure that the Antifederalists soon dubbed him "His Rotundity." This preoccupation with decorum made Congress seem almost ridiculous at first, but the need for getting down to more serious business soon sobered it up. The Constitution offered few suggestions on procedure, though it was clear enough on objectives, and the times were making their own persistent demands.

New York was the capital of what was still a weak nation—a nation beset by foreign and domestic debts, surrounded by enemies, harassed on its borders by hostile Indians, on the sea by bold pirates, and in foreign ports and foreign waters by unfriendly navies. Nor was there unity at home.

First Federalist Measures. During its very first session Congress dealt with each of the tasks the Constitution empowered it to handle. One of its earliest acts, however, was to pass and submit to the states, in September, 1789, the first ten amendments, constituting the promised Bill of Rights (see p. 136). These amendments were ratified by December, 1791.

The government's most urgent need was for money to cover its day-to-day expenses, and Madison hoped to raise the necessary funds by means of a modest tariff bill, which he submitted to the House of Representatives even before Washington was inaugurated. Debate, however, delayed its passage until July 4, 1789. In its final form, the act set up a tax of about 8½ per cent on the value of certain listed imports. But of course no revenue could be collected until inspectors, weighers, collectors, port surveyors, and other personnel had been appointed. The new tariff was designed to benefit American carriers as well as to bring money to the federal treasury. Goods imported in American ships were taxed at a rate 10 per cent lower than goods arriving in foreign ships. An act passed later in the year put tonnage duties of 6 cents per ton on American ships entering American ports and 50 cents per ton on foreign ships.

While the House was occupied with debate on the tariff, the Senate began to work on what was to become the Judiciary Act of September 24, 1789. This act helped cement the federal system by spelling out the procedure by which federal courts could review and, if necessary, declare void, state laws and state court decisions involving powers and duties delegated by the Constitution to the federal government. It also specified that the Supreme Court be manned by a chief justice and five associate justices. The system of federal courts was to be completed by three circuit courts and thirteen district courts. The circuit courts, when sitting, were to have a three-man bench consisting of two federal supreme court justices and one district court judge. The district courts, the lowest in the federal system, were to have but one judge. Attached to each district court were to be United States attorneys and their deputies to serve as federal prosecutors, and United States marshals and their deputies to serve as federal police.

The executive had been one of the weakest links in the old Confederation. Yet the three executive departments created under the Confederation in 1781—Foreign Affairs, Treasury, and War—continued for a time to function unchanged under the new government. Not until July, 1789, did Congress create the new Department of State to manage foreign relations. The new War Department was set up soon after; the Treasury not until September.

While the House and the Senate busied themselves with such basic measures, the President considered appointments to the positions he knew must be created. Washington wanted to surround himself with only

Federal Hall, Wall Street, New York City, 1789.

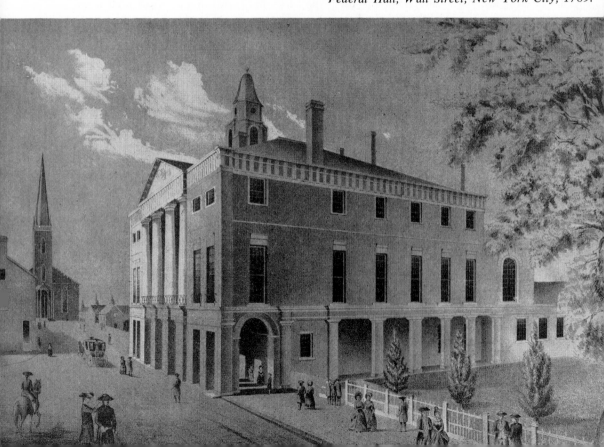

the best men available, but he preferred not to appoint an opponent of the Constitution even to a lesser office when a sympathizer could be found. Washington also considered it politically expedient to spread his appointments among the states. Thus General Henry Knox of Massachusetts, one of the army's most outspoken opponents of the old Congress, became Washington's Secretary of War. To Edmund Randolph of Virginia went the Attorney-Generalship. To the Treasury, Washington named Alexander Hamilton of New York. John Jay of New York, in charge of foreign affairs for the old Congress, continued to direct them until 1790, when Thomas Jefferson of Virginia took over. Jay himself became the first Chief Justice of the Supreme Court.

The Funding Program.

Near the end of the first session of Congress, Hamilton was asked to prepare fiscal reports for the session to begin in December, 1789. His first report, on the public credit, was ready on January 9, 1790. This one was followed the next December by his report on a national bank, and in 1791 he reported to the Second Congress on the mint and manufactures.

Hamilton felt that the people looked to the moneyed class for their natural leaders. Thus, he reasoned, if he could bind the capitalists to the new government, the whole nation would be firmly united. This objective had inspired his fight to supplant the old Articles, and it continued to influence his program under the new Constitution.

In his report on the public credit, Hamilton made three major recommendations: (1) that the foreign debt, of about $12 million, including arrears of interest, be repaid by means of a new bond issue; (2) that the domestic debt, made up of many kinds of Revolutionary securities valued in 1789 at about 25 cents on the dollar, be exchanged at its face value, plus back interest, for additional new bonds amounting to $40 million; (3) that the remaining state debts, totaling about $20 million, be assumed by the federal

government and refunded on a similar basis.

Congress enacted Hamilton's proposal for refunding the foreign debt with very little debate. His program for the domestic debt had much tougher going. The plan had become known to certain of his friends before he made his report, and by the time the House took up the bill to implement it, speculators in and out of Congress began surreptitiously buying up old bonds. Included in the issues to be refunded were the certificates with which the Revolutionary veterans had been paid. Large amounts of these certificates, along with other issues, were scattered throughout the hinterland. Eastern speculators dispatched fast boats and fast stages loaded with cash to beat the news to the back country, and there bought up for a song securities that were soon to go up in value. The Antifederalists, led by Madison, cried corruption; but they could offer only a cum-

The first cabinet. From left to right: Knox, Jefferson, Randolph, Hamilton, and Washington.

bersome, hastily prepared bill as an alternative to Hamilton's plan. Their efforts were wasted. Their bill was defeated, and Hamilton's plan won.

This refunding measure was acclaimed by the men in the cities who felt rich enough to share Hamilton's political philosophy or who at least had enough ready money to share its fruits. Most of the newspapers, and the churches and the universities which themselves had become holders of old bonds, supported Hamilton vociferously. The opposition was led by the South, where cash for speculation in securities was scarce.

The South was even more hostile to Hamilton's proposal that the federal government should assume responsibility for paying the state debts. Georgia, which had few debts, and Virginia, which had paid its debts through paper-money issues, objected to such a procedure. To these states, Hamilton's proposal meant that their citizens would be taxed again to pay off the debts of the northern states. When "assumption" came up for a vote in April, therefore, Congress defeated it. After many subsequent failures, Hamilton got Jefferson's support for the measure by offering to locate the new national capital in the South. Thus in July, 1790, "assumption," to the tune of $21,500,000 was approved by Congress. As part of Hamilton's deal, Philadelphia would be the seat of the capital for ten years, starting in 1790. A new site on the Potomac would be ready in 800.

Bank and Excises.   It is "a fundamental maxim, in the system of public credit of the United States," said Hamilton, "that the creation of debt should always be accompanied with the means of its extinguishment." But in practice Hamilton undertook to supply only the means for paying the interest, not the principal of the debt. He did not want to eliminate the bonds which were the moneyed classes' source of income and their collateral for further speculations. The annual interest

on all the new bonds averaged about $2 million yearly for the period 1791-1795, and came to nearly half the government's total expenditures for these years. The government could not raise even this small amount from the tariff of 1789, which was its main source of revenue. Thus, besides successfully urging an increase in the tariff, Hamilton made two more proposals. Both were adopted, but not without further factional strife.

The first of these proposals called for a national bank with a capital of $10 million, one-fifth to be subscribed by the government, the rest by private capitalists. The Federalists, opposed on principle to government paper money, planned to have the Treasury issue only minted gold and silver. Consequently, Hamilton argued that a bank was needed to supply notes that would serve as currency in business transactions; this bank would also assist the government in its short-term borrowing and would serve as a depository for government funds. Finally, by making personal loans, the bank would make it easier for individuals to pay their taxes.

"This plan for a national bank," objected Representative James Jackson of Georgia, "is calculated to benefit a small part of the United States, the mercantilist interests only; the farmers, the yeomanry, will derive no advantage from it." But Hamilton's bill passed the House, 39 to 20. Thirty-six of the favoring votes came from the commercial North, 19 of the opposing votes from the South. In February, 1791, the Bank of the United States was chartered for 20 years with headquarters in Philadelphia, and in December it opened. Ultimately, eight branches were established in port cities from Boston to New Orleans.

In the debate on this bill in the House, Madison argued that a national bank would be unconstitutional. The Constitutional Convention, he insisted, had expressly rejected the proposition that the federal government be empowered to charter companies. When the bill was sent to Washington for his signature, he asked Jefferson and Hamilton for their opinions on its constitutionality. Jefferson supported Madison. But Hamilton argued that since the government had been delegated the power to regulate currency, it had the "implied power" to establish a bank to issue that currency. Washington rejected the Virginians' "strict interpretation" of the Constitution in favor of Hamilton's "broad interpretation."

Hamilton's second proposal was for an excise tax on various commodities, including distilled liquors. This excise was enacted

Hamilton interpreted the uprising as a rebellion and persuaded Washington to lead 15,000 militiamen out to crush the farmers. Hamilton himself went along. Although they found no organized opposition, they captured about a hundred men. Two of them were later convicted of treason and sentenced to death, but eventually they were pardoned by Washington.

Tarred and feathered tax collector, during the Whiskey Rebellion.

in 1791. "The mode of taxation was odious, unequal, unpopular, and oppressive, more particularly in the Southern states," said Representative Jackson. Opposition to the taxes became most violent in western Pennsylvania, where, to save transportation costs on bulky grain, back-country farmers often converted it into whiskey. To the people in this and other regions where hard money was scarce, whiskey had actually become a medium of exchange, and the tax on whiskey seemed to be a tax on money itself. In 1792, Congress relented sufficiently to exempt small stills from the levy. Collections in 1793, however, were spotty, and the next year additional collectors were sent out. The upshot was the so-called "Whiskey Rebellion" of 1794, in which western Pennsylvania farmers attacked the new Federalist jobholders and threatened federal marshals and judges.

The Federalist Crisis. Hamilton's blueprint for converting the United States into a powerful industrial nation was his celebrated Report on Manufactures, sent to Congress in December, 1791. In it he urged the value of industry to the community, and the need for protective tariffs, subsidies, and other aids while industry was in its infancy. Congress gave the report a cold reception.

The merchants in whose hands the money of the country was concentrated remained cool to industrial enterprise for another quarter of a century. For longer than that they opposed protective tariffs, which they felt only taxed and troubled trade. Many merchants joined with the farmers, who also felt unjustifiably taxed, and both groups became increasingly suspicious of Hamilton as more and more of the country's funds were tied up in speculation in the government's new securities. In the spring of 1792, Hamilton's bosom friend, William Duer, described by Madison as "the prince of the tribe of speculators," failed and went to a debtor's cell. Since Duer's bankruptcy left others unable to meet their obligations, many businessmen were ruined. The farmers at the same time were having difficulties of their own, for excellent harvests in Europe had reduced both the demand and the prices for American exports. Businessmen and farmers both blamed Hamilton and the Federalist program for their plight.

To make matters worse, the Federalist administration was having international troubles as well. In the Southwest, Spain continued to contest the Florida border as defined in the Treaty of Paris (see p. 110), and kept pressure on Washington's administration by refusing to open the Mississippi at New Orleans to western shipping. In the Northwest, England continued to hold military posts and to use them to help Canadian fur-trappers against American entrepreneurs. Spain and England, moreover, did nothing to restrain the Indians from systematically molesting American frontiersmen. This situation, coupled with the failure of Washington's own efforts to deal with the Indians on American territory, was doubly depressing to settlers on the borders who had looked to a strong central government for protection.

In 1790, Washington had invited Alexander McGillivray, a half-breed Creek who led the tribes of the Southwest, to come to New York. Here a treaty was drawn up by which McGillivray agreed, in exchange for a substantial yearly pension, to keep peace on the frontier. He abided by this treaty only as long as it took him to get back to Tennessee, where bloodshed was promptly resumed. In the Northwest, Washington tried to use force against the Indians, but with no more

Population Density 1790

Center of Population

Persons per square mile:
☐ Less than 2
◼ Over 90

success than he had won with diplomacy. In 1790 in the Ohio country, the Indians ambushed General Harmer and 1,500 militiamen. In 1791, Governor St. Clair of the Northwest Territory suffered a worse fate. Most of his 2,000 ill-equipped and untrained men deserted even before they had met any Indians, and the rest were trapped and had to run for their lives. It was not until 1794, in the Battle of Fallen Timbers, that the well-prepared General "Mad Anthony" Wayne routed the northwestern tribes, and not until 1795, by the Treaty of Fort Greenville, did these tribes yield most of their Ohio land. At about the same time, local action by John Sevier and James Robertson (see p. 121) quieted the southwestern tribes. The Treaty of Fort Greenville won for the Federalists much less favor on the frontier than their earlier failures had cost them. And for the accomplishments of Sevier and Robertson, the Federalists got no credit at all.

II. THE ORIGINS AND ISSUES OF PARTY POLITICS

Hamilton's ambition for America was greater than that of most of his followers, and his vision far exceeded theirs. Yet his agrarian opponents outstripped him in both ambition and vision. Hamilton had no respect for the men who were opening up the vast reaches of the new country. He despised farmers, and he hated westerners as troublemakers. In his plan to unify the nation, he assigned to both groups inferior roles. In less than a decade after the start of the new government, however, the majority who lived on the land had shown that they counted for more than the minority in the cities, and that votes counted for more than wealth. Thus Hamilton's program and that of the Federalists did not enjoy a very long life. And without Washington's support, it would not have lasted as long as it did.

Rise of the Republican Party.

Political parties in America did not spring into being; we cannot assign specific dates to their beginnings. But the issue of the Constitution divided the country, and during the first years of the new government factional leaders tried to strengthen the opinions and mobilize the votes of the opposing groups. The Federalists at first enjoyed great advantages. Above all, they had a strong, clear program and, in Hamilton, a resourceful, energetic, and uncompromising leader. Most of the well-educated, wealthy men in the country were Federalists; so were most of the newspaper editors, clergymen, and other makers of opinion. Hamilton showed, too, that the Federalists controlled the army, and were quite willing to make use of it. A readymade network of chambers of commerce, units of the Society of Cincinnati, and other going organizations worked for Federalism on the local level, and the party quickly developed a grassroots patronage system to give sine-cures to local party workers. Even in the First Congress, Federalist leaders caucused and corresponded on platforms, candidates, and campaigns as though they were members of an organized machine.

Far from uniting the country, Hamilton's program only heightened existing antagonisms. Every Hamiltonian measure was essentially a northeastern measure: funding, assumption, the national bank, the excise, protective tariffs—all served to divide the South from the North, the West from the East. Every Hamiltonian measure was a capitalist's measure that alienated debtors from creditors, even in the Northeast. Every Hamiltonian attitude was an aristocratic attitude that pleased the "gentlemen of principle and property" and offended the "people of no particular importance."

Jefferson, as much as Hamilton, sought stability and dignity for the new government, but he believed that men "habituated to think for themselves"—American yeomen, in short—were much easier to govern than men (usually city-dwellers, he thought) who were "debased by ignorance, indigence, and oppression." By 1791, Jefferson was convinced that Hamilton and his "corrupt squadron" menaced the country, and he wrote Washington to say so. By then, Jefferson, with Madison's support, had worked out a plan to save the United States in his own way.

To no other people, said a traveler about Americans at this time, were the "smiles and frowns of political government" of so little consequence. How right he was is shown by the vote: hardly one-fourth of those eligible had voted for delegates to the state conventions to ratify the Constitution; the percentage voting for representatives to the First Congress was still smaller. Jefferson's approach to getting out the vote was to teach the people what might happen if they exercised their political rights.

Thomas Jefferson, life mask, at age 82.

"If left to me to decide whether we should have a government without newspapers, or newspapers without a government," Jefferson once wrote, "I should not hesitate for a moment to prefer the latter." He had disapproved of the secrecy of the Constitutional Convention, and his first step in the looming party battle was to enlist the best man available to keep the public informed of what he believed to be the plot of the victors at the Convention. This man proved to be the poet, Philip Freneau, who had been Madison's classmate at Princeton. In October, 1791, Freneau issued the first number of the *National Gazette,* a new Antifederalist paper published in Philadelphia, which was now the capital. Freneau so quickly took the play away from John Fenno, the editor of the Hamiltonian *United States Gazette,* that Hamilton felt obliged to enter the newspaper battle himself.

Serious Antifederalist party work began late in the winter of 1791-1792, when Madison wrote a series of articles for the *National Gazette* in which he gradually developed the position of "the Republican party, as it may be termed."

But Jefferson needed more than a newspaper in the capital from which sympathetic journals in other sections might echo Madison's resounding articles. He needed allies, local lieutenants, grass-roots clubs, and candidates who could afford the time and money to campaign and hold office. Madison, Jefferson's closest ally, often took the lead himself. Others who were soon enlisted included Governor Clinton of New York, who, in opposition to General Schuyler, Hamilton's rich father-in-law, controlled the upstate vote; and Aaron Burr of New York City (Clinton had recently helped Burr defeat Schuyler for the Senate), whose followers in the Society of Tammany, a drinking club and benevolent association, already were hungering for patronage. In Boston, Dr. Charles Jarvis, a protégé of old Sam Adams and John Hancock, led the Jeffersonians. In Philadelphia, the scientists Benjamin Rush, David Rittenhouse, and George Logan joined the Jeffersonian forces, as did many upstate politicos like Thomas Mifflin, Alexander Dallas, and William Maclay. They were soon joined by the brilliant young Swiss, Albert Gallatin, who had settled on the frontier in western Pennsylvania in 1784. John Francis Mercer in Maryland; Willie Jones in North Carolina; James Jackson in Georgia; and James Monroe, John Taylor of Caroline, and William Giles, all of Virginia, filled out the officers' corps of Jefferson's and Madison's new party.

The Republican party was too young to run a presidential candidate in the election of 1792, and in any event its leaders preferred Washington to any other candidate. The Federalists, in turn, were far from ready to risk going on without the President. So Jefferson and Hamilton together persuaded Washington to run again. Once more Washington was elected unanimously; the Republicans, however, had the satisfaction of throwing a scare into the Vice-president, John Adams. Their candidate, Governor Clinton, carried the great states of Virginia and New York, together with North Carolina and Georgia. All told, Clinton polled 50 electoral votes to Adams' 77.

Abroad and at Home.

During Washington's first administration, party lines had been clearly drawn over financial issues and difficulties on the frontier. In his second administration, problems of foreign policy, as Colonel Higginson of Massachusetts said, "not merely divided parties, but moulded them; gave them their demarcations, their watchwords, and their bitterness." Some of these problems were carry-overs from the war with England. But the French Revolution, which began just a few weeks after Washington first took office in 1789, was the source of most of the trouble.

At first, Americans everywhere welcomed the French Revolution. In 1790, when Lafayette sent the key to the Bastille to Washington, the President acknowledged it as a "token of victory gained by liberty over despotism." A year later, the Hamiltonians had aligned themselves with Edmund Burke's condemnatory *Reflections on the Revolution in France,* and the Jeffersonians championed Tom Paine's libertarian response, *The Rights of Man.* The events of the French Revolution prompted John Adams to publish his *Discourses on Davila* in 1791, in which he insisted that nature had made men vain and selfish, and that this was a fact politicians could not safely ignore in setting up governments. The execution of Louis XVI in January, 1793, disgusted most American conservatives, and the Jacobin "reign of terror" that followed confirmed their deepest misgivings about excessive democracy. In the meantime, the French wars against the continental monarchs, who had combined to end the threat of republicanism, had begun in 1792, and early in 1793 they spread to England and Spain.

For weeks, westerly gales kept news of the executions and the wars from reaching America. When all the news flooded in at once, in April, 1793, it strengthened the Hamiltonians in their stand against France. The Jeffersonians, on the other hand, held to their hatred of monarchs and monarchy and voiced their confidence in the people of France against the autocrats of Britain.

News of the French war with England heightened the conflict in American opinion. More important, it created a dispute over foreign policy. The old French treaty of 1778 (see p. 106) provided that the United States must defend the French West Indies in case of an attack on France herself, and also that American ports must receive prizes captured at sea by French privateers and men-of-war. The Girondists, who ruled revolutionary France in 1792, assumed that this treaty remained in force, as indeed it did, and they sent "Citizen" Edmond Genêt as envoy to America to see that it was carried out. Genêt had other instructions as well. He was to organize expeditions from America to detach Louisiana and Florida from Spain, and to outfit American privateers to prey upon British shipping. These enterprises were to be financed with American funds made available by a speed-up in American payments on the old French loan (see p. 112).

Genêt, an attractive and enterprising young man, landed in Charleston, South Carolina, a pro-French stronghold, on April 8, 1793, and, after a warm welcome, went right to work without bothering to present his credentials to the government in Philadelphia. By the time he arrived at the capital, Washington, after consulting Jefferson and Hamilton, had issued his Neutrality Proclamation of April 22, making it clear that the United States would not participate in the French wars. Jefferson had argued that the treaty of 1778 was with the French nation, whatever its government might be, and this interpretation was strictly true in international law. He also urged that since only Congress could declare war, only Congress could proclaim neutrality. Thus a presidential proclamation of neutrality was unconstitutional. He felt, too, that if such a proclamation were actually issued, England should be forced to make certain commercial concessions in return. Hamilton, on the contrary, held that the French treaty had died with the French king, and that neutrality in any case was the only feasible American policy. Jefferson did not persist, and Washington's proclamation followed.

By this time, Genêt had already commissioned enthusiastic Charleston ship captains as French privateers to prey on British shipping; he had also organized a South Carolina military adventure against Spain in Florida, and had induced George Rogers Clark and other Kentuckians to float down the Mississippi and dislodge the Spanish from New Orleans, a mission dear to Kentuckian hearts. The warmth of Genêt's reception had convinced him that the people were with him, whatever the government might do. Thus when Washington received Genêt with forbidding coldness and gave him to understand that the government would no longer tolerate his operations, let alone abet them under the old treaty, Genêt decided to ignore the President and proceed with his revolutionary work on his own.

Even Jefferson was put out by this persistence, and when Genêt, contrary to Washington's express warnings, allowed the *Little Democrat,* a prize ship converted into an armed vessel, to sail as a privateer, Jefferson voted with the President and the rest of the Cabinet to ask for Genêt's recall. By then, Genêt's group had fallen out of favor at home and, fearing for his life, the young envoy decided to remain in America. He married Governor Clinton's daughter and retired to a country estate on the Hudson. The new French administration then sent over a less amateurish representative.

The Profits and Problems of Neutrality.

The war in Europe greatly increased the belligerents' need for food and other materials, and at the same time tied up the commercial ships that might have brought in the needed supplies. This situation opened the way for a boom in the carrying trade of neutrals; as a leading maritime nation, the United States was among the greatest gainers. Since the French, particularly, had only a small fleet, painfully

vulnerable to British attack, they desperately needed neutral assistance. Early in the war, France at last surrendered her monopoly of the French West Indian trade and opened the islands' ports to American ships and American produce—a turn of events that gave great impetus to American commerce.

The British, determined to monopolize world shipping and especially to keep the late rebels down, retaliated quickly. Trade, according to them, was simply an arm of war. They resurrected the "rule of the War of 1756," which held that trade barred to a nation in peacetime could not with impunity be opened to it during hostilities. This meant, specifically, the French West Indian trade. In November, 1793, they decreed that all shipping to or from the French colonies would be subject to British seizure. The Americans had by then swarmed into the Caribbean to serve the French islands, and the British seized about 300 American vessels, abused their passengers, and forced many of their sailors into the British navy.

Even so, American trade continued to flourish. Many ships were captured, but many more slipped through with profits that more than compensated for the great risks involved. And ship losses served as a stimulus to the ship-building industry. By 1794, however, the British had become so brazen that even the Federalists expected war. The United States insisted that neutral ships made neutral goods, but the British enforced the right to search for enemy supplies anywhere in any ship. The United States insisted that a blockade, to be effective, must be enforced by actual patrols of the closed ports. But the British simply announced "paper blockades" and undertook to enforce them on the oceans wherever they found a vessel presumably bound for a forbidden harbor. Food, the United States insisted most firmly, could not be classified as contraband. But the British were more realistic and did not hesitate to capture as prizes ships sailing with food for France and her allies.

Painful as these British measures were to Federalist shippers, it was the Republicans who made the most of them by labeling them affronts by hated monarchists to the American flag. Recalling how effective commercial retaliation had been against the British in the great days of the Revolution, the Republicans now demanded an embargo to keep British ships out of American ports and American ships off the seas, where they were subject to British seizure.

As if to keep American memories fresh, the British in Canada chose this time to incite the Indians to raid the Ohio country, where thousands of Americans were settling. The British also made it clear that they had no intention of relinquishing their armed posts on American territory, which were giving assistance and encouragement to the Indians. Public opinion, aroused over the hot issues of trade and territory, forced the Republicans' embargo through Congress in 1794. It remained in effect for two months.

Jay's Treaty. This action hurt the Federalist merchants' own trade as much as it did British commerce, and when the British, in March, 1794, revoked the harshest of their rules for neutrals, the Federalists decided to resort to diplomacy. On April 16, 1794, Washington named John Jay, now Chief Justice, to go to England and settle the main differences between the two countries. Jay was instructed (1) to get the British to surrender their military posts in the Northwest, (2) to pay for American ships that had been captured illegally, and, (3) to accept and respect the American position on the rights and privileges of neutrals. Jay was also to negotiate the best commercial treaty he could. Failing to get the British to agree on all these points, Jay was to try to get the northern countries of Europe to agree jointly to enforce the rights of neutrals.

Jay had a good case, and the British needed American friendship. But Hamilton nullified these advantages when he informed Hammond, the British minister in New York, that whatever Jay accomplished or failed to accomplish, the United States would not make war on Britain. Hammond lost no time in conveying this information to the British negotiators. The result was an uphill fight for Jay and a very unsatisfactory agreement.

By the Treaty of London (completed on November 19, 1794, and henceforth known in America as Jay's Treaty), the British agreed once more to evacuate their posts in the Northwest, and by 1796 had actually left. But Jay had to barter away a great deal in return. The British could still carry on the fur trade on the American side of the Canadian border and they could still trade with the Indians who were hostile to advancing American settlement. These concessions almost nullified the surrender of the posts and hardly pleased the westerners, who had remained suspicious of Jay ever since his negotiations with Gardoqui (see p. 124). As for the British paying for captured ships, settlement of this issue was left to a future joint commission which would determine what, if anything, was owed. On the rights of neutrals, Jay failed altogether. The Treaty of London said nothing that would keep the British from continuing to stop and search all ships on the seas and to impress their crews at will. The treaty also left the British the privilege of defining contraband goods as best suited their purposes.

Jay's efforts to get commercial concessions were equally abortive. The treaty did assert the so-called "most-favored-nation" principle, by which American goods entering British home ports and British goods entering American ports were to be treated on the same terms as the goods of the nation having the most favorable commercial agreement with each. But the jewel of the British empire, so far as American merchants were concerned, was the British West Indies, and here Jay made his most objectionable arrangement. For the privilege of visiting Indies ports (a privilege limited to small American ships of no more than 70 tons), American cargoes of molasses, coffee, cocoa, sugar, and cotton—the only worth-while British West Indian commodities—had to be carried directly to American ports. World trade in these commodities was denied to American merchants, but the British could continue to carry them anywhere, including American ports. The Senate forced the removal of this provision before it would ratify the treaty.

Jay's whole agreement was so unsatisfactory that Washington hesitated a long time before he even sent it to the Senate. The Senate, in turn, made every effort to keep the terms from the people lest the call for war against Britain become too strong to withstand. The terms did leak out before the treaty was ratified by the Senate on June 25, 1795, by the slenderest possible two-thirds majority. The public response was as expected, and in the intervening months "Sir John Jay" was hanged in effigy throughout the country.

Pinckney's Treaty.   Jay's Treaty did improve American relations with Spain, which by 1795 had withdrawn from the British coalition against the French Revolution. The sight of Americans making peaceable though unsatisfactory agreements with England prompted Spain to try to win the United States to her own side. The result was the Treaty of San Lorenzo, of October, 1795, negotiated by Thomas Pinckney, the American minister in Madrid, and usually referred to in America as Pinckney's Treaty. This agreement settled the northern boundary of Florida at the latitude of 31 degrees. Much more important, Spain consented to open the Mississippi "in its whole length from its source to the ocean" to American traffic and to allow Americans the free use of the port of New Orleans for three years, after which time the arrangement could be renewed.

III.   JOHN ADAMS' ADMINISTRATION

The Election of 1796.   Washington had been so serious about not running again in 1792 that he had asked Madison and others to draw up ideas for a "Farewell Address" to the nation upon his retirement. Early in 1796 he resurrected these papers and turned them over to Hamilton (who had resigned from the Cabinet in 1795) with a request for a new draft. Nothing could deter Washington from leaving his high office. He looked with dismay on the "baneful effects of the spirit of party," but at the same time he took keen satisfaction in many of his accomplishments.

Washington did not deliver his Farewell Address in person; on September 17, 1796, he simply published it in the newspapers. He noted as a "matter of serious concern that any ground should have been furnished for characterizing parties by *geographical* discriminations—*Northern* and *Southern, Atlantic* and *Western.*" In much of his address he urged upon the country the need for preserving "the unity of government which

constitutes you one people." Only toward the end did he discuss foreign affairs; nowhere was there an admonition against all "entangling alliances." Washington actually said:

The great rule of conduct for us in regard to foreign nations is, in extending our commercial relations to have with them as little *political* connection as possible. ... It is our true policy to steer clear of permanent alliances with any portion of the foreign world. ... Taking care always to keep ourselves ... on a respectable defensive posture, we may safely trust to temporary alliances for extraordinary emergencies.

The party strife that Washington deplored was nearing its peak when he retired. The debate in the House over Jay's Treaty had continued well into 1796, and Washington's own decision intensified the conflict by opening up the highest office to the rising political machines. The Federalists had considered Jay as a candidate, but the furor over the treaty killed his chances. The widespread satisfaction with the Treaty of San Lorenzo, on the other hand, made Thomas **Pinckney** a plausible choice. In the end, the Federalists brought out a ticket of John Adams of New England and Pinckney of South Carolina. The Republicans named Jefferson as their standard-bearer, and Aaron Burr of New York for vice-president.

Hamilton and Adams had long since grown cool toward each other, and Hamilton maneuvered to get Pinckney elected president. But his elaborate scheme backfired. Not only did Adams, with 71 votes, win the presidency, but Jefferson, with 68 votes, was second in the balloting and defeated Pinckney for the vice-presidency.

John Adams'
Foreign Policy.

The French had taken much less kindly than the Spanish to Jay's Treaty; bad as it was, they saw in it a leaning of the United States toward the enemy across the English Channel. As a result, the French intensified their attacks on American shipping bound for British ports. By the time of Adams' inauguration in March, 1797, the French had captured about 300 American ships and had manhandled their crews. In the meantime, Washington had recalled the francophile minister, James Monroe, for having told the French first that Jay's Treaty would never be ratified, and then that it would never become operative because Washington would be defeated in the forthcoming election. Washington replaced Monroe with Charles C. Pinckney, whom the French never accepted. Indeed, after Pinckney had been in France the two months allowed to foreigners, the French police notified him that unless he got a permit to remain they would arrest him. He fled to Amsterdam in a rage. By the time news of Pinckney's treatment reached Philadelphia, Adams had become president and the Federalists were clamoring for war with the brutal French.

Adams withstood their demands, but, without querying the French government, decided as one of his first presidential measures to send a three-man mission to France

to get the French to stop their raids on American shipping. Pinckney, ordered back to France, was joined in Paris by the Federalist, John Marshall, and the Republican, Elbridge Gerry. Talleyrand, foreign minister of the Directory that was then running France, was willing to negotiate, but he affronted the Americans by first sending three subordinates to them to seek a bribe of $250,000 in return for his favor. The Americans drew themselves up, wrote out a statement of their position, and sent it to Talleyrand. Gerry's Federalist colleagues now left Paris. Gerry stayed on to parley with Talleyrand, and came home only when Adams demanded that he cease dallying with the revolutionists.

In their correspondence, the American envoys had referred to Talleyrand's three subordinates as X, Y, and Z. When the correspondence became public, an uproar broke out among the partisans of both parties over the so-called "X.Y.Z. Dispatches." Someone cried, "Millions for defense, but not one cent for tribute," a slogan that Pinckney is erroneously supposed to have flung at Talleyrand's emissaries. Congress, with Republican cooperation, did vote millions for the expansion of the army and navy in 1798 and 1799; it also created a separate Navy Department and repealed all treaties with the French. The new army materialized very slowly, to the chagrin of Hamilton, who was aching to lead it into battle. In the next two years, however, the new Navy Department pushed to completion three well-armed frigates that had been under construction, produced 20 other ships of war, and let loose hundreds of American privateers to prey upon the French.

In 1798 and 1799, an "undeclared naval war" raged with France in which American ships took almost a hundred French vessels, though they suffered numerous losses themselves. To the consternation of Hamilton's friends, Adams steadfastly refused to make any use of the army or to ask Congress to make the French war official.

The Alien and

Sedition Acts. At the time of Adams' election, Madison had written to Jefferson: "You know the temper of Mr. A. better than I do, but I have always conceived it to be rather a ticklish one." One thing Adams soon became most "ticklish" about was the Republican taunt that he was "President by three votes." Other partisan attacks on him and his administration aroused him, early in the summer of 1798, to strike out at his detractors.

Adams might easily have overcome his pique; but when the most violent men of his party pushed through Congress a series of measures known as the Alien and Sedition Acts in June and July, 1798, the President grasped the weapons so gratuitously presented. The first of these measures was a Naturalization Act which raised the residence requirement for American citizenship from five to fourteen years. The next two were the Alien Act, which empowered the president in peacetime to order any alien from the country, and to jail for not more than three years any alien who refused to go; and the Alien Enemies Act, by which, in wartime, the president could jail enemy aliens at his pleasure. No arrests were made under either of these acts, but they did scare hundreds of foreigners out of the country.

The fourth measure was the Sedition Act. Its key clause provided severe fines and jail penalties for anyone speaking, writing, or publishing "with intent to defame . . . or bring into contempt or disrepute" the president or other members of the government. Matthew Lyon, an outspoken Irish-born Republican congressman from Vermont, was the first to be jailed under the Sedition Act. During his prison term of four months, his constituents re-elected him. All told, Federalist judges jailed and fined 70 men. Almost all these victims were Republican editors, and many Republican papers had to close down.

Madison called the Sedition Act "a monster that must forever disgrace its parents."

He and Jefferson both recognized it as the start of the Federalist campaign for the presidential elections of 1800, and they quickly set in motion a broad-gauged attack on the whole Federalist philosophy. Their offensive took the form of a series of resolutions for which their allies won the approval of the legislatures of Kentucky and Virginia in November and December, 1798. The resolutions were then circulated among the rest of the states.

Jefferson wrote the Kentucky Resolutions, Madison those adopted in Virginia. Both sets attacked the Hamiltonian "broad interpretation" of the Constitution and developed the solid state rights position that later was used as a justification for nullification and secession. In Jefferson's words, "the several states composing the United States of America, are not united on the principle of unlimited submission to their general government"; that government, in Madison's terms, is but a "compact to which the states are parties." The Kentucky Resolution held that, as parties to the "compact," the states had the right to declare what measures went beyond their agreement and were "unauthoritative, void, and of no force," and to decide what remedies were appropriate. Madison, in the Virginia Resolutions, said that the states together might "interpose" to check the exercise of unauthorized powers. Jefferson, in his Kentucky Resolutions, went even further: he held that the *legislature of each individual state* had this right.

The Election of 1800.

Republican prospects for the election of 1800 were brightened by the growing split in Federalist ranks between the peace-minded Adams men and the Hamiltonians, whose leader still hungered for military glory in a war against France. The Hamiltonians berated Adams most fiercely when, in 1799, the President, on learning that Talleyrand was ready to talk peace, named another three-man commission to negotiate. The commissioners were Oliver Ellsworth, W. R. Davie, and William Vans Murray, who was already in Europe as American minister to the Netherlands. Hamilton's man, Thomas Pickering, was still Secretary of State and boldly delayed the sailing of Ellsworth and Davie.

The three Americans, meeting in France early in 1800, were cordially received by Napoleon Bonaparte, who had taken over from the corrupt Directory. Napoleon would not hear of paying any indemnity to the United States for ships captured by the French unless the Treaty of 1778 (see p. 106) were to be reactivated. This concession the commissioners could not grant. The French then merely confirmed the principle that "neutral ships make neutral goods." Even this slight concession soon became academic, since Napoleon was on the verge of making peace with England and the world, and neutrality would thus become meaningless. The Senate reluctantly ratified the agreement.

Election of 1800

Electoral Vote
☒ Jefferson 73
■ J. Adams 65

For the campaign of 1800, the Federalists named Adams and C. C. Pinckney; the Republicans named Jefferson and Burr. Again the election centered around the fight between the Adams camp and the Hamilton camp. Not realizing that the Republicans had stirred enough voters from their political lethargy to win the election, Hamilton concen-

trated on defeating Adams by means of his own running mate. The idea this time was for the electors from one Adams state to throw their votes away, thereby giving Pinckney a majority. But no one went along with Hamilton, and what was worse, the Republicans polled enough votes to make the maneuver meaningless anyway. But who was to be president? The electoral college gave both Jefferson and Burr 73 votes to 65 for Adams and 64 for Pinckney. According to the Constitution, the House had to decide between the two Republicans. The voting was to be on the basis of states, not of individual representatives, and nine states (out of 16) were needed to win. On the first ballot, Jefferson carried eight states, Burr six, and two were undecided. And so it went for 35 uproarious ballots. On the 36th, representatives from three states finally yielded, and Jefferson was elected. The next Congress put an end to this kind of problem by sending the Twelfth Amendment to the states, which was ratified by September, 1804. This amendment provided that, henceforth, "The electors ... shall name in their ballots the person voted for as President, and in distinct ballots the person voted for as Vice-President."

Although the Republicans had captured the presidency and both the House and the Senate, the country's first great shift in political power was not quite complete. Just before adjourning, in March, 1801, the lame-duck Federalist Congress gave Adams a new judiciary act which relieved Supreme Court and district court justices from riding to the circuit courts, created a whole new group of circuit court judges, and increased the number of district court judges. Adams filled these life-time jobs and other new judicial posts with Federalist sympathizers. Most important, he named John Marshall as Chief Justice of the Supreme Court. Adams was the last Federalist president, but during more than 30 years of Republican political control Justice Marshall continued to hand down Federalist interpretations of the law.

IV. JEFFERSON AS PRESIDENT

The Republicans Take Office. The narrowness of the Republican victory over the Federalists and of Jefferson's own victory over Burr made the new President deeply concerned about the division in the country. The bitterness that attended this division, heightened as it was by the "Federalist reign of terror" under the Alien and Sedition Laws and the partisan clamor of the press during the campaign, made Jefferson anxious to reassure the losers and if possible to win their support. "Let us, then, fellow citizens, unite with one heart and one mind," he said at the very beginning of his inaugural address, the first to be made in Washington. "We are all Republicans—we are all Federalists. If there be any among us who would wish to dissolve this Union or to change its republican form, let them stand undisturbed as monuments of the safety with which error of opinion may be tolerated where reason is left free to combat it."

In naming his cabinet, Jefferson could hardly be expected to choose any Federalists—if, indeed, any of the "Anglican monarchical aristocratical party," as the Republican press described the opposition, could be found to serve his administration. Federalist newspapers called Jefferson's followers "the worthless, the dishonest, the rapacious, the vile, the merciless, and the ungodly." Of the five cabinet positions, nevertheless, Jefferson gave two to New England, where Federalism was most intransigent. A New Englander also got the Postmaster-Generalship, which had not yet attained cabinet rank. The two most important cabinet posts went to the two most important Republicans after Jefferson: James Madison became Secretary of State, and Albert Gallatin became Secretary of the Treasury.

In filling the hundreds of other federal jobs, Jefferson fired few Federalists, but he hired even fewer. Jefferson also refused to recognize many of Adams' "midnight appointments" to judicial positions. One of Adams' appointees, William Marbury, has become famous because of the row he made over getting his job. President Adams signed Marbury's commission as justice of the peace in the District of Columbia so late that it could not even be delivered to him before Jefferson took office. Madison (the Secretary of State in those days was charged with certain domestic duties as well as the conduct of foreign affairs) now refused to deliver Marbury's commission. Marbury in turn asked the Supreme Court to issue an order commanding Madison to do so. The Court, by the Judiciary Act of 1789 (see p. 142), had this power, but it refused to use it. And therein lies the tale.

Before *Marbury* v. *Madison,* each Supreme Court justice had written a separate opinion on each case. The decision was then based on the majority vote, regardless of the different and sometimes contradictory reasoning of each man. But the new Chief Justice, Marshall, changed all this. For the next 33 years, he wrote almost all the important decisions; the other justices simply concurred or dissented as they chose. This arrangement made the court's logic in each case much clearer—and, since it was usually Marshall's logic, all the more overpowering. In his decision in *Marbury* v. *Madison* (1803), Marshall found that the provision in the Judiciary Act of 1789 that granted the Supreme Court the authority to issue such writs as Marbury sought was unconstitutional. The Constitution stated specifically in what actions the Supreme Court had original jurisdiction, and Marbury's complaint was not among them. Hence the Court refused even to hear Marbury's case.

This power of "judicial review," as it has since been called, probably was intended by the framers of the Constitution to be vested in the Supreme Court (see p. 133). But Marshall, in *Marbury v. Madison,* was the first justice to use it to nullify a congressional statute. That this power should have been reinforced by the leading Federalist judge so early in the first Republican administration, and, gallingly, in a case in which the administration was nominally the victor, taunted Jefferson into taking up his war on the "despotic branch." The Republicans reasoned that if Federalist judges could check legislation simply by declaring it unconstitutional, the legislature must have the power to counteract the judiciary. And, Congress held, this was the power of impeachment.

The most conspicuous victim of this policy was the vulnerable Supreme Court Justice Samuel Chase, who had a habit of entertaining juries with anti-Republican harangues. The House impeached him for misconduct in 1805, but he escaped conviction in the Senate. The Republicans did not try this maneuver again. Instead, they looked to the growing popular approval of their program to bring the courts into closer harmony with the election returns.

Jeffersonian Democracy. It is fitting that Jefferson should have been the first president to begin his term in the rude capital on the Potomac. He himself had suggested the layout of Pennsylvania Avenue, and on many other details had advised the French engineer, Pierre Charles L'Enfant, who planned the city of Washington. An Irishman, James Hoban, designed the White House, and an Englishman, B. H. Latrobe (with the American, William Thornton), designed the Capitol.

Adams' Alien Act offered poor hospitality to such men. Jefferson, once he had named his advisers and manned his administration, began by allowing this "libel on legislation" to lapse, and distinguished foreigners were welcomed to the country once more. Next he freed all who had been jailed under the Sedition Act, and recommended to Congress the return of all fines collected under this act and the restoration of a five-year residence requirement (instead of the Naturalization Act's 14-year requirement) for foreigners who wanted to become American citizens. Congress acted favorably on both suggestions.

Having thus righted matters of the spirit, Jefferson turned to matters of the purse. He admonished his Secretary of the Treasury, Gallatin, to keep the finances so simple "that every member of the Congress and every man of any mind in the Union should be able to comprehend them." Jefferson himself undertook to restore true republican simplicity to the government. He halted the expansion of the navy and reduced the size of the army. He dismembered the diplomatic corps, eliminated many tax-collectors, and cut out costly presidential social affairs. Jefferson reported these economies in his first "state of the union" message, which he sent to Congress in December, 1801, instead of delivering it "from the throne," as Washington and Adams had done. He went on to urge that Congress profit by his example.

To forestall waste, Jefferson recommended that funds be appropriated only for specific purposes, rather than in lump sums for the various departments, as had been the practice. He also advised Congress to require annual accountings from the Secretary of the Treasury, something Hamilton would have taken as a personal affront. Such frugality and good management, Jefferson thought, would make it possible for Congress to repeal the hated excise immediately. Commercial prospects, and hence the prospects of revenue from import duties, were so good, Jefferson believed, that even without the excise, payment of the public debt could be speeded up and millions of dollars in interest could be saved.

Another Jeffersonian economy move was entirely unlooked for in New England and must have surprised everyone who thought the President a poor custodian of national honor. This was Jefferson's "Barbary War."

Operating off Morocco, Algiers, Tunis, and Tripoli, Barbary pirates preyed on Atlantic and Mediterranean shipping, and at the same time demanded tribute from European powers. England, who paid tribute herself, often connived with the pirates to keep other nations from encroaching on British trade. When the United States became an independent nation, American shipping proved a particularly attractive target. During the last ten years, Washington and Adams had sweetened pirate treasuries with $2 million, but valuable ships, cargoes, and men were still being lost. Jefferson decided that it might be cheaper to put a stop to such extortion.

In May, 1801, he ordered a navy squadron to sew up the pirates in their home ports. For a navy "supported" by an economy-minded administration, however, this action was more easily ordered than achieved. The war dragged on until 1805, when the Pasha of Tripoli, threatened with the loss of his throne from other quarters, made peace. The United States continued to pay tribute to Algiers until 1815, but at a much lower rate than heretofore.

Jefferson was fortunate in taking office when he did, for American prosperity, owing to the great European wars, was at its crest, and talks leading to the Peace of Amiens of 1802 between France and her enemies were soon to begin. Jefferson was optimistic enough to believe that continuing prosperity would accompany the coming peace. By the end of 1802, he had reason to feel that his optimism had been justified, and in his annual message to Congress in December of that year he reported encouraging progress in discharging the public debt without recourse to objectionable taxes.

Jefferson and the West.   So contented was Jefferson with the trend of events that he wrote in November, 1802, "The path we have to pursue is so quiet that we have nothing scarcely to propose to our Legislature."

He saw no reason to change his conviction, expressed to Congress the year before in his justification of *national* economy, that "the states themselves have principal care of our persons, our property, and our reputation, constituting the great field of human concerns."

Under Adams, Congress had passed the Land Act of 1800 to stimulate the growth of new states. This new measure reduced the minimum purchase allowed in the public domain from 640 acres, as established by an act of 1796, to 320 acres. The act of 1800 retained the old price of $2.00 per acre, but it reduced the minimum down payment from 50 to 25 per cent, and extended the time for paying the remainder from one year to as many as four. By cutting a potential settler's initial cash payment from $640 to $160, this act greatly stimulated migration to the West. Under Jefferson a new act—the Land Act of 1804—speeded migration even more by reducing the minimum required purchase from 320 to 160 acres, thus making the minimum cash payment only $80.

These measures speeded up the settlement of the Northwest Territory, out of which Ohio (admitted to the Union in 1803) was the first state to be formed. Under the Land Ordinance of 1785 (see p. 122), each state created out of the Northwest Territory was to receive from Congress one section of land (640 acres) in every township, the proceeds from the sale of which were to be used to support education in the state. In the act admitting Ohio, Congress specifically made this grant, the first of its kind. The act also provided that 3 per cent of the federal government's income from the sale of federal land in Ohio was to be used to help the state develop public roads—a provision that established a precedent for national aid to transportation.

In the Southwest, Jefferson also tried to promote settlement, but conflicting claims to huge tracts of land near the Yazoo River in present-day Mississippi presented a major obstacle. In 1789, the state of Georgia, which owned this territory until it ceded it to the national government in 1802, sold about

25 million acres of it to speculators. When the buyers failed in their operation, Georgia, in 1795, re-sold much of the same land to other companies at the extraordinarily favorable price of 1½ cents an acre. All but one of the members of the Georgia legislature were in on the second deal. The cry of fraud was immediately raised, and the next year a new legislature rescinded the sale. But in the meantime the companies had sold stock widely, and the owners of the stock demanded delivery of the land.

By 1798, nothing had yet been done to clear up the confusion. At that point, the federal government, exercising its own claims to this land under the 1783 Treaty of Paris, proceeded to organize the Territory of Mississippi. To further this project, Congress recommended that the President set up a commission to settle all the competing claims, but Adams failed to act. When Georgia finally ceded her western lands to the federal government in 1802, the Yazoo stockholders carried their demands along to President Jefferson. He set up a commission which in 1803 recommended that the Yazoo claimants be reimbursed through the sale of 5 million acres of Yazoo land. The commission also recommended that the United States quiet the Indian claim to territory within the boundaries of Georgia, and that the rest of the land ceded by Georgia should itself become a state when its population reached 60,000.

Georgia and the federal government accepted these recommendations, but loud opposition was heard in the House. John Randolph led the fight against compensating the Yazoo claimants, insisting that the precious rights of the sovereign state of Georgia had been forfeited, with Jefferson's connivance, to the benefit of corrupt speculators. On these grounds he successfully opposed payment for more than ten years, and split the Republican party in the process. Randolph was supported by the die-hard state rights Republicans whose philosophy Jefferson himself had buttressed with the Kentucky Resolutions of 1798. Jefferson, however, as he was to make abundantly clear in the purchase of Louisiana, was no stickler for state rights or for a narrow interpretation of the Constitution where America's expansion was concerned.

As late as 1810, the Yazoo issue was still in doubt, but now John Marshall added his resounding voice to the argument. In the case of *Fletcher* v. *Peck,* which grew out of the Yazoo claims, Marshall declared that the Georgia sale of 1795 was a legitimate contract and that the next legislature had no power to break that contract through a rescinding law without the consent of the other party to it. This decision strengthened the position of the Yazoo stockholders and finally, in 1814, with Randolph out of Congress for the time being, Congress awarded them $5 million. Within the next five years, Alabama and Mississippi, both made up of territory ceded by Georgia, were admitted as states.

Late in 1801 Jefferson wrote, "The increase of [our] numbers during the last ten years we contemplate not with a view to the injuries it may enable us to do to others in some future day, but to the settlement of the extensive country still remaining vacant within our limits." On another occasion in 1801, he grew even more expansive: "However our present interests may restrain us within our own limits, it is impossible not to look forward to distant times, when our rapid multiplication will expand itself beyond those limits and cover the whole northern, if not the southern, continent with a people speaking the same language, governed in similar forms and by similar laws." This, as others were to insist later, was America's "manifest destiny."

As early as 1786, Jefferson had tried to bring these "distant times" a little nearer by furthering a fantastic expedition to be led by John Ledyard through Russia, across Siberia and the Bering Straits, and on into the wild North American interior. But the Cossack police caught Ledyard before he crossed Siberia and sent him home. In 1792, Jefferson persuaded the American Philosophical

Society to finance a far-western journey under the leadership of the French botanist, André Michaux. But this venture also failed when the Frenchman showed more interest in his countryman Genêt's political expeditions (see p. 149) than in Jefferson's natural-history ones.

Finally, early in 1803, Jefferson got Congress to make a secret appropriation of money for an expedition across the continent, ostensibly for scientific purposes, but also to find new supplies and new outlets for American fur-trappers and traders. For this venture, Jefferson chose the experienced

explorer, worked west from the Mississippi and discovered the Colorado peak that bears his name. Like Lewis and Clark, he brought back valuable information on the western country.

The Louisiana Purchase.

When Jefferson sent Lewis and Clark into the West, neither he nor anyone else knew the exact boundaries of Louisiana, or of New Orleans, as the whole western country was sometimes called. Spain had held Louisiana from 1762 to 1800, when Napoleon, in a secret treaty, got it back for France, compensating Spain with territory elsewhere. When Jefferson

Captains Lewis and Clark holding a council with the Indians.

Captains Lewis and Clark fighting off an attack by Indians.

wilderness explorer, Meriwether Lewis, who took as his colleague William Clark, the younger brother of George Rogers Clark (see p. 107) and a well-known Indian-fighter and frontiersman in his own right. By the time their party of about 45 men set out for the Missouri River on July 5, 1803, much of the territory they proposed to explore had become American property through the Louisiana Purchase. Lewis and Clark, however, had been commissioned to go well beyond Louisiana in order to discover a route from the Missouri River to the Pacific. They crossed the Rockies at the Continental Divide and traced the Columbia River to its mouth, thereby establishing an American claim to the Oregon country. In 1806-1807, Zebulon Pike, an experienced

learned of this deal, he let the French know that their taking New Orleans might drive the United States into the arms of England. He said at the time: "There is on the globe one single spot, the possessor of which is our natural and habitual enemy. It is New Orleans, through which the produce of three-eighths of our territory must pass to market, and from its fertility it will ere long yield more than half of our whole produce and contain more than half of our inhabitants." Spain—feeble, pacific, and cooperative—he added, might have retained it quietly for years. "But France placing herself in that door assumes to us the attitude of defiance."

Although Napoleon formally re-acquired Louisiana in 1800, he had reasons enough to postpone taking actual possession of it. For one thing, he had not a franc to spare for the costs of occupation. He intended to develop Louisiana into a source of food for the French West Indies, thus ending their dependence on the United States. But he could not proceed with this plan until he had secured his position in Europe, and he was unable to consolidate his position there until 1802. To protect Louisiana from the British, moreover, the French colony of Santo Domingo, in the Caribbean, was essential as a naval base. Unfortunately for Napoleon, a stubborn slave insurrection in Santo Domingo, led by the Negro General Toussaint L'Ouverture, who claimed to have liberated the island from France, was still going on. Worse, the uprising threatened to spread to the rest of the French West Indies

and thus ruin Napoleon's whole vision of a new American empire.

Once Napoleon had settled his European affairs at the Peace of Amiens in 1802, he sent 20,000 men to crush Toussaint and then occupy New Orleans. At this point, Spain withdrew her permission for Americans to use that port. These rights had been won for three years in Pinckney's Treaty of 1795 (see p. 152), and Spain had continued to recognize them until now. In March of 1803, Jefferson sent James Monroe to France as a special envoy with instructions to buy the territory around the port of New Orleans, and also Florida, which Jefferson suspected France might also have taken from Spain.

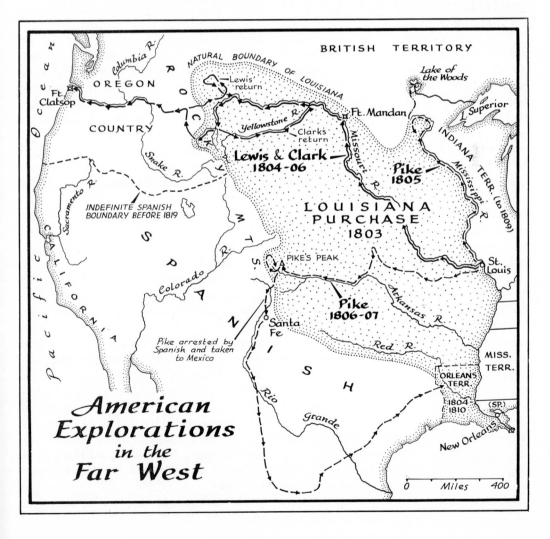

American Explorations in the Far West

Monroe was to work with Robert Livingston, the American minister in Paris. If France refused to sell, Monroe and Livingston were to approach England with the suggestion that she join with the United States in the event of a new war against Napoleon.

Napoleon's campaign against Toussaint turned out badly, for yellow fever and other difficulties destroyed virtually the entire French force. The defeat changed Napoleon's mind about Louisiana and, planning to proceed with the further conquest of Europe instead, he suddenly decided to sell out his American holdings. By the time Monroe arrived in Paris, a staggering offer for the whole Louisiana Territory had been proposed to Livingston, and on April 30, 1803, the deal was closed.

The American envoys were not quite sure what they had bought; the terms said simply that they were to receive Louisiana with the boundaries "that it now has in the hands of Spain." If this seemed vague, said Talleyrand, Napoleon's negotiator, "I suppose you will make the most of it." The final price was $15 million, a fourth of which was to be used to settle the claims of American shippers and shipowners against the French government. The purchase treaty also specified that the inhabitants of Louisiana, most of whom were Catholic, were to become American citizens and were to be protected in the practice of their religion.

To negotiate such a treaty was one thing; to get the money for such a "noble bargain," as Talleyrand called it, was quite another. To begin with, there were many irregularities about the sale. France had never actually taken over the territory from Spain; the French Constitution, moreover, prohibited the disposal of territory without a legislative vote. And the American Constitution did not delegate the power to purchase territory. Jefferson was so troubled on this point that he suggested an amendment to make the treaty legitimate. But, warned that delay might cause Napoleon to renege, Jefferson swallowed his scruples and pushed the treaty through. In November, 1803, the Senate ratified it 26 to 5, and the House appropriated the needed money, 90 to 25. On December 20th, the United States formally took possession. The next year, two territories were made of the Purchase, to be administered according to the procedure outlined in the Northwest Ordinance of 1787. Under these terms, Louisiana, with its present-day boundaries, became a state in 1812.

Florida had not been included in the deal, since Spain had never actually yielded it to France. But Jefferson was far from discouraged. "If we push them strongly with one hand, holding out a price in the other," he said, "we shall certainly obtain the Floridas, and all in good time."

Burr's Conspiracy. The method if not the results of the Louisiana Purchase troubled the Randolph Republicans in the South. But the strongest reaction arose in New England, where the Yankees saw their controlling influence in the new nation completely destroyed by the acquisition of this enormous new territory. So distraught were some of the northerners that they proposed to leave the Union; desperately, they turned to Aaron Burr for help. Jefferson and the Vice-president had broken over the presidential contest of 1800 and the subsequent distribution of Republican patronage, and Burr had been dropped from Republican consideration for the next national election. A few extreme New England Federalists now proposed that Burr, who was then running for governor of New York, should, if victorious, take his state into a new northern confederation. Thus by secession these disgruntled northerners would escape from the rule of the Virginia dynasty. Hamilton helped defeat Burr in the gubernatorial campaign, and the projected confederation collapsed. Embittered by this and other offenses, real and imaginary, Burr challenged Hamilton to a duel on July 11, 1804, in which Hamilton was killed.

The schemes of the "Essex Junto," as

Burr's Yankee conspirators were called, after the Massachusetts county in which they predominated, almost ruined the Federalist party even in New England, and in the November presidential elections of 1804 Jefferson carried every state in the Union but Connecticut and Delaware. The new vice-president was George Clinton, to whom, instead of Burr, Jefferson had entrusted the distribution of Republican "loaves and fishes" in New York.

Jefferson's second inauguration took place on March 4, 1805. Before leaving Washington, the discredited Burr approached the British minister with an offer to detach the western states from the United States in return for half a million dollars. The minister, impressed, conveyed the offer to London, but got no reply. Burr, in the meantime, had gone west, where he talked openly of many different plans, some pro-British, some pro-Spanish, some possibly treasonable. Eventually he got the ear of General Wilkinson, who was in charge of American troops in Louisiana, and of an Irish exile, Harman Blennerhassett, who lived in style on an island in the Ohio River. Burr's ultimate plan for the winter of 1806 was to use Blennerhassett's island as a taking-off place from which to join up with Wilkinson's troops for purposes that were not very clearly specified.

The unscrupulous Wilkinson then double-crossed his wayward accomplice, Burr, and sold out to Jefferson, who had Burr picked up and taken to Richmond for trial. There, John Marshall was sitting as circuit judge. Jefferson tried everything to get his political enemy convicted of treason. But Marshall, who was also Jefferson's enemy, thwarted every move, and Burr finally went free. During the proceedings, Marshall demanded that Jefferson appear in person to give testimony; by refusing, Jefferson set a precedent for future presidents.

Trials of a Neutral. Jefferson's first term coincided more or less with the first years of peace in Europe since the French Revolution. But his second administration became deeply involved in the Napoleonic wars, which were resumed in 1803. By 1805, Napoleon's victory at Austerlitz had given France control of much of the European continent, and Nelson's victory at Trafalgar had given Britain control of the seas. This apparent stalemate led only to an uncompromising war of attrition, with disastrous results for neutrals.

The first new blow against the neutral United States was the decision of a British court in the case of the ship *Essex* in 1805. In 1800, a British court had ruled that American ships could carry goods from the French West Indies to France provided the goods were first landed on American shores, duty-free. This decision had given a great impetus to the so-called "re-export" trade which, by 1805, accounted for more than half of America's booming neutral commerce. In the case of the *Essex,* however, the decision was revoked. The British court now held that French colonial goods could be sent to France only if a duty had been paid on them in America and only if other evidence proved that the goods had not been meant for France in the first place. Any ships that could not produce this evidence to Britain's satisfaction were vulnerable to British capture.

Britain also stepped up its attacks on American commerce, and the impending termination of the 12-year commercial agreement made at the time of Jay's Treaty in 1794 threatened to leave American shipping still more vulnerable. Jefferson took steps to remedy the situation. In 1806, he got Congress to pass a Non-Importation act prohibiting the landing of any British goods that could be purchased elsewhere or manufactured in the United States. With this as a club (the act was not enforced until later), he sent William Pinkney to join Monroe, who was now the regular minister in London, in an effort to make a new commercial treaty and otherwise put an end to British depredations.

In the meantime, as a result of new victories on land, Napoleon prepared to close the entire Continent to Britain, her goods, and her friends, and to blockade the British Isles. For this purpose, he issued the Berlin Decrees of November, 1806. When Pinkney and Monroe negotiated a treaty in London, the British stipulated as a condition of enforcement that the United States must resist these Berlin Decrees. But Jefferson would have nothing to do with such dictation, and he did not even submit the treaty to the Senate. In 1807, Napoleon added the Milan Decrees to the Berlin Decrees, ordering the confiscation of all ships, especially neutral ships, that had visited a British port or might be bound for one. Britain responded with a series of "orders-in-council." The major orders, in January and November, 1807, stated that "all ports and places of France and her allies or of any country at war with His Majesty," were blockaded, and that neutral ships that frequented such ports or sailed toward them did so at their peril.

Impressment and Embargo.   Between 1804 and 1807, the United States lost hundreds of ships to the British alone, who had bottled up the French navy even more successfully than they had blockaded the French ports. Still more obnoxious was the British practice of stopping ships on the high seas to search for and take off alleged deserters from the British navy, the practice known as impressment. The British navy, a harsh institution which had been enormously expanded to fight Napoleon, was characteristically short of men. And the American merchant marine, growing rapidly as a result of the neutral trade, was also eager for new hands. Despite all the losses, American commerce was so profitable that American ship-owners could offer consistently higher wages and better working conditions than the British. Consequently, thousands of British sailors who happened to be in American ports were attracted to American ships. Moreover, the American government was able to meet the

competition of the American merchant marine for sailors to man her warships. In 1807, the frigate *U. S. S. Constitution,* out of a crew of 419, had only 241 who claimed American citizenship, and 149 who admitted to being English. To the beleaguered British, who believed that "Once an Englishman, always an Englishman," this was an intolerable situation.

Britain had practiced impressment, and Americans had complained of it, ever since 1776; after 1804, however, the British redoubled their efforts. In June, 1807, one affront led to violence and almost to war. The new American frigate, *Chesapeake,* was suspected by the British of having a certain deserter on board. As she was sailing near Chesapeake Bay, the British warship, *Leopard,* intercepted her and demanded the right of search. The *Chesapeake's* captain refused, and a few minutes later the *Leopard* fired on her. The *Chesapeake* was so new that many of her guns had not yet been mounted, and her decks were cluttered with gear. She suffered 21 casualties before being boarded by the *Leopard's* officers, who found the deserter they were after and took him off, along with three Americans who had served in the English navy.

To almost everyone but Jefferson, it seemed, this attack meant war. But Jefferson had a policy of his own. He called a special session of Congress in October, which voted an appropriation of $850,000 to strengthen the navy. Only in the regular session in December did he show his true hand. Under a policy that he called "peaceful coercion," he decided to keep American vessels off the seas in order to save ships and men from capture, and to save the country from incendiary insults. Thus deprived of American goods and American carriers, he reasoned, the warring powers of Europe would be forced to recognize neutral, and American, rights. On December 22, 1807, Congress gave Jefferson the Embargo Act, which ruled that no ships were to be permitted to leave United States ports, and no exports were to be shipped out, even overland.

The Embargo Act meant ruin, not to

merce and American ports. In spite of the losses caused by the European wars, between 1803 and 1807 American exports had grown from $55 million to $108 million. By 1808, they had dwindled to the little that could be smuggled out of the country by one ruse or another. It seemed to many that New England's Federalist merchants were the only ones who were being "peacefully coerced" by Jefferson's Republican policy. Actually, all ports suffered alike. In New York, as one traveler reported, "Not a box, bale, cask, barrel or package was to be seen .... The streets near the waterside were almost deserted; the grass had begun to grow upon the wharves." The industries associated with commerce, such as ship-building and sail-making, were also at a standstill, and their artisans were unemployed.

Fourteen months of embargo were enough even for many of the Republicans, and on March 1, 1809, three days before Jefferson's retirement, he was forced to sign an act repealing the measure. He also approved a strong substitute—a Non-Intercourse Act proscribing trade with England and France, but opening it to all other countries. If either England or France, however, would cancel its orders or decrees against American shipping, then the ban would apply only to the other.

Jefferson's Retirement. Jefferson was even more passionate than Washington in wanting to keep America free from Euro-

pean entanglements; his embargo illustrates the extremes to which he would go to accomplish this end. Even more passionate was his compulsion to get Europe out of America, as evidenced by the Louisiana Purchase and his thirst for Florida, to say nothing of his desire for South America and Canada. In spite of all his efforts, however, the United States became increasingly involved in Europe's affairs, and after 1806 Jefferson found himself "panting for retirement."

As early as 1805, Jefferson had written: "George Washington set the example of voluntary retirement after eight years. I shall follow it. And a few more precedents will oppose the obstacle of habit to anyone after a while who shall endeavor to extend his term. Perhaps," he added, foreseeing the possibility of what actually occurred in 1951, "it may beget a disposition to establish it by an amendment of the Constitution."

By the time of the presidential election of 1808, the Republican party was split into various factions; the Federalists, in the meantime, largely because of the effects of the Republican embargo, had recovered some of the ground they had lost. Nevertheless, Jefferson remained the strongest man in the Republican party and in the country. His hand-picked successor, James Madison, won both the nomination and the election. In the electoral college Madison won 122 votes to 47 for C. C. Pinckney, the Federalist candidate.

Readings

A good brief introduction to the problems of getting the new government under way is found in Henry Jones Ford, *Washington and His Colleagues* (1921). This book may be supplemented by John Spencer Bassett, *The Federalist System* (1906), and Leonard D. White, *The Federalists* (1948), and *The Jeffersonians* (1951), the first two volumes of a distinguished series on administrative history. Claude G. Bowers, *Jefferson and Hamilton* (1925), is a colorful account of the period, with a strong Antifederalist bias. Equally good reading on the Federalist side are volumes II and III of Albert J. Beveridge, *The Life of John Marshall* (4 vols., 1916-1919). The biographies of Washington mentioned in Chapter V and of Madison, Hamilton, and Jay mentioned in Chapter VI, each sympathetic to its subject, are all relevant to this chapter. The best biography of John Adams is Gilbert Chinard, *Honest John Adams* (1933). Adams was one of the most cogent thinkers of his day. A fascinating book made up of his marginal comments on the books of his contemporary philosophers is Zoltán Haraszti, *John Adams and The Prophets of Progress* (1952). A good, representative anthology is Adrienne Koch and William Peden, eds., *The Selected Writings of John and John Quincy Adams* (1946). A participant's lively comments on the first Congress are to be found in the *Journal of William Maclay,* edited by E. S. Maclay (1928). Maclay was an Antifederalist senator. His views may be compared with those of the saturnine Fisher Ames, the arch-Federalist from Massachusetts, as disclosed in *Works of Fisher Ames,* edited by Seth Ames (2 vols., Boston 1854).

The standard life of Jefferson is Dumas Malone, *Jefferson and His Times* (2 vols., 1948-1951). Two one-volume biographies merit serious attention: Albert J. Nock, *Thomas Jefferson* (1926), and Gilbert Chinard, *Thomas Jefferson, The Apostle of Americanism* (1929). *Jefferson Himself,* edited by Bernard Mayo (1942), is an imaginative collection of Jefferson's writings in one volume, arranged topically. A useful collection of Jefferson's longer writings is *The Life and Selected Writings of Thomas Jefferson,* edited by Adrienne Koch and William Peden (1944).

One of the classics of all American history is Henry Adams, *History of the United States During the Administrations of Thomas Jefferson and James Madison* (9 vols., 1889-1891). More concerned with Jeffersonian politics than with Jefferson himself is Charles A. Beard, *Economic Origins of Jeffersonian Democracy* (1915), an out-standing work.

Charles D. Hazen, *Contemporary American Opinion of the French Revolution* (1897), remains the most substantial work on this subject. Other aspects of foreign relations may be studied in two books by Samuel F. Bemis, *Jay's Treaty* (1923), and *Pinckney's Treaty* (1926); in Arthur P. Whitaker, *The Mississippi Question, 1795-1803* (1934); and in L. M. Sears, *Jefferson and the Embargo* (1927). An important work written from a Canadian point of view is Alfred L. Burt, *The United States, Great Britain, and British North America* (1940).

THE NATIONAL FOCUS

C H A P T E R   E I G H T

When in 1809 Jefferson turned over to his friend, James Madison, the problems that his embargo had failed to solve, a new generation stood on the threshold of power in the United States. Franklin, Hancock, Washington, and Patrick Henry had died in the 1790's. Between 1803 and 1806, Sam Adams, Hamilton, and Robert Morris followed them. Ready to take their places were men like Henry Clay, John C. Calhoun, and Daniel Webster, all youthful enough never to have been British subjects, many of them eager to found an American empire of their own. The oldest of the group, at 42, was Andrew Jackson. The earlier generation of statesmen had won independence and had established a nation; it became the task of the new generation to knit the country together, to cope with the problems of sectionalism, and to instil a national spirit.

I. OPPORTUNITIES FOR THE NEW GENERATION

When the new leaders appeared on the scene, the United States teemed with opportunities for smart young men. The Louisiana Purchase had doubled American territory. To the east of the Purchase, tens of thousands of Americans were spreading over the land each year. By 1810, more than a million settlers lived across the mountains, most of them in a great triangle with its apex a thousand miles from the coast, at St. Louis. Outside this triangle to the north, Indiana had become a territory, and Illinois had grown into an outpost that was soon to seek admission to the Union. In the South, Alabama, Mississippi, and Louisiana were on the verge of statehood.

In all these new areas, speculators and lawyers were busy with land claims and counterclaims, while farmers were beginning to produce for the market. By 1810, thousands of flat boats were floating down the western rivers, themselves to be broken up into salable lumber at the end of the voyage and to be added to the cargo supplied by farmers, woodsmen, and trappers. Road construction had begun, and men talked of canals and steam power. Fulton had shown the practicability of the steamboat. John Jacob Astor had introduced organization into the fur trade. Yankee ship captains were winning much of the world's carrying trade from the embattled British,

The Clermont *on its first run in 1807* (top) *and as enlarged the next year.*

and transporting goods to all continents and on all the seas (see Chapter IX).

Enterprising southerners, finding their tobacco shut out of European markets, were turning to cotton. Before 1793 only long-staple cotton could be cleansed of its oily seeds at a reasonable cost. But Eli Whitney's gin, invented that year, made it practical to clean the green seeds from the much hardier short-staple boll which could be grown profitably throughout the interior. By 1810, South Carolina and Georgia were producing enough cotton to account for almost one-fourth of all American exports. Innovations in wool production kept up with improvements in cotton. Sheep of the extraordinarily fine merino strain were introduced into America in 1802. By 1810, some 20,000 merinos, along with millions of ordinary sheep raised in Pennsylvania, New York, and New England, were supplying raw wool to a number of new factories and to thousands of spinners and weavers working at home.

Cut off from many supplies by war and embargo, the United States became nearly self-sufficient in many manufactures besides cottons and woolens. By 1810, the value of goods made from the raw products of farm, forest, and sea was placed at almost $200 million annually. Now overland transportation became more necessary than ever. By 1810, almost 200 turnpike companies had been chartered in New England, almost 100 in New York, and about 40 in Pennsylvania; hundreds of miles of good new roads had been built.

Though some critics had predicted that capital would flee the country under a "dangerous" president like Jefferson, capital during the Virginian's terms multiplied as never before—sometimes hindered, but more often prodded by war. Rapidly rising business activity called for expanding credit, more investment. To meet the need, 58 new state banks opened between 1800 and 1811, more than doubling the total. Private banks added to the sources of domestic credit, while foreign bankers, notably the English Barings, extended liberal credit to American merchants.

II. THE WAR OF 1812

The learned and affable James Madison, 58 years old when he took office in March, 1809, was many years older than the enterprising younger generation; but he showed his sympathy with their ideas by appearing at his inauguration dressed unprecedentedly in "a full suit of cloth of American manufacture." In his inaugural address he spoke warmly of the need to promote American industry and "external as well as internal commerce." His Secretary of the Treasury, Albert Gallatin, who shared these attitudes, laid out an ambitious program of federal aid to American enterprise in two reports, one on manufactures and the other on roads and canals.

The Failure of Diplomacy. Yet before such plans could be realized, the nation itself had to be preserved. A few New Englanders, frightened by the Louisiana Purchase and outraged by the embargo, were still talking of returning to the British Empire. Many southerners viewed the closing of American ports to British ships by the Non-Intercourse Act (see p. 165) as a surrender of the southern export economy to New England shipping interests. These southerners might have been glad to see the Yankees leave the Union.

Fortunately England was too busy with her own problems to exploit such divisions. George Canning, who became Foreign Secretary in 1807, instructed David Erskine, the British minister to the United States, to attempt to win from the new president, commitments favorable to the British position. But Erskine suppressed the disagreeable features of his instructions and promised that the British would withdraw the orders-in-council in return for a number of American concessions. To this Madison agreed all too readily, an agreement was signed, and over 600 American ships set sail. But Erskine had promised more than he had been authorized to grant. Canning repudiated the agreement as soon as he saw it, and recalled Erskine, replacing him with Francis J. Jackson, an implacable anti-American, who was hardly capable of settling the serious issues between the two countries. Madison, in the meantime, had been obliged to restore non-intercourse with Britain and to continue it with France.

So, once again, American commerce was stalled. Congress reconvened in December, 1809, and added to the talk of war with inflammatory debate and ill-conceived legislation. One unfortunate measure, effective May 1, 1810, was the so-called "Macon's Bill Number 2," named for the chairman of the House Committee on Foreign Affairs. This act put an end to non-intercourse, but it provided for its revival against France if Britain rescinded her orders-in-council, and its revival against Britain if France rescinded her decrees (see p. 164). Napoleon had his foreign minister write to the American am-

James Madison (1751-1836).

bassador that the French decrees were revoked as of November 1, 1810. Madison, to the consternation of New England, hastened to restore non-intercourse against the British, and Congress confirmed his action with a new enactment in March, 1811.

This maneuvering was "peaceful coercion" again, but it impressed neither England nor France. Napoleon, as many observers in both England and America foresaw, failed to abide by his announced revocation, and French attacks on American commerce continued. At the same time, William Pinkney, the American minister in London, found that the revocation of non-intercourse with France failed to coerce Canning to withdraw the British orders. Soon after, Pinkney was called home. American-British relations now had little chance of improvement, since there was no British minister in Washington and no American representative in London.

The Urge to War.

Popular disgust with the stalemate between America and the belligerents abroad was recorded in the elections of 1810 and 1811, in which the voters unseated most of the Eleventh Congress. The replacements arriving in Washington in November, 1811, included bristling young men from the southern, western, and northern frontiers. Unconcerned with Europe's attacks on American ships, except as affronts to the American flag, these newcomers aimed to extend American territory at embattled Europe's expense.

On the southern frontier, Spain still held the Floridas, an area that had become a haven for runaway slaves and marauding pirates and a home for hostile Indians. By 1810, however, most of the inhabitants of the rich lands of West Florida were Americans who, bemoaning Spain's inability to protect them, revolted and asked to be annexed by the United States. Madison, as eager as Jefferson to acquire new territory, had connived in this uprising. He agreed to annexation in October, 1810, and early in 1812 an armed American expedition set out against weakly defended East Florida. But

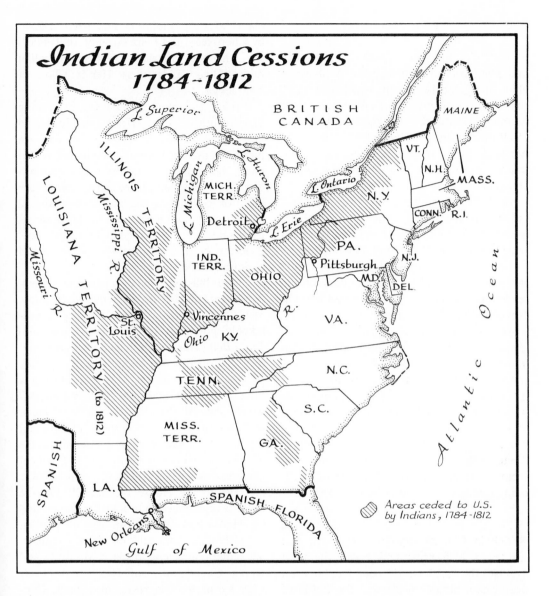

Indian Land Cessions 1784–1812

Areas ceded to U.S. by Indians, 1784–1812

Spain's threat to declare war, and New England's threat to revolt if war came, obliged Madison to recall the troops. This action may have appeased Spain and New England, but it was deemed treachery by the men of the Southwest, who, having tasted the heady wine of expansionism, were thirsting to fight for new lands.

North of the Floridas, on American territory, an Indian war was imminent. Madison shared Jefferson's view that the Indians must be either converted to agriculture or else moved on to the West. Since little time was given to transforming the Indians into husbandmen, sporadic violence between Indian and white increased. Indians all along the frontier were tricked into making grant after grant by treaties they ill understood. Between 1801 and 1810, 110 million western acres had been taken from them in the Ohio Valley. But, having ceded the land, the Indians failed to move along, and settlers occupied much of this land only after the Indians had been driven out.

As the tribes in this region—Creeks, Cherokees, Kaskaskias, Shawnees, and others —were pushed closer and closer to the Mississippi, hostile Sioux and Chippewa tribes in search of furs came south to Wisconsin and Minnesota to hem them in. A Shawnee chief, the great Tecumseh, decided in 1811 that a stand against the frontiersmen must be made. He insisted that the land belonged to all Indians and that individual tribes could not trade away a single acre; he threatened that further settlement would be resisted by consolidated force.

In July, 1811, Tecumseh warned Governor William Henry Harrison of Indiana Territory that he intended to enlist southern tribes for a general defense. This announcement, meant to intimidate Harrison, only inspired him to make a sudden attack on the leaderless tribes once Tecumseh had left. On November 6, 1811, with a thousand soldiers, Harrison arrived at Tippecanoe Creek adjacent to Prophetstown, the central Indian village on the Wabash. Learning of his presence, the braves themselves attacked at dawn on November 7. Harrison's men repulsed them, though suffering heavy losses, and proceeded to burn Prophetstown to the ground. Finding the ruins on his return, Tecumseh mobilized the survivors and swore them to eternal war. By the spring of 1812, many families of would-be settlers were fleeing for their lives to more protected areas.

Frontiersmen had long believed that the British in Canada supplied Tecumseh and his tribes with arms and egged them on against the settlers. Hence frontiersmen everywhere blithely acclaimed the Battle of Tippecanoe as a triumph over the British as well as over the Indians, and explained Tecumseh's retaliation after the battle as part of a British plot. So the cry on the frontiers grew louder for the conquest of all Canada (for how else could the British be eliminated from "Our Continent"?) and for the conquest of all Florida, lest Spain be used as a cat's-paw for Britain's re-entry.

The handful of frontiersmen who brought this borderland cry to the halls of Congress in November, 1811, were promptly branded by the easterners as "War Hawks." Among them were Calhoun, from upland South Car-

olina, whose grandfather had been scalped by Cherokees, and Felix Grundy, of Tennessee, who had lost three brothers in Indian raids. Their leader was Henry Clay, of Kentucky.

Taking advantage of the enmity among older members, Clay's friends quickly elected him Speaker of the House; he in turn promptly used the Speaker's prerogative to name them chairmen of the major committees. Soon they had placed before the House bills for enlisting a big army, recruiting a modest navy, and letting the world know, as Clay said, that "we could fight France too, if necessary, in a good cause,—the cause of honor and independence."

These bills provoked serious argument, but events aided the war party. In May, 1811, the American frigate, *President,* mistakenly pounded the smaller British ship, *Little Belt.* This action, hailed as a great victory, helped dissolve lingering popular fears of "the mistress of the seas." Disclosure a little later of the notorious "Henry Letters," which showed that the British in Canada were looking into the strength of disunion sentiment in New England, also aided the war party. Under pressure in and out of Congress, Madison reluctantly sent his war message to the House on June 1. On the 18th he announced that both the Senate and the House had declared for war on Britain. "I verily believe that the militia of Kentucky are alone competent to place Montreal and Upper Canada at your feet," said Henry Clay during the congressional debates. Congress must have believed him, for when it adjourned on July 6 it had voted no new taxes and only a few new men to carry on the war it had declared.

In his war message, Madison had said nothing about Canada and Florida, and little about the Indian troubles on the frontier. Instead, he stressed the accumulation of intolerable offenses against American citizens, American ports, American ships, and American commerce. He named impressment as the most important cause of the war, and then noted the hovering of British men-of-war in American harbors, the "pretended Blockades," and "sweeping system" of orders-in-council.

The maritime areas, not only in New England but in the Middle states as well, voted against the war mainly because in a conflict with Britain their ships would bear the brunt of the fighting and their commerce the brunt of the cost. The South, which had lost its tobacco market because of Napoleon's Continental System (see p. 164), and which was losing cotton sales because the British could no longer sell their manufactured cotton textiles across the Channel, supported the war. Except in upper New York State and part of upper Vermont, where relations with Canada were close and where trade across the border was favorable, the war had the vociferous support of the exposed frontier.

Two days before Congress declared war, Castlereagh, Canning's successor as British foreign minister, announced the repeal of the orders-in-council. A few days later, Monroe, now Secretary of State, instructed Jonathan Russell, the American *chargé* in Paris who was filling in at London, to arrange an armistice "if the orders-in-council are repealed, and no illegal blockades are substituted for them, and orders are given to discontinue the impressment of seamen from our vessels, and to restore those already impressed." Castlereagh's repeal and Monroe's letter crossed at sea. Neither could have prevented war. Monroe demanded too much; on learning of his offer from Russell, Castlereagh exclaimed, "No administration could expect to remain in power that should consent to renounce the right of impressment, or to suspend the practice." Castlereagh, in turn, offered too little. That strictly maritime concessions would scarcely have been enough to swing the frontier to peace is indicated in a letter written by Andrew Jackson the previous March:

We are going to fight for the reestablishment of our national character, . . . for the protection of our maritime citizens impressed on board British ships of war, . . . to vindicate our right to a free trade, and open market for the productions of our soil now perishing on our hands because the *mistress of the ocean* has forbid us

to carry them to any foreign nation; in fine, to seek some indemnity for past injuries, some security against future aggression, by the conquest of all the British dominions upon the continent of North America.

Preparing for the Conflict. The logic of Jackson's explanation of why the United States fought the War of 1812 was not the first or only thing that was awry about this conflict. Early in 1811, the war party in Congress had allowed the Bank of the United States to die at the expiration of its 20-year charter. This action deprived the government of one of its main fiscal agencies just when its fiscal problems were becoming most acute. Early in 1812, Secretary of the Treasury Gallatin tried to get Congress to vote higher tariffs and various internal taxes to raise money for the impending conflict, but after months of debate Congress postponed action until it reconvened in December. In the meantime, with no bank to lend assistance, only about half of an authorized 6 per cent bond issue of $11 million could be sold. Throughout the war, new taxes were reluctantly voted and expertly evaded; new loans were optimistically authorized and niggardly subscribed.

Madison said the war was to be fought for freedom of the seas, and Jackson said it was to be fought against the "mistress of the ocean." Yet not until six months after war had been declared did Congress appropriate money to enlarge the meager American navy. The army faced a similar plight. "Such is the structure of our society," wrote Henry Clay in 1812, "that I doubt whether many men can be engaged for a longer term than six months." Yet Clay and other War Hawks had voted for an addition of 25,000 men to the regular army (making a total of 35,000), all to be enlisted for five years. Kentucky, Clay's state, had panted for war more hotly than any other; yet in the first two months of the war, only 400 Kentuckians enlisted. In Vermont, which, according to a local correspondent of Madison's, "appeared to wish for war more than . . . other northern states, . . . perhaps not one thousand" were ready to fight. To augment the regular army, early in 1812 the President was authorized to accept 50,000 volunteers for a year's service. But scarcely 5,000 signed up in the following six months. A little later, the President was authorized to call out 100,000 state militia, but few of those who took up arms would follow their officers across the borders of their own states. At the outset of

was the only "tangible" place to engage England, but New England, the logical base from which to launch an invasion of Canada, refused to cooperate and withheld its militia from combat. The South feared that the acquisition of Canada would put slaveholders at a great disadvantage in the government in the future. It would support an invasion "not as an object of war," as Monroe said, but only as a means to force England to yield on impressment, markets, and related matters, and thus bring the war "to a satisfactory conclusion."

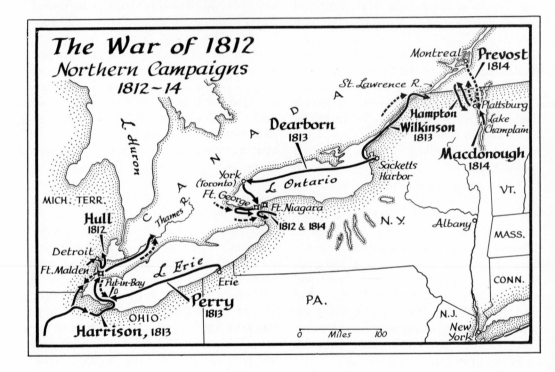

the war, the free population of the United States was about twelve times the population of Canada; yet, according to Henry Adams, two months after the declaration of war, "the Canadian outnumbered the American forces at every point of danger on the frontier."

Strategy on Land and Sea. Confusion in American minds over the objectives of the war muddied the military strategy from the outset. Canada, it was universally agreed,

The West agreed with Jefferson that "the cession of Canada . . . must be a *sine qua non* at a treaty of peace." The trouble here was that the only sure way to conquer Canada was to occupy Montreal, thereby shutting off Canadian supplies to the Indians and closing the main port of entry for British assistance. Given the insignificant forces at the command of American generals, such a campaign would have required the withdrawal of troops from western garrisons and the consequent exposure of the western country to the Indians. For all its hunger for

Canada, the West would not tolerate such a move.

Thus, instead of a quick and concerted push on Montreal with the clear objective of using it as a base for reducing all of Canada, the United States at the opening of the war tried three timid and uncoordinated forays, scattered over almost a thousand miles of border. The first of these, in July, 1812, found General William Hull leading 2,000 men from Detroit into Canada. Meanwhile, Tecumseh had joined the British. Encountering no enemy, and fearful of the Indians at his rear, Hull soon marched back again to find the brilliant Canadian General Isaac Brock, over from Niagara, demanding the surrender of Detroit. Hull yielded, and with his forces was taken prisoner to Niagara.

The second American foray took place early in October. Captain John Wool led an American detachment across the Niagara River and took Queenston Heights; General Brock fell in the battle. New York militia under General Van Rensselaer were expected to follow up this exploit, but refusing to move from their own state, they stood by and watched Canadian forces shoot down most of Captain Wool's men. Meanwhile, far to the east, at Plattsburg on Lake Champlain, General Dearborn prepared at last to move on Montreal. In November, he finally marched north 20 miles, and when the militia decided that was far enough from home, he marched back again.

Before 1812 was over, a new American force under the vigorous direction of General William Henry Harrison stood poised to recapture Detroit. When the Canadians routed a large detachment of Harrison's troops under General Winchester at Frenchtown on the Raisin River, Harrison had to postpone further action, but he was to be heard from later on. Canada thus was not as "tangible" as had been supposed. Far from occupying it—it "will be a mere matter of marching," Jefferson had said—the Americans after six months of fighting found their own frontier pushed back to Ohio.

At sea, another story was unfolding. Statistically, the American navy was no match for the British. In American waters alone, the British had 11 huge ships-of-the-line, 34 frigates, and 52 smaller warships. The United States had 16 ocean-going warships in all, including but 3 frigates, the *Constitution,* the *United States,* and the *President,* to which, before long, a fourth, the reconstructed *Chesapeake,* was added. In the opening months of the war, these ships recorded startling victories over British men-of-war in single-ship engagements. The winter of 1812-1813 found most of the American ships back in harbor. The British, intensifying their blockade of American ports south of New London, Connecticut (they left friendly Rhode Island and Massachusetts ports alone), succeeded in keeping most of these ships bottled up for the rest of the war. But they could not discourage the American privateers. About 500 of them roamed the seas and before the fighting was over had captured more than 1,300 British merchantmen, valued, with their cargoes, at about $40 million.

The End of the War. A week after the American declaration of war against Britain, the Czar of Russia joined Britain in the struggle against Napoleon. As one of his first moves, the Czar tried to settle the differences between his new ally and her old colonies, thereby freeing England for the greater struggle on the Continent. Madison was all for this settlement and immediately dispatched James A. Bayard and Albert Gallatin to St. Petersburg, where John Quincy Adams was already in residence as American minister. The British, however, spurned the Czar's efforts, and the war was fated to proceed.

No one was more eager for peace than Madison; it is not the least of the ironies of this war that in the elections of 1812 he should have found himself the champion of the "war party" against De Witt Clinton of New York, who had been nominated by the "peace party" among the Republicans. The war dominated the campaign. In the election, Clinton, supported by the Federalists as well as the Republicans, carried every northern state except Pennsylvania and Vermont. Madison, however, added to the votes of those states the solid support of the South and West, and Madison won, 128 to 89.

As one manifestation of the new vigor that followed this political victory, Congress authorized the construction of four new ships-of-the-line and six new frigates in December, 1812. None of these ships was completed in time for combat, but elsewhere new warlike steps began to show results. General Hull had been skeptical of holding Detroit without control of Lake Erie, and General Harrison agreed. After Wilkinson's defeat, Harrison decided to wait until the Canadians had been cleared off the water before trying again. The task of taking Lake Erie was given to young Captain Oliver Hazard Perry. Early in 1813, he began to construct a small lake fleet with materials and armament that had been hauled laboriously over the moun-

The Constitution *defeating the* Guerrière.

tains to his headquarters at Presque Isle. In August, 1813, Perry was ready, and on September 10, he found the British squadron in Put-in-Bay at the western end of the lake. Since the British were penned in, the fight was more like a land action, with both sides simply firing away. At the end of the engagement, Perry reported to Harrison, "We have met the enemy and they are ours."

Harrison followed up immediately, chasing the Canadian General Proctor, who had abandoned Detroit on Perry's victory. Harrison caught and defeated Proctor at the battle of Thames River on October 5. Tecumseh perished in this engagement and his Indian forces fell apart. To the east, on Lake Ontario, Captain Chauncey, in collaboration with General Dearborn, raided York (now Toronto), burned the parliament houses (thus giving an excuse for the later burning of Washington), and fled. Control of Lake Ontario had not been established, and without it York was untenable. Still farther east, Generals Wilkinson and Wade Hampton planned a new march on Montreal, but, characteristically, before they had reached the Canadian border they became discouraged and turned back.

In April, 1814, Napoleon abdicated and England was eager for peace, but still, the upstart Americans had to be put in their place. Canada had defended herself valiantly, and now the British prepared to mount an overwhelming offensive. First, they extended the blockade to the New England ports and reinforced it all along the coast, a step that permitted the harassment of American seaboard cities. On one such adventure, emanating from Chesapeake Bay, a British force marched on Washington, routed the hastily mobilized defenders, and, on August 24, set fire to the Capitol and the White House.

Of greater military importance was the three-pronged attack which the British directed successively against Niagara, Lake Champlain, and New Orleans. By mid-1814, the United States had uncovered vigorous new commanders, including General Jacob Brown and his subordinate, Winfield Scott.

"The Battle of Lake Erie," an early nineteenth-century painting showing Perry changing flagships.

Having learned of the British Niagara push before it started, General Brown took the initiative himself. On the fourth of July, he captured Fort Erie, on the Canadian side of the Niagara River; the next day, Scott defeated the British at Chippewa. On July 25, Brown engaged the enemy at Lundy's Lane, near Niagara Falls. He outfought them, but fell back upon learning that strong British reinforcements were on the way.

A month later, 10,000 veterans of Wellington's Napoleonic campaigns arrived at Montreal ready, under Sir George Prevost, to march toward Lake Champlain. Their objective might have been to detach northern New York and New England from the United States and restore them to the British empire.

Whatever their purpose, they failed. The American force at Plattsburg was much smaller than the British contingent, but it had two advantages. First, it was installed in fortifications erected by new army engineers, the first experienced graduates of West Point, which had been established in 1802. Secondly, it was protected by Commodore Macdonough's flotilla on Lake Champlain. Early in September, Prevost moved his fine army toward Plattsburg in coordination with a British flotilla on the lake. Macdonough's men and ships were sorely battered in the ensuing battle of Plattsburg Bay; yet their victory was so complete that Prevost, rather than try a match of arms on land, turned tail.

Plattsburg Bay was the last battle before the Treaty of Ghent. But it was not the last battle of the war. In the Southwest, Andrew Jackson had been campaigning more or less on his own against the Indians, and after routing the Creeks at the battle of Horseshoe Bend in Alabama in March, 1814, he compelled them to yield by treaty many thousands of acres of excellent land. The vigor of Jackson's actions brought him full command of the southwestern theater and the responsibility for checking the British attack in that sector. Aware that the British might use Pensacola in Spanish Florida as a base, Jackson invaded the area and took Pensacola. Then he marched to New Orleans and was ready for the British when they arrived there. The battle between 8,000 British veterans of the Napoleonic campaigns and a rag-tail collection of militiamen, sailors, and pirates, took place on January 8, 1815, fifteen days after the Treaty of Ghent (see p. 179) had been signed. Jackson's rifles and artillery mowed down the assaulting columns of redcoats and routed them. British losses in this unnecessary battle mounted to more than 2,000 casualties, whereas the well-entrenched Americans suffered only 8 killed and 13 wounded. The war was over, and the foundation of Jackson's great popularity had been laid.

The Hartford Convention.

The War of 1812 ended with the federal government impoverished and the public debt standing at $127 million. Public credit had so deteriorated that for wartime securities with a face value of $80 million the government had received no more than $34 million in specie value. Only New England prospered. Since the rest of the country was blockaded, everyone had to come to New England for imports. New England early in the war turned energetically to expand her own textile industry. The number of cotton spindles alone increased from 80,000 in 1810 to 500,000 in 1814; with the introduction of the power loom in 1814, factory production of cotton cloth took a long step forward.

All this activity was reflected in financial trends: while the rest of the country was being drained of specie, the banks of Massachusetts increased their specie hoardings four-fold from the beginning of 1811 to 1814. Yet of $40 million in long-term bonds sold by the federal government in the same period, New England subscribed the niggardly sum of less than $3 million. Add to this financial resistance New England's refusal to employ her militia in the national cause, and it can be seen that her antagonism to the war was in dead earnest.

The Hartford Convention, called by Massachusetts in October, 1814, and assembled the following December, capped what many had come to label New England's treason. Here delegates from Massachusetts, Rhode Island, and Connecticut (with unofficial members from Vermont and New Hampshire) met to air their "public grievances and concerns" and to propose amendments

Southwest Campaign 1813 – 15

0   Miles   100

Huntsville

Jackson against the Creeks 1813–14

Horseshoe Bend Mar. 1814

Vicksburg

MISSISSIPPI   TERR.

Jackson 1814

Ft. Mims

Mobile

SP. FLORIDA

New Orleans Dec.-Jan. 1815

Pensacola Nov. 1814

Pakenham from Jamaica

BRITISH BLOCKADE

Gulf of Mexico

LA.

Battle of New Orleans. Jackson's troops behind the barricades at the left mow down the British formations in the center.

to the Constitution. The "peace party" in New England had coalesced under the uncompromising leadership of Timothy Pickering in 1808 and had clamored all through the war for a separate peace with England. The moderates, led by Harrison Gray Otis, however, got control of the Hartford Convention, issued states-rights pronouncements reminiscent of the Virginia-Kentucky Resolutions of 1798 (see p. 154), and proposed a series of amendments to the Constitution aimed to protect New England against the rising West and to reduce the power of the Virginia dynasty in the South. One amendment would have eliminated the "three-fifths" clause of the Constitution (see p. 132), thus depriving the South of representation based partly on its slave population. Others would have limited the presidency to one term and prohibited the election of successive presidents from the same state.

Ready to reconvene if Congress failed to meet its demands, the Hartford Convention closed just when the war itself was coming to an end. Both events quieted talk of secession. By its hostility to the war and its association with the Convention, the Federalist party doomed itself and opened the way for the so-called "Era of Good Feelings" in domestic politics.

III.   NEW SETTLERS AND NEW TARIFFS

Borders and Boundaries.   Having thwarted invasion from abroad and having survived disunion at home, Madison's administration was eager to turn again to the internal development of the country. But first, issues left over from the indecisive war had to be settled.

Early in 1814, Madison learned that the British were ready to talk peace, and he promptly sent Henry Clay and Jonathan Russell to join Gallatin, Bayard, and Adams at Ghent, in Belgium, where discussions were to take place. But each team of negotiators came to the discussions with an exacting set of demands, the British asking for large territorial gains for Canada and for an Indian buffer state, the Americans for the abandonment of impressment and other objectionable practices. At first it appeared that no meeting of minds was possible. With the discussions deadlocked, the British cabinet sought the counsel of the Duke of Wellington, the hero of the Napoleonic wars, who advised that a successful conclusion of the war would be more costly than most Britishers were willing to endure. At the same time, news arrived of the recent American victories on Lake Champlain and at Plattsburg. The British now gave way, and a treaty was signed December 24, 1814, returning matters precisely to where they had been at the beginning of the war. The treaty did provide that commissions of experts should meet later and settle boundary and fishing disputes. Final borders were not settled until the 1840's, but an agreement in 1818 put to rest for the time being the chief points of dispute.

Until 1815, the British—never wholly accepting the independence of the United States, and retaining some hope of reclaiming the former colonies—had been careless about the Canadian boundary line. The work of the commissions was eventually accepted in good faith by both the United States and Great Britain, but it took some time before relations between them could proceed with friendliness and trust. "That man must be blind to the indications of the future," said Clay in 1816, "who cannot see that we are destined to have war after war with Great

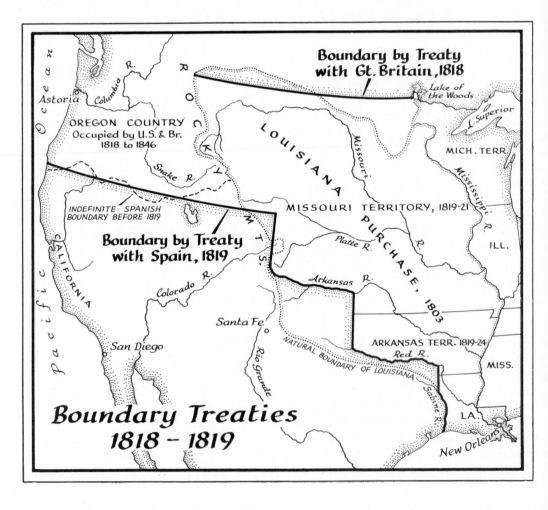

Boundary Treaties 1818 – 1819

Britain." Reflecting Clay's distrust, Congress in 1815 had voted a standing army of 10,000 regulars, greater appropriations for West Point, and $8 million for new warships.

Britain herself watered the ground in which feelings against her grew. There were many occasions for friction. A commercial treaty was arranged between the two countries in July, 1815, which removed discriminations against the commerce of either party in the ports of the other. The stone in the shoe, however, was Britain's insistence that the precious West Indian trade be kept closed to Yankee ships.

From another quarter came more abrasive evidence of ill-will. Nothing had been said about impressment in the Treaty of Ghent or later; after the war, English men-of-war persisted in searching American vessels for British sailors. Shortly after Madison had learned of incidents of this sort on the Great Lakes themselves, news arrived that the British were building new frigates in Canada for lake service. The cost of defense was already great enough, and Madison badly wanted to avoid an armaments race. Early in 1816 he proposed to England that naval vessels of both countries be kept off the Great Lakes. Foreign Secretary Castlereagh, also eager to cut taxes, welcomed the suggestion. To work out a plan, the British representative in Washington, Charles Bagot, met with Richard Rush, acting American Secretary of State, in April, 1817. They made a pact by which each country would henceforth maintain no more than four small armed vessels on the Great Lakes. Except for certain technical changes, the Rush-Bagot agreement was still in force 140 years later.

Anglo-American relations, improved by this evidence of cooperation, soon deteriorated as new disputes flared up in Florida. After the war, ambitious Britishers, among them an old Scottish trader, Arbuthnot, and a young adventurer, Ambrister, convinced the Creeks that their treaty of 1814 with Jackson (see p. 178) was not binding. In 1817, some Seminoles, goaded by Ambrister, taunted a group of Americans onto Creek lands and scalped them. They next ambushed and mas-

sacred reinforcements on their way to Jackson, who had been ordered to punish them. Jackson took his revenge by burning the Indian villages and hanging two of their chiefs. He court-martialed Ambrister, who had started the trouble, and Arbuthnot, who he thought was involved in it, and executed them as well. He then marched on the Spanish in Pensacola, where the Indians had found a haven, ejected the governor, installed his own garrisons, and claimed the territory for the United States.

Many Englishmen demanded war over the execution of their citizens, and many Spaniards were outraged over the invasion of their territory. Congress, meanwhile, where Jackson had enemies, stormed over this wholly arbitrary action of the uncontrollable general. The envious Clay and the outraged Secretary of War, Calhoun, both of whom saw in Jackson a genuine threat to their presidential ambitions, urged that apologies be made to England and Spain. But Secretary of State John Quincy Adams held that Spain had got what she deserved for failing to keep order on American borders. Far from apologizing, he demanded that Spain pay the costs of Jackson's excursion and punish her incompetent officials. Spain, in difficulties over the revolt of her South American colonies, with whom England was already developing an active trade, and unsupported by England, yielded to Adams' demands. After negotiations, she agreed to cede all Florida in ex-

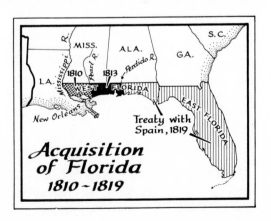

Acquisition of Florida 1810-1819

change for payment by the United States of the $5 million owed to American merchants who had lost ships to Spain during the Napoleonic wars. These and other terms were included in a treaty written in 1819. Because of a revolution in Spain, consideration of the treaty was delayed there until the fall of 1820. The United States Senate ratified the Florida treaty in February, 1821.

Agreement on the northern boundary with Britain and acquisition of southern territory from Spain satisfied the Republican land-hunger for the time being. But the settlement of these lands still hinged on the subjugation or removal of the Indians. Tecumseh's fall cost the northern tribes their leader, and the retirement of England from the Lakes area left them bereft of their only ally and protector. The United States now began a building program in this region. By 1822, older outposts like Fort Wayne and Fort Harrison in Indiana had been restored, and a string of new forts had been built along the Mississippi in Illinois and Wisconsin. To these the government added a line of trading centers where Indians could buy goods below cost; the object was to wean them away from the Canadians, who still sought to trade with them. Having been made tractable by these measures, the Indians in the Northwest Territory agreed, in a series of new treaties, to move across the Mississippi.

In the Southwest, Jackson's victories during the war, and his postwar assaults, cowed the natives. They now were offered what was regarded to be the humane choice of taking up agriculture on the lands where they lived, or moving westward. To the chagrin of the whites, most of the Indians preferred agriculture to moving, and not until after the election of Jackson in 1828 were the "Civilized Tribes" of the Southwest forcibly ejected from their lands.

The Tariff of 1816.   The embargo and other restrictive measures, as well as the War of 1812 itself, gave an immense stimulus to home manufactures by cutting down international trade. As factories were set up in all parts of the United States, even former opponents of American manufacturing became reconciled to it. Thomas Jefferson himself acknowledged, "that manufactures are as necessary to our independence as to our comforts."

But it was one thing to build factories in wartime, quite another to maintain them against foreign competition in peacetime. When the War of 1812 ended early in 1815, Americans rushed to replenish their supplies of European—mainly English—finery and other goods. Imports soared to record heights, and English manufacturers deliberately dumped goods on the American market at bargain prices. "It was well worth while," Henry Brougham told Parliament in 1816 "to incur a loss on the first exportation in order, by the glut, to stifle in the cradle those rising manufactures in the United States, which the war has forced into existence." Petitions rolled in to protect manufacturers against such tactics. In 1816, at Madison's behest, Congress passed a tariff that marked a new turn in American policy. Previously, all tariffs had been imposed primarily to raise revenue; this one was designed to protect home industries.

The measure was not passed without a struggle, and the alignment of forces in the House of Representatives provided a commentary on the distribution of American economic interests. New England's support for the tariff by a vote of 17-10 was a sign of the times. The old trading interests of Marblehead, Newburyport, and Salem lost much of their business as Europe recovered its own carrying trade, and as large-scale migrations from interior New England to the West cut the size of the nearby internal market. But while trading interests took a glum view of the future, younger and more farsighted men were turning their capital into manufactures and laying the basis for the future vigor and glory of Massachusetts. As the old ports declined, new towns came into prominence—Lowell, Lawrence, Chicopee, and Manchester. Boston herself absorbed the trade of the older ports and waxed important as the center of the capital market as well.

In 1816, however, this development was still in its early stages. A substantial minority of New England's delegates, headed by the astute politician, Daniel Webster, still spoke for the commercial interests and fought to keep duties down. The Middle Atlantic states, now in the full swing of the manufacturing development, had relatively fewer mercantile interests to contend with, and supported the Tariff of 1816 by the substantial margin of 42 to 5. The South, despite her commitment to cotton, tobacco, and overseas trade, still numbered in her midst statesmen like the young Calhoun, who sympathized with manufacturers elsewhere and hoped that the South herself might soon have factories to take advantage of domestic cotton supplies. Hence the South Atlantic states opposed the tariff, but with some dissenters

(35 to 16), and the Southwest split 3 to 3. The western states, Ohio, Kentucky, and Missouri, supported local manufactures by 10 to 1.

The 1816 tariff failed in its purpose. British manufacturers evaded it by false invoices and other devices, and kept their American customers by offering lower prices and longer credit than American manufacturers could afford. By 1820, when tariff interests moved once again for a still higher protective measure, New England stood 18 to 17 for protection, the Middle states 55 to 1, and the Northwest 12 to 3. But opposition was stronger in the South and Southwest. The bill passed the House, but it was rejected in the Senate by one vote. A sectional line-up on this issue had begun to appear, foreshadowing the struggles of 1828 and 1832-1833.

IV. THE "ERA OF GOOD FEELINGS"

The Election of 1816. The "Era of Good Feelings" was in fact an interlude of acrimonious local factionalism between the War of 1812 and the beginnings of Jacksonian Democracy. It received its name simply because the absence of a two-party system and a passing moment of harmony caused a magazine editor to use a phrase that has intrigued subsequent historians.

In the election of 1816, when the rest of the country almost unanimously went Republican, many New England Federalists still clung to their old party. To broaden their appeal in the campaign, they nominated Rufus King, a New Yorker who had originally opposed the War of 1812 but later had pleased the patriots by favoring its vigorous prosecution. A more important battle than the election itself was the fight among Republican leaders over their own standard-bearer. William H. Crawford of Georgia had the support of the old Randolph states-rights contingent. But Crawford personally did not oppose Madison's Secretary of State, James

Monroe, who narrowly won in the Republican caucus. Monroe found the election as easy to win as the nomination, and received 183 electoral votes to 34 for King. The Federalist candidates, the last in history, carried only Massachusetts, Connecticut, and Delaware.

Monroe appointed a strong cabinet, of which the ablest member was a New Englander, John Quincy Adams, whose presence as Secretary of State put the conduct of foreign affairs in the hands of a skilled diplomat and appeased the feelings of many New Englanders. At the very beginning of his administration, Monroe made a journey through the northeastern states that was topped by an extremely cordial reception in New England. After this trip, Boston's *Columbian Sentinel* published an article entitled "Era of Good Feelings," in which it noted with pleasure "all the circumstances . . . during the late Presidential Jubilee . . . which attended the demonstration of good feelings." By 1816, the Republicans under Madison had shown so much concern for manufactures and the tariff, for an army and a navy, even for chartering a national bank, that the old issues no longer stood in the way of reconciliation. It seemed as though Virginia and Massachusetts had made peace at last; and indeed, Monroe was re-elected in 1820 with only a single vote (from New Hampshire) cast against him in the entire electoral college.

The Postwar Economic Boom.

While manufacturers struggled to maintain themselves against foreign competition, most of the country enjoyed a brief but heartening period of prosperity. England's textile manufacturing boom, reflected in her massive exports to the United States, brought with it an enormous demand for southern cotton for her tireless machines. The end of the war also revived the European market for southern tobacco. Poor European harvests in 1816 and 1817 added to the demand for western wheat, pork, and beef. With these agricultural staples Americans were able to pay for their record imports of manufactures right after the peace.

This combination of factors drew thousands to the West and Southwest. Between 1810 and 1820, Indiana grew 500 per cent, Illinois 268 per cent, Missouri 237 per cent, and Mississippi 87 per cent. By 1820, Ohio had become more populous than Massachusetts, and the entire West, with about 2,200,000 settlers, had more people than New England. As always in American history, a boom in agriculture brought a boom in land speculation. Spurring on the speculative boom were the 300 or more state and "private" banks that were established after the First Bank of the United States went out of existence in 1811. By 1817, state and private banks had issued $100 million in paper money, much of it unnegotiable even in neighboring communities. Although these "facility notes," as they were called, helped newcomers get started and oldsters to expand, often enough they served only to create an

obligation on which the banker could foreclose simply by withholding further "facilities" at his pleasure. "What," asked the journalist Hezekiah Niles, "is to be the end of such a business?—Mammoth fortunes for the *wise,* wretched poverty for the *foolish.* . . . SPECULATION in a Coach, HONESTY in the Jail."

The Second Bank
and the End of the Boom.

By 1817, the Second Bank of the United States, chartered the year before, entered the business picture. Back in 1814, financiers like John Jacob Astor and Stephen Girard, who had lent large amounts to the government to aid the war effort, had begun agitating for a new United States bank to mobilize the financial resources of the country. But in 1815, though the government had been forced the previous year to suspend payments in specie, a bill for a new bank which passed Congress was struck down by Madison's veto. By 1816, the post-war boom began to make itself felt. Since heavy agricultural exports had failed to match the value of imported goods, scarce specie was drained from the country to pay the balances owed abroad. Most of the gold that remained was in demand to finance land speculation. Thus the government found it increasingly difficult to get acceptable currency for its daily and seasonal needs. Early in 1816, therefore, Secretary of the Treasury Alexander Dallas tailored a bank bill to the requirements of Congress and the President. In April, it passed over the opposition of New England, where the state banks were well-managed and it was not needed. It had the firm backing of Calhoun and Clay.

Like the first national bank, the Second Bank of the United States was chartered for 20 years as the sole depository for government funds. Its capital, reflecting the growth of the country, was placed at $35 million, three and a half times the amount set for the earlier bank. Of this sum, the government was to subscribe one-fifth, or $7 million. Of the remainder, $7 million was to be subscribed in specie and $21 million in the form of securities of the United States. Five of the Bank's 25 directors were to be appointed by the president of the United States; the rest by American stockholders. Foreign stockholders were to have no voice in the Bank's affairs. The Second Bank had the right to establish branches in different parts of the country. Foreseeing competition, however, influential local bankers had persuaded the politicians to write into some western state constitutions provisions against "foreign banks" doing business within their borders.

Ill-managed from the first in the places where it could do business, the new B.U.S. proceeded to justify local fears by outdoing even the state banks in the lavishness of its loans. These were extended in the form of notes that were more acceptable than the notes issued by the local banks. In retaliation, the injured bankers got their states to try to tax out of existence both the branches and the notes of "the monster." In the summer of 1818, the B.U.S. was at last ready with deflationary measures to control the boom. But these measures only made it unpopular with both the people and the local bankers. The sudden contraction of credit prevented many people from keeping up payments on their speculative debts, and before the year 1819 was out, the whole boom collapsed.

Actually, the economic collapse was worldwide. The revival of European harvests after the Napoleonic wars and the weakening of the postwar textile boom combined to create a glut both of wheat and cotton in world markets. But the depression was most severe in the United States and most devastating in the West.

The crisis prompted a number of states to abolish the useless and degrading punishment of imprisonment for debt and to pass liberal bankruptcy laws and laws easing the settlement of contracts. Congress also came to the aid of the West with a new land act in 1820 making it possible for a settler to buy an 80-acre homestead for $100 in cash. The next year it added a Relief Act to assist those people whom earlier credit provisions had got into trouble.

The Role of the Supreme Court.

Against this background of local self-assertion, expanding commerce and invention, internal depression, and quarrels between debtors and creditors, John Marshall issued a series of historic Supreme Court decisions. A veteran of the Revolutionary wars and of Federalist diplomacy, Marshall had been one of the early and outspoken advocates of the Federal Constitution in Virginia, and after the death of Washington he remained the greatest exponent of Federalism in his state. He was not deeply learned in the law, but he had a dominating personality and a command of persuasive logic. As Chief Justice, he imposed his stamp on the Court and usually imposed his will on the form of its decisions. We have already observed how, appointed in 1801 by John Adams, he laid the basis in *Marbury* v. *Madison* (1803) for the Court's power to declare acts of Congress unconstitutional (see p. 156) and how, in *Fletcher* v. *Peck* (1810), he upheld the obligation of contracts against state interference (see p. 159). In a series of subsequent decisions—often the subject of much controversy—he greatly expanded the authority of the Court and the powers of the federal government, limited the scope of action by the states, and defended the sanctity of private contracts against legislative interference.

In 1819, while controversies between debtors and creditors were raging in the states, Marshall handed down two decisions bearing on the rights of contract. Of sweeping importance was *Dartmouth College* v. *Woodward*, which raised the question of whether the charter granted to the college by the legislature could subsequently be changed by the legislature. Marshall decided that the charter was a contract and that it had been unconstitutionally impaired by the legislation in question. Of great importance to colleges, this decision was of still greater importance to business enterprises operating under legislative charters; for it now appeared that these charters, defined as contracts, were secure and substantially unchangeable.

The second decision in 1819, *Sturges* v. *Crowninshield,* dealt with a New York State bankruptcy law. Marshall found that even though Congress was empowered to pass bankruptcy laws, the states could also enact them if Congress failed to exercise its powers. But insofar as the New York law sought to relieve a debtor of the obligation to pay his debt, Marshall found it in violation of the contract clause of the Constitution. Eight years later, however, in the case of *Ogden* v. *Saunders* (1827), Marshall failed for the first and only time to persuade the other justices to follow him in rigidly enforcing the contract laws. Earlier bankruptcy decisions had ruled out state laws impairing debts made *before* these laws were passed. In *Ogden* v. *Saunders,* Marshall wanted to throw out a law impairing debts contracted *after* its passage; but in this case the Court forsook him and upheld a state law of this kind.

In establishing the supremacy of the federal government and the Supreme Court over acts of states, Marshall's regime was a spectacular success. During his 34 years as Chief Justice, the Court acted no less than 13 times to set aside state laws as contrary to the Constitution. In *Martin* v. *Hunter's Lessee* (1816), the Court, speaking through Justice Joseph Story, asserted its supremacy over state courts in interpreting the Constitution. And five years later, in *Cohens* v. *Virginia* (1821), Marshall went out of his way to state this principle in the broadest possible terms.

Two other decisions in 1819 and 1824 clarified and broadened the powers of Congress over matters of decisive economic importance. In *McCulloch* v. *Maryland* (1819), the constitutionality of the national bank was questioned. The state of Maryland had attempted to tax the Baltimore branch of the Bank of the United States out of existence. In broad language, Marshall found that the act creating the Bank was constitutional: "Let the end be legitimate, let it be within the scope of the Constitution, and all means which are appropriate, which are plainly adapted to that end, which are not prohibited, but consist with the letter and spirit of the Constitution, are constitutional." This, one of the most famous sentences in American constitutional law, laid the foundation for a generous interpretation of the implied powers of Congress, as Hamilton had wished. As for the Maryland law taxing the Bank, Marshall found it unconstitutional. "The power to tax," he said, "involves the power to destroy." If the states were allowed to nullify acts of Congress by attacking its agencies, they could "defeat and render useless the power to create." Hence the states do not have the power to "retard, impede, burden, or in any manner control" the operation of constitutional laws passed by Congress to execute powers given to the federal government.

Finally, in the case of *Gibbons* v. *Ogden* (1824), Marshall spoke out on the power of Congress to regulate commerce. New York had granted Robert Fulton and Robert R. Livingston a monopoly of steam navigation in state waters. Aaron Ogden bought from the monopolists the right to run a ferry between New York and New Jersey. When Thomas Gibbons set up a competing ferry, Ogden tried to invoke the monopoly to restrain him from running it. The original grant by New York encroached upon the right of Congress to regulate interstate commerce, but Marshall did not rest content with a narrow assertion of this finding. Instead, he went on to construe the term "commerce" as broadly as necessary, specifically including within it navigation inside the limits of the states. Again, in sweeping language, he excluded the states from acting on such matters when their acts intruded upon the powers of Congress.

V. THE MISSOURI COMPROMISE

The "Era of Good Feelings" had opened in the glow of nationalist feeling inspired by the War of 1812, but conflicts over state rights and sectional aspirations marred it almost from the start. The worst of these clashes took place between 1819 and 1821, when the question of the admission of Missouri to the Union reopened the controversy over slavery. This "momentous question," cried Jefferson in 1820, "like a fire-bell in the night, awakened and filled me with terror."

Slavery had been forbidden in the Northwest Territory by the planners of Jefferson's generation. Thus the first momentous clash occurred just beyond, in the so-called Upper Louisiana Territory, whose settlers applied for admission under the name of Missouri in February, 1819. The "enabling act" to make Missouri a state moved through the

congressional committees in routine fashion. No problems seemed likely to arise until Representative Tallmadge of New York shocked the entire South by offering an amendment to prohibit the introduction of any additional slaves into the new state. He proposed, further, that all children born of slaves in that region be freed when they reached the age of 25.

In 1819, the United States was divided equally into 11 free states and 11 slave states. Although the free states had grown much more populous than those in the South, the southern states could still count on equal representation in the Senate, to which they looked for protection. The Tallmadge Amendment threatened to overthrow this balance of power. After intense debate, the House of Representatives passed the amendment in February, 1819, with a clearly sec-

The Missouri Compromise 1820

tional vote; but the Senate rejected it, and the issue was carried over to the next session, which began in December, 1819.

By then the situation had changed significantly. Maine, which had always been a part of Massachusetts, now asked, with the approval of Massachusetts, for admission as an independent state. There was no chance that slavery would ever become established in Maine. So Maine entered the Union as a free state, and if Missouri was admitted with the privilege of embracing slavery, the old balance in the Senate would be preserved. This settlement of the issue was worked out in a series of measures known as the "Missouri Compromise." Its most significant provision permitted slavery in Missouri, but prohibited it "forever . . . in all territory ceded by France to the United States . . . which lies north of 36°30' . . . not included within the limits of [that] state." President Monroe signed the Missouri Compromise on March 6, 1820.

When Congress took up the matter of approving Missouri's new state constitution, as required by the admitting process, new trouble arose. This constitution provided that the state should never emancipate slaves without the consent of their owners; worse, it contravened the equal privileges and immunities clause of the Federal Constitution by absolutely prohibiting the entrance of any free Negroes into the state. Through the efforts of Henry Clay, Congress finally accepted the state constitution, but not before the so-called "Second Missouri Compromise" required the state legislature to guarantee that it would never deny any of the privileges and immunities of citizens of the United States inside the borders of Missouri.

VI. MONROE AND THE WORLD

Revolt in Spain
and Spanish-America.

Monroe carried his caution over to relations with other nations in the Hemisphere and in the world. In 1810, after Napoleon had invaded Spain, revolts broke out in most of the Spanish-American territory. These revolts had the blessing of Madison, who was then president. By 1816, with the downfall of Napoleon, Spain managed to reinstate a semblance of control in the Western Hemisphere. But she was successfully defied by such Latin-American patriots as José de San Martin, the founder of Argentina, Simón Bolívar, the founder of Venezuela, and Bernardo O'Higgins, the successful dictator of Chile. When these new countries sought American recognition, the United States was negotiating for the purchase of Florida, and Monroe and his Secretary of State, John Quincy Adams, were afraid of displeasing Spain by recognizing them. Henry Clay took a bolder stand, demanding the recognition of these rebels against monarchy, and the support of others who might take up the cudgels of liberty.

Congress did not act on his suggestion; instead it passed a neutrality act in 1818.

In the next five years, great changes took place. By 1822, Peru and Mexico had become independent of Spain, and Brazil had succeeded in throwing off the yoke of Portugal. Revolt had spread to Spain itself. The Quadruple Alliance, which had originally been formed in 1815 by Russia, Prussia, Austria, and Great Britain to keep a watchful eye on any anti-monarchical developments, now determined to enlarge its operations and to crush anti-monarchical uprisings. Against the wishes of the British, who had deserted the Alliance, an Austrian army had been dispatched to restore the king in Naples, and now a French army was to restore the king of Spain. There was even talk of trying to restore Spain's empire in the New World.

The American Reaction.

The threat of possible European intervention in the New World prompted Monroe and Adams to act.

The United States had already granted diplomatic recognition to several of the new Latin-American governments, and in 1823 Monroe and Adams took under sympathetic consideration the suggestion of the new British foreign secretary, George Canning, that the United Kingdom and the United States make a joint protest against any intervention by European powers in the New World.

The interests of the United States in Latin America had become clear. First, there were ideological considerations: a victory there for so-called republicanism was a victory for republicanism everywhere. And there were military considerations as well. The expulsion of European powers from the Western Hemisphere would help keep the United States from becoming entangled in Europe's wars. Finally, there were commercial considerations: Spain's mercantile policy had been extremely monopolistic; her expulsion from the New World would leave the trade of her former colonies open to all comers.

The British also had new commercial interests in Latin America, and they had capital to invest overseas. Having lent money to the revolutionaries, they now looked to the new governments to supply outlets for investment and goods. The British had no desire to help the growth of American interests in Latin America; they simply looked to American support in keeping other powers out, and to their own great navy to keep the Americans subservient. All these circumstances prompted Canning, in August, 1823, to propose to Richard Rush, the American minister in London, a joint Anglo-American protest against the plans of the continental nations.

Canning's proposal was immediately forwarded to Washington. When it arrived, in October, 1823, it became the subject of debate in the cabinet and of profound consideration by the retired Republican patriarchs, Jefferson and Madison. Jefferson, acknowledging that "Great Britain is the nation which can do us the most harm of any one," advised that "with her on our side we need not fear the whole world." He recommended accepting Canning's proposal. Madison concurred—and went even further. He proposed that the joint statement be extended to oppose French intervention in Spain and to protect the current revolt of the Greeks against Turkey, a revolt that had won American sympathy.

But John Quincy Adams disagreed. He feared that Canning was trying to lure the United States into a statement that would seem to be a pledge against future American acquisition of any territory still held by Spain—particularly Cuba. So he urged that the United States act alone and limit its declaration to the Western Hemisphere.

The Monroe Doctrine.

Monroe gradually yielded to Adams' arguments, and in his annual address to Congress on December 2, 1823, he used the words that have since been described as an expression of his "doctrine":

> The political system of the allied powers [of Europe] is essentially different . . . from that of America. . . . We owe it, therefore, to candor and to the amicable relations existing between the United States and those powers to declare that we should consider any attempt on their part to extend their system to any portion of this hemisphere as dangerous to our peace and safety. . . . With the governments who have declared their independence and maintained it, and whose independence we have . . . acknowledged, we could not view any interposition . . . by any European power in any other light than as the manifestation of an unfriendly disposition toward the United States.

Latin America was not the only area of the Western Hemisphere in which European aggression worried Monroe's government. For example, the Russians had been in Alaska for decades. In 1821, the ambitious Alexander I issued a decree declaring that Russian territory extended south to the 51st parallel, and ordering all foreign ships to remain at least 100 miles from the coastline of that territory. This move brought Russia into Oregon, toward which the fur trade had turned American eyes; it also cut off American ships from carrying on the China trade in Oregon furs.

To cover this situation Monroe also asserted "as a principle" in his message to Congress, that the American continents ". . . are henceforth not to be considered as subjects for future colonization by any European powers." As if to buttress the logic and strength of this America-for-Americans policy, Monroe then reaffirmed Adams' stand: "Our position in regard to Europe . . . is, not to interfere in the internal concerns of any of its powers; to consider the government *de facto* as the legitimate government for us; to cultivate friendly relations with it. . . ."

For a long time the Monroe doctrine had little practical meaning. The American press was enthusiastic, Canning irritated, and European embassies quietly annoyed by what they considered to be an arrogant and peremptory action. Latin Americans were well aware that the chief bulwark of their newly won independence was not American good will but the strength of the British navy. To be sure, Russia agreed in 1824 not to extend the southern border of Alaska below 54°40'; but she probably would have done the same thing even without Monroe's pronouncement. Only in later years, when the United States had the stature and the strength to put meaning into the words, did the Monroe Doctrine carry weight in the world.

Readings

Henry Adams' classic *History of the United States,* mentioned in Chapter VII, remains the best general account of the period that culminated in the War of 1812, and its treatment of the war itself is outstanding. Another classic in American historical writing, essential to an understanding of this period, is Frederick Jackson Turner, *The Frontier in American History* (1920). Turner's *Rise of the New West* (1906) should also be read. An unusually perceptive account of the period covered by this chapter is George Dangerfield, *The Era of Good Feelings* (1952). The general works on the West by Billington, Riegel, and Clark, cited in our general bibliography, are all illuminating.

Expansionists of 1812, by Julius W. Pratt (1925), persuasively develops the idea that the origins of the war had less to do with freedom of the seas than with American hunger for Canada and other territory. Alfred L. Burt, *The United States, Great Britain, and British North America* (1940), equally persuasive, takes issue with Pratt's thesis. The best short treatment of the war itself is Francis F. Beirne, *The War of 1812* (1949). The Canadian side is recounted in Charles P. Lucas, *The Canadian War of 1812* (1906). On the war at sea, the most important work is Alfred T. Mahan, *Sea Power in Its Relations to the War of 1812* (2 vols., 1919). On the diplomacy of the war and the peace, Samuel F. Bemis, *John Quincy Adams and the Foundations of American Foreign Policy* (1949), is enlightening. On the Hartford Convention, besides Henry Adams' and Dangerfield's books, see also Henry Adams, *Documents Relating to New England Federalism* (1877), and Samuel E. Morison, *The Life and Letters of Harrison Gray Otis* (2 vols., 1913).

An excellent account of the western panic of 1819 can be found in Volume IV of Beveridge's *Life of John Marshall* (referred to in Chapter VII), which also is best on the performance of the Supreme Court under Marshall in the period just after the panic. On the Court, a short, valuable work is Edward S. Corwin, *John Marshall and the Constitution* (1919). On the Missouri Compromise, see Glover Moore, *The Missouri Controversy* (1953), and F. C. Shoemaker, *Missouri's Struggle for Statehood* (1916).

A useful biography of President Monroe is William P. Cresson, *James Monroe* (1946). On the internal conflicts of Monroe's administration, the old biography by Carl Schurz, *The Life of Henry Clay* (2 vols., 1887), and the more recent, *The Life of Andrew Jackson,* by Marquis James (one-volume edition, 1938) are illuminating. The Monroe Doctrine may best be studied in Dexter Perkins, *A History of the Monroe Doctrine* (1955). Bemis' *John Quincy Adams and the Foundation of American Foreign Policy,* noted above, is also relevant and reliable. For the British side, see C. K. Webster, *Foreign Policy of Castlereagh, 1815-1822* (1925), and H. W. V. Temperley, *The Foreign Policy of Canning, 1822-1827* (1925).

TOWARD
A SECTIONAL
ECONOMY

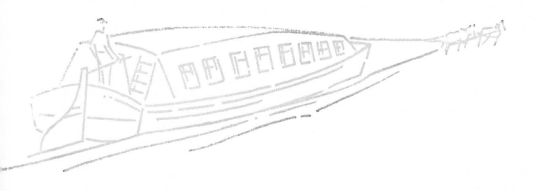

CHAPTER NINE

For 40 years after the Revolution, most of the great issues of American politics sprang from economic matters. Controversies over land policy, tariffs, commercial treaties, currency, the public debt, banks, bankruptcy laws, slave labor, internal improvements—all aroused passions, aggravated social distinc-tions, and inspired fundamental shifts in power and philosophy. Yet for most of this period, such controversies touched the direct interests of relatively few people. Political action may often have involved the future of the nation, but most people felt their own future to be in their own hands.

I. FARMS, FISH, AND FORESTS

In 1815, and indeed for several decades thereafter, the majority of free Americans still lived on family farms in the South as well as in the North. For millions, all but a few family needs continued to be supplied by the husbandry of men and boys, the spinning, stitching, baking, and brewing of women and girls. These people, or their forebears, had come to America partly in search of personal freedom based on economic independence; they remained relatively unconcerned about economic enterprise or growth. Innovations in crops, tools, agricultural methods, and marketing techniques left most of them scornful and skeptical. They traded little and traveled less. Cultivating the land was to them a complete and sanctified way of life rather than a business that fluctuated with the ups and downs of the world and worldly affairs.

The sea with its fish supplied another great natural resource from which many Americans eked out a fiercely independent existence long after the Revolution. Fishermen in most fishing towns went out, like farmers, only for the day. Each had his own boat and brought back his catch for his family, though he might sometimes barter a surplus for grain, clothing, or equipment. At more active fishing centers like Newburyport and Beverly, and on Cape Cod, greater enterprise was shown and voyages were longer and better organized. Nevertheless the rule was that each man supplied his own gear and provisions in return for a share of the catch. The fisherman always preferred going out "on his own hook," a phrase that originated with these Yankees.

One specialized fishing activity—whaling —ranked very high in value of product until after the Civil War, when kerosene supplanted whale oil as an illuminant. Until the War of 1812, just about every New England port had its whaling fleet. After the war, Nantucket Island and New Bedford, Massachusetts, almost monopolized the industry. And after 1820, New Bedford became the whaling center of the world, with perhaps a third of the entire fleet. "New Bedford is not nearer to the whales than New London or Portland," wrote Emerson, "yet they have all the equipments for a whaler ready, and they hug an oil-cask like a brother."

As in farming, fishing, and whaling, few innovations were made in lumbering in the first third of the nineteenth century. In colonial times, American forests had supplied England's navy and merchant marine. After the Revolution, England turned to Scandinavia for timber, but the American industry continued to grow steadily. The home merchant marine was expanding, cities needed more and more new buildings, and steamboats required great quantities of wood for construction and fuel. But until the railroads added their own huge demand for wood for fuel, ties, and rolling stock, and helped to settle the prairies and the plains where there were no trees, lumbering remained the occupation of uncompromisingly individualistic loggers, who supplied timber to widely scattered and independently owned saw mills.

The Indians had taught settlers in America how to grow corn, harpoon whales, and girdle and kill trees before felling them. For more than two centuries, these basic techniques of farming, fishing, and lumbering spread with the gradual development of the country. So did the time-tested methods of making flour, leather, oil, iron ware, and the like. Enterprises specializing in such commodities were organized locally and were carried on generation after generation on a family basis. They offered a living and a way of life; they were marked by stability rather than speculation, tradition rather than innovation.

II. THE FAR WEST:
THE FUR TRADE AND THE SANTA FE TRAIL

Early in the nineteenth century, no one in America was more isolated than the fur-trapper and trader. As the historian Robert Glass Cleland has said, he "started from frontiers at which more cautious pioneers were glad to stop . . . and wandered through the reaches of the outer West with all the freedom of the lonely wind." But, unlike the other primary occupations in America, the fur trade gave a new direction to American life, a new method to American business, and a new spirit to the American economy.

The Fur Trade
and the China Trade.

Fur—mink, otter. lynx, fox, and the ubiquitous beaver, as well as the coarser bear, wolf, deer, rabbit, musk-rat, "coon," and "possum"—had been one of the very first export staples of the colonies. The finer pelts were used for hats, cloaks, and robes; the coarser ones for blankets for man and beast. The Indians, who did most of the actual trapping, traded their valuable furs for tinsel, shoddy, and drink. Consequently, from the start, profits had been large and competition keen. As early as 1700, over-trapping had already exhausted the fur in some areas, and in the next 50 years French traders from Canada and Spanish traders from Mexico, as well as the English colonists, had forced their way a thousand miles inland, far in advance of settlement.

Two thousand miles beyond even the farthest inland fur-trading post in the Mississippi Valley were the sea-otter waters off the Oregon coast. Sea captains from New England and New York, turning to the China trade immediately after the Revolution, discovered an eager market for the strikingly beautiful sea-otter skins (as well as for other domestic furs) among the wealthy mandarins of North China. Here tastes were elegant, the winters frigid, and the dwellings unheated. New Englanders, especially, were attracted to the sea-otter trade because it gave them a product to exchange for the tea, silk, spices, and cheap cottons ("nankeens") of the Orient, which were in such demand at home. The man who made the most of this business, however, was John Jacob Astor, who had emigrated from Germany to New York in 1783. He made his first venture in the China trade in 1800, by which time he had become the leading fur merchant in New York City.

The China trade had opened the eyes of the western trappers and traders as well as the eastern sea captains and merchants, and following the return of Lewis and Clark from their transcontinental expedition of 1806 (see p. 160), a big westward expansion of the fur industry began, with St. Louis as its eastern base. The farther the fur trade reached out from St. Louis, however, the clearer it became that only large, well-financed corporations could afford to engage in it. Trade with the hostile Plains Indians required well-manned and well-armed expeditions. As the distances increased, such expeditions had to be sent out sometimes for more than a year at a time, and that took capital. In 1809, some experienced traders recognized the trend and organized a partnership, the Missouri Fur Company, with headquarters in St. Louis. Similar partnerships were formed in the trapping country itself. All failed, however, mainly because of their members' lack of experience in big business. Speeding their demise was Astor's American Fur Company, a corporation chartered by New York State in 1808 for 25 years and capitalized at $1 million.

In applying for his charter, Astor had stressed the patriotic aspects of his venture. He stated that his aim was to build a string of company posts to the Pacific along the route of Lewis and Clark, thus helping to tame these wild lands for American settlement. He set up his enterprise as a corporation partly to give weight to this great national objective, which, as Astor suggested, could hardly be accomplished by a single individual. But as Astor's friend, Washington Irving, wrote, the entire "capital was furnished by [Astor] himself—he, in fact, constituted the company."

New York granted Astor a charter but not the monopoly he hoped for. Astor nevertheless went to work on the details of his elaborate plan. By 1812, his employees had begun to build a settlement in Oregon, which they called Astoria.

Fur-trading and other enterprises in Canada had looked with hostility on Astor's undertaking, and when the outbreak of the War of 1812 made the Canadians official enemies of the United States, they decided to put an end to the American company. News of the war reached Astoria in January, 1813, along with information that a British warship was sailing toward the settlement. Resistance would have been futile, and Astor's men made the best deal they could, selling out to the North West Company, a Canadian firm, for $58,000.

For a generation thereafter, Canadians kept Americans out of Oregon and monopolized the region's fur. But they did not stop Astor. Deprived of otter skins, as early as 1813 he turned to Hawaiian sandlewood, which was imported in great quantities by the Chinese, who burned it as incense in their joss houses. This traffic and the smuggling into China of opium from the Dutch East Indies and elsewhere sustained American trade with the Orient until the 1830's, when those who had made fortunes in it began to find richer opportunities for their capital in enterprises nearer home. Once the War of 1812 was over, Astor's American Fur Company also set out to capture the fur business east of Oregon by good business methods as well as political maneuvers. Large and efficient

organization made it possible for Astor to give better terms to the trappers who supplied him with furs, to quote lower prices to his customers, and, when necessary, to outdo his rivals in the use of force and graft.

Astor's American Fur Company averaged $500,000 a year in profits until the 1830's, when styles in Europe changed. "It appears that they make hats of silk in place of beaver," Astor observed during a European trip in 1834. By that time, the great fur resources of the country had been almost exhausted. They were the first natural resources to be exploited by the new business methods, and the first to go.

Before it died, the fur trade had opened up vast areas of the West, where other resources have attracted American businessmen ever since. The fur trade had trampled and estranged the Indian, had taught him to drink "fire-water," and had armed him with guns and ammunition. But it also had brought knowledge of rivers, mountain passes, winds, and weather. And it had opened the path of civilization "to that ocean," as Lewis and Clark said of the Pacific in 1805, "the object of all our labours, the reward of all our anxieties."

The fur trade had also nurtured the China trade, which in turn stimulated the development of capitalism in New England and New York. It had made Astor the first American millionaire, and his American Fur Company the first integrated corporation, firm in capitalization, strong in management, aggressive in competition, and active in politics.

The Santa Fe Trail.

Less dramatic than the fur trade, and involving far fewer men and far less capital, was the trade across the Santa Fe Trail. Spain had established the isolated outpost of Santa Fe in the desert of New Mexico early in the seventeenth century, and had supplied it most laboriously from Vera Cruz, 1,500 miles away. Early efforts of Americans to trade at Santa Fe were defeated by Spain's rigid colonial policy (see p. 10), but after Mexico won its freedom from Spain in 1821, the settlement was opened to American traders. The Santa Fe Trail, which ran westward through Kansas Territory from Independence, Missouri, was surveyed by the American army in 1825. For the next 20 years, caravans of American farm wagons trekked across it, hauling all sorts of goods from the East and from Europe. These goods were exchanged at fabulous profits for Spanish gold and silver.

The arrival of the caravan each year was a great event in the Spanish town. Gradually, some of the Americans settled there, while others, noticing the good land along the eastern part of the trail, staked out farms along

the way. When in 1844 Santa Anna, the Mexican leader, closed the trail, Americans viewed his act as interference with their rights and "destiny." The Santa Fe trade never amounted to a great deal financially, and it rarely involved more than a couple of hundred persons a year. But, like the fur trade, it opened a new path across the continent, lured American businessmen into new country, and led to a political and territorial claim that eventually was to be made good by the Mexican War.

III. THE RISE OF THE MIDDLE WEST

Early Settlers. Well to the east of the fur-trappers and traders, but traveling westward over their trails, moved frontier families like Abraham Lincoln's. The typical frontier settler of this period was part backwoodsman, part farmer, and part handyman-carpenter. Thomas Lincoln, the future president's father, was born in the hills of western Virginia in 1778. Four years later, the Lincolns were in Kentucky, where Thomas grew up "a wondering laboring boy," altogether without schooling. In 1806, after Thomas had married the "absolutely illiterate" Nancy Hanks, the Lincolns and Hanks together moved frequently. Abe was born in 1809 in one of their better log huts. By 1816, the whole tribe had gone to Indiana, where they "squatted" on a clearing for a year. For the whole of this first year they lived in that "Darne Little half face camp," a three-sided shelter with two trees for corner posts, and with brush and rough poles for walls. On the open side, which looked south, a fire was kept burning from dawn to dawn. "We lived the same as the Indians," said some Lincoln relatives later, " 'ceptin' we took an interest in politics and religion." The next year, they managed to build a typical log cabin, without floor, door, or window. A roof stuffed with mud and dry grass afforded only nominal protection from the rain.

By the time the War of 1812 broke out,

more than a million people were living in the West. Most of them probably had arrived on foot, their entire possessions on their backs or in wheelbarrows or saddled to a few scrawny cows that had been transformed into beasts of burden. Travelers from abroad noted the characteristic bluish complexion of these settlers, many of whom suffered from forest fever, malaria, milk sickness, and especially the swamp-bred ague. The land was cheap and fertile, but life seemed very hard. "The rugged road, the dirty hovels, the fire in the woods to sleep by, the pathless ways through the wilderness, the dangerous crossings of the rivers"—why, asked the Englishman, William Cobbett, in 1817, did the settlers put up with all this? "To boil their pot in gipsy-fashion, to have a mere board to eat on, to drink whiskey or pure water, to sit and sleep under a shed far inferior to English cowpens, to have a mill at twenty miles' distance, an apothecary's shop at a hundred, and a doctor nowhere." Englishmen, claimed Cobbett, could never survive such conditions. But Americans, as Jefferson said, found it "cheaper to clear a new acre than to manure an old one." So westward they moved.

On the few occasions when these people might see a bit of money—from the chance sale of a hog or a horse to a newcomer who still had coin in his jeans—it would go east to buy salt for curing meat and fish, iron for muskets, lead for bullets, powder for the charge. Usually, though, only a batch of skins could be sent off for payment. Everything else the settlers needed, they made themselves or did without. They used up their capital instead of augmenting it, and even their boys, adept from childhood with rifle and rod, "lit out for the tall timber" on their own.

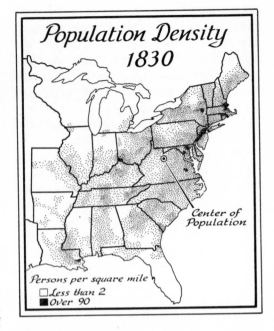

"King Cotton" and the West.

After the War of 1812, the picture in the West changed drastically, though not all at once. The subjugation of the Indians, the departure of the British from the Great Lakes and their military posts, the disintegration of Spanish rule on the Gulf coast—these developments opened up new lands to settlement and made their occupation more secure. The government also furthered settlement by liberalizing its land-sale policies and by showing more tolerance of "squatters."

Were it not for two epochal developments, however, the growth of western wealth would not have been so rapid. The first was the phenomenal rise of King Cotton in the neighboring South (plus large-scale sugar cultivation around Louisiana). The second was

The original cotton gin, 1793.

the introduction of the steamboat to western waters.

Up to 1816, 60 per cent of the nation's entire cotton crop was produced in South Carolina and Georgia, most of it in the piedmont region of those states, to which enterprising planters had moved from the worn-out soils of the tidewater. So intense did cotton-planting become that by 1820 the soil in the piedmont had also been depleted. This area, said one traveler, presented a scene of "dreary and uncultivated wastes . . . half-clothed negroes, lean and hungry stock, houses falling to decay, and fences wind-shaken and dilapidated." From such decay the planters next went into Alabama and Mississippi. The population of these states grew from about 75,000 in 1816 to 200,000 in 1820. By 1830, their combined population exceeded 400,000, even though large planters had been steadily buying up many small farms in the best cotton-producing areas. Similar growth was recorded in the Louisiana sugar country and the sections of Tennessee, Arkansas, and Florida suitable for cotton-planting.

The rapidly increasing cotton production in the new areas is reflected in the growth of New Orleans. Only 37,000 bales of cotton were shipped from this Mississippi port in 1816. In the next six years, the figure soared 435 per cent, to 161,000 bales, and by 1830 it had risen another 266 per cent, to 428,000 bales. Most of this cotton found its way to English textile factories. Some cotton went to continental countries as well, and increasing amounts were sent north to the new textile factories in New England.

It was the Cotton Kingdom's growing requirements in food and work-animals that first gave the slack westerners the impulse they needed to lay down the rod and gun and to think seriously about farming. As markets and prices improved, many farmers then began to thirst for more land. Soon speculation in land became widespread, and some western farmers, for all their prosperity, fell into debt. Now they were forced to concentrate almost as singlemindedly as the planter on cash crops. Southern specialization in cotton spurred western specialization in grain and meat and mules. The marvelous Mississippi River system conveniently tied the two sections together, and the steamboat tightened the knot.

IV.   THE GROWTH OF INTERSECTIONAL COMMERCE

The Transportation Problem.   In colonial America, the ocean had been the most-used path of communication and trade. As farms and great estates were developed along the eastern rivers, these routes also became western business. In 1824, however, John Marshall, in his momentous decision in the case of *Gibbons* v. *Ogden* (see p. 186), dealt the final blow to all monopolies on interstate waters. Fulton's surviving associates (Fulton

A shallow-draft keelboat used to carry goods upstream before the day of the steamboat.

important carriers of people, ideas, and goods. The settlement of the West brought the Mississippi system into use, and the steamboat made it the foremost inland carrier of all. The first western steamboat, the *New Orleans,* was built in 1811 by Robert Fulton, four years after his success with the *Clermont* on the Hudson River. As in New York, Fulton promptly won a monopoly of died in 1815) had been faced with competition before, but now everyone seemed to be entering the steamboat business. By 1830, nearly 200 steamboats were plying the western rivers.

Keelboat rates between Louisville and New Orleans had been about $5 per hundred pounds of freight. By 1820, steamboat rates for this trip were down to $2 per hundred pounds, and by 1842 they had been driven by competition down to 25 cents. Great technological improvements, which were reflected in speedier travel, particularly upstream, helped make even this rate profitable. Another factor was the tremendous increase brought about by the steamboat in the volume of exchange between the South and the booming West. Produce from the free western states came down by steamboat to the levees of New Orleans for shipment overseas or for distribution by coastal vessels to the rest of the South and Southwest and even to the East. And most commodities from abroad or from the East destined for the South and the West were also funneled into this booming port.

The Mississippi system, however, was not as hospitable as it seemed. The Mississippi River itself was full of snags, hidden banks, floating trees, whirlpools, and eddies. Its

tributaries shared most of these impediments and the entire system was infested with pirates. Floods often made navigation especially hazardous; but even worse were the droughts, which greatly narrowed the channels and stranded many steamboats in low water. So dangerous, indeed, were the shallows that most Mississippi traffic came to be bunched in the flood-tide periods of spring and fall. But although this tactic eased the problems of navigation, it increased the problems of marketing. During the flood-tide seasons, the New Orleans market overflowed with produce, and prices fell sharply. It was costly to store the crops until prices rose, and anyway the humidity of the Mississippi Basin spoiled the grain rapidly, making it impossible for shippers to hold their produce off the declining market for very long.

The story of roads is, if anything, worse than the tale of rivers. From the earliest times, many Americans chose to settle down on land several miles away from the nearest water routes. And yet they had to travel to the grist mills, tobacco warehouses, cotton gins, forges, country stores, county courts, and the rivers themselves. As time went on, a network of roads came into use, often following old Indian trails and trapper or trader paths. Only a few of these roads were wide enough for wagon or cart. They ran through dense, dank forests, and usually bristled with tree stumps. In spring and fall, they were likely to be muddy quagmires; in winter, they were frozen into malevolent ruts.

The greatest road-building enterprise of the early years of the Republic was the "National Highway," chartered by Congress in 1806 and built with federal funds. Work began in 1811, westward from Cumberland, Maryland. By 1818, the road had reached Wheeling, Virginia, on the Ohio River. Until 1825, when work was resumed, Wheeling remained the western terminal. By midcentury, the road had been pushed to Vandalia, Illinois, its westernmost point.

The National Highway was an efficient carrier. Other useful roads included the old privately financed Lancaster Turnpike and others modeled after it. The Lancaster "pike"

Mississippi
River System

about 1830

Gulf of Mexico

had been built in 1794 at a cost of $465,000 across the 62 miles from Philadelphia to Lancaster, Pennsylvania. Tolls were collected along the way and the enterprise proved moderately profitable. In the next 30 years, private companies, mostly in New England and the Middle states, built more than 10,000 miles of turnpike. The best of them cost from $5,000 to $10,000 per mile. Many of the turnpike corporations were aided by state and local governments, which bought stock and helped out with proceeds from the sale of government bonds.

Most of the turnpike companies, however, were small and their roads had only local value. They did little to improve the sorry network of country paths. Moreover, they proved to be of little use for carrying heavy agricultural produce, for the high tolls discouraged shippers, who were always hard-pressed for coin. By the 1830's, management and maintenance of the turnpikes had become so costly, and returns were so scanty, that many thousands of miles of turnpikes were abandoned altogether or turned over by private corporations to the states.

The Canal Boom.   Turnpikes, clearly, were not the way for New York, Philadelphia, Boston, or the other eastern seaports to compete with New Orleans for the growing trade of the West. Leaders in these cities turned instead to canals, which were to connect the great waterways with which nature had endowed the American continent.

Canals, however, were harder to build than turnpikes. They cost, not $5,000, but $25,000 a mile; some cost as much as $60,000 and $80,000 a mile. They took not a year or two to build, but seven to ten years. So they presented new problems of finance and labor supply, as well as problems of engineering and management.

People had been talking about canals for decades, but in 1816 there were only 100 miles of them in the United States. Only three canals were more than two miles long; none ran as far as 30 miles. As early as 1810, the New York State legislature had set up a

committee to investigate a canal to the West, and in 1816 De Witt Clinton again raised the issue. He was so convincing that even his political opponents voted for the project— a canal to connect the Hudson River with Lake Erie, 363 miles away. Clinton's canal was to have 83 locks, to cost over $7 million, and to be built with state funds. Construction on the Erie Canal began in 1817, and by 1823 a 280-mile stretch from Albany to Rochester was in operation. So great was the traffic even on this part of the canal that the tolls collected helped to finance the final leg to Buffalo, which was completed in 1825. In 1823, New York had opened the Champlain Canal, connecting the Hudson River and Lake Champlain to the north. In 1825, returns from both projects exceeded $500,000, and in the next nine years, the Erie paid off its total cost of $7 million. Two figures tell the story of the Erie's success: it reduced freight rates between Buffalo and Albany from $100 to $15 a ton, and it reduced the travel time from 20 to 8 days.

Spurred to action, Boston got the Massachusetts legislature to consider a canal to the West in 1825. But the cost of construction through this more difficult terrain seemed so excessive that the plans were dropped. Boston eventually made a connection with the West in 1842 by means of three railroads strung in a line across Massachusetts to the eastern end of the Erie Canal. In 1826, Philadelphia got state approval for its scheme to tap the West, which was even more complicated than Boston's. By the time this system was completed in 1834, it included a main canal and some railroad track and had cost more than $10 million, all of it supplied by the state.

In 1827, Baltimore joined in the competition for western business by projecting the Chesapeake and Ohio Canal. Although the Maryland legislature thought the project visionary, work got underway with private and federal funds. The state legislators turned out to be right, since the canal never got across the broad southern mountains. In 1828,

The locks of the Erie Canal at Lockport, New York, 1836.

work was begun by a private corporation on the Baltimore and Ohio Railroad, the first successful line in America. But the B. & O. did not reach the Ohio River until the 1850's.

Less ambitious east-west projects were completed in almost all the seaboard states by 1840, mostly with public funds. But none proved so successful in tapping the West as the Erie Canal.

The western settlers were as energetic as the easterners in seeking east-west trade. They found that their rich soil could produce more wheat and corn, and that their corn could fatten more hogs, than southern plantations could consume. They were also growing tired of the difficulties of river transportation. In the 1820's these westerners began to lend a sympathetic ear to Henry Clay's program for a high tariff and "internal improvements" (see p. 214). The tariffs, they reasoned, would stimulate the growth of eastern factory towns; the "internal im-

provements," by which they meant the construction of government-aided transportation facilities tying the East and West together, would open such towns to western produce. These "improvements" would also reduce the cost of transporting manufactured goods across the mountains.

Clay's program never was enacted into law, but the western states, led by Ohio, soon embarked on ambitious canal and railroad programs of their own. Between 1825, the year the Erie Canal opened, and 1833, the state of Ohio completed the Ohio and Erie Canal, a 308-mile, $8-million project connecting Portsmouth on the Ohio River with Cleveland on Lake Erie, and, by way of "Clinton's Big Ditch" and the Hudson River, with New York City. Other projects boosted Ohio's canal-building by 1837 to 750 miles. Indiana began building her canal system in 1827, and in the 1830's Illinois, Michigan, and Wisconsin all projected ambitious works which, though interrupted by the Panic of

1837 (see p. 229) and the subsequent depression, eventually were carried to completion.

By 1840, some 3,326 miles of canals, most of them in the North and West, had been constructed in the United States at a cost of $125 million. Private American investors were able to supply only a small fraction of this sum. A considerably larger share came from federal and state subscriptions to the securities of private canal companies. More than half the total was provided directly by the states out of revenues or through the sale of bonds abroad, mainly to Englishmen. The impact of the canals on the economy of the West was as great as expected. The South continued to be a valuable customer of the West, and the Ohio and Mississippi river systems continued to be scenes of intense commercial activity. But the West's connections with the North and East became ever stronger as the canal system developed.

Travel over the turnpikes was slow and expensive; over the canals it was much cheaper, but for four months of the year the northern routes were frozen. The railroad was to free manufacturers and businessmen

from the weather and from the medieval pace of oxen and tow horses. By 1840, there were 3,328 miles of railroad in the United States, almost exactly equal to the canal mileage. But there were only about 200 miles of railroad in the West. By 1838, Illinois, Indiana, and Michigan had sold $12,600,000 worth of state bonds for railroad construction, but they had virtually nothing but the debt itself to show for their efforts. Most of the railroads in 1840 were scattered through the older sections of the country, and only in the Northeast, where Philadelphia and Boston had developed good local rail connections, was there any sort of a railroad system (see pp. 325-326). For some time after 1840, rivers, canals, and turnpikes continued to be the main channels of inland commerce.

The Spectacular Rise of New York City.

In the competition for western trade, then, the East gradually outstripped the South. In the East itself, New York City gradually pulled far ahead of

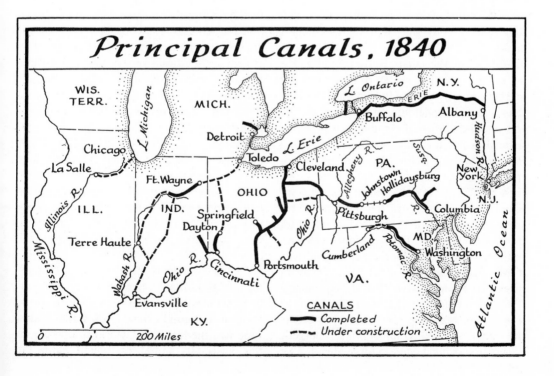

Principal Canals, 1840

Broadway and Canal Street, New York City, 1835.

the rival cities of Boston, Philadelphia, and Baltimore. Nature played a significant part in this success. New York had a far greater hinterland market than Boston; she had a far more serviceable water route to western markets, by way of the Hudson and Mohawk rivers, than Philadelphia and Baltimore; she was also best situated for the coastal trade, since Boston was far to the north, and Philadelphia and Baltimore were too far upstream for easy and inexpensive access. All these advantages in domestic commerce combined to give New York the most favorable situation also as a warehousing area for transatlantic trade. Competition, however, remained keen for a long time, and initially it was enterprise as well as natural advantages that assured New York its supremacy.

Construction of the Erie Canal proved the most progressive step of all; but even before the canal was really under way, energetic New Yorkers had begun to forge ahead. Two

of their innovations proved particularly significant. One was the development of the auction system for disposing of imports. This system was attractive because it assured rapid turnover of goods for cash. Although auctions were held in many American ports, the common practice was to offer goods and then to withdraw them if the bids were unsatisfactory. In New York City, after 1817, auctions were held at which the purchasers were assured that the highest bids would be accepted and that their purchases would be delivered. This assurance made New York the favorite port both for sellers and buyers, who congregated there from all over the country.

The second innovation was the development of transatlantic packets to run on regular schedules between America and Europe, "full or not full." New York's Black Ball Line was the first in the world to operate on this basis. Its initial eastbound ship, the

202

James Monroe, left New York on January 5, 1818, in a snowstorm that "would have been regarded as a valid excuse for delay by any regular trader."

Until this daring scheduling was introduced, ocean commerce often waited upon the whims of the weather and the convenience of ship captains. Irregularity of sailings, indeed, continued to characterize most ocean shipping even after the Black Ball Line began operations. The American merchant marine in this period was second only to the British, and it carried cargo around the world to the Levant, the Baltic Sea, Africa, and the East Indies, as well as to China and India. In an age without wireless communication, there often was no telling when a vessel might sight its home port or what it may have carried or where it may have gone between visits. Still, the so-called "Atlantic shuttle" grew steadily in importance after 1820, when the American West began to feed Europe, and the United States began to offer an expanding market for Old-World manufactures. Boston in particular thrived on the old-fashioned world-wide carrying trade. But New York, by tying America's expanding domestic commerce ever more closely with Europe's expanding industry, grew faster. By 1828, New York's share of the American merchant marine was almost equal to the combined shares of Philadelphia, Boston, and Baltimore.

Dependable auctions and dependable sailings brought businessmen and goods flooding into New York. What the city's merchants needed next was an adequate export staple.

The Erie Canal did wonders in pouring western produce into the city, but even the Canal's volume of wheat, flour, furs, and other commodities was insufficient for New York's needs. So the New Yorkers boldly set out to add the cotton-carrying trade to their other business. In the 1820's, their ships began to follow a new triangular trade route. First they sailed right into New Orleans harbor, or to Mobile, Savannah, and other southern ports. There they picked up cotton and carried it, on the second leg of the voyage, to England and the Continent. Then they exchanged the cotton for manufactures and other goods, which they brought back to New York to complete the triangle.

So successful were the New York merchants in this new trade that by 1830 it was estimated that 40 cents of every dollar paid for cotton went north—almost exclusively to New York—for freight tolls, insurance, commissions, and interest. In 1837, a convention in the South that had been called to sponsor the revival of direct trade with Europe said to southern merchants, "You hold the element from which [the New York merchant] draws his strength. You have but to speak the word, and his empire is transferred to your own soil." But the word was not spoken, and two years later a similar convention declared that "the importing merchants of the South [had become] an almost extinct race, and her direct trade, once so great, flourishing, and rich, [had] dwindled down to insignificance."

V. THE INDUSTRIAL REVOLUTION

The burst of enterprise in the West, the rapid growth of western population, and the growing accessibility of western markets— all gave a strong impetus to the development of industry in the older sections of the country. The concentration on cotton-planting in the South made it a market for textiles that it might otherwise have manufactured for itself. Until western and southern markets

were opened, however, factory industry had a hard time getting started in America.

Difficult Beginnings. As early as 1791, when Hamilton made his Report on Manufactures (see p. 145), he had written, "The expediency of encouraging manufactures in the United States . . . appears at this time to be pretty generally admitted." But he was too optimistic. Hamilton himself helped organize the Society for Establishing Useful Manufactures, chartered by New Jersey in 1791. Capitalized at $1 million, this corporation in the next few years founded the city of Paterson, built numerous buildings to house its works, smuggled in more-or-less skilled British mechanics, and began manufacturing yarn, cloth, hats, and other commodities. By 1796, however, both the works and the town were moribund.

In the first decades of the new nation's life, there was no surplus American labor supply to man new factories. Financiers were happy to keep their capital in the fruitful and accustomed paths of trade, shipping, and land-speculation. The Federalist swells of northern cities with their English commercial connections, or the Republican planters of the South with their English commercial credit, read English books, counted their profit in pounds, and sent their sons to Eton and Oxford. They were more than satisfied with English woolens, linen, china, cutlery, furniture, tools, and hardware. Jefferson himself once apologized to Lafayette for buying English harness: "It is not from a love of the English but a love of myself that I sometimes find myself obliged to buy their manufactures."

Almost from the beginning of colonization, America had its forges, blacksmith shops, flour mills, saw mills, paper factories, tanneries, and even some establishments for spinning woolen or linen fiber, or for finishing or "fulling" home-woven cloth. And as the settlers moved westward, they took their shops along. For some time, Pittsburgh served as a center for pioneers' supplies, especially metal farming implements too heavy to tote over the mountains from the East, or wagon-wheel rims that might have worn out on the journey west. By 1817, there were several Pittsburgh industries that together employed as many as 1,280 workers. In 1810, Lebanon, Ohio, with a population of 300, boasted a wheelwright, three tan yards, four shoe-maker shops, two blacksmith shops, two saddle shops, a nail-maker, and a hatter. Such enterprises were usually part-time activities, carried on in cellars, spare rooms, or outbuildings by farmers and storekeepers, or by lawyers and doctors awaiting clients or patients.

The First
Full-time Factories.

The first full-time factory in America to survive for more than a few years was the cotton-spinning plant of Almy & Brown, Providence merchants. Under the direction of an experienced Englishman, Samuel Slater, this factory began operations at Pawtucket in 1791. It was a tiny affair compared with Hamilton's activities in Paterson. But with the assistance of Almy & Brown's well-established market connections it managed to keep afloat. After the Napoleonic Wars in Europe began in 1799, Americans found it increasingly difficult to get English manufactures. To supply the American market, Slater's mill expanded, and many imitators set up shop. By 1810, perhaps a hundred or more cotton-spinning plants were operating in New England. Most of them were in Rhode Island, where machinists trained at Slater's mill often set up in business for themselves. Few such enterprises were capitalized at more than $10,000. Their managers were inexperienced in keeping account books, handling money or men, or exploiting markets. The banks would have nothing to do with them. These enterprises looked to the poorest local farm families for labor, often employing parents and small children. The thread they spun was given out to home weavers to make into cloth. But Almy & Brown complained in 1809 that "a hundred looms in families will not weave so much cloth as ten . . . under the immediate inspection of a workman."

The Entry of Big Capital.

Although the embargo gave a considerable impetus to domestic manufactures, the War of 1812 was a more significant turning point in their development. Most important, the war's disastrous consequences for the shipping trade turned the attention of men with capital to the promising industrial field. In 1813, great merchants like Francis Cabot Lowell, Patrick Tracy Jackson, and Nathan Appleton organized the Boston Manufacturing Company in Waltham, Massachusetts. This company was as distinct a step forward in its day as Slater's mill had been 22 years before.

establishing their own selling agencies instead of depending on local jobbers, as earlier companies had done.

Large-scale, integrated production enabled the Boston Manufacturing Company to eliminate middlemen and unsupervised domestic workers, and to reduce the time spent in carrying goods from place to place for

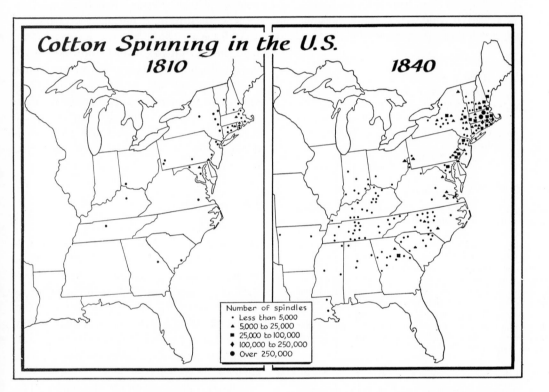

Cotton Spinning in the U.S. 1810 / 1840

Number of spindles
- Less than 5,000
▲ 5,000 to 25,000
■ 25,000 to 100,000
♦ 100,000 to 250,000
● Over 250,000

The Boston Manufacturing Company was organized by men who had proved that they could manage hazardous, large-scale businesses. They invested liberally in the new enterprise, putting $600,000 cash into it in the first six years, and holding as much or more in reserve for operating and emergency expenses. They built the first wholly integrated cotton-manufacturing plant in the world; all operations were under one roof, from the unbaling of the raw cotton to the dyeing and printing of the finished cloth. The founders further integrated the business by

successive processing steps. The managers augmented the economies of this system by introducing power looms and power spindles. They gave constant attention to other improvements in technology, from the design of water wheels and power-transmission systems to the fastness of dyes.

An original scheme for attracting and holding workers was the last of the major innovations of this enterprise. Instead of the children and parents hired by the older mills, the Boston Manufacturing Company took on young women ranging in age from 18 to

22, who were sheltered and fed in the houses that made up the new company town. Here, according to the lights of the organizers, religion was cultivated, educational opportunities were made available in non-working hours, and cleanliness and hygiene were insisted upon. All these devices were calculated to draw to the new enterprise a sturdy, ambitious, hard-working group of young women from respectable farm families. And they succeeded in doing just that. Absenteeism was much lower than in the old Rhode Island

A page from "The Lowell Offering," a collection of articles, poems, and stories, published in 1840 by the girls in the Lowell mills. The girls themselves apparently did not think that they were badly treated.

376   CONCLUSION

of the general character and state of feeling among the female population of this city. They say the Offering, if indeed it be the organ of the factory girls, is not a *true* organ. It does not expose all the evils, and miseries, and mortifications, attendant upon a factory life. It speaks, they say, on only one side of the question ; and they compare us to poor, caged birds, singing of the flowers which surround our prison bars, and apparently unconscious that those bars exist. We however challenge any one to prove that we have made false assertions, and happy indeed are we, if our minds can turn involuntarily to the sunny side of the objects which arrest our gaze. May it not be supposed that we have written of these flowers, because so many assert that they do not exist, and that

"No more for us the violet shall bloom,
Nor modest daisy rear its humble head"?

And perhaps we have written of the bright sky above us, because so many think our sun is always obscured by gloomy clouds.

And who will say that had the Offering been but the medium of the foreboding and discontented, and the instrument for the conveyance of one long, dismal wail throughout the land, that it would have been more useful, or a more correct exponent of the state of feeling amongst us ?

We are not generally miserable, either in point of fact, or in the prospect of a dreadful future. This may be the result of our ignorance—for it should be observed that the objections brought against the manufacturing system, are usually founded on analogies from foreign lands. Neither are we philosophical enough to deduce the long chain of dreadful effects which many think will be consequent upon the simple causes which we see in operation around us. But more than this : we see not how we can be accused of disingenuousness when we have never, either through our Editor, or in any other way, pledged ourselves to disseminate a knowledge of every petty evil and inconvenience of the manufacturing system. The Offering has faithfully sustained its character, as A REPOSITORY OF ORIGINAL ARTICLES, WRITTEN BY FEMALES EMPLOYED IN THE MILLS. In the words of one of our own number, we

"desired to show
What factory girls had power to do."

mills, and industrial discipline was easier to impose.

In the years between 1813 and 1816, Massachusetts alone had chartered over 80 textile-manufacturing companies, most of them small. In other New England states scores more had been chartered, and elsewhere in the country the war emergency and the prospects of war profits led to the establishment of many others. Several of these failed around 1816, when record British postwar exports flooded American markets. Others disappeared during the Panic of 1819 (see p. 185). Yet the Boston Manufacturing Company, which did not begin operations until 1816, proved an immediate and lasting success. In 1817, its able and enterprising management earned for it a dividend of 12.5 per cent. Thereafter annual dividends were even higher. By 1822, dividends totaling 104.5 per cent had been paid to the investors.

Industrial Progress and the Corporation.

The revival of business after the Panic of 1819 began about 1823. In that year, Harrison Gray Otis of Boston wrote: "There has been a curious 'revival' in the spirit of men ... which is quite remarkable. Two years ago our sun had sunk never to rise again. ... All is now reversed and [manufacturing] stocks as well as spirits have risen inordinately. ... It is amazing to see what is done by the puff on one hand and the panic on the other." The opening up of the West and the expansion of the Cotton Kingdom in the South sparked the business upturn. The revolutions against Spain in South America (see p. 189) opened up the first foreign markets for American manufactured goods. After 1826, more and more American manufactures were sent to China to pay for the tea that was being consumed in ever-greater quantities in the United States.

All these changes were reflected in the expansion of the firms that had survived the depression and in the large number of new textile corporations that set up in business during the 1820's and 1830's. Among these new companies were some that were chartered by the same group that had started the Boston Manufacturing Company. Between 1821 and 1835, these men, often referred to as the "Boston Associates," opened nine new companies in Massachusetts and southern New Hampshire, each specializing in a particular textile product on a large scale. More important, during and after the depression these men founded insurance companies and banks to maintain and concentrate the supply of capital; real-estate companies to take over the best factory sites; and water-power companies to control dams and dam sites and harness the power of the great rivers.

The corporation had first been used as a legal device for securing a monopoly by means of a special charter. Astor employed it next as a symbol of prestige. The turnpike and bridge companies used the corporate form mainly to accumulate capital by selling inexpensive shares to numerous subscribers. By the time the canal and railroad companies were being formed, the idea of limited liability had become well established in law and finance. Limited liability meant that the owners of corporation stock were liable for the obligations of the company only to the extent of their own investment, regardless of how great their personal fortunes might be. This protection helped to attract some of the capital required for costly, long-term projects.

The "Boston Associates" used the corporate form for all these purposes, as well as for other purposes of their own. In their hands, the corporation became a device by which a few able men, through ownership of only a fraction of the total stock, could direct the activities of many and varied businesses. The corporate form also made it possible for them to reside in Boston while actual operations were conducted in distant mill towns under the supervision of hired professional managers. Corporate securities, moreover, could be more easily disposed of than investments in partnerships or single-owner businesses. Accordingly, these enter-

prises could look forward to a long life, uninterrupted by the death or withdrawal of investors. Stocks could easily be transferred without seriously affecting the financial structure of a business.

The cotton textile industry was the proving ground for these new techniques. It was the first mature American industry that was geared not to the individual craftsman but to the machine, that was financed not by the owner alone or his bank, but by the accumulated private savings of numbers of people, and that was managed by hired professionals accountable to capitalists living in the great financial centers.

The Early Labor Movement. The corporation gave a tremendous impetus to American economic and social progress, but almost from its inception as a mode of industrial organization its tendency toward harshness in human relations was evident. Before Samuel Slater set up his first mechanized spinning plant in 1791, America had had many "spinning houses" and "spinning schools," the first of which appeared in Jamestown, Virginia, as early as 1646. These schools were set up to provide useful employment for the children of the poor. Slater's factory was modeled on these public institutions, and the children who worked for him were not abused. Many of Slater's imitators, however, were not so charitable, especially when the heat of competition prompted the less efficient firms to seek the road to survival by sweating their workers. By 1810, few of the little spinning corporations chartered in southern New England retained any aspects of philanthropy.

A more striking deterioration in working and living conditions marked the factories and factory towns of the Boston Associates and *their* imitators, especially after the scrupulous founders turned their management over to outsiders whose efficiency was checked in Boston through the medium of financial reports. Here is the way in which an observer in Lowell in 1846 described the factory routine at that time:

The operatives work thirteen hours a day in the summer time, and from daylight to darkness in the winter. At half past four in the morning the factory bell rings, and at five girls must be in the mills. A clerk placed as a watch, observes those who are a few minutes behind the time, and effectual means are taken to stimulate punctuality. This is the morning commencement of the industrial discipline (should we not rather say industrial tyranny?) which is established in these Associations of this moral and Christian community. At seven the girls are allowed thirty minutes for breakfast, and at noon thirty minutes more for dinner, except during the first quarter of the year, when the time is extended to forty-five minutes.

Some years earlier, in 1840, the reformer, Orestes Brownson, said of the Lowell girls who presumably had gone to work long enough to accumulate a dowry or to add to the family income until they married:

The great mass wear out their health, spirits, and morals without becoming one whit better off than when they commenced labor. The bills of mortality in these factory villages are not striking, we admit, for the poor girls when they can toil no longer go home to die.

These comments reflect the conditions that prevailed after the Panic of 1837 had made the corporate managements all the more severe with factory superintendents whose accounts showed too much red ink. But even before the panic, conditions had become so bad in some of the cotton factories that the girls were driven to strike. In February, 1834, a thousand or more Lowell girls walked out in protest against a 15 per cent wage cut. "One of the leaders," reported the *Boston Transcript,* "mounted a stump, and made a flaming ... speech on the rights of women and the iniquities of the 'monied aristocracy' which produced a powerful effect on her auditors, and they determined to 'have their way, if they died for it.' " Actually, the girls went back to work in a few days at the reduced wages—all but the leaders, who were discharged.

There were a few other attempted strikes in the 1830's, but the girls in the New England textile mills and the factory workers in other parts of the country had no unions, no funds, no leadership, and no experience, and their pathetic rebellions almost always ended in quick failure. One of the weapons the corporations used against strikers was the law itself. Until the decision of the Massachusetts Supreme Court in the case of *Commonwealth* v. *Hunt* in 1842, strikers were subject to prosecution for conspiracy under the common law. Thereafter, the legal climate improved. But the change showed only that economic and social conditions were really at the bottom of the workers' weak position. Their main weakness was that for a long time they remained insignificant in numbers in an agrarian society that knew little and cared less about their way of life.

Although little progress was made in organizing American industrial workers until the 1930's, the craft unions have had a much longer history. The skilled crafts themselves, of course, were older than the country itself. The so-called "mechanics" of the eighteenth century and earlier were usually independent artisans who owned their own shops and their own tools, bought their own raw materials, fabricated them for their own customers, and set their own prices. Among them were shoemakers, tailors, blacksmiths, printers, and members of the building trades —bricklayers, carpenters, masons, and so forth. These artisans sometimes employed journeymen who actually journeyed from farm to farm to make shoes, repair houses and barns, and do similar jobs beyond the capacity of the farm family. Below the journeymen were young apprentices, who were often contracted out by their families to an artisan for as long as 20 years.

By the beginning of the nineteenth century, improvements in transportation had opened wider markets to the artisans, some of whom gave up actual hand work to become "merchant capitalists"—that is, businessmen who gathered up larger orders than one artisan and a few helpers could fill, and who began to employ artisans and journeymen to work for them. Others who had never been artisans also entered the different crafts. By the 1820's, competition among merchant capitalists had become so keen that they were forced to cut the wages of their craftsmen. The artisans themselves were further embittered by the loss of their independent status. Another complaint was that their skills were being broken up into a series of simpler tasks which were then given to less well-trained workers who depressed wages all the more.

It was in rebellion against these conditions that the first unions were formed in America. Though the Philadelphia shoemakers had organized as early as 1792, it was not until the middle 1820's that other craftsmen, in defiance of the conspiracy law, turned to united action to save themselves. In New York, Philadelphia, and other large centers, the craft unions combined in city-wide organizations; and in 1834 six such combinations established a "National Trades' Union." In the following three years the membership of the craft unions scattered throughout the country had soared from 26,000 to 300,000, and the unions themselves conducted at least 175 strikes, many of them called to win improvements in conditions, not merely to keep them from growing worse. In 1828, moreover, the Philadelphia unions had created the American Working Men's party to seek, by political means, such improvements as the 10-hour day for themselves and free public education for their children.

The business crash of 1837 crushed the early craft-union movement. Some of the crafts, especially the ones in construction or in specialized fields like printing, managed to maintain a semblance of organization even in the worst years. The crafts that were subject to rising competition from factory production, however, tended to disappear, and their unions and merchant capitalists went with them. Those who made cotton or woolen clothing, carpets, boots and shoes, and iron machinery and other hardware by hand could not long survive an environment of increasing bigness in operations and mechanization in techniques. In such industries, as in the cotton textile industry itself, the smallest firms were beginning to die out, production was being concentrated at the better industrial sites, and commodities were being shipped far and wide to national and international markets.

True, the United States was still many decades away from the time when it would be a mature industrial country linked up by railroads, telegraph, telephone, automobiles, and TV. Large parts of the land still were covered with virgin forests; huge quantities of immensely fertile land still were available almost for the taking. But by 1830 migration to the city was beginning to compete seriously with migration to the ever-retreating West, and it was becoming clear that the Jeffersonian ideal of a society made up of independent and individualistic farmers spread over the whole continent, if not over the whole hemisphere, was not to be realized.

Readings

For a general introduction to this chapter read the imaginative work of Roger Burlingame, *The March of the Iron Men* (1938). Less limited than its title suggests, and excellent reading, is Samuel E. Morison, *The Maritime History of Massachusetts, 1783-1860* (1921). Very informative on the whole economy is George R. Taylor, *The Transportation Revolution, 1815-1860* (1951). A brief presentation will be found in the early chapters of Thomas C. Cochran and William Miller, *The Age of Enterprise* (1942). A seemingly specialized article, but one that is extremely informative, is Guy S. Callender, "Early Transportation and Banking Enterprises of the States in Relation to the Growth of Corporations." This was first printed in the *Quarterly Journal of Economics,* Vol.

XVII, pp. 111-162, and has since been reprinted in a book of readings, *Economic Change in America,* edited by Joseph T. Lambie and Richard V. Clemence (1954).

Herman Melville's *Moby Dick* is a great American novel that presents much fascinating and authentic material on whaling. Informative on the same subject is Elmo P. Hohman, *The American Whaleman* (1928). On the western fur trade, the chapters in Ray A. Billington, *Westward Expansion* (1949), are excellent. The most useful biography of the main figure in the fur trade is Kenneth W. Porter, *John Jacob Astor* (2 vols., 1931). The outstanding work on its subject is Louis C. Hunter, *Steamboats on the Western Rivers* (1949). Worth reading also are James T. Flexner, *Steamboats Come True* (1944), and an older book, *Paths of Inland Commerce,* by A. B. Hulbert (1920). Seymour Dunbar, *A History of American Travel* (4 vols., 1915; one-volume edition, 1937), while here and there out of date in its scholarship, is an absorbing work, comprehensive, spiritedly written, and lavishly illustrated. New York's rise to greatness is superbly set forth in Robert G. Albion, *The Rise of New York Port, 1815-1860* (1939).

The background of the industrial revolution is given in Edward C. Kirkland, *A History of American Economic Life* (1939), and other general economic histories mentioned in our general bibliography, as well as in the works of Burlingame and Taylor mentioned previously. An excellent essay on Hamilton's industrial venture is "The 'S. U. M.': The First New Jersey Business Corporation," by Joseph S. Davis. It is to be found in that author's *Essays on the Earlier History of American Corporations* (2 vols., 1917), which contains other useful essays as well. *The World of Eli Whitney* by Jeannette Mirsky and Allan Nevins (1952) is a first-rate study of the emergence of the industrial spirit.

Caroline F. Ware, *The Early New England Cotton Manufacture* (1931), presents all the phases of America's first modern industry in scholarly fashion. Very informative on the cotton and other industries is Volume I of Victor S. Clark, *History of Manufactures in the United States* (3 vols., 1928). The standard account of the early labor movement is Volume 1 of John R. Commons, and others, *History of Labor in the United States* (4 vols., 1918 and after).

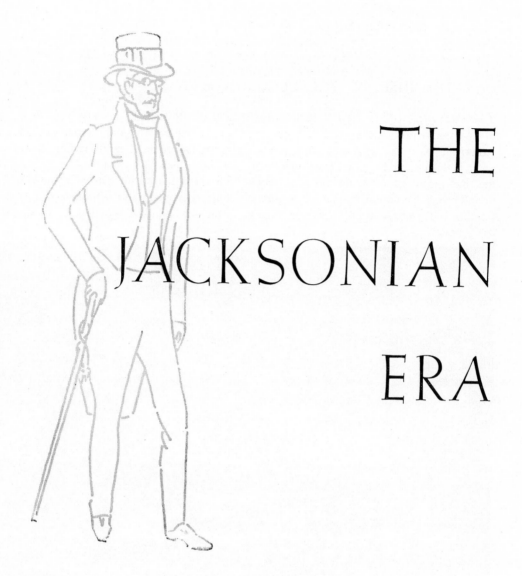

THE

JACKSONIAN

ERA

C H A P T E R T E N

While Monroe's administration was concerning itself with political revolutions abroad and with planning diplomatic strategy for the defense of American interests, American society was being transformed at home. Had the nation not already progressed far toward democracy by 1820, we might almost call the events of 1820-1828 a democratic "revolution."

Though the political and social changes occurred without violence, they did engender intense resentments. The movement culminated in Jacksonian democracy—but Jacksonian democracy was only the high point in a series of changes whose beginnings are buried in the events of the previous century, when the common man in America first exhibited his equalitarian yearnings.

211

I. THE RISE OF THE COMMON MAN

The Meaning of an Era. In the course of the democratic movement, the modern American party system took form; adult white male suffrage became almost universal; the chief means of educating and of agitating or informing the common man—free public schools and a cheap press—became widely ical institutions alone. The new democracy revered military heroes and chose Jackson, a popular general, as its leader: democracy walked hand in hand with nationalism. The new democracy esteemed individualism and enterprise; and although it began by attacking political privileges, it ended by

Election day at the State House in Philadelphia about 1818.

available; politics, once the prerogative of selected leaders, became a career open to talents—and to demagoguery; the modern system of popular election campaigning came into practice; and the spoils system for the distribution of public offices, though foreshadowed earlier, finally took hold and received official sanction.

But the movement which, for want of a better term, we call "Jacksonian Democracy," went far beyond changes in polit-

attacking economic privileges in the interest of broader business opportunities for the enterprising common man. Nor did democracy stop with politics and economics; it affected education and the professions, literature and religion. It spoke in behalf of breaking down "artificial" distinctions between persons, of increasing opportunities, of gaining, or regaining, what was distinctly and natively American. It committed many excesses, but it helped to make modern American life what it is and to underline its differences from English and European politics and social relations.

The Democratic Impulse.

Between 1810 and 1820, six new states entered the Union with constitutions that had no property qualifications for voting. One by one, the older states liberalized the franchise, and even in those states that retained some property test no heavy obstacle barred the adult white male from the polling places. In many states, the broad distribution of landed property had already created an extensive body of voters. But this development only seemed to increase the sense of grievance among those who were denied the privilege of voting.

Even more important than the extension of the franchise was the increasing interest of the common man in exercising that right. In the years before 1824, a period for which we have no reliable election statistics, only small numbers of citizens seem to have bothered to go to the polls. In the election of that year, for instance, hardly more than 355,000 voters were counted in the entire country. But in the next presidential election, as a result of the heightened interest in politics and the expansion of the suffrage, over 1,155,000 votes were recorded. And from 1828 to 1848 the number of those who voted increased 2½ times—a far greater increase than the rise in the population itself.

The liberalizing of voting laws, especially in the western states after 1817, signified among other things that the western settlers had begun to take a keen and active interest in politics. During the period of early settlement, with its self-subsistence and comparative isolation, few federal laws or decisions had had much bearing upon the life of the farmer. But in the period of later settlement, with surpluses to be sold, markets to be sought, and lines of transportation to be secured or improved, the connection between politics and prosperity became obvious. The disastrous Panic of 1819, and the hard times that followed, underscored the

necessity for electing local and national officials who would represent the interests of the majority. Throughout the country the small farmer, the town laborer, and the newly naturalized immigrant no longer accepted as readily as they had in the past the idea that the active functions of government could be entrusted solely to large property-owners, professional men, or educated gentry. The more opportunities the common man saw—and he saw many in this period of astonishing growth—the more eager he became to protect or enlarge his chances through political activity.

The old system of nominating presidential candidates by a "caucus" or meeting of congressmen was also discarded during this period. The caucus, which tended to put the presidential nomination into the hands of an inner party clique, was a nuisance to aspiring politicians; to the public it seemed a symbol of aristocratic rule. There were few to defend it. Growing sectional differences made it

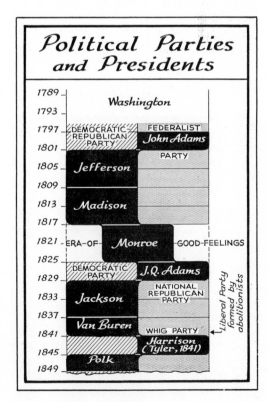

Political Parties and Presidents

1789	Washington
1793	
1797	DEMOCRATIC-REPUBLICAN PARTY / FEDERALIST John Adams
1801	PARTY
1805	Jefferson
1809	
1813	Madison
1817	
1821	ERA-OF- Monroe -GOOD-FEELINGS
1825	
1829	DEMOCRATIC PARTY / J.Q. Adams NATIONAL REPUBLICAN PARTY
1833	Jackson
1837	
1841	Van Buren WHIG PARTY
1845	Harrison (Tyler, 1841)
1849	Polk

Liberal Party formed by abolitionists

difficult for the disintegrating Republican party to agree on a candidate in 1824, and the contestants for the presidency refused to entrust their political futures to the old-fashioned party leaders. Consequently, when an unprecedentedly small Republican caucus, far short of a party majority, named Monroe's Secretary of the Treasury, William H. Crawford, as next in line for the presidency, the other candidates ignored the caucus decision and accepted nomination by the legislatures of their respective states. The credit for developing the national party convention, the modern method of nominating candidates, went to a short-lived minor party, the Anti-Masons (see p. 224), who held the first convention in 1830 and another in 1831 to nominate a candidate for the presidential contest of the following year. The National Republicans (John Quincy Adams men) held their first nominating convention in 1831, and the Jacksonian Democrats held theirs in 1832.

Still another institution gave way before the demand to bring government closer to the people. This was the old system under which presidential electors had usually been chosen by the state legislatures. By 1828, all the states except Delaware and South Carolina had substituted for this system the popular election of members of the electoral college.

The Campaign of 1824

By 1824, the field of aspirants who hoped to succeed Monroe had narrowed down to four: Crawford, the caucus candidate; John Quincy Adams, the representative of New England's aspirations; Henry Clay of Kentucky; and Andrew Jackson. Since the Federalist party had long since withered away, all these men were Republicans; all were nationalists; but each was a sectional candidate who hoped to reconcile the interests of his section with a broad national policy.

Clay and Adams could hardly have stood further apart temperamentally and intellectually. But they both subscribed to the general principles set forth as Clay's celebrated "American System." Clay, hoping to weld together the interests of the prosperous and increasingly commercial farmers of the Northwest with the industrial East, proposed the following measures: (1) a protective tariff to help build American industry; (2) internal improvements, aided financially by the federal government, to facilitate the interchange of western crops and eastern manufactures—these improvements to be financed partly by tariff revenues and the sale of public lands; and (3) a centralized banking system. Clay glowingly pictured an industrial East providing a large market for western produce, which now often went unsold for want of adequate transportation, and an agricultural West providing an expanding market for eastern manufacturing enterprise. Transactions between the sections would be facilitated by a stable credit system underwritten by a national bank. His plan, Clay said, would "place the confederacy upon the most solid of all foundations, the basis of common interest."

It was far less clear what Jackson stood for. Only three years before, he had declared himself unfit for the presidency, and as yet

Henry Clay (1777-1852).

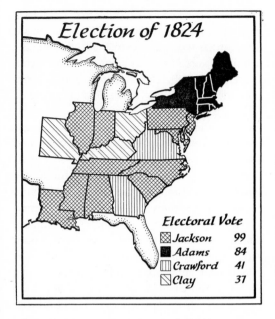

Election of 1824

Electoral Vote

⊠ Jackson	99
■ Adams	84
▥ Crawford	41
◫ Clay	37

he had no policies. But this colorful military figure was popular everywhere with small farmers, with artisans, and with the public in general. Jackson's mass appeal made him the choice of the new type of skilled party politician represented by the New Yorker William L. Marcy, who coined the slogan, "To the victors belong the spoils." Others who backed Jackson as the most likely winner were Marcy's New York colleague, Martin Van Buren, Tennessee's William B. Lewis, and Missouri's Thomas Hart Benton.

Born in upland South Carolina, self-educated and self-made, Jackson had served in the Revolutionary War and had read law before he settled in Nashville in 1788. There he became public prosecutor, raised cotton, served in Tennessee's first constitutional convention, and won elections to both houses of Congress and to the Superior Court of Tennessee—all before 1800. His famous victory at New Orleans in 1815 had made him a national hero, and his unceremonious dealings with the Indians and Spanish in 1818-1821 only heightened his luster among militant nationalists. In Tennessee, strangely, he had not been a "Jacksonian" democrat who stood with small farmers or "leather-shirts." Instead, he had taken the side of the "land barons" or "nabobs," and had favored

the creditors against the debtors. But though his business and legal affiliations linked him with the large propertied interests in Tennessee, in national affairs he appeared as a Jeffersonian. His background was humble, his manners simple and kindly; he was a westerner in the sense that he judged his fellows by their attainments and character rather than by their social background.

This appealing leader did not disappoint his backers among the professional politicians. His vote in the election of 1824 was 153,000 to 108,000 for Adams, 46,000 for Crawford, and 47,000 for Clay. In the electoral college, however, the vote stood: Jackson 99, Adams 84, Crawford 41, Clay 37. The failure of any candidate to secure an electoral majority threw the election into the House of Representatives. Clay, as the least successful candidate, was eliminated from the running, but for this very reason he became particularly important, for if he now swung his own following behind either of the top two contestants, he could in effect choose the victor. Since Crawford, who had suffered a stroke in the later phases of the campaign, was out of consideration, the choice must go either to Adams or Jackson. After a private interview with Adams, Clay lined up his supporters not with his fellow westerner, Jackson (whom he had privately declared he would never vote for), but with Adams, who sympathized with Clay's American System. Thanks to Clay's influence and, to some extent, Daniel Webster's, Adams was elected in the House.

Since Adams, in one of his first presidential acts, named Clay as his Secretary of State (an office then considered the choice slot for the successor to the president), Adams' many enemies immediately deduced that a behind-the-scenes deal had been arranged between the "Puritan" Adams and the "black-leg" Clay. They pointed to Jackson's lead in the popular vote as proof that he should have been elected, and never stopped charging that the election had been **unfairly won by means of a corrupt bargain.**

In fact, the alliance between Clay and Adams, for all their personal differences, was a natural one; but this made little impression on Adams' opponents, who immediately began a four-year campaign against him with the plausible "bargain and corruption" charge on their banners.

Adams' Administration. Adams knew that his term of office had been unfavorably launched. A sensitive and high-minded man, he was worried about taking the presidency with, as he said, "perhaps two-thirds of the whole people adverse to the actual result." Moreover, since his public experience had been mainly in diplomacy rather than in domestic politics, he was out of touch with many of the prevailing tides of public opinion.

In his first annual message, Adams showed his political ineptness by outlining a kind of planned economy for a consolidated nation. At a time when state rights feeling was rising and sectional jealousies were becoming intense, Adams proposed that the government embark on a vast program of internal improvement. He called for the establishment of a national university, federal grants to construct astronomical observatories, the financing of scientific expeditions, the creation of a department of interior, and the standardization of weights. Adams' dream, as he later confessed, was to apply "all the superfluous revenue of the Union into internal improvement" and thereby provide continuous employment for thousands of workingmen while enriching the nation. He attributed the defeat of his plan to the opposition from "the Sable Genius of the South," which was fearful of northern prosperity. But the West also rejected his program as an attempt on the part of the industrial East to keep land prices high and to prevent its labor force from emigrating westward. The country preferred uncontrolled expansion.

Adams also met rebuffs on other counts.

When he revoked a fraudulent treaty signed with the Creek Indians in 1825 and arranged another the next year restoring to the Indians a million acres of good Georgia cotton land, the Georgia officials protested against what they deemed a flagrant violation of state rights. The Georgia governor, George M. Troup, threatened to repel any attempt to enforce the treaty by federal troops. Adams had to back down.

Nor was he any more successful in his handling of foreign relations. The United States had been invited to attend a congress of Latin-American republics in Panama called by Simon Bolívar, the great South American liberator, to discuss common problems. Clay was particularly eager to have America represented, and Adams thought it might be a first step toward the acquisition of Cuba. Adams tactlessly agreed to send delegates without first consulting the Senate. His enemies held up appropriations for the delegates' expenses while attacking one of his

Daguerreotype of John Quincy Adams at his home in Quincy, Massachusetts, a short time before his death.

appointees as "an acknowledged abolitionist" and describing the Latin-Americans "as an ignorant and vicious people." The Panama conference ended without the presence of any representative from the United States.

A more discouraging blow to national prestige resulted from Adams' ill-timed negotiations with the English Foreign Secretary, George Canning. Adams brought pressure against the English government to allow American ships to engage in direct trade with the British West Indies. Canning refused, and took even more drastic measures against American trade. The failure of the Adams administration in this effort became a campaign issue for his opponents.

The Election of Jackson. A concerted campaign against Adams began almost from the minute the election of 1824 was over, and it did not end until the crusty New Englander was unseated in 1828. By 1827, Martin Van Buren, one of the leading spirits in the anti-Adams coalition, wrote to a friend that "the re-election of Mr. Adams is out of the question." Van Buren, an astute New York lawyer and a veteran of politics in his own state since his efforts for Jefferson in 1800, had developed a distaste for Adams, and put his strength on Jackson's side, rowing to his objective, as John Randolph put it, "with muffled oars." Calhoun, too, along with Randolph, Sam Houston, the editor Duff Green, and other politicians at Washington, threw themselves into the Jackson cause, corresponded with committees throughout the country, and provided orators with propaganda about the iniquities of the corrupt bargain, the blunders of the administration, and the virtues of Jackson. Vice-president Calhoun, a former rival who may have suppressed some of his own doubts about Jackson's virtues, agreed to continue as a candidate for the vice-presidency. Very likely he expected that the 61-year-old Jackson would not be a candidate for a second term and would leave the succession to him.

The election of 1828 marked a new high in campaigning activity and a new low in

political dignity. Jackson's supporters introduced a rough-and-tumble carnival spirit into the campaign that persisted in later years. Their offensive against Adams revolved around personal charges designed to portray him as an extravagant and heartless aristocrat: he had cheated the people out of their presidential choice in the previous election; he had taken large sums from the public funds, wasted the people's money on billiard tables and chessmen, and lived a luxurious and dissipated life in the White House. Jackson men paraded with hickory sticks to symbolize the contrasting toughness and angularity of their beloved "Old Hickory," and brandished hickory brooms to signify the need for sweeping the rascals out.

Adams had no gifted managers to run his campaign, and he did not approve of retaliating in kind to the accusations of his opponents. But some of his advocates were far less scrupulous. They assailed Jackson as a ruffian and a duelist, making the most of some of the more arbitrary acts of his military career. Most inexcusably, they branded him as an adulterer. In 1791 he had married Rachel Robards, assuming that her

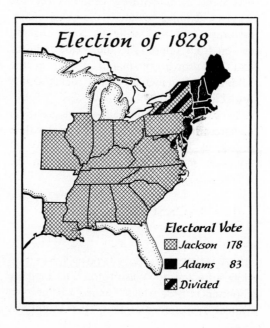

Election of 1828

Electoral Vote
☒ Jackson 178
■ Adams 83
▨ Divided

divorce from her previous husband had been granted. Through a technicality it had not, as Jackson and his wife learned after they had been living together for two years. A second marriage was necessary to make their union legal. This unfortunate incident, long since past, was now revived to discredit Jackson. His sensitive wife, who suffered intensely from the story, died shortly after the election, and Jackson believed that the election scandals had killed her. He never forgave "those vile wretches who have slandered her."

During the campaign year, some of Jackson's supporters concocted an ingenious scheme that hinged on the tariff, an issue over which the friends and enemies of the "American System" were becoming bitterly divided. In 1824, a tariff had been passed that raised most of the duties above the levels of 1820, largely with the support of the industrial Middle states and the Old Northwest, which had faith in the "home market" argument. It had been moderately opposed by New England, which was still heavily interested in commerce, and overwhelmingly resisted by the cotton-raising states, which had given up their hope of becoming manufacturing centers. Yet the 1824 tariff failed to satisfy the rising manufacturers, and the swing of New England capital from shipping to the textile industry and the growth of manufacturing in the Middle states increased the demand for protection.

Now, in 1828, the Jacksonian group in Congress launched a protective tariff whose object, as John Randolph said, was to encourage "manufactures of no sort but the manufacture of a President of the United States." Their plan was to put forth a tariff so high that it could not be passed. They expected that the northeastern manufacturers would balk at the high duties on raw materials, and that their representatives would combine with the shipping interests and the southerners to defeat the bill. Then the Jacksonians planned to claim credit in the North for having supported a protective tariff and in the South for having defeated it. To their surprise, the trick failed, for just enough support was mustered to get the bill through. As Webster said: "Its enemies spiced it with whatever they thought would render it distasteful; its friends took it, drugged as it was." Protectionists felt that it would be better to accept a bad tariff than to abandon the principle of protection. But among its foes the Tariff of 1828 became known as "The Tariff of Abominations."

Jackson's fortunes were undamaged by the backfiring of the tariff scheme. His own remarks on the subject had been astutely vague, though he had spoken of "a careful and judicious tariff" to raise revenue and to help create greater national self-sufficiency. He had no program and needed none. He was the Hero of New Orleans and the spokesman of the common man. The election results justified the optimism of his cohorts, for his popular vote was 647,000 to Adams' 508,000, his electoral-college vote 178 to Adams' 83. Jackson carried the entire South and West, along with Pennsylvania and some of the electoral votes of New York, Maine, and Maryland. Only the older New England states, joined by Delaware and New Jersey, held out solidly against him. In a nation of sections, he had won the closest thing to a national victory that was possible.

II. JACKSONIAN ISSUES

Launching
an Administration. Jackson's inauguration attracted to Washington an immense shouting crowd, which seemed to think, as Daniel Webster said, that "the country is rescued from some dreadful danger." "It was a proud day for the people," wrote the Jacksonian editor, Amos Kendall; but Justice Story reported that to him it looked like

"the reign of King 'Mob.'" The people surged through the streets of the still rude capital city and pressed into the White House as though they were prepared to take it by storm. Many, indeed, felt that the people had in fact captured the center of government at last.

Since Jackson had offered no positive program, many observers wondered what he proposed to do. Who would be his most powerful advisers—the ambitious Vice-president, Calhoun, who hoped to succeed him? Martin Van Buren, his Secretary of State, who found Calhoun rather unpalatable? Or would it be Jackson's personal friends, like Amos Kendall of Kentucky, a journalist who could help him write state papers, and William B. Lewis of Tennessee, one of the members of Jackson's "kitchen cabinet" who stayed at the White House and tendered political advice? What would be the influence of Duff Green, editor of the *United States Telegraph?* Of Francis Preston Blair, the Kentucky editor who hated the Bank? What would Jackson do about the tariff, public lands, internal improvements? How would he manage to keep the support of the divergent sections that had voted for him? Above all, wondered his stoutest enemies, would the arbitrary old general turn out to be a tyrant? Was republican government safe in his hands?

Upon assuming office, Jackson shocked the Adams men by throwing out 919 civil servants among the 10,000 whom he found installed. He has ever since been identified with the "spoils system"—which his political friends preferred to call "rotation in office." Actually, the practice of rewarding one's own partisans with jobs and seizing the spoils of office had long been followed in state politics, and it had not been abhorrent to the Federalists. But the speed and directness with which Jackson replaced office-holders with his own followers seemed to set a precedent for making government, in Adams' words, "a perpetual and unintermitting scramble for office."

Though Jackson did not originate the spoils system, he was among the first to defend it as a positive good. He considered it a reform, a means of rooting out unrepresentative minority groups from government and of preventing the development of an office-holding class. By such persons, he declared in his first annual message, "office is considered as a species of property" and under them government becomes a means "for the support of the few at the expense of the many." He went on: "The duties of all public officers are, or at least admit of being made, so plain and simple that men of intelligence may readily qualify themselves for their performance; and I cannot but believe that more is lost by the long continuance of men in office than is generally to be gained by their experience." To take this position was to place democratic sentiments above respect for expertness in government, but this attitude was widespread in many areas of life during the Jacksonian period and after.

Jackson took a popular stand, too, in his dealings with Congress and the courts. He emerged as a national leader responsible to the electorate as a whole. The presidents before him had been largely content to administer the laws and had been chary in their use of executive authority. But Jackson vetoed more legislation in his two terms of office than had been vetoed by all previous administrations combined. He was the first to take advantage of the constitutional provision allowing the president to kill a measure passed less than 10 days before Congress adjourned simply by withholding his veto (the "pocket veto"). Against the repeated charges of presidential "usurpation" of authority not delegated to him by law, Jackson reasserted his oath to defend the Constitution as he understood it and to fulfill his obligations to the people. He regarded his office as a popular bulwark against "powerful monopolies" and "aristocratical establishments." The "genius of our people," he said, demanded a "plain system" of government, "void of pomp—protecting all and granting favors to none—dispensing its blessings, like the dews of Heaven, unseen and unfelt save in the freshness and beauty they contribute to produce."

That Jackson sometimes interpreted his own prejudices and those of his often rapacious countrymen as the voice of God is more a criticism of his limited outlook than of his sincerity. Nowhere is this better shown than in his Indian policy. Jackson's early career as an Indian-fighter and his sympathy for the planters who coveted Indian lands in Georgia made him a firm believer in the plan to remove all Indian tribes to country west of the Mississippi. Adams had tried vainly to preserve some semblance of decency in arranging for Indian repatriation. After Jackson's election, the Cherokees were removed from their ancestral lands in Georgia despite the fact that they had embraced the white man's ways, owned and operated farms and factories, erected their own schools, and published an Indian newspaper. When Georgia laid claim to all Cherokee lands, the Indians appealed to the Supreme Court for an injunction restraining Georgia from carrying out the order. In *Cherokee Nation* v. *Georgia* (1831) the Court was sympathetic but denied that it had the power to rule on the appeal, since the Indians could not be considered a foreign independent state. However, in *Worcester* v. *Georgia* (1832) the Court ruled that the Cherokees enjoyed not only the protection of the federal government, but also that

Georgia had no jurisdiction in Cherokee territory. Georgia simply refused to heed the decision.

Unfortunately for the Cherokees, the House of Representatives tabled the enforcement order restraining Georgia from evicting the Indians. No federal troops were made available to support John Marshall's decision, and the spoliation of the Indian lands continued. By 1835, only a remnant of Indians retained their lands, and after the subjugation of the Florida Seminoles (1835-1842), millions of fertile acres were opened up for white exploitation.

The Maysville Veto. Jackson showed that he could disregard political expediency when he vetoed a bill for federal aid in the construction of a road between Maysville and Lexington, Kentucky on May 27, 1830, even though he knew that his veto would anger some of his western supporters. Jackson did not object particularly to government aid to internal improvements that would benefit the country as a whole. But the Maysville road lay entirely within Kentucky, and he felt that federal aid to individual states would require a constitutional amendment.

The Maysville veto pleased the South Atlantic states as well as parts of New York and Pennsylvania, but it ran directly counter to Henry Clay's "American System" and sharpened divisions in the Democratic party that were already clearly discernible. The difficult issues that now faced the Jacksonian administration often served as blinds behind which the different sections and their ambitious leaders maneuvered for power. The South, disillusioned by Jackson's intransigent nationalism, angled for western support against the manufacturing Northeast by voting with the West for cheap land. The East courted western support by holding forth the prospect of home markets for western farmers if the West would support eastern manufacturing interests in their demand for a high protective tariff. Presidential aspirants in the North, West, and South were pre-

Removal of Indian Tribes to the West

pared to make concessions to rival sectional interests if only to draw support away from Jackson, whose strength lay in every sector —among the small farmers of the West and South, among aspiring businessmen, and among ardent democrats everywhere.

The old Republican party was breaking up. By 1832, the outlines of two rival parties could be detected—the National Republican or Whig party (as it was to be called), and the Democratic party. The important issues that now came to the foreground must be understood against the background of sectional and party strife.

Public Lands
and the Tariff.

From the 1820's on, the West had campaigned for cheap public lands and for protection for the "squatter" who settled on government land before it had officially been opened to settlement. The frontiersman, who had improved his land during his illegal tenure, demanded the right to buy it at the minimum rate when it was finally placed on the open market. Even the minimum rate of $1.25 seemed excessive to Senator Thomas Hart Benton of Missouri. As early as 1824, Benton had proposed to Congress that unsold government land be gradually reduced from the regular price to 75¢ per acre and then to 50¢. If no takers appeared even then, the land would be given away free to settlers. This proposal came to be known as "graduation."

Easterners regarded Benton's plan as one more scheme to tap their dwindling labor supply; they also recognized that the receipts from the sale of expensive land might quickly pay off the national debt and thereby invalidate one of the principal arguments for high tariffs: the need for additional revenue. Lest a swelling treasury surplus lead to a reduction in tariff schedules, Webster vainly recommended in 1824 that the returns from sales of public land be distributed among all the states according to population. In December, 1829, when Senator Samuel A. Foot of Connecticut urged cutting further land surveys and limiting future buyers to lands already on sale, Senator Benton angrily denounced Foot's resolution as a manufacturer's plot to keep the exploited labor force from emigrating to the western Eden and to "deliver up large portions of new States and Territories to the dominion of wild beasts."

The Southeast had never agitated for cheap land, but its leaders now saw a chance to break up the East-West alliance by supporting western opposition to Foot's resolution. Senator Robert Y. Hayne of South Carolina followed up Benton's attack by suggesting that his own section and the West had grievances in common. In effect, he proposed that the South and the West join in a defensive alliance against the manufacturing East, which was blocking the flow of western immigration and undermining southern prosperity with the protective tariff. As the debate continued, the subject of public lands became lost in a welter of larger and more general issues, constitutional and economic, over which northern and southern statesmen profoundly disagreed. Both the East and the South were wooing the West, the East proposing the scheme of distribution in exchange for western votes for a protective tariff, the South championing western demands in the hope of detaching the West from the "American System." Behind the question of the public domain lay the tariff, and behind the tariff lay the delicate and fateful question of sectional alliances and the control of the Union.

Senator Hayne of South Carolina represented a state whose fortunes had steadily declined since the end of the eighteenth century. In 1829, South Carolina's lands were no longer fertile, nor was Charleston a flourishing seaport. Its planters, faced with competition from the fresh soils of the Southwest, were particularly outraged by tariff rates that excluded British manufactured goods. The high tariff forced planters to pay higher prices for their manufactured goods, bought from protected northern manufacturers. Moreover, it cut their foreign market for cotton, because England would have been able to buy more cotton under a system of free trade. According to South Carolina's greatest statesman, Calhoun, the Tariff of 1828 (see p. 218) reduced the South to serfdom. Northern manufacturers battened on the energies of southern farmers, who were prohibited from competing in the world market. In retaliation against American tariffs, Europe raised barriers against American rice and cotton. No free government, Calhoun argued, would permit the transfer of "power and property from one class or section to another." The tyranny of the majority could be met by the constitutional right of each state to nullify an unconstitutional act of Congress, Calhoun declared in an anonymously published essay, *The Exposition and Protest* (1828). The South Carolina legislature did not act upon Calhoun's nullification solution, but his thesis —"that the tariff is unconstitutional and must be repealed, that the rights of the South have been destroyed, and must be restored, that the Union is in danger, and must be saved" —remained very much alive.

Many of Jackson's supporters sympathized with Hayne's presentation of southern grievances and, by implication, with Calhoun's position. They rejected Clay's "American System" and Webster's industrial clients in New England. However, when Hayne introduced Calhoun's nullification theory into his denunciation of eastern manufacturing interests in January, 1830, the Jacksonians drew back.

Hayne's bitter remarks against the North were answered on January 26-27, 1830, by the "God-like" Daniel Webster, who denied categorically that ultimate sovereignty resided in the state governments. The people, who alone were sovereign, had entrusted sovereign authority to the federal government, and no single state had the right to determine whether or not an act of Congress was constitutional. That privilege was reserved to the Supreme Court. If the people, acting through their state governments, objected to any part of the Constitution, the proper procedure was to amend it. Webster closed his speech with what Senator Benton called "a fine piece of rhetoric misplaced," a vision of two Americas. One was of a land "rent with civil feuds, or drenched . . . in fratricidal blood," the other of a republic "now known and honored throughout the earth, still full high advanced, its arms and trophies streaming in their original lustre." He closed with the famous words that generations of school children were to memorize in the years to come: "Liberty *and* Union, now and forever, one and inseparable."

III. NULLIFICATION

The Jackson-Calhoun Rift. The way Jackson himself would respond to the issues raised by the Hayne-Webster debate might well indicate the response of his western following to the blandishments of the East and South. The administration's position was indicated on March 15, 1830, when Senator Edward Livingston of Louisiana openly spurned both the extreme federalism of Webster and the nullification theories of Calhoun. Taking Jackson's view, he asserted that the people wanted neither "consolidation" (i.e., extreme nationalism) nor disunion. A month later, at a Jefferson anniversary dinner, Jackson in effect corroborated his congressional spokesman. Although inclined toward state rights, Jackson made it clear to the nullifiers that he was first and foremost a nationalist. To Calhoun's dismay, he proposed the toast, "Our Federal Union, it must be preserved." Calhoun's reply was, "The Union—next to our liberty, the most dear."

At this point the breach between Jackson and Calhoun became a factor of great importance in the developing sectional fight. In the spring of 1830, through some of his advisers who disliked Calhoun, Jackson discovered that in 1818, when Calhoun was Secretary of War, he had favored punishing Jackson for his conduct during the Seminole

The young John C. Calhoun.

ing the attacks on his own wife. Martin Van Buren, a widower, took advantage of the situation to ingratiate himself with Jackson by acting cordially to the unconventional but charming wife of his colleague Eaton. Realizing that the social atmosphere of the cabinet would be a liability to the administration, however, Van Buren offered his resignation in the hope that it would compel a complete reorganization of the cabinet. When Eaton's own resignation followed, Jackson called for similar action by the remaining members. In appointing their successors, Jackson ignored the Calhoun men and formed a well-knit, thoroughly Jacksonian group. Van Buren was soon named Minister to England, and Eaton was appointed Governor of Florida Territory. It was obvious now that Jackson regarded Van Buren rather than Calhoun as his successor.

War. Nervously, Calhoun tried to explain himself in an embarrassed letter, but he only convinced Jackson that he had not been entirely candid. "Understanding you now," wrote the unforgiving Jackson to his vice-president, "no further communication with you on this subject is necessary." The breach between the two became final, and members of Jackson's cabinet were forced to decide which one they wanted to support.

The split in the cabinet was intensified by a social dispute that rocked Washington. In 1829, Jackson's Secretary of War, John H. Eaton, had married Margaret O'Neale Timberlake, an ex-barmaid and the daughter of a tavern-keeper whose first husband had died while serving in the navy. Eaton's name had been scandalously linked with hers before their marriage. When Mrs. Calhoun, followed by the wives of other cabinet members, refused to receive Mrs. Eaton, Jackson did not hesitate to defend her, no doubt remember-

Tariff and Nullification. As the election of 1832 approached, it became apparent that the touchy tariff problem could not be evaded much longer. In his message to Congress on December 6, 1831, Jackson recommended that the tariff be revised downward from the level at which the "Tariff of Abominations" had left it. Presumably he hoped to reduce it to a level that would appease the discontented South without antagonizing the Northeast. Good reasons could be given for tariff reduction: the national debt was almost paid off, and the revenue coming in as a result of the 1828 schedules was almost an embarrassment. How could the protectionists justify the 1828 tariff which had brought about sectional bitterness and now threatened to produce an overflowing Treasury? On July 14, 1832, Congress passed a tariff bill that lowered the schedules and removed features that had troubled the manufacturers and the commercial east, but that left the Southerners more agitated than ever. Calhoun hurried home from Washington to propagandize even more effectively than before for the idea of nullification.

In a series of dramatic steps South Carolina moved to put Calhoun's theories into effect. A legislature was elected with members overwhelmingly favorable to nullification. The legislature then ordered the election of a special state convention on the matter, and this body, meeting on November 19, 1832 soon adopted by a vote of 136-26 an ordinance of nullification which declared the tariffs of 1828 and 1832 null and void. The convention also (1) ordered the legislature to prohibit tariff enforcement within the state after February 1, 1833; and (2) asserted that the use of coercion by the federal government in enforcing these tariffs would be followed by secession.

Jackson responded with his famous Nullification Proclamation, drafted for him by Edward Livingston, now Secretary of State, and issued December 10, 1832. Its position on nullification was plain:

I consider, then, the power to annul a law of the United States, assumed by one State, *incompatible with the existence of the Union, contradicted expressly by the letter of the Constitution, unauthorized by its spirit, inconsistent with every principle on which it was founded, and destructive of the great object for which it was formed.*

Jackson warned that the laws of the United States compelled him to meet treason with force, and he appealed to the defenders of nullification to abandon their stand. Privately he spoke with less restraint about "these wicked demagogues" who deserved the gallows. Tension mounted as the Senate passed the "Force Bill" in February, 1833, empowering the President to use the army and navy if rebellious South Carolina resisted federal customs officials.

While the Force Bill was being debated, Henry Clay brought in a new compromise tariff bill calling for a gradual reduction of tariff duties. South Carolina now waited to see what would happen to these two measures. She had already learned that her action would not win the support of other southern states, and that she would have to go it alone.

A belligerent Unionist faction inside her own borders made it clear that she would not enjoy complete unity even at home.

On the day (March 2) the Force Bill became law, Jackson also signed the Tariff of 1833—the outcome of Clay's proposal—which helped to mollify the Carolinians. This tariff provided for a gradual and general reduction over a nine-year period of all duties exceeding 20 per cent. By July 1, 1842, no duties would be higher than that figure. The list of commodities that could be imported free was also enlarged. Even Calhoun, who had resigned as vice-president to be named by the Carolina legislature for the Senate so that he could speak for his state there, voted for this bill. After its passage, South Carolina showed her satisfaction by withdrawing her nullification of the tariffs of 1828 and 1832. But lest it appear that she had backed down on the nullification principle itself, she also passed a new ordinance nullifying Jackson's Force Bill. That law was now no longer needed, and Jackson wisely ignored the attempt of the Carolinians to save face by uttering this last word of formal defiance.

Party Alignments. With Calhoun's defection from the Jacksonian ranks and with Van Buren's emergence as Jackson's potential successor, a new political alignment was shaping up. When Calhoun and Clay temporarily buried their differences, the National Republican party (soon to be called the Whig party) began to emerge. The political situation was further complicated by the rise to national prominence of the Anti-Masonic party, formed in western New York in 1830. William Morgan, a former Mason, had written an exposure of the Masonic order and then had mysteriously disappeared in 1826. Many people assumed that he had been done away with. The resulting agitation against the Masons in particular and against secret societies in general (including Phi Beta Kappa) was skillfully exploited by anti-Jackson politicians. Anti-Masonry, like other enthusiasms emanating from western New York, spread to other states and soon became a formidable movement. The President was an active Mason, but so was Clay, though his "American System" found favor with the Anti-Masons. Clay's refusal to repudiate Masonry embarrassed the Anti-Masons, who wanted him as their candidate. But at last in September, 1831, they found someone who agreed to be their presidential standard-bearer, the distinguished attorney William Wirt of Maryland. Their convention of 1831 was the first convention to nominate a presidential candidate and the first to adopt a campaign platform. The National Republicans then nominated Clay, and the Jack-sonians enthusiastically renominated the President with Van Buren as his running-mate.

At the National Republican convention in Baltimore, held in December, 1831, Jackson was taken to task for his stand on corruption, internal improvements, the Indian policy, and the tariff. But the principal target was his administration's unfriendly attitude toward the Bank of the United States. As it turned out, this question would overshadow all other issues in the 1832 campaign.

IV.. THE BANK WAR

Jackson and the Bank. The Second Bank of the United States had been founded in 1816 (see p. 184) and since 1822 had been managed by the able Philadelphian, Nicholas Biddle. At the outset, it had failed to satisfy critics in every section. By easy-money men, the Bank was blamed for preventing the state banks from issuing sufficient paper currency to carry on the nation's business. State banks, for example, that lent more money than their specie reserves entitled them to lend, discovered that the Bank of the United States would not accept their bank notes at face value. Weak banks that had over-extended their loans might suddenly be presented with large amounts of their own notes to be redeemed in specie. By its watch-dog tactics, the United States Bank helped to maintain financial stability in the country, but many advocates of unrestricted banking —particularly in the West—resented the Bank's power to limit the amount of paper currency in circulation.

Jackson himself had approved of the Bank's deflationary role in 1817, but by 1828 he had come to doubt the Bank's constitutionality and value. It represented for him the spirit of monopoly, and a dangerous convenience at best. His cabinet, however, contained a number of pro-Bank men, and the Bank's services throughout the country made him reluctant to attack it. At first he contented himself with putting pressure on the Bank's president, Nicholas Biddle, to put more administration men on the Bank's payroll. But Biddle's fear that the Bank might be made a part of Jackson's patronage system led him into a highly improper financial relationship with certain opposition members of Congress. After 1829, in order to keep his influence, Biddle began to lend these men money on easy terms and advanced them their salaries without interest. He also curried favor with influential journalists by lending them money at low interest and paying them to put friendly notices about the Bank in their papers. In Congress, Biddle could rely upon the good services of Henry Clay—who saw in the Administration's anti-Bank policy an effective political issue for the National Republicans—and the mighty Daniel Webster, the Senator from Massachusetts, but incidentally the legal adviser of the Bank and one of its directors. Since it was the source of sizable retainer's fees, Webster felt more than a sentimental attachment toward the Bank.

Biddle's tactics only strengthened Jackson's deep-seated prejudices against all banks, and by the middle of 1830 Jackson had decided that the Bank must go. In his second annual message to Congress, December 6, 1830, he proposed that the Bank become a branch of the Treasury Department, "without power to make loans or purchase property."

The Bank issue simmered during the months before the 1832 election. Jackson, underestimating the popular support for his position, would have preferred to keep the Bank out of the campaign. But Webster and Clay now urged Biddle to defy the President and request a new Bank charter long before the old one was due to expire in 1836. They felt confident that both the Senate and the House would comply with Biddle's petition and mistakenly believed that a presidential veto would lose the election for the Democrats. But their knowledge of the public temper was abysmal. Congress did pass the re-chartering bill by a substantial majority. The bedridden Jackson grimly observed to his heir-apparent, Martin Van Buren, "The Bank, Mr. Van Buren, is trying to kill me, *but I will kill it.*"

In his veto message of July 10, 1832, Jackson denounced the Bank as a monopoly from which a privileged few derived enormous advantages. He dwelled upon the danger to the country if the stock, one-third of which was already owned abroad, should pass completely under foreign control (a most unlikely possibility and a negligible danger), and he concluded that the Bank was neither necessary, nor proper, nor constitutional. His reasoning and his facts were certainly disputable, but his closing remarks were eloquent and admirably appropriate for the coming election:

Distinctions in society will always exist under every just government. Equality of talents, of education, or of wealth cannot be produced by human institutions. In the full enjoyment of the gifts of Heaven and the fruits of superior industry, economy, and virtue, every man is equally entitled to protection by law; but when the laws undertake to add to these natural and just advantages artificial distinctions, to grant titles, gratuities, and exclusive privileges, to make the rich richer and the potent more powerful, the humble members of society—the farmers, mechanics, and laborers—who have neither the time nor the means of securing like favors to themselves, have a right to complain of the injustice of their Government.

Nicholas Biddle thought so little of this "manifesto of anarchy" that he had it circulated as pro-Bank propaganda. But Biddle was out of touch with popular sentiment and Jackson was not. In the 1832 election, Jackson won 219 of the 288 electoral votes; Henry Clay, the Bank's champion, got 49.* Some 687,000 ballots were cast for the President, 530,000 for Clay. Jackson's personal popularity probably explains the Democratic landslide, since there is no conclusive evidence that the voters meant to approve his views on the Bank. Nevertheless, after the election, he pressed his war against Biddle's "Hydra of corruption" with typical relentlessness.

The Foes of the Bank.   Jackson's victory had not made him overconfident, nor had it extinguished Biddle's hopes. Anticipating the possibility that federal deposits might be withdrawn for payment on the national debt, the Bank had greatly extended its loans and had spent increasing amounts of money on favorable newspaper publicity. Jackson also became convinced that government funds were not safe in the Bank, though a House investigating committee concluded that they were. For these and other reasons, Jackson's anti-Bank advisers recommended the removal of government deposits from the Bank —some $12 million in all—before Congress could even consider extending its charter.

Not all the members of the cabinet agreed with this drastic proposal. Van Buren urged caution, and Jackson's new Secretary of the Treasury, William J. Duane of Pennsylvania, openly opposed removal of the deposits. Duane had the authority to remove the government funds, but only after he had become convinced that the Bank was unsafe. Neither Duane nor Lewis McLane, now Jackson's Secretary of State, agreed with the anti-Bank extremists among the President's intimates,

* William Wirt's Anti-Masonic supporters joined with the National Republicans in some states and Wirt won only Vermont's 7 electoral votes. In South Carolina, where the nullificationists dominated the legislature, the state's 11 electoral votes were given to John Floyd of Virginia.

and Duane refused to carry out the President's removal order. Jackson finally removed Duane and replaced him with an avowed enemy of the Bank, Roger B. Taney of Maryland, who was more than eager to oblige his chief. A new order (September 26) provided that government funds should henceforth be placed in certain state banks. Anti-Jacksonians immediately dubbed the preferred institutions "pet banks," and implied that their selection was made on purely political grounds. But these banks were at first chosen with care, and the conditions under which they operated were strictly defined. In 1835 and 1836, the Secretary of the Treasury began to abuse his discretion and relax these rules, especially for some newly created western banks. As a result, Congress passed a law in June, 1836, setting firm rules governing the choice of depositories.

In his fight against the Bank, Jackson attracted the allegiance of three interests that agreed on a destructive goal—the attack on Biddle's institution—but not on constructive policies:

1. Perhaps the most influential supporters of the movement against the Bank in its earlier stages were powerful Middle-state banking interests, particularly in New York City and Baltimore. Taney, for instance, who led the fight after Duane's removal, was counsel for the Union Bank of Maryland. Several other anti-Bank men were either still associated with such banking interests or had conceived an unfavorable view of central banking as a result of their experiences as associates of state banks during the Panic of 1819 and after. Men of this sort, substantial business proprietors, agents, or investors, fought the Bank not out of hostility to property but more in the spirit of business rivals who resented the Bank's power and influence.

2. Somewhat similar were the representatives of wildcat bankers in the West and South, and of the land speculators who did business with them. These men felt it would be in their interest to remove the restraining bonds that the central bank put upon their loose practices.

3. A more diffuse group was made up of the small businessmen, proprietors, intellectuals, and professional men who were striving to find a stable place for themselves in the business world and who opposed special privileges for chartered businesses everywhere. To them the Bank of the United States was simply the biggest monopoly among many chartered monopolies, and they responded enthusiastically to Jackson's ringing pronouncements against privilege. Because they spoke the language and shared the feelings of radical democracy, leaders from this group often attracted a following among workingmen. New York, for instance, was the scene of a rebellion in the Democratic party caused by the discontent of such men with the conservative Tammany leaders and the New York bankers, who together dominated the party in that city. The rebels became known as "Locofocos" when, after capturing a Democratic party meeting from the regulars, they found themselves sitting in darkness because the regulars had cut off the gas lights; the rebels then decided to carry on their meeting by the light of "locofoco" matches. The name Locofoco was a symbol of radical politics for years. In truth, the Locofocos were the most resolute enemies of paper money and banks, for workingmen wanted to be paid in hard cash instead of in the often depreciated currency of distant banks. The strongest impulse in Locofocoism, however, was not anti-property sentiment, but an effort to create the conditions, in state and nation, by which small men could enter the race for success, free from the necessity of competing with legally established monopolies of various kinds.

In spite of their common opposition to Biddle, however, these three groups quarreled among themselves. The Locofoco element, taking a radical stand against banks in general, eventually fell out with the state banking elements. To adopt a hard-money policy, and to limit the activities of banks as much as the Locofocos desired, would have tightened credit and exerted a strong deflationary influence. This possibility, once again, ran counter to the wishes and practices of the easy-banking elements of the West and South who were eager to make the most of land possibilities and other speculations through the rapid and unchecked expansion of credit.

Caught between the hard-money Locofocos and the soft-money wildcatters, Jacksonian democracy was unable to follow a consistent course of action and was unable to satisfy the demands of all three interests. The Jackson administration pleased them all when it killed Biddle's move for recharter, and it pleased the Bank's big rivals when it distributed the surplus among the "pet banks." But, as we shall see, it soon disturbed the hard-money men by launching a speculative inflation, and then dashed the hopes of the speculators by adopting drastic deflationary policies. Finally, under Jackson's successor, the administration yielded to one of the chief demands of the Locofocos and drove many of the state-bank supporters into the ranks of the rival Whig party, by removing the federal deposits from all private banks. To understand the last phases of the Bank war, we must review the financial events of 1835-1840.

Boom and Bust.   Not long after the federal deposits were removed from the Bank, Biddle began a campaign to restrict credit artificially, hoping to create such a desperate economic panic throughout the affected parts of the country that public opinion would force Jackson to reverse his policies. Ruthlessly, Biddle called in obligations owed to the Bank. For some months during the winter of 1833-1834, he succeeded in producing all the signs of an economic reversal. But again he miscalculated the political effects. To petitioners who came before him for relief, Jackson insistently replied, "Go to Nicholas Biddle." In time, even segments of the business community appealed to Biddle

to relent, and finally he had to give up his attempt to bring about artificial contraction. Before he launched on this campaign, Biddle's conduct, though occasionally arrogant, had been justifiable. But his attempt to get his way by creating mass suffering brought him into wide disrepute. Historians of finance have pointed out, however, that the Bank in any case would have had to wind up its affairs between 1833 and 1836 and that some shortage of credit would almost certainly have occurred.

When Biddle's artificially encouraged panic came to an end, the American economy almost immediately took off on the opposite tack—toward a dangerous inflationary boom. This boom, characterized by a general expansion in land investment, in cotton and slaves, and in internal improvements, was heightened by the policy of the state banks, which used their resources (in many cases now increased by federal deposits) for purposes of speculation. Released from the restraining hand of the Bank of the United States, the state banks joined freely in the speculative impulse. Where there had been 329 state banks in 1829, there were 788 in 1837. Their circulation of notes increased even more spectacularly—from $48 million to $149 million; and their loans rose from $137 million to $525 million. In the South and West the boom raged with particular fury. Speculators bought land at $1.25 an acre, went to their bank, secured loans by using the land as collateral, and promptly used the loans to buy more land. As long as the boom lasted, these tactics worked very well. Sometimes a speculator sold his land for three times its original cost. The government accelerated the dizzy boom by disposing of large amounts of its own lands; between 1834 and 1836 the annual sales of government land increased from 4,600,000 to 20 million acres. Thus the federal government aggravated the boom not only by making its funds available to banks operating without central restraint but also by throwing its own lands onto the market and by permitting them to be bought with bank paper.

A great many of Jackson's supporters hoped that his bank policies would lead to just such a profitable boom. But others—the so-called hard-money school—objected not only to Biddle's Bank but to many of the looser practices of the state banks. These hard-money Jacksonians looked upon the saturnalia of inflation with deep misgivings and wondered what they had brought about. "I did not join in putting down the Bank of the United States," Benton announced to the Senate, "to put up a wilderness of local banks. I did not join in putting down the paper currency of a national bank to put up a paper currency of a thousand local banks. I did not strike Caesar to make Antony master of Rome." Benton predicted another depression if steps were not taken to check "the present bloat in the paper system." Jackson agreed, but it was now too late to prevent a drastic reaction. On July 11, 1836, he pricked the land boom by issuing his "Specie Circular," which required that all land purchased from the federal government after August 15 be paid for in silver or gold —a provision aimed at speculators. Bona-fide settlers were permitted to use bank notes for an additional four months, provided their purchases were less than 320 acres.

The Specie Circular pleased some of Jackson's hard-money followers, but it was an extraordinary reversal of policy. An economy dangerously inflated by the administration's bank policies was suddenly punctured by Jackson's thrust at the land bubble. Land sales turned sharply downward. In the spring of 1837 stock and commodity prices also broke, and soon the Panic of 1837 was on in earnest. Jackson left office only two months before its onset, and thus escaped political responsibility for the financial inconsistencies of his administration. Having hoped only to deliver the people from oppression, he had instead exposed them to speculation and disaster. As Bray Hammond has observed, "No more striking example could be found of a leader fostering the very evil he was angrily wishing out of the way."

A caricature of the hard times brought on by the Panic of 1837.

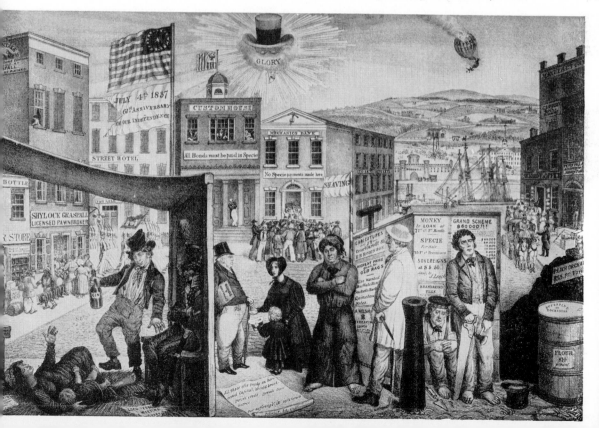

The depression was aggravated by factors other than the land boom and the fiscal policies of the administration. Among them was the international movement of capital. The swollen money market, fed by streams of British capital invested in railroads and state bonds, encouraged many states during the 1830's to embark on wild internal improvement programs based on turnpike, canal, and railroad construction. Most of these schemes were financed by borrowing inflated currency from banks that were organized expressly to lend it for these purposes. The optimistic plans of the states were spurred on still further in the summer of 1836 when it became clear that the federal government was about to distribute to the states some of the $35 million Treasury surplus that had accumulated from tariff revenues and the sale of public lands. A measure sponsored by Henry Clay, and passed in June, 1836, provided that all money in excess of $5 million in the treasury on January 1, 1837, was to be apportioned during the year among the states in accordance with population. The surplus disappeared before payments could be completed, but the measure passed in time to sustain the boom.

It is hard to understand how frontier states with sparse populations and no liquid assets expected to pay back their fantastic debts, but America in these boom days expected miraculous results from improved communications. This was the time, as one cynic observed in 1835, when "faces are shorter, purses are longer, creditors begin to hope, debtors begin to pay." But, with more foresight than his fellows, he anticipated a future of "overtrusting, overtrading, hard times, hard customers, hard creditors, suits, failures, ruin and epidemic woe."

Bank failures in Ireland and Manchester in 1836 brought about the collapse of three large London banks that had extended heavy credits to American speculators. Now British creditors demanded their loans from the overstrained American banks in New Orleans. Cotton prices tumbled and merchants went bankrupt when they were caught with huge supplies of unsold goods bought on credit. The shutting off of British credit at a time when specie had almost disappeared coincided with crop failures and with the weakening of the "pet banks." Banks began to fail everywhere, and English creditors, merchants, and manufacturers were sucked into the financial whirlpool along with the Americans.

Among the events that deepened the depression was the failure in 1839 of Nicholas Biddle's bank, which had been operating since 1836 under a Pennsylvania charter. Biddle, once so hated for his restraints on credit, had advocated a policy of easy credit to meet the depression, but he had not managed his own bank cautiously enough for it to survive. After suspending activities twice, beginning in the fall of 1839, the bank was finally turned over to trustees for liquidation in 1841. Biddle was charged with fraud but was subsequently acquitted. In 1844, at the age of 58, he died a broken man, the victim not merely of his own arrogance, but of the bitterness of American partisan politics and the curious state of American financial thought.

V.   VAN BUREN AND TYLER

The Election of 1836.   When the voters went to the polls in 1836 to choose President Jackson's successor, the panic and depression had not yet begun, and the boom was still in full swing. Only the well-informed knew how much trouble was in the offing, and the surface prosperity helped sustain Jackson's popularity. He had checked nullification, had adopted a democratic and popular position in the Bank war, and had conducted foreign policy with notable success. In 1830, the United States had at last successfully negotiated an agreement with Great Britain whereby American ships could trade freely with the British West Indies. Less smoothly, in July, 1831, the administration had settled American "spoliation claims" against France that had been pending since 1803, and Jackson had shown vigor and determination in collecting the sum. A rebellion by the Texans against the Mexican government in 1836 (see p. 270) required delicate handling, since Mexico rightly suspected the American pretense of neutrality, and New Englanders regarded the move for Texan independence as a slaveholders' plot. Annexation of Texas was out of the question at this time, but Jackson did bring about recognition of the Texas Republic in the last moments of his administration.

For some time before the election, the enemies of his administration had been building up a coalition of forces on the issue of "executive usurpation." The new Whig party, which took its name from the old English and American Whigs who had defended legislative authority against royal autocracy, was an odd coalition. It contained old Adams and Clay men, Anti-Masons, disgruntled Democrats, and moderate anti-slavery men. The unity of these groups consisted almost solely in their common dislike of Jackson. They created a party around which Jackson-haters from all sections—no matter what their politics—could rally. The new party had money, brains, and prestige, an able press, and popular leaders. But its strategists were well aware that they could not hope to beat Jackson's chosen successor, Van Buren, in the usual two-sided contest. Accordingly, they settled on the plan of running a number of candidates each of whom would appeal powerfully to his own section: Daniel Webster to New England; William Henry Harrison of Indiana to the Middle states and the West; Judge Hugh L. White to Tennessee; and Willie P. Mangum to South Carolina, where the presidential electors were still chosen by the legislature. The Whigs hoped to create a situation similar to the one that had occurred in 1824, when the electoral votes were so divided that the election was thrown into the House of Representatives. But Van Buren survived by a narrow margin. He re-

ceived 762,000 votes to a total of 735,000 for his combined opponents. In the electoral college, Van Buren got 170 votes, Harrison 73, White 26, Webster 14, and Mangum 11. For a newly formed party, the Whigs had made a remarkably strong showing, and General Harrison, their candidate, had shown considerable popularity.

The Van Buren Administration.

The problems facing Van Buren when he took office quickly became formidable. Financial panic was in full swing by May, 1837. Banks closed, the price of food and other necessities soared, factories shut down, and severe unemployment with all its attendant miseries gripped the Northeast. Merchants and business leaders besieged the President with petitions to relieve the distress by withdrawing Jackson's Specie Circular, which, they claimed, "had produced a wider desolation" than the cholera epidemic "which depopulated our streets." Conditions were just as bad in the South, where land and slaves dipped sharply in value. But in the West, the full weight of the 1837 recession was not to be felt for several years.

Americans in 1837 (as Van Buren reminded them in a masterly presidential message) had placed their faith in grandiose dreams and the miraculous power of paper currency. Now they blamed Andrew Jackson or the treachery of bankers. Van Buren was given plenty of advice on how to end the economic crisis. Biddle, for example, hinted that now was the time to restore the Bank of the United States. Members of Van Buren's own party offered conflicting solutions. The conservative wing urged him to withdraw the Specie Circular and to continue the state-bank system; the Locofoco anti-Bank wing proposed that the government carry the hard-money crusade even further and remove public funds from all banks, national and state. Only by so doing, they argued, "could the fiscal operations of the United States be placed on such a basis that they may be embarrassed as little as possible by the doings of banks and speculators."

Van Buren favored the radical Democratic proposal and worked throughout his administration to create an "Independent Treasury" system. According to this plan, government specie would be taken from all private banks and would be placed in various sub-treasuries around the country; tariff revenues and receipts from land sales would also be deposited in these storage centers; and government expenditures would be made in cash. Van Buren's scheme, presented to Congress in September, 1837, would have discouraged speculation and protected government funds, but its opponents correctly pointed out that the removal of large sums of specie from circulation would embarrass business.

Opposed not only by the Whigs, but also by conservative Democrats in Congress who were sympathetic to state banking interests, Van Buren had great difficulty getting his Independent Treasury Bill passed. However, during his administration, Calhoun and some of his southern following swung away from the Whig party, to which they had been driven after the feud with Jackson, and returned to the Democrats, whose program seemed more in harmony with their interests. Van Buren had Calhoun's support in the closing phases of this fight. He also succeeded in gaining some support among reluctant western Democrats, who were won over by his position on fiscal and public land policies. Eventually he gained enough support to pass the Independent Treasury Act in the summer of 1840. This "divorce of bank and state," as it was called, was the high water mark of the Locofoco influence in the Democratic party. It was to prove a short-lived triumph.

The Whig Triumph. As the election year of 1840 drew near, it began to appear that the Whig party might find temporary unity on the issue of "executive usurpation." Harrison, who not inaccurately described himself as a "clod-hopper," won the Whig nomination, even though both Webster and Clay had made themselves available. His "victory" over Tecumseh at the Battle of Tippecanoe (see p. 172)—greatly distorted by the Whigs—his Virginia ancestry and western connections, and the vagueness of his political sentiments made him an ideal candidate so far as the astute New York Boss, Thurlow Weed, was concerned. The selection of Harrison and his running-mate, John Tyler of Virginia, who it was hoped would strengthen the Whigs in the South, gave concrete expression to Weed's conviction that principles did not win elections. If the people could not be whipped into enthusiasm over Biddle's bank, they might respond to songs and slogans, ballyhoo and political revivalism.

Van Buren's stock had already fallen as a result of hard times, depressed farm prices, and low wages. The Whigs gleefully chanted their election slogan:

Little Van's policy, fifty cents a day and French soup;
Harrison's policy, two dollars a day and roast beef.

And Whig orators regaled the voters with reports of a perfumed president living in undemocratic luxury at the expense of the taxpayers. One campaign document, on the "Regal Splendor of the President's Palace," presented a picture of Van Buren as a slothful and effeminate oriental potentate sampling French cookery from golden plates and resting after the turtle soup on a "Turkish divan." In contrast to this luxury, the Whigs pointed to the stern simplicity of "Old Tippecanoe." When a Baltimore newspaper taunted the Whigs by saying that Harrison would be perfectly satisfied with a log cabin and a good supply of cider, his managers capitalized on the slur and made the log cabin an effective party symbol. "It tells of virtues," Thurlow Weed declared, "that dwell in obscurity, of the privations of the poor, of toil and danger." The log cabin, this "emblem of simplicity," was far removed from Harrison's gentlemanly origins and habits of living, but the symbol helped to elect him. His popular majority was a good 145,000 out of the 2,411,000 votes cast, and he won 234 electoral votes to Van Buren's 60.

Election of 1840

Electoral Vote
■ Harrison 234
▨ Van Buren 60

A Hollow Victory.   The Whigs, by adopting the same tactics that the Jacksonians had used against Adams in 1828, and by temporarily laying aside party feuds and sectional considerations, had elected their candidate, but they remained as divided as ever. The steadiness and strength of the Whig party lay in a minority of conservatives who were suspicious of unfettered democracy, of the foreign-born and the working classes. In order to succeed politically, however, the party had to lure into its ranks some of the very people it distrusted. Harrison commanded little respect in his own party, and his death one month after his inauguration ended all pretense of party harmony.

Harrison had humbly accepted the guidance of Webster and Clay, but the new incumbent—stubborn, forthright John Tyler—was far more southern than Whig and less susceptible than Harrison to Whig leadership. Prominent among wavering Virginia Whigs, whom the party hoped to keep from breaking ranks, Tyler had served in the Vir-

ginia legislature and in both houses of Congress before his elevation to the vice-presidency, and he had made no secret of his anti-tariff views and his strong dislike for a national bank. Like other men from his section, Tyler opposed government-sponsored internal improvements and stood for state rights and nullification. Yet he kept Harrison's cabinet (which had been hand-picked by Webster) and was willing to compromise with the Whig leaders. He signed a law destroying Van Buren's Independent Treasury System, but on the question of re-establishing a national bank he cheated the Whigs out of their victory.

As a believer in state rights, Tyler twice vetoed Clay's bills to establish a third national bank. After the second veto, almost the entire cabinet resigned at Clay's behest. Only Daniel Webster, who was now engaged in delicate diplomatic negotiations with Great Britain, stayed at his post as Secretary of State.

Just before the cabinet resigned, Tyler put his signature to a measure that marked a great triumph for the West in the field of public land policy. Ever since the earliest days of the Republic, western settlers had agitated for acceptance of the principle of pre-emption. Pre-emption meant that a settler, who took up government land without authorization, should have first chance to buy at the minimum price the land on which he had settled and presumably had made improvements. Otherwise he would have to bid for his "own" land at competitive prices or be evicted from it when it was bought by others. In 1830, 1832, and 1834, under Jackson, Congress had passed a series of temporary bills allowing pre-emption for renewed two-year periods. In 1838 Van Buren, seeking help from the West for his Independent Treasury proposal, had recommended pre-emption again, and in that year the right had been renewed, with safeguards against fraudulent claims. The right of pre-emption was renewed once again in 1840.

In the East, pre-emption was widely felt

to be an encouragement to unlawful and reckless settlement. At least one western leader, Henry Clay, was in sympathy with this feeling, and Clay became an outstanding advocate of the idea of distribution—that is, the proposal that the proceeds of the sales of western lands be in some fair way distributed among the states for their own use. Such a measure would have eliminated land revenues from the Treasury, continued the need for tariffs, and allowed easterners as well as westerners to benefit from the income from land sales. As the campaign of 1840 approached, it became clear that the West would play a mighty role and must be appeased in some way. The Democrats endorsed both distribution and pre-emption, but the Whigs won, partly on the appeal of General Harrison to the frontiersmen and on the ground that he was the friend of the common man. When Clay, in December, 1840, rose to introduce his distribution proposal again, Benton made a counter-move by introducing another pre-emption measure. Now it remained for the Whigs to show the West that their pretensions of friendship for the common man and the humble settler had meaning.

After a long parliamentary struggle, begun under the outgoing Van Buren administration and continued when Harrison and Tyler came in, a compromise was effected in the Distribution-Pre-emption Act which became law in September, 1841. The Act provided that (1) Any head of a family or single male adult could pre-empt 160 acres of government land and then pay the minimum price for it—$1.25—when the land was officially opened to settlement. (2) 500,000 acres were given to each new state for the construction of internal improvements. (3) 10 per cent of the revenues obtained from selling public land were to be returned to the state in whose boundaries the land lay; the rest was to be distributed among the states in proportion to their representation in Congress. Another provision was included to meet the demands of southerners who feared that depletion of the Treasury would provide a good argument for the supporters of a high tariff: (4) If the tariff schedules should exceed 20 per cent, the apportionment of land revenues would be inoperative. When, in August, 1842, a tariff passed which exceeded that level and explicitly repealed the distribution part of the bill, the distribution principle went into discard. But pre-emption survived, a major triumph for the frontier, and a guarantee to the settler that occupying land prior to purchase would no longer be equivalent to trespassing.

The rift between Tyler and the Whig party widened when the President disregarded the advice of his cabinet and vetoed internal-improvement and fiscal bills without bothering to consult his "constitutional advisers." In 1842, Henry Clay managed to push through a tariff bill that raised rates to the 1832 level, but Tyler would go no further in supporting the Whig program.

As the 1844 election drew closer, it was plain that old issues had lost much of their interest, and that Americans were less concerned with banking and finance, the tariff and public land policies, than they were with the expansion of the country and with the issues of slavery and sectional power that such expansion involved. The embattled domains of Jackson and Biddle were dwarfed by the continental empire yet to be won.

Readings

The rise of democratic practices is best traced in an old work, M. Ostrogorski, *Democracy and the Organization of Political Parties* (Vol. II, 1908). The history of suffrage is one of the great neglected areas of American history, but Kirk Porter, *A History of Suffrage in the United States* (1918), gives general information, and special studies by McCormick and Thayer, cited in Chapter III, are helpful on particular states. Administrative aspects of political change, particularly the spoils system, are treated by

Leonard D. White in works previously cited, while a briefer account may be found in Carl Russell Fish, *The Civil Service and the Patronage* (1904).

A fascinating general interpretation of the age is Arthur Schlesinger, Jr., *The Age of Jackson* (1945), though the reader will not want to neglect Frederick Jackson Turner, *The Rise of the New West* (1906), and *The United States, 1830-50* (1935). George R. Taylor, ed., *Jackson Versus Biddle* (1949), has several interesting sources, and includes an indispensable essay by Bray Hammond on the bank controversy, which is a counterpoise to Schlesinger's views. On the bank, see also W. B. Smith, *Economic Aspects of the Second Bank of the United States* (1953), and R. C. H. Catterall, *The Second Bank of the United States* (1903). C. B. Swisher, *Roger B. Taney* (1935), contains a good explanation of the Jacksonian strategy.

The biographical literature is rich and interesting. On John Quincy Adams, see the volumes by S. F. Bemis already cited; on Clay, G. G. Van Deusen, *The Life of Henry Clay* (1937), or the older two-volume work by Carl Schurz, *Life of Henry Clay* (1887); on Benton, the recent biography by W. N. Chambers, *Old Bullion Benton, Senator From the New West* (1956), as well as the older life by W. M. Meigs (1904), and Benton's own recollections, *Thirty Years' View* (2 vols., 1854-1856); on Calhoun, the three volumes by C. M. Wiltse (1944-1951); on Webster, the two volumes by C. M. Fuess (1930); on Van Buren, in the absence of a more adequate study, Holmes Alexander, *The American Talleyrand* (1935), or Van Buren's excellent *Autobiography* (1918); on Harrison, the lives by J. A. Green (1941), and Freeman Cleaves (1939); on Tyler, the work by O. P. Chitwood (1939). Charles Grier Sellers, *James K. Polk, Jacksonian, 1795-1843* (1957) sheds much light on national issues and on politics in Jackson's home state of Tennessee.

The literature on Jackson is full. The old study by James Parton in three volumes (1860) is rich and fascinating, the two-volume work by Marquis James (1933-1937) is colorful, and J. S. Bassett's study is clear and straightforward (1925). Jackson's personal qualities are conveyed in the 6 volumes of his *Correspondence* (1926-1935). A brilliant study of his public appeal is J. W. Ward, *Andrew Jackson, Symbol for an Age* (1953). T. P. Abernethy, *From Frontier to Plantation in Tennessee* (1932), is scholarly and hostile to Jackson, as is William Graham Sumner's *Andrew Jackson* (1882), which is good on financial matters.

Studies that deal helpfully with special problems are the following: On land policy: R. M. Robbins, *Our Landed Heritage, the Public Domain, 1776-1936* (1942); R. G. Wellington, *The Political and National Influence of the Public Lands, 1826-1842* (1914); and G. M. Stephenson, *The Political History of the Public Lands, from 1840 to 1862* (1917). On nullification: Frederic Bancroft, *Calhoun and the South Carolina Nullification Movement* (1928); C. S. Boucher, *The Nullification Controversy in South Carolina* (1916); and D. F. Houston, *A Critical Study of Nullification* (1896). On Indian removal: Angie Debo, *The Road to Disappearance* (1941); and Grant Foreman, *Indian Removal* (1932). On party politics: W. E. Binkley, *American Political Parties: Their Natural History* (1943); Charles McCarthy, *The Anti-Masonic Party* (1902); S. R. Gammon, *The Presidential Campaign of 1832* (1922); E. M. Carroll, *Origins of the Whig Party* (1925); G. R. Poage, *Henry Clay and the Whig Party* (1936); A. C. Cole, *The Whig Party in the South* (1913); and Dixon Ryan Fox, *The Decline of Aristocracy in the Politics of New York* (1919). On southern developments, see C. S. Sydnor, *The Development of Southern Sectionalism, 1819-1848* (1948).

AMERICA
IN FERMENT

CHAPTER ELEVEN

Life in America between 1820 and 1850 seems to modern eyes as puzzling and contradictory as it was rich and various. Bumptious, aggressively nationalistic, prudent and utilitarian, the people were at the same time idealistic, given to nature-worship and to splendid humanitarian outbursts. The upstart Yankee nation appeared serenely confident of a glorious destiny. During the dec-

ades following 1820, its orators and writers saw civilization moving westward and looked back on a "deteriorating" Europe with mingled pity and contempt. Yet not all intellectuals were untroubled about the future. On the surface, society was deceptively open and uncomplicated; in reality, as discerning writers and artists noted, it was elusive and paradoxical.

236

I. THE AMERICAN TEMPERAMENT

A Restless Society.   All observers agreed that Americans worked harder, ate faster, moved around more, and relaxed less than Europeans. In America, Tocqueville wrote,

... a man builds a house in which to spend his old age, and he sells it before the roof is on; he plants a garden, and lets it just as the trees are coming into bearing; he brings a field into tillage, and leaves other men to gather the crops; he embraces a profession and gives it up; he settles in a place, which he soon afterwards leaves, to carry his changeable longings elsewhere.

Nothing seemed finished in this raw republic. "Improvement," both personal and collective, was a national preoccupation. Americans were confirmed tinkerers, whether dealing with machines or institutions. They were on the move, in transit, going from somewhere to somewhere. They were obsessed with speed and impatient of delay. The symbol of the young republic might have been the locomotive that never ceased from its iron labors, or the steamboat that moved men and goods up and down the American rivers—and that frequently blew up.

A Commercial Society.   American society was primarily a business society, materialistic and practical. By the 1820's the businessman already occupied a key position in American society, and the trading spirit permeated American life. Every American, declared the editor of a well-known commercial periodical, was in one sense a trader. The physician traded his "benevolent care," the lawyer his "ingenious tongue," the clergyman "his prayers." One principle motivated the commercial classes, another explained, that enabled them to enrich the country as well as themselves:

Whether it be called avarice or the love of money, or the desire of gain, or the lust of wealth, or whether it be softened to the ear under the more guarded terms, prudence, natural affection, diligence in business, or the conscientious improvement of time and talents —it is still money-making which constitutes the great business of our people—it is the use of money which controls and regulates everything.

But even the severest critics of America usually agreed that there was nothing mean-spirited or sordid in this heroic pursuit of wealth. The prosperous men who followed the success code laid down by Benjamin Franklin (who by this time had become a patron saint) assumed the honors and the responsibilities that went with wealth. Public opinion condoned the drive to be rich, but it also regarded money as an "engine" of benevolence rather than as a good in itself. Many of the merchants, like the public-spirited Abbott Lawrence of Boston, actively supported humanitarian and cultural enterprises and were "even munificent in their donations."

An Idealistic Society.   In spite of their insistence on the practical and the useful and their almost universal contempt for the theoretical and the visionary, Americans were susceptible to every kind of evangelical appeal. They responded emotionally to *causes*. Temperance, world peace, national politics, the Greek Revolution, Hungarian independence, public schools, financial or even dietary panaceas, often distracted the solid citizen from his humdrum activities. "Causes" released dammed-up emotions. This was the the time of missionary crusades to the Pacific Islands and Africa and Asia, of religious revivals in frontier canebrakes, of abolitionist martyrs, of new religions and cults, of pseudo-science and strange delusions. Remarking on the "fanatical and almost wild spiritualism" found in America, Tocqueville surmised that religious enthusiasm naturally expressed itself in a society "exclusively bent upon the pursuit of material objects." A people who made a virtue of common sense, he believed, were likely to display emotional excess whenever they switched abruptly from material preoccupations to spiritual yearnings. Then they were prone to "burst the bonds of matter by which they are restrained" and "soar impetuously towards Heaven." Between 1820 and 1850, the American people attempted a number of such flights.

Democracy and Equality

In our government [declared an orator in 1840], we recognize only individuals, at least among whites; and in social life, the constant effort to do away with the castes produced by difference of fortune, education, and taste. The motto upon the flag of America should be 'Every man for himself.' Such is the spirit of our land, as seen in our institutions, in our literature, in our religious condition, in our political contests.

Democracy meant (to many, if not to all) not only political but social equality. To paraphrase Tocqueville again, men pounced "upon equality as booty" and clung to it "as some precious treasure" they feared to lose. They shunned menial occupations, however well paid, and stoutly resisted any idea or action that might tend to decrease their social prestige.

Yet even as patriots gave lip-service to equality, some Americans saw in the rush to the professions and the declining status of the laboring classes the evidences of a caste spirit. The increase in the number of factory workers, as the industrial revolution got under way, and the growth of an urban population weakened republican simplicity and intensified social distinctions. By the 1830's, a flexible yet well-defined social hierarchy had developed in the commercial

An early nineteenth-century Baptist ceremony—a water color by Paul Svinin.

Northeast and Northwest, as well as in the more class-conscious South.

Distinctions in this socially fluid period depended pretty much on wealth. Although it is impossible to chart the fine distinctions of rank and reputability, successful business leaders and lawyers seem to have occupied the top rungs of society. Clergymen, physicians, and teachers, too, if they were accepted and patronized by the influential, might claim similar status. But below this privileged group stood the bulk of the population, ranging from the moderately well-to-do down to the lowest-paid.

Class lines, to be sure, were flexible. No insuperable barriers prevented the mechanic or the clerk or the farmer—referred to in the press as the "bone and sinew" of the republic—from rising into the élite. Each citizen remained equal before the law, no class demanded special respect from another, and men of all degrees mingled indiscriminately in business. In spite of artificial distinctions, there was no servility. Almost everyone had some stake in the society, and despite the fears of conservatives the American people embarked on no wildly revolutionary course. Events since the Revolution had only confirmed their faith in material prosperity, religion, private property, and the home. Wrapped up in his daily affairs, and schooled to accept the ideas and prejudices of the majority, the citizen usually abided by the "empty phantom of public opinion," which was "strong enough to chill innovators and to keep them silent and at a respectful distance."

Individualism and Cooperation. Although the pre-Civil War era has been popularly regarded as the heyday of rampant individualism, and although the triumphant and self-propelled hero was held up as a model by contemporary orators, the period was also a time of cooperation or of "association." The achievements of the single man have come to overshadow the accomplishments of the group in our folk-lore, but when Tocqueville visited America he was immensely impressed by the fact that "the most democratic country on the face of the earth . . . carried to the highest perfection the art of pursuing in common the object of their common desires."

For the American to pool resources, both material and intellectual, and to throw in his lot with the community in which he worked and lived, simply seemed the most sensible thing to do at the time. A society of "lone wolves" would not have survived. Businessmen joined together to organize banks and insurance companies, or to protect themselves against the competition of foreign merchants. Poor people in the cities sometimes pooled their money to buy up fuel supplies when prices were low. Citizens, hungry for culture, set up mutual improvement clubs, and immigrants formed societies with their own countrymen. Charitable, reform, fraternal, and benefit organizations sprang up naturally in a democracy where there was no fixed ruling class with a tradition of social responsibility to supervise civic undertakings. Associations like these not only satisfied the need for fellowship, but they also gave the individual a sense of belonging to something.

Although some men came together to make frank protests against selfish individualism, most Americans saw no contradiction between their personal ambitions and community welfare. As a newspaper correspondent pointed out in 1834:

In a republic, the prosperity of the country is so intimately blended with that of each individual citizen . . . a citizen may pursue his individual benefit in connection with high consideration of his country's good, without laying himself under any imputation of a want of patriotism, or acting under purely selfish motives.

Another defended associations by pointing out that "Many can accomplish what one cannot." But he added this qualification: "We mean to receive as much as we give, and we ask others to join us on that principle."

Sectarian Rivalry. But if Americans poured their energies into countless societies, often pulling in many directions at once, what was it that kept American society itself together? Many observers during the 30's and 40's were disturbed by this diffuseness, by "lack of a common skeleton." Emerson, in 1847, noted America's "immense resources," but he was also struck by America's "village littleness." Village squabbles and rapacity characterized its policy. America, he concluded, "is great strength on a basis of weakness."

One of the "village squabbles" grew out of sectarian rivalry. During this period, the Americans seemed to be the most religious of peoples and yet the most afflicted by religious bickerings. The United States had always provided a fertile soil for new sects, but in the 30's and 40's, the dissenting churches split repeatedly into rival splinter groups, each claiming the authentic faith. The Baptist and Methodist churches (the fastest-growing denominations between 1800 and 1850) seemed the most susceptible to schisms. But new cults sprang up everywhere, and competition for the souls of immigrants pouring into the Mississippi Valley was fierce and frequently unchristian. Doctrinal differences created a good deal of friction, but the awareness that some denominations considered themselves socially superior to the others also aggravated the dissension. Denominations like the Presbyterians, Congregationalists, Episcopalians, and Unitarians differed in theology and in church organization, but they all drew their membership from the same propertied middle class. Baptists, Methodists, Campbellites, and Universalists were socially a cut below, and the immigrant and Free Negro churches were at the bottom.

Most Protestants, though they squabbled among themselves, shared a common hatred for the Roman Catholic Church. Catholics faced a prejudice deeply rooted in the American past. To prominent ministers like Lyman Beecher, the father of Harriet Beecher Stowe and president of Lane Seminary in Cincinnati, Catholicism still smacked of the sinister rites of the Inquisition and of political autocracy. The gullible readily swallowed crude fictions about Catholic atrocities and sensational "exposés" of Catholic depravity. Sometimes Catholics were insulted and attacked, their churches burned. Anti-Catholic prejudice grew even deeper when foreign immigration began to increase after 1830. During the 1820's, less than half a million Europeans had entered the United States, but between 1830 and 1850 two and one half million poured in. Most of them were from Catholic Ireland, whence they had been driven by disastrous famines during the 40's. Others were from Germany, and again many of them were Catholic.

In 1807, there was but one Catholic bishop in the United States, under whose dominion some 70 priests cared for 70,000 worshippers. By 1830, there were 20 bishops and about 500,000 communicants. In addition, the Catholics had established 6 seminaries, 9 colleges, 33 monasteries and convents, and sizable numbers of schools, hospitals, and other parochial institutions. A Catholic press, starting with the *United States Catholic Miscellany,* first published in 1822, also had come into being, along with a Catholic Tract Society, which had been founded in Philadelphia in 1827 to combat Protestantism as well as to promote the Church.

Yet despite America's looseness and variety, an inner unity—based upon a general acceptance of democracy, property, and religion—held the country together. The intellectual "wild oats" sown during the 30's and 40's, the audacious social experimentation, could never have been permitted in a tradition-ridden or static society—or a society hopelessly divided. True, the idea of the Union was not strong enough to triumph over the passions aroused by slavery, but the social fabric was tough enough to withstand every other strain. Between 1820 and 1850, almost every institution was challenged. Reformers stalked through the land, their pockets bulging with panaceas. Conservatives trembled for the future. But no heads fell and no property was expropriated. Reform could never get out of hand among a people who regarded "temporal prosperity" as the "chief end of existence" and who pur-

sued their material welfare with an intensity that amounted "to a species of heroism."

II. WRITERS AND SOCIETY

Literature and National Culture.   The literature of the period from 1820 to 1850 is both a reflection and a criticism of the prevailing ideas. We read it not only to discover something about popular taste, but also to learn what the most discerning minds had to say about the values and beliefs of their countrymen.

"Men of genius," according to a Boston critic in 1820, were "outlaws" because "for the most part, they want that getting-along faculty which is naturally enough made the measure of man's mind in a young country, where every one has his fortune to make." And yet during the next three decades an intellectual flowering burst forth that has been scarcely equaled by any other generation in our history. In 1802, when Washington Irving began to write, America had no literature and hardly a reading public. When he died, a year before the Civil War began, Emerson, Thoreau, Hawthorne, Poe, Melville, and Whitman had already struck off their masterpieces.

The achievements of these writers seem all the more remarkable when we consider the obstacles that confronted them. After the Revolution, patriots had called for a national literature that would reflect the dawning greatness of the new nation, but the American poets, such as Timothy Dwight and Joel Barlow, who planned mighty and unreadable epics turned out only pale imitations of English literary forms and deferred to English standards of taste. Among the would-be writers, only Philip Freneau and the imaginative Philadelphia novelist, Charles Brockden Brown (1761-1810) possessed more than a minor talent.

Most Americans had no interest in *belles lettres*. And the few who did care preferred the easily obtainable works of popular British authors. Sir Walter Scott, Byron, Bulwer-Lytton, Mrs. Felicia Hemans, and Charles Dickens crowded American authors off the book-shelves. Before the provincial Americans would deign to read their own writers, they had to be sure that the English approved of them. At a time when Americans boasted of their culture, spoke of the decay of learning abroad, and overstated the accomplishments of native American literature, American writers complained of neglect and lamented the absence of a stimulating literary atmosphere. They kept insisting that America had no ancient traditions, no peasants, no knights or kings, no ivy-covered castles, no Gothic churches, no legendary mist.

Deprived of castles, ruins, knights and banditti, American writers also had to reckon with the religiously inspired distrust of literature as literature and the genteel preference for the refined and the ideal. Mrs. Felicia Hemans, a British poet, attracted a large American following because her poetry, according to one admirer, "though never strikingly original . . . is always chaste, always interesting—always ennobling—always good." Such was the taste of the practical, the prudent, and the prudish. The books they liked painted a romantic but decorous landscape, against which heroes spoke in stilted language and heroines remained ladylike in even the most harrowing situations.

Yet the better-known American writers overcame or ignored these cultural handicaps and managed to attract a following. Washington Irving (1783-1859), an urbane New Yorker, was the first professional man of letters who won applause abroad and whose style and temperament made him extremely popular in the United States as well.

His burlesque and almost rowdy *History of New York* (1809) was followed by charming sketches, tales, biographies, and travel books which admirably incorporated his love for the old fashioned, the picturesque, and the ironically sentimental. Irving yearned for Europe (where he spent many years of his life) but in *The Sketch Book* (1819-1820), in *Bracebridge Hall* (1822), and in *A Tour of the Prairies* (1832), he helped Americans to discover their own magnificent landscape and made his Rip Van Winkle and Ichabod Crane household names.

Irving's friend and contemporary, William Cullen Bryant (1794-1878), grew up in the Berkshire Hills of Massachusetts, but he made his career as a poet, newspaper man, and reformer in New York City. Bryant distinguished himself from the lisping imitators of the British by describing American nature cleanly and simply. It was Bryant, as Emerson noted, who "subsidized every solitary grove and monument-mountain in Berkshire or the Katskills . . . every water fowl and woodbird . . . so that there is no feature of day or night in the country which does not, to the contemplative mind, recall the name of Bryant."

An even more illustrious member of the New York group was the novelist, James Fenimore Cooper (1789-1851). He belonged to the old New York Federalist aristocracy, but he was too independent a thinker to fit neatly into any category and retained the manners but not the political philosophy of his class. In Europe, where Cooper lived and traveled and wrote for a number of years, he truculently defended the government and institutions of his beloved America; in America, he berated his countrymen for their bad manners, their chauvinism, their contempt for privacy, and their slavish submission to public opinion. Cooper's early sympathy for Jackson and Jacksonian America soured in the last years of his life, but his thoughtful depiction of republican government, *The American Democrat* (1838), is still one of the best political

essays ever written by an American. What brought him fame both in Europe and America, however, were such novels as *The Spy* (1821), *The Pioneers* (1823), *The Pilot* (1823), and *The Last of the Mohicans* (1826). In the celebrated "Leatherstocking" series, Cooper compellingly evoked the beauty and terror of the American wilderness. Natty Bumppo, or Leatherstocking, the mythic hero of these forest romances, constantly pursuing or escaping from his white or Indian adversaries, embodied the traits of the American hero: strength, humor, resourcefulness, courage, and purity. Cooper, who had served in the American navy, also excelled in describing sea fights and storms and the functional beauty of sailing vessels.

Perhaps the most popular and representative literary figure of this period was the New England poet, Henry Wadsworth Longfellow (1807-1882). Born in Portland, Maine, and educated at Bowdoin College, he had spent several years on the Continent preparing himself to become a professor of modern languages, first at Bowdoin and later (1835) at Harvard College. In his Cambridge study, Longfellow composed volume after volume of mellifluous verse that soon made him famous throughout the world. *Hyperion* (1839), *Evangeline* (1847), *Hiawatha* (1855), and *The Courtship of Miles Standish* (1858) were only some of the better-known titles that delighted the largest audience, perhaps, that any American poet has ever commanded. His sentimentality, his didacticism, his optimism, and his antiquarianism satisfied popular taste. Although no poetic innovator, Longfellow handled all the conventional metrical forms with easy grace and expertly worked his romantic materials (ransacked from every literature) into his well-made stanzas. If his Hiawatha smacked more of Cambridge, Massachusetts, than of the shores of Gitche Gumee, and if the brawny "Village Blacksmith" was a Whig dream of a docile and respectful working man, poems like "The Psalm of Life" expressed without irony the aspirations of middle-class America. From 1839, when his first volume of verse appeared, until his death, Longfellow was our unofficial poet laureate, the first American to make poetry pay, and at his best a minor writer of charm and vitality.

Longfellow and his Boston and Cambridge associates belonged to the coterie of poets, essayists, and historians who contributed to what Van Wyck Brooks has called "The Flowering of New England." The emphasis placed by historians on this regional renaissance has partially obscured the intellectual and artistic activity of other sections. Yet, granting the provincialism and self-satisfaction of New England during this period, its "golden day" was real enough. Boston, Cambridge, and Concord hummed with creativity. No other area contained such a hive of industrious historians and scholars and poets. Much of their culture was thin and bookish, and the great reputations once enjoyed by writers like Lowell, Oliver Wendell Holmes, and John Greenleaf Whittier have deservedly shrunken. But the cumulative output of New England between 1830 and 1850 remains impressive. Today the great names that live on from that time are Francis Parkman, historian; Ralph Waldo Emerson and Henry David Thoreau, essayists and poets; Nathaniel Hawthorne, writer of romances and tales. But we must also return to the less enduring authors if we want to savor that mixture of complacence, idealism, humor, and fervor that characterize the New England mind.

Edgar Allan Poe. Many nineteenth-century New Englanders believed quite sincerely that American civilization was simply an extension of Boston culture. We can understand the irritation of Edgar Allan Poe (1809-1849) when Boston's James Russell Lowell failed to mention any southern writers except Poe himself in his "Fable for Critics," a satirical and amusing poem about the American literati. "Mr. L.," Poe observed at the time, "cannot carry his frail honesty of opinion even so far south as New York. All whom he praises are Bostonians; the other writers are barbarians. . . ."

Born in Boston, a city he sarcastically referred to in later life as "Frogpond," Poe regarded himself as a Virginian. After the death of his actor parents while he was an infant, he grew up in Richmond where his foster-father, John Allan, was a substantial merchant. He attended the University of Virginia until Allan's stinginess and Poe's own gambling debts forced him to leave. His subsequent career included a two-year hitch in the army, a West Point commission, and a court martial in 1831. In between, he managed to publish two volumes of verse (*Tamerlane,* 1827, and *Al Aaraaf,* 1829). But after the West Point fiasco, he became a professional man of letters. Nothing could seduce him from this "most noble of professions," as he once referred to it, but he spent the rest of his short life in the American Grub Street, writing and editing brilliantly for inferior men, and publishing poems, stories, and critical essays that brought him some fame but little income. In his most productive year, 1843, he earned $300. Poetry was his first love, but it was even less remunerative than his tales. The shabby and unrewarding years that he spent with the literary Bohemia of Philadelphia, Baltimore, and New York aggravated his natural instability. He had married his 13-year-old cousin, Virginia Clemm, in 1831. "I became insane," he wrote after her death in 1846, "with long intervals of horrible sanity." In the summer of 1849, he was found lying unconscious in a Baltimore street, and died in delirium at the age of 40.

Poe deliberately appealed to the sensational tastes of his reading public, whose literary preferences he shrewdly gauged, but he disagreed with most of their cherished beliefs and was no apostle of progress. Democracy displeased him, and he wanted no truck with middle-class truths. As a literary critic, Poe performed a tremendous service by attacking American provincialism and by writing cruel but just reviews of bad books. His own poetry and fiction contained most of the weaknesses he unerringly detected in the writings of his inferiors: cheapness, theatricality, bombast, and sentimentality. But in stories like "The Fall of the House of Usher," "The Imp of the Perverse," "The Black Cat," "The Man in the Crowd," and "The Premature Burial"—tales of murderers, neurotics, the near-insane—his vulgarity was redeemed by an extraordinary if sometimes infernal intelligence and intensity. Poe's victims are a far cry from Emerson's self-reliant Americans. The owner of the black cat who sorrowfully cuts out the eyes of his pet, the brother who entombs his sister alive, the lover who pulls out the teeth of his mistress while she sleeps in a cataleptic trance are all victims of dark internal powers; they live in a tormented world far removed from optimistic America.

Yet Poe appealed to the democracy he despised far more than did the self-proclaimed democrat, Walt Whitman. Poe's poem, "The Raven," made him famous throughout America, and it is not true that Poe was neglected in the United States until Europe discovered him. Had he been less unstable, he might have accomplished his dream of becoming the publisher of a successful popular magazine. As it was, Poe perfected, if he did not invent, the detective story, contributed significantly to the genre of science fiction (see his astonishing, "The Narrative of Arthur Gordon Pym"), and profoundly influenced poets and critics of succeeding generations in Europe and America.

Emerson
and Transcendentalism.
The most universal literary figure of his generation was Ralph Waldo Emerson (1803-1882). Boston-born and Harvard-educated, he entered the ministry as his father and grandfather had done before him, but he resigned his pastorate in 1832 because the church forms had become meaningless for him. Thenceforth, he devoted himself entirely to a career of writing and lecturing. *Nature* (1836) contained in condensed form the majority of the themes

he was to treat in his later works. It was followed by two volumes of essays (1841, 1844), *Poems* (1847), *Representative Men* (1850), *English Traits* (1852), and *The Conduct of Life* (1860).

Half Yankee and half yogi, Emerson contained within himself the warring tendencies of his age. Part of him belonged to the practical American world of forms and banks and railroads, and no one celebrated more enthusiastically than he (see his essays on "Wealth," "Power," and "Napoleon") the deeds of powerful individualists. At the same time, Emerson was a mystic and an idealist who looked upon the external world as a passing show and detected an unchanging reality behind it. This shrewd and canny man declared himself to be "part and particle" of God and rejoiced in the unsettling effect his theories had upon his countrymen.

Emerson, like many other Boston intellectuals of his day, had rebelled against the coldness and formality of the Unitarian faith. The Unitarians had repudiated the harsh Calvinist doctrine of human depravity and a vengeful God, but in the process their religion had become chilly and passionless. Emerson wanted to revive the old Puritan fervor without the rigidities of Puritan theology. Quakerism, with its doctrine of the inner light, its gentleness, and its humanitarianism, moved him deeply, and he was drawn to any philosophy that broke down the barriers between mind and matter. In Emerson's youth, the philosophy of the English philosopher, John Locke, was still much in vogue. Locke had held that ideas did not arise spontaneously in the mind, but that they were implanted there by the impressions of the external world acting through the senses. This meant that spirit was subordinate to matter. Emerson's own disposition told him otherwise, and he found support for his idealism in the works of certain continental and Scotch philosophers, oriental poets and sages, and in English romantic poetry.

Transcendentalism, the philosophy associated with Emerson and his sympathizers, was not a systematic faith; it had no creed and it could not be easily defined. To some, the word "transcendentalist" covered "all those who contend for perfect freedom, who look for progress in philosophy and theology, and who sympathize with each other in the hope that the future will not always be as the past." To the journalist and critic, Orestes Brownson, the only common bond shared by the transcendentalists was their opposition "to the old school":

They do not swear by Locke, and they recognize no authority in matters of opinion but the human mind, whether termed the reason with some of them, or the soul with others. They have all felt that our old catechisms need revision, and that our old systems of philosophy do not do justice to all the elements of human nature, and that these systems can by no means furnish a solid basis for a belief in God, much less in Christianity. Some of them . . . *ignore* all philosophy, plant themselves in their instincts and wait for the huge world to come round to them. . . . Some of them reason . . . others merely dream.

Although vague in its outlines, transcendental doctrine was nobly formulated in Emerson's essays and lectures, in which he announced to his fellow Americans that they, too, could speak to God directly without the assistance of churches and creeds. He urged them to be self-reliant and to get their experience at first hand. Every object in the physical world had a spiritual meaning, and those who were capable of seeing that material things were the symbols of spiritual truths might understand nature's purpose. The ability to communicate with God, or the "Over Soul," was given to everyone, but only a small number of poets and scholars and philosophers (Emerson called them men of "Reason") had developed this inborn capacity. From them, other men could learn that only the idea is real, that evil is negative (the mere absence of good), and that a kindly destiny awaited us.

These ideas Emerson expressed in a language that was fresh and audacious. To an audience absorbed in material concerns, he argued against the tyranny of *things* over the *spirit,* and he seemed to speak intimately to any person who read or heard him, encouraging every man to stand up against public opinion and be an individual:

What I must do is all that concerns me, not what the people think. This rule, equally arduous in actual and in intellectual life, may serve for the whole distinction between greatness and meanness. It is harder because you will always find those who think they know what is your duty better than you know it. It is easy in the world to live after the world's opinion; it is easy in solitude to live after our own; but the great man is he who in the midst of the crowd keeps with perfect sweetness the independence of solitude.

A number of Emerson's contemporaries tried to live according to his precepts: Henry David Thoreau as the transcendental adventurer of Walden Pond, Walt Whitman as the democratic poet, Theodore Parker as the minister-reformer, and many others.

Henry David Thoreau.   Henry David Thoreau (1817-1862), like his friend and mentor, Emerson, was a graduate of Harvard College and a resident of Concord, Massachusetts. "He declined," Emerson later wrote of him, "to give up his large ambition of knowledge and action for any narrow craft or profession, aiming at a much more comprehensive calling, the art of living well." Throughout his life, Thoreau gave himself over to self-cultivation and self-exploration. Briefly a teacher and a sometime lecturer, his literary medium was the diary-like record of his intellectual experiences. In *A Week on the Concord and Merrimack Rivers* (1849), *Civil Disobedience* (1849), and especially *Walden*; *or, Life in the Woods* (1854), Thoreau expressed his tart and unconventional opinions about literature, religion, government, and social relations. Many of the reformers were his friends, but he was never a "joiner," distrusted reform movements, and tried to keep himself free from what he called "greasy familiarity." Good fellowship he once described as "the virtue of pigs in a litter, which lie close together to keep each other warm." "Not satisfied with defiling one another in this world," he wrote, "we would all go to heaven together. . . ."

Like most transcendentalists, Thoreau was an unblushing egoist, but he wrote about himself, he said, because he did not know anyone else quite so well. Moreover, his own accounts of how he discovered the miraculous in the common were also suggestions for those men who led "lives of quiet desperation." He asked a generation geared to practicalities, what do the practicalities of life amount to? The immediate things to be done, he said, are trivial and can wait; the wealth of the world is less significant than one true vision:

The ways by which you may get money almost without exception lead downward. To have done anything by which you earned money *merely* is to have been truly idle or worse. . . . There is no more fatal blunderer than he who consumes the great part of his life getting his living . . . you must get your living by loving. . . . It is not enough to tell me that you worked hard to get your gold. So does the Devil work hard. . . . I believe that the mind can be permanently profaned by the habit of attending to trivial things, so that all our thoughts shall be tinged with triviality.

Thoreau advised his countrymen to simplify their private lives and to simplify their government, too, for he was a supreme individualist who regarded the organized state as a threat to true independence. Abolitionist, naturalist, poet, and rebel, and a down-to-earth but subtle writer—he attracted no great notice while he lived. In our day, *Walden* is justly considered a

Portrait of Walt Whitman in 1887 by Thomas Eakins.

literary masterpiece, and its author—who discovered a universe in Concord—is regarded as one of the most original and finest minds of the New England renaissance.

Walt Whitman.

Walt Whitman.   The poet that Emerson predicted in his essay, "The Transcendentalist" (1842), was soon to appear. The "genius" Emerson demanded was Walt Whitman (1818-1892), born on Long Island and a life-long New Yorker. During his formative years, Whitman was a schoolteacher, printer, carpenter, journalist, publisher, and editor. When *Leaves of Grass,* his first volume of poems, appeared in 1855, its undisguised references to the body and sex caused Whitman to be denounced as the "dirtiest beast of his age." The most friendly review described his verse as "a sort of excited compound of New England transcendentalism and New York rowdy." Emerson was the only eminent writer who immediately discerned Whitman's freshness and originality and found (as he wrote to Whitman) "incomparable things, said incomparably well." Whitman continued to revise and add to the *Leaves* until 1892, in addition to publishing other volumes of prose and verse, but the recognition he deserved did not come until after his death.

Whitman's poems, like the essays of Emerson, embody the idea of progress, celebrate the innate goodness of man, and idealize nature; they insist on the spiritual reality that underlies the material world. But Whitman was more passionately democratic than the New Englander, and he looked to the people for his inspiration. Other poets, he said

. . . have adhered to the principle, and shown it, that the poet and the savant form classes by themselves, above the people, and more refined than the people; I show that they are just as great when of the people, partaking of the common idioms, manners, the earth, the rude visage of animals and trees, and what is vulgar.

This belief prompted him to write poems about Negroes and Indians, carpenters, coach-drivers, sailors, and trappers, and to

sympathize with the felon and the prostitute. The love of the masses explains his unprecedented use of common words ordinarily excluded from polite verse ("I recken," "gallivant," "duds," "folks," "blab," "loaf") that give his poetry its peculiar breeziness and toughness. Although he employed a free and unconventional verse form to convey his pictures of American occupations, landscape, and every-day scenes, he was a far more self-conscious artist than he pretended to be. He could be windy and turgid, and his chest-thumping and shouting (what Whitman called his "ego style") is often tiresome, but at his best he wrote lines like

> The carpenter dresses his plank, the tongue of his fore-plane whistles its wild ascending lisp. . . .
>
>   .   .   .
>
> The jour printer with gray head and gaunt jaws works his case,
> He turns his quid of tobacco, while his eyes blurr with the manuscript.
>
>   .   .   .
>
> Of the turbid pool that lies in the autumn forest,
> Of the moon that descends the steeps of the soughing twilight,
> Toss, sparkles of day and dusk—toss on the black stems that decay in the muck,
> Toss to the moaning gibberish of the dry limbs.
>
>   .   .   .
>
> I depart as air, I shake my white locks at the runaway sun,
> I effuse my flesh in eddies, and drift it in lacy jags.
>
>   .   .   .

In his poems, Whitman wrote of the love of comrades, of man for man, but this was to be only a prelude to a larger human brotherhood. He imagined ranks, races, and civilizations commingling, and it was to be America's mission to promote this final fellowship of peoples. At home he saw much in his generation to displease him. His optimism was severely tested by the Civil War, and his faith in America's manifest destiny was shaken by the events after 1865 (see *Democratic Vistas*, 1871), but he never despaired, and he died believing that in the people there existed "a miraculous wealth of latent power and capacity."

The Nay-Sayers.   The writers who swung around Emerson's orbit and shared his vision of nature and reality did not always agree with his optimistic conclusions. Emerson had many trenchant criticisms to make about American politics, business, and culture, but he never squarely faced the problem of evil in the world. An all-wise Power would see to it that wrongs would be righted, or, as Emerson put it in his "Ode to W. H. Channing,"

> Foolish hands may mix and mar;
> Wise and sure the issues are.
> Round they roll till dark is light.

Some of his neighbors, however, were not so sure. Nathaniel Hawthorne (1804-1864) looked for symbols in nature as Emerson did, but his explanations of nature's spiritual meaning were less hopeful, and rather suggested the pessimistic doctrines of his Puritan forefathers. The son of a Salem shipmaster, Hawthorne attended Bowdoin College with Longfellow and a future president of the United States, Franklin Pierce, but his temperament constrained him from accepting the world as complacently as his friends did. Although not the shadowy recluse he has sometimes been made out to be (for Hawthorne was a robust and masculine man who held government jobs and did not shrink from human contacts), his ideas were hardly congenial to Young America. In his tales and sketches, and in his novels—*The Scarlet Letter* (1851), for example—Hawthorne painted a somber moral landscape where men and women were devoured by secret vices. Those who grasped the reality behind the appearance, as Emerson had advised, were more often chilled than uplifted, and the truth turned out very dark indeed. The terrible facts of life exposed by Haw-

thorne mocked the claims of progress, and his reformers and scientists and secret probers (see *The Blithedale Romance*, "Ethan Brand," and "Rappaccini's Daughter") changed into monstrous villains as they searched for perfection.

Hawthorne's friend, Herman Melville (1819-1891), shared Hawthorne's belief in original sin. Melville was a New Yorker. After his father's bankruptcy, he suffered the humiliations of genteel poverty, clerked in a store, and taught school before sailing a whaling ship to the South Seas in 1841. Three years of adventuring in the Pacific provided the materials for two best-selling books, *Typee* (1846) and *Omoo* (1847). His reputation declined, however, as he stopped writing light-hearted sketches of Polynesian life and turned to his private conflicts. In rejecting transcendental optimism, Melville reacted even more strongly than Hawthorne against Emerson's blandness, his easy way of dismissing human misery. Evil, for Melville, resided not merely in the tainted heart, that "foul cavern," as Hawthorne called it; it was a mighty force that hung over the world like a black curtain. In *Moby Dick* (1851), his finest novel and one of America's greatest literary masterpieces, Melville struck through the "paste-board mask" of life. In it, he described the pursuit of a Yankee whaling captain, Ahab, a godlike but ungodly man, after a gigantic white whale that symbolized the beauty, the wickedness, and the mystery of nature. If man were half-divine, as the transcendentalists insisted, he nonetheless faced a tragic destiny. He was incapable of solving the ambiguities of the world. God remained unknowable, progress was an illusion, and the seeker was likely to be fooled by what he saw and what he thought.

Melville's generation could not understand him, nor was it ready to accept his gloomy insights into human destiny. The American credo was a hopeful one. The reading public could not identify itself with Hawthorne's or Melville's heroes, but less hopeful generations found more point in the stricken Ahab and Melville's dark wisdom.

"Kindred Spirits," by Asher B. Durand. The figure on the left is the poet, William Cullen Bryant. His companion is the landscape painter, Thomas Cole, celebrated for his romantic scenes of the Hudson River Valley.

Problems of the Artist.

The division in American society between those who were preoccupied with "stern realities" and those who tried to keep the arts uncontaminated by "dirty facts" was felt by the would-be painter and sculptor as well as the author. The fine arts seemed particularly aristocratic to many sturdy democrats. *The North American Review* in 1825 described them as the products "of corrupt and despotic courts, the flatterers of tyranny, the panders of vice." The sculptor, Horatio Greenough, was not being facetious when he wrote to his friend and patron, James Fenimore Cooper, that "a man may be an artist without being ergo

a blackguard and a mischievous member of society."

It is not surprising that many American artists during this period began their careers as artisans and mechanics. The celebrated sculptor, Hiram Powers, to name but one, started his career in Cincinnati, where he worked in an organ factory, invented a turning lathe, fashioned wax statues, and served as a skilled mechanic before beginning his artistic career. His mechanical ingenuity as well as his ability to model "busts remarkable for their perfect resemblance" accounted for his early reputation. But Powers' most popular work, the "Greek Slave"—the statue that won him international fame—

"Fur Traders Descending the Missouri," by George Caleb Bingham. Sketched from life, the trader in the stern of the dugout, the boy in the center, and the chained fox make a haunting image of a rapidly disappearing occupation.

reveals little influence from his practical apprenticeship. His career swung from the real and the practical to the spiritual, from science and utility to the ideal.

The conception of the fine arts as a branch of mechanics had won favor because it seemed useful and moral. By the late 1820's, however, critics began to insist that the arts had a higher and more uplifting function. Painting, it was said, "like eloquence, poetry, and the other fine arts," exhibited the "higher" and "better" principles of human nature, and tended "to raise the mind above the sordid interest of a merely material life."

A few individualists tried to break down this unhappy distinction between the beautiful and the useful. Emerson argued that an object was beautiful if it had nothing superfluous about it and if it served the use for which it was made. Whitman celebrated the splendor of locomotives, Thoreau defended the functional house, and Horatio Greenough wrote at length about the beauty of sailing ships, well-designed bridges, and machinery:

The men who have reduced locomotion to its simplest elements, in the trotting wagon and the yacht America, are nearer to Athens at this moment than they who would bend the Greek temple to every use. I contend for Greek principles, not Greek things. If a flat sail goes nearest the wind, a bellying sail, though picturesque, must be given up. The slender harness, and tall gaunt wheels, are not only effective, they are beautiful for they respect the beauty of a horse, and do not uselessly tax him.

But views like Greenough's were not common. Most Americans could not agree with Emerson that "Beauty must come back

250

to the useful arts." The successful painter had to satisfy the popular taste for reality—but it had to be reality seasoned with the ideal. Landscape painting, which came into vogue in the 1830's, gave him an opportunity to portray American scenery with a romantic glow. The painter Thomas Cole, friend of Bryant and Cooper, became famous for his poetic renditions of the Hudson River area and the Catskill Mountains. Asher Durand and Thomas Doughty, contemporaries of Cole, also painted America's scenic wonders. By 1860, a distinct school of landscape painters had emerged, and the western country and the Indian had been documented by

tions, and the western rivers—glimpses of urban and rural life. As Whitman was beginning to itemize the occupation and activities of America, lithographers like the famous team of Currier and Ives flooded the country with gay reproductions of forest and farm, railroads, sleigh rides, and boats. Curious citizens trooped to exhibitions of huge paintings, unwound from rollers, that depicted with painstaking accuracy the Mississippi landscape or historical scenes like the landing of Lafayette. John James Audubon, by fusing science and art, pro-

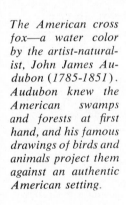

The American cross fox—a water color by the artist-naturalist, John James Audubon (1785-1851). Audubon knew the American swamps and forests at first hand, and his famous drawings of birds and animals project them against an authentic American setting.

artists like George Catlin and Alfred Jacob Miller, who accompanied expeditions into the trans-Mississippi West.

In Jacksonian America and later, painters discovered that a public that preferred museums and circuses to high-flown art could still enjoy the depiction of homely American scenes. *Genre* painting (painted anecdotes) found a more responsive audience than portraits or historical canvases. Artists like William S. Mount, David G. Blythe, and George C. Bingham were the painter-equivalents of the humorists and writers of tall tales. Their paintings recreate for us the atmosphere of minstrel shows, rowdy elec-

duced meticulous studies of bird and animal life.

Yet the ordinary citizen clearly got more enjoyment from "a carnival of wild beasts" than from an exhibit of paintings. The one seemed to him genuine, the other pointless and dull. A few people were really interested in artistic and intellectual matters, and others supported the arts out of a vague sense of duty. But the majority had no interest in "culture." A few art societies made promising starts in the bigger cities, but they soon languished. Since only six art schools had been founded before 1860, American artists either got their training as apprentices or went to the Continent to study. Once trained, they found it hard to reach the apathetic public, and many resented having to depend on the merchant prince who "waxes rich with rise of real estate" but who knew nothing about art.

III.   THE LIVELY ARTS

If moralists had serious reservations about literature and the fine arts, they felt even more strongly about the theater. The most damning criticism of the theater was that it unfitted "mankind . . . for the common concerns of life." Lay-preachers assailed the "vagabond profession" and the indecency of the stage, the "grossness of the characters, and the displays of half-clad females." They pointed with horror to the low comedians who pandered "to the tastes of the basest and most abandoned of our population" with their "vulgar puns and undisguised profanity and obscenity."

Despite these objections, theatrical entertainment became popular during the middle period, and audiences applauded anything from Shakespeare to the broadest farce. Although New York remained the theatrical center, cities in every section supported theaters. Famous stars like Edwin Forrest, James K. Hackett, and Fanny Kemble had national reputations. At a time when the leading statesmen performed in a highly theatrical manner in the public arena, serious drama never made much headway and did not become a dominant cultural force. Instead, burlesque and popular opera ruled the stage. These were extravaganzas punctuated by singing and dancing, and filled with satirical references to the contemporary scene.

Although some theater-goers enjoyed tragedies, especially the more luridly melodramatic plays that gave the shouting, posturing tragedian a chance to display his voice and figure, lighter entertainment was more popular. Minstrel shows like E. P. Christy's, and toe-dancers like the ravishing Fanny Elssler, performed before huge audiences. The nation wanted its entertainment broad, comic, and unintellectual.

To an emotional people fond of sentiment and eloquence, music (especially singing) had a wide appeal. Foreigners might comment on the "barbarity" of American music, but between 1820 and 1860 instrumental and choral performances decidedly improved. Visiting artists from abroad successfully toured the country, and local musical societies in New York, Boston, and elsewhere offered orchestral and choral programs to appreciative if uncritical audiences. The ingratiating ballads of Stephen Foster (1826-1864), one of the first of a long line of northerners to romanticize the "sunny South," were sung all across the land, and opera, introduced about 1825, had some success in a few of the larger cities. A hymn writer like Boston's Lowell Mason (1792-1872), composer of "Nearer My God to Thee" and "From Greenland's Icy Mountains," evoked a more genuine response and grew rich from the sales of his edifying songs. Mason also furthered musical instruction by conducting summer classes for out-of-state teachers.

"The influence and circulation of newspapers," wrote an astonished visitor to the United States about 1830, "is great beyond anything known in Europe. In truth, nine-tenths of the population read nothing else. Every village, nay, almost every hamlet, has its press. Newspapers penetrate to every crevice of the nation." Between 1801 and 1833, the number of newspapers in the country rose from 200 to 1,200, of which only about 65 were dailies; the rest appeared at longer intervals, most of them weekly. During the next decade, the remarkable expansion continued.

Newspapers provided another escape from monotony by featuring, as one paper put it, "robberies, thefts, murders, awful catastrophes, and wonderful escapes." This was an era of rough-and-tumble journalism, when even well-established papers found it difficult to survive. Competition in the larger cities was ferocious. In 1830, New York City's 47 papers had a combined circulation of only 90,000, and only one daily could claim 4,000 subscribers. Enterprising editors reduced the price of their papers to a penny, printed scandalous reports, invented news, and perpetrated hoaxes in order to increase circulation.

Benjamin Day's New York *Sun* pioneered in the new sensationalism, but Day's rival, James Gordon Bennett of the *Herald*, soon surpassed him when he featured the case of a murdered New York prostitute. Bennett also played up the news value of New York society (he headlined his own marriage), and developed circulation techniques that were eagerly picked up by the penny press throughout the country. The expanding circulation created by lurid reporting was made mechanically possible by the invention of new printing presses and improved delivery methods. Advertising men kept up with the spirit of the times by substituting eye-catching copy and pictures for the old, staid announcements. The press, as one reader pointed out, served as a kind of gutter that carried away "all the wanton vagaries of the imagination, all the inventions of malice, all the scandal, and all the corruptions of heart in village, town, or city."

Yet the newspapers did more than merely pander to low tastes. Tocqueville saw them as an important instrument for cooperative action, as painless and indispensable informers of the public: "A newspaper is an adviser who does not require to be sought, but who comes of his own accord, and talks to you briefly every day of the Common weal, without distracting you from your private affairs." The American press, with all its failings, purveyed the information most calculated to interest and instruct a hard-working, politically-minded people. Each paper, in addition to reporting matters of general interest, usually appealed directly to the prejudices and needs of particular

groups. The mercantile interests, religious denominations, and political parties sponsored their own papers, and each editor rode his own private hobby-horse. Papers like the New York *Tribune*, the Cincinnati *Gazette*, the Brooklyn *Eagle*, the Cleveland *Plain Dealer*, the Baltimore *Sun*, and the Philadelphia *Ledger* maintained a fairly high quality. The good editor explained and interpreted pertinent issues, and sometimes made demands upon his readers that few modern editors would attempt. Often he supplemented commercial and political information with useful knowledge and succeeded in raising the level of popular culture.

Magazines sprang up by the dozens in the middle decades, but few of them survived. With no generally accepted literary standards to rely upon, always in danger of offending the prudish, and yet aware of the "vulgar" preferences of their public, the harassed magazine editors had no way to turn. Delinquent subscribers were probably most responsible for the high mortality of periodicals, but the penny press and cheap imprints of pirated English books also reduced their audience. Almost every hamlet bravely launched a literary monthly or quarterly review, but only a few managed to carry on. The *North American Review* (Boston), *The Knickerbocker Magazine* (New York), *Graham's Magazine* (Philadelphia), and *The Southern Literary Messenger* (Richmond), however, did manage to achieve a national circulation. They printed pieces by Cooper, Poe, Bryant, Hawthorne, and Longfellow, as well as by lesser figures, but they provided only a skimpy outlet for American talent.

The "female" audience had its choice of *The Ladies Magazine*, edited by Sarah Josepha Hale, and *Godey's Lady's Book*, with which the former merged in 1836. The latter did more than dictate fashions and rule over morals and manners. Miss Hale, literary editor of the magazine for many years, is best known as the author of "Mary's Lamb," but she published and reviewed intelligently the productions of leading American writers, paid for poems and articles (a significant innovation), and between 1837 and 1849 increased the magazine's circulation from 10,000 to 40,000. The success of *Godey's* and its imitators indicated that American women—the principal consumers of books and magazines—would soon dominate the cultural life of the nation. Their interest was indispensable (for the men were too pre-occupied with mundane affairs to have time for books), but it meant that they were able to impose a kind of petticoat tyranny over American letters and narrowly define the limits of literary propriety.

IV.   EDUCATION: FORMAL AND INFORMAL

Schools.   The religious spirit that had such a powerful effect on literature and the arts in America was felt even more strongly in education. One of the goals of organized religion had always been to create a Christian citizenry. Intellect without virtue, as the saying went, "makes a splendid villain"; what American leaders wanted was a "baptized intelligence." In many respects, education was a secular kind of religious training. Most Americans favored Bible-teaching in the schools because, as the famous Presbyterian minister, Lyman Beecher, expressed it, the Bible gave no sanction "to civil broils, or resistance to lawful authority, but commands all men to follow peace, and to obey magistrates that are set over them, whatever the form of government may be." The Bible would show European immigrants, "extensively infected with Infidelity and Rationalism," that a "land of liberty is not a place to indulge in irreligion and license."

But despite the lip-service paid to Christian, democratic, and practical education, crusaders for public schools faced an apathetic and often hostile public. Men who could afford to educate their own children in private academies saw no reason why they should be taxed to educate the children of the poor. Private and parochial schools, farmers, and non-English-speaking groups joined the conservatives in fighting the free-school movement. It was attacked as a threat to individual liberty, as a radical innovation, as impractical nonsense. Defenders of free public schools replied that the extension of education would reduce poverty and crime, increase productivity, rectify social injustice, and preserve democratic institutions. Every class would benefit, according to one free-school advocate in 1832:

The man who is poor must see that this is the only way he can secure education for his children: The man in moderate circumstances ... will have his children taught for a less sum than he pays at present: The rich man, who will be heavily taxed, must see that his course secures to the rising generation the only means of perpetuating our institutions, and the only guarantee that his children will be protected.

After a campaign in which every conceivable argument was introduced—economic, political, and humanitarian—the leaders of the free-school movement ultimately won their battle. By 1860, most states in the North had installed a tax-supported school program. Credit for this victory must go in large measure to devoted men like Horace Mann of Massachusetts, Henry Barnard of Connecticut, DeWitt Clinton of New York, Calvin Stowe of Ohio, and other pioneer reformers whose investigations and reports did much to educate public opinion. But without support from the urban workingman, the free-school movement would have been seriously weakened; for it was the city worker, deprived of both the leisure and the means to improve himself, who saw in tax-supported schools a way of bettering his chances in the competitive struggle and improving his social status.

The triumph of the free-school advocates destroyed one more vestige of caste in a democratic state, but it did not work the miracles they promised. Education on all levels, in fact, suffered from crippling defects. Low salaries, poor physical equipment, inadequate teacher-training, primitive pedagogy, unmanageably large classes, and a short school term kept standards low.

Throughout the period, educational reformers suggested a variety of schemes to raise the educational level. Battles raged between the classicists and the anti-classicists, the utilitarians and the liberals, and the doctrines of the Swiss educational reformer, Johann Heinrich Pestalozzi, were violently defended and attacked. Pestalozzi's ideas struck at the old-fashioned system of passive learning that ruled in American schools. He declared that all education should proceed from the known to the unknown and the abstract. There was more point, his disciples argued, in teaching a child something about local geography than in making him memorize the rivers of Mesopotamia. Education must be simultaneously mental, moral, and physical. Although Pestalozzi's ideas were influential, conservatives continued to resist efforts to change the system of rote memory drills and corporal punishment. Attempts by American schoolmasters to make education more interesting met with stiff opposition. Thus Samuel Griswold Goodrich's "Peter Parley" geography texts (first published in 1827), which painlessly presented the facts through the eyes of a boy, were regarded as rubbish by the die-hards.

In defense of the critics, it must be acknowledged that many quacks flourished in the profession, and "painless" methods for acquiring a quick education were much in vogue. One disgusted critic in 1829 complained that American youth learns

... Latin and Greek by translations; they study French and Spanish, merely to say that they have studied them; they read history in abridgement, and biography in novels; they learn arithmetic by means of slips of paper, or little stories and counting their fingers; they carry to school large volumes of mineralogy, botany, or conchology; they learn composition by copying other's thoughts and language.

These arguments continued throughout the century and into our own, but in the meantime, the quality of teaching did improve.

The principle of teacher-training had been accepted, largely as a result of the efforts of Horace Mann, who agitated for the so-called "normal schools" for the preparation of teachers, and Henry Barnard, one of the founders of the American Association for the Advancement of Education (1855) and editor of the influential *American Journal of Education*. Teachers' societies sprang up throughout the country, and educational periodicals disseminated the new pedagogical theories.

Restrictions against female education were broken down. Private academies and, later, public schools provided elementary and secondary education to girls by the 1840's, and in 1833 Oberlin College admitted women, the first of the coeducational colleges. Antioch followed suit in 1853, but no state university relaxed its regulations until 1858, when the University of Iowa opened its doors to women.

Classroom of the most prominent girls' school in Boston just before the Civil War.

For the most part, girls' seminaries concentrated on the ornamental accomplishments. The learned woman, or "blue-stocking," was considered a monstrosity:

> If a young lady [declared a writer in 1833] speaks of anything with which the idea of study or research is associated, she is thenceforth looked upon, if not a pretender, at least as an unsexed woman.... We have a feeling... that a learned woman does not fill her true place in the world.... It is thought more creditable for a young woman to possess accomplishments than wisdom—to be sentimental than learned—to *appear* than to *be*.

Yet schools like Mt. Holyoke and Miss Emma Willard's Troy Female Seminary and Catharine Beecher's Hartford Female Seminary did attempt to provide a more substantial intellectual diet for their students.

There were few public high schools until 1840, but during the next two decades the number increased substantially, with Massachusetts, New York, and Ohio taking the lead. High schools offered a more practical kind of education than private schools, and they were available to the poor children of both sexes.

Colleges.   The number of so-called "colleges" increased from 16 in 1799 to 182 on the eve of the Civil War. During those years 412 others had been established but failed to survive. Colleges, said a prominent educator in 1848,

> ...rise up like mushrooms on our luxuriant soil. They are duly lauded and puffed for a day; and then they sink to be heard of no more.... Our people, at first, oppose all distinctions whatever as odious and aristocratical; and then, presently, seek with avidity such as remain accessible. At first they denounce colleges; and then choose to have a college in every district or county, or for every sect and party—and to boast of a college education, and to sport with high sounding literary titles—as if these imparted sense or wisdom or knowledge.

The multiplication of colleges resulted in part from the difficulties and expenses of travel, but sectarian rivalry and local pride were probably the principal causes. Religious control of institutions of higher learning was even more marked than on the elementary-school level, where the influence was only indirect. Each important denomination and many minor ones supported one or more colleges that helped to rekindle the spirit of piety but were of a low grade intellectually. Most of these newly organized colleges were hardly more than dressed-up academies. Students in all but the well-established institutions might enter at 13 or 14, and student discipline was a major problem. The "universities" might better have been described simply as larger colleges. Sometimes they included a theological or law department, but most of the professional schools (law and medicine in particular) were separate institutions.

The curriculum was standard throughout the country. Latin, Greek, mathematics, science, political economy, and moral philosophy offered a solid enough base, but unimaginative methods were used to teach these subjects. The study of the same subjects in colonial colleges had produced gifted leaders. In the mid-nineteenth century learning took the form of tiresome recitations out of textbooks. College teachers got little pay (from $600 to $1200 between 1840 and 1860), and salaries were fixed. Moreover, long teaching hours and poor libraries did not encourage scholarship. In 1839, Harvard's library of 50,000 volumes was the largest in the country; Yale's, with 27,000 volumes, was a poor second. Only 16 other college libraries contained more than 10,000 books.

Before the Civil War, a few notable professors found time to write and experiment, but in general the college atmosphere did not stimulate good work. With sectarianism rampant and political issues explosive, no American college could live up to Jefferson's dream of a higher institution based "on the illimitable freedom of the human mind." Non-denominational colleges in particular were assailed as seats of atheism and aristocracy. Clearly, the "rise of the common man" by no means assured a more liberal education; indeed, it often resulted in intolerance and anti-intellectualism.

The Lyceum.

Verbal support for education did not solve the problem of the urban worker or villager who hungered for the culture he had no time to acquire. Philosophers of democracy like Franklin and Jefferson had insisted that only an educated electorate could sustain a republican government. But how apprentices were to educate themselves after sitting or standing from five in the morning to seven at night was not made clear. One institution that

the Useful Knowledge Society. His *Political Observations Upon the Education of the People* (1825), which went through more than 30 editions within five years after publication, gave a powerful impulse to the cause of popular education. Brougham's plan called for a system of public lectures on the arts and sciences, the formation of societies to discuss non-controversial subjects, the establishment of libraries for workingmen, and the publication of cheap books. His admirers in America put his recommendations into practice, and soon associations for the diffusion of useful in-

Lecturer and his Lyceum audience (about 1838).

seemed particularly designed to meet this problem was the mutual-improvement society that became popular in America during the 1830's and 1840's.

Just as men worked together to organize charity programs and financial undertakings, it was believed that they could educate themselves by organizing cooperative experiments in learning. Mutual-benefit societies, as they were called, seemed admirably suited to the needs of a busy people who had little inclination or opportunity for sustained study, but who were intellectually curious.

This national inclination for mutual improvement was strengthened by the influence of an Englishman, Lord Henry Brougham, leader of the English Whigs and founder of

formation ("lyceums," as they were called) were springing up all over the nation.

A New Englander, Josiah Holbrook, shares with Brougham the honor of inspiring the lyceum movement which got underway soon after Holbrook's recommendations for adult education had been published in 1826. By 1831, a national American Lyceum organization was coordinating the activities of the member groups and publishing its own magazines. Four years later, lyceums could be found in 15 states, and by 1839 the 137 lyceums of Massachusetts alone were drawing some 33,000 citizens. The lyceums sponsored lectures on every conceivable subject —lectures, it was hoped, that might encourage the amateur scientist, scotch dangerous opinions, or merely amuse or edify. Scientific and practical subjects aroused the greatest interest, but figures like Emerson addressed lyceum audiences on such themes as "Wealth" and "Power," and other eminent men discoursed on the live issues of the day.

The roughly 3,000 lyceums established between 1820 and 1860 were centered in New England, New York, and the upper Mississippi Valley, sections where public-school sentiment was strong. In Pennsylvania, where considerable hostility to public schools pre-

vailed, and in the South, where towns were scattered and intellectual interests less encouraged, the lyceum made less impression.

These associations often "confounded a knowledge of useful things with useful knowledge," and provided an education that was both highly superficial and sometimes remote from the very classes for which it was theoretically designed. Yet lyceums helped to bridge the gulf between the learned minority and the community, stimulated and directed new energies, and upheld the ideal of popular culture in a predominantly commercial society.

V. THE REFORMERS

The Reform Spirit.   The spirit of reform, of which the free-school and lyceum movements were only two reflections, pervaded America during the middle period. It derived in part from the general optimism of the times, from faith in the power of cooperation to solve all problems, and also from the desire to hurry on an inevitable but sometimes slow-moving progress. Most reformers were religious people, motivated by an evangelical zeal to promote their particular projects. Some were freakish and wild, insisting that society's salvation lay in the universal acceptance of reform in habits of dress, or in a vegetable diet, or in the abandonment of money. Some believed that the "social destiny of man" lay in new forms of communal society. But reform had its less visionary side as well. During the 1830's and 1840's, a number of men and women devoted their lives to stamping out specific social evils or to supporting particular causes: temperance, the treatment of the insane and the criminal, the education of the deaf, dumb, and blind, and world peace.

Until abolitionism aroused the country after 1830, the movement for "temperance" was the most intense reform activity of all. The excessive mobility of the American population, the break-up of families, the disruption of community life, combined with the loneliness, fatigue, and boredom that accom-

panied the man on the farm or newly arrived in the city—all probably led to an increased consumption of liquor. In 1820, the census-takers declined to list distilling as a separate industry, since it was engaged in by almost everyone in the rural areas. In the cities, saloons were numbered in the thousands.

The temperance movement illustrates what the famous Unitarian minister, William Ellery Channing, meant when he wrote in 1829: "Those who have one great object, find one another out through a vast extent of country, join their forces, settle their mode of operation, and act together with the conformity of a disciplined army." By this time, more than a thousand small temperance societies had arisen separately to combat the national vice of overindulgence. The agitation against drinking had been given a strong impetus by the publication of Dr. Benjamin Rush's *Inquiry into the Effect of Ardent Spirit upon the Human Mind and Body,* written during the American Revolution and very influential in the early nineteenth century. But whereas Rush attacked drinking as bad for the health, the emphasis of the clerical reformers in the next century was moral; to them, drinking was sinful. Temperance became the chief motive for forming library societies, and Bible and Tract societies. In 1826, the activities of these local institutions were coordinated in the

American Temperance Union. By 1830 more than 2,000 "teetotalling" societies had been formed, most of them in the North, and in 1833, these organizations federated to form the United States Temperance Union. A country-wide battle was waged against the "fatal appetite" through evangelical meetings, tracts, pamphlets, and temperance songs. One surviving example of the anti-drinking propaganda of the day is Timothy Shay Arthur's *Ten Nights in a Bar-Room.*

Quarrels between the total-abstinence extremists and the moderate wing weakened the temperance cause, but the movement retained enough strength to force through some kind of prohibition laws in 13 northern states by 1851. Maine led the way in 1846, when, under the influence of the dedicated prohibitionist, Neal Dow, the legislature passed a measure making the sale of liquor illegal. Prohibition made little headway in the South and was not rigorously enforced even in those states that passed laws affecting the sales of stimulants, but liquor was no longer consumed in such heroic proportions. The temperance movement trained a number of men and women in the techniques of reform, an experience that helped them distinguish themselves later in other movements.

Less spectacular but more lasting reforms were achieved by a Massachusetts school teacher, Dorothea Lynde Dix (1802-1887), who led a crusade for more humane and effective treatment of the insane and the feeble-minded. In her *Memorial to the Legislature of Massachusetts* (1834), the result of painstaking investigation, she depicted conditions in asylums throughout the state that were medieval in their barbarity. To the popular mind, insanity was a hideous moral regression into animality, and its victims were whipped and caged and neglected as if they were indeed dangerous beasts. Dorothea Dix discovered maniacs with iron collars around their necks, starved, filthy, and unclothed. During the next 15 years, her influence extended into every section of the country. Eleven states established hospitals for the insane partly as a result of the spotlight she threw on conditions, and before she

died in 1887 she had played an important part in the founding of 21 others.

The Communitarians.

Reform, complete and uncompromising, was the goal of the Utopian visionaries who proposed nothing less than the complete reorganization of society. Filled with the importance of their mission, they lectured to skeptical audiences and conducted short-lived community experiments until their bored, disillusioned, or offended disciples deserted them.

It is now fashionable to debunk the early nineteenth-century communitarians as escapists and nitwits, even as the precursors of twentieth-century totalitarianism. But in pointing out the obvious weakness of the utopian mentality, the method and intent of the Utopians have been misinterpreted. Early American communities, both religious and secular, were efforts to improve society, not escape it. Neither individualistic nor revolutionary, the communitarian wanted immediate reform without violence. Having no faith in independent efforts to meet the problems created by the newly industrialized America, he took what was for him the highly practical step of working through a collective enterprise. Unlike the doctrinaire socialist, the communitarian believed in social harmony rather than in class warfare, voluntary action in place of compulsion. He was experimental and pragmatic in his thinking. In his basic desires, he differed little from his countrymen, as Emerson noted, and his communitarianism was far more congenial to the Americans of the mid-nineteenth century than was scientific European socialism, with its aura of class struggle and irreligion.

The two most controversial socialist experiments during this period were inspired by Robert Owen, a successful manufacturer and industrial reformer from New Lanark, Scotland, and a French socialist, Charles Fourier.

Robert Owen came to America to found a community at New Harmony, Indiana, on a site that he had purchased from a German colony known as the Rappites. Owen believed that man was the product of his environment, and that for a society to be happy and moral, its members must enjoy material equality. A number of gifted European scholars came to Owen's Utopia, and for a time the community offered the best educational instruction in the country, but the rank and file had more than their share of human frailties. According to Timothy Flint, a missionary and novelist, New Harmony attracted

... the indolent, the unprincipled, men of desperate fortunes, moon-worshippers, romantic young men ... those who had dreamed about earthly Elysiums, a great many honest aspirants after a better order of things, poor men simply desiring an education for their children.

A good many people wondered even in 1825 whether Owen's ideas could "keep alive that spirit of liberty and self-respect for one's own opinion, that so peculiarly belongs to the American people." And Owen's experiment did indeed fail after two years, but a large share of the failure of New Harmony can be attributed to the carelessness and imprecision of its founder. Though personally amiable and well-liked (he was one of the few socialists ever to address both Houses of Congress), he had the unhappy faculty of introducing irrelevant issues and needlessly antagonizing American prejudices. Owen's anti-religious views provoked more abhorrence than his fluctuating economic opinions, which Owen always regarded as secondary to his main purpose: the establishment of a rational system of society. Apparently the collapse of his experiment had no effect on the persisting influence of his ethical, educational, and psychological theories. Later socialist communities, disavowing Owen's pet notions about religion and marriage, continued the communitarian idea. In the 30's, a resurgence of communitarian enterprise occurred which was in some ways even more of a dramatic protest against the increasing impersonality of American society.

Owenism had suggested radical working-man's parties, free-thought, and free-love to middle-class Americans. The doctrines of Fourier seemed less dangerous, and during the 1840's were espoused by a talented and respectable nucleus: Albert Brisbane, Fourier's chief propagandist; Parke Godwin, reformer and critic; Margaret Fuller, feminist, famed conversationalist, critic, and one-time editor of *The Dial,* the organ of the transcendentalists; George Ripley, founder of Brook Farm; and many others. Most of them eventually gave up their early radicalism, but for a number of years they broadcast Fourier's theories and made his name familiar throughout the country.

The Fourierists (or "Fury-ites"—as their enemies called them) assumed, as Owen had, that men were naturally good and that society would develop harmoniously under a system of "attractive industry," or "joyous labor." They regarded private capitalism as wasteful and degrading. If men would only abandon the old competitive way and gather in *phalanxes,* or associated groups, they could transform the world into a paradise. What particularly appealed to the Fourierists, many of whom were New England transcendentalists, was the emphasis that Fourier put on the dignity of man, his faith in progress, and what might be called his practical idealism. They rebelled against the coldness and impersonality of the new industrialism and against what they felt was the ferocity of cutthroat competition. To Parke Godwin, for example, competition inevitably ended in monopoly, commercial crises, and the impoverishment of the middle and lower classes. In order to offset this danger, the Fourierists organized over 40 *phalanxes* between 1840 and 1850.

None was successful, but one at least inspired a fascinating novel (Hawthorne's *The Blithedale Romance*) and added some color to the turbulent 40's. This was Brook Farm, organized by a group of transcendentalist intellectuals in 1841. More interested in the Over-Soul than in their bank accounts, they decided to demonstrate the possibility of combining the life of the mind with manual labor. ("After breakfast," Hawthorne noted in his diary, "Mr. Ripley put a four-pronged instrument into my hands, which he gave me to understand was called a pitch-fork; and he and Mr. Farley being armed with similar weapons, we all commenced a gallant attack upon a heap of manure.") The community, which never numbered more than 100, attracted some talented artists and engaging cranks, and about 4,000 annual visitors who came to observe and argue. Before Brook Farm was converted to Fourierism in 1843-1844 and became seriously socialistic, it had all the innocence and charm (as well as the fatal weaknesses) of an intellectual's paradise. Unfortunately, the attempt of its leaders to build a *phalanx* and to practice orthodox "associationism" proved impractical. A disastrous fire ruined the already insolvent community and it closed down in 1847.

Secular communities like Brook Farm failed because the volunteers had neither the knowledge nor the temperament to sustain them. But the communal settlements of the German sectarians—who brought with them a tradition of village cooperation, and who were skillful farmers held together by strong religious ties—showed time and again that the communitarian idea could be made to work. Yet Americans as a rule were too individualistic to sink their private ambitions in such projects.

Abolition.   From the 1830's on, one reform issue grew larger and more portentous until it overshadowed all the others: the anti-slavery cause, or abolition. It had its origin in the late seventeenth century, when humanitarian Puritans like Samuel Sewall and Roger Williams spoke against the ownership of human chattels. The Quakers had long fought the buying and selling of slaves, and in the Revolutionary and post-Revolutionary eras, liberals in every section had deplored slavery as a mortal disease. It was this conviction that inspired the American Colonization Society, founded in 1817 with private, state, and federal support, to establish Liberia in 1822 as a colony for ex-slaves. Unfortunately for the proponents of colonization,

hardly more than a thousand free Negroes were transported to Africa between 1822 and 1830, and the others showed little desire to emigrate. The failure of the colonization plan and the apparent ineffectiveness of those who believed in gradual emancipation encouraged the radical abolitionists to begin a relentless campaign for immediate emancipation.

In 1831, William Lloyd Garrison published his first issue of the *Liberator,* an incendiary periodical of extreme abolitionism; it marked the beginning of the great anti-slavery offensive that culminated 30 years later in the Civil War. Garrison was a Massachusetts journalist, neurotic and wayward yet gentle and humorous, tolerant on occasion yet fanatically uncompromising about his cherished beliefs. Abolition was only one of Garrison's causes. He was an ardent worker for women's rights and international peace, a fervent opponent of capital punishment and imprisonment for debt, but by the 1830's slavery had absorbed his attention. He denounced slavery not because it was inefficient or undemocratic or unjust, but because it was sinful. The Constitution, which guaranteed slavery, he described as "a covenant with death and an agreement with hell," and he publicly burned it.

Garrison's vituperative attacks against the "Southern oppressors" did much to intensify anti-abolition sentiment in the South, but his fanaticism frightened the moderate anti-slavery people, and his refusal to resort to political action minimized his effectiveness. A wiser and more useful agitator was Theodore Dwight Weld of Ohio, who organized and directed the activities of the abolitionist societies in the Northwest. He preferred patient organization to flamboyant pronouncements, and his devoted followers (well versed in the techniques of revival meetings) converted thousands to the abolitionist cause. Before 1850, almost 2,000 societies with a membership that numbered close to 200,000 had been formed, and the talent and conscience of the North had rallied to the anti-slavery standard. John Greenleaf Whittier of Massachusetts became the bard of abolition, but Emerson, Thoreau, Whitman, Longfellow, and Melville also condemned slavery; Boston's eloquent Wendell Phillips thundered against it, and so did famous ministers like Theodore Parker and William Ellery Channing. Distinguished southerners like James G. Birney and the Grimké sisters renounced their slave property and joined the anti-slavery cause.

Public opinion stigmatized the abolitionists as a band of misguided bigots whose activities would destroy the Union if they were left unchecked. Throughout the middle 30's, they were heckled, stoned, tarred and feathered, and lynched. New York, Boston, Philadelphia, Charleston, Richmond, Cincinnati —towns and cities in every section—were swept by riots and mobbings, in defiance, or with the connivance, of the local authorities. Garrison was dragged through the streets of Boston by an angry mob; George Thompson, an English abolitionist, was howled down and threatened; Elijah Lovejoy, an anti-slavery editor in Alton, Illinois, was murdered by a mob in 1837. But the abolitionists would not be discouraged.

Despite the stern repression of the abolitionists in the North, and the constant assurances given to southern leaders that the majority of people in the free states detested the subversive ideas of the *Liberator,* the South grew more and more uneasy. It cried out for penal laws to keep the anti-slavery terrorists under control and threatened sharp economic reprisals if they were not silenced. Southern postmasters confiscated suspected abolitionist literature—lest the slaves be infected with dangerous thoughts and revolt. Southern fears of a slave insurrection and southern resentment against the atrocity stories featured in the abolitionist propaganda made the South magnify the strength of the anti-slavery movement in the North. Its intemperate response, in turn, increased the very anti-slavery sentiment in the North that it sought to allay.

As the sectional conflict deepened, the dream of the millennium that had stirred the hearts of the reformers in the 30's and 40's faded away. The black cloud of slavery that had seemed no larger than a man's hand in 1820 now darkened the land.

Readings

Alexis de Tocqueville's classic, *Democracy in America* (1835) (now available in a number of cheap editions), is a profound analysis of the period covered in this chapter, as well as of American society in general. Among the more useful and readable social histories of the period between 1820 and 1860 are A. F. Tyler, *Freedom's Ferment: Phases of American Social History to 1860* (1944), an account of reform and reformers; R. E. Riegel, *Young America, 1830-1840* (1949), a racy and factual summary of reform movements; Meade Minnigerode, *The Fabulous Forties, 1840-1850* (1924); and E. D. Branch, *The Sentimental Years, 1836-1860* (1934). Relevant chapters in Parrington's *The Romantic Revolution in America, 1800-1860* (see general bibliography), should be consulted as well.

In addition to the works on American literature listed in the general bibliography, the reader should refer to R. L. Rusk, *The Life of Ralph Waldo Emerson* (1949); J. W. Krutch, *Henry David Thoreau* (1948); A. H. Quinn, *Edgar Allan Poe* (1941); Mark Van Doren, *Nathaniel Hawthorne* (1949); Newton Arvin, *Herman Melville* (1950); and Gay W. Allen, *The Solitary Singer: A Critical Biography of Walt Whitman* (1955). F. O. Matthiessen, *American Renaissance* (1941), is a brilliant interpretation of America's literary flowering, and Lewis Mumford, *The Golden Day* (1926), is also revealing. Recent and provocative is R. W. B. Lewis, *The American Adam* (1955), which treats the theme of innocence in American literature.

O. W. Larkin's *Art and Life in America* (1949) covers the history of painting, sculpture, and architecture thoroughly and entertainingly. It should be supplemented by E. P.

Richardson, *Washington Allston* (1948), an interesting discussion of the painter and his times, and A. T. Gardner, *Yankee Stonecutters: The First American School of Sculpture, 1800-1850* (1945).

The history of journalism during this period is well summarized by F. L. Mott, *American Journalism: A History of Newspapers in the United States* (rev. ed., 1950), and A. M. Lee, *The Daily Newspaper in America* (1937). American magazines are discussed in F. L. Mott, *A History of American Magazines, 1741-1850* (3 vols., 1930-1938).

The literature on education is more extensive than exhilarating. Relevant for this chapter are S. L. Jackson, *America's Struggle for Free Schools: Social Tension and Education in New England and New York, 1827-42* (1941), and Paul Monroe, *Founding of the American Public School System* (1940). Merle Curti's *The Social Ideas of American Educators* (1935) contains some excellent chapters on the ideas of the pioneer educators, and L. H. Tharp, *Until Victory: Horace Mann and Mary Peabody* (1953), is a readable story of the education crusade. For the history of colleges, there are informative chapters in R. Hofstadter and W. P. Metzger, *The Development of Academic Freedom in the United States* (1955). The best account of the lyceum movement is in Carl Bode, *The American Lyceum, Town Meeting of the Mind* (1956).

Drama and popular entertainment are adequately discussed in the general works listed above, but specialized studies are available for readers who wish to pursue the matter further. A. H. Quinn, *A History of the American Drama, from the Beginning to the Civil War* (1923), is factual and reliable, as is O. S. Coad and E. Mims, Jr., *The American Stage* (The Pageant of America, XIV, 1929). J. T. Howard, *Our American Music, Three Hundred Years of It* (1946), is a standard account, but this work should be supplemented by C. M. Rourke, *American Humor* (1931), short and brilliantly written, and C. Wittke, *Tambo and Bones* (1930).

The literature of the reform movement during the middle period is enormous, and the following list is partial at best. For the temperance movement, see J. A. Krout, *The Origins of Prohibition* (1925); for prison reform, B. McKelvey, *American Prisons: A Study in American Social History Prior to 1915* (1936); H. E. Marshall, *Dorothea Dix, Forgotten Samaritan* (1937), describes the story of her crusade, and A. E. Bestor, *Backwoods Utopias: The Sectarian and Owenite Phase of Communitarian Socialism in America, 1663-1829* (1950), is a splendid analysis of the New Harmony experiment. Books on abolitionism alone would fill a library. Recommended for this chapter are G. H. Barnes, *The Anti-Slavery Impulse, 1830-1844* (1933), and Allan Nevins, *Ordeal of the Union* (1947).

MANIFEST

DESTINY

C H A P T E R   T W E L V E

Long before America's aggressive expansion got under way in the 1840's, men had dreamed of a transcontinental nation stretching "from sea to shining sea." But romantic hopes had been checked by the actualities of geography. In 1828, the boundaries established by the Spanish treaty of 1819 (see p. 182) seemed permanent. Only 25 years later, the territory of the United States had been extended to its present-day limits.

The "westward movement" had begun with the first English settlements. It proceeded sometimes slowly, sometimes rapidly, depending upon a variety of circumstances: diplomatic, commercial, technological, and political. The purchase or annexation of new land, the impulse to move on, and the improved facilities for migration provided by canal and railroad transportation stimulated the spirit of expansion. And so, too, did the insatiable land hunger of the southern cotton planters and the northern farmers. All these forces had operated before the Louisiana Purchase threw open vast areas to settlement. What gave the westward movement its special character after 1830 was the evangelical gospel of "Manifest Destiny"—a gospel that both quickened and explained the spread to the West.

The term "Manifest Destiny" came into popular use in 1845, but the idea it embodied was much older. Manifest Destiny implied a determination by "the Father of the Universe" or "the Great Architect" to set aside the American continent "for the free development of our yearly multiplying millions." No outside force, no physical barrier, it seemed, could stop the irresistible drive of the nation to extend democratic institutions and to preserve North America from the sinister absolutism of Europe.

This vision of a mighty people on the march swelled an already inflated national rhetoric and inspired the most ridiculous oratorical displays. But the language of Manifest Destiny, despite its racist, imperialist, and mercenary overtones, sometimes expressed an underlying idealism. New lands wrested from Indians and Mexicans (as expansionists like Walt Whitman fondly anticipated) would strengthen democracy, provide asylum for the oppressed European masses, and strike a blow at world despotism.

But the men in charge of America's diplomatic and military policies in the 40's were not intoxicated by these vague aspirations of Manifest Destiny. They had their eyes fixed on more tangible goals—the domination of the northern Pacific waters and trade with the Orient. To insure America's place in the sun, they felt it would be necessary to gain control of the only three good ports on the Pacific coast: the Strait of Juan de Fuca, leading into Puget Sound, San Francisco's magnificent harbor beyond the Golden Gate, and the Bay of San Diego. California and Oregon had to be added to the still sparsely settled republic if the United States were to secure these ports and prevent rival European powers from gaining a foothold on the West coast. On this point, New England merchants, southern congressmen, and spokesmen for every section—Clay, Webster, Calhoun, and Douglas, among others—were in agreement.

I. DIPLOMACY IN THE TYLER ERA

The Caroline Affair.   England continued to be an object of distrust and sometimes of hate in the 1830's and 1840's, as well as the chief obstacle (so many thought) to America's pre-ordained greatness. Before Tyler assumed office, in April, 1841, Anglo-American relations had been steadily deteriorating, despite the fact that trade between the two countries was valuable to both. The English habit of condescending to the tobacco-chewing vulgarians across the Atlantic irritated the thin-skinned Yankees and kept alive old animosities. English travelers came to America to verify what they already believed, and they found the states as dirty and as disreputable as reported. The failure of American debtors to repay their English creditors after the Panic of 1837 (see p. 230) only confirmed British opinions about American dishonesty. Against this background of mutual disrespect, it is no wonder that even unimportant disputes between the two countries provoked talk of war and retaliation.

In 1837, a petty insurrection flared up in Canada against the Crown and was quickly put down. The insurgents found support across the American border, however, where sympathizers furnished them with arms and supplies. On the night of December 29, 1839, the *Caroline,* a small American steamer ferrying supplies to the rebels, lay

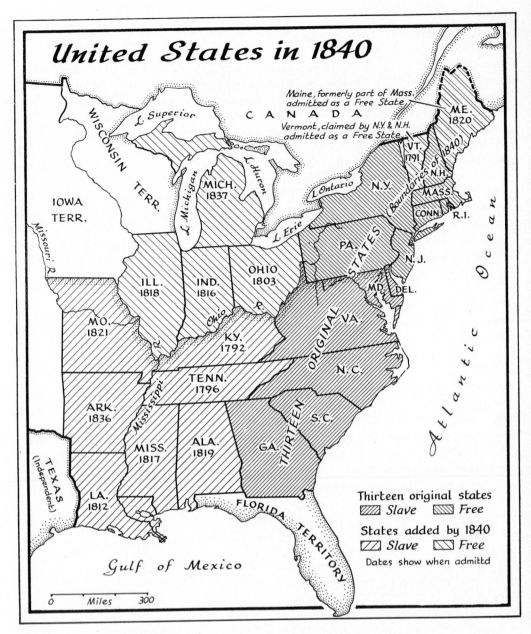

United States in 1840

CANADA

Maine, formerly part of Mass. admitted as a Free State

Vermont, claimed by N.Y. & N.H. admitted as a Free State

L. Superior

L. Huron

WISCONSIN TERR.

L. Michigan

MICH. 1837

L. Ontario

L. Erie

IOWA TERR.

ME. 1820

VT. 1791

Boundaries of 1840

N.H.

N.Y.

MASS.

CONN.

R.I.

MISSOURI R.

ILL. 1818

IND. 1816

OHIO 1803

PA.

STATES

MD.

DEL.

N.J.

MO. 1821

Ohio R.

KY. 1792

ORIGINAL

VA.

ARK. 1836

TENN. 1796

N.C.

Mississippi R.

THIRTEEN

S.C.

TEXAS (Independent)

MISS. 1817

ALA. 1819

GA.

LA. 1812

FLORIDA TERRITORY

Atlantic Ocean

Thirteen original states

▨ Slave   ▧ Free

States added by 1840

▨ Slave   ▧ Free

Dates show when admittd

Gulf of Mexico

0   Miles   300

moored on the state side of the Niagara River. A band of Canadian regulars rowed across, cut the *Caroline's* cable, set fire to the boat, and sank it. During the fracas, one American was killed.

At first the British government refused to acknowledge responsibility for the incident, and the case dragged on. Meanwhile, American partisans organized secretly to cooperate with the Canadian insurgents and to strike a blow against the "tyrants of Britain."

The incident might have been forgotten had not one of the alleged participants in the raid on the *Caroline*, Alexander McLeod, been arrested by New York State authorities in November, 1840, and charged with murder and arson. Lord Palmerston, British Foreign Secretary, now acknowledged that the raid had been officially planned to forestall illegal American aid to the Canadian insurrectionists, and promptly demanded McLeod's release on the ground that any actions he may

266

have committed were done under orders. His execution, Palmerston unofficially warned, would mean war.

But New York's Governor Seward insisted that McLeod face trial in the state courts, though he promised Secretary of State Daniel Webster that if convicted McLeod would be pardoned. Fortunately, McLeod was acquitted, a friendlier ministry took over in England, and Anglo-American relations were spared further strain. Lest similar incidents occur, Webster, with presidential support, drafted a measure (passed by Congress in August, 1842) granting federal jurisdiction in all cases in which aliens were accused of committing acts under the direction of a foreign government.

Anglo-American Parleys. Although the *Caroline* affair ended satisfactorily, other disputes plagued the diplomats of America and Great Britain. The English navy, in its attempts to destroy slave-trading, did not hesitate to stop and search American merchantmen, a practice that was offensive to ardent nationalists, particularly in the South. In 1841, slaves aboard the American brig *Creole* seized the ship and sailed her into a British port in the Bahamas. There they stayed, despite the protests of the ship's owners and the indignation of the southerners. When the British Foreign Secretary sent Lord Ashburton to restore friendly ties between his government and the United States, the *Creole* incident still simmered.

To complicate matters, the inhabitants of northern Maine had begun to glare across the border at their Canadian neighbors. Each claimed the territory that had been in dispute since the signing of the treaty of 1783. Prior to Ashburton's arrival, Maine and Canadian lumberjacks had all but started a small war in 1839 when they clashed over rights to the area around the Aroostook River. Congress grew bellicose and war sentiment spread. But President Van Buren managed to arrange a temporary agreement, and negotiations for a permanent settlement were begun in 1842. The American Secretary of State, Webster,

and the amiable Ashburton, now proceeded to adjudicate old disputes. Webster compromised on the Maine boundary issue and reached an agreement that gave the United States approximately 7,000 of the 12,000 square miles in question. The 5,000 square miles granted to Great Britain were sufficient to protect her communications between Quebec and New Brunswick. Other adjustments were made along the Canadian-American frontier to correspond to new geographical facts unknown to the original negotiators. Webster raised the question of the *Creole* incident, but Ashburton merely promised that henceforth British colonial authorities would not interfere with American vessels "driven by accident or violence" into British ports. Nor would England eat humble pie over the *Caroline* affair. Ashburton "regretted" that "some explanation and apology for this occurrence was not immediately made," and Webster had to make the best of the word "apology."

Extremists in England and America protested that their respective countries had suffered a diplomatic defeat, but the Webster-Ashburton treaty, signed on August 9, 1842, was a model of civilized compromise that paved the way for other peaceful negotiations during the next two decades. Webster

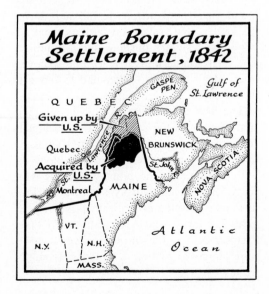

Maine Boundary Settlement, 1842

was able to convince anti-British congress-men to accept the treaty by displaying an old French map supporting the British case, while Ashburton appeased the anti-Amer-icans in Parliament by producing an old English map that clearly proved the Amer-ican claim. Subsequent discoveries showed that the latter was the valid one, but the settlement was well worth the loss of 5,000 square miles.

II. THE TEXAS QUESTION

Obstacles to
Southern Expansion.
By the 1840's, the best lands in the southern Gulf plains had already been occupied, and the finest soils in the "Black Belt" of Georgia, Alabama, and the Yazoo delta were being tilled by slave labor. The smaller and the less successful farmers found themselves frozen out. Unable to compete with the large-scale methods of the big plantations, they faced the alternative of either cultivating less desirable land or starting afresh in some new territory. But their opportunities in the new lands were limited. After the admission of Arkansas in 1836, the only other prospective slave state (under the provisions of the Missouri Com-promise) was the Territory of Florida. Along the northern Mississippi frontier, on the other hand, farmers from Illinois, Indiana, Ohio, and Kentucky began to spill into the newly opened Iowa and Wisconsin country after the removal of the Sauk and Fox tribes in 1833. By 1840, some 43,000 new settlers had found rich farmlands in Iowa, and during the 1830's lumbermen and farmers from ad-joining states were pushing into Minnesota. The small southern planter, with no such vast tracts at his disposal, either had to move to the Far West or turn south toward Mexico.

The first alternative was not encouraging. Immediately to the west lay the "permanent Indian frontier," bounded by the Red River to the south and stretching upward along the 95th meridian to the point where the Mis-souri River bends sharply northward. Here, in the vast stretch of territory popularly re-garded as the "Great American Desert" (see Chapter XIX), the displaced Indian tribes were supposed to live in isolation from the whites.

Although the myth of the "Great Sahara" remained current until the 1870's, more re-liable information about the Great Plains and Rocky Mountain interior gradually filtered through. The expedition of Lewis and Clark (1804-1806) had encouraged fur-traders to explore the new country. In their quest for beaver, they explored inten-sively the areas through which emigrants bound for Oregon and California would soon be passing. By 1840, the trappers were al-ready familiar with trails and mountain passes in the northern and central Rockies, and many of them had moved southward into forbidden Spanish territory, trapping illegally and opening up trade routes between St. Louis and Santa Fe (see p. 194). As the southern frontiersmen learned the best routes westward through the New Mexico country to California, they also discovered that this thinly populated and weakly held empire would offer little resistance to American pene-tration. Tough frontier farmers, mule-drivers, trappers, miners, and bully-boys spearheaded the drive into Texas, Oregon, and interior California. They prepared the way for the main body of settlers from the lower Missis-sippi Valley—sober, decent farmers who be-gan to move into the fertile provinces of Texas.

Colonizing Texas.
Between 1800 and 1820, American traders and filibusters (mili-tary adventurers) established commercial relations with the Mexicans, intrigued with revolutionists, and antagonized the Spanish authorities. In 1819, when the United States obtained Florida from Spain, it yielded its dubious claims to the Mexican province of

Texas, much to the irritation of frontier politicians, who argued that "the Great Engineer of the Universe" had fixed the Rio Grande as a natural dividing line. After Mexico had won her independence from Spain, the Mexican authorities invited Americans to settle in Texas. The man who had pioneered the American colonization of Texas, Connecticut-born Moses Austin, had obtained a land grant from the Mexican government, but he died in 1821 before he could colonize his tract. Later, in 1823, the Mexican government validated this grant for Austin's son, Stephen, who offered to the Mexican authorities a plan for attracting additional settlers. Other promoters, or *empresarios,* received similar concessions.

Mexican officials had hoped that the occupation of Texas by white Americans would protect their own country from Indian raids and from possible aggression by the United States. But they soon realized that they had miscalculated. Between 1820 and 1830, about 20,000 Americans with approximately 2,000 slaves had passed into Texas, but only a few Mexicans had settled there. European immigrants seemed to prefer the more stable society of the upper Mississippi Valley; and settlers from the lower Mississippi frontier predominated. Most of them were law-abiding people, but rougher elements, particularly in eastern Texas, aroused the fears of the Mexicans. The Texans, on their side, resented their lack of self-government. As a part of the state of Coahuila, the province was under the thumb of the Mexican-dominated state legislature. At last, after an *empresario* named Haden Edwards quarreled with the authorities over land titles, his brother, Benjamin, proclaimed the Republic of Fredonia, and staged a short-lived rebellion in 1826.

In 1830, Mexico stopped further American immigration, passed other restrictive measures, occupied the province with troops, and reconsidered her whole colonization policy. American settlers had failed to become Catholics, as they were required to by the provisions for settlement established by the Mexican authorities; they had ignored a Mexican prohibition against slave labor by substituting a thinly disguised "indenture" system; and they had settled along the coasts and boundaries reserved by law for Mexicans.

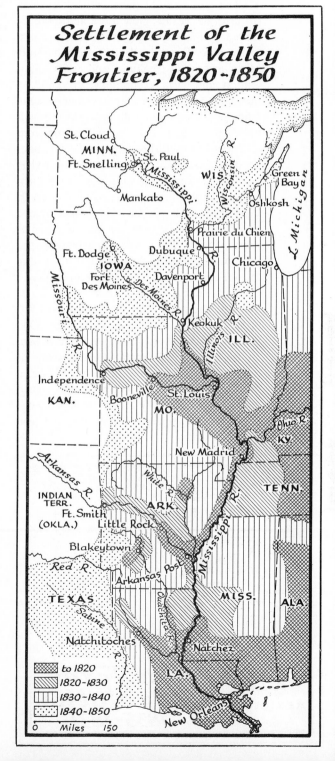

Settlement of the Mississippi Valley Frontier, 1820-1850

Relations between the Mexican government and the Texans had been growing steadily worse since 1826. Attempts by the United States to purchase Texas in 1827 had only confirmed Mexican fears of a Yankee plot to seize the territory by force. In turn, the Texans grew more and more irritated by the Mexican government's refusal to separate Texas from the preponderantly Mexican state of Coahuila, and by its immigration and tariff restrictions. In 1832, a Mexican revolution brought General Santa Anna to power, and a full-scale Texan revolt followed in 1836. The uprising sprang from a demand for reforms rather than for independence, but Santa Anna's threat to exterminate the Americans in Texas drove them to declare their independence on March 2, 1836. Before the Texan leaders had agreed on military strategy, two of their companies were wiped out: 188 died defending the Alamo Mission in San Antonio (among them such half-legendary figures as David Crockett, James Bowie, and William B. Travis), and more than 300 were massacred at Goliad after they had surrendered. One month later, on April 21, 1836, General Sam Houston surprised Santa Anna's army at San Jacinto Creek and decisively defeated him. The captured Mexican general signed a treaty guaranteeing Texan independence and fixing a vague boundary line between the two countries. Although the Mexican government promptly repudiated the treaty, its refusal to recognize the independence of Texas mattered little.

Recognition of Texas.

Sympathy for the insurrectionists had been widespread throughout the United States, particularly in the South and the Northwest where their cause was identified with the struggles of the underprivileged. As one Ohio supporter declared in 1835:

The Texans are mostly composed of the poorer classes of society: men whom misfortunes have driven from our country; men who have gone there at the instance of the invitation of the Mexican Government, on the full assurance of the protection of that government; in the hope and expectation of being able to retrieve their shattered fortunes, and procure bread for their suffering families.

Behind the rant and the fury, the cheap boasts about "the generous anglo-saxon blood" triumphing over the "blood thirsty barbarians of Mexico," was the feeling that the "Texians" had fought the war of humanity and democracy.

In the Northeast, however (where support for the Texan cause was less marked), and among northern Whig circles, the Texans' request to enter the Union after Santa Anna's defeat was interpreted as a slave-owners' plot. From five to seven states, it was pointed out, might be carved out of the huge Texas domain, thus insuring southern control of Congress. Opponents of recognition protested so vehemently that even President Jackson did not recognize Texas as a sister republic until just before he left office in 1837.

Throughout Van Buren's administration, pressure for annexation built up in the United States. The Texas Republic, denied admission to the United States and menaced by an unforgiving Mexico, naturally sought support elsewhere, and England seemed the likeliest protector. Britain, in turn, preferred an independent Texas that would export cotton and import British manufactured goods on a free-trade basis, but she also opposed

The Texas Revolution 1835-1836

slavery. In 1844, the American government learned that Lord Aberdeen of the British Foreign Office was urging the Texan government to abolish slavery.

That Texas might link herself commercially and politically with Great Britain was a frightening prospect to both northern businessmen and southern planters. American commerce would suffer as a consequence, but far more dangerous in southern eyes was the possibility that the abolition of slavery in Texas as a result of British pressure would invite violent insurrection in the slave states and would halt southern expansion. Calhoun went so far as to discount Britain's humanitarian motives and accused her of trying to reduce the productivity of Texas by pressuring her into substituting free labor for slave.

Sam Houston, the President of Texas, cleverly encouraged American fears until the annexationists were ready to do almost anything to bring Texas into the Union. Ex-President Jackson warned in 1843 that Texas must be obtained, "peaceably if we can, for-

cibly if we must," and President Tyler worked tirelessly to bring about annexation before his successor reached the White House. In April, 1844, Tyler submitted a statehood treaty to the Senate, drawn up by Secretary of State Calhoun, but northern opposition voted it down. In February, 1845, however, after the expansionists had triumphed in the 1844 presidential election, Tyler succeeded in persuading both houses of Congress to pass a joint resolution favoring annexation. This resolution made unnecessary the two-thirds vote in the Senate required for treaty ratification. Texas was offered statehood if she would agree to submit a proper constitution, assume her debts, and agree to the possible subdivision of her territory into not more than four states. In return, she would be permitted to retain her public lands, and slavery would be permissible under the terms of the Missouri Compromise. Texas became a state on December 29, 1845.

III. POLK'S DIPLOMACY

The Election of 1844. By opposing the annexation of Texas, Van Buren had destroyed his chance of becoming the Democratic presidential candidate in 1844. In his place, the Democrats nominated the ardent expansionist, James K. Polk of Tennessee, who was committed unreservedly to the annexation of Texas and the reoccupation of Oregon up to 54° 40'. The Whigs nominated Henry Clay on a platform that ignored the Texas question altogether. Unfortunately for Clay, the evasion did not pay off. Failing to gauge the strength of annexationist sentiment, he had joined Van Buren a few days before his nomination in opposing the admission of Texas. Now Clay tried to hedge by protesting in the so-called "Alabama Letters" that he would be willing to accept the admission of Texas if it could be done "without dishonor, without war, with the common consent of the Union, and upon just and fair terms."

This announcement only angered the anti-slavery voters. It did Clay little good in the expansionist South and West and may have cost him New York. Polk, a "dark horse" Democrat with years of experience in Congress, defeated Henry Clay and James G. Birney (candidate of the anti-slavery Liberty party) by conducting a frank "Manifest Destiny" campaign. His electoral vote was 170 to 105 for Clay, his popular vote 1,337,000 to Clay's 1,299,000. Had Clay captured 5,000 more votes in New York (where the Liberty party gathered 16,000) he would have won that state's 36 electoral votes and the election. Every western state except Ohio supported Polk, and the Democrats won a majority in both houses of Congress.

Stubborn, hard-working, and honest, Polk managed to accomplish a great deal during his single term in office. He disliked high tariffs, abolitionists, nullificationists, and office-seekers, and his very lack of imagina-

An 1846 lithograph of James K. Polk, entitled "Freedom's Champion."

The Oregon Question.

In the 1844 presidential campaign the Oregon boundary dispute with England had been as heated an issue as the annexation of Texas. Indeed, the voters seemed more excited by American claims to the Oregon Territory than by slavery itself; and as extremists in both countries began to rattle their sabres, talk of war was heard again. On three earlier occasions, Great Britain had refused to accept a boundary line at the 49th parallel. In 1843, expansionist American politicians demanded all the Oregon Territory up to 54° 40′, but England insisted on a line north of the Columbia River. Polk in his inaugural address had claimed that America held title to all the Oregon Territory.

tion kept him from being sidetracked from his goals. A good Jacksonian Democrat, though far more tactful and even-tempered than his great predecessor, Polk believed in strict construction of the Constitution and in the principle of appointing good party men to office. And he usually got what he wanted. He signed the Walker Tariff of 1846, which drastically reduced rates and embodied the principle of tariff for revenue only. The South and the West approved the new tariff, but industrialists in the Northeast, many of them Democrats, were furious. (Polk referred to them in his diary as "capitalists and monopolists" who derived "enormous profits" from the 1842 tariff.) His restoration of the Independent Treasury (or Sub-treasury) system (see p. 232), a campaign promise fulfilled despite strong Whig opposition, provoked no lasting discord, nor did his popular solution of the long-pending Oregon dispute.

Moreover, in his first annual message to Congress he elaborated the Monroe Doctrine by making some assertions that have often been called "the Polk Doctrine": (1) "The people of *this continent* alone have the right to decide their own destiny." (2) The United States cannot allow European states to prevent an independent state from entering the Union. (3) No European colony or dominion should, without American consent, be established anywhere in North America.

Actually both countries had excellent claims to Oregon. English traders had begun to exploit the Oregon country in the late eighteenth century, and by 1788 Boston merchants were buying sea-otter pelts from he Indians on the Oregon coast and selling hem for enormous prices to the Chinese. American control over the coastal trade was ess decisive than British domination of the nterior. After John Jacob Astor's Pacific ur Company was forced out by the British North West Company (see p. 193), British ur-traders had no competitors for a full generation. A merger of the North West Company and the Hudson's Bay Company n 1821, and the arrival of the formidable nd wily John McLoughlin to take control of ur-trade operations, assured British supremacy in Oregon. The American Congress lost nterest in Oregon, and only a few enthusiastic politicians and businessmen kept the issue efore the public.

In 1834, a party of Methodists headed by ason Lee settled in the Willamette Valley. ee became more interested in accelerating nigration to Oregon than in saving Indian ouls, however, and was replaced a decade ter by another missionary whose concerns ere less worldly. In the meantime, Marcus Whitman, a Presbyterian, established a mison near Fort Walla Walla in 1836, and in

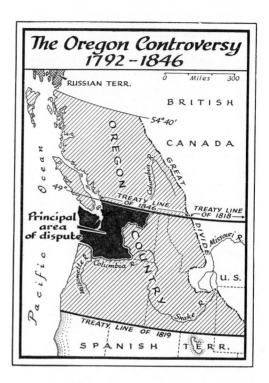

"What? You young Yankee-noodle, strike your own father!" Contemporary cartoon on the Anglo-American dispute over Oregon.

1840 the Jesuits sent out Father De Smet, who founded a Catholic mission the next year.

The Protestants made little headway with the Indians of the Oregon region, whose resistance to the Gospel was sometimes rather violent. Marcus Whitman, his wife, and 12 others in the mission were massacred in 1847 by a disgruntled tribe. The persistence of the missionaries had at least a secular significance, however, for their reports did attract attention to Oregon's agricultural possibilities. In 1843, the first large migration, a thousand strong, headed over the Oregon Trail to the new country. Starting from Independence, Missouri, the "Great Migration" followed the Platte River through Fort Laramie, where the emigrants rested, and then continued to South Pass. After a short stop at Fort Bridger, the caravan passed into the Snake River Valley and moved by stages to the Columbia, and thence to Fort Vancouver, slightly over 2,000 miles from Independence.

The success of the 1843 expedition proved to doubters that an overland trek to Oregon was possible. Hundreds soon followed by

273

wagon, and a few by ship via Cape Horn. Francis Parkman's *Oregon Trail* (1849) provides an unforgettable picture of the emigrant caravan, "with its heavy white wagons creeping on in slow progression," and the emigrants themselves, "tall awkward men, in brown homespun; women, with cadaverous faces and long lank figures." To Parkman, who observed these people at firsthand during a journey from St. Louis to Fort Laramie in 1846, they were "the rudest and most ignorant of the frontier populations; they knew absolutely nothing of the country and its inhabitants; they had already experienced much misfortune, and apprehended more." And yet these "yellow-visaged Missourians" and their "care-worn, thin-featured" wives made good settlers when they reached the Northwest.

In 1843, the Americans in Oregon organized a provisional government in the face of Canadian opposition. Back in the East, politicians began to thunder about America's higher claims to Oregon. The issue, they said, had nothing to do with "musty records and the voyages of old sea captains." Even if England had both history and law on her side, it was "our manifest destiny to overspread and to possess the whole of the continent which Providence has given us for the development of the great experiment of liberty." More menacing to the British authorities than gusty talk in the East were the brawling American frontiersmen themselves. The presence of these unruly settlers together with the depleted supply of fur-bearing animals along the Columbia River, made the English less unwilling to accept a boundary line at the 49th parallel. British hostility, furthermore, had decreased with the reduction of American tariff rates in 1846. Interested in keeping American markets and in avoiding war at a time when they were disturbed by a sharp internal conflict over the Corn Laws, the English were ready to agree.

Congress, on the brink of war with Mexico (see p. 278), now backed down from the aggressive "54 40 or Fight" slogan that w[as] so popular with the expansionists. Preside[nt] Polk himself had no stomach for an Angl[o-] American conflict. Four months after his ele[c-] tion, he had admitted the danger of pressi[ng] for the whole of Oregon and the desirability [of] obtaining a compromise at the 49th parall[el.] Above the line, he had been reliably inform[ed] by Buchanan, the land was unsuitable f[or] agriculture; below it lay "the entrance of t[he] Straits of Fuca, Admiralty Inlet, and Puge[t] Sound, with their fine harbors and rich su[r-] rounding soil." The ultra-expansionists in h[is] party saw the struggle over the Oregon line [as] the last-ditch stand of democracy against mo[n-] archy, but to the commercial-minded in [all] sections of the country Oregon was the "k[ey] to the Pacific." Amidst dreams of trade wi[th] the exotic East, the war sentiment agai[nst] England died away. Better to compromi[se] than to risk conflict, the merchants felt, esp[e-] cially when a concession to the British [in] Oregon might speed America's effort [to] secure the even more valuable Californ[ia] ports. In the meantime, the British Forei[gn] Secretary, Lord Aberdeen, was talking t[he] language of peace in England. As early [as] 1844, he had outlined a compromise su[b-] stantially the same as the one that was fina[lly] adopted.

At last, on June 15, 1846, the Oreg[on] Treaty was signed, a treaty that proved a[d-] vantageous to both countries. The line dra[wn] along the 49th parallel to Puget Sound a[nd] from there to the Pacific through the Stra[its] of Juan de Fuca was simply an extension [of] the Canadian-American boundary that h[ad] been fixed in 1818 as far as the Rocki[es.] The territory north of the Columbia, thou[gh] it was clearly British by right of settleme[nt,] fell into the American sphere. England [re-] tained Vancouver Island and navigati[on] rights on the Columbia River.

The Mormons.   Less than a year af[ter] the signing of the Oregon Treaty, a sm[all] wagon train led by one of the most rema[rk-] able leaders and organizers of his day[—] Brigham Young—followed the Oregon Tr[ail] along the north side of the Platte. Arriving at Fort Bridger, Young rejected the advice of experienced pioneers to continue onward to the rich Willamette Valley. Instead he led his party through mountain and desert to what was considered to be the uninhabitable plains around Great Salt Lake below the Wasatch Range. A larger body followed the advance expedition, and by 1847 some 4,000 people—mainly New Englanders but many of them recent arrivals from old England—were laying the foundations for a religious community in this isolated part of Mexican territory.

These adventurous and dedicated folk were known as Mormons. The founding of their sanctuary in the Great Basin culminated a period of wandering that had started in western New York during the 1820's. It was there in 1823 that Joseph Smith, a visionary Vermonter, had discovered the golden plates on which was printed the Book of Mormon. Published in 1830 after its miraculous revelation, the Book of Mormon proved to be a composite of mythology and prophecy. It gave currency to the ancient legend that the Indians were descendants of the lost tribes of Israel and enjoined the followers of Joseph Smith to convert them from their heathenish ways. On the basis of this revelation, Smith founded the Church of Jesus Christ of the Latter-Day Saints in 1830. Mormonism spread into the Western Reserve, and at Kirtland, Ohio, the distinctive patterns of Mormon community living—markedly similar to the seventeenth-century New England settlements—took shape.

The financial collapse of 1837 (see p. 230) ruined the Mormon community in Ohio and forced an exodus to Missouri, but the Missourians, despising the "Saints" as a set of thieving Yankees, abolitionists, and heretics, cruelly expelled them in the winter of 1838. The fortunes of the Mormons improved after they crossed the Mississippi to Nauvoo, Illinois in 1839, and their settlement there thrived. But misfortune befell them again when Joseph Smith's encouragement of plural marriages (he had received a revelation to this effect in 1843) alienated the monoga-

mists of the sect and infuriated the non-Mormon inhabitants. When the anti-Smith faction among the Mormons attacked him in their newly established newspaper, Smith smashed their press. For this offense, the civil authorities threw him and his brother into jail. From here they were taken by a mob and lynched in 1844.

Two years later, a new leader, Brigham Young, having decided that Mormonism would never be tolerated inside the boundaries of the United States, took the drastic step of migrating to the Salt Lake Valley. Here, encircled by mountain and desert, this brilliant colonizer created a theocracy superbly organized for survival. The Salt Lake community was cooperative rather than competitive. Since its very existence depended on controlling the limited water supply brought in by the mountain streams, Young devised an irrigation system that distributed water equitably to the whole community. He and his advisers parceled out land, laid out new communities, regulated commerce and industry, and experimented in social planning. The Mormon state of Deseret (later changed to Utah by Congress) was probably the most successful communitarian project in American history.

Remote as the "Saints" were, they did not enjoy their self-contained existence for very

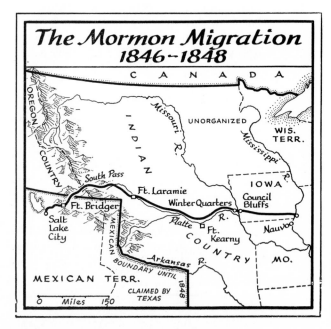

The Mormon Migration 1846–1848

View of Salt Lake City (1853).

long. Mormon legend relates that the Valley of Salt Lake had been revealed to Young in a dream, but his spiritual guides did not inform him that an American-Mexican war, fought during the Mormon migration, would bring his community once more under United States jurisdiction. Furthermore, the Mormon state lay athwart one of the routes to California and, willy-nilly, was involved in the expansionist drive to the southern Pacific. The Mormons were not the only people in the country who were governed by heavenly dictates. All Americans, it seemed, had the responsibility "to redeem from unhallowed hands a *land* above all others favored of heaven, and hold it for the use of a people who know how to obey heaven's behests."

California. California had been loosely held by Spain since the middle of the eighteenth century. A number of missions, managed by Franciscan friars and protected by small garrisons, had been planted by the Spaniards for the double purpose of converting the Indians and preventing British and Russian penetration down the California coast. These missions Christianized and trained thousands of Indians and owned great herds of cattle. In theory, they were tem-

porary establishments set up to teach the Indians agriculture and the household arts. After completing this task, the Franciscans were expected to move on to new fields and allow the regular clergy to take over. The mission lands would then be broken up and distributed to private owners. But who was to decide when this primary stage was over? Even before the establishment of the Mexican Republic in 1825, anti-clericals had opposed religious authority in the provinces. With independence won, the liberals, opposed to the monopolistic aspects of the mission system, and officials and land-speculators hungry for plunder, pressed for the secularization of the missions. By 1834 they had their way. Half the mission lands passed immediately into private hands, and the other half was soon lost to landsharks. At the outbreak of the Mexican War in 1846, the Indians had hopelessly degenerated and hardly any vestige remained of the Franciscan mission system.

About this time, the Mexicans were becoming aware of American intrigues to annex California. For the past 25 years, American whalers had stopped at the ports of Monterey and San Francisco, and New England traders had exchanged textiles, cutlery, and firearms —everything "from Chinese fire works to

276

English cart-wheels"—for hides and tallow. Richard Henry Dana, Jr., whose classic *Two Years Before the Mast* (1840) contains the best account of California life in the 1830's, considered the Mexicans "an idle thriftless people" incapable of making anything, bad bargainers, and suspicious of foreigners. "Indeed," he wrote, "as far as my observation goes, there are no people to whom the newly invented Yankee word of 'loafer' is more applicable than to the Spanish Americans." Dana succumbed to the charm and elegance and pride of these people, but he made clear the reasons for their lack of defense against the Americans who pushed into the valleys of California between 1825 and 1846. During these years, fur-traders, deserters from sailing ships, and emigrants from the Oregon and Mississippi frontiers began to buy up large tracts of California land and to monopolize commerce and industry. For the Americans, the most effective and knowledgeable figure on the coast was Thomas O. Larkin, who settled in Monterey in 1832 and later became a confidential agent of the American government. His counter-

part in the interior was Captain John A. Sutter, a Swiss-American with ingratiating ways. Sutter erected a fort in the Sacramento Valley in 1839 and set up a little trading empire of his own. Both Larkin and Sutter encouraged and aided American emigrants to settle in California.

Although California had not been an issue in the 1844 campaign, it soon became identified in the popular mind with Oregon. Americans who had taken the various routes to California (see map, p. 278) had widely publicized this lush region—none more eloquently than the witty Larkin, who described the pleasures of "hunting wild Deer and dancing with tame Dear." By the summer of 1845, interest in California was keen, and expansionist talk about a mighty nation extending from sea to sea became common. The expansionists warned Polk to take over California before the British stepped in. Polk himself aired plans for a transcontinental railroad to link the harbors of fabulous California with the Mississippi Valley. San Francisco, all agreed, was the most valuable prize in California; twenty times more valuable, thought Daniel Webster, than Texas.

Yet the United States had no claims to California, as she had to Oregon; and American-Mexican relations, strained by the annexation of Texas, hardly favored the American purchase of California. With reason, Mexico suspected that the United States had designs on the coveted territory. The American government had tried unsuccessfully to buy California during Jackson's and Tyler's administrations, and in 1842 Daniel Webster was rebuffed by the British when he sought their help in forcing Mexico to sell California in return for concessions in the Anglo-American dispute over Oregon. In the same year, an American naval officer, Commodore Thomas ap Catesby Jones, who had been mistakenly informed that the United States and Mexico were at war and that the British were planning to seize California, sailed into Monterey and captured the city on October 20, 1842. Discovering his mis-

- Settlements
+ Missions

San Francisco
Santa Clara
San José
Monterey
San Joaquin
San Antonio
San Luis Obispo
MOJAVE DESERT
Santa Barbara
San Gabriel
Los Angeles
SAN JACINTO MTS.
San Diego
Colorado R.
Pacific Ocean

Spanish Settlements in 18th C. California

Routes to California

take, he promptly apologized to the Mexicans, but the significance of this hostile gesture was plain enough. At the time of Polk's election, reports came from Larkin that Britain was preparing to oppose American expansionist plans in California. The President hurriedly sent a representative, John Slidell, to Mexico in November, 1845, with an offer to buy New Mexico and California—and with instructions to pay as much as $40 million if necessary. The recently installed Mexican regime could not consider the offer because of the popular disapproval that such a transfer would create. It invoked a diplomatic technicality as an excuse to refuse to receive the frustrated and disgusted Slidell, who in turn wrote Polk that nothing could be done

with the Mexicans "until they shall have been chastised."

Cooperating with Spanish-speaking Californians who favored American intervention, the United States now tried to encourage a "spontaneous" rebellion through a plan worked out by the canny Larkin. The scheme might have succeeded had a party of mountain men led by the flamboyant John C. Frémont (ostensibly "exploring" for the United States) not interfered. Frémont antagonized the Californians who had favored American annexation and set up his own "Bear Flag" Republic with the assistance of a handful of settlers on July 5, 1846. In the meantime, the United States had declared war against Mexico.

IV. THE MEXICAN WAR AND ITS RESULTS

War with Mexico. Polk had hoped to avoid a war if California could be acquired by purchase. But the failure of Slidell's mission, and Mexico's refusal even to discuss the sale of New Mexico and California, led

him to think seriously of taking more drastic steps. A long-standing dispute over the southern boundary of Texas—both countries laid claim to the territory between the Nueces River and the Rio Grande—provided an occasion for trouble. In January, 1846, immediately after hearing from Slidell about his failure, Polk ordered General Zachary Taylor to move from his base near Corpus Christi and take up a position on the Rio Grande (see map, p. 280). This order was carried out by the end of March. Ostensibly, Taylor was sent to protect Texans from a possible Mexican attack. But Polk seems to have had more than this in mind. Such a show of force might cause the Mexicans to reconsider their refusal to negotiate; but, failing that, the presence of American troops on soil claimed by both sides might cause an incident that would give Polk an excuse for a declaration of war.

Even before the news of hostilities arrived, Slidell's return early in May with his discouraging report seems to have led the impatient Polk to decide to send a war message to Congress. But before his message was delivered, news came that the Mexicans had attacked one of Taylor's patrols on April 25, 1846. On May 11, Polk sent his message. Without the news of these hostilities, a declaration of war might have been hotly contested; but the shedding of American blood on what the United States claimed to be its own soil put Congress in a mood to act without lengthy debate. By May 13, Congress had agreed to declare war by a vote of 40 to 2 in the Senate and 174 to 14 in the House.

Although support for the war was more enthusiastic in Mexico than in the United States, Mexican optimism was unwarranted, to say the least. To be sure, the Americans were not unanimously in favor of the war. New England reformers like James Russell Lowell, Theodore Parker, and Ralph Waldo Emerson opposed it with satire and thundering invective. The indignant Emerson wrote:

> Behold the famous States
> Harrying Mexico
> With rifle and with knife!

But although the Northeast withheld moral and financial aid and supplied only 7,930 recruits, the rest of the country was far more enthusiastic. Some 20,000 southerners and 40,000 westerners enlisted, and the war was quickly won.

Taylor captured Monterrey on September 24, 1846, and defeated a Mexican force of 15,000 men under General Santa Anna at Buena Vista on February 23, 1847. Lest one Whig general gain too much popular acclaim, President Polk appointed another, General Winfield Scott, to command an expedition against Mexico City. Landing at Vera Cruz on March 9 with about 10,000 men, Scott overcame tough Mexican resistance and took the Mexican capital on September 14, 1847. In the meantime, an army under Colonel Stephen W. Kearny, starting from its base at Fort Leavenworth, Missouri, captured Santa Fé and moved on to California. There Kearny joined with American naval units and with Frémont's men to establish American rule. By January 13, 1847, all Mexican forces in California had surrendered.

When news of the victories at Buena Vista and Vera Cruz reached Washington, Polk decided to try to arrange a peace with the Mexican leaders. For this mission, Secretary of State James Buchanan chose the State Department's chief clerk, Nicholas P. Trist, who had been consul at Havana and knew the Spanish language. Trist was instructed to demand the Rio Grande boundary and the

OREGON COUNTRY

IOWA

U.S.-MEXICAN BOUNDARY BY
THE ADAMS-ONIS TREATY, 1819

ILL.

**Kearny
1846**

Ft. Leavenworth

Great Salt Lake

MO.

Bent's
Fort

**MEXICAN CESSION
1848**

San Francisco

Monterey

Colorado R.

Santa Fé

Arkansas

R.

ARK.

**Stockton
1846-47**

Los Angeles

Red R.

MISS.

Kearny, '46

San Diego

Gila R.

**T E X A S
ANNEXED, 1845**

Sabine R.

LA.

El Paso

New Orleans

U.S.-MEXICAN BOUNDARY
BY THE TREATY OF
GUADALUPE-HIDALGO, 1848

Rio Grande

Nueces R.

Corpus Christi

Pacific

Ocean

**Taylor
1846-47**

Monterrey

BUENA VISTA

Santa Anna

Matamoros

Gulf of

Mexico

Tampico

**The Mexican War Campaigns
1846-1848**

**Scott
1847**

Vera Cruz

Mexico City

Puebla

Santa Anna

0   Miles   400

---

cession of New Mexico and California, and
was authorized to offer to assume payment
of the claims of Americans against Mexico
and an additional sum of $15 million. The
latter provision was presumably meant to
satisfy the American conscience by giving
the annexations the character of a purchase.

When General Santa Anna refused to accept Trist's terms, the American envoy was
ordered back to Washington. Now Polk and
his cabinet began to consider a prolonged
occupation of Mexico, the annexation of New
Mexico and California without payment, and
a levy on the people of Mexico to pay the
costs of occupation. Some people in and out
of the cabinet even began to talk of a permanent annexation of all Mexico. Once again
Manifest Destiny was called upon to justify
such an idea. "We believe," said the New
280

York *Herald,* "it is a part of our destiny to
civilize that beautiful country and enable its
inhabitants to appreciate some of the many
advantages and blessings they enjoy."

Strange as it may have seemed to the New
Englanders and free-soilers, who accused the
South of promoting the war to win more
slave territory, the movement to annex all
Mexico was strongly opposed by southerners
in both major parties. They knew that free-
soilers would insist on keeping the territories
out of the Union or making them free. Some,
like Calhoun, feared the strong centralized
government that would surely grow out of
the effort to administer a conquered empire.

With these objections, Trist agreed. Feeling that annexation of Mexico would be
disastrous for the United States, and well
aware that the Moderate party, which had

just come to power in Mexico, would be more reasonable than any other, he ignored his instruction to return and pressed on with his negotiations. On February 2, 1848, he signed the Treaty of Guadalupe Hidalgo. In it he secured the Rio Grande boundary, Upper California (including the much-desired port of San Diego), and New Mexico. He agreed that the United States would assume Mexican obligations to Americans up to $3.25 million and would pay Mexico $15 million.

Astonishing as Trist's behavior was, Polk's, upon receiving the treaty from his unauthorized envoy, was even more so, for he accepted it. After all, it conformed to Trist's original instructions, and it would be inconsistent to repudiate it. Moreover, to do so would excite violent criticism in Congress, where the Whigs held a majority in the House of Representatives. So Polk sent the treaty to the Senate, where it was passed, with a few changes, on March 10, 1848, by a vote of 38 to 14. The revisions were accepted by Mexico in May, and a war that had become increasingly unpopular was ended.

The treaty, which marked the height of American expansion, did not give the United States the whole of Mexico, but it did add over 500,000 square miles of territory to the already enormously extended continental domain. All in all, the United States did very well indeed, though Trist failed to acquire 54,000 square miles along the southern New Mexico border, a strip of land that offered the best route for a southern Pacific railroad. Five years later, in 1853, the "Gadsden Purchase"—named for the United States minister to Mexico, James Gadsden—remedied this oversight, at a price of $10 million.

The War's Legacy.

As Polk's term of office drew to a close, the President proudly noted in his diary the accomplishments of his administration: (1) the annexation of Texas, (2) the settlement of the Oregon boundary dispute "which preceding administrations," he wrote, "had been endeavoring to settle for more than thirty years," (3) tariff reduction, (4) the establishment of the Independent Treasury, and (5) the doubling of United States territory. To this blunt and conscientious man, the bickering that now flared up between supporters of slavery and abolitionists was simply unpatriotic and illogical. He could neither have written nor appreciated the observation of another famous diarist, Ralph Waldo Emerson, who wrote in his journal as American soldiers stormed into Mexico: "The United States will conquer Mexico, but it will be as the man swallows the arsenic, which brings him down in turn. Mexico will poison us."

The symptoms of this poisoning were swift to appear. Even before the close of the war with Mexico, the unimaginative Polk was already reporting this disturbing event in his diary:

Late in the evening of Saturday, the 8th, I learned that after an exciting debate in the House a bill passed that body, but with a mischievous and foolish amendment to the effect that no territory which might be acquired by treaty from Mexico should ever be a slaveholding country. What connection slavery had with making peace with Mexico it is difficult to conceive.

The amendment referred to by Polk had been offered by David Wilmot of Pennsylvania to a bill proposing an additional $2 million for the purchase of more land from Mexico. Although Polk could see no connection between making peace with Mexico and slavery, there were plenty of Americans in both the North and the South who could. Although Wilmot's "Proviso" failed in 1846, it let loose the virus of conflict. From this year on, the question of whether the newly acquired territory would be slave or free was hotly debated.

The Wilmot Proviso raised a new constitutional problem as well. Did Congress have authority to determine whether or not slavery might exist in territory obtained by the United States? Those who said yes could point out that Congress had exercised this power on a number of occasions since 1789 when it confirmed the clause in the Ordinance of 1787 (see p. 122) that excluded slavery from the Northwest Territory. The Constitution (Article IV, Section 3) plainly conveyed such an authority in the clause: "The Congress shall have power to dispose of and *make all needful rules and regulations* respecting the *territory* or other property belonging to the United States. . . ." (Italics added.)

To the statesmen of the South, it was equally plain that Congress did not possess the power to determine the status of slavery in the territories. In territorial matters, they insisted, Congress only acted as the agent of the states, which, together with the federal government, "jointly [owned] the Territories." It obviously followed that Congress could not pass a law forbidding a citizen from taking his slaves into the new territories. The southerners pointed out that the word in Article IV, Section 3, was "territory," not "territories," and that the word "property" clearly meant land. This clause did not give Congress the right to interfere with slave property guaranteed by the Constitution. Only the inhabitants of a territory could decide whether to admit or exclude slaves; and then only when they finally drew up a state constitution.

A less legalistic solution came from the national-minded West. This theory was the doctrine of "popular sovereignty," which was enthusiastically propounded by Lewis Cass of Michigan and Stephen A. Douglas of Illinois. According to their arguments, there was a long-established precedent in America that communities were the best judges of their own interests. Congress had not interfered with the original states when they drew up their constitutions. Why then should Congress interfere with the domestic questions of a territory before it obtained statehood? Let the new territories be set up with the question of slavery left unsettled, and then permit the people to decide for themselves. This argument made good sense up to a point, but the popular sovereignty proponents were not always clear precisely when a territory should decide this momentous question.

So the debate continued. But the issue of whether the Missouri Compromise line (see p. 188) would be extended to the Pacific remained unsettled, with the South insisting that the sectional balance of free and slave states must be maintained. Oregon's petition for a territorial government was held up in Congress for several years before the southern members grudgingly acquiesced, on August 13, 1848, in the organization of the Oregon territory without slavery. But no clear-cut decision was reached on the territories to be carved out of the Mexican cession below the Missouri Compromise line of 36° 30'.

Neither the Democratic nor the Whig strategists were eager to face up to the slavery issue with the presidential election of 1848 drawing near. The northern Democrats were badly split between the strong anti-slavery men, who were reluctant to sacrifice their principles for party harmony, and the regulars, who were working for compromise and party unity. In New York, the anti-slavery Democrats, or "Barnburners" (they were alleged to be willing to "burn down" the Democratic "barn" in order to get rid of the pro-slavery "rats"), clashed with the conservative Democrats, or "Hunkers" (those who "hunkered" for office). And the party was similarly divided in the New England states. The regular Democrats triumphed at the Baltimore nominating convention and chose the "popular sovereignty" candidate, Lewis Cass of Michigan, on a platform that scrupulously ignored the critical issue of the extension of slavery.

Anti-slavery Whigs were equally dissatisfied when their party passed over controversial stalwarts like Daniel Webster and Henry Clay and nominated the "Hero of Buena Vista," General Zachary Taylor, as the presidential candidate. Nor were they reassured by the free-soil sympathies of the vice-presidential candidate, Millard Fillmore of New York. As a result, some of the prominent Whig leaders decided to bolt the party and throw their support to a free-soil presidential candidate.

Shortly after Taylor's nomination by the regular Whigs, a Barnburner convention meeting in Utica nominated Martin Van Buren for president. Free-soilers rallied in other sections in the early summer of 1848, and a national Free Soil party convention, composed of dissidents from the old parties, gathered at Buffalo in August. It drew up a platform opposing the extension of slavery in the territories and calling for free lands to bona fide settlers. Its watchword was "Free soil, free speech, free labor and free men." Van Buren became the candidate of the Free Soil party after a fusion of Barnburners and "Conscience" Whigs threw him their support. The highly respected Charles Francis Adams of Massachusetts was chosen as his running-mate.

The 1848 election itself aroused little popular enthusiasm. Neither Taylor nor Cass appealed particularly to his respective party, and the voting was light. Taylor captured the populous states, winning 1,360,000 votes to Cass' 1,220,000. The Free-soilers polled only 291,000 votes, but they absorbed enough Democratic support in New York to give that state's electoral vote to Taylor, and enough Whig support in Ohio and Indiana to give those states to Cass. The Free Soil

issue. Southern extremists now had fresh grounds on which to convince the moderates and Unionists in their states that a southern party must be formed to oppose northern aggression.

The Compromise of 1850.

Sectional tensions relaxed for a moment when the exciting news of gold discoveries in California spread across the nation early in 1848. From all over the world, men began to converge on the California gold fields. Some risked the perilous voyage around the Horn or the portage across Panama (see p. 320). Others took the overland route through Salt Lake City, thereby enriching the Mormons who sold supplies to the miners at fabulous prices. As the gold-fever swept through the country, Americans of every class and occupation dropped whatever they were doing and headed for the Pacific coast. To Henry Thoreau, already launched on his own spiritual pilgrimage in Concord (see p. 245), the rush to California was a shocking reflection

Street scene in San Francisco in the winter of 1849.

party also elected nine congressmen. Most important of all, it had demonstrated the potential strength and disruptive power of a purely sectional party. Henceforth, there could be no slurring over of the slavery

of American materialism: the "world's raffle," he called it.

What a comment, what a satire on our institutions!... And have all the precepts in all the Bibles taught men only this? and is the last and most admirable invention of the human race only an improved muck-rake? Is this the ground on which Orientals and Occidentals meet? Did God direct us to get our living, digging where we never planted,—and He would, perchance, reward us with lumps of gold?

But Thoreau's bitter comments passed unnoticed, and his anti-materialistic logic made no sense to the motley crowd of adventurers flocking into California. By 1849, California had a wild and violent population of over 100,000, and old towns like San Francisco and Sacramento had mushroomed into jerry-built cities with muddy streets. Conditions were chaotic. Prices skyrocketed to fantastic heights and the gambling spirit infected everyone.

Polk had retired before a deeply divided Congress could decide California's future. Taylor, the new President, was blunt and well-intentioned, but politically inept. He recommended that California and New Mexico draw up their own constitutions and decide without congressional direction whether or not slavery should be excluded from their territories. But tempers in Congress were too short to accept such a matter-of-fact recommendation, and southern Whigs now began to assail the President. All the signs pointed toward the breaking up of the old national parties and the forming of new sectional parties. California, New Mexico, and the Mormon state of Deseret accepted Taylor's invitation to draw up their own constitutions, and all forbade slavery. Now Calhoun's warnings about the impending extinction of the South seemed about to be borne out. Many southerners began to talk fatalistically about the continuing hostility of the North and the certainty of secession, and prepared to take an uncompromising stand before Congress. Should slave depots be banned in the District of Columbia? Should the Fugitive Slave Law be tightened? Must Texas, a slave state, yield part of its western land to the proposed territory of New Mexico? Southern unity in defense of slavery had never been so strong.

President Taylor had no constructive proposals to offer. In a message to Congress he simply advised that body to avoid "exciting topics of sectional character,"—this at a time when senators and representatives carried Bowie knives and Colt revolvers, and Washington newspapermen seriously discussed the possibility of bloody violence in the House. Clearly the South had no intention of allowing California to enter the Union as a free state unless it received important concessions in return. The South would secede rather than accept the Wilmot Proviso.

Henry Clay, 73 years old but still a powerful and persuasive speaker, understood the mood of the South. He refused to dismiss the passionate southern oratory and talk of secession as the mere vaporizings of a minority, and he loved the Union. On January 29, 1850, when ill-will between the sections had reached a climax, Clay recommended to his Senate colleagues that the following resolutions be adopted: (1) that California be admitted as a free state; (2) that the territorial governments set up in the remainder of the Mexican cession (Utah and New Mexico) decide for themselves whether slavery should be permitted or abolished; (3) that the western boundary of Texas be fixed as to exclude "any portion of New Mexico;" (4) that in return for this concession, the United States would assume that portion of the public debt of Texas contracted before annexation; (5) that slavery within the District of Columbia would not be abolished without the consent of Maryland and the residents in the District, and "without just compensation to the owners of slaves within the District"; (6) that slave-trading be prohibited in the District of Columbia; (7) that a stricter fugitive slave law be adopted; and (8) that "Congress has no power to promote or obstruct the trade in slaves between the slaveholding States."

Clay's proposals appealed to the conservative southern planters and to northern businessmen, whose prosperity depended on political stability. The proposals also touched the hearts of nationalists in every section,

Henry Clay, the "Great Pacificator," addressing the Senate in 1850.

whose concern for the Union rose above the claims of state and party. Fanaticism flourished in the North and the South, and was not unknown in the West. But unionist sentiment was stronger west of the Alleghenies than in either of the older sections. In the West, as a Cincinnati editor observed in 1835,

Necessity compels us to lay aside sectional, political, and religious differences—and to unite as brothers—we are taken away from the local prejudices, and accidental influences which at home would have bound us down to one eternal routine of thought and action, and brought us into contact with strange beings in a strange land—we find them human beings like ourselves, torn like us, by the effect of circumstances away from the sphere of their early association; we need their society, their friendship, their confidence, their help; at any rate we are forced to endure their company—and like reasonable folk, we make the best of it.

It was not just an accident, then, that two of the great political leaders of the compromise forces were westerners: Henry Clay of Kentucky and Stephen A. Douglas of Illinois. In the months of dramatic debate that followed Clay's proposal, Daniel Webster also contributed his oratory to the cause of the compromisers. But the measure could not have passed without the aid of moderates in both national parties who represented the nation's desire for conciliation.

The battle for the Compromise of 1850 was one of the most bitterly contested in congressional history; whether it would be passed or defeated remained doubtful until the very end. Opposed to Clay and his compromisers were: (1) The angry and suspicious President Taylor, firm in his conviction that California must be admitted to the Union without any provisions, and prepared to treat even moderate and Union-

285

loving southerners as traitors if they protested. (2) Fiery secessionists like Jefferson Davis (Mississippi), Robert Barnwell Rhett (South Carolina), and Louis T. Wigfall (Texas)—contemptuous of compromise and certain that Clay's plan was simply a disguise for the ambitions of a brutal North. Nothing but a sweeping away of all prohibitions against slavery in the newly acquired territories would satisfy them. (3) Extreme anti-slavery men and radical free-soilers like William H. Seward (New York), Salmon P. Chase and Joshua Giddings (Ohio), and Charles Sumner (Massachusetts), who stood pat on the Wilmot Proviso and appealed to the "Higher Law" above the Constitution. Congress might permit the existence and diffusion of slavery, but in the sight of the "Higher Law"—the law of God—slavery could never be justified.

Each of these statesmen spoke for his respective section. Only Daniel Webster openly broke with his free-soil constituents. On March 7, 1850, he backed his old rival, Henry Clay, and even defended the clause

Daguerreotype of Daniel Webster (about 1851).

that called for stricter enforcement of the Fugitive Slave Law, Massachusetts humanitarians accused Webster of making another bid for the presidency and never forgave him. He had failed, Emerson thought, to stand up "for New England and for man against the bullying and barbarism of the South." John Greenleaf Whittier painted Webster in a powerful poem, "Ichabod," as a fallen and tarnished hero. Walt Whitman linked him with "deformed, mediocre, snivelling, unreliable, false-hearted men" who "insulted" and "betrayed" the country. Theodore Parker, the radical Boston clergyman, could not find words strong enough to show his disapproval of what Webster had done:

When he will do such a deed, it seems to me that there is no such life of crime long enough to prepare a man for such a pitch of depravity; I should think he must have been begotten in sin, and conceived in iniquity . . . that the concentration of the villainy of whole generations of scoundrels would hardly be enough to fit a man for a deed like this!

Webster's stand offended the moral convictions of his section, but he had a truer understanding of the crisis than did his sincere but ill-informed critics. Neither could understand the motives of the other. To Webster the politician, the scruples of reformers like Emerson, Lowell, Thoreau, Longfellow, Bryant, and Parker meant nothing, and he dismissed these men as a noisy minority. But Webster failed to realize that thousands of moderate free-soilers in the northern states shared his critics' revulsion against returning fugitive slaves. By 1850, the moral disapproval of slavery was no longer confined to abolitionists and fanatics.

For the moment, however, Webster's efforts helped to dissipate the clouds of disunion, and other eloquent men carried on the fight until Clay's compromise proposal won out. Stephen A. Douglas was a host by himself. He convinced Congress that the Southwest was unsuitable for slave labor, and whipped the compromise through after the exhausted Clay had been forced to retire. Friends of the compromise had failed to win passage of Clay's "omnibus" proposals in a single package bill, but they succeeded in passing five separate measures that embodied the main features of the original draft. Final passage became certain after President Taylor, unyielding in his opposition, died suddenly early in July, 1850, and was succeeded by the moderate Vice-president, Millard Fillmore. Despite his free-soil sympathies, Fillmore had favored the compro-

their admission to the Union. Slave-trading, but not slavery, was prohibited in the District of Columbia. Finally, an extremely severe fugitive slave law was passed, with many northern congressmen abstaining from the voting.

The nation exulted when news of the compromise became known. Celebrations were held all over the country, politicians

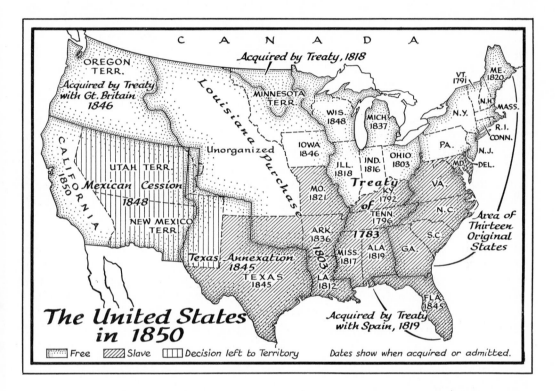

The United States in 1850

☐ Free   ▨ Slave   ▥ Decision left to Territory   *Dates show when acquired or admitted.*

mise all along. As President, he repudiated Seward and the other opponents of the proposal and eased the way for the passage of the acts that collectively became known as the Compromise of 1850.

California entered the Union as a free state, and the western boundary of Texas was fixed where it is today, at the 103rd meridian. Texas received $10 million for giving up her claims to New Mexico. Two new territories, New Mexico and Utah, were created, with the proviso that the question of slavery be left for the people themselves to decide in their constitutions at the time of

forgot old injuries, and talk of secession quieted down. But the respite did not last for long.

The Election of 1852. The results of the 1852 presidential election seemed to reflect a national yearning for sectional tranquillity and moderation. Franklin Pierce, the Democratic candidate, easily defeated his Whig opponent, General Winfield Scott, of Mexican War fame. Pierce carried a total of 27 states and won 254 electoral votes, recording a plurality over Scott of 214,000 votes.

Scott came out ahead in only four states: Massachusetts, Vermont, Kentucky, and Tennessee. The Free Soil party made a far poorer showing than it had four years earlier when disgruntled Whigs and Van Buren Democrats had made it a significant minority party. The "Barnburners" had returned to the fold by 1852.

On the surface, the solid Democratic vote and the decline of the sectional Free Soil party seemed to indicate the triumph of moderation, but the evidence was deceptive. An ominous sign of the trouble ahead was the breaking up of the Whig party, which foreshadowed a greater disruption to come. Whig strength was declining in the South precisely because the party represented a national rather than a sectional outlook. With the deaths of Webster and Clay in 1852, no leader of national stature remained to hold the Whigs together. The Democrats still stood as a great national party, to be sure, but the influx of southern Whigs into the Democratic ranks overweighted the influence of the South on party policy. Although revolution and violence had been temporarily forestalled, the ugly contradictions between North and South had not been resolved. A number of northerners had no intention of abiding by the Fugitive Slave Law, because it offended a "Higher Law." Many southerners were prepared to secede from the Union if the recovery of fugitive slaves was hindered. In both sections there were many intelligent people who neither expected nor wanted the Union to last.

And yet moderates, both in the North and in the South, knew how close the country had come to civil war. During the next decade, they did everything possible to prevent misunderstandings and to cool the ardor of single-minded abolitionists and southern "fire-eaters," as the ardent secessionists were called. For a time, love of the Union, economic prosperity, and the sagacity of party leaders held the nation together, but the sectional rift had widened too far to permit a genuine reconciliation. Even without the slave problem, North and South had much to disagree about. But the issue of slavery made cool and objective arbitration of other sectional differences far more difficult. Whereas thorny issues like the tariff or public lands could be debated and compromised, the slavery issue defied solution. It touched the emotions of too many people too deeply. By 1850, many northerners saw it as a black cloud that obscured the southern landscape; in the South, slavery had become a way of life. It could not be eliminated without disrupting the entire society that sustained it.

Readings

General accounts of Manifest Destiny are available in the diplomatic histories, already cited, by T. A. Bailey, S. F. Bemis, and J. W. Pratt. See also the relevant parts of Bemis, ed., *American Secretaries of State* (10 vols., 1927-1929). The background for this period is thoroughly discussed in R. A. Billington's excellent *Westward Expansion* (1949). Norman A. Graebner has written an important work on the expansionist movement, *Empire on the Pacific* (1955), while Bernard De Voto's *The Year of Decision* (1943) is a fine popular history of the events of 1846. Albert K. Weinberg's *Manifest Destiny* (1935) is comprehensive on American ideas on expansion. Henry Nash Smith, *Virgin Land* (1950), is an imaginative study of Americans' conceptions of the West and its place in their destiny. An excellent recent review of this whole expansionist period may be found in R. A. Billington, *The Far Western Frontier, 1830-1860* (1956).

In addition to Chitwood's life of Tyler, cited in Chapter X, biographical material of value may be found in E. I. McCormac, *James K. Polk* (1922); M. M. Quaife, ed., *The Diary of James K. Polk* (1910); A. C. McLaughlin, *Lewis Cass* (1899); Allan Nevins, *Frémont* (2 vols., 1928), revised as *Frémont: Pathmarker of the West* (1955); R. F. Nichols, *Franklin Pierce* (1931); A. D. H. Smith, *Old Fuss and Feathers* (1937), a life of Winfield Scott; Holman Hamilton's two volumes on Zachary Taylor (1941-1951), or the one-volume study by Brainerd Dyer (1946); and C. B. Going, *David Wilmot, Free Soiler* (1924).

On Texas and the Mexican War, see R. N. Richardson, *Texas, the Lone Star State* (1943); G. L. Rives, *The United States and Mexico, 1821-1848* (2 vols., 1913); J. H. Smith, *The Annexation of Texas* (1911); E. C. Barker, *Mexico and Texas, 1821-1835* (1928); E. D. Adams, *British Interest in Texas* (1910); J. W. Schmitz, *Texan Statecraft* (1941); J. H. Smith, *The War with Mexico* (2 vols., 1919); and J. D. P. Fuller, *The Movement for the Acquisition of All Mexico, 1846-48* (1936). A popular history of the war is A. H. Bill, *Rehearsal for Conflict* (1947).

On Oregon and California, besides works by Graebner, De Voto, and Billington, cited above, see R. G. Cleland, *Early Sentiment for the Annexation of California* (1915); M. C. Jacobs, *Winning Oregon* (1938); J. S. Reeves, *American Diplomacy under Tyler and Polk* (1907); J. W. Caughey, *History of the Pacific Coast* (1933); J. Schafer, *History of the Pacific Northwest* (1905); O. O. Winther, *The Great Northwest* (1947); and Francis Parkman's fascinating *The California and Oregon Trail* (1849), often called *The Oregon Trail*. No effort to understand the Oregon settlement is quite complete without reference to a series of articles by Frederick Merk published in *The American Historical Review* in 1924 and 1932 and in *Agricultural History* in 1934.

On the Mormons, see B. De Voto, cited above, and Nels Anderson, *Desert Saints* (1942); and the two readable biographies of Mormon leaders, M. R. Werner, *Brigham Young* (1925), and Fawn Brodie, *No Man Knows My History: The Life of Joseph Smith* (1945).

On the Compromise of 1850, the biographies, already cited in Chapter X, of Webster, Calhoun, and Clay are helpful. See also George Fort Milton, *The Eve of Conflict: Stephen A. Douglas and the Needless War* (1934); U. B. Phillips, *Life of Robert Toombs* (1913); R. H. Shryock, *Georgia and the Union in 1850* (1926); J. T. Carpenter, *The South as a Conscious Minority* (1930); and A. J. Beveridge, *Abraham Lincoln* (1928), Vol. II. There is a good general account in Channing's *History*, Vol. VI, and a masterful discussion by Allan Nevins in *Ordeal of the Union*, Vol. I, chapters 8-10.

THE
SOUTHERN
NATION

C H A P T E R   T H I R T E E N

o many northerners in the years just before the Civil War, the South was a barbaric kingdom where (as Richard Hildreth, a New England historian, expressed it) "aristocracies of the sternest and most odious kind" ruled over battalions of black slaves and kept millions of debased landless whites in economic and political subservience. This image of Dixie, perpetuated by later historians, appeared in abolitionist tracts, but even allegedly impartial observers like the English economist, J. E. Cairnes, reduced slave society to "the slaves on whom devolves all the regular industry, the slaveholders who reap all its fruits, and an idle and lawless rabble who live dispersed over vast plains in a condition little removed from absolute barbarism." Recent historians, how-

290

ever, have shown that southern society had a far more complicated social structure than these loose classifications indicate. Most authorities generally agree that the average southerner was neither the patrician nor the "poor white," but the small-propertied in-

dependent yeoman who worked his land more often than not without the assistance of slaves, or labored side by side with one or two of them.

I. DIXIE: THE PEOPLE AND THEIR WAY OF LIFE

The People.   Since the yeoman farmer was not as picturesque or as articulate as the southern gentry, he has received less attention than the planters, whose baronial mode of life has been elaborately though sometimes inaccurately recorded. But our view of the prewar South would be seriously distorted if we did not take into account the millions of "plain folk" (as the historian Frank L. Owsley refers to them) who made up the bulk of the small slaveholding and non-slaveholding farmers. From this substantial group came mechanics, storekeepers, overseers, and hired laborers, but most of them made their living from growing a variety of subsistence crops (grains and cereals, sweet potatoes, sorghum cane) and from raising livestock. Yeoman whites could be found tending farms adjacent to the large plantations in the cotton and tobacco country, but they predominated in the upland South—in eastern Tennessee, western North Carolina, northern Georgia, Alabama, and Mississippi, and in the sandy coastal areas.

Seen through the candid but critical eyes of Frederick Law Olmsted, who traveled through the southern hinterlands in the early 1850's, the living standards of the yeoman whites seemed distinctly low when compared with those of northern farmers. And yet, though Olmsted complained of wretched cookery, vermin-filled beds, and rude manners, he also noted that white farmers worked alongside their Negro field hands, and in general he presented a picture of a sturdy, proud, and friendly people. "If you want to fare well in this country," he was told in northern Alabama, "you stop to poor folks' housen; they try to enjoy what they've got while they ken, but these yer big

planters they don' care for nothing but to save." Riding through an area of thin sandy soil, Olmsted reported that it was

. . . thickly populated by poor farmers. Negroes are rare, but occasionally neat, new houses, with other improvements, show the increasing prosperity of the district. The majority of dwellings are small log cabins of one room, with another separate cabin for a kitchen; each house has a well, and a garden enclosed with palings. Cows, goats, mules and swine, fowls and doves are abundant. The people are more social than those of the lower country, falling readily into friendly conversation. . . . They are very ignorant; the agriculture is wretched and the work hard. I have seen three white women hoeing field crops to-day. A spinning-wheel is heard in every house . . . every one wears homespun. The negroes have much more individual freedom than in the rich cotton country, and are not infrequently heard singing or whistling at their work.

The Way of Life.   Even ardent secessionists admitted that the South lagged behind the North industrially and commercially. Statistics on land values, education, illiteracy, immigration, and newspapers suggested that the South was backward in almost every other category as well. Travelers from the North or abroad usually contrasted the well-tended villages and cities of the free states with the untidy, rude look of the slaveholding South. Southerners had two responses to such criticisms: either they attributed the South's backwardness to northern chicanery, or else they defended the southern way of life as something uniquely good that could not be measured by the values of Yankee hucksters.

Southern society was more homogeneous than northern, more settled and conservative in its way, and less exposed to the social and intellectual agitation that kept the North in a perpetual ferment. To the novelist, John De Forest, who lived with the "Southrons" immediately after the war, they seemed as different from the people in New England as the Spartans were from the Athenians. "They are more simple than us," he wrote, "more provincial, more antique, more picturesque; they have fewer of the virtues of modern society, and more of the primitive, the natural virtues; they care less for wealth, art, learning, and the other delicacies; they care more for individual character and reputation of honor." De Forest's remarks about simplicity applied less to the tiny fraction of planter grandees or the "poor whites" than to the substantial yeomanry of small farmers and middling planters who, as we have seen, made up most of the white population in the South. For these people, life was much the same in both the older and the newer regions. Social activities centered around the church, the plantation, the county court, the market towns, and the village taverns. Life seemed slower and more stable than in the North, and the atmosphere of the frontier lingered longer.

The southerners were an outdoor people. Their everyday pursuits and amusements placed a premium upon the manly virtues and accounted for the fighting qualities the southern troops demonstrated so effectively during the Civil War. Before secession, De Forest declared, "Southerners were, in a sense, already veterans." The South was an area of expert marksmen, bold horsemen, formidable brawlers, and relentless duelists. The violence of southern life has no doubt been exaggerated, but the "Arkansas toothpick" (as the Bowie knife was sometimes called) was one of the principal instruments for settling differences in the rougher sections. Even in the older and more settled regions the code of honor prevailed.

The history of the Tillmans, a South Carolina family, is a saga of violence. Benjamin Ryan Tillman, the first, was an indus-trious but lawless planter who gambled as hard as he worked, killed a man in 1847, and died of typhoid fever two years later, aged 46. His wife, Sophia—a commanding, efficient, practical southern matron, niggardly and sagacious—bore him three daughters and seven sons. Thomas, the oldest son, was killed in the Mexican War. The second, George Dionysius Tillman, might have served as the hero of a Faulkner novel. (Faulkner speaks of the "glamorous fatality" of southern names.) This erratic and intelligent young man spent a year at Harvard, read law, and served in the state legislature. On two separate occasions, he fought and wounded his opponent; shortly after, he killed a third man during a card game. George fled the country, filibustered in Cuba, and returned in 1858, repentant, to spend two luxurious years in the local jail. Another son, handsome and ill-tempered, was killed by two brothers whose family he had insulted, and still another son was slain over some domestic quarrel.

Despite such occasional violence in the South, travelers found the people hospitable and friendly. Social intercourse was conducted more ceremoniously than in the North—especially among the well-to-do—but the yeomanry everywhere exhibited an engaging neighborliness and sociability.

The life of the slave-owning squirearchy was scarcely more complicated than the existence the yeomanry led. A very few of the gentry lived extravagantly, but most of them, especially in the older states, experienced the cares that went with ownership of property and had little time to enjoy anything more than the simple pleasures of rustic society. Hunting, horse-racing, card-playing, visiting, and perhaps an annual summer pilgrimage to the mountains or the sea to escape the heat, pretty well exhausted their recreations.

What one southern writer, John Pendleton Kennedy, referred to as "the mellow, bland, and sunny luxuriance" of old-time Virginia society is delineated in the pages of his own *Swallow Barn, or a Sojourn in the Old Dominion* (1832), and in Susan

Dabney Smedes' charming account of her father, Thomas S. G. Dabney of Virginia and Mississippi, the *beau ideal* of the southern planter. Humane, upright, generous, and courteous, such hard-working and practical gentlemen as Dabney had little in common with the fire-breathing "Southrons" and self-designated "Cavaliers" who appear in the romances of William Alexander Caruthers and Nathaniel Beverley Tucker. Sick slaves, the price of cotton, and unreliable overseers were subjects too unliterary for southern romancers. For an authentic picture of plantation society, we must turn to the plantation diaries and account books, with their records of the hazards, anxieties, and disappointments that plagued the gentleman farmer. It was not julep-drinking and amiable dissipation that toughened the southern temper but harsh and crushing responsibility. "Managing a plantation," as Mrs. Smedes observed, "was something like managing a kingdom. The ruler had need of great store, not only of wisdom, but of tact and patience as well." Nor was the planter's wife exempt from irksome domestic duties.

II. AGRICULTURE AND SLAVERY

Agriculture. Among other reasons, slavery took root in the South because African Negroes provided a cheap and available labor force to grow the staple crops. Introduced in the early years of the seventeenth century, slavery had become a permanent institution by the time Congress closed the slave trade in 1808. At that time, about 1 million slaves were owned in the United States. Others were subsequently smuggled in, but most of the slaves who were transported to the newly opened lands in the Southwest came from slave populations already established in the older states of Virginia, Maryland, North and South Carolina, and Georgia. By 1820 the total number of slaves in the United States had risen to 1,538,000. Thirty years later, there were 3,204,000, and on the eve of the Civil War there were about 3,953,000.

The slave population in the ante-bellum South was not evenly distributed. In the upland country that was unsuited for staple crops, like the southern hill country and the Ozarks, slaves were a rarity. But they were numerous in areas that were better suited to the plantation method of crop production: in the rice flats along the coastal areas of South Carolina and Georgia; in the sugar fields of Louisiana and Texas; and in the cotton plantations of the middle and lower South. The heaviest concentration of Negroes after 1850 was in sections of Virginia, South Carolina, and Kentucky, and in the rich belts of farmland in Alabama, Mississippi, and Louisiana. In some counties and parishes, slaves made up two-thirds of the total population. According to the 1850 census, one-third of the people residing in the 15 states of the South were Negroes.

Slaves were employed extensively in the Virginia and Maryland tidewater tobacco fields until about 1800. Then, because of soil exhaustion and erosion in the tidewater, tobacco culture spread into the Piedmont and thence westward across the upper South. Before mid-century, this newer area of the South was producing more tobacco than the old. Tobacco plantations were ordinarily smaller than rice, cotton, or sugar plantations; in fact, many of them were simply farms of about 5 acres with few slaves or none at all. Although tobacco production required the most painstaking supervision, most observers agree that slavery took a milder form in the tobacco states than it did in the lower South.

Crops like tobacco and hemp, which were confined almost entirely to the upper South between 1820 and 1860, did not require large cash outlays and could be grown with a modest labor force. Rice and sugar, on the other hand, were produced on large "agricultural factories" manned by gangs of slaves. Rice-growing was limited to relatively small

Rice culture, near Savannah, Georgia.

areas in South Carolina, Georgia, Louisiana, Texas, and Arkansas. Only rich planters could afford the heavy capital expenditures that were required in growing and harvesting the crop. The same was true of sugar. Only the owners of the large plantations in the rich delta lands of Louisiana and to a lesser extent in the alluvial soils of southeastern Texas and coastal Georgia could afford the costs of sugar-milling equipment. They were able to compete with the more favorably situated West Indian producers only because of the high tariff duties on imported sugar.

But it was the cotton plantations that absorbed the greatest number of slaves in the ante-bellum South. By 1835, cotton culture had spread from the Atlantic seaboard states into the Gulf states, and had superseded rice and tobacco as the chief staple crop. As early as 1820, the cotton crop was more valuable than all the other southern crops combined. Since it required little capital, a small acreage, and few slaves to make a profit, cotton-growing promised high rewards to the lucky and the efficient.

Untrained labor easily mastered its operations, and the demand for Negroes increased as the new western lands were converted to cotton plantations.

By 1850, the Gulf area had become the greatest cotton-growing region in the world. And here it was that the slave system could be studied in its most mature form. Labor on plantations of from 1,000 to 2,000 acres (the most efficient size) was reduced to a series of routine operations with the slaves divided into plow and hoe gangs under the direction of "drivers" and "overseers." Relations between master and slave were of necessity more impersonal on the large plantations than on the smaller ones, and discipline was more strict. The well-run plantation "factories," which often became self-sufficient units producing corn, peanuts, and livestock in addition to cotton, were serviced by a corps of slave carpenters, shoemakers, masons, and weavers. Necessities that could not be provided by the plantation were purchased at wholesale prices. Large-scale agriculture made it easier for the big planter to market his staple crops and enabled him to practice other economies that were denied to the small farmer. Wealthier planters, moreover, were more likely to be interested in conserving the soil, more willing to experiment with new techniques in fertilizing, plowing, and crop rotation.

Slavery. The enormous literature about slavery, and the welter of northern and southern myths and counter-myths, make it difficult to get an objective look at that institution as it existed in the ante-bellum South between 1820 and 1860. Northern abolitionists painted its iniquities in the most lurid colors, holding up the plantation as part concentration camp and part seraglio. Equally distorted was the southerners' idyllic vision of the plantation where innocent slaves, untroubled by the anxieties that weighed down the northern wage-slave, labored happily in the fields for "dear old Massa."

Attempts to defend the "peculiar institution" (a contemporary term used in referring to slavery) as a good in itself were not impressive. Its very existence mocked the republican principles that American orators proclaimed to benighted Europe. But slavery was one of those historical accidents for which no single person or group can be blamed.

What were the facts? First, there is the question of who the slave-owners were. A decade before the Civil War, the white population of the South was 6,184,477, of whom some 347,525 were listed as slave-owners. This group, together with their families, probably included less than one-third of the southern whites. In 1860, the number of slave-owning families had declined to about one-fourth of the total white population.

Among this minority of slave-owners, moreover, only a few had more than ten slaves, and most owned less than five. In 1850, for example, approximately 8,000 people owned 50 or more slaves, 254 owned

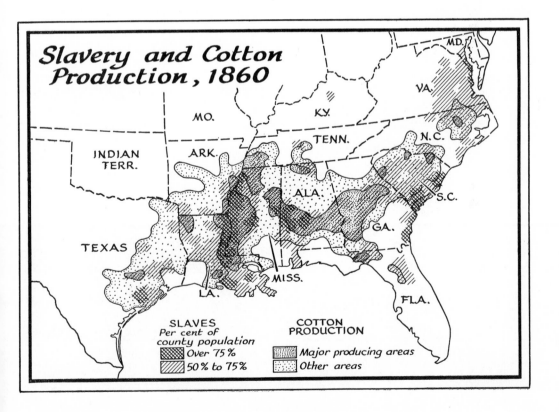

Slavery and Cotton Production, 1860

SLAVES
Per cent of county population
Over 75%
50% to 75%

COTTON PRODUCTION
Major producing areas
Other areas

200 or more, and only 11 in the entire South owned 500 or more. The cotton nabobs, whose vast plantations and splendid mansions have featured so magnificently in post-war romances, never amounted to more than 1 per cent of the white population. The small planters, who had from 1 to 20 slaves, and who lived at best in crude simplicity, made up 23 per cent. Yeoman farmers, with no slaves at all, composed the remaining 76 per cent.

Despite this unequal ownership and the negligible number of slaves in certain regions of the upper South, the vast majority of southerners after 1830 would not consent to the abolition of slavery. Their reasons varied according to class, region, and occupation.

1. The heavy concentration of Negro slaves in the South created a serious problem in race-relations. Anti-slavery northerners living in states where Negroes comprised only a tiny fraction of the population had no inkling of what it was like to live in South Carolina or Mississippi where Negroes out-numbered whites. The total Negro population of the 16 free states in 1850 was under 200,000. In 1860, each of five southern states had twice that number of Negroes.

2. It was a common belief in the pre-war South that the Negro would only be harmed by being given his freedom. And this conclusion was strengthened by reports about the condition of free Negroes in the North. Everywhere in the free-soil states, even in the centers of abolition, Negroes were abused and discriminated against politically, economically, and socially, and some northern states even refused to admit them across state lines. In the South, free Negroes were often worse off, especially after the growing fear of slave insurrections made them objects of suspicion.

3. White workers in southern cities, like most northern workingmen, did not want to see slavery abolished. Negro competition, whether slave or free, threatened their security, and they often refused to work with Negroes, who underbid them and lowered their social status. Race prejudice was particularly strong among immigrant groups, like the Irish, who performed menial jobs

Negro quarters, South Carolina plantation, 1862.

Sorting cotton in South Carolina, 1862.

too dangerous for high-priced slaves. In general, white workers opposed any steps to improve the Negro's lot.

4. Small planters, linked to the gentry either by kinship ties or by common interest, felt that their chances of rising in the world would be jeopardized by abolition. They and many of the yeoman farmers, who were too poor to own any slaves, looked forward to the time when they would be masters of a larger plantation. Hence, anti-abolition sentiment was strong in many areas where the slave population was small.

5. Finally, a small body of impoverished southern whites, disease-ridden and shiftless, fanatically supported slavery as a way of preserving what little status they had. "They are said," wrote the northern observer, Frederick Law Olmsted, "to 'corrupt' the negroes, and to encourage them to steal, or to work for them at night and on Sundays, and to pay them with liquor, and to constantly associate licentiously with them. They seem, nevertheless, more than any other portion of the community, to hate and despise the negroes." In turn, these "crackers"

or "sand hillers" were despised by gentry and Negroes alike. But when the time came, the "poor whites" fought for slave property they did not own, and for a class that looked upon them with contempt.

The Slave's World. It is risky to generalize about the lot of the Negro in the ante-bellum South, because it depended upon so many factors: age and sex and the nature of his employment; the region in which he worked; the size of the farm or plantation or town in which he lived; the character and disposition of his master; and his own temper and personality. Undoubtedly the conditions on some of the rice plantations, situated in malarial districts and managed by overseers for absentee owners, were inhumane. In general, the slaves on the cotton and sugar plantations in the lower South were more harshly treated than their fellows further north, but there is abundant testimony to show that the cruel master was the exception—not the rule. It was the southern refusal to educate the Negro, to

297

develop his potentialities and to acknowledge his manhood, that seems most regrettable in retrospect.

Abolitionists sometimes exaggerated the brutalities of slavery, but they did not have to invent stories of whippings, brandings, mutilations, and murder. The custom of flogging recalcitrant Negroes was widespread. Some planters set their dogs on runaway slaves, and hundreds of authentic records testify to the brutal retaliation that was meted out to Negroes who struck white men or who committed misdemeanors. Some were burned alive; others were starved, shot, or hanged. Slave-owners who killed their slaves often escaped punishment, for Negroes had no rights in court.

The claim that Negro slaves were contented, that their happy-go-lucky temperament enabled them to adjust to their menial position, and that they did not respond to slavery as white men would have done is contradicted by documented evidence. They tried and sometimes succeeded in buying their freedom. Failing this, they ran away from their masters or resorted to a variety of devices—feigned sickness, self-mutilation, simple loafing, and sometimes outright rebellion—to escape forced servitude. Slave revolts always remained a possibility in the ante-bellum period. One serious conspiracy of slaves—organized by a free Negro, Denmark Vesey, in Charleston, South Carolina —was crushed in 1822. In 1831, a vision-inspired Negro preacher, Nat Turner, led an abortive but bloody slave insurrection in Southampton County, Virginia, in which 57 whites and about 100 Negroes were killed.

The abolitionists did not err, then, in reporting harrowing anecdotes of broken slave families, the horrors of the slave marts, the lax marriage arrangements between slaves that were encouraged by the slave-owner, and other ugly features of the system. But they often passed over the difficulties of the planter's position. Obviously, it was to the interest of the slaveholder to protect his human property against bar-barous punishment and excessive work. Since it required the nicest judgment to maintain a balance between laxness and severity in the management of the slaves, the best of masters had to apply methods of discipline that might be offensive to his own inclinations. Given the plantation system, he had to rely on the assistance of overseers, who often could produce a profitable crop only by driving the slaves and ignoring the owner's admonitions. The kindliest slaveholder, either as a buyer or seller, was sometimes forced to break up Negro families. In short, the slaveholder was frequently victimized by the system.

But there is a brighter side of the picture. Even some of the anti-slavery men acknowledged that ordinarily the slaves were adequately housed, clothed, and fed. The slave's diet of pork, corn-meal, molasses, and greens was coarse and monotonous, and the slave quarters were unhygienic by modern standards. But the poor-white farmers lived no better. Slaves worked no longer than many northern agricultural and industrial laborers and, in areas where the "task" system was employed, a slave might complete his assigned chores by early afternoon and spend the rest of the day as he chose. Progressive planters encouraged their slaves to cultivate truck gardens and to keep pigs and chickens for their own use or to sell. Incentive payments, holidays, and entertainments alleviated the drudgery on some plantations, and where the work became too exacting the slaves developed their own slow-down techniques. House-servants found life much easier than field hands, and some gifted slaves were rewarded with positions of trust and responsibility. It seems true enough that many white southerners treated their slaves affectionately and that many slaves responded to this treatment with loyalty and devotion.

The Rewards and Costs of Slavery.
Many southerners felt that their failure to develop manufactures was more than made up for by

the profits of slavery. In addition to being a benevolent social institution, slavery, they argued, also paid dividends; and the splendid incomes enjoyed by successful planters seemed to prove it.

But in both North and South before 1860, men questioned whether slavery was really financially profitable and predicted its peaceful disappearance if the hotheads would only forget about it. Others were just as sure that slavery was economically sound, and the debate still continues today. It is not a simple bookkeeping problem, since many aspects of slavery cannot be measured accurately in dollars and cents.

On the debit side, the risks of managing a plantation were numerous and often fatal. Natural blights and disasters, slave mortality, and the maintenance of the aged and the young cut down profits. To make matters worse, the cost of Negroes soared in the 40's and 50's. Where a male field hand had sold for about $300 in the 1790's, the price had jumped to $1,000 in 1840 and to $1,200 or more by 1860. The planter necessarily found that a heavy proportion of his capital was tied up in the inelastic property of slaves.

A truly successful plantation was the exception. Only the most fertile and skillfully managed were consistently profitable, and often intelligence and solicitude for the welfare of the Negro slaves were not enough to make plantations successful. Lacking incentive, the ordinary slave was an inefficient worker and a constant source of worry to his master. The situation of Senator James H. Hammond of South Carolina was not unusual. After years of planning and experimenting, in 1857 this conscientious planter moodily reflected on the probable outcome of his life's work.

I must sell everything that can be sold. The slaves who for all my life have been my associates, friends, and faithful co-laborers. Every tie with them must be broken, for no one will perpetuate them as I had fondly hoped. I must let my marled and drained lands, the true labour of my life, go to ruin.

This dismal view of plantation slavery has been contradicted by other observers who believe that the hazards of the system were more than offset by its advantages over free labor, and who deny that slavery must bear the responsibility for all the ills of southern agriculture. Much of the soil exhaustion, they say, was only indirectly connected with slavery; it was primarily the result of ignorance and short-sightedness. Scientific husbandry was perfectly possible in a slave society, as was shown in the 1850's when

A slave auction in Virginia.

worn-out lands in Virginia and Maryland were restored. As early as 1833, Edmund Ruffin—the South's greatest expert on soil chemistry before the war—showed his countrymen how corn and wheat yields could be substantially increased by neutralizing acid soil with fertilizer.

Would slavery have persisted after the lands suitable for staple crops had been used up? Many southern and northern men in ante-bellum America believed that nature confined it to a restricted area and that slavery would not outlast the century. It has been argued since, however, that the expansion of the railroads would have brought fresh lands into easy reach of the migrating planter, and that industry might well have absorbed the surplus slave population. A good number of slaves were already working in tobacco processing, in Virginia iron works, in other industries, and in railroading before 1860. Hence it has been argued that slavery was not a dying institution.

Profitable as slavery was to some individual planters, it was socially disastrous for the South. "It may seem a paradox, and yet it is true," declared a North Carolinian in 1853, "that a community of planters may grow rich while they are impoverishing and depopulating their country." Slavery discouraged diversity in agriculture, accelerated the flow of southern yeomanry to the free-soil states, and created an illusory prosperity. The tremendous profits made possible by exploiting virgin soils and by the demand for cotton never returned to the community in the forms of internal improvements or banks or factories. Instead, the planters plowed back their profits into more land and additional slaves.

Finally, there were the human costs. For the Negro, the physical and psychic injuries that resulted from his enforced servitude were obviously immense, but the penalties that slavery imposed upon the whites were almost as disastrous. Although slavery was not the only explanation for the existence of "poor whites" in the South, it produced social conditions that helped to account for their degradation. Their illiteracy, their disdain for manual labor, and their prejudices were in large measure the result of slavery. This was the conclusion of one bitter southerner, Hinton Rowan Helper, whose sensational and propagandistic book, *The Impending Crisis of the South: How to Meet It* (1857), made slavery "the root of all the shame, poverty, ignorance, tyranny and imbecility of the South." Although his widely publicized analysis—abusive and violent—grossly distorted the southern picture, it contained some uncomfortable truths that were hardly answered by calling its author a "miserable renegade."

III. THE SOUTHERN ECONOMY

The South lagged behind the North economically and culturally for some reasons that had nothing to do with slavery. The North had a more invigorating climate, a balanced agriculture, richer natural resources, and better harbors. Slavery kept white immigrants out of the South and lowered the dignity of manual labor, but it is hardly likely that the predominantly agricultural economy of the South would have been different, slavery or no slavery. Devoted to the plantation life, southerners as a rule failed to develop the business skills needed to market their crops advantageously.

The planter relied upon commission merchants, or "factors," to sell his crops. These factors, who resided in port cities or in interior market towns, shipped the produce northward or directly to Europe for a commission. They also sold supplies to the planter, advised him when to sell his crop, bought slaves for him, and performed personal services. Frequently, the planter fell so deeply in debt to his factors that they could dictate the kind of crop they wanted consigned to them for payment. The factor system therefore increased the concentration on cotton, since this was the safest cash crop, and restricted the most lucrative commercial activity to the seaboard cities and to a few interior entrepôts like Memphis. A good many of the factors were New Englanders, backed by New York capital. They were often criticized by the planters for charging high brokerage fees (up to 2½ per cent for selling a crop and from 2½ to 10 per cent for buying supplies). A more valid reason for the planters' constant indebtedness was the business organization that permitted New York commercial interests to tap the profits from southern exports.

The South lost heavily because of its disdain for commerce and its business backwardness, whereas New York profited enormously. Cotton enriched the northern ports, and by 1852 it was sustaining over a million tons of trans-Atlantic shipping. Some 40,000 American seamen were employed in the cotton trade, and it created a variety of specialized occupations for northern labor. By the time the South became aware of its negligence in the 1830's, New York had perfected a trading system that continued to flourish until 1860, despite southern attempts to break it.

Bad transportation, inadequate banking facilities, and unstable marketing conditions were in part the products of the South's predominantly agrarian economy. They were the penalties inflicted upon a people who measured success in terms of land and slaves rather than in terms of industrial growth and the arts of trade. Before the Revolution and the rise of the northern factory system, the South had engaged in household manufacturing. The section possessed the water power, the raw materials, and the white labor to develop its industries after 1800. But as the cultivation of staple crops became the chief occupation below the Mason and Dixon line, the advocates of manufacturing in the South ran into a wall of inertia.

Southerners were perfectly familiar with the invidious contrasts drawn by their own representatives between the busy, contented North—enterprising, public-spirited, pros-

perous—and the indolent, poverty-stricken southern country. Many of them nevertheless feared the effects of introducing factories into an agrarian slave society and harbored the old distrust for cities that Jefferson had expressed so vividly in his *Notes on Virginia.* Would not an unstable white proletariat in the South plant a dangerous anti-slavery element in the heart of a slave society?

Other practical obstacles also stood in the way of southern manufacturing. The surplus capital that did not end up in the pockets of northern middlemen was usually plowed back into land and slaves. And then there was the question of who would man the factories even if they were constructed. Southern whites preferred farm work to factory employment, and prejudice against recruiting Negroes for industry was as widespread as it was illogical. Some felt (although there was evidence in some southern factories to the contrary) that a Negro working in a factory was already half-free; others believed that Negroes were not capable of mastering machinery.

In spite of all these doubts and apprehensions, the apathy toward manufacturing began to decline during the 1820's and 1830's when the controversies over the tariff made the South acutely conscious of its dependence on northern industry. Groups of Georgians and Virginians petitioned their legislators to encourage cotton manufacturing, and the planters were invited to throw off their "degrading vassalage" to the North, to build their own factories, to employ the hitherto unproductive poor whites, and to restore the glory of their section by keeping southern wealth in the South. As one enthusiast expressed it:

How different will be the aspect of things in the whole South, when this tide of wealth is dammed up within our own borders, and made to roll back among our own people; and when our immense capital is employed by our own merchants in establishing a direct trade between our own Southern ports and our customers all over the world. ... The arts will revive, manufactures will spring up around us; our agriculture will rear its drooping head, our commerce will expand, mechanic labor, meeting with ample rewards will pour in upon us, and emigration [*sic*], no longer discouraged by the uninviting aspect of our country will flock to our shores.

Not until the 1840's, however, did the arguments for building up southern manufactures begin to take hold. This decade was a time of falling cotton prices and economic stagnation in the South Atlantic states, and the people were in the mood to listen to a thoughtful Charleston businessman, William Gregg. His *Essays on Domestic Industry* (1845)—written after a tour of the New England mills—pointed the way to an economic and moral rehabilitation of the poor whites through industrial employment. Gregg's proposals, embodied in his own model factories run along the lines of the Lowell plan (see p. 208), contained nothing offensive to southern prejudices. Gregg did not advocate the use of slave labor for manufacturing. He did not demand tariff protection, since the coarse variety of cotton cloth produced in the South did not compete with foreign textiles. His program was applauded by the growing number of nationalists (already looking ahead to southern independence) who wanted a strongly industrialized South when the great day came. Another influential group backed the industrial program for precisely the opposite reasons; they hoped that factories would make the South prosperous and that prosperity would remove the chief cause of sectional animosity.

Once industrial pioneers like William Gregg had demonstrated that cotton mills in the South could be made to pay, textile manufactures increased rapidly between 1845 and 1860; but the operators faced many hazards. Southern mills had to contend with falling prices for finished cotton goods, labor problems, fierce Yankee competition, and a dearth of surplus capital. Between 1850 and 1860, the number of industrial workers in the South increased only from 164,000 to 189,000. On the eve of the Civil War, the South was producing less than 10 per cent of the nation's manufactured goods. In 1860, the Lowell mills alone operated more spindles than the combined factories of the South.

Although textiles, the iron industry, tobacco manufacturing, flour milling, and lumbering made headway in the ante-bellum South, manufacturing remained wholly subordinate to agriculture and commerce. Efforts to revive the southern carrying trade fared little better than the promotion of factories. At the numerous commercial conventions held between 1830 and 1860, the southern imagination was fired with rhetorical visions of teeming cities, happy artisans, and bustling marts. But the steamship lines that were to provide direct communication with Europe, the railroads that were to tap the western markets, the trade that was to spring up with South America, and the cotton factories that were to turn New England into a desert, rarely got beyond the planning stage.

IV. THE MIND OF THE SOUTH

Culture. The ante-bellum South produced some admirable types, but opinions have differed widely over the range and depth of its culture. Measured by conventional standards —illiteracy rates, public schools, museums, the fine arts, and publishing—the South lagged behind the North. To the Bostonian, Henry Adams, the southerners he met at Harvard between 1854 and 1858 seemed incredibly archaic, sunk in a simplicity beyond the comprehension of the most unsophisticated New England student.

Adams' sweeping provincial generalization was belied by history. Calhoun, a brilliant though somewhat doctrinaire analyst, was one of a number of acute thinkers in the South who reasoned only too well. But the claim of impassioned pro-slavery men that the South had erected a superior culture on a slave base was no less mistaken. Intellectual novelties were not welcomed in the South, and the arts got little encouragement; old ways and old ideas retained their hold longer in this agrarian society, and intellectual pursuits were largely confined to an upper-class minority. There was no counterpart, for example, of the educated New England rustic or the self-taught Yankee artisan, and little reverence for education. An agricultural people was more likely to produce soldiers, orators, and politicians than artists and poets.

The Reform Spirit. The Puritanical temper of the old South discouraged liberal and transcendental religious speculation as well as the yeasty fads and visionary doctrines that flourished in the North. So-called "Northern fanaticism" (much exaggerated by fiery southern patriots) could not take root in a society where both clergy and press remained constantly alert to "socialism, or to social equality, nihilism, communism, or to infidelity in any of its shapes or shades." Because few European immigrants settled in the South, alien ideas usually came by way of the North. In the southern mind, all "isms" were tinged with abolitionism—feminism, transcendentalism, Fourierism, and the rest. And there were good reasons for this belief. Before abolitionism absorbed all their energies, northern reformers like Garrison, Theodore Parker, Theodore Weld, and Horace Greeley were interested in temperance reform, world peace, women's rights, socialism, farm-labor schools, and mutual benefit societies. But the South spurned extravagant reforms of all kinds. Feminism outraged the southern ideal of womanhood. Experiments like Frances Wright's plantation in Nashoba, Tennessee, where Negroes and whites were to live happily together, failed completely. Some southern mavericks—notably the aristocratic Grimké sisters, Angelina and Sarah, of Charleston—turned abolitionist or succumbed to other enthusiasms, but they were the exceptions.

Yet the repudiation of Yankee cranks and panaceas did not mean that the South was immune to the humanitarian influences that touched most Americans in the 30's and 40's. The rise of evangelical religion was accompanied by a concerted effort to check frontier brutalities and to discipline breaches of moral conduct. In the South, as elsewhere, criminal codes were humanized, prison reforms were introduced, and improvements were made in the treatment of the insane. Dorothea L. Dix was one Yankee reformer whom the South loved and cherished. Her visit to Tennessee and North Carolina in 1847-1848 brought immediate action, and the asylum that was opened in Raleigh, North Carolina, in 1853 bore her name. During the same period, schools for the deaf and dumb patterned after northern models were established in a number of southern states. Perhaps the most enthusiastically supported reform movement in the pre-war South was the temperance cause. Backed by religious and political leaders, temperance societies sprang up everywhere to the accompaniment of parades and petitions and the publicized testimony of reformed drunkards.

Anti-Slavery Sentiment. Until the antislavery crusade in the North gathered momentum in the early 1830's, a number of southerners criticized slavery or apologized for it, and looked forward to its ultimate extinction. Many years before slavery aroused the humanitarian zeal of the North, southern men and women who knew slavery at first hand had listed its baneful effects on the whites. In the eighteenth century, William Byrd II complained that slaves by their very presence "blow up the pride and ruin the industry of the white people, who seeing a rank of poor creatures below them, detest work for fear it should then make them look like slaves." During the Revolutionary period, southern leaders like Washington, Jefferson, Madison, and Henry were well aware of the incongruity of slavery in a republic dedicated to the principles of the Declaration of Independence. The declining value of tobacco lands and the surplus of Negroes in the upper

South probably heightened the readiness of these men to consider abandoning slavery.

As late as 1817, southerners dominated the American Colonization Society, which was headed by George Washington's nephew. In Virginia, abolition was seriously argued in 1829, when a new state constitution was being drafted, and again in the legislature of 1831-1832. The second debate followed on the heels of Nat Turner's insurrection. The anti-slavery group not only played up the constant threat of slave revolts but also raised many of the arguments against slavery that northern abolitionists were later to use: that slavery was wedded to the destructive one-crop system so injurious to the land, that the presence of slaves discouraged immigration to the South, that slavery kept the South poor. "Wherefore, then, object to slavery?" asked one of the delegates in 1832. "Because it is ruinous to the whites, retards improvements, roots out an industrious population—banishes the yeomanry of the country—deprives the spinner, the weaver, the smith, the shoemaker, the carpenter, of employment and support."

The Defense of Slavery.

During the 1830's, the pro-slavery forces in the South launched their counterattack first against the southerners opposed to slavery and then against the northern emancipationists. They sought to prove that slavery was not cruel and immoral, that it enriched rather than impoverished the South, and that it provided the base for a superior culture.

In order to correct abolitionist distortions and present slavery as an idyllic and humane institution, they felt obliged to combat the popular dissatisfaction with slavery as a system and to demonstrate that it was sanctioned by religion, political economy, science, and culture. They had to justify slavery constitutionally and show that it fostered a genuine and classical form of democracy as distinct from the "mongrelized" industrial democracy of the North. Southern professors, ministers,

jurists, scientists, and journalists provided the intellectual ammunition for the pro-slavery attitude.

A spate of books and pamphlets was written to prove that the Bible authorized slavery, that the Negro belonged to a degraded race, that he was physiologically as well as morally inferior to whites, that men were not born free and equal, and that talk about inalienable rights was so much nonsense. George Fitzhugh's *Sociology for the South; or, The Failure of Free Society* (1854) and *Cannibals All! or, Slaves Without Masters* (1857) managed to include most of the familiar arguments of the day.

The slave system, as it appeared in Fitzhugh's artful descriptions, was a kind of benevolent socialism. In the South, he claimed, capital and labor were not divorced. The fierce exploitation of one class by another, which characterized the cruel and cannibalistic laissez-faire economy of the North, was blessedly absent. He contrasted the hideous conditions in northern and British industrial cities and the miseries of the white slave or "hireling" with the blissful life of the plantation Negro, nurtured and guarded from cradle to grave. Northern capitalism, he declared, led to the impoverishment of the masses and to revolution. No such danger threatened the South. Here was a stable society, resting upon a slave base, a "mud sill," * to quote a current phrase. All whites were socially equal, and the leisure class confined themselves to the tasks of government and to culture. Fitzhugh even called upon northern conservatives to accept slavery as a fact, to join with the slaveholders in their efforts to maintain a stratified society, and to repress the social upheavals in the free states that Fitzhugh attributed directly to unregulated capitalism.

Although Fitzhugh's extreme views were not typical, his exuberant and irresponsible

---

* "The lowest sill or timber of a structure as a house or bridge." Thus, according to Senator James H. Hammond of South Carolina: "In all social systems there must be a class to do the mean duties, to perform the drudgery of life . . . such a class . . . constitutes the very mud-sill of society and of political government."

pronouncements made an impression in the North and fostered misunderstanding. Everyone's attention focused on slavery, some seeing it as a curse and some as a blessing, but other problems that were just as important in understanding the ills and promise of the South were obscured. It was convenient for the northerner to ascribe soil exhaustion, illiteracy, and economic instability to slavery alone, just as it was convenient for the southerner to attribute the social and economic backwardness of his region to greedy northern middlemen and to the high tariffs. Both attitudes grossly oversimplified the southern problems.

Education. The extension of the suffrage raised the threat of an "ignorant and debased" electorate in the South as it did in the North. Public education in the slave states was almost nonexistent, and its advocates faced even greater obstacles than did northern educational reformers. Even a Horace Mann could not have made much headway in the thinly populated rural areas of the South that lacked the necessary wealth or incentive to provide for public schools. Here the rich planters resisted taxation for public schools, and those who would have benefited from free education felt it bore the stigma of charity. Until the 1840's, the private rural elementary ("old-field") schools and academies sufficed for those with the interest and income to attend. There were some 2,700 academies in the South by 1850, over two and one half times the number in New England and 600 more than in the Middle states. But the quality of education in these preparatory schools fell below the standards of northern schools, and only a minority attended them. The rate of illiteracy tells the story. The 1850 census showed that 20 per cent of southern whites were illiterate as against 3 per cent in the Middle states and less than 1 per cent in New England. With the exception of Kentucky and North Carolina (where a state tax provided funds for public schools), public education made little headway in the South.

The state of higher education compared more favorably with the North, but here statistics need qualification. Southern families who could afford it sent their sons to Princeton, Harvard, Yale, and the University of Pennsylvania rather than to their own state universities or to the southern denominational colleges that had multiplied between 1820 and 1860. At the same time, a greater percentage of young men in the South were receiving college training than in the North. In 1840, 2,857 students (a considerable number of them southern) were enrolled in 19 New England colleges, while 6,608 attended 80 southern colleges. Twenty years later, there were 25,882 students in the South out of a white population of 7,400,000. In the North, with 19 million inhabitants, the combined college attendance was 27,408. The University of Virginia, South Carolina College, and for a brief period Transylvania measured up to the standards of the best northern colleges and universities.

As anti-northern sentiment intensified in the 1840's and 1850's, southern leaders made strenuous efforts to throw off the intellectual yoke of the Yankees. Conventions passed resolutions urging that southern youth be educated at home by native teachers, and that textbooks coincide with "the educational wants and the social condition of these States, and the encouragement and support of inventions and discoveries in the arts and sciences, by their citizens." It was particularly galling for southern students to be given biased northern texts. One book, for example, spoke of the upper-class southerner's addiction to drinking and gambling. Another described slavery as "that stain on the human race, which corrupts the master as much as it debases the slave." Such agitation against importing poisonous alien doctrines apparently did not halt the sale of northern books. An organized appeal to preserve southern youth from contamination kept some students at home who normally would have gone north to college, but the campaign did not succeed very well. Yale's southern enrollment fell noticeably between 1850 and 1860, but Harvard's and Princeton's remained about the same.

Literature. Although no literary flowering occurred in the South that was in any way comparable to New England's, during the ante-bellum period a number of talented writers published fiction, poetry, and essays of high quality. Edgar Allan Poe has long been accepted as one of America's greatest writers (although his "southernism" has been ignored or denied). But Poe's contemporary, William Gilmore Simms, is hardly known.

Southern writers were exposed to the same romantic currents that stimulated the literary renaissance in the North. They too had to combat the national indifference to literature and the contempt for the writer. But the problems of the southern authors were magnified by conditions that were peculiar to their section.

So long as the older and better-educated families dominated southern culture, the literary tastes and standards that prevailed were those of cultivated amateurs. These men believed that professional writing was not a suitable occupation for a gentleman. They enjoyed biography and history and shared the national enthusiasm for English authors, but they gave little practical encouragement to their own writers. The "highbrows" of Charleston, according to the poet, Paul Hamilton Hayne, who grew up among them, were great devotees of the classics but read little else. They might admire their distinguished townsman, Simms, but they did not buy enough of his books to please him. "The South," Simms wrote to a friend in 1847, "don't care a d—n for literature or art. Your best neighbor & kindred never think to buy books. They will borrow from you & beg, but the same man who will always have wine, has no idea of a library. You will write for & defend their institutions in vain. They will not pay the expense of printing your essays."

Northern writers, to be sure, faced the same difficulties. The cultural level throughout the country had probably been lowered by the broadening of the democratic audience, and observers had already begun to note a marked taste for the sensational and the sentimental. Southern writers, however, had an even less literate public to write for and practically no publishing facilities. Southern college graduates were often well-informed and intelligent, but politics, agriculture, and sports of the field absorbed their attention. When, for patriotic reasons, southern writers published in the South, their books sold poorly. Well-written magazines like the *Southern Literary Messenger* might praise their works, but only the approval of the more numerous and better-printed northern periodicals had cash value. Southern writers resented their dependence on northern publishers, periodicals, and critics. They felt discriminated against and accused northern reviewers of puffing Yankee mediocrities and ignoring southern genius. Without northern publishers and a northern audience, however, such popular writers as Poe and Simms would not have fared as well as they did. Simms' conclusion about his countrymen seems just: "We are not, in fact, a reading people. We are probably, at best, only the pioneers for those, who will atone to letters and the arts hereafter, for our grievous neglect." The brilliant renaissance of southern letters in our century has borne out the prophecy of this harried pioneer writer.

As sectional animosities grew more bitter, southern writers found themselves in a dilemma. According to the Charleston poet, Henry Timrod, any truthful account of the South antagonized northern readers, and southern readers were quick to detect any lapse in local pride. A writer who tried to deal honestly with the problem of slavery risked the displeasure of those who sniffed the air for the taint of abolitionism. Writers were expected to fight with their pens and to uphold the southern gospel against such intellectual incendiaries as Ralph Waldo Emerson. The South wanted a regional literature free of ideological impurities and true to the ideals of a slave society, but it failed to support its own propagandists.

In the light of these peculiar circumstances, what can be said of the literary achievements of the old South? Taken as a whole, southern writers did not depict the agrarian society as accurately or as fully as they might have. Nowhere is slavery or the Negro treated meaningfully in ante-bellum southern fiction, and there is hardly a novel, a short story, or a poem that presents in memorable form what might be called the "Southern-ness" of the South.

Had southern writers chosen to write realistically of southern life, it is likely that they would have gone unread; southerners, like the majority of other American novel-readers, preferred romances in the manner of Scott or Bulwer-Lytton. Simms, their most prolific and widely known novelist, had to stifle his realistic inclinations or else tuck realism into his works almost surreptitiously. His stories of colonial and Revolutionary South Carolina (*The Yemassee,* 1835) and his border romances laid in the rambunctious Southwest (*Richard Hurdis,* 1838; *Border Beagles,* 1840) make concessions to the romantic school of Scott. Simms contributed his full share of wooden heroes, whose lips curl and whose eyes flash, and of doll-like ladies who speak in stilted phrases. But his low-life characters, his traders, tavern-keepers, squatters, and poor whites, are real. He was the only southern novelist before the war who depicted the yeomanry and the riff-raff believably. His novels, loosely and carelessly written though they are, capture the violence and gustiness of the southern frontier, and his fondness for brutal detail makes him seem at times a precursor of the twentieth-century school of southern naturalists.

The most faithful portrayers of the southern folk were not idyllic recorders of plantation life like J. P. Kennedy or angry secessionists like Nathaniel Beverley Tucker, whose novel, *The Partisan Leader* (1836), described a divided America some years before secession occurred. The plain people of the South are revealed more graphically in the sketches of the southern humorists, most of them journalists, doctors, sportsmen, and lawyers. They wrote of "frolics," quilting parties, horse-swaps, gander-pullings, camp-meetings, and fights, and their "tall tales" provide a vivid panorama of the frontier South. Augustus Baldwin Longstreet's colorful descriptions of rural Georgia were justly praised by Poe as masterpieces of reporting. Johnson Jones Hooper invented a fabulous rascal, Simon Suggs, whose motto, "It's good to be shifty in a new country," summed up the spirit of the raw Alabama hinterlands. The Cumberland Mountain country inspired another frontier humorist, George Washington Harris.

A "Conscious Minority."

After 1831, abolitionist assaults against slavery heightened the southerners' sense of isolation and drove their public men and their intellectuals into truculent defense of southern institutions. Against such biting attacks as Theodore Weld's *American Slavery as It Is* (1839) and its fictional counterpart, Harriet Beecher Stowe's *Uncle Tom's Cabin* (1852), the South replied with pro-slavery arguments, fiery proclamations in defense of state rights, and a rallying of public opinion against anyone in Dixie whose loyalty to southern ideals was suspect. "Unreliable" professors were removed from southern colleges; free discussion of slavery was quashed; newspapers kept silent on the dangerous subject. Before 1860, the South had insulated itself against anti-slavery thought.

The man whose career symptomized the southern shift from nationalism to sectionalism was John C. Calhoun. Starting as an ardent defender of positive government, a constitutional "loose constructionist," he ended as the apostle of nullification after he had become convinced that northern industrial interests were enslaving the agrarian South.

Calhoun loved the Union too much to advocate secession, and yet he became convinced that existing constitutional safeguards could not protect a minority from a rapacious majority capable of taxing it out of existence. In his final reflections, *A Disquisition on Government* (1851) and *Discourse on the Constitution and Government of the United States* (1851), Calhoun proposed his theory of "concurrent majorities," which would grant any interest group (in effect, a section like the South) the right to veto an act passed by the majority (in effect, Congress). Calhoun's solution, in other words, was nothing less than a rationale for minority veto of a majority act. It was a device whereby a section out of power could protect its property against a section in power "by dividing and distributing the powers of government."

Like his northern opponents, Calhoun was often misinformed, unrealistic, and parochial in his thinking, but his clearly reasoned speculations pointed up the threat of majority tyranny in a democracy. Unfortunately, he spoke in behalf of a wasteful and outmoded labor system, and he did not carry over his defense of political minorities to intellectual minorities. He shared a large part of the responsibility for the throttling

John C. Calhoun (1782-1850).

of independent opinion in the ante-bellum South. His appeal to southern honor, his inflammatory speeches on southern wrongs, kept the South constantly agitated, and after his death in 1850 his devoted followers kept the emotional fires burning.

Readings

For a short convenient summary of the ante-bellum South, Clement Eaton's *A History of the Old South* (1949) is balanced and readable. This work can be supplemented with useful summaries by R. S. Cotterill, *The Old South* (1939), and F. B. Simkins, *A History of the South* (1953). Allan Nevins, *Ordeal of the Union* (2 vols., 1947), and *The Emergence of Lincoln* (2 vols., 1950), contain richly documented material on almost every aspect of the southern scene. The case for the southern yeomanry is made in F. L. Owsley, *Plain Folk of the Old South* (1949). Another aspect of the life of the ordinary southerner is treated in L. E. Atherton, *The Southern Country Store, 1800-1860* (1949). J. H. Franklin, *The Militant South, 1800-1861* (1956), is an illuminating and freshly documented discussion of southern militancy and violence. Indispensable as well as extraordinarily interesting are F. L. Olmsted's records of his trip through the South, *The Cotton Kingdom,* which has been edited by A. M. Schlesinger (1953). Other revealing glimpses of southern life can be found in Susan D. Smedes, *Memorials of a Southern Planter* (1887); F. P. Gaines, *The Southern Plantation: A Study in the Development and Accuracy of a Tradition* (1924); and F. B. Simkins, *Pitchfork Ben Tillman* (1944).

L. C. Gray, *History of Agriculture in the Southern United States to 1860* (2 vols., 1933), is the definitive work on ante-bellum southern agriculture and a key book for an understanding of the South. This work together with W. E. Dodd, *The Cotton Kingdom* (1921), and U. B. Phillips, *American Negro Slavery* (1918), and *Life and Labor in the Old South* (1929), should be compared with Nevins' work, previously cited.

Of the controversial literature about the world of the slave, in addition to some of the above-mentioned books, the reader should consult such standard works as J. H. Franklin, *From Slavery to Freedom: A History of American Negroes* (1947); Frederic Bancroft, *Slave-Trading in the Old South* (1931); and Kenneth M. Stampp's *The Peculiar Institution* (1956), a new and vigorous examination of slavery. Harriet Beecher Stowe's *Uncle Tom's Cabin* (1852) is available in many editions and should be read with such books as L. M. Blackford, *Mine Eyes Have Seen the Glory* (1954), an admirable picture of an anti-slavery Virginia lady.

R. R. Russel, *Economic Aspects of Southern Sectionalism, 1840-1861* (1924), is an excellent summary of the southern economy with valuable material on the South's nascent industry. Broadus Mitchell, *William Gregg, Factory Master of the Old South* (1928), is a biography of an important southern industrial pioneer.

A valuable commentary on southern culture is Clement Eaton's *Freedom of Thought in the Old South* (1940). The pro-slavery defense as well as related intellectual material is covered in an excellent volume by A. O. Craven, *The Growth of Southern Nationalism, 1848-1861* (1953). Other pertinent volumes on this subject are W. S. Jenkins, *Pro-Slavery Thought in the Old South* (1935), and Harvey Wish, *George Fitzhugh: Propagandist of the Old South* (1943). D. R. Fox's *Ideas in Motion* (1935) contains an illuminating essay, "Cultural Nationalism in the Old South." Jay B. Hubbell, *The South in American Literature, 1607-1900* (1954), is the most comprehensive and valuable survey of southern literature. The collected *Letters* (1952-1955) of William Gilmore Simms are full of interesting material on the life of the southern writer, and several chapters in Van Wyck Brooks, *The World of Washington Irving* (1944), are provocative.

THE EXPANDING NORTH

CHAPTER FOURTEEN

At the end of 1854, after a decade of unprecedented expansion, a brief depression befell the American economy. The stock market crashed, tens of thousands of factory workers suddenly were unemployed, prices of western produce tumbled, and land values collapsed. The depression was short-lived, but the recovery that began in 1855 raised the speculative fever to such a pitch

that a new and more resounding crash occurred in 1857 from which there was only a halting recovery until the war boom of the 1860's. All sections of the country suffered except the South, and all sectors of the economy became depressed except the culture of cotton. "The wealth of the South," announced that section's leading economist, J. D. B. De Bow of New Orleans, "is permanent and real, that of the North fugitive and fictitious."

Never was thinking more wishful and more wrong. The South's economy, though prosperous, lacked the vitality and variety of the North's; and the ups and downs in northern values reflected the dynamism of industry that would soon make the United States the richest country in the world. Perhaps we should speak of industrial*ism* rather than of industry alone, for it was the spirit of machine production that was at work, and it became as pervasive in market-oriented agriculture and steam-powered water and rail transportation as in the factories themselves.

I. PEOPLING THE "MIDDLE BORDER"

Mechanized agriculture first became important in the United States on the free family farms of the northern prairies and the eastern edges of the unforested Great Plains. This extremely fertile country, Hamlin Garland's "Middle Border," spread from upper Indiana and Illinois northward to central Wisconsin and Minnesota and westward through Iowa and upper Missouri to the eastern townships of Kansas and Nebraska. Even more than the southern coastal plains themselves, this level, lush terrain invited the large-scale corporate type of farming that characterized much of the area in the twentieth century. But its early settlers were mainly independent small farmers from the neighboring East and immigrants from the British Isles and the continent of Europe.

Driven by debt during the world-wide depression of the early 1840's, tens of thousands of farm families in the Ohio Valley and the country bordering Lake Erie and Lake Michigan sold their cleared and cultivated homesteads to newcomers with capital. Drawn by the government's liberalized land policy (see p. 234) to try again on the distant frontier, they settled Iowa in such numbers that it became a state in 1846, and Wisconsin so heavily that it was admitted to the Union in 1848. By 1860, hundreds of thousands of other American farm families, including "shoals" of Yankee abolitionists, had helped to treble the population of these new states. Minnesota, moreover, had grown large enough for statehood by 1858. The admission of Kansas was delayed until 1861 only for political reasons, not for lack of population (see p. 349). Nebraska and even the Dakotas to the north were also becoming inhabited.

During this period, widespread economic distress abroad had been accompanied by political repression and religious persecution. Among the worst sufferers were the Irish Catholics, who were especially hard hit by the potato crop failure and the famine that followed in 1845 and 1846. In the decade that ended with the business panic of 1854, about 1,300,000 Irish had fled the Emerald Isle for the United States. For all their attachment to the "old sod," they usually were too poor even to move inland from the coastal cities in which they landed. Some of them did go west as laborers with canal and railroad-building crews, and of these a few eventually were attracted to the soil. Second in numbers to the Irish were the 940,000 Germans who arrived in this decade, followed by about 375,000 Englishmen, Welshmen, and Scots. A few thousand Scandinavians also came, the heralds of a large migration later in the nineteenth century, along with small contingents of Dutch, Swiss, Belgians, French, and Czechs.

All told, between 1844 and 1854 almost 3 million immigrants braved the Atlantic crossing to America. Most of the newcomers shunned the opportunities and other attractions of the land of cotton. Some of the thousands who were crowded into cotton ships on the return voyages from English cotton ports landed at New Orleans and stayed in that port. Others transferred their few belongings right to Mississippi River steamboats and proceeded to non-slave country.

Most of the immigrants were young adults. As industrial and construction workers, farmers, farm laborers, or domestic servants, they immediately swelled the working force of the free North. A great many also came in family groups. Among these were middle-class businessmen, lawyers, doctors, scientists, and journalists, who brought new skills and new learning to western cities like Cincinnati and St. Louis, and to such aspiring frontier towns as Chicago and Des Moines. More numerous were the rural "reading families," who were readily identified by their bookish preparation for life in the New World, and other agricultural family groups, who sometimes were led to America by their old-country pastors. These families characteristically headed for the prairies and the plains. By 1860, they made up 30 per cent of the population of Wisconsin and Minnesota and were almost as numerous in the other Middle Border states.

So determined were these religious newcomers to preserve their old way of life in the wilderness that they sometimes segregated themselves in a "New Germany," a "New Norway," or a "New Bohemia." But many quickly caught a vision of a brighter future which gradually weakened their commitment to the homeland and to the past. "The prairies," said the son of one of the English immigrants of the 1850's, "possessed a charm created by beauty instead of awe." The Illinois landscape, he recalled, "was an inspiration," while the land of Iowa and Kansas "sloped upward toward the West, giving to the mind an ever-increasing sense of hope and power."

As long as the cotton planters kept their labor system from the Lord's free soil, these western pioneers as a rule were not for meddling with slavery. For their own labor supply they raised large families, held their sons and daughters tethered strictly to the land,

Grim conditions of travel in the hold of an immigrant ship.

Pioneer wagon train crossing the Platte River in Nebraska, 1859.

and invested in machines to multiply their productivity. Mingling occasionally with the rest of the religious mysticism and pseudo-science of the times was a belief that iron poisoned the earth, and some of these new settlers were as wary of iron and steel implements and machines as of abolition itself. But they could not long withstand the competitive force of innovation and the sweeping tide of progress.

II. THE AGRICULTURAL REVOLUTION

Breaking the Sod. For most of the decade and a half before the Civil War the settlement of the free West ran ahead of the extension of the railroad. Pioneer families traveled on foot, on wagons, and on river and Great Lakes boats. Groups of families might settle a particular region, but, since the quality of the soil varied even within a single 640-acre section and the pioneer had the pick of the land, farms might be a day's travel or more apart. Another incentive to isolation was the settler's hope of adding more land to the quarter-section with which he usually started. This optimism only strengthened his habitual view of strangers as interlopers.

Having prayerfully picked his site and registered it, a farmer would build a one-room log cabin or, in treeless country, a hut constructed of slabs of sod, and a barn of the same material. Meanwhile, he would turn his few sheep, cows, and oxen to graze on the wild buffalo grass and fence them out as best he could from the kitchen vegetable garden, the care of which became one of the numerous responsibilities of his wife. Once he got his main fields fenced in, at a cash outlay of $1 or $1.25 an acre, he would begin the laborious round of cultivation. The plow the pioneer brought with him, though it took two men to handle and four oxen to pull, would hardly scratch the heavily matted, grass-rooted virgin sod. At a further cost of $1.75 to $2.50 an acre he would have to hire professional "breakers," teams of men with massive plows drawn by 8 to 12 oxen, who would cut the first shallow furrows on the prairies and the plains. In subsequent seasons, the farmer and his family could plow and plant without help.

313

An acre or at most an acre and a half a day—perhaps 40 acres in a whole 160-acre quarter-section—was the capacity of this manpower, this ox-power, and this equipment. And men who moved their families to the prairies and the plains with the idea simply of re-establishing an independent way of life were satisfied to do as well as this. In the belief, dearly cherished in the United States, that the tiller of the soil was of all creatures closest to God—a belief that gave a Christian base to the Jeffersonian ideal of a democracy of farmers—they tended to resist changes that offered only a greater material reward for their labors.

And yet the sheer fertility of the Border's soil, superficially cultivated though it was by backward methods and with outmoded tools, soon inundated the pioneers with surplus crops. Many, of course, welcomed the opportunity to market their crops for cash. And even the more idealistic always needed money to pay old debts and to buy the usual bare necessities like salt, ammunition, harness, and boots and to maintain their wagons and other equipment. Every farmer, or at least every farm wife, even on the treeless plains, also aspired to move from crude log cabins or crude sod huts to neat frame dwellings with appropriate furniture and a touch of color in a table covering, a window curtain, or a picture on the wall. Money was needed for such "improvements," and until the crash of 1857 money was crying to be made. The crash, indeed, reminded many how deeply they had sunk in the sin of covetousness, and in 1858 a new sweep of revivalism in the West recalled backsliders to religion and the church. The conversions were usually impermanent, however.

Expanding Markets.   For all the Christian traditionalism of the "New Germanys" and the "New Norways," and the often terrifying isolation of the American settlements, the prairie farmers in this Age of Progress were in fact the vanguard and the support of a world-wide business surge. In Europe in this period, industrialism was spreading, the remaining serfs were being freed from their ties to the land, cities were growing rapidly, tariffs on agricultural imports were coming down, the exchange of currencies was being simplified. Accompanying these social changes were the revolutions, famines, and wars that cast so many immigrant families on American shores for asylum and a fresh start. All these circumstances set up a huge demand for foodstuffs which the virgin American West, manned so largely by the immigrants themselves, could plentifully supply.

Nor was the business ferment restricted to Europe. After 1844, American ships and vessels of other nations enjoyed enlarged rights in the treaty ports of China; in 1854, Commodore Matthew Perry, with a fine show of American naval power, opened up the "Hermit Kingdom" of Japan to American trade; in 1856, Siam broadened the privileges accorded 20 years before to American exporters; and all this stirring in the Pacific warmed our interest in salubrious Hawaii. The Orient never took American farm produce, but Oriental trade helped make the American merchant marine the largest in the world and its home ports booming metropolises. And here, as in the great cities of Europe, landless multitudes had to be fed.

From the beginning of the westward movement, corn was always the frontier settler's first marketable crop. Easily transformed into fattened hogs (pigs commonly were turned loose right in the corn fields to "hog down" the ripened ears), corn could be made to walk to market when other transportation was lacking. Corn was also suitable winter feed for beef cattle, which could be walked even farther than hogs. For human consumption, corn was distilled into a potable and packageable "likker," and was eaten off the cob, baked into bread, and prepared in many other ways. In their famine years of the late 1840's, the Irish devoured American corn. But they never developed a taste for it, and corn never won a stable or significant export market. In the United States, on the other hand, corn bread and pork practically made up the national diet.

As late as 1849, Tennessee and Kentucky had led in the production of corn-fed hogs. Ten years later they had fallen behind Indiana and Illinois. By then, Missouri and Iowa (along with Texas) had become the leading cattle states. In the production of corn itself, Illinois had risen to first place; Missouri had passed Tennessee and Kentucky; while Iowa, Kansas, and Nebraska were making noticeable inroads in the market. American corn production reached 838 million bushels in 1859, an increase of 40 per cent in ten years, and most of the gain was supplied by the Middle Border states.

Wheat was far more selective than corn in soils and climate, and even in suitable latitudes it grew best on land that had already produced a corn crop. In 1849, Pennsylvania, Ohio, and New York were the leading wheat states. By 1859, though the country's total wheat production had soared 75 per cent to a record 173 million bushels, each of these three states produced less wheat than it had a decade earlier. Illinois, Indiana, and Wisconsin had moved to the head of the wheat states; and in succeeding decades, to show the momentum of wheat's westward surge, first Iowa, then Minnesota, then Kansas, and then the Dakotas entered the ranks of the leaders.

Acre for acre, wheat paid better than

corn, over which it had advantages both in marketing and production. Unlike corn, wheat was eaten all over the world. Less bulky than corn in relation to value, it could bear high transportation costs more easily. It also stood shipment better. Finally, on the open prairies and plains, where land was plentiful and hired labor scarce, wheat production responded magnificently to improved tools and the application of labor-saving machinery.

Mechanized Farming.   The western farmer's first need in the way of equipment was a new plow. Back in 1837, John Deere, an Illinois blacksmith, had produced the first American steel plow, and by 1858, after making many improvements in it, he was manufacturing 13,000 a year. Light enough for one strong man to sling over his shoulder, Deere's plows nevertheless were the first to cut deep, clean furrows in the prairie sod. Nor did it take vast bovine strength to draw them, and the weaker but faster-moving horse began to supplant the ox on western farms.

Everyone needed plows. More striking improvements were being made in machines especially designed for wheat-growing. Even before Deere's first success, Cyrus Hall McCormick of Virginia (1834) and Obed Hussey of Ohio (1833) had patented practical

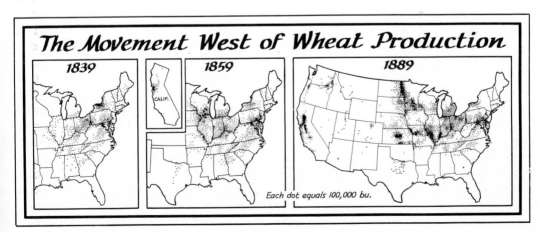

The Movement West of Wheat Production

1839   1859   1889

CALIF.

Each dot equals 100,000 bu.

steel-toothed reapers. One man with Mc-Cormick's horse-drawn machine could do the work of five with scythes. Sales lagged, however, until 1848 when McCormick (while Hussey languished in the East) moved his plant to Chicago and headed his demonstrators toward the western frontier. Ten years later, McCormick was manufacturing 500 reapers a month and still failing to meet the demand.

At first, entire neighborhoods had to be mobilized to harvest the vast quantities of wheat the reaper cut down. But in the 1850's work was progressing on mechanical wheat-binders, which in the next decade would eliminate much of the harvesting army. In the 1850's, mechanical threshers were already in use, and, according to the Census Report of 1860, they were 60 per cent more efficient than "the old flail mode."

In 1800, the average American farmer spent about $15 to $20 for his tools, and the equipment the emigrants carried west in the 1840's was not worth much more. By 1857, the *Scientific American* was recommending that every farmer who had 100 acres of land should have machinery worth about $600. Many wheat farmers got along with less. But the vast expansion of wheat production could not have taken place had not most farmers sloughed off their traditional methods and adopted mechanized techniques. By the time of the Civil War, about $250 million had been invested in farm implements and machines, an average of about $120 for each farm in the country. For the wheat farms of the prairies and the plains, the average investment was much higher.

Farming as a Business. Once the western farmer had committed himself to machinery, he found his life greatly altered. The most disturbing change came from his discovery that he was suddenly in the grip of forces over which he had less and less control. His key machines, for example, such as reapers and threshers, could speed the pro-duction of wheat but they could do little else. The fact that they were usually purchased on credit and that the debt had to be paid off in cash further narrowed his range of choice. For wheat, the specialty of the new machines, was also the cash crop *par excellence*. Even when wheat prices fell, as they did in 1854, the wheat farmer could no longer grow other crops or even return to subsistence agriculture. Indeed, he was forced to grow more wheat than ever in order, at lower prices, to get as great an *aggregate* cash return as before. Increasing his wheat production also often involved breaking or buying new land, either of which would plunge him only more deeply into debt. Then he would need still larger crops in order to acquire the cash to maintain the payments on his larger obligations.

The continuous round of specialization, mechanization, and expansion in the free West gave a momentum to wheat production that was a priceless boon to the world. There were other aspects of wheat farming on the prairies and the plains, however, which hardly helped the farmer. The steps between the wheat-grower and the ultimate urban consumer seemed to multiply disastrously with distance. All along the line, weighers, graders, storage-elevator operators, rail and water carriers, warehouses, local haulers, insurers, money-lenders, and speculators—the whole urban apparatus of finance and distribution—exacted tribute from the farmer.

The world-wide collapse of prices in 1857 staggered the wheat farmer in ways to which the subsistence farmer was largely immune. Debts went unpaid, the threat of foreclosure and indeed foreclosure itself soured his prospects, and his mind turned once more to the free frontier. In 1858, western wheat farmers began attending other meetings besides religious revivals. From such meetings arose broad denunciations of conspiratorial "trading combinations," monopolistic elevator and railroad operators, and grasping money-lenders. The farmer's special place in God's plan was given renewed publicity, and farmers themselves were urged to "assert not only their independence but their supremacy" in society. On the constructive side were vague proposals for farm cooperatives and arguments for the state and federal controls that were to become so much a part of political agitation in the United States in later decades.

Out of it all, before the Civil War, came two specific demands. One was for agricultural colleges to educate farm youth in farm science and to afford them broader educational opportunities as well. These colleges were to be set up by the federal government and financed by federal land grants. The second demand was for free homesteads— free of payment and free of slaves—on the remainder of the public domain. Over southern opposition, Congress enacted a land-grant college bill in 1859, only to have President Buchanan veto it. In June, 1860, he vetoed a homestead bill that would have made western lands available at 25 cents an acre. In the elections later that year, the West, crying the slogan "Vote Yourself a Farm," helped carry the country for Lincoln, fully aware that his policy of no extension of slavery to the territories might carry the country to war.

The Agricultural Revolution in the East.

Right up to the outbreak of the Civil War southern planters remained active customers of the western farmers, but the great bulk of western grain and meat flowed to the Northeast. So great did this volume become that the agricultural revolution in the West forced upon the East an agricultural revolution of its own.

Let the West "supply our cities with grain," William Buckminster of Massachusetts said as early as 1838:

We will manufacture their cloth and their shoes. [Our farms] shall find employment in furnishing what cannot so well be transported from a distance. Fresh meats, butter, hay, and the small market vegetables must be supplied by the farmers of N. England.

What Buckminster had foreseen developed with a rush in the following 20 years—not only in New England but also on the more friendly soil of other eastern states. Two items that Buckminster did not enumerate became the most profitable of all—milk and fruits.

Dairying, once a routine chore in most households, urban or rural, had become big business by 1850. In that year, the Harlem Railroad brought about 25 million quarts of milk into New York City. Every other sizable city in the East had developed its own "milk shed," a nearby expanse of pasture land where carefully bred and carefully tended herds of cows were reared especially for milk production.

Fruit orchards were as common as pastures in the East. But after 1840, the growing of apples and peaches was expanded and given scientific care. Strawberries, blackberries, and many varieties of melons also added interest and nourishment to the urban American's diet. The tin canister or the "tin can," an English invention that became widely used in America in the late 1840's for packaging perishables, enlarged the market for such products and even extended it to men at sea.

Speeding the eastern agricultural revolution was a revival of scientific farming. An earlier movement, which had been restricted to gentlemen farmers, had died in the 1830's. But after 1845, when success or failure hinged increasingly on special knowledge and up-to-date processes, eastern dirt and dairy farmers took a keen interest in information about climate, soils, fertilizers, methods of cultivation, and the idiosyncrasies of different crops. Agricultural associations, fairs, magazines, books, courses, and schools all multiplied in the East in the 1840's and 1850's.

Railroads and water routes between the East and the West encouraged each section to produce specialties of its own. Railroads and water routes in the East and especially in New England so covered the land that these sections could specialize in perishables with the assurance that their produce would be speeded to city markets.

III.   THE PEAK OF WATER TRANSPORTATION

By the time of the outbreak of the Civil War, the railroad had become the dominating factor in the economy of the free North and a powerful influence on the general welfare of the entire nation. But the railroad had to fight for ascendancy, and during the period of its rise other avenues of exchange and other forms of transport were helping to build up the country.

The Revival of Foreign Trade.

One of the most important developments of the 1840's and 1850's was the revitalization of our foreign trade. During the depression that followed the crash of 1837, our foreign trade had fallen to a point well below the level even of the early years of the Republic. In 1843, our combined imports and exports were $125,250,000, a trough never touched in the preceding 30 years. Then began an almost continuous rise which saw this figure multiplied five and a half times by 1860, when it reached a record $687,200,000. Almost every year in this period, our imports exceeded our exports. Eighty per cent of the half-billion dollars in gold taken from the California gold mines before 1857 was sent abroad to pay the difference. Helping to keep the difference down was the rapidly increasing export of western wheat and flour.

One of the most significant aspects of the revival of foreign trade was its effect on immigration. Without vast fleets of merchantmen plying the Atlantic between Europe and America, the millions of newcomers to the United States in the late 1840's and in the 1850's could never have found passage to the New World. Seventy-five per cent of American commerce, and an even greater proportion of the immigrant traffic, was carried in American sailing ships.

The average westward crossing by sail from Liverpool, England, to New York took about 33 days. Steamships, which had been used in ocean commerce since 1838, could make this westward crossing in the 1850's in about 10 days. But they were unreliable and excessively costly to operate. As late as 1899, all ocean steamships carried sails for auxiliary or emergency power. By 1860, steamships, most of which were British, had captured but a tiny fraction of the world's ocean commerce.

The Surge of Domestic Commerce.

Far surpassing even our record foreign trade both in volume and rate of growth in the decade and a half before the Civil War was American domestic, or internal, commerce. The vitality of foreign trade itself contributed significantly to this development. The mere collection at American ports of domestic cotton and cotton goods, and tobacco, wheat, flour, corn, pork, timber, and other commodities for export gave a great deal of business to our home carriers. Similarly, the need to distribute to the vast and sprawling interior the increasingly voluminous imports landed at a few great coastal cities added steadily to the demand for domestic transportation.

But domestic commerce was far more than an adjunct of foreign trade. As the American population grew—and it grew with phenomenal rapidity in the free North in the 1840's and 1850's—the home market naturally expanded. As different regions began to specialize in particular commodities, the need for exchange among them increased. Exchange itself was made easier by larger amounts of gold being mined in California and by better credit achieved through expansion of the banking system. Between 1851 and 1860, the money in circulation in the United States, including specie and banknotes, rose 9 per cent per capita. But the importance of this increase to trade had become even greater than the figure itself indicates, for such devices as the telegraph and the railroads helped to speed up communication in business transactions and thus accelerated the collection of business bills. These changes permitted the actual money in circulation to be used many more times in a single year than heretofore; and since

goods hauled by the railroads and canals combined.

The most glamorous phase of coastal commerce was the era of the clipper ship. The clippers were the most daring commercial sailing vessels ever built. Their designers, among whom Donald McKay in East Boston, Massachusetts, was the unchal-

Clipper ship Syren, *1851.*

the amount of money itself was rising rapidly, the whole pace of domestic commerce quickened. Between 1843 and 1860, while American foreign trade grew five and a half times, domestic trade grew ten times. By 1860, domestic carriers were hauling goods worth at least 15 times the value of goods carried across the seas in both directions, or about $10 billion.

The Clipper Ship Era.

Before the railroad boom of the 1850's, water carriers almost monopolized domestic commerce; and of these carriers the oldest and for a long time the most successful were the coastal sailing ships. In 1852, the value of goods carried by American coastal vessels (the coastal trade was closed by law to foreign ships) was three times the value of

lenged master, drew out the ordinary three-masted packet ships to extraordinary lengths and then reduced the ratio of beam to length so drastically that traditional shipbuilders were dazed. The result was the most graceful hull that ever took to sea. The hulls were topped with the tallest masts available, and on these masts was mounted the largest spread of canvas ever to challenge a captain's courage. The captains themselves were selected from among the most relentless "drivers" of the day. Probably the most famous of the clipper ships was McKay's aptly named *Flying Cloud.* Launched in the summer of 1851, she made a day's run of 374 miles during her maiden voyage—"the fastest day's run," writes the historian Robert G. Albion, "yet made by a ship—nearly forty miles better than any steamship travelled in a single day up to the Civil War." Yet

McKay soon outdid himself. In 1854, his *Lightning* flew 436 miles in one 24-hour stretch on her maiden voyage.

The first genuine clippers were built in the early 1840's with an eye to shortening the seemingly everlasting voyage to the Orient, where trade, as we have seen (p. 314), had begun to take a promising turn. From China and India, clippers sometimes sailed to Liverpool and London, and on arrival so astonished the British that they ordered ships of their own built in America for the Atlantic run.

But the greatest use of the clippers came with the growth of gold mining in California, between about 1851 and 1856. The designers of the clippers had sacrificed cargo space to speed, and for the limited cargo the clippers could carry their owners had to charge higher rates than most shippers could afford. To the California adventurers, however, money was no obstacle and speed was everything. Ships arriving at San Francisco in the summer of 1850 from Boston and New York had averaged 159 days for the journey around the Horn. The next summer, *Flying Cloud* arrived from New York after a voyage of 89 days, 21 hours, a record that stood until she herself reduced it by 13 hours three years later. It was for this "coastal" trade that most of the great clipper ships were built, and for them voyages of 100 days or less were not unusual.

Unfortunately for the clippers, they were beaten at their own game just about the time they themselves seemed to have perfected it. Even before the gold rush to California, New York steamship operators had organized a route to the West coast over which they could make the voyage in four or five weeks as against the clippers' best time of three months. This route was intended initially to serve the settlers of Oregon, but by the time of the first actual voyage in January, 1849, news of the California gold discoveries had spread, and San Francisco promptly supplanted Oregon as the main objective of the business. The steamship route involved a difficult portage across the Isthmus of Panama, which discouraged many travelers and made the handling of heavy freight almost impossible. But in 1855 after many engineering difficulties had been overcome, a Panama Railroad was completed by which the Isthmus could be crossed comfortably and efficiently.

Even before the Panama Railroad was built, this steamship route had become so successful that as early as 1851 Cornelius Vanderbilt, who had made his fortune as a ship operator in New York waters and was already the richest man in the country, entered into the competition. Instead of Panama, he used a more northerly passage across Nicaragua. In 1855, Vanderbilt himself was challenged by still other New Yorkers. With the objective of annulling Vanderbilt's privilege of transit across Nicaragua, these adventurers went so far as to support William Walker in his efforts, which proved successful, to take over the government of that small country. Vanderbilt retaliated by hiring agents to raise a force among neighboring Central American states large enough to overwhelm Walker's government. This tactic effectively ended the Nicaraguan episode. But the Panama crossing continued to be operated profitably right up to 1869, when the first transcontinental railroad was opened to through traffic. Long before that, many of the surviving clippers, their magnificence quite tarnished, had sunk to the status of tramps sailing random sea routes with random cargoes under alien flags.

Sea-going commerce to California by sail or steam accounted for only a small fraction of the vast American coastal commerce during the late 1840's and the early 1850's. But it effectively tied the East and West coasts to one another and made a single, throbbing organism of the free states. One consequence of this development was the ever-greater importance northerners attached to east-west inland carriers. Influenced by the new ideas, Congress decided in 1853 to have the army survey routes for a transcontinental railroad. This decision stirred a

Mississippi River steamboat commerce.

hornet's nest of sectional controversy, and not until the South left the Union in 1861 were the first transcontinentals chartered. By 1853, however, many lesser transportation enterprises had begun to meet the expanding needs of inland commerce. So successful did they prove that the coastal carrying trade, inescapably rigid and roundabout in its routes, suffered a precipitous decline. The outbreak of the Civil War found it with little business left besides carrying cotton from New Orleans or Mobile directly to New England, a remnant of a once remarkable commerce to which (with the unsavory exception of cotton smuggling during the conflict) the war itself also put an end.

The Steamboat Crisis. One of the major factors in the success of the coastal trade had been the great volume of goods brought down to Atlantic and Gulf of Mexico ports by the navigable rivers with which the United States was so lavishly endowed. The largest amount of river traffic, of course, had developed on the Ohio and Mississippi River systems (see map, p. 198), which profited both from the expansion of the free Northwest and the extension of cotton culture into the Southwest. All told, about 750 steamboats plied the western rivers in the 1850's, and the traffic they carried climbed to its historic peak in that decade. Most spectacular, perhaps, was the boom on the upper Mississippi, where sleepy St. Paul was transformed into a bustling port by settlers sending first furs, then lumber, and then wheat, downstream. An immense traffic in passengers helped to swell the bulk of river commerce. Most of these passengers were emigrants, but among them also were many other Americans characteristically on the go.

321

Yet if the coastal trade suffered from having to traverse too great distances, the river trade, which characteristically moved north and south, suffered from the problem of direction. As early as 1851, total river commerce, though itself at the peak of its prosperity, had fallen to but one-twentieth of the total domestic commerce, judged by the value of goods carried. In that year, the upstart canals and the rising railroads each carried goods worth three times the goods transported on all the rivers of the country. The relative share of the western rivers in the commerce of their section, where competitive means of transportation were as yet less well developed than in the East, no doubt stayed at a higher figure; but the fight to maintain this share proved less successful with each succeeding year.

In order to compete with their better-located and technologically more advanced rivals, the river men began cutting their rates to the bone. That was bad enough. At the same time, they competed so fiercely among themselves for a worthy part of the traffic saved by rate-cutting that every one of them became saddled with suicidally rising costs. Never was western steamboat travel so speedy, so luxurious, so gilded with gaudy inducements as in the middle 1850's. But the river men themselves grew only more and more depressed. Races among river steamboats were once one of the joys of competition and lent sparkle and spirit to river scenes. Under the business pressure of the 1850's, competitors sought literally to knock one another out, and collisions, explosions, and fires took a sharply rising toll of property and lives.

Some river men acknowledged that they were their own worst enemies and tried to force others to join with them in combinations to control the deadly craze for speed. They also sought by agreement to keep up passenger fares and freight charges. Nothing worked, however, and the majority, while defending their own God-given natural waterways, were forced eventually to concede that they could not compete with man-made canals and railroads.

Completing the Canals. One of the great limitations on the growth of river traffic, even where the rivers flowed in the right direction, was their inability to follow settlers when they homesteaded at any distance from river bottom lands. At first, the river men hoped that just as they fed the business of the coastal carriers, so inland canals would serve as feeders to hungry river craft. And in many eastern states the canals actually did perform this function. None, of course, performed it better than the Erie Canal itself, which poured a flood of western commodities into Hudson River boats at Albany.

And yet so far as the western rivers and river ports were concerned, the Erie, in concert with the Ohio canals and others completed in the West before 1837, took trade away. By 1838, Buffalo, at the Erie's western end, was receiving more grain and flour annually than New Orleans itself. Once canal construction began again in the West in the 1840's (there was little more canal building in the East after 1837), virtually every project was aimed at reinforcing the diversion of western trade from the Mississippi system and toward the North and the East.

The first of the later canals to be completed was the Miami and Erie, which in 1846 began to suck Ohio River commerce at Cincinnati north to Lake Erie at Toledo. In 1853, the Wabash and Erie Canal reached even farther down the Ohio to tie Evansville, Indiana, to Toledo. In 1848, Illinois completed the Illinois and Michigan Canal, connecting Chicago on Lake Michigan with La Salle on the Illinois River. This river reached the Mississippi above St. Louis, and quickly drew so much Mississippi traffic northward that by 1850 Chicago, as yet without a single railroad connection, had roared to greatness as a port.

Much of the traffic of the canal system originated right along the routes of the canals themselves, where vigorous market towns quickly arose. By reversing the direction of traffic on such rivers as the Ohio, the Illinois, and the northern Mississippi, the canals also transformed these proud streams into feeders. As the canals flourished, such rivers were enabled to compensate somewhat for the sharply declining rate of growth of their downstream runs.

In the decade and a half before the Civil War, paralleling the rivalry of the free states and the slave for control of the West itself, a struggle took place between the Mississippi River system and the Great Lakes for control of western commerce. By the 1850's, the canals had swung the victory irrevocably to the Lakes. Two canals, one of which was foreign-built and neither of which had anything to do with the great north-south river system, added to the Lakes' supremacy. The first was the Welland Canal, built by the Canadian government to join Lake Erie with Lake Ontario, and thence by way of the St. Lawrence River to connect the Northwest with the East at Quebec. In the late 1850's, vessels laden with western goods made the through voyage from Chicago all the way to Liverpool, England, by this route.

The Welland Canal was needed to circumvent Niagara Falls. The second Great Lakes canal was the Sault-Ste. Marie, popularly known simply as the Soo Canal. This one was needed to get around the turbulent St. Mary's Falls, which prohibited passage between Lake Superior and Lake Huron. After two years of incredible construction feats under the guidance of engineer Charles T. Harvey, the Soo was opened in April, 1855, just in time to catch the massive flow of iron ore from the Marquette Range of northern Michigan to the mills of Pittsburgh, Cleveland, and Chicago. Northern wheat also found an outlet through the Soo.

Placed at $150 million in 1851, the value of goods carried by Great Lakes vessels quadrupled in the following five years. This growth reflected the growth of the canals that turned traffic away from the South. But it also reflected the rise of the western Great Lakes country itself as a power and a prize.

IV.   THE TRIUMPH OF THE RAILROAD

Problems and Progress.   The striking extension of the canal system in the late 1840's and the 1850's should serve to remind us that the railroad was not so obvious an improvement over other means of inland transportation as we might suppose. Practical steam locomotives had been invented in England and the United States years before 1829, when their commercial feasibility was first established. As late as 1848, the board of directors of the Pennsylvania Railroad declared that "railroads must be used exclusively for light freight."

Before the coming of the railroad, all means of transportation were open to the individual. The farmer, for example, could drive his wagon, his pigs, and his cattle over the public roads or sail his own boat on the rivers or the sea. Even without the chaos of such random individual use, movement over the rails presented a formidable problem until systems of operation were devised later in the nineteenth century that operated with reasonable safety.

Efficient railroad equipment and construction methods also were slow in coming. Even after steam locomotives had become practical, sails were used to propel cars over some lines, and as late as the middle 1840's some horses were still being used. One of the more persistent problems of steam locomotion was how to generate enough power for the engine to pull a string of cars as well as to move itself. Power often could not be increased without adding to the locomotive's weight; and heavier locomotives made more difficult such related problems, novel in themselves, as the construction of road beds, the laying of track, and the strengthening of bridges to withstand the mounting burdens placed upon them. The limits of grades and curves were other matters that were not solved without the loss of many lives through accidents.

One of the great questions of railroad construction was the material to use for rails. Before this problem was settled by the perfection of the steel rail in the 1870's (see Chapter XX), rails were usually made of wrought iron. Shaped cross-sectionally like an inverted "T," their broad base was easily attached to wooden railroad ties by means of simple spikes. On busy routes wrought-iron rails lasted hardly longer than three months (compared with a steel rail's life of 15 *years* or more), and service was disrupted when a rail had to be replaced. Often the time for replacement was signaled only by a costly wreck caused by broken track.

The distance to be left between the parallel rails of a railroad was an issue that took longer to settle than the manufacture of the rails themselves. As late as 1865, eleven different gauges of track—usually devised by state and local railroad promoters to keep competitors' rolling stock off their lines—marred the continuity of the railroad system in the North. Even "through" shipments had frequently to be transferred from car to car before they arrived at their destinations, and "changing trains" was one of the many nuisances of passenger travel.

Yet the American railroad network, 30,000 miles long in 1860, had become one of the marvels of the world. In that year, American passenger trains exceeded a rate of 20 miles an hour, though only at mortal peril to travelers, and freight trains averaged about 11 miles an hour.

Railroads in the East. Of the 3,328 miles of railroad track in the United States in 1840, a meager 200 miles lay rusting in the West, mute testimony to the debts and disappointed hopes of Michigan, Indiana, and Illinois (see p. 201). The rest of the mileage was shared almost equally by the Northeast and the old South. No railroad linked these two sections south of Washing-

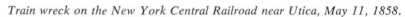

Train wreck on the New York Central Railroad near Utica, May 11, 1858.

ton, and neither section had succeeded in thrusting a line across the Appalachian barrier to the Ohio or Mississippi valleys. The 1,470 miles of track in the South in 1840 included the Baltimore & Ohio, which had made the most determined effort to reach the West by rail but had fallen far short of its goal.

In 1840, there were 1,670 miles of railroad track scattered through the Northeast in every state but Vermont. Pennsylvania, with about one-third of all the northern railroad mileage, was the nation's leader. Most of Pennsylvania's railroad mileage was restricted to the northeastern part of the state, where small lines, privately built, had begun to haul anthracite to barges on nearby rivers and canals. So jealous was the state government of its canal system to the West, that even when it did grant a charter in 1846 to the privately financed Pennsylvania Railroad Company allowing it to build a line from Harrisburg west to Pittsburgh, the legislature required the new company to pay the state's canal administration 3 cents for each ton-mile of freight hauled.

Second to Pennsylvania in railroad mileage in 1840 was New York State. Most of its roads were in the Albany-Troy-Schenectady region at the eastern end of the Erie Canal, or on a line west of that region roughly paralleling the canal itself. By 1842, seven different railroads strung across the state offered a kind of through route between Albany and Buffalo. But these roads cooperated poorly, and in any case until 1851 the state, in an effort similar to Pennsylvania's to protect its canal investment, forbade them to carry freight except when the Erie Canal was frozen over or otherwise closed to navigation. In 1840, New York City had but a single tiny railroad, the New York and Harlem, which connected the metropolis with the independent town of Harlem seven miles to the north.

Of all the states, Massachusetts probably had participated least in the speculative activity of the 1830's, and her major industries, such as shipbuilding and textile manufacturing, were among the first to recover from the crash of 1837. Soon Boston's capitalists were seeking new investment opportunities. None attracted them more than railroads. So intense was railroad construction in Massachusetts after 1845 that by 1850 almost every town of 2,000 persons or more in the state was served by a railroad. During those same few years, 2,200 miles of track were laid in New England, considerably more than in any other section. Boston was the hub of the entire New England railroad network; more important, by means of rail connections with the Welland and Erie canals, she had become a vigorous competitor for western trade. To further this trade, Boston capitalists under the leadership of John Murray Forbes began investing heavily in the late 1840's in railroads in distant western states.

Baltimore was as free as Boston from the prior claims of any state canal systems to western traffic, and in 1842 the promotors of the Baltimore and Ohio Railroad began gathering new capital with an eye to pushing their road over the mountains to Wheeling, West Virginia, on the Ohio River. The B. & O. reached Wheeling in 1853.

The enterprise of Boston and Baltimore jolted Pennsylvania and New York out of their complacent confidence in canals. The Quaker state granted its niggardly charter to the Pennsylvania Railroad in 1846, only after Pittsburghers had taken tentative steps to tie their city to the oncoming Baltimore and Ohio. The Pennsylvania was opened from Philadelphia to Pittsburgh in December, 1852, months before the B. & O. itself reached Wheeling. Five years later, the Pennsylvania bought out the state canal system and the short railroad lines the state itself had built to feed the system traffic, and henceforth it dominated the transportation structure of the commonwealth.

New York City was much nearer than Boston to the eastern end of the Erie Canal. To meet Boston's offer of railroad service there, New York merchants chartered the Hudson River Railroad in 1846.

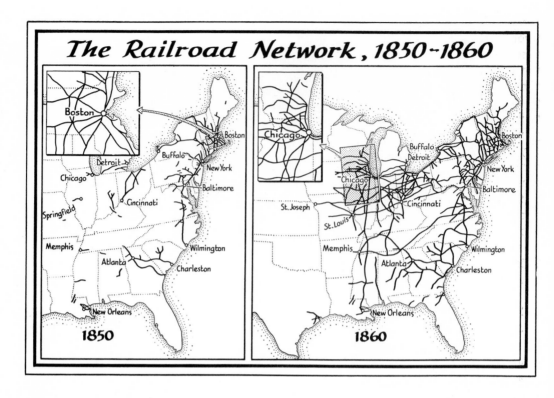

The Railroad Network, 1850-1860

1850

1860

This road was opened between New York City and East Albany in 1851. The next year, a second route was made available by extending the old New York and Harlem Railroad to the Albany vicinity. In 1853, under the direction of Erastus Corning, an iron manufacturer and former Mayor of Albany, the seven independent railroads strung out from Albany to Buffalo were consolidated into the New York Central Railroad. In conjunction with the Hudson River Railroad, the Central could offer a continuous water-level route from New York to the West.

In the early 1850's, another New York railroad became the fourth—along with the B. & O., the Pennsylvania, and the New York Central—to offer through railroad transportation to the West. This road was the Erie. By 1851, the Erie had completed the longest single railroad line in the country, which ran from Piermont on the Hudson to Dunkirk on Lake Erie, 460 miles away. In the next few years, the Erie was opened all the way from Jersey City to Buffalo.

By March, 1852, 10,800 miles of rail-road (about three times the mileage of a decade earlier) had been completed in the United States, and an additional 10,900 miles were under construction. Most of the completed roads either were in the Northeast or connected that section with waterways beyond the Appalachians. With few exceptions these railroads started in great cities, traversed rich and populous territory, and promised to return considerable profits to the investors early in the game. Although most of the roads had state and local government assistance, they were financed largely by private subscription to railroad corporation stock.

Railroads in the West. Most of the railroads built in the 1850's were in the West,* and by 1860 that section, with 11,000 miles of track, had more railroads than the Middle states and New England combined. The western roads faced entirely different conditions from those in the East.

* Ohio, Indiana, Illinois, Missouri, Michigan, Iowa, Wisconsin.

326

Private investment capital was scarce, population thin, and corporation stock difficult to sell. Before 1850, the federal government had given about 7 million acres of the national domain to road and canal companies to assist them in building transportation facilities in thinly settled areas. Such land grants provided their recipients with property that they could sell or mortgage in return for the immediate cash needed for construction and for operational expenses in the first few years. The initial congressional land grant for railroad construction was made in 1850 for the benefit of a system of railroads to run north and south from Chicago to Mobile, Alabama. The grant actually was made by Congress to the states the roads were to cross (except Tennessee and Kentucky, where the federal government owned no land), with the understanding that the states would give the land to companies chartered by them to build and operate the lines. All told, the first grant ran to 3,736,000 acres, 2,500,000 of them in Illinois, the only state actually to build its part of the system.

This first congressional land grant provided a 200-foot-wide right-of-way for the track itself, together with the even-numbered sections (640 acres) of land to a depth of six miles on either side of the line. The government retained the intervening odd-numbered sections for sale at a later date. This grant became the model for most of those made to other western railroads in the following years, though some roads received their lands directly, without the intermediation of the states. By 1860, Congress had granted 18 million acres in 10 states for the benefit of 45 different railroads. With these lands as collateral, the fortunate roads were able to market first-mortgage bonds through investment bankers in Wall Street, in New York City, to American and foreign investors. The invention of the first-mortgage bond and the development of investment banking greatly speeded western railroad development.

A north-south road in Illinois had first been planned in the 1830's by ambitious businessmen in Cairo, at the southern tip of the state, in order to divert to themselves from St. Louis the business of the thriving Mississippi River mining town of Galena, in Illinois' northwest corner. This project collapsed in 1837. When it was revived in the late 1840's, the far-seeing Stephen A. Douglas, then a congressman from Chicago, proposed that the project be extended eastward from Galena to his city. By thus gaining for Chicago a rail connection with the upper Mississippi River, Douglas hoped to draw from St. Louis not only Galena's business but the business of the whole booming Mississippi Valley and the newly opened plains beyond. For this big idea he sought southern support by offering to link his road with Mobile, which craved a connection of its own with the Mississippi River in order to outstrip New Orleans. It was Douglas who, with southern votes, carried through Congress the first momentous railroad land grant.

Once Illinois had received its share of the grant, a great contest took place in the state legislature in 1851 for the charter of the company that would actually get the land with which to finance the construction of the Illinois part of the road. The victors were a group of New York capitalists allied with the Bostonian, John Murray Forbes. They called their company the Illinois Central. Construction soon got underway, and by 1858 Galena at last was linked by rail with Cairo, and Chicago was linked with both cities.

Forbes had already become seriously interested in other western railroads. In 1846, for example, he and associated Boston financiers had bought from the state of Michigan the defunct Michigan Central, which before the crash of 1837 had been headed toward Chicago from Detroit. They immediately began to push completion of this line. In 1850, meanwhile, a group of New York promoters entirely separate from the Illinois Central crowd had captured the Lake Shore and Michigan Southern Railroad, which, over a more southerly route, paralleled the Michigan Central and tapped a much richer territory. In 1851, just when the Illinois legislature was debating the Illinois Central charter, both Michigan lines had reached the eastern Illinois border and their managers converged on the Illinois legislature for the right to enter the Windy City. This battle was a stand-off, neither side gaining Illinois' consent for building on its territory. But as an active member of the Illinois Central, Forbes at least had a grip on land over which his Michigan Central might proceed. Taking its corporate life in its hands, the Michigan Central built its line to Chicago without permission in 1852, and got away with it.

The Michigan Southern financiers did not come away empty-handed. On the contrary, by acquiring a road, which they renamed the Chicago and Rock Island, they not only got a roundabout entry to Chicago from the east, but they also got the first direct route from Chicago west to the Mississippi River on which the town of Rock Island was situated. This route was opened in 1854.

The contest did not end there, for the Forbes group promptly began the construction and assembling of the lines that by 1856 had grown into the Chicago, Burlington & Quincy Railroad, the first to penetrate the state of Iowa from the east. By then, Forbes' Michigan Central had also made agreements with the New York Central to carry the latter's cars all the way to Chicago and, by way of the Burlington, to points west. Not to be outdone, the Michigan Southern people made arrangements with the Erie Railroad and the intervening lines that had been constructed in Ohio in the 1850's for a route that ran from Jersey City through Chicago to Rock Island.

Before 1852, though it had two little local lines, Chicago did not have a single railroad connection. By 1856, it had become by far the major railroad center of the nation. Almost 2,500 miles of track radiated from it to the East, the South, and the West, and tapped the traffic of 150,000 square miles.

By 1860, a total of 5,000 miles of track terminating in a dozen different railroads extended Chicago's connections all the way to the Missouri River at St. Joseph, Missouri. By then, the Mississippi River had been crossed in twelve places, nine of these places serving roads running out of Chicago. A mere three carried railroads into St. Louis, among them lines working in conjunction with the Pennsylvania and the B.&O. These easterly trunk lines also had connections with Chicago.

By 1860, Ohio, which was criss-crossed by north-south roads linking the Ohio River and Lake Erie and by east-west roads linking the Ohio Valley with New York and Chicago, had become the leading railroad state in the country with nearly 3,000 miles of track. Illinois was a close second, and Indiana was fifth after New York and Pennsylvania. Missouri, which had 4 miles of railroad in 1850, had 817 a decade later; Wisconsin, which had 20 miles in the earlier year, had 905 miles by 1860; Iowa, which had not a single mile of railroad in 1850, built 655 in the next ten years.

All over the West the railroad knocked out the canal systems and decimated river traffic. The railroads were faster than canal barges or steamboats. They ran everywhere that traffic warranted and many places where traffic was only a promise for the future. Moreover, railroad spurs could be laid right to factory doors and warehouses. Speeding their triumph, also, were the competitive practices of their managers. Where they had water rivals, the railroads cut their rates even below cost to capture the available traffic. They recouped their losses on such runs by charging all the traffic would bear at non-competitive terminals.

Two waterways survived railroad competition. One was the Great Lakes route, where such heavy freight as wheat and iron ore could still be carried more efficiently by water. The other was the Erie Canal. The continued use of both waterways reflected the massive volume of the east-west trade, which needed every carrier available to meet the demands of the rising population of the western farms and the eastern cities. As for the east-west railroads themselves, the Census of 1860 said, "So great are their benefits that, if the entire cost of railroads between the Atlantic and the western States had been

levied on the farmers of the central west, their proprietors could have paid it and been immensely the gainers."

V. THE ADVANCE OF NORTHERN INDUSTRY

Industry and the Union. "Could the Union endure?—that," writes Allan Nevins, "was the anxious, all pervading question that faced the politicians" of the 1850's. "Could a truly national utilization of the country's resources be achieved?—that was the major question confronting business leaders." The steamboat and clipper-ship operators, and the canal- and the railroad-builders had done everything they could to further this "truly national utilization." But their work, by drawing the East and the West closer together, seemed only to broaden the chasm between the free states and the slave. The spread of manufacturing in the free states, while the South concentrated ever more single-mindedly on growing cotton, made still clearer the differences in the opposing sections' ways of life.

In the 1850's, the North was almost unanimous in the belief that the country's growth would proceed apace even if the South should desert the Union. In the North in the 1850's, writes Nevins, "the underlying forces of the industrial revolution were simply irresistible." Among them he notes the country's natural resources, the movement of immigrants into the labor force, the energy and inventiveness of the people, the flow of capital from California gold mines and from abroad, government friendliness to industrial objectives as shown in tariff policies and low taxes, and government subsidization of transportation. All these, he writes, "combined like a chain of bellows to make the forge roar."

Industry and Farming. And yet we should not lose sight of the fact that the roar of industry even in the North had only begun to be heard. As late as 1860, the richest men

in the North with few exceptions were merchants rather than industrialists. Among them were H. B. Claflin, who had built up a great wholesale drygoods business on the modern principle of mass sales at the lowest possible unit profit; A. T. Stewart, one of the creators of the American department store, whose retail emporium later became John Wanamaker's in New York; and Charles L. Tiffany, who made his fortune selling jewelry and silverware to other rich merchants who could afford them. A large amount of early railroad enterprise and capital was supplied by China traders like John Murray Forbes and his mercantile relatives and friends who made up the "Forbes group"; and by importers and financiers like George Griswold, Jonathan Sturges, and Morris Ketchum, who headed the New Yorkers in the Illinois Central project.

The stock-in-trade of all these men had been manufactured goods not from American factories or handicrafters but almost exclusively from abroad. The narrow limits of our domestic industrial progress before 1860 are suggested by the urgent missions the North itself had to send to Europe at the outbreak of the Civil War to purchase arms and woolen cloth for uniforms. These purchases, like the imports of the previous peaceful years, were paid for largely by the export of our vast agricultural surpluses, which even during the years of "irresistible" industrial progress were growing faster than the product of industrial establishments.

The first fairly accurate census of American manufactures was taken in 1850. The results were doubly dramatic, for they showed (1) that the products of American industry had just passed $1 billion in value, and (2) that this figure was a few million dollars more than the value of all agricultural products, including cotton. In the next ten years, as the Census of 1860 showed, American manufacturers had pushed their production almost to $2 billion. The exact figure was $1,885,862,000. This was an advance that merited the plaudits manufacturers received. Yet by 1860, agriculture seemed to have regained the leadership it had lost ten years earlier, for its commodities were now valued at $1,910,000,000.

The growth of manufacturing and the growth of agriculture, of course, reinforced one another. As industrial cities grew, their landless populations provided expanding markets for farm products. As the number of farms increased, farm families provided an expanding home market for domestic manufactures. Yet it is remarkable how closely related to agriculture itself large segments of American manufacturing still remained. One of the great industries of 1860 was the making of lumber from the virgin forests that still covered much of the land of the country. Lumber production that year was evaluated by the Census at $105 million, about equal to the value of cotton textile production itself. Far higher than either in value were the flour and meal produced by the milling industry. Its output in 1860 was placed by the Census at nearly $250 million—more than one-eighth of the nation's entire industrial production. The distilling of spirits, the brewing of beer, the tanning of leather, and the packing of meat also were growing fast.

All these industries were to be found in the cities of the East, but it was in the West that their greatest volume was produced by factories growing yearly in size and output. The scale of their operations, however, was not the only modern characteristic of leading western factories. By the 1850's, many lumber mills had begun to specialize in the machine production of barrel staves or shingles or railroad ties. Specialization and mechanization characterized other industries as well, none more than meat-packing. This industry had also developed to a high degree

the modern principle of utilizing by-products. The hams and shoulders of hogs would be packed as meat. The rest of the flesh might then be rendered into oil, which was in demand as a lubricant and illuminant. The bristles were used for brushes, the blood for chemicals, the hooves for glue. What remained of the animals was made into fertilizer.

Another modern feature of meat-packing was the use of inclined tables down which each carcass would slide past a stationary worker who was responsible for removing a particular part. This "continuous-flow" method remains one of the key principles of the modern assembly-line technique. In the milling of flour, mechanical conveyor belts were achieving the same "continuous flow" economies. One of the great industries of the West was the manufacture of agricultural machinery. Here mass production by means of the assembly of interchangeable metal parts was perhaps more advanced than in any other industry in the United States.

Progress in Invention. At the 1851 "world's fair" that was held at the Crystal Palace in London, few exhibits won greater admiration than the American display of farm devices. Everything from road-scrapers and sausage-stuffers to currycombs and hay-rakes "bore off the palm" for their "ingenuity, utility, and cheapness." Few of these inventions were ever patented, and to hardly any can the name of the inventor be applied.

Non-agricultural inventions still were far less numerous than agricultural ones, but they helped swell the number of patents issued by the United States Patent Office each year after the opening of the office in 1790. In 1835, a record number of patents, 752, had been issued; in 1860, 4,700 were granted. Most, no doubt, went to the inventors of the different devices. But some went to promoters of unsung inventors' work.

One of the great inventions of the nineteenth century was the electric telegraph, for which Samuel F. B. Morse, the painter, received the first American patent in 1840.

But his contributions to the device, which was perfected for commercial use in the United States in 1844, were far more promotional than mechanical. Back in 1831, Joseph Henry, one of America's superlative scientists, and later the first director of the Smithsonian Institution in Washington, rang a bell by transmitting an electric impulse to it over a mile of wire. This accomplishment was built on a century's growth of electrical knowledge with which Morse had scarcely a nodding acquaintance. In 1837, Henry made the idea behind his feat available to the English inventor, Charles Wheatstone, who proceeded forthwith to furnish his homeland with telegraph service. The significant American contribution to telegraph operation was the now universally used "Morse Code," but Morse himself designed neither the apparatus nor the alphabet. Much more of the credit belongs to his partner, Alfred Vail.

It was Morse who prodded Congress into making a financial contribution to the telegraph's development in 1843 and who staged the famous tableau on May 24, 1844, in the Supreme Court chambers in Washington, from where he sent the message, "What hath God wrought?" to Vail in Baltimore and then received it back. Immediately public interest in the telegraph was kindled and companies began bidding for the rights. In 1860, the United States had 50,000 miles of telegraph wire. In 1861, a transcontinental telegraph was opened.

In England the telegraph was used first to improve control of railroad traffic, an application that came later in the United States. The American telegraph was first used to send business messages and public information. Its effect on the newspaper business was enormous. By the time the telegraph had been perfected, the "penny press" dominated American journalism, and printing machinery had been developed that could produce 1,000 newspapers an hour. Now the demand was for at least 10,000 an hour. This resounding figure was achieved in 1847 with the cylindrical press developed by Richard March Hoe. Steady improvement thereafter in the press and other printing equipment enabled the newspaper to keep pace with the people's rising requirements for "hot news," advertising, and printed entertainment.

Of all the new patents, two in manufacturing itself perhaps merit special mention: (1) the vulcanization of rubber, and (2) the sewing machine. "India" rubber (most of which came from South America, though the East Indies supplied some) had a seemingly unique imperviousness to rain, snow, and mud. But when exposed to heat, products made from it melted, clung, and collapsed. It was Charles Goodyear, a stubborn, sick, impoverished Yankee, who after years of effort finally arrived at the proper mixture of raw rubber, chemicals, and heat by which rubber goods might be made stable at all ordinary temperatures. This process was called "vulcanization," and was patented by Goodyear in 1844. A profitable rubber-goods industry quickly arose, licensed under Goodyear's patent. Goodyear himself died in 1860, leaving debts of $200,000.

Before the advent of the automobile, rubber was used mainly in making boots and shoes. Elias Howe's sewing machine, patented in 1846, also gave that industry a boost. Howe's machine aroused little interest in America until 1851, when Isaac Merrit Singer entered the picture. An important mechanical inventor in his own right, who had made many improvements in the sewing machine's operation, Singer's main contribution was the invention of installment selling. This idea he sold by mass advertising. Working up a mass market in this way, he proceeded to mass-produce the machines, using assembly-line methods. By 1860, a total of 110,000 sewing machines had been made, largely for home use but also for factories. Almost all boots and shoes were now factory-sewn. Another great industry to emerge as a result of the sewing machine was the men's ready-made clothing industry.

Many of the leading inventions of antebellum days led to the development of entirely new industries not only for the manufacture of the new devices themselves, but also for their employment. This situation attests to the genuine creativity of American society. But it also suggests that our industrial condition was itself not very mature. Only in the manufacture of cotton and woolen goods did the United States have an advanced factory industry. Here spectacular new inventions were no longer to be looked for, but a continuous round of invention had very telling consequences. About textile manufacturing, Victor S. Clark, the historian of American industry, has this to say:

At the opening of the [nineteenth] century the owner of a factory thought that he had done well if from the day he purchased his cotton or wool to the time he sold his goods no more than a year elapsed. Within a few years machinery had so accelerated manufacturing that in its ordinary course goods often reached buyers a few days after the raw material from which they were made was received at the factory.

The speeding-up of production was more marked in the cotton-goods industry than in woolens. In both, new machines like the Crompton loom, which permitted the weaving of patterns, and new applications of chemistry, which led to improved dyes of many colors, added to the variety of factory-made cloth. Middle-class consumers now had a wide range of styles and qualities to choose from at prices importers no longer could match. Women became increasingly conscious of fashion, and as annual changes became mandatory to keep up with the Joneses, the demand for factory-made textiles grew. In 1860, the cotton-goods industry ranked second to milling in value of product. This category, of course, included the value of the raw materials. In "value *added by manufacture,*" the cotton-textile industry was the nation's leader.

The Iron Industry.   The whole cycle of invention from the simple steel plow to the Hoe press and the sewing machine gave a great boost to the American iron industry. The new reapers and threshers, and the rakes

and seed drills, all had their iron and steel parts. By 1860, about 3,500 steamboats had been built for western rivers alone, all of them requiring iron sheets for the original boilers and replacements. The hulls of the clipper ships were themselves reinforced with iron forms. The telegraph was strung entirely with iron wire until copper began to replace it in the 1860's. By 1846, John A. Roebling, the future builder of the Brooklyn Bridge, had begun to use wire rope in bridge suspension. Four years later, James Bogardus, an imaginative New Yorker, erected the world's first completely cast-iron building. Cast iron buckled under strain; but when wrought-iron beams began to be rolled for building construction, the invention of the skyscraper was in the offing. The first wrought-iron building was New York's Cooper Union, erected in 1854. Machinery for the manufacture of textiles and for other manufacturing industries also required growing amounts of iron. For machines that made machines, iron, of course, was indispensable.

By far the biggest user of iron in the 1850's was the railroad. As early as 1860 more than half the iron produced in the United States went into rails, locomotives, wheels, axles, and hundreds of other parts of the railroad's stationary equipment and rolling stock. The railroads, moreover, had by far the most extensive machine shops in the country; these shops not only made parts and repairs but also made their own iron and steel tools and machinery.

To supply the needs of a society turning to industry, many important changes were introduced into the American manufacture of pig iron and the many iron forms into which the pig eventually was shaped. In the refining of iron ore and the manufacture of iron products, as in so many other industrial processes, heat is the key element. One of the fundamental changes in iron manufacture after 1840 was the accelerated shift from wood and charcoal (half-burned wood) to anthracite and coke (half-burned soft coal) for fuel. The new combustibles were able to attain far greater temperatures than the old, and hence speeded up production. A second great change was the more frequent employment of rolling mills in place of the hand forge for shaping iron forms. The improvements in iron-making were reflected in a four-fold increase in the production of pig iron between 1842 and 1860, its annual volume on the eve of the Civil War having risen to 920,000 tons.

Yet one of the most striking things about the American iron industry in the 1850's remains its slow development rather than its rise. In 1860, the United States mined less iron ore and manufactured less pig iron than Britain had 20 years earlier. Britain's coal production in 1860 was five times the output of United States mines, and even little Belgium mined 60 per cent as much coal as Americans did.

In 1856, Abram Hewitt, America's leading iron manufacturer, said in an address: "The consumption of iron is a social barometer by which to estimate the relative height of civilization among nations." At that time, America's consumption of iron only suggested how far we had yet to go to catch up with the industrial nations of the day. Certain scattered incidents, of interest because of their relation to enormous changes later, underline the immaturity of our industrial spirit. As early as 1829, for example, drillers had brought in an oil gusher in Kentucky; but it only terrified and angered the workmen, who had been looking for salt. Two years later, Joseph Henry had worked out the essentials of the electric dynamo; but many decades passed before his "philosophical toy," as he called his electromagnetic machine, found practical employment. In 1847, William Kelly, an ironmaster of Kentucky, had discovered the essential process for the mass production of steel; but scarcely anyone was apprised of this until the Englishman, Henry Bessemer, sought American patents in 1856 for a similar process and the machinery for its employment. Even so, it was another 15 years before Bessemer steel began to be produced in large commercial quantities in the United States.

VI. INDUSTRY AND SOCIETY

By 1860, invention and industry had begun to transform the face of America and the character of its people. But the majority of farmers and the commercial elements in the cities had reason enough to misjudge both the force and the imminence of the revolution taking place on their doorstep. Three years before, in 1857, the country had suffered a severe economic decline. But there had been panics in the past, notably in 1819 and 1837, so there was nothing in the mere occurrence of the Panic of 1857 to suggest that a revolution was taking place.

Yet there were new elements in the crash of 1857 which indicated something of the changes America had undergone in the preceding 20 years. For one thing, unemployment during the depression that followed the panic was far greater than in any previous depression. By 1857, factory employment had risen to 1,300,000, and together with construction laborers made up an industrial working force of almost 2 million persons.

The working and living conditions of industrial laborers had never been worse than in the 1850's. Strikes on railroad projects and in factories became especially numerous in 1853 and after. But not even the craft unions had recovered from the crash of 1837 (see p. 209). The unskilled hands had no spokesmen and no organization. Factories, moreover, had become centers of petty tyranny ruled by foremen, and long hours helped to drain the spark of leadership and self-interest required for reform. As the industrial cities became increasingly crowded, living conditions became so bad that workers preferred to put in long hours in the factories, sheltered and among friends, rather than spend the time at home. Under these circumstances, the crash of 1857, which threw hundreds of thousands out of work, was necessarily more brutal than any earlier ones.

By 1857, more than a billion dollars had been invested in manufacturing, most of it in factory buildings and costly machinery. Another billion had been invested in railroads, two-thirds of it in the seven years just preceding the crash. These were also new elements in the panic picture. Earlier panics had been precipitated largely by the absorption of capital in land-speculation at prices far in advance of any reasonable expectation of return. By 1857, overinvestment in productive facilities was very important in bringing about the stringency of funds.

The source of funds for these investments introduced still another new element, which was to balloon in importance in later years. This new feature was speculation in corporate stocks and bonds. Purchases often were made with mere token down payments eked out with loans at high interest from New York banks. These banks often paid interest themselves to depositors in whose number was included so many other banks that in the late 1850's 70 per cent of the entire country's bank reserves were on deposit in New York. In times of financial emergency, country banks would seek to withdraw some of their funds. New York banks then would have to call in the loans made with the country deposits. In times of speculation and financial stringency, this action was likely to set up a snowballing of failures among borrowers caught short.

On August 24, 1857, the New York branch of the leading bank in Ohio, the so-called Ohio Life Insurance and Trust Company, discovered that its treasurer had embezzled most of its funds and was forced to close its doors. The parent bank in Ohio soon failed; news of the failure caused a run on the New York banks and by October 13 all but one of them had closed down, as had most of the banks throughout the country.

There was enough about this crash to confirm conservatives in their belief that American finance had not changed much since 1837. There had been huge land-speculations in the 1850's, the number of banks in the country had expanded rapidly, and their loans had grown faster than their numbers. But American industrial overexpansion lay at the bottom of the trouble. From the crash, fortunately, industrialists learned valuable lessons.

In the 1860's, most leading businessmen remained merchants, but the businessmen with the future on their side already were industrial corporation executives, often administrators for absentee owners or scattered stockholders. For profits, such men could no longer look to the lucky voyage or the fortunate speculation or the simple soundness and progress of the country. Profits would come henceforth from strict attention to management—from cautious financing, careful bookkeeping, enhancement of labor productivity, adaptability to changing markets. Profits promised to grow enormously beyond the dreams of speculative avarice; but they

Run on a New York bank during the Panic of 1857.

were as likely as not to be made up of mountains of pennies and fractions of pennies, and they were likely to disappear if constant attention was not given to such insignificant sums.

The lure of speculation did not die; the unsettled conditions during the Civil War cre-

ated a speculator's paradise. But American industrialists had learned something of the industrial discipline itself, and the North—and ultimately the nation—was the stronger for it.

Readings

Most of the books suggested in the reading list for Chapter IX are important for the subjects dealt with in this chapter. One might note from that list as particularly relevant and engaging the works by Roger Burlingame, Samuel E. Morison, George R. Taylor, Thomas C. Cochran and William Miller, Louis C. Hunter, Seymour Dunbar, Robert G. Albion, Caroline F. Ware, Victor S. Clark, and John R. Commons. To these, for this chapter, should be added Allan Nevins, *Ordeal of the Union* (2 vols., 1947), especially Volume II, chapters I and V-VIII; Arthur C. Cole, *The Irrepressible Conflict, 1850-1865* (1934); and Edward W. Martin, *The Standard of Living in 1860* (1942).

The writings of Hamlin Garland on the Middle Border are full of interest. The reader might start with *A Son of the Middle Border* (1917). A moving account of pioneer life in Illinois is Francis Grierson, *The Valley of Shadows* (1948). For the immigrants, Marcus Lee Hansen, *The Atlantic Migration, 1607-1860* (1940), is indispensable. Somewhat less formal is the same author's *The Immigrant in American History* (1940). A more general account of immigration is Carl Wittke, *We Who Built America* (1939). On the relation of the farmer to God and the soil, an illuminating book is Henry Nash Smith, *Virgin Land* (1950). The best work on northern agriculture is Percy W. Bidwell and J. I. Falconer, *History of Agriculture in the Northern United States, 1620-1860* (1925).

The basic book on American trade is Emory R. Johnson, and others, *History of Domestic and Foreign Commerce of the United States* (2 vols., 1915). One of the best business biographies, and relevant to shipping, is Wheaton J. Lane, *Commodore Vanderbilt* (1942). The classic work on the clipper ships is Arthur H. Clark, *The Clipper Ship Era, 1843-1869* (1910).

An excellent introduction to railroad history is Frederick A. Cleveland and Fred W. Powell, *Railroad Promotion and Capitalization in the United States* (1909). A newer and unusually important book is Alfred D. Chandler, Jr., *Henry Varnum Poor: Business Editor, Analyst, and Reformer* (1956). The classic work on New England railroads is Edward C. Kirkland, *Men, Cities and Transportation, 1820-1900* (2 vols., 1948). Many individual roads have had their history written, usually without distinction. Two first-rate books on railroads and western lands are Paul W. Gates, *The Illinois Central Railroad and Its Colonization Work* (1934); and Richard C. Overton, *Burlington West* (1941). Thomas C. Cochran, *Railroad Leaders, 1845-1890: The Business Mind in Action* (1953), fulfills the promise of its subtitle excellently.

Besides the volumes by Burlingame and others suggested at the head of this list, illuminating works on American industry and invention in this period include the imaginative *Made in America,* by John A. Kouwenhoven (1948); and on the iron industry, Allan Nevins, *Abram S. Hewitt, With Some Account of Peter Cooper* (1935). Waldemar Kaempffert, ed., *A Popular History of American Invention* (2 vols., 1924), is very informative. The more recent *American Science and Invention, A Pictorial History,* by Mitchell Wilson (1954), is an exciting compilation. An important book on a badly neglected figure is Thomas Coulson, *Joseph Henry, His Life and Work* (1950). On the conditions of labor, a basic account is Norman Ware, *The Industrial Worker, 1840-1860* (1924). On banking and the money market, see Margaret G. Myers, *The New York Money Market* (1931); Leland H. Jenks, *The Migration of British Capital to 1875* (1927); and the work by Alfred D. Chandler, Jr., referred to above among the books on railroads. Much the best account of the ups and downs of economic life is Walter B. Smith and Arthur H. Cole, *Fluctuations in American Business, 1790-1860* (1935).

A VIOLENT DECADE

C H A P T E R   F I F T E E N

The turbulent 50's began in compromise and ended in secession. At the beginning of the decade North and South, like two bellicose nations, watched each other uneasily. While responsible statesmen, of whom there were too few, tried desperately to find ways of reconciling sectional differences, powerful forces seemed to be pulling the sections apart.

The most divisive force was slavery, charged with double mischief because it was at once a profoundly exciting moral problem and a system of property and labor. Northern abolitionists looked upon slavery as a sin. To the southerners, it was the linchpin of their civilization, the agency of their material well-being, and the only alternative to the catastrophe of "mongrelization." While abolitionist agitators in the North and sectional chauvinists in the South ˙created an atmosphere of heightened hostility, businessmen and promoters (often as indifferent to moral issues as the agitators were inspired by them) followed the main chance, speculated, organized enterprises, settled land, and sought profits without regard to sectional aims. Unfortunately the promotional impulse, so long a common force in American life, could not go its own way without encountering the agitational impulse and adding rancor and heat to the conflict. In the organization of territories, in the settlement of disputed areas like Kansas, the promoters did not stop considerately while compromising politicians tried to work out satisfactory arrangements. Instead, they plunged in and made workable arrangements doubly difficult to achieve.

I. A HOUSE DIVIDED

In the past, political leaders had been able to mediate between the sections whenever the slavery issue threatened to upset the balance of power between them. The Constitutional Convention, for example, had devised the "three-fifths compromise." And the next generation, increasingly aware of maintaining the nice balance between the sections, had negotiated the Missouri Compromise. More recently, the great generation of leaders that was just passing from the scene had exerted themselves to the utmost before settling the issues between the sections with the Compromise of 1850.

Now, with the final settlement of the continent plainly foreseeable, the lands that were left seemed fated to become free territory, thus depriving the South of the equality in the Senate which had so long seemed to guarantee its defenses. What was to prevent the expanding North from overrunning the territories, carving out more and more new states, and ultimately amassing enough political strength to abolish slavery throughout the Union? What constitutional guarantee would be left if the North were to become overwhelmingly strong? In the days when the Mexican question was in the limelight, a few southerners had toyed with the idea of a Mexican conquest that would make possible the setting up of many new slave states; but most thoughtful southerners had followed Calhoun in shrinking from the tremendous responsibilities of such an undertaking. Cuba still intrigued many southerners as a possible source of power, profits, slaves, senatorial votes, and sectional gratification. But the failure to gain control over Cuba in 1854 left many southerners feeling that the only line of action was to try to force slavery—against the probabilities of nature and economics and the determination of free-soilers—into the new territories that were being organized in the West, and to give these territories a southern and pro-slavery complexion. Should that attempt fail, why not strike out for southern independence while the physical strength of the two sides was still almost equal, rather than wait for the North to become overwhelmingly powerful?

The earlier spirit of compromise had been nourished by powerful institutional bonds between the two sections. Even more effective than the old ties of sentiment and trade and religion were the intersectional political parties, in which leaders from North and South could sit down as cronies and pass easily from the planning of party strategy to the settlement of sectional differences. During the violent decade of the 50's, however, these bonds of union, one by one, loosened and broke apart. First the Whig party disintegrated early in the decade, the victim of its own inability to find a common ground and to meet the divisive force of slavery agitation. Then, at the end of the decade, the Democratic party, split between Douglas and Buchanan factions and unable to hold together ardent southerners and advocates of popular sovereignty, broke up during the election of 1860. When Lincoln, the candidate of a thoroughly sectional party, was elected president with a minority of the popular vote, the Union toppled.

Between 1820 and 1860, a raw and heterogeneous society had been forming and expanding rapidly. The enormously complicated problems created by the social and economic transformation of the times were beyond the capacities of American leaders to solve. Slavery became the explosive issue that divided the sections, but behind this emotion-stirring symbol was a more important cultural fact: the North and the South did not think alike. "I fear Northerner and Southerner are aliens," a young South Carolinian remarked in 1860, "not merely in social and political arrangements, but in mental and moral constitution. We differ like Celt and Anglo-Saxon, and there is no sufficient force in 'a government of opinion' to keep us together against our will." On one essential he was right: the emotional climate in the 50's was not favorable to tolerance. The noble ideals of both sections—the dreams of a southern nation purged of northern vulgarity and greed, and the humanitarian visions of northern reformers—were finally swallowed up in the bloodiest war of the nineteenth century.

II. THE WEDGES OF SEPARATION

Pierce and Slavery.   Franklin Pierce of New Hampshire, the fourteenth President of the United States, lacked the qualities of leadership that were desperately needed during his administration (1853-1857). Good-humored, affectionate, magnetic, and universally well-liked when he took office, he quickly revealed himself (in the words of a contemporary) as "a vain, showy, and pliant man." Although he wished to restore national harmony, he failed to gauge the strength of the contesting forces, free and slave, that sought to dominate his government. Pierce might have succeeded in a sim-

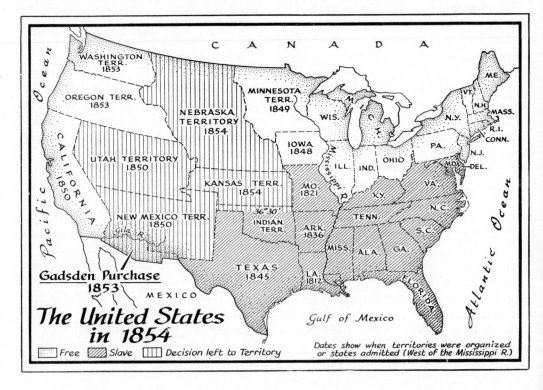

Gadsden Purchase 1853

The United States in 1854

☐ Free   ▨ Slave   ⊞ Decision left to Territory

Dates show when territories were organized or states admitted (West of the Mississippi R.)

pler agrarian age, but he was a misfit in 1853.

Most Americans in 1852 hoped that passage of the Compromise of 1850 would stifle slavery agitation once and for all, but extremists on both sides of the Mason and Dixon line did their best to keep it flaming. During Pierce's fateful administration, the slavery issue was ominously reopened. The North had gagged at the provision in the Compromise of 1850 requiring the return of fugitive slaves, and many northern states passed "personal liberty" laws deliberately intended to hamper the recovery of runaways. Actually, the number of slaves who managed to escape (most of them from the border states) was comparatively small. In 1850, for example, slightly more than 1,000 out of a total slave population of over 3 million ran away, and not all of them crossed over to the free states. But the South regarded the northerners' cooperation with the fugitives as one more proof of a plot to ruin southern prosperity and as conclusive evidence of northern hostility to southern institutions. Northerners, on the other hand (even those who disliked Negroes almost as much as they respected property), now began to condemn slavery as an archaic institution inimical to free labor and national progress.

The person who singlehandedly did more to arouse a national hatred of slavery than any other American was the novelist, Harriet Beecher Stowe. A New Englander who had lived close to slavery in the border city of Cincinnati, Ohio, she wrote her *Uncle Tom's Cabin* (1852) in the belief that once the South recognized the sinfulness of slaveholding, the Negroes would be freed. The sensational incident, humor, and pathos of this powerful tract was calculated to appeal to a vast audience in the North, particularly the women, who responded emotionally to the heart-breaking episodes of Negro mothers forcibly separated from their children. Even southern matrons wept at these passages, and one distinguished Virginia lady, whose five sons fought in the Confederate army, hid a copy of *Uncle Tom's Cabin* under her bed throughout the Civil War. Mrs. Stowe's

A poster advertising Uncle Tom's Cabin.

novel sold 300,000 copies during its first year of publication, and thousands of Americans knew the story in its dramatized version. One young southerner in 1853, after reading Mrs. Stowe's novel, observed that it

... greatly tended to open the widening breach between the two sections, to inflame one-half of the nation against the other, to produce disunion and to stir up a civil war, a war in comparison with which all the bloody scenes of History would be but Child's play; can any *friend* of the human race, or any *friend* of the Negro desire such an issue?

The northern resistance to slavery, quickened by *Uncle Tom's Cabin,* showed itself in widespread flouting of the Fugitive Slave Law. In Chicago and Detroit, federal officers trying to reclaim fugitive slaves were almost mobbed. In Boston, Theodore Parker, the preacher and abolitionist, helped a Negro couple escape to England and brought so much popular pressure to bear upon the southerners who had come North to bring the fugitives back that they were glad to

339

return to Georgia. In 1851, a mob in upstate New York rescued a Missouri slave named Jerry from the law, and in the same year only the use of force prevented a crowd of Bostonians from stopping the extradition of another fugitive slave, Thomas Sims. As it was, the recapture of Sims cost his owner $5,000. The South considered these and other incidents as clear violations of its constitutional rights and responded with countermeasures. A vociferous minority demanded the reopening of the African slave trade. A more influential group of southern leaders, supported by northern well-wishers (including Pierce himself), agitated for the acquisition of Cuba, which would have opened up a large and profitable slave territory.

Cuba had been eyed by American expansionists for some time. In 1848, Spain had haughtily turned down Polk's offer of $100

Stephen A. Douglas (1813-1861).

million for the island, but the expansionist Pierce administration tried again. Spain had already been alarmed by two filibustering expeditions launched against Cuba from the American mainland in 1850 and 1851. Offended by these events and by the provocative behavior of the American minister to Spain, Pierre Soulé, Spain again rejected offers of purchase. In 1854, a naval incident at Havana gave Pierce an excuse to press the question again, even though it was plain that a war over Cuba—given the excited state of popular feeling—would split the country and the Democratic party. At the behest of Secretary of State Marcy, Soulé met to discuss the matter with James Buchanan, the Minister to England, and John Y. Mason, minister to France, at Ostend and Aix la Chapelle in Belgium, and drew up what has come to be known as the Ostend Manifesto, October 15, 1854.

Despite its name, the "Manifesto" was no public declaration but rather a confidential dispatch to Marcy that became known only because enemies of the administration in the House of Representatives insisted on its publication. The three diplomats had recommended that the United States offer $120 million for Cuba and, if the offer was rejected, should seize it on the ground that Spain's control of it gravely endangered "our internal peace and the existence of our cherished Union." The diplomats were merely advising Marcy to do what he already contemplated; what he had hoped for from them was not this truculent suggestion, but an estimate of how the European powers would react to American aggression in Cuba. When the contents of the dispatch became known, free-soilers denounced it vigorously—the New York *Tribune* called it a "Manifesto of Brigands"—and Marcy had to repudiate its proposals. The incident suggested that there was not enough domestic support for expansion into Cuba to press that line of action as a solution for southern discontents.

The Kansas-Nebraska Act.

The question of slaveholding in the western territories and future states had stirred up controversies before the turbulent 50's, but the Missouri Compromise and the Compromise of 1850 had been workable adjustments. It was the unhappy distinction of the Pierce administration to witness the passage of the Kansas-Nebraska Act, a measure that rekindled the sectional controversies temporarily allayed by the earlier compromises. So many issues, open and concealed, lay behind the Kansas-Nebraska Act that any short account is likely to oversimplify it. Railroads, private political ambitions, sectional bargaining, slavery, all played a part, and so did the ever-mounting pressure of settlers to move into the unoccupied and fertile Nebraska country.

The central figure in this drama was Senator Stephen A. Douglas, New England born, but by 1850 the idol of his Illinois constituents whose aspirations he so thoroughly embodied. Douglas had been an ardent supporter of land-grant aid to railroads and the opening up of new territory to western settlers. He had been instrumental in promoting the Illinois Central Railroad, had invested in Chicago and Minnesota real estate, and as early as 1848 had been interested in a central or northern transcontinental railroad that would link the Pacific with a Chicago or Minnesota terminus. Before such a railroad could be built, however, the Nebraska Territory would have to be organized for settlement.

The proponents of the central and northern routes were challenged by the claims of competing promoters of a transcontinental line to the south. A government-sponsored survey showed that a southern route along the Mexican border (with Memphis, New Orleans, or some other Mississippi port as a terminus) offered fewer physical obstacles than the northern routes, and the proposed southern line became even more practical when the United States bought a strip of territory from Mexico in 1853—the Gadsden Purchase (see p. 281). In order for Douglas to win support for a bill to organize the Nebraska Territory, he had to make concessions both to the southern group and to the Missouri advocates of a central route to the Pacific, who wanted St. Louis as the terminus. Two facts were plain in 1854: Congress would help build only one transcontinental route, and the pro-slavery men—particularly those in Missouri—would not even consider the construction of a road through territory forever closed to slavery. Such was the situation on January 23, 1854, when Douglas, after preliminary discussions with his southern colleagues, introduced in the Senate his bill to organize the Nebraska Territory.

Douglas' bill called for the organization of two territories, Kansas and Nebraska, to be divided at the 40th parallel. The decision to create two territories was made on the insistence of some Iowa congressmen, who feared that a single territory would assure the laying of the railroad through the southern-dominated Kansas valley at the expense of the free-soil settlers in the valley of the Platte. The Kansas-Nebraska Act, as finally passed on May 30, 1854, included two important provisos. First, it declared "that all questions pertaining to slavery in the territories, and in the new States to be formed therefrom, are to be left to the people residing therein, through their appropriate representatives." Second, the act expressly repealed the Missouri Compromise (since the new territories lay above the line 36° 30') and abandoned the idea that Congress could exclude slavery from the territories. In brief, the Kansas-Nebraska Act said that the residents of the two territories were to put "popular sovereignty" into practice and decide for themselves about slavery in their future states. But the act was silent on the question of just when this decision should be made in the progress of these territories toward statehood.

Douglas had predicted that his action would raise "the hell of a storm," and he was right. Just what prompted him to risk such a storm is still a matter of conjecture, but a number of considerations seem to have influenced him. Contemporaries charged that he was courting the South's support in a bid for the presidency. Historians have also pointed out that the plan to construct a transcontinental railway demanded the organization and settlement of much of the intervening territory. Douglas, the argument goes, who was associated with real-estate and railroad interests in Chicago, had reasons to make arrangements that would lead to the adoption of a Chicago terminus. However, Douglas had originally favored the construction of three transcontinental roads and by no means insisted upon a Chicago terminus.

But there is evidence that other considerations, probably even more important, were in his mind. The Pierce administration was floundering, and the territorial question stood unsettled. Douglas seems to have felt that his policy would fulfill the desires of the Northwest, provide leadership and cohesion for the Democrats and a workable solution for the territorial problem, and at the same time legitimately advance his own presidential plans. As the historian Allan Nevins has put it: "It seemed to him the most practical policy, and perhaps the fairest, to abrogate the Missouri Compromise, throw the area wide to slaveholder and Northerner alike, and let the popular will decide." Douglas was convinced that "in that climate, with its productions, it is worse than folly to think of its being a slaveholding country." If nature and economics would in the end keep slavery out of this territory, he felt that free-soil principles could triumph there without resort to the device of congressional exclusion, which was so exasperating to southerners. Reasonable northerners, he apparently assumed, would accept this solution; reasonable southerners would yield to fate so long as they were not wantonly provoked.

But most Americans did not accept this solution quietly. To be sure, the South wanted to repeal the Missouri Compromise line, and southern congressmen backed Douglas heartily; but, as we shall see, the South did not in the long run reconcile itself to the idea of a free-soil victory through popular sovereignty. To many southern newspapers, the Kansas-Nebraska Act seemed "barren of practical benefit" and calculated to aid the abolitionist cause. And in many parts of the North the reaction was immediately hostile. Latter-day critics of Douglas insist that he looked upon slavery as a matter of dollars and cents, that he felt it could and should be established where it was profitable and abandoned where it did not pay. His partisans have denied this charge. But apparently he was incapable of realizing that to millions of men slavery was an issue charged with moral dynamite. He was soon reminded of the true state of affairs, however, for Whigs and free-soil Democrats in the North denounced the measure violently. Salmon P. Chase, a free-soil Senator of Democratic background, drafted an "Appeal of the Independent Democrats in Congress to the People of the United States," which was signed by a half-dozen congressmen. In this appeal, Chase attacked the Kansas-Nebraska bill as a

. . . criminal betrayal of precious rights; as part and parcel of an atrocious plot to exclude from a vast unoccupied region immigrants from the Old World and free laborers from our own States, and convert it into a dreary region of despotism, inhabited by masters and slaves.

The measure fractured both parties. Northern Democrats split up into Pro-Nebraska and Anti-Nebraska Democrats, and the northern and southern Whigs were hopelessly rent. A thrill of excitement passed over the people of the North, and free-soil leaders shrewdly exploited it. Douglas said he could have traveled from Boston to Chicago by the light of his burning effigies. Throughout the country, anti-Nebraska men began to form a new political organization, which came to be known as the Republican party.

Trouble in Kansas. Did the new territories have the power either to prohibit or legalize slavery before framing their constitutions and before seeking statehood? According to Douglas' theory of popular sovereignty, they did. The South disagreed. No territory could decide this question, southern spokesmen declared, until it became a state. Until then, it could not keep slaves out. As settlers began to move into the fertile country of the Platte, only recently cleared of Indians, this touchy question passed beyond the stage of debate.

The Nebraska Territory lay wholly within the free-soil orbit, but Kansas, adjacent to the slave state of Missouri, had been earmarked for slavery by southern backers of the Kansas-Nebraska Act. It is probable that under normal conditions, Kansas would not have attracted many southern emigrants, for it lay too far to the North. Arkansas, Louisiana, and Texas were the natural outlets for southern expansion, and planters thought twice before transporting valuable slave property at great cost into a region that was unsuited for cotton cultivation and that might ultimately resolve for free labor. Moreover, the average southern emigrant lacked the ready cash to buy good land, which sold from $5 to $10 an acre. Emigrants coming into Kansas via the Missouri River (use of the steamboat was at its height) were more likely to have sufficient capital. Throughout the period from 1854 to 1860, the overwhelming majority of Kansans came from the northwestern states, very few from New England or the South; and yet hot-headed men from North and South, spurred on by partisan newspaper editors and politicians, succeeded in turning Kansas into a battleground. The situation in Kansas was complicated by hordes of newcomers who were often indifferent to slavery but were eager to make profits from the speculative bubble in real estate and willing to take advantage of the slavery controversy to cover up the less savory part of their activities. As historian Roy Nichols has observed, "No one will ever know how much of the political uproar was due to gangsters and racketeers."

The conflict was started by the pro-slavery Missourians, who suspected the abolitionists of plotting to use Kansas as a bridgehead from which to launch an attack against slavery in the Southwest. They publicized the activities of the New England Emigrant Aid Company and other groups organized between 1854 and 1855 to finance free-soil migrations to Kansas and to "beard oppression in its very den." Was not Kansas, the Missourians asked, the natural colony of Missouri? Were not the New England emigrant aid societies violating the principle of popular sovereignty? To forestall the Yankee "serfs," "paupers," and "cut-throats," Missourians saw to it that the Kansas territorial legislature was made up of only pro-slavery men.

On the day on which the territorial legislators were elected, March 30, 1855, thousands of what the abolitionist press described as "bar-room rowdies," "blacklegs," and "border ruffians" poured into Kansas from Missouri. Slightly more than 2,000 men were registered to vote, but over 6,000 ballots were cast. Andrew H. Reeder, a Democrat from Pennsylvania who had been appointed Governor of the Kansas Territory by Pierce, tried to disqualify eight of the thirty-one members who had been elected irregularly, but his attempt at impartiality was not appreciated by the vacillating President. Overriding Reeder's vetoes, the new legislature passed a series of savagely repressive laws that prescribed the death penalty for anyone aiding a fugitive slave or inciting conspiracy. Simply to question the legality of slavery in Kansas carried a sentence of two years at hard labor. Unfortunately, Reeder became involved in land-speculation at this point, and Pierce used this pretext to dismiss him. With Reeder's removal, it looked as if the pro-slavery men had triumphed, but free-soil elements in Kansas refused to acknowledge the pro-slavery government. They named Reeder as a territorial delegate to Congress. In the fall of 1855, they met in Topeka and drew up their own constitution; in January, 1856, they elected a legislature and governor.

With two rival governments established, Kansas was now ripe for conflict. Troublemakers on both sides rashly provoked each other, and both the northern and the southern press played up the iniquities of "border

ruffians" and "abolitionist fanatics." The Missourians took up arms, and the free-staters equipped themselves with rifles that had been shipped to Kansas with the blessings of the celebrated Brooklyn clergyman, Henry Ward Beecher; hence they were known as "Beecher's Bibles." Occasional disorders punctuated the uneasy truce. Then in May, 1856, a force of pro-slavery men led by a United States marshal raided the Kansas town of Lawrence in search of some free-soil leaders who had been indicted for treason by the pro-slavery legislature. Fortified by alcohol, the raiders burned down the hotel and destroyed some homes and free-soil printing presses. This celebrated "sack of Lawrence" was blown up to horrendous proportions by the northern newspapers. Although it had taken only two lives, it produced a bloody sequel. John Brown of Osawatomie, a fanatical abolitionist who was soon to become better known, gathered together six followers, rode into the pro-slavery settlement at Pottawatomie Creek, and wantonly hacked five men to death. He acted, so he said, under God's authority. But his sacred vendetta started a guerrilla war that was to take over 200 lives.

John Brown (1800-1859).

In the meantime, the excitement in Kansas had infected the United States Congress. Order clearly needed to be restored, but the free-soilers refused to go along with Douglas' proposal to admit Kansas as a state as soon as the pro-slavery Kansas legislature had drawn up a constitution and the territorial population had reached the point where it was entitled to one representative. Anti-slavery men like William H. Seward of New York and John P. Hale of New Hampshire argued that only the constitution that had been written in Topeka in 1855 expressed the will of Kansas. On May 19, 1856— shortly after the "sack of Lawrence" but before news of it had reached Washington— Charles Sumner, Senator from Massachusetts, rose to speak on "The Crime Against Kansas."

Blessed with many natural gifts—learned, handsome, and eloquent—Sumner was not an abolitionist of the Garrison variety. But he had a lofty conception of his own uprightness and could be egotistical and stubborn. His Kansas speech, which lasted two days, was a vituperative tirade against the "harlot slavery," especially against the "murderous robbers" of Missouri, "hirelings picked from the drunken spew and vomit of an uneasy civilization." Sumner aimed his choicest epithets at Senator Andrew P. Butler of South Carolina, the man who (said Sumner) "with incoherent phrases, discharged the loose expectoration of his speech." This insulting outburst induced Butler's nephew, Preston Brooks, Representative from South Carolina, to avenge his uncle, his state, and his section —all with one act of violence. Two days later, as Sumner sat at his desk in the Senate Chamber, Brooks struck him repeatedly over the head with a cane and injured him so severely that Sumner remained an invalid for the next three and a half years. The assault on Sumner by "Bully" Brooks, together with the news from Kansas, increased the sectional tension and helped to shape the issues of the coming presidential campaign.

Splintering Parties. Before Pierce's term expired, the old parties had begun to break apart. Pierce had aggravated sectional

Out of the troubles of the old intersectional parties rose a new third party, the American party, a composite of anti-Catholic and anti-foreign groups whose origin dated back to the early 1840's. Stemming from "The Order of the Star-Spangled Banner," the American party raised its patriotic standard in the late months of 1852. Since secret regulations required its members to pretend they "knew nothing" when they were pressed for information about their organization by the curious, they soon became known as "Know Nothings." Their stand against the unassimilated masses of Irish and German immigrants who had collected in the cities proved popular.

Brooks' attack on Sumner.

strife and had divided his party by fostering the Kansas-Nebraska Act. Disgruntled anti-slavery Democrats now fused with free-soil remnants of the deeply divided Whig party. By 1854, events had forced many southern Whigs—the future Confederate vice-president, Alexander H. Stephens, for example— into the Democratic camp. Not until the Reconstruction period following the Civil War were the former southern Whigs— never entirely comfortable among the Democrats—able to re-form their ranks and seize control of the party they had so reluctantly joined.

Know Nothingism made considerable headway, since it appealed to some people of all classes in various occupations and sections. It was true that immigrants threatened American wage-earners, burdened tax-payers, and offended zealous Protestants. Although only a few of them had settled in southern cities, southerners supposed that the annual arrival of nearly 400,000 immigrants in other regions of the United States would weaken their section politically. Some politicians in both the North and the South hoped that the issue of immigration and Americanization might be made to supersede the slavery issue and that the American, or "Know Nothing" party, by focusing on the new problem, might be the instrument with which to unite a divided people. The American party served as a haven for stranded Whigs, who did not wish to join either the Democrats or the newly formed Republicans; it appealed to temperance men, who associated Catholics with grog-shops; and it seemed attractive to northern anti-slavery men, who disapproved of the pro-slavery sentiments of many Irish-Americans. Finally, plain snobbery and the fatal attraction of secret hand-clasps and mysterious passwords probably helped the Know Nothings along. But the party declined after its first successes in Massachusetts and in other northern states in 1854. The decision of the national convention to support the Kansas-Nebraska Act split the party in two, and most of the Know Nothings ended up as Republicans or Democrats. Even during its heyday, many Americans, among them an Illinois politician named Abraham Lincoln, deplored the intolerant philosophy of Know Nothingism. Soon this "stupendous and far-reaching leprosy," as an Alabama statesman called it, was nothing more than an ugly memory.

The Republican party came into being almost spontaneously in 1854. It has a number of alleged "birthplaces," and no single leader or group of men can claim sole credit for its organization. One firm principle brought its members together: the determination to keep slavery out of the territories and the belief that Congress had the right to do so. Otherwise, like most other large political parties in American history, its ancestry and composition were mixed. Free-soilers, of course, flocked into it, as did "conscience Whigs"—i.e., Whigs whose dislike of slavery was strong. Anti-Nebraska Democrats also joined in good numbers. So eventually did many Know Nothings and some outright abolitionists. A prohibitionist wave was sweeping the country, and the ranks of the so-called temperance movement furnished many Republican recruits. Oddly enough, into this party with its Know-Nothing and temperance elements came a considerable number of German immigrants, whose opposition to slavery was stronger than their distaste for teetotalers and nativists.

The economic backgrounds of the Republican party were similarly diverse. At first the party was intensely idealistic, but after 1858 its appeal became increasingly economic. Businessmen—like the iron-makers of Pennsylvania—were won to the party, more in 1860 than in 1856, because of its support for a high tariff. Workingmen too were attracted—some because they felt a high tariff benefited them as much as their employers, but many because the Republicans contrasted the simple democracy of their party with the aristocratic snobbery of slaveholders and defended free labor against slave labor. Finally, the Republicans' commitment to free public land (fulfilled in the Homestead Act of 1862) attracted western farmers and settlers. Between 1856 and 1860, the Republicans buttressed their moral appeal with an appeal to specific economic issues like the homestead and the tariff.

Although the Republicans opposed the extension of slavery, only a small portion of them were abolitionists, and it is questionable whether more than a minority ever had a strong humanitarian interest in the well-being of the Negro. What they wanted was free soil, not freed slaves; the welfare of the common white man, rather than the advancement of the Negro. For many of them, free soil meant excluding the free Negro as well as the slave from the territories in order to protect white labor from the competition of either slaves or freedmen.

Buchanan's Election.   The presidential campaign of 1856 raised to a higher pitch the political hysteria that had already been stimulated by almost continuous electioneering. The American people were given no chance to cool off, to reflect on the real issues. Now, in 1856, with secession in the air, they had to choose between the tired and faction-ridden Democratic party, the young and vigorous but obviously sectional Republican party, and the unimpressive American (Know Nothing) party.

In choosing a presidential candidate, the Democrats passed over Douglas and named a shrewd and conservative Pennsylvanian, James Buchanan, who had 40 years of political and diplomatic experience behind him. "Old Buck" was soon to be despised in the North as a "Dough-face," the name given to "a northern man with southern principles." But he did not deserve all the vilification he subsequently received. Cautious and narrowly constitutionalist in his thinking, and temperamentally unsuited for leadership in a time of crisis, he was nevertheless an honest man and a lover of the Union. Buchanan had been serving as American minister to England during the hectic Pierce administration, and had stayed out of party squabbles. His discretion paid off when the Democrats chose him as their leader, and the well-oiled party machine, aggressive and generous, handily defeated his Republican opponent, the glamorous soldier-explorer, John C. Frémont, The American party candidate, ex-President Millard Fillmore, ran a poor third.

But although Buchanan won 174 votes in the electoral college, to Frémont's 114 and Fillmore's 8, his popular vote was only 45 per cent, against Frémont's 33 and Fillmore's 22 per cent. Had the Republicans captured Pennsylvania and Illinois, the results would have been different. Hence the Democratic victory did not completely reassure the South. The new party had shown extraordinary strength; Buchanan's position on popular sovereignty was evasive; and southern politicians did not relish the widely held northern assumption that a popular majority in the territories might exclude slavery.

The new President did not even experience the brief spell of good will that his predecessor had enjoyed in 1853. A few days after Buchanan's inauguration, the Supreme Court handed down its opinion in the case of *Dred Scott* v. *Sanford*. At last the country had an answer to the long-debated question of whether Congress could lawfully exclude slave property from the territories.

The Dred Scott Case. Dred Scott, a slave, had been taken by his master in 1834 from Missouri to the free state of Illinois and from there to the Wisconsin Territory (present-day Minnesota), where he stayed until his return to Missouri several years later. The anti-slavery group who backed his suit for freedom hoped to prove that Dred Scott's sojourn in free Illinois and in a territory where slavery was made illegal by the Missouri Compromise had made him a free man. Scott lost his suit in the Missouri Supreme Court. His backers, in order to test the case in a federal court, then contrived to have Scott sold to a New York citizen named Sanford, whereupon Scott brought suit against Sanford in the United States Circuit Court.

The Dred Scott case finally reached the Supreme Court in 1856 and was decided March 6, 1857. The justices might simply have dismissed it on the grounds that Scott was not a United States citizen and hence was not entitled to sue in the federal court. Or, falling back on an earlier Supreme Court decision (*Strader* v. *Graham*, 1851), they might have ruled that Scott's residence in a free state suspended his slave status only temporarily. But the Court knew that Buchanan was seeking a showdown and a settlement of the territorial status of slavery. Buchanan had even gone so far as to indicate his desire to Justices Catron and Grier while the case was pending. Moreover, the justices seem to have concluded that so much public expectation and concern had been aroused that all the questions in the case should be discussed.

In his opinion (six colleagues concurred in part and wrote separate opinions), Chief Justice Taney made three basic assertions: (1) Since Negroes had been viewed as inferior at the time the Constitution was adopted, its makers did not intend to include them within the meaning of the term "citizens." Therefore, the right of citizens of different states to sue in the federal courts did not apply to Negroes. (2) Dred Scott did not become a free man by virtue of the provisions of the Missouri Compromise, because the Missouri Compromise was unconstitutional. (3) So long as Scott had returned to Missouri, his status was in any case determined by Missouri laws. By those laws he was a slave, not a citizen, and thus had no right to sue in federal court. Therefore the Supreme Court must dismiss the case for lack of jurisdiction.

Although the Republicans found other aspects of this decision highly provocative, what excited them most was the Court's finding that the Missouri Compromise (already repealed by the Kansas-Nebraska Act) had always been unconstitutional. This conclusion Taney drew from the due process clause of the Fifth Amendment: "No person shall be . . . deprived of life, liberty, or property without due process of law." The prohibition against taking slave property into the territories Taney found to be a violation of this clause. Thus Congress had no right under the Constitution to exclude slavery from the territories.

But if this position were to be accepted, then the fundamental objective for which the Republican party had been organized was unconstitutional. Moreover, if Scott was not a citizen in Taney's opinion, it had not been necessary for Taney to go beyond this finding and to pronounce against the Missouri Compromise. Did not the fact, moreover, that President Buchanan had pleaded for obedience to the decision before its promulgation suggest a conspiracy between him and some of the justices? The decision convinced abolitionists and free-soilers that the Court had pronounced for property rights against human rights. Republicans, among them Abraham Lincoln, decided that they would oppose the principles of Taney's decision and work peaceably to secure a new judicial ruling. Even the Douglas men were troubled about what effect the ruling would have on the principle of popular sovereignty. For if Congress did not have the constitutional power to exclude slavery from the territories, then neither did the territorial legislatures, which existed by congressional authorization.

"Bleeding Kansas." The question of Kansas also plagued Buchanan's administration from the start. The wounds of "Bleeding Kansas" had been stanched when Pierce sent the capable John W. Geary of Pennsylvania to govern the strife-torn territory in the summer of 1856. Geary's resolution and fairness brought immediate results, but he incited the hatred of the pro-slavery bloc when he asked the territorial legislature to repeal a whole series of undemocratic statutes it had passed in its first flurry of power. Compelled to flee for his life, Geary returned to Washington, where Buchanan accepted his resignation with relief. Geary's reports on the Kansas situation and on the machinations of the pro-slavery leaders angered northerners of all parties. They particularly alarmed Douglas, who realized that the Kansas legislature was balking the popular will. But Douglas was cheered by Buchanan's appointment of Robert J. Walker of Mississippi as Geary's successor.

Walker, able and courageous, had accepted the governorship of the Kansas Territory with the assurance that under no circumstance would Kansas be granted statehood until a majority of the Kansas voters had freely ratified the state constitution. When he reached Kansas in the spring of 1857, he quickly learned (1) that the pro-slavery men, knowing that their government would be overthrown by the preponderantly free-soil electorate, would not countenance a free election, and (2) that they proposed to deal with him as they had with Geary. In June, a rigged election for delegates to a new constitutional convention (from which the free-soilers deliberately abstained) led to the choice of the pro-slavery delegates. In October, the convention met in Lecompton,

Kansas, and drew up a constitution that actually guaranteed slavery. Kansas citizens were not allowed to pass on the constitution as a whole but were given only the privilege of deciding whether, in the future, slaves were to be admitted or kept out. Even if they voted to keep slavery out, slave property already in Kansas was to be protected. Again the free-soilers abstained from voting.

Buchanan, eager to create party harmony, found himself in a quandary. He could back Walker and submit the Lecompton Constitution to a popular election, or he could support the admission of Kansas under the Lecompton Constitution and please the South. He chose the second course, and Walker, whose firm and impartial program he had originally agreed to support, thereupon resigned.

Buchanan's decision angered Douglas and his followers, because it violated Douglas' conception of popular sovereignty. In asking Congress to accept an unrepresentative constitution, Buchanan not only outraged the majority of Kansas voters, but also irrevocably split his party. Douglas, convinced that the majority of Kansans wanted a free state, fought powerfully and brilliantly against the administration bill to admit Kansas as a slave state. To the accusation that he was destroying the Democratic party, he replied: "What if I do differ from the President? I have not become the servile tool of any President to receive and obey his instructions against my own judgment and sense of right." The bill, despite Douglas' opposition, was carried in the Senate, but it lost in the House when the Douglas men joined with the Republicans to defeat it. The stalemate was broken in May, 1858, when Congress passed a bill (the English Bill) that would grant Kansas immediate statehood together with a government land grant if her voters decided to accept the Lecompton Constitution, or that would continue territorial status if they decided to reject it. The Kansans overwhelmingly voted down the Lecompton Constitution, 11,812 to 1,926. Here the matter rested until 1861, when Kansas entered the Union as a free state.

The Panic of 1857 At the peak of the Kansas excitement, the country experienced a short-lived but disastrous panic, the result of inflation, overextension of credit, overexpansion of railroads and manufacturing, land-speculation, unsound banking, and European wars. During the next two years, 1858-1859, a severe depression settled over the industrial Northeast and the agricultural Middle West. Commerce and manufacturing came to a standstill, and the misery that spread among the unemployed was greater than at any previous time in America's history (see p. 333). Only in the South were the effects of the financial hurricane negligible, a fact that confirmed the South's faith in cotton and underscored the advantage to be gained by dealing directly with European firms unaffected by the fluctuations of the New York money market.

The Panic of 1857 had important political consequences as well. It furnished the Republican party with two issues of immense importance in the presidential campaign of 1860—free homesteads of 160 acres, and a higher protective tariff. The protection issue alarmed the South because it threatened the great victory that had been won in 1857, when Congress enacted the lowest tariff since 1812. The Republican strategy was to capture the votes of manufacturers, particularly the ironmakers of Pennsylvania and New Jersey, who were convinced that low tariff duties had created the economic crisis. At the same time the Republicans courted the farmers, who wanted free land.

Lincoln vs. Douglas. As depression gripped the country, a Republican convention met in Springfield, Illinois, on June 16, 1858, and nominated Abraham Lincoln as their senatorial candidate to run against the Democrats' formidable Senator Douglas. Here is how Lincoln described himself about this time: "It may be said I am, in height, six feet four inches, nearly; lean in flesh, weighing on an average one hundred and eighty pounds; dark complexion, with coarse black hair and gray eyes. No other marks or brands recollected." Lincoln was clean-shaven during this period. His lank frame, careless manner of dressing, and rugged yet sensitive face were not so well known as they soon would be, but in Illinois he was already a popular figure. He had come there after a boyhood in Kentucky and Indiana and had somehow managed to educate himself, prosper as a lawyer, become a leader of the Illinois Whigs, and serve one term in the United States House of Representatives. Much has been made of Lincoln's melancholy, his penchant for telling funny stories, and his instinctive goodness. Less well known are the traits that struck some of his contemporaries: his coldness and precision when examining a problem, and his political craftiness.

Lincoln at the time of his debates with Douglas.

The speech in which Lincoln accepted the 1858 senatorial nomination echoed the apprehensions of the free-soil states. He observed that the slavery crisis had grown worse each year. "In my opinion," he said, "it will not cease until a crisis shall have been reached and passed. 'A house divided against itself cannot stand.'" One side or the other would have to prevail. "Either the opponents of slavery will arrest the further spread of it, and place it where the public mind shall rest in the belief that it is in the course of ultimate extinction; or its advocates will push it forward till it shall become alike lawful in all the States, old as well as new, North as well as South." Taney's recent Dred Scott decision suggested, Lincoln said, that soon the Supreme Court might force even the free states to accept slavery.

This address, known to the country as the "House Divided" speech, was carefully studied by Senator Douglas and furnished the basis for his attacks against Lincoln. The seven Lincoln-Douglas debates that followed went beyond local issues and touched on questions affecting Americans everywhere. Douglas, who admired Lincoln personally, stigmatized him as a sectionalist whose "house-divided" philosophy would end in "a war of extermination." Why, Douglas asked, did the Republicans say that slavery and freedom could not peaceably co-exist? Lincoln replied that his party did not propose to interfere with slavery where it already existed, nor did he wish to enforce social equality between Negro and white, as Douglas alleged. But, in keeping with the Republican program, he flatly opposed the further extension of slavery. And then, at Freeport, Illinois, Lincoln asked Douglas a momentous question: "Can the people of a United States territory, in any lawful way, against the wish of any citizen of the United States, exclude slavery from its limits prior to the formation of a State constitution?" To answer this question, Douglas either had to abandon his popular sovereignty or defy the Dred Scott decision.

Douglas answered that the people of a territory could take this step, in spite of the

Dred Scott decision. Slavery could not exist for a day, he explained, if the local legislature did not pass the necessary laws to protect and police slave property. Therefore, merely by failing to arrange for slavery, a territorial legislature, without formally banning it, could make its existence impossible. His realistic answer kindled further opposition to him in the South, and widened the split in the Democratic party, as Lincoln had expected when he put the question. Douglas won the senatorial election despite Lincoln's plurality vote, since inequalities in legislative apportionment permitted Douglas' supporters to dominate the state legislature. But the war between Douglas and Buchanan's southern-dominated administration left the Democratic party more divided and ineffective than ever before.

John Brown's Return. The most electrifying and portentous event to occur during the sectional controversy was John Brown's raid on Harpers Ferry. On October 16, 1859, John Brown (see p. 344) and 18 of his followers captured the federal arsenal at Harpers Ferry, Virginia. Brown's wild scheme was nothing less than to foment a slave revolt by distributing the captured military stores to the Negroes, who he mistakenly believed would rally around him. Eminent northern reformers had known about the plan, and although they did not incite Brown to deeds of violence, they did provide him with money and weapons ostensibly intended

for anti-slavery partisans in Kansas. Brown's exploit, which embarrassed his humanitarian well-wishers, might have been passed off in normal times as the act of an unbalanced mind. But coming as it did after a decade of violence, it produced a furious reaction.

To southerners haunted by the threat of a slave insurrection, Brown's raid seemed part of a great conspiracy hatched by the abolitionists. Throughout the South, vigilante groups beat up and banished anyone who was suspected of anti-slavery sympathies, and dangerous books were publicly burned. In such a charged atmosphere, the moderates chose to keep silent. But Governor Wise of Virginia did nothing to calm the excitement; instead, he encouraged hysteria by attributing the raid to northern plotters. At the same time, huge meetings in New York, Boston, and elsewhere, organized by northern conservatives, attacked John Brown and his methods. Seward, Lincoln, Douglas—men of all parties—joined in this condemnation. But when Wise rejected the plea of Brown's relatives and friends that Brown was insane, he insured Brown's martyrdom. The bravery and dignity of Brown on the scaffold touched millions of people who had abhorred his deeds.

By convincing many in the South that the entire North was implacably hostile to slavery, the John Brown episode weakened further the frayed ties that held North and South together.

III. THE FINAL CRISIS

Lincoln's Election. The months before the presidential campaign of 1860 were packed with dramatic incidents, political and otherwise. In 1859, a few American intellectuals were reading a disturbing book by an English naturalist named Charles Darwin (*The Origin of Species*), which showed how new species had been evolved by natural selection rather than by special acts of God. Ordinary people were absorbed in such

matters as the visit by a delegation from Japan (celebrated in verse by Walt Whitman), an Anglo-American prize fight that was stopped in the 37th round, the landing of a new British "Leviathan," the *Great Eastern,* the arrival of the Prince of Wales, and the collapse of a factory in Lawrence, Massachusetts, which killed or injured hundreds of workers. But politics overshadowed all other concerns as Republicans and southern Democrats sought to capture the Speakership of the House for their respective parties. In the contest, some congressmen rose to speak armed with pistols as protection against attack.

In April, the Democratic convention assembled at Charleston, South Carolina, the heartland of secession, where the uncomfortable weather was soon matched by the rising political temperature. Southern extremists had resolved to insist on a slavery plank in the party platform declaring that neither Congress nor a territorial government could abolish slavery or impair the right to own slaves. Northern Democrats, hoping to nominate Douglas, were willing to accept the rulings of the Supreme Court on the Dred Scott case, but they were equally firm for popular sovereignty and unwilling to support an out-and-out guarantee of slavery. "We cannot recede from this doctrine," a spokesman for Douglas insisted, "without personal dishonor, and so help us God, we never will abandon this principle." The debate over the platform brought the questions of the slavery plank and popular sovereignty to the floor of the convention. When it became evident that the convention would not vote for a plank advocating federal protection of slavery in the territories, most of the delegates from eight southern states withdrew. Douglas, lacking the necessary two-thirds of the ballots, failed to win the nomination, and the convention adjourned. When the Democrats met again in Baltimore on June 18 with the Douglas men in the majority, the southern delegates again bolted the convention. The convention then proceeded to nominate Douglas on a popular-sovereignty platform, and the southern wing of the party, convening on June 28 in Baltimore, chose John C. Breckinridge of Kentucky (himself a moderate) to represent the southern position on slavery in the territories. The final break-up of the Democratic party was an event of sweeping importance—and not only for the Democrats. The last link in the Union—a great political party with

powerful followings in both North and South —had snapped.

In contrast to the demoralized Democrats, the Republicans met in Chicago on May 16, buoyant and confident after the Democratic fiasco at Charleston. Although, as it turned out, the catastrophe at Baltimore all but insured the victory of their own nominee, the delegates took pains to select a candidate who held moderate views on slavery. The most impressive leader was William H. Seward. But he had a perhaps undeserved reputation as an extremist because he had spoken of the "irrepressible conflict" between North and South. The unsavory reputation of his backer, Thurlow Weed, was also a handicap. Two other possibilities were Salmon P. Chase of Ohio and Edward Bates of Missouri. But it was Abraham Lincoln, strongly supported by the Illinois and Indiana delegations and acceptable to both East and West, who finally won the nomination on May 18.

The Republican platform made a shrewd appeal to powerful economic interests and at the same time sounded a high moral tone. It included planks for a protective tariff, free homesteads, a Pacific railroad, and the rights of immigrants. It denounced the disunionism and slave philosophy of the South and denied the power of either federal or territorial governments to legalize slavery in the territories—an answer to Douglas' popular-sovereignty contention. Practical politicians knew that to win the election, Pennsylvania and either Illinois or Indiana would have to go Republican. The tariff was a bid to the iron interests in Pennsylvania; Abraham Lincoln was a lure to the Indiana Hoosiers and the men of Illinois. But a resolution (passed over powerful conservative opposition) calling for a reaffirmation of the Declaration of Independence indicated the idealism of the rank-and-file Republicans if not of the convention managers.

To complicate the campaign even further, a fourth-party candidate had been nominated a few weeks before Lincoln's victory at Chicago. On May 9, the Constitutional Union party assembled in Baltimore. This new party, composed of the conservative remnants of defunct parties, appealed only to fading loyalties, especially among old-line Whigs in the border states. It chose John Bell of Tennessee and Edward Everett of Massachusetts as candidates in the coming election. The Union party hoped to win the border states and to awaken Unionist sentiment in the others. Four parties, each representing a sizable portion of the electorate, now contended for power.

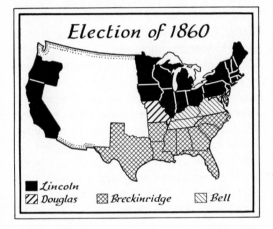

Election of 1860

■ Lincoln
▨ Douglas   ▩ Breckinridge   ◩ Bell

Abraham Lincoln became president of the United States with the support of a minority of the voters. He received 1,866,000 popular votes and 180 in the electoral college. Douglas received 1,375,000 and 12 electoral votes—carrying only Missouri and winning half the electoral vote of New Jersey. Breckinridge, carrying the Deep South and Delaware and Maryland, had 847,000 and 72 in the electoral college; Bell, with three border states, had 590,000 and 39.

Secession. A minority, sectional candidate had become president of the United States. Southern leaders had warned that a Republican victory would be followed by secession—for, as the Governor of South Carolina had put it, the election of a sectional northern candidate would "inevitably destroy our equality in the Union, and ultimately reduce the Southern states to mere provinces of a consolidated despotism, to be governed by a fixed majority in Con-

gress hostile to our institutions and fatally bent upon our ruin."

These expectations perhaps supply the best answer to the question, Why did the South secede? An informed southerner could hardly have imagined that the election of Lincoln would lead to the immediate abolition of slavery in the states in which it had always been legal. Lincoln gave assurances that he had no such intentions; and even if he had, his party did not control the Senate. Moreover, the Supreme Court was still composed, as it had been in the days of the Dred Scott decision, of five southern and four northern justices. The Republicans had won the presidency but not the other arms of the federal government.

Many southerners, of course, were not well informed, and looked upon Lincoln as nothing but "the daring and reckless leader of Abolitionists." Even those who realized that Lincoln was no abolitionist saw reasons for answering his election with secession. For one thing, the South's sentimental attachment to the Union had become weak. Southerners felt that the Yankees looked upon them with contempt, that a man like John Brown was cheered on and even subsidized in his efforts to destroy an institution without which they felt they could not continue to live. More important to many intelligent southerners than the immediate results of Lincoln's election were its probable consequences. The balance of power between the sections now seemed to have turned permanently against the South. In the decade of the 1850's, three free states (California, Minnesota, Oregon) had been added to the Union, but no new slave state had come in to counterbalance them. The North was growing visibly and rapidly in industry, in population, in transportation. It had linked itself firmly to the Northwest by railroad connections. It was winning the new territories. Would it not ultimately become strong enough to act directly against slavery and to destroy the civilization of the Old South?

To understand secession, moreover, it is important to remember that few men in the South anticipated its melancholy aftermath. It was by no means certain that the North would go to war to keep a reluctant South in an unhappy Union. Few believed that if war came—and some thought it would—the struggle would be so long and disastrous, the outcome so unfavorable to the South. Many southerners imagined that the will to fight (in what they thought of as the crass commercial civilization of the North) would be weak; that foreign sympathy, the commercial power of cotton, and southern sympathizers inside the North, would discourage the Union forces from persisting very long in a futile fight.

Instead of a long and disastrous war and ultimate defeat, many southerners dreamed of new theaters of power and expansion, new opportunities for enterprise. No longer would the South be drained of its resources by paying taxes and tariffs that chiefly benefited the North. No longer would it pay tribute to northern banking and shipping interests. It would trade directly with Europe, doing its own financing and carrying, its own buying and selling, even much of its own manufacturing. Perhaps the slave trade would revive and bring in more cheap labor. Cuba, Santo Domingo, Mexico, perhaps even territories in Central America, awaited development by enterprising men. A greatly enlarged southern Confederacy might be created to realize all these possibilities. And all this could be done only if the incubus of the North were shaken off.

This, at least, was what many southerners thought, and had been thinking for the last few years. On December 20, 1860, South Carolina took the initiative to bring this thinking to fruition. A convention in that state formally repealed South Carolina's ratification of the Constitution and withdrew from the Union. On this occasion, unlike the nullification crisis of Jackson's time, South Carolina had the support of her sister states. By February 1, 1861, five other states of the Deep South (Mississippi, Florida, Georgia, Alabama, Louisiana) had seceded, and on that day Texas followed. Four border and fringe states (Virginia, North Carolina, Tennessee, Arkansas) waited until after the firing on Fort Sumter before withdrawing. Three others (Maryland, Kentucky, Missouri) had powerful secessionist movements but were prevented from seceding by the prompt and forceful interference of federal authorities.

The wish for secession, however, was far from unanimous in the South. Although South Carolina's convention voted for it overwhelmingly, there was powerful resistance elsewhere in the Deep South, notably in the conventions of Georgia and Alabama, and in the popular vote for delegates in Louisiana. Significant minorities in every southern state opposed secession; and influential commercial and banking interests in urban areas only reluctantly came to support it. The border states waited until after the firing began, and faltered even then. Virginia seceded by a convention vote of 88 to 55, Arkansas had a popular majority against secession, and in Tennessee the legislature acted in favor of the Confederacy before the people had a chance to express themselves. The most important pocket of opposition came from the mountainous areas of western Virginia, which in 1861 withdrew from the mother state and in 1863 was admitted as the separate state of West Virginia, loyal to the Union cause.

Even before the process of secession had gone far enough to include the states of the upper South, a convention of six cotton states met at Montgomery, Alabama, on February 4, 1861, to form a new government, which they called The Confederate States of America.

Compromise Fails. The secession of the South, which began promptly after Lincoln's victory, took place while James Buchanan was still serving out the closing months of an unhappy administration. Thus, at a moment of the greatest urgency, the occupant of the White House was a "Lame Duck" president, a man without the power to make commitments that would be good for more than a few weeks. Although he declared that secession was unconstitutional, he opposed coercive action and urged compromise largely on southern terms. While he talked of conciliation without bringing forward a plan imaginative enough to capture attention, others tried to restore the Union. Significantly, the two main compromise proposals came from the border states, where men knew that if secession was followed by war their land would become a battleground.

The most seriously considered of the compromise proposals was the Crittenden plan, drawn up in December and presented to a conclave of distinguished senators called the "Committee of Thirteen," which attempted to work out a solution. The plan, put forward by Senator John J. Crittenden of Kentucky, included the following: (1) Slavery was to be banned in the territories north of the line 36° 30'. (2) But it was to be established and maintained under federal protection south of that line. (3) Future states were to come in as they wished, slave or free. (4) Congress was not to abolish slavery in any place under its jurisdiction that was surrounded by slave states—the District of Columbia, for example. (5) The Fugitive Slave Law was to be enforced, and when enforcement failed because of the action of northerners, the United States was to compensate the slave-owner out of funds collected from the county in which the fugitive was aided. (6) Congress was earnestly to recommend the repeal of the states' personal liberty laws, which were intended to aid fugitive slaves. (7) No further amendment was ever to be made to the Constitution that would authorize Congress to touch slavery in any of the states.

This comprehensive program failed because it could not win outright support from determined southerners or from the Republicans. The southern leaders refused to accept it unless it was also endorsed by the Republican party. Lincoln himself, though he favored enforcement of the Fugitive Slave Law and was willing to accept a constitutional amendment protecting slavery where it then existed, was totally opposed to any compromise on the exclusion of slavery from the territories. To a friend in Congress he wrote: "Entertain no proposition for a compromise in regard to the extension of slavery. The instant you do they have us under again: all our labor is lost, and sooner or later must be done over." The clause in the compromise proposals that protected slavery perpetually against abolition in any territory "hereafter to be acquired" south of the 36° 30' line (except where a state wished to emancipate its own slaves) seemed like an invitation to further southern expansion into Cuba or Mexico. Thus, the combined intransigence of the Republicans and the southerners thwarted the Crittenden proposals. A similar body of proposals was produced at a peace convention that met at Washington on February 4, 1861, but its suggestions received little support when they were discussed in Congress two days before Lincoln's inauguration. The hope of compromise flickered out when the delegates from six states of the lower South met in Montgomery, Alabama, to form the Confederacy during the five weeks following February 4, 1861.

Steps to War. Abraham Lincoln took his oath of office with secession an accomplished fact, with compromise all but abandoned, with the Southern Confederacy in being, and with important Union properties in the hands of the Confederate states. In his inaugural address, conciliatory yet firm, he emphasized his determination to save the Union. He had, he said, neither the right nor the inclination "to interfere with the institution of slavery in the States where it exists." As President, he was bound to enforce federal regulations in all the states, hold government property, and "collect the duties and imposts." But in performing these acts, he said, "there needs to be no blood-

shed or violence; and there shall be none unless it be forced upon the national authority." After pointing out that "physically speaking, we cannot separate," and that many of the problems that had troubled the states under the Union would continue to exist between two separate nations, he closed with an eloquent appeal to old ties and affections.

One of Lincoln's most pressing problems was what to do about federal forts on Confederate soil, notably the garrison under Major Robert Anderson at Fort Sumter in the harbor of Charleston. Buchanan, in a special message of January 8, 1861, had refused to recognize the legality of secession and had threatened to meet with force any effort to obstruct federal authorities or to seize federal property. Undaunted, South Carolina fired on a federal ship as it attempted to land supplies, men, and arms at Fort Sumter on January 9. The vessel returned without completing its mission, and Buchanan made no reprisal. Three months later, the Confederacy had seized federal

forts, post offices, and customhouses throughout the South, leaving under federal control only Fort Sumter and three other forts off the coast of Florida. On March 5, the day after Lincoln's inauguration, he was given a letter from Major Anderson, reporting that Fort Sumter could be reinforced only with the aid of 20,000 men and a large naval force, and in effect recommending its evacuation.

Lincoln was now in a serious dilemma. What should he, what could he, do about Fort Sumter and Fort Pickens in Pensacola Bay? If he retreated, as his Secretary of State, Seward, and his military advisers suggested, he would have made the first step toward recognizing the power if not the legality of the Confederacy and might have wrecked his party. But if he made an attempt by sheer force to fortify either of the garrisons, he would risk blood-letting and would appear as the aggressor. Sensing that there would be popular support for forcing a decision, he took action that involved neither of these alternatives. He attempted to provision Fort Sumter peacefully, and notified the South Carolina authorities that he had dispatched an expedition carrying supplies for this purpose.

Now the decision was shifted to the Confederate authorities. If they allowed Sumter to be provisioned, the fort would stand indefinitely in the mouth of one of their few good harbors, a threat to their prestige throughout the world. If they attacked a peaceful expedition bringing food to Major Anderson's men, they would be put in the position of firing the first shot. The southern general, Pierre G. T. Beauregard, was ordered to request Major Anderson to surrender. Anderson, loath to fight and short of supplies, promised to evacuate by April 15, unless he was relieved or ordered to remain. But the Confederates refused to wait, and began to bombard the fort in the early morning of April 12. Without the support of the navy's most powerful warship, the *Powhatan* (which failed to escort the provision ships as a result of official bungling), the relief expedition could land neither men nor supplies, and Anderson surrendered on the 13th. Hostilities had begun.

The attack on Fort Sumter strengthened Lincoln's support throughout the North. The Confederacy stood branded before most of the North as the aggressor, and it became easier than ever to portray the war as a *defense* of the Union. Lincoln's call for 75,000 volunteers met with an enthusiastic response in the North, but it helped to spur the border states into joining the Confederacy.

There was some desire in the North to "let the erring sisters go in peace." After April 12, however, the profound undercurrent of sentiment for the Union built up over 70 years of national existence created a widespread demand to fight. But as in the case of the southern secessionists, few of the northerners who supported the attempt to force the South back into the Union realized how costly the effort would be, how many of their fathers and brothers would lie dead on Civil War battlefields before the states were again united.

The Great Failure. A few months before the fall of Sumter, a thoughtful New Yorker, George Templeton Strong, asked himself: "Why *do* the people so furiously rage together just now? What has created our present unquestionable irritation against the South? What has created the Republican party?" Before 1850, he noted, few people had paid any attention to abolitionist propaganda. The North had been indifferent rather than hostile to slavery. But the issues growing out of the Compromise of 1850 forced the North to reconsider the slavery question. "It opened our eyes to the fact that there were two hostile elements in the country, and that if we allowed slaves to enter any territorial acquisition, our own free labor must be excluded from it." Such doubts were troublesome, he said, but they might have slumbered had not Douglas, with southern assistance, repealed the 1820 Compromise:

That was the fatal blow. Then came the atrocious effort to enforce slavery on Kansas by fraud and violence, with the full support of old Buchanan and his Southern counselors, the brutal beating of the eloquent and erudite Sumner with the cordial approbation and applause of the South, the project to revive the slave trade, and (a little earlier) a sentimental romance, *Uncle Tom's Cabin,* that set all Northern women crying and sobbing over the sorrows of Sambo. The Fugitive Slave Law stimulated sectional feeling by making slavery visible in our own communities, and above all, the intolerable brag and bluster and indecent arrogance of the South has driven us into protest against their pretentions, and into a determination to assert our own rights in spite of their swagger.

To Strong, these were the steps that led to disruption of the nation. His feelings were shared by many fervent Unionists after Beauregard's cannon had reduced Fort Sumter. His catalogue of events also helps to explain why Democrats, who predicted disaster should the Republicans win, now protested their loyalty to Lincoln; and why pacifists insisted that their opposition to war did not mean condoning rebellion. Although many northerners fought Lincoln's war measures then and later, others regarded the preservation of the Union as a holy crusade and were prepared to give their lives if necessary for this sacred cause.

Readings

A number of challenging volumes provide the general background of the "violent decade." Particularly important is Allan Nevins' impressive and well-balanced *The Emergence of Lincoln* (2 vols., 1950), which continues the story begun in his *Ordeal of the Union*. A. O. Craven, *The Coming of the Civil War* (1942); R. F. Nichols, *The Disruption of American Democracy* (1948); and H. H. Simms, *A Decade of Sectional Controversy* (1942), offer differing explanations of the sectional schism. A short and incisive study is D. L. Dumond, *Anti-Slavery Origins of the Civil War* (1939). On the complexities of the Kansas-Nebraska Act, Roy F. Nichols' article in the *Mississippi Valley Historical Review*, September, 1956, is of exceptional interest.

American expansionism in the 50's is thoroughly analyzed by Nevins in the work cited above. Also valuable is Basil Rauch, *American Interest in Cuba, 1848-1855* (1948). The Kansas issue has aroused a considerable amount of controversial writing. To Nevins' excellent summary should be added two books by J. C. Malin, *John Brown and the Legend of Fifty-Six* (1942), and *The Nebraska Question, 1852-1854* (1953). Also important are P. W. Gates, *Fifty Million Acres: Conflicts Over Kansas Land Policy, 1854-1890* (1954), and C. Vann Woodward's essay on John Brown in Daniel Aaron, ed., *America in Crisis* (1952).

For parties and politics, the general works cited above are sufficiently detailed, but the following are also recommended. For the Buchanan administration, P. G. Auchampaugh, *James Buchanan and His Cabinet on the Eve of Secession* (1926); for the Know-Nothing movement, R. A. Billington, *The Protestant Crusade, 1800-1860* (1938), and W. D. Overdyke, *The Know-Nothing Party in the South* (1950); for the background and origins of the Republican Party, A. W. Crandall, *The Early History of the Republican Party, 1854-1856* (1930), and J. A. Isely, *Horace Greeley and the Republican Party, 1853-1861* (1947).

The Dred Scott Case is discussed in detail by C. B. Swisher, *American Constitutional Development* (1943), and in his biography of Taney cited earlier; Nevins' summary of the case is excellent. See also Vincent Hopkins, *Dred Scott's Case* (1951). G. W. Van Vleck, *The Panic of 1857: An Analytical Study* (1943), is an examination of that crisis.

The story of Lincoln's emergence has been dealt with by a number of historians besides those cited above. R. H. Luthin, *The First Lincoln Campaign* (1944), is important. A. J. Beveridge, *Abraham Lincoln, 1809-1858* (2 vols., 1928), and A. C. Cole, *The Era of the Civil War* (1919), contain interesting information. For a concise and perceptive account of the Harpers Ferry episode, see C. Vann Woodward's essay on John Brown, cited above. The secession movement is admirably chronicled in A. O. Craven, *The Growth of Southern Nationalism, 1848-1861* (1953). Ollinger Crenshaw, *The Slave States in the Presidential Election of 1860* (1945), adds an important link to the story; and secession itself is the theme of D. L. Dumond, *The Secession Movement, 1860-1861* (1931), and U. B. Phillips, *The Course of the South to Secession* (1939). For Lincoln's role, see David Potter, *Lincoln and His Party in the Secession Crisis, 1860-1861* (1942). K. M. Stampp, *And the War Came: The North and the Secession Crisis, 1860-1861* (1950), analyzes the northern position in general; and P. S. Foner, *Business and Slavery: The New York Merchants and the Irrepressible Conflict* (1941), describes the attitude of businessmen in the North toward slavery and secession. For a private view of the crisis, *The Diary of George Templeton Strong* (4 vols., 1952), splendidly edited by Allan Nevins and Milton H. Thomas, is strongly recommended.

CIVIL WAR

C H A P T E R   S I X T E E N

In retrospect, the civil struggle between 1861 and 1865 takes on an almost legendary hue, and its famous protagonists resemble the heroes of the Trojan War. Each side displayed a courage and audacity scarcely exaggerated in the romantic postwar accounts, but the crisis also produced its full share of fraud, cruelty, vindictiveness, and hysteria—symptoms of what one contemporary called "a most putrescent state of the national blood."

When the war began, the United States was still agrarian in mind if not in fact. Its institutions and culture were still rooted in a pre-industrial era. When the war ended, the outlines of America's iron age, plainly discernible before 1860, had become much sharper. The northern victory preserved the

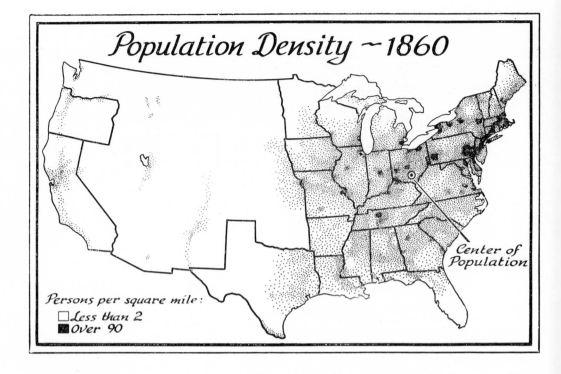

Population Density ~ 1860

Center of Population

Persons per square mile:
☐ Less than 2
▓ Over 90

Union and, despite the colossal bloodletting and destruction, left the North economically stronger than it had been five years before.

But the war left psychic wounds that have not completely healed after the passage of almost a century.

I. UNION AND CONFEDERATE PROBLEMS

The North and the South. In 1861, the northern population far exceeded the southern. The 23 Union states numbered about 22 million inhabitants, as against 5.5 million whites and 3.5 million Negroes in the 11 seceding states. In 1860, there were more than 4 million white males between the ages of 15 and 40 in the North; there were less than a million and a half in the South. Between 1861 and 1865, the Confederacy could raise, all told, an army that has been estimated at about 850,000 to 900,000 men, as against an estimated 2 million put in uniform by the North. The significance of the North's superior manpower became plain during the closing years of the war when the Federal armies, despite terrible casualties, seemed to grow stronger with every defeat.

In economic as well as human resources, the North also enjoyed a tremendous ad-

vantage. The Confederate army was ill-equipped. It lacked sufficient weapons, drugs,

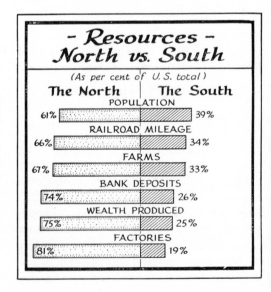

– Resources –
North vs. South

(As per cent of U.S. total)

The North		The South
POPULATION		
61%		39%
RAILROAD MILEAGE		
66%		34%
FARMS		
67%		33%
BANK DEPOSITS		
74%		26%
WEALTH PRODUCED		
75%		25%
FACTORIES		
81%		19%

shoes, food, and the other essentials for war. The Union military machine, on the other hand, faced few such shortages after the early stages of the war. Some 80 per cent of American factories and most of the nation's mineral deposits were located in the North, and the North greatly surpassed the South in the production of grain, pork, beef, horses, and mules. Most of the nation's skilled workers lived above the Mason and Dixon line. In 1860, the South had slightly less than 9,000 miles of railroad track. Important strategic centers were poorly linked, and the food-producing states of Texas and Arkansas, west of the Mississippi, had no railroad communication at all with the rest of the Confederacy. The products of the North's diversified farms and factories could be transported on 21,000 miles of railroad track that intersected the free states and pointed conveniently southward.

How was it that a section inferior in manpower and economic resources, almost without financial facilities (for most of the banking was concentrated in the North), and operating under a makeshift government could withstand northern power for so many years and even threaten to overthrow it? The southern will to resist does much to explain it, but the South also had other real advantages. Southerners were accustomed to outdoor life and the use of firearms. They were more familiar with the battlegrounds of the war than the northern invaders were, and they did not have to expend their limited manpower on garrisoning captured cities, holding conquered territory, or transporting supplies over vast distances. Although southern railroads were for the most part undeveloped, those in Virginia were of great strategic importance in the defense of Richmond and, indeed, of the entire South. Finally, Jefferson Davis, the president of the Confederacy, had better generals from whom to choose his military commanders than did Lincoln. General Robert E. Lee and his brilliant lieutenants seemed more than able to make up for the South's material deficiencies. For two years, they defeated the numerically superior armies that opposed them.

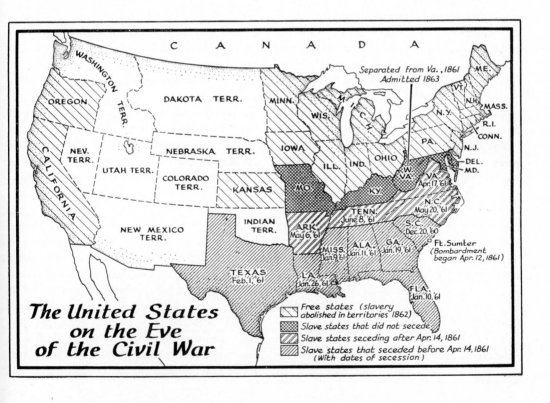

The United States on the Eve of the Civil War

Free states (slavery abolished in territories 1862)
Slave states that did not secede
Slave states seceding after Apr. 14, 1861
Slave states that seceded before Apr. 14, 1861 (with dates of secession)

When southerners thought of their military prospects, they had before them the hopeful example of the American Revolution, won against seemingly greater odds. They knew that strategically they would be on the defensive, and that merely to maintain their existence was a less demanding military goal than the North confronted, for the North's task was one of conquest and subjugation. They knew, too, that opinion about the war in the North was divided, and they hoped that northerners would soon grow weary of the fighting.

The Southern Republic. The Confederacy produced better soldiers than statesmen. The leaders of the new southern nation had the appalling and perhaps hopeless task of welding 11 high-spirited states into an effective working organization. To maintain the shaky system of southern transportation, finance, and industry would have required an administrative genius that was rare among southern leaders.

Jefferson Davis (1808-1889), President of the Confederacy.

A convention of delegates from six seceding states met in Montgomery, February, 1861, to draft a provisional constitution very similar in structure to the federal Constitution, but containing significant modifications. As might be expected, the new constitution unequivocally recognized state sovereignty, but it said nothing about the rights of nullification and secession. It explicitly protected private property in slaves and guaranteed the right to take them into any state in the Confederacy, but it did not legalize the African slave trade. It prohibited protective tariffs and internal-improvement appropriations. Another innovation was the provision limiting the office of president to a single term of six years, and the elimination of congressional "riders" by permitting the president to veto specific terms in a bill without having to throw out the entire measure.

After drafting their constitution, the Confederate delegates elected Jefferson Davis of Mississippi as their provisional president and Alexander H. Stephens of Georgia as their provisional vice-president. Davis, born not more than 100 miles from Lincoln's birthplace in central Kentucky and raised in Mississippi, was educated at Transylvania University and at West Point. He had distinguished himself in the Mexican War and had been a highly competent Secretary of War under Pierce from 1853 to 1857. Although he had opposed the Compromise of 1850 in the Senate and had revealed secessionist leanings, by 1853 he had become an ardent expansionist who envisaged a united nation dominated by the South. Elected to the Senate again in 1857, Davis' vigorously pro-southern stand linked him with the anti-Douglas wing of his party, but he had not welcomed secession and regarded the hasty action of South Carolina and his own state with misgivings. Davis' personal integrity and conscientiousness, and his attachment to the whole southern nation rather than to one particular state, made him a logical choice for the presidency.

But he lacked the depth and human understanding of Lincoln, fussed with petty details, and quarreled with his subordinates.

The brilliant Stephens proved no help to the harassed Davis. Sick and neurotic, a stickler for state rights and civil liberty, he broke dramatically with Davis over the issues of conscription and civil liberties. Davis' impermanent cabinet (he made numerous changes in it during the war) was an undistinguished body chosen partly on the basis of state affiliations. The most able member was the Attorney General (and later Secretary of War and Secretary of State), Judah P. Benjamin, a lawyer from Louisiana. Although Benjamin was widely disliked, Davis trusted him above all his other advisers.

Against Davis' will, the Congress in May, 1861, voted to move the Confederate capital from Montgomery to Richmond. There, for the duration of the war, it wrangled and palavered, and although it granted Davis some of his requests, it failed to pass adequate tax laws or to control inflation. Even worse, the feuds between pro-Davis and anti-Davis congressmen weakened southern morale. Davis and his fellow realists insisted on a rigorous prosecution of the war even if certain constitutional rights and state prerogatives had to be temporarily abandoned. He and his supporters recognized that conscription laws had to be passed if southern armies were to be kept in the field. The anti-Davis faction, on the other hand, were strict state rights adherents who strongly resisted any attempt on the part of the Confederate government to go beyond the limited authority granted to it by their constitution. Davis could neither placate the state-rights group nor yield gracefuly when his measures miscarried, and his chilly manner antagonized his opponents. After 1863, when southern strength was waning, relations between Davis and his Congress steadily grew worse. Confederate leaders seemed unable to mobilize their economic resources; they lacked the will and the manpower to fight the kind of massive war carried on by the Unionists.

Few people, either in the South or in the North, anticipated a long war. Volunteers for the Confederate armies enlisted in a holiday spirit, and many of the first to be captured admitted that the war was completely different from what they had expected. In April, 1862, the Confederate Congress passed the first conscription act in American history (the North followed a year later), which drafted men between the ages of 18 and 35 for three years. The law outraged the state-rights elements and seemed to confirm the slogan that was popular both below and above the Mason and Dixon line: "It's a rich man's war and poor man's fight."

If a man had enough money, he could escape the draft by paying for a substitute; owners or overseers of more than 20 slaves were exempted (this was the most bitterly resented provision), as were ministers, college professors, government and state civil servants, and members of selected trades and occupations. Later laws remedied some of these abuses and extended the age limit from 18 to 45, and then from 17 to 50. Resistance to conscription centered in the hilly regions of Alabama, Georgia, and Mississippi, but it was by no means confined to these areas. Local-minded governors like Joseph E. Brown of Georgia and Zebulon B. Vance of North Carolina either opposed conscription or objected to the way it was administered. Desertions from the Confederate army increased alarmingly after 1863, especially among the troops from non-slaveholding sections. The total number of Confederate deserters through the war amounted to well over 100,000. Union army desertions were much greater in number, but since Union manpower was far superior, they were of less consequence.

The disintegration of the Confederacy was further hastened by economic collapse. Unwisely, the Congress failed to pass a realistic tax law until the spring of 1863. Meanwhile, the Confederate treasury issued over a billion dollars' worth of unsecured promissory notes, to be honored two years after the end of the war. These notes totaled more than twice the amount of paper money issued by the Union government during the same period. Together with the currency issued by state governments, cities, and corporations, this flood of Confederate notes brought about the most onerous inflation since the Revolution. Hoarding and speculating also were rampant, and city crowds sometimes plundered foodshops. Confederate troops had to live on short rations despite the government's impressment of all kinds of supplies and the increased use of substitute foods, and the families of the fighting men often suffered grievously at home. The failure of southern transportation, manufacturing, and agriculture was partly administrative. But it would have been too much to expect an almost exclusively agricultural society, broken up into self-conscious states suspicious of centralized power, to wage war in the manner of the industrial North.

Lincoln as President. By temperament and character, Abraham Lincoln was better fitted for the terrible ordeal of presidential responsibility than was Jefferson Davis. Patient, tolerant, flexible, and crafty, he knew when to press an advantage and when to give in with good grace. Nathaniel Hawthorne, who met the President in 1862, recognized the master strategist and manipulator behind the mask of "Honest Abe":

> The whole physiognomy is as coarse a one as you would meet anywhere in the length and breadth of the States; but, withal, it is redeemed, illuminated, softened, and brightened by a kindly though serious look out of his eyes, and an expression of homely sagacity, that seems weighted with rich results of village experience. A great deal of native sense; no bookish cultivation, no refinement; honest at heart, and thoroughly so, and yet, in some sort, sly—at least, endowed with a sort of tact and wisdom that are akin to craft, and would impel him, I think, to take an antagonist in flank, rather than to make a bull-run at him right in front.

Throughout his term of office, Lincoln was savagely handled by the majority of the newspapers and abused by the politicians of both parties. Nor could he be called a popular president with the electorate. "Half-witted usurper," "the head ghoul at Washington," "political coward," "an awful, woeful ass" were only some of the choicer epithets applied to him by his critics.

Lincoln's cabinet represented the disparate interests that had made his election possible. Like the Republican party itself, it was divided between idealists and opportunists, conservatives and radicals, former Democrats and old anti-slavery Whigs. William H. Seward, affable and competent, blundered occasionally as Secretary of State, but on the whole he performed ably. Gideon Welles, a Connecticut Democrat, made an excellent Secretary of the Navy even though he had had no practical naval experience. Montgomery Blair, member of a politically powerful family, served as Postmaster General, and Edward Bates of Missouri, a "favorite son" in 1860, was made Attorney General. Lincoln reluctantly accepted Simon Cameron of Pennsylvania as Secretary of War. Slippery and corrupt, Cameron had been the candidate of the high-tariff interests and the "favorite son" of an important Pennsylvania political faction that had boomed him for the presidency in 1860. He continued his grafting ways while in the cabinet, and Lincoln was relieved when he found a way of kicking him upstairs by making him American Ambassador to Russia in January, 1862. His successor, Edwin M. Stanton, turned out to be a vigorous and capable war minister but also a troublemaker. As controversial and as complex was Salmon P. Chase of Ohio, the much-maligned and much-adored Secretary of the Treasury. A conscientious, efficient, and honest administrator, he soon lost confidence in Lincoln (whom Chase was too pompous and humorless to understand) and intrigued for the presidency with Lincoln's enemies while he was still in the cabinet.

Extraordinarily adroit in managing his sometimes touchy cabinet members, Lincoln was also a master tactician in party management. Since there was no permanent civil-service group, the victorious party ordinarily swept out the appointees of the defeated. After his election, Lincoln (to quote Gideon Welles' candid diary) had to deal with "A host of ravenous partisans from Maine to California." Lincoln cleaned house by removing 1,195 out of the 1,520 presidential appointees—the most sweeping purge since the founding of the Republic. He also labored so painstakingly in selecting loyal Republicans for federal jobs that idealistic critics accused him of frittering away his time in low political shenanigans while the nation was breaking apart. But Lincoln knew what he was doing. Patronage was the cement that bound together the fragments of the party. The Republicans had to be fused, the disgruntled soothed, the party's friends rewarded. Individual talent and qualifications seemed less vital at the moment than political necessities. Lincoln had to be expedient rather than just; he had to appease the quarreling factions so that he could get on with the war. Yet Lincoln did not lower the tone of American public service, and in his foreign appointments—which included the diplomat Charles Francis Adams, Sr., the historians John L. Motley and Richard Hildreth, and the writer William Dean Howells—his choices were considerably better than those of his predecessors.

Lincoln was not successful in obtaining bipartisan support and never completely won the allegiance even of those "War Democrats" who collaborated with the Republicans during the emergency. Many thousands of so-called "Peace Democrats" systematically opposed Lincoln's war policies, protested against his alleged tyranny, and discouraged enlistment. The "Copperheads" (as the antiwar Democrats were called) were less sinister than their nickname implied and perhaps less annoying to Lincoln than some of the members of his own party. Some of them, however, like the Ohio Congressman, Clement L. Vallandigham, were serious troublemakers. Convicted by a military court in 1863 for treasonable language, Vallandigham was saved from a jail sentence by Lincoln's decision to ship him down to the Confederacy. He re-

turned to Ohio before the war was over but not before he had conducted an unsuccessful campaign for the governorship of his state from Canadian headquarters. Copperhead sentiment remained strong in Ohio, Illinois, and Indiana, and in the last two states prowar governors were seriously hampered by the Copperhead legislatures. Rumors of traitorous plots by Copperhead secret societies like the "Knights of the Golden Circle" were rife in the closing years of the war, but these groups were not an effective "fifth column."

The Republicans in and out of Congress soon split into two groups: the Conservatives, who ordinarily supported Lincoln's moderate and pragmatic policies, though they often took issue with the President on specific measures; and the Radicals, whose antisouthernism sometimes reached fanatical proportions.

The Radicals.   The Radicals differed among themselves on such matters as the tariffs, the homestead law, and federal subsidies for a transcontinental railroad, but agreed on a vigorous war policy and were willing to employ any strategem against slavery. Benjamin F. Wade, Senator from Ohio, was a Cromwellian figure, as brutal as he was brave, and a great decrier of presidential usurpation. Of the same temper was Zachariah Chandler, Senator from Michigan, whose dislike of Lincoln's policies, if not of the man, were constant. To Gideon Welles, Chandler was "vulgar and reckless . . . a noisy partisan," but others found him "fearless" and "uncorruptible." Thaddeus Stevens of Pennsylvania dominated the Republicans in the House. By threats and sheer personal force, he whipped recalcitrants into line and distinguished himself in debate with his genial ferocity.

When the Republicans got Congress to establish the Joint Committee on the Conduct of the War (December, 1861), whose function it would be to scrutinize the war effort, they gained an effective instrument of propaganda. Under the leadership of Wade, and sparked by such zealots as George W. Julian of Indiana and "Old Zack" Chandler, the Committee probed into the military conduct of the war, worked against generals suspected of being lukewarm on Negro rights, jammed through legislation to confiscate Confederate property, carried on secret hearings, and blackened reputations. By permitting the results of its investigations to leak out to newspapers like Horace Greeley's New York *Tribune* and the Chicago *Tribune,* the Committee was able to slant the political and war news.

The Radicals feared that the Conservatives would be too lenient with the slaveholders. "If the rebellion should suddenly collapse," Charles Sumner wrote, "Democrats, copperheads, and Seward would insist upon amnesty and the Union, and 'no questions asked about slavery.' God save us from any such calamity." To forestall this dread possibility and to maintain Republican supremacy, the Radicals pushed hard for the immediate emancipation of the Negroes. Against Lincoln's wishes, they agitated for the rooting out of all Democrats from the civil and military arms of the government, the use of Negro troops (some 186,000 were actually recruited before the end of the war), and the confiscation of rebel property.

In August, 1861, the Radicals forced through the first confiscation act, calling for the seizure of all property involved in any way with "insurrectionary purposes." Thaddeus Stevens revealed the spirit of its backers when he declared that if the complete destruction of the South was the price for preserving the Union, "so let it be." It was better, he thought, to turn land over to the Negroes than to allow the South to "perpetrate the destruction of this people through our agency." The next year (July, 1862) Congress passed the more sweeping but hardly enforcible second confiscation act. The property of Confederate officials was to be confiscated without warning, and the property of those aiding rebellion (technically, anyone residing within the rebellious states no matter what his politics) was to be confiscated after a 60-day warning. Negroes owned by any rebel were automatically declared free forever. Lincoln, who told the Radicals that "the severest justice may not always be the best policy," reluctantly signed the bill after Congress had removed some of the more objectionable features.

The Radicals, then, hampered Lincoln's attempt to set up a harmonious Union coalition, but their distaste for the President and his policies was shared by many Conservatives. It is misleading to think of the Radicals as a well-drilled opposition systematically checkmating the administration. What have sometimes been described as the Radical "plots" against Lincoln were simply the acts of men who were passionately concerned with defeating the South. They compelled the cautious Lincoln to make the war an antislavery crusade as well as a struggle to preserve the Union. He may have chafed occasionally under their pressure, but he continued to work with even the most extreme Radicals and remained genuinely fond of Charles Sumner, who constantly badgered him for moving too slowly toward emancipation.

II. BATTLEFRONTS

Opposing Strategies. When the Civil War began, the United States had no army to speak of, no military tradition, no corps of well-trained and experienced officers. The Mexican War had been too brief and too easy to provide much experience for regular army men, and since 1846 the military profession could not compete with the glittering attractions of law, politics, or business. West Point in the 1840's and 1850's was a backward academy where the fledgling officers who would soon be commanding opposing armies studied outmoded military texts. The oracle of the tacticians, as the historian David

Donald has shown, was Napoleon's military historian, Baron Henri Jomini, whose maxims on the art of war were at first applied by the Civil War generals. Jomini laid down such principles as the superiority of the offensive against the defensive, the necessity for massive concentration of troops against the enemy's weakest point, the futility of constructing entrenchments and earthworks, and the importance of seizing the enemy's capital city.

After a few years of war on a scale that dwarfed any of Napoleon's campaigns, the American commanders had to adjust their tactics to the realities of long-range rifles, railroads, and an advanced industrial technology. The most successful officers on both sides soon abandoned conventional tactics and adopted a new technique of warfare that boiled down to the art of finding your enemy and destroying him. The spade became as important an instrument as the gun, and common soldiers learned that their survival depended on the skill and speed with which they could fortify their positions.

Both the Confederates and the Federals adapted themselves to the new conditions, but the North was more radical in its military experimentation than the South, perhaps because it had the industrial means. Lincoln changed the Union command time and again until he discovered the winning combination; the South kept substantially the same military leadership throughout the war. Encouraged perhaps by its initial victories and the brilliance of its individual commanders, the Confederacy found less reason to modify its way of making war.

From the outset, the Confederates lacked superiority in men and matériel, their ports were exposed to naval attack and blockade, and their government was unrecognized by foreign powers. Diplomatic recognition by England and the continental nations was assured, they felt, by Europe's dependence on cotton and by the promise of an extensive free market for manufactured goods. And yet they had to win quickly if the southern republic was to survive at all. They could not stand a war of attrition. Hence in 1861, some southern strategists wanted to carry the war into the North, believing, with good reason, that a series of crushing Union defeats might create a peace movement in the North and topple Lincoln's administration. In 1861, the South was optimistic, partly because it was convinced that the North could not produce soldiers to match its own.

President Davis, however, refused to permit an all-out invasion, although the Confederates managed to stab into the North four times before the war was over. It would have been politically risky to consolidate the southern forces that were parceled out over the sprawling Confederacy, since no Confederate state was willing to denude itself of troops. The dispersal of southern armies fighting under independent and uncoordinated commands may have cost the South its chance for a quick victory.

Northern strategists were faced with even greater problems. To crush the rebellion, the North had to cut off vital southern imports, prevent the border states from furnishing men and supplies to the Confederates, destroy the southern armies, and seize vital transportation points. Instead of trying to capture and hold southern territory, northern generals eventually learned to reduce the southern capacity for making war. The government, at first imperfectly, but later effectively, blockaded Confederate ports and occupied most of them by 1864. Quite early in the war, the Union armies seized control of vital river arteries in the West, and after capturing the key railroad centers they ravaged the southern interior with total war. By 1865, the shattered but still undefeated Confederacy had literally nothing to fight with. Successful in the eastern sector, the Confederate government apparently never recognized the importance of the western campaigns that dismembered the South and assured the collapse of the Confederacy.

The War: First Phase. In the spring of 1861, General Winfield Scott, a 74-year-old

Virginian who had fought in the wars of 1812 and 1846 and was now physically decrepit, was in command of the Union forces. Because Scott knew that trained armies did not spring up overnight, he advocated a strangling blockade of the South and the fortifying of key northern cities until the Union army was ready to invade the Confederacy. The proximity of the new Confederate capital in Richmond, however, and the prospect of putting a quick end to the rebellion, encouraged Horace Greeley and the congressmen who agreed with him to cry, "Onward to Richmond." In response to such pressure, Union leaders prematurely attacked the Confederacy in the First Battle of Bull Run, the first important engagement of the Civil War.

On July 21, General Irvin McDowell with about 30,000 green troops met a Confederate army of 24,000 (equally green) holding the railroad junction of Manassas, which connected the Shenandoah Valley with Richmond (see map, p. 374). The Confederate general, Pierre G. T. Beauregard, reinforced by the soldiers of Joseph E. Johnston and bolstered at a critical point by General Thomas J. Jackson's "stonewall" defense, finally routed the Federals at the stream of Bull Run. Fashionable ladies and congressmen in a holiday mood had accompanied McDowell's ebullient troops to observe the discomfiture of the rebels, but they were engulfed by the demoralized regiments of three-month volunteers retreating into Washington. The capital lay open to the Confederates, but, according to Johnston, they were too overwhelmed by their victory to pursue their advantage. They did, however, bag a New York congressman who had strolled too near the battle. The defeat at Bull Run ended northern complacence and led to the appointment of 34-year-old George B. McClellan as General-in-Chief of the Union army. McClellan fortified Washington, and reorganized and trained the "grand Army of the Potomac." He was convinced that God had "placed a great work in my hands."

While McClellan drilled and inspected his army of 130,000 troops in Washington, the spotlight of the war turned to the West, where Union prospects appeared brighter. An offensive in the West by river and land routes became possible by early 1862 after a hitherto neutral Kentucky finally decided for the North.

A month after the defeat of the Federals at Bull Run, a campaign to drive Confederate troops out of Missouri temporarily failed when General Nathaniel Lyon lost a hard-fought battle to a state military force under General Sterling Price, a former Missouri governor, at Wilson's Creek on August 10, 1861. Lyon was killed in this action, and southern Missouri remained in Confederate hands until a Union victory at Pea Ridge, Arkansas, on March 6-8, 1862, gave the Federals control of the state. John C. Frémont succeeded Lyon as commander of the western theater with headquarters at St. Louis, but his bungling policies led to his dismissal and the appointment of the bookish Henry W. Halleck. "Old Brains," as Halleck was not too accurately named, had a reputation as a strategist and was technically in charge of western military operations, but he actually owed his success to two of his subordinates, Brigadier General Ulysses S. Grant and Rear Admiral Andrew H. Foote.

Foote had been in charge of a gunboat flotilla on the Mississippi. The objective of Grant and Foote was to get behind the army of General Albert Sidney Johnston, which blocked the way of Union General Don Carlos Buell in eastern Kentucky. To accomplish this end, and to free loyal eastern Tennessee from Confederate control, they had to capture Fort Henry on the Tennessee River, and Fort Donelson, 15 miles away, which dominated the Cumberland River. Fort Henry fell on February 6, 1862, before a combined army and gunboat assault, and Fort Donelson surrendered on the 16th with 15,000 troops. As Grant's army moved into southern Tennessee to join forces with Buell, who was pushing down from Nashville, A. S. Johnston struck at Grant's army at Shiloh on April 6. Though beaten on the first day, Grant's army

General Grant and his aides in the field.

recovered when Buell's troops arrived on April 7. Together, they forced the Confederates to retreat to Corinth, Mississippi. General Johnston was killed in this engagement.

Johnston's death at Shiloh hurt the Confederacy, but an even greater catastrophe was in the making. A Union fleet commanded by David G. Farragut smashed through the fortifications below New Orleans and forced that city to surrender at the end of April. By June 6, Foote's formidable fleet of armored steamboats, mortar boats, and rams pushing down the Mississippi had subdued Fort Pillow, taken the fortified Island No. 10, and destroyed the Confederate river fleet at Memphis (see map, p. 375). Only Vicksburg and Port Hudson blocked Union control of the entire Mississippi River.

Grant's victories brought national attention to this hitherto obscure West Point graduate, a veteran of the Mexican War, whose career between 1846 and 1862 had not been remarkable. He had resigned from the army as a captain in 1854, and for the next seven years had proved his incapacity for civilian life by failing as a businessman. When the Civil War broke out, Grant demonstrated his leadership and dogged courage. Starting out as a colonel in an Illinois regi-

ment of volunteers, he won quick promotion, and at Halleck's recommendation was made a brigadier general in the summer of 1861. Even before Shiloh, Halleck, a jealous armchair general, had censured his aide, and after that battle accused him of being drunk. Grant did drink too much, a failing he shared with a great number of civil servants and officers on both sides, and he was unusually sensitive to even small amounts of alcohol, but he was not drunk at Shiloh. The nation had been shocked by the terrible casualties of this prophetic battle (approximately 13,000 were lost on the Union side), and Grant's critics, besides Halleck, tried to have him removed. But Lincoln replied to them: "I can't spare that man—he fights."

The War: Second Phase. In the eastern sector, the Union forces remained inactive during the fall of 1861. Not until April, 1862, did the cautious McClellan begin to move his well-drilled army. "McNapoleon," as the Radicals derisively called him, magnified his obstacles and treated Lincoln rudely. But, though he was excessively prudent and given to making grandiloquent announcements, his strategy was sound enough, and his anger at the constant interfer-

369

ence by politicians was justified. McClellan, counting on support from the Union navy, proposed to attack Richmond from the East via the Virginia peninsula between the York and the James rivers. At the same time, another Union army under General McDowell was to strike at Richmond from the north.

Naval operations in the Chesapeake Bay were menaced by the Confederate ironclad, the *Virginia* (constructed in the Norfolk navy yard from an abandoned Union frigate, the *Merrimac*). On March 8, 1862, this awesome craft had destroyed or damaged three Union men-of-war and had been prevented from opening up the bay to the Confederacy the next day only by the dramatic appearance of a Union ironclad, the *Monitor*. This "cheese-box on a raft," as it was called, was designed by a Swedish engineer, John Ericsson. The two ironclads fought their historic duel with neither able to sink the other, but the *Virginia* was compelled to retreat to Norfolk and did not dare venture out again. When McClellan began his campaign, the presence

General Robert E. Lee (1807-1870).

of the *Virginia* at Norfolk kept the Union navy from coming to his assistance. Only after McClellan's troops, 100,000 strong, had pushed slowly up the peninsula did the Confederates abandon Norfolk and destroy the *Virginia.*

But the thrust up the peninsula got nowhere. McClellan failed mainly because he was sluggish and irresolute in his operations, but his plan for a two-pronged attack on Richmond fell through partly because the administration decided to keep McDowell's army as a screen between the Confederate army and Washington. The brilliant and aggressive strategy of the Confederate generals also began to tell. "Stonewall" Jackson now aroused fears in Washington by invading the Shenandoah Valley and by defeating in separate actions the Union commanders who opposed him before he rejoined the main Confederate army at Richmond (see map, p. 374). When Joseph E. Johnston was wounded while opposing McClellan's advance, his command fell to the greatest military figure of the South, Robert E. Lee.

"Marse Robert" Lee combined gentleness and tact with extraordinary military daring. He had been offered the leadership of the Union armies after Sumter, but he had refused—not because he approved either of secession or slavery, but because he was loyal to Virginia. Some critics feel that Lee was so concerned with defending his native state that he never developed a coordinated strategy. Others blame his failure to provide adequate supplies for his armies, an oversight that kept him from exploiting his victories, and his habit of giving too much independence to his subordinates. So long as such brilliant corps commanders as Jackson and James Longstreet served under him, Lee's confidence was rarely misplaced. But in the later stages of the war his junior officers were less remarkable.

On June 26, 1862, Lee boldly attacked the Union army, which had advanced to within a few miles of Richmond, and during the fierce Seven Days' Battle that followed McClellan was forced to retreat over the ground he had gained with so much effort. As McClellan fell back, he inflicted heavy losses on Lee's troops and his position was by no means untenable. But Lincoln decided, under pressure from the Radicals, to call off the invasion, to subordinate McClellan, and to appoint the undistinguished Halleck as General-in-Chief of the Union forces. This move proved to be a serious mistake. It permitted Lee to move northward and defeat the boastful General John Pope, McDowell's successor, at the Second Battle of Bull Run (August 29, 30). By now, the Union soldiers were feeling bitter and discouraged. "So long as the interests of our country are entrusted to a lying braggart like Pope," one of them wrote, "we have little reason to hope successfully to compete with an army led by Lee, Johnston, and old 'Stonewall' Jackson." Once more McClellan assumed command of the disorganized Union army in the East.

Lee now decided to cross the Potomac, capture much-needed military supplies at Harpers Ferry arsenal for his ragged veterans, and induce Maryland (and perhaps the other border states) to cast their lot with the Confederacy. Should all go well, France and England might decide to recognize the southern republic and perhaps actively to intervene. Lee's plans miscarried. The Marylanders did not welcome his invading army, and although 25,000 of his men under the command of "Stonewall" Jackson did capture the garrison of 11,000 Federals at Harpers Ferry and large amounts of material, he had to divide his army to do so. Unluckily, a copy of Lee's marching orders fell into Union hands, and McClellan, learning that Lee had split his forces, launched an assault against the Confederates on September 14. At Antietam on September 17, both the Federals and the Confederates suffered grave losses, but Lee's outnumbered troops had to fall back. Had McClellan pressed his advantage, he might have turned a small success into decisive victory, but without continuing the battle he permitted the exhausted Confederates to retire across the Potomac (see map, p. 374). Lincoln observed that McClellan had the "slows" and in November, 1862, again relieved him of his command.

The victory at Antietam, thin though it was, provided an occasion for Lincoln to issue his Emancipation Proclamation. Since the outbreak of the war, the abolitionists had bombarded him with demands that he free the slaves, but Lincoln knew that such an act would alienate the border states, whose support was crucial to Union success. In 1861, Lincoln's first thought had been to preserve the Union even though slavery was left un-

A southern version of Lincoln composing the Emancipation Proclamation, assisted by sundry devils.

"Of that many-threaded drama with its sudden and strange surprises, its confounding of prophecies, its moments of despair...the interminable campaigns, the bloody battles, the mighty and cumbrous and green armies...with over the whole land...an unending, universal mourning-wail of women, parents, orphans—the marrow of the tragedy concentrated in those

The Battle of Fredericksburg by Thomas Nast

Army Hospitals—those forming the untold and unwritten history of the war—infinitely greater (like life's) than the few scraps and distortions that are ever told or written. Think how much, and of importance, will be . . . buried in the grave, in eternal darkness."—WALT WHITMAN disturbed. But when his advisers assured him that Negro emancipation would win friends abroad and encourage enlistments at home, the military advantages that might accrue from such a step persuaded him to take it. In July, 1862, Lincoln accepted the view he had so long opposed, "that it was a military necessity, absolutely essential for the salvation of the nation, that we must free the slaves or be ourselves subdued." On September 22, the President announced that after January 1, 1863, all slaves in the rebellious states should be declared free. The Proclamation did not actually emancipate the Negroes, since it was obviously inoperative in states still controlled by the Confederacy, and it did not apply to areas loyal to the Union. It did, however, give a moral impetus to the war effort and create sympathy for the Union cause in England. Many northerners, already disheartened by military failures and fearing that the Proclamation would lengthen the war, registered their disapproval in the fall elections of 1862. The Democrats cut deeply into the Republican majority in the House and elected a governor in New York.

The year 1862 ended tragically for the Union side. General Ambrose Burnside, Lincoln's choice to replace McClellan, was savagely beaten at Fredericksburg by Lee's well-entrenched army on December 13. Burnside retreated across the Rappahannock River with a loss of about 13,000. His defeat prompted a Radical attack against the President and Secretary of State Seward, with Chase secretly in league with the Radicals. Lincoln cleverly engineered a move by which Seward remained in the cabinet with Chase's reluctant support. But the administration's prestige sank to its lowest point in May, 1863, when "Fighting" Joe Hooker, the darling of the Radicals, fought a four-day battle at Chancellorsville against an army less than half the size of his own. Lee and Jackson split their army, outflanked the Federals, and drove them back across the Rappahannock with substantial losses. Chancellorsville was the high point of Confederate success in the eastern theater, but its cost was excessive. Besides more than 10,000 southern casualties, Lee lost his ablest aide when Stonewall Jackson was mortally wounded by his own pickets early in the battle. Jackson's absence was to be keenly felt in the greatest battle of the war, which was now looming.

Lee, in the flood tide of his success, proposed to invade Pennsylvania and Maryland with an army of about 75,000 men. Be-

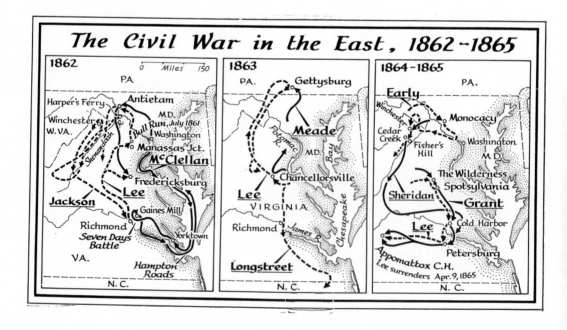

The Civil War in the East, 1862-1865

tween June 15 and 25, he moved his army over the Potomac and prepared to march on Harrisburg. The bulging granaries of Pennsylvania would feed his hungry troops, and a smashing victory might at last result in foreign intervention. George G. Meade commanded the Union army that met Lee's advance at Gettysburg. He had succeeded Hooker, who had quarreled with Halleck and had resigned his command. For three days, July 1-3, 1863, Meade's men repelled gallant Confederate assaults. Finally, Lee's shattered troops pulled back across the Potomac after Meade, despite Lincoln's urging, failed to counterattack. "Our army held the war in the hollow of their hand," Lincoln said later, "and would not close it." But Gettysburg ended the myth of Lee's invincibility. His forces had suffered about 28,000 casualties.

On the heels of the Gettysburg victory came the thrilling report that Grant, now in charge of the western armies, had taken Vicksburg after a harrowing six weeks' siege, on July 4, 1863. Five days later, Port Hudson, the last Confederate stronghold on the Mississippi, surrendered, and Lincoln was at last able to write his memorable words: "The Father of Waters again goes unvexed to the sea."

The Confederate army west of the Mississippi was now cut off, but another commanded by General Braxton Bragg still operated in central Tennessee. A bloody but inconclusive action had occurred at Murfreesboro from December 31, 1862, to January 3, 1863; and it was eight months before a new Union advance began under General William S. Rosecrans in the summer. In a seesaw contest, the Federals first pushed Bragg's army back and occupied the impor-

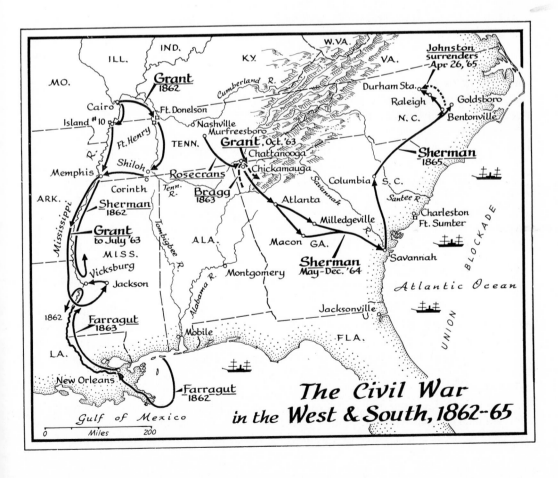

The Civil War in the West & South, 1862-65

tant railroad center at Chattanooga on September 9. A fierce battle then shaped up at Chickamauga on September 19-20, where only a brave stand by the troops of General George H. Thomas prevented a Union rout. Both sides lost heavily, and the battle ended with the Union army bottled up in Chattanooga. Grant, who in October had been placed in command of the Union armies operating between the Alleghenies and the Mississippi, ordered Thomas to take over from Rosecrans and moved swiftly to raise the siege. On November 25, units from the armies of the Potomac, the Cumberland, and the Tennessee, led by the most tested of the Union officers—Grant, Sherman, Sheridan, and Thomas—won a spectacular victory. Bragg's army broke up, and the Federals drove a wedge between the Confederates in the east and in the Mississippi Valley. The Battle of Chattanooga prepared the way for Sherman's march to the sea, which shattered the morale of the South.

Europe and the War. The Union victories at Gettysburg, Vicksburg, and Chattanooga ended any possibility of European intervention in the war on behalf of the South. Before Sumter, southern leaders had been convinced of Europe's absolute dependence on American cotton. After 1861, as cotton stockpiles abroad were used up, the Confederate Republic confidently awaited recognition from the European governments and the collapse of the Union blockade. This "King Cotton" strategy was based on wishful thinking. England, the largest purchaser of raw cotton from the South, had large surpluses of unsold cotton goods on hand in 1861 and enough raw cotton to last until 1862. India and Egypt furnished other sources of supply. Hence the southern policy in the first years of the war—to starve the English and French textile mills by imposing a cotton embargo—did not win favorable foreign intervention. When the South decided to resume its cotton exports to Europe in 1862, the Union navy had bottled up its ports.

The English, as it turned out, had no more need for northern wheat than they had for southern cotton (since they obtained their wheat supplies elsewhere). But other economic considerations helped to insure British neutrality and to offset such sympathy as England's upper classes had for the Confederate cause. Northern purchases of English munitions and the war's disastrous effect on the American merchant marine provided practical reasons for non-intervention. Even without these economic considerations, the English government dared not defy the Union blockade and deny to the North a weapon England had historically relied upon in her dealings with other nations. Nor was the English government unaware of the pro-Union sentiment among the British working class and middle class—a sentiment that Lincoln's Emancipation Proclamation did much to enhance.

English friends of the South in and out of Parliament, however, brought considerable influence to bear in favor of the Confederacy. On May 13, 1861, Queen Victoria issued a proclamation of neutrality, which gave the Confederacy belligerent rights. Charles Francis Adams, the Union minister at London, found the atmosphere chilly, especially after a Union warship, in November, 1861, forcibly removed from the English vessel *Trent* two Confederate commissioners bound for London. These commissioners, John Slidell and James M. Mason, were finally released in response to British protest, and were permitted to resume their journey to England.

But American and English truculence did not disappear. When the Confederate propagandist, Henry Hotze, arrived in England, he found the majority of the English press supporting the Confederacy, and added his own sheet, *The Index,* to the pro-southern chorus. The nobility and what Adams called the "wealthy commercial class" hoped and worked for the defeat of the North, and financed the building of commerce raiders for the Confederates. These raiders were vessels ostensibly designed for peaceful use but actually intended to prey upon Union shipping after the Confederates had armed them in non-English ports. The most famous of the raiders, the *Alabama,* sailed from Liverpool in July, 1862, against the protests of Minister Adams. Before she was sunk by a Union cruiser two years later, her commander, Admiral Raphael Semmes, had taken 62 northern ships valued at more than $6,500,000.

By early 1863, the British cabinet began to doubt the future of the southern cause, and British officials now put aside any thought of interposing in the American struggle and giving full recognition to the Confederacy. Even before Adams' threat that the release of two powerful warships commissioned by the Confederates was tantamount to a declaration of war, the British government had taken steps to buy them for its own navy. Confederate defeats and English fears of becoming involved in a war with the North prevented the pro-southern elements in England from doing much more than showing their sympathy for the Confederate cause.

The same was true in France, where Napoleon III openly championed the southern cause but feared to antagonize the Union government without the assurance of English support. As early as October, 1861, Napoleon had tried to promote a joint Anglo-French effort to aid the Confederacy by breaking the blockade. One reason for his concern was his involvement in Mexico. He had hoped to restore the monarchical principle there; and in 1861, when the Mexican government proved unable to pay its foreign obligations, he took advantage of the failure by arranging a joint Anglo-French-Spanish military expedition to Mexico. The British and Spanish soon withdrew, but the French Emperor kept his troops on Mexican soil. After hard fighting with the Mexican patriot and reformer, Benito Juarez, he installed Maximilian, brother of the Hapsburg emperor of Austria, as his puppet ruler. Had Napoleon succeeded in Mexico, he might have given valuable aid to the Confederacy. But the French failed to gain firm control of the country, and, after a strong protest by Secretary of State Seward, retired completely from the venture in 1866-1867.

Southern diplomacy had failed conclusively. England and France refused to give direct aid to the Confederacy by recognizing its government or by breaking the Union blockade. Russia was alone among the great powers in showing friendliness to the Union from the first. The visit of two Russian fleets to Union ports in 1863 was felt to be a gesture of good will to the North. Actually, Russia feared a war with Britain and France, and her "friendly" visit was primarily a maneuver to keep her fleet from being penned up in the Baltic.

Grant Takes
Command. While the Confederacy carried on its fruitless negotiations with European governments and slowly starved as the blockade tightened around it, its will to fight gradually weakened. Defeatists in the Confederacy spoke of their president as a "miserable, stupid, one-eyed, dyspeptic, arrogant tyrant." But war-weariness attacked the North as well. Lincoln and his measures were opposed in many areas, but especially in large cities like New York where the Democratic working-class voters, encouraged by the anti-administration press, opposed the draft laws of 1863. The new conscription act permitted a man to pay for a substitute if he could find one, or to escape military duty entirely for a fee of $300. The whole conscription program provoked a serious riot in New York City. In July, 1863, a mob set fire to buildings and attacked free Negroes. The draft riot lasted four days, took an undisclosed number of lives, and destroyed over a million dollars' worth of property.

Thus when Grant, in March, 1864, became supreme commander of all the Union armies, it seemed imperative for him to end the war by November, or at least to present the Union with some convincing victories before it next went to the polls. Fortunately for the Union, the South was no longer capable of launching an offensive. The Federals held the important communication centers in the West and were ready to lay waste the interior of the Confederacy from Mississippi to Virginia. Grant, the scrubby, round-shouldered Union leader, so unlike the popular conception of the conquering general, had planned a large-scale campaign to be carried out simultaneously in the western, southern, and eastern theaters. Grant himself was to move toward Richmond with the Army of the Potomac, engaging Lee's army while other Union commanders took the offensive in other theaters of action. Sherman, in Tennessee, was to move into Georgia and take Atlanta; another army would raid the Shenandoah Valley, and still another would repeat McClellan's maneuver and approach Richmond and Petersburg from the Peninsula.

The first reports of Grant's campaign were not encouraging. The Army of the Potomac, commanded by Meade and Grant, fought a number of bloody but indecisive battles on the route to Richmond with Lee's heavily outnumbered troops. Much of the fighting took place in the "Wilderness," a thickly forested area in Virginia where the dense undergrowth made conventional tactics impossible. Checked in the Battle of the Wilderness on May 5 and 6, 1864, Grant advanced toward Spotsylvania, where a murderous battle was fought before the Confederates were forced to retreat. By the end of May, Grant had pushed southward to Cold Harbor, and on June 3, he ordered a suicidal assault against Lee's entrenched soldiers. The enormous losses suffered by the Federals in this and other engagements aroused strong resentment in the North against Grant "the Butcher." But by June, two things had become clear to the Union strategists. First, the Union side was better able to stand a war of attrition than were the Confederates, since southern losses were irreplaceable. Second, a well-entrenched army obtained a tremendous advantage over an assaulting force.

Grant's obvious course now was to cross the James and approach Richmond from the rear. He might have taken the Confederate capital had the thoroughly incompetent General Benjamin F. Butler proceeded up the James and cut communications between Richmond and the well-fortified city of Petersburg, 20 miles to the south. Even with Butler's army helplessly wedged in its base at Bermuda Hundred, Grant almost succeeded in reaching Petersburg before Lee could garrison it, but his subordinates failed him. Nothing remained but to lay siege to the Confederate capital. In its defense, Lee tried to re-enact a diversion that Stonewall Jackson had carried out successfully in 1862. He sent Jubal Early with 17,000 men to attack in the Shenandoah Valley and to menace Washington. Only a skeleton army had been left to man Washington's bristling fortifications. Early's advance was checked at Monocacy for 24 hours by a small army of raw troops led by General Lew Wallace. Early reached the outskirts of Washington, but reinforcements from Grant arrived in time to drive him back. The next month, September, General Philip Sheridan followed Early into the Shenandoah Valley with an army of 55,000, whipped him badly at Winchester and Fisher's Hill, and after a near-disaster at Cedar Creek on October 19, rallied to expel the Confederates from the Valley. Sheridan then systematically devastated the area, one of the granaries of the South (see map, p. 374).

Since May, 1864, General William Tecumseh Sherman, in command of the three veteran Union armies in the West, had been fencing with a small but powerful Confederate army led by the redoubtable Joseph E. Johnston. In a series of flanking movements, he pushed Johnston toward Atlanta. Jefferson Davis now replaced Johnston with the impetuous but less-skilled John Bell Hood, who failed to beat off Sherman's troops now besieging Atlanta. After six weeks of fighting, Sherman wired to Halleck on September 3, "Atlanta is ours, and fairly won."

III.   COSTS AND CONSEQUENCES

The Election of 1864. Sherman's present to the Republican party came at a time when Lincoln had despaired of being re-elected, when some of his advisers were urging him to make peaceful overtures to Richmond, and when others were pressing him to withdraw from the presidential campaign for the benefit of the party. Actually, Lincoln's political situation was not so desperate as both he and his friends believed.

If the Radicals had agreed on one candidate, they might have prevented Lincoln's renomination. But some of them backed Chase, whose bid for the presidential nomination collapsed in March, 1864, and others favored the publicity-minded and breezy Benjamin F. Butler, "as full of poison gas," Lincoln remarked, "as a dead dog." The Radicals also considered John C. Frémont, who was nominated by an anti-Lincoln convention held in Cleveland, Ohio, on May 31 and later withdrew. Yet all their intriguing left Lincoln in control of the election. His backers held key positions in the national executive committees, and he easily won the nomination at the convention of Republicans and War Democrats (the Union party) meeting at Baltimore in June. Andrew Johnson of Tennessee, the vice-presidential nominee, belonged to that branch of the Democratic party that supported Lincoln and the war.

When the Democrats met at Chicago in August, a hodgepodge (to quote Gideon Welles) of "Whigs, Democrats, Know-Nothings, Conservatives, War men and Peace men, with a crowd of Secessionists and traitors to stimulate action," promptly chose McClellan for president after the bid of Governor Seymour of New York fizzled out. The Democrats counted on Lincoln's alleged unpopularity, enhanced, they believed, by a July draft proclamation for 500,000 additional troops, and also by the ground-swell of anti-war sentiment. The "war failure" plank in the Democratic platform, drafted by Vallandigham, declared that four years of war had not restored the Union, that hostilities should cease, and that the "Federal Union of the States" should be re-established on the old basis. This was nothing less than an armistice offer. McClellan, after serious soul-searching, decided to reject this plank and to commit himself to continuing the war until the southerners agreed to rejoin the Union.

After Sherman's victory at Atlanta and the defeat of the Democrats in the October local elections, Lincoln knew he would win. His confidence was not misplaced. His electoral vote in November was 212 against McClellan's 21, and the Republicans assumed control of Congress and most of the state governments.

In obtaining 55 per cent of the votes cast, Lincoln this time won by a convincing majority. Undoubtedly he benefited from the soldier vote, which in some places was unscrupulously manipulated by the Republican leaders, but he was also able to capitalize on the blunders of the divided Democrats. Had the Democrats offered a more sensible program to the voters than an ambiguous peace platform, they might have won. But the presence of peace advocates and Copperheads in the Democratic party seemed to justify the Republican charge that Democrats upheld disunion.

To Appomattox. Shortly after the election, Sherman's perambulating soldiers (or "bummers"), having burned a large part of Atlanta, marched on toward Savannah, while his lieutenants, John M. Schofield and George H. Thomas, the "Rock of Chickamauga," annihilated Hood's army near Nashville. Sherman's army lived off the land, pil-

Union soldiers resting in the trenches at Petersburg.

laged freely, and destroyed railroads and bridges. "We have covered a strip 60 miles wide on our trip here [one of Sherman's men wrote] and although there may be a few houses left there are mighty few fences, and from what I saw of it I don't think it would be a good place for a man to start a farm or a factory." At Savannah, Sherman obtained supplies from a Union fleet, and went on to capture the city on December 21. His invasion cost Georgia, by his own estimate, some $100 million in military resources, $80 million of it "simple waste and destruction." Sherman had indeed, as he wrote, brought "the sad realities of war to those who have been directly or indirectly instrumental in involving us in its attendant calamities." There was something terrible in his laconic observation, "To realize what war is one should follow our tracks."

Sherman resumed his destructive course in January, 1865, moving north from Savannah to North Carolina. Columbia, South Carolina, which was occupied by the Federals on February 17, was either delib-

erately or accidentally burned, and Sherman's army advanced into North Carolina with little or no opposition from the remnants of the Confederate forces. Wilmington and Charleston, the last Confederate seaports, had fallen, but the South was not yet willing to yield. Attempted negotiations at Hampton Roads (February 3, 1865) broke down when Davis refused to discuss peace until southern independence was guaranteed. Lincoln's answer was to continue the war. Long-besieged Petersburg fell at last, and Lee pulled out of untenable Richmond only to find his retreat cut off. Surrender terms were worked out on April 9, and on that day Lee officially yielded to Grant at Appomattox Court House (see maps, pp. 374, 375).

The magnanimous Lincoln had urged both Grant and Sherman to give the defeated Confederates "the most liberal and honorable terms." Grant complied with Lincoln's request. Any Confederate soldier who established his claim to a horse or mule was permitted to take it home with him, and officers could retain their side arms. As the Confederates stacked their guns, one Union officer observed that the Federals kept an awed silence "as if it were the passing of the dead."

Davis fled from Richmond but was caught in Georgia and imprisoned. Held for two years, he finally was released and permitted to retire. The terrible war was over, and the North could at last take stock of its costs and consequences.

The Balance Sheet. The Civil War caused more death and destruction than any previous war in modern history. No other war had been fought on such a grand scale or had employed with such deadly effect a technology designed for peacetime. This first modern war saw the employment for tactical purposes of the railroad, the telegraph, and the balloon. American ingenuity, stimulated by the war, created the railway gun, the electrically exploded torpedo, the Gatling gun, the repeating rifle, and more efficient cannons. The results could be seen in the casualties. Over 110,000 Union soldiers were killed in action out of the 360,000 lost from all causes. Total deaths in the Confederate armies came to 258,000, of whom 94,000 died in battle. Disease killed more men than bullets, since antiseptics were unknown. And hundreds of thousands of men were permanently disabled. It has been estimated that the war cost the North close to $4 billion in initial outlays and several billions more for pensions and other payments later on. For the nation as a whole, the price of the war ultimately came to $20 billion.

The war had almost destroyed southern society, but in the North the wholesale bloodletting and waste seemed only to stimulate the survivors. After a momentary depression in 1861, caused by the South's repudiation of a $300 million debt to northern businessmen, the splurge of government buying led to an economic resurgence. Agriculture boomed, even though thousands of farm workers were fighting with the Union armies. Their places were filled by some of the 707,000 immigrants who entered the country between 1860 and 1865, and by

women and children. The widespread use of labor-saving machinery on the farms not only met the needs of national consumption but helped to produce grain and corn surpluses for export. Cheaper transportation rates and high prices also contributed to farm prosperity.

The growing demand for farm machinery as well as for the "sinews of war" led to American industrial expansion. The enormous military consumption of ready-made clothing, leather goods, blankets, and war materials was made possible by new inventions and the expansion of factories. Of necessity, iron, coal, and copper production boomed during the war years, and arms factories sprang up everywhere. After the discovery of oil in Pennsylvania in 1859, its extraction became a major enterprise. By 1865, the army had all the petroleum it needed for lubricants and large quantities were being exported. The war years also saw a lumbering boom in the Great Lakes region and in New England, and the exploitation of the gold and silver mines in Nevada and Colorado. After 1859, thousands of newcomers traveled west to the mining towns and helped produce tons of the precious metals so vital to the Union cause.

This war prosperity had its harsh and corrupt aspects. Industrial wages, for example, did not keep up with living costs (between 1860 and 1862 wages rose 10 per cent, prices 50 per cent), and it seems probable that the average worker earned less in real wages after the war than he had in 1860. Those who lived on fixed incomes were hit especially hard by inflation. At the same time, the war produced a crop of vulgar millionaires and war profiteers. Windfall gains on war contracts also stimulated speculation, particularly on the New York stock market. Here, *Harper's Monthly* reported in 1864, "The number of brokers has more than quadrupled in a few months. . . . Aggregate business in the city of New York alone, has arisen from twenty-five to more than a hundred millions a day."

Yet in spite of the dishonesty and waste, and the decline in public morality that often occurs at such times, the war on the civilian front was by no means ignoble or socially disastrous. The consolidation of industry and finance was accompanied by a corresponding consolidation of labor; between 1863 and 1865, ten national unions were organized. Medical and relief organizations complemented the work of Surgeon-General William P. Hammond, who had reorganized the military medical service and built up a system of field and base hospitals manned by enlisted personnel. Civilian organizations also performed impressively. The United States Sanitary Commission consolidated local societies that had been organized for soldier relief, raised money by holding large fairs, and made private homes and hospitals available for wounded and convalescent soldiers. The Commission spent $25 million to provide tobacco, food, medicine, and the like, for soldiers, and performed other services that the Army Medical Bureau had not the means to undertake. Clergymen sent out by the United States Christian Commission supplied the soldiers with Bibles and religious services in addition to food and medicine.

Lincoln's Achievements.

Many of the economic gains won during the war were made possible by the acts of the Republican Congress, free at last from the agrarian opposition of the South. The Republicans had come to power with the support of the industrial Northeast and the farmers of the Northwest. Lincoln, in his first message to Congress, declared that the purpose of government was "to elevate the condition of men—to lift artificial weights from all shoulders; to clear the paths of laudable pursuit for all; to afford all an unfettered start, and a fair chance in the race of life."

His administration cleared the paths for business enterprise by the following enactments: (1) It passed the Morrill Tariff in 1861, which raised tariff rates to their 1846 levels, and it continued to revise the tariff schedules upward throughout the war. (2) In 1862, it voted to build the long-debated transcontinental railroad (see p. 341). With no southern claims to worry about, it selected a route from Omaha to Sacramento, and the two companies involved (the Union Pacific and the Central Pacific) were to receive 30 million acres of public land and generous cash loans. (3) It created a national banking system that was congenial to northern capitalists. The National Bank Act of 1863, which was materially revised the next year, required that banks applying for federal charters convert one-third of their capital into government bonds. In turn, the banks could issue banknotes in amounts up to 90 per cent of the bonds' market value, and could also draw interest from them. This measure stabilized paper currency by driving out of circulation the notes of private wildcat banks; paper currency issued by state banks also disappeared after Congress levied a 10 per cent tax on all state bank notes in 1865. The substitution of national bank notes for the thousands of different kinds that had formerly circulated made it much easier to carry on business transactions.

Nor did the Lincoln administration neglect the farmers. The Homestead Law passed in 1862 opened up the public domain to adult citizens or to those who declared their intention of becoming citizens. Only men who had borne arms against the United States were excluded. Every applicant was to receive title to 160 acres after five years' residence. Subsequent acts liberalized the law even further. Farmers also benefited from the Morrill Land Grant Act, for which Jonathan B. Turner, an Illinois educational and agricultural reformer, had long agitated. The Morrill Act, first proposed in 1857 and vetoed by Buchanan in 1859, was passed in 1862. It donated public lands to the states and territories to provide colleges for agriculture, the mechanical arts, and military science. This act played an important part in the founding and maintenance of many state colleges and universities.

The Republican administration succeeded

less well in financing the war, although the difficulties faced by Secretary of the Treasury Chase were not all of his own making. In 1861, the Treasury was empty, largely owing to the Panic of 1857 and the cut in government revenues caused by the Tariff Act of 1857. Chase, together with many others, felt that the war would soon be over. He recommended that a $320 million budget be provided by raising the tariff rates slightly, by instituting a low income tax, and by borrowing $240 million. But these measures were plainly inadequate for a war that was destined to cost billions. Although the people were willing and ready to be taxed, no workable system of excise taxes or graduated income tax was devised in time to pay for the mounting war costs. Chase distrusted bankers and paper money, but soon he had to rely on both. The bankers subscribed to government bonds at the outset of the war when Union hopes were high, but they became increasingly unenthusiastic about bond issues whose interest rates seemed too low and whose sale they were not permitted to administer. Chase tried to sell bonds directly to the public, but he did not succeed until 1862 when a private banker, Jay Cooke, was put in charge of the program. The 1862 bond campaign, carried on with high-pressure publicity, sold $400 million worth of bonds to the public.

The most criticized fiscal measure of the administration was the issuing of $450 million of treasury notes, unsupported by gold, known as "greenbacks." Chase hated to resort to this "war necessity," but no other source of funds seemed available in 1862, a most critical period of the war. Debtors were permitted to pay their obligations in greenbacks, but import duties and interest on bonds still had to be paid in coin. Greenbacks fluctuated in value depending on the fortunes of war. At one point they sank to 39 cents on the dollar. Furthermore, the greenbacks raised prices, caused disastrous fluctuations in the price of gold, stimulated corruption and extravagance, and added about $600 million to the cost of the war. At the war's end, the question of whether the greenbacks should be withdrawn from circulation precipitated a passionate and angry debate.

Lincoln's Death.   By 1865, the pattern of a new industrial society was already discernible, for the war had made inevitable the age of enterprise that was to follow. But the political future of America was by no means irrevocably fixed. Hence the assassination of Lincoln in Ford's Theater in Washington, April 14, 1865, was one of the incalculable events that may very well have changed the immediate course of American history. Lincoln, shot by the mentally unbalanced actor, John Wilkes Booth, had formulated a reconstruction policy that clashed with the plans of the Republican Radicals. He had charged

The last photograph of Lincoln, taken four days before he was assassinated.

the nation to act "with malice towards none, with charity for all," and had acknowledged the guilt of the North as well as the South for "the bondsman's two hundred and fifty years of unrequited toil." But before his assassination, he had already sensed strong congressional opposition to his lenient theories.

What Lincoln might have done to mitigate the errors of the postwar period is anyone's guess. His death, however, transformed a president patronized by his friends as "a well-meaning, sagacious, kind-hearted, ignorant, old codger" (to quote George Templeton Strong) into a saint. *"Death,"* wrote Strong, "has suddenly opened the eyes of the people (and I think the world) to the fact that a hero has been holding high place among them for four years, closely watched and studied, but despised and rejected by a third of the community, and only tolerated by the other two-thirds."

Readings

The best single account of the Civil War (as well as its origins and aftermath) is J. G. Randall, *The Civil War and Reconstruction* (1937); but the reader should also consult C. R. Fish, *The American Civil War* (1937), and G. F. Milton, *Conflict: The American Civil War* (1941).

Northern industrial potential is measured in E. D. Fite, *Social and Industrial Conditions in the North During the Civil War* (1910). On the financial and industrial history of the wartime South, read J. C. Schwab, *The Confederate States of America, 1861-1865* (1901). Clement Eaton, *A History of the Southern Confederacy* (1954), also contains an excellent summary of southern resources on the eve of the war.

The founding of the Confederacy is clearly discussed in the work of Eaton, cited above, and in E. M. Coulter, *The Confederate States of America, 1861-1865* (1950). A more detailed account as well as an excellent portrait of the Confederate president is B. J. Hendrick, *Statesmen of the Lost Cause: Jefferson Davis and his Cabinet* (1939).

Of the many books on Lincoln, the following are recommended: detailed and authoritative are J. G. Randall's *Lincoln, the President: Springfield to Gettysburg* (2 vols., 1945), and B. P. Thomas, *Abraham Lincoln* (1952). Original and illuminating is David Donald's *Lincoln Reconsidered* (1956). More information on Lincoln and his cabinet can be found in the *Diary of Gideon Welles* (3 vols., 1911), and in David Donald, ed., *Inside Lincoln's Cabinet: The Civil War Diaries of Salmon P. Chase* (1954). Lincoln's troubled relations with his party are discussed in D. M. Potter, *Lincoln and His Party in the Secession Crisis* (1942); T. Harry Williams, *Lincoln and the Radicals* (1941); and H. J. Carman and R. H. Luthin, *Lincoln and the Patronage* (1943). Copperheadism is described in Wood Gray, *The Hidden Civil War* (1942).

Moving and authoritative accounts of Civil War action may be found in four books by Bruce Catton: *Mr. Lincoln's Army* (1951), *Glory Road* (1952), *A Stillness at Appomattox* (1954), and *This Hallowed Ground* (1956); and in the four volumes of Carl Sandburg's *Abraham Lincoln: The War Years* (1939).

A vast literature exists on the military aspects of the Civil War. A short and handy summary is Fletcher Pratt's *Ordeal by Fire: An Informal History of the Civil War* (1935); and a superb picture history with sharp and penetrating comments is *Divided We Fought: A Pictorial History of the War* (1952), edited by David Donald. Donald's essay on Jomini, cited in the text, is included in his *Lincoln Reconsidered*. T. Harry Williams, *Lincoln and His Generals* (1952), treats an interesting phase of the war, as does K. P. Williams, *Lincoln Finds a General: A Military History of the Civil War* (4 vols., 1949-1956). A classic account of the campaigns and a revealing study of a great general is *The Personal Memoirs of U. S. Grant* (2 vols., 1885-1886). These memoirs should be supplemented by L. A. Coolidge's *Ulysses S. Grant* (1917). The southern side of the war is reported as richly as the northern. A classic work is D. S. Freeman's *R. E. Lee, A Biography* (4 vols., 1934-1935), and *Lee's Lieutenants* (3 vols., 1942-1944). Readers will find many biographies of the other celebrated generals on both sides (Sherman, Hooker, Thomas, Banks, Sheridan, Meade, Pemberton, Forrest, Jackson, Hood, and Sickles, among others); but for the ordinary man's role in the war, see B. I. Wiley's *The Life of Johnny Reb* (1943), and *The Life of Billy Yank* (1952). Important parts of the war are treated in A. B. Moore, *Conscription and Conflict in the Confederacy* (1924), and in Benjamin Quarles, *The Negro in the Civil War* (1953). Also relevant here is W. B. Hesseltine, *Civil War Prisons: A Study in War Psychology* (1930).

The diplomatic aspects of the war are covered in the general histories previously cited, but F. L. Owsley, *King Cotton Diplomacy* (1931), should not be overlooked. Economic matters are also covered in the general works already mentioned. E. P. Oberholtzer, *Jay Cooke, Financier of the Civil War* (2 vols., 1907), is especially important.

For a picture of life behind the lines, *The Diary of George Templeton Strong* (cited earlier), makes fascinating reading and gives a good picture of the work of the civilian relief organizations. War-time Washington is colorfully described in Margaret Leech, *Reveille in Washington, 1860-1865* (1941), and southern civilian life is presented in B. I. Wiley, *The Plain People of the Confederacy* (1943), and in his *Southern Negroes, 1861-1865* (1938).

RECONSTRUCTION AND THE SOUTH

C H A P T E R   S E V E N T E E N

Most of the wars of the nineteenth century were waged for limited objectives, by professional forces, between nations that rarely questioned one another's sovereignty. The American Civil War, unlike the others, was a struggle for survival, engaged in by an entire people, and with the question of sovereignty at its very heart. For the Confederacy to succeed, the Union had to be destroyed. For the Union to survive, the Confederacy had to be obliterated. The Union survived. The men in blue, said one southerner late in 1865, "destroyed everything which the most infernal Yankee ingenuity could devise means to destroy; hands, heart, fire, gunpowder, and behind everything the spirit of hell, were the agencies which they used."

I. THE CONQUERED SECTION

In the North the $4 billion in direct wartime expenditures gave an impetus to industry. The prosperity, however, did not extend to all lines of enterprise. The cotton textile industry, for example, broke down; the merchant marine and the shipbuilding industry suffered losses from which they did not recover until World War I; railroad building was sharply retarded. Yet, as John Sherman wrote to his brother, General William T. Sherman, in 1865, wartime expenditures by the federal government lifted the hopes of businessmen in the North. "The close of the war," he said, "with our resources unimpaired gives an elevation, a scope to the ideas of leading capitalists, far higher than anything ever undertaken in this country before. They talk of millions as confidently as formerly of thousands."

Direct Confederate expenditures for the war exceeded $2 billion, and expenditures by the individual southern states added many millions more to the total cost. But in the South these outlays were an utter loss in an utterly losing cause. Only a few southerners had managed to accumulate capital during the war. Some of them had succeeded in running cotton through the northern blockade. Some had preyed very profitably on Yankee shipping. Others had been canny enough to demand gold or goods from their neighbors in payment for food and clothing. Still others had managed to cling to their property despite Union arms or Confederate levies. But most of the South was impoverished. At the end of the war, each of the boys in blue went home at government expense with about $235 in his pocket. The boys in gray turned homeward with their pockets empty. Some of Lee's soldiers, writes the historian, Dixon Wecter, "had to ask for hand-outs on the road home, with nothing to exchange for bread save the unwelcome news of Appomattox."

Fighting had occurred in only a relatively few sections in the South, but in these areas the destruction was likely to be complete. Writing of Columbia, South Carolina, believed by many to have been the most beautiful city in North America, one traveler said in September, 1865, that it was

... a wilderness of ruins. ... Its heart is but a mass of blackened chimneys and crumbling walls. Two-thirds of the buildings in the place were burned. ... Not a store, office, or shop escaped; and for a distance of three-fourths of a mile on each of twelve streets there was not a building left.

Nor had the rural areas escaped. Five years after the war an English traveler described the Tennessee Valley country:

The trail of war is visible throughout the valley in burnt-up gin-houses, ruined bridges, mills, and factories ... and in large tracts of once cultivated land stripped of every vestige of fencing. The roads, long neglected, are in disorder, and ... in many places ... impassable.

Southern river ports and coastal harbors were put out of commission. Levees were destroyed or neglected, and floods washed out miles of farm land.

But the South lost even more in non-military damage. Slaveless white farmers, when they took up arms, had to leave their lands, buildings, and tools in charge of the women and the old folks, who could not care for them properly. Many of the large plantations had also fallen into ruin. Half of the South's agricultural equipment had been wrecked. Every third horse and mule had died, wandered off, or been taken by Union or Confederate foragers, so that after the war men and women often harnessed themselves to the old plows in order to prepare their fields for planting. Perhaps worst of all, as far as the future was concerned, the South's labor system was utterly disrupted.

In the midst of the disorganization of

Columbia, South Carolina, at the end of the Civil War.

southern life, few suffered more than the ex-slaves. The problem of free and footloose Negroes had been forced upon the Union armies and the Union government early in the war, as slave territory was occupied and as Negro families fled to the shelter of the Union lines. Eventually, scores of Negroes were corralled in Union "contraband camps," which were so flimsy, filthy, and crowded that death from epidemics, exposure, and crime soon claimed as many as 25 per cent of the inmates. Private philanthropy, first organized in the North in 1862, supplemented these early official measures with somewhat happier results.

When the Emancipation Proclamation of January 1, 1863, sharply focused attention on the problem of free Negroes, Congress began to consider bills to establish a bureau for their care. Not until March 3, 1865, however, did Congress create, as part of the War Department, the Bureau of Refugees, Freedmen, and Abandoned Lands—or, simply, the Freedmen's Bureau. This agency, which was to operate for only one year after

the end of the war, was authorized to issue "provisions, clothing and fuel . . . for . . . destitute and suffering refugees and freedmen." The commissioner at its head was empowered to set aside land within the Confederacy which "shall have been abandoned" or confiscated, and to assign at a fair rent "to every male citizen, whether refugee or freedman . . . not more than forty acres of such land."

At first, the Freedmen's Bureau did nobly. But once the full flush of liberty struck the Negro, the rate of migration soared and the Bureau became hard-pressed. In the summer of 1865, more than 20,000 ex-slaves flocked into Washington. Greater numbers congregated in Charleston, New Orleans, Memphis, and other southern cities. Without resources themselves, these cities could do nothing but increase the number and size of their already overtaxed "contraband camps." Death and disease rates among the inmates soared during the first two years after the war, and in some camps a third of the Negroes died.

The white farmers and planters often fared little better than the ex-slaves. Famine struck many parts of the South as early as 1862, and the disruption of the transportation system prevented people in the more fortunate areas from sending food to their starving neighbors. In 1862, statewide systems of relief were set up in all the Confederate commonwealths, but by 1865 even these had collapsed in the general ruin. Moreover, the 1865 harvest was extremely lean, so that, as one official of the Freedmen's Bureau reported, it was "a common sight, an every-day sight . . . , that of women and children, most of whom were formerly in good circumstances, begging for bread from door to door." So widespread and so persistent was the economic desolation in the four years after the war that the Freedmen's Bureau alone issued almost 21 million rations, about 6 million of which went to impoverished whites.

Perhaps the heaviest blow to the stricken South was the moral cost of war and defeat and ultimately of Reconstruction. The losses in youth and talent hurt beyond measure. Among the survivors, purpose, morale, and aspiration lagged. In Georgia, in 1865, one reporter noted that "aimless young men in gray, ragged and filthy, seemed, with the downfall of the rebellion . . . to have lost their object in life." In Mississippi alone it was estimated that there were 10,000 orphans. A Virginia planter, shorn of all the wealth he had planned to distribute by earlier wills, wrote this last testament in 1866:

I give and bequeath to my. . . descendants throughout all generations, that bitter hatred and everlasting malignity of my heart and soul against . . . all the people north of Mason and Dixon's line, and I do hereby exhort and entreat my children and grandchildren . . . to instill in the hearts of . . . all their future descendants from their childhood, this bitter hatred and these malignant feelings. . . .

The war crippled all the agencies of social control in the South. Church buildings were demolished, their congregations scattered. The school system simply ceased to exist. Colleges went bankrupt and were abandoned. Policemen, sheriffs, courts, judges— all the instruments of law enforcement— could scarcely be found. Heartless bands led by ex-Confederate guerillas like Jesse and Frank James roamed the countryside, refusing to give up the war against the victors and their society. "Our principal danger," said one observer, "was from lawless bands of marauders. . . . Our country was full of highwaymen . . . the off-scourings of the two armies and of the suddenly freed negro population."

As late as 1879, a journalist remarked that the migrants who were leaving the Old South for Texas had "no progress in them, no love for adventure, no ambition." Those who stayed behind, though often the most stable persons in the community, were often the most discouraged. "These faces, these faces," cried a northern observer in 1873 on a visit to New Orleans: "One sees them everywhere; on the street, at the theater, in the salon, in the cars; and pauses for a moment struck with the expression of entire despair."

II. THE ECONOMIC TROUGH

In many countries devastated by war—or by plagues, earthquakes, and similar disasters—the greater the damage the stronger have been men's efforts to recover. But in the South after the Civil War the problem was not simply to rebuild or restore. The war had piled social chaos on economic ruin.

The lowly "blacks" had suddenly risen to the status of free, and disconcerted, men. Upland farmers and hill-country "white trash," in turn, were suddenly challenged on the one hand to aspire to the planter's old power, and on the other were faced with the possibility of being leveled down to the status of ex-slaves. From such disparate groups the South had to build an entirely new society.

Transport and Markets. One of the most pressing economic problems facing the South after the war was how to revive trade and transportation, and here the Union government lent a helping hand. By June, 1865, all restrictions on the exchange of commodities between the former enemies were withdrawn, and goods began to move north and south. In June and July, by calling off the blockade of Confederate ports, the government freed southern crops for export. When the federal government returned the railroads it had taken over, it canceled all charges for bridges it had built or repaired and for all roadbed and track it had laid or restored.

River transport was at least as important to the South as railroads, but here the northern contribution was niggardly. Congressional appropriations for river and harbor improvements in 1866 ran to $3,500,000, but only $75,000 was earmarked for the South, where the need was greatest. To keep its roads in repair, the South was left entirely to its own devices. But southern resources were far too meager to cope with the problem, and apathy soon set in. The best road near New Orleans, for example, was kept in condition more for the purpose of horse-racing than for hauling.

Capital. The South needed capital far more urgently than it needed markets and transportation. And here the action the federal government took was disastrous. Despite Confederate government bans on cotton culture so that the land could be used to grow much-needed cereals and grain, and despite the capture or destruction of existing cotton stocks by the Union army, some southern planters had managed to accumulate considerable reserves of cotton. By selling these at the incredibly high prices that existed in 1865, they planned to get enough capital to restore the land, buildings,

and equipment to their former productivity. It so happened that the Confederate government had its own stores of cotton, which were estimated in 1865 at 150,000 bales. At the end of the war, the Union administration ordered all Confederate government assets confiscated. The zeal of the Treasury agents assigned to this work was stimulated by the promise of a commission of 25 per cent on all goods they rounded up. So attractive was this reward that the agents (and some local citizens posing as agents) raided private as well as public warehouses and, according to one estimate, collected 3 million bales of cotton and large quantities of other commodities in the bargain.

Most of what the legitimate agents took from the South they sold on their own account, making fortunes in the process. On what they turned over to the Treasury, the federal government realized about $34 million, much of which was eventually returned to some 40,000 southern claimants. But this amount was only a small fraction of the loot, and in any case it was returned too late to alleviate the pressing need for capital. Many thousands of southerners were never compensated for their losses.

The federal government completed its attack on southern capital in 1865 and 1866 with a system of confiscatory taxes. A levy of 25 per cent was placed on the sale of any private property, and a shipping tax was imposed on all goods transferred. A so-called revenue tax completed the burden. The revenue tax on cotton ranged from 2 to 3 cents a pound. In three years, this tax alone drained away more than $68 million from the South—far more than the total amount spent on relief and reconstruction by all northern agencies, including the army, the Freedmen's Bureau, and private philanthropic organizations.

Share-Cropping and the Crop Lien. The South's precarious capital position was weakened further by the development of the share-cropping system of cotton culture and the crop-lien system of finance. Before the war, most of the great southern plantations had been heavily mortgaged. After the war, hard-pressed creditors began demanding interest and principal payments on these mortgages, and many planters tried to forestall fore-closures by selling part of their land in order to finance cultivation of the rest. Others leased out acreage for a money rent. But obviously there was not enough money around to sustain these expedients.

Under share-cropping, the land was di-vided into many small holdings, rather like small independent farms, but actually parts of single plantations. Gaining even a small plot for himself was a big step forward for the Negro, for it enabled him to break away from the labor gang of slavery days and to move, however precariously, toward in-dependence and personal responsibility. In other respects, however, the familiar routine of the prewar South was usually re-enacted on the postwar plantations. Planters paid no wages for labor; landless workers paid no rent for land. Instead, planter and laborer shared the crop they produced together.

But planters and croppers could not even get their crop planted unless the local mer-chant advanced them seed and equipment (and personal necessities like food and clothing). And for these advances, the mer-chant demanded a first lien on the cotton the growers and workers themselves were to share.

For his own stock-in-trade, the local mer-chant had to seek credit from northern suppliers. Risks in the South were so great that these suppliers demanded high prices for the goods they sold directly and high in-terest for credit they extended. In addition, oppressive fees were charged for transpor-tation, insurance, and other commercial services. All these charges the merchant passed on to the landlords and croppers whose liens he held. Usually the cotton crop proved to be worth less than the growers' debts. Their inability to pay left the merchant at the mercy of his own creditors in the North, who drained from the defeated sec-tion whatever fluid funds it had left.

Labor and Land.   The South drifted into the catastrophic share-cropping and crop-lien systems in part because the area was starved for capital, and in part because these systems seemed to offer a solution to the labor problem. Immediately after the war, many planters tried to hold on to their newly freed workers by offering them keep and cash. To protect the Negroes from being packed off as soon as the crops were in, the Freedmen's Bureau insisted, often over the objections of the illiterate and suspicious freedmen themselves, that the working ar-rangements be confirmed by written con-tracts. In the hope that the Negroes would stay at least until the harvest was over, the planters usually had been willing to sign. A typical contract stipulated that the planter pay wages of $10 to $12 a month, less the cost (determined by the planter) of "quarters, fuel, healthy and substantial rations." In exchange, the freedman agreed "to labor . . . faithfully . . . six days during the week, in a manner customary on a plantation."

But this wage system, like the land rental system, failed for lack of money. Frequently, though, planters withheld wages even when they had the money. The freedmen "have universally been treated with bad faith," wrote General W. E. Strong from Texas in 1866, "and very few have received any compensation for work performed."

The conduct of the Negroes themselves often did not help matters. Most Negroes, to be sure, followed the prewar pattern as faith-fully as their old masters. As one of the planters said, "They really have an attach-ment to the place and that is about the only definite feeling . . . that they have." But once emancipated, many Negroes resented having to work "in a manner customary on a plantation." Many of them took to the road just as soon as the crop was ready to be picked and lived off the country. Others wandered off in search of their scattered families; still others left in order to rid themselves of the families they had.

Perhaps the strongest drive that set the

Negroes wandering was land-hunger. As early as 1862, Lincoln had talked seriously of colonizing freed Negroes on land captured by Union forces; subsequently, various Union generals had taken over conquered territory and made it available to ex-slaves on easy terms. Since many of the new farmers did well, others were eager for a chance to get land of their own. The establishment of the Bureau of Refugees, Freedmen, and Abandoned Lands right after the war, and speeches by zealots like Thaddeus Stevens demanding confiscation of large southern estates for the benefit of the freedmen, raised the Negroes' hopes of "forty acres and a mule." But nothing ever came of such hopes.

The widespread failure of the wage system led to other experiments. Georgia, Alabama, and other states set up labor bureaus to bring northern farm workers and European immigrants to the southern plantations, but most of the available workers preferred taking up western homesteads over going South to work for wages. Reasoning that the freed Negroes might work better under northern supervision, many planters tried using Yankee managers on their lands; but the northerners usually failed for want of experience.

A harsher device, which remained in operation for a long time after the war and Reconstruction, was embodied in the so-called "Black Codes," which all the ex-Confederate states except Tennessee adopted in 1865 and 1866. These codes, based in part on the prewar laws governing free Negroes in the South, and on the vagrancy laws of the North, attempted to define the legal position of the freedmen. They granted Negroes the right to sue, to give evidence in court, to go to school, to have marriages sanctified and respected, and to have apprenticed children protected by the state. But nowhere could Negroes hold office, vote, serve on juries, or bear arms. In some states, the codes permitted Negroes to hold property, to work at any jobs they could hold down, and to quit a job freely. But in most states, Negroes were prohibited from working as artisans, mechanics, and in other capacities where they competed with white labor, and they could not leave their jobs except under stated conditions.

The vagrancy laws were the most oppressive provisions included in the codes. In Georgia, for example, the law said that "all persons wandering or strolling about in idleness, who are able to work and who have no property to support them," might be picked up and tried. If convicted, they could be set to work on state chain gangs or contracted out to planters and other employers who would pay their fines and upkeep for a stated period.

The wages set for convict labor were far below the rates prevailing in private employment, and the money was paid to the state rather than to the convict. The system not only saved the state the cost of the convict's upkeep, but also brought in money. The vagrancy laws varied in severity of language and strictness of enforcement. In the deep South, where the Negroes were most numerous and the plantations most severely disrupted, the laws were harshly administered and led to what many in the North believed to be a return to involuntary servitude.

None of these methods of securing and holding labor worked so effectively as sharecropping. But we have already mentioned that share-cropping, when combined with the crop-lien system, had some very serious drawbacks. The worst of them stemmed from the lien-holding merchant's constant need for cash to meet his own obligations, and his insistence, on that account, that croppers grow nothing but the great cash crop—cotton. Constant overproduction became the rule and cotton prices tumbled. Not until 1872-1875 did the South regularly produce a cotton crop as large as the typical crop harvested in the pre-war years, about 3.5 to 4 million bales. During most of the years after 1869, cotton brought an average of 15 cents a pound. By 1890, cotton production had doubled, and the price had fallen to 8½ cents. In 1894, production reached a record high of 10 million bales, and the price sank to a record low of 4½ cents. Falling prices and mounting debts sapped whatever spirit of enterprise might have survived the social conflicts and legalized abuses of the time.

The White Farmer and the "New South."

At the outbreak of the Civil War, eight times as many Negroes as whites had been employed in growing cotton, most of them concentrated on the newer plantations of the rich Gulf plain and the Mississippi Valley. After the war, many of these Negroes had become share-croppers and continued to work these once-excellent lands. The independent small farmers of the South had lived mainly off subsistence farming or had grown other crops than cotton for local markets. But now they too needed credit from the local merchants to get their lands back into production and their homes and barns repaired. And, as in the case of the croppers, the merchants dictated that the white farmers also grow nothing but cotton. At first, the white farmers gave the merchant a lien on their forthcoming crops. As debts mounted, the merchant demanded a mortgage on the farmer's land as well; and as the cotton market deteriorated, the merchant ultimately foreclosed. Some white farmers managed to beat the trend and become large land-owners and even merchants. But most of them went under.

The independent white farmers had learned early to look on share-cropping as a Negro institution. When they lost their land, they tried working as tenants on rented land, but lack of cash eventually forced them into share-cropping. Those who refused to give up their independence were relegated to the poorest land, from which their offspring began drifting to the towns. By the 1880's, many of the white farmers had lost virtually everything but their pride of race. It was to restore employment and ambition to white farm youth that the idea of the "New South" was born—a South in which the Negro "hands"

would "keep their place" growing cotton and tobacco in the hot sun while the whites found remunerative work in textile and tobacco factories, iron and steel mills, and other industrial enterprises. The movement to save the South through industrialism took on the guise of a crusade. "The stagnation of despair," wrote the New Orleans *Times-Democrat* in 1881, "has by some magic transformation, given place to the buoyance of hope, of courage, of resolve. The silence of inertia has turned into joyous and thrilling uproar of action. We are a new people. Our land has had a new birth."

Unfortunately, industrialism didn't work. "It was one thing," writes the historian of the "New South," C. Vann Woodward, "to hail the arrival of industrial South Carolina, the cotton-mill state, in 1900; another to point out that . . . only 3.6 per cent [of its people were employed] in manufactures . . . while 69 per cent . . . were still employed in agriculture." Agricultural workers were no better off than they had been 20 years earlier. Industrial laborers (by 1900 the labor force was preponderantly women and children) were paid less per hour than cotton brought per pound. Average wages of $2.50 for a work week that averaged 70 hours were considered high. Actually, few workers ever saw any money. Most of the factories were in new mill towns, and everything in the towns—school, church, police, stores, and factories—was owned by the industrial promoters. The workers had no alternative but to buy at the company store, where their debts soon outran their wages. They became as firmly tied to the company as the share-cropper was to the supply merchant. In a few areas of the South, notably in northern Alabama where there were rich coal and iron deposits, northern capital had developed large-scale industrial activity. But even in these areas the white workers were slavishly treated and profits flowed away from the South.

III. PRESIDENTIAL RECONSTRUCTION

Lincoln's Program. While the South was trying to reconstruct itself, many in the North were trying to reconstruct the Union. That aim, indeed, had been the avowed object of northern military activity during the war. As early as July 22, 1861, the House of Representatives, with only two dissenting votes, had adopted the Crittenden Resolution, which stated, "This war ... is waged ... to defend and maintain ... the Union ... and ... as soon as these objects are accomplished the war ought to cease." Three days later, the Senate adopted the Johnson Resolution, which was similar to Crittenden's.

In 1862, when much of Tennessee, Louisiana, and North Carolina had fallen to Union arms, Lincoln hastened to appoint military governors—among them Andrew Johnson of Tennessee—to pave the way for the establishment of civil administrations in these states and to bring them back into the Union fold. By December, 1863, when Arkansas was brought under control, Lincoln had a full-scale "reconstruction" program ready. Promulgated by presidential proclamation, this program became known as the "ten per cent plan."

Lincoln's plan excluded from participation in politics all high military and civil officers of the Confederacy or its states. To all other Confederates who would take a loyalty oath, a general amnesty would be granted and any confiscated property would be restored. As soon as 10 per cent of a state's 1860 electorate had sworn allegiance to the Union and had agreed to comply with Union laws and proclamations, such as the Emancipation Proclamation, the state could proceed to write a new constitution, elect a new state government, and send representatives and senators to the United States Congress.

Lincoln's theory held that the Union was indestructible and that states could not break away from it even though their people might rebel. Rebellious citizens could be restored to citizenship by presidential pardon, and then could set about manning the newly loyal state governments. This was the foundation of Lincoln's program for restoring the southern states quickly and smoothly to their "proper practical relation with the Union." "Finding themselves safely at home," he said, "it would be utterly immaterial whether they had ever been abroad."

The Radical Program. Congress, however, had no intention of letting the South off so lightly. The House after the war was dominated by Thaddeus Stevens of Pennsylvania and the Senate by Charles Sumner, the doctrinaire anti-slavery leader from Massachusetts. Stevens had cast one of the two votes in the House against the Crittenden Resolution of 1861, and Sumner had refused to vote for the Johnson Resolution in the Senate. To these determined men, the war had been fought to free and elevate the slaves. They were not opposed to "reconstruction" of the Union, but they had terms of their own which they would not surrender even if reconstruction itself were sacrificed.

Stevens had championed the Negro all his life. He would not sign the new constitution of the state of Pennsylvania in 1837 because the constitutional convention had rejected his urgent demand that Negroes as well as whites be given the suffrage. Fond as he was of children and over-generous in their support, he refused to give one cent to the Home for Friendless Children in his own city of Lancaster when the institution declined to accept Negro youngsters on the same basis as white.

Stevens was determined that his ideas of social equality, though advanced even for the North, be forced upon the proud planters.

The whole fabric of southern society [he declared] *must* be changed. ... The Southern states have been despotisms, not governments of the people. It is impossible that any practical equality of rights can exist where a few thousand men monopolize the whole landed property.... If the South is ever to be made a safe republic let her lands be cultivated by the toil of the owners or the free labor of intelligent citizens. This must be done even though it drive her nobility into exile. If they go, all the better.

Surely the crimes of the South, said Stevens, "are sufficient to justify the exercise of the extreme rights of war—'to execute, to imprison, to confiscate.' "

And Sumner added his insistent voice: "If all whites vote, then must all blacks.... Without them the old enemy will reappear, and ... in alliance with the Northern democracy, put us all in peril again."

In opposition to Lincoln's 10 per cent policy, Stevens and Sumner and their militant minority of Radical Republicans (see p. 365) drew up the Wade-Davis Bill, which they rammed through Congress in July, 1864, an hour before the session ended. This bill would have required a *majority* of citizens, not just 10 per cent, to swear loyalty to the Union before an acceptable state government could be established in a seceding state. It also prescribed that new state constitutions in the South must abolish slavery, repudiate state debts, and disfranchise ex-Confederate leaders.

The Radical strategists intended by this bill to commit the Republican party to the Radical reconstruction program in the impending presidential elections. But Lincoln permitted the Wade-Davis Bill to die by a pocket veto and issued a proclamation justifying his action. The Radicals replied with the Wade-Davis Manifesto of August, 1864. "The President," it declared, "by preventing this bill from becoming a law, holds the electoral votes of the rebel States at the dictation of his personal ambition. ... A more studied outrage on the legislative authority of the people has never been perpetrated." It went on: "The authority of Congress is paramount and must be respected." The manifesto did not deter Lincoln and most Republicans from joining with all comers, including Democrats like Andrew Johnson from the ex-Confederate state of Tennessee,

to form the Union party and to sweep the elections of November, 1864 (see p. 379).

Most of the Radical leaders had come around to supporting Lincoln in the campaign because they did not want to smash the Republican party machinery, which they hoped eventually to control. Once the elections were over, however, they lost no time in demonstrating that they still opposed Lincoln's conciliatory policy. In January, 1865, Congress passed the Radical-sponsored Thirteenth Amendment. Ratified the following December, this Amendment declared that "Neither slavery nor involuntary servitude ...shall exist within the United States." In February, 1865, Congress refused to admit

Thaddeus Stevens (1792-1868).

CONGRESSIONAL SURGERY   LEGISLATIVE QUACKERY

DOCTOR NORTH TO PATIENT SOUTH — HELP YOU! OF COURSE! WE WILL FIRST, WITH YOUR ASSISTANCE, TAKE YOU OFF YOUR LEGS, & THEN FIX YOU UP NICELY ON THESE CONSTITUTIONAL AMENDMENTS —   SOUTH "CANT SEE IT"

A conservative view of Stevens' Radical prescription for "reconstructing" the South.

members from Louisiana, though Lincoln had declared that state "reconstructed." Just before the lame-duck session ended on March 3, 1865, Congress created the Freedmen's Bureau to help Negro refugees and to protect the freedom of ex-slaves.

On April 14, 1865, just five days after Lee's surrender at Appomattox, Lincoln was assassinated. At his last cabinet meeting, the President, according to his Navy secretary, Gideon Welles, had called it "providential" that "the rebellion was crushed just as Congress had adjourned. . . . If we were wise and discreet, we should reanimate the States and get . . . the Union reestablished before Congress came together in December." Lincoln's death heartened the Radicals. "Johnson, we have faith in you," exclaimed jubilant Ben Wade. "By the gods, there will be no trouble now in running this government."

Andrew Johnson, a self-educated tailor, had always been as outspoken an enemy of

the cotton planters as Stevens himself. More than once during the war he had referred to them simply as "traitors." Thus the Radicals expected to have a sympathizer in the White House. But even if he turned antagonistic, they felt that he would prove only a small threat to their plans. Johnson had none of Lincoln's stature, none of the prestige that Lincoln had earned in winning the war. He was also tainted as a man from the rebel state of Tennessee. Since Johnson had few claims on the people and none on the Republican party, he was unlikely to win popular or partisan support for any stand he might take. Lincoln's cabinet, moreover, which, perhaps foolishly, Johnson kept intact, contained a strong Radical contingent led by Secretary of War Edwin M. Stanton, who lost no opportunity to embarrass his new chief.

But Johnson moved more swiftly and independently than the Radicals anticipated. His well-known devotion to the Union might have given them a clue to his feelings. Of all the southern senators in 1861, Johnson alone had refused to abandon his seat. Among his cabinet advisers he looked not to Stanton but to moderates like William H. Seward and Gideon Welles, who supported his efforts to restore the United States to national unity.

Early in May, 1865, Johnson recognized Lincoln's 10 per cent governments in Louisiana, Tennessee, Arkansas, and Virginia. He next appointed military governors to the seven states that had not yet complied with Lincoln's 10 per cent plan. On May 29, he offered executive amnesty to citizens of these states except high Confederate military and civil officers and citizens worth more than $20,000. These people had to make personal application for amnesty to the president. The "whitewashed" electorate— that is, those who benefited by the amnesty offer—were then to elect members to a constitutional convention in each state, which would abolish slavery, rescind the state's secession ordinance, adopt the Thirteenth Amendment, repudiate the state war debt, and call an election for a new state government. Worse than the generous amnesty, as far as the Radicals were concerned, was Johnson's permitting the suffrage for this election to be determined by each state rather than by Congress. The Negro, clearly, was not going to get the ballot in the South any more than in most states in the North.

By the winter of 1865, all the seceding states but Texas had complied with Johnson's terms, and their sincerity was confirmed by the reports of investigators Johnson had sent to find out if the South actually did accept the judgment of arms. One investigator, however, Carl Schurz, found that "there is as yet among the southern people an *utter absence of national feeling* [Schurz's emphasis] . . . and a desire to preserve slavery in its original form as much and as long as possible." But Johnson received this report with "great coldness," and only at Sumner's urging did Schurz decide to make it public.

IV. CONGRESS AND PRESIDENT JOHNSON

The Storm Breaks. When Congress met in December, 1865, it was faced with Johnson's executive coup. Trouble developed quickly. The restored southern state governments had played into the hands of the Radicals by their prompt adoption of the rigorous Black Codes. Stevens improved the opportunity thus offered when he said in September, "Let all who approve of our [principles] tarry with us. Let all others go with copperheads and rebels. Those will be the opposing parties."

As their first move, the Radicals set up the Joint Committee of Fifteen—six senators and nine representatives—to scan the qualifications of the men elected in the southern states and to review the whole presidential reconstruction plan that had brought such "traitors" to the very threshold of Congress. These men were never permitted to take their seats. Without them, Congress proceeded early in 1866 to enact a bill continuing the Freedmen's Bureau, which was gradually becoming an instrument of Radical policy. Johnson, believing that the future care of the Negroes had better be left to the state legislatures, vetoed the bill. The Radicals succeeded in overriding the veto in the House, but in the Senate they failed to get the required two-thirds vote.

In March, 1866, Johnson vetoed a civil rights bill which forbade states to discriminate among their citizens on the basis of color or race, as they had in the Black Codes.

But by now a sufficient number of Conservative senators were ready to join the Radicals in defense of congressional prerogatives, if not of Radical principles, and both houses overrode the President. A few months later, in July, 1866, the Radicals succeeded in pushing through a second Freedmen's Bureau bill over Johnson's veto.

The Radicals were showing their parliamentary mettle as well as their political policy. The real test developed over the Fourteenth Amendment. Radical leaders themselves had qualms about the constitutionality of their Civil Rights Act, and feared that another Congress might easily repeal it. A civil rights amendment would set the constitutionality issue at rest and would also make repeal much more difficult. The Fourteenth Amendment, perhaps the most far-reaching amendment ever added to the Constitution, passed Congress in June, 1866. The first of the measure's four major sections in effect declared that Negroes were citizens, and then prescribed that:

No State shall make or enforce any law which shall abridge the privileges or immunities of citizens of the United States; nor shall any State deprive any person of life, liberty, or property, without due process of law; nor deny to any person within its jurisdiction the equal protection of the laws.

The second section did not give Negroes the vote, but it penalized any state for withholding it. Such a state's representation in Congress was to be reduced by the same proportion that those deprived of the vote bore to the "whole number of male citizens twenty-one years of age in such State." * Third, the amendment disqualified from office, unless Congress specifically lifted the disqualification by a two-thirds vote, all Confederates who before the war had taken a federal oath of office. Finally, the amendment guaranteed the Union debt and outlawed the Confederate debt and any claims for compensation for loss of slaves.

The Radicals demanded that the southern states ratify the amendment before they could be represented in Congress. Johnson advised the states not to ratify, and all but Tennessee followed his advice. When the last of the rejections arrived, James A. Garfield of Ohio declared: "The last one of the sinful ten has at last with contempt and scorn flung back into our teeth the magnanimous offer of a generous nation. It is now our turn to act."

---

* This provision, like all others of the Amendment, of course applied to northern as well as southern states. By 1866, only six northern states had as yet given the Negro the right to vote. In no northern state, however, was the Negro population large enough to bring about a reduction in actual representation in case Negro suffrage was withheld.

The Radicals Ride.

The Fourteenth Amendment was rejected while the congressional elections of 1866, the first national elections since the close of the war, were taking place. The amendment had drawn the issue clearly between the President and Congress. Between August 28 and September 15, Johnson made his unfortunate "swing around the circle," visiting key cities on behalf of congressional candidates who favored his policy. Many people considered such campaigning unseemly for a president, and all the more so in Johnson's case, since he was often indiscreet as an impromptu political speaker. The more he talked the more the Radicals made fun of him. Fodder for the Radicals' own campaign was supplied by violence in the South, which reached its peak during a riot in New Orleans on July 30 over Radical efforts to force Negro suffrage on the state of Louisiana. Negroes and whites clashed and 41 men were killed.

The Radicals used such incidents to pound home the intransigence of the Confederates. As if to underscore the need for vigilance, Union veterans completed the organization of the Grand Army of the Republic just before the elections, and in November, 1866, the G.A.R. held its first national encampment in Indianapolis. The Radicals made a big play for the soldier vote, and reminded businessmen what a threat to high tariffs, hard money, and the national debt the

The Negro votes amidst hostile onlookers in Washington, D.C.

South's return to national power would be. Delighted with the South's rejection of the Fourteenth Amendment, the Radicals worked hard for a sweeping victory that they might interpret as a mandate for even severer measures. Indeed, they sought to win enough seats to give them two-thirds majorities in both houses so as to insure the enactment of their measures over the presidential vetoes they anticipated.

So convincing was the Radicals' victory that even before the new Congress met they were able to marshal all the votes they needed to proceed with a virtual revolution in the government. Ordinarily, the new Congress would not have convened until December, 1867, unless called into special session by the President. One of the first acts of the old Congress, on January 22, 1867, was to take it upon themselves to call the new Congress into session on March 4, the day the old Congress was required by law to adjourn. Having insured Congress' uninterrupted presence in Washington, the Radicals moved to concentrate all power in congressional hands.

Their initial and most comprehensive measure was the so-called First Reconstruction Act, which was passed over Johnson's veto on March 2, 1867 (supplementary Second, Third, and Fourth Reconstruction Acts elaborated its language and filled out its enforcement machinery). By the terms of this act, all existing southern state governments except that of Tennessee, which had been accepted back into the Union in 1866, were declared illegal. The South was organized into five military districts, each under a general to be named by the president. Each general was to have an armed force at his command to help him maintain martial law if necessary. The general's main task was to arrange for an election of delegates to a new constitutional convention in each state, an election that was to be based on universal adult male suffrage, Negro and white, except for those who had been disfranchised for serving in the Confederate government. The convention would then establish state governments in which Negroes could vote and hold office. As soon as the new governments convened, they were to ratify the Fourteenth Amendment as a condition for their return to the Union and the acceptance of their representatives by Congress.

By June, 1868, all but three states—Mississippi, Texas, and Virginia—had been "re-

President Johnson on his "swing around the circle," 1866.

constructed" by Congress in time to participate in the presidential elections that year, though in some of them armed forces remained to protect Republican rule for as long as ten years more. The three recalcitrant states were re-admitted in 1870. In that year, Georgia, whose reconstruction had been suspended because of the expulsion of Negro members from her legislature, was also readmitted for the second time.

Two years after the end of hostilities and a year after Johnson, in 1866, had officially declared the war over, the first Reconstruction Act cast the South back into a subjugated status. The Radicals proceeded next to protect their program from the Supreme Court. In the case of *ex parte Milligan* (1866), which arose over Lincoln's suspension of *habeas corpus* in Indiana during the war, the Supreme Court had held that if military rule "is continued *after* the courts are reinstated, it is a gross usurpation of power." When the first Reconstruction Act was passed, southern courts were open, and the Act deliberately defied this decision. When, in *ex parte McCardle,* the constitutionality of this act was challenged, the Radicals attached a rider to a minor bill, withdrawing appellate jurisdiction from the Court in *habeas corpus* matters. Johnson vetoed the whole bill, but the withdrawal measure was then passed over his veto, in March, 1868. The Court had already put *ex parte McCardle* on its schedule but, against the judgment of two justices, the majority yielded to the Radicals, allowed the case to be quashed, and the First Reconstruction Act survived.

Having successfully defied the Supreme Court, the Radicals next set about eliminating the Executive. Two measures had been passed at the same time as the First Reconstruction Act, in March, 1867, with this end in view. The first, the Tenure of Office Act, declared that the president could not remove federal officers who had been appointed with the consent of the Senate without first getting the Senate's consent to their removal. The second, the Command of the

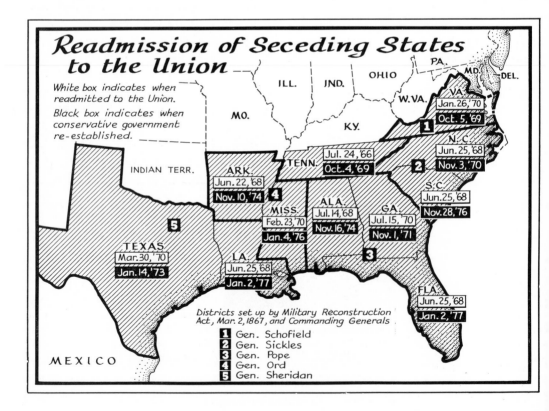

Readmission of Seceding States to the Union

White box indicates when readmitted to the Union.

Black box indicates when conservative government re-established.

State	Readmitted	Conservative gov't re-established
VA.	Jan. 26, '70	Oct. 5, '69
N.C.	Jun. 25, '68	Nov. 3, '70
S.C.	Jun. 25, '68	Nov. 28, '76
TENN.	Jul. 24, '66	Oct. 4, '69
ARK.	Jun. 22, '68	Nov. 10, '74
ALA.	Jul. 14, '68	Nov. 16, '74
GA.	Jul. 15, '70	Nov. 1, '71
MISS.	Feb. 23, '70	Jan. 4, '76
TEXAS	Mar. 30, '70	Jan. 14, '73
LA.	Jun. 25, '68	Jan. 2, '77
FLA.	Jun. 25, '68	Jan. 2, '77

Districts set up by Military Reconstruction Act, Mar. 2, 1867, and Commanding Generals

1 Gen. Schofield
2 Gen. Sickles
3 Gen. Pope
4 Gen. Ord
5 Gen. Sheridan

Army Act, forbade the president to issue orders to the army except through the General of the Army, General Grant. These measures left the president at the mercy of Radical office-holders and divested him of his constitutional role as commander-in-chief. But the Radicals were not satisfied. When, in defiance of the Tenure of Office Act, Johnson tried to remove Secretary Stanton in February, 1868, the President was impeached in the House. From March 5 to May 16 his trial raged in the Senate, which was presided over for the occasion by Chief Justice Chase. At the end, 7 Republicans deserted the Radical leadership of their party and joined 12 Democrats to make the vote 19 against conviction. Thirty-five voted for it, one short of the two-thirds needed to carry.

Squaring Accounts Abroad.

Few presidents in our history have been as tormented by domestic issues as Andrew Johnson. To his credit, however, he made no effort to distract the public from domestic problems by the time-honored strategy of venturing into foreign quarrels. This was not because he lacked opportunity; on the contrary, many suitable occasions had been thrust at him over which the public itself seemed quite ready to respond to militant leadership. One of these involved Napoleon III's adventure in Mexico, which had arisen, ironically, from the French Emperor's efforts to divert his own people from his frustrations and failures at home.

The French were still in Mexico in 1866 when Grant and other generals urged Johnson to throw them out by force. The President, however, preferred the advice of his Secretary of State, Seward, who proceeded gently to remind Napoleon of American interests and asked him to withdraw. Fearful of a reunited United States near Mexico and a newly aggressive Prussia on his European borders, Napoleon reluctantly consented. The last French troops left Mexico in the spring of 1867. The French puppet, Maximilian, by then had grown enamored

of his imperial role and attempted to reign without French military support. Later that year the Mexicans executed him and regained control of their troubled land.

The French irritant had been removed, but now evidences of anglophobia began to appear. Northerners in particular had long nurtured a dislike of Great Britain, a dislike that was fed by events during the Civil War. From the first, Britain had viewed the war not as a domestic conflict but as a struggle between sovereign belligerents. She had permitted three Confederate cruisers, *Alabama*, *Shenandoah*, and *Florida*, to be built in British ports and then, while her ship-owners looked on with open satisfaction, had allowed them to put to sea, take on arms, and then harry the Union merchant marine. Confederate agents had also found safe harbor in Canada, where they mounted attacks on Vermont and New York.

This Canadian activity had ceased with the end of the war, but in 1866 northerners were again reminded of the problems British control of Canada could involve. That year, the Fenians, or the Irish Revolutionary Brother-Republics, an organization of Irish-Americans in New York, began a series of assaults on Canada with the bizarre hope of capturing the country and holding it as a hostage until the British gave Ireland its independence. The Irish vote had become an important factor in northern politics, and how to retain it while discountenancing adventures of this sort presented a ticklish problem to Johnson's administration. But rather than yield to the temptation of supporting or even condoning Irish violence, the administration chose to give Great Britain a lesson in neutral conduct by taking stern measures against anyone who used American bases for foreign intrigues.

Early efforts to settle American claims arising out of England's encouragement of rebel raids on Union shipping showed that the American example was lost on the United Kingdom's leaders. At first, Britain refused even to receive Seward's proposals, and resentful Americans began to eye the Fenian escapades as something worth joining if only to make Britain see the light. By 1869, however, Europe itself was in turmoil because of Bismarck's expansionist policies, and Britain wanted American friendship in the imminent competition with Germany. In January that year the two countries signed a treaty, the Johnson-Clarendon Convention, for arbitrating all claims they had against each other.

Although this treaty had many defects, the administration was satisfied with it as a peaceful solution of the issue; but because of the absence of an apology and of all reference to indirect damages, under Sumner's leadership the Senate rejected the treaty in April by a resounding vote of 54 to 1. Seward's claims—known by the over-all name of the *"Alabama* claims"—had amounted to around $15 million. Senator Sumner, on the ground that Britain's wartime actions had prolonged the war and had cost the Union dearly, now began to agitate for additional "indirect claims" against Britain, which some estimated at more than $2 billion. Sumner suggested that Britain's withdrawal from North America, leaving neighboring Canada ripe for American annexation, would go far toward paying the bill. But the elections of 1868 were looming, and the matter rested there. In the Treaty of Washington, signed in 1871, a new settlement was arranged. When the tribunal of arbitration acted in 1872, the "indirect claims" were thrown out, and the *Alabama* claims were settled for Seward's old figure of $15 million.

While avoiding armed conflict with foreign enemies, Johnson's administration carried through successful negotiations with foreign friends. Among these was Russia, which had favored the Union cause from the start. In March, 1867, the Russian minister in Washington offered Seward a chance to purchase Alaska. An ardent expansionist, Seward jumped at the opportunity. The final price was $7,200,000, and part of the $200,000

was used by the Russian minister to speed the purchase appropriation bill through the hostile House of Representatives. Seward also had the United States occupy the uninhabited Midway Islands in the Pacific and, looking to the future when a much-talked-of canal across Central America would be dug, he negotiated an agreement with Nicaragua permitting the United States to cut across that neck of land.

The Election of 1868.

In the presidential election of 1868, the Radicals succeeded in having General Grant nominated by the Republicans. Grant had no known political principles, although in 1856 he had voted for the Democrat, Buchanan, and in 1860 he had favored Douglas. Johnson himself had such faith in the General that at one point in his controversies with Stanton, in August, 1867, he had suspended the Secretary and had named Grant as acting head of the War Department. At that time, Johnson had already decided to remove Stanton altogether. Anticipating senatorial objections, he had arranged with Grant either to cling to the office even if the Senate upheld Stanton's claims, or to inform Johnson beforehand of his desire to quit so that the President might appoint someone who would keep Stanton out. Grant must have misunderstood, for he held the place until the Senate upheld Stanton and then yielded the office to the suspended Secretary. Johnson naturally felt he had been betrayed and his personal relations with Grant deteriorated. The General, meanwhile, his own ambitions fired by Radical flattery and by the people's undiminishing acclaim whenever he appeared in public, became easy game for Johnson's political enemies. The Radicals simply wanted a winner, and Grant appeared to be just that.

Johnson himself sought the Democratic nomination, but the party turned instead to an untainted if unenthusiastic northerner, former Governor Horatio Seymour of New York. With foreign affairs relegated to the background, the Democrats tried to make a campaign issue of cheap money. During the war, to supplement the bond issues sold by the government to finance the conflict, a total of $450 million in greenbacks had been printed and put into circulation. During and after the war, the greenbacks fluctuated widely in value, but they always held below the value of gold and hence were popular with long-term debtors like farmers who wanted cheap money with which to pay their fixed mortgage obligations. The farmers' creditors naturally opposed the greenbacks, as did those other businessmen whose ordinary transactions depended for success on a stable currency.

On behalf of business, Congress had passed a measure in 1866 providing for the gradual retirement of greenbacks, and in the next two years almost $100 million worth had been withdrawn. To curry favor with the farmers of the West, the Democrats now adopted a platform plank advocating the reissuance of these greenbacks to redeem war bonds which did not specifically require redemption in gold. Since the author of this plank was George H. Pendleton of Ohio, the party's vice-presidential candidate in 1864, this "soft money" proposal became known as the "Ohio Idea."

The Republicans scotched the Ohio Idea in the strongly Union-minded West by arguing that redemption of war bonds in anything but gold smacked of rebel repudiation of a sacred debt that had been contracted to preserve the Union. At the same time, the Republicans promised business that they would extend redemption ". . . over a fair period" so as not to disturb the business credit structure, and that when the time came, all bondholders would be paid in gold. Having thus dealt with the complex problem of money, the Radicals proceeded to keep before the public the main political issue—Radical Reconstruction.

In the elections of 1866, the Republicans had had great success "waving the bloody shirt," a tactic that involved reviling the Democratic party as the standard-bearer of rebellion, Negro repression, and financial repudiation. "In short," cried Oliver Morton, the Radical governor of Indiana, in a typical "bloody shirt" foray, "the Democratic party may be described as a common sewer and loathsome receptacle, into which is emptied every element of treason North and South, and every element of inhumanity and barbarism which has dishonored the age." In 1868, and in many elections thereafter, such tirades served as the staple of Republican oratory and Republican appeals.

Yet this steady fire did not really scatter the opposition. In 1868, against a weak opponent, Grant was elected with a popular plurality of 310,000 votes. He clearly would not have done that well had the Union League Clubs not helped deliver the vote of about 700,000 Negroes who had been given the ballot in seven hastily reconstructed southern states.

The Union League Clubs had been organized in the North in 1862 to spread Union propaganda. Gradually they extended their wartime activity to captured southern territory, where they continued their propaganda activities and engaged in philanthropic work. By 1867, more than 80 chapters of the League were operating in South Carolina alone, and estimates indicated that most of the Negroes in the state were enrolled as members. "I can't read, and I can't write," one Negro said. "We go by [League] instructions."

The part the Negroes played in winning the election—or rather the fact that Negroes in certain states like Louisiana and Georgia had been prevented from casting their votes—prompted the Radicals to strengthen the Fourteenth Amendment's provisions protecting the Negro franchise. When Congress convened early in 1869, it promptly passed the Fifteenth Amendment, which provided that: "The right of citizens of the United States to vote shall not be denied or abridged by the United States or by any State on account of race, color or previous condition of servitude." This amendment was sent to the states in February, 1869, and was declared ratified in March, 1870.

V.   THE DAY OF THE CARPETBAGGER

When Grant accepted the nomination of the Republican convention in May, 1868, he wrote, "Let us have peace." Many men in the country, recalling his magnanimous surrender terms to Lee, thought that the turmoil and vindictiveness of Radical Reconstruction might be nearing an end. The death of Stevens, the most uncompromising of the Radicals, in August, 1868, and the defeat of Ben Wade for the Senate, gave substance to this hope.

But Grant lacked political perception and his administration was easily dominated by such surviving Radicals as Senator (formerly Governor) Oliver Morton of Indiana, Senators Zachariah Chandler of Michigan, Simon Cameron of Pennsylvania, and Roscoe Conkling of New York, and Congressman General "Ben" (Benjamin Franklin) Butler of Massachusetts. Untinged by the abolitionist idealism that had marked the Stevens-Sumner leadership, these men had ample partisan reasons—chief among them the wish to protect wartime tariff, railroad, and banking legislation from attack by returning southerners—for keeping ex-Confederates disfranchised and the Negro voters safe in the Republican camp. Their success in getting the Fifteenth Amendment passed at the very beginning of the new session of Congress in 1869 attested to their strength in the federal government.

Assisting the new Radical leaders in accomplishing their aims in the South itself were the Radical carpetbaggers who had poured into the defeated section after the passage of the First Reconstruction Act of March, 1867, and who, under the protection of the military, had virtually taken charge of politics. In the seven states reconstructed in 1868, 10 of 14 United States senators, 20 of 35 congressmen, and 4 governors were recently-arrived carpetbaggers. The others, with few exceptions, were southern "scalawags" who rode to office on Radical coattails but eventually broke with the carpetbaggers on the race issue. The few exceptions were Negroes.

Carpetbaggers as Reformers. Most of the South's new leaders, like those in the North during this period, were openly self-seeking. Many, however, especially among the carpetbaggers who had arrived earliest, were genuine reformers who were as serious as Stevens and Sumner in trying to help the freedmen become useful citizens, economically independent and politically on a par with whites. Often enough the objectives of the reformers were not in conflict with those of the self-seekers, and under carpetbag rule significant political and social advances were made in the South which benefited both races.

Many of these gains grew out the provisions of the new southern state constitutions written by the "black and tan" conventions, as the southerners branded the assemblages called by the Radical generals. These constitutions often were modeled on copies of liberal constitutions brought from the North. They contained provisions abolishing imprisonment for debt and eliminating property qualifications for voting and office-holding. Representation in the state legislatures and in Congress was reapportioned, with the more populous districts getting a fairer share. Above all, most states provided for public-school education for Negroes and whites.

The ballot, though at first misused, was a notable step forward for the freedman. Office-holding, though also abused, was another significant advance, but it was not so widely shared as the term "black reconstruction" might imply. Only in South Carolina, in 1868, did Negro legislators outnumber whites, 88 to 67, but the sessions were not controlled by Negroes. In other state legislatures, Negroes made up sizable minorities, but the white politicians always dominated the proceedings. One mulatto, P. B. S. Pinchback, became lieutenant-governor of Louisiana; but none rose to higher positions in state government. Several Negroes became congressmen and two became United States senators. Others were appointed to administrative posts, where they did well.

Next to giving the vote to Negroes, nothing offended the South more than efforts to give them schooling. The slogan, "Schooling ruins the Negro," expressed the general belief. As early as July, 1865, Carl Schurz had noted instances of Negro schools being burned and of teachers and students being threatened. By 1877, 600,000 Negroes were enrolled in southern elementary and secondary schools. By then, several colleges and universities had been established by the Freedmen's Bureau and by northern churches and philanthropic agencies. In the opinion of southerners, "the teachers, ignorant, fanatical, without self-poise, proceeded to make all possible mischief." Still, the foundations of Howard, Fisk, and other leading Negro universities were laid in these years. Night schools for adults also flourished. "The great ambition of the older people," said Booker T. Washington, "was to try to learn to read the Bible before they died."

Corruption and Reaction. Many southern leaders actually found little fault with the Radicals' tariff, railroad, and money policies, and felt that the Republicans could trust the South sufficiently to give its spokesmen a voice in national affairs once again. Southern whites also felt that by 1868 they had made every concession that a vanquished nation (as they thought of themselves) ought to have been asked to make by the victors in the late war. The South had disbanded the remnants of its army, repudiated the Confederate debt, renounced secession as a constitutional device, and accepted the

Thirteenth Amendment abolishing slavery. None of these concessions had been made gracefully, but they had been made. When the Radicals began to court the Negro vote to insure protection for their national legislative program, southerners balked at what they called "barbarization of the South" by the enfranchisement of the "inferior race," and were ready, if not to resume the war, at least to resort to armed violence and terror.

The mere existence of the carpetbag governments within their borders seemed insulting and shameful to many southerners. But carpetbag corruption made the affront even harder to bear. "Corruption is the fashion," said Governor H. C. Warmoth of Louisiana, who on a salary of $8,000 retired with a personal fortune of $500,000 after four years of governing his state. "I do not pretend to be honest, but only as honest as anybody in politics." Pickings were far better in the North than in the South, and political boss William Marcy Tweed of New York (see p. 428) demonstrated what an expert could do before he was jailed in 1872. All the carpetbag governments were corrupt, yet they were not as bad as they seemed on the surface.

Between 1868 and 1874, the bonded debt of the 11 Confederate states grew by over $100 million. But this enormous sum was not itself evidence of crime. To raise money, the southern states had to sell bonds in the North, where southern credit was so poor that investors often demanded a 75 per cent discount from the bonds' face value. Thus for every $100 worth of bonds sold, a southern state might actually receive only $25. Many of the social reforms of the Reconstruction legislatures, moreover, were expensive, as was the relief that had to be extended to the starving and homeless.

Nevertheless, much of the debt was corruptly incurred, though not necessarily by carpetbaggers. A large part of it was piled up through the sale of state bonds to back southern-sponsored railroad enterprises that never built a mile of track, or to aid companies that merely distributed as profit the money they received. Carpetbaggers were more likely to busy themselves with more traditional forms of graft. A considerable portion of the debt was created, for example, by politicians who won large contracts for construction or printing, and then supplied little of the services or goods that the contracts called for. Public funds also were spent for personal furniture, homes, carriages, jewelry, liquor, leather goods, and the like. But such conspicuous corruption probably cost the least.

Taxes to pay for carpetbag government exenditures and to service the rapidly growing debt fell most heavily on the oppressed planters, who before the war had been able to pass taxes on to other groups in the South. Business firms escaped with small levies, and personal taxes were low and could be easily evaded.

The growing public debt and the unequal taxation aroused the ire of the former leaders of the South. But the majority of the people complained most bitterly about the gross conduct, the bizarre legislative sessions, the flamboyant or slovenly dress, and the posturing of the new political leaders, Negro and white. Negro militia roamed the southern countryside and sometimes shot up city streets. Negro legislatures were something

new on the face of the earth, and travelers came from Europe and the North to watch them in action. What the visitors expected to find in a society so recently up-ended is not clear, but their reactions often matched the horror of the southerners themselves. Rubbed into the unhealed sores of the war, this kind of "reconstruction" completed the moral rout of the South. Sidney Lanier, the poet, said during this period in a letter north, "Perhaps you know that with us of the young generation in the South, since the war pretty much the whole of life has been merely not dying."

Other southerners found different outlets for their feelings. The keystone of carpetbag rule, they realized, was the Negro's vote. To end it, thousands banded together in the Ku Klux Klan, the Knights of the White Camelia, and other secret organizations. Between 1867 and 1869, hooded or otherwise incognito, these bands roamed the South, shot, flogged, and terrorized Negroes and their supporters, burned homes and public buildings, attacked Reconstruction officials, and, under the guise of keeping order (which, indeed, sometimes needed keeping), perpetrated other acts of violence dedicated to the maintenance of white supremacy. Some of these organizations got completely out of hand and devoted themselves entirely to random violence and pillage.

VI.   THE RETURN TO WHITE SUPREMACY

Radical Repression. The Radical leadership in the federal government did not permit the activities of the violent white organizations to go unnoticed. Two acts in particular were passed in order to put them out of operation. One was the Force Act of 1870; the other was the Ku Klux Klan Act of 1871. The Force Act was designed to insure that the Negro suffrage guaranteed by the newly ratified Fifteenth Amendment would not be infringed and to strengthen enforcement of the Fourteenth Amendment in relation to other privileges

and immunities of the freedmen. It established heavy fines and jail penalties for offenses under either amendment. More important, the Force Act gave to federal courts controlled by carpetbaggers, rather than to southern state courts, original jurisdiction over all cases arising out of the amendments.

In spite of the Force Act, the Democrats made notable gains in the mid-term elections of 1870, and by the following year southern whites had recaptured the governments of Tennessee, Virginia, North Carolina, and Georgia. Attributing these successes to violence, the Radicals in Congress pushed through the Ku Klux Klan Act of 1871 to give federal courts original jurisdiction in all cases arising out of conspiracies or terrorism against freedmen. This act also empowered the president to suspend *habeas corpus*, to declare martial law in any terrorized community, and to send in troops to maintain order.

Within a short time, about 7,000 persons were indicted under these two acts, and although few were convicted or even tried, the personal harassment served to smother political activity among the whites. In October, 1871, to convince remaining skeptics that the Radicals still meant business, Grant declared nine counties of South Carolina, where the Klan was especially active, to be in rebellion and placed them under martial law. An investigation by a congressional committee presently placed its seal of approval on the President's militancy.

The South Carolina episode marked the peak of forceful repression of southern whites. Upon many in the North, Radical excesses in their own section (see p. 426) had already begun to pall. Testimony offered at the few trials of persons indicted in South Carolina and elsewhere, and evidence inadvertently publicized by the congressional investigating committee's report, disclosed the severe political and social disabilities which the Radicals had fastened upon the southern states and which were retarding their recovery. Under mounting pressure, Congress passed a liberal amnesty act in May, 1872, which restored voting and office-holding privileges to all southern whites with the exception of a few hundred of the highest surviving Confederate dignitaries. In the same year the Freedmen's Bureau, the protector of the Negro's rights, was permitted to go out of existence.

The Election of 1872. The fact that 1872 was a presidential election year no doubt prompted the Radicals to make these concessions. One feature of the 1872 presidential campaign was the "Liberal Repub-

lican" movement. The Liberal Republicans' major aim was to unseat Grant. The movement had begun in Missouri, where a faction led by Carl Schurz and B. Gratz Brown had overthrown the Radical regime in 1870 and elected Brown to the governorship and Schurz to the Senate. Years earlier, Schurz, as we have seen, had favored imposing a vindictive reconstruction program on the defeated South. But by 1870, he had come to realize that the Radical carpetbaggers in Missouri were mainly corruptionists who used the Negro vote only to maintain their tyranny over the local whites. He had also been alienated by the selfishness and partisanship of the leading Radicals in Grant's administration (see p. 426), and he was no longer willing to coerce the southern whites simply to maintain the Conklings and Chandlers in office. Grant was the main prop of the Conkling and Chandler type of Radical Republicanism, so, the Liberal Republicans reasoned, Grant must go. When they realized that they had no chance to nominate a regular Republican candidate in his place, the Liberal Republicans left their party. On May 1, 1872, the Liberal Republicans assembled at Cincinnati, organized a new Liberal Republican party, chose a ticket, and wrote a platform for the coming presidential campaign.

To the new standard rallied discontented Republicans of every stripe. Some of them, who had lost out in contests for patronage with the Conklings and Chandlers, had as great contempt for "reform" as Conkling himself. Others had opposed the whole Radical program on tariffs, railroad land grants, and other national issues (see p. 424). Many northern Democrats also joined the Liberal Republican movement, hoping thereby to win their way back into the national political scene without having to bear the treasonous label of their own party.

The weakness of the Liberal Republicans became obvious at their first meeting. The "regular" Republicans were firmly behind Grant, upon whose military reputation they leaned so heavily, but the "liberals" fell out on every issue except their opposition to the President. Their greatest failure was their inability to nominate a candidate who clearly represented their thinking. Instead, after heated disputes, they settled on a compromise standard-bearer, Horace Greeley. B. Gratz Brown was nominated for the vice-presidency. Greeley was a strange choice. Editor for more than 30 years of the renowned New York *Tribune,* he had supported as many contradictory political positions as were represented in the Liberal Republican convention. Most recently, however, as befitted a man who had long been an abolitionist, Greeley had been an outspoken Radical. Worse, he was a staunch high-tariff man, an enemy not only of free trade, but of foreign relations of any kind. Worse still, he was universally known as a crackpot, as a man whose energy always

outran his judgment. His nomination made a joke of the whole Liberal Republican campaign.

If Greeley's nomination was a misfortune for the Liberal Republicans, it was a tragedy for the Democratic party. Its only chance to gain national power was to support Grant's opponents. Yet Grant's opponents had nominated Greeley, who in 1866 in the *Tribune* had publicly branded the Democrats as "the traitorous section of Northern politics." The Democrats swallowed their pride and named Greeley as their own standard-bearer. This move made the election fight very easy for Grant and the Radical machine. The General was re-elected by a majority of 763,000 and carried all but six states.

The "Solid South."

The "Solid South." After the election, Grant made conciliatory gestures toward the South, refraining particularly from using federal troops in local southern affairs. En-

A "Liberal Republican" view of Grantism, 1872.

couraged by Grant's turnabout, southern leaders in states still under carpetbag rule became more determined than ever to "redeem" their states through their own efforts. After 1872, the "Red Shirts" in South Carolina and the "White Leagues" and similar organizations in other states picked up where the Klan had left off. With the demise of the Freedmen's Bureau, southern planters and merchants also began threatening to eject share-croppers and Negro laborers from their land and to burden them with other economic sanctions if they showed any desire to vote. Many Negroes themselves had had their fill of northern domination and proved more than willing to cooperate with their new masters. Still another factor speeding the "redemption" of their states by white southerners was the growing inability of the carpetbaggers to make their scalawag collaborators get along with Negro officials. Their disagreements prompted more and more scalawags to cast their lot with the "white supremacy" advocates. Many businessmen themselves were growing tired of Radical excesses in the North as well as in the South, and after the Panic of 1873, when northern capitalists began looking south for investment opportunities, they also aided the white "redeemers."

By the time of the election of 1876 (see p. 427), only three states, South Carolina, Louisiana, and Florida, remained in Radical hands. But even in these three states the Radicals had recently suffered defeats in the local elections and clung to their offices only with the aid of federal troops. When President Hayes withdrew the troops in 1877, Radical control collapsed. The Radicals had aimed to make the South solid for the Republican party, but they succeeded only in keeping the South solidly Democratic. Once returned to control in the South, moreover, the Democrats used every available device to keep southern politics solidly white.

White supremacy was abetted by a series of Supreme Court decisions, starting with the case of *United States* v. *Reese* in 1876 and ending with the *Civil Rights Cases* of 1883. In the first of these cases, the Court struck at the efficacy of the Force Act. In the Civil Rights Cases, the Court ruled that the federal government had no jurisdiction over such matters as social discriminations directed by private persons or organizations against persons of a different race or color.

The Court's rulings opened the way to passage of Jim Crow laws that segregated Negroes from whites in public places, and to the establishment of poll taxes and literacy tests that were rigged to disqualify Negroes who might risk trying to mark a ballot. For some time after the end of Reconstruction, however, Negro voting remained a part of the southern political picture. In many communities it was impossible for a Negro to vote, but in others the white politicians competed for Negro support, marshaled Negro voters on election days, and on occasion courted their votes with promises of constructive measures that would be of real advantage to them. In the late 1880's and early 1890's, when agricultural depression caused discontented farmers to be pitted against industrialists, railroaders, credit merchants, and conservative political leaders, it seemed possible that poor white and Negro farmers would join together politically to unseat white conservatives. Popular leaders like Tom Watson of Georgia now began to preach cooperation among poor farmers regardless of race. Faced with the prospect that the Populist movement (see Chapter XXI) would seriously threaten their position, conservative white Democrats successfully revived the race issue to keep Negro and white farmers apart. In the course of this reaction, they strengthened devices like the poll tax and literacy requirements that were meant to prevent Negroes from voting. Mississippi took such steps in 1890; she was followed by South Carolina in 1895 and Louisiana in 1898. Other states fell in line, and by 1910 the Negro was effectively disfranchised in eight states. Thus at the turn of the century, the Negro's position in the South reached its lowest point since the days of the Black Codes.

Readings

Postwar conditions in the South are described in detail in Walter L. Fleming, *The Sequel of Appomattox* (1919), and Allan Nevins, *The Emergence of Modern America, 1865-1878* (1927). These two works should be supplemented by some of the eye-witness accounts of travelers who visited the region after the war and noted the destruction that had taken place. Sidney Andrews, *The South Since the War* (1866), and Robert Somers, *The Southern States Since the War, 1870-1* (1871), are interesting reports by two of these observers. A variety of first-hand material is readily available in Walter L. Fleming, *Documentary History of Reconstruction* (2 vols., 1906). The general histories of Reconstruction mentioned below discuss the economic plight of the postwar South. More revealing are "Book Two" of W. J. Cash, *The Mind of the South* (1941), and two books by C. Vann Woodward: *Tom Watson: Agrarian Rebel* (1938), and *Origins of the New South, 1877-1913* (1951).

The standard older accounts of Reconstruction are William A. Dunning, *Reconstruction, Political and Economic, 1865-1877* (1907), and Dunning's *Essays on the Civil War and Reconstruction* (1904). More recent and more comprehensive is J. G. Randall, *The Civil War and Reconstruction* (1937), and more recent still, E. M. Coulter, *The South During Reconstruction, 1865-1877* (1947). William B. Hesseltine, *The South in American History* (1943), and Francis B. Simkins, *A History of the South* (1953), are general histories of the section by men who have written in detail on the Reconstruction period. Unusually well-balanced are Francis B. Simkins and Robert H. Woody, *South Carolina During Reconstruction* (1932), and James W. Garner, *Reconstruction in Mississippi* (1901). Among Negro historians, outstanding are the brilliant but strident W. E. B. DuBois, *Black Reconstruction* (1935), and the scholarly, restrained John Hope Franklin, *From Slavery to Freedom* (1947). A stimulating study of the Negro in American life is Gunnar Myrdal, *An American Dilemma: The Negro Problem and Modern Democracy* (2 vols., 1944). Some aspects of the situation of the Negro in the South are dealt with by C. Vann Woodward in *The Strange Career of Jim Crow* (1955). On Andrew Johnson, the reader should consult George Fort Milton, *The Age of Hate: Andrew Johnson and the Radicals* (1930); on Thaddeus Stevens, A. B. Miller, *Thaddeus Stevens* (1939), and R. N. Current, *Old Thad Stevens* (1942).

The fullest account of national politics during Reconstruction is in Matthew Josephson's *The Politicos, 1865-1896* (1938). A valuable special study is Howard K. Beale, *The Critical Year: A Study of Andrew Johnson and Reconstruction*, which focuses on the elections of 1866. On foreign affairs during Johnson's administration, the relevant chapters in the general diplomatic histories by Bemis, Pratt, and Bailey should be read. On Grant's administration, the most informative work is Allan Nevins, *Hamilton Fish: The Inner History of the Grant Administration* (1936). More sprightly but more superficial is Don C. Seitz, *The Dreadful Decade, 1869-1879* (1926). The definitive work on the reform movement of the early 1870's is Earle D. Ross, *The Liberal Republican Movement* (1919). Relevant also are the early chapters of Eric F. Goldman, *Rendezvous with Destiny* (1951). *Carl Schurz: Reformer*, by Claude M. Feuss, and *"Boss" Tweed: The Story of a Grim Generation*, by Denis Tilden Lynch, are also worth reading. The definitive work on the election of 1876 is C. Vann Woodward, *Reunion and Reaction* (1951).

NATIONAL
PROGRESS AND
POLITICS

C H A P T E R   E I G H T E E N

Although the Union was politically reconstructed by 1876, for many decades after the Civil War the South remained an agrarian society hostile to or envious of the industrialism and material progress of the North. Many northern spokesmen, on the other hand, regarded their victory in the war as proof that their industrial civilization was superior to the South's agrarian economy, and they were outraged by the defeated sec-tion's refusal to embrace their philosophy and their goals. In October, 1866, James Russell Lowell, writing on the situation in the South, asked in Boston's *North American Review:*

Is it not time that [southerners] were trans-planted at least into the nineteenth century, and, if they cannot be suddenly Americanized, made to understand something of the country which was too good for them . . . ?

At about the same time, Governor John A. Andrew of the Bay State insisted that southerners must never be readmitted to the Union "until their ideas on business, industry, money making . . . were in accord with those of Massachusetts."

All the southern states had in fact been readmitted to the Union long before they had swallowed Andrew's reconstruction prescription. But according to Andrew's way of thinking, the war had not yet ended, and many other people, southerners as well as northerners, shared his view. As late as 1880, Edwin L. Godkin, editor of the influential New York weekly, the *Nation*, wrote: "The South, in the structure of its society, in its manners and social relations, differs nearly as much from the North as Ireland does, or Hungary, or Turkey." Godkin went on:

The conversion of the Southern whites to the ways and ideas of what is called the industrial stage in social progress, which is really what has to be done to make the South peaceful, is not a more formidable task than that which the antislavery men had before them fifty years ago.

Godkin still believed that the North should approach the South in a manner "which persuades men and not that which exasperates them." Others in the North were no longer so optimistic or so patient. A week after Godkin's observation, Whitelaw Reid, editor of the New York *Tribune,* wrote:

To us the principles to which [southerners] cling are heresies not to be entertained after such bloody refutation as they have had. . . . [Yet] no facts, no statistics, no arguments can make them comprehend that the Northern masses are their superiors, intellectually, physically, numerically and financially.

Reid had recently sent a corps of reporters south to study the region's slow material recovery. "Manifestly something is wrong," concluded Reid. "Economic laws are violated in some way." What he prescribed was a new "infusion of Northern blood."

I. THE LAND OF OPPORTUNITY

The Capitalist Impulse. Massachusetts' ideas about business, industry, and money-making had enjoyed widespread acceptance outside the South long before actual hostilities between the North and the South had begun (see Chapter XIV). As early as the 1840's, Abbott Lawrence, a rising Yankee cotton manufacturer, wrote to a competitor: "If you are troubled with the belief that I am growing *too rich,* there is one thing that you may as well understand: I know how to make money, and you cannot prevent it." At about the same time, the young Philadelphia financier, Jay Cooke, was writing his parents in Ohio: "Through all the grades I see the same all-pervading, all-engrossing anxiety to grow rich. This is the only thing for which men live here."

During the war, inducements to enterprise had become greater than ever before, and the materialist frame of mind had grown more pronounced. "Such opportunities for making money," wrote Judge Thomas Mellon of Pittsburgh in 1863, "had never existed before in all my former experience." That year his oldest son James, then a young lawyer in Milwaukee, had written home asking for permission to enlist. The Judge ordered, "Don't do it. It is only greenhorns who enlist. Those who are able to pay for substitutes do so, and no discredit attaches." And he added:

It is not so much the danger as disease and idleness and vicious habits. . . . I had hoped my boy was going to make a smart, intelligent business man and was not such a goose as to be seduced from his duty by the declamations of buncombed speeches.

The Judge carried the day, and indeed he himself resigned from the bench in 1870 to go into business again.

By 1870, a spectacular business boom was under way in the North, which ultimately overwhelmed the old morality, the religious spirit that had flourished under it, and the humanitarian impulses that this spirit had nourished. The vogue of Herbert Spencer in succeeding decades made the triumph of materialism complete. Spencer was a self-taught, keen-minded Englishman who wrote a long series of books beginning in the 1860's to show how the Darwinian theory of evolution in nature also worked in the evolution or "progress" of society.* Spencer took Darwin's botanical and biological demonstrations and transferred them to the social sphere. For the "Social Darwinists" who became his disciples, the Darwinian "struggle for existence" was represented by business competition, "natural selection" became laissez faire, and the "survival of the fittest" was demonstrated by the way giant business creations like John D. Rockefeller's oil "trust" swallowed up many smaller, weaker competitors in their rise to the top. The progress of society demanded that these complex industrial organisms be left entirely to their "natural" bent.

When Andrew Carnegie first read Spencer, he recalled in his *Autobiography,* "Light came as in a flood and all was clear." Carnegie, who was raised in Scotland in a radical and rather intellectual environment, had been brought to America in 1848 at the age of thirteen. Twenty years later, still some years before he launched the steel enterprises that were to make him one of the richest men in the entire world, he had noted for his own guidance:

Man must have an idol—the amassing of wealth is one of the worst species of idolatry—no idol more debasing than the worship of money.... To continue much longer overwhelmed by business cares and with most of my thoughts wholly on the way to make more money in the shortest time, must degrade me beyond the hope of permanent recovery.

* Charles Darwin's *Origin of Species* was first published in 1859. Before very long it had touched off a revolution in every field of human thinking and human belief. Americans responded to Darwinism as if they had had a deep latent need for it. For a discussion of its impact on American religion, education, science, politics, and reform movements, see Chapter XXIII.

But reading Spencer helped resolve his doubts. "Not only had I got rid of theology and the supernatural, but I had found the truth of evolution. 'All is well since all grows better' became my motto, my true source of comfort."

John D. Rockefeller, Jr., also drew spiritual strength from natural law. In an address to his Sunday-school class he once said:

The growth of a large business is merely a survival of the fittest.... The American Beauty rose can be produced in the splendor and fragrance which bring cheer to its beholder only by sacrificing the early buds which grow up around it. This is not an evil tendency in business. It is merely the working-out of a law of nature and a law of God.

The Railroads.   Many northerners, believing that industrialism and progress were akin to natural law, tried to convince southerners that the secret to economic recovery lay in following northern industrial practices. But most northern businessmen were anxious to get on with subduing the rest of the continent and saw no need to justify progress in philosophical terms.

Railroad construction and railroad operation dominated the post-Civil War period. During the war, about 4,000 miles of track had been laid down, almost all of it in the free states. In 1865, the railroad track in the country totaled approximately 35,000 miles. By 1873, this figure had been doubled, but only 5,000 miles of track had been built in the South during this period. Most of the construction took place in the Northwest and in the East, where trunk lines running between the Mississippi Valley and the Atlantic were being rapidly completed and a tight network of feeder lines was being opened. Some of this construction connected independent lines, which in turn were consolidated into large companies that offered coordinated service over wide areas.

One of the great railroad consolidators and operators of the postwar period was Commodore Vanderbilt. Vanderbilt had made his

Jay Gould (1836-1892).

fortune in steamshipping, but the decline in sea-borne commerce during the Civil War prompted him to begin investing in railroads in 1862. By 1869, through a series of stock manipulations, he had bought control of the New York Central and the two more or less parallel lines that connected it with New York City, the Hudson River Railroad, and the Harlem Railroad. This maneuver gave Vanderbilt control of a through route from New York City to Buffalo.

In the midst of the negotiations for the New York Central system, Vanderbilt had tried to capture the Erie Railroad, which loomed as a competitor to his new combination. But his efforts were forestalled by the maneuvers of the Erie management, led by the unscrupulous Daniel Drew and his wily lieutenants, Jay Gould and Jim Fisk. The "Erie War," one of the great *cause célèbres* of the postwar decade, had begun in 1866 when Vanderbilt quietly began trying to buy up a controlling bloc of Erie stock in Wall Street. Aware of his intention, the Erie management began printing more and more Erie securities and releasing them in the stock market, where the eager Commodore unwittingly gobbled them up. At last he and his agents realized what was

happening. For more than a year the opposing sides battled for the road on the stock exchange, in the courts (where each sought injunctions obstructing the operations of the other), and in the state legislature (where each side sought to load investigating committees with cooperative politicians).

In 1868, a settlement finally was worked out in which Vanderbilt retired from the fray, but his price for withdrawing was so high that it emptied the Erie treasury. Drew also retired from the Erie at this time, bequeathing the well-milked road to Gould and Fisk. In 1869, Gould testified in court about Erie stock and stated that: "There is no intrinsic value to it, probably; it has speculative value; people buy and sell it, and sometimes they get a little too much." By applying the lessons of stock manipulation they had perfected during the Erie War, Gould and Fisk were able to make their first millions out of the road, bankrupt though it remained. Through the Erie they also played for bigger game, which included manipulating President Grant himself (see p. 423).

His failure to acquire the Erie may have soured the aging Commodore on expanding his railroad holdings any further, but prodded by his son, William H., he turned next to the Lake Shore and Michigan Southern, which he acquired in 1870. This link gave the New York Central system a magnificent, wholly owned through route of 965 miles from New York to Chicago by way of Cleveland and Toledo. In 1870, the Vanderbilts entered into working agreements with other roads that extended their operations all the way to Omaha, and by 1877, the year the Commodore died, the New York Central had also gained entry into Detroit and Toronto over the Michigan Central and its connections.

Commodore Vanderbilt was more than just a railroad-builder. He was also one of the ablest railroad managers of his time. Under his and his son's direction, the Central's lines were double-tracked; heavier and sturdier rails were used; the road bed, bridges, and embankments were rebuilt to make them last and to provide greater safety for passengers; rolling stock was greatly improved; and the Central's engines were made speedier. The Commodore built the first Grand Central Terminal in New York, and cut in half the passenger-service running time between New York and Chicago to 24 hours.

In the 1870's, the Pennsylvania Railroad, guided by its masterful vice-president, Thomas A. Scott, had also built and bought up numerous lines to give it wholly owned through routes from Philadelphia to St. Louis and Chicago by way of Pittsburgh and Indianapolis. In 1871, the Pennsylvania finally gained access to New York City itself by acquiring most of the railroads that ran across New Jersey. The B.&O. meanwhile had extended its construction to Cincinnati, which became a leading western railroad terminal. But by failing to make a connection with New York City during this period, the B.&O. fell far behind the Pennsylvania, the New York Central, and even the Erie in trunk line competition.

With men like Vanderbilt and Tom Scott directing great railroads, competition was incessant, ingenious, and unscrupulous. Competitive points like Chicago, Cleveland, and New York profited greatly from the slashing of railroad rates and the rivalry over speed and other services. Points like Pittsburgh, where the Pennsylvania monopolized rail service, were treated, as Allan Nevins says, "with outrageous insolence." But it remained for buccaneers like those in charge of the Erie, who had other ways of making money out of railroads, to keep transportation service in complete turmoil. Formal peace proceedings had no more ended the Erie War than Appomattox had the Civil War. In 1870, competition between the Erie and the New York Central drove Commodore Vanderbilt to slash his rates for carrying livestock between Buffalo and New York to $1 a head. Jim Fisk retaliated by plunging heavily on livestock purchases in Buffalo, shipping his cattle to New York over the Central, and making a handsome profit on the transaction. It was reported that Vanderbilt "swore horribly" on learning of the stratagem.

The Transcontinentals. Much more spectacular than the railroad-building in the older sections of the country was the construction of the transcontinentals in the West. In 1862, Congress, after a decade of surveys, debates, discussions, and sectional threats, had finally chartered the Union Pacific to build across the continent westward from Omaha, Nebraska. Soon after, it had granted to the Central Pacific, a corporation chartered by California in 1861, the right to build eastward from Sacramento. To both companies Congress made unprecedentedly large land grants. In addition, the companies were to receive loans for each mile of track actually laid, amounting to $16,000 per mile on level ground, $48,000 in mountain country, and $32,000 in intermediate territory.

Despite all the fanfare over the charters and the land grants, both companies experienced great difficulty in raising the money to begin the actual construction that would make them eligible for the government loans. Having failed to dispose of more than a few shares of stock in all San Francisco, Charles Crocker of the Central Pacific, early in 1863, went to Virginia City, Nevada, the mining El Dorado (see p. 445). This is what he reported:

They wanted to know what I expected the road would earn. I said I did not know. . . . "Well," they said, "do you think it will make 2 per cent a month?" "No," said I, "I do not." "Well," they answered, "we can get 2 per cent a month for our money here," and they would not think of going into a speculation that would not promise that at once.

The Union Pacific, promoted mainly by eastern capitalists, had little better luck in New York, Boston, or elsewhere, and by the end of 1863 the whole enterprise was threatened with collapse. The next year, while the railroads' agents were spending at least half a million dollars in Washington trying to get the government to relax its terms, Congress agreed to double the land grant for each road. More important, it agreed that its loans to the roads should be secured only by a second mortgage. This provision made it possible for the roads to issue their own first-mortgage bonds backed by their land grants as collateral. These bonds were much more attractive securities than the stock that the roads had offered earlier. But even so the bonds had to be sold at a discount. For an $111 million issue of first-mortgage bonds, for example, the Union Pacific realized but $74 million.

The actual building of the Union Pacific was carried through not by the corporation chartered by Congress but by a separate construction company which enjoyed the imaginative and ambiguous name, Crédit Mobilier. At its head was Congressman Oakes Ames of Massachusetts, who superintended the Union Pacific's legislative work. A similar construction company had been organized by the California "Big Four"—Crocker, Leland Stanford, Collis P. Huntington, and Mark Hopkins—to build the Central Pacific.

Construction companies had been used earlier in the century to finance the building of canals, but the stakes this time were much higher and the procedure more vulnerable. A congressional investigation of the construction of the transcontinentals later reported that, by means of companies like these, "the persons who under the guise of a corporation that was to take the contract to build the road held complete control of the corporation for which the road was to be built." This investigation disclosed that the Crédit Mobilier ultimately was paid $73 million by the Union Pacific for an estimated $50 million worth of work completed. The difference went to the men who acted as directors of *both* companies. Similarly, the "Big Four's," construction company was paid $121 million for work evaluated at $58 million.

The chance to make huge fortunes before any track was open to traffic impelled the promoters to push the construction of the roads as quickly as possible. Under the superb direction of its chief engineer, General Gren-

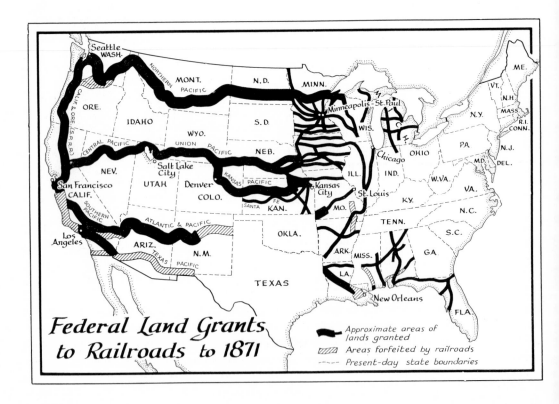

Federal Land Grants to Railroads to 1871

Approximate areas of lands granted
Areas forfeited by railroads
Present-day state boundaries

ville M. Dodge, the Union Pacific construction crews, made up largely of Civil War veterans and Irish immigrants, located, laid, and equipped 568 miles of road in a single year. All told, the Union Pacific laid 1,086 miles of track. The Central Pacific, its construction crews manned mainly by Chinese coolies, laid 689 miles. In the spring of 1869, the two lines approached one another, and on May 10 they were joined by golden spikes at Promontory Point, near Ogden, Utah. The engineering problems had been at least as trying as the financial ones, and, though both roads had to be almost completely rebuilt some years later, the feat of crossing the wild Plains and the forbidding mountain ranges remains one of the great engineering accomplishments in history.

Before the crash of 1873, three other transcontinentals had been chartered and enriched by the federal government—the Northern Pacific in 1864, the Atlantic and Pacific in 1866, and the Texas and Pacific in 1871. Of these three railroads, only the Northern Pacific was ever completed to the coast, and its arrival was long delayed. By 1872, the other two, along with their land grants, had fallen under the control of the Central Pacific's "Big Four." In an effort to control all California railroading, this group also acquired the Southern Pacific Railroad, a company that had been chartered in California in 1865 to connect San Francisco and San Diego. After 1876, they began pushing the Southern Pacific east through the two best mountain passes, through Needles in California and Yuma in Arizona, thereby controlling the access routes leading into California as well as the lines within the state itself.

By 1865, about $1 billion had been invested in American railroads. By 1873, this figure had risen to $3.7 billion. In 1867, the railroads had done about $330 million worth of business; by 1873, they were doing over $500 million worth. Along with this growth came many improvements in service and safety. George M. Pullman built the first sleeping car in 1864, and four years later George Westinghouse introduced the air

brake. By 1875, the refrigerator car had been developed, especially to carry meat from the Midwest to eastern cities. During these years of improvement, a standard-gauge rail was adopted throughout the country, coal-burning engines replaced wood-burners, and the changeover from iron to heavy steel rails was completed.

Industry. Railroad expansion and railroad improvement, of course, had a great deal to do with the surge of northern industry after the war. Actual railroad construction expanded the market for all kinds of goods ranging from steel for rails to meat and blankets for construction crews. Railroad financing, in turn, so familiarized the public with investment procedures that industrial corporations as well as railroads found ready takers for the securities they were offering for sale in the rising money markets of the country. Railroad financing also drew large amounts of foreign capital to America. Foreign capital not only helped build the railroads, but also made it possible for industrialists like Carnegie, Armour, and Rockefeller to use their profits to expand their enterprises and to exploit profitable by-products, fully confident that others would supply the wherewithal for transporting their commodities to market and for supplying them with raw materials.

But railroad development itself only confirmed the spirit of optimism and enterprise that dominated the victorious North after the war. "Everybody and everything's goin' places," observed an Indiana farmer in the late 1860's. In 1869, David A. Wells, the Special Commissioner of Revenue in the federal government, reported:

Within the last five years, more cotton spindles have been put in operation, more iron furnaces erected, . . . more steel made, more coal and copper mined, more lumber sawed . . . , more houses and shops constructed, more manufactories . . . started, and more petroleum collected, refined, and exported than during any equal period in the history of the country.

And the country was still only midway through the industrial boom that would see even the fabulous accomplishments of the late 1860's overshadowed before the Panic of 1873 called a temporary halt to northern progress.

Nowhere was the spirit of opportunity, enterprise, and growth more evident than in the newest industry of all, the production and refining of petroleum. In the 1850's, whale oil, then the world's chief commercial illuminant, had become so scarce that its price threatened to reach $5 a gallon. Petroleum seepages had been noted in many parts of the world for centuries and, as "rock oil," petroleum had gradually gained a mystical reputation as a medicine. In the United States, early in the 1850's, Samuel M. Kier, a manufacturer in Venango County in western Pennsylvania, had set about collecting the oil from local seepages and had marketed it as a cure-all. But Kier had also begun to refine some of this oil into kerosene. He designed lamps in which to burn kerosene conveniently, and he advertised the product widely enough to prepare a market for it.

But Kier did not know how to locate supplies large enough to meet what was beginning to be a tremendous demand. The first practical steps in this direction were taken by a young Dartmouth graduate, George H. Bissell, who in 1857 sent the bombastic "Colonel" E. L. Drake to the oil region around Titusville, Pennsylvania, to begin the first deliberate attempt to drill for oil. Such a novel enterprise encountered great scorn and great difficulties, but in August, 1859, "Drake's Folly" gushed in. Twentieth-century drillers sometimes go down two miles and more for oil. Drake most laboriously got down to 69½ feet, and his first well yielded 20 barrels of crude oil a day.

Oil is appropriately known as "Black Gold," not only for the huge fortunes it has made for many people, but also for the lure it has had for them. By 1864, wildcatters, as oil prospectors were called, had covered the district about Titusville with so many oil derricks that annual production exceeded 2 million barrels. By 1872, the oil fields covered 2,000 square miles in Pennsylvania, West Virginia, and Ohio, and total production had soared to 40 million barrels. Of this massive total, John D. Rockefeller's Standard Oil Company was already refining no less than one-fifth.

Rockefeller was born in 1839 in the hamlet of Richford, New York. At the age of 20, he and Maurice B. Clark, an Englishman, had entered into partnership as wholesalers of grain, hay, and meat in Cleveland. The business flourished during the Civil War, and by the time the war ended Rockefeller had accumulated a personal fortune of nearly $50,000. Two years earlier he had invested in a small refinery in Cleveland and in 1865 he was ready to devote all his time to the growing oil business. He dissolved the partnership with Clark and set up a refinery with Samuel Andrews, an experienced oil-refining technologist.

Rockefeller saw early that an efficient refinery could be built for as little as $50,000, and that an industry into which entry was so cheap and easy must be intensely competitive. In order to outdo all rivals, he and Andrews started with $200,000. Moreover, they located their first plant away from the raw materials in the oil fields—where skilled labor and bank credit were scarce and markets distant. They chose the rising city of Cleveland. In 1867, they added Henry M. Flagler as a partner, and won additional backing from Stephen V. Harkness, a rich Ohio brewer and distiller. In 1870, these men, and John's brother, William Rockefeller, organized the Standard Oil Company with a capital of $1 million. These funds supplied the wherewithal for a triple attack on the competition, which was located mainly in the oil regions and in Cleveland, Pittsburgh, and New York.

First, Rockefeller spent heavily to make his plants the most efficient in the country so that he could undersell all competitors and still make sizable profits. Often enough, he would sell his products well below cost in

Oil Creek, Pennsylvania, 1865.

selected markets in order to ruin a competitor and then recoup his losses by charging higher prices than ever before once he had the market to himself. Second, with his volume of business steadily increasing, Rockefeller approached the railroads with a demand that he be permitted to pay lower freight rates than any of his competitors. Railroad rates nominally were public and equal, but Rockefeller's scheme included a plan whereby the roads would return to him secret rebates from the established charges. And since railroad competition in Cleveland was so intense, those who wanted Rockefeller's business—and everyone did—complied.

By these means, by 1872, the Standard Oil Company had almost eliminated all competition in Cleveland and had gained control of about 20 per cent of the refining facilities of the country. Rockefeller now took the

third step in his ambitious program to bring the entire industry to book. This step involved him in the notorious South Improvement Company, which Tom Scott of the Pennsylvania Railroad had chartered in 1870 with the grandiose idea of eliminating cut-throat competition among the railroads by bringing as many rival lines as possible under one management, his own. Scott had done little with his scheme before 1872, by which time Rockefeller had developed similar "pooling" ideas to eliminate the cut-throat competition that continued to plague the oil industry. Many of the refineries in Pittsburgh, New York, and other centers had already been shaken by Rockefeller's competitive tactics. What Rockefeller needed was a kind of club to brandish at the holdouts. No better bludgeon could have been invented than discriminatory freight rates on

419

oil shipments, which a railroad pool such as the one Scott had in mind could enforce.

The South Improvement scheme was finally worked out in January, 1872, among the Erie, the New York Central, and the Pennsylvania and their affiliates on the one hand, and the Standard Oil Company leaders on the other. It involved a series of steps: (1) The South Improvement Company was reorganized as an oil company headed by Standard Oil chiefs; (2) the railroads were to be permitted to double their charges for hauling crude oil and oil products; (3) the South Improvement Company alone was not to be charged the increase; (4) more than that, the South Improvement Company and not the railroads was to receive—as "drawbacks"—most of the increase paid by Standard's competitors; (5) the railroads were to report daily to the South Improvement Company on all shipments made by competitors, informing the company of the amount, quality, price, and destination of the oil involved; (6) to keep tabs on these reports the South Improvement Company was to have access to all the railroads' books. In exchange, the railroads received a small part of the rate increases and the promise that the South Improvement Company would distribute its patronage as evenly as practicable over the heretofore ruinously competitive railroad lines.

Word of this bold proposal leaked out, and the South Improvement scheme was publicly abandoned, though Rockefeller's position as a shipper and financier had become so strong that he did get rebates and drawbacks from some of the more vulnerable lines after all. The business panic of 1873 also weakened the refiners who had already overextended themselves trying to compete with Rockefeller, and in the next few years he was able to buy their plants at very low prices. By 1879 he had cornered about 95 per cent of the refining capacity of the country and had captured almost the entire world market for his products. Rockefeller himself said a bit later:

This movement [toward monopoly] was the origin of the whole system of modern economic administration. It has revolutionized the way of doing business all over the world. The time was ripe for it. It had to come, though all we saw at the moment was the need to save ourselves from wasteful conditions. . . . The day of combination is here to stay. Individualism has gone, never to return.

Rockefeller was not the only one in the oil industry to employ sharp tactics. Samuel Downer, a leader in refining before Rockefeller so outdistanced the field, once said to Henry Flagler: "Flagler, I am opposed to the whole scheme of rebates and drawbacks —without I'm in it!" Most of the refiners were "in it" if they could exert enough pressure on the railroads to let them in. Nor were rails and oil the only industries where the drive toward monopoly was overwhelming the smaller firms. The burst of enterprise in the United States after the war drew hundreds of thousands of young men into new manufacturing enterprises and other fields. In a single year, 1870, the number of business firms in the country rose from 430,000 to 600,000, and as the business boom continued, the rate of new entries rose. Production soon outran demand, and prices of many commodities began to fall. Rockefeller was not the only one to see that unrestricted competition was likely to bring ruin to all. But he was one of the first to discern what had to be done and to act with a boldness bordering on lawlessness. Others often went to the wall.

Signs of trouble in the American economy began to appear by 1871, when the number of business failures reached 3,000. By 1872 more than 4,000 additional firms had collapsed. A clue to their difficulties may be found in the fact that during the boom period from 1868 to 1873 the volume of American bank loans had grown seven times as fast as bank deposits. The entire economy was being strained to sustain the boom. Two accidental tragedies made the strain almost unbearable. One was the spectacular Chicago fire of 1871, which cost insurance companies $200 million. The second was a great fire in Boston in 1872, which absorbed another $73 million in insurance funds. The crash, which many men like Rockefeller had foreseen and prepared for in their own enterprises, began on September 8, 1873, when the New York Warehouse and Securities Company went into bankruptcy. The greatest shock came ten days later with the failure of Jay Cooke and Company, the most famous banking house in the country. On September 20, "to save [Wall] Street from utter ruin," the New York Stock Exchange suspended all trading for ten days. Shock gradually gave way to profound depression as railroads halted construction and defaulted on their bonds, and as mills closed down and threw half the factory population out of work. As late as 1876-1877 over 18,000 business firms failed.

To many people the crash of 1873 was

sheer tragedy. To businessmen like Rockefeller and Carnegie, who understood both the normal rhythm of capitalist ups and downs and the basic soundness of the country, however, it simply spelled opportunity for investment and expansion. "The man who has money during a panic is a wise and valuable citizen," said Carnegie. After the crash, many of those who had bought stock in his early iron and steel enterprises became desperately short of cash. "So many of my friends needed money," Carnegie explained later about the years 1874-1878, "that they begged me to repay them. I did so and bought out five or six of them. That was what gave me my leading interest in this steel business."

II. THE BUSINESS OF POLITICS

Grantism.   On observing the Washington scene early in 1869, young Henry Adams, son of Lincoln's ambassador to Great Britain and grandson and great-grandson of early presidents, remarked that "the progress of evolution from President Washington to President Grant was alone evidence enough to upset Darwin." An organism as simple as Grant, thought Adams, "had no right to exist. He should have been extinct for ages."

In fact, however, Grant was no throwback but very much a product of his time. A failure in business himself, he was infatuated with business success. He wanted to make A. T. Stewart, the department store king and a lavish contributor to his campaign fund, Secretary of the Treasury; but it was discovered that a law of 1789 forbade persons engaged in commerce to hold that post. The Senate stubbornly refused a request by Grant that Stewart be excepted from the law, and Stewart's name had to be withdrawn. In Washington, Grant was frequently entertained by Henry Cooke, whose business it was to report to his financier brother, Jay, what he could learn at the nation's capital. Fond of the horseracing at Saratoga

Springs, New York, Grant, in the summer of 1869, accepted the use of Commodore Vanderbilt's private car to travel there. He once described Jim Fisk as "destitute of moral character"; yet, as President, he saw nothing wrong in using Fisk's sumptuous boats, dining publicly with Fisk and Gould, and otherwise enjoying the hospitality of the Erie looters while making them privy to the country's financial affairs.

Grant's political appointments were hardly likely to keep the President's businessmen associates from using the information they collected. In making his appointments, the President, of course, turned first to his old army friends, most of whom were as innocent of the ways of politics as their chief. Grant's White House staff, it was said, had "nothing but uniforms." General Horace Porter became Grant's private secretary. The assistant secretary, in the key position of making up Grant's daily visitor list and controlling access to the President, was his former military aide, the foppish Colonel Orville E. Babcock. These men dominated Grant's "Kitchen Cabinet." With three exceptions, his regular cabinet was made up of men who frightened people by their very obscurity. The three exceptions were Secretary of State Hamilton Fish, who served through Grant's two administrations; and Secretary of the Interior Jacob D. Cox, and Attorney-General Ebenezer Rockwood Hoar, both of whom were supplanted in a little over a year by more pliant souls.

The Kitchen Cabinet made most of the decisions on the appointment of federal job-holders, among whom Grant's relatives and neighbors, and retainers of the Kitchen Cabinet itself, were numerous. Federal patronage had grown enormously with the growth of government activity during and after the war, and in dispensing it men like Babcock (on the example of the President himself) often ignored the tradition of consulting the party's senators from the various states. This practice angered senatorial leaders and quickly cost Grant the support of such senators as Charles Sumner and Carl Schurz, and Lyman Trumbull of Illinois, an old favorite of Lincoln's. Alienated also were some of the less-principled patronage-mongers in Republican states like New York and Pennsylvania, who resented being shortchanged on political jobs in favor of Babcock's Radical Republican cronies—Roscoe Conkling, Simon Cameron, Zachariah Chandler, and their ilk. These men had been among Grant's original backers for the Republican nomination, and they did not intend to be deprived of the spoils of victory by men who were as dishonest as themselves, any more than by reformers.

Schurz and Trumbull were among the leaders of the movement for federal civil-service reform, which the enormous wartime rise in patronage had inspired. It was their aim to place federal job-holding on a merit basis, with candidates selected by objective examinations and not by political friends. But the Conklings and Camerons found it easy to mobilize congressional opposition whenever civil-service legislation loomed. When Secretary of the Interior Cox tried to staff his department with men chosen on merit, he won only the indignation of Grant himself, who removed Cox and put the Interior Department under Columbus Delano, a former Ohio congressman who, long before, had discovered how to dispense patronage for political ends.

Even worse than Grant's handling of major appointments and patronage in the ranks was the way he allowed himself and his great office to be used by the corruptionists who surrounded him. A notorious instance was his insistence on the annexation of Santo Domingo in 1869. After a long and bloody struggle, Santo Domingo had won its independence from Spain in 1865. The country was exceedingly rich in minerals, timber, and fruit, and had all the requirements for the successful production of coffee and sugar. Capable of supporting a population of millions, it was settled by a mere 150,000 persons. Clearly it was ripe for exploitation.

Among those who hungrily eyed Santo Domingo were a couple of discreditable Massachusetts promoters, friends of Congressman "Ben" Butler, who included him in their scheme to make a fortune in the small country. Butler brought Orville Babcock into the project, and Babcock persuaded Grant to send him to Santo Domingo. Babcock found Santo Domingo in political confusion, but was able to negotiate a treaty of annexation with one of the groups competing for power. On Babcock's return, Grant submitted the treaty to the Senate. Attorney-General Hoar denounced Babcock's treaty-making as illegal, but Grant was so determined to back his secretary and the latter's colleagues in the venture that he removed Hoar from office. In order to gain southern Democratic votes for the treaty, Grant proceeded to name a southerner as Attorney-General. Such tactics only heightened the opposition, which was led by Senator Sumner, Chairman of the Senate Foreign Relations Committee. Sumner's denunciation of the entire "deal" defeated the treaty in 1870. For his pains, the Conklings and Camerons the next year stripped Sumner of his committee post and practically read him out of the Republican party.

Another notorious event occurred on "Black Friday," September 24, 1869. For months before that date, Fisk and Gould had been plotting to gain control of the gold supply of the country that was not actually held in government vaults. To insure success they persuaded Grant, at one of their social meetings, to promise not to release any government gold that fall. Their argument was a characteristically devious one which the President, no doubt, did not understand. Yet, assured of Grant's cooperation, Fisk and Gould went to work buying gold. Between September 20 and September 24 the price of gold (quoted in terms of the currency dollars required to buy $100 in gold) rose from 140 to 163½. Gold was not used in ordinary business transactions, but it was used by banks and merchants for settling international balances and for other limited purposes. As the price of gold soared, bankers and merchants made frenzied efforts to raise the growing amount of cash they needed to buy it. Stocks and bonds were sold, debts called in, and a genuine panic was created. Advised of the severity of the situation, Grant finally ordered the Secretary of the Treasury, who had not been in on the President's promise, to release $4 million of government gold to New York banks. This broke the corner, but the whole maneuver only widened the gulf between Grant and respectable Republicans.

The Lobbies and Legislation.

Grant, no doubt, was personally innocent of corruption. As a victorious general he had become accustomed to receiving the lavish patronage of the rich. Before his candidacy for the presidency, a group of millionaires headed by A. T. Stewart had presented him with a fully furnished mansion in Philadelphia. Another group, including Hamilton Fish, had helped pay off the $100,000 mortgage on Grant's Washington home. Still another, made up of "fifty solid men of Boston," had equipped this home with a $75,000 library. Many of these men had made fortunes on war con-

tracts, but in Grant's eyes they had also contributed handsomely to winning the war. Now they were sustaining the postwar business boom, which brought such marvelous achievements as the completion of the transcontinental railroad. Suppose their accomplishments did require forcing special-interest legislation through Congress? No one in the postwar epoch could be pure and progressive at the same time.

To those who would point a finger, moreover, Grant could reply that he had inherited a government already far gone in corruption. The competition for war contracts and the fight for other wartime legislation covering protective tariffs, land grants, and the money system, had made lobbying a full-time occupation. Men like John Lord Hayes, who represented the woolen manufacturers, and James M. Swank, who spoke for the iron and steel interests, spent almost all their time cultivating legislators in wartime Washington. After the war they simply stepped up their activities. Just before concluding four years in Congress in 1873, Job Stevenson of Ohio told his colleagues that "the House of Representatives was like an auction room where more valuable considerations were disposed of under the speaker's hammer than in any other place on earth."

Few political favors were more valuable than the tariff. One justification offered for the high wartime protective tariffs of 1862 and 1864 had been the need to compensate American manufacturers for the high internal taxes they were required to pay at each step in the production process. Otherwise, foreign competitors, who of course were not shackled by American internal taxes, would swamp the American market. After the war, the internal taxes were promptly repealed. But the tariffs, instead of being lowered, were pushed higher and higher, and the prices of protected goods went up with them. "Why sir," protested Representative John A. Kasson of Iowa in 1866, "you are protecting the American people until they will not be able to buy one solitary thing that is protected if this goes on."

Such protests checked across-the-board increases, but representatives of special interests swarmed into the very halls of Congress to press their particular needs. By 1870, writes Ida Tarbell, a historian of protection, "the tariff was a conglomeration of special favors." The situation is indicated in this comment by General Robert C. Schenck, Representative from Ohio from 1863 to 1871: "Sitting here as a friend of protective tariffs for eight years, I have voted aye or nay as those who got up the tariff bills have told me."

Many railroad men were among the growing number of outspoken opponents of protection, for the special tariff on steel rails in 1870 appreciably raised the cost of railroad construction and soured them on the whole protective philosophy. Other railroad men took the opposite view. John N. Denison, Chairman of the Board of the Chicago, Burlington & Quincy, for example, told his associates in 1872 that given a start behind tariff walls, manufacturers of steel rails would soon be producing them "as cheap in our country as anywhere." And indeed they were, later on. Denison also argued that manufacturers of other protected goods, stimulated by the rising prices the tariffs made possible, would be shipping in ever-larger volume over the railroad lines.

Railroad men like Denison supported tariffs for others, but they opposed all efforts by Congress to legislate in areas where their own immediate interests were concerned. After the Union Pacific and Central Pacific railroads had received their government loans, Congress annually considered legislation that would have provided for their eventual repayment. The transcontinentals fought this legislation stubbornly and successfully. It was on one such occasion, in the session of 1867-1868, that Congressman Oakes Ames distributed shares in the Crédit Mobilier among senators and representatives "where they will do the most good to us."

The revelation of his sales of stock just before the presidential election of 1872 simply added one more scandal to the Republican record under Grant. The Central Pacific spent large sums in Washington for lobbying year after year. Other railroads, meanwhile, were getting fresh land grants directly from Congress or from western states to which Congress granted the public domain for railroad subsidies. The last congressional grant was made in 1871, bringing the total distributed to the railroads directly or through the states to 160 million acres, valued conservatively at $335 million.

The railroads were also using their immense wealth and power to buy favorable sites from state and local governments for urban rights of way and terminals and to lessen the tax burden on their vast properties. More important, as opposition to railroad rate policies spread among farmers and other shippers, the railroads managed to thwart most political efforts to regulate rate-making (see pp. 463-464, 498).

The Manipulation of Money. Northern financiers, speculators, and creditors and their political friends also shared in the "Great Barbecue," a phrase coined by the literary historian Vernon L. Parrington to describe the postwar boom period. The Republican platform of 1868 had pledged that the government's entire war debt would either be redeemed in gold or refunded with new government bonds redeemable in gold. On March 18, 1869, both houses of Congress adopted a resolution pledging the government to carry out this platform plank. This pledge itself sent the market value of all war bonds soaring and brought substantial profits to speculators in government securities. Laws enacted later to implement the pledge then offered even broader speculative opportunities. These laws, it should be said, proved salutary so far as the government's credit was concerned. Forced during the war to offer interest as high as 6 per cent, the victorious national government was now able to refund 6 per cent bonds with new ones carrying only

5 and 4 per cent interest. Later on, the government was able to borrow for as little as 2½ per cent. Yet the new laws permitted the Secretary of the Treasury to redeem or refund the old bonds more or less at his pleasure, and this flexibility of action introduced a fatal uncertainty into finance which served as a torch to speculative fireworks.

Rumors, hot tips, and cloakroom gossip about Treasury activities flowed between Washington and New York and other financial centers, often causing mad flurries in the money markets. Even the men closest to the government were not above sending out "sure things" over the telegraph to their financial friends around the country, in order to get a share of investment projects that ordinarily would have been much too rich for them. Enemies and innocent bystanders, on the other hand, were often hurt. Wall Street, in the early 1870's, openly charged that the Secretary of the Treasury, George S. Boutwell, often made moves "conspicuously more advantageous to certain 'friends of Government' among speculators . . . than to men engaged in legitimate business."

Yet "legitimate businessmen" were not left completely out in the cold. What this group most wanted was a stable currency, so that the profits of contracts entered into one month would not be wiped out the next by changes in the volume, and hence the value, of money. The volume of money, under the National Banking Acts of 1863 and 1864 (see p. 382), was very closely tied to the volume of government bonds. The new 5 and 4 per cent bonds could not be redeemed by the Secretary of the Treasury at his pleasure. They had a fixed life for as long as 30 years. How well this feature was regarded by the business community is indicated by the fact that the new bonds rose as much as 25 per cent over their face value almost as soon as they were issued.

From time to time, the Supreme Court used its weight to rock the monetary boat. In 1869, in the case of *Hepburn* v. *Griswold,* the Court decided belatedly that Congress could not simply declare paper money legal tender when it had no gold behind it—as

Congress had done in 1862 and 1863 when it first created the greenbacks. This decision sent the greenbacks fluttering downward in value. Then, in 1871, the Court reversed itself. In the Legal Tender Cases of that year (*Knox* v. *Lee* and *Parker* v. *Davis*), it said Congress *could* declare paper money legal tender.

Congress also manipulated the currency occasionally. In February, 1873, for example, it passed a Coinage Act that ended the traditional minting of silver coins. At this time the commercial price of silver was higher than the price the mint itself put on a silver dollar, and little silver was offered for conversion into coin. After the business crash later that year, however, while silver production in western mines kept growing, the commercial price fell off. The silver kings then began offering their metal to the mint. When they found that silver had quietly been demonetized, they set up a long loud howl, calling the Coinage Act "the Crime of '73." As such, the act became an important issue in politics later on (see p. 486).

Early in the depression, when debtors were scrambling for currency with which to fend off their equally hard-pressed creditors, Congress yielded to public pressure with a bill returning enough greenbacks to circulation to bring their face value up to $400 million. Grant, however, kept the volume of currency stable by vetoing the bill. In 1875, with the emergency over, Congress recovered from its lapse. That year, after a decade of agitation, it passed the Resumption Act under which, for the first time since the war, the government became obliged to resume paying specie on demand for all its paper currency, greenbacks included. This action soon placed the greenbacks on a par with gold-backed paper. The act also required the government to resume withdrawal of greenbacks on January 1, 1879 (withdrawal had been checked in 1868), until the amount in circulation was stabilized at $300 million. For the stable-currency forces, this act was a distinct triumph.

III.   REFORM AND RECONSTRUCTION

Republican Rifts.   During Grant's campaign for re-election in 1872, Roscoe Conkling told a receptive New York audience: "If the name and the character of the administration of Ulysses S. Grant have been of value to the nation, no one knows it so well as the men who represent the property, the credits, the public securities and the enterprise of the country." These men truly were in debt to the Republican party, and as a group were to become its staunchest backers over the years. Yet there were many businessmen who had begun to grow restless over the ceaseless exactions of the Radical Republicans who controlled the party. Conkling himself was a particularly nasty thorn in their flesh.

In 1867, Conkling had gained control of the patronage in the New York City Customs House, where thousands of people now worked at administering the complex and detailed customs procedures that the wartime and postwar tariff acts had set up. Until 1874, these tariff acts empowered customs appraisers to condemn entire shipments for fraud on the basis of the slightest, often accidental, infraction, and to make their condemnation stick by getting a court to confirm it. Half of the ultimate settlement extracted from the importers went to the government; the other half—an irresistible temptation—was divided among informants, appraisers, and the lawyers, often including Conkling himself, who had taken the required court action. Much of this money found its way to the Republican party treasury. Other Radical leaders, such as John A. Logan in Illinois and Oliver Morton in Indiana, controlled the spoils-hungry internal revenue collectors in their respective states.

Merchants and traders cried out against Grant for permitting such extortion to continue, and they were joined by most of the old-line Republicans. Senators Sum-

ner, Schurz, and Trumbull, ex-ambassador Charles Francis Adams, and ex-cabinet members Cox and Hoar watched with dismay as the last vestiges of Republican idealism evaporated before the party's new materialistic orientation. They were appalled at the coarseness of Grant's business associates, the plotting of his closest advisers, and the special-interest legislation promoted by his cronies in Congress. Adding their voices to the swelling tones of criticism were newly influential independent journalists like Godkin of the *Nation* and George W. Curtis of *Harper's Weekly,* and, in the Middle West, Horace White of the *Chicago Tribune* and Murat Halstead of the *Cincinnati Commercial.* All were Republicans; but all felt that the party of free soil and free men had clearly become the party of adventurers.

The vogue of Social Darwinism and the material accomplishments of such enviable optimists as Commodore Vanderbilt and John D. Rockefeller may have combined to inhibit the tendency toward reform among Grant's more philosophical opponents. But others were ready to attack the spoilsmen through civil-service legislation and to fight the "tariff robbers" by organizing free trade leagues. Still others were alienated by Grant's policy toward the South. Even old Radicals like Carl Schurz, when he saw how the new Republican leadership was using the Negro vote, began to demand the end of coercive measures against the defeated section, and the return of freely elected southerners to the councils of the nation.

As early as 1870, as we have already seen (p. 407), Schurz led a Republican revolt in his state of Missouri that overthrew the Radicals' carpetbagger regime. As the presidential elections of 1872 approached, Schurz took the lead in transforming his Liberal Republican party in Missouri into a national party dedicated to unseating the tarnished President. The Liberal Republican campaign turned out to be a fiasco, but the spirit of reform that had inspired the movement grew stronger as the hard times that followed the Panic of 1873 persisted, and as the true extent of the corruption under Grant became known.

Even while the campaign of 1872 was in progress, news of the first major Grant scandal—the Crédit Mobilier affair (see p. 424)—was breaking. Grant survived these untimely revelations, but they foreshadowed the history of his second term. After the business crash of 1873, each new announcement of scandal struck with added force, and after the Democrats captured control of the House of Representatives in the elections of 1874, the momentum of investigation and prosecution increased. Two affairs struck close to Grant himself. One was the uncovering of the "Whiskey Ring" in St. Louis, which had defrauded the government of millions of dollars in internal revenue charges. Deeply involved in the fraud was Orville Babcock, who was saved from imprisonment only by Grant's incessant interference in his trial. The second affair led to the impeachment of Grant's third Secretary of War, W. W. Belknap, who, since his appointment in 1870, had been "kept" by traders in Indian Territory under his jurisdiction. The ultimate outrage to both the reformers and the public was the "Salary Grab Act" of 1873 by which Congress raised its own salaries 50 per cent from $5,000 to $7,500 and made the raise retroactive for two years, thereby voting each and every member a virtual gift of $5,000. This act also raised the salary of the president, the cabinet members, and the Supreme Court justices.

The Election of 1876. All this was grist to the political mill, which was grinding out preparations for the presidential election of 1876. With the approach of the national nominating conventions, dissension again began to divide the Grand Old Party, as the Republicans had taken to calling

themselves. The "Stalwarts," the group of callous, hard-boiled professionals closest to Grant, were open and frank in their commitment to the spoils system and wanted Grant to run for a third term. They looked with contempt upon those they called the "Halfbreeds" in the party who, though serving corporate wealth no less faithfully than the Stalwarts, balked at flagrant stealing and paid more attention to the business of government. The Halfbreeds had not deserted to the Liberal Republicans in 1872, but some of them, like James Garfield of Ohio, had a lurking preference for civil-service reform.

The leader of the Halfbreeds, Congressman James G. Blaine, seemed a likely choice for the Republican nomination. Although he labored under the handicap of having no war record, his well-publicized hostility to England made him attractive to the Irish, and he was an astute campaigner. Blaine's chances were ruined, however, by a dramatic revelation, made early in 1876, impugning his honor. As Speaker of the House from 1869 to 1875, Blaine had sometimes aided railroads and, like many of his colleagues, had benefited personally from his services to them. Now some incriminating letters had come to light that involved Blaine in shady negotiations with the Union Pacific, and although Blaine declared his innocence before the House, his refusal to disclose the full text of the letters left little doubt that he had behaved improperly. Even so, he might still have won the nomination if he had not denounced the Stalwarts as "all desperate bad men, bent on loot and booty," thus incurring the hatred of the formidable Senator Roscoe Conkling. When the Republican convention met in Cincinnati, Blaine could not escape the retribution of Conkling and the Republican old guard. Balked in their attempts to renominate Grant, they threw their support to Rutherford B. Hayes, the Governor of Ohio.

By 1876, the Democrats had been out of office for 16 years. Eastern, southern. and western Democrats differed on important matters, such as money policy, the tariff, and federal subsidies for internal improvements. But hunger for the long-awaited spoils of office now united them temporarily. Republican scandals, hard times, and the public's hankering for reform all worked to their advantage. Responding to the national demand for virtue in public office, the Democrats nominated Samuel J. Tilden, a rich corporation lawyer, cultivated and crafty, who had won a national reputation as a reform governor of New York. Tilden appealed to many conservative businessmen who had grown tired of Radical extortions and who also shared his hard-money views. But his greatest claim to the nomination was the fame he had won all over the country in 1872 by sending Boss Tweed, the notorious head of Tammany Hall, to the penitentiary.

During the three preceding years, the Tweed Ring had looted New York City's government of no less than $100 million.

All signs pointed to a Democratic success in the election of 1876—even the Republican candidate, Hayes, privately predicted his own defeat. But political signs are not always reliable. For one thing, no one knew how the South would vote. Since the Republicans still waved the Bloody Shirt and repeated hysterical warnings about "rebel rule," it seemed natural that the South would ally itself with the northern Democrats. But many of the southern leaders who had taken over political control after the departure of the Federal troops were former Whigs and had never been comfortable in the Democratic party. As harbingers of a new industrialized and business-minded South, they often found the Republican economic program more attractive than Democratic economic policies, and they particularly resented the failure of

An "awfully riled" Uncle Sam beating down corruptionist ideas of a third term for Grant in 1876.

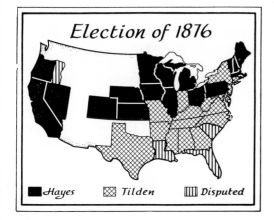

Election of 1876

■ *Hayes*   ⊠ *Tilden*   ⊞ *Disputed*

northern Democrats to support their requests for land grants and other federal subsidies to southern railroads.

The attitudes of the Whiggish southern Democrats were not lost on Hayes' political managers. Eager to create a southern Republican wing to offset the losses the party had suffered in the North, the Republican bosses showed themselves ready to cooperate with the South. One group in particular caught their eye. This group was made up of southerners who, along with powerful northern railroad interests led by Tom Scott of the Pennsylvania, were seeking federal subsidies for a new transcontinental line to link Texas with the Pacific. No political bargains were struck between Hayes' managers and the railroad cabal before the election, but it was understood that if Hayes won, the government might look kindly on supporting "internal improvements of a national character."

First reports of the election results seemed definite enough. The Democratic candidate, Tilden, had a plurality of 250,000 votes, and the press proclaimed him as the new president. But Republican strategists suddenly awoke to the fact that the returns from Louisiana, Florida, and South Carolina, the three states still under carpetbagger control, had not yet come in because of election irregularities. These states, together with Oregon (one of whose three electoral votes was claimed by the Democrats on a technicality), held a total of 20 disputed electoral votes. Tilden needed only one 'of

them to win; Hayes needed all to gain the 185 electoral votes required for election. Although both parties had resorted to the most bare-faced skullduggery, evidence now indicates that Tilden deserved Florida's four electoral votes and Hayes the others. In 1876, however, Congress had to decide which of the double set of returns reported by the three states should be accepted—the Democratic count or the Republican.

Amid threats and talk of insurrection, the two parties agreed to decide the election by turning the problem over to a congressional commission made up of five representatives, five senators, and five Supreme Court justices. Party affiliations were equally divided, except for one independent justice, David Davis. Unfortunately for Tilden, Davis accepted a nomination to the Senate before the commission met, and an avowed Republican, Justice Joseph P. Bradley, replaced him. The Republican majority of eight then voted unanimously for Hayes.

A conference between Democratic and Republican leaders at Wormley's Hotel in Washington was popularly supposed to have averted a Democratic filibuster aimed at forestalling Hayes' designation. The Democrats here agreed to accept Hayes if the Republicans would promise to withdraw federal troops from Louisiana and South Carolina. Actually, Hayes had already promised to pull the troops out. What placated the Southern bloc was a pledge made by party leaders before the Wormley conference to include southerners in the new cabinet, to give them some control of local patronage, and to grant subsidies to southern railroads. As one Washington correspondent put it, "It is thoroughly understood here by Southern men, that Mr. Hayes means, if he should become President, to cut adrift from the carpet-baggers and make an alliance with respectable party leaders of Whig antecedents in the South." In exchange for all this, southern leaders, Democrats though they nominally were, and Democratic though the new House of Representatives was to be, agreed to vote for the Republican, James A. Garfield, as Speaker.

Very soon after Hayes' inauguration, it became clear to the South that the new administration would fail to fulfill its promise of railroad subsidies. Unfortunately, one reason for the Republican defection on this score was the failure of the southern leaders in the House to deliver enough Democratic votes to give the promised speakership to Garfield. Thus the compromise by which a new return to armed conflict was averted broke down almost at its very first test. The North immediately reverted to the thesis that the South had not been reconstructed. At the time the agreements leading to Hayes' victory had been made, northern Republican newspapers had written warmly of the South's return to statesmanship and nationalism. By 1877, they had returned to the old theme that "the spirit of rebellion still lives and is liable at any moment to be again entrenched in arms." At the same time Republican politicians once more brought out the tattered bloody shirt that had carried them to so many electoral victories in the recent past.

The South and the Nation. In *Origins of the New South,* C. Vann Woodward compares the South's position in the Union before the Civil War with her status in the reconstructed Union as of 1912. "For almost fifty of the seventy-two years between the inauguration of Washington and that of Lincoln," he writes, "Southern men held the presidency, and for sixty of those years a Southern chief justice presided over the Supreme Court." Between 1861 and 1912, on the other hand, "no Southerner, except Andrew Johnson, served as President or Vice-President, nor did one achieve so much as the nomination of a major party for either office. Of the 133 cabinet members appointed during that period, only 14 were from the South, and of the 31 justices of the Supreme Court, only 7."

While the South thus remained a section in much more than a geographical sense alone, the rest of the nation drew farther and farther away from it. The movement of textile factories from New England to South Carolina and other southern states late in the nineteenth century did tend to break down economic barriers; the discovery of oil in Texas with the coming in of the great gusher at Spindletop in 1901 marked an even more important milestone in the weakening of the South's pervasive agricultural tradition; but not until World War II and the immense prosperity that followed it, was the South as a whole brought firmly into the orbit of industrialism and national business enterprise. The wartime demand for manpower, and the demand for industrial labor during the prosperous postwar years were among the most important factors that helped to open opportunities for southern Negroes. One of the major consequences of the South's own prosperity was the weakening of segregation in many of its areas and its own contribution, on that account, to ending one of the most unfortunate anomalies of American life in both the North and the South.

IV.   THE CENTENNIAL EXPOSITION OF 1876

After the Panic of 1873, as after the Panic of 1857, the South had good reason to question northern boasts of industrial progress and the superiority of industry over agriculture as a way of life. Each successive American panic seemed to be the herald of a more brutal depression; and even had enough been known about economics to permit the application of effective remedies, the prevailing philosophy dictated that the sickness of the business system be permitted to run its course, whatever the cost in suffering and starvation. The depression of the 1870's reached its depths in 1878 when,

The central aisle of the main exhibition building, Philadelphia Centennial Exposition, 1876.

even after all the bankruptcies of the last five years, more business firms failed, and failed with greater liabilities, than in 1873 itself. Yet by 1878 businessmen like Carnegie and Rockefeller knew that the time for resumption of full-scale activity and indeed for massive expansion was nearing. Two years before, the public at large had had a chance to review the remarkable progress of the country in the preceding century and had come away with a vision of another remarkable epoch in the offing.

The Centennial Exposition that opened in Fairmount Park, Philadelphia, for a five-month run on May 10, 1876, was the sixth in a series of fairs that had been held dur-ing the last 25 years in London, Paris, Vienna, and other cities abroad. It was the first world's fair ever to be held in the United States. The fair's promoters were affronted by the reluctance of France, Germany, and other continental countries to risk shipping their art treasures across the sea for Americans to admire, and their enthusiasm was dampened somewhat by visitors who criticized the architectural style of the Exposition buildings. The boast that the Main Exposition Building was the largest in the world hardly helped matters, since it had no other discernible distinction. Still there were many features of the Exposition that drew praise. Crowds flocked to the

431

foreign pavilions to marvel at the beautiful exhibits of English furniture, German porcelain, jewels and shawls from India, lacquers from Japan, and ivory carvings from South Africa. The exhibition of America's own painting, moreover, was good enough to call forth a glow of national pride. For the first time, millions of Americans could view at first hand the works of John Singleton Copley, Gilbert Stuart, Washington Allston, and other distinguished painters of an earlier epoch, as well as the work of contemporaries like Winslow Homer, Thomas Moran, and Eastman Johnson.

The most auspicious exhibit was housed in Machinery Hall where the magnificent Corliss engine, which could generate the power of 1,600 horses, dominated the show. Sewing machines of all models also were prominently displayed. Of great interest to visitors was the exhibit of western ores and the mining processes by which they were taken from the earth. Even more engaging for some was the display in the Woman's Pavilion, which was devoted to work produced *by* women, not simply for them. The agitation for "women's rights" had increased during the 1870's as women saw Negroes getting the ballot and other civic privileges

while they themselves remained deprived of these rights. The display, showing the remarkable advances women had made in textile design, medical practice, and household manufactures, was calculated to give those who scoffed at the feminist movement food for thought.

But perhaps the most cheering feature of the entire Exposition was the number of visitors. The railroads, hungry for business of any kind, offered greatly reduced rates to Philadelphia, and all other means of transportation were strained by the demand. On a single day, Pennsylvania Day, a record 275,000 persons visited the Fair. All told, more than 10 million admissions to the Fair were counted, of which 8 million were paid admissions. The gross receipts were approximately $3,800,000, a figure that far exceeded even the most optimistic estimates. The Exposition had been planned well in advance of the business crash of 1873. Though the country soon was in the throes of the depression, the promoters had proceeded boldly with their plans. And the response of the country to the show justified all their plans and efforts. Prosperity was still a long way off, even after the Exposition closed; but its success was a heartening manifestation of the people's confidence in themselves.

Readings

Many of the books cited for Chapter XVII are also helpful for this chapter. An excellent general survey of the Reconstruction years is Allan Nevins, *The Emergence of Modern America, 1865-1878* (1927). Illuminating reading is to be found in the chapters on this period in Henry Adams, *The Education of Henry Adams* (1918).

On Social Darwinism, Richard Hofstadter, *Social Darwinism in American Thought* (rev. ed., 1955), is particularly comprehensive. Among Herbert Spencer's own works, a good place to start is with *First Principles* (1864), and *The Study of Sociology* (1874). A lucid account of the "Erie War" and related railroad developments appears in Charles Francis Adams, Jr., and Henry Adams, *Chapters of Erie and Other Essays* (1886). *Railroads: Their Origin and Problems* (1878), by Charles Francis Adams, Jr., though old, remains one of the best introductions to railroad history in this period. The best biography of Cornelius Vanderbilt is Wheaton J. Lane, *Commodore Vanderbilt* (1942). An amusing book is Bouck White, *The Book of Daniel Drew* (1910). On the western railroads, the most useful general account is Robert R. Riegel, *The Story of the Western Railroads* (1926). Good reading is Oscar Lewis, *The Big Four* (1951). The authoritative account of John D. Rockefeller and his enterprises is Allan Nevins, *John D. Rockefeller* (2 vols., 1940, rev. 1954). Sympathetic to the plight of the other oil producers and excellent on the spirit of the early oilmen is Ida Tarbell, *The History of the Standard Oil Company* (2 vols., 1904, one-volume edition, 1950). An interesting account of the early days of the industry is P. H. Giddens, *The Birth of the Oil Industry* (1938).

Of the works on Grant's administration cited for Chapter XVII, the ones most relevant to this chapter are Allan Nevins, *Hamilton Fish* (1936); Matthew Josephson, *The Politicos* (1938); and Earle D. Ross, *The Liberal Republican Movement* (1919). A good biography of Grant is William B. Hesseltine, *Ulysses S. Grant, Politician* (1935). On Grant's early life, an excellent study is Lloyd Lewis, *Captain Sam Grant* (1950), the first volume of a large work halted by Lewis' death, but scheduled for completion by Bruce Catton. A study of broader interest than its title suggests is Ida Tarbell, *The Tariff in Our Times* (1911). On money problems, a good starting point is Davis R. Dewey, *Financial History of the United States* (1936 ed.). A classic study is Wesley C. Mitchell, *A History of the Greenbacks* (1903). Henrietta M. Larson, *Jay Cooke, Private Banker* (1936), is good on its subject.

On the election of 1876 and the conditions surrounding it, the most interesting works are the two by C. Vann Woodward, already noted: *Reunion and Reaction* (1951), and *The Origins of the New South* (1951).

TAMING THE WEST

C H A P T E R N I N E T E E N

Only about half of the United States, geographically speaking, had been engaged in the sectional conflicts of the 50's, in the Civil War, and in the travesty and tragedy of Reconstruction. As late as 1860, not a single state, except Texas, had been set up on the vast plains beyond the Mississippi Valley, roughly between the 95th and 104th parallels. Farther west, in the forbidding mountain country of the Rockies and the Sierras, and in the Great Basin between these ranges, political organization by the white population had hardly begun. News of the great events of the Civil War often failed to reach the men who roamed this distant wilderness—and even those who heard the news were not always interested in it.

I.   THE CONQUEST OF THE PLAINS

The Plains and the Indians. In the 1540's, the Spaniard Coronado had described the enormous western plains as "uninhabited deserts." And from 1820 to 1858 Americans found it labeled in their geography books as the "Great American Desert." This uncharted expanse, which extended well into Mexico and Canada, was as boundless and unbroken as the ocean. Even more discouraging was the almost complete absence of trees for fuel, houses, fences, or shade. Only the lightest rains fell here, but violent hail storms and crushing falls of snow as dry as sand periodically afflicted the region, driven by winds that often surged to gale velocity. Sucked dry in their passage over the lofty snow-crowned mountains to the west, these winds brought extremes of heat and cold to the plains, and the few rivers were alternately parched and frozen.

As late as 1856, the *North American Review*, referring to elaborate surveys that had been made for transcontinental railroads, said:

We may as well admit that Kansas and Nebraska, with the exception of the small strip of land upon their eastern borders, are perfect deserts, with a soil . . . forever to unfit them for the purposes of agriculture. . . . We may as well admit that Washington Territory, and Oregon, and Utah, and New Mexico, are, with the exception of a few limited areas, composed of mountain chains and unfruitful plains; and that, whatever route is selected for a railroad to the Pacific, it must wind the greater part of its length through a country destined to remain forever an uninhabited waste.

Horace Greeley's judgment three years later was even more discouraging. After his overland journey from New York to San Francisco in 1859, he said, "The desert is steadily enlarging its borders and at the same time intensifying its barrenness."

For white men whose outlook had long been conditioned by the forests, rivers, rainfall, and rolling hills of western Europe and eastern America, here was a country to be crossed as hastily and as warily as possible. Most of the people who journeyed to the woodlands and watercourses of Oregon and California, starting with the 'forty-niners and ending with the first passengers of the transcontinental railroads 20 years later, avoided the "desert" altogether. If they could, they went by clipper ship around the Horn. Other travelers sailed to Panama, made a portage across the Isthmus, and sailed again up the Pacific coastal waters (see p. 320). Relatively few undertook to cross the "desert" by wagon train. So strewn were the plains with the wrecks of conveyances, the carcasses of cows and oxen, and the graves of loved ones that this area merited its awesome reputation. Of one region around Nevada, Mark Twain exclaimed, "The desert was one prodigious graveyard."

Yet the arid, treeless plains, like the high mountain ridges and the clear mountain streams that the western trappers plied so successfully, actually teemed with life. Hundreds of millions of jack rabbits and "prairie dogs" (really rodents) fed on the prevalent grass; and tens of millions of wolves and coyotes fed on the rabbits and the "dogs." Most significant and most picturesque were the great herds of buffalo. "Of all the quadrupeds that have lived upon the earth," wrote W. T. Hornaday, a nineteenth-century expert on buffaloes, "probably no other species has ever marshalled such innumerable hosts as those of the American bison. It would have been as easy to count or to estimate the number of leaves in a forest as to calculate the number of buffaloes living at any given time during the history of the species previous to 1870." The American buffalo herd in the 1850's or 1860's has been estimated at 12 million head. The Plains

Indians lived off the buffalo. His flesh provided their food, his skin their clothing, his hide the sheltering cover of their tepees. Their daily life revolved around the buffalo hunt, and their ritual and worship were dedicated to its success.

For centuries, the Plains Indians had hunted the buffalo inefficiently on foot, and the herds multiplied. Then, in the sixteenth century, the Spaniards brought the horse to the American continent, and during the next 200 years hundreds of thousands of horses wandered north over the Great Plains. By the time Americans began crossing the "desert" in the nineteenth century, the Indians had long since made the wild horses their own. The horses had greatly increased the Plains Indians' hunting range, and, by carrying them to lands that belonged to other tribes, had intensified tribal warfare. A mounted Indian was also a much more efficient hunter, and the buffalo herds steadily diminished. As time went on, tribal wars for the possession of the precious beast became more frequent and bloody. To survive, the Indians grew steadily more nomadic, more violent, and more hostile to trespassers of any kind.

George Catlin, who spent almost all his mature life painting pictures of the Plains Indians, said of the Comanche tribe:

I am ready, without hesitation, to pronounce the Comanches the most extraordinary horsemen that I have seen yet in all my travels, and I doubt very much whether any people in the world can surpass them. . . . Comanches . . . in their movements . . . are heavy and ungraceful; and on their feet, one of the most unattractive and slovenly-looking races of Indians that I have ever seen; but the moment they mount their horses, they seem at once metamorphosed,

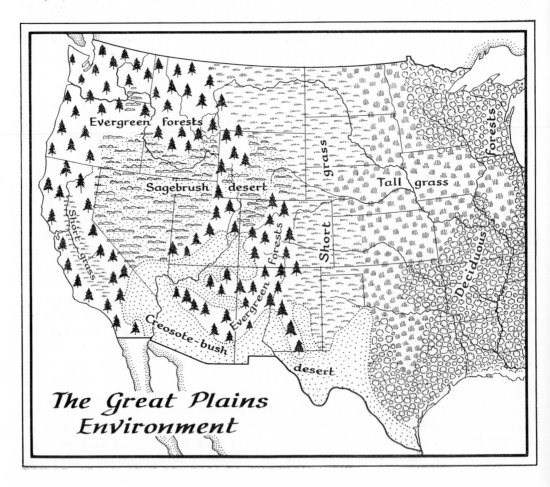

The Great Plains Environment

and surprise the spectator with the ease and elegance of their movements. A Comanche on his feet is out of his element, and comparatively almost as awkward as a monkey on the ground . . . ; but the moment he lays his hand upon his horse, his *face* even becomes handsome, and he gracefully flies away like a different being.

Other riders of the plains—the Sioux, Cheyenne, Pawnee, Blackfeet, and Crows— were nearly as proficient horsemen as the Comanches. A little to the south, the rather less nomadic but equally fearsome Osage, Kiowas, Iowa, Omaha, and related tribes also took well to the horse and the hunt. In the Southwest, on the more authentic desert of Arizona and New Mexico, rode

both hands free, one to feed and the other to release his bow, and shooting under the neck or belly of his mount while remaining virtually invisible himself, the Indian would circle madly, frighten ill-trained army horses with his curdling yells, and thus render "any certain aim with the revolver impossible, while his arrows [were] discharged at horse and man more rapidly than even a revolver [could] be fired." At 30 yards, an Indian fighter galloping at full speed could keep six or eight arrows in the air and on the target, each delivered with sufficient force for the entire shaft to penetrate the body of a buffalo.

Comanche "cavalry exercise," sketched by George Catlin.

the formidable Navajos and Apaches. These Indians, said Catlin, "all *ride* for their enemies, and also for their game." They carried a short bow, no more than two and a half or three feet across and superbly adapted to shooting from horseback, a quiver of a hundred barbed arrows, a long spear, and (in warfare) a circular shield fashioned from the hide of buffalo neck. These shields were so carefully smoke-cured and hardened that they could even deflect bullets that struck at an angle.

But more important than his equipment was the Indian himself. "We were surprised, incredulous, almost offended," said visitors to Kansas in 1854, "when a young officer . . . deliberately asserted that our mounted men, though armed with revolvers, were in general not a match in close combat, for the mounted Indians, with their bows and arrows." Riding alongside his horse, with

Not all the Indians of the West were as violent and efficient as the fighting tribes of the plains. In the poor but protected areas of the Great Basin, for example, there lived agricultural and essentially peaceful tribes, such as the highly civilized Hopi and Zuñi, who built their pueblos into the Basin's cliffs. To the north and west, on the so-called Columbia Plateau, were ugly and primitive tribes like the Utes, Shoshones, and Snakes, who never took up agriculture but eked out a living by eating reptiles, rodents, vermin, grasshoppers, and, as Mark Twain said, "anything they can bite." Westernmost of all were the despised "Digger Indians" of California, who subsisted on roots, tubers, and seeds that they literally dug out of the earth. Mark Twain found them "the wretchedest type of mankind I have ever seen." Completing the Indian population were the sad remnants of the Five Civilized Tribes of the

East who had been forcibly removed to Oklahoma country (see p. 220), and other "woods Indians" who had been pushed west. Both groups soon fell prey not only to government neglect but also to the "horse Indians" of the plains, who were as implacably opposed to their presence as they were to the encroaching whites.

In 1860, about 225,000 Indians shared the "desert" and the mountain country, which had been providentially reserved, as Zebulon Pike said, for "the wandering and uncivilized aborigines of the country." Their companions were the buffalo, the wild horse, the jack rabbit, and the coyote. But the white man could not be excluded altogether. Scattered over the future Dakotas, Montana, Idaho, Wyoming, Colorado, New Mexico, Arizona, Utah, and Nevada, were about 175,000 whites—probably 90 per cent of them male. Their numbers were soon increased by Civil War deserters from both the North and the South. Except for the 25,000 Mormons settled in Utah (see p. 275), these whites, like the Indians themselves, kept on the move. They prospected for precious metals, hunted buffalo, trapped martens and beavers, drove cattle and sheep, guided and sometimes misguided emigrant trains bound for California and Oregon, scouted for the army, hauled overland freight and mail, gambled, drank, and wenched when occasion offered, and traded and fought with the Indians. Some of them, like Kit Carson and Jim Bridger, were as free on a horse and as sharp on a trail as any Indian.

While inhabitants of older sections of the country were making the United States a powerful newcomer among the great nations, and were keeping abreast of developments in science, philosophy, literature, and the arts, the Wild West was living an extraordinary life of its own—a life that has entered profoundly into the American spirit and mythology. Even before the Civil War was over, the pattern of cowboys, rustlers, and roundups, of six-shooters and branding irons, warpath and council fire, wide-open mining towns and posses and sheriffs, had imposed itself on the Great American Desert. After the war, it became so firmly implanted in the American consciousness that it is still visible to this day.

Yet the Wild West had but a short life. After 1890, only Utah, Arizona, New Mexico, and Oklahoma had yet to become states. The older culture of the East had fully asserted itself over the West; the railroads had long since spanned the continent and had opened connecting lines in the new mining, cattle, and farming areas of the "desert." Mining, cattle-raising, and even farming had come conspicuously under the control of great corporations financed by eastern and foreign capital. By 1890, the Indian wars were over; the army had been withdrawn from the western forts; the frontier itself was officially declared closed.

Removing the Indians.
Commenting years later on the disease that had wiped out the Wampanoags and other tribes in Massachusetts within a decade after the arrival of the *Mayflower,* Cotton Mather said: "The woods were almost cleared of those pernicious creatures, to make room for a better growth." From the very beginning of white settlement in North America, the paganism of the natives served to justify Christian violence.

The white migration to Oregon in the late 1840's, the surveys for transcontinental railroads starting in 1853, the organization and settlement of the Kansas-Nebraska region in 1854, and the Colorado Gold Rush of 1858 convinced the Indians of "the fatal tendency of their new environment." If further evidence was needed, it was furnished by the attitude of the United States government. Demands from traders, travelers, and explorers for protection against the Indians prompted the army in the 1840's and 1850's to establish a line of forts on the plains. In 1851, the policy of maintaining "one big reservation" on the whole expanse of the "desert" ended, and treaties were made with the Plains Indians forcing them onto reservations that (1) deprived them of their traditional hunting grounds, and (2) crowded them onto the lands of other tribes who resisted their presence.

In the meantime, the administration of Indian affairs, which had previously been a function of the army, was given in part to the new Bureau of the Interior, created in 1849. The resentment caused by the new reservation policy among the Indians was fanned into rebellion by the maladministration of this new department. From the first, its officials were extremely corrupt; they made large fortunes by supplying the reservation Indians with shoddy of all sorts, by cheating them of their lands, and by selling them forbidden liquor. Many westerners took part in the Bureau's dealings with the Indians and naturally supported it. But the army was reluctant to yield its power to civilian politicos. Moreover, since army garrisons brought a great deal of money and business into the West, many western merchants wanted the troops to stay. Between corrupt administrators and touchy soldiers, the Indian was either starved on the reservations or killed in the open country. In the 1850's, one western settler wrote:

It was customary to speak of the Indian man as a Buck; of the woman as a squaw. . . . By a very natural and easy transition, from being spoken of as brutes, they came to be thought of as game to be shot, or as vermin to be destroyed.

The treaties of 1851 and after curtailed Indian lands and permitted the government to build roads and railroads across Indian preserves. As always, these treaties were made only with nominal Indian leaders and rump groups. Most of the Indians were never consulted; if they raised their voices in protest, they were ignored. But it was one thing to set aside Indian reservations, and another to force the Indians onto them and to keep them there under the guns of the army. Trouble was constantly brewing. In 1862, when regular army units were recalled from the plains for Civil War service, and were replaced by inexperienced recruits, the earliest of the Indian wars on the plains broke out.

That year a small band of irresponsible Sioux youths murdered five whites near a reservation in the vicinity of New Ulm, Minnesota. To forestall retaliation, the Sioux, under Little Crow, took to the warpath, killed hundreds of settlers, and burned their farmhouses. The militia finally overwhelmed them and 38 warriors were hanged. Running conflict between the Sioux and the army continued until late in 1863, when Little Crow himself was killed. The Sioux lands in Minnesota were confiscated, and the remnants of the tribe moved elsewhere. Two years later, the government tried to build a road along the Bozeman Trail from Fort Laramie, Wyoming, north to Bozeman, Montana. This road would have cut across the best hunting grounds of the western Sioux tribes. Red Cloud, chief of the western Sioux, led his warriors in harassing the work. In 1866 they ambushed and destroyed a small force under Captain W. J. Fetterman, who had been sent out to see a wood train through. Thereafter their attacks forced the abandonment of the project.

To the south, warfare with the Cheyenne and Arapaho tribes had been raging since 1861, when miners claimed their Colorado lands. This phase of the Indian wars came to a climax in 1864, when Colonel John M. Chivington massacred about 450 men, women, and children in a Cheyenne encampment at Sand Creek. The Indian response was equally bloody. Brutality on both sides increased until 1868, when, at Washita, in Oklahoma, the regular army under Colonel George A. Custer defeated a small force of Cheyenne and Arapaho warriors. Cheyenne Chief Black Kettle was killed and the Cheyennes were subdued.

Scores of other battles took place between the army and the Indians, and between Indians and marauding whites. But the Sioux and Cheyenne wars convinced a parsimonious Congress that the cost of subduing the Indians was too great and that the rate of

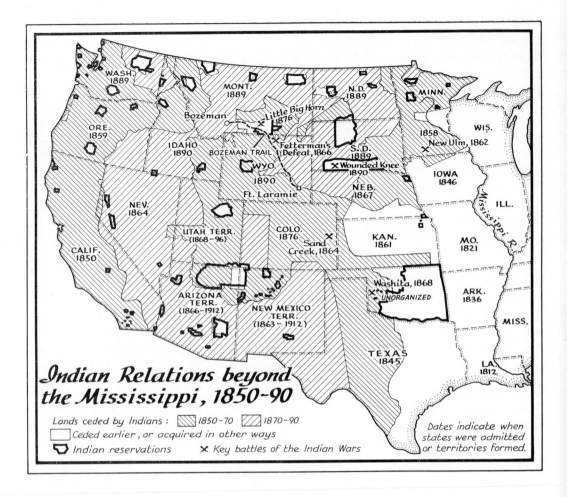

Indian Relations beyond the Mississippi, 1850-90

Lands ceded by Indians: [hatched] 1850-70 [hatched] 1870-90
[blank] Ceded earlier, or acquired in other ways
[symbol] Indian reservations   X Key battles of the Indian Wars

Dates indicate when states were admitted or territories formed.

subjugation was too slow. Thus, in 1867, peace commissioners were sent westward to convince the tribes to move to selected reservations, one in the Black Hills of Dakota, the other in present-day Oklahoma. By 1868, treaties to this effect were forced upon the war-weary Indians. General Sherman wrote:

> We have now . . . provided reservations for all, off the great roads. All who cling to their old hunting grounds are hostile and will remain so till killed off. We will have a sort of predatory war for years—every now and then be shocked by the indiscriminate murder of travelers and settlers, but the country is so large, and the advantage of the Indians so great, that we cannot make a single war end it. From the nature of things we must take chances and clean out Indians as we encounter them.

As Sherman predicted, between 1869 and 1875, over 200 pitched battles were waged

between the army and the Indians. The nature of these conflicts may be deduced from a statement of General Francis A. Walker, Commissioner of Indian Affairs, in 1871: "When dealing with savage men, as with savage beasts, no question of national honor can arise. Whether to fight, to run away, or to employ a ruse, is solely a question of expediency." On the reservations, meanwhile, a new civilian Board of Indian Commissioners, created in 1869, tried to convert the Plains Indians to agriculture on inadequate land. By eking out the pitiful crops with bonuses, annuities, and other doles, these commissioners made the Indians increasingly dependent, and pauperization completed what the army had left undone.

In the 1870's, violence continued to flare as the Indians were kept on the new reservations only with great difficulty, and as the whites, with equal difficulty, were kept off them. Moldy flour, spoiled beef, and moth-eaten blankets made up the typical fare supplied to the reservation Indians by the commissioners. The Sioux in Dakota were further enraged by the encroachment on their reservation of Northern Pacific railroad crews, and by the influx of prospectors when gold was discovered in the Dakota Black Hills in 1875. In 1876, war broke out again. It was during this conflict that Colonel Custer made his famous "last stand" against Crazy Horse and Sitting Bull in the Battle of the Little Big Horn on June 25, 1876. The Sioux annihilated Custer, but shortages of ammunition and food forced them to scatter. An ill-timed attack on a wagon train gave away the location of the largest group of Indians, and their capture in October, 1876, ended the war. Sitting Bull fled to Canada, but, facing starvation, he returned in 1881.

In Oregon, the Nez Percé tribe, whose religious leaders urged them to drive out the whites, took to the warpath against encroaching miners in 1877. Until they succumbed to starvation and disease, the Nez Percé, under Chief Joseph, led 5,000 government troops on a wild chase over Oregon and Montana. In the 1880's, the Apaches in New Mexico went on a prolonged rampage until their chief, Geronimo, was captured in 1886.

What finally destroyed the Indians was the extermination of the buffalo herd. The building of the Union Pacific in the late 1860's cut the herd in two and left the southern bisons at the mercy of every railroad worker, miner, adventurer, and traveler. Since a stampeding herd was capable of overturning a train, buffalo-hunting became a regular feature of railroad-building. "Buffalo Bill" Cody got his reputation by killing some 4,000 buffalo in 18 months as a hunter for the Kansas Pacific Railroad. As railroads continued to open, buffalo-hunting became a popular and devastating western "sport." In 1871, the fate of the remaining herd was sealed when the sport changed into a business. In that year, a Pennsylvania tannery discovered that it could process buffalo hides into commercial leather; the hides, which had hardly been worth retrieving before, suddenly became worth $1 to $3 apiece. Between 1872 and 1874, the annual carnage of buffalo averaged 3 million, and by 1878, the southern herd had vanished. In 1886, when the National Museum wanted to mount some samples of the once teeming beasts, it found only about 600 of the northern herd left, deep in the Canadian woods.

When Columbus discovered America, probably 1 million aborigines lived on the continent to the north of Mexico. These natives were grouped in more than 600 distinct tribes, few of which numbered

The mass slaughter of the buffalo on the western plains in the early 1880's.

more than 2,000 persons. With the coming of the horse, small groups broke off from their tribes to hunt independently, and only once a year, in the summer, did they reunite for the sacred Sun Dance. This ritual, which lasted for four days, centered around offerings to the buffalo. In 1884, the Sun Dance and other Indian religious practices were prohibited by the government, but in 1890 the Sioux went ahead with the dance on their reservation in spite of the ban. When government troops appeared, the Indians fled. The troops followed, and in the "battle" of Wounded Knee massacred the half-starved remnants of what had once been a fierce tribe of warriors. By this time, hardly 200,000 Indians remained in the United States.

Three years before Wounded Knee, in 1887, Congress had enacted the Dawes Act, which remained the government's basic Indian policy until 1934. This act broke up tribal autonomy even on the reservations. It divided up reservation land and gave each family head 160 acres to cultivate. After a probation period of 25 years, he was granted full rights of ownership and full citizenship in the United States. In 1924, the United States granted full citizenship to all the Indians in the country. The Dawes Act, a dramatic reversal of former Indian policy, was the result of widespread humanitarian opposition to the extermination policy that had been conducted by the army and the Interior Department. Yet the act did little to benefit remaining Indians. In dividing the land, the poorest was usually given to the Indians, and the best was sold to white settlers. And even where they had good land, inexperience with ownership and with legal matters left the individual Indians vulnerable to the same kind of sharp practice that had cost them so dearly in making tribal treaties. Again and again, they were tricked into selling their best holdings. More disastrous still, they had neither the tradition nor the incentive to cultivate the land they retained. Great numbers of them became paupers, though there were a few exceptions—like the handful of Indians who held onto their oil-rich Oklahoma lands.

The Indian Reorganization Act of 1934 again reversed Indian policy. Under men like John Collier, who had lived much of his life among the Navajos, the Office of Indian Affairs succeeded in restoring tribal land-holding and tribal incentive on a wide scale. Collier's administration turned the "vanishing Americans" into one of the fastest-growing groups in the population of the United States. By 1955 their number had reached 400,000.

II. THE LAST FRONTIERS

The Mining Country. The plains and mountains of the West, as we have seen, were far from being desert wastes; they pulsated with plant, animal, and human life. The 30 years after the Civil War were to reveal that this country was also rich in agricultural and mineral wealth, the enormous extent of which has even yet to be appraised accurately. The most productive of the earth's wheat lands, once the secret of cultivating them had been discovered, stretched across the Dakotas and eastern Montana. In the more westerly parts of these states, in large areas of Wyoming, Colorado, and Texas, and even in sections of Nevada, Utah, and Arizona, seemingly boundless grazing lands lay ready to feed the cattle and sheep that would supply most of America's and the world's beef, mutton, hides, and wool. Other parts of the plains and the mountains held some of the world's largest and purest veins of copper and iron ore, some of the world's most extensive deposits of lead and zinc, and valuable seams of coal. Beneath the earth in Texas (and elsewhere in the West, as time proved), were incredibly large fields of petroleum and natural gas.

For centuries, nature had developed and stored these riches. But for generations the forest-oriented nation had even less use for them than did the Indians who roamed the western lands. Americans had plenty of land elsewhere; their need for coal as a fuel and for iron in construction remained small, since the older settled areas were still well supplied with wood. Copper was almost useless to a nation with little use, as yet, for electric wire. The supply of Pennsylvania petroleum, which was burned almost exclusively as an illuminant rather than a fuel, was more than adequate for a nation still awaiting the automobile. In mid-nineteenth century, the traditional channels of investment continued to reward American capital well enough, and men of means were content to leave to prospectors with little standing and less credit the job of searching out new wealth. And the prospectors cared little about the future requirements of organized society; they followed, unflaggingly, only the most ancient of lures—the precious metals, gold and silver. Anything else they regarded as a disappointment and a nuisance.

The early prospectors for gold in California had a fine code and fine camaraderie. "Honesty was the ruling passion of '48," one of them wrote. "If an *hombre* got broke, he asked the first one he met to lend him such amount as he wanted until he could 'dig her out.' The loans were always made and always paid according to promise." A year later, however, the California crowds had thickened:

Hordes of pickpockets, robbers, thieves, and swindlers were mixed with men who had come with honest intentions. . . . Murders, thefts, and heavy robberies soon became the order of the day. A panic seized that portion of the diggers who had never before been out of sight of 'marm's chimbly.'. . . Most of them presented the appearance of traveling armories; yet it was evident they wouldn't shoot. But men were to be found who had ridden the elephant of this world all their lives and well knew the course we had to pursue under the change of affairs. Whipping on the bare back, cutting off ears, and hanging soon became matters of as frequent occurrence as those of robbery, theft and murder.

Conditions grew steadily worse in California during the 1850's as the fabulous discoveries at Sutter's Fort and elsewhere in the San Joaquin and Sacramento valleys were thoroughly staked out and some of the best locations began to run thin. In a single decade, miners extracted hundreds of millions of dollars in gold from these hills and streams, much of it by the crudest placer-mining methods. All a man needed was a shovel to throw "pay dirt" into a washing pan, a little water in which to swirl the dirt so that the mud and gravel were separated from the grains of gold, and some kind of tool to scrape the grains from the bottom of the pan. The "cradle" was an improvement over the crude washing pan, for it had cleats to catch the gold, and it could be rocked with one hand while dirt and water were fed in with the other. The "sluice box" offered a still more efficient method. A long wooden box, called a "long Tom," with openings at one end and cleats at the other, was placed so that the flow of a fast-moving stream could be diverted through it. The miner then shoveled dirt into the box, let the water carry it away, and collected the gold that was caught in the cleats.

With these methods a man could take $50 a day from a rich lode. But by the end of the 50's, the pickings in California had become slim. Plenty of gold remained, but it was buried under enormous deposits in hills that had to be blasted away, or was locked in tough veins of quartz that had to be tunneled and worked with costly equipment and teams of men.

Blasting and quartz-mining required more capital and business ability than most of the prospectors had. Those who managed to strike it rich usually gambled away their "dust" or squandered it in other ways. When the surface gold ran out, a few took up more stable occupations; some became miners for the growing corporations, and others even became farmers. But tens of thousands continued to make "prospectin' " a way of life. The call of gold became too strong to resist, and ears were tuned to every murmur of new strikes. Distance and inaccessibility meant nothing: Australians, South Americans, Africans, and Europeans—all had come to California. Soon they were taking Californians back with them to prospect in their home countries. Gold-fever was a disease from which thousands suffered all over the world. Few ever got over it, and fewer still got rich. But taken together, these prospectors gave a great impetus to the wealth of nations and to the flow of trade.

The most persistent rumors in the late 1850's whispered of gold and silver in Colorado and Nevada. Even on the way to California in 1848 a pair of adventurers, Captain John Beck of the Oklahoma country and W. Green Russell of Georgia, had seen signs of gold around the South Platte River in northeastern Colorado. In 1858, having sold out in California, they decided they would lose nothing by looking further into Colorado. Others followed, but Russell and Beck, in July, 1858, staked out the first claim in the Pike's Peak region near present-day Denver. Soon the eastern newspapers were full of news about the Colorado strikes, and before the end of 1858 the cry "Pike's Peak or Bust" echoed through the land. By June, 1859, over 100,000 "yonder-siders" from California and "greenhorns" from Kansas and points east had made the trek to Colorado. Tall stories kept the gold bugs coming, but the truth soon became known: there was gold around Pike's Peak, but very little of it.

The trek homeward began, only now the wagons carried the slogan, "Pike's Peak and Busted." Some of the prospectors, as in California, stayed on to try their hand at farming and grazing and to lay the foundations for Colorado's future economy.

In May, 1859, John H. Gregory made a new Colorado strike in an area west of Denver that became known as Gregory Gulch. By June, the 5,000 people congregated there in new Central City were much more richly rewarded than the Pike's Peak contingent. Among them was George Pullman, the future builder of Pullman cars, who is said to have got the idea for his sleeping cars from the miners' double-decked bunks. The mines around Boulder to the north were opened soon after those at Central City. In the early 1870's, rich beds of silver were successfully prospected near Leadville, and a bit later gold was found in the region of Cripple Creek. These discoveries, coupled with the vigorous growth of Denver as a commercial center, spurred the drive for statehood, and in 1876 Colorado was honored with admission to the Union as the "Centennial State."

As in Colorado, rumors of precious metals in Nevada had persisted throughout the 1850's. After the 1859 failure in Colorado, the Nevada rumors became magnified into a sure thing, and the mob poured in. Among the hopeful prospectors was John W. Mackay, who was to make a fortune from the fabulous Comstock Lode. Many rich veins of silver and some deposits of gold were uncovered in Nevada in 1859, and in the spring of that year the Comstock Lode on Davidson Mountain was struck. In a few months, 20,000 men—with their horses and

The Mining Country

Dates indicate beginning of gold and silver mining operations
······ Present-day boundaries

mules, their picks, shovels, and pans, their whiskey, cards, and camp-following women —swarmed into the wild country and established never-to-be-forgotten Virginia City. In the next four years, about $15 million in gold and silver was taken from the Comstock Lode alone, but this was only "placer" pickings. The lode was as rich in silver as in gold. In 1868, Mackay and his new partners, James G. Fair, James C. Flood, and William S. O'Brien, got their first grasp on Comstock property, and took over $150 million from their mines. The yield of the entire Comstock Lode, over a period of 20 years, came to $306 million.

The discovery of the Comstock Lode in 1859 set others looking for deposits in the adjacent country, and by 1861 Nevada had several settlements and a population that was perhaps larger than it has ever been since. Organized as a territory in that year, Nevada became a state in 1864—the first in the mountain country.

Each year, as the mining boom echoed through the West and as the Civil War raged in the more settled parts of the country, new recruits were being drawn to prospecting from deserters of both armies and from footloose or ambitious civilians all over the world. The cry of "Gold!" in 1860 on the reservation of the Nez Percé Indians in present-day Idaho soon brought 15,000 miners into that country, which was still in Washington Territory. By 1863, the Territory of Idaho had been carved out, with Boise as its center and with Montana and much of Wyoming still included in it. The Boise district alone claimed as many as 25,000 hopefuls—a number that soon fell off sharply, as it did in most of the other mining towns. The census of 1870 reported only 15,000 in the whole Idaho Territory, which by then had been somewhat reduced in area.

In Montana, in 1864, gold was discovered

"Sunday Morning in the Mines," painted by Charles C. Nahl, 1872.

in Last Chance Gulch. During the next six years, Last Chance Gulch (present-day Helena) grew to 20,000 persons, and more than $100 million in gold was taken from the neighborhood mines. Here is how one resident described this typical mining town in 1864, after its first three months of existence:

This human hive, numbering at least ten thousand people, was the product of ninety days. Into it were crowded all the elements of a rough and active civilization. Thousands of cabins and tents and brush wikiups . . . were seen on every hand. Every foot of the gulch . . . was undergoing displacement, and it was already disfigured by huge heaps of gravel, which had been passed through the sluices and rifled of their glittering contents. . . . Gold was abundant, and every possible device was employed by the gamblers, the traders, the vile men and women that had come in with the miners . . . to obtain it. Nearly every third cabin in the town was a saloon where vile whiskey was peddled out for fifty cents a drink in gold dust. Many of these places were filled with gambling tables and gamblers. . . . Hurdy-gurdy dance-houses were numerous. . . . Not a day or night passed which did not yield its full fruition of fights, quarrels, wounds, or murders. The crack of the revolver was often heard above the merry notes of the violin. Street fights were frequent, and as no one knew when or where they would occur, every one was on his guard against a random shot. . . . Sunday was always a gala day. . . . The stores were all open. . . . Horse-racing was among the most favored amusements. Prize rings were formed, and brawny men engaged in fisticuffs until their sight was lost and their bodies pommelled to a jelly. . . . Pistols flashed, bowie knives flourished, and braggart oaths filled the air, as often as men's passions triumphed over their reason. . . . All classes of society were represented at this general exhibition. Judges, lawyers, doctors, even clergymen, could not claim exemption. . . .

In the Southwest, where the Spanish had lived for centuries, deposits of precious metals had long been known. But it was not until 1862 that the western prospectors turned their serious attention to the gold and silver of Arizona and New Mexico. By 1863, Arizona had grown populous enough to become a territory. The lasting monument to its placer-mining history is the reputation, which persists even to this day, of Tombstone, one of the most violent towns of the epoch.

The era of the prospectors' West was drawing to a close when, in 1874, gold was discovered on the Sioux reservation in the sacred Black Hills of South Dakota. Here Deadwood grew to rival Tombstone.

Although the mining country was wide open and offered a haven to every kind of refugee from society, it early developed its own legal code. This code applied not only to personal crimes, but also to such matters as claims, assays, and water rights. Enforcement was difficult, however, and throughout the 50's and early 60's Congress was pressed to extend justice to the West. It finally responded to the demands in 1866, but only by declaring that the mining country was free to all, "subject to local customs or rules of miners in the several mining districts." This attitude put a premium on vigilantism. But the gradual settlement of the West eventually brought about the establishment of more formal government agencies, which were strengthened by increasingly effective transportation and communication facilities.

And yet it was these very facilities that offered the last opportunity to western desperadoes. Before the railroad penetrated the Wild West, freight was hauled to the mining camps and other settlements by trains of "prairie schooners" run by express companies like Russell, Majors, and Waddell, and Wells, Fargo. The overland mail was also carried by these companies and, in the short but exciting period of 1860-1861, by the Pony Express. Until they were supplanted by the transcontinental telegraph in October, 1861, the Pony Express riders made the 2,500-mile run between St. Joseph, Missouri, and San Francisco in the incredible time of ten days.

Before the completion of the transcontinental railroads, express and mail holdups were daily affairs in the West. Thereafter, the headline "Great Train Robbery" became a regular feature of western news. But in 1881, even this phase of wild western life was brought under control. In that year, the railway and express companies joined the Governor of Missouri in placing such a high price on the heads of Jesse and Frank James that one of their own men shot Jesse in the back for the reward. In Oklahoma country in the 1890's, the notorious Dalton brothers re-enacted some of the bloodiest of the Jameses' exploits, but by then the West had generally become a safer place.

The Cattle Kingdom. The violence of the mining camps and mining towns kept the more staid and settled members of American society out of the western country for a long time. And the violence of the trail, the range, and the cow town kept them off the Great Plains. In the cattle kingdom as in the mining country, the population was almost wholly male, but the monotony was relieved in the towns by the usual coveys of obliging women. Tombstone and Deadwood had nothing on Dodge City, Kansas, the "Cowboy's Capital," where 25 men are said to have been killed during the town's first year of existence.

Ranching and cow-punching came into American life with the annexation of Texas in 1845. Long before, Mexicans had designed the bit, bridle, saddle, and spurs, the lariat, chaps, and five-gallon hat of the traditional cowboy; for centuries they had broken broncos, grazed calves, roped steers. But they were too careless to use the branding iron. When Americans from Mississippi, Alabama, and Tennessee began to trickle into Texas in the 1820's, many of them simply put their brands on what they deemed to be wild herds and set themselves up as cattle kings.

Over the years, many Mexican horses and cattle had broken away from Mexican herds to wander northward across the grassy plains. As Americans moved across Indiana and Illinois and into the plains as trappers, traders, soldiers, adventurers, or 'forty-niners who never went on to California, they too acquired herds of horses and cattle. Thus began the range cattle industry in Kansas and Nebraska, which supplied beef and fresh horses to emigrants going west, and also fed mining camps and railroad crews. Compared with the herds of Texas, however, these northern herds were insignificant.

In the 1850's, some of the more enterprising Texas ranchers undertook to drive their cattle westward to the Colorado and California markets, or northward to Illinois. But these drives proved uneconomical. The herds and the herders were easy prey to the Indians, and many of the steers that reached their destination were maimed and lame. Almost all of them were too muscular, thin, tough, and light-weight to command a price that would cover the cost of the venture. While the cattlemen awaited the opening of more accessible markets, their herds multiplied. By the time of the Civil War, nearly 5 million longhorns, all of them owned but most of them unbranded "mavericks," were crowding even the almost limitless Texas range.

As soon as the war was over, Texas ranchers began looking with renewed interest for markets. When they learned that steers, which sold for no more than $3 or $4 a head in Texas, would command as much as $40 a head in the northern markets, they decided to try the drive north. By this time a new factor had come into play: the railroad. In 1865, the Missouri Pacific was opened from Kansas City to Sedalia, Missouri. Before 1865, the ranchers had driven their cattle directly to the abattoirs. In the spring of 1866, they were ready for the first of the "long drives" to a railroad town, from which the railroad would haul the cattle to great city markets. Before fall, some 260,000 head of cattle had hit the trail for Sedalia.

As a business venture, this first drive was a failure. The trail to Sedalia wound through unfamiliar forests, which made the longhorns of the open range stampede. And it crossed over new Missouri farm land, where protesting "nesters," as the cowboys called the settlers, came rushing out with their guns. Moreover, most of the horse Indians, though nominally on their reservations, still roamed the plains. In the end, only a few of the Texas

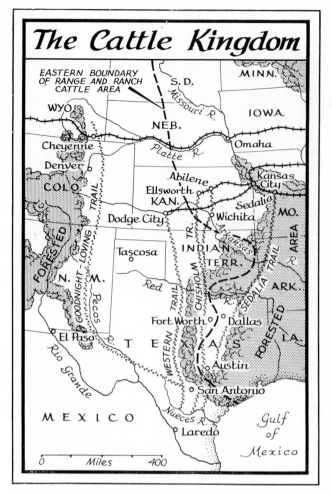

The Cattle Kingdom

EASTERN BOUNDARY OF RANGE AND RANCH CATTLE AREA

S.D.

MINN.

WYO.

Missouri R.

IOWA

NEB.

Cheyenne

Omaha

Denver

COLO.

Platte R.

Abilene

Kansas City

Ellsworth

KAN.

Sedalia

MO.

Dodge City

Wichita

Tascosa

INDIAN

TERR.

ARK.

N.M.

Red

Pecos R.

Fort Worth

Dallas

Rio Grande

T E X A S

FORESTED

LA.

El Paso

Austin

San Antonio

MEXICO

Nueces R.

Laredo

Gulf of Mexico

GOODNIGHT-LOVING TRAIL

FORESTED

WESTERN TRAIL

CHISHOLM TRAIL

SEDALIA TRAIL

Arkansas R.

0 Miles 400

and barns, stables, pens, and loading chutes. In 1868, Abilene received 75,000 head of cattle, and the figure boomed to a peak of 700,000 in 1871, the record for a long time to come.

Gradually, the Kansas Pacific was extended westward across Kansas, and with each advance a new cow town sprang up. Wichita and Ellsworth, Kansas, which succeeded Abilene, received over a million head between 1872 and 1875. Next came the fabulous Dodge City, to which another million head were driven between 1876 and 1879. In the meantime, on the Union Pacific route, first Cheyenne and then Laramie became important cattle-receiving railheads.

The "long drive" has become a romantic chapter in the fable of the West, but it was actually more hazardous than glamorous. The cowboys went out in groups of six, working for $24 to $40 a month. Equipped only with cow ponies, lassos, and six-shooters, they tried to keep safe and under control a thousand head of hungry, thirsty, touchy steers for two months of grueling travel. "It was tiresome grimy business for the attendant punchers," writes one of the veterans of the drive, "who travelled ever in a cloud of dust, and heard little but the constant chorus from the crackling of hoofs and of ankle joints, from the bellows, lows, and bleats of the trudging animals."

Since even the drive to the nearest railhead did grown steers little good, it became the practice in the 1870's to drive young Texas steers out to graze on the northern range in western Kansas and Nebraska, and in Colorado, Wyoming, Montana, and the Dakotas—the area where the buffalo herds were being obliterated. With the buffalo went the Indians' food supply, and with the food supply went the Indians themselves. Now the northern "feeders" could buy longhorns and other breeds, and fatten them on the lush grass of the open public range until they were ready for market at four to five years of age. As time went on, the best cows and bulls were culled from the herds, and the breeds were constantly improved. The open-range cattle industry came into its own after

steers ever got to Sedalia. But those that did brought $35 a head, a price that encouraged many ranchers to try again next year.

By that time, an enterprising Illinois meat-dealer, Joseph G. McCoy, realized that he could make a fortune if he could establish a convenient meeting point for northern buyers and Texan and western breeders. In working out his scheme, he approached, unsuccessfully, the Missouri Pacific Railroad for special low rates on bulk shipments of cattle to the East. Then he turned to the Kansas Pacific, which was advancing through Kansas. This time he was successful, and he set about devising a link farther east. The Hannibal and St. Jo Railroad, which ran from Kansas City to Chicago, was the answer. McCoy then chose Abilene, Kansas, on the Kansas Pacific route, as a meeting place for ranchers and packers. There he built a hotel,

1878, when the distressing Panic of 1873 had run its course and beef prices had revived. For the next seven or eight years, it was one of the most profitable industries in the country.

Like the isolated mining centers, the range too had to make its own laws. Here the need for water was vital, and "range rights" along a stream became the most precious part of a cattleman's ranch. Local regulations had the force of law in determining the extent of each man's or company's "range rights," but claims often had to be backed up with the six-shooter. Even where the ranchers respected one another's territory, the cattle did not. Here again rules had to be established for recording brands and for disposing of "mavericks." Rustling, of course, became very common, and could be resisted only with the greatest difficulty. Since the ranches covered as many as 30 or 40 square miles, they could not be policed efficiently. It was easy enough to spirit the cattle away, and, once in possession, rustlers found it simple to alter the brand markings.

The enforcement of rude justice was one

of the main objectives of the numerous stock-growers' associations that were organized on the plains in the 1870's. Eventually, these groups developed a hidden government in the territories that were being cut from the range. One of their more important business objectives, however, was to forestall competition by making it very difficult for newcomers to become members, and by making it dangerous for them to operate without joining up. These objectives grew out of an awareness of the speed with which the range, endless though it seemed, could become disastrously overstocked.

In spite of all the stock-growers' efforts, news soon leaked out about how five-dollar steers could be transformed into property worth $45 to $60 a head, with only the investment of four years of free grazing. Prospective ranchers flocked in, like the prospectors hurrying to the mines. So many young steers were bought for grazing that between 1882 and 1884 as many were shipped north to the range as were shipped east to the

Texas longhorn cattle arriving at Dodge City, Kansas, 1878.

market. When anticipated profits actually materialized, ranchers and large investors set up corporations to buy more and more steers and graze them on the free range.

Profits of 40 and 50 per cent were common in the early 80's. By 1885, however, the range had finally become overcrowded, and the disastrous winter of 1885-1886, followed by a blistering summer, destroyed most of the feed and cattle. The steers that did find their way to market were of such poor quality that beef prices crashed, despite the intense shortage. It was at this time that the sheep herders began to cross the range in large numbers. Their flocks, which tainted the water and made the atmosphere noxious to cows and cowboys alike, ate not only the grass but the roots themselves, leaving in their wake wide swaths of barren range. To add to the stock-growers' misery, the farmers began homesteading the plains and fencing in the open range. Many of these farmers kept their own herds on fenced fields, where they could control breeding more carefully and regulate the feed. The beef that they produced was far higher in quality than any

that could be produced on the open range. In 1882, range beef commanded $9.35 a hundred pounds in Chicago; by 1887, the price had fallen to $1.90.

The cowboys were beginning to sing mournfully:

> I little dreamed what would happen
>> Some twenty summers hence
> When the nester came with his wife
>> and kids,
>> His dogs and his barbed-wire fence.

The West had indeed changed. One open-range cowboy working on a fenced-in ranch had this to say in the late 1880's:

I remember when we sat around the fire the winter through and didn't do a lick of work for five or six months of the year, except to chop a little wood to build a fire to keep warm by. Now we go on the general roundup, then the calf roundup, then comes haying—something that the old-time cowboy never dreamed of—then the beef roundup and the fall calf roundup and gathering bulls and weak cows, and after all this a winter of feeding hay. I tell you times have changed.

The end of the open range brought an end to the last frontier.

III.   THE FARMER ON THE PLAINS

Settling the Land.   "These fellows from Ohio, Indiana, and other northern and western states," an old trail-driver complained in the 'seventies, "—the 'bone and sinew of the country,' as politicians call them—have made farms, enclosed pastures, and fenced in water holes until you can't rest; and I say D—n such bone and sinew!" Although the cattlemen were just on the verge of their greatest boom, revolutionary agricultural developments were to make that boom their last. Perhaps the most important of these changes was the development of barbed-wire fencing, first patented by three different inventors in 1874. One cattleman expressed the feelings of all when he wished that the "man who invented barbed wire had it all around him in a ball and the ball rolled into hell."

Although the Homestead Act of 1862 (see p. 382) opened the West to free settlement under liberal conditions, much of the best land was appropriated before the homesteaders could get to it. And certain other circumstances, having to do with both the law and the land itself, further restricted the act's usefulness. For example, the quarter-section (160 acres) offered by the act, though suitable for the Mississippi Valley, and lavish for New England (the two areas from which most of the proponents of the measure came), was either too large or too small for the arid, treeless plains. For the small settler, the cost of breaking enough of the 160 acres to get a paying crop, plus the cost of irrigation, buildings, equipment, taxes, and hired help, were prohibitive; in 1871, the Department of Agriculture estimated that wood fencing alone for such a farm would cost $1,000. For the large farmer or farming corporation, on the other hand, willing to use the costly new machinery so well fitted to the broad expanse of the plains, a quarter-section hardly justified the investment.

Belated recognition of these problems prompted the passage of the Timber Culture Act of 1873. On the theory that trees brought rain, this act offered an additional quarter-section to the settler who would put at least 40 acres of it into timber. Settlers failed to comply with the terms of the act, however, and it was repealed in 1891.

Two other measures, passed ostensibly to stimulate settlement of the West by farmers, actually worked to keep them out. One was the Desert Land Act of 1877. This act allowed a settler to occupy 640 acres on payment of 25 cents an acre; the holder could win clear title to the land in three years for an additional payment of $1 an acre, provided he could prove he had irrigated the plot. Thousands of farmers agreed to try to irrigate the land, but the job proved too difficult and most of them gave up long before the three years had expired. The Desert Land Act was really a ruse used by the cattlemen to win private title to the once-open grazing range. They registered thousands of acres in the names of cowhands and then, to prove that they had irrigated the land, they got the cowhands to testify that they "had seen water on the claim."

The second measure was the Timber and Stone Act of 1878, an attempt by the lumbermen to wrest public lands for themselves. It offered a maximum of 160 acres of rich timber land—land "unfit for cultivation"—in California, Nevada, Oregon, and Washington at $2.50 an acre, "about the price of one good log," as the historian Ray Allen Billington has commented. Since even aliens who had done no more than file their first citizenship papers were eligible for these grants, a land-office business was set up right in the waterfront courthouses. In return for on-the-spot bonuses ranging from $10 to $50, thousands of alien seamen were induced to register claims and then to sign them over to lumber-company agents.

All told, between 1862 and 1900, 80 million acres were registered under the Homestead Act, and this figure includes many dummy registrations used by speculators in accumulating large holdings. During the same period, railroads, land companies, and states receiving grants of federal land under the Morrill Act of 1862 (see p. 382) sold at least five or six times as many millions of acres to settlers. For these lands they charged from $2 to $10 an acre, a fair enough range for the best sites near transportation facilities and markets. The purchasers, moreover, often got credit for equipment as well as land from companies that were eager to sell.

After 1868, when the Union Pacific was nearly ready for passengers, Kansas and other states on the edge of the frontier were placarded with railroad advertisements calling their lands "Better than a Homestead." Henceforth every land-grant railroad had both its Land Department and its Bureau of Immigration. In the 1870's, the Union Pacific and the Burlington railroads each spent over $1 million in advertising their lands abroad, often in spectacular fashion. Other railroads and land companies advertised nearly as widely, and most of them had London offices and agents scouring the Continent for settlers. Their efforts were supplemented by bureaus of immigration that were set up by the western states that had land to sell, and by steamship companies that were engaged in the transportation of immigrants to the New World.

These land-sales campaigns were remarkably successful. According to the 1880 census, 73 per cent of Wisconsin's population was of foreign parentage, 71 per cent of Minnesota's, 66 per cent of the Dakotas', and 44 per cent of Nebraska's. Thereafter, "American fever" rose to epidemic proportions all over Europe. In the ten-year period from 1880 to 1889, a record total of 4,640,000 European immigrants landed in the United

States; in 1882 alone, almost 650,000 came in. Large numbers of these immigrants remained in the teeming ports of entry, and thousands of others got no farther west than the mills of Pittsburgh and Cleveland (see p. 479). But millions of them found their way to the farmlands of the plains. Between 1860 and 1900, the land held by American farmers more than doubled, from 407 to 841 million acres, and the proportion of land actually under cultivation rose from 40 to almost 50 per cent.

Plains Farming. Before the new settlers of the plains could transform the country into farmland, they had to overcome many forbidding obstacles. Since they were unable to build even rude log cabins on the treeless plains, their first shelters were dank and dark sod huts. The lack of wood also presented a fuel problem in a region that covered some of the coldest parts of the United States. At first, the settlers burned dried buffalo dung; then hay became a common fuel, in special stoves designed to burn it slowly. But nothing proved really satisfactory until the railroads brought coal out to the plains.

The dryness of the region, which increased as settlers moved farther and farther west, offered even greater difficulties, especially to families who settled at a distance from the infrequent rivers. Mechanical well-digging equipment was not in use until the 1880's. Even when wells could be dug the necessary 200 or 300 feet, there remained the problem of getting the water to the surface. Windmills that harnessed the power of the strong prevailing breezes promised to provide an answer in the 1870's, but other approaches to the problem helped matters before windmills became cheap enough for the average farmer. The water shortage made life hard, and especially retarded wheat-growing. One solution, which is still rather undependable and costly, was "dry farming." With this system, a field is harrowed after each precious rainfall in order to retard evaporation and help the roots to store whatever water they have captured.

The scarcity of water was only one of the problems involved in cultivating this virgin land. The tough sod of the plains, as we have seen, resisted the old-fashioned plow. John Deere's steel plow (see p. 315) was a great improvement, but it remained expensive. In 1868, James Oliver of Indiana began the improvements in the chilled-iron plow which by 1877 had made it a cheap, versatile, and efficient tool. As time went on, the plowshares were mounted on a sulky and their number was increased, so that several furrows could be cut at once. The way was open for the mechanical tractor of today. By 1874, grain drills had been designed to mechanize planting. In a region battered by hail storms, wind storms, and sudden frosts, however, the factor that limited a farmer's production was not how much he could plant but how much he could harvest. Speed and labor-saving economy were essential. The "cord binder" supplied the first satisfactory answer (see p. 316). This device permitted two men and a team of horses to harvest 20 acres of wheat a day. Whereas the old-time eastern farmer dared not plant more than eight acres of wheat in a season, by 1890 one western farmer could count on harvesting 135 acres.

But there had to be a revolution in the grain industry before such a wheat harvest became worth while. Eastern wheat farmers grew soft-kernel winter wheat, which was traditionally milled by grinding the husks between two millstones. Easterners usually planted their crop in September or October, and harvested it in June or July. The first farmers in Wisconsin and Minnesota found that the early winters killed the seed before it could sprout. And on the open plains, the winters proved even more severe. Moreover, the moisture needed for the soft winter wheats was lacking here.

Spring wheat, planted in May and harvested before the first frosts, had been known to farmers before 1860. But the known varieties lacked hardiness and, worse, their tough husks could not be milled economically. In

Frederic Remington sketched this picture of his Kansas ranch in 1883.

the 1860's, after a long journey from Poland via Scotland and Canada, a new type of hard spring wheat appeared on the plains, and by the end of the decade a new process for milling the hard grain had been brought over from Hungary. This process employed a series of revolving rollers instead of the old mill-stones. In 1872 or 1873, settlers from the Crimea introduced into Kansas a hard *winter* wheat known as "Turkey Red." This too became commercially manageable through the new milling process.

Both these hard wheats soon proved profitable to the millers and popular with the bakers. The new milling process, perfected by the development of chilled-steel corru-gated rollers in 1879, permitted a much higher yield of good flour, and the high gluten content permitted more bread to be made from it than from equal amounts of soft-wheat flour. In 1879, Illinois, the lead-ing wheat state for 20 years, was still in first place; but by 1899 it had fallen out of the first ten, which were dominated by the hard-wheat states of Minnesota, the Dakotas, Kansas, California, and Nebraska. Oklahoma and northern Texas also were being rapidly developed.

During the 1870's, the farmers grew more and more insistent in their demands that the ranchers fence in their cattle; the ranchers either urged the "nesters" to move out alto-gether, or else demanded that they bear the high cost of building fences to keep the cattle out. This sharp hostility between the groups often led to open gun battles on the plains. When fencing became cheap enough for the farmer to buy, the days of the rancher were numbered.

Joseph F. Glidden, one of three independ-ent holders of the patent on barbed wire, set up the first barbed-wire factory in DeKalb, Illinois, in November, 1874. The next year, Glidden's eastern supplier of ordinary wire bought a half-interest in the firm and in 1876 began mass production. That year, 3 million pounds of barbed wire were sold at about $20 per hundred pounds; within four years, sales had zoomed to 80 million pounds, and the price had been cut to $10 per hundred. By 1890, the price was down to $4, and much of the arable land of the plains had been fenced in, most of it for wheat-growing.

After a disastrous series of grasshopper invasions in the early 1870's, everything conspired to make the new wheat country appear to be the El Dorado that the adver-tisements pictured. After 1875, Europe suf-fered one famine after another, and the widespread hardship was heightened by the Russo-Turkish War of 1877-1878, which closed Russia's ports and left the rest of the Continent increasingly dependent on Ameri-can grain. All the great improvements in American farm technology coincided with the opening of the new European market—

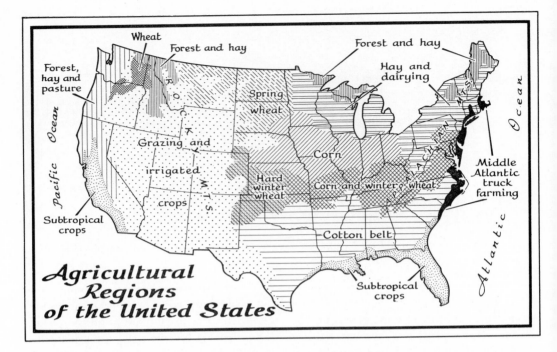

Agricultural Regions of the United States

a market that was to continue to expand, since the countries of western Europe were turning away from farming toward industry, and the populous manufacturing cities that were growing up had to be fed. Then there was the chance factor that for eight years before 1886 the plains enjoyed such plentiful rainfall that the characteristic aridity of the region appeared to have ended.

So American agricultural production boomed. And with the seemingly limitless demand, prices remained steady. Over the whole decade from 1866 to 1875, the average annual price of wheat had been $1.24; in the following decade the average price was still 92 cents. Such prices encouraged

expansion; it became the fashion to take over more and more good land before the next fellow got it, by mortgaging one's farm to the limit. And the banks themselves, as optimistic as the rest, interpreted this limit liberally.

Wise heads knew that the West was riding for a fall; over-production in the United States by the mid-1880's, the entry of India and Australia into the world wheat market, the revival of Russian wheat production, the rise of tariff barriers in Europe, all were ill omens. Yet just as buffalo had drawn the Indian to the virgin West, as gold had drawn the prospector, and grass the rancher, so wheat had drawn the farmer. But he alone had come to stay.

Readings

Ray A. Billington, *Westward Expansion* (1949), has informative and admirably organized sections on each of the themes discussed in this chapter. Useful also is Allan Nevins, *Emergence of Modern America, 1865-1878* (1927). Walter P. Webb, *The Great Plains* (1931), and James C. Malin, *The Grassland of North America* (1948), are two extraordinarily imaginative studies that add greatly to our understanding of the relationship between the natural environment and social life.

Literally millions of words have been written about the Indians. A moving account of Indian life is found in John C. Collier, *Indians of the Americas* (1947). A more specialized study is Helen Hunt Jackson, *A Century of Dishonor* (1881), which is a passionate indictment of Indian policy to that date. Informative also are Paul Radin,

The Story of the American Indian (1927), and G. B. Grinnell, *The Story of the Indian* (1895).

The standard study of the mining country is T. A. Rickard, *A History of American Mining* (1932). Useful also is W. J. Trimble, *The Mining Advance into the Inland Empire* (1914). More colorful are Glenn C. Quiett, *Pay Dirt, a Panorama of American Gold Rushes* (1936), and Charles H. Shinn, *The Story of the Mine* (1896), which is mainly the story of the Comstock Lode. Shinn also wrote a solid work called *Mining Camps: A Study in American Frontier Government* (1885; reprint 1948). Mark Twain, *Roughing It* (2 vols., 1872), is the great writer's stirring account of Nevada days. J. V. Frederick, *Ben Holladay, the Stagecoach King* (1940), is informative on transportation before the coming of the railroad, as are Arthur Chapman, *The Pony Express* (1932), and LeRoy R. Hafen, *The Overland Mail, 1849-1869* (1926).

Three sound general works on the cattle kingdom are Ernest S. Osgood, *The Day of the Cattleman* (1929); Edward E. Dale, *The Range Cattle Industry* (1930); and Louis Pelzer, *The Cattlemen's Frontier* (1936). On the cowboy himself, Andy Adams, *Log of a Cowboy* (1903), and P. A. Rollins, *The Cowboy* (1922), are well worth reading. Enlightening on the bad men and the coming of law and order to the West is Wayne Gard, *Frontier Justice* (1949).

Fred A. Shannon, *The Farmer's Last Frontier: Agriculture, 1860-1897* (1945), is a scholarly analysis of the settlement of the West and the transition from ranching to farming. On the distribution and sale of the western domain, useful accounts may be found in Roy M. Robbins, *Our Landed Heritage* (1942); B. H. Hibbard, *A History of the Public Land Policies* (1924); and Aaron M. Sakolski, *The Great American Land Bubble* (1932). On pioneer farm life, Everett Dick, *The Sod-House Frontier, 1854-1890* (1937), and Mari Sandoz, *Old Jules* (1935), present detailed and dramatic stories. Very revealing also are the novels of Ole Rölvaag, especially *Giants in the Earth* (1929), and Willa Cather's *O Pioneers!* (1913), and *My Ántonia* (1918).

AN INDUSTRIAL NATION

C H A P T E R   T W E N T Y

In the year 1890, the Superintendent of the United States census made one of the most unnerving announcements in American history:

Up to and including 1880 [he wrote] the country had a frontier of settlement, but at present the unsettled area has been so broken into ... that there can hardly be said to be a frontier line. In the discussion of its extent, its westward movement, etc., it cannot, therefore, any longer have a place in the census reports.

Throughout its history the open spaces of the American continent had stood as evidence to the world of free opportunity in American society. Now civilization had closed the moving frontier and an epoch in American life was ending. Yet the United States survived the closing of the land frontier, and its rate of industrial growth thereafter completely overshadowed the progress that had been made in all the preceding decades of conquest in the West.

456

I.   NEW FRONTIERS FOR OLD

To many Americans, the announcement by the Superintendent of the census was hardly news. As early as 1881, the New York *Tribune* printed a letter from a correspondent who wrote that America's resources had all been claimed, and who advised, "The nation has reached a point in its growth where its policy should be to preserve its heritage for coming generations, not to donate it to all the strangers we can induce to come among us." The following year, in response to organized agitation in many parts of the country, Congress took its first tentative steps toward sealing the ports of the United States against foreign settlers (see p. 479). Foreigners themselves also seem to have sensed the decline of American confidence in expansion and opportunity. In 1880, 1881, and 1882, a record number of immigrants had reached the United States each year, and in the three years combined nearly 2 million newcomers had entered the country. Thereafter, though the annual figures showed ups and downs more or less corresponding with the business cycle, immigration fell off to a 20-year low of 229,000 in 1898. This shrinkage can hardly be attributed to the enforcement, which was spotty indeed, of the early exclusion acts.

So closely had Americans and immigrants associated land with freedom and space with opportunity, that few were aware of the new frontiers that were beckoning American enterprise and ingenuity just when the last of the old frontiers was disappearing. In the 1880's, free farm land was growing relatively scarce, the open range had been fenced in, much of the virgin forest had been reduced to unsightly stretches of stumps or burned-over deserts, and fabulously rich mining regions of the recent past were marked only by ghost towns.

Yet once Americans had breached the new frontiers of science, technology, and business management, the resources of the country were made to yield wealth and riches far beyond the dreams even of the most optimistic prospectors and promoters of the 1860's and 1870's. The old frontier had pitted men against raw nature, and its extension westward had brought more casualties than Americans care to count. The new frontiers more often pitted man against man, more often demanded the leadership of the few and the discipline of the many. The casualties on the new frontiers usually were counted in business defeats and financial failures rather than in deaths, but these casualties were often as harrowing as those that had marked the breaching of the frontiers of old. The conquests on the new frontiers insured the United States world industrial supremacy.

II.   THE RAILROADS AND THE PUBLIC

The Network Completed.   The movement of Americans to the West in the later decades of the nineteenth century often ran ahead of the railroad, just as it had in the decades before the Civil War. The fact that the last frontier was disappearing in the 1880's did not mean that the newer settlements were as yet in close touch with the rest of the country. Plenty of open space still remained to be conquered by transportation and communication. As railroads were extended westward, they once again quickened the business activity of the entire country and spurred new railroad building in the older sections as well.

On the eve of the Panic of 1873, there were about 70,000 miles of railroad in the United States. In the next 20 years, though two periods of depression had intervened, an unbelievable 100,000 more miles of track were laid, bringing the total on the eve of the crash of 1893 to about 170,000 miles. By this time, the development of our railroad grid was virtually completed. By 1900, another 23,000 miles of rail had been laid, mainly to fill out the existing systems.

Much of the western railroad building in the 1870's and 1880's was undertaken by old-fashioned plungers of the Huntington-Gould school, who were determined to make their fortunes by any means other than providing efficient service. They bribed congressmen and local officials in order to get lavish land grants and other government assistance; they operated construction companies that channeled exorbitant construc-

tion charges into their own pockets; they speculated on Wall Street in the securities of their own and competitive roads; and they promoted flimsy, fly-by-night enterprises parallel to important lines and then threatened the latter with such severe competition that they would be forced to buy out the new enterprises at the promoter's own price.

The unrivaled master of these tactics was Jay Gould himself. After selling out his Erie securities for millions in cash on the eve of the Panic of 1873, Gould soon began buying up the depressed securities of the Union Pacific. Having won virtual control of this great transcontinental by 1878, Gould proceeded to buy up other western roads, including the shaky Kansas Pacific, which paralleled the Union Pacific from Denver east to Kansas City. By threatening to extend the Kansas Pacific west from Denver to

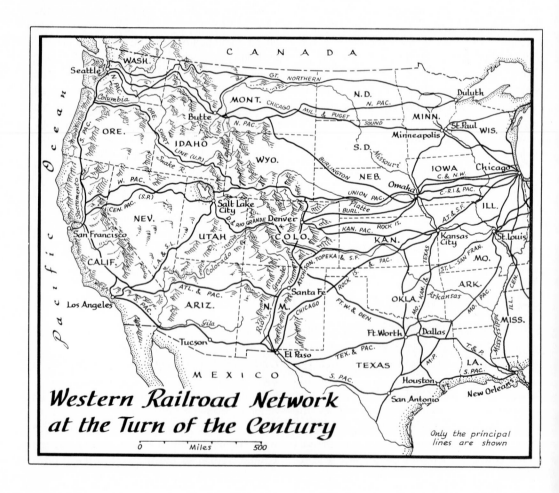

Western Railroad Network
at the Turn of the Century

0   Miles   500

Only the principal lines are shown

Salt Lake City, where it would find the Central Pacific ready to carry its cars all the way to California, Gould early in 1880 forced the directors of the Union Pacific to buy the Kansas Pacific from him. He had bought into the Kansas Pacific at under $10 a share; he sold out at over $90. Having unloaded the Kansas Pacific, Gould also foisted on the Union Pacific, on terms no less favorable to himself than the Kansas Pacific deal had been, many of his other western roads.

While he was milking the Union Pacific for his personal profit, Gould began quietly selling off his own U.P. stock at high prices before news of the true state of the road's gutted finances could leak out. Before ridding himself of his remaining U.P. shares in 1883, Gould set up a number of new branches which were paid for by the issuance of $10 million in new Union Pacific stock between 1880 and 1883. A goodly portion of the proceeds from these issues found its way to Gould's pocket through a quarter-interest he held in the construction company that built one of the new branches, the Denver & South Park. In speaking of this branch, a later president of the Union Pacific told a congressional investigating committee in 1887: "The chief source of revenue . . . was in carrying men and material into Colorado to dig holes in the ground called mines, and until it was discovered that there was nothing in these mines, the business was immense."

Gould's toying with the Union Pacific appears only to have engaged his right hand. With his left, he pushed his way into Huntington's Southern Pacific. His weapon was a pasted-up system of southwestern roads, the key parts of which were the Missouri Pacific, which tied Kansas City to St. Louis, where it met the Pennsylvania and other trunk lines running to the Atlantic; the Missouri, Kansas and Texas (well-known as the "Katy" line), which ran from near Kansas City to Dallas; and the Texas and Pacific, which since 1877 had been building west from Dallas toward El Paso. By 1881, El Paso had become the Southern Pacific's eastern terminal. Faced with the threat that the Texas and Pacific might cut off his path through Texas, Huntington hastened to make a traffic-sharing and rate-fixing agreement with Gould in 1881. Thereafter Gould himself played an increasingly important role in the development of the Southern Pacific's power in California.

Gould's own system, meanwhile, dominated the Southwest to the east of California. Most of the roads that made up this system had been poorly constructed, and throughout the 1880's Gould added many miles to them that were of no better quality. In fact, they had been laid mainly to provide Wall Street with signs of activity and progress. By 1890, Gould was in control of about 9,000 miles of railroad in the Southwest, nearly half the total mileage of the section, and he held the shippers of his domain in bondage.

The other major system in the Southwest was the Atchison, Topeka, and Santa Fe, which had been chartered by Kansas in 1859 with the modest aim of connecting Atchison, Kansas, with the state capital at Topeka. As a result of an extensive land grant in 1863 and the railroad construction craze after the Civil War, the Santa Fe's promoters gradually acquired transcontinental ambitions. It was to shut the Santa Fe out of California before it reached Needles on the Arizona border, that the Southern Pacific had grasped the two best southern passes through the Sierras in 1881 (see p. 417). In 1883, the Santa Fe was permitted to enter California over Southern Pacific track on terms favorable to the Huntington-Gould coalition. In 1885, the Santa Fe worked out a route of its own to San Diego; but its freedom was short-lived, for the following year its charter fell to Huntington and Gould. Under their aegis, the road was quickly consolidated with others, and by 1888 it had made connections with far-off Chicago. By then, the Santa Fe had grown into a 7,000-mile system. More striking was the fact that 2,000 of these miles had been built between 1886 and

Railroad building on the Great Plains in the 1870's.

1888, not to meet any transportation needs but simply to saturate strategic railroad territory and to kill off the competition of the roads already there.

The Union Pacific and the old Central Pacific occupied the central transcontinental route, and the Southern Pacific and the Santa Fe held two southerly routes. But the great Northwest was also the scene of vast transcontinental enterprises. One of these, the Northern Pacific, was as speculative as any. Although in 1864 the promoters of the Northern Pacific received the most lavish of all federal land grants, running to some 40 million acres, they failed to attract construction capital. Not until 1869, when the buoyant Jay Cooke took up the charter, was progress made. Even so, construction had scarcely got under way when the Panic of 1873 crushed the House of Cooke and all its works. Construction was resumed under new auspices in 1875; but only after Henry

Villard had captured the Northern Pacific in 1881 was it pushed onward to Portland, Oregon, and then, by 1883, to Tacoma, Washington.

An educated German, Villard had come to America in the 1850's and had found his way into finance through journalism. In the middle 1870's, he had become attracted to the Oregon region, and with old-country financing proceeded to develop its resources and transportation. In 1879, he organized his holdings in the Oregon Railway and Navigation Company. At that time, the Northern Pacific was approaching Oregon, and its backers hoped to reach Portland the cheap way by tying in with Villard's existing track. The next year, however, they interested the New York bankers, Drexel, Morgan and Company, in their project and floated a $40 million bond issue with which to finance construction of their own entry into Villard country. On seeing a prospective collaborator turn into a threat, Villard began to fight fire with fire. Working up a $20 million fund of his own, he proceeded to capture the Northern Pacific itself by means of extraordinary yet well-concealed Wall Street maneuvers.

Thereafter, though construction of the Northern Pacific progressed, Villard dissipated its resources in financial fights during which he was alternately in and out of control. Among his enemies were Huntington and Gould, who considered the entire West coast, if not indeed the entire West, as their private bailiwick. In the background, moreover, sat James J. Hill, who had ideas of his own about the Pacific Northwest and how to build and run a railroad.

Hill had come to St. Paul from Canada as a young man in 1856, and at the end of 20 years had risen no higher than a transportation agent handling the transshipment of Mississippi River cargo between the United States and Canada. He had also become something of a town character—"that Hill," as he was called—with all his talk about the future of the Northwest. Hill's chance came after the crash of 1873 had left the grandiosely named St. Paul and Pacific Railroad—it ran only about 200 miles west from St. Paul—in bad shape. After biding his time, Hill with his tall talk won the help of Canadian financiers in acquiring the road in 1878. In 1889, it took the name of Great Northern. By then, with little government assistance, Hill and his backers had pushed construction 2,775 miles west through Minnesota, North Dakota, and Montana, and up to Winnipeg in Canada. In 1893, the Great Northern reached Puget Sound, Hill's goal from the start.

The Great Northern paralleled Villard's Northern Pacific to the south. When Villard's road reached the West coast in 1883, Hill was not nearly so discouraged as some of his partners. "I think the time is at hand," he wrote, "when railway property generally will be tested by its capacity to pay net earnings. . . . I think the Northern Pacific will have its greatest trial when . . . its finances are no longer sustained by sales of

bonds, but all payments must be made from earnings." Hill was right.

From the very start, Hill had insisted on constructing the Great Northern track and roadbed with the best materials available. He had also chosen to build around mountains rather than over them. Not only did this approach greatly reduce the cost of construction (an objective abhorred by the construction-company type of promoter, whose purpose was to spend as much as possible), but it also reduced operating costs once a road was built. The Great Northern's long trains and heavy trainloads, which neither the track nor the mountainous routes of other western roads could carry, became the wonder of the railroad world. The proof of Hill's policies came in 1893 when the Great Northern alone of all the transcontinentals survived the crash and the depression that followed.

In the next decade, the Great Northern not only acquired the Northern Pacific—which had been reorganized with the aid of J. P. Morgan in 1898—but with Morgan's collaboration Hill had also gained control of the strategic Chicago, Burlington & Quincy, the best entry to Chicago from the west. The Burlington acquisition touched off a bitter fight between Hill and Edward H. Harriman, as great and thorough a railroad man as Hill himself, who had eyed the Burlington for his own purposes. As a young man, Harriman had worked his way up in Wall Street and was thoroughly attuned to its operations. In the 1880's, he had gained control of the Illinois Central, and in 1895, with Illinois Central support, he had won control of the Union Pacific. In 1900, at Collis Huntington's death (Gould had died eight years earlier), Harriman acquired 45 per cent of the stock of the Southern Pacific. Harriman's backers were the bankers, Kuhn, Loeb and Company, who themselves enjoyed the financial confidence of the Rockefeller Standard Oil crowd, which had long been looking for likely outlets for its millions. Thus the stage was set and the parts assigned—Kuhn, Loeb; Rockefeller; Harriman; and the National City Bank versus Morgan, Hill, and the First National Bank—for the great financial contests of the twentieth century, with control of the western, and indeed the national, railroad network as the prize.

Reform and Regulation. While Hill was giving the railroad men of the Far West lessons in railroad construction, management, and responsibility—lessons they were reluctant to learn—some of the roads in the older sections had also begun to mend their lines and their ways. Speculative and selfish management, of course, persisted for a long time. One of the worst examples was the so-called Richmond Terminal system, which, between 1881 and 1891, had built and consolidated a network of southern railroads embracing over 8,500 miles of track. The leading figure in the manipulation of this system was a small-time Jay Gould named Calvin S. Brice. A little farther to the north was the B. & O., which for years before going into receivership in 1896 had been paying excessive dividends to the Garrett family (owners of most of the stock) even while traffic languished and the track and rolling stock fell apart. Nor were the Garretts too proud to keep a false set of books for the benefit of the inquisitive—minority stockholders included. Still farther north, the episode of the West Shore Railroad unfolded.

The West Shore had been built in the most shoddy fashion on the west shore of the Hudson simply to blackmail the Vanderbilts into buying it at an exorbitant price to forestall competition with their own New York Central. By 1885, it was ready for business. Vanderbilt appealed to J. P. Morgan to find a way out of the difficulty. Morgan discovered that the Pennsylvania Railroad had had a hand in encouraging the West Shore adventurers, but he also found that Vanderbilt had secretly pushed the Philadelphia and Reading to compete with

the main line of the Pennsylvania. Morgan settled the issue by arranging for the Central to buy out the West Shore at cost and to sell to the Pennsylvania the Central's interest in the Philadelphia and Reading.

Such incidents and some even worse continued to crop up in railroad history. More important were the great improvements, extensions, and legitimate consolidations that marked many of the eastern and midwestern railroads before the crash of 1893. The most far-reaching improvement of all was the introduction of the steel rail. As late as 1880, though Carnegie and others had been producing steel rails in massive quantities for almost a decade (see p. 467), only 30 per cent of the American railroad mileage was made of steel. By 1890, the proportion had climbed to 80 per cent. Steel rails could bear ten or fifteen times the weight of iron rails and still last twenty times as long. They made possible the use of stronger locomotives, larger freight cars, and speedier schedules, and assured safer and more reliable service.

A related development was the double-tracking and quadruple-tracking of thousands of miles of busy routes. In this undertaking, the New York Central showed the way, but the Pennsylvania, the Erie, and the Illinois Central were not far behind. These lines also laid much new track in order to extend their service to an ever-widening list of cities and towns that were growing busy enough to warrant railroad service. After 1875, moreover, "through service" at last began to take on the smoothness and co-ordination that had merely been promised in earlier years. In addition, clean and often elegant dining cars were added to many long-distance passenger trains, sleepers were continuously improved, and terminals and stations, once open sheds or mere platforms, were becoming carefully planned architectural façades for roads that had begun to take pride in their names and emblems.

Yet none of these improvements seems to have muffled the cry for railroad regulation and reform which swept across the country especially after the Panic of 1873, and which gathered new intensity after 1884 when another panic forced many speculative roads to the wall. It is usually believed that the farmers of the West, who were so dependent on the railroads to get their produce to market and to get it there in season, led the demand for railroad regulation. And so they may have (see p. 496). But many other elements in American society made the cry for reform almost universal.

In the late 1870's and throughout the 1880's, *average* railroad freight rates were steadily pummeled down by the fierce competition for traffic. The trouble was that the *average* rates included suicidally low ones at some railroad junctions, and compensatory high ones where the absence of competition made it possible to charge what the traffic would bear. This satisfied no one, least of all the railroads. Among shippers at competitive points, any attempt to raise the low rates aroused animosity; and any attempt to eliminate competition by agreements—or "pools"—among the roads serving such points, or by their consolidation, was likely to produce an angry outcry. Naturally, shippers at monopoly points where the rates were high suffered in competition with shippers more favorably located. The most antagonistic of these shippers were situated at monopoly points along railroads that terminated at competitive points. These shippers often had to pay more for short hauls along a small portion of the road than shippers at the terminals paid for long hauls across the road's entire length.

As we have seen in connection with John D. Rockefeller and the Standard Oil Company, the railroads often were willing to make special concessions to powerful shippers, usually in the form of rebates from the posted rates. But the secrecy by which this practice had to be carried on was a burden even to those who profited from it; to those who were discriminated against, the practice was a fence upon which their little enterprises often were impaled.

Rate policy was only one source of enmity to the railroads. Another was their dividend policy. Always eager for capital, the roads sought to maintain liberal dividend payments in order to attract investors. The investors, in turn, were always eager for a quick and bountiful return. In the early 1880's, rash railroad managements sometimes paid dividends as high as 100 per cent; often they paid somewhat lower dividends even when the roads failed to earn them. Such policies could lead only to the end of both the dividends and the investments. When this happened, the investors cried that they had been tricked and cheated.

The unsavory way in which many of the leading railroads had won their charters from Congress and state governments, and their land grants and other assistance as well, added many disinterested persons to their list of enemies. Still others were alienated by the fierce armed wars that sometimes flared up between roads fighting for a favorable mountain pass or other piece of ground, and by the Wall Street manipulations that frequently caused unexpected flurries in the entire market and brought ruin to innocent investors as well as to those who tried to outsmart the insiders by speculating in railroad securities.

Beginning as early as the 1860's, all these circumstances had brought vociferous and swelling demands for railroad investigations, railroad reform, railroad regulation. The first railroad regulatory commission was set up in Massachusetts in 1869, with Charles Francis Adams, Jr., at its head. It had no punitive powers but only the right to investigate and make public any railroad abuses. Thereafter, reformers in most of the other states tried to win legislation setting up similar bodies or stronger ones. The railroads fought this growing agitation by spending large sums of money and employing some of the country's best legal talent. "War," said the English commentator, James Bryce, in the 1880's, "is the natural state of an American railway towards all other authorities." In this war, as the reformers complained, the railroads enlisted "the ablest [attorneys] in the United States, all of them paid out of the people's money. . . ." This open flouting of the people's government, this open corruption of all the channels of political practice, would have been enough in itself to raise the protest against the railroads to irresistible levels.

Despite railroad opposition, by 1880 fourteen states had copied the Massachusetts regulatory commission of 1869. Other states had enacted even more severe measures. But the railroads had attacked most of them successfully through action in the state and federal courts, and it had become clear that state regulation was not the answer to the problem. As Congressman James B. Weaver of Iowa said in Congress in 1880, the railroad corporations

. . . are citizens of the State for all other practical purposes; but, when a controversy arises under the law as it now stands, the corporation has only to go into the State Court and there set forth the fact that it is a foreign corporation, organized under the law of Massachusetts or some other State, and the cause is removed to the Federal Court.

In this same year, the legislature of Mississippi petitioned Congress to "provide . . . adequate means of . . . regulating the tariff and freight rates on all railroads . . . in the United States."

Pressure for federal regulation mounted until, in 1886, two events made it virtually impossible for the federal government to postpone action any longer. One was the decision of the Supreme Court in the Wabash case, in which the justices upset earlier decisions favorable to state regulation of railroads, and which forbade any state henceforth to set rates even within its borders on railroad traffic entering from or bound for other states. The second event was an investigation into railroad practices conducted by a committee of the United States Senate headed by Shelby M. Cullom of Illinois. The Cullom Committee was anything but a radical group; but its report scorched railroad management

in general as "extravagant and wasteful," especially in the "reckless strife for competitive business." On the other hand, it also condemned the efforts of the railroads themselves to join together in pooling arrangements aimed at reducing competition.

The Wabash decision had made it imperative for the federal government to take some action in regulating railroads. But the report of the Cullom Committtee helped little in pointing toward a consistent policy. Free competition, in its eyes, had grown monstrous. On the other hand, efforts to check it seemed, if anything, even more antisocial. The Interstate Commerce Act, derived largely from the findings of the Cullom Committee, in a sense got around this dilemma. Signed by President Grover Cleveland on February 4, 1887, the Interstate Commerce Act forbade the usual railroad competitive practices, such as granting rebates to favored shippers and charging higher rates for non-competitive short hauls than for competitive long ones. And it also forbade the railroads' self-regulating practices, such as agreements to pool traffic and maintain high rates. At the same time, the act made almost no provision for enforcing its prohibitions.

President Cleveland showed his good faith by appointing excellent men to the Interstate Commerce Commission set up to administer the act. But the act gave these men no power except to issue "cease and desist" orders that could be enforced only through the courts. The result was that railroad lawyers, exceedingly adept at this sort of thing, tied up the Commission's orders for years with every kind of court-room delaying tactic, while the railroads themselves continued freely to engage in the practices that were under attack. At the end, moreover, the railroads usually won. Between 1887 and 1905, the Supreme Court heard 16 cases under the Interstate Commerce Act, and in 15 of these it upheld the railroads rather than the Commission.

The Interstate Commerce Act was not a complete failure, however. It clearly affirmed the right of the federal government to regulate private interstate business, and it supplied a foundation upon which a system of increasingly effective regulation could be built in the twentieth century.

Before the turn of the twentieth century, it was not the government but private bankers who brought the chaotic railroad system to book. This development was a consequence of the railroads' own history. With few exceptions, the great American railroads, especially those in the West, had been extravagantly financed by means of bond issues. Interest on these bonds placed a great strain on railroad revenues, leaving little for the maintenance and expansion of service in good years and no reserves when the "progress of the country" faltered from time to time. Efforts to raise new funds brought railroad management hat in hand to the offices of financiers like J. P. Morgan, who had solid connections in the English money market, and Jacob Schiff, head of Kuhn, Loeb, who had connections with Rothschild and other banking houses on the Continent. The bankers themselves learned early that the investment of their clients' funds in railroad securities was extremely hazardous unless the bankers themselves controlled, or at least had representation on, railroad boards of directors. Once entrenched, they ran matters to suit themselves. Since most of the railroads fell under the control of a relatively few bankers, the way was opened for the elimination of cutthroat competition by means of understandings (or threats) made in Wall Street.

The administration of the railroads by the bankers was no panacea; often enough Morgan himself burdened the railroads he controlled with heavier bonded indebtedness than they had when he took over. Nevertheless, the bankers usually installed as presidents of their roads men with long experience in the actual operation of railroads rather than in promotion alone. They also improved accounting methods and instituted stricter financial and managerial controls. The bankers made a good profit for themselves out of handling railroad securities and resurrecting bankrupt properties. But they also improved service so that the lines could handle the enormously expanded traffic that rapidly growing agriculture and industry thrust upon them.

III.   THE INDUSTRIAL DISCIPLINE

Steel.   Next to oil refining, the manufacture of steel and steel products was the most spectacular of all American postwar industrial developments. Before the war, steel had been a rare and costly metal, which could be produced only in quantities of 25 to 50 pounds by processes that took weeks to complete. As early as 1847, William Kelly of Kentucky had discovered a simple method by which tons of excellent steel could be made in a matter of minutes; but nothing much was heard of his discovery until ten years later, when Kelly contested the application of an Englishman, Henry Bessemer, for an American patent on a process similar to his own. The patent controversies soon were straightened out; yet as late as 1867 only 2,600 tons of what has since become known as Bessemer steel were produced in the United States. Five years later, Andrew Carnegie, fresh from his long experience in railroading and the building of steel railroad bridges, entered the steel manufacturing industry. But he put off adopting the Bessemer process. "Pioneering doesn't pay a new concern," he said; "we must wait until the process develops." A trip to England the next year finally convinced Carnegie of the practicality of the new process, and on his return he could talk of nothing else.

In 1873, Carnegie organized a new firm, Carnegie, McCandless & Company, and built the greatest steel plant in the world, the J. Edgar Thomson Steel Works, near Pittsburgh, shrewdly named after the presi-

TESTING RAIL

ROLLING A RAIL

SAWING A RAIL

THE CONVERTERS

WATCHING THE CONVERTERS

Casting ingots.

Heating ingots.

Bessemer steel manufacture.

of great intimacy with Thomson, Tom Scott, and other railroad kings such as Vanderbilt, Huntington, and Gould, Carnegie ignored the depression of the succeeding years and "went out," as he said, "and persuaded them to give us orders" for steel rails. By 1879, American steel production had risen to 930,000 tons, three-fourths of it in the form of steel rails. Almost all these rails were manufactured by the Carnegie company. By 1890, American steel production had taken another spectacular leap to an annual figure of over 4 million tons. By that time, three other giant steel enterprises had arisen or were on the verge of completing their consolidation out of numerous smaller companies: the Tennessee Coal and Iron Company in the South, the Illinois Steel Company in the Middle West, and the Colorado Fuel and Iron Company in the mountain region. The "Pittsburgh district," however, continued to dominate steel production, and Carnegie was acknowledged to have "almost absolute control" of the steel business there.

Carnegie's success sprang in part from his own abilities as a salesman. But he also had a vision of big business that far outstripped the thinking of any of his competitors, and he had the energy and discipline to bring his vision to fruition. Other steel men (like the wildcatters in oil) often lived off their profits in the grand style, but Carnegie, like Rockefeller, constantly plowed back his own and his company's earnings into the expansion, integration, and modernization of the enterprise. Before he sold his company and retired in 1901, Carnegie had acquired immense holdings in the fabulous Mesabi ore lands of Minnesota, from which as much as 85 per cent of America's entire iron ore needs in the twentieth century have come. He also bought up Pennsylvania coal fields and scattered limestone quarries, and the coke business of Henry Clay Frick, taking Frick himself, an excellent manager, into partnership. Ore, coal, limestone, and coke are the basic raw materials for the manufacture of steel; to insure their regular delivery to his plants, Carnegie also invested heavily in ore ships and railroad cars. Beyond all this, Carnegie was one of the first industrialists to employ a full-time scientifically trained chemist to study and control the tricky metallurgy of steel in order to produce a more uniform and satisfactory product. He introduced sound cost-accounting, and developed a successful incentive pay system for executives and workers alike.

At about the same time that Kelly and Bessemer had discovered the Bessemer steelmaking process, other inventors were developing the open-hearth method, which had two important advantages over Bessemer production. The open-hearth furnace could attain a higher temperature than the Bessemer converter; yet it was easier to draw samples from it for testing during actual production. The greater heat broke down the elements of iron more thoroughly than a Bessemer converter could, and the easy testing gave the worker greater control in recombining them or mixing them with alloying metals.

As experience with steel grew, and as metallurgy furnished more precise explanations for faults and accidents, the quality of steel improved. Bessemer steel was especially satisfactory for steel rails. But when steel came into greater demand for other uses—in skyscraper construction, in high-speed factory machinery, in the manufacture of automobiles—the finer open-hearth steels became more popular. By 1910, two-thirds of American steel production was open-hearth.

Science and Centralization. While Andrew Carnegie was extending his control over the steel industry, John D. Rockefeller and his colleagues were widening their control over oil. Transportation, as we have seen (p. 419), was one of the key factors in the competition among oil companies. At first, oil and refined products were carried in barrels, and Rockefeller had gained a jump on the field by manufacturing his own barrels at a cost far below their purchase price. Then, when the railroad tank car supplanted the barrel, Rockefeller was highly successful in gaining special privileges from the railroads. In the 1870's and 1880's, the oil pipe line was perfected and brought into wide use, especially for carrying crude oil from the producing regions to the refineries. It was not long before Rockefeller's Standard Oil Company had used its enormous power to gain a virtual monopoly of pipe-line transportation from the Pennsylvania and neighboring oil fields.

A more daring and original move made late in the 1880's protected and extended the Standard Oil Company's position. Petroleum production in Pennsylvania and neighboring oil regions had hit an all-time peak in 1882, but the Pennsylvania oil fields were not bottomless, and thereafter oil men began to worry that the entire industry would dry up with the decline of Pennsylvania's resources. So alarmed were they that within a few years, John D. Archbold, Rockefeller's own closest and most trusted associate, quietly began to sell off his Standard Oil stock at 75 cents on the dollar. In 1885, a great new oil field was discovered near the town of Lima in western Ohio, and soon after another great field was found just across the Indiana border. The difficulty, however, was that the oil produced here, though richer than Pennsylvania's in some respects, was contaminated with excessive sulphur, an odoriferous ingredient that earned for this product the name "pole cat oil," or "skunk juice."

By 1887, Lima-Indiana oil had become a drug on the market. But Rockefeller decided that a way could surely be found to remove its stench. By threatening to go it alone if need be, he forced the Standard Oil directors to organize the Ohio Oil Company in 1887 with the purpose of monopolizing production in this new oil region, and then he hired a team of chemists to make its products marketable. In a short time they succeeded. Now Standard Oil was in a posi-

tion to keep newcomers from the new source of supply, and also from the markets in the Mississippi Valley and beyond.

Increasingly, in the late nineteenth century, science was becoming the servant of industry in the production of other commodities besides steel and oil. Labor shortages during the Civil War had driven many manufacturers to invest in the newest, most efficient labor-saving machinery almost regardless of its initial high cost; and the demand for goods during the immediate postwar boom justified continued investment in the new and often revolutionary equipment that science was making possible. The Panic of 1873, itself induced in part by industry's over-expansion and over-investment in machinery, brought a pause. But it was followed by a 20-year period during which the prices of most commodities fell almost steadily. This state of affairs put a premium on the use of the most efficient machinery to keep production costs down, and it also stimulated manufacturers to rethink the processes by which many commodities were being produced. Engineering, which had been largely limited to problems of transportation such as bridge construction and railroad surveys, was now brought into the manufacturing plant. We have already noted the prewar use of interchangeable parts in the fire-arms and farm-machinery industries, and the use of assembly-line techniques in meat-packing (see p. 330). In the 1870's and after, both techniques became highly refined and began to be applied in new industries.

The continuing mechanization of factories and the specialization of workers made it possible to reduce the cost of production greatly. Yet there was a catch. So high was the initial investment now required to build and equip modern plants in many industries, that economies of production were realized only when plants were operated at or near capacity. If plants produced fewer items than they were geared for, the cost of each item rose remarkably. On the other hand, if they produced at capacity, their volume was so great that the market would be flooded and the price of their output would fall. Every source of hope for new markets in the postwar era—the opening of a new railroad line, a boom in immigration, a burst of exports, a rise in the tariff—led to the further expansion and mechanization of factories. But each new development soon ran its course and left behind idle plant and equipment—usually purchased with borrowed money on which interest had to be paid.

This situation became a constant hazard of American business life in the 1880's. As the *Bulletin* of the American Iron and Steel Association said in 1884, "Indeed it might almost be rated the exception for half the works in condition to make iron to be in operation simultaneously." The National Association of Stove Manufacturers reported in 1888: "It is a chronic case of too many stoves and not enough people to buy them." The same year, the National Millers Association bemoaned the situation in its industry: "Large output, quick sales, keen competition, and small profits are characteristic of modern trade." Then it continued:

We have the advantage in our business of always being in fashion; the world requires so much bread every day, a quantity which can be ascertained with almost mathematical accuracy. . . . But our ambition has overreached our discretion and judgment. We have all participated in the general steeplechase for preeminence; the thousand-barrel mill of our competitor had to be put in the shade by a two-thousand-barrel mill of our own construction; the commercial triumph of former seasons had to be surpassed by still more dazzling figures. As our glory increased our profits became smaller; until now the question is not how to surpass the record, but how to maintain our position and how to secure what we have in our possession.

As a result, many independent plants in heavily mechanized industries were forced to close down. In 1880, for example, the country had almost 2,000 woolen mills; by 1890, there were only 1,300. The 1,900 manufacturers of agricultural implements in 1880 had been reduced to 900 a decade later. During the same ten years, three-fourths of the manufacturers of leather goods went out of business.

A second and equally fateful consequence was the movement toward pools, trusts, and holding companies. The objective in each case was for one or a few firms to control the output, prices, and market areas of entire industries so that a satisfactory level of profits could be assured to the survivors.

Pools, which had long been known to industry, were essentially agreements among competitors to restrict output, maintain prices, and divide markets. They usually were created in emergencies, and they usually collapsed when the emergency passed. Pools enabled independent entrepreneurs to retain a semblance of individuality and to express it if need be. When the pools failed, they were usually supplanted by trusts, of which the first in this epoch was the one organized by Rockefeller in 1879 and reorganized in 1882. "Its success," said a New York legislative committee that investigated it in 1888, "has been the incentive to the formation of all other trusts or combinations."

In forming a trust, the stock of many competing companies is turned over to a group of trustees agreed upon by the combining companies; in exchange for such stock, trustee certificates are issued. Ownership of the stock remains in the original hands, but management of the enterprises represented by it is concentrated in the hands of a single board of trustees. In the decade after the founding of the Standard Oil Trust, there appeared the Cottonseed Oil Trust, the Salt Trust, the Sugar Trust, the Leather Trust, the Cordage Trust, and many others. Not all were strictly "trust" arrangements, but the tag was pinned to any large combination whose objective was to restrain cutthroat competition. An example was the so-called "Sugar Trust," of which Judge Barrett of the Supreme Court of New York said:

It can close every refinery at will, close some and open others, limit the purchases of raw material, artificially limit the production of refined sugar, enhance the price to enrich themselves and their associates at the public expense, and depress the price when necessary to crush out and impoverish a foolhardy rival.

Pools and "trusts" seemed to be the answer to problems of brutal competition abroad as well as in the United States. In Germany in particular, the cartel, which was essentially a large pooling arrangement with more or less severe penalties for backsliders, became the characteristic method of controlling production, marketing, and prices. In Europe, such arrangements usually had the overt sanction of the state. In the United States, where free competition had become the accepted path to progress, the government for a long time was forced to give tacit sanction to consolidations of every sort while at the same time seeming to impose restraints on their monopolistic tendencies.

The major effort at restraint before the twentieth century was the Sherman Antitrust Act, which passed Congress in July, 1890, with scarcely a murmur of dissent. Earlier, many states had enacted "antitrust" statutes, which were no more effective against "foreign" corporations (that is, those chartered in other states) than state regulation of interstate railroads had been. In 1886, moreover, the Supreme Court seemed to have ended the right of states to regulate private business corporations when it declared that the Fourteenth Amendment applied to corporate "persons" as well as to human ones, and that under this amendment no state could "deprive any person of life, liberty, or property, without due process of law." With the states thus weakened, critics of the "trusts" demanded federal regulation. The Sherman Antitrust Act sounded severe. It made combinations in restraint of trade illegal, subjected perpetrators to heavy fines and jail sentences, and ordered that triple damages be paid to persons who could prove injury by such combinations. Few courts, however, sustained any of the actions brought under the act. "What looks like a stone wall to a layman," commented the humorist, Finley Peter Dunne, "is a triumphal arch to a corporation lawyer."

The Sherman Act did prompt many groups of companies to give up specific "trust" arrangements and to merge into simple huge corporations which dominated their industries at least as thoroughly as the trusts had. In other industries, the holding company device was employed. The holding company was an independent corporation which owned enough stock in other companies to control their policies effectively. Dodges such as these neutralized the Sherman Act for a time. And even when the act was greatly strengthened later, it succeeded only in harassing companies that had been forced together by the pressures of competition; it did not eliminate combinations of these companies.

The Tools of Control. In many American industries during the 1880's and early 1890's, of course, hand labor persisted as of old and investment in machinery was small. In such industries, competition was likely to be less severe than in those where machines demanded maximum production at all times. Similarly, the "trust" movement affected these industries very little. New plants continued to be built, and expanding markets usually absorbed their products at profitable prices. The "trusts" that were organized in the United States in the 1880's and early 1890's were insignificant compared with those that appeared after the crash of 1893 (see p. 577).

Still, new large-scale enterprises were appearing with increasing frequency in the American economy and creating many new problems of administration. Among these were the sheer mechanical problems of transmitting directions and policies from central boards of directors in large cities to many scattered plants, and of getting back reports of plant operations. Then there were the problems of raising large amounts of money quickly and cheaply in order to fight or buy out new competitors or to rebuild obsolescent plants and renew obsolescent equipment. In time, the mechanical problems were solved by the invention or improvement of office machinery and methods; and the financial problems were solved by new specialists in the money markets, mainly the growing insurance companies and the investment bankers (see pp. 577-578).

Among the new mechanical devices were the office typewriter, which first appeared in 1867 and was steadily improved thereafter, and the office adding machine, which was made practical in 1888. Both set in motion the mechanization of the office that was to make such huge strides when electronic equipment became common after World War II. More fundamental were the expansion of the telegraph and the development of the telephone. By 1878, Western Union owned 195,000 miles of telegraph routes and controlled 80 per cent of the telegraph business. In 1881, at a cost of nearly $25 million, the company proceeded to buy out its two rising competitors, the American Union Company and the Atlantic and Pacific. This accomplished, President Norvin Green of Western Union declared to his stockholders:

Successful competition with your Company is improbable if not actually impossible.... Competition may be a popular demand, and it may be good policy on the part of your Company to indulge competing lines between the principal points. This would not materially interfere with remunerative dividends.

But secure as Western Union seemed in 1881, two years later a strong new rival loomed. This was the Commercial Cable Company, partly owned by John W. Mackay, the Comstock Lode millionaire. A disastrous rate war with Western Union began in 1886, and the following year both companies were ready to call it quits. They did not merge, but they did agree to end all competition in rates.

In 1876, Alexander Graham Bell patented the telephone he had invented the year before. In 1877, Western Union, which first scorned Bell's invention as an "electrical

toy," decided it had better enter the field. Backing a rival patent by Elisha Gray, it organized the American Speaking Telephone Company and proceeded to use all its political influence to block the Bell Company from winning franchises from local communities. The Bell Company, under the direction of Theodore N. Vail, was not awed by its great rival and proceeded to sue Western Union for infringement of patents. Bell's case was so good that Western Union settled out of court in 1879. By then, Western Union had hastily set up some 56,000 telephones in 55 cities, and Bell paid handsomely for this equipment and the accompanying franchises.

During the 1880's, the Bell Company was beset by competitors, all of whom it ultimately bought out at a total cost of $225 million. In this and later decades, constant improvement was made in the telephone instrument and in the wires, and new patents kept the Bell Company invulnerable to competition. One of the major innovations was the development of long-distance telephone service, beginning in 1884. To expand this business, the Bell directors set up

Bell's first demonstration of the telephone, Boston, March 10, 1876.

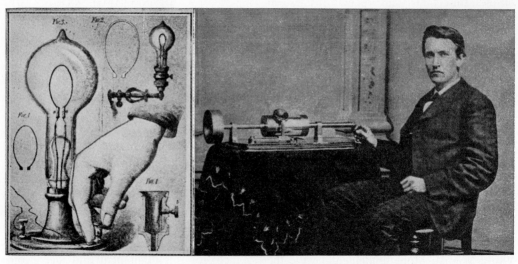

One of Thomas A. Edison's earliest incandescent bulbs, 1880, and the young inventor with his first phonograph, 1877.

a new corporation, the American Telephone and Telegraph Company. In 1900, A.T. & T. became the over-all holding company of the entire Bell system, with a capitalization of $250 million. In that year, 1,350,000 Bell telephones were in use in the United States. Service still cost New Yorkers $240 a year for a private phone. At such rates, the American Telephone and Telegraph Company's profits were the envy of industry.

While Bell and others were experimenting with the telephone, Thomas A. Edison was experimenting with electric lighting. The earliest commercial use of electricity had been in communication, and until the 1880's its use was still restricted to telegraphy and the telephone. Then, in 1879, Edison perfected a reasonably priced incandescent bulb. In 1882, he succeeded in building the first central electric power station, the Pearl Street station, in New York City. From this station, he distributed current to 85 buildings wired to receive it. This was direct current, which Edison persisted in believing to be the only feasible commercial current. Yet direct current could be transmitted great distances only at great cost. Alternating current, on the other hand, made it possible, with the use of transformers, to take direct current from a power plant, step up its volt-

age a hundred times for transmission over any distance desired, and then step it down again for practical use.

In collaboration with William Stanley, George Westinghouse, the inventor of the railroad air brake and other devices, developed the first generators and transformers to make alternating current practical. Before it could be used for mechanical power, however, a suitable motor had to be devised. In 1888, Nikola Tesla, a Serbian immigrant, who had arrived in America but four years earlier, perfected a simple, inexpensive motor employing alternating electric current. Westinghouse bought Tesla's patent soon after and made alternating current famous by using it to illuminate the World's Fair in Chicago in 1893. In the following two years, Westinghouse succeeded in harnessing the great water power of Niagara Falls, and carried the current generated there a distance of 20 miles, which was considered an incredible feat.

Electricity revolutionized American business and American life even more than cheap steel did; but the great era of electricity was to be the twentieth century. In the nineteenth century, the United States and the world still depended mainly on water and steam for power.

IV.   THE CONDITIONS OF LABOR

The Factory World.   By 1860, $1 billion had been invested in American industry, and the factories and shops that made up our industrial community produced goods that year valued at about $1.8 billion. By 1890, the capitalization of industry had soared to $6.5 billion, and the annual value of industrial production approached $10 billion. These are simply crude indices of the transformation of the United States in a short 30 years from an essentially agrarian nation to one of the leading industrial nations of the world. This transformation brought undreamed-of wealth to the country at large and to hundreds of individuals who made the concept of the millionaire the hallmark of American progress. On the other hand, it wiped out thousands of individual, independent businesses; and although their owners often started new enterprises, these were likely to be less rewarding in terms of profit and personal satisfaction. Many other former owners were forced to become employees of national corporations, where some found wider scope for their talents while the rest languished in their new and unaccustomed bureaucratic environment. This transformation from an agrarian to an industrial economy placed these corporations more or less at the mercy of a handful of eastern bankers and promoters. The massive concentration of American industry in a relatively few hands has been largely a twentieth-century phenomenon; yet it had already progressed far enough by the year 1890 to make it the target of the Sherman Antitrust Act and of the public agitation that forced that act's adoption.

Accompanying the transformation of American business life in the period from 1860 to 1890 was a 300 per cent rise in non-agricultural employment, compared with a rise of but 50 per cent in the number engaged in agriculture. By 1890, more than 4,600,000 persons worked in American factories, and another 3 million were divided equally between construction industries and transportation. In the last two decades of this 30-year period, the fierceness of business competition kept the prices of essential commodities falling. At the same time, the wages paid unskilled non-agricultural workers remained virtually fixed at $1.25 to $1.50 a day. Skilled workers were paid twice that and more. Since such fixed money wages could buy more and more goods at progressively falling prices, it would appear that industrial labor was constantly improving its situation. In fact, however, industrial workers, skilled and unskilled, were often harder hit than the expropriated independent businessmen.

One of the major factors that forced industrial concerns into pools, trusts, and consolidated giant corporations was their inability to keep their expensive machinery going all the time. Translated into the worker's terms, this meant that although his daily rate of pay remained unchanged, the number of days he worked in any year was likely to fluctuate violently. Few industrial workers had job security, except for skeleton staffs of highly skilled labor. After trusts or giant corporations came into control in many industries, moreover, their first step often was to shut down the less efficient plants, making no provision for the workers who were thereby displaced. Under such conditions, some areas became blighted by more or less permanent unemployment, or by the exodus of workers who could pay the cost of moving to more likely places.

One of the conditions making periodic unemployment a certainty in some industries was the tendency to keep factories in operation for excessively long hours when demand was high. Work-weeks ranging from 60 to over 80 hours were common; and the seven-day week was the rule in steel and paper mills, oil refineries, and other highly mechanized plants. Advances in technology, in turn, accelerated the pace of industrial production, and where this occurred the human worker was expected to keep up. Rapidly operating machines greatly increased the physical danger of factory work; and long hours and the accompanying fatigue ran up the toll in accidents, injuries, and deaths.

Another consequence of advancing technology was that the machines themselves did more and more of the skilled work. Skilled labor remained in great demand in unmechanized crafts, in the operation of certain complex machine processes, and in the setting up and maintenance of the machines themselves. But in general the old skills gradually were broken down, work tended to become little more than an endless series of identical and monotonous movements devoid of personal satisfaction, and skilled craftsmen were leveled to the status and the pay of the unskilled. Bossing them all in large plants, moreover, were likely to be brutish and tyrannical foremen, who were answerable to their superiors only for the speed, quantity, and cheapness of production.

Outside the factory the worker's life was likely to be no happier. Many worked for organizations like the Pullman Company in Chicago or the textile mills of the South, which owned their own towns, required their employees to live in them, and supplied town services at exorbitant rates. The big cities themselves rarely made any provision for the industrial workers that the new factories brought swarming in. Housing, sewage, water supply, schools, police and fire protection all broke down, and disease, crime, and illiteracy spread steadily (see Chapter XXII). Underscoring the brutality of the workers' new environment was the fact that many of them had so recently come from the farms, where sunlight and fresh air were taken for granted, where food was usually plentiful, and where fish, meat, fowl, and fruit were often to be had simply for the catching, hunting, or picking.

Unionization and Industrial Warfare.

The mass of American industrial laborers in the late nineteenth century did not always endure their hardships meekly, and they had patrician and middle-class allies who sought through legislation and other means to bring about reforms like the eight-hour day, workman's compensation for industrial accidents, mandatory safety provisions for dangerous jobs, and the recognition of labor's legal right to engage in collective bargaining. Yet many decades elapsed after the Civil War before these gains became effective (see Chapters XXV and XXVIII).

We have already described how the panics of 1837 and 1857 had brought about the collapse of the national labor organizations of their day. After the Civil War, a number of new efforts were made to organize labor nationally, of which two (before the advent of the A.F.L. in 1886) are worth noting. The first was the National Labor Union formed in Baltimore in 1866 by delegates from many local organizations and from a medley of reform groups interested in labor's welfare. In 1872, this union grew ambitious enough to form a Labor Reform party and to run a candidate in the presidential election. Most of its other efforts were as impractical as this one, however, and although at one time it claimed a membership of nearly 650,000 it failed to survive the business crash of 1873.

As miscellaneous in its membership and as unfocused in its aims was the Noble Order of the Knights of Labor, organized in 1869 by Uriah S. Stephens, a Philadelphia tailor. The Knights' principal aim was to unite the whole country—except for liquor dealers, lawyers, gamblers, and bankers—into one big union to engage in the production and distribution of goods on a cooperative rather than a capitalistic basis. The Noble Order made little headway until Terence V. Powderly, a Scranton, Penn-

The Haymarket riot in Chicago, 1886.

sylvania, machinist, became "Grand Master" in 1878. An extremely energetic organizer, Powderly traveled all over the country recruiting enthusiasts for the cooperative idea, and established more than 30 cooperative enterprises under the Knights' auspices. Though they opposed strikes and violence, Powderly and the Knights got their big break when unions affiliated with them struck against Jay Gould's Missouri Pacific Railroad in 1885 and forced Gould to rescind a wage cut and rehire hundreds of union men he had fired. Success here raised the Knights' standing so high that before the year was out membership had grown from about 100,000 to more than 700,000.

Powderly, however, soon had reason to believe that nonviolence was the best policy after all. On "May Day," 1886, Knights of Labor unions and many other labor groups totaling 340,000 men went on strike as a demonstration to promote legislation for the eight-hour day. In Chicago, where a long strike against the McCormick Harvester Company was in progress, the demonstration was followed by a series of outdoor meetings addressed by enthusiastic anarchists. At a meeting in Haymarket Square on May 3, a bomb was thrown at the police, killing one officer and injuring many more. A riot followed, and before it was put down seven

policemen and four civilians had been killed. The bomb-thrower was never found, but eight anarchists were accused of murder for inciting the incident, and seven of them were sentenced to death. The sentences of two were changed to life imprisonment, and together with the eighth man they were freed six years later by Illinois Governor John P. Altgeld, who accused the sentencing judge of having acted with "malicious ferocity."

The Haymarket riot outraged the general public, and although the Knights of Labor had had nothing to do with it, their participation in the earlier demonstration identified them in the public mind with the anarchists' work. Skilled workers within the organization shared the public's revulsion, and they began to desert the Knights in large numbers. The organization suffered also from growing administrative problems and internal dissension, and it shrank almost to extinction in a few years.

The American Federation of Labor was an entirely different kind of national labor organization. Its members were not workers as such, but national craft unions affiliated in a way similar to the manner in which the states of the United States were associated. The A.F.L. imposed certain standards on member unions. It insisted on the rigorous collection of regular dues to provide each union and the Federation itself (which took a share) with adequate funds in case of costly strikes. It insisted on the unions' hiring full-time salaried organizers to enlarge and discipline their memberships. It undertook to settle all issues of jurisdiction that arose when two or more member unions tried to organize workers in the same or similar fields, and it sought to protect its members from raids by non-affiliated rivals.

The A.F.L. had no political aspirations and little faith in reform legislation. Its dominating aim was to force business to engage in collective bargaining with member unions on such everyday issues as wages, hours, and working conditions. An essential goal was the establishment of the "closed shop"—that is, a shop that would agree to employ only members of A.F.L. affiliates. Gradually, initiation fees were pushed up in order to give the A.F.L. complete control over certain crafts by virtually closing entry to them. But this was a later development. At first, the Federation aimed to expand rather than restrict its membership.

Between 1886 and 1892, the A.F.L. gained the affiliation of unions with some 250,000 members. Progress in making collective-bargaining agreements was also satisfactory. One of the feathers in the A.F.L. cap was a contract it negotiated with the Carnegie Steel Company in 1890. In 1892 and 1894, however, the A.F.L. became involved in two violent and losing strikes which retarded union progress.

The first of these strikes was incited by the Carnegie Steel Company itself when, with Carnegie in Europe, President Henry Clay Frick tried to cut wages. The Amalgamated Association of Iron and Steel Workers, an A.F.L. member, refused to accede to Frick's proposal, and on July 1, 1892, Frick anticipated a walkout by closing down the great Homestead plant and hiring 300 Pinkerton detectives to protect it. When the Pinkertons arrived by barge on July 6, they were overwhelmed by an army of angry workers. Frick then requested the governor of Pennsylvania to call out the state militia to preserve order. Only after five months did the workers begin to go back to their jobs on company terms. But by then they had lost more than the strike. Public sympathy had been with them at first; but when an anarchist (who had nothing to do with the strike) tried to assassinate Frick, unionist sentiment declined.

The year after the Homestead strike, business fell into a severe depression that lasted

Miners burning the Pinkerton barges during the Homestead strike, 1892.

until 1898 (see p. 502). As a result, millions were thrown out of work, wages were drastically cut, and violent labor disputes broke out frequently. The most important of these was a strike against the Pullman Company, which ran a company town near Chicago. In 1894, Pullman laid off a third of his men and cut the wages of the rest by as much as 40 per cent. At the same time, he kept up the rents and prices the workers had to pay for company houses and for provisions at company stores. In protest, the Pullman workers quit. The year before, a fiery railroad worker, Eugene V. Debs, had organized the American Railway Union, which was open to all railroad workers, skilled and unskilled alike, and had promptly enlisted a membership of 150,000. Now Debs helped the Pullman strikers with money. He also got his members to boycott all Pullman cars by cutting them off the trains on which they worked. When the boycotters were fired, virtually all the railroad men west of Chicago went on strike, and with the railroads at a standstill hoodlums began to derail and loot all the rolling stock they could find.

The railroads, leery of Governor Altgeld, who had released the Haymarket riot anarchists, appealed directly to federal agencies for the use of federal troops. The Constitution permitted the use of such troops in a state only at the request of the governor or the legislature. President Cleveland ultimately found a way around this limitation and ordered the army to protect the mails. His justification lay in the fact that Attorney-General Olney had ordered an injunction against the strikers to be issued by a federal court in Chicago; and Cleveland's act was to insure that the injunction be obeyed. When the troops proceeded not only to protect the mails, but also to break the strike, Debs protested. Arrested under the terms of the injunction, Debs and other strike leaders refused to post bail and were sent to jail. Their trial for contempt months later resulted in a six-months' sentence for Debs.

The Pullman strike was a failure, but it had several interesting sequels. Debs spent

his time in jail reading radical literature and emerged a dedicated socialist. The federal courts had acted openly for the first time as strike-breakers while a labor dispute was in progress. The court injunction had been used before in labor disputes, but only on the traditional legal ground of protecting property that could not later be restored; its great value was the right it gave to the court to jail breakers of an injunction without granting them a jury trial. In the Pullman strike, a federal court had issued a labor dispute injunction for the first time under the novel terms of the Sherman Antitrust Act. The Court forbade strikes as conspiracies in restraint of interstate commerce. This was a departure that placed the injunction at the service of business whenever other grounds were lacking.

The Homestead strike and the Pullman strike disclosed the chasm that was opening up between big corporate business on the one hand and the mass of workers on the other. Yet just as corporations insisted on being treated before the law as if they were actually private persons no different from the flesh-and-blood individuals who worked for them, so the workers seemed to hold to traditional individualism and to forego the advantages of organization. Industrial labor had ample reason to rebel in the 1890's; yet for all the prominence given to labor warfare and labor organization, the vast majority of workers in the factories remained unorganized and docile. By 1898, their number had soared to more than 17 million. Yet of this vast number, a mere 500,000 were members of labor unions. The law was still far from protecting the welfare of American workers, but they themselves seemed scarcely to have awakened to the opportunity of looking out for themselves.

The "New Immigration."

In the decades after the Civil War, great corporations had begun to pre-empt for themselves such basic areas of economic activity as mining, lumbering, transportation, communication, and manufacturing. As the scale of operations grew and as technological requirements became more complex and more costly, the amount of capital needed for a new company to gain a firm foothold in an industry naturally rose. Opportunities for small, new enterprises in these areas thus began to decline just at the time when the large corporations had begun to recruit masses of unskilled labor to carry on their monotonous, often exhausting tasks.

A great deal of this labor came from the American farms. With the new industrial giants like Rockefeller and Carnegie as their models, farm boys swarmed into the industrial cities with the expectation of working for just a few years before scaling the heights of enterprise on their own. In Europe, a similar movement from rural to urban life was under way, of which the migration of millions to the cities of the United States was but a part. Americans and Europeans alike clung to their belief in free opportunity for the individual; if hard work alone would not insure power and fortune, there was always the chance that a lucky break would come their way and transform them into real-life Horatio Alger heroes. The Alger stories, which had their greatest vogue in the 1870's and 1880's, sustained among the youths of those decades a belief in economic opportunity that faded only when they had grown to frustrated and impoverished manhood.

The belief in individual opportunity no doubt accounted for much of the indifference of American workers to the attempts of unions to recruit them into their ranks. Another cause of indifference was the farm boys' complete ignorance of such ideas as organization and institutional discipline. A third factor was that opportunity of a kind usually did exist: a sweeper or shoveler might rise to be a machine operator, an operator to be a foreman, a foreman to be a section superintendent. And opportunities of this sort might be endangered by union membership and union activity. Another major factor was the steady and systematic introduction of foreigners into factory work. Each new influx—first the Irish, then the Italians, then the Poles, Hungarians, Lithuanians, and others from central and southeastern Europe—tended to start at the bottom and then to be pushed upward as inexperienced newcomers arrived. Gradually the native American workers tended to monopolize the top of the "blue shirt" hierarchy and to look down upon the strangers in their midst. The idea of uniting with the immigrants in common action against common oppression grew increasingly distasteful. Henry Clay Frick was only one of hundreds of American industrialists who had their agents scour Europe for cheap and ignorant labor in order to make their plants into veritable Babels and to impede effective labor organization.

European immigration to the United States reached its nineteenth-century peak in 1882, when almost 640,000 newcomers were admitted (see p. 452). Swelling the tide that year were the all-time record arrivals of Germans (250,600) and Scandinavians (105,300), and a total from Great Britain (103,000) that was exceeded in only two other years and then by just a few thousand. Immigration was resumed on a rising scale just after the turn of the century, and in the decade that ended with the outbreak of World War I in 1914 it broke all previous records. But by that time, it was made up largely of people from areas that had sent very few emigrants to the United States during the nineteenth century. The year 1882 is a kind of watershed between the so-called "old immigration" from Britain, Germany, and western Europe, and the so-called "new immigration" from central and southeastern Europe.

The old immigration had had its quota of illiterates and had supplied much of the unskilled labor for American industry and for mining and construction crews; but it had also included millions of farmers and large numbers of skilled artisans, businessmen, and professional men, who tended to travel on to the rising cities of America's "inland empire." The new immigration was made up of poorer people, less well educated, who were often corralled in Europe by tricky American agents of industry, land-grant railroads, and steamship companies, and then victimized after they had landed in the incredible, bewildering world of the United States. By 1910, such immigrants, along with Negroes migrating from the South, made up two-thirds of all the workers in 21 major branches of American industry. By then, they had become inured to the hardships of factory life and city slums, which together had conspired to turn many of their children into illiterate delinquents and criminals. Most of these immigrants remained in the port cities in which they landed or in the factory towns to which they were herded on arrival. They tended to associate with their own countrymen, to segregate themselves from Americans and others, to huddle in ever-more crowded tenements and slums. The conditions of their life often made them hostile to the American institutions around them, which seemed to offer no protection and no way out. This hostility, in turn, was gradually reciprocated by the Americans over whom the irresistible tide of immigration swept.

The earliest federal measure to restrict immigration to our shores was passed in May, 1882, in response to a long-standing demand of West coast agitators to exclude the Chinese (see p. 485). This act forbade Chinese to enter the United States for a decade, a suspension which subsequent legislation extended and which an act of 1902 made permanent.

More significant than Chinese exclusion was an act of 1882, by which Congress voted to limit immigration from Europe. This act placed a 50 cent tax on each immigrant arriving in American ports, the returns from which were to make up an immigrant welfare fund. More portentous were provisions that specifically denied entry to alleged lunatics and idiots, convicts, and persons likely to become public charges. The spread of Darwinian ideas about the "hereditary character of pauperism and crime," as one social worker put it in 1880, lay behind the middle-class agitation that led to the passage of this act. Henceforth, first organized labor and then the business community itself began to agitate for the extension of exclusion and ultimately for a strict limitation on the number of newcomers admitted each year. Organized labor was determined that American jobs be held for American workers; whatever the unorganized optimists in the labor force might think of American opportunity, the organized firmly believed in holding on to what they had. In 1885 the Knights of Labor had succeeded in getting Congress to forbid the importation of contract laborers after Hungarians and Italians had been imported under contract the previous year to be used as strike-breakers. Businessmen joined the agitation for immigration restriction after measuring the gains of having an unrestricted supply of new workers against the costs of the "foreign ideas" of socialism, anarchism, and the like, which seemed to be spreading in the 1890's and with which all immigrants were supposed to be infected.

The agitation for immigration restriction took many forms, but it was not until well into the twentieth century that general restriction was successfully imposed by Congress. Until that time, the United States seemed to have prospered as no other nation in history under the policy of free entry that had been hers since the Revolution and that had settled the colonies long before independence had been won.

Readings

A comprehensive survey of the economic history of the period covered in this chapter is Ida Tarbell, *The Nationalizing of Business, 1878-1898* (1936). Thomas C. Cochran and William Miller, *The Age of Enterprise* (1942), should also be consulted. Two short and perceptive books are those by John Moody in the Yale Chronicles series: *The Masters of Capital* (1919), and *The Railroad Builders* (1919). Roger Burlingame, *Engines of Democracy* (1940), stresses invention and technology, but is written with a fine grasp of the whole economic environment. Very illuminating on the competitive situation in the 1880's is David A. Wells, *Recent Economic Changes* (1890). Matthew Josephson's *The Robber Barons* (1934), though reflecting more of the spirit of the 1930's than the 1880's, still is useful and interesting. Scholarly studies of the business community are to be found in William Miller, ed., *Men in Business* (1952). The most comprehensive study of the Sherman Act is H. B. Thorelli, *The Federal Antitrust Policy* (1955).

Indispensable for an understanding of the details of early railroad manipulation and consolidation is Stuart Daggett, *Railroad Reorganization* (1908). A later scholarly summary will be found in the opening chapters of E. G. Campbell, *The Reorganization of the American Railroad System, 1893-1900* (1938). William Z. Ripley was an outstanding railroad expert, and two of his books merit special study: *Railroads: Rates and Regulation* (1912), and *Railroads: Finance and Organization* (1915). One of the most original books on railroad history is Thomas C. Cochran, *Railroad Leaders, 1845-1890* (1953). On the western railroads, see Robert E. Riegel, *The Story of the Western Railroads* (1926). On anti-railroad agitation, a scholarly study is Lee Benson, *Merchants—Farmers—and Railroads* (1955). Railroad leaders have not been happy in their biographers, but we may note as useful J. B. Hedges, *Henry Villard* (1930), and J. G. Pyle, *The Life of James J. Hill* (2 vols., 1917).

Three books, none completely satisfactory, tell the story of Andrew Carnegie: one is his *Autobiography* (1920); the second is J. H. Bridge, *The Inside History of the Carnegie Steel Company* (1903); the third, the official biography, *The Life of Andrew Carnegie*, by Burton J. Hendrick (2 vols., 1932). Herbert Casson, *The Romance of Steel* (1907), is a better book than its title might suggest. Very useful on the post-Civil War history of steel are Vols. II and III of Victor S. Clark, *History of Manufactures in the United States* (1928).

Besides Nevins' life of Rockefeller, referred to earlier, two books deal in detail with the later history of the oil industry: Ralph W. and Muriel E. Hidy, *Pioneering in Big Business, 1882-1911: History of the Standard Oil Company (New Jersey)* (1955), and Paul H. Giddens, *Standard Oil Company (Indiana)* (1955). For the story of consolidation and integration, see Eliot Jones, *The Trust Problem in the United States* (1921), and H. R. Seager and C. A. Gulick, Jr., *Trust and Corporation Problems* (1929).

The standard labor history is John R. Commons, and others, *History of Labour in the United States* (4 vols.; see especially for this period Volume II). A useful short account is Herbert Harris, *American Labor* (1939). More detailed is Norman Ware, *The Labor Movement in the United States, 1860-1895* (1929). Henry David, *History of the Haymarket Affair* (1936), is excellent on its subject and related issues. Terence V. Powderly, *Thirty Years of Labor* (1889), and *The Path I Trod* (1940), are interesting autobiographical accounts by the "Grand Master" of the Knights of Labor. The best account of the formation and policy of the A.F.L. is Samuel Gompers' autobiographical *Seventy Years of Life and Labor* (2 vols., 1925). A useful biography of Eugene V. Debs is Ray Ginger, *The Bending Cross* (1949).

Especially good on the "new immigration" is Oscar Handlin, *The Uprooted* (1951). Other valuable general studies of immigration include Carl Wittke, *We Who Built America* (1939), and I. A. Hourwich, *Immigration and Labor* (rev. ed., 1923). Indispensable to an understanding of the immigrant's reception in the United States in the later nineteenth century and the beginnings of immigrant restriction is John Higham, *Strangers in the Land* (1955).

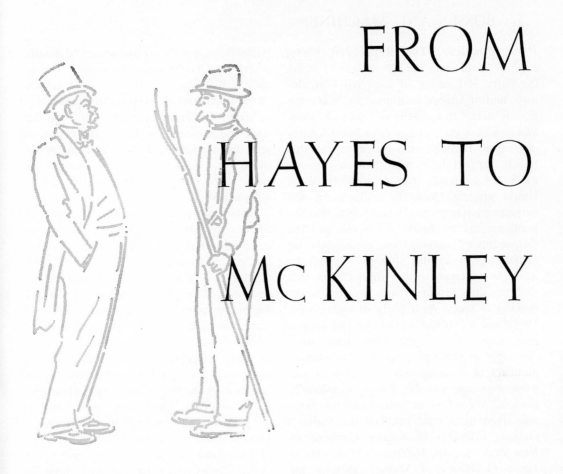

FROM HAYES TO McKINLEY

C H A P T E R   T W E N T Y - O N E

Looking hard at his country after the Civil War, Walt Whitman acknowledged that America's technical achievements, the "beating up the wilderness into fertile farms ... her railroads, ships, machinery," were causes for rejoicing. Yet he lamented that with all this "unprecedented materialistic advancement—society, in these States, is canker'd, crude, superstitious, and rotten. Political, or law-made society is, and private, or voluntary society, is also." Whitman's words were harsh, but honest.

Other thoughtful men shared Whitman's low opinion of politics and politicians during the postwar years. Henry Adams considered the politician a dog who needed the discipline of a stick. "One might search the whole list of Congress, judiciary, and executive dur-

481

ing the twenty-five years 1870 to 1895," he wrote in 1905, "and find little but damaged reputations. The period was poor in purpose and barren in results." Neither the Republicans nor the Democrats provided the leadership that was so badly needed.

I. BOSSES AND MACHINES

Party Politics. The Republican party, carefully exploiting the advantages of being the party of Lincoln, of the Civil War victory, and of Union, continued to "wave the bloody shirt," to keep the war wounds open, and to accuse the Democrats of being a party of treason. Through such appeals it was able to win support from many citizens outside the South, especially from the veterans of the Union armies. Until the collapse of the carpetbag governments in the South, the Republicans, as the heirs of Lincoln and the proponents of emancipation, made good use of the Negro vote. But after 1877, when the white South lapsed into a solid Democratic section, this resource was worth almost nothing to them. As a party of high tariffs, liberal aid to railroads, and, for the greater part, sound money, the Republicans were also able to win the support of substantial numbers of businessmen. The eastern and western wings of the party occasionally clashed over economic issues, and the party was riven by a feud between the Stalwart faction (followers of Roscoe Conkling of New York) and the Halfbreeds (followers of James G. Blaine of Maine). But on the whole it was able to compromise its differences and act as a reasonably disciplined organization.

The Democrats, despite the "treason" label, were far from a weak opposition. After the collapse of the carpetbag governments, they dominated the South. In many of the great cities, their leaders, particularly the Irish bosses, able and systematic organizers of the immigrants, developed powerful machines with strong patronage systems and a broad mass following among the newcomers to the country. And although the Democrats had less support from business than the Republicans, they appealed to many segments of business, especially in commerce and finance, where high tariffs were unpopular. The so-called "Bourbon" or conservative Democrats of the South and Midwest wielded a powerful influence in party councils, and, together with the segments of the party connected with finance in the East, managed for the most part to hold down the more radical sections of the party that flourished in the developing West.

Since both parties were run by conservatives, they differed on the details, not on essentials, of such important issues as monetary policy, tariffs, civil service, and railroad regulation. For this reason, political discussion was of only mild interest. At bottom, the parties were two great well-matched machines struggling chiefly for the spoils of office—for the jobs that could be handed out to party supporters and for the graft that came with the power to make political decisions affecting the development of business.

Although the Democrats lost control of the presidency when Lincoln was elected in 1860 and did not regain it until the election of Cleveland in 1884, the two parties retained almost equal strength throughout the last three decades of the nineteenth century. In no election from 1876 to 1896 was the winning side's share of the popular vote greater than 50.8 per cent. In two elections, 1876 and 1888, the Republican victor was elected with fewer popular votes than his Democratic opponent. Such narrow margins of victory put the politicians on their mettle, and their reluctance to discuss the great issues caused them to make the most of emotional appeals and to exploit scandals and corruption.

The men who controlled the outcome of presidential elections were not the candidates themselves so much as the bosses and party leaders who planned the strategy, engaged in political horse-trading, and brought in the votes. Until the Civil Service Reform Act was passed in 1883 (see p. 488), the bosses were active politicians and war leaders like Zachariah Chandler of Michigan and Oliver P. Morton of Indiana. They filled their campaign chests by assessing state and federal employees whose jobs depended on their party loyalty. By the mid-80's, a new kind of boss had emerged whose methods were as quiet and efficient as those of the businessmen he served. By making the sale of offices more difficult, the Civil Service Reform Act weakened an important source of campaign revenues. But private industries—steel corporations, oil and sugar refining companies, and railroads—now came forward with money for political expenses in return for special favors and protection. Shrewd party managers like Matthew Quay of Pennsylvania, Thomas C. Platt of New York, and Marcus Alonzo Hanna of Ohio represented their big-business clients efficiently and saw to it that their political donations were wisely spent.

As might be expected, the national and state governments during this period were quick to respond to the demands of special interests—to the lobbyists and favor-seekers who expected to be paid for their contributions. Determined business interests also made their influence felt in the party organizations, the primaries, and the conventions. As William Graham Sumner noted in 1889, the plutocracy * always entered "the contest with a small body, a strong organization, a powerful motive, a definite purpose, and a strict discipline, while on the other side is a large and unorganized body [the reform element], without discipline, with its ideas undefined, its interests illy understood, with an indefinite good intention." This observation sums up many of the economic and political contests that occurred between 1876 and 1896.

Reformers.   Any period of rapid change, like the years between 1870 and 1900, naturally brings with it a great many social ills and produces a wide variety of grievances affecting several classes of the population. Voices calling for reforms were always heard during these years, but they called for different things and announced their intentions in different tones. It was partly because of this lack of unity among reformers that conservatives held such firm control over national affairs during the greater part of these decades. Indeed, the reformers were a motley crew. On the left were advocates of special panaceas like Henry George's single tax and Edward Bellamy's Nationalism, who had wide intellectual influence in the long run but little immediate following and limited political impact. Only slightly more respectable were the monetary reformers, who sought to cure all industrial and agrarian ills with some form of inflation, whether through greenbacks or free silver. A roughly parallel but even weaker strain of reform was represented by the Knights of Labor, who were hardly a labor movement at all in the modern sense. More successful than any of these were the Grangers, who sought a variety of solutions for the transportation and credit problems of farmers, but whose following was strong chiefly in a few states of the Midwest.

The most respectable of all the reformers were the Mugwumps and intellectual liberals. The typical Mugwump was by no means a radical. In fact, his desire for change went no

---

* "A plutocrat is a man who, having the possession of capital, and having the power of it at his disposal, uses it, not industrially, but politically; instead of employing laborers, he enlists lobbyists. Instead of applying capital to land, he operates upon the market by legislation, by artificial monopoly, by legislative privileges; he creates jobs, and erects combinations, which are half political and half industrial; he practices upon the industrial vices, makes an engine of venality, expends his ingenuity, not on the processes of production, but on knowledge of men, and on the tactics of the lobby. The modern industrial system gives him a magnificent field, one far more profitable, very often, than that of legitimate industry." William Graham Sumner, *The Conflict of Plutocracy and Democracy,* 1889.

further than civil-service and tariff reform, and he was likely to be a firm advocate of sound money. Boss rule, labor organizers or "walking delegates," "socialistic" legislation —all provoked his disdain or anger. At the same time, the Mugwump despised the aggressive nouveau riche, the plutocrat who had usurped his social leadership since the Civil War. He felt out of place in an America dominated by millionaires, and he shared the scorn of Henry Adams for vulgarians who shut him out of his rightful heritage. The typical Mugwump belonged to a class that acted responsibly toward its inferiors and took its duties seriously. He was Protestant and Anglo-Saxon and was linked by habitat or culture with New England. His heroes were Washington, the Adamses, Webster, and Clay; his spokesmen were E. L. Godkin, the free-trade editor of the *Nation,* and the high-minded George W. Curtis, editor of *Harper's Weekly;* his favorite cartoonist was Thomas Nast; his favorite politician, the Liberal Republican Carl Schurz. He understood the basic economic issues of his day no better than did the plutocrats and the spoilsmen he assailed, and he had, perhaps, even less faith in the masses. But he helped to keep alive the ideas of political morality and the sacredness of the public trust at a time when the men in power ignored them. The Mugwumps and their allies attracted a following among many solid and respectable citizens, but they had slight appeal for the great mass of Americans, especially the recent immigrants, and little talent for political organization.

Moreover, the various reform groups had little use for each other. The Mugwumps, for example, thought the more radical reformers were dangerous. Labor reformers had few points of contact with the agrarian movements. Even the agrarian movements, the strongest of all, were handicapped by problems of timing. The Grangers drew much support from farmers in such midwestern states as Illinois, Iowa, and Minnesota in the 1870's and early 1880's. But by the time the states farther west, like Kansas, Nebraska, and the Dakotas, had been drawn into the orbit of agrarian protest along with the South, the older farm states had solved enough of their transportation and credit problems to become relatively contented and conservative.

Finally, the reformers had had little experience with the techniques of solving social problems through national legislation. Yet the economy had become a national unit. The conception of control of business through federal commissions was new, and even when farm and business groups prevailed on Congress to pass regulatory legislation like the Interstate Commerce Act of 1887 and the Sherman Antitrust Act of 1890 (see pp. 464, 470), these laws were poorly drafted and for many years were slackly administered.

II.   THE REPUBLICAN ERA

Hayes' Administration. In 1877, the newly elected President Hayes, war veteran, Congressman, and Governor of Ohio, was an earnest and honest executive, generous, humane, and superior to the run-of-the-mill politician. But he was hardly the man to guide the nation through the difficult years of rough-and-tumble politics that were ahead.

In September, 1876, the Springfield (Massachusetts) *Republican* had asked in an editorial, "Which candidate can most successfully resist the bad conduct and overcome the bad character of his own party?" Hayes tried his best to do just that after the election. In choosing his cabinet, he ignored the old gang of patronage-dispensers and appointed honest and capable men. It took courage for Hayes to make the civil-service reformer, Carl Schurz, his Secretary of the Interior. And it took courage for him to tangle with the formidable Stalwart, Roscoe Conkling. But although Hayes managed with the help of his experienced and wily Secretary of the Treasury, John Sherman, to take New York's political machine away from the Conkling supporters, he failed to fulfill his campaign promise of "thorough, radical, and complete" reform. Many good Republicans refused to go along with Hayes' order forbidding federal office-holders to manage political organizations or to pay "assessments for political purposes." They agreed with Conkling's contemptuous comment on reformers: "They forget that parties are not built up by deportment, or by ladies' magazines, or gush!"

The Democrats did their best to whip up dissension between Stalwarts and Halfbreeds, and they worked tirelessly to discredit Hayes' administration. The attempt of an anti-administration congressional committee in 1878 to dig up new evidence proving that "His Fraudulency" (as Conkling called Hayes), or "Rutherfraud," had stolen the presidency backfired suddenly when the Republicans discovered that Tilden supporters had tried to bribe some of the Republican electors in the disputed states during the election deadlock. No more successful was the Democratic effort to repeal the Force Act passed in 1870 during the Reconstruction period to control southern elections (see p. 406). Hayes regarded this move as an attempt on the part of Congress to dictate to the President. When the Democrats attached their repeal measures as riders to appropriation bills on seven occasions, Hayes responded with seven vetoes and ultimately compelled Congress to pass these appropriations without riders.

Hayes' aggressive handling of the violent railroad strikes that flared up in 1877 met with no opposition from Congress. In July, after repeated slashes in pay, trainmen of the Baltimore & Ohio struck. The rioting that followed spread into Pittsburgh, Chicago, and other parts of the Middle West. Soon the strikers and their sympathizers were fighting pitched battles with state militias, burning railroad property, and molesting trains. When four state governors begged Hayes for federal troops, he felt it his constitutional

duty to oblige; troops were sent to Martinsburg, West Virginia, and to Pittsburgh. Only once before, during Jackson's administration, had government forces intervened in a struggle between private industry and its employees, and Hayes took this fateful step with some misgivings. He shared none of the vindictiveness of the anti-labor people who applauded his action, although he had only the simplest notions about the causes of the social unrest that marked the early part of his administration. His veto in 1879 of a bill restricting the number of Chinese passengers on ships bound for the United States was also widely interpreted as an anti-labor gesture. Although Hayes disapproved of the Chinese "labor invasion" that had been stimulated by mining and railroad corporations, he felt that the bill violated the spirit of the Burlingame Treaty of 1868 with China, which gave Chinese unlimited immigration rights. Workingmen's parties in the West condemned him, but Hayes followed the correct diplomatic procedure of negotiating a new treaty with China in 1880 that gave the United States the privilege of regulating or suspending Chinese immigration to America. In 1882, Congress closed off Chinese immigration for ten years.

In currency matters, Hayes lived up to his reputation as a hard-money man. He had strongly backed the Resumption Act of 1875 (see p. 425), which called for the resumption of specie payments after January 1, 1879, and the reduction of greenbacks in circulation. In 1877, Secretary of the Treasury John Sherman of Ohio began to build up a gold supply to pay for the retirement of the greenbacks. Returns from the sale of bonds raised the gold reserve, and so did a favorable trade balance made possible by bumper American harvests and European crop failures. Even before 1879, the greenback, which had sunk as low as 38 cents during the war, was worth 100 cents, and on January 1 of that year, with $200 million worth of gold in the Treasury, no one bothered to redeem his greenbacks.

To the agricultural producers who comprised a majority of the population, the Resumption Act simply meant fewer dollars and lower prices. During the war, when the market was strong, they had been prosperous; but the postwar deflation put an end to the good times, especially for debtors in the South and West. A wheat farmer, for example, may have borrowed $1,240 in 1871 when its purchasing value was 1,000 bushels of wheat; four years later, the $1,240 he repaid to the lender would have bought 1,320 bushels of wheat. Cotton-growers borrowed when cotton was worth 16.5 cents a pound and paid their creditors when it had dropped to 9.9 cents. Naturally, many farmers saw a correlation between low prices and the shortage of money in circulation; so they turned to the nascent Greenback party, whose program called for an increase in the currency. The Greenbackers had caused only a slight ripple in the election of 1876, but in the elections of 1878 they elected 14 congressmen and polled 1,060,000 votes. This was the high point of the movement, however, for the trade revival that began in 1879 brought a measure of prosperity to the disgruntled farmers and small entrepreneurs. The party ceased to exist after 1884.

But another cheap-money panacea began to gather strength during Hayes' administration: the movement for the unlimited coinage of silver. In 1834, Congress had fixed the ratio of silver to gold in the dollar at 16 to 1 —that is to say, there was 16 times as much silver by weight in the silver dollar as there was gold in the gold dollar. Until 1849, this ratio adequately measured the value of the two metals, but the flood of gold mined during the gold rush (see p. 283) reduced its value to the point where the 16 to 1 ratio undervalued silver. Owners of silver found it more profitable to sell it on the open market as a metal than to present it to the mint for coinage. So no one protested when Congress adopted a new coinage law in 1873 that ended the minting of silver dollars, which had long been out of circulation.

Had the price of silver not fallen sharply after 1873, the demand to restore the coinage of silver might never have arisen. The discovery of new deposits of silver in Nevada, Colorado, and Utah, however, together with new refining methods, lowered its price. By 1878, the old ratio of 16 to 1 clearly undervalued gold. It became worth while again to offer silver for coinage. The inflationists, balked by the reduction of greenbacks, began to urge the government to coin silver dollars again, charging that a sinister group of bankers had engineered the "Crime of '73," as the coinage law of 1873 was now called. Thousands came to believe that the unlimited coinage of silver would work as effectively as greenbacks to increase the money supply, raise prices, and make it easier for debtors to meet their obligations.

The first important test for the silver inflationists in Congress came in November, 1877, when Richard ("Silver Dick") Bland of Missouri introduced a bill in the House of Representatives for the unlimited coinage of silver at 16 to 1. This was clearly an inflationary measure that was intended to drive gold out of circulation. The silver dollar in 1877 was worth about 89 cents and was dropping in value. Bankers warned Hayes that the passage of the Bland Bill (which would permit the debtor to pay his creditor in depreciated currency) amounted to debt repudiation and that capitalists would never buy government bond issues in gold if silver became legal tender. Hayes agreed, but he knew that if he vetoed the bill Congress would override him. He was rescued from his dilemma when the original Bland Bill was quietly emasculated in the Senate by Iowa's smooth-talking William Allison. The amended Bland-Allison Bill (passed in 1878 over Hayes' veto) substituted "limited" for "unlimited" coinage of silver. It required the Treasury to buy not less than $2 million and not more than $4 million worth of silver every month. In the end, these controlled silver purchases did not drive gold out of circulation or raise prices, since silver coin and treasury notes were redeemable in gold. And so matters rested for 12 years.

The Election of 1880. Hayes lost the chance to dominate his party when he announced after his nomination that he would serve only one term. Although he brought dignity and honesty to the presidency and helped to heal sectional bitterness, his hopes for reform had not materialized. By 1879, his old enemy, Conkling, had recaptured his authority in New York, had routed the civil-service reformers, and was plotting to renominate the pliable Grant for a third term. "Blaine from Maine" and John Sherman of Ohio made themselves available for the Republican nomination.

Their strategy seemed good. But this time the big men of the Republican party lost out to a "dark horse" at the Chicago convention. Although the Stalwart bosses joined forces, they failed to pass a convention ruling requiring each state delegation to cast its entire vote for the majority candidate—a device that would have assured Grant's nomination for a third term. Yet they were strong enough to eliminate Blaine. After a long convention deadlock between Blaine and Grant, the Sherman and Blaine delegates nominated James Abram Garfield of Ohio and (to appease the Stalwarts) Chester A. Arthur as his running-mate. Then the convention framed a platform that came out boldly for veterans' pensions and Chinese exclusion, but that was characteristically vague on the really controversial issues of the tariff and civil-service reform.

The Democrats, wracked by schisms, nominated an honest but politically inexperienced Civil War hero, General Winfield S. Hancock, after the aged Tilden had refused to run again. Their platform called for a tariff for revenue.

Garfield squeaked into office with a plurality of only 9,464 votes out of a total of almost 9 million cast. His large electoral majority of 214, against Hancock's 155, was the result of victories in two pivotal states (Indiana and New York), which had been carried by good Republican discipline and plenty of hard cash. After the election, Conkling and his friends expected recognition for their pains.

The new President had reached the political top after a brilliant Civil War career and an arduous apprenticeship in the House. Although he had narrowly escaped disgrace in the Crédit-Mobilier scandal, he was a man of some integrity who had an instinctive dislike for the coarse-grained professionals. He disapproved of Grant, and he broke with Conkling immediately by giving the most lucrative patronage post in the United States, the position of the Collector of the Port of New York, to an anti-Conkling Republican, W. H. Robertson. Pressure on behalf of Conkling by other senators did not budge the stubborn Garfield, and by holding up all other appointments he forced the Senate to confirm Robertson. Conkling and the junior senator from New York, Thomas Platt, promptly resigned their seats and went to Albany to win state vindication. But the New York legislators shilly-shallied and finally refused to re-elect them. This blow was the beginning of the end for the Stalwarts. In the meantime, post-office frauds that took place during Hayes' administration were uncovered by Garfield's Postmaster-General. Prominent Stalwart politicians and post-office officials (two of whom had been active directors of Garfield's campaign) were indicted for issuing fraudulent contracts to stagecoach lines carrying mail in the Far West.

James Blaine, Secretary of State, was more than pleased with Garfield's conduct and confidently looked forward to an auspicious administration. This hope was dashed in July, 1881, when Garfield was shot down as he entered the Washington depot by a Chicago lawyer, Charles Guiteau, who had become unbalanced by his failure to get a European consulship. As the assassin fired his pistol into Garfield's back, he exclaimed, "I am a Stalwart and Arthur is President now." Garfield died two months later and Chester A. Arthur, a prominent member of Conkling's political entourage, became president. No one missed the irony of the Republican drama—that Arthur, a Stalwart and an associate of Roscoe Conkling, had succeeded the very man who had rebuffed Conkling. But Arthur did not submit to Conkling's influence, as had been predicted, and though he filled his cabinet with Stalwarts, his administration saw the beginning of civil-service reform.

Until Garfield's assassination, the cause of civil-service reform had languished. In 1871, Senator Carl Schurz of Missouri had succeeded in pushing through a law setting up a Civil Service Commission, and Grant had appointed the ardent reformer, George W. Curtis, editor of *Harper's Weekly,* to head it. But the attempt of Curtis and his friends (E. L. Godkin and Thomas A. Jenckes, a Rhode Island congressman) to end the "spoils system" and to base federal appointments on merit alone got nowhere. Professional politicians were convinced that party assessments won elections and that parties were held together by dividing up political spoils. Hayes had also tried to remove federal job appointments from politics, and so had Garfield. But Garfield's death accomplished what neither he nor the civil-service reform associations had been able to do: it provided the cause with a martyr.

In 1883, President Arthur signed a civil-service act (the Pendleton Act) that for the first time set up machinery to protect federal officeholders from the reprisals of party politicians. Three civil-service commissioners, to be appointed by the president, were given authority to draw up practical competitive examinations "testing the fitness of applicants for the public service now classified, or to be classified." The practice of assessing federal office-holders for campaign contributions was prohibited, nor could any federal employee be fired for purely political reasons. The Pendleton Act put more than 15,000 government employees (about 12 per cent of the total) on the civil-service list, and it gave the president power to extend the coverage. In succeeding administrations, the classified list was continuously expanded. (By the time of Woodrow Wilson, over 70 per cent of federal employees were classified,

and in recent years the figure has reached over 85 per cent.) Although the Pendleton Act did not end the dunning of the many federal job-holders who were still unclassified, it did force party bosses to turn more and more to big business for their campaign funds.

All in all, Arthur conducted himself creditably during his time in office. He did not draw back from prosecuting the culprits in the post-office frauds, even though two of them were prominent Republicans. He won a slight reduction in tariff duties in 1883, and he held off pork-barrel raids on the Treasury. He was never able, however, to throw off the taint of his earlier associations so far as the reformers were concerned, and his independence as president displeased the old guard. Consequently, the Republican convention in 1884 passed him over and chose instead that perennial presidential aspirant, James G. Blaine.

The Democrats Return.   Blaine had the attributes that make for a successful president: an unblemished family life, a magnetic presence, oratorical power, a lucid if not powerful mind, and political shrewdness derived from many hectic years in the House. Genial and vindictive by turns, he hated the Stalwarts and despised upstart reformers, whom he labeled as "conceited, foolish, vain, without knowledge." Although he inspired adoration among his followers (he was their "Plumed Knight" *), his dubious financial connections (see p. 427) deprived him of his highest ambition. During the 1884 campaign, one of the dirtiest in American history, the Democrats revealed the full scope of Blaine's financial indiscretions, and held Blaine up to scorn before his fellow Americans as a corruptionist and liar.

The Liberal Republicans, who had opposed Blaine's nomination, found themselves in a quandary. Should they "follow a noble im-

* So labeled in Colonel Robert Ingersoll's eloquent tribute before the Republican Convention, June, 1876.

pulse," as Carl Schurz put it, and desert the orthodox wing of the party? Young Republicans like Henry Cabot Lodge and Theodore Roosevelt wavered and then rationalized their decision: they would be of more service to the cause of reform inside the party rather than outside it. The more dedicated reformers, like the university presidents Charles W. Eliot of Harvard and Andrew D. White of Cornell, the preacher Henry Ward Beecher, and a number of lesser lights, decided to follow Schurz out of the party. Having taken this step, these "Mugwumps," as they were called, came out for the 1884 Democratic nominee, Grover Cleveland.

Cleveland, a relatively new man in politics, had attracted notice as a reform mayor of Buffalo, New York, in 1881 and as governor of the state from 1882 to 1884. Blunt, honest, and steadfast, he had guarded the public treasury like a bulldog, believed implicitly in hard money, and never deviated in his defense of property rights. Unsentimental machine politicians managed Cleveland's campaign, which was almost as heavily subsidized by the corporate wealth of the country as was the Republicans'. The bankers knew he was sound on the gold question, and

This anti-Blaine cartoon contrasts the upright Cleveland with "liar" Blaine, tarred with the brush of corruption.

Cleveland enjoyed more than ordinary confidence among businessmen.

In their campaign, the Democrats straddled the tariff issue, and the Republicans came out for high protection. But otherwise the two party platforms were much alike. "No one," Henry Adams wrote to an English friend, "talks about real interests. By common consent they agree to let these alone." Instead, the Republicans dug up and gleefully publicized the fact that the bachelor Cleveland had acknowledged paternity of an illegitimate child. And the Democrats unearthed new letters proving that Blaine, while Speaker of the House, had used his influence in favor of certain railroads. Republicans paraders marched down the streets shouting

> "Ma, Ma! Where's my Pa?"

while the bolder Democrats retorted,

> "Gone to the White House,
> Ha, Ha, Ha!"

Shortly before election day, the Democrats capitalized on two episodes that seriously damaged Blaine's candidacy. In pledging support for Blaine, the Reverend Samuel D. Burchard, a spokesman for a New York delegation of clergymen, observed that the Democratic party's "antecedents have been rum, Romanism, and rebellion." Apparently Blaine was not listening when these fatal words were uttered. But a Democratic reporter was, and he quickly informed Irish voters that Blaine had not rebuked the minister for his insulting allusion to their drinking habits and religion. On the same day, Jay Gould and other "money kings" tendered a lavish testimonial dinner to the Republican candidate which was described in the Democratic press as "The Royal Feast of Belshazzar Blaine." Pulitzer's *World* was the most eloquent:

> While Blaine and his millionaire admirers were feasting at Delmonico's last night, thousands of children in this great city whose fathers labour twelve hours a day, went to bed hungry and many of them supperless. Mr. Blaine was at home in the midst of the Monopolists and Millionaires last night. He loves them and they admire him. From Rum, Romanism, and Rebellion at the Fifth Avenue Hotel, Mr. Blaine proceeded to the merry banquet . . . where champagne frothed and brandy sparkled in glasses that glittered like jewels.

The "Plumed Knight" lost New York by 1,149 votes, and New York turned out to be the decisive state in the election. Cleveland's popular plurality was only 23,000 votes out of the 10-million-odd cast. Some experts believed that the votes won by the Prohibition candidate and by the Greenback nominee, the notorious Benjamin F. Butler, were responsible for Blaine's defeat. Others credited Cleveland's victory to Mugwump support or to the clergyman Burchard's impolitic words. Whatever the cause, the Democrats had come back to the White House after 24 years.

Cleveland's First Term.

On assuming office in 1885, Cleveland ran head-on into the same dilemma that had embarrassed Hayes and Garfield. Committed though he was to civil-service reform, he dared not ignore the interests of his party. By lengthening the civil-service list, he antagonized the party regulars; and by replacing hundreds of Republicans who held unclassified jobs with "deserving Democrats," he offended the Mugwumps who had deserted their own party to vote for him. "Your attempt to please both reformers and spoilsmen," Carl Schurz wrote to Cleveland in 1886, "has failed." The Republican majority in the Senate, attempting to curb the presidential appointive power, then tried to evoke the old Tenure of Office Act, passed by the Radicals during Johnson's administration. This act required the president to give good reason for removing an office-holder before the Senate would confirm a replacement. But Cleveland simply continued to make appointments until at last the Senate complied.

Little noteworthy legislation was passed during Cleveland's term except for the Interstate Commerce Act (see p. 464), which became law in 1887. Cleveland, whose acts were characteristically negative, stubbornly foiled a series of pension grabs inspired by the Grand Army of the Republic, a powerful organization of Civil War veterans. He vetoed pork-barrel appropriations and recovered 81 million acres that were being held illegally by powerful railroad corporations and lumber and cattle interests. Violent labor disturbances during 1886 (see p. 475) prompted him to propose that government machinery be set up to arbitrate labor disputes. The conservative press criticized this recommendation and Congress refused to accept it, but in 1888 a law was passed permitting voluntary arbitration and creating a president-appointed commission with the power to investigate and conciliate disputes.

Cleveland's most courageous act was his decision to push for a lowering of the tariff in spite of the warnings of his able and business-wise Secretary of the Navy, William C. Whitney. Although Cleveland was unimaginative and often short-sighted, his often-quoted response to the Democratic politicians who advised him to soft-pedal the tariff issue is typical of the man: "What is the use of being elected or re-elected if you don't stand for something?"

Tariff Issues. Civil War protectionists, like Vermont's Justin Morrill, had advocated tariffs as a way of nursing infant industries "into perennial vigor." Morrill had urged "moderate and steady discrimination in their favor, so long as their condition makes it proper, so long as there is a probable chance of ultimate success." A decade after the Republicans passed the Morrill Tariff in 1861, the idea of "moderate" discrimination for revenue and protection had been replaced by the idea of protection for protection's sake. So each important industry now felt obliged to organize a lobby and put pressure on Congress for special handouts. When moderate protectionists objected, according to one enemy of the tariff lobbies, they were "immediately assailed with accusations of corrupt and unpatriotic motives."

Tariff lobbyists in Washington during Grant's malodorous administration, together with the hordes of other plundering favor-seekers, turned the Capitol into a political sink.

Before 1870, anti-protectionists had pointed out that excessive protective duties did not always restore sick industries. Moreover, they did much harm. A tariff on salt had permitted salt manufacturers to combine, limit production, and triple the cost to the public in nine years. Pig-iron producers had won enormous bonuses as a result of high duties, but related industries, like shipbuilding, had been ruined as a consequence. To free-traders and moderate protectionists, high tariffs simply raised the prices of consumer goods, bestowed unwarranted benefits on a few industries, promoted monopoly, and encouraged foreign countries to retaliate.

Between 1865 and 1890, the struggle in Congress between the low-tariff and high-tariff men continued. Each side had its able champions: William D. "Pig-Iron" Kelley of Pennsylvania, whose devotion to high schedules amounted to a religion, and the witty S. S. "Sunset" Cox of New York, who spoke for free trade. The tariff reformers (many of them Liberal Republicans) made slight gains in 1872, but it was not an easy job for a large body of congressmen subject to the never-ending pressure of the lobbyists to draw up an equitable and workable tariff. The protectionists seized upon the devastating financial panic of 1873 to justify an increase in tariff rates in 1875, and from that point on the low-tariff men made little headway in either party. Able free-trade publicists kept the issue before the country, however, and when the Republicans in 1883 decided to make protection a campaign issue, the "education" of the nation proceeded apace. By this time, powerful tariff lobbies and industries demanding protection were so thoroughly entrenched in the Senate that tariff reform was virtually impossible—as the 1883 tariff demonstrated.

President Arthur had appointed a bipartisan tariff commission in 1882 to study the tariff schedules and to recommend changes. The commission, although it contained protectionist members, drew up a tariff bill that eliminated complicated schedules, reduced the rates on certain raw materials, and cut the tariff revenues by 20 per cent. After the proposed bill had been overhauled by House and Senate committees, it bore no resemblance to its original form. In fact, lobbyists representing hundreds of interests and trades saw to it that the rates were raised instead of lowered, and the practice of log-rolling prevented any reasonable adjustment. A wool congressman, for example, would agree to vote for higher iron rates if an iron congressman would cast his vote for an increase in the wool tariff. As a result, both rates would go up. Astute friends of the trusts and combinations in the Senate —men like Republican Nelson W. Aldrich of Rhode Island and Democrat Arthur P. Gorman of Maryland—adroitly scuttled any liberalized tariff bill that managed to slip by their co-workers in the House, and for a long time they foiled a growing demand for lowered tariffs.

President Cleveland did not want to establish free trade, as his critics charged, but only to make the tariff less exorbitantly protective. The treasury surplus, which had become dangerously swollen as a result of heavy tariff receipts, drew currency out of circulation at a time when additional amounts of money were needed to serve an expanding economy. Cleveland felt that the solution was not to give away the surplus to the states, as Blaine proposed, but to reduce it by scaling down the tariff rates. This he called for in an important message (December, 1887) devoted almost entirely to the case for tariff revision, in which he attacked excessive protection as a bane to the farmer and laborer and as a cause of monopoly. Shortly before the nominating conventions in 1888, the House passed the Mills Tariff Bill, which established moderate reductions, but it was revised upward in the Senate and finally buried. Republican protectionists decided to make the tariff the leading issue in the coming campaign.

The Harrison Administration.

Cleveland was renominated in 1888 by the Democrats without opposition, and the Republicans, accepting Blaine's decision not to run again, chose a conservative corporation lawyer, Benjamin Harrison of Indiana. Hostile cartoonists sometimes portrayed Harrison, a man of no remarkable talent, as a dwarf wearing a hat many sizes too big for him. In addition to being the grandson of President William Henry Harrison, "Young Tippecanoe" had other useful qualifications: a good war career (he had achieved the rank of brigadier general), some political experience (one term in the Senate), and a stanch faith in high tariffs and sound money.

The Republicans, under the astute management of National Party Chairman Matthew Quay of Pennsylvania, carried on a masterly campaign. They made the tariff the leading issue and charged that Cleveland's "free-trade" policy would ruin American manufacturing and betray the American workingman to the "pauper labor" of Europe. Many employers reinforced these warnings with threats of mass unemployment should the Democrats win. Even the Knights of Labor (see p. 474) succumbed to this argument and endorsed Harrison's candidacy. Where tariff "education" failed to convince, cash often persuaded. John Wanamaker, the Philadelphia department store millionaire, had raised large sums for the G.O.P., which were spent judiciously in the right states. The Republicans resorted to bribery of the most brazen sort in the key states of Indiana and New York.

Of great help to the Republicans in the last days of the campaign was a widely publicized letter written by the British minister in Washington to a Republican who had represented himself as an English-born American seeking advice on how to vote in the coming election. Which candidate, he asked, would be more friendly to England? The minister foolishly replied that Cleveland was to be preferred, and it is thought that his letter, immediately headlined in the press, swung many Irish-American votes (traditionally Democratic) to Harrison. Cleveland's popular vote topped Harrison's by more than 100,000, but Harrison had an electoral majority of 65. A switch of only about 6,500 votes in New York would have given Cleveland that state's votes and the election.

During the next four years (1889-1893), President Harrison—pious, chilly, and honest—was overshadowed by the men around him. His cabinet had already been determined by party leaders before he took office. Blaine became Secretary of State once more, and the other posts were filled by businesslike representatives from the East and West, including the merchant, John Wanamaker, as Postmaster-General. The banker, Levi P. Morton, was vice-president. Harrison promised to carry out the civil-service law that had been passed in 1883 (the Pendleton Act), but his own henchmen indulged in a wholesale dismissal of Democratic postmasters before the President could intervene. The civil-service commissioners whom he had named then placed the newly appointed officials on the classified list, forever free from Democratic retribution. Young Theodore Roosevelt, one of the commissioners, made himself obnoxious to the Republican professionals by trying to make the commission, as he wrote in 1889, "a living force." The "spoilsmen," however, regarded elections as wars to be won by hook or by crook and scorned what Conkling had called the "snivel service."

The conservatives were invincible in the Senate, where the friends of the railroad, lumber, oil, sugar, steel, silver, copper, and public-utility interests held sway, but they were at times strongly challenged in the House. The Speaker of the House, Thomas B. Reed of Maine, was an impressive parliamentarian who coolly abrogated old House rules in order to expedite House business and established new ones that gave him dictatorial power in controlling debate. The "Reed Rules" ended the obstructions

President Harrison (in this cartoon burlesque of Poe's famous poem, "The Raven") sits uncomfortably before the bust of his grandfather, whose hat he has been unable to fill. "Raven" Blaine, perched atop the bust of "Old Tippecanoe," croaks "Nevermore," forecasting Harrison's defeat in 1892.

that had long held up House business and permitted the majority party to govern without being hamstrung by the opposition tactics of a partisan minority.

Under the sardonic and genial direction of "Czar" Reed and his allies in the Senate, the Republicans during Harrison's administration began to subsidize their political friends and distribute to their deserving partisans the treasury surplus that had embarrassed past administrations.

Civil War veterans and the managers of protected industries had contributed greatly to Cleveland's defeat, and their reward was the "billion-dollar Congress." Gigantic handouts were the order of the day. The Dependent Pension Act, passed in 1890, provided pensions for any disabled veteran even though his disability had no connection with the war, and for the widows of veterans. By 1893, the number of pensioners had risen from 676,000 to 970,000, and the cost of paying them from $81 million to $135 million annually.

Having provided for the war veterans, Congress on October 1, 1890, enacted the McKinley Tariff, the highest thus far in American history. William McKinley, Republican Representative from Ohio, equated his tariff measure with national prosperity, "the great comforts to the masses," and "the safety and purity and permanency of our political system." In effect, it was a prohibitive tariff that excluded rather than limited foreign imports, raised the price of many necessities, and enriched protected industries. Earlier tariffs had "nourished" the so-called "infant industries." The McKinley Tariff had the distinction of protecting them before they were even born. Tin-plate, for example, had been imported cheaply from abroad up to this time, and the heavy duty imposed on it in 1890 was simply a bounty to would-be manufacturers who now proceeded to invest heavily in domestic tin-plate mills. The protectionists hoped to placate the farmers by taxing the entry of certain farm products (eggs, potatoes, bacon, barley) that were imported in very small quantities. To soothe the sugar-refiners, they put raw sugar on the free list, a provision that incidentally eliminated a large source of the tariff revenue. The McKinley Bill compensated the hitherto protected American sugar-growers by giving them a bounty of 2 cents a pound. Understandably, Secretary of State Blaine feared that European nations whose manufactured goods were shut out by the new tariff barriers would not buy the American farm surplus. Although he failed to introduce the kind of reciprocity terms he wanted, he succeeded in inducing the Senate to accept an amendment giving the president authority to remove certain items from the free list if the countries that produced them placed discriminatory duties on American goods.

The McKinley Tariff helped solve the problem of the treasury surplus but infuriated the western voters, who resented being penalized for the benefit of eastern manufacturers. And the passage of the loosely framed and slackly administered Sherman Antitrust Act in July, 1890 (see p. 470), ostensibly aimed at curbing monopolies, failed to appease them. Blaine's warning to McKinley that the protective features of his tariff "will protect the Republican Party only into speedy retirement" was soon borne out.

Western Republican congressmen had supported the eastern wing of the party on the McKinley Tariff, and in return the easterners reluctantly cooperated with the western silver Republicans to pass the Sherman Silver Purchase Act of 1890. This bill provided for government purchase of 4.5 million ounces of silver bullion a month (approximately the total output of the western silver mines), against which the Treasury would issue notes redeemable in gold and silver coin. Debtors in the rural South and West hoped that the Silver Purchase Act would produce a more abundant currency, but the price of silver declined and the resulting inflation for the next few years was slight. Neither the extreme inflationists, who were pressing for unlimited coinage of silver, nor the anti-inflationists, who were fearful of any tampering with the gold standard, were satisfied.

The Harrison administration's "giveaway" program did not sit well with the voters, as the elections of 1890 unmistakably showed. The Republicans lost control of the House and their majority was cut down in the Senate. The Democratic upsurge, which was in part a reaction to the McKinley Tariff, foreshadowed Harrison's eclipse in the presidential election of 1892 and the return of Cleveland. Harrison had displeased eastern financial interests by failing to veto the Silver Purchase Bill, and he had antagonized the reformers in his party by tolerating the spoils system. Moreover, his coldness and his suspicious nature discouraged an enthusiastic personal following, such as Blaine enjoyed, from developing around him. In 1892, Cleveland received 5,556,000 votes to 5,176,000 for Harrison. Narrow though his margin was, it represented the most decisive presidential election victory since 1872.

Labor unrest, culminating in the bloody Homestead strike in the summer of 1892 (see p. 476), aided the Democratic candidates. But even more telling was the decline of Republican strength in the trans-Mississippi West and the rise of the People's party (more familiarly known as the Populist party), which had been founded two years before. The Populist candidate, General James B. Weaver of Iowa, received over a million votes and captured four states in the 1892 election. Both major parties feared that a powerful third party was in the making, although neither was ready to incorporate the Populist program into its party platform.

III. THE AGRARIAN REVOLT

Backgrounds. Between 1870 and 1890, the western farmer—faced with rising costs and falling prices, and driven frantic by the effects of drought, insect pests, and other hazards of nature—became convinced that he was the victim of political and economic persecution. Certainly he was not getting his fair share of America's vaunted prosperity.

The agricultural depression slowly settling upon the Mississippi Valley and the rural South was in part a result of the mechanical and communications revolution that had transformed the diversified farm into an agricultural factory and the jack-of-all-trades farmer into a business specialist. Farm prices had zoomed up during the Civil War and immediately after. With improved machinery and an apparently unlimited supply of land, the farmer began to raise single crops of corn and wheat and to extend his acreage. In the 30 years between 1870 and 1900, four hundred and thirty million acres of new land were settled. One consequence of this expansion was a vastly increased output of wheat and corn that had to compete in the world market with cereals grown in the developing territories of Argentina, Australia, and Canada. American producers, whose prosperity depended more and more on foreign exports, found themselves trapped. The fresh lands of the West, improved machinery, and access to new markets made possible by the railroad had encouraged them to overextend their operations. When their long-anticipated prosperity failed to materialize, the farmers sought desperately for explanations and remedies.

A persistent decline in farm prices from 1870 to 1897 was the most disheartening symptom of rural ills and the main source of agrarian bitterness. Wheat sold for 95 cents a bushel in 1880; for 83 cents in 1890; and for 50 cents in 1895. Between 1870 and 1895, corn prices declined about 50 per cent, and cotton prices fell about 37 per cent. Tobacco, hogs, sheep, butter, and cheese were all caught in the same downward spiral. A temporary recovery took place in 1890-1891, but prices nose-dived again in 1895-1896 to hit the lowest levels ever reached between 1865 and the 1920's.

To make matters worse, most western and southern farmers were heavily in debt to eastern creditors. Beginning in 1881, land-speculation (encouraged by the railroads, politicians, and the press) sent land prices skyrocketing in Kansas, Nebraska, Missouri, and the Dakotas. "Haste to get rich," as one Kansas official remarked later, "has made us borrowers, and the borrower has made booms, and booms made men wild, and Kansas became a vast insane asylum covering 80,000 square miles." Much of the western farmer's trouble could be blamed on the get-rich-quick spirit that encouraged his reckless borrowing, but his difficulties were made acute by agencies and institutions for which he himself was not responsible and by natural forces over which he had no control.

Southern farmers labored under greater handicaps than farmers in any other section of the country. The vast majority of them were sharecroppers or tenant farmers whose virtual enslavement to the supply merchant preserved the worst features of the prewar one-crop system, and made it more pervasive than ever (see p. 392). By the 1880's, the typical southern farm was small and unmechanized, devoted to producing a cash staple of cotton or tobacco and nothing else. The exceptions were the rice plantations on the coast of Louisiana and Texas, the sugar plantations in Louisiana, and the truck farms along the southern coastal plain.

The "Bourbon" leadership that had taken over the South after 1876 included the old plantation gentry (many of them former Confederate officers), the merchants, and the new class of industrialists. Their social position and their anti-Reconstruction record made them politically acceptable to the mass of white farmers, but they showed more interest in financial speculation than in agriculture and were content to leave the dirt farmers in virtual peonage. Of more interest to Bourbons like Henry W. Grady, editor of the Atlanta *Constitution,* and to other propagandists for the New South were the opportunities for manufacturing textiles and tobacco, building railroads, establishing cotton exchanges, and improving marketing facilities. In short, the post-Civil War gentry had become industrial-minded, and the old agrarian convictions were kept alive only by the dirt farmers.

As cotton prices dipped sickeningly from about 15 cents a pound in the 1870's to 7 cents a pound in the early 90's, and as taxes and debts mounted, these destitute and neglected men accused the Bourbons of selling out to the Yankee capitalists who financed the extortionate southern railroads. By the 1880's, the agrarians had lost their apathy and responded to the fiery appeals of their new leaders, who were by no means the fanatical yokels their enemies made them out to be, but solid men of property and education.

The Farmer's Plight.

In *The Octopus,* Frank Norris' novel about California wheat-growers, the railroad is likened to "a gigantic parasite fattening upon the life-blood of an entire commonwealth." And so thousands of farmers came to regard it. The railroad had been heralded in the trans-Mississippi West as an agency of progress, and the states, counties, and municipalities through which it passed had contributed millions of dollars to help construct it. The coming of the railroad did enhance land values, and it did connect the western farmers with hitherto inaccessible markets. But it also increased the number of farmers who were competing for these markets. And the longer the distance between the farm and the markets, the smaller the farmer's profit.

Yet American farmers rarely took these facts into consideration. Those who lived west of Milwaukee and Chicago knew only that sometimes they had to give up one bushel of wheat or corn to pay the freight on another. Railroad officials justified the high rates (farmers called them "extortionate") by pointing out that traffic from the western states was highly seasonal and almost entirely one-way, and that freight cars had to be sent back empty from the eastern terminals. Farmers countered with the accusation that the carriers charged "all the traffic will bear" in order to pay dividends on their watered stock. The stiffest freight rates, moreover, were paid by farmers living in the very areas that had subsidized the railroads by exchanging county bonds for this same over-capitalized stock. The railroads, they charged, had repaid this confidence by favoring one locality over another, by discriminating between large and small shippers, by resorting to rebates and pools (see p. 463), and by forcing farmers to store their grain in railroad-controlled elevators and warehouses. Everyone knew that railroads bought and sold legislatures, awarded free passes to favored persons, hired the most skillful lawyers, and exhibited a public-be-damned attitude toward anyone who challenged them.

Attempts to regulate freight and storage rates had already been made before the founding of the Patrons of Husbandry in 1867. This enterprising society of farmers, organized into state or local "granges," came into being in 1867 after its founder, Oliver H. Kelley, had been moved to do something

to improve the social and cultural opportunities of American farmers. A semi-secret society, it took no open part in political activities. With the onslaught of the 1873 depression, however, its members (perhaps 1,500,000 by 1874) began through associated political clubs to agitate for cheaper transportation, tax adjustments, easier credit terms, and a reduction of fees to middlemen; and they helped to consolidate anti-railroad sentiment in Iowa, Wisconsin, Illinois, and Minnesota. Together with the merchants and shippers, the Grangers (as they came to be called) and other farm groups pushed through legislation to regulate the activities

The "good life" of the farmer that the Grangers hoped to restore.

of railroads and grain-elevator companies. In some states, the legislatures fixed maximum rates for intra-state traffic. Other states set up commissions either with discretionary power to determine railroad rates or with the privilege of making recommendations.

The railroads fought regulation in the courts on the grounds that public rate-fixing was nothing less than legalized confiscation and that no state might regulate interstate commerce. In 1877, the Supreme Court denied these contentions in decisions involving eight "Granger" cases. The most important of these cases, *Munn* v. *Illinois,* established the principle of state regulation on the ground that owners of property "in which the public has an interest" must necessarily "submit to be controlled by the public for the common good. . . ." In other cases, the Court upheld the right of the state to regulate rates on commodities moving across its boundaries. The Court declared, finally, that the question of whether the rates were confiscatory was a legislative matter that could not be reviewed by the Court.

In the next two decades, a more conservative Court reversed certain parts of the Granger rulings. It held in the Wabash case in 1886 that a state could not determine rates on interstate traffic or otherwise interfere with it. Although later decisions hampered public regulation, the Granger cases had established a vital precedent: the legitimacy of public control over the great corporations. The railroads refused to accept this interpretation and continued to run their business as they had in the past. But the Granger cases, although they could hardly have been responsible for a decline in freight rates that began as early as 1873, may have helped bring about a more conscious effort on the part of the carriers to court the public's good will.

Public opinion ultimately forced the major political parties to enact federal legislation regulating railroads after state regulation of interstate traffic had been nullified by the Supreme Court. Federal legislation took the form of the Interstate Commerce Act of 1887, which forbade rebates, pooling agreements, and other railroad abuses, but lacked effective enforcement provisions (see p. 464).

One of the farmer's most legitimate complaints was that he had to carry an unfair tax burden. Before the era of railroads, corporations, and utilities, personal property consisted pretty much of land and livestock on which it was relatively easy to assess a property tax. But with the growth of financial and industrial institutions, new kinds of personal property came into existence—stocks and bonds. Stocks and bonds were less visible kinds of property than cows and barns and were easier to conceal. As a result, the tax burden began to fall more and more oppressively on the American farmer, whose possessions were wide open to the view of the tax assessor. It was this situation that prompted an Ohio governor to declare in 1887: "The great majority of personal property in this state is not returned, but entirely and fraudulently withheld from taxation."

Thus taxation fell upon the small and medium-sized property-owners who were least able to afford it, whereas great corporations and their wealthy owners either escaped taxation entirely or succeeded by fraud in scaling down their assessments by hundreds of thousands of dollars. The railroad owners, who were especially adept at undervaluing their property, paid no taxes on their extensive land grants; yet the owners of mortgaged farms were often taxed for more than their property was worth. And farmers could not pass the tax along to the consumer, as the monopolists could.

The protective tariff constituted still another kind of tax, although many farmers in the North were seduced by the arguments of the protectionists into supporting it. Free trade, traditionally espoused by the South, was still identified with the perpetrators of rebellion, and the tariff propagandists succeeded in convincing many people that high tariff rates and patriotism were one and the same thing, and that protection assured the farmer a reliable home market for his crops.

Southern farmers had long recognized that high tariff rates excluded cheap foreign manufactures and forced the American farmer to sell his products at a disadvantage in a competitive world market. But northern farmers often failed to see that mounting tariff revenues in effect granted a federal subsidy to the men who were most vociferous in defending competition and laissez faire and who consistently fought any program to raise farm prices and to reduce farm costs. Only gradually did the western farmer come to understand how the tariff (to quote one Iowa representative) taxed "every prominent necessity of life, food, fuel, shelter, and clothing," and why (as a tariff commission

Unfortunately, the farmers' penchant for regarding complicated business procedures as the conspiracies of evil men blinded them to their own lack of managerial skill, organizing ability, and technical information. Too often they rallied behind some economic cure-all and ignored legislation that might have revised the tax system, regulated transportation, or lowered the outrageous tariff rates. Politically and economically, they simply were no match for the business and financial leaders, nor could they agree for very long among themselves on any program of reform.

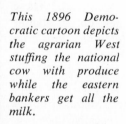
This 1896 Democratic cartoon depicts the agrarian West stuffing the national cow with produce while the eastern bankers get all the milk.

report concluded in 1882) he paid a tax of from 33.5 to 60 per cent on these necessities and others.

But if farmers were uncertain at times about the pros and cons of tariffs, they soon came to realize that they were subject to the protected industries, the trusts that were "mothered" by the tariffs. Southern farmers paid tribute to the jute-bagging, cottonseed-oil, tobacco, and fertilizer trusts. And northern farmers discovered that farm machinery, tools, binding twine, staple foods, building materials, and clothing—anything from kitchen utensils to umbrellas—were controlled by combinations. The trust became the ugly symbol of the conscienceless "Money Power," and the frustrated farmers saw the hand of the trust in the policies of both major parties.

Origins of Populism.   For 30 years, disgruntled farmers had been complaining about farm conditions to their state and national governments. But by the early 90's, the railroads, trusts, and banking interests were enjoying greater power than ever before, and farm prices were still dropping. Many Republicans and Democrats now turned in desperation to the People's party—an amalgam of the old "out" groups—ex-Grangers, Greenbackers, Single-Taxers, Bellamy Nationalists, Socialists, and Trade Unionists—whose separate attempts at reform had only partly succeeded or had failed entirely.

The roots of the People's party, which was organized in 1890, were firmly planted in American history. Comparable farmers' movements go back at least as far as Shays' rebellion, and farm societies and clubs had been demanding government relief long before the Civil War. Although orators liked to speak of the farmer's distaste for "speculative adventures" and the "simple grandeur of his rural estate . . . exempt from all complexity of business relations," matters like credit and indebtedness, the price of fertilizer, and the costs of transportation were all too real to him. After 1865, farm organizations attempted persistently though unsuccessfully to solve these nagging problems.

The immediate origins of Populism can be traced to the new farmers' organizations that sprang up in the late 80's to supplant the Grange. One was the powerful Farmers' Alliance and Industrial Union (better known as the Southern Alliance). The other was the National Farmers' Alliance in the Northwest (the Northwest Alliance). The Southern Alliance had well over a million members by 1890, far more than the Northwest Alliance had; together, these two great regional societies formed the most powerful body of farmers in American history. Although each of the groups had its special problems and programs, and although they disagreed on such questions as Negro membership, organizational structure, and methods of political action, their objectives were much the same. Besides government ownership of railroads and telegraph facilities, they wanted a more plentiful money supply and easier credit for the farmer.

One scheme to expand credit for the marketing season—the so-called "sub-treasury" plan—was proposed by C. W. Macune, a Southern Alliance newspaper editor. Let the government set up a sub-treasury office and warehouse, Macune recommended, in every country that offered for sale more than $500,000 worth of farm products annually. Farmers who deposited non-perishable crops in these government warehouses or elevators would receive as a loan until the time of sale United States Treasury notes in amounts up to 80 per cent of the local market value of their stored crops. This loan was to be repaid when the crop was sold. The plan, later incorporated into the agricultural program of the Democrats in the 1930's, had the double advantage of allowing the farmer to hold his wheat or corn until he could get the best price, and of increasing the supply of legal tender.

This scheme, as well as other Alliance demands, was passed off as "hayseed socialism" by the eastern conservatives, but they could not ignore the political prairie fire that began to rage in the southern and Plains states between 1887 and 1890. Southern Alliance men, working at first through the Democratic party, elected three governors and won control over the legislatures of eight states. Candidates sponsored by the Northern Alliance on an anti-monopoly platform were less successful in the grain states of the Northwest, but their gains were still impressive. There were no Alliance political parties as such, but where Alliance men were not trying to capture one of the two major parties they formed third parties of their own. These parties had different names, but in Kansas (where drought had reduced the corn crop from over 158 million bushels in 1885 to 55 million in 1889, and where over 75 per cent of the farms were mortgaged) the name People's party was adopted. Members of this party, and others like it, became known as "Populists" (the foes of the "Plutocrats"), who advocated public ownership of the railroads, free silver, and cheap credit.

By 1890, the radical farmers of the Northwest were eager to start a new party, even though the members of the Southern Alliance held back for fear that a split between the voters in the South would threaten white supremacy. The third-party men called for a convention in May, 1891, and into Cincinnati came a swarm of Alliance farmers, relics of defunct parties, ambitious politicians, and visionaries with private recipes for salvation. Knights of Labor men came too, for by this time the Knights' membership lay principally outside the large industrial cities in the smaller communities closely tied to a rural economy. The convention postponed until the following year the question of whether to start a third party, but in the meantime the Cincinnati delegates drew up a People's party platform calling for unlimited coinage of silver, direct election of senators, the nationalizing of banks, government ownership of railroads and utilities, the prohibition of foreign ownership of land, postal savings banks, and an eight-hour day.

A year later, in St. Louis, on February 26, 1892, the People's party was officially founded by a convention of representatives from every farm group in the United States, the most important of whom were the Southern Alliance leaders who had held off from the Cincinnati meeting. After adopting the Cincinnati platform, the St. Louis delegates called for a presidential nominating convention to meet in Omaha in July. At this convention, representatives of every reform program of the past three decades chose James B. Weaver of Iowa and a former Confederate general, James Field of Virginia, as the presidential and vice-presidential candidates. The platform was about the same as the one accepted at St. Louis, but it contained additional demands for the secret ballot, the sub-treasury plan, and a single term for the president and vice-president.

The Populist Mind. Populist leaders in the 90's ranged from sober-minded farmers to flamboyant fanatics. They bore wild-sounding names like "Sockless" Jerry Simpson of Kansas and David H. "Bloody Bridles" Waite of Colorado. And their orators, one of whom was the "Kansas Pythoness," Mary Ellen Lease (who advised her audiences to "Raise less corn and more hell"), spoke with a vehemence that shocked respectable easterners. The first Populist conventions, unbossed and spontaneous, resembled religious revivals more than party caucuses. Populist rhetoric was grandiloquent, studded with such expressions as "pitiless oppression," "the blood-hounds of money," "scheming, purse-proud foreigners," and "the altar of Mammon." Populist spell-binders sometimes injected into their attacks on the bankers and railroads a note of violence and illiberality that clashed with their idealistic objectives.

Nowhere is the Populist mentality better demonstrated than in a widely read novel, *Caesar's Column* (1889), written by one of the most prominent Populist leaders, Ignatius Donnelly. Donnelly had been active in Minnesota politics after the Civil War and later became a brilliant and influential orator for the Alliance. During his three terms in Congress, he spent his spare hours in the Library of Congress, where he digested the enormous store of odd learning that was to appear in his popular scientific treatises. One of his books proved the existence of Plato's fabled Atlantis; another that the world had once collided with a comet; a third that Bacon had written Shakespeare's plays. In each of these books, he was obsessed by conspiracy or violence. And in *Caesar's Column,* the Populists' fear of fraud, their hatred of international bankers, and their suspicion of urban parasites are fused into one of the most violent and horrifying novels in American literature. Its theme appeared in the preamble to the People's party platform that Donnelly wrote in 1892:

A vast conspiracy against mankind has been organized on two continents; and it is rapidly taking possession of the world. If not met and overthrown at once, it forebodes terrible social convulsions, the destruction of civilization, or the establishment of an absolute despotism.

Like Bellamy, Donnelly projected his novel into the future, but his New York locale bore no similarity to Bellamy's transformed Boston. Donnelly pictured society as divided into a small plutocracy, incredibly corrupt and soulless, and a brutalized proletariat. He showed that progress and poverty had developed simultaneously, and actually described the bloody revolution that had been predicted so often in the 1880's. Donnelly's apocalyptic book reflected the rage and suppressed violence of his era. The villains who provoke the violence he piously deprecated but obviously enjoyed, are the "plutes," the "cultured spoilers of the many."

Populism was far from the "lawless, irresponsible, incendiary" thing that the eastern press described it as being. But when the Populists seized upon certain stereotypes—

the banker, the middleman, Wall Street—to symbolize the forces of exploitation, they dangerously oversimplified the causes of their plight and provided a strategy for the less innocent demagogues of the future.

IV. THE BATTLE OF THE STANDARDS

Cleveland's Second Term. President Cleveland, who began his second term in 1893, had little sympathy with Populism and its advocates. His hard-money views and innate conservatism seemed proof to the radicals in the South and West that the Democratic party, no less than the Republican, represented big business exclusively. "The crowd," declared one southern Populist, "that takes their politics from Alexander Hamilton is the crowd we have got to beat. Cleveland is our Hamilton," said another, the slave to "the financial kings of the country."

One of the most disastrous panics in American history inaugurated Cleveland's second term, and the resulting depression hung on for four years. By the end of 1893, more than 600 banks had gone under and over 15,000 businesses had failed. Many railroads, including giants like the Union Pacific and the Northern Pacific, had gone into receivership.

The overexpansion of transportation and industry seems to have been the principal reason for the collapse of 1893. But the long agricultural slump that began in 1887, the reduced purchasing power of a large section of the farm population, irresponsible speculation, the decline in the gold reserve, and the unstable economic conditions abroad that forced foreign investors to sell their American securities—all fed it. Democrats placed the blame on Harrison's "billion-dollar Congress" and on the McKinley Tariff that lopped millions off the annual tariff revenues. Conservative businessmen and politicians blamed the Silver Purchase Act, which, they said, weakened the currency, stimulated the hoarding of gold, and destroyed business confidence. Even the withdrawal of foreign investment, they argued, had been prompted

by European fears that America was going off the gold standard.

Whatever the causes of the panic, Cleveland saw only a few weeks after he had taken office that he would have to act quickly if the Treasury was to continue to redeem in gold all types of currency presented to it. The gold surplus he had built up during his first administration had begun to drain away in Harrison's term and was continuing to fall alarmingly. The McKinley Tariff had sharply reduced tariff revenues, and what with the huge payments to veterans, unfavorable trade balances that drained off the gold to Europe, and the monthly purchases of silver under the terms of the Silver Purchase Act (see p. 494), the financial picture grew steadily darker. By April, 1893, the gold reserve had dropped below the $100 million that was considered the minimum amount required to secure the issues of treasury notes and greenbacks.

Cleveland's first thought was to repeal the Silver Purchase Act, which permitted holders of silver certificates to exchange them for gold. With some hesitation, he called for a special session of Congress to amend the act in the summer of 1893. "Gold" Democrats and Republicans closed ranks against the inflationists in both parties and enacted the repeal in October. Repeal of the Silver Purchase Act checked, but did not stop, the flow of gold from the Treasury. Owners of gold and silver certificates, suspecting that the government would soon be unable to redeem currency in gold, began a run on the Treasury. Had the Treasury been permitted to retire their notes from circulation, the government's plight would not have been so desperate. But the law required the Treasury to re-issue these notes immediately, which meant that the same currency might be presented to the Treasury for redemption in gold many times.

By February, 1894, the gold reserve had shrunk to $65.7 million. Frantic efforts to replenish the Treasury by means of a series of bond issues to banking syndicates did little to help matters, for the government was simply getting back the gold it had paid out to redeem paper currency. To meet the crisis, Cleveland was forced in February, 1895, to borrow $62 million in gold from the Morgan and Belmont banking syndicate on terms decidedly unfavorable to the government. The syndicate netted more than $7 million in the transaction, and Cleveland was denounced by the inflationists as a tool of Wall Street. But the bankers did go abroad to secure half of the gold they supplied, and Morgan did succeed in slowing down the drain of gold to Europe. In January, 1896, the government floated another loan, this time popularly subscribed, which brought the gold reserve up to $128 million. The crisis was at last over, and, with confidence restored, the gold in government reserves became increasingly plentiful.

Cleveland's resolute defense of the gold standard aggravated agrarian discontent in the West and South as much as it heartened the financiers, and it probably destroyed any hope of getting mass support for tariff reform. The Democrats, fulfilling a campaign promise, had passed a tariff bill in the House drawn up by William L. Wilson of West Virginia. Wilson's bill provided for a modest reduction in rates and included, as a concession to the Populists, a 2 per cent tax on incomes over $4,000. When the bill reached the Senate, a Democratic-Republican coalition of protectionists led by Senator Gorman of Maryland restored most of the cuts that had been made in the House. The sugar interests saw to it that high rates were placed on both refined and raw sugar, and the iron and coal interests successfully prevented their products from going on the free list. In all, the Wilson-Gorman Tariff, which became law in August, 1894, without Cleveland's signature, was a triumph for the lobbyists. Cleve-

land regarded it as a disgrace to his party and acceptable only as an improvement on the even higher McKinley Tariff of 1890.

The glee of the Populists over the income tax provision in the tariff was short-lived, for in 1895 the Supreme Court in a 5-to-4 decision declared it unconstitutional. Joseph H. Choate, who argued the case against the government, raised the specter of communism and held up the income tax as a blow at widows and orphans. The majority of the Court agreed, but its decision was narrowly constitutional. It ruled that direct taxes could only be apportioned among the states on the basis of population, not on the basis of personal wealth, and that the income tax violated the "direct tax" clause of the Constitution (Article I, Section IX, paragraph 4).

The Election of 1896.   As Cleveland's second term drew to a close, the American mood was growing more sullen. Thousands of unemployed roamed the country, sometimes traveling in large gangs. Since the government offered no relief to the destitute, agitators began to propose schemes for solving the problem of unemployment. The activities of one agitator—General Jacob S. Coxey of Massillon, Ohio—convinced some frightened property-holders in 1894 that a revolution had actually begun.

To employ the jobless and to end the depression, Coxey proposed that Congress appropriate a half-billion dollars to be distributed at the rate of $20 million a month for a gigantic road-building program. Unemployed men would be paid $1.50 for an eight-hour day, and local public works would be financed by government loans to communities offering non-interest-bearing bonds as security. To dramatize his program, Coxey and his lieutenants planned a march on Washington. Soon "armies" all over the country were heading for the Capitol. Coxey's army actually arrived, but it was speedily dispersed after Coxey and a few of his leaders were arrested for stepping on the grass.

The other armies were turned away. But by this time unemployment had become a well-aired national issue—an issue on which the Populists hoped to capitalize.

The silver issue, however, crowded out all others from the popular mind. The heavy propagandizing of the western silver interests had begun to tell, and the farmers who had been demanding inflation for years saw the "conspiracy" against silver as another evidence of Wall Street treachery. When William H. Harvey published his *Coin's Financial School* in 1894, he gave the silverites an ideal little handbook that reduced the complicated details of money and banking to terms that laymen could understand. Through skillful use of diagrams, cartoons, and simple questions and answers, Professor Coin (the name of Harvey's spokesman) "proved" that the unlimited coinage of silver would guarantee prosperity and make other reforms unnecessary; only "a conspiracy of Goldbugs barred the way."

Harvey described the country as "distracted," with "tens of thousands . . . out of work," the jails, workhouses, and insane asylums filled, half-starved men marching on Washington, riots and strikes prevailing throughout the land. Whether exaggerated or not, these conditions were probably reflected in the elections of 1894, which showed Cleveland's declining popularity in areas where he had once been strong. The Republicans won overwhelming control in the House (244 to 105), and the Populists, whose vote in two years had increased by 42 per cent, elected six senators and seven congressmen. Even more ominous for Democratic prospects, anti-administration Democrats in the South like Benjamin R. Tillman of South Carolina viciously attacked Cleveland. "When Judas betrayed Christ," Tillman charged, "his heart was not blacker than this scoundrel, Cleveland, in deceiving the Democracy." He promised his constituents that he would take a pitchfork to Washington and prod the "old bag of beef" in "his old fat ribs."

These Democratic dissensions naturally pleased the Republicans, who now predicted an easy victory in the presidential election of 1896. They failed to realize that party discontent was not entirely confined to the Democratic rank and file. Many Republican voters as well were receptive to a third party.

In June, 1896, the Republican convention, meeting in St. Louis, chose William McKinley of Ohio as its presidential candidate. McKinley, the sponsor of the tariff of 1890, had served as governor of Ohio between 1891 and 1895. He owed his nomination very largely to his friendship with the Ohio businessman and party boss, Marcus Alonzo Hanna. In 1896, Hanna—king of Great Lakes shipping, banker, and street-railway magnate—dominated Ohio politics. Blunt and unsentimental, he managed the political fortunes of his friend, McKinley, with a skill that drew applause from rival bosses. Months before the Republican convention, Hanna had captured a majority of the delegates by persuasion and money, and McKinley's nomination on the first ballot came as no surprise.

The only opposition to McKinley in the East had come from the gold men who feared that he was not sound on the money question. "Nobody," declared the New York Republican boss, Thomas C. Platt, "can look at McKinley's record and read the flabby things he has said without perceiving that he has no fixed opinions, but has been turned and twisted by changing public opinion." McKinley had voted for the Bland-Allison Act in 1878 and the Silver Purchase Act of 1890, but he had no passionate attachment to silver. The astute Hanna would have preferred McKinley to straddle the currency issue in order to keep the silverite Republicans from bolting the party, but he was willing to accept a sound money plank in return for eastern financial support. "We are . . . opposed to the free coinage of silver," the Republican declaration read, "except by international agreement with the leading commercial nations of the world, which we pledge ourselves to promote, and until such agreement can be obtained the existing gold standard must be preserved." After the adoption of this "sound-money" plank, a small bloc of silver Republicans led by Senator Henry M. Teller of Colorado walked out of the convention.

To the Democrats, the silver issue was heaven-sent. The Democratic National Committee adhered to the gold standard, but others saw a chance of absorbing the Populists and winning the election in 1896. At the Democratic convention in Chicago, which met shortly after the Republican convention, the silver majority routed the "gold bugs"— as the gold-standard men were called. Western and southern Democrats repudiated President Cleveland, ignored Missouri's Richard P. Bland, and nominated instead a 36-year-old Nebraskan, William Jennings Bryan. John P. Altgeld, whose pardon of the Haymarket rioters in 1893 and handling of the Pullman Strike (see p. 477) had made him anathema to conservatives everywhere, wrote the platform, which came out flatly for unlimited coinage of silver at the ratio of 16 ounces of silver to 1 ounce of gold.

Bryan's nomination was not the unpremeditated act of an inspired convention, nor was he an unknown. He had already distinguished himself in and out of Congress as an eloquent orator, and his friends had been working for his nomination since April. No other aspirant possessed his qualifications: he was a long-standing Democrat who could appeal to the West and South; he did not bear the anarchist stigma, as Altgeld did, yet he sounded enough like a Populist to win Populist votes. His celebrated speech delivered at the Democratic convention in which he attacked the apostles of gold and defended the claims of the agrarian West, seems a little bombastic when read today, but it caught the Biblical fervor of the Populist crusade: "You shall not press down upon the brow of labor this crown of thorns, you shall not crucify mankind upon a cross of gold."

The Populists, who held their convention at St. Louis in August, were now faced with a dilemma. To fuse with the Democrats by supporting Bryan would mean political ex-

tinction; but to wage a separate Populist campaign would only split the silver vote and hand the election to the Republicans. Most of the delegates approved of Bryan, but the southern Populists strongly opposed fusion with the Democrats, with whom they had been fighting bitterly for years. The fusionists, however, could point out that the Democratic platform did demand the unlimited coinage of silver; it did attack Cleveland's deals with the bankers; it did recommend stricter railroad regulation and a constitutional amendment to make an income tax possible. Against the wishes of the die-hards, the delegates nominated Bryan for president, but they could not stomach the Democratic vice-presidential candidate, Arthur Sewall, a rich Maine banker. In his place, they nominated the fiery Georgian, Thomas E. Watson. Even before the election of 1896, many disillusioned Populists and reformers were disgusted by the overemphasis on silver and the playing down of the more radical reforms in the People's party platform.

The election of 1896, one of the most dramatic and poignant in American history, demonstrated the superiority of a well-financed and masterfully organized campaign against a campaign that relied more on emotion than on cash. Bryan, handicapped by two running-mates who detested each other, and strapped for money to finance his campaign, subordinated most of the Populist issues in order to play up the free-silver question. The redoubtable Hanna, in the meantime, was extracting contributions for McKinley's campaign (variously estimated from $3 million to more than $15 million) from financial and industrial interests. According to Brooks Adams, grandson of John Quincy Adams and brother of Henry, Hanna moved his forces like a squad of policemen against a mob. To Adams, the fight of the Populists was as impressive as it was futile:

A rising of miserable bankrupt farmers, and day labourers . . . have made the greatest fight against the organized capital of the world that has ever been made in this century—or perhaps ever. No money, no press, no leaders, no organization. Amidst abuse, ridicule, intimidation, bribery—against forces so powerful and so subtle that they reach the bravest and most honest men in the country.

But the Bryanites, abandoned by the conservative eastern Democrats, vilified by the press as raving anarchists, abused by ministers and professors, were decisively repudiated at the polls. McKinley's plurality was over 600,000, the largest any presidential candidate had achieved since Grant defeated Greeley in 1872. He won 271 electoral votes to Bryan's 176 and captured former agrarian strongholds in the Northwest. Even Iowa, Minnesota, and North Dakota went Republican.

In retrospect, Bryan's defeat seems almost inevitable. A rise in wheat prices immediately before the election may have reduced farm discontent somewhat, although other farm prices did not rise until after November. No doubt the flood of propaganda, the pressure that employers put on industrial workers, and the identification of Bryanism with anarchy and revolution had something to do with McKinley's success, but there were even more obvious causes. Bryan's support outside the Great Plains and the Rocky Mountain states was spotty. Older farm areas in the Northwest, with a more diversified agriculture, opposed him, and the urban workers

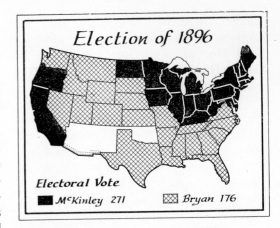

Election of 1896

Electoral Vote
■ McKinley 271   ▧ Bryan 176

failed to provide the mass support Bryan hoped for. A hodge-podge party of dirt farmers, socialists, reformers, political opportunists, and cranks, held together by common grievances, inexpertly led and poorly financed, had been crushed by what John P. Altgeld (himself a target for Republican mud-slingers) called "a combination of forces such as had never been united before and will probably never again be." But Republican slush-funds do not explain why Bryan failed so badly in the industrial East. McKinley won, according to the famous Kansas editor, William Allen White, because "he could unite to a political solidarity the American middle class."

Republican Prosperity. It is doubtful that McKinley's election in 1896 restored prosperity, as the Republicans claimed, but

The symbol of Republican prosperity—"the full dinner pail"—that figured in the election of 1900.

the defeat of Bryan—"the wretched, rattle-pated boy, posing in vapid vanity and mouthing resounding rottenness," as the New York *Tribune* so unkindly described him—soothed the fears and raised the confidence of those who stood to gain most from protective tariffs and sound currency. The Republican administration immediately passed the Dingley Tariff Bill in 1897, which raised schedules above the rates set by the Wilson-Gorman Tariff of 1894 and even above the McKinley Tariff of 1890. Fortunately, deflation was halted and the money supply was increased by new sources of gold that poured in from the Klondike, South Africa, and Australia, and by the introduction of a cheap cyanide process for extracting gold from low-grade ore. Good harvests at home, crop failures abroad, and high farm prices extinguished social discontent. When the Republicans finally passed the Currency Act of 1900, which officially made the gold dollar the unit of value and required all paper currency to be redeemable in gold, the free-silver "heresy" was fast waning.

"Republican prosperity" became a key issue in McKinley's successful campaign for re-election in 1900 (see p. 564). The Republican slogan of "The Full Dinner Pail" seemed an appropriate symbol for a resurgent America.

And yet before long, the various radical planks in the Populist program that had been neglected for silver in 1896 were enacted into law: railroad legislation, direct election of senators, the income tax, an expanded currency and credit structure, the initiative and referendum, postal savings banks, and some features of the sub-treasury plan. Thus the doctrines of Populism outlived the party. Moreover, the McKinley victory did not long quiet the forces of protest. At the end of the century, the American people, far from being complacent, eagerly welcomed the revelations of a buzzing hive of reformers who probed into every cranny of American economic and political life. The country was on the threshold of a remarkable era of reform.

Readings

There is still no adequate political history of this period in spite of many valuable biographies of its leading figures and numerous monographs on its political, economic, and cultural phases. Matthew Josephson, *The Politicos, 1865-1896* (1938), is a lively, informative, but slanted survey. E. F. Goldman, *Rendezvous With Destiny: A History of Modern American Reform* (1952), is a good introduction to the reformist spirit of the period; and Richard Hofstadter's *The Age of Reform: From Bryan to F.D.R.* (1955) contains an analysis of the agrarian mind and middle-class reform. The reader will also find useful interpretations in W. E. Binkley, *American Political Parties: Their Natural History* (1943), and colorful background material in contemporary memoirs like H. T. Peck, *Twenty Years of the Republic, 1885-1905* (1906), and J. G. Blaine, *Twenty Years of Congress* (2 vols., 1884-1886). For a lively personal commentary on affairs from 1868-1898 by an interested observer, the reader should consult *The Letters of Theodore Roosevelt,* edited by E. E. Morison, J. M. Blum, and J. J. Buckley (Vol. I, 1951).

A good one-volume biography of Hayes is H. J. Eckenrode, *Rutherford B. Hayes, Statesman of Reunion* (1930). R. G. Caldwell, *James A. Garfield, Party Chieftain* (1931), and G. F. Howe, *Chester A. Arthur* (1934), are satisfactory accounts of these statesmen. Blaine's career is well summarized in his own book, cited above, and in D. S. Muzzey, *James G. Blaine, A Political Idol of Other Days* (1934).

The financial and administrative aspects of the 1870's and 1880's have been covered fairly well. A. D. Noyes, *Forty Years of American Finance* (1909), is a good general account. The ups and downs of Greenbackism are treated in F. E. Haynes, *Third Party Movements Since the Civil War, with Special Reference to Iowa* (1916), and D. C. Barrett, *The Greenbacks and the Resumption of Specie Payments, 1862-1879* (1931). The struggle for civil-service reform is told in C. R. Fish, *The Civil Service and the*

Patronage (1904), and in great detail in A. B. Sageser, *The First Two Decades of the Pendleton Act* (1935).

For studies of men and issues during the Cleveland era, see H. J. Ford, *The Cleveland Era* (1919); the solid biography, *Grover Cleveland: A Study in Courage* (1932), by Allan Nevins; and W. A. Robinson, *Thomas B. Reed, Parliamentarian* (1930). To the works by Taussig and Stanwood on the tariff, cited in the general bibliography, should be added an admirably lucid story by Ida M. Tarbell, *The Tariff in Our Times* (1911). Two useful accounts of the history of federal pensions are J. W. Oliver, *History of the Civil War Military Pensions* (1917), and W. H. Glasson, *Federal Military Pensions in the United States* (1918).

There is a large and ever-growing literature on agrarian unrest and Populism. A standard factual history is C. C. Taylor, *The Farmers' Movement, 1620-1920* (1953). More pertinent for this chapter and indispensable for understanding the farmers' revolt is F. Shannon, *The Farmer's Last Frontier* (1945). S. J. Buck, *The Granger Movement* (1913), and *The Agrarian Crusade* (1920), cover the history of the Grangers; and the standard work on Populism is J. D. Hicks, *The Populist Revolt* (1931). C. Vann Woodward's *Origins of the New South, 1877-1913* (1951) has an excellent survey of the populist revolt in the South; and the same author's remarkable *Tom Watson, Agrarian Rebel* (1938) offers a clue to the mentality of southern reformer turned demagogue. Other important studies dealing with Populism are C. M. Destler, *American Radicalism, 1865-1901* (1946); R. B. Nye, *Midwestern Progressive Politics: A Historical Study of Its Origins and Development, 1870-1950* (1951); and H. B. Merrill, *Bourbon Democracy of the Middle West, 1865-1896* (1953).

G. H. Knoles, *The Presidential Campaign and Election of 1892* (1942), is a good introduction to the events of the period prior to the election of 1896. The story of the currency issue is related in the financial histories listed in the general bibliography; but F. B. Weberg, *The Background of the Panic of 1893* (1929), also should be consulted. D. L. McMurry, *Coxey's Army* (1929), sketches the industrial unrest which led to the march on Washington; and A. L. Lindsey, *The Pullman Strike* (1942), is a detailed study of that event. Altgeld's role in this strike is told in H. Barnard, *"Eagle Forgotten," The Life of John Peter Altgeld* (1938); and Debs' part is portrayed in biographies by Ray Ginger, *The Bending Cross: A Biography of Eugene Victor Debs* (1949), and M. Coleman, *Eugene V. Debs, A Man Unafraid* (1930).

The best life of the Republican master-mind, Mark Hanna, is Herbert Croly's *Marcus Alonzo Hanna* (1912), which also throws much light on the men and issues of these years. There is no satisfactory biography of McKinley, although the reader may be interested in the portrait of McKinley presented by W. A. White, *Masks in a Pageant* (1928), and by Josephson in *The Politicos*. M. R. Werner, *Bryan* (1929), is readable but not very searching. On Bryan, see also Paxton Hibben, *Peerless Leader* (1929).

THE

CITY

C H A P T E R   T W E N T Y - T W O

In Europe the idea of the "city" had always implied a center of power and of learning, religion, and art. The city—Athens, Rome, Paris, London, Milan, Moscow—was a place of palaces and kings and aristocrats, of universities and great churches, of architects, sculptors, painters, poets, philosophers, scholars, and doctors. The city had its cruel and seamy side; but in essence it was the heart and nerve center of the state. "When we get piled upon one another in large cities," Thomas Jefferson cautioned in 1787, "we shall become corrupt as in Europe, and go to eating one another as they do there." A century later, the prejudice against urban life still lingered, but some Americans were beginning to realize that a democratic society could be maintained even under the conditions that Jefferson had found so threatening.

509

I.   THE CITY AND ITS PROBLEMS

In America, as the historian Carl Bridenbaugh has said, the first urban centers were "cities in the wilderness." As late as the 1830's, America's rural population continued to grow much faster than the urban population. Thereafter, the expanding city imposed itself on America's agrarian consciousness mainly as a problem. In the 1850's, northern moralists had already begun to shudder at the "immense accumulations of ignorance and error, vice and crime" in their cities, and southern propagandists tried to demonstrate the superiority of their own way of life by contrasting the sturdy yeomanry of Dixie with the urban proletariat above the Mason and Dixon line. As American cities grew into metropolises in the later nineteenth century, they began to cast a spell over the country. But most Americans no doubt shared the puzzlement of one observer in 1895 over the readiness of farm people to "leave the country where homes are cheap, the air pure, all men equal, and extreme poverty unknown, and crowd into cities" where they seemed to find "in the noises, the crowds, the excitements, even in the sleepless anxieties of the daily struggle for life, a charm they are powerless to resist."

Growth of the City.   In 1840, only one-twelfth of the American population lived in cities of 8,000 or more. By 1860, the proportion of city-dwellers had grown to one-sixth, and by 1900 to one-third, of the population. In 1900, more than 25 million Americans were living in cities, most of them in the metropolises that had grown so lustily in the preceding 50 years. In 1850, New York City and independent Brooklyn together had a population of 1,200,000. By 1900 (after official consolidation in 1898), their population had soared to over 3 million. In the same period, Philadelphia rose from

560,000 to 1,300,000, Pittsburgh from 67,000 to 450,000. Most spectacular of all was the development of Chicago. Starting out in 1831 as a muddy trading post on the prairie with 12 families and a meager garrison as its only inhabitants, Chicago had grown to 30,000 by 1850; 500,000 by 1880. In the next 20 years, its population soared to 1,700,000, a figure that placed it far ahead of Philadelphia and second only to New York in size. No other city quite matched the speed of Chicago's rise. But striking in its own right was the sudden thrust forward of places that had scarcely existed in 1860. Denver, a small mining camp on the eve of the Civil War, had 134,000 persons in 1900. In the same period, Minneapolis grew from 2,500 to 200,000; Los Angeles from 5,000 to 100,000. Birmingham, Alabama, was not founded until 1871, but in 1900 it had 38,000 inhabitants.

The rapid growth of American cities after the Civil War was but one reflection of the enormous increase in the scale and the pace of American business enterprise (see Chapter XX). The development of Pittsburgh and Birmingham were attributable directly to the expansion of the iron and steel industries, that of Minneapolis to the rise of the grain trade and flour-milling. Chicago had risen to eminence first as a wheat port, then as a railroad center, and then as the meat-packing center of the world. Industry and trade gave such a boost to its business activity that it also became the financial center of the West. Its credit facilities, moreover, drew a great variety of new industries and new distributing enterprises, such as the Marshall Field store. Philadelphia and New York profited largely from the development of the commercial ties that had been established fairly early in their histories, and also from new industries—such as the manufacture of ready-to-wear clothing, which was boosted by the needs of the armed forces for uniforms during the Civil War. All over the country, opportunities were opening up for city work—in factories, in department stores, in journalism, in banking and insurance, in the administration of interurban and local transportation, and in the management of other city services.

The cities needed new workers by the millions, and other inducements impelled men to leave their accustomed habitations to fill the need. So great had the efficiency of American agricultural machinery become in the decades after the Civil War, especially in the production of wheat, that even though the demand for food throughout the western world was growing, the increased demand could be met by a relatively small increase in the number of men working on the land. Farm youths by the millions found that farming no longer needed them. Many of them moved in their teens or early manhood to nearby boom towns, and hundreds of thousands ventured long distances to the richer opportunities of the great cities. Attracted, perhaps, by the lurid descriptions of the dangers and temptations awaiting the raw country boy in the wicked city, they found in urban life what they had pined for in the country: domestic conveniences, music, art, and popular entertainment.

The millions of immigrants who crowded into the cities before the turn of the century were not so fortunate in adapting to their new life. In the 1880's alone, more than 5 million Europeans landed on American shores, most of them from central and eastern European countries. Many of them were peasants who had come in response to the glowing promotional literature of steamship and railroad companies, which held out the promise of low-priced farms in the West. Only a small proportion of the newcomers, however, ever found the means to acquire land of their own. Thousands moved west as railroad construction workers, and many others were recruited by heavy industry to take over unskilled jobs in the sweltering steel plants, foundries, and textile mills. These people were strange to city ways, and

to the American tongue and American life in general.

By 1900, three-fourths of Chicago's population was foreign-born, and the proportion of foreign-born in New York City was by far the highest in the country. Greater New York's Italian population in the 1890's equaled that of Naples; its German population equaled that of Hamburg. Twice as many Irish lived in New York as in Dublin, and thousands of Russians and Polish Jews, Hungarians, Bohemians, Greeks, and Syrians formed communities in American cities. The flood of arrivals alarmed many native-born Americans, who had become concerned, as one of them confessed in the 1890's, "at the prospect of adding enormously to the burden of the municipal governments in the large cities, already almost breaking down through corruption and inefficiency." Such critics failed to recognize the enormous contributions that these new Americans were making to the prosperity and culture of their adopted country.

The Shame of the Cities. The immigrant problem only aggravated the difficulties of city government with which the Americans were already struggling. The large cities had grown up without plan. Their affairs were ordinarily administered by merchants, lawyers, and bankers who put their faith in rising land values and trusted others to look out for themselves. Most city-dwellers took at best a half-hearted interest in civic projects that did not immediately affect their own pocketbooks or pleasure. City development lay in the hands of real-estate operators who cut up the land into rectangular lots divided by a gridiron of streets and who gave little thought to reserving desirable sections for public use. City authorities seldom considered zoning, and allowed landowners to erect factories, shops, and business offices wherever they pleased. Industrialists polluted the streams and rivers, and unthinkingly turned ideal residential areas into slag-heaps. In an age of laissez faire, when planning was out of fashion, the convenience of businessmen determined the shape and the life of the city.

The cities did provide some services, however—if only those that were absolutely necessary. Gas mains were constructed; water supplies were maintained; police and especially fire protection was made available; garbage was regularly collected; transportation and lighting of a sort were supplied. But facilities for recreation and health were provided only as afterthoughts, if at all. Living quarters for the working population were especially bad, usually lacking space, ventilation, and plumbing. American cities became increasingly pockmarked with slums and infected with vice and crime. The very size and impersonality of cities soon discouraged attempts to improve conditions.

By the middle 1880's, the poor administration of American cities had become, according to one observer, James Bryce, "the one conspicuous failure in the United States." A prominent educator announced in 1890 that "with few exceptions, the city governments of the United States are the worst in Christendom—the most expensive, the most inefficient, and the most corrupt."

In his celebrated study, *The American Commonwealth* (1888), Bryce discussed some of the causes of city mismanagement that he had extracted from a report drawn up by a New York commission in 1876. He listed them as follows: (1) crooked and incompetent officials, (2) the "introduction of State and national politics into municipal affairs," and (3) the control of local affairs by state legislatures unfamiliar with the processes and needs of city government. Then he added a comment of his own:

. . . In great cities we find an ignorant multitude, largely composed of recent immigrants, untrained in self-government; we find a great proportion of the voters paying no direct taxes, and therefore feeling no interest in moderate taxation and economical administration; we find able citizens absorbed in their private busi-

nesses, cultivated citizens unusually sensitive to the vulgarities of practical politics, and both sets therefore specially unwilling to sacrifice their time and tastes and comfort in the struggle with sordid wire-pullers and noisy demagogues.

Bryce's comments begged some interesting questions, but they contained a great deal of truth.

In most American cities, power resided in the mayor, in the single- or double-chambered city council, or in independent boards. These agencies determined how municipal funds should be spent, what streets needed to be paved, and where new parks and streets would be laid out. They granted franchises for street railways, let out contracts for building sewers, bought fire-fighting equipment, and granted monopolies to public utilities. Most of these activities were entrusted to hand-picked committees, and unscrupulous political bosses found it easy to place their henchmen in key positions where they could mulct the city treasuries of millions of dollars. The career of Boss William M. Tweed, leader of the corrupt Tammany ring which robbed New York City of more than $100 million between 1869 and 1871, is a classic example of municipal fraud, but lesser thieves plundered other American cities just as thoroughly. In Philadelphia, Chicago, Cincinnati, St. Louis, Minneapolis, and San Francisco, politicians perfected the fine art of "boodling," defined by a contemporary as "the corrupt disposal of public property by the representatives of the people in return for a price paid not to the public but to their dishonest representatives."

Reformers attributed the success of the political bosses and their corrupt machines to what one of them called the "typical immigrant . . . a European peasant, whose horizon has been narrow, whose moral and religious training has been meager and false, and whose ideas of life are low." To native-born reformers, the immigrant became a kind of scapegoat for conditions that had already begun to develop before his unhappy arrival. Yet it is true that the sheer multitude of newcomers heightened the city's difficulties.

The unassimilated foreigner living in the

slums and ignorant of American democratic practices voted dutifully for the city bosses who speeded up his naturalization proceedings, gave him donations at Christmas, found city jobs for him or his sons, encouraged his ethnic customs, and mediated with the law when he or his children got into trouble. Many had carried with them to America feudal notions of government—the idea that aristocrats were bound to be the rulers—and could not think of themselves as active participants in public affairs even after they had become American citizens. Reform programs that sought to reduce taxes hardly touched the average immigrant's life, for he had no property to tax. He was suspicious of reforms to improve the efficiency of city administration, for "efficiency" in government might very well mean that he would be dropped from the city payroll. Fearful of change, the peasant-immigrant disliked the very sound of "reform"; and the reformer, lacking any notion of the immigrant's real needs and desires, further alienated himself by attacking the very men to whom the immigrant felt most loyal—the political bosses.

But the immigrant was only one part of the story. Even the well-educated native voter was taken in by the politicians, who cleverly exploited party loyalties and merged non-political local issues with national political ones. Many honest and respectable men, rather than endanger their national party, chose to support the corrupt machines. Or they tolerated government by the bosses on the grounds that it was good for business; or that, despite its high cost, it worked well; or that it protected the industrious citizen from the irresponsible mob. Businessmen found it easy to deal with the machine when they wanted a franchise, a right of way, or a subsidy, and they discovered that they could avoid supervision and annoying restrictions at the cost of a few well-placed bribes. Only when the depredations of the political rings became too outrageous did respectable citizens organize for "good government."

As a result of the public's political apathy and the domination of local and state governments by political and business connivers, the costs of city building projects and municipal services were enormously high. Boss Tweed's famous Court House in New York City cost millions more than its estimated $3 million, and Philadelphia's politicians fleeced the city in the process of transforming it (to quote a citizens' petition in 1883) into "the worst paved and worst cleaned city in the civilized world," renowned for its stinking sewers and undrinkable water. By the end of the century, Chicago had become the greatest railway center in the world, with lines running in from every direction, but the hundreds of miles of track that cut across the city at random snarled up traffic and caused shocking accidents.

The American city from the 70's through the 90's, smoke-ridden, filthy, and overcrowded, clearly deserved the condemnation of its many critics, domestic and foreign. But some progress was made in solving the technical problems that inevitably arose as city boundaries expanded and as city populations increased.

Technical Advances.   To relieve traffic congestion and to carry thousands of urban workers to and from their jobs, a swifter and more reliable vehicle was needed than the horse-cars, omnibuses, and cabs that had sufficed for a simpler society. In 1880, there were 18,000 streetcars in the United States hauled by 100,000 horses and mules. These cars had been in operation for 20 years. Besides being too slow (their maximum speed was about six miles an hour), they were dirty and uncomfortable. Here is how one disgruntled traveler described the horrors of riding on a crowded horse-car:

Sixty people packed into a box so closely that no man can tell which legs are his own and which his neighbor's, their heads buried in the dark concave above, breathing an atmosphere of fifty overfull or over-empty stomachs, mingled with the stench of rotting straw, the steam of reeking garments pervaded with fumes of bad rum and worse tobacco or the pungent odors of undigested corn beef and cabbage. . . .

One answer to the smelly horse-cars was the steam-driven elevated railroad, which had been experimented with as early as 1867 in New York City and came into actual use during the 70's. Horse-car companies fought the new lines bitterly, and citizens complained of the discharges of soot and smoke that poured through their windows, and the hot ashes that dropped on their heads. But the gradual abandonment of the elevated steam railroads had nothing to do with the discomforts they produced. It simply became too expensive to construct elevated structures capable of supporting heavy loco-motives—the only kind powerful enough to draw a long train of cars at adequate speeds. A new and cheaper method had to be found to transport people who were forced by overcrowding to live farther and farther from their work.

The most promising innovation was elec-tric traction, developed by Frank Julian Sprague, whose successful system in Rich-mond in 1887 proved its practicability in large cities. In getting his system into opera-tion, Sprague first had to solve difficult tech-nical problems. He invented the first satis-factory car-motors, trolleys, wires, and cars, and devised a scheme for regulating the movement of cars so that traffic jams would not clog the lines.

The men who owned and operated steam railroads in the great cities had invested a great deal of capital in their enterprises and were extremely reluctant to switch to the new method, but eventually they had to yield. Clearly, electric trolleys surpassed in every way the steaming, stinking, clangorous coal-burning locomotives, and they did not re-quire the old networks of elevated track that cut off air and light. The electric lines needed no heavy locomotives, since each car had its own power. The cars could be run singly or in trains; they could be switched easily; and repair problems were cut to a minimum.

Besides providing the energy for trans-portation vehicles, electricity also solved the problem of lighting American cities. Flicker-ing gas lamps gave way to the improved arc lamps in 1879, and interior lighting by elec-tricity became commercially feasible after Thomas A. Edison's improvements in the incandescent bulb the same year (see p. 472). Improved lighting made possible the night-shift, and factories began to run 24 hours a day. Churches introduced electric lighting, and electric signs lit up a few streets —in anticipation of the "Great White Way" of the modern city. Gas, however, was by no means driven out as an illuminant. In 1885, an Austrian, Auer von Welsbach, invented a conical gas mantle that produced an intense diffused light, and for many years the gas lamp was more widely used for interior lighting than the electric bulb.

New inventions that bore directly on busi-ness activities were successfully adapted to city needs—the electric tram, the incandes-cent bulb, and the telephone (in practical use by the 80's). But in dealing with such matters as water supply, waste-disposal, and street-cleaning, which had once been handled fairly well, American cities grew less and less conscientious. By 1870, the disposal of waste had reached a critical stage in the larger cities, where sanitation methods scarcely differed from those employed in the villages of a century before. Not one Amer-ican city filtered its water, even though the indiscriminate dumping of sewage and gar-bage into streams often polluted the supply. Even in the last decades of the century, deaths from typhoid fever in Chicago and Philadelphia were scandalously high. Be-tween 1880 and 1900, cleaner streets, purer water, and more efficient methods of fire-fighting made the American metropolis more livable, yet it retained many of its ugly and brutal features. European travelers who visited the states at the end of the century frequently commented on the sordidness of the New York and Chicago slums, "the mud, the dirt, the filth, the stinking humidity, the nuisances, the disorder of these streets," and they sometimes wondered whether the miser-

The interior of a New York tenement.

able ragpickers, the Pittsburgh steel-workers living in "humble wooden dwellings, smoke-begrimed, dirty, miserable, barn-like structures," might not better have remained in Europe.

Urban Housing. Technical improvements gradually made life in the city safer and more comfortable as time went on, but all city-dwellers—no matter what their wealth or station—put up with annoying inconveniences. The very rich, in their own privileged world, escaped most of the annoyances that plagued the poor. But even with their armies of servants, their equipages, their expensive balls and dinners, and their fondness for display, the city millionaires often lived in mansions situated near the slums and gasworks and slaughterhouses, and breathed the same sooty air as their employees. They disfigured their houses with pointless ornamentation, and filled them with expensive knickknacks. In middle-class dwellings throughout the country, the interiors were dark, crammed with overstuffed and befringed furniture, and decorated with bad paintings and reproductions. The bulk and clutter of Victorian living suited a generation that over-ate, whose women attached bustles to the back of their dresses, and who lived what might be described as upholstered lives. The bad taste of the rich and respectable percolated down the social scale.

The very poor lived under conditions that were scarcely endurable. The tenement slum, which had made its first appearance in the early nineteenth century, spread over metropolitan America like a disease after 1865. Open sections of the city were swallowed up by factories. Then, as the native middle class withdrew to sections protected from industry and aliens, their old houses were converted into tenements. Dozens of people crowded into rooms that had once been occupied by a single family and that lacked even the most primitive sanitary facilities. Landlords, driven on by ever-rising ground rentals, built on every available inch of space, leaving no room for grass or trees. The ghettos and slums that infested the cities were cut off physically and spiritually from the better quarters.

In 1879, the "dumb-bell tenement," so-called because of the shape of its characteristic floor plan, was introduced as the model housing unit in New York City.This structure was an improvement over the old tenements, since it provided fireproof stairways and one toilet for every two families in place of the old cellar or outdoor privies. Each room also had a window opening to the outside. Nevertheless, the rows of long five- or six-story buildings, built on a 25-foot lot and extending 90 feet to the rear, quickly became pest-houses—sunless, airless, and ill-smelling. Instead of solving New York's housing problem, they simply postponed a thorough-going tenement reform. By 1894,

about 39,000 tenement houses of this kind had been built in New York City, and thousands of citizens lived in dwellings that were considerably worse. A city commission in that year drew up a disheartening report on families housed in fire-traps, without bathtubs, toilets, running water, or backyards.

New York's slums were the worst in the nation, but wretched conditions prevailed in other cities as well. The report of a federal commission in 1894 listed the slum population of Baltimore at about 25,000, Philadelphia at 35,000, and Chicago at about 162,000. Conditions similar to those found in the slums of Washington, D. C., and Boston's South End could be duplicated in almost every major city of America.

II. URBAN REFORMERS

The Humanitarians. One way to deal with city slums was simply to move away from them, and many prosperous middle-class families during the 70's and 80's did escape to the sunlight and air of the suburbs. Fortunately, though, not everyone took this way out. A corps of reformers, philanthropists, and churchmen (moved by moral considerations and sometimes by a fear of social revolution) worked by themselves or in groups to help the city unfortunates.

A vision of a kind of garden city had been born as early as the late 1850's, when Calvert Vaux and the great landscape architect, Frederick Law Olmsted, planned Central Park in New York. At this time, many people considered parks aristocratic, un-American, and un-businesslike, but this prejudice disappeared in later years. Between 1872 and 1895, Olmsted and his disciples laid out parks in Boston, Washington, Buffalo, Detroit, Rochester, and elsewhere. Although the parks did not transform the industrial metropolis into an Eden, they at least preserved a vestige of nature in a world of stone and steel.

During these same years, social workers began to investigate the casualties of urban life: the slum-dweller, the criminal, the sick,

and the helpless. The traditional view had attributed their poverty and misfortunes to personal weakness, but by the late 70's urban reformers had begun to realize that the causes of poverty were complex, and that material success was not a matter of individual virtue. Sickness, the death of the bread-winner, unemployment, and low wages, clearly created more paupers and criminals than either alcoholism or laziness. The city poor needed practical aid more than they needed sermons. Moreover, the task of administering poor relief had become so vast that private charities working independently could no longer do the job properly. In 1877, Buffalo became the first city to coordinate its relief organizations. A decade later, 25 associated charities throughout the country had cut out much of the inefficiency and duplication that had marred the work of earlier social agencies.

The overpopulated city, it was pointed out in the 1890's, swells the number of the classes most exposed to agitation and discontent, intensifies the danger of social upheaval, and widens the growing chasm between the classes. To bridge the gulf between social classes in the cities, reformers established settlement houses in the poorer districts where neighborhood families could mingle without regard to race or nationality or religion. In 1886, the country's first settlement house was set up by Stanton Coit in New York City. Encouraged by the example of the famous Toynbee Hall in the East London slums, social workers soon carried the idea into other cities. To dedicated women like Jane Addams in Chicago's Hull House (founded in 1889), and Lillian Wald, who organized the Henry Street Settlement in New York's lower East Side in 1893, the people in the slums were "potentially useful citizens who simply needed help." Women like Jane Addams, wrote the municipal reformer, Frederic Howe, saw the "city in the light of the home. The vice, the saloon, the schools, the libraries, the water, gas, and transportation questions are to her questions of the family, of the child, questions of comfort, of happiness, of safety." Jane Addams put it somewhat differently.

The settlement [she wrote] is an attempt to relieve . . . the overaccumulation at one end of society and the destitution at the other; but it assumes that this overaccumulation and destitution is most sorely felt in the things that pertain to social and educational advantages. It must be grounded in a philosophy . . . which will not waver when the race happens to be represented by a drunken woman or an idiot boy.

In Boston, Cleveland, and Pittsburgh, young college men and women put Jane Addams' philosophy into practice. They formed clubs for boys and societies for wayward girls, transformed settlement houses into a combination of day-nursery, men's club, school, gymnasium, and employment bureau, and campaigned resolutely for improved sanitary regulations, better housing, and penal reform.

The scientific approach to social welfare did not slow down the crusade against intemperance and the saloon, however, for this movement began to gather increased momentum after the heavy-drinking years of the Civil War. The Prohibition party, which ran its first national ticket in 1872, proved ineffective against the saloon interests, and most Americans stuck to the old parties. But

"Bandit's Roost," a cross-section of New York slum life, photographed in 1888 by Jacob Riis.

a powerful new organization took shape in 1874 with the founding of the Women's Christian Temperance Union. Led by Frances E. Willard, a former educator whose creed was "No sectarianism in religion, no sectionalism in politics, no sex in citizenship," the W.C.T.U. propagandized against liquor and the people who made and sold it. Its stated policy was "mental suasion for the man who thinks and moral suasion for the man who drinks, but legal suasion for the drunkard-maker."

A recruit of dubious value to the prohibition cause was Carry A. Nation of Kansas, a six-foot, 175-pound fanatic who carried on a personal vendetta against the saloon. She was arrested some 30 times for smashing saloons with her hatchet and for disturbing the peace in the principal American cities. In 1893, with the founding of the Anti-Saloon League, the prohibition movement gathered momentum, and by the middle of the 1900's its branches in 40 states were

517

working closely with other temperance organizations throughout the country.

Frances Willard and many other women temperance leaders were as zealous in the fight for woman suffrage as they were in the crusade against drinking. Agitation for the political rights of women had sprung up even before the Civil War, and the most famous women in American life had spoken in its behalf. In 1869, suffrage groups formed the National Woman Suffrage Association, with Elizabeth Cady Stanton as president. Not unreasonably, the women argued that they were just as entitled to the vote as former slaves were. By 1896, Wyoming, Colorado, Utah, and Idaho had given women full suffrage rights, but no federal amendment was passed until the next century.

The Churches. The response of the churches to slums and poverty was at first halting and indecisive. Few ministers had any firsthand knowledge of tenement life in the industrial cities, and most of them were out of touch with the tenement dwellers. Even before the Civil War, American clergymen had reported a falling off of working-class attendance in their churches, a trend that continued in the postwar decades. As class divisions became sharper, the workingmen's demands for shorter hours and for government regulation of working conditions met with little sympathy from church leaders. "Whatever you suffer here from injustice of others," they reminded him, "will turn to your account hereafter. Be quiet. Whatsoever your hands can find to do, do it, and be content with your wages. God will take care of the rest." But as religious writers released more and more exposés of city conditions during the 1870's, the churches began to modify their naive disregard for the facts of city life.

The Social Gospel movement, which burgeoned during the last two decades of the century, was organized by socially conscious ministers from various denominations and rested on the conviction that man is born "in a sinful society, which fact is the cause of deep evil." Christ, the Social Gospelers believed, came to "establish a new environment" as well as "to save rebellious men." Hence all Christians ought to be social reformers.

Some liberal clergymen went no further than to advocate moderate reforms in wages, housing, and working conditions. The more radical, however, did not want to preserve the economic system; they wanted to reform it from the bottom up. Ministers like Washington Gladden, R. Heber Newton, Henry Codman Potter, and Walter Rauschenbusch boldly defended the demands of trade unions and wrote and preached against the economic philosophy of the Social Darwinists (see pp. 529-530). Gladden's *Applied Christianity* (1886), and Newton's *The Morals of Trade* (1876), expressed the Social Gospel ideal that Christian solutions existed for all social problems, and that contrary to the Social Darwinians, the remedying of social ills was neither impractical nor impossible. By the 1880's, theological seminaries were offering courses in social Christianity and social ethics.

Yet despite its influence, the Social Gospel movement was confined to a minority of intellectuals and did not touch the vast majority of American churchgoers in the rural areas. In general, churches like the Baptist and Methodist, whose membership consisted largely of artisans, shopkeepers, and farmers, preferred to keep the old emphasis on individual responsibility for sin. The fact that many of the newly rich were Baptists and Methodist laymen (John D. Rockefeller was a prominent Baptist elder, Daniel Drew a fervent Methodist) may also help to explain why their churches did not quarrel with the status quo. Indeed, most of the influential American clergymen themselves were orthodox in their economics even when they were unorthodox in their theology.

Henry Ward Beecher, one of the most celebrated ministers of his day, preached a liberal theology and repudiated (as his sisters, Harriet and Catharine, had done) the hell-fire and damnation doctrines of his famous father, Lyman Beecher. At the same time, he upheld the economic views of his wealthy Brooklyn congregation and sanctified the cult of business success. He condemned the eight-hour day, insisted that poverty was a sign of sin, and urged that strikers be put down with violence if necessary. These sentiments were so deeply appreciated by his national following that not even the scandalous story of adultery brought out in the widely publicized Beecher-Tilton divorce trial could extinguish the intense loyalty of Beecher's following.

Although social Christianity caught the imagination of middle-class intellectuals, most city-dwellers turned to the itinerant evangelists who ignored economic and political issues and preached the "old-time religion." In 1870, Dwight L. Moody, a former shoe salesman from Boston, teamed up with the singer Ira D. Sankey to launch a mighty campaign for saving souls that reached millions of people. Moody preached a simple but powerful message; Sankey sang the tender old hymns, "Saved by Grace," "Almost Persuaded," and "Safe in the Arms of Jesus," with such compelling sweetness that thousands were melted into grace. From Chicago, where Moody had evangelized successfully in the "Little Hell" on the North Side, Moody and Sankey carried the question "Are You a Christian?" to England. Having silenced the scoffers there, they went on to Brooklyn, New York, Boston, and to every large city in the country. The Chicago Bible Institute for Home and Foreign Missions, founded in 1889, was only one of many monuments erected to the achievements of this great evangelist.

The evangelist spirit was more tangibly expressed in the Young Men's Christian Association, founded as an American offshoot of an English society in 1851, and the Young Women's Christian Association (1858). Both associations were dedicated to "the physical, mental, social, and spiritual benefit" of their members and of men and women everywhere. By 1897, the Y.M.C.A. had 263,298 members in the United States and the

Y.W.C.A. about 35,000. Another importation from England was the Salvation Army, organized by a Wesleyan Methodist, "General" William Booth. This army of Christians devoted themselves to feeding and sheltering the city's unfortunates and restoring their souls. After the first American branch was established in 1880, the Salvation Army's "slum brigades" penetrated into the tenement areas and "skid rows" of the great cities. Its methods were hardly scientific, for it ignored the basic causes of urban sickness. Yet the soldiers of General Booth brought much comfort and relief to the neglected poor.

More well-to-do city-dwellers (owing, it was sometimes suggested, to the hectic pace of urban living) required a different sort of spiritual balm. This was provided by a remarkable woman, Mrs. Mary Baker Eddy, whose *Science and Health* (1875) contained the basic doctrines of the Church of Christ, Scientist, a sect that numbered 35,000 by 1900. In brief, Mrs. Eddy taught that "Disease is caused by the mind alone" and that "Science" (another name for the wisdom of God) had been revealed to man by His Son, Jesus Christ. Christ showed how the Mind (the equivalent of God, Truth, or Spirit) could overcome sickness and disease. "Mind constructs the body, and with its own materials instead of matter; hence no broken bones or dislocations can occur." Christian Science had obvious connections with older theologies, but no one before Mrs. Eddy had announced the unreality of death and pain and sin as demonstrable science. Her message appealed to many Americans, particularly to city-dwellers, for whom science had come to have a magical significance.

The activities of the Protestant churches hardly touched the great mass of the Roman Catholic urban proletariat, whose church was well prepared by tradition and experience to cope with poverty. The Catholics had increased from roughly 6 million in 1880 to 12 million in 1900, largely as the result of heavy immigration from Italy and eastern

Europe. This influx of Catholic immigrants brought to the surface all the anti-Catholic prejudice that had been latent since the days of the Know Nothing movement (see p. 345), and it revived old fears of a Vatican plot against America. The American Protective Association, a secret society formed in 1887 to exploit the bigotry of the rural Middle West against the influence of Roman Catholicism in labor and politics, capitalized on these fears. The A.P.A. warned that a concealed army of 700,000 papal soldiers was ready to take over the American government, even though at this very time Catholic leaders like Cardinal James Gibbons of Baltimore and Archbishop John Ireland of St. Paul were championing political democracy and accepting the separation of church and state. The A.P.A. quickly spread to the cities, but since it rarely appealed to influential people it lost its impetus after 1896.

III.   EDITORS AND ARCHITECTS

Urban Journalism.   Even before the Civil War, writers and editors had discovered that crusades against civic corruption or private iniquity not only improved the moral tone of the public but also paid off in sales. In 1858, *Frank Leslie's Illustrated Newspaper* conducted a sensational campaign against New York milk-producers accused of selling milk from diseased herds, and succeeded in arousing such a widespread public clamor that the state legislature in 1861 was forced to prohibit the sale of milk from cows nourished on the waste products of distilleries. A decade later, *Harper's Weekly,* edited by George William Curtis and featuring the savage cartoons of Thomas Nast, led the fight to overthrow New York City's corrupt Tweed regime. This crusade trebled *Harper's Weekly's* circulation, which by 1872 had reached 160,000. Henry and Charles Francis Adams' revelations in the *North American Review* of Jay Gould's financial piracies, the Congregational minister Josiah Strong's denunciation of slums, mass immigration, and despotic capitalists in his book *Our Country* (1885), and W. T. Stead's uncompromising and lurid reports of Chicago wickedness (*If Christ Came to Chicago!,* 1894) were other highly moral treatments of controversial or scandalous subjects that evoked a wide response.

Civic vice proved such a popular subject that newspaper editors, to give a jolt to circulation, began to invent "causes" of their own or to feature crime in highly indignant "human-interest" stories. Recent arrivals from the farm were particularly responsive to stories that seemed to confirm their suspicions about life in the "wicked city." Reporters who were able to "crash" the lavish entertainments of the rich and to describe them from the inside, or who were able to draw a tear by authentic reports of the sordid experiences of the poor, brought a new inidividuality and a new glamor to newspaper careers.

These new methods in journalism helped to increase the daily circulation of newspapers from 2,800,000 in 1870 to 24 million in 1899. Increased revenue from subscriptions and sales, and above all from advertising, permitted greater editorial independence from political pressure and freed the newspapers to become powerful manipulators of public opinion.

Joseph Pulitzer, owner of the St. Louis *Post-Dispatch* and later of the New York *World,* exemplified the new type of publisher in the many schemes he devised to promote circulation. Combining the crudest sensationalism with effective exposés of civic corruption, Pulitzer's *World* lived up to the promise of its owner to publish a "journal that is not only cheap but bright, not only bright but large, not only large but truly democratic . . . devoted more to the new than the old world, that will expose all fraud and sham, fight all public evils and abuses." The

World introduced colored comics and exploited all the inventions that were revolutionizing publishing during this period: improved newsprint made from wood pulp, the Linotype machine (1886), typewriters, telephones, and the telegraph. These improvements, together with the *World's* superior news coverage, sensational stories, liberal crusades, solid editorials, and promotional stunts, produced a startling rise in circulation. Two months after Pulitzer took over in May, 1883, he had doubled the original circulation of 20,000. By the fall of 1884, the *World* claimed 100,000 readers, and in 1886 it claimed 250,000.

Pulitzer's methods were quickly copied by papers in other large cities and by ruthless competitors in New York itself. E. W. Scripps' papers in Cleveland, St. Louis, and Cincinnati successfully employed Pulitzer's techniques. But it was William Randolph Hearst, fresh from Harvard and backed by his father's millions, who outdid Pulitzer himself in sensational journalism. One result of the fierce rivalry among the newspapers of the day was the appearance of "yellow journalism," a name that derived from the yellow ink used in colored comics but that came to stand for flamboyant and lurid journalistic practices. The "yellow journalists" cynically exploited any cause in order to build up circulation.

Conservative editors were quick to criticize "yellow journalism," but the only effective answer was to produce a good newspaper that sold widely. Adolph S. Ochs demonstrated that this could be done when he took over the moribund New York *Times* in 1896, cut its price to a penny, introduced new features, and revived its circulation. Soon it became widely known for its trustworthy coverage of foreign and domestic news.

The magazine, too, was profoundly influenced by the social and economic forces that transformed the American newspaper. When Congress on March 3, 1879, passed a postal act granting second-class mailing privileges to magazines, the circulation of periodicals increased even more spectacularly than the circulation of newspapers. *McCall's* (1870), *Popular Science* (1872), *Woman's Home Companion* (1873), *Good Housekeeping* (1885), *Cosmopolitan* (1886), *Collier's* (1888), *National Geographic* (1888), *Vogue* (1892), and *Outdoor Life* (1898) were only a few of the magazines that benefited from the new postal act. By and large, these magazines, as well as the old-established monthlies like *Harper's, The Atlantic, Scribner's*, and *The Century,* appealed to the tastes and the moral code of the middle-class urban reader. Whether designed for the businessman, the housewife, or the child, the periodicals of the period were well produced and well illustrated.

In the last decade of the century, magazines of opinion became more sensational in their methods and focused more attention on controversial current issues—a tendency that foreshadowed the muckraking magazines of the early 1900's. New techniques in printing and heavier subsidies from advertisers lowered the price of magazines so that by 1900 hundreds of thousands of families were regular magazine subscribers and 50 or more magazines boasted circulations of over 100,000.

Cyrus H. K. Curtis' *Ladies Home Journal* was the most spectacular success of all. Founded in 1883, it reached the million mark 17 years later, largely through Curtis' promotional efforts. He advertised heavily, hired a brilliant managing editor, Edward Bok, and filled his magazine with features calculated to fascinate feminine readers avid for advice on how to bring up their children, decorate their homes, and preserve their health. Bok bought the fiction of the most popular American and English writers, and paid them well for their stories. Soon this "monthly Bible of the American home" had become a national force which, among other accomplishments, influenced American domestic architecture, led a campaign to force municipal authorities to clean up their cities, and pioneered in the crusade against patent medicines.

The Urban Landscape. M u c h h a s been made of the ignorance and vulgar display of the tastemakers of the Gilded Age. We hear of plutocrats who bought "old masters" especially manufactured for them in Paris studios, or of the millionaire steel baron who, hearing of a famous artist named Copley, told his secretary to get in touch with him "to paint the kids." Then there is the caricature of Henry C. Frick seated on his Renaissance throne under a baldacchino and immersed in a copy of the *Saturday Evening Post;* and of William H. Vanderbilt, out to buy only "the best and most costly" paintings in the world. Anecdotes like these reveal the tastelessness of the nouveau riche, but they do not explain the bad architecture and the bad painting of the Gilded Age itself, or the failure of its genteel critics, polite and conventional, to appreciate the possibilities of art in an industrial age.

Realistic writers conceived the modern industrial city as a kind of hell. The Chicago heroine of Hamlin Garland's *Rose of Dutcher's Cooly* (1895), for example,

... looked out across a stretch of roofs, heaped and humped into mountainous masses, blurred and blent and made appalling by smoke and plumes of steam. A scene as desolate as a burnt-out volcano—a jumble of hot bricks, jagged eave-spouts, gas-vomiting chimneys, spiked railings, glass skylights, and lofty spires, a hideous and horrible stretch of stone and mortar, cracked and seamed into streets. It had no limits and it palpitated under the hot September sun, boundless and savage. At the bottom of the crevasses men and women speckled the pavement like minute larvae.

To Henry Blake Fuller, author of *The Cliff-Dwellers* (1893), the Chicago landscape was weird and fantastic:

This country is a treeless country—if we overlook the "forest of chimneys" comprised in a bird's eye view of any great city, and if we are unable to detect any botanical analogies in the lofty articulated iron funnels whose ramifying cables reach out wherever they can, to fasten wherever they may. It is a shrubless country—if we give no heed to the gnarled carpentry of the awkward frame-works which carry the telegraph, and which are set askew on such dizzy corners as the course of wires may compel. It is an arid country—if we overlook the numberless tanks that squat on the high angles of alley walls, or if we fail to see the little pools of tar and gravel that ooze and shimmer in the summer sun on the roofs of old-fashioned buildings of the humbler sort. It is an airless country—if by air we mean the mere combination of oxygen and nitrogen which is commonly indicated by that name. For here the medium of sight, sound, light, and life becomes largely carbonaceous, and the remoter peaks of this mighty yet unprepossessing landscape loom up grandly, but vaguely, through swathing mists of coal-smoke.

The novelist Henry James, returning to New York City at the turn of the century after many years abroad, described with amazement the changes that had occurred since his boyhood. What he found was something "impudently new." He was struck by the "multitudinous sky-scrapers standing up to view, from the water, like extravagant pins in a cushion already overplanted, and stuck in as in the dark, anywhere and anyhow." A gigantic office building hung over old Trinity Church like an avalanche; the "vast money-making structure quite horribly, quite romantically justified itself, looming through the weather with an insolent cliff-like sublimity." What better symbol could there be for the "growing invisibility of the churches"? The office building ("huge constructed and compressed communities, throbbing, through its myriad arteries and pores, with a single passion") and the world it signified were not, James thought, without grandeur, but he clearly preferred the architectural monuments of Europe.

And yet, in spite of all its ugliness, the Gilded Age saw some striking gains in American building. It took a different kind of imagination than James possessed to see the originality and beauty in America's bridges, causeways, railroad stations, grain elevators, viaducts, warehouses, and office buildings. Brooklyn Bridge, conceived by John Roebling in 1869 and built by his son Washington Roebling between 1869 and 1883, performed a practical function. It connected Manhattan Island with Long Island, carried tremendous loads, and eased the ferry-boat congestion. But its unadorned steel structure was also beautiful.

Many of the skycrapers of the period revealed a similar functional beauty, fulfilling what a pioneer Chicago architect called the "ideals of modern business life, simplicity, stability, breadth, dignity." High ground rents had made the maximum use of space in business districts imperative, and the vertical, soaring office building seemed to escape from the city's limited dimensions. Such buildings were made possible by the electric elevator, which was perfected in the 80's, and by cheap steel, which replaced the customary bulky masonry walls or stone columns of business buildings with a light, strong "cage." James Bogardus, a New York architect, had designed buildings with supporting iron columns in 1847, but it was not until the 1860's that the needs of industrial America compelled even the architectural aesthetes, men trained to regard iron as beneath the dignity of the artist, to work in iron and glass.

Henry Hobson Richardson, a great architectural innovator, borrowed boldly from traditional forms in building his railroad stations, warehouses, and office buildings, but he stamped his personality on every building he designed, and his mature work was never derivative. He was one of the first architects in America to accommodate himself to American conditions, to consider the purpose of his houses, libraries, and warehouses as more important than their façades. He would not promise that a finished building would conform to a client's "ideas of beauty and taste," but the huge seven-story granite Wholesale Store that he designed in 1885 for the Chicago merchant Marshall Field had a simplicity and beauty of its own. "Four-square and brown, it stands," wrote Richardson's contemporary, the architect Louis Sullivan, "in physical fact, a monument to trade, to the organized commercial spirit, to the power and progress of the age, to the strength and resource of individuality and force of character."

The first steel-skeleton skyscraper—the Home Insurance Building in Chicago, designed by William LeBaron Jenney and completed in 1885.

Richardson, an audacious experimenter in masonry construction, died before steel-frame construction came into general use. But under his influence a group of architects who helped to rebuild Chicago after the fire of 1871 perfected the skyscraper and combined the beautiful and the purposeful in an exciting way. Men like John W. Root, Daniel Burnham, William L. Jenney, and (in his early designs) Louis Henri Sullivan created an architecture that reflected admirably the spirit and function of modern business. The skyscraper that emerged after decades of experimenting turned streets into canyons, shut out the light and air, increased congestion, and could be made to seem grandiose and vulgar. But at its best it embodied what Horatio Greenough many years before had

523

The dream city (1893)—a view of the Columbian Exposition.

called "the principle of unflinching adaptation of forms to function."

The Dream City.

In 1876, a centennial exposition at Philadelphia had convinced the world of America's economic, if not her artistic, maturity. Aesthetically, the exhibits of domestic furnishings and fine arts and the buildings that housed them were without distinction. What the Gilded Age regarded as "good taste" in 1876 could be summed up as a fondness for the overstuffed, the exotic, and the ornate. America's chief contribution lay in what William Dean Howells described as "the superior elegance, aptness, and ingenuity" of its machinery. "It is still in these things of iron and steel," Howells wrote, "that the national genius most freely speaks; by and by the inspired marbles, the breathing canvases, the great literature; for the present America is valuable in the strong metals and their infinite uses."

The World's Columbian Exposition, held in Chicago from May to October in 1893, did not fulfill Howells' prophecy, but the 21 million Americans who visited it did catch a glimpse of a white city rising miraculously from the shores of Lake Michigan. The Exposition is no longer regarded as the architectural awakening many once thought it was, and it showed little evidence that the artistic timidity current in 1876 had abated. Nevertheless, as one observer noted, it was "the climacteric expression of America's existence." It dramatized the tremendous progress that had been made in American industry, organizational skill, and inventiveness.

The idea of a world's fair to commemorate the discovery of America was conceived by Congress in 1889. Washington, St. Louis, and New York all contested for the privilege of housing the fair, and New York was so certain of success that investors actually bought up unoccupied land north of Central

524

Daniel Aaron, *Men of Good Hope* (1951); and A. M. Schlesinger, *The American as Reformer* (1950).

The most recent study of American poverty is R. H. Bremner, *The Discovery of Poverty in the United States* (1956). Jacob Riis, *How the Other Half Lives* (1890), is a famous report of slum conditions and their social implications, as is his *The Battle With the Slums* (1902). Another classic on this subject is Jane Addams, *Forty Years at Hull House* (1935). For an account of the Women's Christian Temperance Union, see Mary Earhart, *Frances Willard: From Prayers to Politics* (1944).

The church's part in urban reform is well told in A. I. Abell, *The Urban Impact upon American Protestantism, 1865-1900* (1943), and in Henry May's solid monograph, *Protestant Churches and Industrial America* (1949). The Social Gospel movement is the theme of C. H. Hopkins, *The Rise of the Social Gospel in American Protestantism, 1865-1915* (1940). Beecher's extraordinary career is sardonically chronicled in Paxton Hibben, *Henry Ward Beecher, An American Portrait* (1927), and briefly in C. M. Rourke, *Trumpets of Jubilee* (1927). The celebrated Beecher-Tilton story is told by R. Shaplen, *Free Love and Heavenly Sinners: The Story of the Great Henry Ward Beecher Scandal* (1954). Some of the more important books dealing with evangelism are W. W. Sweet, *Revivalism in America, Its Origin, Growth, and Decline* (1944); G. Bradford, *D. L. Moody, A Worker in Souls* (1927); and G. C. Loud, *Evangelized America* (1928). For the Y.M.C.A., see C. H. Hopkins, *A History of the Y.M.C.A. in North America* (1951). The histories of Christian Science are biased pro and con. Favorable and official is Sibyl Wilbur, *The Life of Mary Baker Eddy* (rev., 1913); and critical is E. F. Dakin, *Mrs. Eddy: The Biography of a Virginal Mind* (1929). The best one-volume account of the Catholic Church is Theodore Maynard, *The Story of American Catholicism* (1941). Msgr. John Tracy Ellis gives an excellent brief survey in *American Catholicism* (1956). The best treatment of anti-Catholic sentiment is in John Higham's *Strangers in the Land* (1955).

For the story of journalism, consult the works of F. L. Mott, previously cited, and W. G. Bleyer, *Main Currents in the History of American Journalism* (1927). J. W. Barrett, *Joseph Pulitzer and His World* (1941), is relevant here, as is Edward Bok, *The Americanization of Edward Bok* (1920).

In addition to the works of Mumford, cited above, the story of American architecture is covered in W. A. Starrett, *Skyscrapers and the Men Who Build Them* (1928); John Kouwenhoven, *Made in America: The Arts in Modern Civilization* (1948); and T. F. Hamlin, *The American Spirit in Architecture* (1926). For the World's Columbian Exposition, see the account in Larkin's *Art and Life in America*.

MINDS IN
TRANSITION

CHAPTER TWENTY-THREE

Historians have invented a number of epithets—none of them complimentary—to describe the decades that followed the Civil War. The most familiar is the term "Gilded Age," which was taken from the title of a novel by Mark Twain and Charles Dudley Warner. In this exposé of political corruption, the authors caught the cynical spirit of the new plutocracy. But they also reflected the prevailing mood of hope and adventure. Vast resources were on hand to be developed, and thousands of practical men felt they could do the job if the government would permit the laws of competition to operate without interference. The only artificial aid they needed was a high tariff.

The conservative faith was sanctioned by the makers of public opinion. Great edu-

528

cators and leading editors supported laissez faire, popular ministers praised the art of making money as a form of public service, and leading economists persuasively defended the laws of competition. The defenders of orthodoxy drew on every realm of faith and knowledge to support their

arguments. Even the ideas of Charles Darwin, so radical in many of their implications, were at first seized upon enthusiastically by conservatives who ingeniously adapted them to their own purposes.

I. CONSERVATISM AND DISSENT

Social Darwinism. Darwin published his momentous book, *The Origin of Species,* in 1859. In it he argued that the species of life all around us, far from having been created by separate acts of God in seven days, had gradually evolved, over millions of years, out of lower orders of life through the operation of the principle of "natural selection." According to Darwin, all forms of life were engaged in an unceasing "struggle for existence" in a constantly changing natural environment. Although some died, the fittest—those whose physical variations had enabled them to adapt to changing conditions—would survive, and would pass on to their offspring their favorable characteristics. Over long ages of time, such accumulating changes would develop entirely new species.

Darwin's ideas frightened and outraged Biblical fundamentalists and offended some leading scientists as well. Darwin's theory of how new species arose, for example, was condemned as blasphemous nonsense by Louis Agassiz, Harvard's great naturalist. More remarkable, however, was the readiness with which Americans in general embraced the new ideas.

After Agassiz died in 1873, no other leading scientist remained to deny the theory of evolution. Darwin's popularizers in America—men like the Harvard botanist, Asa Gray, and the historian and lecturer, John Fiske—came to the rescue of religion in a way that pleased liberal thinkers. Fiske saw nothing anti-religious in the belief that man was the result of a long evolutionary process. To him it seemed a marvelous proof of Providence. The Darwinian, said Fiske, "recognizes the slow and subtle process of

evolution as the way in which God makes things come to pass. . . . He sees that in the deadly struggle for existence which has raged through aeons of time, the whole creation has been groaning and travailing together in order to bring forth that last consummate specimen of God's handiwork, the Human Soul."

But it remained for the English philosopher, Herbert Spencer, to reconcile the Darwinian theory with American optimism. His "synthetic philosophy," as he called it, explained the new biology in terms that the ordinary man could understand. Spencer believed that evolution was not merely change but progress. Ultimately, the process would culminate in a state of existence where "evil and immorality must disappear." For God, Spencer substituted the "Unknowable," thus satisfying thousands of Americans who no longer held to a literal interpretation of the Bible but who did cling to a faith in a supernatural agency.

Spencer's ideas took the United States by storm. By 1900, about 350,000 copies of his books had been sold in America, a fantastically high figure for difficult sociological and philosophical works to attain. These books must have been read by millions. No saint ever had more devoted disciples than Spencer had in Edward Livingston Youmans and John Fiske. Beginning in the late 1860's, these two apostles spread the gospel of Social Darwinism throughout the country via magazine articles, popular books, and lectures. Harvard in 1869 and Yale, Johns Hopkins, and other universities in the 1870's, adopted the Spencerian philosophy in teaching religion and the biological and social sciences.

Even the churches succumbed. In 1867, Henry Ward Beecher of Plymouth Church in Brooklyn (see p. 344), said that he found "arising in the studies in Natural Science a surer foothold for [his evangelical] views than they ever had." Fifteen years later he pronounced himself "a cordial Christian evolutionist," and acknowledged Spencer as his intellectual foster father of many years' standing. "Men have not fallen as a race," Beecher exclaimed. "Men have come up." For evidence he had only to turn to his rich, satisfied congregation. His parishioners were more secular perhaps than the Puritans of old but they were no less certain of their elect status, as evidenced by their possession of the good things of life on earth.

As we have noted (Chapter XVIII), American businessmen in particular appreciated the application of Spencer's evolutionary ideas to social and economic practices. To Spencer, success in business demonstrated superior ability to adapt to circumstances, and failure implied inferior ability. He felt that the intrusion of the state into economic and social spheres only interrupted the process by which impersonal nature rewarded the strong and eliminated the unfit. So Spencer opposed poor relief, housing regulations, public education, and even laws to protect consumers from medical quacks.

He also wrote that society, if it changed at all, must move with millennial slowness, and that the attempts of reformers to hurry it along were both mischievous and futile. "We can only wait," declared E. L. Youmans, "for evolution. Perhaps in four or five thousand years evolution may have carried men beyond this state of things."

The most original thinker among the American Darwinians was William Graham Sumner, a Yale sociologist and political economist, who preached an American brand of Social Darwinism that was more rigorous and less optimistic than Spencer's. Sumner, like Darwin and Spencer, accepted the theory of T. R. Malthus that population increase outstrips food supply, but unlike Spencer he did not feel that the pressure for food or the struggle for life made for inevitable progress. For Sumner, life was a grim business, a constant struggle, and it was "root, hog, or die." He scornfully dismissed the sentimentalists who invented nostrums to preserve the unfit, and he hailed the millionaires as products of natural selection. Reformers were meddlers engaged in an absurd effort to make the world over; their victim was the "forgotten man" who worked hard, minded his own business, and paid taxes for the upkeep of the improvident. Unlike many professed Social Darwinists, Sumner was consistent in his individualism and, to the dismay and even rage of other conservatives, he opposed government handouts in the form of high tariffs. Nor had he any sympathy for the racists and imperialists who glorified the Anglo-Saxon stock and who cited Darwin to justify American expansion at the expense of "inferior" peoples.

The Dissenters.   Like the conservatives, the critics of society tried to use Darwinism to strengthen their case. They criticized Spencerians for drawing unjustified parallels between nature and society and for neglecting the power of the human mind to shape the environment. They accepted *The Origin of Species*, but rejected as unscientific and unchristian the Social Darwinists' notion that man's situation was just like the animals' and that natural selection in biology justified laissez faire in economics. "The fact is," concluded the reformer, Henry D. Lloyd, "these hypothetical economists . . . have substituted assumption and dogma for a Darwinian patience in accumulating facts and reserve in generalization."

One of the most outspoken antagonists of Spencer and his American school was the largely self-taught sociologist, Lester Ward. Born in Joliet, Illinois, in 1841, Ward had to struggle for a hearing and did not obtain an academic position until 1906. In the meantime, he worked in factories, fought in the Civil War, learned ten languages, made important contributions to the science of botany, and served as chief paleontologist for the United States Geological Survey. Unlike Spencer, Ward at first commanded no appreciative audience (*Dynamic Sociology*, 1883, his first major work, sold only about 500 copies in ten years). Not until the 90's did his ideas begin to take hold.

In his writings, the most readable of which is *The Psychic Factors of Civilization* (1893), Ward countered the prevailing theory that "neither physical nor social phenomena are capable of human control" with the assertion "that all the practical benefits of science are the result of man's control of natural forces." Ward pointed out that nature was uneconomical and wasteful. Its value to mankind depended on its being governed by what he called "telic" forces (forces originating in the human mind) as against blind and directionless "genetic" forces. Man's duty, then, in both the natural and the social sciences, was not to imitate nature but to dominate it. Far from assuring the survival of the fittest, competition often prevented it. Ward emphasized the superiority of selective breeding over natural breeding by pointing out that vegetables and fruit from an artificially cultivated garden were far superior to those that grew untended. Because Ward believed in social planning, he welcomed the intervention of government—"one of these artificial products of man's devising"—in social matters. A democratic government operating in the interests of all would permit a truer individualism by cracking down on the monopolies that strangled economic opportunities. "Those who dismiss state interference," Ward declared, "are the ones who most frequently and successfully invoke it."

Ward's assault on Social Darwinism was backed by another group—they might almost be called secular evangelists—who also denied that progress arose from competition and from the resulting removal of the unfit. The social upheavals they witnessed from the 1870's through the 1890's seemed too urgent for them to accept Spencer's fatalistic pronouncement that man-made reforms were useless and that only time would solve social problems. They saw little that was beneficial in the struggle for existence.

To the reformer Henry George, the Spencerian philosophy sinned against the divinity of man by treating him like "a thing, in some respects lower than the animal," and failed to explain why it was that some peoples progressed while others did not. George rejected Spencer's talk of the "survival of the fittest" as specious and maintained that progress depended upon human association and equality that unleashed the creative powers of man. When inequality prevailed, association stopped and civilization declined.

What was the cause of this inequality? George thought he had found the answer. Born in Philadelphia in 1839, he had left for California in 1857, where he observed a civilization in the making. The frontier society, simple and equalitarian, had quickly been transformed into a wealthy and class-stratified society. As George put it, "The tramp comes with the locomotive, and almshouses and prisons are as surely the marks of 'material progress' as are costly dwellings, rich warehouses, and magnificent churches."

George felt that progress was accompanied by poverty because of the iniquitous system of private land ownership. The value of land, he thought, was largely a matter of social accident. For example, the high cost of land in metropolitan New York was "not because of what its owners had done." Rather, it was "the presence of the whole great population" that made it worth millions of dollars an acre. If this was true, the land-speculators who bought up land inexpensively and waited for it to rise in value did not deserve to reap a profit that they had not really earned. Since land took on value because of the people who lived on it, George argued, this unearned rent ought to return to the public in the form of a "single tax" on land values. He would leave the husk of ownership in private hands but would socialize the "kernel"—rent. George thought that the single tax on land would make other taxes unnecessary and would promote "the

Golden Age of which poets have sung and high-raised seers have told us in metaphor!"

George set down his theory in *Progress and Poverty*, and his influence spread throughout the world. The book's appeal lay partly in its rhapsodic style and in the skill with which George reduced economic complexities to language that everyone could understand, and partly in its central theme that material progress without social justice leads to despotism. George continued to develop his theme in subsequent books. He edited a newspaper, spoke frequently, and narrowly missed being elected mayor of New York City in 1886. He ran again in 1897 but died five days before the election.

George's contemporary, Edward Bellamy, also rejected the conservative fatalism of the Social Darwinists, but, unlike George, Bellamy concentrated his attack on the competitive system itself in his Utopian novel, *Looking Backward* (1888). Bellamy's radicalism had something in common with the communitarian experiments of Fourier and his American disciples (see p. 260) and with the Social Gospel movement. As a journalist and fiction writer in Chicopee, Massachusetts, Bellamy had long been troubled by the suffering and poverty he had observed in industrial America. In *Looking Backward*, he penned a vision of an ideal society flowering in the year 2000 whose beauty, tranquillity, and efficiency contrasted vividly with the smoky and strike-ridden America of the 80's. The Golden Age had dawned after the nationalizing of the great trusts and the "substitution of scientific methods of an organized and unified industrial system for the wasteful struggle of the present competitive plan with its countless warring and mutually destructive undertakings."

The millions of Americans who read Bellamy's charming tale were impressed by his amiable and persuasive tone and delighted by the vision of his immaculate and gadget-filled city of the future. Amazed by the impact of his book, Bellamy concluded that the American people might be persuaded to put

his theories into practice. "Nationalism," as he called his system, was not a class movement. It rested on the idea that all people

... are victims in mind, body, or soul, in one way or another, of the present barbarous industrial and social arrangements, and that we are all equally interested, if not for ourselves, yet for our children, in breaking the meshes which entangle us, and struggling upward to a higher, nobler, happier plane of existence. ...

"Nationalist" clubs sprang up throughout the country. "Nationalist" magazines advocating such measures as public ownership of railroads and utilities, civil-service reform, and government aid to education were widely circulated. Before Bellamy's death, Nationalism had been absorbed by the agrarian reformers, but it had accomplished its purpose of presenting socialist ideas and programs in terms that were acceptable to a large American audience.

Bellamy and his co-workers deliberately avoided the word "socialism," for, as he wrote to Howells,

In the radicalness of the opinions I have expressed I may seem to outsocialize the Socialists, yet the word socialist is one I could never well stomach. In the first place it is a foreign word itself and equally foreign in all its suggestions. It smells to the average American of petroleum, suggests the red flag with all manner of sexual novelties, and an abusive tone toward God and religion, which in this country we can at least treat with decent respect.

Bellamy knew his public. "Socialism," "anarchism," and "communism" (in America the terms were interchangeable) were words that evoked uneasiness or rage in most Americans. Anarchists protested that they were "simply unterrified Jeffersonian Democrats," and socialists denied that they intended a violent overthrow of society. But the majority of Americans turned away from these exotic systems. One organization, the Socialist-Labor party, founded in 1877, upheld the doctrines of Karl Marx, but most of its tiny membership was foreign-born, and its influence on American reform was negligible. Under the influence of its leader, a doctrinaire Marxian theoretician, Daniel De

Leon, the Socialist-Labor party entered the presidential race in 1892 but obtained only 21,000 votes. When De Leon attempted to disrupt the American Federation of Labor and the Knights of Labor, his authoritarian methods provoked a revolt in his party, and in 1899 a faction broke away to form the Socialist party under Eugene Debs.

Orthodoxy Challenged. The social ideas of such "underground" theorists as George and Bellamy and Henry Demarest Lloyd found little support in universities, where orthodox economics was firmly fixed in the early postwar years. American students learned that inequality in wealth produced the incentives without which progress was

impossible; that labor's wages depended upon the number of men competing for jobs who shared in a "wage fund" that no artificial regulation could modify; and that competition was the only way for free individuals to satisfy their own needs and to work for "the greatest good of the greatest number." Only in an unregulated society could the natural economic laws function properly.

These sentiments, held by the leading academic social scientists, began to be challenged in the mid-80's by a group of younger scholars, many of whom had been trained in German universities. Economists like Richard T. Ely, John R. Commons, and Edward Bemis grew increasingly critical of

Portrait of Thorstein Veblen (1857-1929), by Edwin B. Child.

laissez faire and considered far more sympathetically than had their predecessors the idea that the power of the state might legitimately be used to improve society. Under the leadership of Ely, the younger economists and some liberal clergymen founded the American Economic Association in 1885. The A.E.A. declared itself in favor of "the positive assistance of the state," and, while recognizing "the necessity of individual initiative in industrial life," it held that "the doctrine of laissez faire is unsafe in politics and unsound in morals."

Younger sociologists had also broken out of the Spencerian straitjacket by the 1890's. Whereas Spencer had seen society as composed of separate individuals each operating independently of one another, the new sociologists like Albion Small, Charles H. Cooley, and E. A. Ross argued that the individual personality was shaped by social institutions that were in turn amenable to social control. In *Sin and Society* (1907), Ross tried to show that the new conditions of corporate society demanded a new code of morality that required the soulless corporation to take full responsibility for its antisocial acts.

The younger social scientists differed in their economic and political programs, but by and large they all distrusted a static view of the universe, absolute laws, and fixed conceptions. Society, they felt, was constantly changing and had to be examined as process and growth. Consequently, they turned to the historical past in order to understand the present and looked for relevant facts in the other disciplines that would help to illuminate their own.

Foremost among the academic rebels (and as unconventional in his personal life as in his thinking) was Thorstein Veblen, who critically re-examined the accepted truisms of conservative economics in the light of the new evolutionary method. The son of Norwegian immigrants, the Wisconsin-born Veblen had absorbed some frontier Populism before he completed his training at Yale (where he studied under Sumner) and at The Johns Hopkins University. Always remote, always the type of renegade whom he once described as "a disturber of the intellectual peace," he concealed his feelings behind a heavily ironic and polysyllabic style, and sardonically spoofed the sacred beliefs of his society.

The well-to-do leisure class, according to Veblen, was not the most biologically fit. The millionaires were not, as Sumner had insisted, "a product of natural selection," nor were they socially useful. The captains of enterprise and the lesser businessmen sabotaged the industrial machine, because their concern—unlike the interests of the productive technician or engineer—was primarily financial. In his most widely read book, *The Theory of the Leisure Class* (1899), and in a number of other volumes, Veblen discussed the habits and thoughts of the upper class as if he were reporting the behavior of a primitive tribe, and introduced ethical, psychological, biological, and anthropological observations not to be found in conventional economic studies. Although he wrote as a detached neutral, above the battle of the market place, he envisaged a community of "masterless" men organized under a technical élite and freed from what he considered to be the depredations of wasteful business saboteurs. These ideas seemed merely whimsical in the early 1900's, but Veblen's influence grew during the 1920's and reached its peak after the disastrous breakdown of the American economy in 1929.

II. NEW LINES OF THOUGHT

The Philosophers. What chiefly distinguished pre-Darwinian science from post-Darwinian science, as Veblen pointed out, was the way in which the scientist looked at his facts. The Darwinian did not care whether his observations harmonized with older formulas, with long-treasured ideals, with fixed beliefs. He accepted evolution because he was less concerned (as the philosopher John Dewey remarked) "in what or who made the world" than in "what kind of world it is anyway." This, said Dewey, was "the intellectual transformation effected by the Darwinian logic." But the transformation did not occur immediately, for the "Darwinian logic" clashed with an older one deeply embedded in the American mind.

Before the Civil War, the prevailing philosophy in the United States was known as Scottish or "common-sense" realism. The Scottish philosophy was an adaptation of some of the insights and methods of Enlightenment thought to the needs of Protestant, mainly Calvinist, religion; and it was the standard philosophy taught in the denominational colleges by such men as the Reverend James McCosh of Princeton, the Reverend Noah Porter of Yale, and their followers. It supposed that man possessed a God-implanted faculty which enabled him to arrive at the truth. As Newton had formulated the laws of the universe, so other men could formulate natural laws of politics, economics, and ethics. In the hands of most of the common-sense philosophers, these laws had a way of turning out to be justifications of the status quo and of conservative ways of thought.

In the 1870's and after, German idealism, particularly as developed by Hegel and his followers, made inroads upon the Scottish school. Hegel had seen the whole course of history as the working out of divine purpose according to certain general laws of change. But since Hegelians looked upon the present state of affairs as an inevitable stage in historical development, Hegelianism served as well as the Scottish philosophy to justify existing conditions. Its chief element of novelty lay in the fact that it taught reverence for the state, and preached that the individual could be truly free only by subordinating himself harmoniously to the development of his national government and the institutions of his society. This school, which originated in the work of non-academic philosophers in St. Louis, received strong support from William T. Harris, who became United States Commissioner of Education in 1889.

Possibly the most influential and certainly the most readable of the American idealists was Josiah Royce, a brilliant Californian who taught at Harvard from 1882 until his death in 1916. Royce defended the idealistic belief in an absolute mind, but unlike the more orthodox Hegelians, he found a larger and more active place for the individual in the universe. Royce preached a social ethic in which the greatest good was not to be found in aggregate happiness but in unification and harmony. He believed that through the principle of loyalty many individuals could be brought together into the unity of a single life, and he built a large part of his later philosophy around this theme of social cohesion.

But a new school of philosophy appeared toward the end of the century that regarded the concerns of the idealists as irrelevant. The "pragmatists," as they came to be known, repudiated fixed systems of belief and evaluated ideas in terms of their consequences. The forerunners of pragmatism, Chauncey Wright and Charles Peirce, were both remarkable thinkers (Peirce was probably the most original technical philosopher America has ever produced), but neither received much credit for pragmatism's subsequent development. Two other men, William James and John Dewey, broadened and humanized pragmatism from a method of thinking into a philosophy of action.

William James, the brother of the novelist Henry James, had revolted from the determinism of Herbert Spencer and from all systems of thought that left no place for chance or human will. In the late 60's, he had gone through an emotional crisis that almost destroyed him. He emerged from this ordeal with an intense will to believe and with a conviction that the purpose of thinking was "to help change the world." As a philosopher and psychologist at Harvard

University, James developed his case against the "awfully monotonous" Spencerian universe, wrote a brilliant exposition on the active role of the mind (*Principles of Psychology,* 1890), and later expounded his views on pragmatism. The pragmatist, wrote James

... turns away from abstraction and insufficiency, from verbal solutions, from bad *a priori* reasons, from fixed principles, closed systems, and pretended absolutes and origins. He turns towards concreteness and adequacy, towards facts, towards action and towards power.

He regards theories as *"instruments, not answers to enigmas."* Pragmatism "has no dogmas, and no doctrines save its method," James said; it is a method for arriving at the truth. Pragmatism appealed to America's preference for facts over theory, but when James declared that "the true is the name of whatever proves itself to be good in the way of belief, and good, too, for definite, assignable reasons," he laid himself open to the charge that pragmatism was only a high-sounding name for vulgar expediency: anything is good that works.

John Dewey (1859-1952).

The same charge was later leveled at John Dewey's "instrumentalism," another version of the pragmatic philosophy. Starting out as an idealist, Dewey had been converted to pragmatism in the 1890's after reading James, but soon the disciple began to influence the master. Far more than James, Dewey believed in the intelligence as a tool for social reform, and he had less interest in the private struggles of the individual mind than in the interactions between men and the community. The mind, he said, "is at least an organ of service for the control of environment," and he called upon philosophers to stop speculating on what were for him meaningless quibbles and to turn to politics, education, and ethics. Like Ward, George, and other social dissenters, Dewey was an early critic of laissez faire, Social Darwinism, and commercialism. In arguing that life need not be accepted passively, but could be shaped by man, Dewey laid a philosophical groundwork for the program of liberal reformers. He also applied his ideas to education, which he felt should be intimately related to the rest of life and which he thought could be made into an instrument for social reform. In the early decades of the twentieth century, Dewey's "progressive" theories of learning began to influence American education and provoked a controversy that still rages today between his followers and their critics.

The Law and Social Theory.

The Darwinian influence also transformed old conceptions of the law. The preceding generation had commonly believed that the law was something handed down from on high, and that judicial decisions were inevitable, logical interpretations of constitutions or statutes. Oliver Wendell Holmes, son of the poet, and a friend of William James, served on the Massachusetts Supreme Court and then on the United States Supreme Court from 1902 to 1932. To him, the law was part of the social process, an outcome of social views and political compromises. Even the decisions of judges, he demonstrated in his book, *The Common Law* (1881), arose out of prejudices and preconceptions. As Roscoe Pound, another legal scholar, wrote in 1910, "Public thought and feeling have changed, and, whatever the law in the books, the law in action has changed with them."

Among practitioners who did most to change the law in action was Louis D. Brandeis, a Boston lawyer-reformer, who was eventually appointed to the Supreme Court by Woodrow Wilson. Brandeis believed that since the social beliefs of judges did color their judicial decisions, they ought to support their rulings not merely with legal arguments but also with the economic and social facts relevant to the case. In a famous brief presented in the case of *Muller* v. *Oregon* (1908), he defended the constitutionality of a ten-hour law governing the work of women in Oregon laundries, and showed with overwhelming evidence from physicians, factory inspectors, social workers, and other competent observers that the number of hours women worked affected their health and morals and hence the well-being of the entire community. The preceding generation had usually been content not to go behind the text of the laws to the texture of social reality, but Brandeis persuaded the Court that the facts of social life should be taken into account.

Even the supreme law, the Constitution itself, became an object of skeptical study. The political scientist, Arthur F. Bentley, concluded in his book, *The Process of Government* (1908), that all law was the result of struggles among interest groups, and that constitutions were merely a special form of law. Another writer, J. Allen Smith, argued in *The Spirit of American Government* (1907) that the framers of the Constitution of the United States had intended not to realize democracy but to check it. In *An Economic Interpretation of the Constitution* (1913), the brilliant Columbia historian, Charles A. Beard, laid critical hands upon the sacrosanct document and upon the generation of the Founding Fathers, by discussing at length the economic interests of the framers. Such works, though sometimes exaggerated in tone and inexact in scholarship, released the critical mind from its shackles and induced a whole generation of social scientists to set about re-examining the precepts of their society and assessing the possibilities of reforming it.

The Historians. Evolutionary ideas also had a strong influence on historical theory in America. The analogy between biological development and the emergence of social institutions was too obvious to be missed, and by the 1880's some historians were convinced that history could be transformed into an exact science once the laws of history had been ascertained. The popular lecturer John Fiske pursued this course of thought for a wide general audience, tracing America's political development from its earliest stages to its present complexity. And a school of American historians, under the influence of Herbert B. Adams of The Johns Hopkins University and John W. Burgess of Columbia, professed to see the origins of American democracy in the primitive tribes of Germany. Inspired by the racist views of English historians like E. A. Freeman and by the swelling expansionist sentiment, they made the Anglo-Saxon race the originators and the preservers of freedom. "By that race alone," one of them wrote in 1890, "it [freedom] has been preserved amidst a thousand perils; to that race alone is it thoroughly congenial; if we can conceive the possibility of the disappearance among peoples of that race, the chance would be small for that freedom's survival. . . ." The young Theodore Roosevelt and the even younger novelist, Frank Norris, saw the westward expansion as merely a continuation of an Anglo-Saxon drive that had begun in the swamps of Germany.

To Frederick Jackson Turner, Wisconsin-born and trained at Johns Hopkins, the conquest of the American frontier was part of an evolutionary process. But as he argued in his immensely influential essay, "The Significance of the Frontier in American History" (1893), American democracy did not originate in the German forests but in the American forests. The European settler eventually conquered the New World wilderness, but during his long struggle the conqueror was himself transformed by his environment, stripped of his civilized garments, and forced to adapt himself to new conditions or to perish. Wrote Turner:

> The advance of the frontier has meant a steady movement away from the influence of Europe, a steady growth of independence on American lines. And to study this advance, the men who grew up under these conditions, and the political, economic, and social results of it, is to study the really American part of our history.

The closing of the frontier that Turner noticed in 1893 had, he believed, dangerous implications for America. The frontier had created the American character; from it had sprung the toughness, resourcefulness, individualism, and versatility that made America great. Turner had misgivings as he contemplated the new industrialized and urbanized civilization that now overlay the once-savage wilderness, but he remained hopeful that America, because of its frontier heritage, would escape the social evils that plagued the tired civilization of Europe.

Optimistic faith might sustain a buoyant middle-westerner like Turner, but to Henry Adams and his brother, Brooks—the descendants of presidents—the future looked much blacker. Throughout his life as political observer, journalist, professor, novelist, and traveler, Henry Adams had been fascinated by historical forces and had often lived close to the men who made history; his meticulous and often brilliant account of the Jefferson and Madison administrations and several historical biographies showed that he could write history as well. But as he grew older, he took pleasure in demonstrating to his own satisfaction that history is not progress but degradation. Thus he could maliciously observe in his famous autobiography, *The Education of Henry Adams* (1907), that America's decline could be measured by contrasting Washington with Grant. In *Mont-Saint-Michel and Chartres* (1904), he contrasted the spiritual vitality of the Middle Ages (the age of unity), symbolized by the cult of the Virgin, with the destructive violence of industrial civilization (the age of multiplicity), symbolized by the dynamo. Drawing a very dubious analogy from physics, he concluded that the constantly accelerating dissipation of energy would ultimately end in the destruction of human civilization, and he even calculated the possible dates of this cosmic debacle.

Brooks Adams shared his brother's pessimism, but for a short time he allowed his hopes to be stirred by the possibility of America's forging ahead in the competition among nations. By 1912, however, he agreed with Henry that America could not adapt itself quickly enough to changing conditions and that its leaders lacked the will and the imagination to convert the United States into a disciplined state.

III.   EDUCATION

The Higher Learning. In *The Theory of Social Revolutions* (1913), Brooks Adams accused the American universities of turning out narrow, half-educated specialists who lacked the breadth of mind needed to administer a complex, centralized economy. And Thorstein Veblen's *The Higher Learning in America* (1918) savagely pilloried the American universities as temples of "intellectual quietism" run by "captains of erudition" for the production of salesmen. Beginning in the 1890's, reformers complained about the alleged dictatorship of the plutocrats over the universities, about professors being tried for economic heresies and dismissed from their posts for offending conservative founders or trustees. They could cite the cases of Richard T. Ely at Wisconsin, whose books were denounced as "utopian, impracticable or pernicious" by one of the state regents who tried unsuccessfully to have him thrown out; of Edward T. Bemis, fired from the University of Chicago for attacking the railroads and the Gas Trust; of E. A. Ross, dismissed from Stanford for holding opinions offensive to the late founder's wife. But it was by no means true that academic freedom was stifled even during the troubled 1890's, or that university presidents (as Veblen implied) invariably knuckled under to big business. Since 1865, universities had become bigger and bigger, and they had become bureaucratized in the process. But more to the point, they had vastly improved in quality.

Between 1870 and 1900, higher education had been advanced by public and private donations. Under the terms of the Morrill Act (1862), the federal government had offered large land grants to any state that would found a college in which "agriculture and the mechanic arts" were taught. By 1868, Wisconsin, Minnesota, California, Texas, Massachusetts, and New York had established land-grant colleges, many of them co-educational. Other colleges and universities were set up through private philanthropy. Ezra Cornell, for example, who made a fortune from the electric telegraph, founded Cornell, which opened its doors in 1868. Stanford (1891) and Vanderbilt (1873) were the educational heirs of two railroad millionaires, and the University of Chicago (1891) received $34 million from the oil magnate, John D. Rockefeller. The Johns Hopkins University (1876) bore the name of a wealthy Baltimore banker and railroad executive; Carnegie Institute (1896) in Pittsburgh, the name of a multimillionaire steel man who believed it was the duty of men of wealth to spread culture.

The prewar colleges had confined themselves pretty much to non-utilitarian subjects —the classics, mathematics, and theology— but the postwar institutions responded to the demand for a business and technical education that would prepare university graduates

Charles W. Eliot, President of Harvard from 1869 to 1909.

for life in an industrial society. The prestige of science had risen so high (another result of the Darwinian revolution) that changes in the curriculum, the increasing emphasis on research, and the liberation of higher education from a narrow sectarianism had to be accepted. By the end of the century, a number of university scientists had won international reputations: Harvard's mathematician, Benjamin Peirce (the philosopher's father); the paleontologists O. C. Marsh of Yale and E. D. Cope of Pennsylvania; Albert A. Michelson of the University of Chicago (who made important discoveries in molecular theory and measured the velocity of light); and, above all, Josiah Willard Gibbs of Yale, one of the great original minds of his age, whose work in theoretical physics and physical chemistry paved the way for the theory of relativity and for other scientific advances.

Thanks to men like Charles W. Eliot of Harvard, a new kind of university emerged in which undergraduates "elected" courses from a greatly expanded curriculum instead of being "compelled to an unwelcome task." Harvard graduate schools were created, scholarly faculties were assembled, and administration was centralized. Between 1869 and 1900, Eliot also pushed through a drastic reformation of Harvard's medical and law schools. Pre-medical students, who had formerly obtained degrees with a minimum of course and clinical work, were now required to study three full years in medical school, to work in laboratories, and to take examinations. C. C. Langdell, Dean of the Harvard Law School, abolished the textbook and introduced a system whereby the law student got his knowledge by examining specific cases.

Eliot's theories—especially his "elective system," which permitted less serious undergraduates to choose an unrelated group of subjects and to avoid the difficult courses—provoked some opposition, but most universities accepted it along with the broadened curriculum and the new emphasis on commercial and scientific subjects. The founding of The Johns Hopkins University, for example, gave a strong impetus to diversified courses and furthered specialized research. Many of its faculty members had studied in Germany, and they proceeded to train a corps of teachers in the exacting methods of German university scholarship. The requirements of industry and finance were met by the technical schools that mushroomed during the last half of the century, and by institutions like the Wharton School of Finance, connected with the University of Pennsylvania (1881).

Not all the innovations that transformed the universities and colleges in the last half of the century, however, were intellectual. The introduction of organized sports like baseball, basketball, and football (a rougher American version of the original English rugby) aroused an almost fanatical concern for competitive athletic contests both inside and outside the schools, and encouraged what the poet T. S. Eliot was later to call the "decadent athleticism" of American life. By the 1890's, intercollegiate football had become a mass spectacle attended by crowds amounting to thirty or forty thousand, and critics were already protesting against its brutality and its professional emphasis. Here are the impressions of a shocked Frenchman watching the game between Harvard and the University of Pennsylvania in 1893:

> The signal is given and the play begins. It is a fearful game, which in itself points to the differences between the Anglo-Saxon and the Latin world—a game of young bulldogs trained to bite, to rush upon the quarry, the game of a race made for wild attack, for violent defense, for implacable conquests, and desperate struggles. . . . The entire object of the game is to throw an enormous leather ball, which each side holds in turn. All the excitement of this ferocious amusement is concentrated in waiting for this throw. He who holds the ball is there, bent forward. His companions and his adversary likewise bend down around him in the attitude of beasts of prey about to spring. All of a sudden he runs to throw the ball or else with wildly rapid movement hands it to another, who rushes off with it.

So far as educational opportunities went, women remained "second-class citizens" even after the war. A few colleges (Antioch, Oberlin, Iowa) were co-educational before 1860, but the traditional prejudice against higher education for women broke down only after business and professional jobs were opened up to them that had hitherto been restricted to men. By 1880, most of the important midwestern universities had opened their doors to women, and women's colleges like Vassar, Smith, Wellesley, and Bryn Mawr—founded between 1865 and 1875—were preparing their graduates for the professions.

Gains in
Public Education.
Progress in public education after 1865 was reflected in the steady lengthening of the school term, a

higher dollar expenditure per pupil, a declining illiteracy rate, and compulsory school-attendance laws. The old prewar academy that had once monopolized American secondary education gave way after 1870 to the modern public high school. Although the old-fashioned pedagogical methods, with their emphasis on corporal discipline and rote learning, remained the rule rather than the exception, new ideas from abroad changed the aims and the content of public education. School curricula were widened to include history and literature, as well as vocational and commercial courses, and greater stress was laid on preparing the child to meet the challenge of his social environment.

Between 1870 and 1910, the number of public high schools increased from 500 to more than 10,000, and a high-school education had begun to be what a grammar-school education had once been—the normal expectation of great numbers of young Americans. During this 40-year period, the total number of pupils attending public schools increased from 6,871,000 to 17,813,000. In 1870, only 57 per cent of the eligible children had been attending schools. Moreover, the schooling became increasingly rigorous. The average number of days in the school-year rose from 132 to 157, and the per capita appropriations of funds for education more than doubled. Illiteracy declined from 17 per cent of the population in 1880 to 7.7 per cent in 1910. Toward the end of the period, the average American was receiving six years of formal education. Interest had also risen in pre-schooling for the very young. The first kindergarten was established in St. Louis in 1873, and by the end of the century there were about 3,000 in the country. Advances in public education were more marked in the cities than in the country areas, and more impressive in the Northeast than in the South and West. The carpetbag governments in the South had laid the groundwork for public-school systems, but the return of the conservatives to power in the mid-1870's saw a falling off in appropriations. Even the grants of northern philanthropists like George Peabody could do little to eliminate illiteracy or overcome the prevailing apathy toward public education that was traditional in the South.

Modest in their programs, but performing an indispensable service, were the Negro vocational and normal schools that sprang up after 1865. Both white and Negro leaders had come to realize that so long as the ex-slave remained illiterate, he would remain a slave in fact if not before the law. Education would equip him for better jobs, increase his self-respect, and develop his natural aptitudes. The Hampton Normal and Agricultural Institute (1870) pioneered in vocational training for Negroes. Its most famous graduate, Booker T. Washington, became the head of a normal school at Tuskegee, Alabama, in 1881, and was soon recognized as the educational leader of the Negroes.

Casting down your bucket among my people [he told influential whites], helping and encouraging them . . . to education of head, hand, and heart, you will find that they will buy your surplus land, make bloom the waste places in your fields, and run your factories. While doing this you can be sure in the future, as in the past, that you will be surrounded by the most patient, faithful, law-abiding and unresentful people the world has ever seen.

Such docility infuriated militant Negroes, and today Booker T. Washington's attitude toward Negro-white relations is repudiated by the majority of his race. Nevertheless, his services to his people should not be minimized. If Washington prepared his students for agriculture, domestic service, and the lower-paid factory jobs, it was simply because better jobs were not open to them.

Popularizing Culture. For those who had finished their limited schooling and still hungered for more learning, a number of privately sponsored agencies came into being that provided a varied, though usually diluted, intellectual fare. The men who launched these experiments in popular culture were prompted by both idealistic and mercenary motives, but their efforts helped to bridge the gap between the intelligentsia and the average man.

A highly successful venture in popular learning began in western New York in 1874 with the establishment of the Chatauqua Assembly by an Ohio businessman, Louis Miller, and a Methodist bishop, John H. Vincent. Its original purpose was to train Sunday-school teachers during the summer months, but like the old lyceum movement (see p. 257), the Chatauqua soon expanded into wider fields. Before long, the Chatauqua Literary and Scientific Reading Circle had become a national organization with study circles and a corps of eminent lecturers who spoke to audiences throughout the land. Other more commercial "Chatauquas" (as these traveling lyceums came to be called) grew out of the pioneer endeavor; and educational entrepreneurs, capitalizing on the craving for self-culture, organized correspondence schools and published "libraries" of cheap books that were sold either by subscription or distributed through department stores and mail-order houses. Middle-class women found an outlet for their cultural interests in the "literary" clubs (later to be satirized by Edith Wharton in *The Custom of the Country* and by Sinclair Lewis in *Main Street*), which were united into the General Federation of Women's Clubs in 1889.

IV.   THE WRITER AND HIS WORLD

The Writer: 1870-1900. The year 1865 was a dividing point between old and new America. Hawthorne and Thoreau were dead, Emerson was past his prime and retiring more and more into himself, and Melville was living virtually forgotten in prison-like anonymity. Of all the writers who belonged to the "Golden Day" and who wrote after Appomattox, only Walt Whitman still sounded his "barbaric yawp over the roofs of the world."

The industrialized and urbanized America that emerged in the 70's and 80's was not a congenial subject for the older American writers. Perhaps a measure of their uneasiness is the curious fact that many of them gave themselves over to recalling a pastoral America precisely at that moment when country people were flocking to the cities. Already conscious of their lost heritage, these writers tried to strengthen their spiritual ties with the past. The result was the so-called "local color" movement in American fiction. Writers like Bret Harte, Joel Chandler Harris, Sarah Orne Jewett, and George Washington Cable tried to capture the "native element" of distinctive sections—the California mining country, the New England village, the southern plantation, the Kentucky and Tennessee mountains. Theoretically, the local colorist did not rule out the city:

The local movement will include the cities as well [wrote the local colorist, Hamlin Garland, in 1894], and St. Louis, Chicago, San Francisco, will be delineated by artists born of each city, whose work will be so true that it could not have been written by anyone from the outside. The real utterance of a city or a locality can only come when a writer is born out of its intimate heart. To such a one, nothing will be "strange" or "picturesque"; all will be familiar, and full of significance or beauty. The novel of the slums must be written by one who has played there as a child, and taken part in all its amusement; not out of curiosity, but out of pleasure seeking. It cannot be done from above nor from the outside. It must be done out of a full heart and without seeking for effect.

With few exceptions, however, the local colorists stuck to what they considered to be the authentic part of America—the village, the small town, the farm—and lovingly recorded the variations in dialect and the manners and customs of an older and rapidly disappearing America.

Mark Twain (1835-1910)—the pen name of Samuel L. Clemens—belonged by temperament to the local-color tradition and was regarded in his own day as a regional author.

But he was a writer of far greater dimensions than the local colorists. In many respects, Mark Twain was the most revealing figure in post-Civil War American literature and the man who best combined the virtues and defects of the period he so caustically analyzed. Born in Hannibal, Missouri, he had been a reporter, river pilot, and popular lecturer before he made his first success with *The Innocents Abroad* (1869), a wild and absurdly funny account of a junket through Europe and the Near East. Other novels, essays, and sketches followed in rapid succession.

Mark Twain wrote prolifically about everything from Christian Science to Andrew Carnegie and penned historical romances and pessimistic fantasies. But his best works, *The Adventures of Tom Sawyer* (1876), *Life on the Mississippi* (1883), and *The Adventures of Huckleberry Finn* (1884), all derive from the days when he lived close to the great river. It was his loyalty to the simple republican America of his boyhood that partly accounts for his rage over the betrayal of democratic ideals in the Gilded Age. "In my youth," wrote Twain, "there was nothing resembling a worship of money or of its possessor, in our region." It took people like Jay Gould, he said, "to make a God of the money and the man":

> The gospel left behind by Jay Gould is doing giant work in our days. Its message is "Get money. Get it quickly. Get it in abundance. Get it dishonestly if you can, honestly if you must."

And yet Twain shared the Philistinism and provincialism of the society he entertained, enjoyed "striking it rich," speculated recklessly, and always wrote with an eye on his large audience. As he put it:

> I have never tried in even one single instance to help cultivate the cultivated classes. I was not equipped for it by native gifts or training. And I never had any ambition in that direction, but always hunted for bigger game—the masses.

In his own subtle way, however, Mark Twain was a moralist who looked upon mankind with exasperation (because of its cruelty, credulity, and pigheadedness), and with compassion (because it was not to blame). *Huckleberry Finn* is an ironical attack against social hypocrisy, false respectability, and the canons of success—all bound up in the "civilization" from which Huck is trying to escape. In renouncing civilization, Huck remains true to his natural goodness without denying human depravity or his kinship with the wicked. As Mark Twain wrote: "I am the whole human race without a detail lacking . . . the human race is a race of cowards; and I am not only marching in that procession but carrying a banner."

William Dean Howells (1837-1920), a friend of Mark Twain, was born and reared in Ohio and had come to literature (as so many of his contemporaries had) through the printer's office and the newspaper. A campaign life of Lincoln earned him a consular appointment in Venice. After his return from Italy in 1865, he became a magazine editor in Boston and later in New York, wrote at least 40 works of fiction, a number of plays, and volumes of criticism. By 1900, many of the younger writers considered him the dean of American letters.

Howells, the leader of the school of "realists," wanted to deal directly with the sober realities of American life. "Realism," as Howells used the term, simply meant "the truthful treatment of commonplace material." The romanticism permeating the popular literature of his day was immoral, in Howells' opinion, because it corrupted American taste and falsified life. In place of sensational tales or "lies," Howells wanted to create a fiction that maintained "fidelity, not merely to the possible, but to the probable and ordinary course of man's experience." Let fiction, he said,

> . . . cease to lie about life; let it portray men and women as they are, actuated by the motives and passions in the measure that we all know; let it leave off painting dolls and working them by springs and wires; let it show the different interests in their proportions; let it forbear to teach pride and revenge, folly and insanity, egotism and prejudice, but frankly own these things for what they are, in whatever figures and occasions

they appear; let it not put on fine literary airs; let it speak the dialect, the language, that most Americans know—the language of unaffected people everywhere—and there can be no doubt of an unlimited future, not only of delightfulness but of usefulness, for it.

Howells vehemently championed literary realism in the works of other writers and practiced it effectively in his own novels. Rejecting the stock figures of romance, he wrote about self-made businessmen (*The Rise of Silas Lapham,* 1885) and the class gradations in urban society. He was fascinated by travel, religious mysticism, ethical problems, and social reform. Settling in New York in 1885, he saw at firsthand the competitive strife and extremes of social inequality that had long disturbed him. His *A Hazard of New Fortunes* (1890) implicitly condemned the mindless struggle for wealth, the paradox of Fifth Avenue luxury and East Side squalor, and the degradation of the republican dream.

Although Howells' friend, Henry James (1843-1916), allied himself with the realists, he could not find enough material for fiction in what he regarded as the bleak American scene. He was born in New York, but he had spent a good deal of his youth in Europe and could never find his roots in American soil. After a half-hearted attempt to study law at Harvard, James gave himself entirely to literature, and from 1875 until his death he did most of his writing abroad. Because he visited his native land so infrequently, and because so many of his novels and short stories have a European setting, James has been considered by many critics to be outside the main currents of American literature. Actually, his international plots deal almost exclusively with Americans, and from his foreign vantage point he discerned a good deal about the character of his countrymen that escaped the American writers who remained at home.

Like Hawthorne, by whom he was profoundly influenced, James liked to place his Americans in what he called "morally interesting situations." He subjected his traveling businessmen (*The American,* 1877), his sensitive and intellectually curious heroines (*The Portrait of a Lady,* 1881), his artist heroes, hungry for culture (*Roderick Hudson,* 1876), to moral tests that they either passed or failed. America remained for him —with all its artistic sterility—a land of innocence and promise; Europe was beautiful but decadent. James was not only a superb technician and psychologist; he was also a social historian who recorded impressionistically but truthfully the moral cracks and strains in the upper-class society he so minutely depicted.

As a result of the realists' efforts, the young writers who came of age in the last two decades of the century could experiment even more boldly than their predecessors in literary realism. Although it no longer took courage to portray a society committed to railroads, stockyards, real estate, and Wall Street, the new literary school that evolved

Henry James, with the English dramatist, James M. Barrie, on his right.

went much further than the realists in describing the seamy and brutal aspects of American life. "Naturalism," as the new movement was called, derived its inspiration from French novelists like Emile Zola, who believed that literature should be governed by the same scientific laws that guided the physiologist. Man's fate was determined by heredity and environment, by inward drives and external circumstances over which he had no control. Theoretically, the naturalist writer put down objectively what he saw. No matter how disgusting or shocking it was, he remained icily impersonal.

In America, naturalists like Stephen Crane and Frank Norris never matched the frankness of the French school, but they dealt with themes that Howells (who always had his eye fixed on the young girl reader) did not care to touch. In *Maggie, A Girl of the Streets* (1893), Crane wrote of the seduction and suicide of a New York slum girl; in *The Red Badge of Courage* (1895), he reproduced convincingly the animal fear of a young Civil War recruit under fire and his psychological recovery. In all his tales and sketches of derelicts and soldiers, of frightened, abandoned people, Crane suggests that men must struggle without guidance from the supernatural. Nature is like the ocean or the snowstorm.

Norris, a less able writer than Crane and more given to melodrama, disliked the kind of realism Howells represented, because it dealt with the commonplace, with "the tragedy of the broken tea cup." Norris had a fondness for huge supermen with "primordial" jaws, and he loved to describe the clash of titanic natural forces. Many of his books were spoiled by exaggerated violence and sensationalism, but in *McTeague* (1899), the story of a man's reversion to brutishness, he displayed a power that was new in American fiction. In his best-known novel, *The Octopus* (1901), Norris presented an epic struggle between the California wheat-growers and the railroad. The seeming radicalism of this book was considerably diluted by Norris' message that the wheat and the railroad represented natural forces, each

governed by the law of supply and demand. "Men have only little to do in the whole business."

In Jack London, many of the themes of Frank Norris' writing were repeated, notably the tendency to exalt the brutal while at the same time offering moral judgments on the brutality of the whole social order. Born in 1876, and thrown on his own resources at an early age in the tough waterfront environment of Oakland, California, London became a hobo and a seaman, among other things, before settling down to write. His literary career lasted only 18 years, but in its course he turned out over 50 books. He died in 1916, burnt out by his exertions and by the rage against life that expressed itself in his work.

London embraced a naturalistic social philosophy, in which he preached, at one and the same time, a despairing doctrine of the subordination of man to the impersonal forces of nature, and the hopeful teachings of socialism. He never succeeded in reconciling these antagonistic ideas, but he wrote a good deal of literature that successfully expressed one or the other, and he was one of the most widely read writers of his time, as well as a figure of some importance in the American socialist movement. His most interesting writings are his autobiographical novel, *Martin Eden* (1909), in which he tells of the bitterness of a proletarian youth who aspires to respectability and a literary career, and his novel of social struggles, *The Iron Heel* (1907), in which he portrays a bitter fight to the death between the exploiting and the exploited classes of society. Such books as these expressed his social idealism, but at bottom he was more interested in the spectacle of brute struggle. His greatest success, a book about pack dogs in the Yukon, *The Call of the Wild* (1903), gloried in details of animal conflict.

The writings of Theodore Dreiser reflected a naturalism that was even more uncompromising than that of Crane, Norris, or London. But in Dreiser, the replacement of the good and the bad by the strong and the weak was accompanied by a deeper feeling for character and a profound, almost maternal, tenderness. Dreiser was born in Terre Haute, Indiana, of German immigrant parents, in 1871. His early life in a family of 13 children was filled with squalor and hardship. After years of drifting from one unsatisfactory job to another, Dreiser spent several years as a newspaperman in Chicago, St. Louis, Cleveland, and Pittsburgh, where he saw at firsthand the hard side of city life. His experiences inspired him with the idea of treating the life of a great American metropolis as realistically as Balzac had treated Paris.

Dreiser had to battle against the restrictions set by the tradition of polite literature, and his position was not secure until the 1920's. His first novel, one of his best, *Sister Carrie,* was published in 1900 and then quickly withdrawn because many persons objected to its frankness. In a style criticized for its clumsiness, it tells of a young girl who comes to Chicago from a small western town and succumbs in succession to the blandishments of a vulgar but generous salesman and then to a restaurant manager. Sister Carrie takes a grip on her own fortunes, and in the end becomes a successful actress. The greatest chapters of the book, one of the most remarkable sequences in American letters, trace the gradual deterioration of her second seducer, Hurstwood, who drifts toward complete ruin while Carrie is winning success.

Although Dreiser is always compassionate toward his characters, it is seldom clear whether he is complaining about harsh human society or about the harshness of life itself. His characterization of an adventurous business tycoon (patterned after a Chicago traction magnate, Charles T. Yerkes) in *The Financier* (1912) and *The Titan* (1914) could be taken either as a naturalist's comments on the waste and immorality of life itself or as a part of the Progressive protest against rapacious business. Dreiser's hero, Frank Cowperwood, has his image of life fixed in his mind as a boy when he visits the aquarium and sees a lobster devour a squid:

Things lived on each other—that was it. Lobsters lived on squids and other things. What lived on lobsters? Men, of course! And what lived on men? he asked himself. Was it other men? . . . He wasn't so sure about men living on men; but men did kill each other. How about wars and street fights and mobs? He had seen a mob once. It attacked the *Public Ledger* building as he was coming home from school. His father had explained why. It was about the slaves. That was it! Sure, men lived on men. Look at the slaves.

Cowperwood grows up with the touch of Midas in his business dealings and the touch of Don Juan in his love life. In his pursuit of money and women, he is ruined once but boldly builds a whole new career. Toward him Dreiser maintains a mixed attitude of condemnation and approval, but basically he condones Cowperwood. Like the less successful organisms—like the squid who are eaten—Cowperwood is merely a product of nature, but a more interesting product than most of the others. In a self-consciously moral period, however, like the Progressive era in which these volumes first appeared, it was impossible for many Americans to read the Cowperwood novels without finding in them an indictment of the whole order of unchecked greed that the Progressive reformers were trying to tame.

The Little Renaissance.   The generation that came of age in 1912 was less provincial than the preceding one, thanks to the influence of cultural cosmopolites like the critic James Gibbons Huneker, whose essays on art, literature, and music opened the European continent to American intellectuals during the first decade of the century. The works of the German philosopher Friedrich Nietzsche, with their cult of the supreme individual, the Superman, came into vogue; and iconoclastic English writers—George Bernard Shaw, H. G. Wells, Samuel Butler—served as literary gods. The new artist-rebels who dominated the American cultural scene between 1912 and 1917 often differed from one another in political philosophy, social background, and aesthetic principles, but they agreed in their dislike for the genteel tradition, and they expressed their revolt in the magazines, books, and manifestoes that appeared during these exciting years. As one magazine editorial put it, the aim of this "league of youth" was to be "freely experimental, skeptical of inherited values, ready to examine old dogmas, and to submit afresh its sanctions to the test of experience."

Typical of the so-called "little renaissance" of these years was the feminine nonconformist, Mabel Dodge, a wealthy and talented lady of advanced views who opened her ample Fifth Avenue apartment to rebels of every persuasion. At her famous evenings, the guests discussed such themes as socialism, anarchism, women's rights, poetry, penology, birth control, sex, religion, labor— anything, in short, that came under the heading of "opinions." No idea or institution was immune from critical discussion. To these iconoclasts and to many inhabitants of Greenwich Village, now the favorite haunt of the "intellectually emancipated," the magazine *The Masses,* founded in 1911 and brought to life in 1912 under the editorship of the brilliant Max Eastman, expressed the correct attitude toward art, politics, and morals. Although editorially committed to socialism, *The Masses* reflected a peculiar anarchism and paganism. It preached, above all, human freedom and what one of its editors, the poet and novelist Floyd Dell, called the "play spirit"; it was both passionately reformist and refreshingly gay.

Putting aside old definitions, the league of youth launched an attack against artistic conventions that had created a sterile "highbrow" culture on the one hand and a vulgar "lowbrow" culture on the other. In defense of artistic freedom, a group of poets calling themselves the "Imagists" revolted against the tyranny of old poetic forms and prescribed "poetic" vocabulary and subject matter. Amy Lowell, Ezra Pound, and others advocated verse that presented hard, clear poetic outlines in concentrated images. In the same spirit, a group of artists and friends

of modernism sponsored an exhibition of modern art in the New York Armory in 1913 that attracted thousands of spectators and provoked a violent debate between the traditionalists and the radicals. Rebellious literary critics like Van Wyck Brooks were determined to produce a culture that truly represented American democracy and that at the same time embodied the best of European culture. No social revolution was possible, Brooks believed, until "a race of artists, profound and sincere, have brought us face to face with our own experience."

Before America's entrance into World War I in 1917 had stilled this creative surge, a number of poets, novelists, playwrights, and critics had contributed to what Van Wyck Brooks called "America's coming of age." H. L. Mencken, editor, entertainer, moralist, and terrible excoriator of boobs, had written some of his most virile essays against cultural intolerance and had begun work on the first edition of his *The American Language.* John Macy (*The Spirit of American Literature,* 1913) criticized American letters for being a pale derivative of Europe's. Randolph Bourne, one of the noblest and most dedicated of the young writers, blamed college professors for ignoring the cultural contributions of the melting pot and for failing to take advantage of the "usable past." Poets like Robert Frost, Carl Sandburg, Vachel Lindsay, and Ezra Pound became known in America and England; Eugene O'Neill, at home with the anarchists and bohemians of Greenwich Village, wrote his first important plays for the Provincetown Players; and Sherwood Anderson, inspired by the work of the American expatriate, Gertrude Stein, published his first novel.

World War I ended this "joyous season." Bourne, opposed to America's participation, found all outlets for writing closed to him. John Reed, poet, war correspondent, and revolutionist, ended up in Russia reporting the October uprising and after his death became a patron saint of the Communist party. *The Masses,* symbol of joy and liberation, was banned, and the bold experimental thinking that had marked the five preceding years was no longer tolerated by public sentiment.

It was strangely appropriate that a book should appear in 1918 that darkly summed up the years between Appomattox and America's declaration of war against Germany. *The Education of Henry Adams* had been in private circulation since 1907. Finally made available to the American public in 1918, it expressed the skepticism and pessimism that had already begun to settle upon the intellectual world and that would carry on into the 20's. Adams—historian, novelist, and prophet—confessed that he had not been able to adjust to the civilization of the dynamo that opened up after the Civil War. A future yawned "where order was an accidental relation obnoxious to nature," and meanwhile he found himself a stranger in his own country, hating the politicians and capitalists who ran it, and yet knowing, as he put it, "that he must accept the regime." Perhaps his disillusion with the democratic experiment indicated his own failure to accommodate himself to American society, but his mood was contagious. Soon other American intellectuals would share his feeling that the nation's best years were long past.

Readings

Post-Civil War intellectual history is discussed in Merle Curti's *The Growth of American Thought* (1943), in Ralph H. Gabriel's *The Course of American Democratic Thought* (rev. ed., 1956), and in Henry S. Commager's *The American Mind* (1950). More specialized treatments of ideas between 1865 and 1920 are Richard Hofstadter, *Social Darwinism in American Thought* (rev. ed., 1955); M. G. White, *Social Thought in America* (1949); Eric F. Goldman, *Rendezvous with Destiny* (previously cited); Daniel Aaron, *Men of Good Hope* (1951); and Charles Page, *Class and American Sociology: From Ward to Ross* (1940). Perry Miller, *American Thought: Civil War to World War I* (1954), is an excellent anthology of the leading thinkers of the period and is prefaced by a first-rate introduction.

A good biography of William Graham Sumner is yet to be written. A. G. Keller, *Reminiscences* (*Mainly Personal*) *of William Graham Sumner* (1933), conveys the flavor of the man, but Sumner himself must be read to be appreciated. The standard work on Ward is S. Chugerman, *Lester F. Ward: The American Aristotle* (1939). C. A. Barker, *Henry George* (1955), is now the standard biography; but G. R. Geiger, *The Philosophy of Henry George* (1931), should be consulted. A. E. Morgan, *Edward Bellamy* (1944), is a good introduction to Bellamy; a more critical judgment of his utopianism may be found in Lewis Mumford, *The Story of Utopias* (1922). The most detailed life of Veblen is Joseph Dorfman, *Thorstein Veblen and His America* (1934). Also recommended is David Riesman, *Thorstein Veblen, A Critical Interpretation* (1953), a less laudatory but searching analysis. Veblen's *The Theory of the Leisure Class* (1899) is available in inexpensive editions, and his *Absentee Ownership* (1923) should not be overlooked. R. B. Perry, *The Thought and Character of William James* (2 vols., 1935), is an excellent introduction to James. For Dewey, see Sidney Hook, *John Dewey* (1939), an admirable study. Oliver Wendell Holmes best reveals himself in *The Mind and Faith of Justice Holmes,* edited by Max Lerner (1943), and in his remarkable correspondence, *Holmes-Pollock Letters* (2 vols., 1941), and *Holmes-Laski Letters* (2 vols., 1953), both edited by M. D. Howe. For Brandeis, see A. T. Mason, *Brandeis: A Free Man's Life* (1946).

H. H. Bellot, *American History and American Historians* (1952), is a useful survey of American historical writing, which can be supplemented by W. H. Jordy's *Henry Adams: Scientific Historian* (1952), informative and well-written.

Some books on higher education are listed in the general bibliography. In this field, the institutional histories of the University of Wisconsin by Merle Curti and Vernon Carstensen, of The Johns Hopkins University by J. C. French, of Cornell by Carl Becker, of Harvard by Samuel Eliot Morison, and of Yale by George W. Pierson are of especial value. See also the biography of Charles W. Eliot by Henry James, III, and the autobiography of Andrew D. White.

The story of the expansion of primary and secondary schools is covered by Cubberley and Knight (see general bibliography) but pertinent for this chapter are such studies as S. C. Parker, *A Textbook in the History of Modern Elementary Education* (1912); C. W. Dabney, *Universal Education in the South* (2 vols., 1936); M. E. Curti, *The Social Ideas of American Educators* (1935); T. Woody, *A History of Women's Education in the United States* (2 vols., 1929); and H. K. Beale, *Are American Teachers Free?* (1936). The story of the Chatauqua movement is told in V. and R. O. Case, *We Called It Culture: The Story of Chatauqua* (1948).

Only a few books dealing with the literary history of the period can be mentioned here. The last two volumes in Van Wyck Brooks' history of the writer in America, *New England Indian Summer* (1940), and *The Confident Years, 1885-1915* (1952), are fresh and evocative. Edmund Wilson, *The Shock of Recognition* (1955), is brilliantly edited and contains unusual selections. Entertaining and illuminating is the collection of Mark Twain's posthumous writings edited by Bernard De Voto, *Mark Twain in Eruption* (1940). Everett Carter, *Howells and the Age of Realism* (1954), is valuable not only as an analysis of Howells, but also as an insight into his literary contemporaries. Alfred Kazin, *On Native Grounds* (1942), is a stimulating account of American writing since 1890.

BEYOND CONTINENTAL FRONTIERS

For more than a thousand years the history of European man has been the history of expansion. To explain his impulse constantly to push outward the frontiers of the known world would be to explain his nature. Duty moved him as much as daring, the word of God as much as the spirit of adventure, faith as much as science. He was impelled to spread "civilization," but also to escape from it. The quest for freedom and personal independence urged him on as much as the pursuit of knowledge. Power lured him as strongly as trade, pride as strongly as profit. In the story of this quest, the European discovery, exploration, and settlement of America was but one chapter. America's own continental and oceanic expansion added exciting new chapters to the story.

550

I. BACKGROUND FOR EXPANSION

The Contest

for the World.   For almost four centuries after the discovery of America, the New World was the scene of the most acute rivalry among the European nations. By the eighteenth century, this rivalry, especially the phase between England and France, had spread to India and other parts of the Orient. England's victory over Napoleon in 1815 put her far ahead in the contest for empire, and the onset of the Industrial Revolution in England thrust her beyond the reach of all comers for a century.

But the Industrial Revolution also spread throughout Europe, and after the world-wide fall in prices following the international Panic of 1873, competition for world markets became increasingly intense. The wealth created by the new industrialism gave a fresh impetus to imperial ambitions that had been checked since Waterloo. France, Belgium, Holland, Russia, and above all Bismarck's newly unified Germany, each sought "a place in the sun." They were soon to be followed by Italy and westernized Japan. Latin America, the islands of the Pacific, the interior of Africa and China, indeed all the world, became once again the stage of the imperial drama. Out went western explorers, missionaries, travelers, traders, engineers, inventors, politicians, generals, and admirals, bearing England's "White Man's Burden," France's *mission civilisatrice,* and rising Germany's *Kultur.*

Like England, most of the late-comers, once the growth of their own industrial systems had become stable and their profits modest, sought channels for more fruitful investment in the booming railroads and industries of the United States. And by the 1890's, the United States itself was ready to shoulder the "expansionist destiny" of the Anglo-Saxon race, to join "the Christian nations," as an American missionary said, who "are subduing the world, in order to make mankind free."

In 1885, in *Our Country,* a book that sold 175,000 copies soon after publication, the Reverend Josiah Strong declared that "the Anglo-Saxon, as the great representative of these two ideas . . . civil liberty . . . and pure *spiritual* Christianity . . . is divinely commissioned to be, in a peculiar sense, his brother's keeper." The Anglo-Saxon stock, Strong went on to say, has been "strengthened in the United States," and from here "this race of unequalled energy, with all the majesty of numbers and the might of wealth behind it . . . having developed peculiarly aggressive traits, calculated to impress its institutions upon mankind, will spread itself over the earth."

The Expansionist Spirit.   Expansionism

was, of course, not a new idea in America. Even before the Revolution, the colonists had protested against the mother country's policy of restricting settlement to the area east of the Appalachians. Once free, the United States expanded westward astonishingly fast, until by 1853, with the Gadsden Purchase (see p. 341), it had completed its continental course to the Pacific. But even that was not enough. Canada continued to tempt American expansionists for many decades after the War of 1812. Charles Sumner, as we have seen, tried to claim Canada from the British just after the Civil War as payment for his fantastic demands under the *Alabama* claims (see p. 402). It was Sumner's remarkable three-hour speech which helped persuade the Senate to ratify the Alaska Purchase treaty of 1867, thereby removing, as he said, "one more monarch from this continent." Seward, who had negotiated the Purchase, shared with Sumner the hope that Alaska would henceforth form the northern arm of a giant American pincer movement to eliminate the British monarch as well as the Russian by squeezing Canada into the American fold. In 1891, James G. Blaine said he expected that Canada would "ultimately seek . . . admission to the union."

Nor did the ambitions of expansionists stop with Canada and Alaska. Commodore Perry in the 1850's thought it "self-evident" that the United States would have to "extend its jurisdiction beyond the limits of the western continent." And Blaine, as Secretary of State in 1881, had Hawaii in mind when he observed that the spirit of American enterprise "would not be slow to avail itself of openings of assured and profitable enterprise even in mid-ocean."

Americans, as Lewis Cass once said, had "a capacious swallow for territory." They also had a sublime confidence that their superior endowments qualified them to rule over allegedly inferior peoples. Jefferson himself had prescribed Anglo-Saxon property institutions and American agriculture to the Indians, whose remaining choices were to move on or die. In 1848, another expansionist wrote: "The Mexican race now see in the fate of the aborigines of the north their own inevitable destiny. They must amalgamate or be lost in the superior vigor of the Anglo-Saxon race."

Yet until the 1880's postwar Americans were predominantly concerned with developing their immense homeland rather than with adding territory, with developing their home markets rather than their exports, with building up their home railroads and factories rather than their overseas investments. After 1865, the American merchant marine, for almost a century among the greatest in the world, almost disappeared from the seas; as late as 1914, 90 per cent of our imports and exports were carried in foreign bottoms. Similarly, the navy, once as strong as the merchant marine, and in skill and spirit second to none on the oceans, was reduced by the 1880's to a small number of wooden sailing hulks, which were worse than useless in an age of steel and steam.

Business Imperialism.

Business Imperialism.   Although Americans had little enthusiasm for overseas adventures before the Civil War, the United States sometimes became involved in such undertakings. In the 1840's, the United States had acquired "most-favored-nation" treaty rights in China. In the 1850's, after Commodore Matthew C. Perry had opened Japan, Townsend Harris, the first American consul there, negotiated a treaty of friendship with the Shogunate and became the chief adviser to the inexperienced Japanese government in its early international relations. In 1856, while a "guano craze" was sweeping American agriculture (guano was a rich fertilizer made from the excrement of sea fowl), the United States government had permitted American naval officers to raise the American flag on Pacific islands rich in guano deposits. By 1880, some 50 small islands had thus become "appurtenances" of the United States.

The rapid settlement of Oregon and California before the Civil War also gave a great impetus to two phases of American expansionist policy: (1) It stimulated renewed interest in a canal across the Isthmus of Panama, which would avert the tremendously long sea voyage around Cape Horn, and led to the signing of treaties with Nicaragua and Colombia for building routes across the Isthmus. (2) It heightened American interest in Pacific possessions. When the transcontinental railroads were built after the war, both points of interest received greater attention.

In the Caribbean region, furthermore, men like Minor Keith and Daniel Guggenheim were laying the foundations for private American empires in the 1870's. Keith started by building railroads in Costa Rica and then, in typically imperialist fashion, converted the economy of the little country to the production of bananas in order to supply the railroads with freight. A once simple and self-sufficient economy was thus diverted to the production of a single staple and was left at the mercy of the market for that one product. This venture was the beginning of the United Fruit Company. The Guggenheims began operating copper and silver mines in Mexico and South America, thus laying the foundation for the family's extensive foreign interests.

Only in two areas did the growth of overseas enterprise deeply involve the American government. One of these was Samoa, in the southern Pacific; the other was Hawaii, in the northern Pacific. Events in Cuba in the 1860's and 1870's also engaged American attention, though little was to be done about them for another 25 years.

Samoa, well-known to Pacific mariners as early as the 1830's, took on special interest for Americans after the completion of the first transcontinental railroad in 1869. The fine harbor at Pago Pago promised to provide an effective way station for Pacific commerce, and a treaty of 1878 gave Americans harbor privileges there. But both Great Britain and Germany also had privileges in the island, and for a time it appeared that the three powers might clash. In 1889, Bismarck called a conference of the three that established a tripartite protectorate. Ten years later, after the first arrangement proved unsatisfactory, the islands were divided between the United States and Germany, the Americans retaining Pago Pago harbor. For withdrawing her claims, Great Britain received title to the Gilbert and Solomon Islands, previously held by Germany. Small though the Samoan issue was, Secretary of State Walter Q. Gresham saw its significance when he said that it was "the first departure from our traditional and well established policy of avoiding entangling alliances with foreign powers in relation to objects remote from this hemisphere."

The Hawaiian Islands, the nearest land in the Pacific to the western coast of the United States, had long interested Americans. Missionaries had settled there as early as 1820, and Hawaii had become an important link in the China trade and the northern Pacific fur trade. In 1842, Daniel Webster, as Secretary of State, announced that the United States would be "dissatisfied" if any European power threatened the Islands' independence. In 1854, the Pierce administration accepted an offer from the Hawaiian king to negotiate a treaty of annexation, but the final draft proved mutually unsatisfactory.

After 1850, Hawaii became an important center of sugar production, and after 1876, when a reciprocity agreement between the United States and the Islands admitted Hawaiian sugar into the United States duty-free, sugar-growing boomed. When the time came for renewing this agreement, the United States Senate in 1887 recognized the growing strategic importance of Hawaii and insisted on an amendment giving the United States exclusive use of Pearl Harbor as a coaling and repair station for its naval vessels. The McKinley tariff of 1890 hurt Hawaiian sugar producers when it admitted other foreign sugars duty-free and gave United States growers a bounty of two cents a pound. The Hawaiian economy suffered and Island interest in annexation grew.

By 1890, the greater part of Hawaiian sugar production was controlled by Americans or descendants of American settlers. Three years earlier, an uprising led by Hawaiian-born white businessmen, not planters, had imposed a constitution on the corrupt government of King Kalakaua (and his successor, Queen Liliuokalani) providing for ministerial responsibility. Nativist Hawaiians quickly grew resentful of the new government, and when the Hawaiian economy suffered after 1890, trouble brewed.

Queen Liliuokalani's active resistance to the operation of the 1887 constitution drove the white businessmen and lawyers into a second rebellion in 1893, which received the support of the American minister, John L. Stevens, and took place under the protective eyes of troops landed from an American cruiser. The new government won immediate recognition from Stevens and rushed a commission to Washington to negotiate a treaty of annexation. This treaty, sent to the Senate by the retiring President Harrison, was still under discussion when Grover Cleveland was inaugurated. Suspicious of Stevens' impropriety in Hawaii, Cleveland sent a former Democratic Congressman, James H. Blount of Georgia, as a special commissioner to Hawaii to investigate the situation. Secretary of State Gresham, in summarizing Blount's report for Cleveland in October, 1893, charged that Stevens, by his abuse of the authority of the United States, had done a great wrong to a "feeble but independent State". Cleveland tried to restore the Queen, but the Provisional Government was adamant, and in 1894 wrote a constitution, proclaimed a Republic, and confirmed Sanford B. Dole, as president.

Cleveland could hardly declare war on the new government, but he would not accede to its desire for annexation. It was not until 1897, under McKinley, that a new treaty of annexation was worked out. The Senate, reflecting popular discontent with American imperial ventures, rejected the treaty. But the public temper changed during the Spanish-American War (see p. 562), and in July, 1898, Hawaii was annexed.

Blaine's Diplomacy. Individual American citizens, then, had often forced a reluctant or uninterested government to become involved in their aspirations, ambitions, and enterprises, in distant and foreign lands. But not all American statesmen were cool to imperialist ventures. One of the most sympathetic American statesmen was James G. Blaine, who served as Secretary of State during 1881 under Garfield and Arthur, and again from 1889 to 1892 under Harrison. Like Clay, Blaine was a perpetual aspirant for the presidency who never satisfied his ambition; and like Clay he used the power and prestige of lesser offices to push an aggressive and spirited diplomacy, especially in Latin America. He hoped not only to keep European governments out of the sister republics to the south, but also to further American influence and commercial interests in the area. Even during his brief tenure of office in 1881, he tried to encourage interest in a Panama canal and intervened in Latin-American affairs both to fend off European influences and to settle disputes among Latin-American countries.

Latin America still had strong religious and nationality ties with Spain and Portugal, and strong commercial ties with Britain. In the 1870's, Germany too began to seek Latin-American markets for German goods and German capital. Blaine wanted to turn Latin-American trade and development toward the "Big Sister" to the north, and in 1881 he issued invitations to a Pan-American conference. Acceptances were still coming in when Garfield's assassination caused the conference to be canceled. When Blaine returned to office in 1889, he addressed himself more eagerly than ever to the subject of Latin-American trade—about which most Latin Americans, and most North Americans, too, remained quite indifferent.

In 1889, Blaine picked up the threads of his original scheme and organized the first Pan-American conference in Washington. Delegates from 18 nations met and formed the Pan-American Union, but they accomplished little else. Blaine wanted to produce goods for the world—at least for the American world. In the 1880's, he realized that the United States was importing staples—coffee, hides, sugar, and wool—from Latin America that were twice the value of Latin-American imports from the United States. In effect, the Latin Americans were selling in the United States and buying in Europe. Worse, well over 85 per cent of Latin-American produce was entering the United States duty-free. Blaine's Pan-Americanism was aimed at getting at least equal treatment for American goods in Latin America. But the Latin Americans could see no advantage for themselves in satisfying Blaine. When the delegates to the 1889 conference failed to grant tariff concessions to the United States, Blaine showed his hand by threatening to retaliate by putting tariffs on Latin-American goods.

Blaine succeeded in incorporating this retaliation into the McKinley Tariff Act of 1890, under its so-called "reciprocity" provisions. In effect, the act said that the United States would reciprocate for good treatment abroad; in fact, it meant that we would also reciprocate for poor treatment. Some Latin-American countries yielded to this threat; few, however, increased either their trade with the United States or their tenderness toward American advances.

As part of his policy, Blaine also advocated a new and powerful American navy. In 1881, the United States ranked about twelfth among the nations of the world in naval power. That year, with Blaine's approval, the Secretary of the Navy, William H. Hunt, persuaded Congress to set up the Naval Advisory Board. As it turned out, the work of the Board was largely to maintain at public expense the agitation for increased naval appropriations. Though Blaine was soon out of office, this first step led to others. In 1883, Congress appropriated funds for the famous "White Squadron" of four new steel ships equipped with steam power and a full rigging of white sails. But these vessels constituted only a token navy, since they had no armor. The establishment of the Naval War College at Newport in 1884 gave further impetus to "big navy" propaganda. It was at Newport that Captain (later Admiral) A. T. Mahan gave the lectures that eventually became the heart of his series of books on seapower in history, the earliest of which was published in 1890.

Between 1883 and 1890, Congress authorized the building of nine new cruisers, and construction began on the first modern American battleship, the *Maine*. Then came the Naval Act of 1890, the result of a report from a Naval Policy Board that Secretary of the Navy Benjamin F. Tracy had set up to investigate the whole naval expansion issue. Heretofore, to calm foreign anxieties over American naval expansion and modernization, the navy had been described officially as consisting of "seagoing coastline battleships." Now the fiction of coastline defense was officially abandoned, and the

idea of a "navy second to none" began to emerge. Tracy's Naval Policy Board acknowledged that the United States had "no colonies nor any apparent desire to acquire them," that its foreign trade was "carried in foreign vessels," and that its manufactures competed "with those of other nations in but few markets." But the Board also urged the construction of 200 modern warships. Although Congress did not go that far, under successive appropriations it authorized the construction of many battleships, cruisers, gunboats, and torpedo boats, and also the maintenance of three naval yards.

Having prevailed upon Congress to take steps that gradually made the United States a respected naval power, expansionists turned next to the resurrection of the merchant marine. In 1891, they persuaded Congress to enact the Ocean Mail Subsidy Act, which by increasing federal payments for carrying overseas mail encouraged the construction and operation of new vessels. In addition, the reciprocity provisions of the McKinley Tariff Act stimulated exports, as did the provision of an act of 1891 that empowered the president to raise tariffs against European countries that did not give most-favored-nation treatment to American meat products.

Toward the end of the century, the position of the United States in world trade was greatly improved, as Blaine had hoped. Between 1870 and 1900 American imports had almost doubled; in the same period American exports had almost tripled. The crash of 1893 simply encouraged American businessmen to look more aggressively for foreign markets. Chambers of commerce of the large exporting centers, the National Association of Manufacturers, diplomatic representatives, and consular officials all increased their efforts. Senator Albert J. Beveridge of Indiana put it aggressively in a speech delivered in April, 1898:

American factories are making more than the American people can use; American soil is producing more than they can consume. Fate has written our policy for us; the trade of the world must and shall be ours. We will establish trading-posts throughout the world as distributing-points for American products. We will cover the ocean with our merchant marine. We will build a navy to the measure of our greatness. Great colonies governing themselves, flying our flag and trading with us, will grow about our posts of trade.

The Martial Spirit.

While the United States was girding both her navy and her factories to serve the growth of foreign trade, a series of diplomatic incidents occurred that threatened to throw the United States into war. These incidents also did much to create the martial spirit that some leaders had begun to desire. The first incident arose over the Canadian fisheries.

American fishing rights in Canadian waters had been settled by treaty in 1871. But the United States, finding the settlement irksome, notified Canada that it would terminate the treaty on July 1, 1885. Canada retaliated by taking American fishing vessels found in her waters after that date. "Wherever the American flag on an American fishing smack is touched by a foreigner," declaimed Henry Cabot Lodge, then a young congressman from Massachusetts, "the great American heart is touched." The Detroit News was more explicit. In February, 1887, it boasted, "When the next war closes, there should be but one flag floating from the Rio Grande to the pole." The News then added,

We do not want to fight,
But, by jingo, if we do,
We'll scoop in all the fishing grounds
And the whole Dominion too.

Cleveland's administration proceeded to negotiate a treaty with Britain to end the fishing controversy. But the election of 1888 was impending, and Republican senators killed the treaty to prevent the Democrats from gaining votes for having made the settlement. A working arrangement between the two countries prevented further trouble.

Within the next two years, another controversy with Britain over the seal fisheries in the Bering Sea area came to a head. In fishing for seal, Canadians used methods that threatened to exterminate the herd. To protect their own catch, American revenue cutters began to seize Canadian fishing schooners in the Bering Sea after 1886. Canadians protested vigorously, and the resultant diplomatic intercourse only heightened the ill feeling. When rumors spread in 1890 that British warships were policing the North Pacific, war talk again was heard. "The thing to do," explained the Sioux City Journal, is to "shoot any British ship which is in those waters." Cooler heads again prevailed, and an arbitration treaty was ratified in February, 1892. The arbitration court eventually decided against the United States on all disputed points.

A third episode brought the country yet a little closer to outright war. During a revolt against the president of Chile, which had broken out in 1891, a rebel steamer arrived at San Diego, California, trying to buy arms. The American ambassador in Chile had openly sided with the Chilean president, and now the United States detained the rebel ship. The revolutionists, nevertheless, won out. National hostility flared up against the United States, and in October, 1891, an incident occurred that almost ignited the fuse. The captain of the U.S.S. Baltimore, then in Valparaiso, permitted his crew of over a hundred to go ashore unarmed. Soon a riot broke out between them and some Chileans in which two American sailors were killed and many others imprisoned.

Chilean apologies were slow in coming, and President Harrison hinted that he might invite Congress to declare war. Other prominent people in the United States were bursting to take up the cudgels. Among them was Theodore Roosevelt, whose intimates thereafter were to taunt him as "the Chilean Volunteer." Just in time, a full apology arrived to calm American feelings, and Chile eventually agreed to pay $75,000 to the families of the dead sailors and to the men who had been injured in the fracas.

The most serious of these hazardous affairs brought the United States closest to war in 1895. This incident involved the boundary between British Guiana and neighboring Venezuela in South America. A contested area separated the two countries, and after 1876 Venezuela tried to get American help in urging Britain to settle the boundary line. Discovery of gold in the region heightened the conflict, and Venezuela broke off diplomatic relations with Britain in 1887. The United States offered to act as mediator, but Great Britain rejected the proposal. The last American mediation effort was made in July, 1895, by Richard Olney, Cleveland's Secretary of State. In a note to Lord Salisbury, the British Foreign Minister, Olney reminded him of the non-colonization clauses of the Monroe Doctrine, and proceeded to invite Britain to leave America altogether. "Three thousand miles of intervening ocean make any permanent political union between a European and an American state unnatural and inexpedient," Olney wrote. Then he added:

Today, the United States is practically sovereign on this continent, and its fiat is law upon the subjects to which it confines its interposition. Why? It is not because of the pure friendship or good will felt for it. . . . It is because, in addition to all other grounds, its infinite resources combined with its isolated position render it master of the situation and practically invulnerable as against any or all other powers.

Olney closed with a suggestion of "peaceful arbitration."

Salisbury took his time in replying. When he did, in November, 1895, he rejected arbitration and proceeded to remind the United States explicitly that the Monroe Doctrine was not recognized in international law and did not apply to boundary disputes. Cleveland made the Olney-Salisbury interchange public in December, when he himself further fired opinion by a message to Congress. In it he asked for funds to finance a commission to determine the actual boundary between British Guiana and Venezuela, and then added the inflammatory assertion that "it will . . . be the duty of the United States to resist by every means in its power, as a wilful aggression upon its rights and interests" any efforts by Great Britain to grasp any territory that the United States, after investigation, found of right to be Venezuela's.

Congress cheered these fighting words and voted for the fact-finding commission. Twenty-six governors promptly pledged their support. If war came, said Theodore Roosevelt, he hoped he might "have a hand in it myself." "The bankers, brokers, and anglomaniacs generally," he moaned to his sympathetic friend Lodge, seemed to favor "peace at any price. . . . Personally I rather hope that the fight will come soon. The clamor of the peace faction has convinced me that this country needs a war."

Since the Venezuelan boundary dispute coincided with mounting silverite aspirations for action against the alleged center of the "gold power," it was much more inflammatory than any of the earlier episodes had been. But the peace parties eventually won out both in the United States and Great Britain. Cleveland's proposal for a boundary commission gave Americans time to simmer down, since nothing could be done until the commission reported. Britain, meanwhile, was growing increasingly concerned over the rise and rivalry of Germany. Cooler English heads refused to be drawn into a dispute with the United States, which itself had become a power strong enough to be courted. Thus in February, 1897, Great Britain and the United States negotiated a treaty turning the dispute over to international arbitration. In 1899, a final settlement was made. Roosevelt and his friends had to wait for their war, but not for long.

II. WAR AND EMPIRE

The Cuban Crisis. As the Venezuela affair passed into history, the young inflammables on the American scene found a new incident to exploit. This new incident was the Cuban insurrection against Spain, which had begun in 1895.

For decades, America had been interested in Cuba. Before the Civil War, southerners had hoped to extend the Cotton Kingdom to the island; after the settlement of California and Oregon had led to serious discussion of a canal through Central America, many northerners had also become interested in acquiring Cuba as a base from which to defend such a canal. The isolationism of the post-Civil War generation quieted the issue; and when the Cubans rebelled against Spanish rule in 1868, Americans looked on indifferently. This rebellion dragged on for ten sickening years. Then, having lost many men and spent large sums to crush the Cubans, Spain agreed to undertake serious reforms. The Cubans made two major demands: (1) emancipation of the slaves on the island, and (2) self-government for the island's inhabitants. Spain actually took another ten years before freeing the slaves, and she postponed granting autonomous government indefinitely. But for a time, Cuba was quiet.

By 1895, the Cuban situation had changed, however. After the emancipation of the slaves, large amounts of European and American capital had moved in, bringing modern methods to the island, especially in the production of sugar. At the same time, Europe had greatly enlarged its own sugar production, and the United States gradually became Cuba's main market and source of capital. An executive agreement with Spain in 1884, which removed the American duty on Cuban sugar, further stimulated sugar production in Cuba. Between 1889 and 1894, sugar production on the island jumped from

630,000 to 1,050,000 tons. But suddenly, events conspired against Cuban prosperity. Europe's production of beet sugar became so great that the world price of sugar fell. The Panic of 1893 and the following depression pushed the price down even more. Finally, the Wilson Tariff of 1894 restored a 40 per cent duty on sugar. Raw sugar commanded a price of 8 cents a pound in 1884. In 1895, the price had broken to 2 cents, and the Cuban way of life broke with it.

When insurrection started again in 1895, American interests were inevitably threatened. To quell the rebels, Spain sent over her best general and 200,000 men, but the Spaniards could not cope with the insurgent leaders and their guerilla followers, who had taken to the hills. The rebels also mounted attacks against American property in order to force the United States to intervene to protect her interests. At this point, the Spanish government decided to change commanders, and in January, 1896, sent the notorious General Valeriano Weyler to Cuba where he soon earned the nickname "Butcher."

Weyler turned Cuba into a series of concentration camps into which he drove the guerillas. The rest of the population he forced into other concentrated sectors guarded by troops. Since few could work, few could eat. Starvation, disease, and death decimated the population.

During all this time a Cuban junta, which had been organized in New York, kept agitating for American intervention and Cuban autonomy. At the same time, Joseph Pulitzer of the New York *World* and William Randolph Hearst of the New York *Journal* started a spirited circulation battle, each trying to outdo his competitor in printing gory stories of Spanish brutality. Mahan, Roosevelt, Lodge, Beveridge, and others, in turn, whipped up the war spirit. "Today," said Beveridge in 1896, "the issue is national life. Are the American people a nation, or are they an aggregation of localities? Is the Stars and Stripes the flag of a vital nation . . . of an invincible people?" In June, 1897, Theodore Roosevelt said in an address before the Naval War College: "Cowardice in a race, as in an individual, is the unpardonable sin, and a wilful failure to prepare for danger may in its effects be as bad as cowardice."

But President Cleveland would not be stampeded. He feared, as he said in 1896, that "there were some outrages upon both sides, if the truth were known." By March, 1897, however, McKinley had become president on a platform that called for Cuban independence. By the end of that year, even he was convinced of Spain's good intentions in offering reforms. Hope was raised by a change in government in Spain. Weyler was replaced by a new general who was ordered to end the concentration-camp system.

War might still have been averted had not a chance series of events occurred. On February 9, 1898, a letter stolen from the Havana post office fell into the hands of Hearst's New York *Journal*. In it, Dupuy de Lôme, the Spanish minister to the United States, characterized McKinley, after his first message to Congress in December, 1897, as "weak and a bidder for the admiration of the crowd, besides being a would-be politician who tries to leave a door open behind himself while keeping on good terms with the jingoes of his party." This was a private letter, but Hearst made it as public as possible. Spain disavowed any evil intent on her minister's part, and De Lôme himself resigned as soon as the letter was published. Things still might have calmed down had not the *Maine* incident followed in less than a week.

The *Maine* had been sent to Havana late in January, 1898, when the American consul-general there cabled that American property and persons were in danger. Spain was assured that the ship's visit had no aggressive purpose, and when the *Maine* arrived late in January its officers and men

were entertained by the Spanish General, Blanco. Then on February 15, the *Maine* apparently hit a submarine mine, and two officers and 258 members of the crew were lost. An immediate official inquiry left the causes of the explosion uncertain, but Congress appropriated $50 million for national defense just the same. Captain Sigsbee of the *Maine* had wired right after the disaster that "Public opinion should be suspended until further report." But it was not long before the cry "Remember the *Maine*" was whipping up the country.

War with Spain.   At the head of the war party was Theodore Roosevelt, who, as Assistant Secretary of the Navy, seized upon the temporary absence of Secretary John D. Long to take charge of affairs. Roosevelt, in consultation with Lodge, who was now a senator, lost no time in cabling Commodore Dewey, in command of the Pacific squadron near Hong Kong: "Keep full of coal. In the event of declaration of war Spain, your duty will be to see that the Spanish squadron does not leave the Asiatic coast, and then offensive operations in Philippine Islands." In the meantime, politicians, intellectuals, and publicists such as John Hay, Ambassador to London, Senator Beveridge, Whitelaw Reid, editor of the New York *Tribune*, and Walter Hines Page, editor of the *Atlantic Monthly*, joined Roosevelt and Lodge in keeping the pressure on McKinley. They were supported by many free-silver men, who had disliked Cleveland's caution and who hoped that a war would give a fresh impetus to inflation.

But peace still had many strong and well-placed partisans in the cabinet, in Congress, in the Republican party, and among substantial business groups. And these men prevailed upon the wavering McKinley to make every effort to avoid war. Accordingly, the State Department cabled a series of demands to Spain on March 27, of which the most important was the demand for an armistice

EDITION FOR GREATER NEW YORK.

NEW YORK JOURNAL
AND ADVERTISER.

The Journal will give $50,000 for information, furnished to it exclusively, that will convict the person or persons who sank the Maine.

The Journal will give $50,000 for information, furnished to it exclusively, that will convict the person or persons who sank the Maine.

NO. 5,572. Copyright, 1898, by W. R. Hearst. NEW YORK, THURSDAY, FEBRUARY 17, 1898.—16 PAGES. PRICE ONE CENT In Greater New York and Jersey City. Elsewhere TWO

DESTRUCTION OF THE WAR SHIP MAINE WAS THE WORK OF AN ENEM

$50,000!

$50,000 REWARD!
For the Detection of the
Perpetrator of
the Maine Outrage!

The New York Journal hereby offers a reward of $50,000 CASH for information, FURNISHED TO IT EXCLUSIVELY, which shall lead to the detection and conviction of the person, persons or government criminally responsible for the explosion which resulted in the destruction, in Havana, of the United States war ship Maine and the loss of 258 lives of American sailors.

The $50,000 CASH offered for the above information is on deposit with Wells, Fargo & Co.

No one is barred, be he the humble but misguided seaman eking out a few miserable dollars by acting as a spy, or the attache of a government secret service, plotting, by any devilish means, to revenge fancied insults or cripple menacing countries.

This offer has been cabled to Europe and will be made public in every capital of the Continent and in London this morning.

The Journal believes that any man who can be bought to commit murder can also be bought to betray his requisites. **FOR THE PERPETRATOR OF THIS OUTRAGE HAD ACCOMPLICES.**

W. R. HEARST.

Assistant Secretary Roosevelt Convinced the Explosion of the War Ship Was Not an Accident.

The Journal Offers $50,000 Reward for the Conviction of the Criminals Who Sent 258 American Sailors to Their Death. Naval Officers Unanimous That the Ship Was Destroyed on Purpose.

$50,000!

$50,000 REWARD
For the Detection of the
Perpetrator of
the Maine Outrage!

The New York Journal hereby offers a reward of $50,000 CASH for information, FURNISHED TO IT EXCLUSIVELY, which shall lead to the detection and conviction of the person, persons or government criminally responsible for the explosion which resulted in the destruction, at Havana, of the United States war ship Maine and the loss of 258 lives of American sailors.

The $50,000 CASH offered for the above information on deposit with Wells, Fargo & Co.

No one is barred, be he the humble, but misguided, seaman who acts out a few miserable dollars by acting as a spy, or the attache of a government secret service, plotting, by any devilish means, to revenge fancied insults or cripple menacing countries.

This offer has been cabled to Europe and will be made public in every capital of the Continent and in London this morning.

The Journal believes that any man who can be bought to commit murder can also be bought to betray his requisites, **FOR THE PERPETRATOR OF THIS OUTRAGE HAD ACCOMPLICES.**

W. R. HEARST.

POWDER MAGAZINE

MINE

WIRE

NAVAL OFFICERS THINK THE MAINE WAS DESTROYED BY A SPANISH MINE.

George Eugene Bryson, the Journal's special correspondent at Havana, cables that it is the secret opinion of many Spaniards in the Cuban capital that the Maine was destroyed and 258 of her men killed by means of a submarine mine, or fixed torpedo. This is the opinion of several American naval authorities. The Spaniards, it is believed, arranged to have the Maine anchored over one of the harbor mines. Wires connected the mine with a powder magazine, and it is thought the explosion was caused by sending an electric current through the wire. If this can be proven, the brutal nature of the Spaniards will be shown by the fact that they waited to spring the mine until after all the men had retired for the night. The Maltese cross in the picture shows where the mine may have been fired.

Hidden Mine or a Sunken Torpedo Believed to Have Been the Weapon Used Against the American Man-of-War---Officers and Men Tell Thrilling Stories of Being Blown Into the Air Amid a Mass of Shattered Steel and Exploding Shells---Survivors Brought to Key West Scout the Idea of Accident---Spanish Officials Protest Too Much---Our Cabinet Orders a Searching Inquiry---Journal Sends Divers to Havana to Report Upon the Condition of the Wreck.

Was the Vessel Anchored Over a Mine?

BY CAPTAIN E. L. ZALINSKI, U. S. A.

(Captain Zalinski is the inventor of the famous dynamite gun, which would be the principal factor in our coast defence in case of war.)

Assistant Secretary of the Navy Theodore Roosevelt says he is convinced that the destruction of the Maine in Havana Harbor was not an accident. The Journal offers a reward of $50,000 for exclusive evidence that will convict the person, persons or Government criminally responsible for the destruction of the American battle ship and the death of 258 of its crew.

The suspicion that the Maine was deliberately blown up grows stronger every hour. Not a single fact to the contrary has been produced.

Captain Sigsbee, of the Maine, and Consul-General Lee both urge that public opinion be suspended until they have completed their investigation. They are taking the course of tactful men who are convinced that there has been treachery.

Washington reports very late that Captain Sigsbee had [...] as a hidden mine. [...] all day the naval officers in cabling instead of the usual Am[...]

"Who Destroyed the Maine?"—Hearst's front page, February 17, 1898.

The Spanish War in the Pacific, 1898

further "offensive operations in Philippine Islands," and by the time the first contingent of 2,500 arrived on June 30, British, French, Japanese, and German men-of-war were swarming around the Philippines seeking to protect their nationals. The German force was much the strongest, and Dewey was suspicious of it. But it had no aggressive designs, though stories of its supposed threats began to circulate in America and aroused concern over the new imperial power. By July 25, about 11,000 American troops had landed in the Philippines, under General Wesley Merritt. Supported by Filipino insurrectionists under Emilio Aguinaldo, whom Dewey had helped arm, Merritt took Manila on August 13.

By then, indeed, the "splendid little war," as Hay called it, had already come to a close in the West Indies. On April 29, a Spanish fleet under Admiral Cervera had sailed west from the Cape Verde Islands, destination unknown. American coastal cities panicked and demanded naval protection. A patrol fleet was established to satisfy eastern politicians, and the main American fleet under Admiral Sampson and Commodore Schley tried to seek out Cervera before he got to Cuba, where they decided he was headed. They could not locate him, however, until he was safely in Santiago harbor, where Sampson bottled him up. A military expedition was now planned to capture Santiago overland and force Cervera out under the fleet's waiting guns.

On June 14, a poorly equipped expeditionary force of 17,000 men under General William Shafter finally left Tampa, Florida. Typical of this army was the First Volunteer Cavalry Regiment, the "Rough Riders," who had no horses. Shafter and his men reached Santiago on June 20 and took six days to disembark. The Spaniards had 200,000 men in Cuba, but only 13,000 in Santiago. And of these, because of problems of transport and supply, only 1,700 could be mobilized to meet the Americans. The Spaniards were well trained and well armed, however. After

in Cuba until October 1. Four days later, the Spanish government, fearful of losing face at home, agreed to everything but the truce. Spain finally heeded the pleas of the American minister and agreed to an armistice on April 9. But the delay was disastrous. Prodded by the press and the war enthusiasts, McKinley was already at work on a militant message to Congress, which he delivered on April 11. Congress interpreted the message as a demand for war. McKinley's deliberate omission of a direct reference to Spain's capitulation, which he had been aware of for two days, made this interpretation easier. A formal declaration of war followed on April 25, effective as of April 21.

On April 27, the duly warned Commodore Dewey in Hong Kong raised steam and on the night of the 30th sailed into Manila Bay. The next morning, after giving the famous order, "You may fire when you are ready, Gridley," Dewey blasted the small and antiquated Spanish fleet that was sitting there. Admiral Montojo, the Spanish commander, lost all his ships and 381 men; American casualties were 7 wounded sailors. News of the victory arrived in America on May 7.

Dewey lacked the necessary men to take

a two-day battle, which saw Roosevelt lead the Rough Riders up San Juan Hill on July 1, the American attack petered out. "We are within measurable distance of a terrible military disaster," Roosevelt admitted in a letter to Lodge.

Luckily for Shafter, the Spaniards were even more spent, and on July 3 Cervera decided to escape if he could. The American fleet was awaiting this move, but expected Cervera to try to get away at night. When he left in broad daylight, the American fleet was so snarled in its own tracks that he almost escaped, but the overwhelming American firepower finally destroyed his wooden ships. Of Cervera's men, 474 were killed or wounded. The American fleet suffered little damage and had but one man killed and one wounded. On July 17, General Linares surrendered Santiago to the Americans, and on July 25 General Miles made a triumphant if belated march through Puerto Rico. By July 13, the Spanish government had already begun to seek a peace treaty, and on August 12 hostilities were declared over. The next day, Manila fell.

All told, the United States had lost 5,462 men in the four months of hostilities, of whom only 379 fell in combat. The rest died from disease and other causes. In money, the immediate war cost was about $250 million. Spain's losses in the fighting were much higher, and in addition she lost the remnants of her once imposing New World empire. Confirmation of her loss was to be found in the peace treaty, on which formal meetings began in Paris on October 1. In December, the treaty was signed. Ratification by the Senate, however, was another matter.

America's First Empire. In the 1890's, the frontier had been declared officially closed, and the continent had been conquered and now cradled a business civilization. But business itself was in deep trouble. The depression that began in 1893 was the most severe in the country's history. The tendency toward the centralization of industry in the 1880's already appeared to have closed the door of opportunity to rising young men, and in the 1890's centralization went on at an accelerated pace. Business itself contracted and opportunities seemed to vanish. This state of affairs mortified the souls of ambitious young intellectuals imbued with patriotism, and it constricted the hearts of poor young men who had fled the suffering farm for the lures of the city. The first group raised the banner of conquest and empire, and the second group seemed ready to march behind it.

The United States clearly had no territorial ambitions at the outbreak of the war. Congress' war resolution had stated that Cuba ought to be free and independent, and if Spain failed to grant independence instantly McKinley might use the armed forces of the United States to win Cuba's freedom from Spain. Then followed a fateful amendment, offered by Senator Henry M. Teller of Colorado, that the United States pledge herself to leave Cuba in control of the Cuban people.

While the war with Spain was in progress, American policy toward the acquisition of territory began to change. On July 6, 1898, Congress adopted a joint resolution annexing

The Spanish War in the Caribbean, 1898

Hawaii to the United States. Two weeks later, in stating terms for an armistice in the war, McKinley demanded the cession of Puerto Rico and of Guam. He stipulated, moreover, that the United States was to occupy the "city, bay, and harbor of Manila pending the conclusion of a treaty of peace." "By our code of morality," McKinley had said earlier, annexation of territory "would be criminal aggression." By July, along with the rest of the country, he was becoming less abstemious. "We must keep all we get," he said; "when the war is over, we must keep what we want."

While America's negotiators were preparing to make the treaty with Spain, American hunger for the Philippines kept growing. First it was only Manila; then, on September 16, the negotiators were instructed by McKinley to take nothing less than the island of Luzon. By October 26, the whole archipelago was being demanded. When Spain demurred, an ultimatum was issued on November 21, to which Spain capitulated. "There was nothing left for us to do," the

President explained to a group of Methodist ministers later, "but to take them all, and to educate the Filipinos, and to uplift and civilize and Christianize them, and by God's grace do the very best we could by them as our fellow men for whom Christ also died."

The final treaty, insuring the freedom of Cuba and granting to the United States the Philippines (for a payment of $20 million), Puerto Rico, and Guam, was signed on December 10. In the debate on ratification in the Senate, the annexation of the Philippines became the main issue. Many people in the country had opposed the war from the start; and in November, 1898, they mobilized in the Anti-Imperialist League and employed every available propaganda technique to defeat annexation even if it meant defeating the treaty. Opposed to them were the brash young men of the war party, flushed with victory and determined to enjoy its fruits. Late in 1898 the American consul in London wrote to McKinley: "If

McKinley tailoring a suit of "expansion cloth" for Uncle Sam as anti-imperialists look on.

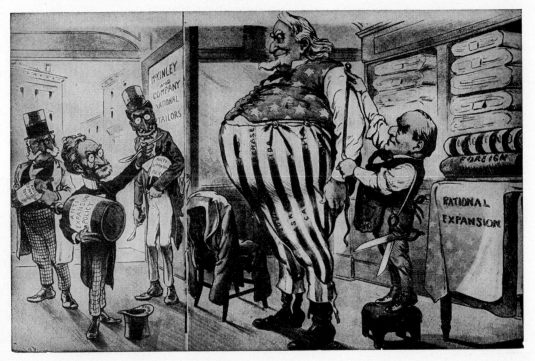

what I hear and what I read is true there is a tremendous party growing up for expansion of territory, especially by the younger and more active elements in the country." What he read was true.

On February 6, 1899, the Senate narrowly ratified the treaty by 57-27—only two votes above the required two-thirds. The decision was influenced by the reaction of the Filipinos themselves. For on December 21, 1898, while the debate in the Senate was at its peak, McKinley had ordered the War Department to extend the military occupation of Manila to the entire Philippines. This move served to touch off a Filipino insurrection, which promptly took the lives of American soldiers and no doubt swayed Senate votes. The insurrection, led by Emilio Aguinaldo, lasted three sordid years and cost more than the war with Spain itself. Before it was put down, American forces had to resort to the same concentration-camp method that the Spanish had used to combat the guerillas in Cuba. Thus a movement that had started as an effort to liberate the Cubans ended in a drive to subjugate the Filipinos.

Nor, indeed, were the Cubans actually liberated. General Leonard Wood remained in Cuba as military governor until May 20, 1902, and then Cuba was forced to subscribe to the so-called Platt Amendment. General Wood accomplished important reforms: he inaugurated an excellent sanitation program, set up a school system, rebuilt Havana, put the island's finances on a stable basis, and kept peace while a convention sat to draw up Cuba's new constitution. The General's presence in Cuba gradually became suspect, but the United States, despite the Teller Amendment, was not yet prepared to yield the islands fully.

The Platt Amendment to an army appropriations bill of 1901 solved the dilemma for the United States. This amendment limited Cuba's treaty-making powers, its right to borrow money, and its control over such internal matters as sanitation. Moreover, according to its terms Cuba could not refuse to sell or lease lands wanted by the United States for coaling or naval stations, nor could it permit any other power to gain a foothold on its territory. Finally, the amendment gave the United States at its own discretion the right to intervene in Cuba "for the protection of life, property, and individual liberty." The United States required the incorporation of the Platt Amendment in any constitution drawn up by Cuba, and also stipulated that Cuba make a permanent treaty with the United States reiterating the amendment's terms.

The war with Spain had ushered the people of the United States into a new era. The conflict itself, the problems of the peace treaty, the pacification of Aguinaldo's rebels, and the shackling of free Cuba all kept the issue of the new imperialism constantly before the public. In the midst of all the discussion and debate, the election of 1900 took place. Many issues were involved, including the old problems of the gold standard and the protective tariff. The Democratic candidate, William Jennings Bryan, had been instrumental in securing some Democratic votes for the treaty of peace in the Senate. Unsympathetic to the treaty himself, he still urged its support, partly to protect his party from the imputation of wanting the war renewed, and partly to get the whole issue of imperial expansion into the campaign. In the election, McKinley and the Republican party won an even more substantial victory than they had in 1896. Many interpreted the verdict as a victory for imperialism. When McKinley was assassinated a few months after his inauguration in 1901 and Vice-president Theodore Roosevelt became president, the imperialist camp had reason to expect that expansionism would be further encouraged.

In 1901, in the so-called Insular Cases, the Supreme Court added its sanction to the assent of the executive and the people. In these cases, the Court held, essentially, that the Constitution did not follow the flag, that the rights of United States citizens did not automatically belong to the people of the territories. In particular, the Court decided that Puerto Rico was "territory appurtenant . . . but not a part of the United States," and that Congress could determine afresh many of the civil rights of the "native inhabitants. The Court also decided, in a 1903 case arising out of the denial of trial by jury to the Hawaiian people, that Hawaii had not been incorporated into the United States when it was annexed; and that therefore it was lawful to continue to follow the existing criminal procedure in the islands instead of substituting procedures laid down for Americans by the Federal Constitution.

Yet Americans were not entirely comfortable in the role of colonizers or empire-builders. Cuba, instead of being kept as an open dependency, was made relatively free, and ultimately even the Philippines were promised independence. When President Mc-Kinley sent William Howard Taft to the islands in 1900 as chief of the Philippine Commission, the beginnings of independent self-government were laid down and many other reforms in the land system and in transportation and sanitation were begun. By 1907, the Filipinos had gained the right to elect the lower house of the legislature, and in 1916 the Jones Act gave them virtual autonomy over their domestic affairs. Some of this ground was lost during the 1920's, but in 1934 the Tydings-McDuffie Act provided for independence after ten years. The Filipinos agreed to the ten-year provision in 1936. Fortunately, when the islands were recovered from Japan during World War II the Filipinos finally achieved their independence, as originally planned, on July 4, 1946.

III.   THE ORIENT

The "Open Door."   The war with Spain and the acquisition of the Philippines and Hawaii helped to enhance an American awareness of the Far East that had been growing for a long time. For imperial powers, the great prize in the Far East was the relatively impotent and passive country of China, which at the turn of the century was beginning to be staked out into spheres of influence by various imperial powers. At the beginning of the new century, Japan had occupied Korea, France was established in Kwangchau Bay, Germany held a 99-year lease on the port of Kiaochow and had been granted special rights on the Shantung Peninsula, Britain held Hong Kong, and Russia held Port Arthur and claimed special privileges in Manchuria. It was clear that if China were to be totally dismembered, American hopes for further trade with that country would be disappointed. The problem posed to the United States was to find a way of achieving and maintaining equal trading rights in China without risking war and without becoming a party to further partition.

McKinley's Secretary of State, John Hay, attempted to meet this problem in September, 1899, when he sent his memorable "Open Door" notes to England, Germany, and Russia, and later to Japan, Italy, and France, inviting them to agree to three points. First, no nation was to interfere with the trading rights or privileges of other nations within its sphere of influence. Second, Chinese officials would be permitted to collect duties under the existing tariff, which granted the United States most-favored nation privileges. Third, no nation was to discriminate against nationals of other countries in levying port dues and railroad rates.

The response to Hay's note was not as whole-hearted as he might have wished. Although none of the recipient nations was willing to put itself in the position of openly bullying China, none was prepared to make important concessions. Each in replying thus evaded Hay's request. With the exception of Russia, they stated that they approved in principle, but could not commit themselves until all the others had accepted. Hay saved himself from a fiasco by calmly announcing on March 20, 1900, that the powers had all granted "final and definitive" consent to his request. The only power that cared to challenge this audacious bluff was Japan. Although there has been a good deal of comment about the "Open Door" principle, it is noteworthy that it represented only the most limited of demands and that it was hardly more than a publicity gesture. Hay had not proposed that the great powers cease to make inroads upon China's territorial integrity; he had merely tried to persuade them all to declare that they would respect each other's trade rights within their own spheres of influence.

Hardly had the negotiations over the "Open Door" notes been concluded when a group of fanatical Chinese nationalists, the Boxers, rose up against foreigners in China, launched upon a course of widespread murder and pillage, and surrounded and besieged the foreign diplomatic corps in Peking. An international rescue force, to which the United States contributed 2,500 soldiers, set out from Tientsin toward Peking to relieve the besieged international garrison.

It was just this sort of military action that had led to total partition elsewhere, but the United States and Britain moved to prevent the extension of spheres of influence this time. John Hay sent a note to the powers declaring that the policy of the United States government was to seek a solution which would "preserve Chinese territorial and administrative entity" and "safeguard for the world the principle of equal and impartial trade with all parts of the Chinese Empire." This announcement went further than the Open Door notes insofar as it actually spoke out for the territorial integrity of China and for commercial equality not merely in the spheres of influence but in all parts of the Chinese empire. Eventually, Hay obtained the consent of the participating nations to

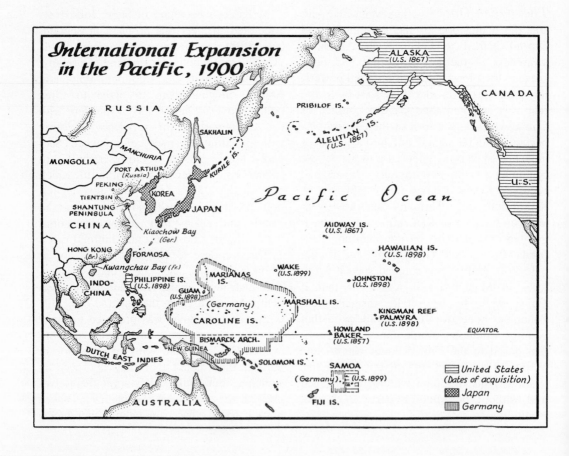

International Expansion in the Pacific, 1900

accept a money indemnity from China rather than grants of territory. The share of the United States, which was almost $25 million, was larger than necessary to meet damages; the unexpended balance was later returned to China, and was used by that country to educate Chinese students in the United States.

Americans felt that Hay had achieved a major diplomatic victory in preventing further partition. The New York *Nation* called it "a splendid instance of American sagacity winning a peaceful victory." What had made the settlement possible, however, was the unwillingness of the European powers at this time to launch themselves upon a scramble in China that might touch off a general war.

Roosevelt and Japan.

Roosevelt and Japan.   The succession of Theodore Roosevelt to the presidency in September, 1901, seemed to promise a period of aggressive foreign policy. Roosevelt, only 43 at the time he took the oath of office, was as vigorous as he was young, and by temperament as belligerent as he was vigorous. He had built his public reputation partly on his service during the Spanish-American War, and had preached for some years the importance of what he called "the soldierly virtues." "No triumph of peace," he had told the Naval War College in 1897, "is quite so great as the supreme triumphs of war. . . . The men who have dared greatly in war, or the work which is akin to war, are those who deserve best of the country." Roosevelt felt that American interests could be maintained only if the nation increased its strength and actively extended its influence throughout the world. But except for his aggressive conduct in acquiring the Panama Canal territory (see p. 570), his policies were more moderate than his pronouncements.

Roosevelt's first major move was prompted by the Russo-Japanese War of 1904-1905. Japan, encouraged by a treaty of alliance signed with Great Britain in 1902, felt free to try to drive the Russians out of Manchuria, where the two nations had fallen into rivalry. In the United States, suspicion and fear of the power of the czar had been traditional, whereas Japan, a seemingly small nation, enjoyed some degree of sympathy and was looked upon as a counter-weight to Russia in the Far East. But Japan's early and overwhelming victory persuaded Roosevelt that Japanese expansion was a far more important threat than it had been imagined. In 1905, therefore, when the Japanese, finally exhausted by the very efforts that had led to their victories, secretly asked Roosevelt to mediate the struggle, he successfully insisted that the Japanese respect the Open Door policy.

Having won Japanese acceptance of this demand, Roosevelt invited Japanese and Russian delegates to meet at Portsmouth, New Hampshire, on August 9, 1905. The Japanese, among other things, demanded a huge money indemnity, together with the Russian island of Sakhalin. The Russian government balked, and eventually the Japanese, warned by Roosevelt against pressing their demand for money, gave up on this issue and accepted the southern half of Sakhalin. Japan had emerged from the war as the dominant power in the Far East and had won a number of specific gains. Throughout the discussions, Roosevelt's mediation was helpful; but the Japanese people, who had counted on winning an indemnity for tax relief, considered Roosevelt responsible for their failure to get it, and the results of his intervention disappointed and displeased the Japanese.

Another disruptive issue between Japan and the United States was the treatment of Orientals on the Pacific coast, where prejudice against Japanese had long existed and where the startling Japanese victories in the Far East gave rise to a great deal of anxiety about the "yellow peril." In October, 1906, the Board of Education of San Francisco passed an order segregating the 93 Japanese children in the city in a separate school. The news of this action stung Japanese racial pride and prompted a number of

Japanese newspapers to call for drastic action. Roosevelt was furious over California's provocation, but the American federal system gave him no jurisdiction over the California public schools. Only after denouncing the San Francisco action in his annual message of 1906 as a "wicked absurdity," and after bringing a great deal of pressure to bear on local authorities, did Roosevelt succeed in getting the action reversed. In return, he promised the nervous Californians that the Japanese immigration that had alarmed them would be curbed. After some negotiation, the Japanese accepted the Gentleman's Agreement of 1907-1908, in which the Japanese government promised to issue no more passports to Japanese workers emigrating to the United States mainland.

Having mollified the Japanese, Roosevelt feared that they might interpret his behavior as a sign of weakness. He was anxious, he wrote to a friend, "that they should realize that I am not afraid of them and that the United States will no more submit to bullying than it will bully." As a demonstration of American strength, he decided to send the American fleet around the world on a practice cruise. Although some feared that this nautical exercise would be considered an aggressive gesture, the American fleet was welcomed with such enthusiasm in Japan (Japanese school children took the trouble to learn to sing the Star-Spangled Banner in English to greet the sailors) that the voyage was considered a great success and Japanese-American relations continued to improve.

Outstanding Japanese-American differences were negotiated on November 30, 1908, with the signing of the Root-Takahira Agreement. An executive agreement rather than a treaty, the arrangement bound only the Roosevelt administration and the current government of Japan. Both powers agreed: first, to maintain the status quo in the Pacific area; second, to respect each other's possessions in that area; third, to uphold the Open Door in China; and finally, to support by peaceful means the "independence and integrity of China." This agreement was widely hailed in the American press, but the Japanese interpreted it as a concession to their special interests in Manchuria.

Roosevelt's successor, William Howard Taft, continued to encourage the United States to seek its place as a world power. He and his Secretary of State, the corporation lawyer Philander C. Knox, embarked upon a policy of encouraging foreign investment and trade, a policy that became known as "Dollar Diplomacy." As Taft once put it, "This policy has been characterized as substituting dollars for bullets. It is one that appeals alike to idealists of humanitarian sentiments, to the dictates of sound policy and strategy and to legitimate commercial aims."

Imposing as this explanation sounded, the policy brought unimpressive results, particularly in the Far East. One of the favorite projects of Taft and Knox was to win participation for a group of American bankers in a consortium of British, French, and German bankers, which was planning a railroad in central and southern China. After exerting pressure on the other powers, the Taft administration won the admission of American bankers to the consortium, but the bankers themselves showed little interest in using their investment as a wedge to extend American influence in the Far East. Secretary Knox also tried to check Russian and Japanese influence in Manchuria by financing China's purchase of the Manchurian railroads in which these two powers were interested. His effort only aroused the suspicion and animosity of Russia and Japan, drove the two together, and irritated American bankers whose capital Knox hoped to conscript for this diplomatic move. These efforts brought Taft a stern letter of disapproval from Roosevelt. "I utterly disbelieve in the policy of bluff," Roosevelt admonished him. "I do not believe in our taking any position anywhere unless we can make good."

IV. PANAMA AND THE CARIBBEAN

The Panama Canal. When the Spanish-American War ended, the United States had interests in both the Caribbean and the Pacific, and the increasing range of her activities brought about a renewal of an old dream—the construction of an isthmian canal. Strategic considerations as well as trade pointed to the desirability of such a canal. A battleship moving from the Atlantic to the Pacific had to make the long voyage around South America—three times the distance that would have been necessary had there been a canal. By the Clayton-Bulwer Treaty of 1850, Britain would enjoy equal rights with the United States in any canal that was constructed. The first step, clearly, was to win English consent to a change in these terms. Troubled by the hostilities aroused against her by the Boer War, Britain agreed to revise the treaty. After one draft was rejected in the Senate because of a clause prohibiting the United States from fortifying the projected canal, the second draft, the Hay-Pauncefote Treaty, was concluded in 1901. The treaty gave the United States a free hand to build, control, and, by implication, to fortify an isthmian canal. In return, the United States promised that the canal would be open without discrimination to the commercial and fighting vessels of all nations.

Two routes were possible for the canal, one through Panama, the other through Nicaragua. Years before, a French canal company, led by Ferdinand de Lesseps, had gone bankrupt trying to dig a waterway through Panama, which was owned by the Republic of Colombia; but in 1902 the Senate voted to repeat the Panama effort. By threatening to come to an agreement with Nicaragua, Secretary Hay was able to drive a hard bargain with Tomás Herrán of Colombia in a treaty approved in March, 1903. The United States, for a cash payment of $10 million and a yearly payment of $250,000, was to receive rights to a canal zone six miles wide across the Isthmus. But the Colombian government, which resented some of the terms of the arrangement, now refused to ratify the treaty and aroused the violent animosity of

Roosevelt throwing dirt from the Panama Canal on Bogotá, the capital of Colombia.

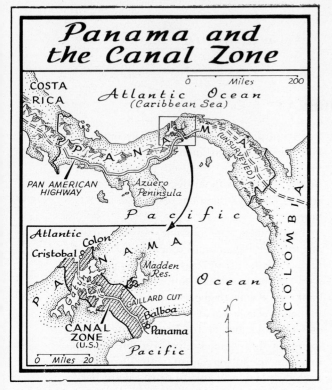

Panama and the Canal Zone

COSTA RICA

Atlantic Ocean
(Caribbean Sea)

0   Miles   200

PAN AMERICAN HIGHWAY

PANAMA (UNSURVEYED)

Azuero Peninsula

Pacific

COLOMBIA

Atlantic

Colon

Cristobal

PANAMA

Madden Res.

Ocean

GAILLARD CUT

CANAL ZONE (U.S.)

Balboa

Panama

Pacific

0   Miles   20

to seize the Panama railroad and to prevent the landing of any armed force within 50 miles of Panama. This order cut the Colombian troops off from the revolutionary area, and the revolution took place quietly. Washington promptly recognized a minister from the new republic of Panama and a treaty was signed at once giving the United States the desired strip for $10 million and $250,000 a year.

Roosevelt has been much criticized for his complicity in the Panamanian revolution, but he defended himself by remarking: "If I had followed traditional conservative methods I should have submitted a dignified state paper of probably 200 pages to Congress and the debate would be going on yet; but I took the Canal Zone and let Congress debate; and while the debate goes on the canal does also." Roosevelt's aggressive behavior and remarks created many enemies for the United States throughout Latin America, although it did speed up the completion of the canal somewhat. Within a decade, under the direction of Colonel George W. Goethals, an army engineer, and thanks to the feats of sanitation achieved by Colonel W. C. Gorgas, an army medical officer, the canal was finished. On August 15, 1914, the first ocean steamer passed through it.

In 1914, the Wilson administration, desiring to placate Colombia and win good will in Latin America, concluded a treaty with Colombia that apologized for the part played by the United States in the Panamanian revolution and set aside $25 million to be paid to Colombia to soothe her wounded feelings. Roosevelt's friends in the Senate would not abide this slur upon his conduct and the treaty was shelved. Later, in 1921, after Roosevelt's death, the treaty minus the apology at last passed the Senate by a vote of 69 to 19, and Colombia received its indemnity in full.

Roosevelt, who felt that the "black-mailers of Bogotá" must not be allowed "permanently to bar one of the future highways of civilization."

Roosevelt was determined to have the canal site on whatever terms were necessary. The French company, which had agreed to sell the site of its earlier efforts to the United States for $40 million, was anxious to close the deal. Furthermore, the people of Panama were growing restless, fearing that if the United States did not soon construct the canal on their soil it would turn to Nicaragua instead. Several parties concerned thus arrived at the conclusion that a revolution in Panama would be extraordinarily convenient both for those in the United States who wanted a Panama site and for the French company as well. So, under the leadership of its ingenious adventurer-lobbyist, Philippe Bunau-Varilla, the French company fomented a revolution in Panama against the Colombian government. This revolution could not have succeeded without the cooperation of the American navy. On October 30, 1903, the *U.S.S. Nashville* was ordered, in case of rebellion,

The Caribbean Area. The construction of the Panama Canal, by giving the United States a great new enterprise to protect from potentially hostile powers, heightened American involvement in the Caribbean. The political and financial instability of the smaller Caribbean republics posed an especially touchy problem. A large part of the national debts of such republics, in the form of government bond issues, was held by European financiers. If the failure to make payments on these bonds provoked intervention by European powers, some European state itching for an opening wedge for imperialist expansion might simply move in with the idea of staying indefinitely.

To avert this danger, President Roosevelt declared in his message to Congress on December 6, 1904: "Chronic wrong-doing . . . may in America, as elsewhere, ultimately require intervention by some civilized nation, and in the Western Hemisphere the adherence of the United States to the Monroe Doctrine may force the United States, however reluctantly, in flagrant cases of such wrongdoing or impotence, to the exercise of an international police power." The statement that the United States might intervene in the Western Hemisphere in order to prevent intervention there by European powers is called the Roosevelt Corollary to the Monroe Doctrine.

The first application of the Roosevelt Corollary came in 1905, when the Dominican Republic found itself unable to pay its debts. After a show of force by the United States, the Dominican government had to invite the United States to step in and take control. The foreign debt was scaled down and transferred from European to American bankers, and a certain percentage of customs collections was allocated to pay Dominican debts. Cuba also drew the attention of the Roosevelt administration in 1906, when revolutionary disturbances prompted the administration to land troops to restore order. They were not withdrawn until 1909.

Intervention in Latin America continued under the administration of President Taft. Taft and Knox hoped that the financial administration set up for the Dominican Republic might become the model for further intervention in the Caribbean and hoped that the pursuit of Dollar Diplomacy would enable American bankers not merely to protect the Panama Canal, but also to build up a financial empire. To this end, Secretary Knox persuaded American bankers to in-

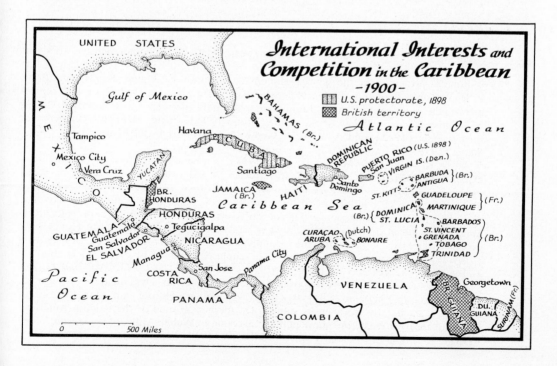

crease their interest in the debt of Honduras and to put capital into the National Bank of the Republic of Haiti.

The outstanding instance of Dollar Diplomacy took place in 1911, when a revolution broke out in Nicaragua and American bankers took charge of the country's finances. In 1912, American marines were landed to prevent further upheavals. This armed intervention in the territory of Caribbean neighbors aroused great hostility to the United States throughout Latin America.

Woodrow Wilson, who succeeded Taft in 1913, declared himself unalterably opposed to imperialist policies and promised that the United States would "never again seek one additional foot of territory by conquest." But the rise of international tension that came with the outbreak of World War I in 1914 made the American government more vigilant than ever in the Caribbean, and while President Wilson busied himself with more important problems of foreign policy the State Department and the Navy Department continued to intervene. The purchase of the Virgin Islands from Denmark in 1917 was a result of the desire for more Caribbean naval bases. More spectacular was the intervention in Haiti, which began in 1915 in response to violent revolutionary disturbances that culminated in the assassination of the Haitian president. The country was then occupied by American marines, who did not leave until 1934, and a new constitution for the Haitian Republic was imposed upon it by the Navy Department. The Wilson administration occupied the Dominican Republic again in 1916, after a conflict between the Dominican government and American officials, and also intervened in Cuba in 1917. The most acute problem to be confronted by the Wilson administration in Latin America, however, arose over troubled relations with Mexico (see p. 603). But even this problem was forced into the background by the advent of World War I. For a hundred years after 1815, the United States had escaped involvement in Europe's wars. But the expansionist history of the late nineteenth and early twentieth centuries had once more tied America's destiny to the fate of the Old World.

Readings

Parker T. Moon, *Imperialism and World Politics* (1926), is a comprehensive work that places the problem of imperialism in a world setting where it belongs. The American side is broadly presented in the general diplomatic histories by Bailey, Bemis, and Pratt. B. H. Williams, *Economic Foreign Policy of the United States* (1929), is a useful supplement to the other general books. Illuminating, but more specialized, are Samuel F. Bemis, *The Latin American Policy of the United States* (1943); Tyler Dennett, *Americans in Eastern Asia* (1922); and A. Whitney Griswold, *The Far Eastern Policy of the United States* (1938).

Albert K. Weinberg, *Manifest Destiny* (1935), is a penetrating study of the American expansionist urge; *Our Country*, by Rev. Josiah Strong (1885), and a series of books beginning with *The Influence of Sea Power upon History, 1660-1783* (1890), by Alfred T. Mahan, were very influential in nurturing the imperialist urge in their own day. The thinking underlying American expansionism is clearly set forth in Richard Hofstadter, *Social Darwinism in American Thought* (rev. ed., 1955). Read also Hofstadter's essay, "Manifest Destiny and the Philippines," in Daniel Aaron, ed., *America in Crisis* (1952), Chapter VIII. A severe yet scholarly criticism of expansionist thinking and its consequences may be found in Charles A. Beard, *The Idea of National Interest* (1934), a book that reflects the isolationist thinking of its own time.

The Rise of American Naval Power, 1776-1918, by Harold and Margaret Sprout (1939), is a scholarly work on its subject. On the background of the Spanish-American War and the war itself, the most popular account is Walter Millis, *The Martial Spirit* (1931). An important scholarly work is Julius W. Pratt, *Expansionists of 1898* (1936).

Entertaining chapters will also be found in Henry F. Pringle, *Theodore Roosevelt: A Biography* (1931), and Matthew Josephson, *The President Makers, 1896-1919* (1940).

A comprehensive study of the American postwar empire is Julius W. Pratt, *America's Colonial Experiment* (1950). On the Panama Canal, two books tell the story: Gerstle Mack, *The Land Divided* (1944), and Dwight C. Miner, *The Fight for the Panama Route* (1940). On the Caribbean in general, Dexter Perkins, *The United States and the Caribbean* (1947), and Dana G. Munro, *The United States and the Caribbean Area* (1934), are enlightening. Interesting also is Henry F. Pringle, *Life and Times of William Howard Taft* (2 vols., 1939). On Mexico, stimulating reading may be found in Ernest H. Gruening, *Mexico and Its Heritage* (1928). On the Far East, see Tyler Dennett, *John Hay* (1933); Fred H. Harrington, *God, Mammon and the Japanese: Horace N. Allen and Korean-American Relations, 1884-1905* (1944); and John K. Fairbanks, *The United States and China* (1948).

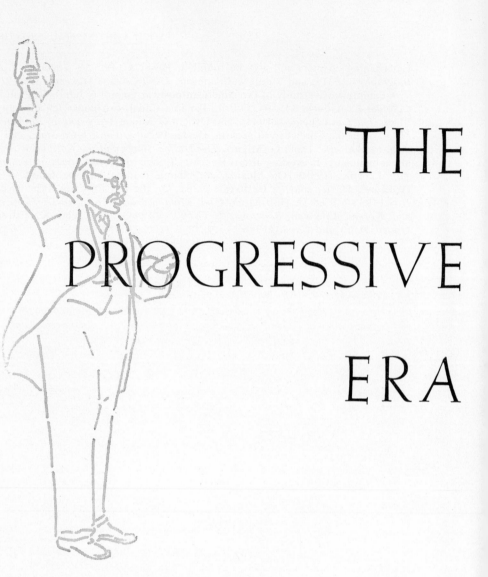

THE
PROGRESSIVE
ERA

C H A P T E R   T W E N T Y - F I V E

The years from the beginning of Theodore Roosevelt's presidency to the outbreak of World War I are generally known as the Progressive era, an age that was dominated by a passion for social progress and for reform in politics, business, and morals. The preceding generation had devoted its energies to settling the continent, building new industrial plants, and making money.

The Progressive generation set out to reform what it considered the most serious abuses in the society it had inherited. Out of this impulse arose both the Square Deal of Theodore Roosevelt and the New Freedom of Woodrow Wilson, as well as a host of other reforms that were not, strictly speaking, a part of either program but that won the support of men in both major parties.

I.   SOCIAL AND ECONOMIC PROBLEMS

Progressivism Defined.   What was Progressivism? As its name implies, the movement was founded on the notion that further progress toward social justice was possible, indeed necessary. Different Progressives pointed out different approaches, but most of them had the same goals: to make political life more democratic, to make economic life fairer and more competitive, and to make social life more moral and more just. Many Progressives hoped that they could cleanse and purify American society. They hoped to broaden opportunities for the common man, to eliminate special privilege and favoritism. Some of them feared that without a concerted effort in this direction, American society would fall victim to plutocracy, and that its traditional forms of democratic government would wither and disappear.

For most Progressives, the biggest threat to political democracy came from corrupt machine politics and big business. But they were also aware of other evils festering beneath the surface of a society that outwardly seemed to be healthy and prospering. They realized, for instance, that despite increases in national income and in the comfort of the working classes, the wealth of the nation was unequally distributed and the poorest Americans lived at a shameful level of existence. According to one estimate, the wealthiest 1 per cent of the families of the nation in 1910 owned about 47 per cent of the national wealth, and each year received about 15 per cent of the national income.

At the bottom of the social scale was a class of workers who were plagued by unemployment, were huddled into hideous slums, and were vulnerable to all sorts of diseases. Millions of workers toiled at their machines for 54 to 60 hours a week, some for as long as 72 hours or more. Industrial accidents brought tragedy, and then poverty, to an extraordinarily large portion of the working class; even in 1913, after safety measures had been adopted by many industries, 25,000 workers were estimated to have been killed on their jobs and 700,000 gravely injured. Women and children worked long hours in factories, fields, and mills, most of them unprotected by legislative regulation or by union organization. The millions of immigrants who filled the cities lived under the most trying conditions, with little chance of becoming first-class citizens. The American Negro—victimized by his heritage of slavery, terrorized and voteless in the South and neglected in the North—challenged the conscience of every informed and humane American. The Progressive generation was more sensitive than Americans had ever been before to the persistence of these problems and to the need for remedying them.

Throughout the years from 1870 to 1900, various voices had been raised on behalf of reform; in some respects, Progressivism continued in more practical form the criticisms and demands those voices had made. Most of the reformers from 1870 to 1896 had contented themselves with intellectual criticism or futile agitation, but after 1900 reformers became increasingly active in practical politics and began to achieve practical results. The age of Henry George, Edward Bellamy, and James B. Weaver was followed by the age of Robert M. La Follette, Theodore Roosevelt, and Woodrow Wilson.

The Business World.   No single force can account for this remarkable flowering of the reform spirit at the turn of the century, although the changes in economic organization that had been taking place since the end of the Civil War had a great deal to do with it. Particularly important was the growth of the corporation as the dominant form of business organization. Before the Civil War,

Sweatshop workers in a small gas-lit factory, 1900. It was against such conditions that the Progressives crusaded.

practically all American businesses had been run by individuals or partners, and the size of a business had been limited by the amount of money an individual or a few partners could raise among themselves. The corporation, as a device by which the savings of thousands of persons could be drawn upon to finance a single enterprise, was not unknown in those early days, but it was confined to only a few types of enterprises— banking, insurance, transportation, and a very few manufacturing firms. After the Civil War, however, as the scale of industrial activity grew, the corporation rapidly became the leading form of organization in American industry.

The giant enterprises that emerged during the Gilded Age—the oil and steel companies, the railroads, the great manufacturing and mining concerns, and the huge public utilities —were too numerous and too large to be financed by wealthy individuals. So a domestic investment market developed, making it possible to recruit the savings of great numbers of persons to underwrite such enterprises. By 1900, tens of thousands of Americans owned corporate securities; at the close of the Progressive era in 1917, hundreds of thousands. In 1899, a total of 66 per cent

576

of all manufactured goods were corporation-made; ten years later, the figure had risen to 79 per cent.

The large corporation's envelopment of business meant that most investors no longer managed their own capital; they simply owned stock in large organizations over whose affairs they had little control. A larger and larger proportion of the capital of the country belonged to investors of this sort, and corporation officials were exposed to extraordinary temptations in handling other people's money. Reorganizations, mergers, and other devices, though at times planned for sound enough business reasons, could also be manipulated by shrewd promoters for their own special benefit, which often ran counter to the best interests of the stockholders. Much of the business consolidation, though itself improvidently carried out, was in fact undertaken to avoid the waste and insecurity arising from unbridled competition. Many citizens, however, could see in all these maneuvers only a threat to opportunity and democracy. To the man of modest means, the potential investor, and the ambitious new entrepreneur, the big corporation seemed to be an obstacle that shut him out from the most profitable avenues of enterprise or confronted him with overwhelming competition. To the employee, the corporation meant that he must work in a world of impersonal, mechanized, bureaucratized, and standardized relationships, rather than in the world of personal employer-employee contact that traditionally had characterized American business. In the long run, the corporation would be able to offer its employees many more advantages and benefits than the small businessman, with his small-scale operation, could afford. But in the Progressive era, such benefits were neither available nor imminent.

For the economy as a whole, the large corporation had sweeping significance, for it meant that men who controlled a few strategic businesses could create vast economic empires. An investment banking firm like J. P. Morgan & Co., for example, could extend its control by consenting to lend money to a corporation or to sell its securities if the corporation would agree to make room for a Morgan man on its board of directors. Since the banker-director then controlled the corporation's supply of new money, he could play a decisive role in the corporation's affairs. The president of the New York, New Haven and Hartford Railroad, Charles S. Mellen, once admitted that his board of directors "used to vote as a rule pretty near where Mr. Morgan voted. . . . There were strong men on the New Haven Board other than Mr. Morgan, but I do not recall anything where Mr. Morgan was determined, emphatic, insistent—I recall no case in which he did not have his way."

During the ten years that followed the Panic of 1893, the corporate economy began to consolidate very rapidly. During this panic, the two leading Wall Street investment houses, J. P. Morgan & Co., and Kuhn, Loeb & Co., concluded that much of the chaos in railroading was caused by lack of organization and excessive competition. So they began to consolidate bankrupt roads. The idea proved so rewarding that J. P. Morgan next turned his attention to industry. When rivalry between Andrew Carnegie and other steelmakers threatened to precipitate a price war

in the steel industry. Morgan stepped in and took the initiative in forming the billion-dollar United States Steel Corporation. After his quick rise to power in the steel industry, Morgan looked to other fields, acquired new industries, and secured positions for his partners and representatives on the boards of directors of many more corporations.

Morgan's opportunities arose largely because of the cutthroat competition among highly mechanized companies that threatened to destroy each other in their efforts to keep their costly machinery working full blast. The depression that started in 1893 made this kind of competition all the more severe and encouraged the consolidation of competing firms with the assistance of investment bankers. The return of prosperity in 1897 made it still easier for the bankers to float the new issues of securities needed to finance consolidation. Between 1898 and 1904, the number of consolidations reached a peak that was not to be attained again until the 1920's.

In 1904, when John Moody published his famous survey, *The Truth about the Trusts,* he listed 318 great corporations that had been organized, or were in the process of being organized, by January of that year. The United States Steel Corporation, the Standard Oil Company, Consolidated Tobacco, Amalgamated Copper, the International Mercantile Marine Company, and the American Smelting and Refining Company all were incorporated during the last years of McKinley's administration and the first administration of Theodore Roosevelt. During the same period, consolidations were taking place in the telephone, telegraph, gas, traction, and electric power and light industries.

At the peak of the economy stood the two great financial empires organized by the House of Morgan and by the Rockefeller Group. The basis of J. P. Morgan's power was his long-established supremacy in the investment banking field, capped by his firm's ownership of the National Bank of

Commerce and part ownership of the First National Bank of New York City. In addition, Morgan controlled many other regional banks. His firm also spoke with a powerful voice in such national corporations as United States Steel, International Harvester, and General Electric. It dominated a series of railroads, of which the largest were the Great Northern, the Northern Pacific, the New Haven, and the Erie—all told, a significant portion of the railroad capital of the country. A prized plum for any investment banking house was control of a large insurance company, which would provide excellent markets for securities. Morgan controlled New York Life and Mutual Life, and in 1910 his interests bought control of Equitable Life.

The Rockefeller Group, which had been formed to channel the vast surplus profits of Standard Oil into other industries, included, besides the oil firm, the financial resources of Morgan's rival in the investment field, Kuhn, Loeb & Co., which was led by Jacob H. Schiff. The Group also controlled the National City Bank, the Hanover National Bank, and the Farmers Loan and Trust Company, as well as the Union Pacific, Southern Pacific, and nine other railroads that were under the astute and aggressive management of Edward H. Harriman.

There were other financial empires, but at the turn of the century the two giants dominated the country's business life. In 1900, they locked horns in a momentous battle over the control of the major transcontinental railroads. James J. Hill, a Morgan ally, controlled the two northernmost lines, the Great Northern and the Northern Pacific. Harriman and Kuhn, Loeb & Co., on the other side, controlled the two southernmost systems, the Union Pacific and the Southern Pacific. Both groups were trying to buy the Chicago, Burlington & Quincy, which commanded the best connections with Chicago. When Hill's roads bought the Burlington in 1901, Harriman and Schiff mounted an ingenious counterattack by trying to buy control of Hill's own Northern Pacific. The

battle between the two factions in the New York Stock Exchange sent Northern Pacific stock soaring and precipitated a market boom and crash that made a few fortunes but ruined thousands of unoffending investors. By the time the smoke had cleared, Harriman and Schiff owned the majority of Northern Pacific shares, but Hill and Morgan still held the majority of the crucial voting stock. It had been a costly experience, and the two sides agreed to compromise. They formed the Northern Securities Company, which now controlled Hill's lines. Harriman and Schiff were given minority representation on its board of directors. Harriman was also given a voice in the control of the Burlington.

This spectacular clash, and the size and fame of the competitors, had focused a great deal of attention on the combination, and soon made the Northern Securities Company a logical choice for prosecution by President Theodore Roosevelt. The masters of the great combinations, however, had decided that unity was more sound than competition, even between giants. This lesson was reinforced in 1907, when the two groups had to act together to stem a stock-market panic. After 1907, the two groups tended to merge through interlocking directorates and the purchase of stock in each other's companies.

In 1913, the Pujo Committee of the House of Representatives, which had been working for two years to unravel the financial affairs of these two combinations, released a report showing that persons who belonged either to the Morgan or the Rockefeller interests held the following strategic business and financial positions:

One hundred and eighteen directorships in thirty-four banks and trust companies having total resources of $2,697,000,000 and total deposits of $1,983,000,000.

Thirty directorships in ten insurance companies having total assets of $2,293,000,000.

One hundred and five directorships in thirty-two transportation systems having a total capitalization of $11,784,000,000 and a total mileage (excluding express companies and steamship lines) of 150,000.

Sixty-three directorships in twenty-four producing and trading corporations having a total capitalization of $3,339,000.

Twenty-five directorships in twelve public utility corporations having a total capitalization of $2,150,000,000.

In all, 341 directorships in 112 corporations having aggregate resources or capitalization of $22,245,000,000.

Here, then, was a combine that controlled more than three times the assessed value of all the property in the 13 southern states, more than the assessed value of all the property in the 22 states west of the Mississippi River! In the presence of such power, what would become of American free enterprise? How could political freedom itself survive?

The New Barbarians? But the Progressives, troubled as they were about the social and political consequences of business power and the future of American society, also resented the huge personal fortunes the financiers had accumulated and the flamboyant way they sometimes spent their money. In the old America—in the United States as it existed, say, down to 1870—quite a few men had accumulated modest fortunes, but there were very few poor people and very few millionaires. During the 1840's, for instance, there were probably fewer than 20 millionaires in the entire country. By 1892, the New York *Tribune* could publish the names of 4,047 men who reputedly were millionaires. And in 1893, a statistician of the Census Bureau estimated that 71 per cent of the country's wealth was held by 9 per cent of its families.

The new millionaires were extraordinarily rich, impressively numerous, and often uncultivated and crude. In the older America, the wealthy class had consisted mostly of merchants with long-established places in their communities, good educations, philanthropic interests, and cultivated tastes. Such men did not entirely disappear after the end of the Civil War, but their influence waned before the new self-made men, whose business and political methods were rough and aggressive, and whose minds and tastes were

coarse. "If our civilization is destroyed, as Macaulay predicted," wrote the reformer Henry Demarest Lloyd in his *Wealth against Commonwealth* (1894),

it will not be by his barbarians from below. Our barbarians come from above. Our great money-makers have sprung in one generation into seats of power kings do not know. The forces and the wealth are new, and have been the opportunity of new men. Without restraints of culture, experience, the pride, or even the inherited caution of class or rank, these men, intoxicated, think they are the wave instead of the float, and that they have created the business which has created them. To them science is but a never-ending repertoire of investments stored up by nature for the syndicates, government but a fountain of franchises, the nations but customers in squads, and a million the unit of a new arithmetic of wealth written for them. They claim a power without control, exercised through forms which make it secret, anonymous, and perpetual. The possibilities of its gratification have been widening before them without interruption since they began, and even at a thousand millions they will feel no satisfaction and will see no place to stop.

The mere existence of "robber barons," whether or not they made others poor and themselves rich, was a provocation to the rest of society. Their swollen fortunes made men of more modest means feel small and insignificant. Their lack of scruples put men of principle at a disadvantage. Even their charities and philanthropies—for they were sometimes generous—seemed over-conspicuous and designed to throw other men's generosity into the shade. The follies that they and their families indulged in were in keeping with their immense means: monstrous and ugly houses, squads of retainers and mistresses, fantastic extravagances of all kinds. With wonder, and with growing indignation, poorer men and women read lavish newspaper reports of the exotic antics that occupied the rich set during and after the 1890's —the party at which the guests, all on horseback, rode their mounts into a luxurious hotel; the dinner at which cigarettes rolled in hundred-dollar-bills were passed out to the guests and smoked after the coffee; the dinner at which each guest found in one of his oysters a magnificent black pearl; Harry Lehr's memorable dog dinner at which his friends' dogs were invited to sup on rare dainties; the opening in 1892 of the Vanderbilts' Marble House at Newport, which with its furnishings cost $9 million; the $200,000 ball given by the James Hazen Hydes in 1905.

Was it to defend such goings-on, men wondered, that the wealthy went into politics? The defiant Frederick Townshend Martin, brother of the New York millionaire, Bradley Martin, seemed to answer a belligerent yes to that question. "We are the rich," he declared in *The Passing of the Idle Rich* (1911):

we own America; we got it, God knows how, but we intend to keep it if we can by throwing all the tremendous weight of our support, our influence, our money, our political connections, our purchased senators, our hungry congressmen, and our public-speaking demagogues into the scale against any legislation, any political

platform, any Presidential campaign, that threatens the integrity of our estate. . . . Truly I can say that wealth has no politics save its own interests.

Men whose political impulses were basically quite conservative feared that boasts like this would provoke the public into dangerous political extremes. Many of the reforms sponsored by enlightened conservatives like Roosevelt were intended to put an end to this continual provocation. Roosevelt wrote to William Howard Taft in 1906 about the problems of American political leadership for the next quarter of a century:

I do not at all like the social conditions at present. The dull, purblind folly of the very rich men, their greed and arrogance, and the way in which they have unduly prospered by the help of the ablest lawyers, and too often through the weakness or short-sightedness of the judges or by their unfortunate possession of meticulous minds; these facts, and the corruption in business and politics, have tended to produce a very unhealthy condition of excitement and irritation in the popular mind, which shows itself in part in the enormous increase in the socialistic propaganda.

II. THE POPULAR SOLUTIONS

The Muckrakers. "Muckraking" got its name from a speech made by President Theodore Roosevelt in 1906 about the work of the journalists who were exposing the sordid aspects of American society. "In Bunyan's *Pilgrim's Progress*," he said, "you may recall the description of the Man with the Muck-rake, the man who could look no way but downward with the muck-rake in his hands; who was offered the celestial crown for his muck-rake, but would neither look up nor regard the crown he was offered, but continued to rake the filth on the floor."

Roosevelt condemned the muckrakers, even though he agreed that many of their charges were true, because he feared that their widely read exposures were becoming irresponsible and would arouse dangerous discontent. But the muckrakers insisted that the American people would not fight for

necessary reforms until they had been fired with indignation. And the way to create indignation was to report every ugly fact that could be found under the surface of American life.

Muckraking, or rather the idea of "digging up dirt," did not begin in 1900. For several decades before, a visiting English journalist, W. T. Stead, and a number of local reporters, had written sad and sordid stories of the sort that made the muckrakers famous. And what the reporters had been unable to find out, the novelists had been quick to imagine. What was new after the turn of the century were the popular magazines that spent large sums so that the muckrakers could get information and that provided them with a nationwide audience. Before the 1890's, there were no mass-circulation magazines in the United States. Limited audiences—usually about 130,000—bought the staid and respectable old family magazines like the *Century, Harper's, Scribner's,* and the *Atlantic.* These periodicals were usually edited by literary men affiliated with one of the book-publishing houses. They sought to make their journals the repositories of polite literature of the day, and their goal was to publish nothing that might offend the young daughters of their respectable subscribers. They even shied away from discussing controversial political issues.

During the 1890's, a group of enterprising magazine promoters brought out a wholly new kind of popular magazine that was patterned not after books but after newspapers, sponsored not by publishing houses but by promotion-minded businessmen. The new magazines sold for only half as much as the older journals; they used a much livelier type of article or story, and they were heavily illustrated. They quickly reached audiences of from 400,000 to a million and more persons. Some of them, like *Munsey's, The Saturday Evening Post,* and the *Ladies' Home Journal,* remained impeccably conservative in their outlook; but others, like *McClure's, Everybody's, Cosmopolitan, Collier's,* and the *American Magazine,* became exposé magazines.

Publishers and editors learned that the American public wanted to hear about the corruption in American life, and they were quite ready to meet the demand. Recruiting a band of extremely able reporters—Ray Stannard Baker, Ida M. Tarbell, Lincoln Steffens, Burton J. Hendrick, Charles Edward Russell, and others—they supplied them with facilities that no reporters in the history of journalism had ever before enjoyed. S. S. McClure, for instance, estimated that the research for the famous articles Ida M. Tarbell wrote in 1904 about Standard Oil cost $4,000 each, and that Lincoln Steffens' essays on corruption in American cities cost $2,000. With backing like this, the reporters were able to probe into court records, locate witnesses, and dig up mountains of facts. Earlier writers had relied partly on the public record and partly on guesswork, but the new

muckrakers named names and recounted misdeeds in sensational detail; and the new magazine promoters made them a national influence.

Hardly any sphere of American life escaped the muckrakers' prying eyes. Perhaps the most famous muckraking enterprise was Lincoln Steffens' series on American cities. He investigated Philadelphia, Pittsburgh, Minneapolis, St. Louis, and other cities, and found them all suffering from the same ills: bribery by businessmen, corrupt and shrewd party bosses, political collusion, special privilege, organized vice, venal police, and apathetic citizens. Ida Tarbell's almost equally famous exposé of Standard Oil retold the story of the pitiless methods by which that huge combine had been built. Charles Edward Russell exposed the beef trust, Thomas Lawson exposed Amalgamated Copper, and Judge Ben B. Lindsey attacked Colorado politics. The novelist David Graham Phillips wrote a series about the Senate, which he portrayed as a club of millionaires who put private interests (including those of its members) above the public welfare. John Spargo's *The Bitter Cry of the Children* described the appalling conditions of child labor in the United States; George Kibbe Turner exposed prostitution and the white slave traffic in his *Daughters of the Poor;* Ray Stannard Baker discussed the treatment of the Negro in his *Following the Color Line.* Gustavus Myers, a socialist writer, rewrote American history with a muckraking pen in his *History of the Great American Fortunes* and drew upon old court records and other forgotten materials to show the extent to which American enterprise had thrived on exploitation, dishonesty, and unearned profits.

In a few areas, muckraking had a direct and distinctly wholesome effect. Upton Sinclair's *The Jungle,* a nauseatingly realistic exposure of Chicago food-packing methods, had a great deal to do with the passage of pure-food legislation by Congress; and Burton J. Hendrick's *The Story of Life Insur-*

ance stimulated the regulation of the great New York life insurance companies during the governorship of Charles Evans Hughes. Once the muckrakers had done their work, the average citizen could no longer imagine that American life was pure and innocent. He had been put in possession of an overpowering list of names and dates and facts, and had been confronted with a challenge: What, as a citizen, would he do about such conditions?

City and State Reform. The Progressive movement originated on the local level and spread from the cities to the states and ultimately to the federal government. The movement for municipal reform began during the 1890's, when many new city reform organizations were founded. In 1894, for instance, Tammany Hall was overthrown by New York reformers, and in Chicago, as an aftermath of the attention drawn to the city's corruption by the Columbian Exposition of 1893, a reform movement put Carter Harrison into the mayor's office and did much to clean up the city. In 1901, Tom Johnson, a colorful figure who had been a great railway operator and manufacturer, and who had been converted to reform by reading Henry George, was elected Mayor of Cleveland, an office he held until 1910. Although Johnson failed to win acceptance of his entire program, he did secure tax reforms and made Cleveland one of the nation's best-governed cities. His work, along with that of Samuel ("Golden Rule") Jones of Toledo, set an example for other local reformers, such as Newton D. Baker, who succeeded Johnson in Cleveland; Mayor Hazen Pingree, in Detroit; Brand Whitlock, who succeeded Jones in Toledo; Emil Seidel, the socialist mayor of Milwaukee; and others.

Legally, the cities were the creatures of the state legislatures, a relationship that complicated problems for the municipal reformers. Local bosses who were defeated in municipal contests often turned to their allies

in the legislatures, and with their help undid the work of the reformers. When Tom Johnson was trying to break the monopoly of local trolley utilities in Cleveland, for example, his opponents persuaded the Ohio legislature to throw new obstacles in his path by altering the city's municipal code. Local reformers often were forced to tackle the state machines in order to extend home-rule privileges for their cities.

One of the first, and perhaps the greatest, of the state reformers was Robert M. La Follette, who was elected governor of Wisconsin in 1900. La Follette ousted the strong Republican state machine, established his own, made advances in the regulation of railroads and public utilities, and reformed the tax system of the state. In California, Governor Hiram Johnson fought an epic battle with the railways and eventually brought them under state supervision. In New York, Charles Evans Hughes, who was elected governor in 1906, fought for the regulation of utilities and for the direct primary. His election as governor was in part the result of his work in exposing the unscrupulous practices of insurance companies. Other state leaders fought battles with the bosses and the corporations and introduced a variety of reforms: Hazen Pingree, who from being Mayor of Detroit became Governor of Michigan, Woodrow Wilson in New Jersey, James M. Cox in Ohio, William S. U'Ren in Oregon, Joseph Folk in Missouri, Charles B. Aycock in North Carolina, and "Alfalfa Bill" Murray in Oklahoma.

By bringing about changes in municipal and state government, the Progressives hoped to cripple the power of the political machines, put the control of affairs more directly into the hands of the citizens, and increase the efficiency of government. In trying to achieve these goals—which were in some respects inconsistent—they met with only limited success. To improve municipal government, they insisted that the mayor and council should be replaced by a commission of administrators without party affiliations. This idea originated almost by accident in 1900, when Galveston, Texas, was flooded by a tidal wave.

The city council proved completely incompetent to meet this emergency, so the legislature set up a five-man commission to govern the city. The scheme worked so well that it began to be imitated in other cities in Texas and finally in the country at large. By 1914, over 400 cities, most of them small or middle-sized, had adopted this system of local management, though now the commissioners were elected by the voters. Although the commissioners were supposed to be experts in city management, they sometimes lacked the experience required to do the job well.

Another disaster—a flood at Dayton, Ohio, in 1913—resulted in a modification of the idea. Under the new system, political authority was vested in a small body of commissioners, but they in turn appointed a city manager, who usually was in fact an expert, to administer the departments of city government. The manager was responsible to the commissioners for his work. This system made it possible to combine expert management with democratic control. By 1923, more than 300 cities had adopted this method of government.

More ambitious reforms in the mechanics of government were sought through the state legislatures. The reform most generally advocated, and perhaps the most important, was the direct primary. Reformers hoped that the direct primary would insure the selection of abler and more independent candidates by leaving the choice of candidates to the people themselves, rather than to the machines. By 1916, some form of the direct primary had been adopted by all the states except Rhode Island, Connecticut, and New Mexico. The initiative—a reform that permitted the public to propose legislation—was adopted in several states, as was the referendum, which allowed the voters to pass on measures that had already been passed by the legislatures. Such devices were particularly popular in the western states. The recall of public officers through popular vote, another reform device, received widespread support as a means of getting rid of unsatisfactory officials before their terms of office expired. To the con-

servatives, the most radical and objectionable proposal of all was for the recall of judges. This measure gained strength because many court decisions throughout the land were invalidating social reforms. Seven states, all west of the Mississippi, adopted such measures, although nowhere were they invoked. Theodore Roosevelt aroused a great deal of criticism during the 1912 campaign when he suggested, as an alternative to the recall of judges, the recall of judicial decisions. Only one state, Colorado, adopted such a device, but it was declared unconstitutional in 1921, eight years after its enactment. Short-ballot laws, intended to simplify the voter's problems when he went to the polls, were adopted in many cities; and corrupt practices acts, intended to prevent or punish graft and the excessive use of funds in elections, were adopted in most of the states. The Seventeenth Amendment provided for one of the changes most in demand among reformers, the direct election of United States senators by the people. This amendment was passed by Congress in 1912 and ratified by May 31, 1913.

Although the reformers succeeded in translating a great many of their political reforms into law, they were often disappointed by the results. Party machines found ways to manipulate the political process despite the direct primary. Initiative and referendum were cumbersome devices and often misfired. Recall was used only rarely. And nothing could prevent money from influencing politics, even though some of the grosser practices could be eliminated or punished more severely. All too often the outbursts of reform lasted for only a short time, or depended on the personality of one outstanding reformer for their survival. The bosses eventually came filtering back, perhaps somewhat more careful but still powerful. Reformers had to console themselves with occasional victories and with the thought that, without the threat of reform uprisings from time to time, the machines might have done even more harm to the public.

Social Legislation. The Progressives had more success in their attempts at social reform, particularly in the state legislatures. As city-dwellers became aware of slum conditions and the distress of the working class, philanthropic reformers took it upon themselves to make increasing use of the power of the states to protect exploited workers. Some progress in legislating against child labor had already been made in almost half the states by 1900. In 1914, after a concerted drive by child-labor reformers, every state but one had set a minimum age, usually 14, at which a child could be employed in industry. Other prohibitions prevented night work and employment in dangerous occupations. By 1930, a total of 41 states had laws limiting or regulating child labor. Efforts at the federal level did not fare so well. In 1916, under the urging of Woodrow Wilson, Congress passed the Keating-Owen Act, which prohibited the shipment in interstate commerce of goods made in factories, mines, and quarries that employed children under specified ages. In 1918, however, in the case of *Hammer* v. *Dagenhart,* the Supreme Court declared the Keating-Owen Act unconstitutional on the ground that it invaded the police powers of the states, and attempted to use federal control of interstate commerce to achieve other ends.

The campaign to protect women in industry also resulted in a number of state laws limiting the weekly hours of female labor. Between 1896 and 1908, a number of states, led by New York and Massachusetts, had limited the work-week for women to 60 hours. In 1908, the Supreme Court decided the case of *Muller* v. *Oregon,* in which an employer had challenged a state law limiting the daily hours of women's work to ten. The Court was impressed by the arguments of the distinguished lawyer, Louis D. Brandeis, who was retained by the reformers to argue for the constitutionality of the disputed law. By deciding in favor of the constitutionality of the Oregon law, the Court not only justified Brandeis' confidence in his unconventional brief, but also opened the way to further legislation in this area.

In the nine years after 1908, some 39 states either enacted new legislation governing women's work or strengthened existing laws. Limitations on the hours of work were supplemented by laws establishing minimum wages. Between 1912 and 1923, a total of 15 states adopted minimum wage rates intended to secure to women workers a decent standard of living. In 1923, however, the Supreme Court, speaking through Justice George Sutherland in the case of *Adkins* v. *Children's Hospital,* found unconstitutional a law passed by Congress to regulate the wages of women in the District of Columbia. The Justice argued that prescribing minimum wages for grown women deprived them of their freedom of contract, and asserted that there was no proved relationship between hours of work and health or morals. Since this decision was a precedent that affected state laws as well, it put an end for a time to any further state reform along these lines.

Insurance against industrial accidents, another objective of reformers, occasioned a considerable amount of legislation. Traditional common-law practice had left unprotected the families of workers who were injured or killed at their jobs. In order to collect compensation from employers, dependents or survivors had to go to court—in itself a costly undertaking—and prove that the victim of the accident had not willingly assumed the risks of his job, that neither he nor any fellow-worker had contributed to the negligence that caused the accident, and that the accident was the sole fault of the employer. In short, the burden of all the risks of industry had been thrown onto the shoulders of the workingmen and their families. After 1909, a number of states adopted accident insurance systems, and by 1920 all but five of the states and territories had fallen into line.

The Progressives also succeeded in establishing a certain amount of public responsibility for the support of children and old people. States had always accepted some responsibility in this direction by providing public almshouses or by administering occasional relief in the homes of the recipients. But not until 1911 did the states begin to accept the idea that it would be better to aid dependent children in their own homes than to place them in institutions. During that year, the states began to pass mothers' assistance acts which set up public agencies to grant relief or financial help to working mothers with dependent children. By 1913, eight states had adopted this innovation; others followed, until by 1930 all but four states had fallen into line. These acts helped widows with dependent children, as well as families left destitute by divorce, desertion, or the illness or incapacity of the bread-winner.

In 1914, the states began to pass legislation to provide help for the aged poor in their own homes. Arizona began the practice, though the state supreme court found the law unconstitutional. Urged on by the American Association for Old Age Security, however, thirteen states passed such measures during the 1920's. In most cases, persons 65 years old and over were made eligible for pensions amounting to as much as $30 a month.

Women's Suffrage. Women played an important part in the Progressive movement, as they had more than half a century before in the abolitionist drive. Many of their demands were made on behalf of others, but some of them were intended to improve the legal position of women themselves. By the beginning of the twentieth century, the working woman was a common figure in American life. In 1910, 8,076,000 women worked in factories, offices, and schools, and a few had entered the professions. Women's contacts with life outside the home had given them a better understanding of social problems and a glimpse of their own potentialities as citizens. Since the 1840's, a small advance guard had argued that women as well as men deserved the right to vote. But the voices of such suffragist leaders as Susan

B. Anthony and Elizabeth Cady Stanton had not been heeded by enough of their fellow-women to make much of a stir. Progressivism, which had effected reforms in many areas of special concern to women, such as child labor, now encouraged women to demand their political rights. "We have no platform," said the president of the General Federation of Women's Clubs in 1910, "unless it is the care of women and children and the home, the latter meaning the four walls of the city as well as the four walls of brick and mortar."

The political enfranchisement of women gained increasing support until it could not be held off any longer. By 1898, four states, Wyoming, Colorado, Utah, and Idaho, had granted full voting rights to women, and many other states permitted them to vote for certain officers, such as members of school boards. A women's suffrage amendment was passed by the state of Washington in 1910, which led a number of other states to consider the enfranchisement of women. In 1912, women's suffrage became an issue in the presidential campaign. Taft and Wilson, the candidates of the major parties, evaded it. But Roosevelt (who had hitherto been opposed to it) and the Progressive party endorsed the proposal. The election of Wilson brought to the White House a man of conservative southern views on the position of women in society, but women went right on agitating. By 1914, a total of 11 states had granted the vote to women. But progress had been slow, and dissatisfied partisans now decided to concentrate on a campaign for a federal amendment. A huge petition was prepared for Congress with 404,000 signatures, and a lobby was opened in Washington. Some women, like Mrs. Carrie Chapman Catt and Dr. Anna Howard Shaw, preferred quiet techniques of gradual education and propaganda. Others, following the lead of Alice Paul, patterned their strategy after the English suffragists and engaged in dramatic demonstrations and picketing. Eventually, even Wilson was persuaded to give women's suffrage faint-hearted endorsement. The active and sacrificing role played by women in World War I strengthened their demand, and finally, in June, 1919, the Nineteenth Amendment passed Congress by a narrow margin. The amendment was ratified in August, 1920, in time for women throughout the country to take part for the first time in a presidential election.

Prohibition. During the fight for ratification of the Nineteenth Amendment, another debate was going on over a proposed prohibition amendment, and the same sides were often found in conflict in both debates. The two issues were intimately linked, for many women enthusiastically favored the prohibition of alcoholic liquors. On the other side, the saloon and liquor interests had long been connected with machine politics in American cities, and the Progressive assault on the machines encouraged many "temperance" advocates to feel that their hour had also struck. Political agitation for prohibition had been going on in the United States since the early nineteenth century, but after more than a half-century of campaigning, only five states—Kansas, Maine, North Dakota, New Hampshire, and Vermont—were legally dry in 1898. The liquor business, however, was in retreat. The disreputable old saloons were under fire, and many Americans who themselves drank began to feel that the experiment of outlawing liquor might be worth trying.

Three organizations carried on the active battle for prohibition: the Women's Christian Temperance Union, the Temperance Society of the Methodist Episcopal Church, and the Anti-Saloon League. In earlier years, prohibitionists had tried unsuccessfully to work through an independent Prohibition party; with the organization of the Anti-Saloon League in 1893, however, they at last had an agency powerful enough to carry their cause to victory. The Anti-Saloon League worked not as a party but as a lobby to put pressure on politicians in both major parties, a task at which it was unusually successful. After it had begun its concerted drive about 1907, state after state in the West and South fell into the prohibition column. In March, 1913, the Webb-Kenyon Bill, passed over President Taft's veto, prohibited the shipment of intoxicating liquors into any state, territory, or district where they were intended to be used in violation of the local laws. Encouraged by this success, the prohibitionists introduced a national prohibition amendment in Congress in December, 1913, and though the measure failed, the ground had been laid for ultimate victory. Wartime conditions, popular resentment against German brewers, and the need to conserve the materials used in distilling gave prohibitionists their long-awaited opportunity to make national prohibition a part of the Constitution. The Eighteenth Amendment passed Congress in December, 1917, was ratified in January, 1919, and went into effect in January, 1920. It soon became one of Progressivism's most controversial legacies to the next generation.

III.   REPUBLICAN PROGRESSIVISM

Theodore Roosevelt and Progressivism.   For many historians, the Progressive era begins with the first administration of Theodore Roosevelt, and some have written as though his sudden entry into the White House after President McKinley's assassination in 1901 was it-

self the cause of the Progressive ferment. In fact, Roosevelt's relations to Progressivism were not so simple. He could hardly have created the Progressive movement by himself, and in some respects he followed its course instead of leading it, restrained it instead of urging it on. Yet to many of his contemporaries, Roosevelt did symbolize Progressivism, and was its leader and outstanding spokesman. Few presidents have projected their personalities so vividly and with such success to the American public. Few have been so popular over a period of so many years.

Roosevelt was born in 1858, the son of a New York City banker and importer, and the heir of a long American family tradition. Like many men of his age and class, he was offended by the crass materialism of the new millionaires and by the corruption of ordinary politics. For a time, he seemed to be simply another well-meaning but ineffectual Mugwump reformer. But Roosevelt had determined to enter into the rough-and-tumble of politics in his own way, and he broke with the reformers in 1884, when he decided to support the tainted James G. Blaine for the presidency rather than join the Mugwump bolt from the Republican party. He began his office-holding career with three terms as an assemblyman in the New York legislature, then ran for the mayoralty of New York City in 1886 and served as a member of the Civil Service Commission under Presidents Harrison and Cleveland from 1889 to 1895. In 1895, he returned to his native city as president of the New York City Board of Police Commissioners, an office in which he amused the newspapermen and the public by the novel and dramatic ways in which he sought to reform and discipline the corrupt police force. McKinley appointed him Assistant Secretary of the Navy, but he left his desk to fight in the Spanish-American War. His feats on the battlefield added to his popularity, and in 1898 he was elected governor of New York. But Boss Tom Platt found him uncooperative and the machine politicians were happy to remove him by helping nominate him for vice-president on the successful McKinley ticket in 1900 (even though Mark Hanna complained: "Don't any of you realize that there's only one life between this madman and the White House?"). In September, 1901, an assassin mortally wounded McKinley at Buffalo, and

Theodore Roosevelt in a characteristically aggressive speaking pose.

Roosevelt became president of the United States.

Theodore Roosevelt's outstanding quality was his energy. Historian, hunter, rancher, and warrior, as well as politician, he possessed an uncommon desire to leave his mark upon the world; and it seemed unlikely that he would continue the tradition of passive government set by his predecessors. His conception of the presidency and of executive leadership was, like his personality, aggressive. He believed that American democracy needed to be invigorated and that politics could be made honest only by a strong responsible leadership.

Although vague about what policies should be adopted, he had no doubt that something was wrong with the moral tone of American political life. Above everything else he was a moralist and a preacher, and he once re-

587

ferred to the White House as "a bully pulpit." His strong-sounding speeches on behalf of Progressivism were one of his outstanding contributions to the movement, for he whipped up Progressive sentiment even when he was not sure how to realize it in action. In spite of the sharp flavor of his speeches and essays, in domestic affairs he was fundamentally disposed toward moderation. He believed the great mass of middle-class Americans to be virtuous. He deplored the social callousness of men of great wealth, but he feared radicalism and agitation. He was an ardent nationalist, and he saw in devotion to the nation and to the public welfare an answer to the extremes both of complacent plutocracy and radical agitation. Yet he brought to this abstract loyalty a shrewdness in practical politics, an ability to deal with other politicians, and a remarkably intuitive sense for the workings of the popular mind.

The Square Deal.   Roosevelt did not believe that the great corporations could be broken up, but he realized that the widespread unrest that corporate power had created must be taken seriously. In 1902, he made his first positive and dramatic move when he ordered Attorney-General Philander C. Knox to bring suit to dissolve the Northern Securities Company (see p. 578). The Northern Securities Case proved an excellent way of dramatizing the vigor of the new administration. The struggle between the Hill-Morgan and the Harriman-Kuhn, Loeb interests had become notorious, partly because of the financial panic it precipitated. And the Northern Securities Company itself had attracted a great deal of notice and a great deal of hostile criticism. Since it involved some of the greatest moneyed interests in the country, the announcement of the suit aroused speculation that Roosevelt was about to assault the mightiest of the financial giants. Indeed, Wall Street was alarmed as never before, and J. P. Morgan himself made an unprecedented trip

to Washington to find out if Roosevelt really intended to launch a general attack upon his interests.

The suit dragged on for almost two years. Then in 1904 the Supreme Court handed down a verdict that was greeted as a great triumph for the President and for the anti-trust principle. By a vote of 5 to 4, the Court ruled that the combination must be broken up. Although this success was only technical, the suit reversed a decision rendered nine years earlier in the case of *E. C. Knight* v. *The United States,* and opened the way to other prosecutions. Roosevelt hailed the result as "one of the great achievements of my administration. . . . The most powerful men in this country were held to accountability before the law." Later, Roosevelt ordered more prosecutions. One suit was brought against the "Beef Trust," a combination of packing companies, and others against Standard Oil and the American Tobacco Company. These actions dragged out for a long time in the courts and for the most part had rather indecisive results. They did not halt the wave of business consolidation, but they did keep alive the possibility that a particularly conspicuous or ruthless firm might find itself confronted with a costly prosecution. In 1903, in accordance with Roosevelt's strong belief in publicity and information, a Bureau of Corporations was set up in the new Department of Commerce and Labor. The Bureau was authorized to investigate the affairs of interstate corporations, and it provided valuable information on several industries that were in time made subject to prosecution.

Another display of Roosevelt's vigor and independence came in 1902 on the labor front. In May, a bitter strike by the United Mine Workers union under the leadership of John Mitchell broke out in the anthracite coal fields. The workers won public sympathy, partly because of the stubbornness of the mine-owners and partly because of the publication of an arrogant statement by George F. Baer, president of the Reading Railroad and spokesman of the mine-operators. Baer announced that the interests of the miners would be protected "not by the labor agitators but by the Christian men to whom God in His infinite wisdom, has given control of the property interests of the country."

As the strike carried on through the summer and early fall, however, it appeared that eastern cities would face serious coal shortages during the coming winter. Pressure for decisive action grew, and in October, President Roosevelt called Mitchell and the operators to a White House meeting. Mitchell agreed to arbitrate the dispute, but the operators declared that they would never come to terms with the U.M.W. Roosevelt then made secret plans to have the United States army take over the mines and operate them on behalf of the government. He also persuaded J. P. Morgan to try to get the operators to arbitrate before the impending seizure became necessary. The mine-operators agreed, on one condition: that no labor official could serve on the commission of arbitration. Here Roosevelt's sense of humor came to his rescue. He appointed a former president of one of the railroad unions to the commission as an "eminent sociologist." The mine-operators did not demur, and the commission went to work. Ultimately, the mine-workers won a nine-hour day, a 10 per cent wage increase, a permanent board of conciliation, and the right to select check-weighmen. It was the most decisive, the most impartial, and the most satisfactory intervention that had ever been undertaken by an American president in a labor dispute. It added greatly to Roosevelt's prestige, and strengthened the public's conviction that the White House was at last occupied by a man who could deal successfully, and in the public's interest, with the great masters of capital.

By 1904, when the time came to campaign for the presidency in his own right, Roosevelt had become more popular than ever. The only Republican who might have given him serious opposition, Senator Mark Hanna of Ohio, died in February of that year, and in June, Roosevelt was nominated without opposition by the Republican convention. The Democrats, after having failed twice with their radical leader, William Jennings Bryan, surrendered to the conservative wing of their party and nominated an obscure and colorless figure, Judge Alton B. Parker of New York, to oppose Roosevelt. Parker rested his campaign on the charge that Roosevelt had in effect blackmailed leading capitalists to contribute large sums to his support. Large sums had indeed been contributed by a number of capitalists—among them Harriman, Morgan, the Rockefeller interests, and some of the New York insurance companies—who evidently did not share the widespread feeling in Wall Street that Roosevelt was a dangerous man. But the money had not been exacted from these men by anything resembling blackmail, and the public was more impressed by Roosevelt's record and his vigorous campaign speeches than it was by Parker's charges. Roosevelt himself was worried enough by Parker's claims to instruct his campaign managers (to no effect) to return some of the large donations. Roosevelt was both pleased and surprised by the election results, for he received 7,623,000 votes to Parker's 5,077,000, one of the most smashing victories in the history of presidential campaigns.

President at last in his own right, Roosevelt continued to act with energy and confidence during his second term (1905-1909). During these four years, his major achievements involved railroad regulation, the protection of consumers, and the conservation of natural resources, a project close to his heart.

Railroad regulation held the spotlight in Roosevelt's second administration, much as anti-trust action had dominated his first. The Interstate Commerce Act (see p. 464) had proved a complete disappointment, partly because administrations since 1887 had neglected to make much use of it, but largely because the Supreme Court's narrow interpretation of the powers of the Commission rendered it almost helpless. In 1903, in response to pressure from the railroads themselves, Congress passed the Elkins Act, making it illegal for railroads to depart in practice from their published freight rates, and making shippers as well as railroads liable for punishment for infractions. This measure struck at the practice of rebating, which the railroads themselves had come to regard as a major nuisance. The Elkins Act, however, failed to give the Interstate Commerce Commission any power to fix rates, which was what farmers and businessmen wanted most.

In 1906, under Roosevelt's prodding, Congress passed the Hepburn Act, under which the first really effective regulation of railroads by the federal government began. This measure failed to go far enough to satisfy ardent reformers, but it did authorize the Commission, when a complaint was received, to set maximum rates and to order railroads to comply after 30 days. An amendment introduced by Senate conservatives authorized the district courts to issue suspensive injunctions against the I.C.C.'s decisions, but quick appeal was authorized to circuit courts and the Supreme Court, the only agencies that were empowered to reverse the Commission's rulings. These courts were also instructed to presume the Commission's rulings sound until evidence was massed to the contrary, thus throwing the burden of proof upon the railroads and their lawyers and reducing the chances of judicial setbacks for the Commission.

The Hepburn Act also extended the I.C.C.'s power to include regulation of storage, refrigeration, and terminal facilities, and sleeping-car, express, and pipe-line companies. (In 1910, the act was further extended to include telephone and telegraph companies.) The Commission was authorized to settle disputes between railroads and shippers and to impose a standardized accounting system upon all railroads. Strong Progressives like Senator La Follette were dissatisfied because the bill did not give the Commission power to evaluate the physical properties of the railroads and the actual cost of their services. Without such knowledge. it was impossible for the Commission

to set rates that were intrinsically reasonable. Few, however, denied that a forward step had been taken. Within two years, shippers made more than 9,000 appeals to the Commission, and a great many rates were revised downward.

Of less importance in the extension of governmental regulation over business was the passage of measures controlling foods and drugs. Investigations conducted by Dr. Harvey W. Wiley, a chemist in the Department of Agriculture, and other scientists, had shown that undesirable adulterants and preservatives were being widely used in canned foods. Dr. Wiley prevailed upon Roosevelt to recommend pure-food legislation in his annual message for 1905. The packing interests put up furious resistance against any interference with their long-standing right to prepare food free from supervision. Then in 1906 Upton Sinclair, the socialist muckraker, published his shocking novel, *The Jungle*, which described the revolting practices current in the Chicago stockyards. Public opinion was aroused by the book, the resistance of the food-packers was broken, and in June, 1906, a federal meat-inspection law was passed. Muckraking by Samuel Hopkins Adams exposed the dangers of patent medicines and their misleading and exaggerated advertisements. In 1906, Congress responded by enacting a Pure Food and Drugs Act to control such practices. This law did not give full protection to consumers, but it did strike at some of the worst abuses.

In approaching the problem of conservation of national resources, Roosevelt acted boldly and with originality. The American people had recklessly wasted their magnificent natural resources from the very earliest days of settlement. Over three-fourths of the original forest land, for instance, had been appropriated and carelessly exploited by private interests. Although some timber lands had been set aside under Harrison, Cleveland, and McKinley, exploitation of the forests was still going on at an alarming rate when Roosevelt took office.

An amateur naturalist and an outdoor man

with a taste for natural beauty, Roosevelt took an intelligent interest in the conservation problem from the start. In accordance with the Forest Reserve Act, passed in 1891, he set aside almost 150 million acres of unsold government timber land in various parts of the country as a forest reserve, and closed to public entry about 85 million additional acres in Alaska and the Northwest in order to give the United States Geological Survey a chance to study mineral and water resources in these areas. He turned over the supervision of the national forests to the Secretary of Agriculture, who put an able conservationist, Gifford Pinchot, in charge. In 1907, Roosevelt called federal and state officials and many private persons to a national conservation conference, which became a center from which a great deal of information about the conservation problem flowed out to the American public. A National Conservation Association was established to carry on with this work. All these activities checked some of the despoiling of the public domain, but waste went on at a rate far too great to be coped with by such measures. Little further progress was made in conservation until Franklin Delano Roosevelt came to office in 1933.

In the fall of 1907, a financial panic struck the country and darkened the last days of Roosevelt's administration. For several months, business was slack and unemployment was severe. Several railroads went bankrupt and 13 banking institutions in New York City were forced to close down. Roosevelt feared that his entire reputation as president might be spoiled if a long depression were to follow his departure from office. Industrialists and Wall Streeters had been trying to persuade him that the developing panic could be stemmed by permitting the United States Steel Corporation to acquire control of the Tennessee Iron and Coal Company. The securities of this firm were held by numerous brokerage houses, which in turn might fail if the securities were not underwritten. Roosevelt, frightened, gave his consent and by this action implied that United States Steel would be immune from anti-trust prosecution. How much this action had to do with turning the trick it is hard to say. Perhaps of greater importance was the work of Secretary of the Treasury George B. Cortelyou, who relieved the currency stringency by an emergency issue of Panama Canal bonds on terms both generous and reassuring to the bankers. In any event, the panic was stemmed and prosperity quickly returned.

The Panic of 1907 and Roosevelt's decision to check it had two important consequences for American politics: (1) Financial authorities began to search for ways of strengthening national finance, a search that led to the Aldrich-Vreeland Act of 1908, and the Federal Reserve Act of 1913 (see p. 599). (2) Groundwork was laid for the later breach between Roosevelt and Taft, for in 1911, when Roosevelt's successor launched upon a prosecution of the United States Steel Corporation, Roosevelt took it as a rebuke to his 1907 decision, and the gulf between Taft and Roosevelt widened.

The Taft Regime. At the end of his second term in 1908, Roosevelt bowed to the tradition that no president should seek a third term. The unchallenged leader of the Republican party, he chose his friend and Secretary of War, William Howard Taft, to succeed him. Taft, a member of a long-established and well-to-do Cincinnati family, had been a circuit-court judge, an unusually able Governor of the Philippines, and administrator of the Canal Zone before he joined Roosevelt's cabinet. The jovial Taft held the retiring president's confidence. Since the Democrats had fared far worse under a conservative candidate in 1904 than they ever had under Bryan, they returned once more to Bryan, the "Great Commoner." But the Progressive reforms made under Roosevelt had left Bryan without a vital issue. After a listless campaign, Taft was elected by a vote of 7,679,000 to 6,409,000.

Although Roosevelt and Taft had imagined

that their views were in harmony, Taft tended to be more conservative than his predecessor. He lacked Roosevelt's talent for dramatizing such sympathies as he had with Progressivism. Above all he was unwilling to tussle with the conservative Old Guard Republicans in the Senate, with whom Roosevelt had had to bargain for every Progressive measure. Though not by plan or design, the majority of the Republican party now began to drift back toward conservatism, while an active and able minority struck off on the road toward insurgency.

Taft, however, did not disappoint the Progressives at every turn. In his one administration, he instituted about twice as many prosecutions under the Sherman Act as Roosevelt had in two administrations. Such prosecutions as the Standard Oil and American Tobacco cases, begun under Roosevelt, were also carried to successful conclusions. Taft recommended, to no avail, that Congress act to end stock-watering, and to take other strong measures aimed at regulating corporations. Failing in these efforts, he began proceedings for the dissolution of 46 corporations under the Sherman Act. His two leading cases, against International Harvester and United States Steel, were failures, but many others succeeded.

In 1911, however, after the Supreme Court had ordered the dissolution of the oil and tobacco monopolies, the government accepted plans to re-establish the constituent companies. Shares in the new companies were distributed among stockholders in proportion to their previous ownership in the dissolved holding companies. Even though these arrangements caused the Progressives to doubt that the dissolutions were meaningful, the legal possibility of effective anti-trust prosecution was clearly established by the time Taft left office.

What Congress accomplished in the field of railroad regulation during the Taft administration was done less by the President and his supporters than by the Progressives in both parties. Despite the success of the Hepburn Act in dealing with specific rate complaints, nothing prevented railroads from making over-all rate increases. After 1908, the railroads issued so many legal challenges to the Interstate Commerce Commission that the dockets of the circuit courts quickly became overcrowded. As a remedy, the administration introduced a new bill, which became a battleground between Taft and the Progressives. As it was finally passed, the Mann-Elkins Act of 1910 represented a victory for the Republican insurgents. The act empowered the Commission to suspend general rate increases, and to take the initiative in revising rates. A Com-

William Jennings Bryan, a fabulous campaigner and a powerful influence on American Progressivism.

merce Court was established to speed up the judicial process by hearing appeals directly from the Commission. All these terms were substantially in line with Taft's desires. But the insurgents also pushed through a provision forbidding railroads from acquiring competing lines, and added another that put telephone, telegraph, cable, and wireless companies under the Commission's control. Further, the physical evaluation of railroad property as a basis for rate-making, which was considered vital by the Progressives, and which they had not been able to get into the 1910 bill, was enacted in 1913 during the last months of the Taft administration. The Physical Evaluation Act required the I.C.C. to assess the value of all property owned by every company under its jurisdiction, and specified the manner in which this assessment was to be made. Such valuations were to be taken as prima-facie evidence of the value of the property. Now the Commission could fix rates not on the basis of watered stock, but on the true value of operating properties.

The Sixteenth Amendment, which set up a federal income tax, and the Seventeenth Amendment, which provided for the direct election of United States senators, were both passed during Taft's administration. Both were ratified by the states in 1913. During Taft's term, Congress also created a postal savings bank and a parcel post service, set up a Department of Labor (by dividing the Department of Commerce and Labor instituted by Roosevelt), and established a Federal Children's Bureau. New Mexico and Arizona, two territories with Progressive leanings, were admitted as states.

Except for his anti-trust policies, however, President Taft was not closely identified with the Progressive measures that were adopted in his administration. The first policy over which he disappointed the Progressives was the tariff. Tariff revision had been one of the unresolved problems of the Roosevelt administrations, and the Republicans had promised action on it in their platform of 1908. Taft called Congress into special session in March, 1909, to take up the matter, but proposals for downward revision met with strong opposition from the spokesmen of special interests in the Senate. Senator Nelson Aldrich and his colleagues set about reworking the measure that had been introduced into the House, and the final bill not only failed to reduce duties but actually raised them slightly. At this point, a group of Republican insurgents— La Follette of Wisconsin, Dolliver and Cummins of Iowa, Beveridge of Indiana, Clapp of Minnesota, and Bristow of Kansas—rallied to fight against this betrayal of the party's campaign pledge. But the Payne-Aldrich Tariff passed with only slight concessions to the insurgents. Taft offended them not only by signing the bill, but also by referring to it in a speech in Winona, Minnesota, as the best tariff the Republican party had ever passed.

Taft also outraged the Progressives by helping to quash a rebellion of insurgent Republicans against the iron rule of the Speaker of the House, "Uncle Joe" Cannon. Many Democrats joined the Republicans in a move to replace Cannon. But the Speaker successfully appealed to Taft, and Taft's support, together with the defection of many of the Democrats, temporarily saved Cannon's hide. Early in 1910, however, a determined thrust led by George W. Norris of Nebraska resulted in Cannon's removal from the rules committee, which meant that he no longer had power to appoint members of standing committees. Although Taft did not object to Cannon's defeat, neither did he give the insurgents any word of encouragement. Thus he lost a chance to mollify them.

Republican unity, already shaky, really began to break down during the excitement over the Pinchot-Ballinger affair. The trouble began when the Chief Forester of the Department of Agriculture, Gifford Pinchot, heard from Louis Glavis, an investigator for the Interior Department, that Secretary of the Interior Richard A. Ballinger had agreed to let the Guggenheim interests have reserved coal lands in Alaska. Pinchot encouraged Glavis to appeal to Taft and himself issued a statement denouncing Ballinger. Taft chose to believe Ballinger's denials rather than Glavis and authorized Glavis' dismissal from the Department of the Interior. Pinchot carried on with the attack until he, too, was removed. Congress investigated the Interior Department and, though Ballinger was not found guilty of misconduct, he showed under the sharp questioning of Louis D. Brandeis, that he had no interest in conservation policies. Taft did believe in conservation, and through executive action he had continued and extended Roosevelt's policies on oil and coal lands. But after his support of Ballinger and his rejection of Pinchot, it was easy to persuade people that he was against conservation.

This series of minor disagreements and major misunderstandings between Taft and the insurgents broke into open warfare after March, 1910, when Taft began to use presidential patronage to build up conservative Republicanism in the Midwest. The congressional elections of that year showed clearly that the party could not afford to lose Progressive support in the country. The House of Representatives went Democratic for the first time since 1893, and many Democratic governors were elected. After a long spell out of power, it seemed that the Democrats would have an excellent chance to recapture the presidency in 1912, and also that the insurgents might capture the Republican party and repudiate Taft.

The Insurgent Challenge. The most obvious man to lead the Republican insurgents was Senator Robert M. La Follette of Wisconsin. La Follette was no Johnny-come-lately to the Progressive cause, nor was he a mere speech-maker or agitator. He had been active in Republican politics since 1880 and had been working for Progressive measures for many years. After three terms in Congress, he had served four years as Governor of Wisconsin, where he built up a

clean and stable Progressive political machine and enacted such Progressive measures as tax reform, railroad control, and direct primaries. He was probably the first political leader in American history to make extensive use of what has come to be called a "brain trust." A graduate of the University of Wisconsin, La Follette had built his first political successes upon the loyalty of old school friends. Later, many members of the liberal-minded faculty of the University of Wisconsin provided him with advice and information. In Washington, he made careful research into economic and social problems before he formulated legislative proposals. His speeches were well delivered and crammed with facts and statistics. He had been prominent in the insurgent revolts in Congress and commanded admiration throughout the country. Some of the most ardent Progressives wanted to put him forward as a presidential candidate to challenge Taft, but others, feeling that he could not be nominated or elected, preferred Roosevelt.

Roosevelt himself proceeded cautiously. At the beginning of Taft's administration, he had gone off on a hunting trip to Africa, presumably a gracious gesture to remove himself from the scene. After a triumphal tour through Europe, he returned to New York in 1910, where he was greeted enthusiastically. He had been watching the Taft administration from a distance and had become increasingly displeased with the way things were going. Taft's conduct in the Ballinger affair dismayed him, and he was personally offended by Taft's prosecution of United States Steel. But most disturbing was his feeling that he had bequeathed a strong party to his successor and that it had been allowed to go to pieces.

At first, Roosevelt refrained from making any move that would publicize his estrangement from Taft. But on August 31, 1910, he delivered a famous address at Osawatomie, Kansas, in which he came out for a number of Progressive, anti-administration reforms. His espousal of the popular recall of state-court decisions that nullified social legislation, and his accusation that the federal judiciary was obstructing the popular will, shocked conservatives throughout the nation. Nonetheless, Roosevelt did not openly announce his candidacy for a third term, and Senator La Follette felt—though he was never able to prove it—that Roosevelt had promised to support him. Roosevelt himself seems to have believed that 1912 would be a Democratic year, and that he might well wait until 1916 to lead a rejuvenated Republican party to victory. However, on February 2, 1912, Senator La Follette, tired, ill, and troubled by the serious illness of one of his daughters, collapsed while delivering a major speech. The many Progressive Republicans who had been waiting to switch to the more formidable Roosevelt took this as an occasion to desert La Follette. In February, 1912, at Roosevelt's instigation, seven Republican governors publicly wrote the ex-President, urging him to announce his candidacy. Less than two weeks later he asserted, "My hat is in the ring."

A savage fight followed. La Follette's support dwindled to a small group of die-hards, and Roosevelt and Taft were left to struggle for the Republican party's nomination. When the party met at Chicago in June, there was an angry contest over 254 delegates' seats. After the Taft supporters had appropriated almost all the contested seats, Roosevelt's delegates refused to carry on and finally stormed out of the convention hall.

Renominated on the first ballot by an overwhelming majority, Taft was left in possession of a broken party.

Roosevelt's "Bull Moose" followers, so named from Roosevelt's statement that he felt "fit as a Bull Moose," hastily organized and met in convention, again at Chicago, with an enthusiasm that has probably never been equaled by the delegates of any party. William Allen White, the Kansas journalist and one of the bolters, described his own and the crowd's frenzy by saying, "Roosevelt bit me and I went mad." The convention bellowed with enthusiasm when Roosevelt shouted "We stand at Armageddon and we battle for the Lord." The delegates paraded around the hall singing "Onward Christian Soldiers" and adopted a platform calling for the adoption of almost all the long-proposed social reforms: the initiative, referendum, and recall, the recall of judicial decisions, workmen's compensation and social insurance, minimum wages for women, women's suffrage, child-labor legislation, and federal trade and tariff commissions to regulate business.

In the meantime, the Democrats, heartened by the Republican split, had been going through a party battle of their own. Bryan, still a great power in Democratic ranks, had announced that he would not run again.

Young Robert M. La Follette brings his message to the people at Cumberland, Wisconsin, during his campaign for governor in 1897.

Among the leading aspirants for the nomination were Woodrow Wilson, the Progressive Democratic Governor of New Jersey and a relative newcomer to party politics; Champ Clark of Missouri, Speaker of the House of Representatives and a political veteran; and Oscar W. Underwood of Alabama, a tariff reformer and the leading southern spokes-man. Clark led in the early balloting, and for a time the Wilson forces despaired. Finally, Illinois and then the Underwood forces switched to Wilson, and the New Jersey Governor won on the 46th ballot. The Democratic platform, though neither so comprehensive nor so advanced as the Bull Moose platform, also called for a variety of reforms; it was particularly outspoken in demanding business and tariff reform.

IV.   DEMOCRATIC PROGRESSIVISM

Woodrow Wilson and Progressivism.   Although they could hardly have known it when they nominated Wilson, the Democrats had chosen a man who was to become a figure of world-wide importance. Wilson, born in Virginia in 1856, was 55 at the time of his nomination. Having lived almost all his early years in the South, and having been in his mature life a student of English ideas and English statecraft, Wilson combined a flair for politics and a respect for high statesmanship. He had been educated for law, but finding practice in Atlanta, Georgia, distasteful, he turned to academic life. He attended graduate school at The Johns Hopkins University during its great early days, wrote a distinguished book on congressional government, and took his Ph.D. in 1886. After some years of teaching and writing in political science and history, an experience that left his aspirations for great achievements still unsatisfied, Wilson became president of Princeton University in 1902. There he attracted attention by criticizing the expensive and aristocratic eating clubs, which he proposed to replace with a form of student organization closer to the Oxford-Cambridge pattern. Although he failed to realize all his reforms at Princeton, which were educational rather than democratic in inspiration, his efforts made him conspicuous as a "democratic" spokesman at a time when people were looking for vigorous leaders. In 1910, the Democratic bosses of New Jersey, seeking a candidate who would give them a respectable front, offered Wilson the nomination for governor. Once elected, Wilson surprised the bosses by repudiating their backing and by espousing a variety of reforms that brought him ardent support from New Jersey Progressives. During the first legislative session of his term, he won a primary and elections law, a corrupt practices act, workmen's compensation, utilities regulation, school reforms, and an enabling act giving New Jersey cities the right to adopt the commission form of government (see p. 582).

As a person, Wilson was a bundle of paradoxes. Outwardly cold and forbidding, he was in fact extraordinarily intense. His great reputation in domestic politics was based upon his achievements as a reformer, yet his ideas displayed a deep sense of tradition and great reverence for the past. He was an innovator who sought to restore a social order that had long been dead, a southerner raised on southern and English doctrines of laissez faire who lived to advance the welfare state, a man of essentially aristocratic temperament who became a spokesman of world democracy.

That Wilson should have been successful in politics is indeed remarkable, for though he had personal and intellectual distinction, he lacked the equally necessary practical qualities. He was an excellent speaker, with a remarkable ability to sense the needs and express the demands of large segments of the American public. His speeches were rhythmic (someone once said that you could waltz to them), clear, and dignified. He was an impressive if not an electrifying campaigner. But offstage he was ill-suited to the give and take of American politics. His intense personality expressed itself largely in terms of ideals and principles, not in personal loyalties. He was too rigid to be compromising. ("Government," he wrote during his earlier days, "is too serious a matter to admit of meaningless courtesies.") To continue to be so high-principled and yet to engage in practical politics meant that Wilson had to deceive himself continually, a self-deception that some of his critics have mistaken for hypocrisy. He was too concerned with general principles and ideals to be patient with the practical details of politics or protocol. As president, he left patronage to his Postmaster-General and made the elementary political mistake of taking no senator to the peace-making at Paris (see p. 621). Like Roosevelt, Wilson's basic political goals were the goals of moderation. Like Roosevelt, he disliked the selfish plutocracy and distrusted the radicals and agitators of the extreme left. He felt at home with the moderate reformism of the American middle classes and understood with particular poignancy the feelings of the small entrepreneurs, who found themselves edged aside in the world of great corporations.

Wilson's greatest asset in the 1912 campaign was the split in the Republican party. The three-cornered contest soon narrowed

down to a struggle between Wilson and Roosevelt. Since both Roosevelt and Wilson campaigned as Progressives, a large part of the campaign turned upon the trust issue, the one point on which they seemed clearly to disagree. As Louis D. Brandeis put it, the issue was between regulated competition (Wilson's position) and regulated monopoly (Roosevelt's). Wilson asserted that the great business combinations were too powerful to be regulated, that they would instead control the very government that tried to impose regulations upon them. He pointed to the presence of such big-businessmen as the millionaire, Frank Munsey, and the Morgan partner, George W. Perkins, among Roosevelt's financial backers as evidence that the Progressive party's position on the trusts was acceptable to the organizers of trusts. The only possible line of action, Wilson insisted, was to restore true competition to business and for the government to take vigorous action to suppress unfair and illicit competition.

Roosevelt countered with the claim that Wilson's conception of economic life was archaic. To restore competition as it had once existed in America would be undesirable, for it would deprive the country of the advantages and economies of large-scale organization. Further, it would be impossible, for it would be an attempt to reverse the natural processes of economic evolution. What was needed was a thorough and consistent attempt to distinguish between good businesses and bad and to subject businesses guilty of unfair practices to public exposure and to regulation for the best interests of the country.

Probably not many voters followed all these arguments. Instead, they voted in 1912 in accordance with their traditional allegiance, their preference for personalities, or on other issues. Wilson, with 6,293,000 votes, or slightly less than 42 per cent of the whole electorate, swept most of the states and held an overwhelming majority in the electoral college. Roosevelt, with 4,119,000

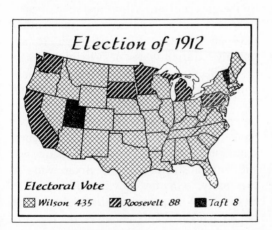

Election of 1912

Electoral Vote

⊠ Wilson 435   ▨ Roosevelt 88   ▣ Taft 8

votes, carried only six scattered states; Taft, with 3,484,000, carried only Vermont and Utah. The Democrats captured the House and won a working majority in the Senate. Thus, when Wilson took office in 1913, promising a "reinterpretation of democracy," it was with excellent prospects for a constructive administration, for he had a united party to work with and a large bloc of Progressive Republicans to support Progressive measures.

The New Freedom.   The years of Wilson's two administrations, 1913-1921, were extraordinarily fruitful in significant reform legislation. First on the docket was the tariff, a long-postponed reform over which Wilson called a special session of Congress. A bill sponsored by Representative Oscar Underwood proposed to cut the Payne-Aldrich Tariff, which, on the average, levied duties of 37-40 per cent, down to about 29 per cent, a modest but constructive downward revision in line with Democratic platform promises. The bill passed the House, but in the Senate it ran into the usual combination of special interests. For a time it seemed about to go the way of preceding efforts at reform. Then Wilson took an unusual step. One May 26 he issued a public statement denouncing the lobbyists working to defeat the bill—the "great bodies of astute men [who] seek to create an artificial opinion and to overcome the interests of the public for their private profit." His appeal sounded the signal for a general attack on lobbyists and made it easier for the measure to pass. Senator La Follette and other Progressives undertook an inquiry into lobbying and ingeniously forced senators to reveal whether or not they had any property themselves that might be affected by the tariff. Passed in September, 1913, the Underwood Tariff effected the first satisfactory downward revision since the Civil War. In addition to reducing general levels, it put several items on the free list. The bill also included an income tax, which was intended to supply the revenue lost through tariff reduction. A tax of 1 per cent was levied on incomes of over $4,000, and an additional graduated surtax ranging from 1 to 6 per cent was levied on higher incomes.

Financial reform was next in line. The need for banking reform was recognized by both conservatives and reformers; American financial resources were insufficiently mobile, American credit too inelastic. The brief Panic of 1907 (see p. 591) had resulted in the Aldrich-Vreeland Act of 1908, which allowed banks to issue emergency currency against state and municipal securities and commercial paper; but both sides deemed this measure unsatisfactory. A commission under the chairmanship of Senator Aldrich had reported in favor of establishing a great central bank with branches dominated by the leading banking interests. The Democrats denounced this proposal in their 1912 platform, but they agreed with the commission's judgment that there were many defects in the banking system, including "an unhealthy congestion of loanable funds in great centers" and an undesirable "concentration of surplus money and available funds in New York."

Beyond this agreement, the Democrats were themselves divided. The more conservative among them wanted a decentralized reserve system, free from Wall Street but still owned and run by private interests. Bryan's supporters wanted a reserve system and a currency supply owned and controlled by the government. Wilson had to step carefully to get a bill written that would have any chance of being passed. Representative Carter Glass of Virginia brought in a bill that proposed 20 reserve banks under private control but without central direction. Wilson insisted on providing for a central governing board on which bankers would have only minority representation. But this modified measure was still not satisfactory to the Bryan wing of the party. On the advice of Louis D. Brandeis, Wilson agreed that there should be no banking representatives on the pro-

President-elect Wilson and President Taft at Wilson's inauguration. Taft is obviously pleased to be free of presidential duties, and the cares of office have not yet fallen upon Wilson.

posed Federal Reserve Board and that all notes of issue should be obligations of the federal government. Short-term credit facilities for farmers were also provided to meet the demands of the agrarian critics of the bill.

As it was finally passed, then, the Federal Reserve Act of December 23, 1913, set up 12 regional banking districts, each with a Federal Reserve Bank. The Federal Reserve Banks were owned by the member banks of the Federal Reserve System. Member banks were required to subscribe 6 per cent of their capital to the Federal Reserve Bank. The regional banks of the system did not engage directly in banking; instead, they acted as the agents and servants of the member banks. The system was placed under the direction of the Federal Reserve Board, consisting of the Secretary of the Treasury, the Comptroller, and six other persons appointed by the president. A new currency was created: Federal Reserve notes, issued by the Reserve Banks to member banks and secured by commercial and agricultural paper and a 40 per cent gold reserve. Since it would vary somewhat in proportion to outstanding commercial transactions, this currency was intended to be flexible. All national banks were required to join the system, and state banks also were eligible to join. By 1923, the

Federal Reserve System embraced 70 per cent of the banking resources of the country.

In the end, even the bankers who had opposed it with the Bryan modifications had to admit the value of the Federal Reserve System. It created a currency that was both flexible and sound. It established a system by which the excessive concentration of reserves in a few financial centers was rendered mobile. It left banking a private business, but under central governmental direction.

As amended by the agrarians, the Federal Reserve Act was also supposed to improve agricultural credit facilities. But this provision was not properly carried out. In May, 1916, however, the Federal Farm Loan Act was passed, creating a Federal Farm Loan Board and 12 regional Farm Loan banks patterned after the Federal Reserve System. The banks were authorized to lend sums to cooperative farm loan associations, on the security of farm lands, buildings, and improvements, up to 70 per cent of the value of these assets. Loans were to be on a long-range basis, interest was not to be more than 6 per cent, and profits were to be distributed to the members of the subscribing farm-loan associations. Within 14 years, over 4,000 farm-loan associations had been established, and over $1 billion in farm mortgages was outstanding. In 1916, another bill was passed for the benefit of farmers—the Warehouse Act—which authorized licensed warehouse operators to issue warehouse receipts against farm products deposited with them. Farmers could use these warehouse receipts as negotiable paper. This measure embodied the essential features of the sub-treasury scheme proposed by the Populists in 1892 (see p. 500).

After the Federal Reserve Act was passed, Wilson went on to fulfill his promise to provide anti-trust legislation. By the fall of 1914, Congress had passed two measures to extend the regulation of business. The Federal Trade Commission Act, passed in September, was intended to prevent rather than punish unfair trade practices. It created a new commission of five men to replace Roosevelt's Bureau of Corporations (see p. 588). The measure outlawed, but did not try to define, "unfair" trade practices. The Federal Trade Commission was authorized to investigate corporations engaged in interstate commerce, to look into alleged violations of anti-trust laws, and to issue "cease and desist" orders against corporations found guilty of unfair competitive methods. If that recourse failed, the Commission could bring the accused corporations to trial. During Wilson's administration, 379 cease and desist orders were issued, and a few dissolutions of trusts were initiated in cooperation with the Department of Justice. Even so, Progressives felt that the Commission was not using its powers vigorously enough, and the Republican administrations of the 1920's found ways of turning it into an instrument of business consolidation.

The second anti-trust law requested by Wilson was the Clayton Act, passed in October, 1914, which was supposed to supply the legal basis for vigorous anti-trust action. It prohibited a number of business practices: price discrimination that might lessen competition or create monopoly; tying contracts —that is, contracts that forced purchasers to refrain from buying the products of competitors: the acquisition by corporations of stock in competing concerns; and the creation of interlocking directorates in corporations and banks over a specified size as measured by capitalization. Officers of corporations were made liable for prosecution if they violated these provisions. Labor unions as such were not to be construed as illegal combinations or conspiracies in restraint of trade, and labor injunctions were forbidden except when necessary to prevent "irreparable injury to property, or to a property right." But the Clayton Act was passed on the eve of war, and during wartime, anti-trust action was of necessity greatly curtailed. During the conservative regimes of the 1920's, moreover, a series of Supreme Court decisions nullified the provisions of the act that had been intended to protect labor unions.

A few other measures completed the legislative accomplishment of the Wilson administrations. The La Follette Seamen's Act, passed in March, 1915, without Wilson's sponsorship, raised the safety requirements on American ships and, by abolishing the crime of desertion, released American merchant seamen from bondage to labor contracts upon their return to American ports. The Smith-Lever Act of 1914 provided millions of dollars for home-demonstration work for farmers throughout the country and later made a significant contribution to American agricultural progress. The Smith-Hughes Act of 1917 subsidized vocational and agricultural education and finally rounded out the program that had been begun during the Civil War with the land-grant colleges. A workman's compensation act was extended to federal employees, and the Adamson Act of 1916 established an eight-hour day for workers on all interstate railways. The Revenue Act of 1916 included provision for a tariff commission. The Keating-Owen Child Labor Act (see p. 584) was passed the same year. Finally, Wilson pleased Progressives throughout the nation when he appointed the distinguished liberal lawyer, Louis D. Brandeis, to the Supreme Court on January 28, 1916.

It is hard to tell exactly what effect the New Freedom would have had upon the economic and social life of the nation had it been continued. But certain things are clear: (1) the New Freedom represented the climax of the Progressive movement; (2) Wilson felt that his promises had been substantially fulfilled; and (3) the movement toward reform had come to a halt. Even as early as December, 1914, Wilson had pronounced the program of business regulation "complete" with the passage of the Clayton Act, and had promised businessmen that "the

road to ungrudged, unclouded success" at last lay open. When Wilson entered the presidential campaign of 1916, he could point to a substantial record of legislative achievement. The legislative program of the New Freedom, however, was largely nullified by administrative negligence, by wartime conditions, and at length by the conservative reaction during the 1920's.

Readings

In his *Farewell to Reform* (1932), John Chamberlain interprets Progressivism from the standpoint of the depression era. Interpretive works written from the standpoint of the 1950's are Eric Goldman, *Rendezvous with Destiny* (1952), and Richard Hofstadter, *The Age of Reform* (1955). Louis Filler, *Crusaders for American Liberalism* (1939), deals with muckraking and other critical thought; and C. C. Regier, *The Era of the Muckrakers* (1932), is still useful. Harold U. Faulkner surveys the period briefly in *The Quest for Social Justice, 1898-1914* (1931).

Among writings of contemporaries, Herbert Croly's *The Promise of American Life* (1909); Walter Weyl, *The New Democracy* (1912); and Walter Lippmann, *Drift and Mastery* (1914), are all important and provocative. Frederick Lewis Allen, *The Lords of Creation* (1935), deals with businessmen in this era; and Lincoln Steffens, *The Shame of the Cities* (1904), is a representative and influential muckraking work. Such novels as Brand Whitlock, *The Thirteenth District* (1902); Theodore Dreiser's *The Financier* (1912), and *The Titan* (1914); and the various novels of Winston Churchill (the American writer, not to be confused with his more famous British namesake) reveal a great deal about the spirit of Progressivism. *The Autobiography of Lincoln Steffens* (2 vols., 1931), and *The Autobiography of William Allen White* (1946), are absorbing.

The autobiographies of both Theodore Roosevelt and Robert M. La Follette are well worth reading. H. F. Pringle's *Theodore Roosevelt* (1931) remains the best biography of its subject; it can be profitably supplemented with George Mowry, *Theodore Roosevelt and the Progressive Movement* (1947). A fascinating source is *The Letters of Theodore Roosevelt* (8 vols., 1951-1954), edited by Elting Morison, and others. For a keen analysis of Roosevelt's presidency, see J. M. Blum, *The Republican Roosevelt* (1954). The standard biography of Taft is Henry Pringle's (2 vols., 1939), while La Follette's story is well told by Belle Case and Fola La Follette (2 vols., 1953).

The first volume of Arthur Link's biography-in-process of Woodrow Wilson, *The Road to the White House* (1947), is an excellent study of Wilson's career up to 1912. The second volume of this major work, *Wilson, The New Freedom* (1956), covers the period from Wilson's election to November, 1914, and carefully analyzes the legislation of the New Freedom. These two volumes may be supplemented by the same author's *Woodrow Wilson and the Progressive Era* (1954). Wilson's book, *The New Freedom* (1913), is a brilliant expression of Progressive ideals. Wilson is analyzed briefly and skillfully in two recent books: J. M. Blum, *Woodrow Wilson and the Politics of Morality* (1956), and John A. Garraty, *Woodrow Wilson* (1956). See also A. T. Mason, *Brandeis* (1946).

A number of special works are helpful. Among these, Harold U. Faulkner, *The Decline of Laissez Faire, 1897-1915* (1951), is good on economic changes. George E. Mowry, *The California Progressives* (1951), is an excellent study. Among biographies, P. C. Jessup, *Elihu Root* (2 vols., 1938), deals with a counselor of Roosevelt; John A. Garraty, *Henry Cabot Lodge* (1953), with one of Roosevelt's friends. Claude Bowers, *Beveridge and the Progressive Era* (1932), is good on the Senate Progressives; N. W. Stephenson's *Nelson W. Aldrich* (1930), on the conservatives.

THE FIRST WORLD WAR

C H A P T E R   T W E N T Y - S I X

"It would be the irony of fate if my administration had to deal chiefly with foreign affairs," said Woodrow Wilson before he left New Jersey to go to Washington. His remark proved prophetic. Before his election in 1912, he had been chiefly concerned with the domestic problems of the nation. He neither expected nor desired to become involved in international affairs and could

hardly anticipate that the greater part of his administration would be concerned with a world war. Yet he had hardly taken office before he was faced with a problem in United States-Mexican relations more serious than any since the Cuban crisis of 1897-1898. In some respects his conduct in the Mexican crisis foreshadowed the attitudes he took toward the First World War.

602

I. MEXICO AND MORAL DIPLOMACY

For some time, Mexico had been in a state of revolution. In May, 1911, President Porfirio Diaz, a dictator who had ruled the country for a third of a century by strength of arms, was overthrown by a coalition of revolutionaries, led by the liberal idealist, Francisco Madero. Peons who hoped to gain ownership of their lands, Mexican patriots who resented the privileges enjoyed by foreign investors in their country, and middle-class Constitutionalists who hoped to establish a free and lawful regime for their people, had united to depose Diaz. But they were unable to organize a new regime rapidly and securely enough to protect themselves from counterrevolution.

In February, 1913, General Victoriano Huerta, head of the Mexican army, organized a successful counterrevolution and coldly arranged the murder of Madero. Shocked by the assassination, Wilson refused to recognize Huerta's new regime, a stand which encouraged the revolutionary forces that seethed in Mexico. Wilson adopted a policy of "watchful waiting," hoping that Huerta would fall as Diaz had fallen. But most European governments recognized the new regime. Moreover, American business interests that had invested perhaps as much as a billion dollars in Mexican mines, oil fields, smelting plants, railroads, and rubber plantations, urged Wilson to change his policy. The President refused on the ground that the Mexican regime was not a free government resting on law and the consent of the governed. "We can have no sympathy," he said, "for those who seek to seize the power of government to advance their own personal interests or ambition."

In effect, Wilson declared that his policy was to refuse recognition to any government whose moral course and internal constitution the American government did not approve. This was a highly moral position, but it was attended by serious practical difficul-

ties. It threw upon the United States the dubious responsibility of deciding whether or not a foreign government was a moral one. There was always the danger, when an "immoral" foreign regime survived, that the United States would either lose prestige by being forced to retreat from its non-recognition policy or would have to intervene actively to uphold that policy, even at the risk of war.

Wilson therefore found himself driven to intervene in Mexican affairs and to increase the risk that American military forces would have to be used to support his policy. He was able to persuade the British government, which had a strong interest in Mexican oil, to withdraw support from Huerta in return for a rash American promise to protect British concessions in Mexico. He also offered support to the dissident Constitutionalist troops in Mexico, led by Venustiano Carranza. But here he was rebuffed, for even Carranza's followers did not want to be identified with unpopular American influence. Nonetheless, in February, 1914, Wilson revoked an embargo on arms to Mexico that had been established by President Taft, hoping that this move would help the Constitutionalists get the weapons they needed to overthrow Huerta. When Huerta's regime withstood the challenge, Wilson found himself unable to redeem the pledge he had made to Mexico and to the world that he would guarantee constitutional government in that country.

On April 9, 1914, an incident occurred that gave Wilson an excuse for forceful American intervention. The paymaster and crew of an American vessel, the *U.S.S. Dolphin,* were arrested by a colonel in Huerta's forces for landing their whaleboat behind Mexican lines at Tampico without authorization. Although the Americans were promptly released by a superior officer, who apologized, Admiral Henry T. Mayo, commander of an American squadron, demanded a more elaborate apology in the form of a 20-gun salute to the American flag. Wilson supported Mayo, but Huerta taunted Wilson by asking, in effect, how a government whose existence was not even recognized could be called upon to apologize. Huerta further demanded that the Americans give a 20-gun salute to the Mexican flag. Wilson regarded Huerta's reply as an insult to the nation's dignity and asked Congress for authority to use armed forces to obtain redress.

While Congress debated the President's request, news reached Washington that a German steamer was about to arrive at Vera Cruz with a load of ammunition for the Huerta government. Without waiting for congressional approval, Wilson ordered the navy to occupy Vera Cruz, and a landing was carried out by American marines with only moderate losses on April 21. Wilson wanted only to prevent the arrival of supplies that would be used against American forces if hostilities broke out. But to the Mexicans and to the world at large, his action appeared to be a heavy reprisal for a trifling incident. After this action, his idealistic language and his declarations on behalf of peace seemed hypocritical. Even Carranza and his followers resented the landing, threatened war, and demanded an immediate evacuation of Vera Cruz. Wilson had hoped to seize Vera Cruz and blockade the Mexican coasts without risking a general war. Now it seemed that he might have to fight both the Constitutionalists and the supporters of Huerta.

At this critical point, the "A.B.C." powers —Argentina, Brazil and Chile—stepped in and offered to mediate the dispute. Wilson seized upon this opportunity to escape from the difficulties of the situation, and in May, 1914, the United States and the "A.B.C." powers met at Niagara Falls to try to work out a settlement. The new constitutional government for Mexico that the members of this conference proposed was unacceptable to Huerta; but, unable to secure arms or credit from European nations, who were strengthening their own armed forces, his regime collapsed. In August, 1914, Carranza took over the presidency, and in October, 1915, the United States gave the new Carranza government *de facto* recognition. During the next six years, Mexico, divided between Carranza's government and new rebel forces under Pancho Villa, remained a land of disturbance and disorder. In March, 1916, General John Pershing was sent across the Rio Grande to pursue Villa, who had made repeated raids across the border into American territory. Only in March, 1917, when Pershing's expedition was withdrawn and the Carranza regime was finally given legal recognition by the United States, did the difficulties arising from Mexican-American skirmishes and from the presence of American troops on Mexican soil come to an end.

Wilson had come perilously close to provoking an unwanted war, but his Mexican policy had not been a complete failure. He had in the end succeeded in fending off European powers that would have supported Huerta and in contributing to the downfall of a dictatorial regime. But his Mexican experience showed that a president, even with the best intentions toward a foreign people, might through his very idealism become involved in embarrassing difficulties and arouse the suspicions of the very people he meant to help. The diplomacy of the European war repeated this lesson on a grander scale. Here Wilson faced a problem far more difficult, achieved something perhaps more noteworthy, but finally met tragic defeat.

II. THE ROAD TO WAR

War and Propaganda. The outbreak of World War I in the summer of 1914 surprised the American public. But years of economic rivalry, armament races, balance-of-power politics, and nationalistic outbursts had provoked a series of crises that threatened to involve the Continent in a general war and had left Europe, in 1914, divided between two sets of nervous allies: the Triple Alliance, comprising Germany, Austria-Hungary, and Italy; and the Triple Entente, comprising France, Russia, and Great Britain.

On June 28, 1914, the Archduke Franz Ferdinand, heir to the Austro-Hungarian throne, was shot by an assassin at Sarajevo in the province of Bosnia. Austria, aroused by the chronic agitations of the Slavic peoples, claimed that the Serbian government had known of the impending assassination and had done little to prevent it. The Austrian government presented the Serbian government with a series of exorbitant demands that actually involved a surrender of inde-

pendence. When Serbia refused to meet one of these demands, Austria, assured of the diplomatic backing of her German ally, declared war. Russia, the leader of the Slavic world, was convinced that she could not afford to stand by while Serbia was crushed. She began to mobilize her armies, a signal to all the war offices of Europe that a general conflict was about to begin. Germany, determined to move more rapidly than the enemies that stood on either side of her, and knowing that the French and Russians were bound by an alliance, declared war on Russia and then on France in the opening days of August.

Europe in 1914

The Balkans on the Eve of World War I

It had long been the plan of Germany's military leaders, in the event of a general war, to move first against France, in the hope that France could be struck down quickly while Russia was still mobilizing her vast but unwieldy armies. Although bound by treaty to respect the neutrality of Belgium, the Germans struck at France through Belgium in an attempt to outflank the French armies. When Belgium was invaded, England declared war against Germany. A general war had begun in full and terrible force, and the old Europe that had maintained a precarious balance among the major powers since the end of the Franco-Prussian War (1871) now seemed bent on its own destruction.

Although the United States had occupied a place of some prominence in world affairs since the Spanish-American War, it was still a provincial nation in 1914, poorly informed about the transactions of Europe's chancelleries. Americans were surprised by the coming of the war, and, even more, relieved not to be involved. "Our isolated position and

freedom from entangling alliances," said the *Literary Digest,* "inspire our press with the cheering assurance that we are in no peril of being drawn into the European quarrel." But to wish to remain at peace was not the same as to feel completely neutral toward the war. Although President Wilson appealed to the people in the early days of the war to be "impartial in thought as well as in action," even he was far from neutral. Moreover, there were in the United States over 32 million people who were foreign-born, or the children of one or two foreign-born parents. More than 8 million Americans might have some sentimental attachment to Germany, and there were more than 4,500,000 whose Irish loyalties pitted them against the British cause. Millions had other loyalties that disposed them to favor other belligerents.

But most of the people sympathized with Great Britain, France, and their allies. Since the turn of the century, Anglo-American relations had been consistently friendly. Ties of language and literature bound the cultivated classes of both countries; bonds of trade and finance united parts of their business communities. For France there was a widespread, though somewhat vague, sentimental enthusiasm that dated back to the days of Lafayette. For "poor little Belgium" there was of course great sympathy. Germany, on the other hand, had been regarded with suspicion by many Americans at least since the accession of Kaiser Wilhelm II in 1888, who was given to grandiose and alarming pronouncements about Germany's imperial ambitions. The martyrdom of Belgium only confirmed a widespread idea that the German government was ruthless and unprincipled. So, despite self-congratulatory newspaper editorials that expressed relief at our not becoming involved in the war, the passions of the country were deeply engaged. "America," said George Bernard Shaw, "to judge by some of its papers, is mad with British patriotism, Polish nationality, and Belgian freedom."

Both sides in the struggle attempted to plead their cases with the American public, the Germans largely to counter hostility, the

British and French to intensify friendly feelings. In this war of words, the advantage lay decidedly with the Allies. Since the British controlled the Atlantic cables, they could censor all war news emanating from Europe except for wireless dispatches, and their skillful propaganda was based upon a sound understanding of the American mood. The British worked quietly and effectively through the influential agencies that formed American opinion—newspaper publishers and editors, movie-makers, prominent writers, teachers, and college presidents. As Sir Gilbert Parker, the Canadian novelist who took charge of British propaganda, later explained: "We asked our friends and correspondents to arrange for speeches, debates, and lectures by American citizens, but we did not encourage Britishers to go to America and preach the doctrine of entrance into the war."

By comparison, German propaganda was inept. It varied from complicated and rather legalistic explanations of Germany's position to violent denunciations of the Allies that had little effect on Americans who were not already sympathetic to the cause of the Central Powers. Moreover, German propaganda had greater obstacles to overcome. To Americans filled with the moral idealism of the Progressive era and raised on repeated denunciations of lawlessness and oppression at home, nothing could explain away Germany's violation of the Belgian neutrality she had so solemnly sworn to respect. As Count Bernstorff, the German Ambassador in Washington, admitted, "The Belgium question was the one which interested Americans most and which was most effective in working up American opinion against us."

Allied propagandists conjured up a terrible picture of German rape, plunder, and cruelty in Belgium, most of which was later proved false, but much of which was readily accepted in America. The war at sea also favored the public-relations work of the Allies. By 1916, the Allied blockade of Central Europe brought hunger and malnutrition to women and children, but this slow process of attrition was hard for the Germans to dramatize. German submarine warfare, on the other

hand, caused dramatic and terrible sinkings at sea, which struck horror into the hearts of everyone. As the weeks went by, it became apparent that the Allies were winning the battle for American opinion, already so favorably disposed to them.

Freedom of the Seas. As in the Napoleonic wars a century earlier, the war at sea drew the United States into serious difficulties with both sides. But the problems that had arisen from the British blockade a hundred years before, acute and acrimonious though they were, had never brought the same threat of American intervention as the problems that now arose out of German submarine warfare. One of the earliest wartime disputes between the United States and Britain arose over the definition of contraband—that is, those goods which in international law cannot be supplied to one belligerent nation by a neutral without risk of lawful seizure and appropriation by the other side. Early in the war, the British arbitrarily redefined contraband to embrace *all* articles of importance—including foodstuffs, hitherto not designated as contraband—that might give direct or indirect aid to the enemy. (The British in the beginning exempted cotton, however, to conciliate the South and to avoid building up pressures upon the Wilson administration from that quarter.)

A second source of friction between Britain and America arose from the liberties the British were taking with the traditional right of visit and search. It had always been permissible under international law for a belligerent vessel to stop and visit a neutral merchantman to search for contraband, and either to release it if none was found, or to send it to a prize court for legal action if contraband was aboard. The British insisted that the task of searching a large modern vessel had become too complicated for them to observe the usual procedure any longer. Instead, they often insisted on conducting neutral vessels to port for a thorough examination, a procedure that caused long delays and imposed great economic losses upon American shippers. Although wartime shipping remained profitable, and although the British paid for many of the cargoes they confiscated, their behavior was widely resented in American shipping circles and within the Wilson administration.

A third source of trouble stemmed from the way the British conducted their blockade. The British intercepted not only American ships bound for Germany, but also those destined for neutral countries near enough to act as entry points to German markets. A system of rationing imports for neutral countries was worked out by the Allies under which these countries were forbidden to import substantially more than they had before the war.

In November, 1914, the British government declared the North Sea a military area and mined it so thoroughly that no neutral vessel could pass through without first stopping to receive British directions on how to navigate past the mined zones. This was a radical departure from earlier international practice; but to all complaints against her violations of international law, Britain replied that she was fighting for her life, and that she could not be bound by notions of maritime law framed under earlier and far different conditions of marine technology and warfare.

The Wilson administration did not accept the British position without complaint. A number of sharp protests were sent to London in which the case against British practices was forcefully argued from the standpoint of tradition. In the summer of 1916, the British government announced that British subjects were forbidden to trade with any of a blacklist of 85 persons or business firms in the United States that were suspected of giving aid to Germany. At this point, American tempers were sorely tried. Wilson professed himself "about at the end of my patience with Great Britain and the Allies. This blacklist business is the last straw. . . .

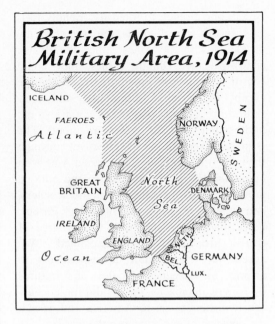

Can we any longer endure their intolerable course?"

In spite of the irritation from such conflicts, there seems no reason to believe that the United States ever really considered going to war against the Allies. American grievances were not pressed to the breaking point. The chief reasons for American restraint were the prevailing sympathy for the Allies and the widespread fear in the United States that a German victory would be dangerous to American interests. This feeling was predominant in the Wilson administration, where many officials believed that the defeat of Britain and the possible destruction of the British fleet, or its control by the military leaders of Germany, would pose a threat to the United States. "England is fighting our fight," declared Wilson at one point to his secretary, Joseph Tumulty. And when some members of his cabinet urged him to embargo exports to England early in 1915, he replied: "Gentlemen, the Allies are standing with their backs to the wall fighting wild beasts. I will permit nothing to be done by our country to hinder or embarrass them in the prosecution of the war unless admitted rights are grossly violated." If the Germans should succeed, he once told the British ambassador, "we shall be forced to take such measures of defense here which would be fatal to our form of Government and American ideals." Many thoughtful men throughout the country agreed.

A second reason for American restraint was the profitable trade that the United States was carrying on with the Allies. American trade with the Central Powers, cut off by the British blockade, sank from $169,289,000 in 1914 to $1,159,000 in 1916; but during the same period trade with the four great Allied countries, England, France, Italy, and Russia, rose from $824,860,000 to $3,214,480,000. When the war broke out, the United States was suffering from a business depression, still in its early stages but nevertheless quite severe. Huge war orders quickly restored American prosperity and put the country back to work.

Soon the administration was confronted with a vital decision. Formerly a debtor nation, the United States had suddenly become a creditor. Old American debts to the Allied powers had been paid off by the sale of war goods. Now the Allies, no longer the suppliers of capital for American industrial development, had to call for loans from America to finance further buying. If these loans were denied, it seemed clear that the Allies might be defeated, Americans would lose their profitable war business, and the United States would lapse back into depression. Unemployed workers would stalk the streets, cotton farmers in the Democratic South would suffer from a severe drop in prices, the demand for war trade would be taken up by the Republicans, and Wilson's administration might be defeated at the polls. So, although the State Department, under Secretary William Jennings Bryan's urging, had originally discouraged American bankers from making private loans to the Allied governments, it now substantially reversed its position and permitted the war loans to go on.

As time passed, the United States came to have a tremendous economic stake in the Allies' ability to pay back these loans. Many years afterward, a muckraking senatorial committee headed by Senator Gerald Nye charged that the war had been fought by America to assure the safety of bankers' loans and munition-makers' profits. The facts of the situation do not bear out this narrow accusation, nor can primary responsibility be laid upon any group of businessmen. But it is true that the United States was confronted with the alternative of (1) writing off war trade and risking a very serious depression, with everything that that entailed (including the possible emergence of a war party far less responsible than the Wilson administration), or (2) carrying on its war trade with the aid of loans and sustaining its wartime prosperity at the cost of an intimate economic liaison with the Allies. After a brief period of hesitation, the Wilson administration chose the second course. And the administration seems to have acted in full accord with American public opinion. The tides of trade and the tides of sympathy were both pulling in the same direction.

Submarine Warfare.   No such restraints deterred the United States from making a full assertion of its rights in the face of German submarine warfare. The submarine was one of those technological developments that raise new questions of international law and morality. A frail craft, the submarine, once surfaced, could easily be sunk by the light deck guns of armed merchant vessels. Submarine commanders therefore could not follow the established practice of halting an enemy merchant ship, ascertaining its identity, and providing for the safety of its passengers and crew before sending it to the bottom. To operate a submarine at maximum effect and in least danger, its captain had to hit and run, without troubling about whether he had accidentally struck a neutral ship and without worrying about the fate of the passengers. This was a kind of warfare that was hard to justify. But the Germans argued that it was no more inhuman than the long-run effects of the Allied food blockade upon innocent civilians and offered to change their submarine tactics if the blockade were lifted. When the German government announced on February 4, 1915, that it was setting up a war area around the British Isles in which all enemy ships were to be destroyed without warning, and in which it was clear that neutral vessels would not be safe, the stage was set for a prolonged controversy with the United States that eventually provided the occasion for war.

Early in 1915, when more and more Allied merchant vessels were being sunk, it became evident that the lives of Americans

German Submarine War Zone, Feb. 15, 1915

traveling on belligerent ships were in great danger. The German government issued warnings about that danger, but American citizens continued to travel on Allied ships. Secretary of State Bryan urged that the President forbid Americans to take this risk, but Wilson took a firm stand on the ground that these travelers were simply exercising a traditional right.

On May 7, 1915, the unarmed British liner Lusitania was sunk with the loss of 1,198 passengers, including 128 Americans. Although the ship was carrying rifle cartridges and other contraband, the shocking toll of lives among women and children dramatized the submarine issue. "The torpedo that sank the Lusitania," declared the New York Nation, "also sank Germany in the opinion of mankind." Some Americans demanded that the United States go to war, but Wilson opposed the idea. "There is," he said in a public address, "such a thing as a man being too proud to fight. There is such a thing as a nation being so right that it does not need to convince others by force that it is right." Militant Americans raged at Wilson's caution, calling it cowardice, but the administration refused to do more than send three vigorously worded notes of protest to Germany. (The second of these, indeed, came so close to being a threat of war that Secretary of State Bryan, who wanted peace at any reasonable cost, resigned rather than sign it. He was replaced by the ardently pro-British Robert Lansing.) Nine months after the sinking, Germany acknowledged responsibility for the loss of American lives and agreed to pay an indemnity. The dispute had not been finally settled when the United States went to war.

Further sinkings took place and further American protests led to German assurances that the conduct of submarine warfare would be seriously modified. In March, 1916, however, an unarmed French ship, the Sussex, was torpedoed and several Americans on board were seriously injured. Wilson considered this attack a violation of the assurances given by the German government, and he warned Germany that unless she immediately abandoned her "present methods of submarine warfare against passenger and freight-carrying vessels, the Government of the United States can have no choice but to sever diplomatic relations." Faced with this threat of diplomatic rupture and war, the German government capitulated, and on May 4, 1916, gave to the United States what has commonly been referred to as the Sussex pledge: henceforth no more merchant vessels would be sunk without warning—provided that the United States also held England accountable for her violations of international law. Wisely, Wilson decided to ignore this proviso and accept the pledge. For nine months after the *Sussex* pledge, American relations with Germany were comparatively undisturbed. Wilson had succeeded in forcing the Germans to place crippling restrictions on their most powerful maritime weapon.

Mediation and Preparation. W i l s o n was not unreservedly optimistic about America's chance of staying out of the war if it continued much longer. Convinced that the best way of avoiding entry into the war was to end it, he made efforts to mediate. In January, 1915, and once again a year later, he sent his personal adviser, Colonel Edward M. House, on peace missions to Europe. In 1915, House found that the goals of the belligerents were too far apart for him to do anything to help. In 1916, House, with Sir Edward Grey, the British Foreign Secretary, drew up a memorandum of an understanding in which House indicated that Wilson, on hearing from England and France that the opportune moment had arrived, would summon a conference to end the war. House went beyond his instructions and indicated that should the Allies accept this proposal, and should Germany refuse it, the United States would *probably* enter the war against Germany. Should Germany accept the proposal, the United States would cooperate with the Allies in attempting to force her to accept a reasonable settlement. This was by no means a binding pledge of American participation, but it gave the Allies the clear impression that the United States was morally committed to their side. Nothing came of the proposal, for it was hard to convince either side of the necessity for a peace conference so long as both sides held hopes of victory.

Discouraged by the failure of these negotiations, Wilson gave way to the agitation for preparedness that many persons, including Theodore Roosevelt, had urged. Preparedness parades were held throughout the nation. To the horror of peace-minded Progressives, the army, the navy, and the merchant marine were all expanded. But in espousing preparedness, Wilson appropriated what might have been an important vote-winning issue for the Republicans in the coming presidential election.

Wilson entered the presidential campaign of 1916 with a double program of peace and preparedness. Four years earlier, he had been elected with a minority of the popular vote only because normal Republican strength had been split between Roosevelt and Taft (see p. 597). Now the Republicans named an attractive candidate, Associate Justice Charles Evans Hughes of the Supreme Court. It was hard to see how Wilson could be re-elected, and all the early indications pointed to a restoration of the Republican preponderance that had marked the period before 1912.

Hughes had been free from all responsibility for national policies and from making pronouncements upon them, and he tried to maintain this position throughout the campaign. He straddled the neutrality issue and tried to make capital of Wilson's Mexican policy and his capitulation to the railroad workers in backing the Adamson Act (see p. 600). Hughes' candidacy proved unexciting, and the Democrats dubbed him Charles "Evasive" Hughes. Although no longer split between conservatives and insurgents, his party was seriously divided between war-minded and pacifistic (or pro-German) elements.

The Democrats, on the other hand, made much of the fact that Wilson had wrung the *Sussex* pledge from the German government without the use of force, and pounded away with the slogan, "He kept us out of war." Wilson's domestic reforms and his success in keeping the country at peace while maintaining traditional American rights stood him in good stead. He won the votes of a great many supporters of the Progressive party, as well as of labor, farmer, and anti-war groups. In the end, the election hung on the votes of the Far West. Wilson carried California by almost 4,000 votes, and with it enough votes in the electoral college to give him a majority. In the popular vote he led narrowly, 9,129,000 to 8,538,000.

America Goes to War. Soon after his re-election, Wilson made still another attempt to arrange a peace. On December 18, 1916, he sent a note to all the belligerent governments asking them to state the terms that would satisfy them. Unfortunately, the note seemed merely to echo a statement issued a week earlier by the Germans, in which they said they were willing to discuss peace. The Allies were deeply offended by the timing of the overture, which came at a moment when Germany's fortunes in the war were at a high point. Moreover, the terms called for by the two sides were altogether irreconcilable.

Wilson followed this gesture by making a speech before the Senate in January, 1917, that was in effect an appeal to the world. He expressed his own conception of a just and lasting peace and outlined his ideas for a League of Nations to maintain world peace. "It must be a peace without victory," for, he asserted prophetically,

Victory would mean peace forced upon the loser, a victor's terms imposed upon the vanquished. It would be accepted in humiliation, under duress, at an intolerable sacrifice, and would leave a sting, a resentment, a bitter memory upon which terms of peace would rest, not permanently, but only as upon quicksand. Only a peace between equals can last.

Most Americans greeted this speech with enthusiasm, but to the Allies it seemed to be a withdrawal of the informal sympathy and accord they had come to expect from the United States.

The echoes of Wilson's appeal hardly had died away when the entire situation was transformed by an announcement from the German government on January 31, 1917, that German submarines would again be ordered to sink all vessels on sight, armed or unarmed, within a specified zone around the British Isles and in the Mediterranean. Thus the *Sussex* pledge was revoked, and Wilson had to make good on the warnings he had issued earlier. When the German war leaders changed their submarine policy, they knew full well that they risked almost certain war with the United States, but they had chosen to take that risk. They reasoned that the United States was, in a sense, already engaged in the war against them economically; and they assumed it would take America many months to get its military forces to the battlefronts, by which time they would have knocked Britain out of the war by cutting off her food supply. The decision was a desperate gamble, but it came very close to succeeding in the summer of 1917.

Wilson responded to the German move by breaking off diplomatic relations, but he still hoped to avoid war. He next called upon Congress to authorize him to arm American merchant vessels. When this proposal was blocked in the Senate by a filibuster led by Senator La Follette of Wisconsin, Wilson's aides discovered an old statute of 1797 that authorized the president to arm vessels without congressional sanction. Wilson then settled back to await further developments. He was reluctant to move more rapidly than public opinion would permit, and he still hoped that some turn in the situation would make it possible to avoid war.

In the meantime, at the beginning of March, public opinion itself took another sharp turn against the Central Powers as the result of an incredibly melodramatic incident. British naval intelligence had intercepted a coded message from German Foreign Secretary Zimmermann to the German Ambassador in Mexico, informing him of the German decision to resume unrestricted submarine warfare. The message instructed Zimmermann to propose to Mexico that, in the event of war between the United States and Germany, the Mexicans and Germans should make an alliance and wage war together, and that Germany would support Mexico in an effort to recover "the lost territory in New Mexico, Texas, and Arizona." Wilson, outraged at the terms of the note, at first hesitated to release it because he knew that it would inflame public opinion. But, after holding it for almost a week, he decided to make it public in order to create further support for his armed-ship bill.

American sentiment for drastic measures against Germany rose immediately upon release of the note on March 1, 1917.

One of the last brakes against entering the war on the side of the Allies was removed as a result of the March revolution in Russia, which replaced the czarist regime with a provisional republican government. With this tyrannical ally of the Western Powers deposed, it was now easier to describe the war against the Central Powers as a war against autocracy. At the same time, sinkings of American ships began in the Atlantic, with five going down in March alone.

To take the final step toward war was something that a man of conscience like Wilson could not regard lightly, and he decided on it only after a terrible struggle with himself. More than once during the closing days of March, 1917, he asked his close associates, "What else can I do? Is there anything else I can do?" He foresaw that waging a great war would tax to the utmost, perhaps even destroy, American tolerance for dissent and the American system of constitutional government. To Frank Cobb of the New York *World,* he confessed what was on his mind:

He said that when a war got going it was just war and there weren't two kinds of it. It required illiberalism at home to reinforce the men at the front. We couldn't fight Germany and maintain the ideals of Government that all thinking men shared. He said we would try it but it would be too much for us.

"Once lead this people into war," he said, "and they'll forget there ever was such a thing as tolerance. To fight you must be brutal and ruthless, and the spirit of ruthless brutality will enter into the very fibre of our national life, infecting Congress, the courts, the policeman on the beat, the man in the street." Conformity would be the only virtue, said the President,

and every man who refused to conform would have to pay the penalty.

He thought the Constitution would not survive it; that free speech and the right of assembly would go. He said a nation couldn't put its strength into war and keep its head level; it had never been done.

"If there is any alternative, for God's sake, let's take it," he exclaimed.

But Wilson could see no alternative, and on the following day, April 2, 1917, he went before Congress to read the war message that had been lying on his desk as he spoke to Cobb. He reviewed the history of the submarine controversy and asserted that the United States was fighting for the rights of neutrals, for international law, and for security from ruthless autocracy. "The world must be made safe for democracy." This was not a quarrel with the German people but with their imperial government. He urged the American people to fight "without rancor and without selfish object," and concluded:

It is a fearful thing to lead this great peaceful people into war, into the most terrible and disastrous of all wars, civilization itself seeming to be in the balance. But the right is more precious than peace, and we shall fight for the things which we have always carried nearest our hearts,—for democracy, for the right of those who submit to authority to have a voice in their own governments, for the rights and liberties of small nations, for a universal dominion of right by such a concert of free peoples as shall bring peace and safety to all nations and make the world itself at last free.

Two days later, on April 4, 1917, the war resolution passed Congress by a vote of 82 to 6 in the Senate and on April 6 by 373 to 50 in the House. The United States was at war.

III. WINNING THE WAR

The War at Sea. America's participation in the war demanded of her two things she had never done before. The nation had to send vast numbers of men to fight against

a great power 3,000 miles away, and it had to organize its entire continental economy for one purpose.

In the spring of 1917, the allied cause

This picture of a World War I convoy moving at full speed through the submarine zone was taken from a British dirigible balloon. Many submarines were sunk by bombs dropped from such dirigibles.

was faring badly almost everywhere. A huge French offensive on the Aisne River had broken down, with terrible losses; several important French bankers and politicians were discussing possible peace with Germany. Defeatism was growing among the common soldiers, and ten French divisions actually had mutinied. On the Western Front, the Allies barely held their own, and elsewhere their situation was far from encouraging. In the Balkans, a carefully prepared offensive had not only failed to make much headway but was even being pressed back toward Salonica by the Bulgarians, Germans, and Austrians. In the Russian armies, warweariness was growing rapidly. Tired of an oppressive regime that had given them the most incompetent leadership, the masses of the Russian people opposed any government that would not call a halt to the war.

Worst and most urgent of all, the German submarine campaign was an outstanding success. Sinkings of Allied merchant vessels had averaged almost 570,000 tons per month in February and March and reached 881,000 tons in April. And the numbers of German U-boats were growing. In April, England had enough grain on hand for only six or eight weeks. Admiral Jellicoe, First Sea Lord of the Admiralty, told American Admiral William S. Sims, to the latter's dismay, that "it is impossible for us to go

614

on, if losses like this continue. . . . The Germans . . . will win unless we can stop these losses—and stop them soon."

Although it was to be many months before the United States could throw any substantial numbers of troops into the conflict, the navy was ready to help cope with the emergency. Clearly a change in defensive tactics had to be made. Many naval officers had argued that greater safety could be achieved through the convoy system, in which a fleet of merchant vessels is guarded by an escort of cruisers and destroyers. But the Allies had not yet adopted convoys. Captains of merchant vessels preferred to go it alone, relying on their speed and their ability to dodge torpedoes. They insisted that it was impossible to organize a large number of steamships into a stable convoy where each ship had to hold a fixed station. But under Sims' urging, the convoy system was adopted, and was put into operation with impressive results. Allied monthly shipping losses fell from 881,000 tons in April to 289,000 tons in November. Not one American troop-transport ship carrying American doughboys to the Western Front was sunk, and in this unprecedented transfer of men, not a single life was lost. By the end of the war, the United States also had contributed a fleet of over a hundred small subchasers, had put 500 planes to work spotting enemy U-boats, and had taken the initiative in laying a tremendous mine barrage across the North Sea which eventually closed that area as an exit for submarines. In all, more than 2,000 American vessels of all sizes had been thrown into the conflict.

Mobilizing America. Although the power of the navy could make itself felt almost immediately, the task of raising, equipping, training, and transporting a large army took time and careful planning. When the declaration of war was adopted, the combined strength of the Regular Army and the National Guard was about 378,000 men, trained or partially trained, who could become the officers and non-coms of the new army created by a national draft. On May 18, 1917, Congress passed a Selective Service Act, requiring all men between the ages of 21 and 30 (it was extended later to 18 and 45) to register for military service. Registrants were separated into five classes of eligibility, headed by able-bodied unmarried men without dependents. It was from this group alone that the nation drew all the 2,810,000 men actually drafted for service in the army. The order in which men were called up was determined by a complicated lottery system. To train them, 32 camps and cantonments were hastily thrown up, mostly in the South. By the end of the war, 4,800,000 men and women were under arms in the army, navy, and marine corps.

To support her military and naval operations and to contribute to the financing of her Allies, the United States had to mobilize her economic strength. Although some experts recommended that this immense effort be financed on a pay-as-you-go basis, with wartime profits and earnings taxed to the utmost, the government resorted to borrowing on a large scale. The total cost of the war from April, 1917, to June, 1920, was estimated at about $32.8 billion, of which about one-half was raised by four Liberty Loan drives in 1917-1918 and the rest through taxes. Rather than sell bonds through bankers, as the Civil War government had sold them through Jay Cooke (see p. 383), the administration decided to launch intensive campaigns to sell directly to small buyers as well as to large investors. Volunteer salesmen were recruited, rallies and entertainments were held, and Liberty Loan posters were widely distributed. Social pressure was used to sell bonds, and reluctant buyers were scorned as slackers or German sympathizers. Each loan was handsomely over-subscribed. Taxes were levied on a variety of luxuries—transportation, gasoline, amusements and entertainments, and alcoholic beverages. During the war, the basic income-tax rate was raised and new corporation taxes were imposed.

To organize the nation's resources for war, a task for which Wilson had no satisfactory precedent, he set up an over-all planning board, the Council of National Defense, consisting of six members of the cabinet and an advisory commission of seven civilians. Under the general supervision of this Council, six huge wartime agencies devoted themselves to specific tasks of economic mobilization. The Emergency Fleet Corporation, created in April, 1916, under the United States Shipping Board, attempted to build new ships to meet the U-boat threat. Not until the summer of 1918, however, did the government have enough ships on hand to transport the A.E.F. to France.

The Food Administration, ably headed by Herbert Hoover, undertook to supply civilians and combatants and to conserve food resources. Hoover successfully publicized a national campaign to plant war gardens and to adopt wheatless and meatless days. Through the purchases of the Grain Corporation and other activities of the Food Administration, he set a high price on wheat and other products that induced farmers to expand their acreage and their operations to the utmost. Similarly, a Fuel Administration meted out coal and oil supplies; a Railroad Administration consolidated the railroads of the nation and, without removing them from private ownership, operated them as a single system; the War Trade Board licensed foreign trade and kept American supplies from reaching enemy powers.

A body of vital importance, the War Industries Board, under the direction of Bernard Baruch, exercised dictatorial powers over the American economy, determining what materials manufacturers could and could not use, what new products they must make and what familiar ones they must temporarily drop, and which manufacturers could have first access to limited materials and to transportation facilities. Great savings were effected by minute regulations that covered everything from the number of trunks that traveling salesmen could carry to the styles of pocket knives that could be made and the number of stops elevators could make. Immense strides were made through standardization. For instance, the number of sizes and styles of plows was reduced from 376 to 76, the number of colors of typewriter ribbons from 150 to 5. As a result of over 1,200 such economies, Americans not only conserved labor and material for the war effort, but also learned a great deal about the advantages of standardization and planning.

One of the seven civilian advisers of the Council of National Defense was Samuel Gompers, President of the American Federation of Labor and spokesman of the forces of trade unionism. Gompers announced that the American workingman stood behind the war, but called upon the government to make sure that the war did not become an occasion for profiteering or for exploiting labor. In March, 1918, the War Labor Conference Board, which had been set up by the Secretary of Labor as an advisory agency, drew up a set of guiding principles for the administration. Labor was to pledge not to strike. In return, it was assured of the right of collective bargaining, the maintenance of the eight-hour day, where existing law required it, and other privileges. A National War Labor Board was set up in 1918 to mediate and conciliate labor disputes, and a War Labor Policies Board handled questions arising over hours of labor and working conditions. The number of strikes had risen from 1,405 in 1915 to 4,359 in 1917, and the number of persons involved in strikes more than doubled. The American Federation of Labor increased its membership from 1,996,000 in 1913 to 2,726,000 in 1918.

Actually, labor shared in the wartime prosperity, though not so spectacularly as farmers and businessmen. The demand for labor was great, and in some industries wages rose even faster than prices. In the most favored industries, like manufacturing, mining, and transportation, it is estimated that workers were enjoying real earnings as much as 20 per cent higher in 1918 than in 1914. For all wage-earners, however, the rise in real earnings was closer to 4 per cent. As is usual in periods of rapid price rises, salaried employees had a bad time, losing perhaps as much as one-third of their pre-war purchasing power.

Neither businessmen nor farmers neglected the possibilities opened to them by wartime demand. The War Industries Board, unwilling to delay production by lengthy negotiations over terms with contractors, gave up the traditional practice of competitive bidding on war contracts and negotiated on the basis of cost-plus contracts. These contracts guaranteed the contracting firm a profit ranging from 2½ to 15 per cent of the cost of production, and enabled some businessmen to take advantage of the government by padding their costs. Despite higher taxes, corporations were able to increase dividend payments substantially, pay much larger salaries to executives, and still pile up profits. Large personal fortunes increased. In 1914, there were only 5,000 personal incomes in the $50,000 to $100,000 a year tax brackets; by 1918, there were 13,000. Progressive tax policies cut deeply into these incomes, however, and a larger proportion of the tax burden was shifted during the war from the lower to the higher income brackets.

Encouraged by the government and lured by high prices, farmers were ready and willing to expand their acreage. The price of wheat, for instance, rose from $1.43 a bushel in 1916 to $2.16 in 1919. During the same period, the harvested acreage rose from 53,510,000 to 73,700,000 acres, the total crop from 634,572,000 to 952,097,000 bushels. Farmers bought up or rented all the land they could get their hands on and stretched their resources to the utmost. They helped to feed the country and its Allies and lined their pockets in the process. The real income of farm operators was 29 per cent higher in 1918 than it had been in 1915. But soon after the war had ended, the farmers found themselves overextended and over-competing in a market that had collapsed.

The High Cost of Hatred. The administration attempted to mobilize the American mind as well as American resources. Something in this direction probably had to be done, for a great many Americans sympathized with the Central Powers, others had mixed feelings, and many others were indifferent. Less than two weeks after war was declared, Congress established the Committee on Public Information, which Wilson put under the direction of George Creel, a journalist who had once been a prominent muckraker. To keep the fires of patriotism burning brightly, Creel conscripted many scholars and journalists and ministers, who went eagerly to work to show the country how abominable and depraved the Germans were and how their depravity was manifested in German history and culture.

Various high-powered propaganda efforts by the C.P.I. and other agencies seem to have been all too successful. Pacifists, anti-war socialists, and alleged sympathizers of the Central Powers were persecuted throughout the country. In a few places, German books were burned, and amateur spy-chasers conjured up enemies of the war effort. Pacifists were beaten and tortured. Meetings of socialists, pacifists, and liberals were raided; left-wing labor leaders and socialists were tarred and feathered. In Butte, Montana, a crippled IWW organizer was dragged from his bed by masked men, taken to a railway trestle, and hanged. A judge sentenced an adolescent girl to a 20-year imprisonment for criticizing the war. Thousands of Americans did and said things they were later ashamed of. Wilson's prediction that the country might lose its constitutional liberties altogether was not borne out, but his warning that the people would lose all understanding of tolerance proved tragically correct.

German-Americans suffered particularly from this outburst of wartime intolerance, although the overwhelming majority of them accepted the necessity of war once it had begun. The German language was dropped from schools throughout the country, German books were removed from libraries, and individual Germans were discriminated against. The distinguished violinist, Fritz Kreisler, was denied the right to give a concert by the mayor of a New Jersey town. A peak of silliness was reached when sauerkraut was renamed "liberty cabbage" and the dachshund was rechristened the "liberty pup."

Intolerance was made official by the passage of the Espionage Act of June, 1917, and the Sedition Act of May, 1918. The Espionage Act prescribed a fine of up to $10,000 and a prison term of 20 years for anyone who interfered with the draft or attempted to encourage disloyalty. The Sedition Act set the same penalty for anyone who obstructed the sale of United States bonds, incited insubordination, discouraged recruiting, or who would "wilfully utter, print, write or publish any disloyal, profane, scurrilous, or abusive language" about the American form of government, the flag, or the uniforms of the services, or who would bring the form of government or the Constitution into contempt, or "advocate any curtailment of production in this country of any thing necessary or essential to the prosecution of the war." Over 1,500 persons were arrested and imprisoned for disloyalty under these laws, including the socialist leader, Eugene Debs. More than 450 conscientious objectors were sent to military prisons. Only a few Americans protested that this was a strange way to conduct a war for liberty and democracy.

The War on Land. As the months passed, American troops slowly began to make their presence felt on the field of battle. The few contingents that arrived in Europe the summer of 1917—the 1st Infantry Division landed in France in June—were token forces sent to bolster the morale of the French and English armies, and they were thinly distributed along the front in order to gain the greatest possible psychological effect. The first time a major force of the American army entered battle was in October, 1917, near Toul, east of Verdun. In March, 1918, when the Germans were mounting the massive spring offensive that was intended to deliver the crushing blow to the Allies, there were about 300,000 American soldiers in France, and more were arriving every day. Between March and October, 1,750,000 Americans landed in France, and by the end of the war a total of 2,079,880 men had been carried to Europe, together with more than 5 million tons of supplies. In April, 1918, the Germans enjoyed a numerical superiority on the Western Front of over 320,000 infantrymen. By November, fresh American troops had given the Allies a preponderance of over 600,000 men. Of the troops sent overseas, about 1,400,000 saw fighting service, all but a few of them on the Western Front in France. (Small numbers were employed in Italy, in Belgium, and in Siberia after the Russian Revolution.)

Despite all the mobilization efforts at home, the American army was never entirely supplied with American arms and ammunition. American field artillery units were largely equipped with French 75 mm. field guns, and the American program for airplane production developed so slowly that American aviators were forced to fly foreign-made aircraft. American industry was so ill-prepared to meet the problems of armored tank production that its contribution in this sphere was negligible. British transport ships carried more American troops to Europe than did American vessels.

Of necessity, large numbers of American troops were thrown into battle without thorough training, but they played a decisive and strikingly independent role in the last eight months of the war. The Allies hoped to use American troops as replacements, and to brigade them with French or British units instead of having them take separate places in the lines. But General Pershing, the American Commander, opposed this policy, feeling that the Allies had grown too defense-minded and that the Americans would be more successful conducting independent offensive operations. Hence the greater part of the American army took its place in the lines as a separate force under Pershing's command, subject, however, after April, 1918, to the over-all supreme command of Marshal Foch of France.

American Operations on the Western Front, 1918

American riflemen of the 166th Regiment picking off German soldiers on the edge of Villers, France, July 30, 1918.

Americans received their first major test when they were assigned to help repulse a menacing German thrust toward Paris, which by May 30, 1918, had reached Chateau Thierry on the Marne, only 50 miles from the French capital. On May 31, the Second American Division and several regiments of marines went into action in support of French colonial troops. They forced the Germans back across the Marne, and from June 6 to 25 gradually cleared Belleau Wood of enemy forces. In July, when the German General Staff made its last great effort to break through to Paris between Rheims and Soissons, 85,000 Americans were engaged in the successful effort to throw the Germans back.

In its first major assignment as an independent force, the American army launched an attack upon the St. Mihiel salient, a German bulge protruding sharply into the Allied lines across the Meuse River

southeast of Verdun. Pershing sent American troops against both flanks of the salient, and with some support from the French reduced it in a two-day engagement in mid-September, 1918. An American army of half a million troops was employed. At the cost of 7,000 casualties, it captured 16,000 German prisoners and over 400 guns, and established a new threat to the fortified center of Metz. By Foch's orders, however, the American army was not sent on toward Metz but was shifted westward and down the Meuse River, through the Argonne Woods toward Sedan, with the object of taking that city and cutting the strategically important Sedan-Metz railroad.

The Meuse-Argonne engagement was one of the fiercest battles in American military history. Together with the French forces on that front, the Americans captured more than 25,000 prisoners and a great deal of equipment, but at a high cost in casualties.

619

This offensive, part of a coordinated drive against the Central Powers all along the Western Front, in Italy, in Greece, and in Palestine, helped bring Germany and her allies to their knees. At the end of September, Bulgaria surrendered. Turkey followed in October and Austria in November. Finally, on November 11, Germany, with her armies everywhere in retreat, her navy on the verge of general mutiny, and her civilian population hungry, exhausted, and dangerously discontented, gave up resistance and signed an armistice.

The war was not over, since terms of peace had yet to be worked out, but the fighting was at an end. American losses—48,000 killed in battle, 2,900 missing in action, 56,000 dead of disease—were light in comparison with the losses the other great powers had suffered since 1914. Russia counted 1,700,000 battle deaths, Germany 1,800,000, France 1,385,000, Britain 947,-000, and Austria-Hungary 1,200,000. But America's losses were heavy in proportion to the length of time she had been in the war and the numbers of troops she had sent into battle. Americans had had more than a mere glimpse of the horrors of the gigantic struggle.

IV. LOSING THE PEACE

The Fourteen Points. While his administration was waging a zealous propaganda campaign on the home front, Wilson himself was beaming propaganda messages to the enemy peoples to persuade them to give up the struggle. When the United States was still a neutral, he had appealed for "peace without victory" and had brought hope to a world already weary of conflict. When the United States went to war, he kept asserting that the war was being waged not against the German people but against their government. During the war, he had emphasized that neither punitive damages nor territorial gains were the Allies' real objectives, but rather the destruction of autocratic governments and a settlement that would bring permanent peace. On January 8, 1918, he set forth a program for peace in a speech to Congress that embodied his famous Fourteen Points, which he called "the only possible program." Briefly summarized, his proposals were as follows:

I. Open covenants of peace, openly arrived at.

II. Absolute freedom of navigation upon the seas in peace and in war.

III. The removal, so far as possible, of all economic barriers among the nations consenting to the peace.

IV. Guarantees that national armaments will be reduced to the lowest point consistent with domestic safety.

V. An impartial adjustment of colonial claims giving equal weight to the interests of the populations concerned and to the government whose title is to be determined.

VI. The evacuation of all Russian territory.

VII. The evacuation and restoration of Belgium.

VIII. All French territory should be freed, the invaded portions restored, and the wrong done to France in 1871 in the matter of Alsace-Lorraine should be righted.

IX. Readjustment of Italian frontiers along clearly recognizable lines of nationality.

X. The peoples of Autria-Hungary should be accorded opportunity for autonomous development.

XI. Rumania, Serbia, and Montenegro should be evacuated, occupied territories restored, Serbia accorded free and secure access to the sea. The Balkan States should be constituted along historically established lines of nationality.

XII. The Turkish portions of the Ottoman Empire should be assured a secure sovereignty, the other nationalities under Turkish rule should have autonomous development. The Dardanelles should be open to the commerce of all nations under international guarantees.

XIII. An independent Polish state should be erected and should be assured a free and secure access to the sea.

XIV. A general association of nations must be formed under specific covenants for the purpose of affording mutual guarantees of political independence and territorial integrity to great and small states alike.

The Fourteen Points made Wilson a moral hero in the eyes of the western world. To people everywhere, tired of the sacrifices and the horror of the war, Wilson's words promised that a new and better world would emerge out of the ashes of conflict. Peoples struggling for national freedom and self-determination were heartened. Liberals were pleased with his espousal of open diplomacy and the lowering of trade barriers. The nations that had borne the burdens of armaments and taxation rallied with hope to the idea of a reduction of armaments. Even the Germans, who distrusted British sea power, found merit in the proposal for freedom of the seas. Men everywhere hoped that a League of Nations might be set up that would prevent a recurrence of the horrors they had experienced. Throughout the world, men of good will toasted the health of the American President. The common people almost worshiped him. On a visit to Italy, George Creel found in a peasant's mountain cabin a shrine with a wax figure of a patron saint on one side and a picture of Wilson on the other.

Two ideals and two leaders motivated those people who felt that somehow a better order must emerge from the ruins. In the East, the ideal was international communism, whose spokesman was Lenin; in the West a revitalized liberal democracy provided the inspiration, and Wilson was its patron saint. In a sense, the effort to make peace was a race between these ideals, but in the end neither was to win a complete victory.

Yet as Wilson's reputation grew in the rest of the world, he was meeting with increasing opposition at home. Wartime hatreds had inclined many Americans to favor a strong peace, and they opposed Wilson's ideas. Those who believed that we never should have entered the war in the first place could hardly be expected to rally behind him. And as the end of the war drew near, partisan politics again became acute. For years the followers of Theodore Roosevelt in the Republican party had been listening to his angry denunciations of Wilson, whom Roosevelt considered a weakling, a coward, and a fraud. "Let us," preached Roosevelt, "dictate peace by the hammering guns and not chat about peace to the accompaniment of the clicking of typewriters."

In October, 1918, facing the off-year congressional elections, Wilson was troubled by the thought that his role as peace-maker would be greatly weakened if the American people repudiated his party at the polls. Accordingly he issued a fatal appeal to the voters, asking them to express their approval of his leadership by voting for Democratic representatives and senators. This was a serious mistake, for it alienated many Republicans who had strongly supported Wilson's war policies. At any rate, the voters, irritated by domestic discontents as well, returned Republican majorities to both houses of Congress, and Wilson went to Paris in December, 1918, at the head of the American peace delegation as a man seemingly repudiated by his countrymen.

Wilson further angered the members of the opposition party when he failed to appoint any outstanding Republican leader, or indeed any member of the Senate from either party, as a member of the Peace Commission that went with him to Paris. There were eminent Republicans, men like William H. Taft or Charles Evans Hughes or Elihu Root, who could have been counted on to support internationalist views. But the only Republican appointed to the Peace Commission was the able career diplomat, Henry White, who had retired from active political life almost a decade before. The composition of the Peace Commission encouraged the suspicion that Wilson did not want to be accompanied by a strong and independent delegation.

The Big Four interrupt their labors to pose for a memorable picture. Left to right: Lloyd George, Orlando, Clemenceau, and Wilson.

Peace-Making: 1919. The Paris Peace Conference, which met from January to June, 1919, was not a meeting between the Allies and the defeated powers, but rather a conference among the Allies to decide what terms they would impose upon the vanquished. The Big Four—England, France, Italy, and the United States—made the important decisions. England was represented by David Lloyd George, the British Prime Minister, an alert and able politician who had won a general election the preceding December on a campaign calling for strong punitive measures against Germany. France was represented by its Premier, Georges Clemenceau ("The Tiger"), a determined watchdog of French interests and French security who cared about little else. Vittorio Orlando, the Italian Prime Minister, concerned himself chiefly with Italian territorial gains at the expense of Austria. Italy had entered the war for her own benefit after a period of candid bargaining with both sides, and had been promised concessions by the Allies in one of a series of secret treaties made during the war. When it became clear that all Italy's demands would not be met, Orlando

withdrew from the conference, and the Big Four became the Big Three.

Wilson took a program to Paris based upon three cardinal principles: self-government, free trade, and peace. Self-government—that is, self-determination for the peoples of Europe and to some extent even for the peoples of colonial countries—would alleviate discontent and serve the principle of democracy. Free trade would mollify national rivalries and broaden prosperity. Peace would be underwritten by a system of mutual guarantees of territorial integrity, protected by the League of Nations and backed by the threat of common action against an aggressor. Wilson knew that the sufferings the French, British, and Italians had endured during the war would make it difficult for him to persuade his allies to forget purely national grievances and aspirations long enough to support his program. He told one of the experts who accompanied him to Paris that "we would be the only disinterested men at the Peace Conference, and that the men whom we were about to deal with did not represent their own people." The second part of this assertion typified the kind of miscalculation to which Wilson was prone, for the Allied peoples shared only too fully in Clemenceau's single-minded concern for security and in Lloyd George's demand for vengeance.

Wilson was soon driven into a long, sometimes acrimonious, and only partially successful effort to persuade the Allies to forget the harsh terms they wanted to impose. After some compromises had been made, the Treaty of Versailles was signed by the Germans on June 28. It contained the following chief provisions: Germany was stripped of all her colonies and commercial rights in Africa and the Far East. Alsace-Lorraine was to be returned to France, and the Saar Basin was given over to French exploitation for 15 years, after which a plebiscite was to decide whether the region should remain under international control, or go to France or to Germany. Germany had to pay an immediate indemnity of $5 billion, agree to sign a blank check for future reparations, and to pay large amounts of livestock and other goods as reparations to Britain, France, and Belgium. Her standing army was reduced to 100,000 men, conscription was forbidden, the manufacture and purchase of war materials were virtually barred, and frontier fortifications were torn down. She was to pay shipping damages on a ton-for-ton basis by ceding most of her

Europe in 1920

existing merchant marine and new maritime construction. Among the terms that rankled in the German mind for years were the requirements that part of her territory be cut off by the creation of the "Polish corridor" and that the Rhineland be occupied for 15 years.

These harsh terms were a far cry from the lenient ones Wilson had called for, but he had succeeded in moderating many of the Allies' demands, and he thought that he must make some concessions in order to win support for his proposed League of Nations. "It is a very severe settlement with Germany," he said in September, 1919, "but there is not anything in it that she did not earn." Germany would almost certainly have imposed at least as harsh terms upon the Allies if she had won. A year earlier, at Brest-Litovsk, when the Russians had sought peace, the Germans had dictated exorbitant terms. They had partitioned the Russian Empire, and had exacted tremendous territories inhabited by millions.

The terms of the Versailles Treaty did not satisfy Clemenceau, who consented to them only in return for a separate alliance among Great Britain, the United States, and France to act jointly against any future attacks on France. Wilson consented, though he might have expected that a commitment which violated so openly the American tradition of avoiding European alliances would be, as indeed it soon was, rejected by the United States Senate.

It was the League of Nations that he expected would really underwrite the security of France and of all nations, and, after much effort, he persuaded the Allies to include this League in the Treaty. The Covenant of the League set up a permanent Secretariat with headquarters at Geneva, a Council of nine members, and an Assembly. The Council consisted of one representative each from the United States, Great Britain, France, Italy, and Japan, and four others chosen by the Assembly. The Assembly had a voting representative from every member nation.

A Permanent Court of International Justice was also set up at the Hague.

The members of the League—all nations and self-governing dominions were eligible —pledged themselves "to respect and preserve as against external aggression the territorial integrity and existing political independence" of all other members; to recognize the right of each member nation to bring to the attention of the Assembly or the Council any matter involving a threat to international peace; to give publicity to treaties and armaments; to submit to inquiry and arbitration disputes threatening international peace, breaches of treaties, and questions of international law; to refrain from war until three months after the decision of the arbiters; to refrain from war with nations complying with the decision of the League; and, when called upon by the League, to employ military, naval, and economic sanctions against nations that resorted to war in violation of their League agreements.

The Council was empowered to make plans to reduce armaments and mitigate dangers arising from the private manufacture of armaments; to investigate disputes brought before it by member or non-member nations; to give publicity to treaties; to establish an International Labor Bureau with some control over conditions of labor, health, drugs, arms and munitions, and international moral standards; and to exercise mandates—that is, supervised protectorates —over the colonies taken from Germany and Turkey.

Since the Treaty of Versailles governed only the settlement with Germany, other treaties had to be made with her allies. The Treaty of St. Germain with Austria attempted to guarantee that she would not initiate or consent to union with Germany. The Treaty of Trianon, signed by Hungary in 1920, drastically reduced the borders of the old Magyar kingdom. The Treaty of Neuilly, governing the Bulgarian settlement, trimmed her pre-war borders. The Treaty of Sèvres with Turkey stripped her of almost all her non-Turkish territory, but Turkish nationalists prevented its ratification; in the Treaty of Lausanne, contracted in 1923, Turkey won better terms.

The Fight for the Treaty.

When Wilson returned to try to win the Senate's consent to the Treaty of Versailles, he faced the most difficult task of his career. The election of 1918 had given the Republicans control of the Senate, and Wilson's sworn foe, Senator Henry Cabot Lodge of Massachusetts, had become Chairman of the Senate Committee on Foreign Relations. German-Americans throughout the country felt that Germany had been lured to the Peace Conference by false promises and then had been betrayed. Italian-Americans were dissatisfied with Italy's share of the peace spoils. And Irish-Americans were angry over Wilson's failure to raise the issue of Irish independence at Paris. All these groups provided important cores of anti-League and anti-Wilson sentiment. Liberals were disappointed with the harshness of the treaty, if not with the League itself. Many Americans were dubious about promises to use American arms in what they felt were other nations' disputes. In the Senate, a strong group of "irreconcilables" representing extreme isolationist views—William E. Borah, Philander C. Knox, Hiram Johnson, Robert M. La Follette, and others—gathered their forces for a last-ditch resistance to Wilson.

Wilson still felt that he could carry the people with him and put the League through, and there is every evidence that the majority of the public favored American membership in the League. More than the necessary two-thirds of the senators were willing to vote for some form of League membership, although tact and flexibility were required to get the treaty ratified. But Wilson was in an uncompromising mood. When the French Ambassador, Jusserand, assured him that the Allies would gladly accept American membership with reservations that would satisfy the doubts of an influential group of Republican senators, he said flatly:

"Mr. Ambassador, I shall consent to nothing. The Senate must take its medicine." He consistently refused to consider modifications in the Covenant of the League that might have made it acceptable to the men who were holding out against it.

Through the summer of 1919, the Senate and the nation at large debated and discussed the League. As the weeks passed, it became apparent that the tide of public opinion was turning against the League, and Wilson decided to take his case to the country. Although he was exhausted by many months of grueling work, and had fallen ill with influenza in Paris, he set forth in early September on a nation-wide speaking tour of the sort that is usually attempted only in presidential campaigns. In a 22-day trip covering 8,000 miles, he delivered 37 lengthy speeches, participated in about a dozen parades, and addressed innumerable small audiences from the rear platform of his train.

In the meantime, the Senate fell to fighting over a series of 14 reservations sponsored by Senator Lodge. Superficially, the purpose of these reservations was to limit American obligations to the League, but in fact Lodge seems to have hoped that they would stimulate a debate that would end in making American participation impossible. By the time the Lodge reservations were introduced, Wilson had suffered a physical breakdown and had been forced to cancel the rest of his trip and return to Washington for absolute rest. Early in October, he suffered a stroke that left him half-paralyzed, and from that point on he was unable to carry on his side of the debate. He had appealed to "all true friends of the treaty" to spurn the Lodge reservations. They were rejected in November, 1919, but a resolution to ratify the treaty without any reservations also failed, by a vote of 53-38.

So much sentiment for the League remained in the country and the Senate, however, that the issue was brought up again in March, 1920. The Wilsonian Democrats were still under instructions from their sick leader to reject the treaty so long as reservations were attached. Some of them broke with his instructions and voted for the treaty, and it received a small majority, 49-35. But this was far short of the constitutional two-thirds.

The League of Nations, along with the Treaty of Versailles, was defeated. Wilson had gambled for total victory and had achieved total defeat. Legally, the war with Germany did not end for the United States until July 2, 1921, when Congress passed a joint resolution declaring that hostilities were over and reserving to the United States the rights and privileges of a victorious power.

The Election of 1920.   Even with the treaty dead in the Senate, Wilson did not give up hope. The election of 1920, he announced, must be "a great and solemn referendum." The people themselves would now vote directly on the issue. But it has never been possible to make an American presidential election a clear referendum on any issue of foreign policy, and 1920 was no exception.

The Republicans, deprived of their leader by the death of Theodore Roosevelt early in 1919, turned to a relatively obscure candidate, Senator Warren Gamaliel Harding of Ohio. When the Republican convention at Chicago seemed about to go into a deadlock between the supporters of Theodore Roosevelt's friend, General Leonard Wood, and Governor Frank O. Lowden of Illinois, a group of seasoned politicians met in a smoke-filled room in the Blackstone Hotel and settled upon Harding as a man they could control. Formerly the editor of the Marion (Ohio) *Daily Star,* Harding had served only one term in the Senate. He was a pleasant, pliable man who had quietly opposed the League during the fight over the treaty. To run against him, the Democrats nominated another Ohioan, the popu-

lar and progressive Governor James M. Cox, who had not been closely identified with the Wilson administration and who was acceptable to the bosses of the big city machines. As his running-mate, Cox was given young Franklin D. Roosevelt, who had been Assistant Secretary of the Navy under Wilson.

Cox, impressed with Wilson's personal gallantry, waged his campaign on the League issue, but Harding and the Republicans were so ambiguous on the subject that it was impossible to be sure what they proposed to do. The Republican platform condemned the Covenant of the League but Harding promised vaguely in a series of speeches delivered on his front porch to work for the creation of "an association of nations." Irreconcilables like Borah and Johnson supported him as an enemy of the League, while a group of 31 prominent Republicans who believed in the League signed an appeal for his election as the best way of assuring America's ultimate entry into a satisfactory world organization.

Had an overwhelming majority of Americans been persuaded of the League's value in 1920, it seems unlikely that the Republican technique of avoiding the issue would have been successful. In fact, there appears to have been an immense reaction against Wilson and everything he represented—against the idealism and self-criticism of the Progressive era, against reform, the war, political intensity, self-sacrifice, and personal discipline. In addition, those who had been troubled by America's entry into the war, by the conduct of the war, or by the high prices, taxes, hysteria, and repression that came with it, were against Wilson or anyone who might inherit his mantle. Cox was crushed at the polls, 16,152,000 to 9,147,000, getting only 34.1 per cent of the popular vote. No major-party candidate in the history of American elections had ever been defeated so badly. But, as a contemporary observer remarked, Cox was beaten "not by those who dislike him but by those who dislike Wilson and his group." The New York *World* wrote: "The American people wanted a change, and they have voted for a change. They did not know what kind of a change they wanted, and they do not know today what kind of a change they have voted for." Warren Harding, who was in many ways an average American, had stated that "America's present need is not heroics but healing; not nostrums but normalcy; not revolution but restoration." Educated citizens laughed at the candidate's unwitting coinage of a new word for normality, but voters thought they knew well enough what he meant. And yet what was it that was normal? The old days of McKinley and Hanna that the reformers had worked so hard to supersede? Or some still older and still more golden days of the earlier nineteenth century? The "moral over-strain" of the Progressive era and the tensions and hysteria of the war that followed it had blurred former standards of the normal and the good. Like the peoples of Europe, who suffered from the same problems even more acutely, the people of the United States were entering an era that they could hardly be expected to understand. The world that the Progressives had so confidently tried to reform had been shattered by the war.

Readings

Several of the volumes dealing with Wilson and his policies cited in the preceding chapter are also relevant for the war period and immediately after.

Both Sidney B. Fay, *Origins of the World War* (2 vols., 1930), and Bernadotte E. Schmitt, *The Coming of War* (2 vols., 1930), survey the backgrounds of the European struggle. America's entry is discussed thoroughly by Charles C. Tansill, *America Goes to War* (1938), and interestingly by Walter Millis, *The Road to War* (1935), both from an isolationist point of view. A more sympathetic view toward Wilson is taken by Charles Seymour in *American Diplomacy during the World War* (1934). Preston W. Slosson, *The Great Crusade and After, 1914-1928* (1930), discusses the war experience. Thomas A. Bailey deals with peace-making and the fate of the Versailles Treaty in *Woodrow Wilson and the Lost Peace* (1944), and *Woodrow Wilson and the Great Betrayal* (1945). See also John Garraty, *Henry Cabot Lodge* (1953). For a general account of the war period, see F. L. Paxson, *American Democracy and the World War* (3 vols., 1936-1948).

On the Mexican problem, see J. F. Rippy, *The United States and Mexico* (rev. ed., 1931). Harley Notter, *The Origins of the Foreign Policy of Woodrow Wilson* (1937), is a thorough work.

H. C. Peterson, *Propaganda for War* (1939), and Harold Lavine and James Wechsler, *War Propaganda and the United States* (1940), are among more recent studies of wartime propaganda, though Arthur Ponsonby's *Falsehood in War Time* (1928) still is an interesting piece of work. See also George Creel, *How We Advertised America* (1920). Elting E. Morison, *Admiral Sims and the Modern American Navy* (1942), and J. G. Harbord, *The American Army in France, 1917-1918* (1936), deal respectively with naval and military aspects of America's participation in the war. Coercion at home during the war is dealt with in Zachariah Chafee's *Free Speech in the United States* (rev. ed., 1941). On a special aspect of wartime intolerance, Carl Wittke, *The German Americans and the World War* (1936), is informative.

Harry R. Rudin, *Armistice, 1919* (1944), discusses the end of the fighting, while Paul Birdsall, *Versailles Twenty Years After* (1941), is a re-estimation of the peace. D. F. Fleming, *The United States and the League of Nations, 1918-1920* (1932), is favorable to Wilson. On the election of 1920, both J. M. Cox, *Journey Through My Years* (1946), and S. H. Adams, *Incredible Era* (1939), are helpful.

FROM NORMALCY TO DEPRESSION

C H A P T E R   T W E N T Y - S E V E N

In many ways, public life in America during the 1920's was like the Progressive era turned upside down. The Progressives had thrilled again and again to idealistic rhetoric, but to many sensitive men and women of the postwar generation, all idealism was suspect.

"I was embarrassed," says Lieutenant Henry in Ernest Hemingway's postwar novel, *A Farewell to Arms*, "by the words sacred, glorious, and sacrifice and the expression in vain. We had heard them, sometimes standing in rain almost out of earshot, so that only the shouted words came through, and had read them, on proclamations, now for a long time, and I had seen nothing sacred, and the things that were glorious had no glory and the sacrifices were like the stockyards in Chicago, if nothing was done with the meat except to bury it .... Abstract words such as glory, honor, courage, were obscene .... " Although Hemingway expresses here his disillusionment with the language of wartime idealism, his words might well be taken as his generation's rejection of the whole of Progressive morality.

I. COMPLACENCY AND SCANDAL

The New Temper. After the war, there was a widespread feeling that the old moral issues had been meaningless, that public morality and idealism, self-sacrifice and self-restraint, were neither so realizable nor so important as the Progressive politicians and publicists had claimed. These issues had not lost ground in a general public debate, but they had lost the center of attention and had become increasingly ignored. Americans turned from the effort to reform society to the effort to make money from its growth. They relaxed their criticism of businessmen, and accepted business leadership not merely in practical affairs but in morals and philosophy as well. And they voted for the politicians who spoke for business leadership. "What we want in America," said Harding in 1920, "is less government in business and more business in government." Harding's successor, Calvin Coolidge, summed it up by saying, "The business of the United States is business." Hence the policies of the 1920's expressed a desire, except in certain limited areas, to withdraw from governmental efforts to control, limit, or regulate the activities of business. Economic action by the government was usually confined to measures that would aid business and give businessmen a free hand in the development of the country. The age of reform had passed, and America was now in an age of acquisition and enjoyment—or so it seemed.

The Republican party, whose leaders were to preside over the political life of the nation for 12 years, had been deprived of its idealistic wing by the estrangement of the Progressive insurgents (see p. 593) and by the death of Theodore Roosevelt. It was left in the hands of Old Guard professionals in the Senate and of the great business interests who supplied its campaign funds. Men of this kind, seeking a president they could control, had chosen Warren Gamaliel Harding in 1920 to be the first president of the Republican restoration.

Harding himself was not a businessman, nor even a politican practiced in representing big-business interests. He was a plain American, a simple, easy-going, hard-drinking, small-town newspaper editor whose genial ways had led him into political life. Handsome, generous (he quietly pardoned Eugene Debs), and unpretentious, he became extravagantly popular; but he had neither the training nor the insight to carry out positive policies or to prevent the disaster that his associates brought upon his administration.

To Harding, politics was chiefly a game one played to reward personal loyalties. He promised the country to bring its "best minds" to Washington as his advisers—a promise he redeemed in part by making such outstanding men as Charles Evans Hughes Secretary of State, Herbert Hoover Secretary of Commerce, and Henry C. Wallace Secretary of Agriculture. But he also brought with him a group of local cronies, neither scrupulous nor competent, who eventually came to be known as the "Ohio gang." And it was with these cronies, who played poker and drank with him in the White House, that Harding felt most at home. The Ohio gang made the Harding administration synonymous with corruption and scandal. Perhaps what was most significant of the era, however, was not that this should have occurred in Washington, but that it should have made so little impression upon the minds of most Americans.

The Harding Scandals. The lesser scandals of the Harding administration can be recounted briefly. Charles R. Forbes, adventurer and one-time deserter from the army, who had so charmed Harding that he had been put in charge of the Veterans' Bureau, was eventually discovered to have disposed of nearly $250 million in graft. Forbes had made a practice of taking kickbacks from contractors and suppliers who dealt with the Veterans' Bureau, and of buying materials at outrageous prices. In 1925, he was sent to Leavenworth Prison. The office of Colonel Thomas W. Miller, the alien property custodian, whose job was to supervise the valuble German patents and other properties confiscated during the war, was found to have parted with governmental

caped conviction in the courts. His henchman, Jesse Smith, who conducted a sort of clearing-house for the graft of the Ohio gang, had committed suicide in 1923.

The most spectacular of the Harding scandals was the famous Teapot Dome Affair. Since 1909, when the conservation movement was in full swing, three tracts of oil-rich government land had been set aside for the future needs of the navy. These reserves had been placed under the jurisdiction of the Secretary of the Navy, but early in 1921 President Harding, by executive order, had transferred them to the custody of the Secretary of the Interior, Albert B. Fall. Fall, who was intimately acquainted with representatives of certain large oil interests, welcomed the opportunity to do favors for his friends at considerable profit to himself. Within less than a year after he was given

Wilson and Harding at Harding's inauguration. The ailing Wilson shows his bafflement and frustration, while Harding smiles amiably.

properties for far less than they were worth, and to have favored the clients of a few skilled lobbyists. Miller was eventually convicted of conspiracy to defraud the government. Harry Daugherty, Harding's Attorney General, was dismissed by President Coolidge in 1924 when some of his improprieties were revealed. Although the Senate found Daugherty guilty of misconduct in the sale of liquor permits and of pardons, he es-

power to dispose of the oil reserves, he secretly leased one of them, the Teapot Dome Reserve, to Harry F. Sinclair's Mammoth Oil Company. Some months later, he secretly leased another, the Elk Hills Reserve, to Edward F. Doheny's Pan-American Petroleum Company. These arrangements were made without competitive bidding.

Under the terms of these leases, the government was to receive certain amounts of oil as royalties from the private operators in return for the privilege of exploiting the reserves. For his favoritism, Fall received some $223,000 in Liberty Bonds from Sinclair, along with a herd of cattle for his ranch, and received a "loan" of $100,000 from Doheny. Fall's sudden wealth attracted the interest of vigilant senators, and after long investigations by a committee headed by Senator Thomas J. Walsh of Montana, the tangled story of these sordid arrangements was unraveled. Both leases were ultimately voided by the Supreme Court. Secretary of the Navy Denby was driven by public criticism to resign from office. Fall was convicted of accepting a bribe, fined $100,000, and sentenced to a year in prison, though oddly enough both Doheny and Sinclair were acquitted of having bribed him. Eventually, however, Sinclair served a double term in prison for contempt of the Senate in refusing to answer questions put to him by the Committee on Public Lands, and also for contempt of court because he had hired private detectives to shadow the jury at his trial.

Long before the scandals were known to the general public, Harding had found out about some of them. From the very beginning, the presidency overwhelmed him. "I knew this job would be too much for me,"

he once moaned to a friend. Exhausted by the tasks of his office, tormented at the thought that he had been betrayed by his friends, and horrified at the realization that disclosures about to be made were bound to destroy his reputation, Harding sank rapidly under his burdens. In the summer of 1923, returning from a visit to Alaska, he fell ill with what was diagnosed as ptomaine poisoning. This attack was followed by pneumonia and finally by what appeared to be a stroke of apoplexy. On August 2 he died, and the entire nation, still ignorant of the scandals soon to discredit his administration, went into mourning as deep and genuine as had been accorded to any public figure since the time of Lincoln. Only later, when the graft scandals and Harding's personal indiscretion were revealed, did his reputation decline. It was eight years after his death before a president could be induced to come to Marion, Ohio, to dedicate the Harding Memorial which the public, with affectionate generosity, had lavishly subscribed shortly after his death. And even then, the speech that President Hoover made was an uncomfortable attempt to show that Harding had been betrayed by those whom he had trusted.

II. AN AGE OF INTOLERANCE

The Red Scares. The wartime spirit of intolerance carried over into the postwar period. During the months we were actually engaged in the war, Americans had grown accustomed to conformity and the suppression of dissent. While the war lasted, intolerance had been directed mainly against those persons who were suspected of sympathizing with Germany and the Central Powers, but now it embraced a wider variety of persons —foreigners in general, Negroes, Jews and Catholics, radicals or suspected radicals, and strikers.

In large part, the new wave of fear could be traced to the American reaction to the

Bolshevik Revolution in Russia, even though only a handful of Americans sympathized with the Bolsheviks. In part, the scare arose out of the immediate postwar economic cycle and the labor activities that attended it.

During the war, trade unions had grown enormously in strength and militancy; many workers had joined them in an effort to protect themselves against rapidly rising prices. In the short-lived postwar boom of 1919 and 1920, prices continued to shoot upward. No longer under the restraint imposed by the wartime emergency, workers were able to back their wage demands with new vigor and power. In 1919, there were

3,630 strikes, involving 4,160,348 workers. Particularly bitter were the unsuccessful 1919-1920 strike against the United States Steel Corporation and the 1919 dispute in the bituminous coal industry. Most of the strikers were seeking higher wages or shorter hours, demands quite familiar in the history of American trade unionism, but some began to call for new and more fundamental changes. The railroad workers, for instance, endorsed the widely discussed Plumb Plan, which called for continued government management of the railroads with labor participation, and the United Mine Workers demanded nationalization of the coal mines.

Conservative employers used the general fear of Bolshevism and radicalism as a weapon to oppose the demands of labor. Actually, the avowed adherents of communism and anarchism could not call upon the support of more than a fraction of 1 per cent of the adult population of the country, but in the general hysteria this fact was overlooked.

A few startling provocative acts, presumably committed by anarchists, gave the color of truth to fears that were already prevalent in 1919. A time bomb was discovered in the Mayor of Seattle's mail; another bomb exploded and blew off the hands of a Georgia senator's house servant. No less than 36 bombs addressed to persons in high places, including J. P. Morgan, John D. Rockefeller, and Justice Holmes of the Supreme Court, were discovered in various post offices. A bomb was exploded just outside the home of Attorney-General Palmer in Washington. In September, 1920, when the Red scare was beginning to simmer down, it was given new life by a tremendous explosion at the corner of Broad and Wall streets in the heart of New York's financial section, which killed 38 persons and injured hundreds. The criminals were never discovered, though there

Smoke still hangs in the air after the Wall Street explosion of September 16, 1920, which did so much to keep the Red scare alive.

was evidence indicating that alien anarchists were behind the deed. But now it was much easier for Americans to believe in the exaggerated reports of radical influences, and to look upon all dissenters, however peaceful their programs, as potential exponents of violence. The growing fear of radicalism rapidly brought about a climate of opinion hostile to all critical thought.

A. Mitchell Palmer, Wilson's Attorney-General and once a reformer, took the initiative in a nation-wide crusade against the labor movement and radicals, real or alleged. In 1919, to a chorus of applause from the press, he issued an injunction restraining leaders of coal unions from doing anything to further a strike, although the law under which he acted had been drafted under the stress of wartime conditions. He then launched a series of raids to round up alien members of the Communist party for deportation. In the course of these raids, which took place on New Year's Day, 1920, federal agents arrested over 6,000 men, many of whom turned out to be neither aliens nor communists. One-third of the men arrested were later released. The raids were followed by a flood of high-powered propaganda, which urged the public to take drastic action against the Reds. Eventually, 556 aliens were deported.

One event that occurred during the red scare of 1920 was to haunt the American people for almost seven years. In April, 1920, at South Braintree, Massachusetts, a factory paymaster and his guard, carrying a payroll, were killed by two robbers. A few weeks later the police arrested two alien Italian anarchists, Nicola Sacco and Bartolomeo Vanzetti, for the murders. In 1921, the two were brought to trial before Judge Webster Thayer and a jury and were found guilty. At first the trial attracted only slight attention, but as protests against the verdict began to be made throughout the country and throughout the world, more and more Americans began to question its validity. The actual evidence against the men was slight, and the suspicion grew that they had been found guilty not because they had committed the crime but because of the prejudice against their political convictions. Moreover, the conduct of the trial judge was subject to question, and Governor Fuller of Massachusetts appointed an investigating committee to look into the matter. The committee concluded that the trial judge had been guilty of a "grave breach of official decorum," but in spite of this, it said, justice had been done.

As the issue dragged out over a period of years, the dignified demeanor of the condemned men and their continued quiet devotion to their beliefs made it increasingly hard for many people to believe that they were ruthless murderers. When they were finally electrocuted in 1927, amid a new wave of world-wide protests, millions were convinced of their innocence, and millions more were convinced that, guilty or innocent, they had not been given a fair trial. The truth in the case has never been finally determined, but there can be little doubt that the protest against it helped to free the public from the mood of intolerance that had set the stage for the trial.

Anti-Foreign Sentiment. In the wake of the war, there arose a vague and indiscriminate anti-foreign feeling. One result of this feeling was a drastic change in the nation's historic immigration policy. For years before the war, many liberals and labor sympathizers had been complaining that immigration was becoming a threat to the American way of life in general and to the workers' standard of living in particular. From 1897 to 1914, a total of 2.9 million immigrants had entered the United States from northern Europe, but 10.2 million had arrived from southern and eastern Europe. Americans were used to the northern Europeans, but they received the immigrants from the new areas with less hospitality, claiming that they were alien to the living standards, the "racial" stock, and the political folkways of the United States.

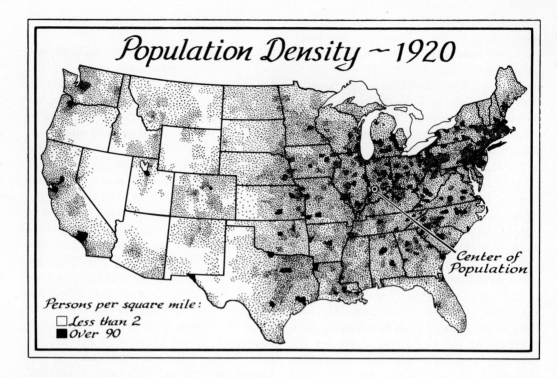

Population Density ~ 1920

Persons per square mile:
☐ Less than 2
■ Over 90

Center of Population

This rising distrust of aliens, fed by the mistaken belief that there were many radicals among them, paved the way for a reversal of the old liberal conditions of admission to the United States.

In 1921, Congress adopted a drastic new immigration policy. Each European nation was assigned a quota (most Asiatics were already barred) based on 3 per cent of the number of its nationals resident in the United States in the base year, 1910. During the next few years, immigration from northern Europe did not increase, but immigrants from the other areas filled their quotas. So Congress pushed this policy still further with the National Origins Act of 1924, which cut the quota to 2 per cent and shifted the base year back to 1890, when the ratio of north Europeans in the American population had been much higher than it was in 1910. After 1927, the entire quota from all European nations was set at 150,000, with each country allotted the same proportion of this total that its nationals represented in the American population of 1920. (This provision in fact went into effect only in 1929.) Under these laws, the United States, which

during the years before the war had been accustomed to receiving from three-quarters of a million to a million immigrants from Europe each year, cut its arrivals to between 147,000 and 169,000 during the years 1925-1930. From 1931 to 1938, when the effects of the depression were added to legal restriction, only 12,000 to 62,000 immigrants entered the country each year.

Closing the immigration gates by no means put an end to the ethnic animosities caused by the recruiting of American labor from a great variety of stocks. It did, however, cut off one of the world's great migrations, that epic movement of peoples to American shores that had begun in the seventeenth century and continued for 300 years.

After the Red scare had died down somewhat, the most important symptom of the nation's rising spirit of intolerance was the revival of the Ku Klux Klan. The Klan of Reconstruction days had been dead since the 1870's (see p. 406). The new Klan was founded in Georgia in 1915 and was dedicated to preserving the racial and ideological purity of "Anglo-Saxon" Protestant America against the incursions of foreigners generally, and of "foreign" ideals, but particularly against Negroes, Catholics, and Jews. After 1920, the organization expanded rapidly, and at its peak in 1924, its membership was estimated at around 4,500,000 (it claimed 6 million), concentrated in the small towns of the South, the Middle West, and the Pacific coast. Wearing nightshirts and carrying out terroristic night raids, the Klan burned fiery crosses to advertise its presence, flogged or kidnaped Negroes and whites alike, set itself up as an enforcement arm for prohibition, acted as a moral censor, made and unmade local politicians, discouraged strangers and union organizers, and made life miserable for some Catholic and Jewish businessmen. Klan leaders justified these extra-legal efforts by insisting that alien forces were taking America out of the hands of the old Anglo-Saxon stock and putting it into the hands of the new immigrants and their children.

By 1924, the Klan's political influence was so great that the Democratic national convention spent many anguished days debating a resolution to condemn the Klan by name, and became hopelessly divided between the Klan and anti-Klan factions. Finally, a riot of financial and sexual scandal in the Klan-dominated state of Indiana served to disillusion the rank-and-file members, many of whom were sincerely if misguidedly idealistic. Liberal-minded Americans everywhere rallied to fight the Klan, and its influence declined rapidly.

Prohibition. Prohibition, a troublesome political issue during the 1920's, was another aspect of the struggle between two visions of morality and two ways of life. Drinking was considered to be the pre-eminent vice of immigrants and of corrupt city life. Nationwide prohibition itself was a product of the moral idealism of the Progressive era and of the stresses of the war. The Prohibition Amendment (see p. 586) was supplemented by the Volstead Act of October, 1919, which defined intoxicating liquor as any beverage

containing over one-half of 1 per cent of alcohol. In January, 1920, prohibition went into effect, and a long, expensive campaign to enforce it began.

Making drink illegal had two immediate effects. For many people, liquor now took on a glamour it might not otherwise have had, and illegal drinking became an adventure. Putting outside the pale of the law a personal habit that millions of Americans would not give up also opened a vast new field of illegal activity to gangsters and bootleggers. Most of the old saloons were eliminated, but in their place came the covert "speakeasy." The bartender and the legitimate brewer were gone, but instead there came a horde of undesirables engaged in the illegal manufacture of beer and liquor, much of it extremely bad, some of it actually poisonous. Gangsters like Al Capone built empires of vice upon the sale of beer and liquor. Corruption spread from the lucrative illegal liquor business into the ranks of the police and the prohibition agents. For the ordinary workingman, liquor was hard to get; but for many people, bootleg or bathtub gin became a staple of every party.

Criticism of the prohibition experiment grew louder and louder. Most of it arose within the Democratic party, which appealed more strongly than the Republicans to those elements in the population for whom drinking was an immemorial social custom. It became an issue in the campaign of 1928, when Al Smith proposed to do away with national prohibition and return the problem to the states. Herbert Hoover, not yet ready to claim success for the Eighteenth Amendment, described it as "a great social and economic experiment, noble in motive and far-reaching in purpose."

After his election in 1928, Hoover appointed George W. Wickersham of the New York Bar to head a group of 11 distinguished Americans to examine the enforcement problem. In January, 1931, when the results of this inquiry were published, they gave more comfort to the critics of prohibition than to its advocates. In frank and full detail, the Wickersham Commission rehearsed the failures of enforcement, the prevalence of crime and corruption. But, confusingly enough, the majority of the Commission recommended that the experiment be given a further trial. The Commission seemed to be recommending that prohibition was a failure which should be steadfastly continued. As a contemporary columnist put it:

> Prohibition is an awful flop.
> We like it.
> It can't stop what it's meant to stop.
> We like it.
> It's left a trail of graft and slime,
> It's filled our land with vice and crime,
> It don't prohibit worth a dime,
> Nevertheless, we're for it.

In 1932, for the second time, the platform of the victorious Democrats called for abandonment of federal prohibition; and in December, 1933, enough states had ratified the Twenty-First Amendment to repeal the Eighteenth. The control of liquor was thus returned to the states, of which only seven elected to continue prohibition within their borders. By the 1950's, not one state totally barred the sale of beer, whisky, or wine, although some states left with localities the right to ban sales of such beverages within their jurisdictions.

Fundamentalism. A major sign of the popular fevers of the 1920's was the increasing aggressiveness of religious fundamentalists—that is, those groups and sects that favored a literal interpretation of Biblical Christianity and resisted all attempts to modify theology in the light of modern scientific discovery or Biblical criticism. The fundamentalist's opposition to science, like the prohibitionist's crusade against drink, represented the effort of a minority to shore up its scheme of values through the agencies of the law. The tide of knowledge and of belief seemed to be running against the funda-

mentalists, but in some parts of the country they were numerous and powerful. They leveled their heaviest attack against the doctrine of evolution; into the legislatures of nearly half the states they introduced bills to prevent the teaching of Darwin's theories in the public schools. In Tennessee and Mississippi, they succeeded in getting their laws passed.

The Tennessee statute made it unlawful for schools or universities, supported in whole or in part by public funds, "to teach any theory that denies the story of the Divine creation of man as taught in the Bible, and to teach instead that man has descended from a lower order of animals." To test the validity of the law, a young high-school teacher in Dayton, Tennessee, John Thomas Scopes, arranged to be prosecuted for violation of the act. His trial in July, 1925, dramatized the battle between fundamentalism and modernism for the entire nation. Brilliant and nationally famous lawyers, Clarence Darrow, Dudley Field Malone, and Arthur Garfield Hays, took up the case for Scopes, while William Jennings Bryan, an ardent fundamentalist, acted as counsel for the prosecution. Reporters came from all over the nation to cover the trial, and religious revivalists converged upon Dayton to preach to curious crowds, concerned over the fate of religion. The climax of the trial came when Bryan took the stand to testify and was subjected to grueling and pitiless questioning by Darrow, who exposed serious gaps in Bryan's thought and learning. The presiding judge mercifully cut the questioning short, but Bryan died just a week after the trial. Scopes was found guilty and fined $100, though later his fine was rescinded on a technicality. Superficially, the fundamentalists had won their point, since the anti-evolution law had been upheld. But they had been held up to ridicule, and the modernists began to take on some of the militancy and unity that the fundamentalists alone had shown before.

As the forces of intolerance were not always unopposed, so their invasions of freedom were not always successful. So respectable and beloved an American as the Emporia newspaper editor, William Allen White, fought unremittingly against the Ku Klux Klan in his native state of Kansas. And when the New York State Legislature expelled five duly elected socialist members on the ground that socialism was "absolutely inimical" to the interests of the state, Charles Evans Hughes, later to become Chief Justice of the Supreme Court, made a dignified protest against the hysteria behind the act, as did the New York Governor, Alfred E. Smith. Some of the most searching philosophical statements on the ideal of freedom of speech were made by Justice Oliver Wendell Holmes, particularly in the dissenting opinions he formulated during his career on the Supreme Court.

III. THE POLITICS OF PROSPERITY

The Election of 1924. H a r d i n g seemed to represent prosperity, expansive and corrupt. His successor, Calvin Coolidge, seemed to represent prosperity, frugal and scrupulous. Unlike Harding, Coolidge was sparing of words and emotions. He had first come into national prominence in 1919, when as Governor of Massachusetts he had dramatically broken a strike of Boston policemen. The strike, a protest against the refusal of the police commissioners to recognize a union organized to raise the extraordinarily low wages paid to policemen, had left Boston all but defenseless against disorders. Since it came at a moment of widespread labor strife and universal fear of "radicalism," it aroused general public hostility. After a call from Boston's mayor, Coolidge called out the state guard to restore order. When President Samuel Gompers of the A.F.L. protested because some of the leaders of the policemen's union were fired for their organizing activities, the Governor replied with a memorable and characteristic statement: "There is no right to strike against the public safety by anybody, anywhere, any time." This sentence, despite his inept handling of the situation, established Coolidge almost instantly as a national hero and led to his nomination for the vice-presidency in 1920.

When Harding died, in August, 1923, Coolidge's oath of office was administered to him by his father in their simple Vermont farmhouse by the light of an old-fashioned kerosene lamp. Almost immediately, people began to regard this lean and silent New Englander as a man who would be a vigilant custodian of the nation's affairs, and it was Coolidge's good fortune to come into office at the beginning of a boom period that soon began to be called "Coolidge prosperity." The postwar depression was coming to an end, and the nation was entering upon the seven good years that preceded the 1929 crash. By 1924, when Coolidge ran for the presidency in his own right, prosperity was in evidence almost everywhere.

By the summer of 1924, Coolidge's nomination was a foregone conclusion, and it took the Republican party only three days to nominate him and his running mate, Brigadier General Charles G. Dawes. The Democrats, already handicapped by "Coolidge prosperity" and public apathy toward the Harding scandals, handicapped themselves even more by displaying their bitter internal party division. One faction of the party, whose candidate was William Gibbs McAdoo, Wilson's Secretary of the Treasury and his son-in-law, found its strength in the rural, Protestant, and Prohibitionist segments of the party. The other faction, whose candidate was Alfred E. Smith, New York's popular governor, drew upon the city machines and appealed to Catholic voters, who were strongly opposed to Prohibition. After a furious battle over the question of whether the Democratic party should condemn by name the anti-Catholic, anti-Jewish, and anti-Negro Ku Klux Klan (it was decided not to do so), the Smith and McAdoo forces became locked in a sullen deadlock that lasted 16 days in the broiling heat of New York City. More than 100 ballots were taken. In the end, when it became clear that the party was so badly wrecked that the nomination was worthless, the delegates settled upon John W. Davis. Originally from West Virginia, Davis was a dignified and impeccably conservative New York corporation lawyer. To ease the heart-burnings of more reform-minded Democrats, the convention nominated as his running mate William Jennings Bryan's brother, Charles.

The chief note of novelty in the 1924 campaign was provided by the third-party candidacy of Robert M. La Follette. In 1922, the Conference for Progressive Political Action had been organized by leaders of discontented farmers, officials of the Railroad Brotherhoods (whose members were particularly aroused by the railroad strike of 1920), intellectuals and liberals who hoped to keep alive the spirit of Progressivism, and a few socialists. This organization fostered La Follette's candidacy on an independent Progressive party ticket. The party's platform demanded government ownership of railroads, abolition of the injunction in labor disputes, relief for farmers, a popular referendum for the declaration of war in cases other than invasion of the United States, and other reforms. Senator Burton K. Wheeler, one of the leading investigators in the Teapot Dome Affair (see p. 630), bolted from the Democratic party to accept the Progressive vice-presidential nomination.

During the campaign of 1924, both major parties tended to concentrate their fire on La Follette rather than to debate the issues with each other. The Progressive candidate was charged with encouraging the radicalism that had become such a bogy in the public mind. In the election, Coolidge received 15,-725,000 votes, Davis 8,386,000, and La Follette 4,822,000. The general lack of interest in the campaign was shown by the fact that only a little more than half the eligible voters went to the polls. But perhaps the most striking lesson of the election was the unchallengeable domination of the Republican party. The size of Coolidge's majority, after that won by Harding in 1920, showed that the customary two-party struggle in American politics had ceased to exist. The Republican leaders had a free hand, and, as Coolidge remarked in his inaugural address of March 4, 1925, the public mood showed "a state of contentment seldom before seen."

Economic Policies.   This state of general public contentment made possible the conservative economic policies adopted by the postwar administrations. Even the Wilson administration, in its closing months, had adopted policies which indicated that the Democratic party, in spite of its prewar progressivism, had turned somewhat to the right.

The chief exception to this trend was the solution to the railroad problem. One of the first questions confronting the nation's policy-makers after the war was what should be done with the railroads taken over by the government during the war. Should they be returned to private management? If so, under what terms and with what restrictions? One solution, the so-called Plumb Plan, was proposed by the general counsel for the Railroad Brotherhoods, Glenn E. Plumb, who wanted the railroads to remain under federal ownership and to be managed jointly by representatives of the government, the operators, and the unions. Congress took a different tack, adopting a measure that involved neither full private management nor government ownership, but a considerable increase in public regulation.

In February, 1920, Congress passed the Esch-Cummins Transportation Act. This act empowered the Interstate Commerce Commission to evaluate all railroad properties and to fix fair rates and a fair return to investors. All earnings over 6 per cent were to be split between the railroads and the government, and the government was to use the pool thus established for the relief of weaker roads.

(This feature of the act was repealed in 1936 and the money collected from the more prosperous roads was returned.) A Railway Labor Board was set up to mediate labor disputes. (Later, in 1926, when it appeared that the Board had failed to establish labor harmony in railroading, it was replaced by other boards of mediation and arbitration less closely linked to the federal government.) The Interstate Commerce Commission was given power over railroad finances to protect the investing public. Moreover, after years of attempts at antitrust prosecutions, the railroads were now authorized and indeed encouraged to plan combinations that would make their operations more efficient, and some lines did consolidate.

Private businessmen were more pleased with the way Congress decided to dispose of the wartime merchant marine. The Merchant Marine Act of 1920 provided for handsome mail subsidies to shipping companies. The Shipping Board was authorized to sell government-owned merchant ships to private companies on very generous terms, and a preferential tariff was set on goods imported in American vessels. In 1928, the Jones-White Act provided for even greater mail subsidies and set aside $250 million to be used for making construction loans to private companies. It also eased the terms governing the purchase by private companies of vessels not yet sold by the government.

When the Republicans returned to power, they swung sharply away from wartime fiscal practices. During the 1920's, the tax policies of the three Republican administrations showed a great deal of continuity. For one thing, the Secretary of the Treasury from 1921 to 1932 was the immensely wealthy Andrew Mellon, whom Herbert Hoover once called "the greatest secretary of the Treasury since Alexander Hamilton." A more cynical critic remarked that he was the only Secretary of the Treasury under whom three presidents had served. Mellon was the head of a huge aluminum trust and the owner of oil wells, coal mines, distilleries, steel mills, utility companies, and banks. He was a formidable power in Pennsylvania politics and a lavish contributor to the coffers of the Republican party. His views on the tax problem suited his financial position, and Congress tended to follow his lead. Despite the $24 billion national debt inherited from the war, Mellon favored tax reductions on the ground that they would encourage business enterprise. "Anybody knows," he once said, "that any man of energy and initiative can get what he wants out of life. But when that initiative is crippled by legislation or a tax system which denies him the right to receive a reasonable share of his earnings, then he will no longer exert himself and the country will be deprived of the energy on which its continued greatness depends."

The Revenue Act of 1921 repealed the wartime excess profits tax and reduced the surtax, but a revolt of Senate progressives staved off major cuts. The Act of 1924 raised exemptions in the lower tax brackets, reduced the general rate of taxation, and even permitted rebates on what was called "earned income." These reductions were followed by other slashes in 1926, 1928, and 1929. Despite the falling tax rates, the prosperity of the country made it possible to reduce the federal debt to $16,900,000,000 by 1930. By leaving great untaxed sums in the hands of businesses and private individuals, however, Mellon's tax policies probably encouraged the dangerous speculative activities that preceded the stock market crash of 1929, for these sums augmented an existing surplus of capital funds that could not find sound investment outlets.

As taxes went down, tariffs went up. In 1922, duties were increased to a second level by the Fordney-McCumber Act. This high tariff checked postwar international trade, led other countries to adopt a policy of retaliatory tariffs against the United States, made repayment of war debts in goods more difficult than under the old law, and induced some American manufacturers to build branch plants abroad because they could no longer sell American-made products in foreign markets. Nonetheless, higher tariffs continued to be popular in the United States, and the Hawley-Smoot Tariff bill of 1930 again increased the rates on some commodities. A petition from more than a thousand economists urged President Hoover to veto the measure, but with no effect. The tariff struck hard at American trade, for a score of countries imposed additional retaliatory tariffs against American products during the next two years.

Republican admiration for business efficiency led the administrations of the 1920's to abandon another Progressive policy: the crusade to break up big business and impede business consolidation. As Secretary of Commerce under both Harding and Coolidge, Herbert Hoover encouraged businessmen to cooperate with one another by sharing information, by accepting codes of fair practice, and by standardizing products to eliminate the welter of wasteful confusion in sizes and types of industrial and consumer goods. In some respects, the codes of fair practice, some 200 of which were put into operation, anticipated the codes later adopted under Franklin D. Roosevelt's N.R.A. (see p. 656). Unhampered by the threat of anti-trust prosecution, businessmen in the 1920's engineered a series of consolidations that resembled those their predecessors had carried out from 1898 to 1904. Between 1919 and 1929, thousands of firms disappeared through mergers. In the field of public utilities alone, 3,744 firms were swallowed up, and comparable consolidations took place in banking, transportation, and trade. By 1933, some 594 corporations owned 53 per cent of all corporate wealth in the country; the remaining 47 per cent was owned by over 380,000 smaller concerns.

While business was consolidating and gaining influence, the organized labor movement was marking time or even losing ground. The serious strikes that had hit the steel, coal, meat-packing, and railroad in-

dustries from 1919 to 1922 had failed. Increasingly, employers recruited workers into company unions, whose members numbered over a million and a half by 1929. Employers also launched an open-shop drive, and succeeded in keeping labor unions out of most lines except the traditionally organized skilled crafts. The membership of the American Federation of Labor, which had stood at a high of 4,078,000 in 1920, fell off to about 3,000,000 in 1923, where it remained until 1929. Throughout the 20's, workers were enjoying modest annual improvements in their standard of living, and strikes tapered off along with union membership.

In the 1920's, 34 states liberalized workmen's compensation laws, but unions and social legislation fared badly in the courts. In *Duplex Printing Press* v. *Deering* (1921), the Supreme Court handed down a decision stipulating that the Clayton Act (see p. 600) did not legalize the secondary boycott and that workers resorting to such boycotts were subject to injunctions. In the same year, in *Truax* v. *Corrigan,* an Arizona law protecting workers from injunctions in certain situations was declared unconstitutional. *Bailey* v. *Drexel Furniture Company,* which was decided in 1922, decreed that child labor could not constitutionally be regulated by a discriminatory tax levied on products manufactured by child labor; and in 1923, in *Adkins* v. *Children's Hospital,* the Court struck down an act of Congress establishing minimum wages for women and children in the District of Columbia. Only in 1932, after the depression had created a new political mood, did the forces of labor succeed in reversing the tide and pushing through Congress the Norris-LaGuardia Act against labor injunctions. This measure President Hoover reluctantly signed.

The Power Problem.   During the war, it became clear that something had to be done to insure the government a steady supply of nitrates that could be used in making explosives. To meet this need, the government set up two nitrate plants at Muscle Shoals on the Tennessee River in northern Alabama, and work was begun on a power dam, which later was named the Wilson Dam. At the end of the war, work on the dam ceased, and further funds for the entire development were cut off in the House. Disturbed by this action, Senator George W. Norris of Nebraska, chairman of the Senate's Committee on Agriculture, insisted that the Tennessee River projects represented an immense wasted asset, and that something must be done to complete the construction and bring the plants and the power dam into operation. Norris had a good case, for the two idle plants and the unfinished dam so far had cost the government $145 million.

The government decided to solve the problem by leasing the sites for private development. Henry Ford made an offer for them that captured the public imagination but that also raised the distressing thought that the Tennessee Valley might fall into the hands of a single millionaire, who was noted for his personal crotchets and petty tyrannies. A minor speculative boom began in the lands around the Valley as soon as Ford made his offer, but Congress hesitated to take positive action. Widespread opposition among utilities militated against the efforts that were being made to preserve the project as a public power plant.

Finally, in 1928, Norris introduced a bill allowing the distribution and sale of power from Wilson Dam and authorizing the manufacture and distribution of fertilizer. This measure attracted widespread support from agricultural areas. It passed both houses of Congress in May, 1928, was killed by Coolidge's pocket veto, and was only re-passed long after Hoover's election. But Hoover opposed the sale of public power, and in 1931 vetoed the proposal in a famous message which emphasized his opposition to putting the government into business. "I hesitate," he wrote,

to contemplate the future of our institutions, of our country, if the preoccupation of its officials is to be no longer the promotion of justice and

equal opportunity but is to be devoted to barter in the markets. That is not liberalism, it is degeneration. . . . Muscle Shoals can only be administered by the people upon the ground, responsible to their own communities, directing them solely for the benefit of their communities, and not for purposes of pursuit of social theories of national politics.

And there the matter rested until the Roosevelt administration adopted an entirely new policy with the establishment of the Tennessee Valley Authority in 1933 (see p. 665).

Agriculture. The nation at large faced an even more serious problem: agricultural distress. The benefits of "Coolidge prosperity" had failed to reach many of the country's farmers. True, some of the farmers who dealt in special products—dairymen, vegetable truck farmers, and fruit farmers—had won their share of the general prosperity by taking advantage of the shift in the nation's dietary habits or of their proximity to growing cities. But producers of staple crops—wheat, cotton, and corn—never managed to recover from their over-expansion during the war period (see p. 617). They had greatly increased their acreage, productivity, and production just before the domestic market slumped. Foreign markets were cut by competition from Canadian, Australian, and Argentine wheat, and from Brazilian, Egyptian, and Indian cotton, as well as by foreign retaliation against American tariffs. Women were wearing more rayon and less cotton, and the very changes in eating habits that favored the truck farmers hurt the growers of staple crops. Farm prices collapsed, and net farm income shrank from $8,368,000,000 in 1920 to $2,285,000,000 in 1932.

Republican leaders insisted that higher tariffs were the only remedy for the farmer's plight. But since the farmer was an exporter and had to compete in the world market, the higher duties imposed on agricultural products by the tariffs of 1921, 1922, 1924, and

1926 brought him only verbal benefits. When foreign countries hiked their own tariffs in retaliation, the farmer's loss of export markets was all too real.

A strong farm bloc grew up in Congress in response to the distressed cries of the farmers. But the McNary-Haugen Bill, which embodied a complicated scheme to aid farmers, was twice defeated in Congress, then passed in 1927 and again in 1928, only to be vetoed both times by President Coolidge. In 1923, the Federal Intermediate Credit Act (or Agricultural Credits Act) represented a new approach to the farm problem. Private investors were authorized to set up corporations to lend money to farmers. Twelve intermediate credit banks, each with $5 million in capital subscribed by the government, were established to liberalize credit for farmers and for agricultural cooperatives. In 1929, during Hoover's administration, the Agricultural Marketing Act was passed, which created the Federal Farm Board to encourage the organization of agricultural cooperatives. The Board was given a fund of $500 million for loans to cooperatives and was authorized to create corporations to control agricultural surpluses and to insure cooperatives against losses. This act did stimulate the growth of cooperatives. Only after the outbreak of the depression, however, did the Federal Farm Board try to use its resources to bolster prices by buying surpluses, and even then it was unsuccessful.

"Coolidge Prosperity."   The farmers were not the only Americans who were excluded from the general prosperity. Workers in a few specialized industries, such as textile manufactures (particularly in New England), coal mining (which was now a sick industry), and shoe and leather manufacturing, also suffered. But most industries, and the nation at large, were booming. Many industries made great gains in productivity. National income rose from $54,200,000,000 in 1919 to $87,200,000,000 in 1929. Perhaps the most significant figures concern the rise of the automobile. In 1919, there had been 6,771,000 passenger cars on the roads. In 1929, there were 23,121,000. Along with the new cars came extensive road construction, garages, filling stations, roadside restaurants, and all the apparatus of tourist life, as well as an increased demand for fuel, metals, glass, and rubber. Radio, advertising, refrigeration, chemicals, films, and telephones also shared in the new prosperity that was being nourished by consumer demand for new luxuries and amusements. Between 1922 and 1927, the purchasing power of wages increased at a rate of more than 2 per cent a year. At the top of the economic pyramid, large and middle-sized fortunes multiplied rapidly. Americans were spending, but they were also saving. A surplus of capital soon became available for investment in the stock market. Hundreds of thousands of people began to speculate, and the prices of stocks began the upward movement that continued, though with a few spectacular interruptions, until the fatal crash of 1929.

Although "Coolidge prosperity" was unevenly distributed, and in important respects insecure, it reached enough Americans to create a widespread feeling of contentment and confidence. Little sympathy was felt for those who did not manage to cut themselves a slice of the American cake; it was widely believed that only personal failure to seize opportunities could be responsible for those groups or individuals who were not sharing in prosperity's benefits.

Complacency prevailed in both political parties. In the summer of 1929, John J. Raskob, the millionaire chairman of the Democratic National Committee, declared:

If a man saves $15 a week, and invests in good common stocks, and allows the dividends and rights to accumulate, at the end of twenty years he will have at least $80,000 and an income from investments of around $400 a month. He will be rich. And because income can do that, I am firm in my belief that anyone not only can be rich, but ought to be rich.

If Raskob was right, America was well on its way to surpassing all other economic societies, for it was about to dispense with poverty altogether. This was, indeed, the opinion of the newly elected President. "We in America," Hoover said, "are nearer to the final triumph over poverty than ever before in the history of any land .... We have not reached the goal, but given a chance to go forward with the policies of the last eight years, we shall soon with the help of God be in sight of the day when poverty will be banished from this nation." At the height of prosperity, millions of Americans saw no reason to doubt Hoover's words.

The Election of 1928. The election of 1928 reflected the triumph of the complacent mood. Gone was the lingering discontent that four years earlier had caused almost 5 million Americans to vote for La Follette (see p. 638). The candidates of both major parties agreed with the business philosophy that had come to dominate the nation's outlook. Calvin Coolidge, in an announcement whose precise meaning has never been fully agreed upon, stated that he did not "choose to run" for the presidency in 1928. Taking him at his word, the Republicans nominated his Secretary of Commerce, Herbert Hoover.

For his excellent relief work during and after World War I, Hoover had long enjoyed the reputation of a humanitarian, a liberal of sorts, and an excellent administra-

Election of 1928

Electoral Vote
■ *Hoover 444* ▨ *Smith 87*

urban wet, and anti-Catholic bigotry was invoked against Smith in an underground campaign that reached every corner of the nation and attained particular influence in the rural areas and the South. Many Protestants of the sort who supported the Ku Klux Klan believed that Smith's election would bring the Pope to Washington to take over the government. To such voters, appeals against bigotry made little impression. In the light of Hoover's initial advantages, it seems unlikely that any Democratic candidate could have beaten him. But his smashing victory over Smith convinced many Catholics that bigotry had been responsible for Smith's defeat, and it left a lasting wound. Hoover won by a vote of 21,391,000 to 15,016,000, carrying all but eight states and including, for the first time since Reconstruction, five states of the solid South.

IV. THE POLITICS OF DEPRESSION

"Hoover Depression." Late in October, 1929, hardly more than seven months after Hoover's inauguration, a panic broke out in Wall Street, the first of a series of terrible shocks that plunged the nation into a deep depression. Exactly what touched off the panic is not clear even now. But one fact partially explains the frightening dimensions the crash quickly assumed. A great many people had acquired more stocks than they had cash to cover. They had bought on "margin"—that is, on credit from their brokers—and speculators who were frightened by the first drop in prices hastily began to unload. Before very long the trickle of selling became a torrent. Stocks were thrown onto the market so fast that prices plunged faster than the stockmarket ticker could report them. At one point, the tickers were a full two hours behind current prices. The frantic selling went on for several days, and the value of stocks listed on the New York Stock Exchange declined over one third, from $87 billion to $55 billion. Hundreds of thousands of people with capital invested in the market had been transformed from solid citizens into debtors or paupers.

At first, many optimists made a forlorn effort to deny that the collapse in speculative values had very much bearing upon the underlying business of the country, and to assert that the stockmarket liquidation represented a loss only in inflated paper values. But prices dropped sharply, factories curtailed production or closed their doors, employers cut wages, men were thrown out of work, trade slackened, prices dropped still further—and the American people found themselves in a major economic disaster. In 1931, 7 million workers were unemployed.

Economists began to wonder what had plunged the country from the pinnacle of prosperity to the depths of depression. Soon they identified some of the unhealthy forces that had been at work under the prosperous surface of the 1920's. For one thing, widespread distress had robbed farmers of much of their purchasing power. Moreover, for a period of prosperity, unemployment had been relatively high—it had rarely been less than 1,000,000, and in 1928 it had risen to 1,800,000. The world economic situation had also been precarious. European nations had depended on American credit for the imports they needed to restore their battered economies and to stabilize foreign exchange, but they could not repay their debts by shipping goods to the United States because they were shut out of American markets by our high tariffs. And American manufacturers, in turn, could no longer sell in Europe. The American and European economies were so closely linked that the depression soon became world-wide.

Domestic prosperity had not been evenly distributed. Throughout the 20's, the level of wages and consumption had risen slowly and steadily, but had been outdistanced by the great leaps in profits, savings, and investment. The productivity of the American worker had been stepped up enormously. Between 1919 and 1929, output per worker increased by 43 per cent—compared with an increase of only 30 per cent during the much longer period from 1890 to 1914. But the worker's income, improved though it was, was not sufficient for him to purchase enough of the goods he was turning out, and other groups in the population were too quickly satisfied to keep the demand for these goods on a level with production. (In theory, prices should have fallen with the sharp increase in productivity, but in fact they remained fairly stable.) As President Hoover put it, "The debacle . . . was largely contributed by a failure of industry to pass its improvement (through labor-saving devices) on to the consumer." The maldistribution of wealth contributed to the imbalance between savings and sound investment. A study made later by the Brookings Institution showed that in 1929, 42.4 per cent of the families had incomes of less than $1,500 a year. The 24,000 families that had an income of over $100,000 each in 1929 had a *total* income over three times as great as the *total* income of the 5.8 million poorest families. The extensive savings of the rich were invested in producing goods that the modest incomes of the less fortunate were unable to buy. Savings, which had piled up out of all proportion to the opportunities for legitimate (i.e., not highly speculative) investment, had gone into speculative activity in the stockmarket. All America had been living on futures, and the bubble had burst at the first sign that the future was not unclouded.

The Hoover Policies. Many observers decided that the depression had been touched off by a failure of confidence. To restore and maintain confidence, they argued, would restore prosperity itself. President Hoover, who insisted that the country suffered more from "frozen confidence than from frozen securities," went to great lengths to build up the public's confidence. But his assertion that "the fundamental business of the country, the production and dis-

As the depression deepened, long breadlines such as this one became a common sight in American cities. Men this side of sign are assured a five-cent meal.

tribution of commodities, is on a sound and prosperous basis," and his prediction that a return of prosperity was just around the corner, came to have an increasingly hollow ring. His political opponents turned these phrases into sharp-edged weapons of mockery. The Republicans had once claimed as "Coolidge prosperity" a prosperity that Coolidge had done nothing to protect. So now the Democrats began to pin the label "Hoover depression" to a crash that Hoover had not brought about.

Hoover did more than just try to brighten the public mood. He gave strong support to the Agricultural Marketing Act of 1929, which was intended to encourage farm cooperatives and to strengthen farm credit. In 1930, when the fall in wheat and cotton prices was beginning to assume the proportions of a catastrophe, a Grain Stabilization Corporation and a Cotton Stabilization Corporation were created under the Federal Farm Board with power to buy in the open market in the hope of raising prices. These corporations did help to keep prices up for a time, but soon they found themselves with warehouses full of apparently unmarketable surpluses of wheat and cotton, surpluses that hung over the open market like heavy clouds. Late in 1931 and early in 1932, both agencies were forced to acknowledge defeat and suspend further purchases, and staple prices continued to sink.

Hoover also developed a program to help industry and labor. Early in 1930, Congress granted him over $700 million to be used to erect public buildings, improve rivers and harbors, and build public roads. As Secretary of Commerce, Hoover had been interested in the possibility of using public construction as a kind of balance wheel for the trade cycle, on the assumption that increased public expenditure would help to stem trade decline and ease unemployment in bad times, and that decreased expenditures would put a brake on economic booms in prosperous times. As President, he spent over two and a quarter billion dollars on public construction. His attempt to use federal funds to stem depression went well beyond what any former president had done.

Early in the depression, Hoover tried to use voluntary agreements to stem the tide of recession and to reduce suffering. He called a series of conferences among industrialists and labor leaders in which he pointed out that a succession of wage reductions would be disastrous, since each reduction would cause a further contraction in the market, and might lead to bitter industrial strife. He urged employers to hold off wage reductions, and that when reductions became absolutely imperative, they be made only in proportion to the decline in prices. In this way, employed workers would not suffer an accompanying decline in purchasing power and living standards. Many industrialists made an earnest effort to comply with the President's suggestions, and actually succeeded in maintaining wage rates. But they could not keep men at work when no market existed for the goods they made, and layoffs continued to increase. By 1932, there were about 12 million unemployed in America.

At last, Hoover was forced to abandon his policy of using voluntary agreements rather than governmental devices for coping with the depression. To have allowed the decline in prices to go on indefinitely might have bankrupted great manufacturing and utility corporations and railroads, and ultimately the insurance companies, building and loan associations, savings banks, and philanthropic institutions. Toward the end of 1931, it appeared that many of these institutional investors might lose everything. At this point, Hoover called on Congress to create the Reconstruction Finance Corporation, which was authorized to lend large amounts to banks, railroads, life insurance companies, and other business organizations to keep them from going under. During 1932, the Reconstruction Finance Corporation lent $1,500,000,000 to more than 5,000 business concerns. The agency was continued and expanded under the New Deal.

By 1931, the depression had become severe in Europe, first in Central Europe and then in the Atlantic nations. In September, 1931, Great Britain was forced to abandon the gold standard. Hoover was convinced that the burden of paying inter-governmental debts was one of the greatest obstacles to world trade and world recovery. So in June, 1931, he proposed that the nations accept a one-year moratorium on the interest and principal payments of such obligations. This proposal was accepted by the 15 governments involved. A more drastic step would have been to cancel the obligations outright. This would have meant that the United States, the principal creditor, would have to cancel the war debts owed to her. Although many businessmen in the United States supported this step as a move that would restore world trade, it was generally unpopular and

Life among the unemployed, 1931. Many large cities had similar encampments of unusable men.

was not taken. But when the moratorium ended in 1932, only five governments made their payments to the United States, and in the following year all but Finland made only token payments.

Despite Hoover's efforts to curb the depression, the results of the mid-term congressional elections of 1930 made it clear that he was rapidly losing the confidence of the country. The Democratic leaders in Congress were waging a successful campaign to place the blame for the depression on him. Hoover, who had never had the gift of courting popularity, was now portrayed as callously indifferent to the fate of the jobless and the stricken. Much was done to quicken this impression in the summer of 1932 when the "Bonus Army," a band of over 12,000 jobless veterans, marched to Washington in hopes of persuading the Congress to make a veterans' bonus appropriation. They were

driven out of the city with tear gas and bayonets by an army detachment acting on the President's order and led by General Douglas MacArthur.

The Campaign of 1932. As the campaign of 1932 approached, the Democrats' prospects of recapturing the presidency after 12 Republican years were rapidly improving. The most promising aspirant to the Democratic nomination was Franklin D. Roosevelt, Governor of New York. The child of well-to-do and socially well-established parents, he was a fifth cousin of Theodore Roosevelt, whose niece he had married. He had become a figure of some national prominence as Assistant Secretary of the Navy under Wilson, and had been Cox's vice-presidential running mate in the Democratic campaign of 1920. During the early

1920's, Roosevelt had been crippled by an attack of poliomyelitis, but with great courage and resolution he had returned to public life.

Although politically identified with Alfred E. Smith—whose name he had placed in nomination at the convention of 1924—Roosevelt had managed to remain on good terms with both quarrelsome factions in the Democratic party. Even in 1928, a year of defeat for his party, he had run well ahead of his ticket and was elected governor of New York; he was overwhelmingly elected to a second term in 1930. After a lively contest with the supporters of Al Smith, Roosevelt was nominated by the Democratic convention of 1932, with John Nance Garner of Texas, Speaker of the House and a leading Hoover critic, as his running mate. Dramatically, Roosevelt flew to Chicago to accept the nomination in person. "I pledge you, I pledge myself," he told the delegates, "to a new deal for the American people." The Republicans gloomily renominated Hoover and loyally adopted a platform praising the efforts he had made to cope with the unprecedented disasters of the depression.

The chief issue in the campaign of 1932 was the cause of the depression. Hoover maintained that it was an aftermath of World War I, the result of world-wide conditions which the United States could hardly have been protected against. Without denying that the depression was in fact a world-wide affair, Roosevelt insisted that it was also the outcome of important flaws in the domestic economy of the country. In one of his speeches, he asserted that the country had

Election of 1932

Electoral Vote
Roosevelt 472   Hoover 59

reached a point at which the relations between government and business must take a new tack. Hoover warned that an excess of governmental zeal would destroy liberty. ("You cannot extend the mastery of government over the daily life of a people without somewhere making it master of people's souls and thoughts.") But Roosevelt called for novel governmental methods to meet novel conditions. "A glance at the situation today," he declared, "only too clearly indicates that equality of opportunity as we have known it no longer exists." "As I see it," he continued, "the task of government in its relation to business is to assist the development of an economic declaration of rights, an economic constitutional order."

The results of the election were not difficult to foresee. More voters were heartened by Roosevelt's promises than were impressed by Hoover's warnings. Roosevelt received 22,821,000 votes, Hoover 15,761,-000. The Democratic candidate carried all but six states. His party won an overwhelming majority in both houses of Congress, taking the House by 310 to 117 and the Senate by 60 to 35.

Readings

The political history of the 1920's has been written by Harold Faulkner, *From Versailles to the New Deal* (1950), and the economic history by George Soule, *Prosperity Decade* (1947). Karl Schriftgiesser, *This Was Normalcy* (1948), gives an acidulous account of the Republican regimes, while Samuel H. Adams has written of the Harding scandals in his *Incredible Era* (1939). The developing depression is followed by Gilbert

Seldes in *The Years of the Locust* (1933), while John K. Galbraith has written a fascinating brief study of the 1929 debacle called *The Big Crash* (1955). Hoover's policies have been defended by W. S. Myers and W. H. Newton, *The Hoover Administration* (1936), and in *The Memoirs of Herbert Hoover: The Great Depression, 1929-41* (1952). Frederick Lewis Allen's account of the 1920's, *Only Yesterday* (1931), is unusually interesting. Herbert Hoover gives succinct expression to the business philosophy of the 1920's in *American Individualism* (1922), while J. W. Prothro analyzes it in *Dollar Decade* (1954).

Election campaigns can be studied in Kenneth C. MacKay's *The Progressive Movement of 1924* (1947), which concentrates on La Follette; R. V. Peel and T. C. Donnelly, *The 1928 Campaign* (1931); and the same authors' *The 1932 Campaign* (1935).

The intolerance of the 1920's can be traced through J. P. Clark, *Deportation of Aliens from the United States* (1931); Chafee's *Free Speech in the United States,* already cited; G. L. Joughin and E. M. Morgan, *The Legacy of Sacco and Vanzetti* (1948); J. M. Mecklin, *The Ku Klux Klan* (1924); N. F. Furniss, *The Fundamentalist Controversy, 1918-1931* (1954); and R. K. Murray, *Red Scare* (1955). On the closing of the gates, see R. L. Garis, *Immigration Restriction* (1927), and the last chapter of John Higham, *Strangers in the Land* (1955).

Prohibition is interestingly covered in Herbert Asbury, *The Great Illusion* (1950), and Virginius Dabney, *Dry Messiah: The Life of Bishop Cannon* (1949). Some of the intellectual atmosphere of the age is suggested by Joseph Wood Krutch, *The Modern Temper* (1929), and much of its tone is captured by F. Scott Fitzgerald in his novels, the best of which is *The Great Gatsby* (1925).

For farm problems, see Theodore Saloutos and John D. Hicks, *Agricultural Discontent in the Middle West, 1900-1939* (1951), which is exhaustive, or John D. Black, *Agricultural Reform in the United States* (1930), which is shorter. Farm bloc politics are discussed by R. B. Nye in *Midwestern Progressive Politics* (1951), and in Grant McConnell, *The Decline of Agrarian Democracy* (1953).

There is no fully satisfactory biography of Alfred E. Smith. The best is Henry F. Pringle, *Alfred E. Smith: A Critical Study* (1927), which can be supplemented by Smith's own *Up to Now* (1929), and by Emily Smith Warner's biography of her father, *The Happy Warrior* (1956). The religious issue in the election of 1928 is objectively studied by E. A. Moore in *A Catholic Runs for President* (1956). William Allen White's *A Puritan in Babylon* (1938) is a superb biography of Coolidge. Hoover can best be followed through the volumes of his rather defensive *Memoirs.* A great deal of light is shed upon the politics of the 1920's by two volumes of Frank Freidel's definitive biography, *Franklin D. Roosevelt.* Volume II, *The Ordeal* (1954), covers the period to 1928; Volume III, *The Triumph* (1956), carries Roosevelt down to his election in 1932. Among other useful biographies are B. C. and Fola La Follette's study of Robert M. La Follette (2 vols., 1953); G. W. Norris, *Fighting Liberal* (1945); T. A. Huntley, *John W. Davis* (1924); and C. O. Johnson, *Borah of Idaho* (1936).

THE NEW DEAL

CHAPTER TWENTY-EIGHT

In his inaugural address of March 4, 1933, Roosevelt spoke eloquently of the difficulties confronting his administration in its earliest hours.

Values [he declared] have shrunken to fantastic levels; taxes have risen; our ability to pay has fallen; government of all kinds is faced by serious curtailment of income; the means of exchange are frozen in the currents of trade; the withered leaves of industrial enterprise lie on every side; farmers find no markets for their produce; the savings of many years in thousands of families are gone.

More important, a host of unemployed citizens face the grim problem of existence, and an equally great number toil with little return. Only a foolish optimist can deny the dark realities of the moment.

These conditions, he went on, were not the result of material failures or the lack of nature's bounty; they were the result of mental and moral failure, of greed and incompetence. But the nation was on the verge of a new restoration of ethics in which "mere monetary profit" would be replaced by higher values. "The money changers have fled from their high seats in the temple of our civilization." Yet new moral values would

not be enough. "This Nation asks for action, and action now." The chief task was to put people to work, which could be done in part by government itself, "treating the task as we would treat the emergency of a war."

I. MEN AND IDEAS

When Roosevelt took over the helm, he stripped the decks for action, and action was his strong point. A man of enormous self-confidence, with few fears about new undertakings, he came into office at a time when Americans were eager to welcome a man of his type. Buoyant, charming, self-assured, Roosevelt himself was the New Deal's greatest asset. When the Democratic convention nominated him in 1932, he had struck a note of novelty and originality by flying to Chicago and addressing the delegates in person. Hardly a profound man, he was nonetheless open-minded, eager to tackle the difficult problems ahead, and prepared to do things in a new way. During its early days, many people spoke of the New Deal as an attempt at economic planning, but it would be more accurate to call it a period of economic experimentation.

Roosevelt was not systematic in his thinking, as Hoover tried to be, and his mind did not run toward consistency in policies or tidiness in administration. Although the primary problems the nation faced were economic, Roosevelt's art was not economics, but politics. He was gifted in dealing with people, privately or in the mass. Blessed with a good voice, he could read a speech beautifully. In an age of radio, he was the first American politician to develop a first-rate radio personality. This asset he exploited to great effect from time to time by giving "fireside chats," nationwide broadcasts in which he made his listeners feel that he was discussing important problems with them on a man-to-man basis.

Hoover had been trained in private business and administrative jobs and had never played a distinctively political role before the 1928 campaign. But Roosevelt was a seasoned political professional, who had been accustomed to dealing with other politicians and with the people for more than 20 years. Brought up as a political leader in the badly divided Democratic party of the 1920's, he knew how to keep friends on both sides of a political fence. And when his tact failed him, as it occasionally did, it was only because he had decided to play a strong part. With the possible exception of the public power issue, he had not given deep thought to the great national economic questions at the time of his nomination, but he had devoted a great deal of attention to the problem of how to weld and use a political coalition.

Though hardly a passionate person, he was warmhearted and deeply moved by the plight of the destitute. He was firmly convinced that every underprivileged interest had a legitimate claim upon the sympathies of the government. He did not always know how to translate this sympathy into constructive policy, but he felt instinctively that the farmers, the unemployed, the homeowners, the workingmen, and the small businessmen, all had a right to be helped, and that in some measure the needs of all must be met. In many ways, the history of the New Deal is the history of a gigantic effort to provide something for everybody.

It has been said that there was not one but several New Deals. And certainly the range of Roosevelt's policies was matched by the variety of his advisers and associates. Outstanding among them was his first Postmaster-General, James A. Farley, an astute professional politician and former supporter of Al Smith, who carried in his mind a card-index of prominent Democrats throughout the country. Of great influence at first in the administration of relief, then in more general policies, was Harry Hopkins, an Iowa-born social worker, whose humane sense for the needs of those on relief made him a hero to liberals, but whose penchant for partisan politics made him a villain to the opposition. For Secretary of Agriculture, Roosevelt chose another Iowan, Henry A. Wallace, an experienced plant-breeder and agricultural editor, whose father had served in the same post under Coolidge and Harding. Harold L. Ickes, a crusty Chicago reformer and one-time supporter of Theodore Roosevelt, was put in charge of the Department of the Interior. The Secretaryship of Labor went to Frances Perkins, New York Industrial Commissioner, who served as the first woman cabinet member. As Secretary of State, Roosevelt chose Cordell Hull of Tennessee, a dignified professional politician who represented the South's traditional interest in lower tariffs. William H. Woodin, a conservative industrialist who enjoyed the confidence of businessmen, was made Secretary of the Treasury. When Woodin resigned after giving yeoman service during the urgent bank crisis of 1933, he was succeeded by Henry Morgenthau, Jr., an old friend of the President's. After 1939, a great many cabinet changes were made.

An important feature of the New Deal was the recruitment of a "brain trust" to counsel the President on technical matters and to help draft his speeches. Robert M. La Follette, as Governor of Wisconsin, had had the benefit of advisers from the University of Wisconsin, and Al Smith in New York had also drawn on expert personal counsel. But nothing like the brain trust had been known in the history of the presidency. Most prominent in this group was Raymond Moley, a Columbia professor, who helped to organize it. An expert on criminal justice, Moley had been an adviser of Roosevelt's in New York. He was among those who believed that recovery must be sought through economic nationalism. In time, he became disappointed with the President's policies and wrote a highly critical book about his experiences, *After Seven Years*. From Columbia, Moley brought with him A. A. Berle, Jr., and Rexford G. Tugwell, experts respectively on problems of corporate finance and agriculture. Later, such

Franklin D. Roosevelt and Herbert Hoover at Roosevelt's inauguration.

able lawyers as Thomas B. Corcoran and Benjamin V. Cohen worked on legislation to protect investors. When brain-trusters began to influence matters of highest policy and of broad political consequence, they fell into conflict with some of the professional politicians on Capitol Hill, who resented their closeness to the President. And some of the brain-trusters became the target of heavy criticism from the press, especially Tugwell, who was unjustly accused of extreme radical tendencies. In this way, the brain-trusters served the President not only as advisers, but also as lightning rods, for they attracted much of the public criticism that might otherwise have fallen on him.

Although the New Deal was not founded upon any fundamental all-embracing theory, its leaders' opinions about what should be done to effect recovery differed from the notions that were held by the men who had preceded them. Hoover's approach to the problem of recovery had been to allow the deflation to take its course, except when it seemed dangerous or prejudicial to recov-

ery. But the New Deal resorted to direct action on a number of fronts, particularly with mild currency inflation and with the attempt to "prime the pump" of private business through public investment. No less wide was the difference between this administration and the preceding one on the question of relief. Hoover had stayed close to traditional means of administering relief, even when confronted by unprecedented suffering, and his action was limited by his own constitutional and political scruples. But the New Deal tried to shape relief policies to the measure of the human needs it had to meet. The authors of the New Deal were not troubled by any inhibitions about the role the federal government should play. Finally, the Hoover administration had shown little interest in making the economic crisis an occasion for reforms. But the New Deal began with limited reforms in a few areas and then, after public pressure for change became apparent, went in for reforms on a big scale and in an adventuresome spirit.

II. THE SEARCH FOR RECOVERY

The Banking Crisis.   At the very moment of his inauguration, President Roosevelt had to deal with a crisis of extraordinary urgency. The entire banking system of the nation was on the verge of collapse. Even in prosperity, American banking practices had been irregular; in depression they were disastrous. During the depression, the number of bank failures mounted steeply, and in the early months of 1933, the situation reached panic proportions. The failure of unsound banks sent frightened depositors rushing to other banks to withdraw their funds for fear that they too would fail. Eventually, even the soundly managed banks found it hard to meet their obligations.

By March 3, almost half the governors had ordered bank holidays in their states, in the hope of stemming the panic among depositors. By March 4, the morning of

Roosevelt's inauguration, most of the banks in the country had been closed by state action. On March 6, a presidential proclamation suspended all banking operations and gold transactions for four days. While the country waited in tense expectancy, Congress passed the Emergency Banking Act on March 9, which ratified the President's earlier actions and provided steps for reopening the sound banks. Roosevelt delivered a "fireside chat" in which he reassured the people on the soundness of the banking system that was about to emerge from the reorganization.

In the meantime, the condition of the banks was being hastily re-examined. The Reconstruction Finance Corporation advanced funds to distressed banks, the President took over control of foreign exchange transactions, and the Treasury was empowered to call in all gold coin and certificates as a safeguard against hoarding. Before the end of the month, most of the nation's sound banks were being reopened, and the unsound ones were in the process of being permanently closed, with as much return to their depositors as was possible. Within two months of the banking holiday, more than 12,000 banks, with 90 per cent of the country's bank deposits, were back in business. A major crisis had been passed.

The successful solution of the banking problem proved a great asset to the New Deal in the next few months, for it started the new administration off with a claim to public confidence. Moreover, the administration had spurned the more radical solution to which it could have easily resorted— nationalizing the banking system—and had left banking in private hands. For the moment, the suspicion of many conservatives that the New Deal was bent on a revolutionary approach to American economic institutions was quieted, and it became clear to moderate men that the aim of the administration was not to establish a new economic system but to rescue the existing one.

The solution of the banking crisis was followed in June, 1933, by the Glass-Steagall Banking Act, which was aimed at reforming the ill-managed banking system. From the standpoint of the ordinary bank depositor, the most important part of this bill was the creation of the Federal Deposit Insurance Corporation to provide for the insurance of bank deposits and to make impossible a repetition of the frightening experiences of 1932-1933. Out of its capital of $150 million, the F.D.I.C. was authorized to guarantee bank deposits up to $5,000 per depositor, and to reorganize any insured bank that failed. The system proved effective both in protecting depositors and in creating a sense of confidence in the banking system. The Glass-Steagall Act also compelled the divorce of commercial and investment banking, it forbade national banks to maintain securities affiliates, and it provided

for other reforms. The Banking Act of 1935, which followed, greatly increased federal authority over the banking system by empowering the Federal Reserve Board to regulate interest rates.

Another set of early New Deal reforms dealt with the securities market. Senate investigations carried out from 1932 to 1934 showed that bankers had been playing fast and loose with other people's money. These disclosures created a widespread demand for laws that would protect investors from misrepresentation and depositors from having their funds used in risky enterprises. The first reform measure was the Securities Act of May, 1933, passed in response to the President's plea that "every issue of new securities ... shall be accompanied by full publicity and information, and that no essentially important element attending the issue shall be concealed from the buying public." The Securities Act denied the sellers of securities access to the mails unless their securities were registered with the Federal Trade Commission, and it required that information about new stocks be made available to the public. This measure was followed in June, 1934, by the Securities Exchange Act, which created the Securities and Exchange Commission. The S.E.C. was authorized to license stock exchanges and to require the registration of all securities in which the exchanges dealt, to prevent price manipulations by underwriters and market operators, and to cooperate with the Federal Reserve Board in controlling the purchase of securities on margin. Directors and officers of corporations and persons holding more than 10 per cent of the stock of a corporation were required to report dealings in their companies and were forbidden to engage in "short selling"—that is, gambling on a fall in market prices.

Other laws enlarged the S.E.C.'s powers. The Public Utility Holding Company Act of 1935 placed the management of holding companies almost entirely under the supervision of the S.E.C. A provision of the Bankruptcy Act of 1938 empowered the S.E.C. to intervene in corporate reorganizations when more than $3 million was involved. In 1939-1940, another series of laws expanded the powers of the S.E.C. over investment trusts. The over-all effect of these laws was to provide an elaborate system of protection for the American investor. But they also aroused great resentment against the New Deal within the financial community.

Currency Experiments. Much less successful than its banking and investment reforms was the New Deal's effort to spur recovery by manipulating the currency. One wing of the Democratic party, led by a bloc of western senators, urged the administration to launch upon extreme inflationary experiments, involving such old Populist demands as a large issue of greenbacks and the free coinage of silver. Although it resisted these demands, the administration did try to raise commodity prices. A price rise, it was thought, would have three valuable consequences. First, it would make it easier for debtors—farmers, private debtors, and institutional debtors like railroads—to pay off their obligations at dollar value. This, the administration claimed, would be fairer than the existing level because it would be closer to the value the dollar possessed at the time when the debtors borrowed. Second, a moderate price rise would help to reverse the downward trend in business by spurring manufacturers to lay in raw materials, hire workers, and set the wheels of industry in motion. Third, devaluating the dollar would encourage exports. Although most of the other countries of the world had by now abandoned the gold standard, the United States still clung to it. This meant that the American dollar was expensive in terms of foreign currencies, and that it was extremely difficult for other nations to buy in the United States. Inflation—cheaper American money—would remove this barrier.

The authority to pursue a policy of inflation was granted to a reluctant President by Congress on May 12, 1933, in the Thomas Amendment to the Agricultural Adjustment Act. He was empowered (many inflationists in the Senate had hoped that he would be *required*) to issue up to $3 billion in greenbacks or legal tender notes in order to pay federal obligations or to redeem outstanding bonds of the United States. He was also authorized to reduce the gold content of the dollar by as much as 50 per cent, provide for unlimited coinage of both gold and silver at a ratio that he could set, accept a limited amount of silver in debt payments from foreign governments, and issue silver certificates against the bullion thus received. More prudent than many of the act's proponents, Roosevelt, at first, exercised these sweeping powers with great caution. On June 5, however, as a corollary to the desire to benefit debtors, Congress by joint resolution voided any clause in past or future contracts, governmental or private, that required payment of obligations in gold. The constitutionality of this measure was challenged in the courts, but was finally upheld by the Supreme Court in the Gold Clause Cases of 1935.

Up to October, 1933, the administration pursued the modest policy of divorcing the dollar from gold in order to permit its value to sink in terms of foreign currencies. At the outset, this policy forced the administration to make an important decision with respect to its economic foreign policies. The nations of the world had agreed to meet at the London Economic Conference in June, 1933, to try to stabilize international monetary arrangements. But they could do nothing without the cooperation of the United States, and it would be impossible for the United States to cooperate if it intended to keep a free hand to indulge in monetary experiments.

Faced with the choice of seeking recovery either in collaboration with other nations or on a nationalistic go-it-alone basis, Roosevelt chose the latter course. On July 3, he sent to the Conference a radio message which he later admitted "fell upon it like a bombshell." He asserted that it would be "a catastrophe amounting to a world tragedy" if the Conference, which had been called to bring about "a more real and permanent financial stability," should allow itself to be diverted by "a purely artificial and temporary experiment affecting the monetary exchange of a few Nations only." Roosevelt's message wrecked the Conference; but supporters of the New Deal argued that the Conference had been called on a one-sided basis, since the participating nations insisted that the United States abandon further devaluation of the dollar before other nations made any concessions.

After October, 1933, the administration, disappointed by earlier efforts to raise commodity prices, adopted a new theory. The idea was that by purchasing gold at increasing dollar prices, the dollar could be artificially devalued to a point even lower than the level it had reached on the international exchange. Adopted in October, this policy began with purchases of domestically mined gold, but presently it embraced foreign gold as well. Subsequently, against its will, the administration was also forced by a ruthless bloc of western senators to launch upon an extraordinary silver-purchase program. Under the terms of the Silver Purchase Act of June 19, 1934, the Treasury was obliged to buy the entire output of the domestic silver mines at an artificially high price.

Although the technique of bullion purchase avoided the dangers of all-out printing-press inflation, it did not succeed in its main purpose, which was to raise commodity prices appreciably. A temporary rise in prices occurred during 1933, but it was not consistently maintained throughout the year, and it could easily have been caused by other factors. At some cost to the Treasury, but with little benefit to the nation, an abnormally large portion of the world's gold supplies was concentrated in the United States. Neither the hopes of the inflationists nor the exaggerated fears of the die-hard gold-standard advocates (one of whom thought that going off gold meant "the end of Western civilization") were realized. Finally, in January, 1934, the gold content of the dollar was fixed at 59.06 cents, and experiments with dollar devaluation ceased.

Industry and Labor. The mainspring of the early New Deal's program for industry and labor was the National Industrial Recovery Act, an effort to realize the "economic constitutional order" that President Roosevelt had promised during his campaign. This act, passed in June, 1933, was in part the outcome of plans for industrial organization put forward by such businessmen as Bernard Baruch and Gerard Swope, President of General Electric, and by leaders of the United States Chamber of Commerce. And in part it was an attempt by the administration to head off a bill, of which it strongly disapproved, that had been introduced by Senator Hugo Black of Alabama, providing for a limit of 30 workhours a week in factories. Black's measure, which had passed the Senate in April, 1933, and had subsequently been linked with a proposal to impose a minimum wage, frightened conservative industrialists. The National Industrial Recovery Act, then, was an attempt to bring together these two demands: the demands of industrialists for a code of industrial organization that would relieve them of the pressure of anti-trust laws, and the demand of labor for a reduction in hours.

Under the provisions of the act, business was permitted to make sweeping price agreements (which required suspension of the anti-trust laws) and to set production quotas; in return, business was to accept wage agreements in the form of codes of fair practice that would improve the condition of the poorest-paid workers. Each type of business was given the power to draw up its own code. The government reserved the right to accept or reject the codes, or to set up its own when the industries failed to agree, and undertook the task of enforcing them. In Section 7(a) of the act, labor was guaranteed the right of collective bargaining. A National Recovery Administration

(N.R.A.) was set up to administer the codes under the chairmanship of General Hugh Johnson.

"History," President Roosevelt said at the time the N.R.A. was created, "probably will record the National Industrial Recovery Act as the most important and far-reaching legislation ever enacted by the American Congress. It represents a supreme effort to stabilize for all time the many factors which make for the prosperity of the Nation and the preservation of American standards." In fact, the history of the measure was a history of quarrels and disappointments, culminating in early failure and legal repudiation by the Supreme Court.

At the core of the N.R.A. was the paradoxical notion that recovery and stability could be achieved through more or less systematic monopolization, the suspension of technical advances, the limitation of production, and the raising of prices—all qualified by a limited number of modest gains for labor. The model for the N.R.A. had been the wartime organization of industry, with which both President Roosevelt and General Johnson, as wartime administrators, had been familiar. But there was an important difference. Wartime industry had been organized to increase production; the N.R.A. was organized to ration production and to raise prices. At an early press conference, General Johnson explained: "We are going to ask something of an armistice on increased producing capacity, until we see if we can get this upward spiral started. . . . We are going to plead very earnestly . . . not to use any further labor-saving devices or anything further to increase production for the present."

No less than 746 basic and supplementary codes were adopted for the regulation of industry. These codes usually called for minimum prices that could not be undersold, standardization of products and business practices, the filing of fixed price schedules with the government, and the regulation of productive output. False advertising, price discrimination, attacks upon the reputation of competitors, and similar competitive practices were commonly outlawed.

But the hastily drawn codes, with the high prices they frequently embodied, seem to have retarded rather than hastened recovery. Businessmen soon lost their initial enthusiasm. Small businessmen complained that the codes were drawn up by the larger firms in each industry and that they ignored or overrode the needs and operating conditions of the small firms. Workers, who at first rallied enthusiastically to the N.R.A., began to complain that its administrators were taking the side of anti-union employers in labor disputes, and soon the N.R.A. was labeled in union circles as the "National Run Around." At the same time, many employers resented the very existence of Section 7 (a), which guaranteed the right of collective bargaining, and the use that labor leaders had made of its promise to spur labor organization.

Because of internal wrangling and widespread criticism, in the spring of 1934 Roosevelt appointed a National Review Board under the chairmanship of the lawyer, Clarence Darrow, to re-examine the N.R.A. and to report on whether it had discriminated against small business. The Darrow Board, whether judiciously or not, returned a devastating indictment of the entire experiment. At the same time, consumer discontent with price practices engendered by N.R.A. also came to a head. Finally, just when the N.R.A. had reached a new low in popularity, its legality was brought to a test before the Supreme Court. On May 27, 1935, in the case of *Schechter Poultry Corporation* v. *United States,* the Court unanimously found that the National Industrial Recovery Act was unconstitutional on two counts: first, that it improperly delegated legislative powers to the executive; and second, that the provisions of the poultry code constituted a regulation of intrastate, not interstate, commerce. The New Deal's plan for industry and labor, its "economic constitutional order," lay in fragments.

Although the N.R.A. had not promoted economic recovery, a purpose for which it was ill-designed, it had at least offered some kind of program for industry and labor and in some areas had provided a temporary remedy for acute distress. For example, at the time the codes were adopted, some of the most exploited workers in the textile industry had been receiving wages as low as $5 a week. The codes had set a minimum of 30 to 40 cents an hour. The cancellation of the codes threatened, and in many instances brought about, a restoration of earlier conditions. The Supreme Court's nullification of N.R.A. resulted in a new turn in administration policy, and this time the needs and demands of labor were given far more consideration than the plans of businessmen.

The Labor Movement.   Section 7(a) of the N.I.R.A. had specified that employees should have the right "to organize and bargain collectively, through representatives of their own choosing," and to be free from coercion by employers or their agents in the choice of organizations. It had also provided that no employee could be compelled to join a company union as a condition of employment. Its enforcement had been put in the hands of a National Labor Board, which was empowered to mediate, conciliate, or arbitrate disputes. The most important result of Section 7(a) was that aggressive labor leaders in the industrial unions undertook an organizing drive in which they appealed to the sanction of this section. They went to the workers with the argument, impressive at that time because of Roosevelt's high prestige, that "The President wants you to join." Their approach was very successful. Immense gains were made in industries that were already partially organized, and also in new ones, like the automobile and the rubber-tire industries, where there had been no unions before. Total union membership, which had stood

at 2,857,000 in 1933, rose to 3,728,000 in 1935.

Labor was becoming more powerful politically as well as economically. After the nullification of the N.I.R.A. and in response to labor's demands for new guarantees, Congress passed the Wagner-Connery or National Labor Relations Act on July 5, 1935. This law established a National Labor Relations Board (N.L.R.B.) of three members. It re-enacted in almost the same words the collective bargaining guarantees of Section 7(a), but it tightened the restrictions on employers who tried to coerce employees into joining company unions, to dominate outside unions, and to interfere with a worker's decision to join a union. The act provided that the representative of the majority of the employees should be the exclusive bargaining representative of all the employees, and empowered the N.L.R.B. to investigate and certify the proper representatives and to hold supervised elections among employees when there was a dispute over which union should represent them. Businessmen, particularly in the powerful National Association of Manufacturers, protested angrily that this law was one-sided. But under its mantle, labor organization continued. No less than 340 company unions were broken up. Membership in genuine trade unions continued to grow, until in 1941 it had reached the level of 10,489,000.

This remarkable development in labor organization took place at the cost of much upheaval and strife, not only between workers and employers, but also within the ranks of labor itself. For many years there had been a major difference of opinion within the A.F.L. over the issue of industrial unionism. One group of aggressive leaders insisted that the mass-production industries could be organized only by new unions established along industrial lines rather than along the craft lines traditional in the A.F.L. This issue had come to a head in the 1935 convention of the A.F.L. at Atlantic City, when industrial and craft union advocates clashed head-on. John L. Lewis, the determined leader of the United Mine Workers Union,

A clash between strikers and police at the Republic Steel plant, South Chicago, May 30, 1937. Police used guns, tear gas, and clubs to break up a strikers' demonstration. Ten workers were killed.

ended up in a fist fight with William L. Hutcheson of the Carpenter's Union. The majority of the delegates stood for craft unionism. But a few weeks later, the heads of eight A.F.L. international unions formed the Committee for Industrial Organization (C.I.O.), with Lewis as chairman, and announced that they would advise on the best methods for organizing the unorganized. When they were called upon by the A.F.L. to dissolve, they refused, and were suspended. In 1938, the C.I.O. formed a separate organization, the Congress of Industrial Organizations, with power and membership roughly equal to that of the A.F.L. Until 1955, when a merger was at last agreed upon, the American labor movement was split between these two groups.

One of the new methods introduced during the organizing drive conducted by the C.I.O. was the "sit-down" strike. Workers, instead of walking off the job and picketing the plant, went to their posts and stayed at them without working, thus making it harder for scabs to replace them. Sit-down strikes against two great automobile companies, General Motors and the Chrysler Corporation, enabled the C.I.O. to win recognition as the bargaining agent for workers in these plants. An even greater victory followed when the United States Steel Corporation, once the terror of organized labor, accorded

the C.I.O. full bargaining authority for its employees in March, 1937.

The smaller steel companies fought more resolutely against the Steel Workers Organizing Committee. On Memorial Day, 1937, a strike against Republic Steel in Chicago led to a riot in which the police killed ten strikers. Other violent incidents took place in Ohio, at Youngstown, Massillon, and Cleveland. But the mill-owners managed to mobilize both the authority and the public sentiment of local communities against the strikers, and the organizing campaign against "Little Steel" failed for the time being. (Eventually, in 1941, even Little Steel capitulated to the union drive and signed contracts, after the N.L.R.B. had ordered the reinstatement of workers discharged during the 1937 organizing efforts.) When the great organizing campaigns of 1937 were over, 4,740 strikes had taken place, involving 1,860,000 workers. Many new industries had been organized, and the membership of older unions had been greatly increased.

Agriculture. At the same time that Congress set up the program for industry and labor in the N.I.R.A., it also enacted a program for agriculture that followed a broadly similar pattern: prices were to be raised by having farmers restrict production in ac-

659

cordance with some common plan. On May 12, 1933, the Agricultural Adjustment Act was passed, establishing an Agricultural Adjustment Administration (A.A.A.) to carry out its provisions. The stated goal of this measure was to bring farm income back to the level it had reached during the palmy days of 1909-1914. The New Deal planners, including Secretary of Agriculture Wallace, abandoned hope of regaining the lost foreign market and decided to reduce production to the level of domestic demand. The A.A.A. authorized the Secretary of Agriculture to make agreements with farmers by which the farmers promised to cut their production of staple crops and the government in return undertook to give them cash subsidies. The farmers would benefit in two ways. They would receive a higher price for the products they raised, and they would collect cash payments on the contracts they signed with the government. Funds to pay for the program were to come from taxes levied on the processors of farm products—that is, on millers, cotton-ginners and spinners, and meat-packers. At first, the act provided for crop reduction only in cotton, wheat, corn, hogs, rice, tobacco, and milk; later, it was extended to include other products.

Since the A.A.A. did not become law until after the spring planting period in 1933, acreage restriction during the first year of the measure unfortunately had to be replaced or supplemented by the destruction of crops, particularly cotton and hogs. Cotton planters were paid to plow up one-fourth of the growing cotton crop, and more than 6 million young pigs were slaughtered. The spectacle of deliberate destruction in a society in which people badly needed food and clothing aroused sardonic comment from critics of the New Deal on both the right and the left. Newspapers observed that the mules in the cotton fields seemed more intelligent than their masters; trained to avoid spoiling the growing crop, they found it hard to plow along a line that was intended to uproot it.

Many farmers accepted government checks for reducing acreage, and then calmly proceeded to intensify cultivation of the remaining acres. As a result, the net reduction in crops did not amount to nearly as much as the government planners had hoped. Hence in 1934, Congress enacted laws that set up production quotas. The Bankhead Cotton Control Act set quotas for cotton-growers and imposed taxes on those who violated them. The Kerr-Smith Act taxed the sale of tobacco produced by farmers who had not signed A.A.A. tobacco contracts.

Despite criticism that the A.A.A. was coercive, and despite all the ironic newspaper comments about crop destruction, the A.A.A. was successful in a number of important respects. In both 1934 and 1935, more than 30 million acres were taken out of production, in return for which farmers were paid $1,151,000,000. Farm prices did rise considerably. The price of wheat, which was 38 cents a bushel in 1932, rose to $1.02 in 1936. Cotton rose from 6.5 cents a pound to 12.3 cents, hogs from $3.34 per hundredweight to $9.37, and tobacco from 10.5 cents a pound to 23.6 cents. The total realized net income of American farm operators rose from $1,832,000,000 to $5,062,000,000. Many a farmer felt that his head was above water for the first time in years.

On January 6, 1936, in the Hoosac Mills Case (*U.S.* v. *Butler, et al.*), the Supreme Court ruled that the crop-control methods undertaken by the A.A.A. were illegal, because they invaded powers reserved to the states. Moreover, the processing tax could not legally be levied as a part of the plan to regulate and control agricultural production. For the time being, this decision invalidated federal control of agricultural production, and the more obviously compulsory methods for limiting production were labeled unconstitutional.

In February, however, Congress replaced the earlier acts with the Soil Conservation and Domestic Allotment Act, which continued crop restriction under a new legal form. Technically, the plan was intended to increase soil fertility and to conserve re-

A farmer and his sons seek shelter from a dust storm in Oklahoma, 1936. New Deal conservation policies were intended to strike at the land waste that helped make such storms possible.

sources. The A.A.A. was authorized to pay farmers for adopting soil-conservation measures and for reducing soil-depleting crops. Operating on the principle that the great staple crops tend to deplete the soil, the government continued to secure acreage reduction in staples. Instead of the unconstitutional tax on processors, regular congressional appropriations were relied upon to finance the program. However, shortages developed after a drought in 1936 and prices rose considerably. So farmers increased their plantings for the following year, and in 1937 brought in bumper crops. Once again prices sagged.

Congress passed a second Agricultural Adjustment Act in February, 1938, to meet the problem of low prices. This law embodied Secretary of Agriculture Henry A. Wallace's idea of the "ever-normal granary." The government continued the soil-conservation program, but now made payments to farmers who accepted acreage allotments based upon estimates of the normal demand plus a reserve necessary for times of shortage. Farmers who produced more than their allotments received loans on the surplus, which they were expected to store for sale in shortage years. When two-thirds of the producers of any of the five staples covered in the act (corn, cotton, wheat, tobacco, and rice) voted for quotas, the government was empowered to impose a marketing quota and to tax all sales in excess of this quota. If the price of any of the five staples fell below 75 per cent of parity—that is, 75 per cent below the 1909-1914 level—the government could compensate farmers for all or part of the difference with "parity payments." Large amounts were paid to farmers under this measure, but satisfactory conditions did not return to the American commercial farm until the 1940's, when wartime demand once again boosted farm prices.

The basic New Deal legislation for agriculture helped commercial farmers a good

Living conditions of migrant workers at Tulare, California, 1937.

bit, but it did little for share-croppers, farm tenants, and hired farm laborers. Although the commercial farmers had long been organized and influential, the marginal farmers were all but helpless. As the depression wore on, however, people began to sympathize with the underdog everywhere, and some effort was made to help the rural underprivileged who were shut out from the cash benefits of the A.A.A. Farm families were, of course, eligible for federal relief; but in April, 1935, Roosevelt took a step to help them strengthen their position as farmers by creating the Resettlement Administration. Against tremendous obstacles, the R.A. launched a drive on rural poverty. It withdrew 9 million acres of wasted and almost useless soil from cultivation, established new communities in resettlement areas, extended

loans to farmers who could not obtain credit elsewhere, and encouraged cooperative action among farmers who had always insisted on going it alone.

In 1936, Roosevelt appointed a special committee to study the problem of farm tenancy. In the following year, this committee made a comprehensive report not only on farm tenancy, but also on the general problem of American rural poverty. As a result, in 1937 Congress passed the Farm Tenancy Act, which provided loans to share-croppers, tenant farmers, and farm laborers for the purchase of land, livestock, supplies, and equipment. The Resettlement Administration was reorganized as the Farm Security Administration, which by June, 1944, had given financial assistance to 870,000 rural families.

III. RELIEF AND REFORM

Relief. One of the New Deal's most urgent tasks was to provide relief for almost 12 million unemployed, many of whom were on the brink of starvation. Up to this time, the federal government had done little, the theory being that relief should be provided

by private individuals, or perhaps by local and state governments. Hoover's administration had coordinated the country's relief efforts, but he himself felt that if the federal government assumed the relief burden, the recipients would become demoralized. However, the resources of state and local governments and of private agencies had run out long before.

In 1933, the issue was no longer whether the federal government should act—this question had been settled by the 1932 election. The issue now was whether the government should simply make handouts to the poverty-stricken or whether it should provide work relief. In accordance with suggestions made by Roosevelt in an address to Congress in March, 1933, several lines of action were adopted.

The Federal Emergency Relief Administration was set up in May, 1933, with a fund of half a billion dollars to provide direct emergency relief to states and localities. Although the federal government provided the money, the relief itself was to be administered by the states. At first, cash payments were distributed. But the relief administrator, Harry Hopkins, believed firmly that work relief was both psychologically and economically superior to a dole. So the Relief Administration began to experiment with work relief projects, and in time almost half the people receiving relief were put to work on jobs that presumably did not compete with the work of private business. Pay rates began at 30 cents an hour. Ultimately, the F.E.R.A. spent about $4 billion, of which a little less than a third was contributed by states and municipalities, the rest by the federal government.

Another form of relief—the Civilian Conservation Corps—linked together the conservation of natural resources and the needs of unemployed youth. The C.C.C. was established by the President under congressional authorization. Members, young men from 18 to 25, were recruited from cities and sent to work camps built by the War Department, where they were put to work on reforestation, fire-prevention projects, road and dam construction, the control of mosquitoes and other pests, and similar tasks. They were given housing and recreational facilities and were paid $30 a month, of which $22 was sent to their families. By the end of 1941, some 2,750,000 youths had spent some part of their lives in the C.C.C. camps. The value of this program insofar as the morale of the young and the conservation of the nation's resources were concerned was beyond calculation.

The Civil Works Administration, established in November, 1933, was different from the F.E.R.A. in that it was administered from Washington and was devoted entirely to work relief. It quickly put 4 million men to work on a variety of tasks, such as repairing roads and improving schools and parks. Widely criticized by opponents of the New Deal on the ground that it "made work" and that it was spending money on leaf-raking and similar futile efforts, it in fact accomplished a great many useful objectives before it was disbanded in the spring of 1934. Much of its work was absorbed into the expanding program of the F.E.R.A.

Another agency, intended both to create work and to stimulate private business, was the Public Works Administration, established in the summer of 1933 under the administration of Secretary of the Interior Harold L. Ickes. This agency planned needed public works and made contracts with private companies, joining with cities and states to finance the projects that it approved. About half a million of the workers employed were drawn from the pool of the unemployed. School and college buildings, bridges, dams, sewage systems, roads, and hospitals were built and reclamation work was undertaken by the P.W.A. Ickes, wary of log-rolling, corruption, and bogus projects, determined to spend the money allotted to him with the greatest care. Since he was slow to approve plans, it took many months before the pump-priming effects of the P.W.A. began to be felt. By 1939, it had spent about $6 billion, and the country was dotted with buildings planned under its auspices. Its expenditures are generally credited with helping to stimulate the recovery that started to show itself between 1935 and 1937.

Early in 1935, President Roosevelt proposed a reorganization of the entire relief program. Many persons had complained that relief agencies duplicated each others' tasks, and that the government had never tried to distinguish between employable persons who needed relief and the "unemployables" who could not have found work even in good times. Roosevelt now proposed that federal relief be devoted only to employables, leaving the care of others to states and municipalities, and that the federal government provide work relief only. Congress passed the Emergency Relief Act in May, 1935, putting these suggestions into operation. Relief other than the measures undertaken by the C.C.C. and the P.W.A. (these agencies were continued) was consolidated under a new agency, the Works Progress Administration. The W.P.A. was placed under the direction of Harry Hopkins, who held the position until 1939, when he became Secretary of Commerce. From the beginning substantial sums were appropriated for the operations of the W.P.A., and by July, 1941, when its operations ended, it had spent no less than $11,365,000,000. All in all, it provided work for 8 million individuals, and at its peak in November, 1938, 3,-271,000 persons were on its payroll. Among the more than 250,000 projects it undertook were water works, sewage plants, street and highway improvements, hospitals, bridges, municipal power plants, school buildings, and slum clearance.

Nor did the W.P.A. ignore the professional artists whose vocations had been disrupted by the depression and who had come to regard themselves as useless citizens. It instituted various projects in music, the fine arts, and the theater that gave employment to artists and writers (as well as to actors, stagehands, designers, and other workers). By so doing, it provided brilliant and inexpensive entertainment for many people who had never seen a play or attended an exhibition. The Federal Writers Project rescued hundreds of writers from despair and put them to work collecting documents, writing local histories, and making surveys and studies. Finally, the needs of youths with intellectual interests were recognized. The work of the W.P.A. was supplemented by a National Youth Administration, which gave young people between 16 and 25 part-time employment in high schools, colleges, and universities, chiefly at tasks that assisted these institutions in the conduct of their affairs and the management of their offices.

No part of the New Deal drew more criticism than its relief program. Its cost was truly enormous, and the burdens of relief had to be carried by the private sector of the economy. Many critics charged—usually inaccurately—that relief projects were of little or no use and were inefficiently handled. Accusations were made—often justly—that the administration used the relief program for political purposes. Many Americans had no sympathy with the cultural work of the W.P.A., or with the idea that musicians, writers, and artists had as much claim on the community as did workers in other fields. It was said also, and often with truth, that persons with radical and unconventional views were being employed on the cultural projects. Yet few of the critics realized that these cultural projects might provide the beneficiaries with a sense of security, restore their personal pride, and undermine their radicalism. Elsewhere in the world, where intellectuals and artists had been completely neglected and left to make their own way, they had often turned toward fascism or communism.

Other Americans defended the relief program eloquently. The work undertaken by the various agencies had changed the face of America, had tailored its land, improved its cities, and provided it with hundreds of public buildings, which would be urgently needed by coming generations. The enormous expenditures of the relief programs placed a heavy burden on the taxpayers. But the huge amounts of money that swelled the nation's purchasing power seemed to have stimulated the movement toward business recovery that was evident after the middle of 1935. Above all, there was the humane accomplishment. Americans would not let other Americans starve in the midst of plenty. Nor would they let their fellow citizens suffer a devastating loss in pride. Vital to every man's morale is the need to be wanted, the desire to be useful. By providing work and by keeping up the spirits of millions, the relief agencies had tided the nation's spirit over several desperate years.

Public Power. During 1933 and 1934, the work of stimulating recovery and providing relief had kept the administration busy. A few reforms were effected in these early days, as we have seen, chiefly affecting the banking system and the investment market. But not until after the spring of 1935 did the New Deal begin in earnest to reform American life, to change its ways of doing things, and to distribute its income more equitably.

Before it changed direction in the summer of 1935, the single greatest reform effort made by the New Deal was the creation of the Tennessee Valley Authority in 1933.

We have already seen that the Roosevelt administration had inherited the unsolved problem of Muscle Shoals (see p. 641). Long interested in both the power and conservation problems, the new President implemented the old dream of making the Tennessee Valley a great experiment in regional rehabilitation. A law passed in May, 1933, created the Tennessee Valley Authority and empowered it to buy, build, and operate dams in the Tennessee Valley, generate and sell electric power, plan reforestation and flood control, develop the Tennessee River for navigation, withdraw marginal lands from cultivation, and (rather sweepingly) to advance the economic and social well-being of the people of the river basin.

The area affected by the T.V.A. covered seven states and embraced about 40,000 square miles. It possessed vast natural resources, many of them entirely undeveloped. In this region, operating under its board of three directors, the T.V.A. constructed sixteen new dams, partly with the help of

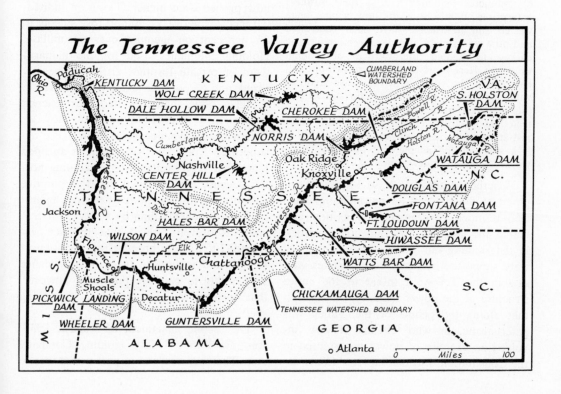

The Tennessee Valley Authority

P.W.A. funds, and took over control of five others. The best known of the new dams, the beautiful Norris Dam northwest of Knoxville, Tennessee, was finished in 1936. It was named after Senator George W. Norris, who had given years of his life to making T.V.A. a reality. By 1940, four dams were generating power, and in the following year over 400,000 users, including homes, farms, and businesses, were being directly or indirectly served. Farms in the region were being supplied on a far greater scale than ever before with electric power at cheap rates. And private companies, under pressure of government competition, were lowering their rates. Land was being redeemed and improved, and the people of the Valley were developing pride in their region and affection for the experiment. David E. Lilienthal, one of the directors of T.V.A., exulted in 1944:

This is the story of a great change. . . . It is a tale of a wandering and inconstant river now become a chain of broad and lovely lakes which people enjoy, and on which they can depend, in all seasons, for the movement of the barges of commerce that now nourish their business enterprises. It is a story of how waters once wasted and destructive have been controlled and now work, night and day, creating electric energy to lighten the burden of human drudgery. Here is a tale of fields grown old and barren with the years, which now are vigorous with new fertility, lying green to the sun; of forests that were hacked and despoiled, now protected and refreshed with strong young trees just starting on their slow road to maturity. It is a story of the people and how they have worked to create a new valley.

Nonetheless, the T.V.A. was heatedly opposed at first by private power companies, who resented government competition and feared the use of a governmental yardstick in determining fair rates. These companies were supported by many conservatives who saw in the T.V.A. a threat to the entire structure of the power industry, or who felt that aiding the people of the Valley was paternalistic, or who felt that T.V.A. involved an exercise of power not granted in the Constitution. But the Supreme Court decided in *Ashwander* v. *Tennessee Valley Authority* (1936) that at no point had constitutional powers been exceeded. Another plan, for a similar development in the Missouri Valley (the projected M.V.A.), was never enacted into law; other hydroelectric developments made under the New Deal—the Grand Coulee and Bonneville dams on the Columbia River, the Hoover Dam on the Colorado River, and the Fort Peck Dam on the upper Missouri—did not incorporate the broad social programs of the T.V.A.

Other Reforms. In August, 1935, the passage of three New Deal measures marked a distinct turn toward reformism and speeded the growing estrangement between the Roosevelt administration and the business class and conservative Americans. One of these measures, inspired by the administration's desire to stop the growth of big business and the accumulation of gigantic individual fortunes, was the Revenue Act of 1935, sometimes called the Wealth Tax Act. Tax rates, which had already been raised by earlier New Deal revenue measures, were now pushed even higher. Taxes on individual incomes above $1 million rose steeply to 75 per cent on incomes over $5 million. Holding companies used for the management of private fortunes also were heavily taxed, and corporation taxes were pushed to a higher point than they had ever reached before. In a reaction to this law, Roy W. Howard, a newspaper-owner who had often supported Roosevelt, wrote him in an open letter that businessmen were becoming hostile because they believed that this punitive measure was inspired more by revenge against political opponents than by a desire for revenue. Roosevelt replied that the act was intended to "create broader range of opportunity" and to impose taxes in accordance with ability to pay. He promised, however, that business would now have a "breathing spell."

The second enactment of August, 1935, was the Public Utility Holding Company Act. This measure was in part a response to revelations that holding companies were be-ing used to exploit investors and to con-trol large investments with relatively modest funds. By purchasing a majority of the stock in an operating company, a holding company could place its directors in con-trol of the operating company. By pyramid-ing one holding company on top of another, an intricate financial structure could be created. And through this structure, which would be understood by the managers but unintelligible to investors, the investors could be milked of their funds. The collapse of the holding-company system erected by Samuel Insull had focused public attention on this evil. Holding companies were par-ticularly prominent in the electric power in-dustry. The 13 largest companies controlled 75 per cent of the entire industry in 1932. The new bill required that holding com-panies which could not, within five years, demonstrate that they had brought about economies in management must be dis-solved. This "death sentence" clause touched off a sharp fight in Congress, and holding companies spent large sums trying to defeat it. At length, after some compromises, the "death sentence" remained in the measure, which was signed on August 28. Its con-stitutionality was questioned, but the Su-preme Court eventually upheld it.

The third August enactment, somewhat less controversial than the others, was the Social Security Act. This measure provided for pensions for the aged and the infirm, for unemployment insurance, and for benefits to dependent mothers and children. The gov-ernment was to pay pensions of up to $15 a month to the poor over 65 years of age, and the states were expected to pay an equal amount. Retirement funds ranging from $10 to $85 a month were to be paid to workers who retired at 65 and who had participated in the plan before their retire-ment. Money for security payments was to be raised by a payroll tax levied equally on employers and employees. By 1940, some 50 million workers were covered by the plan. Most of the states set up old-age pensions and unemployment insurance systems conforming to the provisions of the act. And in most states, a worker who lost his job could col-lect unemployment benefits of from $5 to $15 a week for a period of about 15 weeks while he looked for work.

Two more reform measures were passed in 1937 and 1938, after Roosevelt's re-election (see p. 670). The first dealt with the problem of housing. As early as 1933 the administration had created the Home Owners Loan Corporation with huge re-sources to protect impoverished house-holders from losing their property through mortgage foreclosure. The Federal Housing Administration, created in 1934, lent money mainly to middle-income families for repair-ing old houses or building new ones. The H.O.L.C. had also undertaken housing de-velopment, and had helped more than a million home-owners. But positive action in low-income housing came only with the Wagner-Steagall Housing Act of 1937, which established the United States Hous-ing Authority. The U.S.H.A. was author-ized to make long-term, low-interest loans to state or local public housing agencies to clear slums and construct houses that met its standards. Tenants had to be selected from low-income groups who could not pay rents high enough to induce private housing enter-prises to build dwellings for them.

By 1941, the U.S.H.A. had built new homes for almost 200,000 families, and had torn down more than 78,000 unsafe build-ings. Although these accomplishments met only a small portion of the need for more low-income housing facilities, opposition from real-estate interests made it impossible to expand the program. The stimulation given by the U.S.H.A. to housing and the technical possibilities suggested by its new housing developments were perhaps more important than the actual number of persons it housed.

The last major reform enactment of the New Deal was the Fair Labor Standards Act of June 25, 1938. The outcome of long-standing agitation by liberals in and out of

Congress, this measure had failed to pass Congress on its first try. Finally, after Roosevelt gave it his support, the measure became law over strong opposition from southern Democrats. It applied to firms engaged in interstate commerce, and exempted many occupations, including farm laborers, domestic servants, employees in retail establishments, seamen, and others. But to those to whom it applied, which included most industrial laborers, it aimed to secure a minimum wage of 40 cents an hour and a maximum work-week of 40 hours. And it provided that even these modest objectives should be arrived at only gradually. Beginning at 44 hours, the work-week was to be lowered to 40 hours in three years. Beginning at 25 cents an hour, the minimum

wage was to be raised to 40 cents after eight years. Many Americans were shocked to discover that over 750,000 workers were so poorly paid that they received immediate wage increases when the law first went into effect in August, 1938. The hours of 1,500,000 workers were shortened at the same time.

The law also called for the payment of time-and-a-half for overtime, banned child labor under 16, and limited workers under 18 to non-hazardous occupations. Modest as its requirements were, the law was an important step toward outlawing sweatshop conditions and abuses of child labor. Years afterward, in 1949, when rising prices had wiped out the benefits of the minimum wage increase, President Truman persuaded Congress to raise it to 75 cents, and it was raised still higher under President Eisenhower.

IV. AN AGE OF CONTROVERSY

New Deal Politics. The central art of the New Deal was not economic planning but adroit political maneuver. The steady succession of Roosevelt victories in the presidential campaigns of 1932, 1936, 1940, and 1944 suggests a political power strong beyond challenge, but at no time was the administration actually free from forceful challenges inside and outside the Democratic party. Even the relatively modest policies of 1933-1934 had horrified a large segment of the business community. In those early days, the Roosevelt administration was under constant criticism from business-oriented conservatives who were alarmed at the rapid pace and free spirit of its experimentation, and also from agitators who made themselves the spokesmen of the still discontented masses.

Most formidable of these agitators was Senator Huey Long, who had established a veritable dictatorship in his home state of Louisiana. A skilled and jovial demagogue with a remarkable command of the popular idiom, Long had built up a large following throughout the country, particularly in the

Mississippi Valley, on the strength of a vaguely developed plan to "share the wealth." In 1935, the Democratic National Committee feared that Long might be able to split the Democratic party and hold the balance of power in American politics, with perhaps disastrous consequences for their party in the coming election of 1936. In September, 1935, however, Long was assassinated by a Louisianan who had a personal grievance against him.

Two other demagogues also enjoyed large followings. One was an elderly practicing physician from Long Beach, California, Dr. Francis E. Townsend. In early January, 1935, Townsend announced a plan for a government allowance of $200 a month to every citizen 60 years or over, the cost to be paid by a sales tax. Each pensioner, the ingenious doctor proposed, would be required to spend his entire allowance within the month. This, he thought, would start such a wave of spending that business would boom and make it easy for the rest of the country to bear the cost. Responsible economists dismissed the notion as a crackpot

Three agitators of the depression era meet at a Social Justice Convention at Cleveland, Ohio, in 1936. From left to right: Gerald L. K. Smith, a follower of the late Huey Long; Father Charles E. Coughlin; Dr. Francis E. Townsend.

scheme, but at a time when millions of aged were destitute and desperate, and when many wild schemes were in the air, it had a great popular appeal—at least among persons over 60. Townsend Clubs were organized throughout the country, and their combined membership was believed to be about 3 million in 1935, with perhaps as many as 7 million unorganized supporters.

Another threat came from one of Roosevelt's former supporters, Father Charles E. Coughlin, the "radio priest" whose eloquence in his weekly broadcasts from Royal Oak, Michigan, had brought him an enormous audience. Coughlin raked Wall Street and the international bankers in familiar Populist idiom and demanded "a living annual wage" as well as "nationalization of banking and currency and of national resources."

To discontented Americans, discouraged by the government's failure to get the country back on its feet, men like Long, Coughlin, and Townsend seemed prophets of a social millennium. To those who had watched the rise of dictators abroad, they seemed more like the "forerunners of American fascism," as an able journalist, Raymond Gram Swing, called them. Their activities, coupled with labor's fierce expressions of discontent with the N.R.A., suggested in the spring of 1935

that the mass appeal of the Roosevelt administration, so high in its earliest hours, was about to collapse.

At this point, the administration, which had so far concentrated pretty much on recovery and relief, turned leftward and began to think more and more about the necessity for reform. Dangerous as President Roosevelt might think a man like Huey Long, he recognized that behind Long's agitations, and behind the appeal of Townsend and Coughlin, were real popular grievances that could not be ignored. Privately he spoke of the necessity for doing something "to steal Long's thunder." And a measure like the Wealth Tax was designed, among other things, to do just that. The Social Security Act, with its old-age pension provisions, was expected to take the sting out of the Townsend movement by offering its followers a more responsible substitute for their dreams. The enactment by Congress of these two measures in 1935, together with the passage of the W.P.A. program, the "death sentence" clause for holding companies, and the National Labor Relations Act, was calculated to quiet dissatisfactions among those people who felt that the New Deal had not been "radical" enough. The administration succeeded, but only at the cost of hardening the enmity of great numbers of businessmen, who had hitherto been its supporters or at worst only moderate and hesitant opponents.

By the time the 1936 election rolled around, the nation had moved part way toward economic recovery. Farm incomes were up, millions of unemployed were receiving enough relief to keep body and soul together, and organized labor was making important gains. These groups—the farmers, the unemployed, and the trade unions—together with Roosevelt's great personal popularity, seemed enough to insure the President's victory over any Republican challenger. But the Republicans met at Cleveland in June and condemned the New Deal from stem to stern. "America is in peril," their platform began, and it went on to expand on their belief that the country's liberties were being rapidly destroyed. "We invite all Americans, irrespective of party, to join us in the defense of American institutions." They nominated as their standard-bearer Governor Alfred M. Landon, of Kansas, and named Frank Knox, a Chicago newspaper publisher, as his running-mate. The Democrats renominated Roosevelt and Vice-president Garner by acclamation. A third-party ticket, mustering the discon-

tented to whom Father Coughlin particularly appealed, nominated William Lemke, Republican Congressman from North Dakota, under the banner of the Union party.

Landon was supported by a number of dissaffected Democrats, including Al Smith, and by an organization called the Liberty League, financed by conservative millionaires and dedicated to the proposition that the works of the New Deal were subversive of liberty. Landon was driven into a position where he appeared far less liberal and humane than he actually was, and his campaign soon seemed to be foundering. Moreover, the denunciations of the President by the Liberty League started off at such a shrill pitch that instead of building up to a climax, they veered toward the ludicrous. Landon's association with the ultra-rich supporters of the Liberty League severely handicapped him.

Roosevelt made a trip through the nation in October and defended his policies with vigor and skill before large, well-organized, and enthusiastic audiences. The election ended in a triumph for his cause almost as overwhelming as the victory of Harding over Cox in 1920 (see p. 626). Roosevelt received 27,751,000 votes to Landon's 16,679,000—over 60 per cent of the total popular vote. Landon carried only two

Franklin D. Roosevelt as he was often seen during his presidency. This smile was irresistible to cartoonists.

states, Maine and Vermont. Roosevelt's success in winning over the discontented of the country and diverting them from protest movements was shown in the poor performance of the minor parties: Lemke got only 882,000 votes, Norman Thomas, the socialist, only 187,000, and Earl Browder, the communist, only 80,000. The New Deal had completely broken the forces of independent political radicalism.

In his second inaugural address (January 20, 1937), Roosevelt expressed no complacency over his victory or his achievements. Much remained to be done, he said; the living standards of Americans could be "raised far above the level of mere subsistence."

In this nation I see tens of millions of its citizens—a substantial part of its whole population—who at this very moment are denied the greater part of what the very lowest standards of today call the necessities of life.

I see millions of families trying to live on incomes so meager that the pall of family disaster hangs over them day by day.

I see millions whose daily lives in city and on farm continue under conditions labelled indecent by so-called polite society half a century ago.

I see millions denied education, recreation, and the opportunity to better their lot and that of their children.

I see millions lacking the means to buy the products of farm and factory and by their poverty denying work and productiveness to many other millions.

I see one-third of a nation ill-housed, ill-clad, ill-nourished.

Roosevelt promised that the New Deal would continue to do everything in its power to remedy these conditions. And from that time on, the New Deal engaged in a struggle against the forces, not only within the Democratic party, but also within the federal judiciary itself, that seemed to be preventing it from tackling the grave problems of the nation in its own experimental way.

The Court Fight.   Roosevelt's emphatic endorsement by the people in the election of 1936 was followed almost immediately by his most striking political defeats. The trouble started with Roosevelt's attempt to reform the Supreme Court, which had thrown out so many New Deal measures, and to change the character of his own party. His difficulties were increased by the onset of a sharp business recession in 1937-1938, which damaged his prestige and raised once again the question of whether the administration knew where it was going.

On February 5, 1937, out of a clear blue sky, came a sudden proposal from the President to enlarge the Supreme Court and reform the federal judiciary. He suggested that whenever a federal judge failed to resign or retire within six months after reaching the age of 70, a new federal judge should be appointed. Although the proposal applied to the entire federal judiciary, embracing both district and circuit court judges, it was obviously aimed at the Supreme Court, to which, according to the President's plan, as many as six judges could be added, bringing its membership to a possible 15. At the time of the proposal, six of the judges of the Supreme Court were already 70 or over. Even Roosevelt's associates were surprised when he announced his proposal, for he had apparently consulted no one except his Attorney-General, Homer Cummings, who drafted the bill for him.

Although the announcement came as a shock, the reason behind the bill seemed clear. The people had undeniably approved of the New Deal, but the Supreme Court had been unmistakably, emphatically, and disastrously opposed to its early legislation. Only in the Gold Clause and the T.V.A. cases had it sustained any of the major New Deal legislation that had thus far come before it. In 1935 and 1936, it had struck down the N.R.A. and the A.A.A., which were pillars of the New Deal program. It had turned back a railroad retirement plan and had spurned the Bituminous Coal Act, which was intended to reorganize a sick industry. It had invalidated congressional legislation to protect farm mortgages, and it had thrown out a municipal bankruptcy act. To those who sympathized with the New Deal social program, the Court seemed to be creating a no man's land of legislation where neither state power nor federal power could be brought to bear upon crucial problems. Until the Court could be made more flexible, it seemed unlikely that very much additional legislation could be passed.

To find a suitable way of reforming the Court was difficult. The number of justices had been changed several times during the past, but the present line-up of nine had been fixed for so long that the number almost had the sanction of constitutional authority. A possible alternative to Roosevelt's plan would have been to enlarge the number of judges by constitutional amendment, but to pass such an amendment might have taken many years. An amendment removing or limiting the Court's power to review acts of Congress would also have been difficult to pass and almost impossible to explain, though in theory it would have been a more direct and open attack upon the problem. Roosevelt's plan was a short cut, but it seemed to lack candor. Its real purpose was to change the tenor of the judge's decisions by bringing new blood into the Court; but Roosevelt's assertion that it was intended to help the courts catch up with their business seemed disingenuous.

The "court-packing bill," as it was promptly labeled by the hostile press, aroused a tornado of opposition. The President's opponents, long convinced (quite unjustly) that he was seeking dictatorial powers, found in this measure a vindication of their belief. Even inveterate supporters of the President spoke out against it, and opposition in the Senate was led by Burton K. Wheeler, who had voted for most New Deal measures in the past. Although some distinguished jurists supported the measure, and many of the loyal professionals in the President's party in Congress were prepared to vote for it, it was thrown on the defensive from the very beginning of the debate.

After many months of hearings, the Judiciary Committee of the Senate found against the court bill by a narrow vote of 10 to 8, and turned in a majority report bristling with such phrases as "needless, futile, and utterly dangerous abandonment of constitutional principle," "destroy the independence of the judiciary," and "evasion of the Constitution." But even while the court debate got under way, changes were taking place that were altering the complexion of the Court. One of the most conservative of the judges, Justice Willis Van Devanter, announced his intention to retire, and it became clear that Roosevelt would soon have at least one appointment of his own to make. To this vacancy he appointed a crusading liberal senator, Hugo L. Black of Alabama. Moreover, Justice Owen Roberts, perhaps influenced by the clamor over the Court's ultra-conservatism and by the results of the 1936 election, had begun to vote on the liberal side in some recent cases. ("A switch in time," said a legal wit, "saves nine.") The growing liberalism of Justice Roberts made a vital difference, since the Court had been evenly divided on some important cases.

On March 29, 1937, less than two months after Roosevelt first made his proposal, the Court handed down three decisions that pointed in a new direction. In *West Coast Hotel Co.* v. *Parrish,* it overruled *Adkins* v. *Childrens Hospital* (1923) and in effect reversed one of its own recent decisions on state minimum wage laws, *Morehead* v. *New York ex. rel. Tipaldo* (1936). On the same day, the Court unanimously sustained a revised Farm Mortgage Act of 1935 and the Railway Labor Act as amended in 1934. Far more important for the course of the New Deal was a series of five decisions handed down on April 12 in which the Court upheld the National Labor Relations Act. Six weeks later, in two 5-to-4 decisions, the Court sustained the social security legislation. After March, 1937, the Court almost ceased to declare acts of Congress unconstitutional.

Moreover, the aging justices began to retire—at first the liberals, Brandeis and

Cardozo, but then the conservatives, Sutherland, Butler, and McReynolds. In their places Roosevelt appointed Stanley Reed, Felix Frankfurter, William O. Douglas, Robert H. Jackson, and Frank Murphy—all New Deal supporters. Thus, although Roosevelt's court bill had been buried and all that had been salvaged from it were a few minor reforms of the lower courts, New Dealers could salve their feelings with the thought that they had lost a battle but won the war. Fortunately, both sides in this angry contest found satisfaction in the outcome—Roosevelt's opponents in the overwhelming defeat of his bill, his supporters in the Court's changing attitude and composition. Otherwise the bitterness of the struggle might have lived on. In any case, Roosevelt had lost ground in the battle for public opinion. By placing his hands, with whatever justification, upon the holy of holies in the American constitutional structure, he had lost prestige that could not easily be regained.

Recession. Hard on the heels of the Supreme Court fight came a downward turn in business conditions that anti-New Dealers, perhaps remembering the way the term "Hoover depression" had been used against Hoover in 1932, were quick to call the "Roosevelt recession." The recession seems to have come about partly because the administration, encouraged by signs of business advance, had called for a reduction of expenditures by the W.P.A. and other New Deal agencies. High tax rates, enacted in 1935 and 1936, also seem to have cut private investment, and the accumulation of funds under the social security laws cut purchasing power. The readiness with which this retrenchment started the downward trend suggested that the administration still could not do without its spending policies. Early in 1938, the President and Congress put the spending program back into high gear and increased the outlays of the F.S.A. and the W.P.A. and the lending activities of the R.F.C. Once more recovery began to stir, though the economic level of 1937 was not again reached before the outbreak of World War II.

The onslaught of the recession, although it was more intimately linked to the government's tax and spending policies than to any other event, aroused new concern over the pricing policies of American business as an obstacle to recovery. Once responsible, in the N.R.A., for a comprehensive attempt to organize industry and accept price agreements, the administration now explored an opposite philosophy and began an attack on monopoly. In April, 1938, Roosevelt delivered a message to Congress in which he warned that private power was becoming "stronger than [the] democratic state itself," and argued that the concentration of business power was "seriously impairing the effectiveness of private enterprise." "Big Business collectivism in industry," he warned, "compels an ultimate collectivism in government." Congress responded by authorizing the Temporary National Economic Committee to investigate the facts of American business organization. The T.N.E.C. made a comprehensive investigation, collected 37 volumes of testimony, and published 43 monographs. It carried out a detailed examination of price-fixing, patent monopolies, holding companies, and interlocking directorates.

In 1938, the administration launched a trust-busting program. Ironically, the campaign was put in the hands of Assistant Attorney-General Thurman W. Arnold, who had poured scorn on the anti-trust acts in his satiric book, *The Folklore of Capitalism.* The Antitrust Division of the Department of Justice, now greatly expanded, began a crusade against artificial price-maintenance. The theory behind the program was that the heavy industries enjoyed a semi-monopoly that enabled them to maintain their prices even in bad times, whereas the more competitive industries had to cut their prices drastically. This situation, it was alleged, contributed to the imbalance of the economy, cut purchasing power, and impeded recovery. Arnold launched many prosecutions, but the outbreak of World War II made it impossible to test their long-range economic value.

A final setback to Roosevelt's plans for reform was delivered by the congressional elections of 1938. The Democratic party seemed now to have reached the limits of its capacity for reform. It embraced the conservative South, with its opposition to wage-and-hour legislation and to any change in the status of the Negro, and also included the liberals of the North, who relied for mass support upon the trade unions, the unemployed, and the Negro voters. The southern conservatives were particularly powerful, because through their seniority they were entrenched in the strategic committee chairmanships of Congress. Many of them had fought against the Court reform bill and the Fair Labor Standards Act. In the primary contests leading up to the elections of 1938, President Roosevelt tried to liberalize the party by supporting the liberal opponents of a few of the Democratic conservatives, chiefly in the South. But in the South he was invariably beaten. Only in New York City, where the Chairman of the House Rules Committee, who had obstructed the passage of the Fair Labor Standards Act, was defeated, did he have any success. The fall elections showed that the tide was running against the administration. The Democrats still kept their majorities in both houses, but the Republicans increased their seats in the House from 89 to 164 and in the Senate from 16 to 23.

The country had begun once more, though slowly, to swing toward conservatism. In his annual message of January 4, 1939, Roosevelt announced that the dynamic phase of the New Deal was over: "We have now passed the period of internal conflict in the launching of our program of social reform. Our full energies may now be released to invigorate the processes of recovery in order to preserve our reforms." The flood of innovations had stopped.

An Assessment. The New Deal lasted as a reform movement from March, 1933, to the end of 1938. It is not easy to assess the flurries of legislative and political activity that took place during this five-and-a-half-year period. Although the New Deal program commanded the loyalty of the majority of Americans, as shown by the election results, it was hotly contested at every turn and is still the subject of controversy.

Anti-New Dealers point out that the New Deal was an extremely expensive experiment, that it persistently failed to balance the budget, and that from the fiscal year 1932 to 1940, the national debt increased from $19,487,000,000 to $42,967,000,000. The New Deal had built up a large bureaucracy. It had failed to restore the confidence of the business community that would have been the key to real recovery. Certainly if we test it by its contribution to business recovery, we must judge the New Deal a failure. For in 1939, when all the experiments were over, there were still over 8,700,000 workers who had not been re-employed by private industry. To the opponents of the New Deal, the gains that it achieved were purchased at too high a price in tax burdens, red tape, and unresolved social problems.

Defenders of the New Deal have strong counter-arguments. New Deal policies raised the debt, but they also helped raise national income from $39,963,000,000 in 1932 to $70,829,000,000 in 1939. Furthermore, pro-New-Dealers contend that if unemployment under the New Deal is measured in terms of real human suffering and social waste, it was far less significant than the unemployment of earlier days. The unemployed were no longer left desperate and hopeless, as they had been before 1933, nor were they so idle, for the New Deal had provided useful work for many of them.

Finally, the defenders of the New Deal appeal to intangibles. The New Deal had taken up a people brought to the brink of despair by poverty and failure, and had restored their morale. It had placed on the statute books a number of measures to make life more comfortable and secure, measures that would benefit not only contemporaries, but also millions of Americans yet to be born. After 1936, not even the Republicans quarreled in their party platforms with such reforms as the Social Security Act, minimum wages and hours, improved housing conditions for low-income families, or the insuring of bank deposits. Although the New Deal had created a large class of civil servants to administer its measures, it had never abandoned democratic methods. And it had strengthened democracy by giving millions of Americans the assurance that they had a strong stake in the survival of their own government.

When Roosevelt came into office in 1933, many Americans were flirting with false gods —with thoughts of violence, with doubts about democracy, with political panaceas of the extreme right and the extreme left. The New Deal restored their belief that a democratic people could cope with its own problems in a democratic way. This demonstration was significant for the whole western world. Tyranny ruled in Russia, Germany, Italy, and Japan. But in the most powerful of the western democracies, the people still stumbled, erratic but free, toward the solution of their problems through constitutional and parliamentary means.

Readings

Balanced general appraisals may be found in D. W. Brogan's *The Era of Franklin D. Roosevelt: A Chronicle of the New Deal and Global War* (1950); Dixon Wecter, *The Age of the Great Depression* (1948); and in the earlier work by Basil Rauch, *History of the New Deal, 1933-38* (1944). See also Charles and Mary Beard, *America in Mid-passage* (2 vols., 1939). Economic forces are considered by Broadus Mitchell, *Depression Decade: From New Era through New Deal, 1929-1941* (1947). The best general biography of Franklin D. Roosevelt is the one by Frank Freidel, thus far carried only through the election of 1932 (3 vols., 1952, 1954, and 1956). John Gunther's *Roosevelt in Retrospect* (1950) is a satisfactory one-volume work, but J. M. Burns' *Roosevelt: The Lion and the Fox* (1956) is outstanding. Robert Sherwood, *Roosevelt and Hopkins* (1948), is revealing, as is Frances Perkins, *The Roosevelt I Knew* (1946).

The Public Papers and Addresses of Franklin D. Roosevelt (9 vols., 1938-1941) is an important source. Raymond Moley, *After Seven Years* (1939), is a serious critical document on the early New Deal. Hostile views can be found in the various writings of Herbert Hoover after 1933, especially *The Challenge to Liberty* (1934).

On special policies, see A. W. Crawford, *Monetary Management under the New Deal* (1940), and Merle Fainsod and Lincoln Gordon, *Government and the American Economy*. On labor, see Herbert Harris, *American Labor* (1939), and Edward Levinson, *Labor on the March* (1938). The role of labor is also discussed by Mathew Josephson in *Sidney Hillman: Statesman of American Labor* (1952), while labor leaders are critically examined by C. Wright Mills in *The New Men of Power* (1948). For other special problems, see E. G. Nourse, and others, *Three Years of the Agricultural Adjustment Administration* (1937); H. L. Ickes, *Back to Work: The Story of the P.W.A.* (1935); J. C. Brown, *Public Relief, 1929-1939* (1940); Abraham Epstein, *Insecurity, A Challenge to America* (rev. ed., 1938); Nathan Straus, *The Seven Myths of Housing* (1944); David Lilienthal, *TVA: Democracy on the March* (1938); and Hugh S. Johnson, *The Blue Eagle from Egg to Earth* (1935). Thurman Arnold deals with the conflicting ideologies of the New Deal period in *The Folklore of Capitalism* (1937), and with anti-trust problems in *The Bottlenecks of Business* (1940). On the Supreme Court fight, see E. S. Corwin, *Constitutional Revolution* (1941).

On New Deal politics, several memoirs and diaries are helpful, among them James A. Farley's *Behind the Ballots* (1938), and *Jim Farley's Story* (1948); *The Memoirs of Cordell Hull* (2 vols., 1948); and Harold L. Ickes, *The Autobiography of a Curmudgeon* (1943). Ickes' 3-volume work, *The Secret Diary of Harold L. Ickes* (1953-1954), is amusing, though not always reliable.

FROM

ISOLATION

TO GLOBAL WAR

C H A P T E R   T W E N T Y - N I N E

To achieve isolation, if not from the world as a whole, at least from the quarrels and problems of Europe, was the primary aim of American foreign policy during the years after World War I. Americans traditionally believed that America and Europe were polar opposites, indeed that America's superiority lay in being precisely what Europe was not. America was new, democratic, and, in some vague sense, a "natural" society. Europe was old, aristocratic, artificial, and decadent. Many Americans had parents or ancestors who had fled from persecution or starvation or failure in the Old World. To be fully American, they felt, was to cut themselves off as completely as possible from their European roots.

I.   PEACETIME DIPLOMACY, 1920-1939

America and Europe.   For only a short time, the emergency of World War I and the Progressive idealism formulated by Wilson worked to pull the United States away from its anti-Europeanism. Wilson did not attempt to defy the common American assumption that the United States had virtues the rest of the world lacked, or enjoyed only imperfectly. He himself regarded the United States as the prime example of democratic and representative government. What made him different from the anti-Europeans who preceded him, and from the later isolationists, was his conviction (held by Americans during the period of Manifest Destiny) that the United States ought to foster the growth of America's excellent institutions throughout the rest of the world, or at least the European world. He regarded Europe not as anti-America but rather as a potential America. In his second inaugural address, delivered in March, 1917, before the United States entered the war, Wilson proclaimed that Americans had become "citizens of the world."

After World War I, as we have seen, Americans returned with a vengeance to their more characteristic impulse to withdraw from European affairs. Except among a handful of intellectuals, who looked to Europe for higher cultural standards, the image of Europe among Americans was never more unfavorable than during the 1920's. Europe, it was said, was a broken wasteland, inhabited by quarrelsome people who would always hate each other. None of its countries was capable of sound self-government. Europeans had no character, for they did not even pay their debts. Nations and individuals alike tried to cheat innocent Americans. Europe was the home of alien and unwholesome ideas—bolshevism, anarchism, socialism, and all the other isms. (During the 1920's few Americans had the foresight to condemn fascism as well.)

America and the East.   The prevailing American attitude toward the other theater of world conflict, the Far East, was quite different. Americans had always moved westward, across the continent and toward the Pacific, and since the early nineteenth century there had always been business-men, politicians, journalists, and others who looked beyond the Pacific coast to the Far East for further trade and future empire.

But in the Orient, American aspirations for power ran up against the much more imperious ambitions of Japan, a country that had rapidly been developing its own industrial power during the last three decades of the nineteenth century. Since the Japanese victory over Russia in 1905, Americans had been looking with anxiety on the expansionist policies of Japan. There was talk of "the yellow peril" and of eventual war in the Orient even before World War I, though no crisis had arisen between the United States and Japan serious enough to offer a threat of war.

After World War I, when Japan began to assert herself vigorously at the expense of China, Americans felt no inclination to remain aloof, despite their reluctance to become involved in European affairs. Indeed, after having refused to join the League of Nations, the United States tried in 1931-1932 to lead the nations of the world in a stand against Japanese imperialism in the Pacific. However, American diplomats were no more successful in persuading Europeans to line up against Japan than the Europeans had been in inducing Americans to participate in the collective efforts of Europe.

In the end, the United States could neither maintain its withdrawal from Europe nor hold the line in Asia without resorting to war. When both the European fascist powers and the Japanese war lords began to take the initiative at the same time, events in the two parts of the world became interwoven, and it was no longer possible to maintain separate theaters of action as the American public would have liked. The distress of the European democracies, a growing source of alarm to Americans, was the signal for Japan to strike. Confronted by a vast postwar coalition of hostile powers, the United States was gradually drawn into the global war that began in 1939. But this time, slogans about saving the world for democracy had little appeal to the American public. Americans were simply forced to fight. The threat to their physical survival made those who were not willing to fight *for* democracy at least willing to fight *with* the democracies. What confronted Americans between 1939 and 1945 was not the task of making their political institutions prevail throughout the world, but simply of keeping them intact at home. In candid recognition of this fact, Franklin D. Roosevelt once suggested that World War II be called the "War for Survival."

The Washington Conference. In 1921-1922, a conference on the limitation of armaments was held in Washington in response to (1) the aggressions of Japan in the Far East; (2) the three-cornered naval rivalry among the United States, Great Britain, and Japan; and (3) a rising sentiment in the United States for disarmament. Japan had taken advantage of World War I to strengthen her own position. As one of the Allies, she had seized German holdings in Shantung, China. On January 18, 1915, her government had presented its Twenty-One Demands to China—demands so sweeping in their implications that they in effect called upon China to surrender her sovereignty. Secretary of State Bryan had protested vigorously, but his successor, Secretary Lansing, held conversations with Viscount Ishii in 1917 during which, in return for Japanese endorsement of the Open Door

principle, Lansing had agreed that Japan had "special interests" in China.

Nonetheless, the United States and Japan continued to watch each other guardedly. The strategic Pacific island of Yap became a source of controversy after the war. Wilson had said that the island should be internationalized, but the Japanese, with British support, had received a mandate over it. The distrust that showed itself in American protests over this mandate was borne out by the race toward armaments construction; all three of the great naval powers in the Pacific—the United States, Great Britain, and Japan—had developed ambitious programs for battleship construction; and much talk about a coming Japanese-American war circulated in both countries. Yet a new war was not what the American public wanted. A resolution introduced into the Senate by Senator William E. Borah, calling for a three-power disarmament conference, won wide public approval, and by the end of June had passed both houses of Congress almost without opposition. Despite Japan's reluctance to attend, the conference was finally arranged in the summer of 1921, and in November of that year the representatives of the participating nations assembled at Washington. In addition to the three Pacific powers, France and Italy joined in the disarmament discussions.

The delegates had hardly settled in their seats when they were startled by Secretary of State Hughes, who bluntly proposed that the powers agree to a ten-year holiday in the construction of capital ships, and the scrapping of other ships built or planned. Hughes suggested that the ratio among the navies of the United States, Great Britain, and Japan be left at their current proportions: 5-5-3. Calmly he proposed that the United States scrap 30 capital ships totaling 845,000 tons, and that the other powers follow suit by destroying some 66 ships of their own. The Conference was stunned by this imaginative gesture, and Hughes was applauded in his own country and throughout the world.

The Hughes proposals met strong resistance, but after much discussion the powers agreed to set up a ratio for tonnage in capital ships. The United States, the British Empire, Japan, France, and Italy agreed upon the respective magnitudes of 5-5-3-1.7-1.7. No such agreement was adopted, however, to cover the construction of smaller ships, cruisers, destroyers, and submarines, and at this level naval competition continued as it had in the past. Later, at the London Conference of 1930 called by President Hoover, restrictions were adopted to cover such craft. But in 1934, when Japan notified the other powers that after two years she would no longer be bound by any part of the Washington agreement, the naval race was on again.

One of the problems of the Washington Conference was the old Anglo-Japanese Alliance made in 1902, which the English no longer wanted and of which the United States disapproved. It was replaced at the Conference by a Four-Power Pact among the United States, the British Empire, France, and Japan. The contracting powers pledged that they would keep peace in the Pacific by respecting each other's rights in that area, and that they would consult together when any of these rights seemed to be threatened. The Anglo-Japanese Alliance was abrogated, to the disgruntlement of the Japanese.

The rights of China were the subject of a second agreement that emerged from the Washington Conference. This agreement, the Nine-Power Pact, was concluded on February 6, 1922. The Nine-Power Pact, to which the signatories of the Four-Power Pact as well as China, Italy, Belgium, the Netherlands, and Portugal subscribed, affirmed the "sovereignty, the independence, and the territorial and administrative integrity of China." Between the time of the Conference and the spring of 1923, the Japanese settled the Shantung controversy with China, withdrew the most objectionable of her Twenty-One Demands, conceded to the United States special cable rights on the island of Yap, and consented to an annulment of the Lansing-Ishii agreement.

For the moment, the results of the Conference seemed satisfactory.

Japanese Conquest. Nine years later, Japan struck in the Far East. On the night of September 18, 1931, a provocative incident took place on the Japanese-controlled South Manchurian Railway. Japan seized upon this incident as an excuse to overrun the entire province of Manchuria. Herbert Hoover's Secretary of State, Henry L. Stimson, promptly notified the Japanese that they were violating their treaty obligations. The League of Nations invoked the Kellogg-Briand Pact, which had been signed three years before by Japan, and set up the Lytton Commission to report on the Far Eastern crisis. But the Japanese armies rolled on. By January, 1932, they had crushed all Chinese resistance in Manchuria.

On January 7, Secretary Stimson stated in a note to Japan and China that the United States could not recognize any treaty or agreement in the Orient that infringed its rights, and invoked the Kellogg-Briand Pact once again. This policy—refusing to recognize territorial conquest in Asia—became known as the "Stimson Doctrine," though it had already been enunciated and applied by Bryan. The Stimson Doctrine had no more than moral force, however, so long as arms were not to be used to back it up. Stimson hoped that the British government would associate itself with his action, but the British Foreign Office refused, issuing a statement which, as Stimson later said, could be interpreted by the world, including the Japanese government, as "a rebuff to the United States." The American people, too absorbed in their own domestic problems to care much about Manchuria, did not "give a hoot in a rain barrel" (as a Philadelphia newspaper said) who controlled North China. And the administration, to its credit, refrained from using the incident to distract the public from the woes of the depression.

The situation deteriorated on January 28,

1932, when Japan, stung by a Chinese boycott, attacked not only the Chinese forces at Shanghai but also the defenseless civilian population. For the first time, militant sentiment against Japan began to appear in the United States. Five thousand civic leaders urged an economic boycott against Japan. Others, including President Hoover himself, believed that economic coercion would be an invitation to war. The administration confined itself to making protests wherever American interests in Shanghai were affected.

Stimson, fearing that he would only court another humiliating rebuff if he appealed to the signers of the Nine-Power Pact against Japan, decided to issue a message to the world in an informal way by expressing his views in a letter to Senator Borah, chairman of the Senate Committee on Foreign Relations. In this letter, Stimson asserted that the United States would stand on its treaty rights in the Far East, specifically those recognized in the Nine-Power Pact, and invited other nations to do the same. This move was greeted with strong approval in the American press, and on March 11, 1932, the League of Nations Assembly adopted a resolution using much the same language. Subsequently, the League's Lytton Commission issued a report condemning Japan's actions and refusing to recognize the validity of the puppet regime Tokyo had established in Manchuria as the state of Manchukuo. But as an effort to organize the nations of the world to take action against Japanese aggression, Stimson's statements must be counted as a failure. The nations were not ready to stand firm, and this one long step away from the traditional American policy of isolation came to nothing.

Latin-American Relations.   In its relation with its neighbors to the south, the policy of the United States had long been dictated by two considerations: the protection of American investments and, above all, the protection of the Panama Canal Zone. When anything happened to threaten these interests, the United States was prepared to act, even at the cost of injuring its already unsatisfactory relations with its Latin neighbors. American diplomacy in this area after World War I is the story first of continued intervention followed by a radical revision in policy that established what has come to be called the "Good Neighbor Policy."

A few minor instances of intervention took place in the early 1920's. The United States sent a battleship to Panama in 1921 to speed up the cession of a piece of territory to Costa Rica; American troops were stationed in the Dominican Republic from 1921 to 1924 to protect American financial interests; and marines were landed in Honduras in 1923 to intervene in a revolution. By 1924, the United States was taking an active part in directing the financial policies of ten Latin-American nations, and was prepared to exert financial pressure or land troops if the need arose.

A small force of American marines had been on guard in Nicaragua since 1912 when, at the request of President Adolfo Diaz, the United States had intervened to bring order out of political turbulence. The marines were withdrawn for a short time in 1925, but when revolution broke out again soon afterward, the country was reoccupied, and by 1927 there were 5,000 American marines in the country. President Coolidge had sent the American forces without congressional approval—an action that brought him under attack from both his Democratic opponents and the anti-imperialists. He replied that the United States had a "moral responsibility" in Nicaragua, and insisted: "We are not making war on Nicaragua any more than a policeman on the street is making war on passersby." In April, 1927, Colonel Henry L. Stimson, Coolidge's newly appointed special envoy, arrived in Nicaragua and worked out the terms of an agreement between the rebels and the government under which both sides consented to hold an election the next year, supervised by the American government. The results were generally satisfactory to both groups. But the followers of General Sandino, one of the rebel leaders, refused to be pacified, retired to the hills, and kept harassing American marines until 1933, when the last troops were withdrawn.

American investments in Mexican mineral and oil resources led to a major diplomatic crisis. The Mexican Constitution of 1917 had turned over the ownership of all mineral and oil resources to the Mexican government. American investors feared that this policy might be made retroactive, in which case their properties would be liable to confiscation. When President Calles of Mexico took office in 1924, he announced his desire to make just such a change. The pressure of American oil interests, together with the influence of American Catholics who resented Calles' anti-clerical policy, caused some talk of war in the United States. But in 1927 President Coolidge sent to Mexico his former Amherst classmate, Dwight L. Morrow, a partner in the House of Morgan, with the curt instruction: "Keep us out of war." Morrow proved an excellent diplomat, and his own friendship for the Mexicans was soon returned. Favored by a decision of the Mexican Supreme Court, he worked out a compromise by which American investors could retain the oil properties they had held before the Constitution of 1917 went into effect.

Morrow's success in Mexico heralded a major change in American diplomacy in Latin America. At the Inter-American Conference at Havana in January, 1928, some of the Latin-American countries felt for the first time that they could candidly express to American diplomats their dislike of American interventionist policies. As its southern neighbors grew more proud and independent, and as its world position grew more perilous, the United States could ill afford to make enemies in Latin America. From 1928 onward, American leaders carried out a statesmanlike retreat from policies that were likely to arouse further resentment. At the Washington Conference on Conciliation and Arbitration in December, 1928, the

United States signed treaties of conciliation and arbitration with Latin-American countries that amounted to a promise to refrain from unilateral action. In the same year, President-elect Herbert Hoover made a successful good-will tour of Latin America. He declared in his inaugural address that "we have no desire for territorial expansion, for economic or other domination of other peoples."

In 1930, a memorandum drawn up two years earlier by Under-Secretary J. Reuben Clark of the State Department was released for publication. This historic document repudiated the so-called Roosevelt Corollary of the Monroe Doctrine (see p. 571) and argued for a strict interpretation of that policy. The Monroe Doctrine, Clark said, "states a case of the United States *vs.* Europe, and not of the United States *vs.* Latin America." Events were to show that this was not mere talk. The United States refrained from intervening in a 1929 uprising in Mexico, and followed the same policy the next year in Brazil. In 1932, when El Salvador defaulted on a bond issue, the United States did not, as it had so casually done in the past, intervene to help American bankers recover their losses. In the same year, America withdrew her marines from Haiti and relaxed her supervision of the country's financial affairs.

Franklin D. Roosevelt continued the policy of self-restraint in Latin America, auspiciously begun under Herbert Hoover. In his first inaugural address, Roosevelt hoped "to dedicate this nation to the policy of the good neighbor—the neighbor who resolutely respects himself and, because he does so, respects the rights of others. . . ." The delegates at the 1933 Montevideo Conference of American States, among whom was Secretary Hull, approved a pact asserting that "no state has the right to intervene in the internal or external affairs of another." American intentions were severely tested in Cuba that year, when President Machado was overthrown by revolutionists under the leadership of Ramón Grau San Martin. President Roosevelt did not recognize the new regime until Carlos Mendieta, who was acceptable to American business interests, became president. But in May, 1934, the island was released from its liability to intervention under the Platt Amendment (see p. 564) by a new treaty with the United States. Trade concessions followed this recognition of Cuban autonomy.

Similarly, the United States, by an agreement ratified in 1939, gave up its rights to intervene in Panama and increased its annual payments for canal rights. And when President Cardenas of Mexico began a confiscatory policy toward foreign petroleum interests, the United States refrained from doing anything that could be interpreted as a threat. Compensation to American interests was later amicably arranged by a commission composed of representatives of the two countries.

Under the Good Neighbor policy, the United States also tried to further trade relations with Latin-American countries, and in 1938 created a Division of Cultural Relations in the State Department with a view to encouraging cultural exchange. The campaign to reassure Latin America and to conquer the age-old suspicion of "Yanqui imperialism" gained ground slowly. But as the years wore on, the United States achieved a measure of prestige and friendship in Latin America that would not have seemed possible earlier in the century; and when World War II began, America was assured of friendly and cooperative neighbors in the Southern Hemisphere.

American Isolation. Throughout the 1920's and during most of the 1930's, events in Europe demanded more and more American attention, but they did not command much American sympathy. The dominant anti-Europeanism we have already referred to was reflected in or heightened by many official policies; in shutting off fur-

ther large-scale immigration, for example, and in the tariff warfare aroused by the Fordney-McCumber and Hawley-Smoot bills. The very arguments over allied war debts, which the United States refused to cancel and the European nations refused to pay, reflected a complete breakdown of mutual understanding. The Allies felt that during the war they had suffered more than the Americans in both personal and material losses. If the foe had really been a common foe, why should the United States, which was spared the extensive damages inflicted on her European allies, insist on being repaid? How, in any case, could the Allies repay the United States when they were prevented from selling in the American market? When they tried to link repayment to the reparations they were supposed to receive from Germany, the United States again objected.

From the American point of view, the payment of debts was simply a matter of character. That the European nations were balking, proved exactly what the isolationists had suspected all along—that they were not entirely honest. Calvin Coolidge was reported to have said, "They hired the money, didn't they?"

As for the League of Nations, perhaps nothing represented American sentiment quite so well as Harding's much-applauded remark in 1923 that the United States "does not propose to enter now by the side door, or the back door or the cellar door." True, eminent Americans like John Bassett Moore served on the World Court, the League's judicial agency, and American observers attended sessions of the League, giving their country, as Clemenceau said, representation "by an ear but not by a mouth." And in 1926 the Senate voted to join the World Court, though with so many reservations that the members of the World Court were unable to accept the request. By 1930, the United States had actually taken part in 40 League conferences. But to join the League was unthinkable, and even to suggest the possibility of overt cooperation with the League, as Secretary Stimson did in 1931 over the Far Eastern crisis, was to risk the

wrath of many powerful newspapers throughout the country.

Paradoxically, though the most elementary cooperation with the League had to be
undertaken quietly by successive administrations during the 1920's and 1930's, the
public was ready to give its overwhelming
approval to such a grandiose but essentially
empty gesture as the Kellogg-Briand Pact.
This pact, the product of a great deal of popular agitation in the United States, was first
signed in Paris in August, 1928. The 15
countries that signed it—ultimately other
signers were to bring the total to 62—high-
mindedly renounced war "as an instrument
of national policy," and declared their intention to settle all disputes of whatever sort
"by pacific means." Some Americans scoffed
at the pact as an empty gesture, an "international kiss." But it was extremely popular,
and the Senate ratified it by a vote of 85 to 1.
Time, unfortunately, was to show how little
such a gesture meant without some means
of taking positive collective action against an
aggressor.

Isolationism survived the 1929 crash and
the ensuing depression. Nor did the coming
of the New Deal at first mark a serious reversal of the policies of the Republican administrations. True, high tariff barriers were
lowered. The Trade Agreements Act, approved on June 12, 1934, authorized the
president to lower existing tariff rates by as
much as 50 per cent by agreement with
nations that were prepared to make reciprocal concessions to the United States. And
Secretary Hull's ardent efforts to realize the
promise of this act brought a substantial
lowering of the tariff levels. But in other
respects the New Deal was politically isolationist and economically nationalist. Even
before his nomination in 1932, Franklin
Roosevelt, once a good Wilsonian and a
hardy exponent of the League, allowed himself to be pressured by the Hearst press into
repudiating the League on the ground that
it had not gone in the direction Wilson
wanted. "American participation in the
League," he concluded, "would not serve the
highest purpose of the prevention of war and

a settlement of international difficulties in
accordance with fundamental American
ideals. Because of these facts, therefore, I do
not favor American participation." His decision to pursue monetary policies on a
purely nationalist basis and his disruption of
the London Economic Conference of 1933
(see p. 655) seemed to commit the United
States more firmly than ever to a go-it-alone
policy.

The consequences of the depression and
the accompanying revelations about America's business and financial leaders increased
public skepticism about the honesty and responsibility of the business class. Accordingly, the isolationists of the mid-1930's took
on an anti-business complexion. Men argued
that wars were brought about by those elements who profited by them. In particular,
they maintained, the entrance of the United
States into World War I had been engineered by a conspiracy of munitions-makers
and potential war profiteers and by international bankers who could not afford to see
their loans to the Allies lost through Allied
defeat. In 1934, a Senate Committee headed
by Gerald P. Nye of North Dakota instituted
sensational hearings on the activities of munitions-makers, the so-called "merchants of
death." People reasoned that if the primary
reason for entering the last war had been to
save the trade and investments of a favored
few, then the way to stay out of wars in the
future would be to make it legally impossible
to make money out of trading with belligerents.

The Neutrality Act of 1935, hastily passed
because of the Italo-Ethiopian crisis of that
year, and signed on August 31, provided
that when the president proclaimed that a
state of war existed, it would be illegal to
sell or to transport munitions to the belligerents. Congress placed a sixth-month
limit on the embargo, which did not include
such basic war materials as oil, steel, and
copper. Though he signed this measure, the
President did not hide his feeling that it
would not help keep the country out of war.

In 1936, Congress also prohibited loans to belligerents. In the Neutrality Act of May 1, 1937, it retained the earlier restrictions on loans and munitions and made civilian travel on belligerent ships flatly illegal. The President was authorized to decide when a state of war existed or civil war endangered the peace of the world. When he found such a situation existed, an embargo against exports of arms and ammunition, and against credits was to begin at once. A "cash-and-carry" plan, which was limited to two years (see page 686) empowered the President to require belligerent nations buying non-military goods to pay cash for them and to take them away in their own ships.

One of the assumptions underlying the Neutrality Act was that the United States had no interest in discriminating between the aggressor and the victim in any future war. The isolationists were only concerned with keeping America out of the war by making it unprofitable for us to go in. Although many Americans took comfort from this simple notion, new currents were stirring in the world that shortly were to make the position untenable. Fascism in Italy and Germany and military tyranny in Japan were on the march. The relentless fascist drive for expansion and the brutal fascistic disregard for the rights of individuals and nations soon posed a challenge that the United States could not continue to ignore.

In October, 1935, Premier Mussolini of Italy launched a war of conquest against Ethiopia, aiming to reduce the African kingdom and then colonize it. For a time, it appeared that the League of Nations might impose sanctions against the sale of oil to Italy, but here once again the opportunity to check an aggressor was permitted to slip by. After his quick success in Ethiopia, Mussolini turned to other adventures. In 1936, a fascist revolution broke out against the Republican government of Spain. Mussolini sent Italian troops, planes, and supplies to aid the rebels; and Adolf Hitler sent the insurgents technicians and matériel. Communist Russia sent supplies and "advisers" to the Spanish government, hoping to use the revolution for her own ends.

American opinion was deeply divided over the Spanish war. Liberals and radicals sided with the Spanish government, sent funds and medicine, and even volunteered to fight for it. Fascist sympathizers and many Catholics, attracted by the clerical bias of General Franco's government, supported measures to keep the United States from aiding the Republican government, which it had long since recognized. On January 6, 1937, Congress passed a joint resolution forbidding the export of munitions to either side. This action worked to the disadvantage of the Spanish government, which had resources to buy American arms; and General Franco, the rebel leader, was able to get ample supplies from his fascist allies. In March, 1939, after a cruel and exhausting war, the Republican government was overwhelmed, and all Spain fell under the control of a dictator friendly to Mussolini and Hitler.

II.   WARTIME DIPLOMACY, 1939-1941

The End of Isolation.   The year 1937 marked the beginning of the end for the American policy of isolation. In July, fighting broke out between the Japanese and the Chinese around Peiping, and soon new detachments of Japanese troops were pouring into North China. President Roosevelt responded with his famous "quarantine speech," of October 5, 1937. He told a Chicago audience that although 90 per cent of the population of the world wanted peace, security was being threatened by the other 10 per cent. Peace-loving nations must act together, he asserted:

There is a solidarity and interdependence about the modern world, both technically and morally, which makes it impossible for any nation completely to isolate itself from economic and political upheavals in the rest of the world, especially when such upheavals appear to be spreading and not declining. . . .

When an epidemic of physical disease starts to spread, the community approves and joins in a quarantine of the patients in order to protect the health of the community against the spread of the disease. . . . War is a contagion, whether it be declared or undeclared. . . . We are determined to keep out of war, yet we cannot insure ourselves against the disastrous effects of war and the dangers of involvement. We are adopting such measures as will minimize our risk of involvement, but we cannot have complete protection in a world of disaster in which confidence and security have broken down.

This speech, hotly debated throughout the nation, did not lead to positive action, but it was the first indication of a change from isolation to a policy of collective action against aggressor nations. A year later, speaking before a Canadian audience, Roosevelt declared that "the United States will not stand idly by if domination of Canadian soil . . . is threatened by any other nation." And in January, 1938, he called on Congress to authorize a billion-dollar appropriation for the construction of a two-ocean navy.

In September, 1938, an ominous European crisis arose. Hitler had been demanding that the German-populated Sudetenland of Czechoslovakia be turned over to Germany. It now seemed likely that a general war might break out between the dictatorships and the democracies over Hitler's expansionist policies. At a disastrous conference concluded on September 29 at Munich, Great Britain and France, unprepared to challenge Hitler on the field of battle, bowed to his demands. Prime Minister Chamberlain told the English people that he had secured "peace with honor . . . peace in our time." But this capitulation, a demoralizing blow to the people of the smaller democracies, was followed by proof of what everyone might have known—that there was no bargaining with Hitler. In March, 1939, Hitler violated his Munich pledge to respect the integrity of Czechoslovakia beyond the Sudetenland by swallowing up the rest of the small republic.

Three weeks later Mussolini took over Albania.

In April, 1939, President Roosevelt addressed a letter to Hitler and Mussolini asking them to pledge that they would not attack any one of a list of 31 specified nations for a period of ten years. He proposed an international conference to discuss disarmament and international trade. This sensational appeal won wide approval inside and outside the United States. But it was ignored by Mussolini and turned aside by Hitler, who suggested that the danger of German aggression existed only in President Roosevelt's imagination. In May, 1939, the administration asked Congress to revise the Neutrality Act to make possible economic assistance to Great Britain and France in the event of war. A stubborn group of isolationists in the Senate blocked this proposal. The dictators now had reason to hope that the arms factories of the United States would not be available to the democracies.

On August 22, 1939, the entire world was rocked by the news that the German and Soviet governments had concluded a non-aggression pact. After years of saber-rattling and seemingly implacable hostility to each other, the Nazi and communist totalitarianisms were now in accord. No one could doubt that for the western democracies this was news of the most ominous kind. The first victims of the new alliance were the Poles. Hitler had been demanding the return of the Polish Corridor and Danzig, both of which had been taken away from Germany at Versailles. Backed by Britain and France, the Poles had been sturdily resisting Hitler's demands; but when Germany and Russia signed their pact, the Poles were isolated and all but helpless. Roosevelt cabled appeals to Germany and Italy urging arbitration or conciliation, but in vain. On September 1, the fast, relentless legions of the German army began their march into Poland, and the German air force rained bombs on Polish cities. On September 3, after Hitler had rebuffed demands that he withdraw his troops, France and Britain declared war on Germany. As the law required, President Roosevelt invoked the Neutrality Act against the belligerents. He told the American people in a radio address, "I hope the United States will keep out of this war. I believe that it will. And I give you assurances that every effort of your government will be directed toward that end."

The American public might well have wondered which was the more realistic: this expression of hope and belief in continued neutrality, or Roosevelt's earlier assertion in his quarantine speech that there was "no escape" for the United States from international anarchy and instability "through isolation or neutrality." One thing Roosevelt did *not* do; he did not repeat Woodrow Wilson's appeal for neutrality in thought as well as in deed, for now there could be no thought of such neutrality. "Even a neutral," said Roosevelt, "cannot be asked to close his mind or his conscience." For more than a decade the American people had seen what the fascist powers were capable of. They had heard fascist leaders express their contempt for democratic society and democratic culture. They had seen, in Ethiopia and in Spain, warfare more brutal than the world had ever known before. They knew about the torture of the Jews in Germany—"I myself," Roosevelt said in 1938, "could scarcely believe that such things could occur in a twentieth-century civilization." They had seen the fascist dictators build up huge war machines with which to devour their neighbors. It was fascist aggression, not the peaceful aims of the western democracies, that Americans feared. A public opinion poll taken in October, 1939, showed that 84 per cent wanted the Allies to win, only 2 per cent wanted Germany to win, and 14 per cent had no opinion.

And yet while most of the American people prayed fervently for an Allied victory, they hoped with equal fervor to stay out of the war. They were willing, however, to take the risk of abandoning the neutrality policy.

During the pre-Munich period, only about one-third of the public had favored selling arms to Britain and France in the event of war; but immediately after Hitler violated the Munich agreement, more than two-thirds of the people approved the policy. Drastic changes would have to be made, however, to clear up the confusion in the existing neutrality laws. The democracies could not buy arms in the United States, but they could buy all other important war supplies. Furthermore, the cash-and-carry clause of the 1937 Neutrality Act had expired in May, 1939, leaving American merchant ships free to carry supplies through the combat zones where they would be exposed to Hitler's submarines. These laws neither assured effective aid to the Allies nor provided safeguards to neutrality.

Accordingly, Roosevelt asked Congress to repeal the arms embargo so that arms could be sold to the Allies. But he also asked for authority to prevent American ships from sailing into danger zones so that provocative incidents on the high seas could be avoided. Belligerents must carry their own cargoes. This combination of measures was a compromise: lifting the arms embargo pleased the interventionists, and the restoration of cash-and-carry pleased the isolationists. The proposal was passed on November 3, 1939.

Meanwhile, the debate between isolationists and interventionists went on. The isolationists appealed to a motley group: pacifists and socialists whose main aim was to avoid war; Germans and Irish who hated Britain more than they feared dictatorship; and a few outright fascist sympathizers. This strange set of bedfellows was now joined by the small American Communist party, all-out for non-intervention so long as it was in Russia's interest. The isolationists set up an organization called America First to propagate their point of view. Colonel Charles A. Lindbergh expressed their sentiments when he declared: "In the future we may have to deal with a Europe dominated by Germany. . . . An agreement between us could maintain peace and civilization throughout the world as far into the future as we can see."

Interventionists found their voice in the Committee to Defend America by Aiding the Allies, whose chairman was William Allen White. White replied to Lindbergh that many countries that had tried to be neutral, as Lindbergh advised, had been destroyed: "Hitler's whole philosophy, his idea of government, his economic setup, his insatiable ambitions, all make it impossible for a free country and a free people to live beside Hitler's world enslaved."

The Triumph of Intervention.

During the winter of 1939-1940, the western front was relatively quiet, and many persons assumed that static trench warfare, so familiar in 1914-1918, was about to be repeated. But in April, 1940, Hitler's armies marched into neutral Denmark, attacked neutral Norway, and in a few weeks threw out the British armies that tried to repulse them. In May, Hitler invaded neutral Belgium, Holland, and Luxembourg, and sent his troops smashing around the French defenses, the vaunted Maginot Line. German successes were incredible, nightmarish. On June 10, Mussolini sprang at France from the south, while her armies were reeling back in the north. On June 22, completely crushed, France signed an armistice. The British Empire now stood alone against the force of German arms and the power of the Berlin-Rome Axis. Only the greatest heroism had enabled Britain to rescue the British Expeditionary Force from the Continent by transporting it from Dunkirk, France, to England in every available craft, under pounding from German planes and guns.

During the summer and fall, in a tremendous effort to bring Britain to her knees, Hitler sent clouds of planes against English cities. Bombs poured down on London, Manchester, Birmingham, Plymouth, Dover, and Portsmouth. The town of Coventry became a target for saturation bombings. Tens of thousands of civilians were killed and wounded. But the Royal Air Force fought back with extraordinary courage and skill, destroying hundreds of enemy planes, and by fall it was clear that Hitler's attempt to bomb England into defeat could not succeed. If England was to be subjugated it must be by invasion, and Winston Churchill, a magnificent leader in England's hour of peril, had promised at the time of Dunkirk that invasion would be an extremely costly enterprise for the Germans to undertake.

As Hitler scored victory after victory, Americans began to face the fact that whether they entered the war or not, they would some day have to reckon with the power of the German armies and Hitler's mad ambition. Roosevelt was busy trying to increase American strength and to express American sentiments. In May, 1940, he requested funds from Congress for "at least 50,000 planes a year." In June, he condemned Mussolini's attack on France ("The hand that held the dagger has struck it into the back of its neighbor") and promised not to recognize infringements of French territory. In August, he consulted with the Canadian Prime Minister, Mackenzie King, concerning the defense of the northern half of the Western Hemisphere, and agreed to set up a joint board of defense. Throughout the summer, aid was rushed to the British; military equipment that could not be transferred directly from government to government was sold to American private firms, which then resold it to England.

In September, 1940, a profoundly controversial step was taken when the United States government announced the transfer to Great Britain of 50 over-age destroyers, still usable, and urgently needed to stave off the German submarines. In return, Britain gave the United States sites for naval bases on Newfoundland and Bermuda, and rent-free leases for six sites in the Caribbean and South Atlantic. Since the arrangement was made by executive agreement rather than by treaty, it did not require consent of the Senate. Few denied that the acquisition of the naval sites strengthened American defenses materially, but the President's critics, particularly in the Republican party, were outraged at the method by which the agreement was reached. And there was little doubt that it represented a departure from strict legal neutrality.

The presidential election of 1940 took place with the debate over isolation or intervention still unsettled. In spite of the tradition against a presidential third term, the Democrats, who had no leader remotely comparable to Roosevelt, nominated him again, and chose Henry A. Wallace as his running-mate. The spot-light at the Republican convention was shared by two outspoken isolationists, Senator Arthur Vandenberg of Michigan and Senator Robert A. Taft of Ohio, and by the flashy young District Attorney of New York, Thomas E. Dewey, who then had isolationist leanings. The popular hero of the party, however, was the former president of the Commonwealth and Southern Corporation, Wendell Willkie. The Indiana-born Willkie, who had first come into prominence as an opponent of the T.V.A., possessed a political magnetism comparable to Roosevelt's own. Though not a professional politician, he had a native gift for politics and had captured the hearts of the younger and more liberal elements in the Republican party. In the end, popularity prevailed, and on the sixth ballot Willkie won the nomination from Dewey.

The Republican platform condemned the administrative techniques and over-all results of the New Deal, but refrained from threatening to undo its work or to destroy its basic reforms. The mistake of 1936 was not to be repeated (see p. 670). Willkie carried on a vigorous campaign, discussing the issues on a high level. His position on the war was closer to Roosevelt's than to the stand taken by the die-hard Republican isolationists. He accepted the terms of the destroyer deal, but denounced the method by which it had been taken as "the most dictatorial action ever taken by any President." Lacking a sharp issue to set him off from his opponent, he campaigned at a dis-

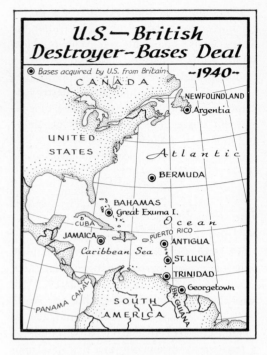

advantage. He was defeated by a popular vote of 22,305,000 to 27,244,000 and an electoral vote of 82 to 449, but he restored the Republican party to a position of vigorous opposition without accepting the views of its isolationist wing, and this was an outstanding personal success. His premature death in 1944 was a great blow to his party and his country.

The election hardly over, Roosevelt revived the debate over foreign policy by proposing the Lend-Lease Bill. In order to furnish economic aid to the British, whose resources were approaching exhaustion, Roosevelt proposed not to lend them money but to lend them arms, which were to be returned or replaced after the war was over. Lend-lease was set forth as a means of keeping the war away from America by strengthening the Allies. But the isolationists could not see it that way. Senator Wheeler of Montana called it the "New Deal's 'triple A' foreign policy—to plow under every fourth American boy"—a remark that Roosevelt branded "the rottenest thing that has been said in public life in my generation." Although the United States had already abandoned the technical pretense of neutrality, the Lend-Lease Bill was fiercely debated as a distinct step toward war, for it committed the United States to the cause of the western democracies. But public opinion favored it, and it was accepted in Congress by a vote of 60 to 31 in the Senate and 317 to 71 in the House. On March 11, 1941, it became law.

During the spring and summer of 1941, the United States edged closer and closer to war in the Atlantic. In March, the United States seized 65 Axis or Axis-controlled ships in American ports. In April, disturbed by Nazi patrols around Greenland, it made an agreement with the governmentless Danish minister in Washington by which the United States was to occupy Greenland temporarily for defensive purposes. In May, Roosevelt urged the French people not to cooperate with the puppet Vichy government the Nazis had set up; proclaimed an unlimited national emergency in the United States; and, when an American merchantman, the *Robin Moor,* was sunk in the South Atlantic by a torpedo, froze all German and Italian assets in the United States. In June, he requested Germany and Italy to close their consulates in the United States on the ground that they were centers of subversive activities. In July, he announced that the United States, by agreement with the Icelandic government, was taking over the defense of Iceland, hitherto in the hands of the British, for the duration of the war, and that the United States navy would keep convoy lines open as far as Iceland. In August, he dramatically met Winston Churchill on a British battleship at sea, where the two statesmen drew up an eight-point declaration, the Atlantic Charter, in which they professed what amounted to common war aims. In September, when a German submarine near Iceland fired two torpedoes at a United States destroyer, the *Greer,* and when two American-owned merchantmen were sunk, Roosevelt delivered a radio talk in which he declared that United States patrols would defend the seas against German "piracy" by striking the first blow at any Axis raiders they encountered. In

October, when an American destroyer, the *Kearney,* was damaged near Iceland in a battle with German submarines, Roosevelt issued a statement in which he asserted, "America has been attacked. . . . The shooting has started." At the end of October, the destroyer *Reuben James* was sunk off Iceland while engaged in convoy duty, and Congress responded in November by removing the most restrictive sections of the Neutrality Act. Now American merchant ships were armed, and they could carry lend-lease supplies direct to England.

Thus, by the fall of 1941 the United States had become an open ally of England without actually being in a state of war. The country became, in Roosevelt's phrase, "the arsenal of democracy," but it was not committed to the all-out mobilization that could come only with full participation in the conflict. What held the country back was not so much the agitations of the isolationists, now a distinctly small minority of the public, but the ultimate reluctance of the average American, even when he was heart and soul for the destruction of Nazi tyranny, to take the final step into another costly war.

While the United States was thus moving ever closer to the conflict, Hitler had changed the entire pattern of the war. In an astounding gamble, he had thrown aside his agreement with Russia and on June 22, 1941, had sent his armies against the Soviet legions. What led him to take this momentous step is uncertain, but it is clear that he gravely underestimated the amount of resistance the Russians would be able to muster. He hoped to win with a few well-calculated blows the wheat of the Ukraine, the oil of the Caucasus, and the greater part of Russia's industrial resources. Then, he seems to have reasoned, the British would recognize that they were at war with an invincible continental empire and would have to come to terms.

His calculations proved wrong. The German armies were greatly superior in quality and equipment, but Russia was vast and cold, and the Russians were tenacious. When winter came, the German armies were still outside Moscow and Leningrad, and Russia was still mustering her energies for resistance. From the beginning, Churchill, while emphasizing the great difference between the political systems of the Soviets and the western democracies, welcomed the Russians as comrades in arms. Alone and bruised at the end of 1940, the British Empire found itself six months later with two powerful allies, one sending supplies and rapidly moving toward open belligerency, the other already locked in deadly combat with the Nazi armies along a thousand-mile front.

It was a strange coalition that had emerged. In the Atlantic Charter, Roosevelt and Churchill had endorsed broad principles that amounted to a reassertion of Wilson's Fourteen Points: no territorial aggrandizement, no changes of territory against the wishes of the people concerned, self-government for all peoples, free access to trade and raw materials, freedom from war, from fear, and from want, freedom of the seas, and the abandonment of war as an instrument of international relations. The fortunes of war now made them the partners of a Soviet dictatorship, until recently Hitler's silent partner, whose adherence to these principles might well be doubted. Many men wondered what would be the outcome of this three-cornered coalition, and what it would do if it won. But the problems of the present were too urgent to allow time for worrying about the possibilities of the future. The crisis facing the United States was rapidly becoming graver than any she had faced in her history.

III. THE WAR AGAINST THE AXIS

Global War. America's indeterminate position in the world struggle was abruptly changed in the early afternoon of December 7, 1941. While most Americans were settling down with their Sunday papers, news came that a strong carrier-borne force of Japanese airplanes had attacked the American naval base at Pearl Harbor in Hawaii. Most of the American aircraft had been destroyed on the ground; the unprotected naval vessels had suffered frightful damage; five battleships and three cruisers were sunk or put out of action and other ships were damaged; over 3,500 casualties had been suffered. The next day, Congress voted to declare a state of war with Japan, and when Germany and Italy declared war on the United States a few days later, Congress responded with similar resolutions against them.

What had happened in the Far East, dazed Americans wondered, to bring about the sneak attack in the Pacific? Since 1937, when the renewal of Japanese aggression in China precipitated Roosevelt's quarantine speech (see p. 684), Japan had been seeking ways of improving her position. As early as December, 1937, when Japanese planes sank an American gunboat, the *Panay,* in the Yangtze River, war had seemed possible; but neither country was ready to fight, and Japan apologized for the attack and paid reparations to the United States.

From then on, the United States followed an ambiguous line. On one hand, Roosevelt refused to invoke the Neutrality Act lest it halt the movement of supplies to the Chinese forces over the tortuous Burma Road. Yet Americans continued to sell large quantities of scrap iron and steel, copper, oil, lead, and machinery to Japan. It would have been possible, after January, 1940, to end this traffic by imposing embargoes on shipments to Japan. But Roosevelt hesitated at first to make this move because he thought it would only cause the Japanese to invade the poorly defended Dutch East Indies in search of the needed supplies. After the fall of France, Britain's weakened position and the defenseless condition of French Indo-China

Pearl Harbor. The battleship Arizona *after the surprise attack, December 7, 1941.*

and the Netherlands Indies presented the Japanese militarists with an irresistible temptation to make new conquests. In July, 1940, Roosevelt went so far as to require licenses for the export of oil and scrap metal, which gave him some control over their sale, and to bar the sale of aviation gasoline outside the Western Hemisphere. These moves the Japanese vigorously protested.

In September, 1940, the Japanese announced that they had signed a treaty with Germany and Italy in which they agreed to attack jointly any power not then a belligerent that should in the future make war on any one of them. It was clear, since Russia was specifically exempted, that this Berlin-Rome-Tokyo Axis was directed against the United States—that it was intended to prevent her from going to war against either the European Axis or Japan.

The first major change in the Pacific situation came after the Nazis attacked Russia and removed the last possibility that sizable Russian forces could be deployed against Japan in the Pacific theater. In July, 1941, Tokyo compelled the helpless French government to grant Japan bases in southern Indo-China. The United States retaliated by freezing all Japanese assets in the United States. Japan reciprocated, and trade between the two countries was all but paralyzed by these hostile actions and by the American embargo policies.

At this low point in Japanese-American relations, a special Japanese envoy, Saburo Kurusu, came to the United States by airplane on November 15, avowedly to try to work out a general settlement of differences. Five days later, he and the Japanese ambassador presented Secretary Hull with a series of Japanese proposals. Tokyo would withdraw its troops from French Indo-China upon the restoration of general peace in East Asia. She would agree with the United States that neither power should make armed advances "into any of the regions in the Southeastern Asia and the Southern Pacific area excepting the part of French Indo-China where the Japanese troops are stationed at present." In return, she expected that the United States would cooperate in securing needed goods for her from the Netherlands Indies, restore commercial relations to the status that prevailed before the freezing of assets, "supply Japan a required quantity of oil," and refrain from actions "prejudicial to the restoration of general peace between Japan and China."

To Americans, these proposals seemed no less than a demand that the United States approve and abet Japan's conquests in Asia. On November 26, the State Department pre-

691

sented a set of counter-proposals. Tokyo was to support the Chinese Nationalist government at Chungking, withdraw all her armed forces from China and Indo-China, and enter into a multilateral nonaggression pact with nations that had interests in the Far East. In return, the United States would grant Japan a favorable trade agreement, unfreeze her assets, cooperate in stabilizing the ratio between the dollar and the yen, and attempt to end American and Japanese extraterritorial rights in China.

On the same day, unknown to the American negotiators, the Japanese carrier force, which had long been preparing and practicing for an attack on Pearl Harbor, set out from its base in the Kurile Islands on its fatal errand. On December 1, the Japanese

dismissed the American demands as "fantastic," but requested that discussions continue, a gesture that can be construed only as a blind for the impending attack. The fleet moving toward Pearl Harbor was not observed, but Washington did receive word of other Japanese troop transports moving in a direction that suggested a possible attack on the Philippines, Thailand, or the Malay Peninsula. Roosevelt, who thought that these movements foreshadowed an attack in the Southwest Pacific, sent a hasty peace appeal to the Japanese emperor on December 6, but on the following day his appeal was answered by the bombs that fell on Pearl Harbor.

Days of Disaster. Disaster after disaster struck Allied arms in the opening

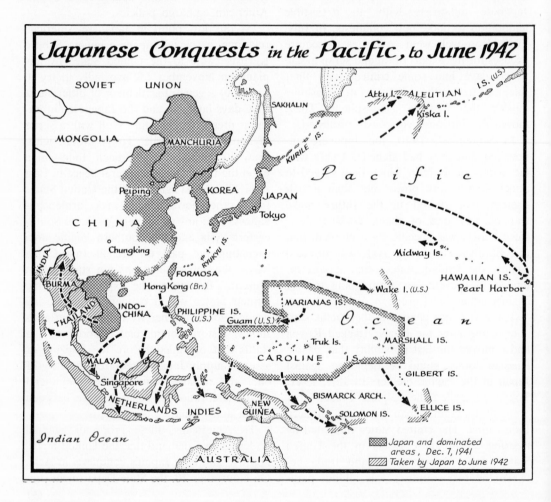

Japanese Conquests in the Pacific, to June 1942

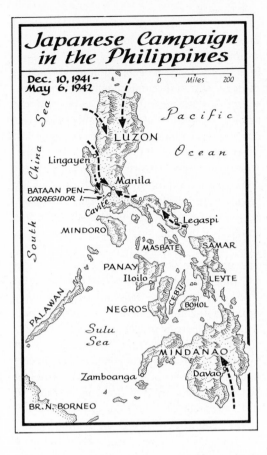

Japanese Campaign in the Philippines

Dec. 10, 1941 – May 6, 1942

weeks of the Pacific war. Immediately after Pearl Harbor, attacks were launched against the Philippines, Wake Island, Guam, Hong Kong, British Malaya, and Thailand. Thailand surrendered immediately, Guam on December 13, Wake Island on December 20, and Hong Kong on December 25. American troops in the Philippines under General Douglas MacArthur made a brave stand on the Bataan Peninsula and on the island fortress of Corregidor, but they too were eventually overwhelmed. Bataan surrendered in April, 1942, Corregidor in May. General MacArthur managed to escape to take command of the United Nations forces in Australia.

In the Southwest Pacific, there was nothing but bad news. On December 10, the Japanese paralyzed the British Pacific fleet's striking power by sinking the battle cruiser *Repulse* and the battleship *Prince of Wales* off Malaya. They swept through Malaya, captured Singapore, the center of British power in Asia, and pushed the retreating defenders out of the Netherlands Indies. They conquered Burma and closed the Burma Road, thereby cutting aid to China down to a trickle.

The anti-Axis forces, in the spring of 1942, had little reason to hope they could win the war in anything less than a long drawn-out struggle, if indeed they could win it at all. To be sure, the peoples of Britain and her Dominions, the United States, Russia, and the portions of China under friendly control outnumbered the population of the Axis powers. Most of the Central American republics declared war against the Axis, and by January, 1942, all Latin America except Chile and Argentina had at least broken off diplomatic relations. But the Axis powers were in a position to draw upon enormous labor resources in the occupied part of Russia and the Southeast Pacific. Hitler and Mussolini controlled the continent of Europe from the Atlantic to the Russian battle lines and from the Baltic to the Mediterranean. France, occupied by the German army, could add materially to the German war potential. Strategic Spain was friendly toward the dictators. Both the Atlantic and the Mediterranean were extremely dangerous for Allied shipping. Since the eastern Mediterranean had become impassable, Allied ships had to take the long route around the Cape of Good Hope to supply British forces in the Middle East. Axis forces occupied North Africa from Tunis to the border of Egypt, and Germany's formidable tank corps, under General Erwin Rommel, seemed on the verge of smashing eastward to Alexandria, closing the Suez Canal, and forcing Turkey to join the Axis. In southern Russia, the Germans were hammering at the Caucasus, and it seemed possible that they might drive through to Iraq and Iran and complete the conquest of the routes to the East, cutting Britain off from her empire. On the Continent, the Axis enjoyed the advantage of interior lines of communication, whereas the Allies had to carry their supplies from great distances over exposed stretches of sea. The United States particularly was waging a long-range war—Tokyo is 5,347 miles from San Francisco. At worst, an Axis victory within a few years seemed a possibility. At best, to some experts a war lasting from 7 to 15 years seemed in the offing before the enemy could be beaten.

Such pessimistic forecasts—it is easy to say in retrospect—neglected some of the assets of the Allies. First, American resources of oil, steel, and many other strategic materials were far greater than those of any other belligerent. American industrial productive capacity, notably in the critical automotive industry, dwarfed that of the rest of the world. These resources were not keyed to war production in 1941, but the change-over was made very rapidly and skillfully. One year after Pearl Harbor, the United States was producing more supplies than all the Axis nations combined.

Second, the internal planning and administration of the democratic countries was vastly superior to that of the dictatorships. Only after the war, when captured German materials revealed how slipshod the vaunted Nazi mobilization was, did men fully realize how superior were the uses that Britain and the United States had made of their resources. It was not superior techniques of industrial organization, but simply the early German start on war preparations and the traditional efficiency of the German army, that had enabled Germany to sweep across Europe in 1940-1941. Democracy, once mobilized, planned much better than dictatorship.

Third, the Axis powers completely failed to coordinate their efforts, whereas the United States and Britain, through their combined Chiefs of Staff and the intimate collaboration of Roosevelt and Churchill, worked together with remarkable harmony, sharing military resources, knowledge, and plans. General George Marshall later wrote:

"It was the most complete unification of military effort ever achieved by two Allied nations." At Washington on January 1, 1942, 26 nations signed a declaration in which they pledged the full employment of their resources to the defeat of the Axis. On the whole, the efforts of this mighty coalition, the United Nations, were well coordinated.

At an early point in their joint effort, American and British military planners made an important over-all decision. They planned to concentrate first on the European Axis forces, and in the meantime to conduct a holding operation in the Pacific. This strategy would enable the United States to concentrate on the nearest target first and to bring immediate aid to two hard-pressed allies, Britain and Russia, before either could be further weakened or knocked out. After the European enemies had been reduced, it would be time to turn upon an isolated Japan and bring her to her knees. This decision was hotly criticized in America by those who wanted to concentrate all effort immediately upon the enemy that had so spectacularly assaulted the United States. But the decision was vindicated by later events.

In the spring of 1942, two important naval victories strengthened Allied hopes that Japan could be held at bay. In May, the Japanese, in an attack on Port Moresby in New Guinea, a center important to American-Australian communications, ran up against an American and Australian fleet of aircraft carriers and cruisers in the Coral Sea. After a somewhat confusing engagement, in which carrier planes did the brunt of the work on both sides, a Japanese carrier was sunk and two others were damaged. Although the United States lost the carrier *Lexington,* the Japanese were forced to retire on May 11, with 15 of their major ships sunk and 20 damaged. Between June 3 and June 6, another naval-air battle took place over Midway Island. Capture of Midway by the Japanese would have made Pearl Harbor almost unusable, but Admiral Chester Nimitz, learning from naval intelligence of the approach of a large Japanese fleet, and having discovered some details of the Japanese plans, met the foe with his carrier planes. After a severe engagement that brought heavy losses to both sides, he sent the Japanese fleet, whose force was much larger than his own, reeling homeward, with one-fourth of its vessels, including four carriers, sunk or damaged. Hawaii was safe, and the United States turned with greater confidence to the war in Europe.

Civilian Mobilization. The attack on Pearl Harbor put an end to the internationalist-isolationist debate in America and created a united feeling that there was nothing to do but go to work and win the war as soon as possible. As even the isolationist Senator Wheeler put it, "The only thing now to do is to lick hell out of them." Differences of opinion continued over the conduct of the war and over coalition strategy, but public support of the war effort was otherwise complete. Americans felt they were fighting not to help Britain or to crusade for world democracy or freedom of the seas or the rights of small nations, but plainly and simply to survive as a nation. Since almost no one doubted the necessity for the war, there was much less intolerance than there had been in World War I, although large numbers of Japanese-Americans were put into internment camps under circumstances that many Americans were later to judge unfair or worse.

The United States set to work energetically to recruit, equip, and train huge armies and transport them to the far-flung battlefields of the war. Selective Service had already been enacted in September, 1940, and an army of 1,600,000 was already in existence in December, 1941. All men between 18 and 45 were made subject to military service. In all, over 17 million men were examined by draft boards. For the first time, women were permitted to serve as volunteers in the armed forces, and by the war's end these auxiliaries of the army, navy, marines, and coast guard numbered 216,000. Counting volunteers, more than 15 million

men and women served in the four services during the war.

Training this huge and ever-mounting force to operate the complicated machines of war and providing it with barracks, food, medical care, clothing, and sufficient entertainment to maintain morale was a remarkably complex task. Even to keep mail flowing back and forth between the armed forces and their friends and families required new techniques of organization. Seven thousand men behind the lines were needed to supply and service the 8,000 fighting men in an infantry division. The demands made upon engineering ingenuity were most exacting. Camps, hospitals, roads, bridges, pipe lines, airfields, and port facilities had to be erected in the far corners of the world. Some men had to learn to work and live in the heat of the tropics, others in the cold of the Aleutians, others to fly at immense speed and at incredible altitudes, still others to care for the new diseases and disorders that accompanied these conditions, as well as to heal the familiar injuries that mechanized war spawns. New devices and techniques were needed: radar apparatus; strangely designed landing boats for amphibious operations that could put men or guns or tanks ashore on beaches under fire; drugs for the control of tropical insects; new treatments for burns and for shattered nerves; surgery for shattered bodies.

Behind this effort stood the mobilized forces of American industry, labor, and science. Industry, under the direction of the War Production Board, swung into high gear, and despite lags and gaps made amazing progress in converting from peacetime to wartime production. Critics of the President had dismissed his words as fantastic and ridiculous when he called for 50,000 planes a year in 1940. But in 1942, over 47,000 military and special-purpose aircraft were built, and by 1944 the figure had gone up to over 96,000. Between July, 1940, and July, 1945, American industry produced over 296,000 planes, 71,000 naval ships of various kinds, 5,400 merchant ships for the Maritime Commission, 2,724,000 machine guns, and 86,000 tanks. Steel mills almost doubled the production levels they had set during the 1930's; output of aluminum increased about 6 times, of magnesium about 40 times. Because Malayan and East Indian rubber supplies had been cut off, an entire synthetic rubber industry had to be established; by 1944, this industry was producing no less than 762,000 tons a year.

American science was as effectively mobilized as American industry. The Americans and British, their scientific personnel greatly enriched by refugees from the racist persecutions of the fascist powers, shared their scientific knowledge to great advantage. In the United States, the Office of Scientific Research and Development, under the direction of Vannevar Bush and President James Conant of Harvard, worked closely with the armed services to meet their needs. Among its more important contributions was a form of microwave detection which made it possible for planes to locate

and bomb submarines that were too deeply submerged to be visible to the human eye.

The most lethal development was the atomic bomb. It was generally known in scientific circles around the world that German scientists were working on atomic fission, and scientists shuddered at the thought that the masters of Germany might work out a nuclear weapon before the Allies could do so. In 1939, three foreign-born scientists, Albert Einstein, Leo Szilard, and Eugene Wigner, warned President Roosevelt of this danger. The long and complicated project was launched in preliminary experiments at the University of California, Columbia University, and the University of Chicago. At Los Alamos, New Mexico, a physics laboratory was set up under the direction of Professor J. Robert Oppenheimer, and some of the world's greatest scientists set to work to translate the preliminary experiments into reality. On July 16, 1945, an experimental bomb was successfully exploded at the Alamogordo air base in New Mexico.

Behind the technicians and the organizers stood a vast and augmented working force. Unemployment melted away, women joined

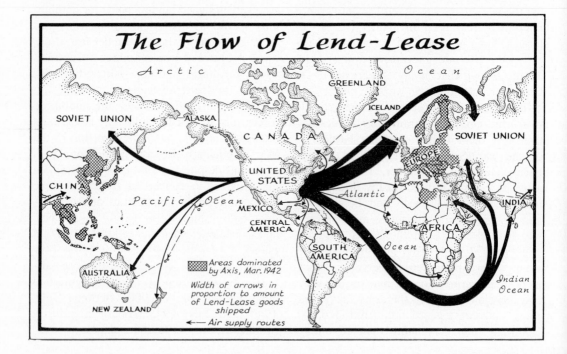

The Flow of Lend-Lease

or replaced men on the assembly lines, key war plants went on day and night shifts, and the average work-week lengthened from 38 to 45 hours. A War Manpower Commission shifted workers into areas where they were most needed, and made other arrangements to insure the most efficient use of manpower. The inducement to take up war work grew strong as average weekly earnings rose from $23.86 in 1939 to $46.08 in 1944. After the Japanese attack on Pearl Harbor, the A.F.L. and the C.I.O. made no-strike pledges. But later, as prices rose and as the most desperate period of the war passed, strikes became quite frequent, though almost entirely in industries not contributing directly to the war effort. Workers were widely criticized for the strikes. But the slogan, "There are no strikes in foxholes," was met with the retort, "There are no profits either." In fact, America was waging war with a sizable sector of the economy still operating free of wartime controls. Profits were piling up, and workers were demanding a greater share in them. Corporate profits after taxes rose from $5,000,000,000 in 1939 to $9,900,000,000 in 1944. Many new fortunes were made during the war years.

Although the farm population decreased during the war (despite draft exemptions for many agricultural workers), farm production soared. In 1945, the output per farm worker almost doubled the level that had been reached during the period from 1910 to 1914, agriculture's golden years. Helped by favorable weather, by the soil rehabilitation program of the A.A.A., and by increased use of fertilizer, farmers produced bumper crops. Between 1939 and 1945, the number of cattle slaughtered rose from 14,621,000 to 21,691,000, hogs from 66,-561,000 to 71,891,000. Corn production rose from 2,580,985,000 bushels to 2,880,-944,000, wheat from 741,210,000 bushels to 1,108,224,000. Farm income doubled. The war showed, too, that a small farm laboring force, working with improved agricultural techniques, could meet the normal needs of the domestic market.

A concerted effort was made by the Office of Price Administration, under the chairmanship of Leon Henderson, to stem inflation. Price ceilings were set on a wide variety of consumers' goods, and a few products, such as sugar, coffee, and meat, were rationed without causing any undue hardship. Prices had already risen about 25 per cent when controls were authorized in January, 1942, and they continued to rise slightly. But serious inflation was avoided.

Once again, agriculture benefited from wartime demand. After ten years of trying to cut down on crops in order to adjust to a small demand, the full productive capacities of agriculture were again released. Farmers were worried, however, that they might in the end face a postwar collapse such as they had experienced in 1920. To protect them against another such calamity, the Price Stabilization Act of 1942 contained some special concessions to farmers. Some commodity prices were to be supported at 90 per cent of parity for two years after the end of hostilities. No price ceilings were to be set on agricultural products until their prices had reached either 110 per cent of parity or the level that existed from 1919 to 1929, whichever might be higher. These arrangements were in effect continued in the Stabilization Extension Act of 1944. The farmers had driven a hard bargain with the government. Some farm prices rose above the ceiling prices paid by consumers, and the government itself was forced to make up the difference. Roosevelt protested, but members of the agricultural bloc in Congress exerted all their influence to make sure that the practice continued.

War expenses were fabulous. By mid-1943, they were running at $8 billion a month, as high as the *yearly* budgets of the peacetime New Deal. In 1945, for the first time in history, the federal government spent over $100 billion. Between 1941 and 1945, the national debt rose from less than $48 billion to $247 billion. Taxes, which were raised along many lines, paid for two-fifths of the cost of the war. After July 1, 1943, employers began to collect income taxes for the government from employees by deducting them from payrolls, a procedure that assured the government of its revenues and kept the workers abreast of their tax liabilities from month to month. When the cost of the war was finally tallied up, the bill came to about $350 billion—ten times the amount World War I had cost us.

Politics were not suspended during the crisis. In the Congressional elections of 1942, the Republicans gained considerable ground by capitalizing on the widespread public discontent with military defeats. But by 1944, the military situation had completely changed, and the Republicans had to contend once again with Roosevelt's popularity. They nominated Thomas E. Dewey, the youthful and vigorous Governor of New York, to run for the presidency. The Democrats, with the third-term tradition shattered ("There is a law against bigamy," quipped a commentator, "but whoever heard of a law against trigamy?"), nominated Roosevelt with little ado. The convention spotlight centered on the choice of a vice-presidential candidate. After a stormy session, Henry Wallace, who was unpopular with the city bosses and the southern conservatives, was finally dropped in favor of Senator Harry S. Truman of Missouri, who had commanded attention as chairman of a Senate committee investigating wartime contracts. Dewey had no sound issue on which to attack, since he and his party had accepted most of the administration's program and foreign policy (including the commitment to a new international organization). He was defeated by a vote of 25,602,000 to 22,-006,000 and by 432 to 99 in the electoral college.

The Democrats' choice of a vice-president proved to be far more important than anyone realized at the time, for Roosevelt was fated to serve less than four months of his fourth term. Worn down by 12 years of strenuous presidential life, he suffered a massive cerebral hemorrhage on April 12, 1945, and died while seeking rest at his winter home in Warm Springs, Georgia. He had been drafting a Jefferson Day dinner speech to be delivered the next week, which he planned to end with the words: "Let us move forward with strong and active faith."

The War in Europe.   It was vital for the democracies to gain mastery of the sea and the air as soon as possible. For months after the United States entered the war, U-boats wreaked havoc along the Atlantic and Gulf coasts, and then in the Caribbean, carrying the war directly to American shores. The threat was urgent, for the rate of sinkings ran extremely high, while the toll of U-boats was relatively low. An entirely new system of convoys was worked out, using a host of light ships, and coastal waters were patrolled by bombers. By April, 1943, the Allies had begun to win the battle with the submarines. But the cost in tonnage and lives lost had been enormous, and the task of manning convoys and merchant ships had been one of the most hazardous of the war.

In the air, supremacy had passed to the RAF during the great air battles over England in 1940. By 1941, when British aircraft production surpassed Germany's, the RAF went on the offensive, returning in kind the terrible attacks that Germany had first inflicted upon British cities. This sustained bombing reached a peak during July, 1943, when a series of raids on Hamburg destroyed more than a third of the port and killed over 60,000 persons. In August, 1942, American airmen joined the British in raids over the Continent, and an active collaboration began. At night, the RAF sallied out, saturating German cities with their bombs, disrupting labor, and unsettling civilian morale. By day, the American bombers, protected by fighter planes, went out for precision bombing of specific targets. Between them, the two forces eventually dropped over 2,600,000 bombs on enemy targets. At one point, there was talk on the Allied side of trying to bring Germany down through air attacks alone, thus avoiding the immense casualties that an invasion of the Continent would almost surely entail. But this notion had to be abandoned. Air attacks never succeeded in biting deep enough into the production of such essentials as planes, submarines, or synthetic rubber. On the other hand, air assaults were devastating in the long run to two priority targets: transportation, and oil and aviation gasoline. When the time came for the invasion of the Continent, Germany was gravely hampered by the disruption of her transport at home and in France, and many of her planes and tanks were immobilized in the final months of the war by lack of fuel.

The first great Allied counter-stroke on land in the Atlantic theater came in North Africa. On November 8, 1942, three Allied forces, two starting from England, one from the United States, landed at various points in North Africa. The expedition had been planned in Washington by Roosevelt and Churchill four months before. The troops were to strike eastward and if possible to join up with Empire forces under General Alexander that had been defending Egypt and Suez from the determined assaults of the Axis tank corps. The operation, if successful, would help reopen the Mediterranean to Allied shipping, provide bases for anti-submarine operations in the South Atlantic, protect the oil fields of the Middle East and destroy the threat to Suez, neutralize Spain, and provide bases for an invasion of Italy. The operation was risky, the planning hasty. Never before in the history of warfare had an amphibious force set out from one side of the ocean, as did the American force from Hampton Roads, Virginia, to land and attack an objective on the other side, over 3,000 miles away.

Nevertheless the landings were carried out successfully. General Henri Giraud, who had escaped from imprisonment in Germany and had agreed to take command of French forces in North Africa, cooperated with the Allies. Far more useful to the Allies was the Vichy Admiral, Jean François Darlan, whose word carried real weight with the French forces. The Allied forces under General Eisenhower moved rapidly eastward over difficult mountain and desert country. In Tunisia, however, they met with powerful opposition, and at the beginning of 1943 Tunisia was still in Axis hands. But Anglo-American forces continued to batter the Germans and Italians from the west, and

High-altitude precision bombing. Daylight raids by American B-17's disrupted transportation on the Continent and knocked out vital refineries, oil-storage depots, and other top-priority targets.

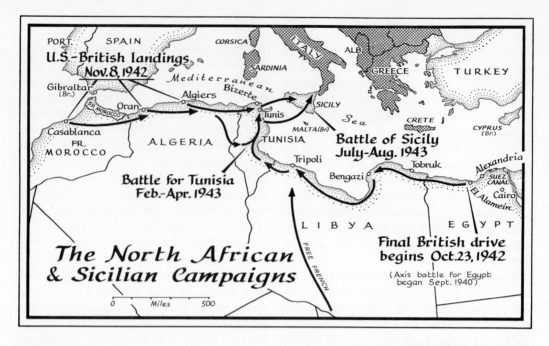

The North African & Sicilian Campaigns

U.S.-British landings Nov. 8, 1942

Battle for Tunisia Feb.-Apr. 1943

Battle of Sicily July-Aug. 1943

Final British drive begins Oct. 23, 1942

(Axis battle for Egypt began Sept. 1940)

0 — Miles — 500

General Alexander's army pushed on from the east.

At this juncture, in January, 1943, Roosevelt, Churchill, and their chiefs of staff met at Casablanca to plan United Nations strategy. The moment was auspicious, for the Russians at Stalingrad had just thrust the Germans back and Alexander had broken Rommel's attack in Africa. The Allied planners decided to invade Sicily and Italy after the Axis had been cleared out of North Africa, agreed to send sufficient forces to the Pacific to take the offensive there, and promised to ease pressure on the Russians by setting up another front in Europe that would engage the enemy armies "as heavily as possible." They also announced that they would be satisfied only with the "unconditional surrender" of all their enemies. This conference heralded a number of strategic war-time meetings among the enemies of the Axis powers (see p. 731).

The North African campaign soon entered its last phase. Rommel, reinforced, launched a powerful counter-offensive that was turned back by the Allies. The Anglo-American forces, now swollen to half a million men, closed in on him near Mareth, smashed his army, and on May 7, 1943,

captured both Tunis and Bizerte. The Axis forces, cut up by swift advances, became demoralized, and surrendered on May 13. They lost 350,000 men in the campaign, and with them Africa and the Mediterranean.

The Italian Campaign

Battleline Apr. 9, '45

Allied landing Sept. 9, 1943

Jan. 22, 1944

British cross here Sept. 2, '43

0 — Miles — 200

The invasion of Normandy. This aerial photograph gives a vivid picture of the magnitude of the landing operation.

The attack on Italy followed as soon as sufficient landing craft could be assembled. Landing on the 10th of July, the British and American forces swept rapidly around Sicily, first investing the coastland and then sweeping in to capture the Axis troops isolated on the island. A large German army succeeded in escaping across the Straits of Messina, but by August 17, when Sicily was cleared, 100,000 prisoners had been taken. Meanwhile, King Victor Emmanuel and members of the Fascist Grand Council had deposed Mussolini and had set up a new government under Marshal Pietro Badoglio, who immediately sued for peace. On September 3, the Italian government signed an unconditional surrender.

Italy was still largely occupied by the Germans. The Allies, although they had succeeded in knocking Italy out of the war,

nevertheless decided to push on up the peninsula. This drive, it was felt, would help Russia by engaging large German armies, as promised at Cairo, and yet at the same time would permit the Allies to move into the Balkans and prevent Russia from overrunning southern Europe when the final push against Germany came. But the Italian campaign was immensely expensive. During the fall and winter months, the American and British armies slogged up the Italian peninsula through mud and snow against stubborn and costly resistance by the Germans, who established line after line that had to be painfully stormed. Not until June 4, just on the eve of the cross-channel invasion, did the Allies enter Rome.

The elaborately planned invasion of the Continent began on June 6, 1944. After a six-week aerial pounding that disrupted com-

701

munications in northern France, the Allied forces were launched from England against the formidable system of artillery, pillboxes, barbed wire, mines, tank traps, and other obstacles that the Nazis had long been preparing. By the end of the first day, under heavy fire in many places, 120,000 men had been landed, some by parachute. By the end of the first week, 360,000 men were ashore and the reconquest of France was under way. By the end of July, over a million Allied troops were fighting in Normandy and Brittany. Paris was recaptured amid great rejoicing on August 24-25. On August 15, landings were also made in southern France, and the Allied forces pushed rapidly up the Rhone. Throughout France, the occupied people rose up against the Germans and as-

sisted the liberators. By October, the Germans had been completely cleared from France, after having lost half a million men, 3,500 aircraft, and great stores of supplies. In the meantime, on the eastern front the Russians had been moving forward into Bulgaria, Rumania, and Finland, had reoccupied much of Poland, and had invaded Hungary, Yugoslavia, Czechoslovakia, and East Prussia.

Germany's situation was now hopeless, but those who expected an early surrender reckoned without the madness of Nazi leadership. Marshal Rommel, who had seen the futility of further fighting and proposed to negotiate with Eisenhower, was removed from his post and forced to commit suicide. The last stages of the war brought some of the fiercest fighting. The Germans launched an unexpected counter-attack in December in

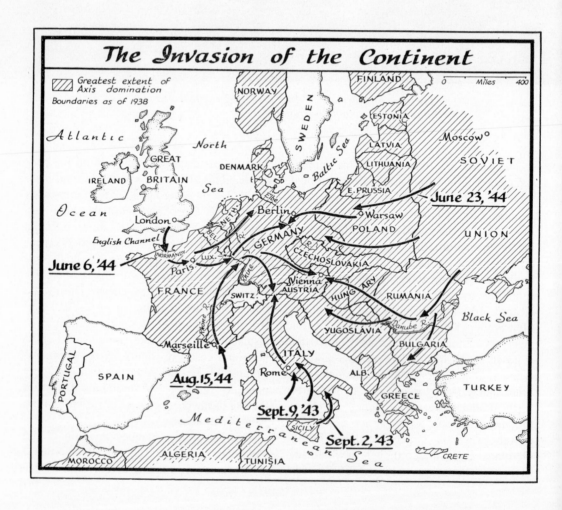

The Invasion of the Continent

the Belgium-Luxembourg sector, which for a time threw the Allied forces off stride, and they made almost every further Allied advance a costly one. But on March 7, 1945, American soldiers broke across the Rhine at Remagen. Other bridgeheads were established, and soon the Allies were streaming into Germany.

"We shall not capitulate—no, never!" Hitler had declared years earlier. "We may be destroyed, but if we are, we shall drag a world with us—a world in flame." As the English and American troops moved into Germany, they caught sight of the war against humanity that had been waged behind the battlefronts of the Third Reich— concentration camps for Jews and Poles and political prisoners, systematic torture, scientific murder on a huge scale, experimentation with human guinea pigs—evidences of a depravity beyond the imagination of civilized men. Amid these ghastly revelations fascism went down to defeat. Mussolini was caught and killed in April by Italian partisans and strung up by his heels alongside his mistress in a public square in Milan. Hitler issued orders, obeyed only in small part, to raze Germany so that the Allies would capture nothing but waste and rubble. "If the German people was to be conquered in the struggle," he had declared a few months earlier, "then it had been too weak to face the test of history, and was fit only for destruction." On May 1, he committed suicide by shooting himself in his shelter under Berlin. On May 7, General Jodl signed an unconditional surrender at Rheims, and on the following day all hostilities ceased. So, in its

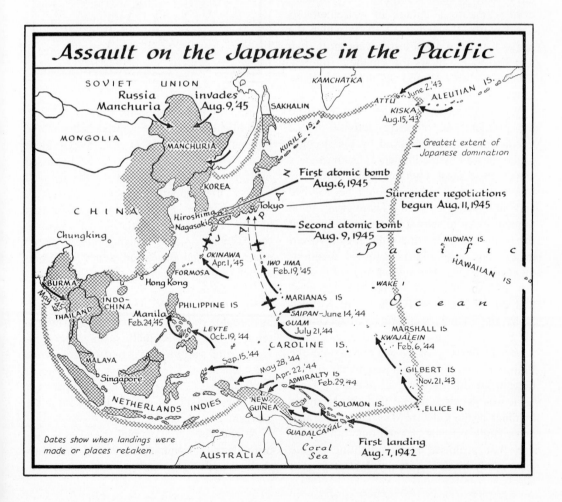

Assault on the Japanese in the Pacific

12th year, ended the Third Reich, destined, according to its Führer, to last for a thousand years, but crushed by the means of violence in which it had put its faith.

Victory in the Pacific.   While great victories were being won in Europe, United Nations forces had not been idle in the Pacific theater, where the brunt of the counter-offensive was carried by American arms. The last echoes of Japanese offensive operations in the Pacific islands were heard in September-November, 1942, when they made a strong effort to retake the island of Guadalcanal in the Solomons, which American marines had occupied in August in an operation extremely costly to the American navy. The second campaign for Guadalcanal came to a climax in a tremendous naval battle, November 12-15, in which the heavy American naval losses were more than matched by the blows the Japanese suffered. The foe pulled out, and the defensive phase of the war was over.

When American strategists first surveyed the problems of offensive activity in the Pacific, they were dismayed by the strength of the foe and by the immense distances over which they must operate. Bases must be found from which Japan could be bombed and ultimately invaded. There was some thought given to setting up the main base on the China coast, but the difficulties involved in securing a foothold there forced abandonment of the idea. Throughout the entire eastern and southeastern Pacific the Japanese had established a vast network of fortified atolls and islands, many of them serving as air bases. An advance toward Japan from Australia by way of New Guinea and the Philippines would be exposed to air operations from this network all along its flank. So it was decided instead that the Japanese holdings in the Gilbert, Marshall, and Caroline islands must be cleaned out—an operation that promised endless fighting of the most costly kind. Eventually, a strategy was

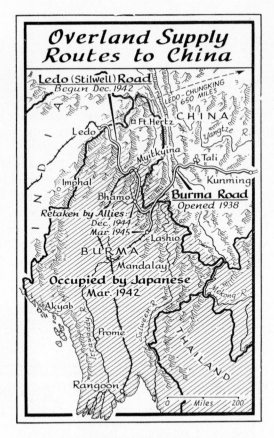

devised to eliminate some of this fighting. The islands were to be approached not one by one in order, but in a series of great leaps. Many of them were to be bypassed and only the few necessary to the over-all success of the operation were to be seized.

In November, 1943, the marines took part of Bougainville, the northernmost island of the Solomons, from which bomber planes escorted by fighters could attack the great Japanese base of Rabaul. With Rabaul neutralized from the air, it was no longer necessary to mount a costly frontal attack against this strongly held bastion. During the same period, the Gilbert Islands were invaded and captured. A particularly fierce engagement on Tarawa, November 21, cost the Second U.S. Marine Division 20 per cent casualties and all but wiped out the Japanese garrison.

At the very end of January, 1944, Admiral Nimitz' command attacked the Marshall Islands. The atoll of Kwajalein was taken in February, and the heavily fortified island of Truk, again too strong to invade, was blasted by planes and ships and then bypassed. In May, amphibious forces recaptured Wake. In mid-June, when the Japanese tried to reinforce the Marianas, the two navies clashed again in the battle of the Philippine Sea. In this engagement, the Japanese carrier groups were wiped out by an American force under Admiral Spruance. In July, the United States attacked the Marianas. By August 1, the Japanese had been cleared out of the main islands there, and American engineers were constructing airfields on Saipan. Japan had suffered her most discouraging setback of the war, for now American bombers could be based close enough to strike at the Japanese home islands themselves.

On October 20, United States troops landed on Leyte in the Central Philippines,

and the navy fell into a major engagement with the Japanese fleet, which cost the enemy so many ships that the United States was left in complete command of Philippine waters. The reconquest of the Philippines—redeeming General MacArthur's dramatic pledge to return to the islands—went rapidly. Manila was retaken on the 23rd of February, 1945, and on July 4, 1946, a Philippine Republic was once again set up.

In the meantime, the Japanese had been losing out on the Asiatic mainland. Though they had delivered a serious blow to American airpower by capturing airbases at Honan, in May, 1944, their forces had to withdraw from southern and central China by the spring of 1945. American planes had organized regular transport flights over the Himalayas and each month 45,000 tons of

Atomic warfare: a sample of the devastation at Hiroshima after the dropping of the first atomic bomb.

supplies had been flown into China. In January, 1945, the new Ledo Road was completed, easing the supply problem. In Burma, in Malaysia, and in the Netherlands Indies, the Japanese were being pushed back. It was growing harder for Japan to supply her troops, for between 1942 and 1944 she had lost 4,300,000 tons of merchant shipping.

Now the last phase of the war began. The bombing of Japan was facilitated by the marines' capture of Iwo Jima in March, 1945. The first of the Japanese islands to be invaded was Okinawa, attacked in April, where deadly resistance made it clear that the final conquest of Japan would be resisted to the last ditch. Suicidal Japanese aviators, the *kamikaze,* drove their bomb-laden planes directly at American ships, sinking 36 of them and badly damaging 158. The island was not taken until late in June.

On July 26, Allied war leaders in conference at Potsdam delivered an ultimatum to Japan: "The alternative to surrender is prompt and utter destruction." Already Japan's cities were being devastated by air attacks. Over 330,000 civilians had been killed and many more injured. Industrial production was rapidly being throttled. But on August 6 the ultimate weapon was used: the atomic bomb was dropped on Hiroshima. Two days later, the Russians declared war and attacked the Japanese in Manchuria. On August 9, a second atomic bomb struck Nagasaki. The Japanese inquired about terms of peace, and upon being assured that the emperor would be allowed to keep his throne, they capitulated. On September 2, they signed the terms of surrender aboard the American battleship *Missouri.*

The war, which at the cost of incalculable suffering had raged for six years in Europe and for almost four years between the Japanese and the United Nations in the Pacific, was over. A dazed world set about the tasks of reconstruction, sobered by the thought of the horrible weapons that would be used in any future world war.

Readings

A general account is given by Allan Nevins in *The United States in a Chaotic World: A Chronicle of International Affairs, 1918-1933* (1950), as well as in the standard general diplomatic histories by Samuel Flagg Bemis, Julius W. Pratt, and Thomas A. Bailey. Robert E. Osgood has attempted to assess the significance of foreign policies in his *Ideals and Self-Interest in America's Foreign Relations* (1953), an important book. On the European scene, Hajo Holborn offers a stimulating interpretation of *The Political Collapse of Europe* (1951), while a satisfactory general account may be found in C. E. Black and E. C. Helmreich, *Twentieth Century Europe* (1950), or in C. V. Easum, *Half-Century of Conflict* (1952).

Brief general accounts of America's participation in World War II are not yet abundant. Readers with leisure will find rewarding reading in Winston Churchill's *The Second World War* (6 vols., 1948-1953), although there are briefer general histories of the war by Francis T. Miller (1945), W. P. Hall (1946), Roger W. Shugg and H. A. De Weerd (1946), and Fletcher Pratt (1950).

On the Washington Conference, see J. C. Vinson, *The Parchment Peace* (1950); on America and Japan, see Forster R. Dulles, *Forty Years of American-Japanese Relations* (1937), and A. Whitney Griswold, *The Far Eastern Policy of the United States* (1938).

The fullest accounts of pre-war American diplomacy are in William L. Langer and S. E. Gleason, *The Challenge to Isolation, 1937-1940* (1952), and the same authors' *Undeclared War, 1940-41* (1953), which is highly favorable to American policies. The same point of view is developed by Basil Rauch in his *Roosevelt: From Munich to Pearl Harbor* (1950). Herbert Feis, *The Road to Pearl Harbor* (1950), which is an excellent account of the coming of the war with Japan, argues a similar thesis. An opposite interpretation permeates such isolationist studies as Charles A. Beard, *President Roosevelt and the Coming of the War* (1941), and Charles C. Tansill, *Backdoor to War: The Roosevelt Foreign Policy, 1933-41* (1952).

Walter Millis, *This is Pearl!* (1947), is a dramatic account of Pearl Harbor. Eliot Janeway, *The Struggle for Survival* (1951), is a summary of economic mobilization. Donald M. Nelson in *Arsenal of Democracy* (1946), and E. R. Stettinius, Jr., in *Lend-Lease, Weapon for Victory* (1944), give some account of war production and lend-lease respectively, while the memoirs of Cordell Hull and Sherwood's *Roosevelt and Hopkins*, already cited, tell much about wartime diplomacy.

The Historical Division of the Department of the Army is preparing a history of army operations in many volumes, of which more than 20 already have been published. Samuel E. Morison has written a nine-volume *History of Naval Operations in World War II* (1947-1954).

THE
CULTURAL
SCENE

CHAPTER THIRTY

An American born in 1890 and still living today has witnessed more advances in human comfort, convenience, and luxury than all the generations that have preceded him. But these years of fantastic technical progress, especially from 1920 to 1950, have not brought as much spiritual comfort as they have physical luxury. The years after 1914 were years of wasting depression, terrible wars, and spiritual disorder.

Much of the story of America and of the world during this period is the story of rapid technological progress accomplished against a dark background of social disorder and moral uncertainty. The twentieth century has brought mass leisure and varied opportunities for cultural advancement and recreation to millions, but changing values and the tensions of modern living have produced a widespread sense of insecurity.

708

I. SOCIAL CHANGE

In 1890, 62.9 million people lived in the continental United States, and by 1950 there were 150.7 million. Inevitably, as the decades after 1920 went by, a higher and higher percentage of this population was native-born. In 1890, almost one out of every seven Americans had been born abroad, but by 1950, the ratio had fallen to slightly less than one in fifteen. We were becoming a nation of city-dwellers. At the turn of the century, 60 out of every hundred still lived in the country, but by 1920 the census for the first time showed that more than half of the population lived in cities.

On the farms, machinery had replaced hand labor to a large extent—so much so that although there were twice as many people in the United States as there had been in 1900, their food was being raised on a slightly smaller number of farms. As the number of farmers declined, an increasingly important place in the population picture was taken by another occupational group, the so-called "new middle class." This stratum, consisting of people who worked in offices and behind counters as salaried salespeople and office help, managers and professionals, grew to be about one-fourth of the whole population, while farmers by 1950 fell to slightly more than one-tenth. More and more women were joining the labor force. By the middle of the century they represented two out of every five white-collar workers and almost one out of every three workers of all sorts.

As machine power took the place of manpower on farms and in factories, the standard of living rose much faster than the population. The use of machines, the growth of industrial research, and the progress of scientific management enabled Americans by 1950 to produce three and one-half times more for each hour of labor than their counterparts had been able to turn out in

1900. National income made an equally remarkable over-all advance. Estimated at about $28.7 billion in 1909, it fluctuated through the years, rising to a peak in 1929 and falling to a low in 1933. But during and after World War II it rose sharply, until by 1953 it had reached $307.7 billion, or more than ten times the 1909 figure.

Not only was income growing, but the achievement of nearly full employment in the years following World War II, as well as changes in tax policy hastened by the New Deal, caused this income to be more broadly and equitably distributed. According to the estimates of the economist, Simon Kuznets, the year 1929 represented a peak for the inequitable distribution of American wealth. But from 1929 to 1946, the top 5 per cent of the nation's individuals and families saw their share in the total national income dwindle by one-half, which meant that the remaining 95 per cent almost doubled its share. In spite of these impressive gains, poverty was still a problem. Even in 1951, a prosperous year, over 17 per cent of all American families received an annual income of less than $1,500.

As labor became more mechanized, more routine, and more specialized, the average job-holder received less gratification from his work; but he also found himself with more free time. Leisure became less of a luxury but more of a problem—the problem of how to escape from the routine of work into recreation that was itself free from routine and genuinely relaxing. In the middle of the nineteenth century, workmen usually put in about 11 hours a day, 6 days a week. Between 1870 and 1910, first the 10-hour day and then the 8-hour day and the five-day week, lightened labor's burden. By 1933, the average work-week had fallen to 39.2 hours. Part of this drop stemmed from the fact that the annual two-week

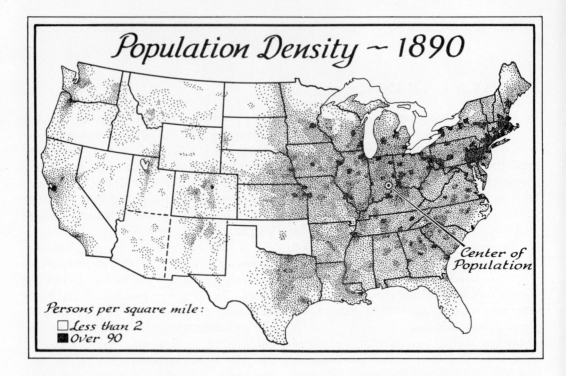

Population Density ~ 1890

Center of
Population

Persons per square mile:
☐ Less than 2
■ Over 90

vacation with pay had become common. Older workers were taking advantage of old-age insurance and industrial pension schemes to retire earlier. New household appliances, prepared foods, and ready-made clothes freed the housewife from many time-consuming tasks. Many of them took jobs—one out of every four married women was either employed or looking for a job during the early 1950's—but even the working woman had leisure to spare, and a new problem to contend with: how to spend it.

II. THE BUSINESS OF LEISURE

In the 1920's, providing amusement for America became a major business. The automobile industry, the radio industry, the movies, and commercialized sports, all boomed. In this era of prosperity, thousands of established businesses expanded and thousands of new ones entered the field, to supply what seemed to be an insatiable demand for amusement and for the equipment that amusements required. In the period of relaxation and prosperity that followed World War II, the great amusement boom of the 1920's was repeated and surpassed.

In 1950, the American people spent about $40 billion on their pleasures—on recreational goods and services, liquor and tobacco, vacations and sports, candies, soft drinks, and sport clothes. This amount was almost five times what they spent for medical care and twice what they paid for rent.

The Movies. The glamorous world of motion pictures was born as a humble peepshow in a penny arcade. A person put a nickel in a device called a kinetoscope (invented by Thomas A. Edison about 1896) and saw tiny figures moving against blurred backgrounds. Edison regarded his invention as little more than a childish toy and soon lost interest in it, but others took up where he left off and soon succeeded in projecting the image upon a screen for the benefit of large audiences. By 1905, more than 5,000

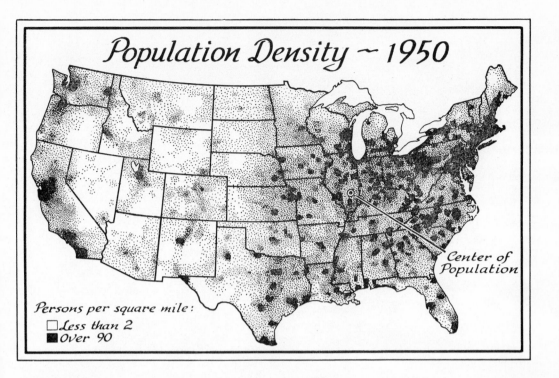

Population Density ~ 1950

Center of Population

Persons per square mile:
☐ Less than 2
■ Over 90

"nickelodeons," housed in converted shops or warehouses throughout the country, were showing rudimentary short films for a five-cent admission.

The peep-shows had prospered by showing short, presumably comic incidents, such as a man sneezing. New films, some as long as a thousand feet, introduced new features. Movie-makers began turning out endless variations on the theme of the chase. Cowboys chased bad men, and city sleuths chased bank robbers. Comedians threw custard pies and slipped on banana peels. The first picture with a plot was *The Great Train Robbery*, made in 1903, and its success was so immediate that every producer turned to thrillers. But for some time there were no stars, no sex, no culture. It was David W. Griffith who finally liberated the movie camera from the themes of the nickelodeon and the techniques of stage filming. His *The Birth of a Nation,* though a partisan and intolerant film about the Civil War and Reconstruction, was grandly conceived, budgeted at an unheard-of $100,000, and directed with imagination. Sweeping panoramas of massed armies, fade-outs, and close-ups of the principals showed what could be done with a camera.

By 1917, the movies had become a multi-million-dollar industry. Hollywood, the film capital, sprang up, complete with all its familiar trappings. Luxurious movie theaters began to replace the nickelodeons, and Americans spent $175 million a year on admissions. The first stars—Charlie Chaplin, Mary Pickford, Marie Dressler—earned fabulous salaries, lived glamorous lives, and attracted the same kind of attention and adulation their counterparts receive today. Color was first used successfully in the 1920's, and the first full-length talking picture, *The Jazz Singer* (1928), whipped up the popular appetite for films as never before. By 1930, the industry had a capital investment of $2 billion, employed about 325,000 people, and collected $1.5 billion in annual admissions. Entertainment was now big business.

Certainly the art of the film was a popular art, and it was the aim of the producers to give the public what it wanted: spectacles like *Ben Hur* and swashbucklers like *The Three Musketeers*, or, more frequently, films

711

Mass leisure. A busy day at Coney Island.

with such titles as *Sinners in Silk* and *Women Who Give*. Although these films promised considerably more than they gave, moralists worried about their effect on the rebellious youth of the 20's and agitated for more censorship. In 1922, film producers decided to forestall public censorship by regulating their own affairs, and hired Will H. Hays, who had been chairman of the Republican National Committee and Harding's Postmaster-General, to head their organization. The Hays code set certain standards governing love-making, décolletage, crime, and profanity; but the larger issue of the distortions this censorship imposes on reality, and the question of what effect movies actually have upon the minds of their audiences, have yet to be solved.

712

Radio. Unlike the movies, whose commercial possibilities were exploited from the first, the early development of radio was haphazard and accidental. In 1920, perhaps 20,000 amateurs listened on home-made sets to wireless telephone messages, sent mainly from ships at sea. As an experiment, the Westinghouse Electric and Manufacturing Company in Pittsburgh began to broadcast music that year. Amateurs in the area responded enthusiastically, and soon a popular demand induced Westinghouse to put the program on a regular basis and to introduce reports of baseball scores in addition to concerts. A Pittsburgh department store began to advertise radio sets, and in December, 1920, the first commercial broadcasting station, KDKA, was set up in Pittsburgh to broadcast the results of the Harding-Cox election.

KDKA was an enormous success; overnight, radio became big business. Within four years, there were 562 stations sending out music, stock-market and news reports, bedtime stories, church services, and prize-fights. "There is radio music in the air, every night, everywhere," a newspaper editor wrote. "Anybody can hear it at home on a receiving set, which any boy can put up in an hour." By 1930, 40 per cent of all American families had radios; by 1950, 95.7 per cent had at least one.

It was highly appropriate that the first station should have been opened to report a political event; now that Americans could listen to political conventions and campaign speeches in their homes, their interest in politics grew. Millions followed the Smith-Hoover campaign of 1928 by radio, and millions more followed the events of the New Deal era by listening to Franklin D. Roosevelt's effective "fireside chats."

As a news medium, radio performs a real service. Although it gives fewer details than the newspapers, it gets news to the public faster. During World War II, when the latest news was a matter of the greatest urgency, battles were reported even as they were being fought. Radio reporting, under the supervision of the Federal Communications Commission, also tended to be freer

from the bias, distortion, and extravagant omissions of which so many newspapers are guilty. During the presidential campaign of 1952, when newspapers in many cities carried only the sketchiest coverage of the Democratic candidate, anyone who wanted to follow both sides of the campaign could hear Adlai Stevenson's speeches or get brief factual summaries of them over the radio.

Once established as a national habit, radio-listening became the object of intensive study by two groups—the advertiser, who paid for most of the entertainment, and the critic of popular culture, who was concerned about the quality of this entertainment. As selling mediums, radio and now television seem to be unsurpassed. The advertiser can reach into the homes of millions of people and pour his message into their ears. And most people, surveys show, tend to accept "commercials" without much resentment as the price they must pay for free entertainment.

The cultural critics of radio have tended to focus their attention on the daytime serial, some 30 of which were broadcast daily in 1950. Gilbert Seldes, one of the most provocative of these writers, calls the "soap opera" "the great invention of radio, its single notable contribution to the art of fiction." As Mr. Seldes points out, the dif-

The first factory-built radio receiver, 1921.

ficulties of putting on a show for a half-hour every week, or for fifteen minutes five days a week, are enormous. Each individual program must be made as easy to forget as possible, so that the same theme, the same story, the same joke can be repeated soon without sounding like the same program.

Television. Television brought into the living room the universal availability of radio with some of the intensity of the movie experience—the spectator sitting in semi-darkness with all his attention fixed on the screen. Experiments with television started during the 1930's, but it was not until after World War II that sets became widely available. Once they did, production jumped from 7,500 in 1946 to 6.5 million in 1950. By January, 1953, 20 million sets were in use in about 40 per cent of all American homes. Perhaps because television networks were developed for the most part by the two big radio networks, programs tended to follow the pattern set by radio. After some hesitation, most of the more successful radio stars, and many of the programs, made the switch to the new medium without noticeable distress.

Certainly both radio and television give their audiences ample reason to complain of the low quality of their material. There have been successful experiments in both mediums with meaningful dramatic presentations, and with educational programs that have won much praise. Whether these experiments will in some measure raise the present dead-level of the majority of programs, or whether the combined limitations of the advertisers, the audiences, and the mediums themselves make improvement impossible, is an open question.

The Spread of Culture. Mechanization did more than simply free people for sun and fun. As Russell Lynes, author of *The Tastemakers* and a well-known critic of popular culture, puts it, the machine introduced "the muses to the masses." Beginning in the 1920's and 30's, but especially after World War II, ways were found to reproduce cheaply and to distribute widely not only the worst, but also the best work of artists, writers, and musicians. In recent years, though flower prints and mountains at sunset continue to ornament many an American living-room wall, reproductions of old masters "suitable for framing" are sold by the hundreds of thousands. Mass-circulation magazines devote page after page to lavish displays of classic as well as modern art. Art appreciation classes are well-attended, and spare-time painting captivates world-famous men like Eisenhower and Churchill. But in spite of the art boom, only a handful of American artists can live by art alone; they teach if they can, but more and more they try their hands at advertising art, which has rarely been successfully combined with creative effort.

For the first time in the history of American publishing, the supremacy of the hardcover best-seller is now being challenged by the infant but already lusty paper-back. Before World War II, although serious books were published in paper covers abroad, notably by Penguin in England, paper-backs in America were for the most part thrillers and mysteries or special editions for textbook use. In 1953, the publishing house of Doubleday & Co. launched Anchor Books, reprints of literary classics and difficult books of classic and contemporary philosophy and criticism priced at about $1. The first titles, many of them long out of print, quickly sold out editions of about 20,000 copies, and the race was on. Other publishers launched their own series, equally serious and equally successful. Paper-backs of all sorts soon took over the front space of half the bookstores in the country, and were sold on newsstands and in railroad and air-line stations as well.

Music has always been somewhat more popular with Americans than other cultural forms. The major cities began to organize symphony orchestras shortly after the Civil

War; grand and light opera have long flourished, and good schools of music have been well patronized. At the turn of the century, when the phonograph first appeared, popular interest increased, but mostly in popular tunes. During the 1920's, radio threatened to make the phonograph obsolete; but in the late 30's interest in classical music revived, and since what a person wanted to hear was not always available on the radio, records began to sell again. After World War II, the combination of hi-fidelity phonographs and long-playing records eliminated the bulky, breakable prewar album and much of the scratchiness and blurring of sound. LP's were an overnight success, and now as never before relatively cheap recordings by serious musicians playing classical and modern compositions are readily available and convenient to play. So are the works of young composers and the performances of young artists.

III. FAITH AND KNOWLEDGE

Religion. The forces that so changed western society in the twentieth century also shook the churches of the world. As the skyscraper over-reached the church spire, the influence of the churches declined. Modern science posed challenges to theology that were met crudely at first, and not until science showed itself to be as much an instrument of destruction as of progress did religion begin to recoup its losses. Over the past 50 years, religion in America has been for the most part on the defensive, but in the face of the advancing secularism of society, there has been a significant resurgence of religious life.

Those who first opposed secularism did so with fire in their eyes. The most vehement of the various movements to bring the people back to the churches was the revival of fundamentalism in the 1920's. The fundamentalists seem to have hated modern influences and feared their ultimate triumph as much as they were moved by deep piety or Christian love. They sought to return to simple acceptance of Biblical Christianity and refused to countenance the findings of modern Biblical criticism. Darwinian science they opposed root and branch. The trial of Thomas Scopes for teaching Darwin's theory of evolution to high-school students (see p. 636) dramatized fundamentalist issues and feelings in an unforgettable fashion.

The religious revival following World War II has dealt with the issues of modern life in a much more positive way, and has had a wider appeal than any of its predecessors. The tremendous number of lives lost in the war, the revelations of Nazi bestiality and Soviet inhumanity, and the fear of atomic annihilation caused men to question the secular articles of faith—belief in human progress and natural goodness—and secular values as well. Millions turned again to religion for comfort and hope. At its best, the tone of this revival was set by theologians like Karl Barth, a neo-orthodox Swiss minister, and Paul Tillich, a refugee from Germany, who emphasized the significance of sin and the folly of glorifying man rather than God. At a more popular level, the religious revival was led by evangelists stronger in emotional appeal than reason.

In the postwar period, the churches regained the ground they had lost. In 1926, 46 per cent of the total population were church members; by 1954, membership stood at 60 per cent—the highest proportion of the population ever reported to be on church rolls. The Baptists in particular made great gains, and there was a proliferation of new Protestant sects, among them the Church of the Nazarene, the Churches of God, the Pentecostal Assemblies, and the Foursquare Gospel Movement. The Catholic churches also benefited from the general revival, although their proportion of the whole population declined slightly, from 36 per cent in 1936 to 33 per cent in 1951.

Much of the Protestants' intolerance of Catholicism seemed to have disappeared, however, and in both social acceptance and political influence Catholicism gained ground. After the decline of the Ku Klux Klan during the 1920's (see p. 635), no movement that made a comparable parade of its intolerance arose. Intense criticism of the Catholic Church continued to be made, but on an intellectual level rather than on the level of persecution and mob violence. Paul Blanshard's *American Freedom and Catholic Power* stirred a strong Catholic counter-attack after its publication in 1949. One issue, moreover, continued to arouse antagonism between Catholics and Protestants. In many northern and mid-western states, bus transportation and lunches were furnished to parochial schools as well as to public schools. Protestants opposed public support for parochial schools, while many Catholics opposed federal aid to states so long as states did not pass part of this aid along to parochial schools. This opposition was interpreted by Protestants as an attempt to undermine the system of public education. In other social efforts, however, such as Community Chest drives, people of differing faiths exhibited a new sense of harmony and cooperation.

Education. Population growth, and the ever-larger demand for the literate skills that was being made by an increasingly bureaucratized society, strained the facilities of public education in America more and more as the century went on. In 1900, most Americans left school after the eighth grade; there were only 630,000 high-school students in the entire country. Fifty years later, the nation's population had doubled and the high-school population had reached 7 million. Between the years 1910 and 1930, the high school had become a genuinely popular institution, and employers began to demand a high-school education as a requisite for many different jobs. Higher education made comparable advances in enrollment. In 1900,

237,000 students were enrolled in colleges and universities; the number rose steadily, until by 1950 there were 2.7 million students, about 30 per cent of the college-age group.

Throughout this period, schools were hard put to keep their curriculums in tune with the demands of rapidly changing times. In the nineteenth century, grammar-school teachers had been expected to do little more than instruct their pupils in the 3 R's. By 1930, grammar schools were offering as many as 30 subjects. High schools had once been expected to offer only an academic course designed to prepare students for college. But as high schools became more popular, many students enrolled who did not expect or want to go on to college, and who had little interest in the conventional courses. Practical and vocational subjects—machine shop, woodworking, sewing and cooking, typing, stenography, and bookkeeping—were introduced. Vocational training provoked an angry controversy among educators, some of whom argued that it was no substitute for the ability to think, write, and speak; others replied that traditional education had been designed for a small minority and did not prepare the majority for life in the modern world. Even greater disagreement arose among educators on teaching methods, especially when the philosopher John Dewey's ideas in this important field slowly gained acceptance after World War I. Advocates of progressive ideas insist that learning informally through actual experience and participation, without formal assignments or teacher-imposed discipline, will encourage initiative, responsibility, and self-discipline. The traditionalists who oppose the progressive plan insist upon the proved value of systematic training in and mastery of basic subjects and skills.

Colleges also changed to meet the needs of swelling enrollments. An entirely new institution, the junior college, answered the needs of students who did not want a full college education but who did want to continue for two years beyond high school. In 1920, there were only 52 junior colleges in the country. By 1950, there were 500. A great many of the junior colleges were sponsored by municipalities that wanted to give their young people wider educational opportunities. Some educators looked forward to the time when as many people would have two years of junior college as had once had a high-school education.

Within the colleges, the sciences and the applied arts gained steadily at the expense of the liberal arts and the humanities. During the 1920's and 1930's, there was a moderate reaction against the disorganized curriculum brought about by the elective system, and many colleges introduced humanities courses. But the increasing demand for technicians and specialists during and after World War II swung thousands of students away from the humanities toward the sciences. Colleges found it hard to mantain staffs in the liberal arts, but they were obliged to expand their science staffs during the early 1950's. And the sciences were overwhelmingly favored in research appropriations. Of the $350 million spent on research by American colleges and universities in 1952-1953, 90 per cent was earmarked for the physical or biological sciences. Thoughtful educators worried lest the nation develop an educated class whose technical skills far surpassed their humanistic understanding.

In the postwar period, a persistent problem among educators was pressure from outside groups bent on interfering with the freedom of the teacher or of the student. High-school teachers had long had to face humiliating restrictions on their personal lives, and college teachers found themselves under fire for discussing subjects that special interests did not want mentioned in the classroom. A battle over freedom in education raged through the University of California from 1949 to 1952. The president and the regents, hoping to protect the university from reckless critics in the state legislature, required faculty members to sign a special loyalty oath in addition to the oath they normally signed as employees of the state. Resentful over being singled out and humiliated in this way, many professors, including men of world-wide repute, refused to sign the oath on the ground that it threw doubt on their loyalty and was an affront to their dignity. Eventually, the oath was rescinded, but not before many distinguished professors had left to take positions elsewhere.

Science and Research.

Research in the natural sciences has flourished in twentieth-century America under the sponsorship of universities, foundations, government, and industry. The role of the university has been primarily to develop new scientific ideas and to train new scientists; government and industry have usually applied the ideas developed in the university, although during World War II and after, their role in original research and in training became increasingly important. In 1930, $166 million was spent on scientific research and development; 14 per cent of this money came from the federal government, 70 per cent from industry, 12 per cent from universities, and 4 per cent from such other sponsors as state governments and private foundations. The contribution of the federal government grew slowly up to 1940, and rapidly thereafter so that in 1941-1945 its share became 83 per cent, that of industry 13 per cent, and that of all other sources 4 per cent. Much of the federal money was administered through contracts with universities, but after 1945 a concerted effort was made to promote scientific research and education by outright grants to universities, by substantial subsidies to research projects, and by direct scholarships, rather than by awarding contracts. A National Science Foundation was set up in 1950 to implement this program and to coordinate the over-all development of American science.

This willingness on the part of Americans to contribute money for the advancement of scientific research and experiment is based on widespread public recognition of the great contribution science makes to our well-being and security in peace and in war. Under these conditions, the process of invention and discovery has prospered as never before in human history. Since the explosion of the atomic bomb, however, the social role of science has been undergoing a re-examination. The question of whether the scientist is to be held responsible for his discoveries, or whether it is proper for him to pursue his investigations without regard for their social consequences, is hotly debated among scientists themselves and among the public at large. Recognition of the intimate relation of social change to scientific growth, emphasized by such recent developments as the use of atomic energy for power and the technological unemployment that might occur as a result of automation in industry, has raised other questions. Whether it is possible to plan scientific research, or perhaps to control it so as to maximize its benefits and minimize the harm it can do, is, however, merely one aspect of the larger question of social planning that so concerns our age. In the sense that the distribution of funds must be planned, many rough predictions about the goals of scientific inquiry are already being made.

For most Americans, the practical applications of research are of more interest than its internal problems, vital as these undeniably are. In recent years, innovations have come thick and fast in every area of life. But to call these innovations "modern miracles" is to misunderstand the painstaking steps by which new scientific facts are added to the existing body of knowledge. As one historian of science, I. Bernard Cohen, has said, "there is a ring of hollow mockery in the expression, 'We live in an age of science,' so long as we continue to describe each new advance in science in terms of 'miracle' or 'magic.' "

The uses to which scientific knowledge has been put are dramatic indeed. New weed-killers, based on principles derived by fundamental research in plant hormones, may rid the world of weeds. In the United States alone, weeds have been estimated to cost the farmer about $3 billion a year, aside from untold back-breaking labor. Radar, developed during World War II but actually stemming from research with radio waves made during the 1890's, has been used with great effect to increase the safety of ship and plane travel. Years of industrial research in the laboratories of the Du Pont Company have produced both synthetic rubber and nylon as well as other synthetic yarns.

One could go on with such a list indefinitely, but of all the benefits modern science has bestowed on man, certainly the most beneficial and the most dramatic have been developments in medical science. New drugs and new surgical techniques have put tools in the hands of doctors that make the treatment of disease a thousand times more effective than it was even 20 years ago. The list of diseases that were once dreaded but have now become relatively minor health hazards is long indeed—among them are typhoid fever, diphtheria, malaria, and puerperal fever. Venereal disease can now be treated with a high expectation of complete cure. Pneumonia, influenza, tuberculosis, and polio are becoming far less formidable. Nothing better illustrates the advance of medical science than the conquest of polio by the Salk vaccine, despite mishaps with the vaccine itself and gross mishandling of its distribution. The wide public response to fund-raising campaigns for research in cancer, heart disease, and a rapidly growing list of other diseases attests to the faith people have in the capacity of research to conquer disease.

The real progress that has been made in medicine is reflected in the fact that the average age of the population and normal life expectancy rose rapidly throughout the half-century. In 1900, the average 20-year-old male could expect to live to be 62. By 1925, his life expectancy was 66; by 1950, almost 70. The median age of the population rose from 22.9 in 1900 to 30.2 in 1950. How to care for the aged and how to increase their span of economic productivity loomed as a growing problem for the future.

The Social Sciences.   In the social sciences, psychology became a great new force. The findings of Sigmund Freud and of his followers and critics were put to use in clinical work; and in psychotherapy, anthropology, sociology, and political science Freud was brought from the clinic to the classroom, the advertising office, and the poll-taker's study. And post-Freudian critics like Harry Stack Sullivan, Erich Fromm, and Karen Horney tried to show how his concepts could be construed in social terms. Freud's emphasis on childhood experiences focused attention on methods of child-rearing, not only in theoretical studies of primitive cultures but also in practical advice to parents. By mid-century, a whole generation of American mothers, few of whom had read Freud, but most of whom had absorbed some of his ideas at second, third, and fourth hand, were busy putting his insights to work, avoiding the mistakes their own mothers had made, and perhaps originating fresh mistakes of their own. Students of society made good use of the Freudian awareness of unconscious motivation, and of such Freudian mechanisms as "displacement" and "sublimation," and of the techniques of analyzing dreams and using projective tests (like the Rorschach) to explain the desires and motives of men. Freudian insights were applied not only to the problems of contemporary society, but also to primitive society, by anthropologists like Ralph Linton and Margaret Mead, and by psychiatrists interested in anthropology like Abraham Kardiner.

Sociology did not emerge as an academic discipline distinct from general courses in the history of civilization until late in the nineteenth century. The first American sociologists, William Graham Sumner, Lester Ward, and Edward A. Ross, were primarily interested in analyzing the structure of society. After 1900, influenced by the work of the philosophers William James and John Dewey, sociologists succeeded in presenting a new picture of man himself as a more complicated structure of tendencies, interests, and habits, and emphasized the interconnection between the individual and the larger society.

Influenced by the humanitarianism of the Progressive era and the political renaissance of the common man, and also by James' and Dewey's emphasis on the effects of environment on behavior, the new sociology was pulled along in the current of pre-World War I reform. Interest in social structure gave way to interest in social ills, although the name given this new branch of social science, social pathology, was derived from biology. Throughout the 20's, academic sociology continued to be tied to social work. It was out of this interest in social problems that the method of the local survey, or community study, emerged, exemplified by such pioneering studies as Robert S. and Helen M. Lynd's *Middletown* (1929), and *Middletown in Transition* (1937). The Lynds were interested in the whole community, however, and not merely in its problem areas.

Although it is aimed at social structure, current sociological inquiry has little in common with the theories of society developed by Spencer or Ward. The ambition of the present-day sociologist is to create a set of scientific theories for the explanation of empirical social phenomena. To this end, there has been a tendency to organize inquiry into cooperative research projects that require large staffs of researchers and interviewers, and an increasing refinement of statistical techniques largely derived from market research. Important volumes compiled by the project method include *The American Dilemma* (1944), a study of the Negro problem in the United States by the Swede, Gunnar Myrdal, and his assistants; *The Authoritarian Personality* (1950), by Theodore Adorno and associates, an analysis of extreme right-wing behavior; and *The People's Choice* (1944), an examination of voting habits by Paul Lazarsfeld and others. One notable exception to this trend has been David Riesman's penetrating study of American character, *The Lonely Crowd* (1950), the most widely read book in the history of sociology. Riesman worked with no staff, but with two collaborators.

Although the main trend in sociology has been to concentrate on the American society, economics has tended to stress the problems of the "international economy," to use Gunnar Myrdal's phrase. American economists have argued that the vigor of the free world depends on a rapid improvement in the economy of underdeveloped areas. And they have tried to work out ways of achieving this improvement with the least possible disruption of the life and traditions of the non-capitalist peoples affected.

Yet economists have also made significant gains in the study of the American economy itself. The vogue of the brilliant English economist, John Maynard Keynes, though he was closely associated with the later philosophy of the New Deal, persisted even after the return of the Republicans to the presidency in 1952. Keynes stressed the futility of expecting the business system itself to work the entire country out of such deep economic distress as we experienced in the 1930's. He recognized the part that the government always played in the total economy and developed the general theory of governmental participation in "economic planning." Many economists have quarreled with Keynesianism since the 1930's; but the Establishment of the Council of Economic Advisers under President Truman in 1946, gave such advisers an official stature of which most economists, whatever their attitude toward "planning," seem to have approved. The Council, indeed, was strengthened under the Eisenhower administration. Between 1952 and 1956, Arthur F. Burns, Professor of Economics at Columbia University and Director of the National Bureau of Economic Research, served as head of the Council. And by employing techniques of research and analysis perfected at the National Bureau (a privately endowed organization that has stressed the study and control of business cycles), he was able to advise the administration most skillfully on economic policies. No one knows whether another severe depression is in the offing in the United States. But economists have accepted the defenses that were built into the economy by planners after the debacle of 1929. And they have studied and managed these defenses with an eye to keeping us on an expanding but safer course.

Historians, unlike the sociologists, did fruitful work without making very much use of staff techniques, or finding it necessary to abandon their traditional individualism. None of the important historical works of the twentieth century, any more than of the nineteenth, was the work of a staff—though individual historians did contribute volumes to continuing projects like the History of American Life Series and the New American Nation Series. The tendency in American history has been toward minute and meticulous research, and an impressive number of monographs have been written which give perhaps more detailed information about America than has ever been available about any country, but offer little in the way of general speculation. Narrative history has also been written by men like Allan Nevins, whose biographies and historical works on a great variety of subjects have been successful with the general public, and Samuel Eliot Morison, biographer of Columbus, historian of Harvard, and chronicler of New England maritime history. William L. Langer has written brilliant studies of diplomatic history and world imperialism, and has edited a series of volumes on the history of modern Europe that show the American historical profession to have numerous first-rate scholars whose interests are not confined to the history of their own country.

IV. MOODS OF THE TWENTIES

In Europe, World War I ended in general despair, with both sides impoverished and exhausted. In America, the war had been a bitter experience, but the country emerged from it into a period of economic prosperity and moral relaxation. What Europeans experienced as despair, Americans felt as disillusion. They felt they were sadder but wiser; not wiser than their prewar selves so much as wiser than the generation of their fathers. As Joseph Wood Krutch said in his widely read *The Modern Temper* (1929), "We know at least that we have discovered the trick which has been played on us and that whatever else we may be we are no longer dupes."

Now, for the first time in America, there appeared a group of writers who thought of themselves as a generation, a "lost generation" united at least in their desire to kick over the traces of a false and misleading past. F. Scott Fitzgerald, in his novel, *This Side of Paradise* (1920), spoke for "all the sad young men" who "had grown up to find all Gods dead, all wars fought, all faiths in men shaken." The preceding generation, and everything it had stood for—progressive reform in politics, material standards of success, conventionality in manners, the genteel tradition in literature—was fair game for the satire that was to become the order of the day. But there was something heady in revolt and in the sudden sense these young writers had of taking over. They proclaimed their lack of faith with boisterous pride, and celebrated the dissolution of the old order with reckless gaiety. Fitzgerald said, "America was going on the greatest, gaudiest spree in history . . . . The whole golden boom was in the air—its splendid generosities, its outrageous corruptions and the tortuous death of the old America in prohibition."

These young American thinkers and writers were disillusioned with many things, but above all with America itself. Paradoxically, the new prosperity and world power of their country produced in them a critical passion unequaled by any of their predecessors. In 1922, a young writer, Harold Stearns, edited a volume, *Civilization in the United States*, which acquired lasting fame as a statement of how American writers felt about the culture in which they lived. The book was an almost unrelieved complaint that mocked its title; the contributors found the United States to be almost without civilization. The theater, according to George Jean Nathan, was "at once the richest theater in the world and the poorest. Financially it reaches to the stars; culturally, with exceptions so small as to be negligible, it reaches to the drains." The American city, Lewis Mumford wrote, was an index of the country's material success and spiritual failure. "Literature," Van Wyck Brooks said, "was simply underdeveloped. The chronic state of our literature is that of a youthful promise which is never redeemed. . . . For half a century the American writer as a type has gone down in defeat." Politics, said H. L. Mencken, was at once corrupt and absurd. "Examine the average congressman at leisure, and you will find that he is incompetent and imbecile, and not only incompetent and imbecile, but also incurably dishonest." The press had been corrupted by advertising and the credulous public made no protest. The universities seemed to have been created, said Professor Joel Spingarn, "for the special purpose of ignoring or destroying scholarship." Business simply showed, said Garet Garrett, "man's acquisitive instinct acting outside of humanistic motives." The American husband, Alfred Kuttner found, "becomes everything in his business and nothing in his home . . . . The wife, on her part, either becomes hysterical or falls victim to religious reformatory charlatanism."

This indictment may sound shrill and overdrawn, but for many intelligent people it expressed the very discontent they felt. This generation had been shown much that was ugly in its society and had come to believe that ugliness was all there was to see. How could one speak of the poise and generosity of the American public mind after the wild chauvinism of the war just past, or during the "red" hysteria that followed it? Where was the boasted moral tone of American politics during the Harding scandals and the Coolidge buffooneries? Americans had always prided themselves on their religious tolerance, but the 20's engendered the bigotry of the Ku Klux Klan and the ugly whispering campaign against Al Smith. Was American justice symbolized by the Sacco-Vanzetti trial? Was the state of free inquiry reduced to the idiocies of the Scopes trial? Was the American attitude toward the amenities of life and toward personal freedom illustrated by prohibition, with its hypocrisies and its stimulation to lawlessness? Was urban life to flourish under gangsterism and machine politics? Surveying such a scene, the intellectuals of the 20's concluded that the United States had indeed reached that state of civilization toward which it had long been tending; unlike the optimistic spokesmen of business, however, who maintained the same thing from another quarter, they found it altogether bad.

Feeling as they did about their country's culture, the generation of the 20's set about finding ways to rebel against it. Unlike the Progressive generation, or indeed their own successors in the 1930's, they did not turn to politics. The Progressive tradition of reform had little to offer them, and by 1920 most of its leaders had dropped out of active politics or had become tired and acquiescent. It seemed hopeless even to think of going into politics when the political life of the country seemed to be beyond the influence of men of good will. Many writers did talk in a rather abstract way about socialism, but the novelist John Dos Passos (see p. 725) (see p. 725) was almost the only one among them to express radical ideas seriously and fervently in his work.

But there were many ways of rebelling ready at hand. Official prohibition made drinking bootleg gin and patronizing speak-easies a defiant gesture, a rebellious thrill. In a complacent and still conventional society, sexual experimentation and the easy-going Bohemian life seemed marvelously daring; flocks of young people left their small-town homes to pursue the artistic life in New York's Greenwich Village. For others, true culture was only to be found abroad, and off they went to Paris, where dollars went a long way and receptivity to new ideas even further. In Paris, those expatriates who had no private means or book royalties to live on got jobs as Paris correspondents for American newspapers, or as editors for small magazines, or managed to sell stories and articles to American periodicals.

Those who stayed at home looked with envy upon their fellows who had escaped abroad. Meanwhile they read with great enthusiasm those critics who were most unsparing of American life. They delighted in the merciless raillery of H. L. Mencken, who raked American culture in the columns of the Baltimore *Sun* and in the lively new periodical, the *American Mercury*. With serious attention, they listened to Van Wyck Brooks' solemn discussions of the limitations of American literature and read his brilliant biographies of Mark Twain and Henry James, in which he tried to show how the great potentialities of these writers had been limited or distorted by the American environment.

From the work of critics like Brooks and Mencken a popular theory of American culture emerged. The great enemy of culture became "the Puritan," a figure that had less to do with the early New England Puritan than with the contemporary evangelical crusader and the Victorian prude. Mencken wrote with irritation of "the old Puritan suspicion of the fine arts as such—the doctrine that they offer fit asylum for good citizens only when some ulterior and superior purpose is carried to them."

As one examines the literature of the 1920's, the unhappy forces so deplored by many writers seem to be focused in the American small town. Many of the expatriates on the Left Bank of the Seine and in Greenwich Village and in the lesser Bohemias of the time came from small towns. Indeed, the literature of the period was a kind of revolt against the village. Sherwood Anderson, in his *Winesburg, Ohio* (1919), wrote of the puzzled loneliness of small-town characters, their need for love, and their ultimate defeat. The poet Edgar Lee Masters had written earlier about the same kind of people, in the bitter tones of his *Spoon River Anthology* (1915). In *Main Street* (1920), Sinclair Lewis denounced the "Village Virus," the cultural poverty of the small midwestern town. Nor was this concern confined to fiction. Thorstein Veblen, in his last and greatest book, *Absentee Ownership* (1923), reviled the country town as "the perfect flower of self-help and cupidity standardized on the American plan," and Robert S. and Helen M. Lynd pitilessly exposed the barren culture of their *Middletown* (1929).

Of all the writers who proclaimed the new generation, none burst upon the world as glamorously or as noisily as F. Scott Fitzgerald, "a kind of king of our American youth." The publication of *This Side of Paradise* in 1920, when he was 24, made him rich and famous overnight. During the next few years, he became not so much a novelist as a celebrity, the living hero of his own novels, and the leading citizen of the glittering, partying, carnival world he had written about in *Tales of the Jazz Age* (1922), *The Beautiful and Damned* (1922), and numerous magazine stories. He dashed off many relatively insubstantial stories about flappers and their swains, although even the least of them are touched with Fitzgerald's great talent for words. But in *The Great Gatsby* (1925), he caught the unexpected poignancy of youth and wealth and success in a profound parable of the despair and waste at the heart of the American dream. In his last books,

William Faulkner (1897-   ).

Tender Is the Night (1934), and the unfinished *The Last Tycoon,* published in 1941 after his death, he wrote ever more skillfully and movingly of the deterioration of that world whose advent he had announced with such bravado.

Like Fitzgerald, Ernest Hemingway wrote his first books in the brittle idiom of the 20's. His *The Sun Also Rises* (1926) was drawn against the background of the Paris expatriates, and *A Farewell to Arms* (1929) was the most famous of the American war novels. But critics soon became aware that Hemingway had developed an economical and evocative style of his own, that he was a dedicated craftsman with a concern for art as passionate as Henry James', and that he was centrally concerned with universal problems of conduct and honor. The true subject of Hemingway's work, "the task of preserving one's self by preserving and refining one's art," became more and more

723

evident in his stories about war and those sports—hunting, fishing, and bullfighting—that have their end in death.

Regarded by some as the greatest of this generation of writers, William Faulkner first attracted attention with a bitter book about the aftermath of war called *Soldier's Pay* (1926). *The Sound and the Fury* (1929), *As I Lay Dying* (1930), *Light in August* (1932), and other books that he wrote in rapid succession established him as a writer of major stature. As he went on to *Absalom, Absalom* (1936), *The Unvanquished* (1939), and *The Hamlet* (1940), Faulkner's reputation as a great commentator on the mind and spirit of the South spread in his own country and in Europe. The world he has created, in an imaginary Mississippi county, Yoknapatawpha, the families of aristocratic Sartorises and poor white Snopeses whose lives he has described with depth of perception and an elaborate rhetoric, have universal significance, and have earned for their creator world-wide acclaim.

V. THE THIRTIES

Even before the stock-market crash and the Great Depression, signs were appearing which indicated that the mood of dapper disillusionment had run its course. The unqualified enthusiasm with which Charles A. Lindbergh was welcomed after his trans-Atlantic flight in 1927 suggested a popular hunger for heroes with no trace of bitterness about them. As the complacency of the prosperous 20's vanished in the face of deepening economic depression, so also did the irritation of the intellectuals and their alienation from the larger public. Scoffing at the insensitiveness and boorishness of America was fair enough in times of prosperity but unthinkable when people were hungry and suffering and demoralized. Expatriates whose revenues had dried up after the beginning of the depression returned from Paris in 1930 and 1931 to find the country stirring with new impulses. Broad humane sympathies traditional in American liberalism were coming back. Personal and aesthetic revolt was being transformed once again into public and political revolt. Writers were thinking less about criticizing their country, more about doing something to save it from deepening disaster. Bohemians became radicals. Business culture, formerly disdained because it was successful, domineering, and complacent, was resented more than ever—but now because it was unsuccessful and improvident.

During the early phases of the depression, while the business index plunged downward and the lines of job-hunters grew longer and more despairing, most discontented Americans supported with increasing enthusiasm the moderate reforms of the New Deal. A few were attracted by more radical proposals. Socialist and communist leadership had never had as much influence in the United States as in most countries of Europe, though the devoted humanitarian socialist leader, Eugene V. Debs, had twice received, in the presidential elections of 1912 and 1920, around 900,000 votes, and Norman Thomas, the party leader after 1928, usually received a respectful hearing from the American public. The New Deal reforms took the wind out of the socialists' sails, and their party almost disappeared after 1932. Communism continued to exert some independent influence, though only a small number of persons ever participated actively in the Communist party or gave it their vote. The largest vote ever received by a presidential candidate on the communist ticket was William Z. Foster's 102,000 in 1932, which represented a small fraction of 1 per cent of the total popular vote. But among writers and readers of serious books there developed in the depression years a brief vogue for what was called "proletarian literature" and for Marxist literary criticism. The disillusion that followed the Nazi-Soviet pact of 1939 (see p.

685) put an abrupt end to this enthusiasm, but not before several books had been written that expressed in fiction the social tensions of the 1930's.

Writers who tried to make their novels into revolutionary tracts achieved nothing of permanent significance, though they wrote voluminously of strikes and political conversions. Three left-wing, though politically independent writers, however, did produce important literature that still conveys some of the urgency and fervor of the 1930's. John Dos Passos had been one of the few writers in the 1920's with a serious interest in radical politics, and the second of his anti-war novels, *Three Soldiers* (1921), forecast something of the social novelist he was to become. *Manhattan Transfer* (1925), was an experiment in the form he was later to perfect in *U.S.A.* (1930-1936), which shuttles between the lives of several characters at various social levels in order to portray the complexity of the mass scene. The three volumes of the *U.S.A.* trilogy, *42nd Parallel, 1919,* and *The Big Money,* ambitiously attempted by this collective technique to portray American society in the first three decades of the century. *U.S.A.* is a massive indictment of America. Its rich and successful characters are corrupt and unhappy; its poor people are frustrated and hopeless. Unlike the orthodox Marxist novels of the period—almost compulsively optimistic about the coming of a new society —Dos Passos sees no grounds for optimism. He indicts life itself, and his hatred of all society is so intense that its salvation is not only unlikely, but undesirable. Dos Passos eventually despaired of the radical movement and was horrified by the development of Soviet communism. He became increasingly conservative in such later works as *Adventures of a Young Man* (1939), and *Number One* (1943), but he seemed to have lost his original creative energy.

No other writer about the American underdog has achieved the broad popularity of the novelist John Steinbeck, who first attracted attention with such works as *Tortilla Flat* (1935), *In Dubious Battle* (1936),

and *Of Mice and Men* (1937). His most imposing work, *The Grapes of Wrath* (1939), was one of the most widely read American books of our time, reaching millions of readers. It has been spoken of as the *Uncle Tom's Cabin* of the depression years, and no work seems more representative of the 1930's. Steinbeck tells the story of the Joads, a family of dispossessed Oklahoma farmers, and describes what happens to these "Okies" after they are driven from their farm and wander to California to look for work among the downtrodden fruit- and vegetable-pickers of the Salinas Valley. Though he treats them with the utmost sympathy, Steinbeck's characters remain vague, almost symbolic. But the horror of their situation is painfully clear.

As Steinbeck wrote of the rural poor, another novelist, James T. Farrell, wrote of a special urban group, the lower-middle-class and working-class Irish among whom he had grown up in Chicago. Here the sources of ruin were moral rather than economic. In his outstanding trilogy, *Young Lonigan: A Boyhood in Chicago Streets* (1932), *The Young Manhood of Studs Lonigan* (1934), and *Judgment Day* (1935), Farrell traced the lives of a people who lacked moral focus despite the ministrations of the Church, who nourished a grievance over their rejection from respectable Protestant society, who fought a losing battle with alcoholism and Puritanism. In his portrayal of what one critic has called "Irish Babbittry," Farrell used a harsh technique to present sordid situations. After his original achievement in the Lonigan trilogy, Farrell seemed unable to do more than repeat the same themes in such works as *Tommy Gallagher's Crusade* (1939), *Ellen Rogers* (1941), and *Bernard Clare* (1946).

Another writer who drew upon personal experience with the same intensity and candor as Farrell, though with far less interest in politics, was Thomas Wolfe. A North Carolinian who came to New York to seek his literary fortunes, Wolfe told the story of his own life in four huge volumes of fiction that totaled more than a million words even after liberal cutting by his devoted editor, Maxwell Perkins. As he wrote to F. Scott Fitzgerald, he belonged with the "putter-inners" rather than with the "taker-outers." In *Look Homeward, Angel* (1929), *Of Time and the River* (1935), *The Web and the Rock* (1939), and *You Can't Go Home Again* (1940), Wolfe spelled out somewhat repetitively the story of his family life, his literary aspirations, and his friendships. Although he was as undisciplined as he was ferociously energetic, he had a gift for the lyrical communication of his own intensity and his longings and a strong feeling for the American scene. "I wrote," Wolfe said,

about night and darkness in America, and the faces of the sleepers in ten thousand little towns; and of the tides of sleep and how the rivers flowed forever in the darkness. I wrote about the hissing glut of tides upon ten thousand miles of coast; of how the moonlight blazed down on the wilderness and filled the cat's cold eye with blazing yellow. I wrote about death and sleep, and of that enfabled rock of life we call the city. I wrote about October, of great trains that thundered through the night, of ships and stations in the morning; of men in harbors and the traffic of ships.

Wolfe died prematurely in 1938, aged 38, and the last parts of his personal saga were posthumously published.

After 1933, when Hitler seized power in Germany, Americans became acutely aware of the menacing shadow of fascism. Both left-wingers and right-wingers feared for a time, though unrealistically, that the early experiments of the New Deal, particularly the N.R.A., would lead to some form of fascism. Americans fought angrily over what official policy should be toward the civil war in Spain, which broke out in the summer of 1936 (see p. 684). The advances of the totalitarian powers caused Americans to look to their defenses and to re-evaluate their institutions by comparing them with institutions abroad. The more they saw of fascism, the more they valued their own culture. And

as the New Deal began to cope more effectively with the depression, their confidence in the recuperative powers of American society began to rise. Thus, as the 30's wore on, American thought tended more and more to move away from the critical attitudes of the 20's toward a greater appreciation of American life and a revival of a kind of literary nationalism.

The critics and expatriates of the 20's had fled from American life, but the Americanists of the 30's rushed back to it and embraced it with unbounded enthusiasm. Everything American took on a new interest and seemed worth reporting, recording, narrating, photographing, and understanding. The critics of the 20's had concerned themselves with the businessmen and the powers-that-were in American society. But the enthusiasts of the late 30's and early 40's concerned themselves with the common man, with his sufferings, his courage, his struggles, his virtues. Photographers from the Farm Security Administration went out to the American land to portray the people who worked upon it, in all their native plainness and dignity. The authors of the various W.P.A. local and regional guides went back to local history lovingly and lingeringly. The reading public showed an immense appetite for reporting and for history that recalled all the details of American reality. As in the days of Whitman, they delighted to hear the very names of American places rolled over the tongue—witness the commentary written for "The River," Pare Lorentz's famous film about the Mississippi Valley:

Down the Judith, the Grand, the Osage,
 and the Platte,
The Rock, the Salt, the Black, and
 Minnesota,
Down the Monongahela, the Allegheny,
 Kanawha and Muskingum,
The Miami, the Wabash, the Licking
 and the Green. . . .

Some of the very men who had been America's most caustic critics rushed to re-embrace their country. Van Wyck Brooks, once the bellwether of the critics, dropped the sharp views that had marked his studies of Henry James and Mark Twain, dropped indeed the critical task altogether, and began to write his immensely successful series of books beginning with *The Flowering of New England* (1936), and continuing with *New England Indian Summer* (1940), *The World of Washington Irving* (1944), *The Times of Melville and Whitman* (1947), and *The Confident Years: 1885-1915* (1952). In these works, Brooks found everything about American writers important and interesting except, perhaps, the failings that he had once attacked so sharply. He became the loving genealogist of American literature, endlessly and affectionately relating all the family gossip.

Other critics followed Brooks. Lewis Mumford found new values in America. Archibald MacLeish lectured American intellectuals for toying irresponsibly with their own disillusionment. John Dos Passos, only recently so unsparingly critical of the American present, wrote a wistful book about the early days of America, *The Ground We Stand On* (1941). Charles A. Beard, whose *Rise of American Civilization,* written with his wife and published in 1927, had been one of the literary monuments of the age of criticism, joined her in writing *A Basic History of the United States* (1944), which dropped or soft-pedaled his old attacks. Beard also wrote a eulogistic analysis of American political practices in *The Republic,* and warned Americans to withdraw into their hemispheric shell and to avoid the contaminations of the Old World with its wars and political intrigues. Sinclair Lewis, after writing an anti-fascist novel, *It Can't Happen Here* (1935), wrote an acquiescent tale about American society in *The Prodigal Parents* (1938), and startled a lecture audience by remarking that he had written *Babbitt* not out of hatred but out of affection. Even H. L. Mencken, the *enfant terrible* of the 20's, settled down to write the pleasantly reminiscent pages of his excellent autobiographical volumes, *Happy Days* (1940), *Newspaper Days* (1940), and *Heathen Days* (1943).

Thus, as the 1930's passed into the 1940's, American writers were becoming reconciled to their country's experience, and were becoming increasingly conservative, first in cultural matters, and then in those political.

VI.   SINCE THE WAR

World War II and the prosperity that followed it made Americans more eager to hold onto what they had and yet increasingly anxious about their chances of doing so. The persistence of the cold war, and the ever-present menace of atomic warfare, disposed them to put up with whatever evils they saw about them for the sake of keeping what they knew was good. Proposals for social reform lost most of their appeal. Men thought less about how they could improve the future and more about whether there would be a future at all. With the sobriety of those who have been told that they have only a short time to live, many turned their attention to the long-range problems of personal life and personal destiny. They looked more and more to religion, the more sophisticated to the religious prophets of the past and present, to Søren Kierkegaard and Paul Tillich, to St. Augustine and Reinhold Niebuhr; the less sophisticated to the works of Norman Vincent Peale or Fulton J. Sheen.

Writers and artists at mid-century were confronted with a paradox. They had won an acceptance and security that Melville or Poe or Whitman would have envied. And yet they found themselves under hostile pressure in a culturally uninviting environment. What use did society have for vision, for criticism, for originality, in an age of television and movies, commercialized sports and comic books? What chance did the liberal arts have in a society whose very educators seemed to be losing faith in the importance of literacy and the intellectual skills? What future was there for a creative artist in a society marked, as one observer put it, by "the decline of attention"?

At mid-century, American creativity—at least in prose writing, though hardly in music or the graphic arts—seemed to have lost its energy. The older writers whose reputations had been established in the 20's or 30's had either stopped writing or were turning out works that added little to their reputations. William Faulkner alone seems not to have lost the strain of his creativity. Hemingway depressed many of his readers with works like *Across the River and into the Trees* (1950). In *The Old Man and the Sea* (1952), his style, once so fresh and widely imitated, seemed to some discerning critics excessively self-conscious. At times he seemed to be imitating himself. F. Scott Fitzgerald and Thomas Wolfe had died, still quite young. Dos Passos no longer wrote novels with his old sweep and vitality. Steinbeck seemed to the more sophisticated critics of the 40's and 50's merely another popular writer, though perhaps more interesting than most. As if they had given up hope for their own generation, many readers and critics of serious literature began to take a fresh look at figures of the past. Many a writer who had

been neglected in his own day was revived—Melville, Hawthorne, Henry James; and foreign writers who in one way or another suited the mood of dismay and anxiety were widely read and discussed—Marcel Proust, Franz Kafka, André Gide.

The younger writers who began to be published in the postwar era seemed to have less to say than their predecessors—or at least less that was new. Most critics regarded successful war novelists like Norman Mailer and James Jones more as entertainers than as serious writers. No novelist wrote of the Second World War as well as Hemingway and Faulkner had written of the First. The standards of writing were generally higher; there seemed to be more dedicated craftsmen than ever, writers who had made a loving study of the uses of English prose. Yet despite the work of such fine and sensitive poets as Elizabeth Bishop, Robert Lowell, and Theodore Roethke, the fiction of Saul Bellow, Truman Capote, Carson McCullers, and J. F. Powers, and the plays of Tennessee Williams, there seemed to be a falling off of creative vitality. Criticizing literature seemed more absorbing than creating it, though much of the New Criticism was doctrinaire or self-conscious, pompous or sterile. Whether the years after 1940 presaged a real decline in creativity, or were merely the trough before a new crest, only the future could tell.

Readings

Frederick Lewis Allen, *The Big Change* (1952), takes an optimistic view of twentieth-century cultural developments in America and defends it entertainingly. Alfred Kazin, *On Native Grounds* (1942), is a critical history of American prose writing since the 1890's. Horace Gregory and Marya Zaturenska, *A History of American Poetry, 1900-1940* (1942), is an intelligent critical work. John I. Bauer's *Revolution and Tradition in American Art* (1951) discusses twentieth-century painting. Herbert W. Schneider's *Religion in Twentieth Century America* (1952) is a fine brief synthesis. F. J. Dewhurst and others, *America's Needs and Resources* (rev. ed., 1955), is a treasure house of information, statistical and otherwise, on almost every aspect of our twentieth-century social history that can be measured. *Recent Social Trends* by the President's Committee on Social Trends (2 vols., 1933), though now somewhat outmoded on many counts, is still interesting and suggestive. David Riesman presents a challenging analysis of American character in *The Lonely Crowd* (1950). For a brilliant and mordant account of the growing white-collar class, see C. Wright Mills, *White Collar* (1951). On the effect of business organization on personality, W. H. Whyte, Jr., *The Organization Man* (1956), is suggestive. The same author's analysis of business propaganda and advertising, *Is Anybody Listening?* (1952), is penetrating and amusing. It is instructive to compare the critical essays on American society in H. E. Stearns, ed., *Civilization in the United States* (1922), with the follow-up volume, *America Now* (1938).

The changing American community is studied by Robert S. and Helen M. Lynd in *Middletown* (1929), and *Middletown in Transition* (1937), and by W. L. Warner, and his associates, in a series of books, which includes *Democracy in Jonesville* (1949). The automobile and its effects are discussed in David L. Cohen, *Combustion on Wheels* (1944). See also Henry Ford's personal story, *My Life and Work* (1922), and the critical biography by Keith Sward, *The Legend of Henry Ford* (1948). Foster R. Dulles has written the most satisfactory account of American recreation and sport, *America Learns to Play* (1940).

On radio and television, Gilbert Seldes, *The Great American Audience* (1950), is a distinguished book of criticism and analysis; see also his *The Public Arts* (1956). Useful but more pedestrian is Charles Siepmann, *Radio, Television, and Society* (1950). Films are dealt with historically by Lewis Jacobs, *The Rise of the American Film* (1939), and psychologically by Nathan Leites and Martha Wolfenstein, *Movies* (1950). Leo Rosten examines the movie colony sociologically in *Hollywood* (1941), as does Hortense Powdermaker in *Hollywood: The Dream Factory* (1950). On book publishing, see William Miller, *The Book Industry* (1949). Russell Lynes writes amusingly on changes in public taste in *The Tastemakers* (1954).

Science is discussed in its social relations by Bernard Barber, *Science and the Social Order* (1952), and by I. Bernard Cohen, *Science, the Servant of Man* (1948). For the impact of World War II on science, see J. P. Baxter, *Scientists Against Time* (1946). On scholarship, see the essays in Merle Curti, *American Scholarship in the Twentieth Century* (1953).

THE AGE OF RESPONSIBILITY

CHAPTER THIRTY-ONE

The foreign policies of the United States during most of its history had been directed toward winning territory on the continent itself, toward acquiring a modest colonial empire to provide an outlet for trade and investment, and toward guarding the American life-line, the Panama Canal. In the twentieth century, especially during and after World War II, the United States was forced into a position of world leadership and world responsibility in order to assure its own security and protect its political system. Americans accepted this new role, even though most of them may have preferred their old continental isolation; for without American strength, actively exerted, the entire system of western political democracy might have broken down or been overwhelmed by totalitarianism. In World War II and in the tense years that followed the peace, America hesitantly and reluctantly assumed her new responsibilities.

I.   DISSOLUTION OF THE GRAND ALLIANCE

From Casablanca to Teheran.   As we have seen, the union of the three major Allied powers during World War II was an uneasy one. Confronted by a common enemy of immense power, the Big Three—the United States, Great Britain, and Russia—joined in a concerted effort against the Axis; but their common purpose did not allay the mutual suspicions that existed between East and West. During the war, a number of conferences were held that involved sometimes two, sometimes all, of the major Allies. These conferences were called primarily to work out wartime strategy, but also involved plans for carrying over Allied cooperation into the postwar world.

At the Casablanca Conference of January, 1943 (see p. 700), Roosevelt and Churchill had agreed on general offensive strategy to be followed during the closing phases of the war, but they had left most of the details unresolved. At the Quebec Conference that followed in August, 1943, the two leaders and their advisers planned the opening of a second front in Europe as well as military operations in the Far East. They also officially recognized the French Committee of National Liberation as the government of Algeria and of the French overseas territories that acknowledged its authority.

The Foreign Ministers of the Big Three—Hull, Molotov, and Eden—further developed their plans at the Moscow Conference of October, 1943. They declared their intention to establish as soon as possible a general international organization of large and small states "for the organization and maintenance of peace and security." A declaration, announced at the close of the conference, promised Austria liberation from Germany. Agreement was reached on the general terms of settlement with Germany; and Italy, which had already surrendered, was promised help in setting up a more democratic government.

But the western powers failed to persuade the Russians to resume diplomatic relations with the Polish government-in-exile in London. Relations between the two governments had been broken off when the Poles accused the Russians of having committed atrocities against them during the Russian occupation of 1939-1941. The question of Poland's future status and future frontiers continued to plague the Big Three throughout the rest of the war and into the postwar period.

In November, 1943, at the Cairo Conference, Roosevelt and Churchill conferred with Generalissimo Chiang Kai-shek on the Pacific war and planned operations in China and Burma. The three powers asserted that they would carry on until Japan surrendered, agreed that certain territories, including Manchuria and Formosa, would be returned to China after the war, and guaranteed the freedom and independence of Korea.

At another major conference, held at Teheran, the capital of Iran, in December, 1943, Stalin for the first time took a personal part in Big Three proceedings. Details of the second front were worked out, and it was decided that the Anglo-American invasion of western Europe would be supported by an invasion of southern France. At the same time, Stalin was to launch an offensive against Germany from the east. Stalin also reaffirmed more positively a previously declared intention to enter the war against Japan.

The decision that the major thrust against Germany should be made directly across the English Channel and that the secondary invasion should strike into southern France was a source of satisfaction to Stalin. For military and political reasons, some of the British leaders had hoped to persuade the Americans to make a diversionary stab into the Balkans when it came time to launch the cross-Channel invasion. The British people, fighting now for more than four years, had suffered heavy losses, and still had vivid memories of the frightful blood-letting of 1914-1918. A Balkan invasion, they thought, would enable them, by deploying only modest forces, to use their sea power and general mobility to better advantage and to keep casualties down. Moreover, they were concerned with a political as well as a military goal: the establishment of an Allied counter-force to Russian influence in the Balkans. The American military chiefs, and with them the President, saw the matter differently. They conceived of the war more strictly in military terms. They wanted to concentrate on winning the war in the shortest possible time by striking directly at the enemy's heart with overwhelming forces.

The Yalta Conference.

In February, 1945, when the Russians were already pressing into Germany and the western Allies had liberated France, the Big Three leaders met at Yalta in the most important of their war-time conferences. At its close, the chiefs of state announced that they had agreed on military plans for the defeat of Germany and for the destruction of Nazism. Although they did not attempt to settle all matters involving Germany's future, they did declare their intention to take the necessary steps to disarm and dismember the Third Reich. For the moment, they agreed that: (1) Germany would be divided into four zones of military occupation, one of which was to be administered by the French, the others by each of the Big Three. (2) Germany would pay reparations (the figure of $20 billion was set as the basis of discussion), and a commission was to be set up in Moscow to work out particulars.

The Big Three also ironed out their differences over postwar international cooperation, and settled the problem of voting procedure in the Security Council of the United Nations organization, which was to be set up in the near future. This agreement, revealed during the following month, specified that the permanent members of the Security Council would have the veto power over all major

The final dinner at the Yalta Conference. In the foreground, Secretary of State Stettinius raises his glass in what appears to be a toast. On the opposite side of the table, from left to right: Stalin, Roosevelt, Churchill, Molotov.

acts of that body. It also provided that the Soviet Union would have three votes in the General Assembly, since the Ukraine and Byelo-Russia were to be recognized for voting purposes as independent nations.*

The Polish issue was the knottiest problem to confront the conferees at Yalta. The Russians insisted that the so-called Curzon line of 1919 (settled at that time as the eastern boundary of Poland) be adopted now, with some small changes. Roosevelt and Churchill agreed, stipulating that Poland should be compensated for the loss of territory in the east by annexations of German territory in the west. More difficult was the question of the government of Poland. Stalin wanted the western powers to recognize the Soviet-controlled Lublin government, but Roosevelt and Churchill refused. In the end, Stalin promised that the Lublin government would be broadened to include democratic elements, and that free elections would be held in Poland. It was clear to the western leaders, however, that they had failed to win this point.

For eastern Europe generally, the Soviets promised "broadly representative governments." They secured the establishment of a new Yugoslav government under Marshal Tito, and agreed that this government would be broadened by including members of the old parliament who had not collaborated with the Nazis.

Besides these publicly announced features of the Yalta Conference, a number of secret agreements were made. Some of these dealt with the repatriation of citizens in liberated areas. One agreement, involving the Far East, was later widely criticized. The Soviets promised that they would enter the war against Japan when the fighting in Europe was over. In return, the United States (with Britain's concurrence) promised: (1) Recognition of

the existing status of the Mongolian Peoples' Republic (Outer Mongolia), which had detached itself from China and had accepted Russian protection. (2) Restoration to Russia of territory and rights held in the Far East before the Russo-Japanese War of 1904-1905, including the return to Russia of the southern half of the island of Sakhalin. (3) The transfer from Japan to Russia of the Kurile Islands. Since these Far Eastern arrangements violated promises that had been made to Chiang Kai-shek at Cairo, his reluctant consent had to be secured, and this unpalatable task was left to Roosevelt.

For the concessions made to Russia at Yalta, Roosevelt was later subjected to a vast amount of criticism in the United States. Some of this criticism, his defenders have replied, rested upon a failure to bear in mind the military situation existing at the time of the Yalta Conference, particularly in eastern Europe. Russia had overrun almost all of eastern Europe, including Poland. For the western Allies to try to bring about the outright liberation of any of this territory would have required that Russia be ousted by force. Presumably this would have meant a third world war following immediately upon the heels of World War II, a development that would have outraged public opinion in Britain and America. Short of exerting force, there was little to do but to extract from the Soviet leaders promises and declarations of good intent, though the western leaders knew that these could not be enforced.

By early 1944, Churchill seems to have become increasingly intent upon checking the spread of communism. Even before the Casablanca meeting, he had proposed to Roosevelt that the western powers "strike at the under-belly of the Axis in effective strength and in the shortest time." The "under-belly" was Italy and the Balkans. On a general Mediterranean front, the Allies might expect cooperation from the Turks and from Greek and Yugoslav guerillas. Possibly at that early date, the goals Churchill had in mind were largely military. But the anti-

* The Russians began by demanding 16 votes for the various associated republics of the Soviet Union, arguing that only this would give them comparable influence with what they felt would be American and British Commonwealth blocs. Roosevelt replied that by the same reckoning the United States should have 48 votes. Of course, it was membership and voting procedure in the Security Council, not in the General Assembly, that mattered most.

communist political objective soon became important in his thinking, for in May, 1944, he sent two memoranda to Foreign Minister Anthony Eden in which he suggested that "we are approaching a showdown with the Russians," and asked, "Are we going to acquiesce in the communisation of the Balkans and perhaps of Italy?" Had a Balkan thrust been undertaken by the Allies, and had Allied armies taken up strategic positions along the borders of the Balkan nations, the countries of central and southeastern Europe would have been encouraged to lean to the democratic camp, an unlikely development should Russian armies alone dominate the region.

Since this strategy had been rejected by the United States, Churchill next tried to restrain Russia by bargaining with the Kremlin. In the summer of 1944, before the Red Army penetrated into the Balkans, he had proposed to Stalin (without informing Roosevelt) that the Balkans in effect be divided into spheres of influence, with the Soviet Union controlling Rumania and Bulgaria and Britain controlling Greece and Yugoslavia. Roosevelt spoke out against the arrangement when he was informed of it, but agreed to give it a three-months trial. In October, 1944, Churchill and Eden visited Moscow and made the arrangement more firm and detailed. This hard-boiled bargaining remained unpalatable to American leaders. Before coming to Yalta, Roosevelt made it clear that he would not be bound by the agreements reached in Moscow and would insist on retaining "complete freedom of action." In repudiating the spheres-of-influence bargain, he was expressing an idealistic view of postwar arrangements that would probably have met with the approval of the American public. The more idealistic arrangements for a democratic eastern Europe that he sought at Yalta were unrealizable in the face of Russian military power. But at Yalta he gave to the Russians nothing in eastern Europe that they did not already hold.

It has been more difficult for Roosevelt's defenders to justify the territorial and other concessions made to Russia in the Far East. To be sure, these concessions rested upon the assumption that Soviet intervention against Japan, which was offered in return, would be of great military value to the western Allies, and that it would save hundreds of thousands of American lives in the Pacific war. But at Moscow in October, 1943, Stalin had already told Hull of the Soviet intention to enter the war in the Far East when Germany was crushed, and it is doubtful that Stalin's reaffirmation of the pledge at Yalta represented any real gain. More important, Russia's intervention was not even needed. The atomic bomb had not yet been tested and proved, but Japan was already on the verge of collapse as a consequence of aerial bombardment and naval blockade. This state of affairs was suggested in intelligence reports that were already available in Washington. Acting on the basis of obsolete information, the Joint Chiefs of Staff at Yalta urged upon Roosevelt the importance of Soviet cooperation against Japan. Thus advised, Roosevelt made his concessions. There can be little doubt, however, that, even without the concurrence of Roosevelt and Churchill at Yalta, Russia would have seized what she wanted on the Asiatic mainland.

In sum, there were two broad lines of action that might have been pursued before Yalta. Britain and America might have committed themselves to the conventional balance-of-power strategy so often employed in the past. Concretely, this course would have involved partitioning the Balkans and eastern Europe, building up Japan and Germany as military powers to act as balances to the Soviet Union, and abandoning at once almost all hopes of postwar cooperation. Though Churchill seems to have favored some features of this strategy, a great body of opinion in both Britain and America looked to another course. This other course involved abandoning the old balance-of-power system—which had not prevented wars in the past—in favor of a concert of interests among the great powers based upon mutual concessions and mutual understanding. Secretary Hull, returning from the Moscow Conference of 1943, avowed his conviction that there would "no longer be need for spheres of influence, for alliances, for balance of power, or any other of the special arrangements through which, in the unhappy past, the nations strove to safeguard their security or to promote their interests." And Roosevelt, returning from Yalta, expressed a similar belief that the old system was dead. Had he failed at Yalta to safeguard the possibility of continued American-Soviet cooperation, he would also have been severely criticized.

In any event, disillusionment set in early. Before long, Roosevelt was growing indignant over what he called "vile misrepresentations" made by the Soviets about Allied policies in Italy, and over Russian attitudes toward the United Nations organization and eastern Europe. On April 1, 1945, less than two weeks before his death, he sent to Stalin a sharp message expressing his disappointment at "the lack of progress made in carrying out . . . the political decisions which we reached at Yalta, particularly those relating to the Polish question." Even before the war was over, the grand coalition was on its way toward breaking up.

Creating the U.N. At Yalta, plans had been drawn up to call a meeting at San Francisco in April, 1945, to draft a charter for the United Nations organization. Even before the war ended, two conferences of experts had drawn up plans for the postwar world. The first conference, held at Bretton Woods, New Hampshire, in 1944, and attended by representatives of 44 nations, set up an International Monetary Fund to stabilize national currencies, and an International Bank for Reconstruction and Development to extend loans to nations that needed economic rehabilitation. The second conference, held at Dumbarton Oaks near Washington, D. C., and concluded in October, 1944, drafted plans for the U.N. Charter. When the San Francisco Conference met in April, 1945, Franklin D. Roosevelt had died, but plans were carried out for setting up the international organization in which he had come to put increasing hope. The delegates, representing 50 nations, witnessed a sharp dispute between the Russians and the western powers. A number of issues were involved, including again the troublesome Polish question. Voting procedure alone almost wrecked the meeting. The Russians interpreted the Yalta agreement to mean that a single power could use the veto to prevent even the discussion of questions whose settlement might require force. Over this interpretation, the Americans threatened to withdraw. But President Truman, acting through Harry L. Hopkins in Moscow, secured an agreement from Stalin that the veto would not be used to choke off discussion. With this understanding, it became possible to complete arrangements.

The charter of the United Nations provided for two major agencies: (1) a General Assembly, in which all nations had one vote —except Russia, which had three. The General Assembly had the power to discuss all questions falling within the scope of the United Nations Charter and to recommend suitable action to the Security Council. (2) The Security Council, composed of eleven members, was to remain in continuous session and to settle international disputes. On this body, the Big Five—the Big Three plus France and China—were to have permanent seats; the other seats were to rotate for two-year terms among the other members. The fundamental initiative and authority in the United Nations rested with the Security Council; the General Assembly served more as a discussion agency. The Assembly was particularly valuable to the small nations as a forum in which they could win a hearing for their views. Four other agencies completed the structure: an International Court of Justice; a Secretariat to coordinate the work of the U.N.; an Economic and Social Council; and a Trusteeship Council to handle colonies taken from Japan and Italy.

Although the U.N. Charter laid the basis for constructive cooperation among its members, the fact that the veto power could be used by any permanent member of its Security Council—a provision that was desired both by the Russians and the Americans— indicated that the Council would be unable to oppose aggression by any of the major powers.

Growing Tensions.   The United Nations held its first meetings in London in 1946, but in time moved to New York City where handsome buildings had been provided as its permanent headquarters. From the beginning the U.N. was split by major disagreements which divided the nations into two blocs, one led by Russia, the other by the United States. Russia began at an early date to use her veto power repeatedly and irresponsibly, and at one point, in a dispute over Iran, Russian delegates walked out of a Security Council session. Russia opposed the creation of an international police force, fearing that it might become a powerful agency for an organization in which Russia would be in the minority. The defeat of this idea dealt a serious blow to the hopes of advocates of collective security.

An important difference arose during 1946 over international disarmament and the control of atomic energy. In June of that year, Bernard M. Baruch submitted to the recently created Atomic Energy Commission of the U.N. a plan for international control of atomic weapons. It called for an international agency that would own and operate all the facilities for mining ores and producing atomic explosives and would have the power to inspect atomic installations in any country to see that all agreements governing the control of atomic energy were being observed. Russia, however, still far behind the United States in atomic research, and fearing that the international authority would be controlled by an American-dominated coalition, countered by proposing an international agreement to abandon atomic warfare. This idea had more significance as propaganda than as an enforceable arrangement. The two sides were so far apart that no agreement could be reached; and later, in 1949, after Russia exploded her own atomic bomb, the United States brought forth its plan again, but with no more success than before.

II.   THE TRUMAN ADMINISTRATION

With the death of Roosevelt in 1945, the leadership of the United States fell to a midwestern American with no experience in world affairs other than his service as an officer in World War I. A small businessman before he entered politics in his home state of Missouri, Harry S. Truman had won himself a good reputation during World War II as chairman of a Senate committee investigating wartime contracts. At first rather overawed by the office he had inherited ("Boys, if you ever pray, pray for me now," he said to reporters when he heard of Roosevelt's death), Truman became increasingly confident as his months in the White House wore on. To his administration fell the burden not only of continuing the search for peace, but also of guiding the nation through the transition period from war to peace.

Demobilization.   At the end of the war, much pressure existed both within the army and among civilians for the return of American soldiers from overseas. The government responded so quickly that for a time it appeared that there might not be enough soldiers remaining in the defeated countries to carry out occupation duties. In May, 1946, the second peacetime draft in American history called for the conscription of men over 18 for one year. But in spite of the draft, rapid demobilization still continued to weaken our military strength; and this development, coupled with the abrupt termination of lend-lease in the summer of 1945, weakened the position of the country in international affairs.

As early as the mid-summer of 1946, the huge American wartime army had been cut to 1,500,000 men, and the navy was down to 700,000 men. The discharged soldiers, eagerly returning home, were aided by the "G.I. Bill of Rights," passed during the Roosevelt administration in June, 1944. This measure entitled veterans to unemployment insurance for a year, guaranteed them government loans for building homes or establishing businesses, and offered them subsidized education in colleges or vocational schools proportionate to the length of their military service.

Economic demobilization was also carried out quickly. Many American businessmen had always been restless under the price controls established by the Office of Price Administration during the war and had argued that inflation could be stopped simply by increasing production and permitting expanding supplies to keep prices down at their normal level. When Congress renewed the Price Control Bill in 1946, and extended the life of the O.P.A. for one year, it crippled the powers of that agency so drastically that Truman vetoed the bill and permitted price controls to lapse on July 1. Soon Congress accepted a second bill, but prices had already got out of hand. In November, all controls except those on rents, sugar, and rice were ended. As a result, sharp inflation set in just when the Republicans were conducting a vigorous campaign to regain control of Congress. This price inflation, combined with a brief but acute meat shortage, caused widespread discontent and seemed to augur ill for the future of the Democrats.

Labor Issues. A further cause for dissatisfaction with the Truman administration arose from a wave of strikes after the end of the war. The most severe were the strikes of the United Mine Workers in April, 1946, which caused President Truman to order the seizure of the mines. Eventually the mine workers made important wage gains. A still more controversial nation-wide railroad strike resulted in such prolonged and fruitless negotiations that President Truman seized the railroads in May, 1946, and asked Congress for drastic powers to save the country from economic paralysis. Only a last-minute settlement, concluded just before the President's appeal to Congress, prevented the passage of unprecedented labor-control measures. After 1946, the wave of strikes receded; during the period that followed, labor-management cooperation reached new heights with the signing of a number of labor contracts that were motivated by a new spirit of social responsibility on the part of both parties. The immediate result of the postwar labor discontent, however, was to arouse dissatisfaction with the administration both within the labor movement and within the ranks of labor's critics.

The congressional elections of 1946 gave the Republican party a majority in both houses of Congress. The Eightieth Congress, convening in January, 1947, passed measures that expressed the general conservative reaction against the New Deal era. President Truman vetoed a tax bill passed by Congress to benefit persons in the upper-income brackets, and his veto was narrowly sustained. But the conservatives won an important victory with the passage in June, 1947, of the Taft-Hartley Act, which deprived labor of some of the gains it had made during the New Deal period. It outlawed the closed shop and a number of union practices that were deemed unfair. It permitted employers to sue unions for broken contracts or for damages inflicted during strikes. It forced unions to accept a 60-day "cooling-off period" before striking, required them to make their financial statements public, forbade them to contribute to political campaigns, put an end to the checkoff system in which employers help collect union dues, and required union leaders to file affidavits that they were not communists before their unions could enjoy privileges under the National Labor Relations Board. Truman vetoed this measure, but this time Congress overrode his veto. Labor leaders denounced the Taft-Hartley Act as a "slave bill," but it did not prevent further substantial gains in union organization. From 1945 to 1952, union membership, including the A.F.L.,

C.I.O., and independent unions, increased from about 14,621,000 to about 17,000,000.

The Election of 1948.   Republican successes in 1946 suggested to most observers that after 16 years the Republican party would almost surely return to power in the presidential election of 1948. Not only did the Republican cause seem resurgent, but the Democratic party was divided. Henry A. Wallace, Secretary of Commerce during the first Truman administration, had attacked the administration's policy of firm resistance to Russian penetration. He had formed a Progressive party which threatened to detach from the Democrats some of the liberal and staunchly pacifist segments of their party. This threatened split seemed enough in itself to guarantee a Republican victory. The Republicans re-nominated their candidate of 1944, Governor Thomas E. Dewey of New York, and adopted a conservative internationalist platform. The Democrats, having no choice and no hope, re-nominated Truman. Their platform denounced the record of the Eightieth Congress and the Taft-Hartley Act, praised the domestic and foreign policies of Roosevelt and Truman, and included a strong civil-rights plank calling for the establishment of a Fair Employment Practices Commission and the enactment of federal anti-lynching and anti-poll tax laws. This last plank em-

bodied a strong appeal to the increasingly important Negro voter.

The domination of the Democratic party by liberal and civil-rights supporters touched off a southern rebellion. A States' Rights Democratic party was formed by insurgent southerners, or Dixiecrats, in July at Birmingham. They nominated Governor J. Strom Thurmond of South Carolina and Governor Fielding L. Wright of Mississippi to head their ticket. It was their hope that they could throw the election into the House of Representatives, where as a bloc they would have great influence in the final choice of a president.

Facing the Dixiecrat split on the right and the Progressive party on the left, Truman's cause seemed hopeless; but the departure of the southerners only increased his appeal to the strategically important Negro voters of the North, while Wallace's campaign, which was quietly manipulated by a small group of communists and their sympathizers, only served to dramatize the fact that the extreme left was also outside the Democratic ranks. While Governor Dewey was conducting a self-confident but extraordinarily vague campaign, President Truman stormed up and down the land vigorously denouncing "the no good, good-for-nothing Eightieth Congress." His approach, not Dewey's, registered with the voters. To the surprise of the world, Truman won in the greatest upset in American political history. When the ballots were counted, he had 24,105,000 popular and 303 electoral votes to Dewey's 21,969,000 popular and 189 electoral votes. Thurmond won the electoral votes of South Carolina, Alabama, Mississippi, and Louisiana. Wallace, whose appeal had faded from week to week, received 1,156,000 popular votes.

The Fair Deal.   Feeling that he had received a popular mandate to carry on what he called his Fair Deal program, Truman now drew up a program of legislation intended to alter the course set by the Eightieth Congress. At most vital points he was blocked by a coalition of Republicans and conserva-

Election of 1948

Electoral Vote
Truman 303
Dewey 189   Thurmond 39

Truman, in a moment of triumph, enjoys evidences of premature optimism in the opposition press.

tive Democrats, but in 1949 and 1950 he secured an amendment to the Fair Labor Standards Act (see p. 667) which increased the minimum wage from 40 to 75 cents an hour. A new Social Security Act was passed in August, 1950, increasing by almost 10 million the number of workers eligible for benefits. A National Housing Act, passed in July, 1949, was another important victory, for it provided large sums to cities for aid in slum clearance and for the construction of over 800,000 units for low-income families. Congress, however, defeated an ambitious plan for stabilizing farm income, the Brannan Plan, and refused to repeal the Taft-Hartley Act as the President wished. Instead, it passed amendments that modified the measure along lines desired by labor. Congress also passed the Twenty-second Amendment to the Constitution, which limited the president to two terms in office. This amendment was finally ratified by the states in February, 1951. As the incumbent, President Truman was specifically excepted from this amendment, which was inspired by long-standing Republican dislike of Franklin D. Roosevelt and by general public suspicion of prolonged presidencies.

III. THE COLD WAR

After 1947, attempts at cooperation between East and West broke down almost completely, and a persistent and ominous hostility prevailed. In the spring of 1946, Winston Churchill, speaking at Fulton, Missouri, had already pointed out that Soviet tyranny was spreading and becoming more implacable. From the Baltic to the Adriatic, he observed, "an iron curtain has descended across the Continent." Bernard Baruch, the perennial adviser to American presidents, made a speech in South Carolina almost a year later in which he observed: "Let us not be deceived—today we are in the midst of a cold war." These two harsh phrases—"iron curtain" and "cold war"—evoke the atmosphere of the divided postwar world.

The Conquered Nations. The tension between East and West affected all aspects of the postwar settlements. At the Potsdam

739

Conference, held in July, 1945, Truman, Stalin, and Prime Minister Clement Attlee (replacing Churchill and representing the new Labour government in England), arrived at an agreement concerning the administration of Germany. They left the management of the country in the hands of an Allied Control Council of American, English, French, and Russian generals in charge of four military zones. The question of Poland's western frontier was also taken up. The Russians had already turned over to the provisional Polish government all German territory east of a line marked by the Oder-Neisse River. The western Allies felt compelled to accept this as a temporary arrangement, after the Soviets reaffirmed that the final determination of the Polish-German frontier would await the peace settlement. Finally, the Potsdam Conference set up machinery to negotiate peace treaties with Italy, Bulgaria, Rumania, Hungary, and Finland. A Council of Foreign Ministers of the United States, Great Britain, Russia, and China was created to work out these treaties immediately, and also was directed to meet regularly four times a year to discuss other problems. The peace treaties were drawn up by the Council of Foreign Ministers and signed in February, 1947. But by the time these various settlements were made, relations between the United States and Russia had deteriorated so hopelessly that no immediate effort was made to draft general treaties of peace with conquered Japan and Germany.

During 1945 and 1946, the leading members of the Nazi hierarchy were brought to trial at Nuremberg before an international military court. They were charged with responsibility for bringing about the war and for conducting it in ways that violated fundamental human decency. The proceedings at this trial revealed to the world the full story of Nazi barbarity. Ten war criminals were executed, two committed suicide, and several others were imprisoned. Other trials in Japan led to the execution of former Premier Tojo and six other war leaders, and further trials resulted in sentences for more than 4,000 other war criminals.

The occupation of Germany provided an additional source of strife between East and West. In 1948, various irritations arising out of the administration of Germany and the reparations issue caused the Russians to order a blockade of Berlin, which, though situated deep in their zone, was jointly administered by Russia and the West. As a result of the blockade, Germans in the western zone of Berlin were threatened with starvation. The Allies met the challenge by developing the "air lift," an ingenious system by which food and supplies were delivered to the city by continuously shuttling cargo planes. In the end, Russia gave in, and in May, 1949, she lifted the blockade on the understanding that the Council of Foreign Ministers would review the whole German problem.

Finding themselves unable to reach a basic agreement with Russia on the status of Germany, the western powers met in June, 1948, and gave their consent to the creation of an unarmed West German state. A German Federal Republic, embracing the three western zones, was set up at Bonn in September, 1949. In the new state, Allied authority was still exercised through a High Commission representing the United States, France,

and the United Kingdom. In the following month, the Soviets established an eastern German state called the German Democratic Republic. Now there were two Germanies, one democratic and tied to the western powers, the other totalitarian and Russian-dominated.

The administration of conquered Japan had been left in the hands of General Douglas MacArthur, though he was offered advice by an Allied Council in Tokyo that included delegates from Russia, China, and England. A Russian request to join in the occupation of Japan was turned down by the United States. Under American direction, a new constitution was put into effect on May 3, 1947, which broke up landed estates and economic monopolies and imposed perpetual disarmament on Japan. Many social reforms were carried out, and the occupation of Japan by American troops proceeded far more smoothly than might have been expected in view of the bitterness of the war just ended. It was not until near the end of 1951 that a general Japanese peace treaty was concluded, to which there were 49 signers (Russia was not included). Japan's "full sovereignty" was restored, but she had to renounce all her island possessions and mandates.

While American policy experienced a mixture of successes and reverses in Europe, in the Orient it received a major setback that had many domestic repercussions. To the intense disappointment of a great many Americans, postwar China passed into the hands of the communist forces. Soon after the defeat of Japan, a strong communist movement, which had been developing in China for over 20 years, began to contest control of the country with the Nationalist government of Chiang Kai-shek. General George C. Marshall went to China in 1945-1946 in an unsuccessful attempt to arrange a peace between these powerful factions, and he returned greatly disillusioned with both sides. By 1950, most of China had fallen under the control of a communist state in close alliance with the Soviet Union, and Chiang had withdrawn to Formosa. A strong faction in the United

States felt that anti-communist forces in China had not been given enough support. But Chiang's government had not won popular backing in China, and the administration concluded that the United States could not afford to prop up a clearly inefficient and allegedly uncooperative regime. In fact, to save Chiang might have required full-scale military intervention. The United States, unlike England and most other major countries, refused to recognize the People's Republic of China, or to consent to its admission to the U.N. Instead, it continued to recognize Chiang's Nationalist government on Formosa.

The Truman Doctrine. President Truman, however, was by no means complacent in the face of growing Russian influence in the world. He chose Greece as the place to call a halt to the spread of communism in Europe. A conservative Greek government, which the British had strengthened so that the country was preserved from conquest by the communists, seemed about to fall early in 1947 when the British ambassador notified the United States that Britain would soon have to withdraw from Greece. In admitting that Britain could no longer bear the burden of resisting communism in that area, the British were implicitly acknowledging the end of their supremacy in the Mediterranean. It became clear that leadership in the defense of the free world, with all the obligations it entailed, would now pass to the United States.

Truman took up the challenge. In March, 1947, he went before Congress to ask for $400 million to assist Greece and Turkey and to protect the Middle East from communism. He also made a bold statement of principle, which become known as the Truman Doctrine:

I believe that it must be the policy of the United States to support free peoples who are resisting attempted subjugation by armed minorities or by outside pressure. . . . The free peoples of the world look to us for support in maintaining their freedoms. If we falter in our leadership, we may endanger the peace of the world —and we shall surely endanger the welfare of this nation.

With the help of Senator Arthur Vandenberg of Michigan, the Republican Chairman of the Senate Committee on Foreign Relations, who had formerly been an isolationist, Truman won sufficient support from Republicans in Congress to get his bill passed in May, 1947. Between 1947 and 1950, the United States spent about $659 million on aid for Greece and Turkey. The economy of Turkey was stabilized and Greece was saved from communist conquest.

The Marshall Plan. A more constructive and imaginative approach to the problems of western Europe was announced by Secretary of State George C. Marshall on June 5, 1947, in a commencement address at Harvard University. Marshall declared that a stable European economy was essential to the preservation of democracy in that area and that the United States was willing to help those countries that would cooperate in pursuing their own recovery. As Marshall put it:

Our policy is directed not against any country or doctrine, but against hunger, poverty, desperation, and chaos. Its purpose should be the revival of a working economy in the world so as to permit the emergence of political and social conditions in which free institutions can exist. . . . Any government that is willing to assist in the task of recovery will find full cooperation, I am sure, on the part of the United States government.

The European powers were quick to take advantage of Marshall's offer. But the Russians and their satellites, who were invited to participate in the plan, soon proved sullenly hostile. Nevertheless, in July, 1947, representatives from a number of non-communist European nations, including Britain, France, and Italy, met at Paris and established a committee that drew up a broad plan for European recovery contingent on large-scale

assistance and loans from the United States. The greater part of their demand was met by Congress in the Economic Cooperation Bill. Isolationists throughout the country opposed the bill, but liberals and internationalists in both parties rallied to its support, as did labor and farm groups. In February, 1948, when a communist *coup* destroyed the democracy of Czechoslovakia, the need for American action became painfully evident. Finally, in April, 1948, Congress passed a bill providing for $5.3 billion for the first 12 months of Marshall Plan aid, thus launching the European Recovery Program (E.R.P.). E.R.P., under which the United States spent about $12 billion, continued for three years and then was supplanted by the Mutual Security Agency.

American aid under the Marshall Plan gave an immense stimulus to economic recovery and provided a formidable barrier against further communist gains in western Europe. It was followed in 1949 by President Truman's "Point Four Program"—so called because it was part of a four-point plan for fighting communism in which he advocated steps to make scientific and industrial knowledge available "for the improvement and growth of undeveloped areas." In 1950, Congress began voting appropriations for this purpose and from 1951 to 1954 authorized nearly $400 million. The Point Four Program began positive efforts to propagate American influence in economically backward areas of the world, not by exporting arms, but by exporting knowledge and skills.

The Atlantic Alliance. As the western nations grew increasingly fearful that Soviet tactics would prevent the United Nations from keeping the peace, they began to feel the necessity of a western European alliance. At Brussels on March 17, 1948, Britain, France, the Netherlands, Belgium, and Luxembourg signed a treaty of economic cooperation and military alliance, a step that inspired further American interest in European efforts. In June, 1948, the Senate adopted a resolution by Senator Vandenberg to the effect that the United States should seek peace through collective defense arrangements, regional or otherwise, with friendly powers. The Vandenberg resolution led to the North Atlantic Treaty, signed on April 4, 1949, by 12 nations of the North Atlantic and western European areas. The contracting parties agreed to settle their own disputes peacefully and to help each other develop their capacity to resist armed attack. Article 5 of this treaty stated that an armed attack upon any member would be considered an attack upon all, and promised that each would go to the assistance of the party attacked by whatever action was thought necessary, "including the use of armed force." This arrangement was to last for 20 years.

To build up the military strength of the nations participating in the North Atlantic Treaty Organization (NATO), Congress passed the Mutual Defense Assistance Act in September, 1949. From October of that year to the end of 1953, the United States supplied almost $6 billion worth of arms and military material to European allies and another $1.7 billion to other countries. During the same period, the European powers spent immense sums on their own defense and greatly enhanced their military forces. The military command of NATO was placed under the direction of General Dwight D. Eisenhower, who was then president of Columbia University.

IV. THE IMPACT OF KOREA

The Korean War.   In 1950, the cold war suddenly grew hotter and more dangerous when on June 25 the North Koreans launched an attack against South Korea. At the Cairo Conference (see p. 731), it had been decided that Korea, which had been held by the Japanese during the war, should be made independent. After Japan's defeat, Russia and the United States had temporarily divided the country into two zones at the 38th parallel, presumably just long enough to receive the Japanese surrender. But the Russians were not prepared to leave so quickly, and the split between North and South Korea persisted. North of the 38th parallel, the government was completely under communist influence, while to the south a western-oriented republic was set up. North Korea was recognized by Russia and its satellites, and South Korea was recognized by the U.N. Assembly and by the United States. When the Russian and American occupying armies withdrew in 1948 and 1949 respectively, the Russians left the North Koreans heavily armed. As a consequence, they were able to slash southward against little resistance when they decided to attack in 1950.

The North Korean invasion posed a painful problem for the democracies, and President Truman showed vigor and courage in meeting it. If the democracies were to permit South Korea to be overrun, as long ago they had permitted Czechoslovakia to fall to the Nazis, the door would be thrown open to a series of incursions by Soviet power in various parts of the world, and the confidence of nations that depended on the United States for security against Russian aggression would be undermined. On June 27, 1950, the Security Council of the United Nations, in the absence of its Soviet members, resolved that the member nations should furnish help to South Korea. On the same day, President Truman ordered American naval and air units to support the South Koreans, and a few days later he ordered ground troops to be sent to the Korean front. Other nations responded to the Security Council's call for help, but American forces comprised about four-fifths of the U.N. forces sent to fight. The U.N. troops in turn were more than matched in numbers by the army South Korea eventually put in the field.

The Korean fighting was as savage and as costly as many of the campaigns of World War II had been. By the end of August,

1950, the outnumbered United Nations forces had been pushed back to a small and precarious bridgehead around the port of Pusan. But new forces were now being thrown in, and in September the United Nations troops, under the command of General Douglas MacArthur, began a counter-drive with a brilliant amphibious landing at the port of Inchon behind the North Korean line. A full-scale offensive followed in November, which rapidly drove the North Koreans back toward the 38th parallel and destroyed a considerable part of the North Korean army. Taking advantage of this moment of superiority, and fortified by a resolution of the U.N. General Assembly calling for "a unified, independent and democratic Korea," U.N. forces pushed across the 38th parallel on October 9, 1951, and pressed on toward the Yalu River, the northern boundary of Korea. But late in November, Red China came to the aid of the North Koreans, threw huge armies into the fray, launched a massive attack against the U.N. armies, and soon thrust them below the 38th parallel, recapturing the South Korean capital of Seoul in the process.

General MacArthur grew increasingly dissatisfied with the restraints imposed upon him by the U.N.'s political strategy of conducting a limited war for limited objectives. He publicly expressed his dissatisfaction with the policies of the U.N. and the administration, complaining especially against the ban on bombing Manchuria, from which supplies were flowing to the North Korean forces. He preferred an all-out effort to win total victory, even at the risk of becoming involved in open war with Red China, a development that many sober observers believed might lead to a world war with the Soviet Union. General Omar N. Bradley, Chairman of the Joint Chiefs of Staff, warned that a major war against Red China would be "the wrong war at the wrong place, in the wrong time and with the wrong enemy." MacArthur's insubordination finally led President Truman to relieve him of his Korean command and of

his control of the occupation forces of Japan on April 11, 1951.

A storm of opposition now broke out from a great many Americans who sympathized wholeheartedly with MacArthur's impatience. MacArthur returned to the United States and eloquently presented his point of view to Congress, but as he toured the country, speaking before a series of rallies, his popularity faded very rapidly. Although it thus seemed that the great majority of Americans were opposed to risking a full-scale war, still the Korean stalemate left feelings of acute dissatisfaction.

The stalemate passed into an uneasy armistice. On June 23, 1951, the head of the Soviet delegation in the U.N. suggested that the Korean conflict might be settled if both parties were willing. This announcement led to armistice negotiations, beginning July 10, 1951, and proceeding with incredible and exasperating delay until July 23, 1953. It proved impossible to settle quickly the location of a cease-fire line, to work out machinery for enforcing the armistice, or to solve the hotly argued question of how war prisoners should be repatriated. The repatriation issue became especially acute when U.N. spokesmen refused to consent to the return of thousands of Chinese and North Korean prisoners who declared their reluctance to go back and live under communism. While the debates went on, the war continued in a somewhat muted form.

The Age of Suspicion.   The increasing tension of the Cold War, which culminated in the Korean conflict, engendered a mood of anxiety and frustration in the American public. Having just finished a long war, Americans were naturally discouraged over their involvement in the indecisive Korean action within only a few short years. The rapid dissolution of the optimistic expectations of international cooperation that had existed toward the end of the war increased their disappointment; and, aware that the Soviets now possessed the atomic bomb, they became increasingly sensitive about threats to their internal security. Even before the Korean War broke out, the case of Alger Hiss, a former employee of the State Department, had attracted wide attention. Accused by a former communist agent, Whittaker Chambers, of having turned over classified government documents to him in 1937, Hiss persistently denied the charges. Since the alleged delivery of the documents had taken place over seven years earlier, Hiss could not, under the law, be prosecuted for violation of security regulations. But he was indicted for perjury, convicted in the second of two trials, and in January, 1950, was sentenced to five years in prison. To the American public, the thought of a trusted official being involved with foreign agents was appalling. The presence of communists in other government posts at various times in the past also came to light.

In September, 1950, Congress passed the McCarran Internal Security Act, which required all members of the Communist party and of Communist-front organizations to register with the Attorney-General, forbade aliens who had been communists to enter the country, and authorized the president to hold communists in detention camps in the event of war. President Truman, charging that this measure punished opinions rather than actions, vetoed it; but the act was passed over his veto. Ten years earlier, in 1940, Congress had passed the Smith Alien Registration Act making it illegal for anyone to teach or advocate the overthrow of any government in the United States by force, or to organize or join any group teaching such a doctrine. In 1949, the Truman administration invoked this act to convict 11 leading Communist party officials. In June, 1951, the Supreme Court, in the case of *Dennis et al. v. U.S.*, upheld the convictions and found the Smith Act constitutional. The communist leaders began serving prison terms of three to five years.

In the spring of 1950, Senator Joseph McCarthy of Wisconsin, who had won a close election four years earlier, made a speech before the Women's Republican Club in Wheeling, West Virginia, in which he charged the State Department with being infested with communists. Originally, he asserted that he had a list of 205 subversives; later he reduced it to 57; and in the end he was unable to substantiate any of his charges. Early in the following year, however, as the new Chairman of the Senate Committee on Government Operation, McCarthy made great capital of the communist issue. Soon the word "McCarthyism" had passed into the language as an expression for reckless and indiscriminate charges of political disloyalty.

One of the most important consequences of the Korean War was a renewed military mobilization. Increasing employment and the decline in the production of civilian supplies sent prices upward. Congress was now

Action in the Korean War. Men of an anti-tank team, United States 77th Infantry, use mine detectors on a road. Machines wait while men clear the ground for advance.

led by men hostile to rigid controls, and President Truman was unable to secure wage and price controls effective enough to hold the line against inflation. As a consequence, prices zoomed to new heights in 1951. Moreover, the discontent over foreign policy aroused by the Korean crisis inspired an effort in Congress to cut European aid drastically. The administration resisted this move, but the Senate passed a resolution in April, 1951, which, after reaffirming the need for maintaining troops in Europe and the importance of the North Atlantic Treaty, nonetheless asserted that no more than four divisions of ground troops could be sent to Europe without the approval of Congress.

The Election of 1952.   As the election of 1952 grew near, it became apparent that the Democrats were losing favor with the public. Concern over Korea, discontent with high prices, nervousness over the loyalty problem, and other grievances arising out of the war situation damaged Democratic prestige. In 1951, a number of petty scandals also came to light involving the use of influence by persons close to the administration, and the Kefauver Committee of the Senate probed into connections between gangsters and political machines in several cities. In addition, financial irregularities were unearthed in the Internal Revenue Bureau. The fact that the Democrats themselves made most of these revelations did not prevent the administration from being branded as corrupt in the eyes of many voters. In 1952, moreover, a threatened steel strike caused Truman to seize the mills avowedly to maintain defense production. But the Supreme Court nullified the President's action, and the strike went on. The union demands were met, but only at the cost of raising steel prices, and again the administration was widely criticized.

The Republicans met in convention at Chicago on July 7, 1952. After a struggle between the isolationists and ultra-conservatives who supported Senator Robert A. Taft, and the party moderates who favored General Eisenhower, the convention nominated Eisenhower. The Democrats needed a new leader, for President Truman had announced in March, 1952, that he would not be a candidate again. Eventually, after a contest with Senator Estes Kefauver of Tennessee, who had gained much renown for his crime investigations, Governor Adlai E. Stevenson of Illinois won the nomination.

Stevenson conducted a vigorous, witty, and unusually eloquent campaign, but he could not overcome the cumulative discontent of recent years and the acute crisis in public sentiment brought about by the Korean situation. In General Eisenhower, moreover, the Republicans had a candidate who was extraordinarily popular with all classes of Americans—indeed, he had been sought earlier as a candidate by the Democrats themselves. Eisenhower managed to satisfy both wings of the Republican party, struck hard at "corruption" in the Truman administration, capitalized on the anxiety over internal security, and, in an effective speech near the end of his campaign, promised to go to Korea as a prelude to bringing about a quick end of the war. At the polls, Stevenson was overwhelmed. Eisenhower received 33,824,000 votes, Stevenson 27,314,000. In the electoral college, the margin was 442 to 89, with the Republicans cutting into the traditionally Democratic South for the first time since 1928. After 20 years, Democratic supremacy had been broken.

V.   THE EISENHOWER ADMINISTRATION

The Korean Settlement.   Eisenhower was a soldier with wide experience in dealing with civilian authorities and in reconciling opposing political and military factions. And as President he was faced once again with the task of conciliation. Having held the support of both wings of the Republican party during the campaign, he now had to decide which would determine his policy. He decided to go along with the moderates at the cost of disappointing the extreme right wing. Far from attempting any drastic reversal of the policies of his Democratic predecessor, Eisenhower embraced many of them. In dealing with the Korean stalemate, he avoided the MacArthur policy of risking all-out war, and continued the Truman policy of seeking peace without total victory. But in this attempt he was more fortunate and more successful than his predecessor had been. He redeemed his dramatic campaign promise in December, 1952, by flying to Korea for a brief visit which itself had no immediate effect on the truce negotiations but which heightened Eisenhower's determination not to allow this drain on American resources to go on any longer than necessary.

On March 5, 1953, Joseph Stalin died in Moscow, and the attitude of the Kremlin toward the West now seemed to take a more promising tack. A new Soviet effort to cultivate influence in the world by adopting milder policies and a milder manner was reflected in the negotiations in Korea, and on July 27, 1953, armistice terms were finally signed. The communists agreed that prisoners who did not want to return to their homeland would be taken care of by neutral countries. A truce line very near the 38th parallel was finally accepted, and both sides withdrew some distance behind the existing battle line. A neutral commission was set up to enforce the armistice terms, and Korea was left a divided country.

In the three years of the Korean War, the United States had suffered more than 140,000 casualties in dead, wounded, and missing, and had spent over $15 billion. In the end, the United Nations had neither won nor lost, so far as the internal balance in Korea was concerned. But the primary purpose for which the war had been launched —to demonstrate that further communist aggression would be met with force—had been accomplished.

Domestic Policies.   The end of the Korean War eased domestic tensions and created an auspicious atmosphere for the success of the new administration. Eisenhower appointed a conservative cabinet in which big businessmen and Taft supporters had a prominent place. The Republican Congress set up a new cabinet post, the Department of Health, Education, and Welfare, to which Eisenhower appointed the second woman cabinet officer and the first from her party, Mrs. Oveta Culp Hobby of Texas.

Despite its conservative complexion, the Eisenhower administration left intact most of the social gains of the New Deal and Fair Deal period. Indeed, in the field of social security it added 10 million persons to the number of those entitled to receive benefits. The chief departures from Democratic policies were the following: (1) The Reconstruction Finance Corporation, created by Herbert Hoover and continued throughout successive Democratic regimes, was permitted to pass out of existence. (2) The price and wage controls imposed during the Korean War were eliminated. (3) The public housing program was limited to one year. (4) Many office-holders were cut from the federal payroll; the budget was drastically reduced from the levels set at the end of the Truman administration; and taxes were cut.

even at the cost of reducing the air force. Foreign aid was also scaled down. (5) The administration turned over offshore oil lands to the states along the Gulf of Mexico, a move that vastly stimulated private rather than federal exploitation of these resources. (6) The administration fostered private rather than public development of hydroelectric power, and passed an act empowering private industry to produce electricity through atomic power. (7) Farm supports were lowered. Faced by large surpluses of farm products that the government had accumulated in an attempt to maintain prices, Secretary of Agriculture Ezra Taft Benson at first reduced the level of price supports from 90 per cent of parity (see page 661), the figure at which the Truman administration had left it, to 75 per cent, and then secured congressional authorization for a flexible scale ranging from 82.5 to 90 per cent. These policies irritated many farmers.

President Eisenhower went to great lengths to pacify right-wing elements in his own party, who were disturbed at the administration's seeming liberalism. He sought the advice and support of Senator Taft, generally the spokesman for the group, and Taft, in turn, threw his great prestige and influence behind many administration measures. But in July, 1953, Taft died, and thereafter the Republican right wing grew increasingly discontented. Right-wingers strongly backed an amendment proposed by Senator Bricker of Ohio to limit the treaty-making powers of the president, a measure that was narrowly defeated in the Senate. Under their influence, Congress refused to revise the Taft-Hartley Act, and it set aside administration plans for a national health insurance system, federal aid to schools, and aid to states for highway construction. It did pass a housing program, but in a limited form. In May, 1954, however, Congress authorized the joint construction with Canada of a St. Lawrence seaway that would make it possible for ocean-going vessels to dock at Great Lakes ports.

Senator McCarthy, the Chairman of the Senate Committee on Government Operation, tried to put himself at the head of the anti-administration forces in the Republican party by bringing against the administration much the same kind of charge he had made against the Truman administration. When he accused the Department of the Army of being "soft" on communism, the Department countered with charges of its own about the Senator's efforts to use his influence improperly within the army. The whole controversy resulted in a prolonged televised Senate investigation of the affair that considerably diminished the Senator's public appeal. In the election of 1954, the usual anti-administration trend of off-year congressional elections again showed itself, and the Republicans lost both houses of Congress, the Senate by the margin of one vote. McCarthy now lost the chairmanship of his committee. Soon afterward, the Senate voted 67 to 22 to adopt a resolution in which he was "condemned" for conduct "unbecoming a Member of the United States Senate, . . . contrary to senatorial traditions," and tending "to bring the Senate into disrepute." Not since 1929 had the Senate so repudiated one of its members.

The Democratic Congress and the Republican administration worked together in reasonable harmony, though little positive legislation was passed. Congress authorized 45,000 new housing units, extended the Reciprocal Trade Agreements Act for three years, whereas the previous Congress had extended it only a year at a time, and raised the legal hourly minimum wage under the Fair Labor Standards Act from 75 cents to $1.00. Labor itself grew stronger in 1955 when representatives of the A.F.L. and C.I.O. agreed to merge their 15 million members and put an end to their 19-year-old feud.

The Court
and Desegregation.
Although foreign affairs continued to claim the greatest attention, at least one domestic event during

Eisenhower's first term would have been considered a revolutionary development at any period in American history—the Supreme Court's decision on segregation in education. This development was the outcome of a series of historical changes. Both world wars had encouraged the migration of Negroes to the North and had created an immense voting bloc of Negro citizens in strategic northern states. During the New Deal era, considerable gains had been made in the direction of equal rights for Negroes, and the developments of World War II had heightened American consciousness of this issue. Negroes were called upon, as they had been in the past, to make the same kind of sacrifice that other citizens made, and many Americans saw the hypocrisy in fighting a war against racism abroad when full rights were being denied to a large segment of the population at home. During the war, Congress created a Fair Employment Practices Committee (F.E.P.C.) to protect workers from discrimination on grounds of race, color, or creed. Other minorities, of course, benefited from this legislation, but it was of particular significance for Negroes. A bill to make the F.E.P.C. permanent was introduced into Congress in 1945, but it was blocked by a filibuster of southern congressmen. Still, many F.E.P.C.'s were set up during this period by state legislatures in the North.

In 1946, President Truman had appointed a Committee on Civil Rights, composed of distinguished citizens of both races, to inquire into the civil rights of minorities. This committee recommended a federal anti-lynching law, the abolition of poll-tax limitations on voting, the federal enforcement of fair employment practices, and the abandonment of segregation on trains and buses and in federally aided housing and education. The threat of a filibuster again cut off the possibility of action on civil rights, but during Truman's administration much progress was made in providing equal opportunities for Negroes in the armed services.

In May, 1954, the Supreme Court, in the case of *Brown* v. *Board of Education of Topeka,* handed down a momentous decision to the effect that the long-existing "separate but equal" school accommodations provided for Negroes in 17 states of the Union were a violation of the Fourteenth Amendment. Long before, the court had ruled in the case of *Plessy* v. *Ferguson* (1896) that providing separate but equal facilities satisfied the Fourteenth Amendment's requirement that the states give "equal protection of the laws." This doctrine had been under attack for many years, and had been partly undermined by the Court in recent decisions. But it was not until the Brown Case that *Plessy* v. *Ferguson* was reversed in unmistakable terms. Speaking for a unanimous Court, Chief Justice Earl Warren said: "We conclude that in the field of public education the doctrine of 'separate but equal' has no place. Separate educational facilities are inherently unequal." Recognizing that a sudden change in the educational practices of the southern states would be tantamount to a social revolution, the Court indicated that a gradual approach to desegregation would be acceptable. Even so, the decision met with as much resistance within the southern states as it did with enthusiasm among Negro citizens and their supporters. In the border states and in the North, considerable progress had been made toward compliance with the Court's decision within two years after its verdict. In the deep South, however, it became clear that compliance, if it came at all, would come only after a series of negotiations and adjustments stretching out over many years.

Foreign Policies.   After the Korean settlement, the efforts of the Eisenhower administration to achieve both peace and security ran into continuing difficulties. In Europe, the effort to build up the strength of the anti-communist bloc led to the eventual rearmament of West Germany. French reluctance had delayed German rearmament by several years, but an agreement was finally reached among the western nations in Paris in the fall of 1954 granting sovereignty to West Germany, admitting her into NATO, and authorizing a German army of 500,000 troops.

After Korea, Far Eastern affairs continued to be a thorn in the side of American policy-makers. Early in 1954, it appeared that French forces fighting against communists in Indo-China (Viet Nam) were in danger of being overwhelmed, and that their defeat might lead to a communist conquest of all Southeast Asia. On July 20, a conference was held at Geneva by delegates from Soviet Russia, Red China, France, Great Britain, and Indo-China, resulting in the division of Viet Nam at the 17th parallel. The northern section of the country was allotted to the communists, and a free election was called for to determine what would happen to the rest. The United States consented to the agreement, but did not participate in working it out.

After this conference, whose results were widely criticized in the United States and elsewhere, Secretary of State John Foster Dulles took the initiative in forming a collective organization in Southeast Asia that would serve as a counterpart to NATO in Europe. His efforts finally led to the signing of a Southeast Asia Collective Defense Treaty at Manila on September 8, 1954. In addition to the United States, the signatories were Australia, New Zealand, Thailand, the Philippines, and the free part of Indo-China. But important Asian powers like India, Burma, Indonesia, and Ceylon refused to join. This treaty did not go so far as the NATO compact; it merely provided that an attack upon one member would be regarded as a threat to the peace and safety of the others. Rather than agreeing, as in NATO, to take up arms against an aggressor, each member of the Southeast Asia Treaty Organization (SEATO) agreed to act to meet the common danger in accordance with its constitutional system. The agreement also provided for economic cooperation to promote economic progress among the member states and called for the establishment of a council on which all members should be represented.

SEATO was formed only after disastrous losses had been incurred in Southeast Asia. When India and Indonesia expressed their suspicion of the treaty as a provocation to aggression, Secretary Dulles replied that the pact was "directed against no government, against no nation, and against no people. It is directed only against aggression." The agreement was supplemented by a verbal promise to the Filipinos that the United States, in its own interest, would respond immediately if the Philippines were attacked, and by a subsequent treaty with the Chinese Nationalist government on Formosa committing the United States to regard an attack on the territory of Formosa, including the Pescadores Islands, as a threat to its own peace and safety. The United States was granted the right to station troops on Chinese Nationalist territory. Both parties also promised that they would attempt to settle by peaceful means any disputes they might become involved in. This meant that Chiang Kai-shek, whom President Eisenhower had threatened in 1953 to "unleash" against Communist China, now promised not to act on his own initiative in bringing about a war with Communist China, in which the United States could easily become involved.

Communist China regarded Chiang's presence on Formosa with American support as a continuing threat to its security, however, and was by no means reassured. Early in 1955, it became clear that Communist China was building up its forces, and its leaders openly began to talk of taking the little islands of Quemoy and Matsu, which were under Chiang's control but which lay just off the Chinese coast. For a time, it seemed that a highly explosive situation was in the making. Early in 1955, President Eisenhower asked Congress for a grant of broad authority to use American armed forces to repel any communist assault on Formosa. By requesting permission from Congress beforehand, he was serving notice that American forces would be used if an emergency

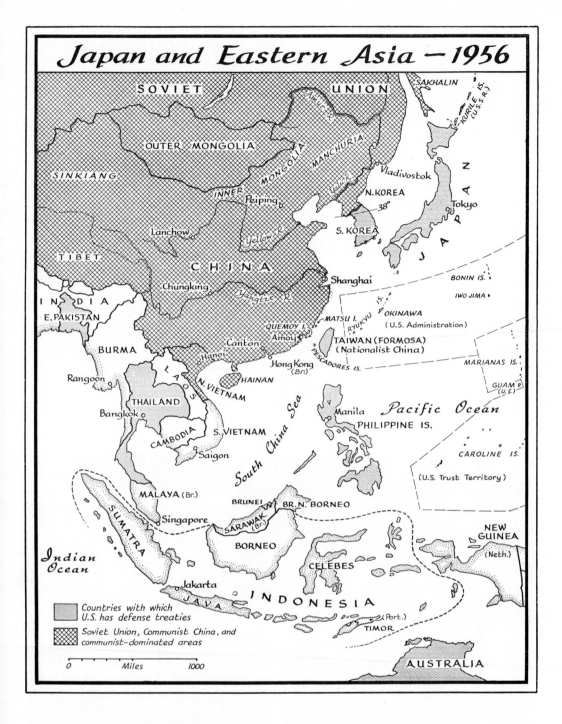

Japan and Eastern Asia — 1956

SOVIET UNION

SAKHALIN

KURILE IS. (U.S.S.R.)

OUTER MONGOLIA

MANCHURIA

Amur R.

SINKIANG

INNER MONGOLIA

Vladivostok

N.KOREA

38°

Tokyo

Peiping

S.KOREA

JAPAN

Lanchow

Yellow R.

TIBET

CHINA

Shanghai

BONIN IS.

IWO JIMA

Chungking

Yangtze R.

I N D I A

E.PAKISTAN

QUEMOY I.

MATSU I.

RYUKYU IS.

OKINAWA
(U.S. Administration)

BURMA

Canton

Amoy

TAIWAN (FORMOSA)
(Nationalist China)

MARIANAS IS.

Rangoon

Hanoi

LAOS

Hong Kong
(Br.)

PESCADORES IS.

GUAM
(U.S.)

N.VIETNAM

HAINAN

THAILAND

Bangkok

South China Sea

Manila

Pacific Ocean

PHILIPPINE IS.

CAMBODIA

S.VIETNAM

Saigon

CAROLINE IS.

(U.S. Trust Territory)

MALAYA (Br.)

BRUNEI

BR.N. BORNEO

Singapore

SARAWAK (Br.)

BORNEO

NEW
GUINEA

(Neth.)

Indian
Ocean

CELEBES

SUMATRA

Jakarta

JAVA

I N D O N E S I A

(Port.)

TIMOR

Countries with which
U.S. has defense treaties

Soviet Union, Communist China, and
communist-dominated areas

0   Miles   1000

AUSTRALIA

arose. In effect, he thus eliminated the necessity for making an executive decision such as Truman had had to make in Korea. Congress responded by giving President Eisenhower the requested authority by a vote of 85 to 3 in the Senate and 409 to 3 in the House. Fortunately, the expected attack on Formosa and the off-coast islands did not develop.

A brief and somewhat deceptive period of relaxation followed this moment of acute tension. The Soviet leaders once again began

751

to smile, and a few stubborn problems suddenly yielded to solution. In May, 1955, the Soviets accepted a treaty in which the Four-Power occupation of Austria, which had existed since the end of World War II, came to an end. The Moscow leaders then came to an understanding with their former protégé, Marshal Tito, who had broken from the Soviet group in 1948, and recognized his independent communist-nationalist regime in Yugoslavia. At about the same time, as though acting by arrangement with Moscow, the government of Communist China began to release American airmen whom it had been holding in prison under sentence as spies since the year before. For the time, visitors were encouraged to enter behind the Iron Curtain.

In June, 1955, the heads of the Big Four powers met in conference at Geneva. Presi-

dent Eisenhower boldly proposed that the Soviets and the United States exchange blueprints of their military establishments and agree to permit mutual aerial reconnaissance over their military installations. Although the Soviets rejected this plan, the friendly spirit of the conference induced a momentary mood of hope. Subsequent events behind the Iron Curtain and in the Middle East, however, soon shattered much of the optimism that had lingered on into 1956.

New developments were shaking Soviet authority and Soviet pretenses. On February 25, 1956, the Russian Communist party leader, Khrushchev, took the occasion of the party's 20th Congress to denounce Stalin as a tyrant and a monster. This sudden attack on the dead dictator electrified the world, stunned Communist parties throughout the West, and caused some satellite leaders to hope that they could expect greater freedom in managing their own coun-

One of the lighter moments of the Geneva Conference, July 19, 1955. From left to right: Soviet Premier Nicolai Bulganin, President Eisenhower, French Premier Edgar Faure, British Prime Minister Sir Anthony Eden.

tries' affairs. Taking advantage of the Russian de-Stalinization campaign, the Polish communists on October 21 named as secretary of their party a Titoist, Wladyslaw Gomulka, and voted to expel Soviet Marshal Konstantin Rokossovsky, who had been a power in Polish affairs since 1949. Gomulka promised that the Red Army would be withdrawn from Poland. His accession was followed by a strong show of Polish determination to resist Soviet pressure. In December, the Russians did grant the Poles some control over Soviet forces based in Poland. In January, 1947, Gomulka received an overwhelming endorsement from the Polish electorate.

In Hungary, however, resistance to Russian authority did not fare so well. Mass meetings and demonstrations between October 20 and 23 brought a turnover in the Hungarian government in which ex-premier Imre Nagy was brought back to power. For a time, the Red Army left Budapest, and Nagy promised free elections. But on November 4, the Russians returned in great force and launched a ruthless nationwide attack to crush the Hungarian revolution. This act, condemned by the U.N. General Assembly, succeeded within five days in subduing most of the armed resistance, although, as 1956 ended, strikes and pockets of rebel resistance continued to harass the new Soviet-sponsored government. The harshness of the Russian action and the plight of Hungarian refugees struck a sharp blow at Soviet pretenses of idealism and weakened its prestige even among former sympathizers.

The Middle East Crisis. Outside the Pacific area, the strategic Middle East at mid-century was the weakest spot in western resistance to communist penetration. Before World War II, this area had been of hardly more than marginal concern to American policy-makers, who had generally been content to think of it as a region in which Britain had special interests and bore a primary responsibility. It was partly because of this attitude that American policy proved so inadequate and inconsistent in the post-war

years when it became necessary for the United States to assume greater responsibility in the region.

The United States had never had territorial ambitions in the Near East, but its vital interests became threatened both by Soviet efforts to curry favor among restless Arab peoples and by Arab nationalism that threatened the interests of the British and French in the area. Both the United States and Britain had an interest in the immense oil resources of the region, and the Suez Canal had always been regarded by the British as their imperial life-line. Because of these interests, the United States faced a grave dilemma: if it supported the efforts of its British and French allies to maintain their Middle Eastern position, it risked arousing the resentment of the Arab nationalists and abandoning its own principled sympathy for colonial peoples throughout the world; but if it deserted its allies to maintain its prestige among the Arabs and other colonial peoples, it might offend Britain and France and undermine the diplomatic unity of NATO. Faced with this problem, the United States under both the Truman and Eisenhower administrations pursued a wavering course, though after 1953 American policy tended steadily to favor the Arab states.

Another dilemma arose from the fierce antagonism between the Arab states and the young state of Israel. As far back as 1917, the British, in the Balfour Declaration, had promised a homeland in Palestine for the Jewish people, and in 1948 the British mandate over Palestine came to an end with the formation of an independent Jewish state of Israel. The neighboring Arab states of Syria, Lebanon, Jordan, Iraq, Saudi Arabia, and Egypt, which during the war had drawn together to form an Arab League, never accepted the new state. They vowed to destroy it, and from the formation of Israel in May, 1948, to July, 1949, the new nation was intermittently engaged in war with the Arab League. Finally an uneasy truce was arranged by the U.N. This settlement was accepted by the Arab states not because they were reconciled to Israel's existence but because they had been unable to subdue her. Sympathy for the large number of Jewish refugees who crowded into Israel after World War II pulled the United States in one direction, while the desire to remain friendly with the Arabs and other colonial peoples pulled the country in another.

The implacable hostility of the Arab nations to Israel induced the United States, Great Britain, and France to issue a common statement on May 25, 1950, to the effect that they would supply arms to either Israel or the Arab states only upon assurance that the arms would not be used for aggression. They also pledged to take action, both in the U.N. and independently, if any of the states of the Middle East should be found preparing to violate frontiers or armistice lines. In 1953-1954, the United States also achieved success in its efforts to assure peace in the Middle East when it mediated a three-year-old British-Iranian dispute touched off by Iran's nationalization of the holdings of the Anglo-Iranian Oil Company.

Beginning in 1953, however, the United States helped pave the way for a series of diplomatic disasters in the Middle East. Secretary of State John Foster Dulles, attempting to strengthen the region against the Soviets, sponsored the Baghdad Pact, finally signed in 1955, which joined Turkey, Iraq, Iran, and Pakistan with Britain in a formal military alliance. But this pact aroused suspicion and hostility all the way from Egypt (which saw its leadership in the Arab world threatened) to India (which was feuding with Pakistan). Accordingly, the United States itself refused to join the alliance it had promoted, and the enterprise became the butt of ridicule and cost the United States much prestige in Asia and the Middle East. Moreover, under pressure from Jefferson Caffery, the American ambassador in Cairo, the British agreed in 1953 to evacuate their posts in the Sudan, to which the Egyptians had objected, and finally, in the fall of the

following year, to withdraw from their base in Suez over an eighteen-month period. Thus, under American pressure, our British ally relinquished its central military base in the Middle East, and with the British withdrawal went the pivot of western power in the entire region.

American efforts on behalf of Egypt were not reciprocated by any growth of friendly feelings on the part of the Egyptians. Instead, in September, 1955, the Egyptians made a deal with the Soviets for the delivery of $200 million worth of Russian and Czechoslovakian military supplies. Now, attempting to forestall the Egyptian shift toward the Russian orbit, Secretary of State Dulles offered the Egyptians American aid in the construction of a major Egyptian project, the Aswan Dam, which was designed to harness the power of the Nile River. Continuing anti-western gestures by the Egyptians persuaded Dulles to cancel this offer seven months later, in July, 1956, at the very moment when Egypt had agreed to accept American terms. One week later, on July 26, Egypt's Premier, Colonel Gamal Abdel Nasser (soon to be made President), nationalized the Suez Canal, which had previously been operated by a company whose stockholders were largely British and French. Though the Canal was not closed to any nation except Israel, this act threatened the flow of supplies from the Middle East and the Orient to Europe and America, represented a powerful implicit danger to the economies of the western European countries, and flatly challenged American prestige throughout the world. Nasser further refused on September 9, 1956, to agree to international control of the Suez Canal by 18 nations that regularly used the waterway.

In October, 1956, Israel, hoping to take advantage of Russia's preoccupation with the crises in Hungary and Poland, and possibly by prearrangement with Britain and France, launched an invasion of Egypt from the east, with the announced objective of destroying the bases from which a number of provocative Egyptian raids had been made on Israeli territory. This action was followed by a sudden Anglo-French invasion of the Suez area from Cyprus. London and Paris announced that their forces would occupy the Canal Zone to insure continued traffic through the Canal. At the U.N., both the Soviet Union and the United States joined in condemning the British and French action, and the General Assembly promptly voted to organize a U.N. police force to supervise a cease-fire.

The threat of Russian intervention, as well as a storm of criticism at home and abroad, induced the British and French to accept the U.N. call for a cease-fire on November 6, and the Israelis, after American

and Soviet warnings, also agreed to withdraw from Egyptian territory. The first detachments of a United Nations Emergency Force arrived in Egypt on November 15, and the last Anglo-French troops were withdrawn on December 22. But at the end of 1956, the Middle East remained an international trouble spot. The Canal was blocked by ships the Egyptians had scuttled during hostilities. The British and French faced an economic and political crisis brought about in large part by a shortage of oil, though the United States began making plans to rush oil from

Europe and the Middle East in 1956

Countries in Western defense system
Members of Arab League
Member of both
Soviet Union and Satellites

its own wells to its western allies. The Egyptians had learned how successfully they could play off the ambitions of Russia against the western powers. And the western alliance had been profoundly shaken.

The Election of 1956.

During the years of his presidency, the enormous personal popularity of President Eisenhower had increased. In September, 1955, however, while vacationing in Colorado, he was stricken with a heart attack, which raised questions about his availability for a second term. His recovery had just passed the point at which he felt he could undertake a second term, when in early June, 1956, he was forced to undergo an operation for ileitis. Inordinately dependent upon Eisenhower's personal popularity, Republican leaders still urged him to run, and at the San Francisco convention in August he was re-nominated by overwhelming acclamation, along with Vice-president Nixon.

The illness of the President and the controversial reputation of his running-mate among many Democrats and some independent voters encouraged the Democrats to feel that they had a chance to win. Adlai E. Stevenson, despite the opposition of ex-President Truman, easily re-won the Democratic nomination in Chicago. The convention then named as his running-mate his opponent of long standing, Senator Estes Kefauver, who had withdrawn from the contest for the presidential nomination before the start of the convention. In vain, the Democratic candidates tried to exploit local areas of economic discontent, notably in the farm belt, to criticize weaknesses and failures in foreign policy, and to capitalize on the President's illness by dwelling on the threat of a Nixon succession. The Republicans countered with a slogan of "Peace, Progress, and Prosperity," and exploited to the full the popularity of their standard-bearer.

Earlier American presidents of comparable popularity had always been re-elected during a period of general prosperity, and Eisenhower proved no exception. Indeed, the intensification of the Middle East crisis and the events in eastern Europe seem only to have added to his strength. When the votes were counted, Eisenhower had beaten Stevenson even more decisively than in 1952. Polling over 34,751,000 votes to slightly more than 25,427,000 for Stevenson, the President received 58 per cent of the popular vote, thus recording the most decisive presidential victory since Roosevelt's defeat of Landon in 1936. In the electoral college, Eisenhower had 457 votes, Stevenson 73. That the President was far more popular than his party was shown once again in the congressional races. The Democrats maintained their 49 to 47 margin in the Senate and increased by two seats their comfortable majority in the House. Not since the time of Zachary Taylor, over a century before, had a president been elected without winning at least one house of Congress for his party.

The Promise of American Life.

Late in 1952, American scientists exploded the first hydrogen bomb, and not long afterward the experiment was duplicated by the Russians. The force of a thermonuclear explosion, already terrifying, had been multiplied beyond belief. Now a single bomb might have more power than all the bombs dropped by the United States during World War II. It was within the power of man to destroy whole societies at a single blow—and at the same time to command infinitely more energy than before for constructive ends.

To exercise the leadership of half the world under such conditions was a more exacting responsibility for Americans than any they had faced in the past. From the time of Columbus, and even before, the history of the New World had been linked with the legendary and the fabulous, with adventure and discovery; and every man who came to America projected upon it his deepest aspirations—his hope or his ambition, his demand for freedom or his desire to be saved. To the western world, America had always been a harbinger of the future, and the development of its life and institutions had been watched for portents of the fate of humankind. Its Revolution had rallied the world to stronger faith in self-government; its democratic institutions had been the hope of egalitarians and the despair of aristocrats; its Civil War had caused men of good will to tremble for the fate of republicanism; its success in organizing a continent under one federal government had

inspired dreams of even broader political unity among men; and the productiveness of its economy had been a model for those who sought the end of poverty. In the twentieth century, it remains for the United States to show whether it can still pioneer on the most demanding of all frontiers—the wise and benevolent use of immense power under conditions at once more precarious and more promising than any the world has known.

Readings

For the wartime conferences, Cordell Hull's *Memoirs* (2 vols., 1948), and Robert S. Sherwood's *Roosevelt and Hopkins* (2 vols., 1948), are of central value, and Winston Churchill's *The Second World War* (6 vols., 1948-1953) gives first-hand information. The break-up of the Grand Coalition is traced by W. H. McNeill in *America, Britain, and Russia, 1941-1946* (1953). The reader will be interested in comparing the evaluations of the Yalta Conference in such standard diplomatic histories as those of T. A. Bailey, S. F. Bemis, and J. W. Pratt, and in reading the various essays in John Snell, ed., *The Meaning of Yalta* (1956). E. R. Stettinius' recollections, edited by Walter Johnson, *Roosevelt and the Russians* (1949), is of special value on Yalta, as is Churchill's final volume, *Triumph and Tragedy*. See also James F. Byrnes, *Speaking Frankly* (1947). Chester Wilmot, in *The Struggle for Europe* (1952), lays a heavy responsibility on Allied handling of the closing phases of the war as a reason for Soviet postwar successes.

On the general background of Russian-American relations, see T. A. Bailey, *America Faces Russia* (1950). Henry L. Roberts has made a thoughtful evaluation of the problems of the cold war in *Russia and America: Dangers and Prospects* (1956).

On Korea, see J. C. Caldwell and L. Frost, *The Korea Story* (1952). R. Rovere and A. M. Schlesinger, Jr., are critical of General MacArthur in *The General and the President* (1951), while Major General Courtney Whitney lauds him in *MacArthur: His Rendezvous with History* (1955).

On America's role in postwar Germany, see Hajo Holborn, *American Military Government* (1947), and E. H. Litchfield, ed., *Governing Postwar Germany* (1953). A balanced account of American-Chinese relations is Herbert Feis, *The China Tangle* (1953). Harold M. Vinacke, *The United States and the Far East, 1945-1951* (1952), covers our relations with Asia, as does Kenneth Scott Latourette, *The American Record in the Far East, 1945-1951* (1952). L. M. Goodrich and E. Hambro, *Charter of the United Nations: Commentary and Documents* (1949), is standard on its subject.

A general account of postwar America may be found in Eric Goldman's *The Crucial Decade: America, 1945-1955* (1956). Various domestic issues are discussed in the following: H. C. Millis and E. C. Brown, *From the Wagner Act to Taft-Hartley* (1950); Joel Seidman, *American Labor from Defense to Reconversion* (1953); and E. R. Bartley, *The Tidelands Oil Controversy* (1953). Crime and corruption are reviewed by Estes Kefauver, *Crime in America* (1951); P. H. Douglas, *Ethics in Government* (1952); Blair Bolles, *How to Get Rich in Washington* (1953); and G. A. Graham, *Morality in American Politics* (1952). On the Eisenhower administration, R. J. Donovan, *The Inside Story* (1956), contains authentic first-hand information. On civil rights and desegregation, see The President's Committee on Civil Rights, *To Secure These Rights* (1947). Important materials on civil rights and civil liberties, including both the Dennis case and the desegregation decision, are assembled and discussed by M. R. Konvitz in *Bill of Rights Reader* (1954).

Satisfactory biographies of recent political figures are, of course, still to be written. Aside from Harry S. Truman's *Memoirs* (2 vols., 1955), the best work on Truman is Jonathan Daniels' *The Man of Independence* (1950). Kevin McCann, *America's Man of Destiny: An Intimate Biography of General Eisenhower* (1952), is a campaign biography by a friend and staff writer. N. F. Busch, *Adlai E. Stevenson of Illinois* (1952), is also a friendly portrait. On Taft, see W. S. White, *The Taft Story* (1954); on Vandenberg, see *The Private Papers of Senator Vandenberg* (1952). Stevenson's *Major Campaign Speeches* (1952) remains a collection of interest. Recent American political behavior is discussed illuminatingly in two books by Samuel Lubell, *The Future of American Politics* (1952; rev. ed., 1956), and *Revolt of the Moderates* (1956), and by Louis Harris, *Is There a Republican Majority?* (1954). The principles of the two major opposing parties are discussed by Dean Acheson, *A Democrat Looks at His Party* (1955), and Arthur Larson, *A Republican Looks at His Party* (1956). The extreme right wing is examined critically in a book of essays edited by Daniel Bell, *The New American Right* (1955).

The loyalty issue is discussed from different points of view by Alan Barth, *The Loyalty of Free Men* (1951); Sidney Hook, *Heresy, Yes—Conspiracy, No* (1953); Nathaniel Weyl, *The Battle against Disloyalty* (1951); and Robert K. Carr, *The House Committee on Un-American Activities* (1952). J. Anderson and R. W. May are critical in their *McCarthy: The Man, the Senator, the "Ism"* (1952), and J. Rorty and M. Decter have written a close evaluation of the evidence in *McCarthy and the Communists* (1954). Alistair Cooke, *A Generation on Trial* (1950), is an account of the Hiss case by a reporter at the trial. Ralph De Toledano and Victor Lasky review the evidence to prove Hiss' guilt in *Seeds of Treason* (1950). The autobiographical *Witness*, by Whittaker Chambers (1952), is a fascinating personal document. Richard B. Morris, *Fair Trial* (1952), evaluates the Hiss and other trials according to traditional American concepts of fair play.

APPENDIX

GENERAL READINGS

This list is meant as a guide to reference works and to general books, some of which may also be found in the chapter bibliographies.

REFERENCE WORKS. *The Harvard Guide to American History* (1954), edited by Oscar Handlin and others, is now the indispensable work of reference. It is a guide not only to historical writings, but also to other reference books in the field. H. P. Beers, ed., *Bibliographies in American History* (rev. ed., 1942), is a guide to the guides. The *Dictionary of American Biography,* edited by Allen Johnson and Dumas Malone (21 vols., 1928-1944), and the *Dictionary of American History,* edited by James Truslow Adams and R. V. Coleman (6 vols., 1940), are comprehensive works on the lives of outstanding Americans and the stories of leading events. *The Encyclopedia of American History,* edited by R. B. Morris and H. S. Commager (1955), is a handy one-volume guide. *Historical Statistics of the United States, 1789-1945,* issued by the United States Department of Commerce (1949), is immensely useful for all kinds of information that can be put into figures, as are the annual volumes of the *Statistical Abstract of the United States,* put out by the same source. For maps, see C. O. Paullin, *Atlas of the Historical Geography of the United States* (1932), and C. L. and E. H. Lord, *Historical Atlas of the United States* (1944).

COLLECTIONS OF SOURCES. J. F. Jameson, ed., *Original Narratives of Early American History* (19 vols., 1906-1917), is superb for colonial times. H. S. Commager, ed., *Documents of American History* (rev. ed., 1949), is a standard work. R. Leopold and A. Link, eds., *Problems in American History* (1952), is an original work which introduces source materials with essays by authorities. *The*

People Shall Judge (2 vols., 1949), edited by the Social Sciences Staff of the College at the University of Chicago is excellent, as is Louis Hacker and Helene Zahler, eds., *The Shaping of the American Tradition* (1947). See also A. Craven, W. Johnson, and F. R. Dunn, eds., *A Documentary History of the American People* (1951), and A. T. Mason, ed., *Free Government in the Making* (1949). Also valuable are J. R. Commons, and others, eds., *Documentary History of American Industrial Society* (10 vols., 1910-1911), good for labor; W. L. Fleming, ed., *Documentary History of Reconstruction* (2 vols., 1906-1907); A. B. Hart, ed., *American History Told by Contemporaries* (5 vols., 1897-1929); T. H. McKee, ed., *National Conventions and Platforms of all Political Parties, 1789-1904* (1904); K. H. Porter and D. B. Johnson, *National Party Platforms, 1840-1956* (1956); Allan Nevins and H. S. Commager, eds., *Heritage of America* (1939); and W. Thorp, M. Curti, and C. Baker, eds., *American Issues* (2 vols., 1941). Oscar Handlin, ed., *This Was America* (1949), and H. S. Commager, ed., *America in Perspective* (1947), are collections of foreign comment. See also R. J. Bartlett, ed., *The Record of American Diplomacy* (1950); G. S. Callender, ed., *Selections from the Economic History of the United States, 1765-1860* (1909); and L. B. Schmidt and E. D. Ross, eds., *Readings in the Economic History of American Agriculture* (1925). Felix Flügel and H. U. Faulkner have edited *Readings in the Economic and Social History of The United States* (1929).

GENERAL WORKS. Comprehensive histories of the United States, covering various extended periods of time, in multiple volumes, have been written by such outstanding historians as Henry Adams, George Bancroft, Edward Channing, Richard Hildreth, Hermann von Holst, James Bach McMaster, Ellis P. Oberholtzer, James Schouler, James Ford Rhodes, and Justin Winsor. The most recent effort is still in progress, Allan Nevins' volumes on the period from 1850 through Reconstruction, of which the first four have appeared, *The Emergence of Lincoln* (2 vols., 1950), and *The Ordeal of the Union* (2 vols., 1947). Other comprehensive histories have been the work of many hands. Albert B. Hart edited the 28-volume series called *The American Nation: A History* (1904-1918). Allen Johnson edited the readable 50-volume *Chronicles of America Series* (1918-1921); Allan Nevins edited 6 supplementary volumes (1950-1951), which carry the history of the nation down to 1945. A. M. Schlesinger and D. R. Fox have edited the excellent 13-volume *A History of American Life* (1927-1948). W. H. Stephenson and E. M. Coulter have edited *A History of the South* in 6 volumes, to be supplemented by 4 forthcoming works. Only the first few volumes have appeared of *The New American Nation Series,* edited by Henry Steele Commager and Richard B. Morris.

INTERPRETIVE STUDIES. Two of

the most famous interpretations are by foreign observers, Alexis de Tocqueville, *Democracy in America,* 2 vols., available in several editions and originally published in 1835, and James Bryce, *The American Commonwealth* (2 vols., 1888). One of the most lively examinations of American history is *The Rise of American Civilization,* by Charles and Mary Beard (2 vols., rev. ed., 1933). Suggestive evaluations by foreign students are D. W. Brogan, *The American Character* (1944), and Frank Thistlethwaite, *The Great Experiment* (1955). American political history is surveyed in terms of the development of political parties in W. E. Binkley, *American Political Parties: Their Natural History* (1943), and in terms of individual leaders in Richard Hofstadter, *The American Political Tradition* (1948). On reform leaders, see Daniel Aaron, *Men of Good Hope* (1951). Various writers examine critical episodes in American history in Daniel Aaron, ed., *America in Crisis* (1952). A stimulating brief interpretation is offered by H. B. Parkes, *The American Experience* (rev. ed., 1953).

CONSTITUTIONAL

HISTORY. Homer C. Hockett, *The Constitutional History of The United States, 1776-1826* (2 vols., 1939), is detailed on the early period. One-volume surveys of the whole field are A. H. Kelly and W. A. Harbison, *The American Constitution* (1948), and C. B.

Swisher, *American Constitutional Development* (1943). The older survey by Charles Warren, *The Supreme Court in United States History* (2 vols., 1937), is still interesting. Benjamin F. Wright, *The Growth of American Constitutional Law* (1942), is a brilliant brief interpretation. A comprehensive annotated version of the Constitution, prepared for Congress under the supervision of E. S. Corwin (1952), is a remarkable reference work that traces Supreme Court decisions on practically every phase of that document.

INTELLECTUAL AND CULTURAL

HISTORY. V. L. Parrington, *Main Currents in American Thought* (3 vols., 1927-1930), though much criticized, is still a standard work. Merle Curti, *The Growth of American Thought* (rev. ed., 1951), is comprehensive. R. H. Gabriel, *The Course of American Democratic Thought* (rev. ed., 1956), deals with the period since 1815. Two standard surveys of philosophy are Herbert W. Schneider, *A History of American Philosophy* (1946), and the briefer work by Joseph Blau, *Men and Movements in American Philosophy* (1952). An exhaustive survey of American literature may be found in R. E. Spiller, and others, *Literary History of the United States* (3 vols., 1948). The third volume, a bibliography, should be supplemented by H. M. Jones, *Guide to American Literature and Its Backgrounds since 1890* (1953). O. W. Larkin's *Art and Life in America* (1949) is comprehensive and profusely illustrated. The standard works on journalism are Frank Luther Mott, *American Journalism* (rev. ed., 1950), and the same author's *A History of American Magazines* (4 vols., 1930-1957). A. M. Lee, *Daily Newspaper in America* (1937), is also an excellent work. E. P. Cubberley, *Public Education in the United States* (rev. ed., 1934), and E. W. Knight, *Education in the United States* (rev. ed., 1951), are standard. Merle Curti, *Social Ideas of American Educators* (1935), is excellent. Richard Hofstadter and Walter P. Metzger, *The Development of Academic Freedom in the United States* (1955), which goes beyond the scope of its title, provides information not found elsewhere about the institutional development of higher education. There are three one-volume surveys of religion: H. K. Rowe, *The History of Religion in the United States* (1924); W. L. Sperry, *Religion in America* (1946); and W. W. Sweet, *The Story of Religion in America* (1920). P. G. Mode has compiled an extremely helpful work, *Source Book and Bibliographical Guide for American Church History* (1921).

LABOR AND IMMIGRATION. The

standard work on labor history is J. R. Commons, and others, *History of Labor in the United States* (4 vols., 1918-1935), though a briefer survey is available in F. R. Dulles, *Labor in America* (1949). See also Selig Perlman's interpretive *History of Trade Unionism in the United States* (1922). Carl Wittke, in *We Who Built America* (1940), has written the most adequate survey of the whole story of immigration, but the interested reader also will want to turn to Marcus Lee Hansen's two books, *The Immigrant in American History* (1940), and *The Atlantic Migration, 1607-1860* (1940), as well as Oscar Handlin's sensitive account of the immigrant experience, *The Uprooted* (1951). John Hope Franklin has written the best account of the Negro in *From Slavery to Freedom: A History of American Negroes* (1948). Anti-immigrant prejudice and its consequences are traced in two good books: R. A. Billington, *The Protestant Crusade, 1800-1860* (1938), and John Higham, *Strangers in the Land* (1955), which carries the story down to 1925. Among the many books on special groups, Carl Wittke, *The Irish in America* (1956), is one of the most informative, while J. A. Hawgood, *The Tragedy of German America* (1940), is an excellent interpretation.

THE FRONTIER AND THE WEST.
Comprehensive one-volume surveys are R. A. Billington, *Westward Expansion* (1949); D. E. Clark, *The West in American History* (1937); and R. E. Riegel, *America Moves West* (1947). The essays by Frederick Jackson Turner in *The Frontier in American History* (1920) are classic. R. E. Robbins, *Our Landed Heritage* (1942), is excellent on the disposition of the public lands. On the Indian, see Clark Wissler, *Indians of the United States* (1940), or Paul Radin, *The Story of the American Indian* (1937). W. P. Webb, *The Great Plains* (1931), is important and interesting. J. C. Malin, *The Grassland of North America* (1947), has many distinctive insights.

DIPLOMATIC HISTORY.
Among surveys in this field, T. A. Bailey, *A Diplomatic History of the American People* (rev. ed., 1955), is the liveliest and most satisfactory treatment of the relationship between diplomacy and public opinion; S. F. Bemis, *A Diplomatic History of the United States* (rev. ed., 1955), is sober and comprehensive; Julius W. Pratt, *A History of United States Foreign Policy* (1955), is good. S. F. Bemis, ed., *American Secretaries of State and Their Diplomacy* (10 vols., 1927-1929), is useful. Dexter Perkins, *History of the Monroe Doctrine* (rev. ed., 1955), is valuable. S. F. Bemis has told the story of *The Latin American Policy of the United States* (1943),

and A. W. Griswold that of *The Far Eastern Policy of the United States* (1938). A. J. Weinberg, *Manifest Destiny* (1935), is a brilliant study in the ideology of American foreign policy. On naval history, see Harold and Margaret Sprout, *The Rise of American Naval Power* (1942). On military developments, R. E. and T. N. Dupuy, *Military Heritage of America* (1956), is comprehensive; Walter Millis, *Arms and Men* (1956), is good on the development of modern warfare; and A. A. Ekirch, Jr., *The Civilian and the Military* (1956), deals with the anti-militarist tradition.

ECONOMIC AND FINANCIAL HISTORY.
Among the general surveys, H. U. Faulkner, *American Economic History* (rev. ed., 1954); E. C. Kirkland, *A History of American Economic Life* (rev. ed., 1951); and F. A. Shannon, *America's Economic Growth* (rev. ed., 1951), are recommended. T. C. Cochran and William Miller, *The Age of Enterprise* (1942), is a general interpretation of industrial America since 1800, while Louis Hacker, *The Triumph of American Capitalism* (1940), deals with the developments from colonial times down to the 1870's. The 3 volumes of Joseph Dorfman's *The Economic Mind in American Civilization* (1946-1949), trace economic thought and economic folklore. D. R. Dewey, *Financial History of the United States* (rev. ed., 1934), is less full than W. J. Schultz and M. B. Caine, *Financial Development of the United States* (1937). On transportation, see B. H. Meyer and others, *History of Transportation in the United States before 1860* (1917), and on travel, Seymour Dunbar's magnificent *History of Travel in America* (4 vols., 1915). On the tariff, F. W. Taussig, *The Tariff History of the United States* (rev. ed., 1931), is standard, but see also F. W. Stanwood, *American Tariff Controversies in the Nineteenth Century* (2 vols., 1903). On taxation, Sidney Ratner, *American Taxation* (1942), is good. On agriculture, E. E. Edwards, "American Agriculture: The First Three Hundred Years," in the 1940 *Yearbook of Agriculture* of the Department of Agriculture is the best short survey, but greater detail may be found in L. C. Gray, *History of Agriculture in the Southern United States to 1860* (2 vols., 1925), and P. W. Bidwell and J. I. Falconer, *History of Agriculture in the Northern United States, 1620-1860* (1925). V. S. Clark, *History of Manufactures in the United States* (3 vols., 1929), is voluminous rather than readable. E. R. Johnson, and others, *History of Domestic and Foreign Commerce of the United States* (2 vols., 1915), is standard on its subject. Henry

David, and others, eds., *The Economic History of the United States* (1945-   ), to be completed in 9 volumes, is good. On technology, Roger Burlingame, *March of the Iron Men* (1938), and *Engines of Democracy* (1940); and Waldemar Kaempffert, ed., *A Popular History of American Invention* (2 vols., 1924), are excellent.

SOCIAL HISTORY.

A. W. Calhoun, *A Social History of the American Family* (3 vols., 1917-1919), is the only book on its subject. On etiquette, see A. M. Schlesinger, *Learning How to Behave* (1946). On high society, Dixon

Wecter, *The Saga of American Society* (1937), is excellent. R. O. Cummings, *The American and His Food* (1940), discusses diet. H. L. Mencken, *The American Language* (3 vols., 1936-1948), is standard and vastly amusing. F. R. Packard, *History of Medicine in the United States* (2 vols., 1931), and Albert Deutsch, *The Mentally Ill in America* (1937), are standard. Blake McKelvey, *American Prisons* (1936), is the primary book on its subject. For sport, see F. R. Dulles, *America Learns to Play* (1940), and J. A. Krout, *Annals of American Sport* (1940). On women, see E. Stanton, S. B. Anthony, and M. J. Gage, eds., *History of Woman Suffrage* (6 vols., 1881-1922), or, more briefly, I. H. Irwin, *Angels and Amazons* (1933).

INEXPENSIVE PAPERBOUND BOOKS

One of the most remarkable and encouraging developments in the American cultural scene during the period after World War II has been the rise in the number of serious books of all kinds available in inexpensive paperbound editions. The following is a selection, necessarily brief, of some of the books available in American history and civilization at prices ranging from 35 cents to $1.65. Paperbound books are widely available in well-stocked bookstores, but can always be ordered directly from the publishers by mail. The number of books available in inexpensive editions grows rapidly. A catalogue of such works, *Paperbound Books in Print,* is issued semi-annually by R. R. Bowker Company of New York City. This list was compiled from the 1956 editons of this catalogue. Many of the following books appear in the chapter bibliographies above; all are relevant to the material in this volume.

Among the useful selections of documents on American history in paperbound volumes are Henry Steele Commager's *America in Perspective* (New American Library), a collection of travelers' commentaries; *A Documentary History of the United States,* edited by Richard D. Heffner (New American Library); *Basic Documents in American History,* edited by Richard B. Morris (Anvil); Benjamin Franklin's *Autobiography* (Pocket Books); *From the Declaration of Independence to the Constitution: The Roots of American Constitutionalism,* edited by Carl J. Friedrich and Robert M. McCloskey (Liberal Arts Press); *The American Revolution: A Short History,* edited by Richard B. Morris (Anvil); *On the Constitution: Selections from the Federalist Papers,* by Hamilton, Madison, and Jay, edited by Ralph

H. Gabriel (Liberal Arts Press); Thomas Paine, *Common Sense and Other Writings* (Liberal Arts Press); *The Marshall Reader,* edited by Erwin Surrency (Oceana); *Social Theories of Jacksonian Democracy,* edited by Joseph L. Blau (Liberal Arts Press); John C. Calhoun, *A Disquisition on Government and Selections from the Discourse,* edited by Gordon Post (Liberal Arts Press); *The Webster Reader,* edited by Bertha Rothe (Oceana); *The Lincoln Reader,* edited by Paul Angle (Bantam); *The Holmes Reader,* edited by Julius J. Marke (Oceana); *The Brandeis Reader* edited by Ervin Pollack (Oceana); and *The Wilson Reader,* edited by Frances Farmer (Oceana).

General accounts of American history or of special periods include John Bartlet Brebner, *The Explorers of North America* (Anchor); Clinton Rossiter, *The First American Revolution* (Harvest); James Franklin Jameson, *The American Revolution Considered as a Social Movement* (Beacon); Edward S. Corwin, *The "Higher Law" Background of American Constitutional Law* (Cornell); Henry Adams, *The United States in 1800* (Cornell), a selection from the author's classic *History of the United States, 1801-1817;* Arthur M. Schlesinger, Jr., *The Age of Jackson* (New American Library), a drastically abridged version; Richard Hofstadter, *Social Darwinism in American Thought* (Beacon); Eric Goldman, *Rendezvous with Destiny* (Vintage); George Kennan, *American Diplomacy: 1900-1950* (New American Library), a practicing diplomat's interpretation; Frederick Lewis Allen, *Only Yesterday* (Bantam); Roger Burlingame, *Machines That Built America* (New American Library); and Richard Hofstadter, *The American Political Tradition* (Vintage).

Special commentaries on American history, politics, and culture number among them Alexis de Tocqueville's great work, *Democracy in America* (2 vols., Vintage); James Fenimore Cooper, *The American Democrat* (Vintage); Thorstein Veblen, *The Theory of the Leisure Class* (New American Library); Woodrow Wilson, *Congressional Government* (Meridian); V. L. Parrington, *Main Currents in American Thought* (2 vols., Harvest); Carl L. Becker, *Freedom and Responsibility in the American Way of Life* (Vintage); Lewis Mumford, *The Brown Decades: A Study of the Arts in America, 1865-1895* (Dover); Wilbur J. Cash, *The Mind of the South* (Anchor).

Among biographical studies, the following will prove helpful: Lord Charnwood, *Lincoln* (Pocket Books); Frederick Lewis Allen, *The Great Pierpont Morgan* (Bantam); Henry F. Pringle, *Theodore Roosevelt* (Harvest); and Robert E. Sherwood, *Roosevelt and Hopkins* (2 vols., Bantam).

Among recent paperbound publications are three works of distinction which cover a great deal of ground: D. W. Brogan, *The American Character* (Vintage); J. T. Ellis, *American Catholicism* (University of Chicago); and Clinton Rossiter, *The American Presidency* (Signet). Other useful titles include a good abridgement of J. T. Collier, *Indians of the Americas* (Mentor); S. E. Morison, *Christopher Columbus, Mariner* (Mentor), a distillation of the author's learning on this subject; J. T. Wertenbaker, *The Puritan Oligarchy* (Grosset's Universal Library); V. W. Crane, *The Southern Frontier, 1670-1732* (Ann Arbor Books); E. S.

Morgan, *The Birth of the Republic, 1763-1789* (University of Chicago); R. B. Morris, ed., *The Basic Ideas of Alexander Hamilton* (Pocket Library), a skillfully selected Hamilton anthology; C. Vann Woodward, *Reunion and Reaction* (Anchor); B. T. Washington, *Up from Slavery* (Bantam), the classic autobiography of the Negro leader; C. F. and Henry Adams, *Chapters of Erie* (Cornell), a great study in early criticism of the modern business order; Basil Rauch, ed., *Franklin D. Roosevelt: Speeches, Messages, Press Conferences, and Letters* (Rinehart); and C. Wright Mills, *White Collar* (Oxford).

Works of literature are too numerous to be specified in detail. Paperbound volumes represent in abundance such standard American authors as Stephen Crane, John Dos Passos, Ralph Waldo Emerson, James T. Farrell, William Faulkner, F. Scott Fitzgerald, Hamlin Garland, Nathaniel Hawthorne, Ernest Hemingway, Henry James, Jack London, Herman Melville, Edgar Allan Poe, John Steinbeck, Henry David Thoreau, Mark Twain, and Walt Whitman.

Among the most notable of the special literary studies are Louise Bogan, *Achievement in American Poetry* (Gateway Books); Van Wyck Brooks, *The Ordeal of Mark Twain* (Meridian); Malcolm Cowley, *Exile's Return,* a literary history of the 20's (Compass Books); Alfred Kazin, *On Native Grounds* (Anchor), a history of American prose writing since 1890; and Constance Rourke, *American Humor* (Anchor).

THE DECLARATION OF INDEPENDENCE

When, in the course of human events, it becomes necessary for one people to dissolve the political bands which have connected them with another, and to assume, among the powers of the earth, the separate and equal station to which the laws of nature and of nature's God entitle them, a decent respect to the opinions of mankind requires that they should declare the causes which impel them to the separation.

We hold these truths to be self-evident, that all men are created equal; that they are endowed by their Creator with certain unalienable rights; that among these, are life, liberty, and the pursuit of happiness. That, to secure these rights, governments are instituted among

men, deriving their just powers from the consent of the governed; that, whenever any form of government becomes destructive of these ends, it is the right of the people to alter or to abolish it, and to institute a new government, laying its foundation on such principles, and organizing its powers in such form, as to them shall seem most likely to effect their safety and happiness. Prudence, indeed, will dictate that governments long established, should not be changed for light and transient causes; and, accordingly, all experience hath shown, that mankind are more disposed to suffer, while evils are sufferable, than to right themselves by abolishing the forms to which they are accustomed. But, when a long train of abuses and usurpations, pursuing invariably the same object, evinces a design to reduce them under absolute despotism, it is their right, it is their duty, to throw off such government and to provide new guards for their future security. Such has been the patient sufferance of these colonies, and such is now the necessity which constrains them to alter their former systems of government. The history of the present King of Great Britain is a history of repeated injuries and usurpations, all having, in direct object, the establishment of an absolute tyranny over these States. To prove this, let facts be submitted to a candid world:—

He has refused his assent to laws the most wholesome and necessary for the public good.

He has forbidden his governors to pass laws of immediate and pressing importance, unless suspended in their operation till his assent should be obtained; and, when so suspended, he has utterly neglected to attend to them.

He has refused to pass other laws for the accommodation of large districts of people, unless those people would relinquish the right of representation in the legislature; a right inestimable to them, and formidable to tyrants only.

He has called together legislative bodies at places unusual, uncomfortable, and distant from the depository of their public records, for the sole purpose of fatiguing them into compliance with his measures.

He has dissolved representative houses repeatedly for opposing, with manly firmness, his invasions on the rights of the people.

He has refused, for a long time after such dissolutions, to cause others to be elected; whereby the legislative powers, incapable of annihilation, have returned to the people at large for their exercise; the state remaining, in the meantime, exposed to all the danger of invasion from without, and convulsions within.

He has endeavored to prevent the population of these States; for that purpose, obstructing the laws for naturalization of foreigners, refusing to pass others to encourage their migration hither, and raising the conditions of new appropriations of lands.

He has obstructed the administration of justice, by refusing his assent to laws for establishing judiciary powers.

He has made judges dependent on his will alone, for the tenure of their offices, and the amount and payment of their salaries.

He has erected a multitude of new offices, and sent hither swarms of officers to harass our people, and eat out their substance.

He has kept among us, in time of peace, standing armies, without the consent of our legislatures.

He has affected to render the military independent of, and superior to, the civil power.

He has combined, with others, to subject us to a jurisdiction foreign to our Constitution, and unacknowledged by our laws; giving his assent to their acts of pretended legislation:

For quartering large bodies of armed troops among us:

For protecting them by a mock trial, from punishment, for any murders which they should commit on the inhabitants of these States:

For cutting off our trade with all parts of the world:

For imposing taxes on us without our consent:

For depriving us, in many cases, of the benefit of trial by jury:

For transporting us beyond seas to be tried for pretended offences:

For abolishing the free system of English laws in a neighboring province, establishing therein an arbitrary government, and enlarging its boundaries, so as to render it at once an example and fit instrument for introducing the same absolute rule into these colonies:

For taking away our charters, abolishing our most valuable laws, and altering, fundamentally, the powers of our governments:

For suspending our own legislatures, and declaring themselves invested with power to legislate for us in all cases whatsoever.

He has abdicated government here, by declaring us out of his protection, and waging war against us.

He has plundered our seas, ravaged our coasts, burnt our towns, and destroyed the lives of our people.

He is, at this time, transporting large armies of foreign mercenaries to complete the works of death, desolation, and tyranny, already begun, with circumstances of cruelty and perfidy scarcely paralleled in the most barbarous ages, and totally unworthy the head of a civilized nation.

He has constrained our fellow citizens, taken captive on the high seas, to bear arms against their country, to become the executioners of their friends, and brethren, or to fall themselves by their hands.

He has excited domestic insurrections amongst us, and has endeavored to bring on the inhabitants of our frontiers, the merciless Indian savages, whose known rule of warfare is an undistinguished destruction of all ages, sexes, and conditions.

In every stage of these oppressions, we have

petitioned for redress, in the most humble terms; our repeated petitions have been answered only by repeated injury. A prince, whose character is thus marked by every act which may define a tyrant, is unfit to be the ruler of a free people.

Nor have we been wanting in attention to our British brethren. We have warned them, from time to time, of attempts made by their legislature to extend an unwarrantable jurisdiction over us. We have reminded them of the circumstances of our emigration and settlement here. We have appealed to their native justice and magnanimity, and we have conjured them, by the ties of our common kindred, to disavow these usurpations, which would inevitably interrupt our connections and correspondence. They, too, have been deaf to the voice of justice and consanguinity. We must, therefore, acquiesce in the necessity which denounces our separation, and hold them, as we hold the rest of mankind, enemies in war, in peace, friends.

We, therefore, the representatives of the United States of America, in general Congress assembled, appealing to the Supreme Judge of the world for the rectitude of our intentions, do, in the name, and by the authority of the good people of these colonies, solemnly publish and declare, that these united colonies are, and of right ought to be, free and independent states: that they are absolved from all allegiance to the British Crown, and that all political connection between them and the state of Great Britain is, and ought to be, totally dissolved; and that, as free and independent states, they have full power to levy war, conclude peace, contract alliances, establish commerce, and to do all other acts and things which independent states may of right do. And, for the support of this declaration, with a firm reliance on the protection of Divine Providence, we mutually pledge to each other our lives, our fortunes, and our sacred honor.

THE CONSTITUTION OF THE UNITED STATES OF AMERICA

We the people of the United States, in order to form a more perfect union, establish justice, insure domestic tranquillity, provide for the common defense, promote the general welfare, and secure the blessings of liberty to ourselves and our posterity, do ordain and establish this Constitution for the United States of America.

ARTICLE I

Section 1. All legislative powers herein granted shall be vested in a Congress of the United States, which shall consist of a Senate and House of Representatives.

Section 2. 1. The House of Representatives shall be composed of members chosen every second year by the people of the several States, and the electors in each State shall have the qualifications requisite for electors of the most numerous branch of the State legislature.

2. No person shall be a representative who shall not have attained to the age of twenty-five years, and been seven years a citizen of the United States, and who shall not, when elected, be an inhabitant of that State in which he shall be chosen.

3. Representatives and direct taxes [1] shall **be** apportioned among the several States which may be included within this Union, according to their respective numbers, which shall be determined by adding to the whole number of free persons, including those bound to service for a term of years, and excluding Indians not taxed, three fifths of all other persons. [2] The actual enumeration shall be made within three years after the first meeting of the Congress of the United States, and within every subsequent term of ten years, in such manner as they shall by law direct. The number of representatives shall not exceed one for every thirty thousand, but each State shall have at least one representative; and until such enumeration shall be made, the State of New Hampshire shall be entitled to choose three, Massachusetts eight, Rhode Island and Providence Plantations one, Connecticut five, New York six, New Jersey four, Pennsylvania eight, Delaware one, Maryland six, Virginia ten, North Carolina five, South Carolina five, and Georgia three.

4. When vacancies happen in the representation from any State, the executive authority thereof shall issue writs of election to fill such vacancies.

5. The House of Representatives shall choose their speaker and other officers; and shall have the sole power of impeachment.

[1] See the 16th Amendment.

[2] See the 14th Amendment.

Section 3. 1. The Senate of the United States shall be composed of two senators from each State, chosen by the legislature thereof,[3] for six years; and each senator shall have one vote.

2. Immediately after they shall be assembled in consequence of the first election, they shall be divided as equally as may be into three classes. The seats of the senators of the first class shall be vacated at the expiration of the second year, of the second class at the expiration of the fourth year, and of the third class at the expiration of the sixth year, so that one third may be chosen every second year; and if vacancies happen by resignation, or otherwise, during the recess of the legislature of any State, the executive thereof may make temporary appointments until the next meeting of the legislature, which shall then fill such vacancies.[4]

3. No person shall be a senator who shall not have attained to the age of thirty years, and been nine years a citizen of the United States, and who shall not, when elected, be an inhabitant of that State for which he shall be chosen.

4. The Vice President of the United States shall be President of the Senate, but shall have no vote, unless they be equally divided.

5. The Senate shall choose their other officers, and also a president pro tempore, in the absence of the Vice President, or when he shall exercise the office of the President of the United States.

6. The Senate shall have the sole power to try all impeachments. When sitting for that purpose, they shall be on oath or affirmation. When the President of the United States is tried, the chief justice shall preside: and no person shall be convicted without the concurrence of two thirds of the members present.

7. Judgment in cases of impeachment shall not extend further than to removal from office, and disqualifications to hold and enjoy any office of honor, trust or profit under the United States: but the party convicted shall nevertheless be liable and subject to indictment, trial, judgment and punishment, according to law.

Section 4. 1. The times, places, and manner of holding elections for senators and representatives, shall be prescribed in each State by the legislature thereof; but the Congress may at any time by law make or alter such regulations, except as to the places of choosing senators.

[3] See the 17th Amendment.
[4] See the 17th Amendment.

2. The Congress shall assemble at least once in every year, and such meeting shall be on the first Monday in December, unless they shall by law appoint a different day.

Section 5. 1. Each House shall be the judge of the elections, returns and qualifications of its own members, and a majority of each shall constitute a quorum to do business; but a smaller number may adjourn from day to day, and may be authorized to compel the attendance of absent members, in such manner, and under such penalties as each House may provide.

2. Each House may determine the rules of its proceedings, punish its members for disorderly behavior, and, with the concurrence of two thirds, expel a member.

3. Each House shall keep a journal of its proceedings, and from time to time publish the same, excepting such parts as may in their judgment require secrecy; and the yeas and nays of the members of either House on any question shall, at the desire of one fifth of those present, be entered on the journal.

4. Neither House, during the session of Congress, shall, without the consent of the other, adjourn for more than three days, nor to any other place than that in which the two Houses shall be sitting.

Section 6. 1. The senators and representatives shall receive a compensation for their services, to be ascertained by law, and paid out of the Treasury of the United States. They shall in all cases, except treason, felony, and breach of the peace, be privileged from arrest during their attendance at the session of their respective Houses, and in going to and returning from the same; and for any speech or debate in either House, they shall not be questioned in any other place.

2. No senator or representative shall, during the time for which he was elected, be appointed to any civil office under the authority of the United States, which shall have been created, or the emoluments whereof shall have been increased, during such time; and no person holding any office under the United States shall be a member of either House during his continuance in office.

Section 7. 1 All bills for raising revenue shall originate in the House of Representatives; but the Senate may propose or concur with amendments as on other bills.

2. Every bill which shall have passed the House of Representatives and the Senate, shall, before it become a law, be presented to the President of the United States; If he approves he shall sign it, but if not he shall return it, with his objections, to that House in which it shall have originated, who shall enter the

objections at large on their journal, and proceed to reconsider it. If after such reconsideration two thirds of that House shall agree to pass the bill, it shall be sent, together with the objections, to the other House, by which it shall likewise be reconsidered, and if approved by two thirds of that House, it shall become a law. But in all such cases the votes of both Houses shall be determined by yeas and nays, and the names of the persons voting for and against the bill shall be entered on the journal of each House respectively. If any bill shall not be returned by the President within ten days (Sundays excepted) after it shall have been presented to him, the same shall be a law, in like manner as if he had signed it, unless the Congress by their adjournment prevent its return, in which case it shall not be a law.

3. Every order, resolution, or vote to which the concurrence of the Senate and the House of Representatives may be necessary (except on a question of adjournment) shall be presented to the President of the United States; and before the same shall take effect, shall be approved by him, or being disapproved by him, shall be repassed by two thirds of the Senate and House of Representatives, according to the rules and limitations prescribed in the case of a bill.

Section 8. The Congress shall have the power

1. To lay and collect taxes, duties, imposts, and excises, to pay the debts and provide for the common defense and general welfare of the United States; but all duties, imposts, and excises shall be uniform throughout the United States;

2. To borrow money on the credit of the United States;

3. To regulate commerce with foreign nations, and among the several States, and with the Indian tribes;

4. To establish an uniform rule of naturalization, and uniform laws on the subject of bankruptcies throughout the United States;

5. To coin money, regulate the value thereof, and of foreign coin, and fix the standard of weights and measures;

6. To provide for the punishment of counterfeiting the securities and current coin of the United States;

7. To establish post offices and post roads;

8. To promote the progress of science and useful arts, by securing for limited times to authors and inventors the exclusive right to their respective writings and discoveries;

9. To constitute tribunals inferior to the Supreme Court;

10. To define and punish piracies and felonies committed on the high seas, and offenses against the law of nations;

11. To declare war, grant letters of marque and reprisal, and make rules concerning captures on land and water;

12. To raise and support armies, but no appropriation of money to that use shall be for a longer term than two years;

13. To provide and maintain a navy;

14. To make rules for the government and regulation of the land and naval forces;

15. To provide for calling forth the militia to execute the laws of the Union, suppress insurrections and repel invasions;

16. To provide for organizing, arming, and disciplining the militia, and for governing such part of them as may be employed in the service of the United States, reserving to the States respectively, the appointment of the officers, and the authority of training the militia according to the discipline prescribed by Congress;

17. To exercise exclusive legislation in all cases whatsoever, over such district (not exceeding ten miles square) as may, by cession of particular States, and the acceptance of Congress, become the seat of the government of the United States, and to exercise like authority over all places purchased by the consent of the legislature of the State in which the same shall be, for the erection of forts, magazines, arsenals, dockyards, and other needful buildings; and

18. To make all laws which shall be necessary and proper for carrying into execution the foregoing powers, and all other powers vested by this Constitution in the government of the United States, or in any department or officer thereof.

Section 9. 1. The migration or importation of such persons as any of the States now existing shall think proper to admit, shall not be prohibited by the Congress prior to the year one thousand eight hundred and eight, but a tax or duty may be imposed on such importation, not exceeding ten dollars for each person.

2. The privilege of the writ of habeas corpus shall not be suspended, unless when in cases of rebellion or invasion the public safety may require it.

3. No bill of attainder or ex post facto law shall be passed.

4. No capitation, or other direct, tax shall be laid, unless in proportion to the census or enumeration hereinbefore directed to be taken.[5]

---

[5] See the 16th Amendment.

5. No tax or duty shall be laid on articles exported from any State.

6. No preference shall be given by any regulation of commerce or revenue to the ports of one State over those of another: nor shall vessels bound to, or from, one State be obliged to enter, clear, or pay duties in another.

7. No money shall be drawn from the treasury, but in consequence of appropriations made by law; and a regular statement and account of the receipts and expenditures of all public money shall be published from time to time.

8. No title of nobility shall be granted by the United States: and no person holding any office of profit or trust under them, shall, without the consent of the Congress, accept of any present, emolument, office, or title, of any kind whatever, from any king, prince, or foreign State.

Section 10. 1. No State shall enter into any treaty, alliance, or confederation; grant letters of marque and reprisal; coin money; emit bills of credit; make any thing but gold and silver coin a tender in payment of debts; pass any bill of attainder, ex post facto law, or law impairing the obligation of contracts, or grant any title of nobility.

2. No State shall, without the consent of the Congress, lay any imposts or duties on imports or exports, except what may be absolutely necessary for executing its inspection laws: and the net produce of all duties and imposts laid by any State on imports or exports, shall be for the use of the treasury of the United States; and all such laws shall be subject to the revision and control of the Congress.

3. No State shall, without the consent of the Congress, lay any duty of tonnage, keep troops, or ships of war in time of peace, enter into any agreement or compact with another State, or with a foreign power, or engage in war, unless actually invaded, or in such imminent danger as will not admit of delay.

ARTICLE II

Section 1. 1. The executive power shall be vested in a President of the United States of America. He shall hold his office during the term of four years, and, together with the Vice President, chosen for the same term, be elected, as follows:

2. Each State shall appoint, in such manner as the legislature thereof may direct, a number of electors, equal to the whole number of senators and representatives to which the State may be entitled in the Congress: but no senator or representative, or person holding an office of trust or profit under the United States, shall be appointed an elector.

The electors shall meet in their respective States, and vote by ballot for two persons, of whom one at least shall not be an inhabitant of the same State with themselves. And they shall make a list of all the persons voted for, and of the number of votes for each; which list they shall sign and certify, and transmit sealed to the seat of the government of the United States, directed to the president of the Senate. The president of the Senate shall, in the presence of the Senate and House of Representatives, open all the certificates, and the votes shall then be counted. The person having the greatest number of votes shall be the President, if such number be a majority of the whole number of electors appointed; and if there be more than one who have such majority, and have an equal number of votes, then the House of Representatives shall immediately choose by ballot one of them for President; and if no person have a majority, then from the five highest on the list the said House shall in like manner choose the President. But in choosing the President, the votes shall be taken by States, the representation from each State having one vote; a quorum for this purpose shall consist of a member or members from two thirds of the States, and a majority of all the States shall be necessary to a choice. In every case, after the choice of the President, the person having the greatest number of votes of the electors shall be the Vice President. But if there should remain two or more who have equal votes, the Senate shall choose from them by ballot the Vice President.[6]

3. The Congress may determine the time of choosing the electors, and the day on which they shall give their votes; which day shall be the same throughout the United States.

4. No person except a natural born citizen, or a citizen of the United States, at the time of the adoption of this Constitution, shall be eligible to the office of President; neither shall any person be eligible to that office who shall not have attained to the age of thirty-five years, and been fourteen years a resident within the United States.

5. In case of the removal of the President from office, or of his death, resignation, or inability to discharge the powers and duties of the said office, the same shall devolve on the Vice President, and the Congress may by law provide for the case of removal, death, resignation or inability, both of the President and

[6] Superseded by the 12th Amendment.

Vice President, declaring what officer shall then act as President, and such officer shall act accordingly, until the disability be removed, or a President shall be elected.

6. The President shall, at stated times, receive for his services a compensation, which shall neither be increased nor diminished during the period for which he shall have been elected, and he shall not receive within that period any other emolument from the United States, or any of them.

7. Before he enter on the execution of his office, he shall take the following oath or affirmation:—"I do solemnly swear (or affirm) that I will faithfully execute the office of President of the United States, and will to the best of my ability, preserve, protect and defend the Constitution of the United States."

Section 2. 1. The President shall be commander in chief of the army and navy of the United States, and of the militia of the several States, when called into the actual service of the United States; he may require the opinion, in writing, of the principal officer in each of the executive departments, upon any subject relating to the duties of their respective offices, and he shall have power to grant reprieves and pardons for offenses against the United States, except in cases of impeachment.

2. He shall have power, by and with the advice and consent of the Senate, to make treaties, provided two thirds of the senators present concur; and he shall nominate, and by and with the advice and consent of the Senate, shall appoint ambassadors, other public ministers and consuls, judges of the Supreme Court, and all other officers of the United States, whose appointments are not herein otherwise provided for, and which shall be established by law: but the Congress may by law vest the appointment of such inferior officers, as they think proper, in the President alone, in the courts of law, or in the heads of departments.

3. The President shall have power to fill up all vacancies that may happen during the recess of the Senate, by granting commissions which shall expire at the end of their next session.

Section 3. He shall from time to time give to the Congress information of the state of the Union, and recommend to their consideration such measures as he shall judge necessary and expedient; he may, on extraordinary occasions, convene both Houses, or either of them, and in case of disagreement between them with respect to the time of adjournment, he may adjourn them to such time as he shall think proper; he shall receive ambassadors and other public ministers; he shall take care that the laws be faithfully executed, and shall commission all the officers of the United States.

Section 4. The President, Vice President, and all civil officers of the United States, shall be removed from office on impeachment for, and conviction of, treason, bribery, or other high crimes and misdemeanors.

ARTICLE III

Section 1. The judicial power of the United States shall be vested in one Supreme Court, and in such inferior courts as the Congress may from time to time ordain and establish. The judges, both of the Supreme and inferior courts, shall hold their offices during good behavior, and shall, at stated times, receive for their services, a compensation, which shall not be diminished during their continuance in office.

Section 2. 1. The judicial power shall extend to all cases, in law and equity, arising under this Constitution, the laws of the United States, and treaties made, or which shall be made, under their authority;—to all cases affecting ambassadors, other public ministers and consuls;—to all cases of admiralty and maritime jurisdiction;—to controversies to which the United States shall be a party;[7]—to controversies between two or more States;—between a State and citizens of another State;—between citizens of different States;—between citizens of the same State claiming lands under grants of different States, and between a State, or the citizens thereof, and foreign States, citizens or subjects.

2. In all cases affecting ambassadors, other public ministers and consuls, and those in which a State shall be party, the Supreme Court shall have original jurisdiction. In all the other cases before mentioned, the Supreme Court shall have appellate jurisdiction, both as to law and fact, with such exceptions, and under such regulations as the Congress shall make.

3. The trial of all crimes, except in cases of impeachment, shall be by jury; and such trial shall be held in the State where the said crimes shall have been committed; but when not committed within any State, the trial shall be at such place or places as the Congress may by law have directed.

Section 3 1. Treason against the United States shall consist only in levying war against them, or in adhering to their enemies, giving them aid and comfort. No person shall be convicted of treason unless on the testimony of two witnesses to the same overt act, or on confession in open court.

[7] See the 11th Amendment.

2. The Congress shall have power to declare the punishment of treason, but no attainder of treason shall work corruption of blood, or forfeiture except during the life of the person attainted.

ARTICLE IV

Section 1. Full faith and credit shall be given in each State to the public acts, records, and judicial proceedings of every other State. And the Congress may by general laws prescribe the manner in which such acts, records and proceedings shall be proved. and the effect thereof.

Section 2. 1. The citizens of each State shall be entitled to all privileges and immunities of citizens in the several States.[8]

2. A person charged in any State with treason, felony, or other crime, who shall flee from justice, and be found in another State, shall on demand of the executive authority of the State from which he fled, be delivered up to be removed to the State having jurisdiction of the crime.

3. No person held to service or labor in one State under the laws thereof, escaping into another, shall, in consequence of any law or regulation therein, be discharged from such service or labor, but shall be delivered up on claim of the party to whom such service or labor may be due.[9]

Section 3. 1. New States may be admitted by the Congress into this Union; but no new State shall be formed or erected within the jurisdiction of any other State; nor any State be formed by the junction of two or more States, or parts of States, without the consent of the legislatures of the States concerned as well as of the Congress.

2. The Congress shall have power to dispose of and make all needful rules and regulations respecting the territory or other property belonging to the United States; and nothing in this Constitution shall be so construed as to prejudice any claims of the United States, or of any particular State.

Section 4. The United States shall guarantee to every State in this Union a republican form of government, and shall protect each of them against invasion; and on application of the legislature, or of the executive (when the legislature cannot be convened) against domestic violence.

8 See the 14th Amendment, Sec. 1.
9 See the 13th Amendment.

ARTICLE V

The Congress, whenever two thirds of both Houses shall deem it necessary, shall propose amendments to this Constitution, or, on the application of the legislatures of two thirds of the several States, shall call a convention for proposing amendments, which in either case, shall be valid to all intents and purposes, as part of this Constitution, when ratified by the legislatures of three fourths of the several States, or by conventions in three fourths thereof, as the one or the other mode of ratification may be proposed by the Congress; Provided that no amendment which may be made prior to the year one thousand eight hundred and eight shall in any manner affect the first and fourth clauses in the ninth section of the first article; and that no State, without its consent, shall be deprived of its equal suffrage in the Senate.

ARTICLE VI

1. All debts contracted and engagements entered into, before the adoption of this Constitution, shall be as valid against the United States under this Constitution, as under the Confederation.[10]

2. This Constitution, and the laws of the United States which shall be made in pursuance thereof; and all treaties made, or which shall be made, under the authority of the United States, shall be the supreme law of the land; and the Judges in every State shall be bound thereby, any thing in the Constitution or laws of any State to the contrary notwithstanding.

3. The senators and representatives before mentioned, and the members of the several State legislatures, and all executive and judicial officers, both of the United States and of the several States, shall be bound by oath or affirmation to support this Constitution; but no religious test shall ever be required as a qualification to any office or public trust under the United States.

ARTICLE VII

The ratification of the conventions of nine States shall be sufficient for the establishment of this Constitution between the States so ratifying the same.

Done in Convention by the unanimous consent of the States present the seventeenth day of September in the year of our Lord one

10 See the 14th Amendment, Sec. 4.

thousand seven hundred and eighty-seven, and of the independence of the United States of America the twelfth. In witness whereof we have hereunto subscribed our names.

[Names omitted]

* * *

Articles in addition to, and amendment of, the Constitution of the United States of America, proposed by Congress, and ratified by the legislatures of the several States, pursuant to the fifth article of the original Constitution.

AMENDMENTS

FIRST TEN AMENDMENTS PASSED BY CONGRESS SEPT. 25, 1789, RATIFIED BY THREE-FOURTHS OF THE STATES DECEMBER 15, 1791.

AMENDMENT I

Congress shall make no law respecting an establishment of religion, or prohibiting the free excerise thereof; or abridging the freedom of speech, or of the press; or the right of the people peaceably to assemble, and to petition the government for a redress of grievances.

AMENDMENT II

A well regulated militia, being necessary to the security of a free State, the right of the people to keep and bear arms, shall not be infringed.

AMENDMENT III

No soldier shall, in time of peace be quartered in any house, without the consent of the owner, nor in time of war, but in a manner to be prescribed by law.

AMENDMENT IV

The right of the people to secure in their persons, houses, papers, and effects, against unreasonable searches and seizures, shall not be violated, and no warrants shall issue, but upon probable cause, supported by oath or affirmation, and particularly describing the place to be searched, and the persons or things to be seized.

AMENDMENT V

No person shall be held to answer for a capital, or otherwise infamous crime, unless on a presentment or indictment of a grand jury, except in cases arising in the land or naval forces, or in the militia, when in actual service in time of war or public danger; nor shall any person be subject for the same offense to be twice put in jeopardy of life or limb; nor shall be compelled in any criminal case to be a witness against himself, nor be deprived of life, liberty, or property, without due process of law; nor shall private property be taken for public use, without just compensation.

AMENDMENT VI

In all criminal prosecutions, the accused shall enjoy the right to a speedy and public trial, by an impartial jury of the State and district wherein the crime shall have been committed, which district shall have been previously ascertained by law, and to be informed of the nature and cause of the accusation; to be confronted with the witnesses against him; to have compulsory process for obtaining witnesses in his favor, and to have the assistance of counsel for his defense.

AMENDMENT VII

In suits at common law, where the value in controversy shall exceed twenty dollars, the right of trial by jury shall be preserved, and no fact tried by a jury shall be otherwise reëxamined in any court of the United States, than according to the rules of the common law.

AMENDMENT VIII

Excessive bail shall not be required, nor excessive fines imposed, nor cruel and unusual punishments inflicted.

AMENDMENT IX

The enumeration in the Constitution of certain rights shall not be construed to deny or disparage others retained by the people.

AMENDMENT X

The powers not delegated to the United States by the Constitution, nor prohibited by it to the States, are reserved to the States respectively, or to the people.

AMENDMENT XI

PASSED BY CONGRESS MARCH 5, 1794, RATIFIED JANUARY 8, 1798.

The judicial power of the United States shall not be construed to extend to any suit in law or equity, commenced or prosecuted against one of the United States by citizens of another State, or by citizens or subjects of any foreign State.

AMENDMENT XII

PASSED BY CONGRESS DECEMBER 9, 1803.
RATIFIED SEPTEMBER 25, 1804.

The electors shall meet in their respective States, and vote by ballot for President and Vice President, one of whom, at least, shall not be an inhabitant of the same State with themselves; they shall name in their ballots the person voted for as President, and in distinct ballots, the person voted for as Vice President, and they shall make distinct lists of all persons voted for as President and of all persons voted for as Vice President, and of the number of votes for each, which lists they shall sign and certify, and transmit sealed to the seat of the government of the United States, directed to the President of the Senate;—The President of the Senate shall, in the presence of the Senate and House of Representatives, open all the certificates and the votes shall then be counted;—The person having the greatest number of votes for President, shall be the President, if such number be a majority of the whole number of electors appointed; and if no person have such majority, then from the persons having the highest numbers not exceeding three on the list of those voted for as President, the House of Representatives shall choose immediately, by ballot, the President. But in choosing the President, the votes shall be taken by States, the representation from each State having one vote; a quorum for this purpose shall consist of a member or members from two thirds of the States, and a majority of all the States shall be necessary to a choice. And if the House of Representatives shall not choose a President whenever the right of choice shall devolve upon them, before the fourth day of March next following, then the Vice President shall act as President, as in the case of the death or other constitutional disability of the President. The person having the greatest number of votes as Vice President shall be the Vice President, if such number be a majority of the whole number of electors appointed, and if no person have a majority, then from the two highest numbers on the list, the Senate shall choose the Vice President; a quorum for the purpose shall consist of two thirds of the whole number of Senators, and a majority of the whole number shall be necessary to a choice. But no person constitutionally ineligible to the office of President shall be eligible to that of Vice President of the United States.

AMENDMENT XIII

PASSED BY CONGRESS FEBRUARY 1, 1865.
RATIFIED DECEMBER 18, 1865.

Section 1. Neither slavery nor involuntary servitude, except as a punishment for crime whereof the party shall have been duly convicted, shall exist within the United States, or any place subject to their jurisdiction.
Section 2. Congress shall have power to enforce this article by appropriate legislation.

AMENDMENT XIV

PASSED BY CONGRESS JUNE 16, 1866.
RATIFIED JULY 28, 1868.

Section 1. All persons born or naturalized in the United States, and subject to the jurisdiction thereof, are citizens of the United States and of the State wherein they reside. No State shall make or enforce any law which shall abridge the privileges or immunities of citizens of the United States; nor shall any State deprive any person of life, liberty, or property, without due process of law; nor deny to any person within its jurisdiction the equal protection of the laws.
Section 2. Representatives shall be apportioned among the several States according to their respective numbers, counting the whole number of persons in each State, excluding Indians not taxed. But when the right to vote at any election for the choice of electors for President and Vice President of the United States, representatives in Congress, the executive and judicial officers of a State, or the members of the legislature thereof, is denied to any of the male inhabitants of such State, being twenty-one years of age, and citizens of the United States, or in any way abridged, except for participating in rebellion, or other crime, the basis of representation therein shall be reduced in the proportion which the number of such male citizens shall bear to the whole number of male citizens twenty-one years of age in such State.
Section 3. No person shall be a senator or representative in Congress, or elector of President and Vice President, or hold any office, civil or military, under the United States, or under any State, who having previously taken an oath, as a member of Congress, or as an officer of the United States, or as a member of any State legislature, or as an executive or judicial officer of any State, to support the Constitution of the United States, shall have engaged in insurrection or rebellion against the same, or given aid or comfort to the enemies thereof. But Congress may by a vote of two thirds of each House, remove such disability.

Section 4. The validity of the public debt of the United States, authorized by law, including debts incurred for payment of pensions and bounties for services in suppressing insurrection or rebellion, shall not be questioned. But neither the United States nor any State shall assume or pay any debt or obligation incurred in aid of insurrection or rebellion against the United States, or any claim for the loss or emancipation of any slave; but all such debts, obligations, and claims shall be held illegal and void.

Section 5. The Congress shall have power to enforce, by appropriate legislation, the provisions of this article.

AMENDMENT XV

PASSED BY CONGRESS FEBRUARY 27, 1869.
RATIFIED MARCH 30, 1870.

Section 1. The right of citizens of the United States to vote shall not be denied or abridged by the United States or by any State on account of race, color, or previous condition of servitude.

Section 2. The Congress shall have power to enforce this article by appropriate legislation.

AMENDMENT XVI

PASSED BY CONGRESS JULY 12, 1909.
RATIFIED FEBRUARY 25, 1913.

The Congress shall have power to lay and collect taxes on incomes, from whatever source derived, without apportionment among the several States, and without regard to any census or enumeration.

AMENDMENT XVII

PASSED BY CONGRESS MAY 16, 1912.
RATIFIED MAY 31, 1913.

The Senate of the United States shall be composed of two senators from each State, elected by the people thereof, for six years; and each senator shall have one vote. The electors in each State shall have the qualifications requisite for electors of the most numerous branch of the State legislature.

When vacancies happen in the representation of any State in the Senate, the executive authority of such State shall issue writs of election to fill such vacancies: *Provided,* That the legislature of any State may empower the executive thereof to make temporary appointments until the people fill the vacancies by election as the legislature may direct.

This amendment shall not be so construed as to affect the election or term of any senator chosen before it becomes valid as part of the Constitution.

AMENDMENT XVIII [11]

PASSED BY CONGRESS DECEMBER 17, 1917.
RATIFIED JANUARY 29, 1919.

After one year from the ratification of this article, the manufacture, sale, or transportation of intoxicating liquors within, the importation thereof into, or the exportation thereof from the United States and all territory subject to the jurisdiction thereof for beverage purposes is thereby prohibited.

The Congress and the several States shall have concurrent power to enforce this article by appropriate legislation.

This article shall be inoperative unless it shall have been ratified as an amendment to the Constitution by the legislatures of the several States, as provided in the Constitution, within seven years from the date of the submission hereof to the States by Congress.

AMENDMENT XIX

PASSED BY CONGRESS JUNE 5, 1919.
RATIFIED AUGUST 26, 1920.

The right of citizens of the United States to vote shall not be denied or abridged by the United States or by any State on account of sex.

Congress shall have the power to enforce this article by appropriate legislation.

AMENDMENT XX

PASSED BY CONGRESS MARCH 3, 1932.
RATIFIED JANUARY 23, 1933.

Section 1. The terms of the President and Vice President shall end at noon on the 20th day of January, and the terms of Senators and Representatives at noon on the 3d day of January, of the years in which such terms would have ended if this article had not been ratified; and the terms of their successors shall then begin.

Section 2. The Congress shall assemble at least once in every year, and such meeting shall begin at noon on the 3d day of January, unless they shall by law appoint a different day.

Section 3. If, at the time fixed for the beginning of the term of the President, the President-elect shall have died, the Vice President-elect shall become President. If a President shall not have been chosen before the time fixed for the beginning of his term, or if the President-elect shall have failed to qualify, then

[11] Repealed by the 21st Amendment.

the Vice President-elect shall act as President until a President shall have qualified; and the Congress may by law provide for the case wherein neither a President-elect nor a Vice President-elect shall have qualified, declaring who shall then act as President, or the manner in which one who is to act shall be selected, and such person shall act accordingly until a President or Vice-President shall have qualified.

Section 4. The Congress may by law provide for the case of the death of any of the persons from whom the House of Representatives may choose a President whenever the right of choice shall have devolved upon them, and for the case of the death of any of the persons from whom the Senate may choose a Vice President whenever the right of choice shall have devolved upon them.

Section 5. Sections 1 and 2 shall take effect on the 15th day of October following the ratification of this article.

Section 6. This article shall be inoperative unless it shall have been ratified as an amendment to the Constitution by the legislatures of three-fourths of the several States within seven years from the date of its submission.

AMENDMENT XXI

PASSED BY CONGRESS FEBRUARY 20, 1933.
RATIFIED DECEMBER 5, 1933.

Section 1. The Eighteenth Article of amendment to the Constitution of the United States is hereby repealed.

Section 2. The transportation or importation into any State, Territory, or possession of the United States for delivery or use therein of intoxicating liquors in violation of the laws thereof, is hereby prohibited.

Section 3. This article shall be inoperative unless it shall have been ratified as an amendment to the Constitution by conventions in the several States, as provided in the Constitution, within seven years from the date of the submission thereof to the States by the Congress.

AMENDMENT XXII

PASSED BY CONGRESS MARCH 12, 1947.
RATIFIED MARCH 1, 1951.

No person shall be elected to the office of the President more than twice, and no person who has held the office of President, or acted as President, for more than two years of a term to which some other person was elected President shall be elected to the office of the President more than once.

But this article shall not apply to any person holding the office of President when this article was proposed by the Congress, and shall not prevent any person who may be holding the office of President, or acting as President, during the term within which this article becomes operative from holding the office of President or acting as President during the remainder of such term.

This article shall be inoperative unless it shall have been ratified as an amendment to the Constitution by the legislatures of three-fourths of the several States within seven years from the date of its submission to the States by the Congress.

PRESIDENTIAL ELECTIONS, 1789–1956

Year	No. of States	Candidates	Party	Electoral Vote	Popular Vote	Percentage of Popular Vote
1789	10	*George Washington*		69		
		John Adams		34		
		John Jay		9		
		R. H. Harrison		6		
		John Rutledge		6		
		John Hancock		4		
		George Clinton		3		
		Samuel Huntington		2		
		John Milton		2		
		James Armstrong		1		
		Benjamin Lincoln		1		
		Edward Telfair		1		
		(Not voted)		12		
1792	15	*George Washington*	Federalist	132		
		John Adams	Federalist	77		
		George Clinton	Democratic-Republican	50		
		Thomas Jefferson		4		
		Aaron Burr		1		
1796	16	*John Adams*	Federalist	71		
		Thomas Jefferson	Democratic-Republican	68		
		Thomas Pinckney	Federalist	59		
		Aaron Burr	Antifederalist	30		
		Samuel Adams	Democratic-Republican	15		
		Oliver Ellsworth	Federalist	11		
		George Clinton	Democratic-Republican	7		
		John Jay	Independent-Federalist	5		
		James Iredell	Federalist	3		
		George Washington	Federalist	2		
		John Henry	Independent	2		
		S. Johnston	Independent-Federalist	2		
		C. C. Pinckney	Independent-Federalist	1		
1800	16	*Thomas Jefferson*	Democratic-Republican	73		
		Aaron Burr	Democratic-Republican	73		
		John Adams	Federalist	65		
		C. C. Pinckney	Federalist	64		
		John Jay	Federalist	1		
1804	17	*Thomas Jefferson*	Democratic-Republican	162		
		C. C. Pinckney	Federalist	14		
1808	17	*James Madison*	Democratic-Republican	122		
		C. C. Pinckney	Federalist	47		
		George Clinton	Independent-Republican	6		
		(Not voted)		1		

PRESIDENTIAL ELECTIONS, 1789–1956 (Continued)

Year	No. of States	Candidates	Party	Electoral Vote	Popular Vote	Percentage of Popular Vote
1812	18	*James Madison*	Democratic-Republican	128		
		DeWitt Clinton	Fusion	89		
		(Not voted)		1		
1816	19	*James Monroe*	Republican	183		
		Rufus King	Federalist	34		
		(Not voted)		4		
1820	24	*James Monroe*	Republican	231		
		John Q. Adams	Independent-Republican	1		
		(Not voted)		3		
1824	24	*John Q. Adams*	No distinct party designations	84	108,740	30.54
		Andrew Jackson		99	153,544	43.12
		Henry Clay		37	47,136	13.23
		W. H. Crawford		41	46,618	13.09
1828	24	*Andrew Jackson*	Democratic	178	647,286	56.02
		John Q. Adams	National Republican	83	508,064	43.97
1832	25	*Andrew Jackson*	Democratic	219	687,502	54.96
		Henry Clay	National Republican	49	530,189	42.38
		William Wirt	Anti-Masonic	7	33,108	2.64
		John Floyd	Nullifiers	11		
		(Not voted)		2		
1836	26	*Martin Van Buren*	Democratic	170	762,678	50.90
		Wm. H. Harrison	Whig	73		
		Hugh L. White	Whig	26	735,651	49.09
		Daniel Webster	Whig	14		
		W. P. Mangum	Anti-Jackson	11		
1840	26	*William H. Harrison*	Whig	234	1,275,016	52.87
		Martin Van Buren	Democratic	60	1,129,102	46.82
		James G. Birney	Liberty		7,069	.29
1844	26	*James K. Polk*	Democratic	170	1,337,243	49.55
		Henry Clay	Whig	105	1,299,062	48.13
		James G. Birney	Liberty		62,300	.23
1848	30	*Zachary Taylor*	Whig	163	1,360,099	47.35
		Lewis Cass	Democratic	127	1,220,544	42.49
		Martin Van Buren	Free Soil		291,263	10.14
1852	31	*Franklin Pierce*	Democratic	254	1,601,274	50.93
		Winfield Scott	Whig	42	1,386,580	44.10
		John P. Hale	Free Soil		155,825	4.95

Year	No. of States	Candidates	Party	Electoral Vote	Popular Vote	Percentage of Popular Vote
1856	31	*James Buchanan*	Democratic	174	1,838,169	45.34
		John C. Frémont	Republican	114	1,341,264	33.08
		Millard Fillmore	American	8	874,534	21.57
1860	33	*Abraham Lincoln*	Republican	180	1,866,452	39.87
		J. C. Breckenridge	Democratic	72	847,953	18.11
		Stephen A. Douglas	Democratic	12	1,375,157	29.38
		John Bell	Constitutional Union	39	590,631	12.61
1864	36	*Abraham Lincoln*	Republican	212	2,213,665	55.08
		George B. McClellan	Democratic	21	1,805,237	44.91
		(Not voted)		81		
1868	37	*U. S. Grant*	Republican	214	3,012,833	52.70
		Horatio Seymour	Democratic	80	2,703,249	47.29
		(Not voted)		23		
1872	37	*U. S. Grant*	Republican	286	3,597,132	55.63
		Horace Greeley	Democratic;			
			Liberal Republican	66*	2,834,125	43.82
		Charles O'Conor	Independent-Democratic		29,489	.45
		James Black	Temperance		5,608	.08
		Thomas A. Hendricks	Independent-Democratic	42		
		B. Gratz Brown	Democratic	18		
		Charles J. Jenkins	Democratic	2		
		David Davis	Democratic	1		
		(Not voted)		17		
1876	38	*Rutherford B. Hayes*	Republican	185	4,036,298	47.87
		Samuel J. Tilden	Democratic	184	4,300,590	51.01
		Peter Cooper	Greenback		81,737	.96
		G. C. Smith	Prohibition		9,522	.11
		James B. Walker	American		2,636	.03
1880	38	*James A. Garfield*	Republican	214	4,454,416	48.31
		W. S. Hancock	Democratic	155	4,444,952	48.21
		James B. Weaver	Greenback-Labor		308,578	3.34
		Neal Dow	Prohibition		10,305	.11
		John W. Phelps	American		700	.007
1884	38	*Grover Cleveland*	Democratic	219	4,874,986	48.49
		James G. Blaine	Republican	182	4,851,981	48.26
		John P. St. John	Prohibition		150,369	1.49
		Benjamin F. Butler	Greenback-Labor		175,370	1.74

* Because of the death of Greeley, Democratic electors scattered their votes.

PRESIDENTIAL ELECTIONS, 1789–1956 (Continued)

Year	No. of States	Candidates	Party	Electoral Vote	Popular Vote	Percentage of Popular Vote
1888	38	*Benjamin Harrison*	Republican	233	5,439,853	47.79
		Grover Cleveland	Democratic	168	5,540,309	48.68
		Clinton B. Fisk	Prohibition		249,506	2.19
		Anson J. Streeter	Union Labor		146,935	1.29
		Robert H. Cowdrey	United Labor		2,818	.02
		James L. Curtis	American		1,600	.01
1892	44	*Grover Cleveland*	Democratic	277	5,556,918	46.07
		Benjamin Harrison	Republican	145	5,176,108	42.92
		James B. Weaver	People's	22	1,041,028	8.63
		John Bidwell	Prohibition		264,133	2.19
		Simon Wing	Socialist-Labor		21,164	.17
1896	45	*William McKinley*	Republican	271	7,104,779	51.02
		William Jennings Bryan	Democratic; People's	176	6,502,925	46.70
		John M. Palmer	Nationalist Democratic		133,148	.95
		Joshua Levering	Prohibition		132,007	.94
		Charles H. Matchett	Socialist-Labor		36,274	.26
		Charles E. Bentley	Nationalist		13,969	.10
1900	45	*William McKinley*	Republican	292	7,207,923	51.61
		William Jennings Bryan	Democratic; Populist	155	6,358,133	45.53
		John C. Woolley	Prohibition		208,914	1.49
		Eugene V. Debs	Socialist Democrat		87,814	.62
		Wharton Baker	People's		50,373	.36
		Joseph F. Malloney	Socialist-Labor		39,739	.28
		Seth H. Ellis	Union Reform		5,698	.04
		Jonah F. R. Leonard	United Christian		5,500	.03
1904	45	*Theodore Roosevelt*	Republican	336	7,623,486	56.42
		Alton B. Parker	Democratic	140	5,077,911	37.58
		Eugene V. Debs	Socialist		402,283	2.97
		Silas C. Swallow	Prohibition		258,536	1.91
		Thomas E. Watson	People's		117,183	.86
		Charles H. Corregan	Socialist-Labor		31,249	.23
		Austin Holcomb	Continental		1,000	.007
1908	46	*William H. Taft*	Republican	321	7,678,908	51.57
		William Jennings Bryan	Democratic	162	6,409,104	43.04
		Eugene V. Debs	Socialist		420,793	2.82
		Eugene W. Chafin	Prohibition		253,840	1.70
		Thomas L. Hisgen	Independence		82,872	.55
		Thomas E. Watson	People's		29,100	.19
		August Gillhaus	Socialist-Labor		14,021	.09
		Daniel B. Turney	United Christian		500	.003

Year	No. of States	Candidates	Party	Electoral Vote	Popular Vote	Percentage of Popular Vote
1912	48	*Woodrow Wilson*	Democratic	435	6,293,454	41.86
		William H. Taft	Republican	8	3,484,980	23.18
		Theodore Roosevelt	Progressive	88	4,119,538	27.40
		Eugene V. Debs	Socialist		900,672	5.99
		Eugene W. Chafin	Prohibition		206,275	1.37
		Arthur E. Reimer	Socialist-Labor		28,750	.19
1916	48	*Woodrow Wilson*	Democratic	277	9,129,606	49.27
		Charles E. Hughes	Republican	254	8,538,221	46.08
		A. L. Benson	Socialist		585,113	3.15
		J. Frank Hanly	Prohibition		220,506	1.19
		Arthur E. Reimer	Socialist-Labor		13,403	.07
		(Various candidates)	Progressive		41,894	.22
1920	48	*Warren G. Harding*	Republican	404	16,152,200	60.36
		James M. Cox	Democratic	127	9,147,353	34.18
		Eugene V. Debs	Socialist		919,799	3.43
		P. P. Christensen	Farmer-Labor		265,411	.99
		Aaron S. Watkins	Prohibition		189,408	.70
		W. W. Cox	Socialist-Labor		31,715	.11
		Robert C. Macauley	Single Tax		5,837	.02
		James E. Ferguson	American		48,000	.17
1924	48	*Calvin Coolidge*	Republican	382	15,725,016	54.05
		John W. Davis	Democratic	136	8,386,503	28.82
		Robert La Follette	Progressive	13	4,822,856	16.57
		Herman P. Faris	Prohibition		57,520	.19
		Frank T. Johns	Socialist-Labor		36,428	.12
		William Z. Foster	Workers		36,386	.12
		Gilbert O. Nations	American		23,967	.08
		William J. Wallace	Commonwealth Land		1,532	.005
1928	48	*Herbert Hoover*	Republican	444	21,391,381	58.21
		Alfred E. Smith	Democratic	87	15,016,443	40.86
		Norman Thomas	Socialist		267,835	.72
		William Z. Foster	Workers		21,181	.05
		Verne L. Reynolds	Socialist-Labor		21,603	.05
		William F. Varney	Prohibition		20,106	.05
		Frank E. Webb	Farmer-Labor		6,390	.01
1932	48	*Franklin D. Roosevelt*	Democratic	472	22,821,857	57.42
		Herbert Hoover	Republican	59	15,761,841	39.65
		Norman Thomas	Socialist		881,951	2.21
		William Z. Foster	Communist		102,785	.25
		Verne L. Reynolds	Socialist-Labor		33,276	.08

Year	No. of States	Candidates	Party	Electoral Vote	Popular Vote	Percentage of Popular Vote
1932 (cont.)	48	William D. Upshaw	Prohibition		81,869	.20
		William H. Harvey	Liberty		53,425	.13
		Jacob S. Coxey, Sr.	Farmer-Labor		7,309	.01
1936	48	Franklin D. Roosevelt	Democratic; American Labor	523	27,751,597	60.83
		Alfred M. Landon	Republican	8	16,679,583	36.56
		William Lemke	Union, Royal Oak; National Union for Social Justice, 3rd Party; Independent		882,479	1.93
		Norman Thomas	Socialist		187,720	.41
		Earl Browder	Communist		80,159	.17
		D. Leigh Colvin	Prohibition; Commonwealth		37,847	.08
1940	48	Franklin D. Roosevelt	Democratic; American Labor	449	27,244,160	54.30
		Wendell L. Willkie	Republican	82	22,305,198	44.46
		Norman Thomas	Socialist; Progressive		99,557	.19
		Roger Q. Babson	Prohibition; National Prohibition		57,812	.11
		Earl Browder	Communist		46,251	.09
1944	48	Franklin D. Roosevelt	Democratic; American Labor; Liberal	432	25,602,504	53.39
		Thomas E. Dewey	Republican	99	22,006,285	45.89
		Norman Thomas	Socialist		80,518	.16
		Claude A. Watson	Prohibition		74,758	.15
		Edward A. Teichert	Socialist-Labor; Industrial Government		45,336	.09
		(Unpledged)	Texas Regulars		135,439	.28
1948	48	Harry S. Truman	Democratic; Liberal	303	24,105,695	49.51
		Thomas E. Dewey	Republican	189	21,969,170	45.12
		J. Strom Thurmond	States' Rights	39	1,169,021	2.40
		Henry A. Wallace	Progressive; American Labor		1,156,103	2.37
		Norman Thomas	Socialist		139,009	.28
		Claude A. Watson	Prohibition		103,216	.21
		Edward A. Teichert	Socialist-Labor; Industrial Government		29,061	.05
		Farrell Dobbs	Socialist Workers; Militant Workers		13,613	.02

PRESIDENTIAL ELECTIONS, 1789–1956 (Continued)

Year	No. of States	Candidates	Party	Electoral Vote	Popular Vote	Percentage of Popular Vote
1952	48	*Dwight D. Eisenhower*	Republican	442	33,824,351	54.94
		Adlai E. Stevenson	Democratic; Liberal	89	27,314,987	44.36
		Vincent Hallinan	Progressive; American Labor		132,608	.21
		Stuart Hamblen	Prohibition		72,768	.11
		Darlington Hoopes	Socialist		18,322	.02
		Eric Hass	Socialist-Labor; Industrial Government		29,333	.04
		Farrell Dobbs	Socialist Workers; Militant Workers		8,956	.01
1956	48	*Dwight D. Eisenhower*	Republican	457†	35,582,236	57.28
		Adlai E. Stevenson	Democratic; Liberal	73†	26,028,887	41.90
		T. Coleman Andrews	States' Rights		275,915	.44
		Harry F. Byrd	Independent		134,157	.21
		Eric Hass	Socialist Labor; Industrial Government		44,368	.07
		Enoch Holtwick	Prohibition		41,547	.06
		Farrell Dobbs	Socialist Workers; Militant Workers		7,805	.01
		Darlington Hoopes	Socialist		2,192	.003
		Henry Krajewski	American Third Party		1,892	.003

† One electoral vote cast for Walter B. Jones.

President	Vice-President	Secretary of State	Secretary of Treasury
1. George Washington ....1789 Federalist	John Adams ....1789 Federalist	T. Jefferson ....1789 E. Randolph ....1794 T. Pickering 1795	Alex. Hamilton ....17. Oliver Wolcott ....17.
2. John Adams ....1797 Federalist	Thomas Jefferson ....1797 Democratic-Republican	T. Pickering ....1797 John Marshall 1800	Oliver Wolcott ....17. Samuel Dexter ....18.
3. Thomas Jefferson ....1801 Democratic-Republican	Aaron Burr ....1801 Democratic-Republican George Clinton ....1805 Democratic-Republican	James Madison 1801	Samuel Dexter ....18. Albert Gallatin ....18.
4. James Madison ....1809 Democratic-Republican	George Clinton ....1809 Independent-Republican Elbridge Gerry ....1813 Democratic-Republican	Robert Smith ....1809 James Monroe 1811	Albert Gallatin ....18. H. W. Campbell ....18. A. J. Dallas ....18. W. H. Crawford ....18.
5. James Monroe ....1817 Democratic-Republican	D. D. Thompkins ....1817 Democratic-Republican	J. Q. Adams 1817	W. H. Crawford ....18.
6. John Q. Adams ....1825 *	John C. Calhoun ....1825 *	Henry Clay 1825	Richard Rush ....18.
7. Andrew Jackson ....1829 Democratic	John C. Calhoun ....1829 Democratic Martin Van Buren ....1833 Democratic	M. Van Buren ....1829 E. Livingston ....1831 Louis McLane ....1833 John Forsyth 1834	Sam. D. Ingham ....18. Louis McLane ....18. W. J. Duane ....18. Roger B. Taney ....18. Levi Woodbury ....18.
8. Martin Van Buren ....1837 Democratic	Richard M. Johnson ....1837 Democratic	John Forsyth 1837	Levi Woodbury ....18.
9. William H. Harrison ....1841 Whig	John Tyler ....1841 Whig	Daniel Webster 1841	Thos. Ewing ....18.
10. John Tyler ....1841 Whig and Democratic		Daniel Webster ....1841 Hugh S. Legare ....1843 Abel P. Upshur ....1843 John C. Calhoun 1844	Thos. Ewing ....18. Walter Forward ....18. John C. Spencer ....18. Geo. M. Bibb ....18.
11. James K. Polk ....1845 Democratic	George M. Dallas ....1845 Democratic	James Buchanan 1845	Robt. J. Walker ....18.
12. Zachary Taylor ....1849 Whig	Millard Fillmore ....1849 Whig	John M. Clayton 1849	Wm. M. Meredith ....18.
13. Millard Fillmore ....1850 Whig		Daniel Webster ....1850 Edward Everett 1852	Thomas Corwin ....18.
14. Franklin Pierce ....1853 Democratic	William R. D. King ....1853 Democratic	W. L. Marcy 1853	James Guthrie ....18.
15. James Buchanan ....1857 Democratic	John C. Breckinridge ....1857 Democratic	Lewis Cass ....1857 J. S. Black 1860	Howell Cobb ....18. Philip F. Thomas ....18. John A. Dix ....18.
16. Abraham Lincoln ....1861 Republican	Hannibal Hamlin ....1861 Republican Andrew Johnson ....1865 Unionist	W. H. Seward 1861	Salmon P. Chase ....18. W. P. Fessenden ....18. Hugh McCulloch ....18.

* No distinct party designations.

Secretary of War	Attorney-General	Postmaster-General †	Secretary of Navy	Secretary of Interior
Henry Knox ....1789 T. Pickering ....1795 Jas. McHenry 1796	E. Randolph ......1789 Wm. Bradford .....1794 Charles Lee 1795	Samuel Osgood ....1789 Tim. Pickering ....1791 Jos. Habersham 1795	Established April 30, 1798.	Established March 3, 1849.
Jas. McHenry .....1797 John Marshall .....1800 Sam'l Dexter ....1800 R. Griswold 1801	Charles Lee ....1797 Theo. Parsons 1801	Jos. Habersham 1797	Benj. Stoddert 1798	
H. Dearborn 1801	Levi Lincoln ......1801 Robert Smith ......1805 J. Breckinridge ....1805 C. A. Rodney 1807	Jos. Habersham ....1801 Gideon Granger 1801	Benj. Stoddert ....1801 Robert Smith ....1801 J. Crowninshield 1805	
Wm. Eustis ....1809 J. Armstrong ....1813 James Monroe .....1814 W. H. Crawford 1815	C. A. Rodney ....1809 Wm. Pinkney .....1811 Richard Rush 1814	Gideon Granger ...1809 R. J. Meigs, Jr. 1814	Paul Hamilton ......1809 William Jones ....1813 B. W. Crowninshield .1814	
Isaac Shelby ....1817 Geo. Graham ....1817 J. C. Calhoun 1817	Richard Rush .....1817 William Wirt 1817	R. J. Meigs, Jr. ....1817 John McLean 1823	B. W. Crowninshield..1817 Smith Thompson .....1818 S. L. Southard 1823	
Jas. Barbour ....1825 Peter B. Porter 1828	William Wirt 1825	John McLean 1825	S. L. Southard 1825	
John H. Eaton .....1829 Lewis Cass ....1831 B. F. Butler 1837	John M. Berrien ...1829 Roger B. Taney ....1831 B. F. Butler 1833	Wm. T. Barry .....1829 Amos Kendall 1835	John Branch ....1829 Levi Woodbury ......1831 Mahlon Dickerson ...1834	
Joel R. Poinsett 1837	B. F. Butler ......1837 Felix Grundy ......1838 H. D. Gilpin 1840	Amos Kendall .....1837 John M. Niles 1840	Mahlon Dickerson ...1837 Jas. K. Paulding 1838	
John Bell 1841	J. J. Crittenden 1841	Francis Granger 1841	George E. Badger 1841	
John Bell ....1841 John McLean ....1841 J. C. Spencer ......1841 Jas. M. Porter .....1843 Wm. Wilkins 1844	J. J. Crittenden ....1841 Hugh S. Legare ....1841 John Nelson 1843	Francis Granger ....1841 C. A. Wickliffe 1841	George E. Badger ....1841 Abel P. Upshur .....1841 David Henshaw ......1843 Thomas W. Gilmer ...1844 John Y. Mason 1844	
Wm. L. Marcy 1845	John Y. Mason ....1845 Nathan Clifford ....1846 Isaac Toucey 1848	Cave Johnson 1845	George Bancroft ....1845 John Y. Mason 1846	
G. W. Crawford 1849	Reverdy Johnson ...1849	Jacob Collamer 1849	Wm. B. Preston 1849	Thomas Ewing 1849
C. M. Conrad 1850	J. J. Crittenden 1850	Nathan K. Hall ....1850 Sam D. Hubbard ...1852	Wm. A Graham ..... 1850 John P. Kennedy 1852	A. H. Stuart 1850
Jefferson Davis 1853	Caleb Cushing 1853	James Campbell 1853	James C. Dobbin 1853	Robert McClelland ..1853
John B. Floyd .....1857 Joseph Holt 1861	J. S. Black ....1857 Edw. M Stanton ...1860	Aaron V. Brown ...1857 Joseph Holt 1859	Isaac Toucey 1857	Jacob Thompson 1857
S. Cameron ....1861 E. M. Stanton 1862	Edward Bates .....1861 Titian J. Coffey ....1863 James Speed 1864	Horatio King ......1861 M'tgomery Blair ...1861 Wm. Dennison 1864	Gideon Welles 1861	Caleb B. Smith .....1861 John P. Usher 1863

† Not in Cabinet until 1829.

President	Vice-President	Secretary of State	Secretary of Treasury	Secretary of War
17. Andrew Johnson ....1865 Unionist		W. H. Seward 1865	Hugh McCulloch ...1865	E. M. Stanton ....1865 U. S. Grant ......1867 L. Thomas ....1868 J. M. Schofield 1868
18. Ulysses S. Grant ....1869 Republican	Schuyler Colfax ....1869 Republican Henry Wilson ......1873 Republican	E. B. Washburne ..1869 Hamilton Fish 1869	Geo. S. Boutwell ...1869 W. A. Richardson ..1873 Benj. H. Bristow ...1874 Lot M. Morrill 1876	J. A. Rawlins .....1869 W. T. Sherman ...1869 W. W. Belknap ...1869 Alphonso Taft ....1876 J. D. Cameron 1876
19. Rutherford B. Hayes.1877 Republican	William A. Wheeler .1877 Republican	W. M. Evarts 1877	John Sherman 1877	G. W. McCrary ...1877 Alex. Ramsey 1879
20. James A. Garfield ...1881 Republican	Chester A. Arthur ..1881 Republican	James G. Blaine ...1881	Wm. Windom 1881	R. T. Lincoln 1881
21. Chester A. Arthur ..1881 Republican		F. T. Frelinghuysen.1881	Chas. J. Folger ....1881 W. Q. Gresham ....1884 Hugh McCulloch ...1884	R. T. Lincoln 1881
22. Grover Cleveland ...1885 Democratic	T. A. Hendricks ....1885 Democratic	Thos. F. Bayard ...1885	Daniel Manning ...1885 Chas. S. Fairchild ..1887	W. C. Endicott ...1885
23. Benjamin Harrison ..1889 Republican	Levi P. Morton ....1889 Republican	James G. Blaine ...1889 John W. Foster 1892	Wm. Windom .....1889 Charles Foster 1891	R. Proctor ...... 1889 S. B. Elkins 1891
24. Grover Cleveland ...1893 Democratic	Adlai E. Stevenson .1893 Democratic	W. Q. Gresham ....1893 Richard Olney 1895	John G. Carlisle ...1893	D. S. Lamont 1893
25. William McKinley ..1897 Republican	Garret A. Hobart ...1897 Republican Theodore Roosevelt..1901 Republican	John Sherman .....1897 Wm. R. Day ......1897 John Hay 1898	Lyman J. Gage 1897	R. A. Alger ......1897 Elihu Root 1899
26. Theodore Roosevelt ..1901 Republican	Chas. W. Fairbanks 1905 Republican	John Hay ....1901 Elihu Root ....1905 Robert Bacon 1909	Lyman J. Gage ....1901 Leslie M. Shaw ....1902 G. B. Cortelyou ...1907	Elihu Root ....1901 Wm. H. Taft .....1904 Luke E. Wright ...1908
27. William H. Taft ....1909 Republican	James S. Sherman ..1909 Republican	P. C. Knox 1909	F. MacVeagh 1909	J. M. Dickinson ..1909 H. L. Stimson 1911
28. Woodrow Wilson ....1913 Democratic	Thomas R. Marshall.1913 Democratic	Wm. J. Bryan .... 1913 Robert Lansing ....1915 Bainbridge Colby ..1920	W. G. McAdoo ....1913 Carter Glass ....1918 D. F. Houston 1920	L. M. Garrison ...1913 N. D. Baker 1916
29. Warren G. Harding ..1921 Republican	Calvin Coolidge ....1921 Republican	Chas. E. Hughes ...1921	Andrew W. Mellon .1921	John W. Weeks ...1921
30. Calvin Coolidge .....1923 Republican	Charles G. Dawes ..1925 Republican	Chas. E. Hughes ..1923 Frank B. Kellogg ..1925	Andrew W. Mellon .1923	John W. Weeks ...1923 Dwight F. Davis ..1925
31. Herbert Hoover .....1929 Republican	Charles Curtis .....1929 Republican	Henry L. Stimson ..1929	Andrew W. Mellon .1929 Ogden L. Mills 1932	James W. Good ...1929 Pat. J. Hurley 1929
32. Franklin D. Roose- velt ....1933 Democratic	John Nance Garner .1933 Democratic Henry A. Wallace ..1941 Democratic Harry S. Truman ..1945 Democratic	Cordell Hull ......1933 E. R. Stettinius, Jr. 1944	Wm. H. Woodin ...1933 Henry Morgenthau, Jr. 1934	Geo. H. Dern ....1933 H. A. Woodring ...1936 H. L. Stimson 1940
33. Harry S. Truman ...1945 Democratic	Alben W. Barkley ..1949 Democratic	James F. Byrnes ...1945 Geo. C. Marshall ...1947 Dean G. Acheson ...1949	Fred M. Vinson ...1945 John W. Snyder 1946	Robt. H. Patter- son ....1945 K. C. Royall .....1947 **
34. Dwight D. Eisen- hower ....1953 Republican	Richard M. Nixon ..1953 Republican	John Foster Dulles .1953	George C. Humphrey 1953	

** Lost cabinet status in 1947.

Attorney-General	Postmaster-General	Secretary of Navy	Secretary of Interior	Secretary of Agriculture	Other Members
James Speed ....1865 Henry Stanbery ..1866 Wm. M. Evarts ..1868	Wm. Dennison .1865 A. W. Randall ..1866	Gideon Welles ..1865	John P. Usher ..1865 James Harlan ..1865 O. H. Browning.1866	Cabinet status since 1889.	*Secretary of Commerce and Labor* Established Feb. 14, 1903.
E. R. Hoar .....1869 A. T. Ackerman .1870 Geo. H. Williams 1871 Edw. Pierrepont 1875 Alphonso Taft ...1876	J. A. J. Creswell 1869 Jas. W. Marshall 1874 Marshall Jewell .1874 James N. Tyner.1876	Adolph E. Borie 1869 Geo. M. Robeson 1869	Jacob D. Cox ..1869 C. Delano .....1870 Zach. Chandler .1875		George B. Cortelyou ......1903 Victor H. Metcalf ...1904-6 O. S.
Chas. Devens ...1877	David M. Key .1877 Horace Maynard 1880	R. W. Thompson 1877 Nathan Goff, Jr..1881	Carl Schurz 1877		Straus ....1907-9 Chas. Nagel ...1909
W. MacVeagh ...1881	T. L. James 1881	W. H. Hunt ...1881	S. J. Kirkwood .1881		(Department divided, 1913)
B. H. Brewster ..1881	T. O. Howe ....1881 W. Q. Gresham 1883 Frank Hatton ..1884	W. E. Chandler.1881	Henry M. Teller.1881		*Secretary of Commerce*
A. H. Garland ..1885	Wm. F. Vilas .1885 D M. Dickinson 1888	W. C. Whitney .1885	L. Q. C. Lamar.1885 Wm. F. Vilas ..1888	N. J. Colman.1889	W. C. Redfield 1913
W. H. H. Miller .1889	J. Wanamaker .1889	Benj. F. Tracy .1889	John W. Noble .1889	J. M. Rusk ..1889	Joshua W. Alexander ...1919 H. C. Hoover...1921
R. Olney ......1893 J. Harmon 1895	W. S. Bissell ...1893 W. L. Wilson ..1895	Hilary A. Herbert 1893	Hoke Smith ....1893 D. R. Francis ..1896	J. S. Morton .1893	H. C. Hoover..1925 W. F. Whiting 1928
J. McKenna ....1897 J. W. Griggs ....1897 P. C. Knox 1901	James A. Gary .1897 Chas. E. Smith 1898	John D. Long ..1897	C. N. Bliss ....1897 E. A. Hitchcock 1899	James Wilson .1897	R. P. Lamont..1929 R. D. Chapin..1932 D. C. Roper...1933 H. L. Hopkins.1939
P. C. Knox .....1901 W. H. Moody ...1904 C. J. Bonaparte .1907	Chas. E. Smith 1901 Henry C. Payne.1902 Robt. J. Wynne.1904 G. B. Cortelyou.1905 G. von L. Meyer.1907	John D. Long ..1901 Wm. H. Moody.1902 Paul Morton ..1904 C. J. Bonaparte.1905 Victor H. Metcalf .....1907 T. H. Newberry.1908	E. A. Hitchcock 1901 J. R. Garfield ..1907	James Wilson .1901	Jesse Jones....1940 Henry A. Wallace ....1945 W. Averell Harriman ....1946 Charles W. Sawyer ....1948 Sinclair
G. W. Wickersham 1909	F. H. Hitchcock .1909	G. von L. Meyer 1909	R. A. Ballinger.1909 W. L. Fisher ...1911	James Wilson .1909	Weeks 1953
J. C. McReynolds 1913 Thos. W. Gregory 1914 A. M. Palmer ...1919	A. S. Burleson .1913	Josephus Daniels 1913	F. K. Lane ....1913 J. B. Payne 1920	D. F. Houston.1913 E. T. Meredith 1920	*Secretary of Labor* Established March 4, 1913
H. M. Daugherty 1921	Will H. Hays ..1921 Hubert Work ..1922 Harry S. New ..1923	Edwin Denby ..1921	Albert B. Fall ..1921 Hubert Work ..1923	H. C. Wallace.1921	W. B. Wilson..1913 J. J. Davis..1921-29 W. N. Doak...1930
H. M. Daugherty 1923 Harlan F. Stone .1924 John G. Sargent 1925	Harry S. New ..1923	Edwin Denby ..1923 Curtis D. Wilbur 1924	Hubert Work ...1923 Roy O. West ...1928	H. M. Gore ..1924 W. M. Jardine 1925	Frances Perkins '33 L. B. Schwellenbach 1945
Wm. D. Mitchell.1929	Walter F. Brown.1929	Chas. F. Adams.1929	Ray L. Wilbur .1929	Arthur M. Hyde 1929	M. J. Tobin....1948 M. P. Durkin..1953
H. S. Cummings 1933 Frank Murphy ..1939 Robt. H. Jackson 1940 Francis Biddle ...1941	James A. Farley.1933 Frank C. Walker 1940	Claude A. Swanson .....1933 Chas. Edison ..1940 Frank Knox ...1940 James V. Forrestal 1944	Harold L. Ickes.1933	H. A. Wallace 1933 C. R. Wickard.1940	James P. Mitchell 1953
Tom C. Clark ...1945 J. H. McGrath .1949 James P. McGranery ...1952	Robt. E. Hannegan ...1945 Jesse L. Donaldson ...1947	James V. Forrestal ....1945 ††	Harold L. Ickes.1945 Julius A. Krug .1946 O. L. Chapman .1951	C. P. Anderson 1945 C. F. Brannan.1948	*Secretary of Defense* Established July 26, 1947. James V. Forrestal 1947
Herbert Brownell, Jr. ..1953	Arthur E. Summerfield .1953		Douglas McKay.1953 Fred Seaton ..1956	Ezra T. Benson 1953	Louis A. Johnson .....1949 George C. Marshall ....1950 Robert A. Lovett ......1951 Charles E. Wilson 1953

†† Lost cabinet status in 1947.

Secretary of Health, Education, and Welfare

Established April 1, 1953.

Oveta Culp Hobby 1953

Marion B. Folsom......1955

JUSTICES OF THE UNITED STATES SUPREME COURT

Name (Chief Justices in Italics)	Service (Term)	(Years)	Name (Chief Justices in Italics)	Service (Term)	(Years)
John Jay (N.Y.)	1789-1795	6	Horace Gray (Mass.)	1881-1902	21
John Rutledge (S.C.)	1789-1791	2	Samuel Blatchford (N.Y.)	1882-1893	11
William Cushing (Mass.)	1789-1810	21	Lucius Q. Lamar (Miss.)	1888-1893	5
James Wilson (Pa.)	1789-1798	9	*Melville W. Fuller* (Ill.)	1888-1910	22
John Blair (Va.)	1789-1796	7	David J. Brewer (Kans.)	1889-1910	21
James Iredell (N.C.)	1790-1799	9	Henry B. Brown (Mich.)	1890-1906	16
Thomas Johnson (Md.)	1792-1793	½	George Shiras, Jr. (Pa.)	1892-1903	11
William Paterson (N.J.)	1793-1806	13	Howell E. Jackson (Tenn.)	1893-1895	2
John Rutledge (S.C.)[1]	1795-1795		Edward D. White (La.)	1894-1910	16
Samuel Chase (Md.)	1796-1811	15	Rufus W. Peckham (N.Y.)	1895-1909	14
Oliver Ellsworth (Conn.)	1796-1800	4	Joseph McKenna (Calif.)	1898-1925	27
Bushrod Washington (Va.)	1798-1829	31	Oliver W. Holmes (Mass.)	1902-1932	30
Alfred Moore (N.C.)	1800-1804	4	William R. Day (Ohio)	1903-1922	19
John Marshall (Va.)	1801-1835	34	William H. Moody (Mass.)	1906-1910	4
William Johnson (S.C.)	1804-1834	30	Horace H. Lurton (Tenn.)	1909-1914	5
Brock. Livingston (N.Y.)	1806-1823	17	*Edward D. White* (La.)	1910-1921	11
Thomas Todd (Ky.)	1807-1826	19	Charles E. Hughes (N.Y.)	1910-1916	6
Joseph Story (Mass.)	1811-1845	34	Willis Van Devanter (Wyo.)	1910-1937	26
Gabriel Duval (Md.)	1811-1835	24	Joseph R. Lamar (Ga.)	1910-1916	6
Smith Thompson (N.Y.)	1823-1843	20	Mahlon Pitney (N.J.)	1912-1923	11
Robert Trimble (Ky.)	1826-1828	2	James C. McReynolds (Tenn.)	1914-1941	27
John McLean (Ohio)	1829-1861	32	Louis D. Brandeis (Mass.)	1916-1939	23
Henry Baldwin (Pa.)	1830-1844	14	John H. Clarke (Ohio)	1916-1922	6
James M. Wayne (Ga.)	1835-1867	32	*William H. Taft* (Conn.)	1921-1930	9
Roger B. Taney (Md.)	1836-1864	28	George Sutherland (Utah)	1922-1938	16
Philip P. Barbour (Va.)	1836-1841	5	Pierce Butler (Minn.)	1922-1939	17
John Catron (Tenn.)	1837-1865	28	Edward T. Sanford (Tenn.)	1923-1930	7
John McKinley (Ala.)	1837-1852	15	Harlan F. Stone (N.Y.)	1925-1941	16
Peter V. Daniel (Va.)	1841-1860	19	*Charles E. Hughes* (N.Y.)	1930-1941	11
Samuel Nelson (N.Y.)	1845-1872	27	Owen J. Roberts (Pa.)	1930-1945	15
Levi Woodbury (N.H.)	1845-1851	6	Benjamin N. Cardozo (N.Y.)	1932-1938	6
Robert C. Grier (Pa.)	1846-1870	24	Hugo L. Black (Ala.)	1937-	
Benjamin R. Curtis (Mass.)	1851-1857	6	Stanley F. Reed (Ky.)	1938-	
John A. Campbell (Ala.)	1853-1861	8	Felix Frankfurter (Mass.)	1939-	
Nathan Clifford (Maine)	1858-1881	23	William O. Douglas (Conn.)	1939-	
Noah H. Swayne (Ohio)	1862-1881	19	Frank Murphy (Mich.)	1940-1949	9
Samuel F. Miller (Iowa)	1862-1890	28	*Harlan F. Stone* (N.Y.)	1941-1946	5
David Davis (Ill.)	1862-1877	15	James F. Byrnes (S.C.)	1941-1942	1
Stephen J. Field (Calif.)	1863-1897	34	Robert H. Jackson (N.Y.)	1941-1954	13
Salmon P. Chase (Ohio)	1864-1873	9	Wiley B. Rutledge (Iowa)	1943-1949	6
William Strong (Pa.)	1870-1880	10	Harold H. Burton (Ohio)	1945-	
Joseph P. Bradley (N.J.)	1870-1892	22	*Fred M. Vinson* (Ky.)	1946-1953	7
Ward Hunt (N.Y.)	1872-1882	10	Tom C. Clark (Tex.)	1949-	
Morrison R. Waite (Ohio)	1874-1888	14	Sherman Minton (Ind.)	1949-1956	7
John M. Harlan (Ky.)	1877-1911	34	*Earl Warren* (Calif.)	1953-	
William B. Woods (Ga.)	1880-1887	7	John M. Harlan (N.Y.)	1955-	
Stanley Matthews (Ohio)	1881-1889	8	William J. Brennan (N.J.)	1956-	

[1] Appointed and served one term, but not confirmed by the Senate.

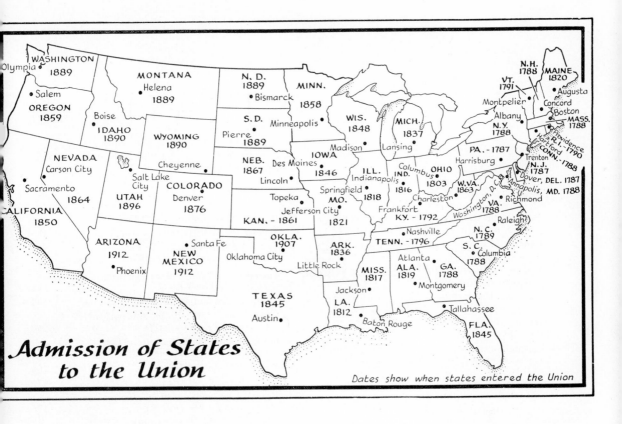

Admission of States to the Union

Dates show when states entered the Union

ILLUSTRATIONS

Abbreviations: *NYPL*—New York Public Library; *NYHS*—New-York Historical Society; *NYPLPC*—New York Public Library Picture Collection.

INDEX

1846   A successful war with Mexico wins the United States enormous new territory but reopens the domestic conflict over the extension of slavery

1850   The compromise over the admission of California as a free state temporarily settles the growing slavery controversy

1854   The Republican party is organized as a sectional party dedicated to the exclusion of slavery from the territories by act of Congress

1857   The decision of the Supreme Court denying the slave, Dred Scott, his freedom angers the growing anti-slavery element in the North

1859   John Brown's raid on the federal arsenal at Harpers Ferry, in order to arm a slave revolt, confirms the South's worst fears

1860   Abraham Lincoln's election as a Republican president prompts South Carolina to lead the South to secession

1861   Civil War begins with the Confederate attack on Fort Sumter

1863   The Emancipation Proclamation frees the slaves in all states "in rebellion against the United States"

1865   Lincoln is assassinated five days after Lee's surrender to Grant at Appomattox

1869   The first transcontinental railroad is completed

1890   The Sherman Antitrust Act (along with the Interstate Commerce Act of 1887) begins the era of federal regulation of "big business"